La Leche League International

THE BREASTFEEDING ANSWER BOOK

Revised Edition

La Leche League International

THE BREASTFEEDING ANSWER BOOK

Revised Edition

by
Nancy Mohrbacher, IBCLC
and
Julie Stock, BA, IBCLC

La Leche League International
Schaumburg, Illinois

La Leche League

INTERNATIONAL

1400 North Meacham Road P.O. Box 4079
Schaumburg IL 60168-4079 USA
847-519-7730
847-519-0035, fax
http://www.lalecheleague.org/

Revised edition, January 1997
Second Printing, March 1997
Third printing, June 1998
First edition, August 1991
Five printings, 40,500 copies
© 1991 and 1996, La Leche League International, Inc.
All Rights Reserved
Printed in the United States of America

"Marmet Technique of Manual Expression,"
© 1978, revised 1979, 1981, and 1988. Used with permission of Chele Marmet.
The Lactation Institute, 16430 Ventura Blvd., Suite 303, Encino, California 91436
USA (818-995-1913)

"Transfer of Drugs and Chemicals into Human Milk," © 1994, American
Academy of Pediatrics. Used with permission.

Cover design by David Arendt.
Book design by Lucy Lesiak Design.
Library of Congress Catalogue Card Number 96-78580
ISBN 0-912500-48-4

To all the women who taught us through their experience that breastfeeding can be a problem-free and joyous process.

Contents

Foreword by Edward Newton, MD   xiii

Foreword to the First Edition by Jan Riordan, EdD, RN, IBCLC
     and Hugh Riordan, MD   xv

Preface to Revised Edition   xvii

Acknowledgements   xix

Introduction   xxi

1
Giving Effective Breastfeeding Help

Using Active Listening   2

Asking Questions   3

Giving Information and Suggestions   5

Respecting Differences among Mothers   7

Helping the Mother Work with Her Doctor   10

When Breastfeeding Doesn't Work Out   13

2
The Breast and How It Works

Breast Anatomy   16

Hormonal Influences   17

3
Breastfeeding Basics

Normal Breastfeeding Patterns   20

During the Early Months   24

The Let-Down, or Milk-Ejection, Reflex   32

Common Questions   34

4
Positioning, Latch-On, and the Baby's Suck

Positioning   46

Latch-On—How the Baby Goes on to the Breast   52

The Baby's Suck   57

If Breastfeeding Hurts—Review the Basics   71

5
Fussy at the Breast and Breast Refusal

The Mother's Feelings   79

Asking Questions and Gathering Information   80

Fussy at the Breast   80

Breast Refusal   101

Persuading the Baby to Take the Breast   104

Refusal of One Breast   106

6
Weight Gain

Normal Growth Patterns during the Baby's First Year   114

Slow Weight Gain during the First Year   116

Rapid Weight Gain during the First Year   136

7
Starting Solid Foods

Determining a Baby's Readiness for Solids   142

How to Introduce Solids   144

What Foods to Offer   146

Foods to Avoid   148

Introducing the Cup   149

8
Weaning

The Mother's Feelings and the Decision to Wean   154

Approaches to Weaning   157

If the Baby Refuses to Breastfeed   166

Physical Changes That Occur with Weaning   167

9
Expression and Storage of Human Milk

Choosing a Method of Expression   170

Basics of Milk Expression   171

Milk-Expression Strategies for Different Situations   178

Storage and Handling of Human Milk   188

10
Employment and Breastfeeding

The Mother's Feelings   196
Milk Expression   200
Home Strategies   209
Feeding Tips for Baby's Caregiver   210
Storage and Handling of Human Milk   212

11
Newborn Jaundice

The Mother's Feelings   222
Causes of Newborn Jaundice and Elevated Bilirubin   223
Why and When Newborn Jaundice May Need Treatment   227
Treatment Options for a Jaundiced Baby   228
Helping the Mother Work with Her Baby's Doctor   235

12
Prematurity

The Mother's Feelings   242
The Advantages of Breastfeeding a Premature Baby   244
Building a Relationship between Mother and Baby   245
The Premie Weighing More Than 1500 Grams (3.3 lbs.)   248
The Premie Weighing Less Than 1500 Grams (3.3 lbs.)   248
The First Nursings   258
The Mother's Diet and Drug Considerations   264
Working with Hospital Personnel   264
Preparing for Hospital Discharge   267
The First Weeks at Home   268

13
Illness—Baby

When the Baby Is Ill   280
Hospitalization of the Breastfeeding Baby   287

14
The Baby with Special Needs

The Mother's Feelings   296
Cardiac Problems   296
Cleft Lip and/or Palate   297
Cystic Fybrosis   304
Down Syndrome   304
Galactosemia   308
The Neurologically Impaired Baby   309
PKU   312

15
Multiples— Breastfeeding Twins, Triplets, or More

Feelings about Having More Than One Baby   318
Advantages of Breastfeeding Multiples   318
Preparations during Pregnancy   319
After Birth—Adjusting to Life with Multiples   320
Breastfeeding Basics   321
Mother Care for the Mother of Multiples   325
Breastfeeding Triplets and Quadruplets 327

16
Relactation and Adoptive Nursing

Talk about Feelings, Goals, and Realistic Expectations   330
Relactation—Stimulating a Milk Supply   333
Induced Lactation—Stimulating a Milk Supply   335
Encouraging the Baby to Take the Breast   338
Making the Transition—How to Be Sure That Baby Is Getting
    Enough   340

17
Pregnancy and Tandem Nursing

Breastfeeding during Pregnancy   344
Tandem Nursing   347

18
Sexuality, Fertility, and Contraception

Breastfeeding and Sexuality   354
Breastfeeding, Fertility, and Contraception   356

19
Nutrition, Weight Loss, Exercise, and Personal Grooming

Nutrition for the Nursing Mother   372
Weight Loss and Eating Disorders   379
Exercise   381
Personal Grooming   382

20
Nipple Problems

Sore Nipples   388
Treatment of Sore Nipples   393
Flat and Inverted Nipples   396
Teething and Biting   402
Thrush   404
Nipple Blisters and Sores   406

21
Breast Problems

Engorgement   414
Mastitis—Plugged Ducts and Breast Infections   418
Breast Abscess   425
Breast Lumps   426
Blood in the Milk   428
Deep Breast Pain   428
Breastfeeding after Breast Surgery or Injury   432

22
Cesarean Birth

The Mother's Feelings   444
Advantages of Breastfeeding to the Cesarean Mother   445
Breastfeeding in the Hospital   445
The First Weeks at Home   449

23
Health Problems— Mother

When Mother Is Ill   452
When Mother Is Hospitalized   467
Chronic Illness or Physical Limitation   471
Postpartum Depression   482

24
Drugs, Vitamins, Vaccines, and Diagnostic Tests

Prescription and Over-the-Counter Drugs   500
Substances of Concern   509
Substances of Abuse   513
Vitamin and Mineral Supplements for Babies   514
Vaccines   516
Diagnostic Materials and Tests   517

Supplements

Transfer of Drugs and Other Chemicals into Human Milk

Drugs That Are Contraindicated during Breastfeeding   526
Drugs of Abuse: Contraindicated during Breastfeeding   526
Radioactive Compounds That Require Temporary Cessation of Breastfeeding   526
Drugs Whose Effect on Nursing Infants Is Unknown but May Be of Concern   527
Drugs That Have Been Associated with Significant Effects on Some Nursing Infants   527
Maternal Medication Usually Compatible with Breastfeeding   528
Food and Environmental Agents: Effect on Breastfeeding   530
Generic Drugs and Corresponding Trade Names   531

The Use of Breast Pumps and Other Products

Alternative Feeding Methods   540
Breast Pumps   546
Breast Shells   562
Creams and Ointments   563
Milk Storage Bags   565
Nipple Shields   566
Nursing Pads   567
Nursing Pillows   567
Nursing Stools   567
Other Products   568

Appendix

About La Leche League   573
Photo Credits   577
Index   579

Foreword

I am honored and grateful to participate in the review and foreword of this edition of THE BREASTFEEDING ANSWER BOOK. My exposure to breastfeeding and La Leche League International has been lifelong. When I was a child, the dinner table and many "free" weekends were filled with the discussion and teaching of breastfeeding by my parents, Michael and Niles Newton. As an adult, my wife, Karen, and my children, Rebeccah and Kimberly, have benefited from and been occupied by my practical, academic, and educational interests in breastfeeding. The evolution of THE BREASTFEEDING ANSWER BOOK has resulted in a practical and scientific expression of attitudes, expectations, and philosophy that reflects the viewpoint of both my parents and myself.

THE BREASTFEEDING ANSWER BOOK provides a wealth of information on the management of breastfeeding. A central theme is recommendations based on well-documented scientific principles and supported by scientific literature. The excellent bibliography provides supportive reading for those who counsel today's well-educated and demanding new mothers.

THE BREASTFEEDING ANSWER BOOK goes beyond the sometimes "hard" scientific support for management of breastfeeding. The book has woven into it the loving experience of millions of nursing mothers who have committed themselves to the philosophy of La Leche League International. The result has been to combine the practical aspects with the scientific research. THE BREASTFEEDING ANSWER BOOK is unique in combining love and science.

As we approach the next millennium, breastfeeding will face increasing challenges in the Western world. Many new mothers will be highly educated with full-time jobs. There will be continued societal pressure to purchase luxury goods and services. Many times her family will be blended or she will be single. In addition to her family, she will be providing support for aging parents. Her obstetrician will have breastfed her own child six weeks or less, and the breast pump will be a culturally accepted substitute for breastfeeding.

These challenges of social isolation, lip service, and technology-dependence are no less of a challenge to breastfeeding success than the disinterest, ignorance, and antagonism of the past. THE BREASTFEEDING ANSWER BOOK provides practical, scientifically based information to meet the challenge. It will be a valuable resource for both the breastfeeding counselor and medical professionals alike.

Edward R. Newton, MD
Houston, Texas, 1996

Foreword

Reprinted from the First Edition

How times change! When our first child was born over three decades ago, there was nothing in our medical or nursing education that was of any use in trying to breastfeed him. As a matter of fact, there was no information at all, and no one to teach us how to breastfeed. We had just moved to the wide-open Southwest to begin an internship and were essentially alone with only each other and a handful of newly found (non-breastfeeding) friends. As a result, Michael was fed at the breast for two months before the milk "ran out." With the next baby we learned a little more on our own, so Nell was breastfed a little longer. But by the time our third baby, Teresa, was born, the first edition of THE WOMANLY ART OF BREASTFEEEDING had found its way to Kansas. That unpretentious little loose-leaf book which cost a whole dollar was a wonderful find. Because of that book, Teresa was breastfed for more than a year and our last three children, Renee, Brian, and Quinn, for even longer.

Now, three decades later, we are grandparents. There are dozens of books on breastfeeding, numerous breastfeeding support groups, and breastfeeding classes. We have made great strides in educating young parents. But the times call for a special book. This book is a "new" approach to breastfeeding counseling. The content offers the reader a concise, practical guide of what to do and why in virtually any breastfeeding circumstance. THE BREASTFEEEDING ANSWER BOOK is intended for the non-medically trained breastfeeding counselor. She can easily locate special breastfeeding situations and appropriate advice to help her determine what course to take to help the breastfeeding family.

Non-medical breastfeeding counselors, such as La Leche League Leaders, are needed now more than ever. During this last decade, the average length of hospital stay following birth has been cut almost in half as the health care industry strives to keep costs down. Women are sent home to grapple on their own. The need is reflected in the fact that, worldwide, babies are getting less time at their mother's breasts and in the knowledge that the traditional support system of female relatives or of the "doula" can no longer be counted on to buoy the new, vulnerable mother in her effort to breastfeed.

Breastfeeding will always be the optimal way to nourish babies. A species-specific "liquid gold," human milk is an overlooked natural resource. This resource is provided in attractive, reusable containers readily available at the right temperature with all the nutrients the baby needs to grow and the protective elements that increase an infant's chances for healthy survival.

Breastfeeding, like childbirth, empowers women. This power is not society's masculine definition of power meaning authority, money, or material goods. It is the power of nurturance, intimacy, and attachment that gives quality and meaning to our lives. When a mother breastfeeds she develops a sense of accomplishment in herself and her abilities. The ability to create and nurture life is a major human event that puts a woman in touch with the essence of being. No events are more vital to humanity than childbearing and breastfeeding—vulnerable links that assure our continuation as a species.

This book is an important tool for those who daily help mothers to successfully experience the beauty of breastfeeding. La Leche League International, drawing on its background and collective experience in helping breastfeeding women all over this planet for thirty-five years, is eminently qualified to present this material.

Jan Riordan, EdD, RN, IBCLC
Hugh Riordan, MD
Kansas, 1991

Preface

The changes in this revised edition of THE BREASTFEEDING ANSWER BOOK reflect the growth in research and practical experience in the field of lactation during the past five years. Our continuing work with breastfeeding mothers, both within La Leche League and as lactation consultants in private practice, has deepened our understanding of the challenges and joys of breastfeeding. Our travels and correspondence have given us the opportunity to hear the questions and concerns of breastfeeding counselors in different regions. We offer thanks to all the women who have shared their experiences and insights.

Although keeping up with the rapidly expanding body of breastfeeding literature has been a major undertaking, it was crucial to this revision. We are grateful for access to the extensive files of breastfeeding research on file at LLLI's Center for Breastfeeding Information.

Our own experience during the past five years along with the experiences of La Leche League International played an essential role in this revised edition. In addition to incorporating research and practical experience, one of our goals for this revised edition was to acknowledge and clarify different attitudes and approaches to breastfeeding problems. The breastfeeding counselor needs to be aware that breastfeeding experts sometimes disagree among themselves about some basic issues. We hope that including these differing viewpoints will give you more strategies to choose from, increasing the odds that you will find one that is perfectly suited to the very individual mother and baby you are helping.

We are gratified that the first edition of this book has been so widely used by La Leche League Leaders and other breastfeeding counselors around the world and hope that this revised edition will be an even more effective tool in helping mothers enjoy their breastfeeding experience.

Nancy Mohrbacher, IBCLC
Julie Stock, IBCLC

Acknowledgements

It gives us great satisfaction to thank the individuals whose help and contributions have significantly enhanced this revised and expanded edition of THE BREASTFEEDING ANSWER BOOK.

Particularly deserving of recognition is Lawrence Gartner, an invaluable contributor to the first edition and an equally vital force in the successful completion of the revised edition. Dr. Gartner's careful reading of the text and generous sharing of his knowledge and insights resulted in significant changes in the presentation and understanding of medical issues related to breastfeeding infants. An outstanding scientist and a generous mentor, Dr. Gartner is well known for his commitment to the support and success of breastfeeding.

Others who contributed meaningfully to the finished manuscript, offering either expertise in medical information or the fine tuning of our words, have our sincere thanks. They are Judy Torgus, Director, LLLI Publications Department, Betty Crase, Director, LLLI Center for Breastfeeding Information, Gene Cranston Anderson, Cheston Berlin, Kathleen Kennedy, Ruth Lawrence, Edward Newton, and Richard Schanler.

Lois Arnold, Allan Cunningham, Judy Hopkinson, Miriam Labbok, Jack Newman, Jan Riordan, Judith Roepke, and Bill and Martha Sears gave generously of their time and expertise to improve the scope and quality of the finished manuscript. We are grateful for their help.

Many others offered nuggets of information that allowed us to more completely present issues of importance to breastfeeding mothers and those who counsel them. Our appreciation is extended to Gere Clark, Lee Ann Deal, Paul Fleiss, Dany Gauthier, Gwen Gotsch, Linn Hodder, Sue Huml, Ruth Lufkin, Judy Minami, Sally Murphy, Martha O'Donnell, Debra Peterson, Cindy Smith, Arnold Tanis, Maryelle Vonlanthen, and Mary Kay Wales.

Last, and certainly not least, Julie wishes to thank Carol Huotari of LLLI's Center for Breastfeeding Information for her patient and positive interest and thoughtful helpfulness in dealing with the issues involved in revising the book. Nancy offers special thanks to Clifford Rot, whose personal and professional support was invaluable to her.

We are grateful to our families and to the many others who have supported us as individuals as well as breastfeeding specialists over the last five years. Our appreciation for their concern and positive input will remain well beyond the lifetime of this book.

Nancy Mohrbacher, IBCLC
Julie Stock, IBCLC

Acknowledgements

Reprinted from the First Edition

This book began as a collective, volunteer effort by many La Leche League Leaders, some of whom are also lactation consultants. The preliminary goal was to provide an easy-to-use guidebook of basic breastfeeding information. Their efforts to compile the basic information provided the essential first step. Thanks to Terri Bloomingdale, Betty Crase, Pam Koehler, Debbie Mix, Edie Orr, and Mary Price for their contributions in getting the book underway.

Other La Leche League women volunteered their administrative and review services as work progressed and the project expanded. The efforts of Suzanne Glennon, Meta Levin, Ruth Lufkin, Susan Meintz Maher, Willow Reed, and Cindy Smith are greatly appreciated.

Special thanks to Judy Minami, Mary Kay Smith, and Sally Tobin, who wrote and reviewed materials during the early stages.

The following members of La Leche League International's Health Advisory Council generously volunteered their expertise and reviewed the final manuscript. We are indebted to Leo Buchanan, Edward R. Cerutti, Lawrence M. Gartner, John W. Gerrard, Robert Jackson, Derrick Jelliffe, Ruth Lawrence, Judith Roepke, Arnold Tanis, and Gregory J. White for their help on this project and their continuing interest in, and support of, La Leche League.

We thank the American Academy of Pediatrics for giving us permission to reprint its "Transfer of Drugs and Other Chemicals into Human Milk."

Thanks also to Judy Torgus, and Gwen Gotsch, who reviewed and edited the final manuscript, and Edwina Froehlich, who offered invaluable suggestions.

Introduction

Everyone agrees breast is best. Breastfeeding is promoted worldwide by UNICEF and the World Health Organization. Here in the United States one of the health objectives for the year 2000 is to increase the incidence and duration of breastfeeding. Yet surveys of new mothers indicate that many mothers who start out breastfeeding give up after a few days or weeks.

One reason for this may be that knowledge about the "how-to's" of breastfeeding is still generally lacking. A mother might believe with all her heart that her milk is best for her baby, but sore nipples make nursing unbearably painful for her. Or early introduction of artificial nipples confuses her baby, causing him to refuse her breast. Who can help such a mother? Will she find the help she needs to continue breastfeeding from her health care professionals, her friends, her family? Will her self-esteem be damaged if she considers herself a failure at breastfeeding? And if she doesn't get the help she needs, will she try breastfeeding again when her next baby is born?

La Leche League has worked for forty years offering information and support to women who want to breastfeed, as well as providing continuing education for health care professionals. As a mother-to-mother organization, almost all of LLLI's publications have been written for the nursing mother. When this book was first published in 1991, it was our first breastfeeding book written for those who help the nursing mother. It was developed primarily as a resource for La Leche League Leaders, however, other breastfeeding counselors—lactation consultants, pediatric nurses, and public health personnel—have also found this book helpful in their work.

In compiling the first edition of THE BREASTFEEDING ANSWER BOOK, Julie Stock and Nancy Mohrbacher worked as a team. Julie came up with the original concept of the book, reviewed the scientific literature, and provided the impetus that kept the book going through its various stages. Nancy did most of the research and writing. For the revised edition, Nancy and Julie developed the overall vision for the project, as well as reviewing the research, revising and updating the information, rewriting an extensive amount of the existing text, and writing the three new chapters.

This book is not meant to be read from cover to cover. It is designed to help answer a mother's breastfeeding questions and for that reason information is sometimes repeated when it applies to different situations. Since most LLL Leaders—and many other effective breastfeeding counselors—come from a lay background, this book is written in non-medical language. This will also make it easier to convey the information to mothers.

Although we **are** aware that babies come in two genders, in this book, we refer to baby as "he," not with sexist intent, but simply for clarity's sake, since mother is unquestionably "she."

Breastfeeding is truly an art and not a science. Answers to questions are rarely simple and straightforward. When a mother asks a La Leche League Leader or other breastfeeding counselor a general question about breastfeeding, more often than not, her response will be, "it depends." To be truly helpful to each nursing couple, individual differences and variations must be acknowledged and respected.

This book explores in depth all types of possible breastfeeding questions—from mildly disturbing to potentially serious and severe—along with a wide variety of possible solutions and approaches. By offering a more complete picture in an easy-to-use format, this book enables the breastfeeding counselor to tailor her suggestions to the individual mother and baby in a wide variety of circumstances. Presenting a broad spectrum of approaches to the breastfeeding counselor can increase the chances that she and the mother will be able to find the most effective way to resolve most problems.

Also important is an appreciation for the many complex issues and feelings that are interwoven with questions about breastfeeding. Breastfeeding is more than just a method of feeding; it is also a way of caring for and comforting a baby. For many mothers, breastfeeding becomes an integral part of their relationship with their baby. So when questions about breastfeeding arise, it is not unusual for them to also involve the mother's feelings about her baby and her feelings about being a mother. A cookbook approach to solving breastfeeding problems—where the same suggestions are routinely given to all mothers—will not do justice to most mothers and babies. What makes giving breastfeeding help so fascinating and challenging is the creativity it requires to find just the right variation that will work in each unique situation.

We hope this book will make this challenge easier for you. It has been sometimes overwhelming—but also a pleasure—to gather under one cover breastfeeding information from so many sources: LLLI publications, other respected books on breastfeeding, research studies, LLL International Conference sessions, and personal experiences. We hope that having this information in one volume will make it easier for you to find just the right bit of information that will make breastfeeding as fun and enjoyable for mothers and babies as it was meant to be.

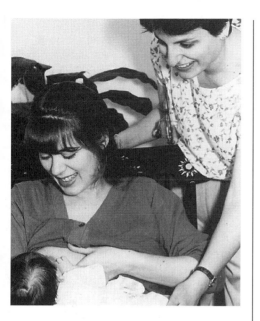

1

Giving Effective Breastfeeding Help

USING ACTIVE LISTENING

ASKING QUESTIONS

GIVING INFORMATION AND SUGGESTIONS

RESPECTING DIFFERENCES AMONG MOTHERS
    Single Mothers
    Adolescent Mothers
    Family or Cultural Breastfeeding Practices
    Cultural Differences
    Economic Differences
    Differences in Parenting Styles

HELPING THE MOTHER WORK WITH HER DOCTOR
    When Suggestions Differ from the Doctor's Advice
    Help the Mother Express Her Feelings and Goals
    How to Help in a Medical Situation

WHEN BREASTFEEDING DOESN'T WORK OUT
    Lasting Impressions

Putting the mother at ease is as important as offering accurate breastfeeding information.

Although accurate breastfeeding information is essential when a woman asks for breastfeeding help, she is also looking for reassurance. The breastfeeding counselor must find a way to put the mother at ease and establish a feeling of rapport. She listens carefully to show that she is really interested in helping the mother. She asks questions to help to clarify the situation. She helps the mother identify her feelings to help her focus on what is important to her. She offers information, makes suggestions, and discusses options, helping the mother weigh the pros and cons. She puts her own feelings and experiences in the background and makes the mother the main focus.

Questions about breastfeeding often involve more complex issues and feelings.

Sometimes a mother calls with a specific breastfeeding question and needs straightforward information. But more often, when a mother calls she begins with a simple question that leads to a discussion of more general topics and complex feelings. Breastfeeding is more than just a method of feeding; it is also a way of caring for and comforting a baby. Breastfeeding often becomes an integral part of a mother's relationship with her baby. So when questions about breastfeeding arise, it is not unusual for them to also involve a woman's feelings about being a mother. Clarifying feelings allows the mother to distinguish her own feelings from the attitudes and opinions of those around her and helps her make decisions with which she will be most comfortable. With calls like this, active listening is a useful tool.

USING ACTIVE LISTENING

Active listening differs from social listening.

Active listening is a learned communication skill, an art. When using active listening, the listener puts herself in the background. She rephrases what the talker has said and attempts to put the talker's unspoken feelings into words. This helps the listener better understand the talker and the talker better understand herself. This is not as easy as it may sound, because the natural reaction in ordinary conversations is for the listener to offer her own point of view, so active listening may take some practice. Sometimes active listening is all that is needed to help a mother clarify her feelings and solve the problem herself.

Rephrasing what the mother has said, identifying feelings, and responding without judging are all aspects of active listening.

There are several aspects to active listening.

Rephrasing what the mother has said lets her know she is being heard and understood and encourages her to continue to talk and to share what is on her mind. It also reassures the breastfeeding counselor that she understands the mother correctly. Summary phrases might begin this way:

> *"Let me see if I am following you. You said..."*
> *"You seem to be telling me that..."*
> *"I hear you saying that..."*

Identifying the mother's feelings. By putting a mother's feelings into words, we can help a mother identify her own feelings.

MOTHER: "My baby refuses to nurse and cries all the time."
COUNSELOR: "You sound very *worried* about your baby."
MOTHER: "Yes, I am worried."

The following phrases can be used to reflect a mother's feelings:

> *"You seem to be feeling..."*
> *"You sound..."*

BASIC INFORMATION   BACKGROUND NEEDED

Accepting differences and responding without judging. Every mother has her own life experiences, beliefs, and parenting style. And mothers who call for breastfeeding help may come from a variety of racial, cultural, religious, and economic groups. It is not necessary to agree with the mother or approve of her choices in order to help her. Active listening can be used even if you do not agree with the mother. It is important that each mother feels free to say what she is thinking without fear of being criticized or judged.

For example, if a mother boasts that her three-week-old baby eats three bowls of cereal a day but wonders why her milk supply seems to be decreasing, it might be tempting to say, "You shouldn't be giving him solids at this age." However true this may be, such a remark would probably make the concerned mother feel criticized and guilty. These negative feelings would make her unable or unwilling to hear anything else that is said.

To really help this mother, it is necessary to recognize and reflect the mother's anxiety. When the mother feels empathy and understanding, she will be more open to suggestion. "You're worried that your milk supply seems to be decreasing. The breast needs to be stimulated often by baby's sucking to maintain or increase milk production. You might consider reducing the solids as much as possible so the baby will nurse more and bring your supply back up again." If the mother is at all receptive, that might be the time to give more specific suggestions on what else she can do to reestablish her milk supply.

ASKING QUESTIONS

Questions should be phrased so they are not threatening or critical and so that they elicit specific information.

It is also important to know how to ask questions sensitively and effectively, so that while information is being gathered the mother feels supported rather than threatened or criticized.

The best questions are those that do not require a simple "yes" or "no" answer and do not put words into the mother's mouth. In general, beginning a question with "what" or "how" will elicit more information. These words will encourage a mother to expand upon her answer. For example:

NOT: "Is the baby breastfeeding well?"
INSTEAD: "How do you feel the baby is breastfeeding?"
NOT: "Is the baby sleeping through the night?"
INSTEAD: "How long does the baby sleep at night?"

Once a mother feels at ease, it is easier to discover what the real problem is. Sometimes the first question or situation a mother raises is not really what's on her mind. It may be just a "test balloon" to see what kind of a person she is talking to and whether she can be trusted with what's really bothering her. One way to clarify the mother's situation before jumping in with suggestions is to ask questions that will give specific information. Then, rather than making assumptions about a situation the counselor can find out the specifics.

NEW MOTHER: "My baby isn't getting enough milk!"
COUNSELOR: "What makes you think he isn't getting enough?"
NEW MOTHER: "But I'm nursing him all the time."
COUNSELOR: "Tell me more about your baby's nursing pattern. About how long does he nurse at each breast and about how long does he go between nursings?"

Questions should be paced according to the mother's emotional state.

Some mothers need to be drawn out more slowly or gently guided in the conversation. A warm, sincere manner and tone of voice will help put an anxious mother at ease. If the mother is crying, reassure her it's all right to cry. Talk until she can get more control, using her name frequently. If she has given you some idea of her problem, try to identify and reflect her feelings before giving any practical advice.

Some breastfeeding problems, such as slow weight gain or a baby who is fussy or refuses the breast, require that you ask the mother many questions to help find the cause. When many questions must be asked, it is important to listen attentively, taking notes and asking the questions in a calm, relaxed manner rather than in rapid succession. A calm and relaxed discussion will put the mother at ease. Some of the questions may deal with sensitive areas, especially if the baby is not doing well, so be sure to word them so they are not threatening to the mother.

Emphasize the normal variations among mothers and babies.

Many mothers worry that they may have caused their breastfeeding problem, that it may be all their "fault." To minimize the mother's tendency to blame herself, make sure she understands that breastfeeding is not a by-the-book procedure; it is an intimate relationship with different dynamics from one nursing couple to the next. (A mother almost always notices differences in breastfeeding when she nurses more than one child.) Although there are general breastfeeding principles that are good to know (for example, the more often and effectively the baby nurses, the more milk there will be), there are no hard-and-fast rules.

Let the mother know that individual mothers and babies respond differently to the same things. For example, if the mother has been giving bottles, tell her that some babies are able to breastfeed and take bottles with no problems at all, while other babies become "nipple confused." If the mother of a slow-gaining baby is asked whether she smokes cigarettes, mention that some mothers smoke and breastfeed with no problems, yet other mothers who smoke have babies who gain slowly.

Look for opportunities to praise the mother for what she is doing right.

If breastfeeding is not going well, the mother may feel especially vulnerable to real or perceived criticism. Breastfeeding difficulties often contribute to a new mother's fragile sense of self-esteem. Be aware of the mother's sensitivity to any questions or comments that may cause her to doubt her capability. And be sure to praise her for what she is doing right.

At least once during every conversation, say something positive, such as, "It sounds to me as though you're doing a wonderful job as a mother." This allays the underlying fear behind many of the mother's questions. In addition to providing the mother with the basic information she needs, positive reinforcement can build a mother's self-confidence.

Find out what the mother sees as the problem.

It is essential to know what the mother sees as the problem so that the mother's concerns can be fully addressed. Ask, for example:

"What do you see as the problem?"
"How would you like to see this resolved?"

Even when a problem is identified that the mother has not been aware of, it is best to address the mother's immediate concern first. A mother may also bring up something that you would consider to be a problem but the mother does not. Keep in mind the old saying, "If it's not broken, don't fix it." If the mother is happy with the way things are, don't suggest that there might be a problem, unless there is a reason to be concerned about the mother's or the baby's health.

When a mother raises many concerns at once, active listening can be more effective than questions in determining where to start.

When a mother has many concerns, rather than starting with a series of questions, identifying and reflecting the mother's feelings will usually offer cues on which direction to go.

MOTHER: "I guess I'm just going to give up breastfeeding. My doctor says John is gaining too slowly and that I shouldn't have to nurse him more often than every three hours. My two-year-old got hold of some aspirin while I was nursing John. I'd been up all night trying to rock John so he'd sleep longer than two hours because I knew I had to tell the doctor he was waking all night and nursing more often than every three hours. The doctor would want me to supplement and I'm just not going to do both. I'm just not!"

Rushing in with information and suggestions is a common response to comments like this, but an even better response would be to express empathy and help the mother clarify what her most pressing need is.

COUNSELOR: "You're bewildered. The baby doesn't seem to be doing as well as you had hoped. You are afraid your doctor will tell you to supplement. Your other little one needs attention—the aspirin incident scared you. Now you really wonder what to do."

This statement recognizes the mother's feelings. Notice the feeling words used: "bewildered," "afraid," and "scared." Each area of concern is mentioned, allowing the mother to indicate which area needs attention first.

MOTHER: "You're right. I feel like such a failure. I don't seem to be able to handle anything. The aspirin incident really upset me. I know what to do about that though. I'll just have to keep my two-year-old with me. I know that's what I'll have to do, but I'm so tired. Being responsible for anyone other than the baby seems to be more than I can bear."

COUNSELOR: "When you're as exhausted as you are now, it seems hard to handle everything, but even as tired as you are, you've come up with a very good plan—keeping your two-year-old with you. You would like to be able to handle this, yet you're not sure whether you can keep yourself and the two-year-old intact."

MOTHER: "That's it. I know the only thing to do is to keep him with me, but I've never had two children. How will I ever manage?"

Who would have guessed that the first thing on this mother's priority list would be suggestions on handling two children? The immediate temptation might be to tell her how to fatten up the baby. Notice how the counselor responds empathetically to this mother until she clarifies her priorities. Even if the mother's feelings had been labeled inaccurately ("bewildered," "afraid," "scared"), the mother would clarify these in her response. In this example, the counselor knew she was on the mark when the mother said, "You're right. I feel like such a failure."

The counselor continues with empathy until the mother says, "I need help with handling two kids. What do I do?" This is the sign that the mother is ready for suggestions because she has specifically asked for information.

GIVING INFORMATION AND SUGGESTIONS

Giving information implies trust; giving advice implies a lack of trust.

Giving information is different than giving advice. Giving information is sharing facts. Giving advice, on the other hand, is telling the mother what to do. Advice conveys the unspoken message that the listener cannot be trusted to act responsibly. Advice begins with phrases such as:

"You should..."
"You ought to..."
"Why don't you...?"
"You should have..."
"Why didn't you...?"
"You shouldn't have..."

This approach is almost guaranteed to raise resistance. Even if the mother asks openly for advice, the outcome is rarely positive. If the advice proves to be helpful, the mother may solve her problem but feel incompetent. If the advice is not helpful, she may reject the person giving it.

Giving information, on the other hand, implies trust and faith in the person who is making the decision. By giving information, making suggestions, and presenting options, you are expressing confidence in the mother's ability to decide what is best for her and her family. This conveys trust, which is the basis of successful counseling.

Present information in a positive way.

Fear is not the best learning tool. Rather than presenting information by saying, "Don't do that, because if you do an awful thing will happen." It is far better to present a fact positively by highlighting the good that will result. For example:

NOT: "If you give solids before the baby is about six months old, he has a good chance of developing allergies."
INSTEAD: "Babies who have only mother's milk until about the middle of the first year after birth develop fewer allergies."

Wording suggestions tactfully may be easier if certain phrases are used.

The cardinal rules of making suggestions are: never say "You must..." and never say "Never." The following phrases are positive ways to offer suggestions:

"Would you like to hear what other mothers have done in a similar situation?"
"How would you feel about... ?"
"Many mothers have found... "

These tactful ways of presenting suggestions leave room for the inevitable exceptions that arise. Some feel awkward at first about consciously wording their suggestions this way but find that with practice it soon comes naturally.

When presenting options, encourage the mother to give her honest opinion and respect her acceptance or rejection of any suggestion.

When presenting options, encourage the mother to respond honestly by saying:

"Do you think these alternatives might work for you?"
"Could one of these options be modified to fit your family?"

Sometimes a mother will reject an option. In that case, show respect for the mother's feelings by acknowledging them. In this example, it has already been suggested that the mother breastfeed her slow-gaining baby more often.

MOTHER: "So, you're suggesting not only to nurse more frequently—whenever the baby wants—but to use both breasts. I believe I can manage that, at least during the day. But what will I do about the nighttime? I really do need some sleep."
COUNSELOR: "You feel good about nursing more often during the daytime, but are still concerned about the nighttime. Have you thought about taking the baby to bed with you?"
MOTHER: "You've got to be kidding! I don't think it's good to have a baby in bed with us. Surely you don't think so, do you?" (The mother's tone of voice reveals her strong rejection of the suggestion.)
COUNSELOR: "While this works well for some families, you are not comfortable with it. Have you thought of using an adult bed in the baby's room and going to him the first time he wakes? If you fall asleep while nursing, at least you would be getting some rest."
MOTHER: "That sounds like it would work, and I certainly would welcome the sleep."

In a complicated or stressful situation, it may be most helpful to start with simple suggestions, go slowly, and offer a little information at a time.

When a mother is having many difficulties or is not handling her situation well, it may be necessary to start with some very simple, specific suggestions that are easy for her to carry out. It may be clear that there are some deep, complicated causes for this mother's problems and that it is unlikely she will be able to resolve them all at once, but sometimes small improvements lead to greater ones. For instance, if the mother is totally exhausted, the simple suggestion of napping with the baby may give the mother renewed strength to face other difficulties.

If a mother raises a number of concerns at once, go slowly, so as not to over-load the mother with too much information. Going slowly and offering a little information at a time also allows the mother to absorb it more fully. By giving the mother time to talk and clarify her needs, she will have the opportunity to give more information about the situation that is causing her concern.

RESPECTING DIFFERENCES AMONG MOTHERS

Single Mothers

When offering suggestions and dis-cussing options, keep in mind that some mothers do not have husbands, partners, or family members to help.

It is important to be sensitive to the individual, family, economic, and cultural differences among mothers.

Be sure to ask the mother about her situation before offering suggestions that involve help from others. For example, if a mother calls and complains about feeling exhausted and overwhelmed, before assuming she has a partner who can help her get some rest, ask her, "Is there someone who might be able to help you with the children while you rest?" If she says no, tailor the suggestions to her situation. For example:

- Keep the children in one room, if possible, so that she can watch them while she has a little quiet time.
- Set aside a time each day when she and all the children will lie down, even if they don't sleep.
- Try breastfeeding the baby lying down at least once a day.

Adolescent Mothers

Adolescents are physically capable of breastfeeding.

Between 12 and 18 months after an adolescent girl's first menstrual period, her breast tissue is developed enough to produce sufficient milk for her baby (de Nobrega 1992). Research on the composition of mothers' milk has found only minimal differences between the milk of adolescent mothers and the milk of mothers older than 19 (Lipsman 1985). One study found the adolescent mothers' milk had higher concentrations of protein and found a difference in types of fatty acids that the researchers attributed to differences in the mothers' diet rather than to age (Brasil 1991).

Adolescent mothers have many things in common with other mothers, but they may have some different concerns and outlooks.

Considerations and Concerns of Adolescent Mothers

Emotional Considerations
- Wants to be treated as an adult, not talked down to or lectured;
- May be fearful or unhappy about the physical changes of pregnancy;
- Peer-oriented but also concerned about the reactions of family, teachers, and the baby's father;
- May be insecure, have a poor self-image, doubt her self-worth;
- Lives for the moment; may have difficulty in planning for the future.

Physical Considerations during Pregnancy
- May have had inadequate prenatal care due to early denial of pregnancy;
- Diet may be erratic or inadequate;
- May be reluctant to gain weight.

Birth Considerations
- May feel threatened and overwhelmed by the hospital environment, poli-cies, and procedures, and may be reluctant to ask for help or ask any questions;
- May not be assertive in arranging for immediate or regular contact with her baby after birth;
- May lack confidence in her ability to care for her baby.

Breastfeeding Concerns

- May be strongly swayed by negative feelings about breastfeeding among female family members;
- May be concerned about how breastfeeding will affect her relationships with others;
- May fear, even more than most mothers, being ridiculed if she is seen breastfeeding in public;
- May be concerned about how breastfeeding will affect or restrict her other activities—how to manage the practical details of breastfeeding while going to school and/or work (expression and storage of milk);
- May be concerned about how breastfeeding will affect her physically—if breastfeeding will affect how soon she returns to her pre-pregnancy weight, if breastfeeding will affect the shape and size of her breasts, if she can smoke cigarettes and breastfeed, if she can breastfeed while taking birth-control pills, if the baby will bite her while breastfeeding.
- May be concerned about how her partner feels about breastfeeding.

Emphasize the advantages of breast-feeding for the adolescent mother.

When talking to an adolescent mother, it may be helpful to emphasize the benefits of breastfeeding to her, such as:

- Breastfeeding gives her something she can do for her baby that no one else can. (This may be especially important to her if she is worried that the baby's grandmother or babysitter will usurp her role as the baby's mother.)
- Breastfeeding right after birth causes her uterus to contract and reduces the flow of blood, helping to prevent hemorrhage and get the uterus back into shape more quickly than if she were not nursing.
- Breastfeeding mothers have been found to lose weight faster without restricting calories.
- Breastfeeding encourages a strong emotional bond between baby and mother and may help increase the mother's confidence in her ability to care for her baby.
- Breastfeeding saves money—not only the cost of formula, but also doctor bills and medications, since breastfed babies have fewer illnesses. The mother herself may miss less school and/or work to care for a sick baby if she breastfeeds.

It is important to be sensitive to the adolescent mother's culture, her possible perception of the breast-feeding counselor as an "authority figure," and other considerations.

When working with teen mothers it helps to try to look at the world through their eyes. They may react negatively to breastfeeding education if it seems too much like school or if breastfeeding pamphlets or books feature photos of older mothers or are written at a higher reading level than they can understand. They may be more sensitive than older mothers to having others touch their breasts or of seeing a breastfeeding counselor demonstrate breastfeeding techniques by touching her own breasts. Unless carefully explained ahead of time, follow-up phone calls from the breastfeeding counselor may be perceived as checking up on the teen mother rather than sincere offers of help. Developing an honest, positive, and supportive relationship with adolescent mothers is essential to effective counseling (Podgurski 1995).

Family or Cultural Breastfeeding Practices

Family or cultural breastfeeding practices should not be discouraged unless it could be harmful to mother or baby.

Breastfeeding practices that have been passed down through the mother's family or are part of her culture may carry more weight with her than suggestions from others. If the mother mentions an unfamiliar practice, ask her more about it. If the practice will not affect breastfeeding or harm the mother or baby, do not make disparaging remarks about it or discourage the mother from doing it. If the practice makes the mother feel more comfortable, it will encourage her to breastfeed. For example:

MOTHER: "While I have been engorged, I have been drinking lemongrass tea, because my mother told me that will help."

BASIC INFORMATION   BACKGROUND NEEDED

COUNSELOR: "There are some other suggestions I can give you for engorgement that have been helpful for other mothers .... "

If, however, the practice could affect breastfeeding or the mother's or baby's health, help the mother to understand why the practice could be harmful.

Cultural Differences

Cultural practices concerning childbirth, breastfeeding, and the postpartum period should be respected.

If the mother is from a different culture, be sensitive to the beliefs and customs of her culture. Each culture has its own outlook on health, medicine, and sexuality, and many cultures recommend specific practices during pregnancy and the postpartum period that the mother may want to follow. For example, a common practice for American Hispanic women is to stay in bed for three days after birth and to avoid eating pork, chili, and tomatoes. Hispanic women are also cautioned to avoid extremes in temperature when they are breastfeeding, because it is believed that cold decreases milk flow and extreme heat makes the milk curdle. So during the coldest days of winter and the hottest days of summer, the mother may be reluctant to go out. In a traditional Hispanic family, the baby may not be breastfed until the third day because the colostrum is considered "unclean." Hispanic women may also be reluctant to breastfeed in the hospital out of modesty (Taylor 1985).

Rather than openly rejecting a mother's custom or belief, take some time to talk to her about it so that it can be considered and respected when offering suggestions. For example, it would be unnecessary to suggest that the Hispanic mother eat pork, chili, and tomatoes. But it may be helpful to talk to her about the value of colostrum and point out that other mothers nowadays nurse their babies right after birth. Suggest reading on the subject for her consideration. It would also be appropriate to offer suggestions on ways to breastfeed modestly in the hospital, such as having the nurse pull the curtain around her bed when she is ready to nurse so that those passing by her room could not see her breastfeeding.

To learn more about cultural beliefs and customs regarding health care, family attitudes, pregnancy, and the postpartum period in various United States' populations, see Meredith Mann Taylor's "Transcultural Aspects of Breastfeeding—USA" (referenced at the end of this section).

Economic Differences

When giving suggestions, offer options that do not involve spending money.

Women breastfeed without any special equipment or paraphernalia in many cultures and in many parts of the world. Some families have tight budgets, and spending extra money may not be practical. If money is limited, suggestions that cost money may be perceived as barriers to breastfeeding. Encourage the mother in her efforts to find low-cost alternatives, and be sensitive to the options she may have. For example:

MOTHER: "I will be returning to work six hours a day three days a week when my baby is three months old, and I'd like some information on working and breastfeeding. My baby will be at a sitter's house, and I will be away from him for seven hours at a time."

COUNSELOR: "You're baby is so lucky you want to continue to give him the benefit of your milk! Many women combine working and breastfeeding. One aspect you'll need to think about is how you will express your milk while you're away from your baby. There are many different methods; some women buy a pump, but others prefer hand-expression. Do you have a preference?"

Differences in Parenting Styles

Some differences in parenting style affect breastfeeding; others do not.

Many mothers are comfortable breastfeeding their baby on cue and allowing the baby to determine the length of the feedings, which is ideal for breastfeeding to go well, but some mothers are not, preferring instead to impose a feeding schedule. Some mothers keep their babies close at night to help get their rest, and willingly continue night nursings through their child's toddler years. Other mothers are firmly committed to having their babies and toddlers sleep in separate rooms and eliminating night nursings as early as possible.

Some differences in parenting style affect breastfeeding and some do not. And the same variation may affect one baby adversely yet have no effect at all on another. If the mother prefers to impose a feeding schedule, for example, she will need to know that this may affect her milk supply, because her milk is regulated by how often and how effectively her baby sucks. She will also need to know that the fat content of the milk increases as the feeding progresses and that if she cuts feedings too short, her baby may not get as much of the fatty hindmilk as he needs and his weight gain may slow down. And she should know that keeping track of her baby's wet diapers, bowel movements, and weight gain will be a good indication of whether or not he is getting enough to eat. Because of individual differences in mothers and babies, a feeding schedule may work well for some but cause problems for others. If the baby's weight gain slows, the mother then has the option of either breastfeeding more often or introducing a supplement.

If strong feelings about the mother's parenting style make it impossible to give her effective breastfeeding help, it may be best to refer her to another breastfeeding counselor.

Some breastfeeding counselors find it difficult to remain objective when they strongly disagree with a mother's choices. When feelings run high, it may help to keep in mind that your primary purpose is to act as a sounding board for the mother. To effectively fulfill this purpose, personal opinions, feelings, and experiences need to be kept in the background, keeping the mother as the main focus. The counselor's job is to help the mother clarify her own feelings and to offer information and options that will help her make an informed choice.

Because a mother's relationship with her baby is of paramount importance, she should be encouraged to make parenting choices with which she feels comfortable. The main message should be how important each mother is to her baby and how breastfeeding can be a wonderful part of this. Each mother should also be left with a feeling of acceptance and a sense of trust in her own judgment. Perhaps, most important of all, the mother's feeling of self-confidence and trust in her own instincts should be enhanced. If the breastfeeding counselor's feelings of disagreement with the mother are so strong that she cannot do this, it may be best to refer her to another breastfeeding counselor.

HELPING THE MOTHER WORK WITH HER DOCTOR

When Suggestions Differ from the Doctor's Advice

If a suggestion differs from the doctor's advice and the baby is healthy, ask the mother if she would like to try the suggestion for a short while before sharing it with her doctor.

If the baby has a health problem or if the mother is reluctant to go against her doctor's advice, suggest she call the doctor and discuss the suggestion before she tries it.

Sometimes a counselor's suggestions may differ from those of a mother's doctor. For example, a doctor may tell a mother not to nurse her slow-gaining baby more often than every three hours. If the baby is healthy and the mother seems comfortable with the idea of nursing more often, suggest she try it for a week or so, or until the next visit to the doctor, and see if the baby's weight gain improves. If she decides to do this, she should be encouraged to tell the doctor that the improved weight gain was the result of more frequent nursing. This way the doctor will learn more about breastfeeding in a positive way.

If the baby has a health problem, encourage the mother to stay in close touch with the doctor, discussing the suggestions you have given her. The doctor may want to monitor the baby's progress while the mother tries new breastfeeding management techniques. For example, if the baby is gaining weight slowly, suggest the mother offer to bring the baby to the doctor's office for regular weight checks every week or two until the doctor is satisfied with the baby's progress. Be sure the mother knows the background that supports your suggestions so she can discuss them with the doctor.

BASIC INFORMATION

BACKGROUND NEEDED

Encourage the mother to be honest with her doctor about what she is doing, as the doctor cannot treat a patient with incomplete information.

When mother and doctor disagree, it is important to keep the channels of communication open and try to separate feelings from facts. Encourage openness and honesty between the mother and her doctor. The health and well-being of the baby are the goals of both mother and doctor. The doctor cannot treat a patient with incomplete or incorrect information. When a mother does not tell her doctor what she is doing, she risks incurring the physician's anger, feeling guilty for disregarding his or her advice, and losing some self-respect by not being honest. Remind her that the doctor needs to know what she is doing since they are working as a team in safeguarding the health of the baby. If the mother feels pressured to hide things from her baby's doctor, suggest instead she seek another medical opinion.

Help the Mother Express Her Feelings and Goals

Suggest the mother express her feelings and preferences to her doctor and, if there is a conflict, offer communication tools she can use to work more productively with her doctor.

It will help the mother to communicate with her doctor if she expresses her feelings and goals. She might say something like, "I want to do everything I can to continue breastfeeding." This may make the doctor more willing to consider different approaches.

Most people, but especially a pregnant woman or new mother, find it very stressful to be in conflict with a doctor. If the doctor advises a treatment that the mother is uncomfortable with, give her the communication tools she needs to come to some agreement with her doctor. The basic tools are tact, honesty, respect, knowledge, and patience.

Suggest the mother think through her approach before she speaks to the doctor. There are many ways she can make her encounter with the doctor more positive. The mother can:

Practice her responses before she talks to the doctor. Offer to take some time to discuss the mother's concerns and to practice with her so she can express them aloud before she talks to the doctor.

Ask the doctor for a complete explanation of the treatment. If the mother is unsure of the reasons for the doctor's recommendations, encourage her to ask him or her to take the time to explain them to her thoroughly. In evaluating the doctor's advice, it may help to ask, "Is this your general policy with regard to my baby's condition or is this specific to my baby?"

Repeat the doctor's statements in her own words. By paraphrasing what the doctor says, the mother can avoid confusion and show the doctor what impact his or her words are having on her.

Share her feelings with the doctor. It is best if a mother has been clear about her feelings from the beginning, but if not, it is never too late to start. A doctor cannot know what an individual mother's preferences and priorities are unless she expresses them. The mother might tell the doctor, for example, "Our family has a history of allergies and I feel strongly about exclusive breastfeeding. Are there treatment options that allow for continued breastfeeding without giving formula?"

Project self-confidence. Writing down questions and concerns in advance may be helpful, as well as being friendly and willing to consider alternatives.

Make statements in a positive way. Another way to foster a friendly atmosphere is to make positive statements, for example, "I would like to try encouraging my baby to breastfeed more often before offering supplements," rather than "I don't want to give my baby supplements."

Try the "broken record" technique. When disagreements arise, the "broken record" technique can be an effective way of getting a message across. The mother simply restates her basic position, calmly and quietly at each opportunity. "I appreciate your concern about her health, but now that she's breastfeeding well, I'd like to monitor her weight for another week before considering other options."

Use tact, give respect, and expect them in return. If a mother feels that her doctor is being judgmental or overly critical, it may be helpful to recognize his or her concern for her baby (for example, "I understand your concern for my baby's health and well-being") but still calmly insist that the doctor offer current medical information to back up opinions. Most physicians are not inflexible and would be willing to meet a mother halfway.

Keep in mind that the ultimate responsibility for the baby's health lies with the parents. Although the doctor is the medical expert, the parents are the ones who are ultimately responsible for the decisions made about their baby. A mother can shift a discussion to emphasize parental responsibility by saying, "You'd like my permission to... ?" or "Your recommendation is...."

If not satisfied, seek a second medical opinion. After discussing her feelings and possible approaches with her baby's doctor, if a mother feels that the doctor is not as supportive of breastfeeding or her feelings as she would like, it is almost always possible to get a second medical opinion.

How to Help in a Medical Situation

When asked about a medical situation, begin by using active listening and asking questions about the doctor's recommendations and the mother's feelings.

When a mother asks about a medical situation that affects breastfeeding, first determine what the problem is, what the doctor has advised, and how the mother feels about what the doctor has said. Answering the following questions may help a mother focus on how she feels about the doctor's recommendations, which is a necessary first step in communicating her feelings to her doctor.

"What did the doctor say?"
"Why do you think the doctor said that?"
"How do you feel about those suggestions?"
"What do you want to do?"

Other ways to help the mother are to give information, not advice, discuss how other mothers have handled the situation, and share written resources.

Other ways to help the mother in a medical situation are:

- quoting accurately and objectively from written resources;
- sharing stories of mothers who have encountered similar situations;
- offering current information pertaining to breastfeeding and her medical situation.

For lay breastfeeding counselors, it is especially important to know the difference between sharing information and giving medical advice.

If the doctor's advice seems questionable, offer the mother help in coming to an agreement with her doctor by using communication skills and by sharing references.

If the doctor recommends a treatment for a health problem that will negatively affect breastfeeding or has been invalidated by research, offer to share references with the mother that she can give to her doctor. Also, keep in mind:

- In a complex medical situation, the mother may not have explained or completely understood everything about her or her baby's condition. First impressions may not be accurate, and there may be more to the situation than is apparent.
- Openly disagreeing with the doctor's advice will not help the mother. In fact, it may confuse her even more. What she needs is help in coming to some agreement with her own or her baby's doctor.

In addition to discussing ways to communicate with her doctor as described in the previous section, the safest approach is to offer to share references with her that she can give to the doctor. For example, if the baby's doctor suggests a course of action that is not backed by current research, say to the mother: "Some doctors do take that approach, but research has shown..." and then ask the mother if she would like a reference to give her doctor.

WHEN BREASTFEEDING DOESN'T WORK OUT

When a mother weans prematurely, it may help to have supportive responses ready.

There will be times when a mother decides not to follow or accept any of your suggestions. A mother may decide to stop breastfeeding before she had planned to. Or the mother may not want to wean but circumstances lead her to believe that she must. Any of these can be disappointing, but it is not helpful to second-guess a mother's decisions. The breastfeeding counselor's job is to help the mother sort out her feelings and suggest possible options, letting the mother make up her own mind. The decisions of whether to breastfeed or not, and how long to breastfeed, are the responsibility of the mother and the baby's father, with input from their health-care professional.

For those times when a mother decides to stop breastfeeding prematurely, it may be helpful to have supportive responses ready. For example:

"That must have been a difficult decision."
"I'm so glad you're enjoying your baby."
"You sound happier, relieved, calmer...."
"If I can be of further help, or if you want more information, please call."

There are still several things you can do for the mother:

1. Affirm the value of breastfeeding for whatever length of time she nursed her baby. Even one nursing at the breast is of value.
2. Acknowledge any grief she's feeling.
3. Let the mother know that maintaining her close relationship with her baby is most important—and express confidence in her ability to continue to give her baby her best.
4. Be tactful. Avoid saying anything that might make the mother feel guilty for "failing." Keep the relationship positive.

Lasting Impressions

When the counseling relationship ends, your last contact with the mother provides one more opportunity to reinforce the mother's sense of competence and self-confidence.

It may be tempting to gauge how well you have done your job by how well breastfeeding has progressed and the decisions the mother has made, but a mother's choices are not an accurate reflection of the quality of help she has received. Each situation is influenced by many individual variables. For example, the mother's health, family situation, desire to breastfeed, support, access to resources, nutrition, and knowledge all affect the progress of breastfeeding. Other important considerations include the baby's health, gestational age, temperament, physical anomalies, and nursing style.

So, how can a breastfeeding counselor know if she has done her job? Even if the mother stops breastfeeding before she had planned to, the best measure of success is how the mother feels about herself and about the breastfeeding relationship. Does she perceive that her feelings were respected? Did you help her feel good about being a mother and meeting her baby's needs in the way that seemed most appropriate to her?

Although one of your goals as a breastfeeding counselor is to provide reliable breastfeeding information, your main message to each mother should be how important she is to her baby and how breastfeeding can be a wonderful part of this. Each mother should be left with a feeling of acceptance. Perhaps, most important of all, each mother should be left with a feeling of self-confidence and trust in her own instincts.

References

Brasil, A. et al. Fat and protein composition of mature milk in adolescents. *J Adolesc Hlth* 1991; 12(5):365-71.

de Nobrega, F. Composition of milk in adolescents. *J Adolesc Hlth* 1992; 13:261.

Illinois Department of Public Health. *Lactation Counselor's Manual.* Springfield, Illinois, 1989.

Lipsman, S. et. al. Breast-feeding among teenage mothers: milk composition, infant growth, and maternal dietary intake. *J Ped Gastro Nutr* 1985; 4:426-34.

Mohrbacher, N. and Torgus, J. eds. THE NEW LEADER'S HANDBOOK. Schaumburg, Illinois: La Leche League International, 1989.

Podgurski, M. Supporting the breastfeeding teen. *J Perinat Ed* 1995; 4(2):11-14.

Riordan, J. and Auerbach, K. *Breastfeeding and Human Lactation*. Boston and London: Jones and Bartlett, 1993, pp. 63-64, 350.

Taylor, M. *Transcultural Aspects of Breastfeeding—U.S.A.* La Leche League International's Lactation Consultant Series. Unit 2. Wayne, New Jersey: Avery Publishing, 1985.

2

The Breast and How It Works

BREAST ANATOMY

HORMONAL INFLUENCES

The breast—or mammary gland—is a complex and efficient organ. Development of the breast begins before birth during the early weeks of gestation, but the mammary gland doesn't become fully functional until the onset of lactation. The breast continues to change under the influence of normal physical processes—such as menstrual cycles, pregnancies, birth, and weaning—through menopause, when the gland begins to atrophy. Knowledge of breast anatomy and function will be helpful in understanding how normal bodily functions and environmental influences affect breastfeeding.

BREAST ANATOMY

Composition of the breast

The breast is a secretory gland composed of the following parts:

- **glandular tissue**, which makes and transports milk,
- **connective tissue**, which supports the breast,
- **blood**, which nourishes breast tissue and provides the nutrients needed to make milk,
- **lymph**, which removes waste,
- **nerves**, which make the breast sensitive to touch and allow the baby's suck to stimulate the release of hormones that trigger the let-down, or milk-ejection, reflex and the production of milk,
- **adipose (fatty) tissue**, which offers protection from injury.

The size of the breasts is determined to a great extent by the amount of fatty tissue present, which has no effect on milk production or the quality of the milk produced.

The enlargement of the breasts during pregnancy and lactation indicates that the mammary gland is becoming functional.

Alveoli

Alveoli are grape-like clusters of glandular tissue in which milk is synthesized from blood.

Alveoli cells secrete milk. They are surrounded by a network of band-like myoepithelial cells, which cause the alveoli to contract when stimulated by the oxytocin released during the let-down, or milk-ejection, reflex. This action expels the milk into the ductules and down into the ducts.

Ductules and lactiferous (mammary) ducts

Ductules are branch-like tubules extending from clusters of alveoli.

Each ductule empties into larger ducts called lactiferous or mammary ducts.

Milk or lactiferous sinuses

The lactiferous ducts widen underneath the nipple and areola to become lactiferous sinuses, where milk collects.

The baby's gums need to be well behind the end of the nipple in order for the lactiferous sinuses to be properly compressed and emptied.

Lobes and lobules

Each mammary gland forms a lobe of the breast, which consists of a single major branch of alveoli, milk ducts, and one lactiferous sinus that narrows to an opening in the nipple (nipple pore). There are fifteen to twenty-five lobes in a breast, and each lobe consists of twenty to forty lobules (a smaller milk duct with its supporting alveoli). Each lobule consists of ten to 100 supporting alveoli.

Nipple tissue

After widening into a lactiferous sinus, the duct narrows again and leads to the nipple opening or pore, although some ducts may merge near the tip of the nipple.

The nipple protrudes and becomes firmer with stimulation. It is flexible and graspable so it will conform to the baby's palate, tongue, and gums during breastfeeding.

BASIC INFORMATION   BACKGROUND NEEDED

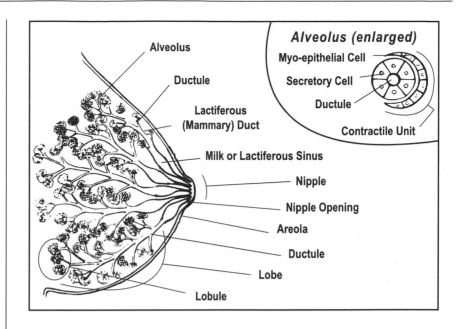

Areola

The nipple protrudes from the center of the darker pigmented area of the breast called the areola.

Since the baby's sight is not fully developed at birth, it is thought that the darkened area may serve as a target to help the baby locate the center of the breast.

Montgomery glands

The areola is also the site of the Montgomery glands—small oil-producing glands that provide lubrication and alter the pH of the skin, thus discouraging the growth of bacteria on the skin of the nipple and areola (Williams 1992).

Montgomery glands enlarge during pregnancy and have a pimply appearance.

Washing the nipples with soap is unnecessary and removes the beneficial oils that are secreted by the Montgomery glands. It may cause drying and cracking, making the nipple and areola more prone to soreness.

Daily rinsing with warm water while bathing is sufficient to keep the nipples clean and preserve the lubricating and anti-bacterial properties of the oil secreted by the glands.

HORMONAL INFLUENCES

Estrogen

The increase in estrogen during pregnancy stimulates the ductule system to grow and become specific. Estrogen levels drop at delivery and remain low for the first several months of breastfeeding.

Progesterone

The increase in progesterone during pregnancy influences the increase in size of alveoli and lobes.

Prolactin

The increase in prolactin and other hormones contributes to the accelerated growth of the breast tissue during pregnancy (Rillema 1994).

Prolactin levels rise with nipple stimulation during feedings.

The pattern of pressure and release caused by the baby's mouth on the mother's areola stimulates the nerve pathways from the nipple to the brain to release prolactin into her bloodstream.

Alveolar cells make milk in response to the release of prolactin when the baby sucks at the breast.

The use of nipple shields, a baby with a weak suck, or improper positioning can alter prolactin levels and hamper the mother's milk supply (Woolridge 1980). Frequent feedings and effective sucking enhance the production of milk.

Prolactin has been referred to as the "mothering" hormone. Together with oxytocin, it may be responsible in part for the intense feeling of needing to be with the baby that many mothers experience.

Oxytocin

Oxytocin contracts the smooth muscle of the uterus during childbirth, after birth, and during orgasm.

After birth, oxytocin contracts the smooth muscle layer of band-like cells surrounding the alveoli to squeeze the newly produced milk into the duct system.

Oxytocin is necessary for a let-down, or milk-ejection, reflex to occur.

Let-down, or milk-ejection, reflex

The let-down, or milk-ejection, reflex is responsible for making the milk available to the baby, particularly the fatty hindmilk. The baby needs this richer, creamier hindmilk for adequate weight gain.

When the baby sucks effectively at the breast, it stimulates the nerve endings in the nipple and areola, sending signals to the mother's pituitary gland by way of her hypothalamus and initiating the secretion of prolactin and oxytocin into the bloodstream. Oxytocin quickly stimulates the band-like myoepithelial cells surrounding the alveoli to contract, squeezing milk into the ducts. The let-down may also occur without the stimulation of the baby's suck (Cobo 1993). Prolactin stimulates the alveoli to produce more milk.

For signs of a healthy let-down, or milk-ejection, reflex and ways to encourage a delayed or inhibited let-down, see "The Let-Down, or Milk-Ejection, Reflex" in the chapter "Breastfeeding Basics."

Publications for Parents

La Leche League International. THE WOMANLY ART OF BREASTFEEDING, 35th Anniversary ed., Schaumburg, Illinois, 1991, pp. 357-60.

References

Cobo, E. Characteristics of the spontaneous milk ejecting activity occurring during human lactation. *J Perinat Med* 1993; 21:77-85.

Lawrence, R. *Breastfeeding: A Guide for the Medical Profession,* 4th ed. St. Louis: Mosby, pp. 59-89.

Rillema, J. Development of the mammary gland and lactation. *Trends Endrocrinol Metab* 1994; 5(4):149-54.

Riordan, J. and Auerbach, K. *Breastfeeding and Human Lactation*. Boston and London: Jones and Bartlett, 1993, pp. 81-103.

Williams, J. Anatomy and physiology of breastfeeding: assessment of the mother. Presented at the International Lactation Consultant Association Conference, Chicago, Illinois, July 1992.

Woolridge, M. et al. Effect of a traditional and a new nipple shield on sucking patterns and milk flow. *Early Human Dev* 1980; 4:357-62.

3

Breastfeeding Basics

NORMAL BREASTFEEDING PATTERNS
    In the Early Days

DURING THE EARLY MONTHS
    Concerns about Milk Supply
    After the Baby Starts Solids
    The Breastfeeding Toddler
    Breastfeeding and Infant Sleep Patterns

THE LET-DOWN, OR MILK-EJECTION, REFLEX
    Signs of a Healthy Let-Down
    Delayed or Inhibited Let-Down

COMMON QUESTIONS
    Pacifier (Dummy) Use
    Leaking Milk
    Spitting Up
    Crying and Colic

NORMAL BREASTFEEDING PATTERNS

Answers to questions about breast-feeding patterns are rarely simple and straightforward.

There is a wide variation in what's normal. This is as true of breastfeeding patterns as it is of other areas of child development and growth. Two different—yet perfectly normal and healthy—children may walk, talk, and get their first tooth at different ages. Their nursing patterns may differ, too. One baby may breastfeed every hour while another baby may breastfeed only every four hours and both may thrive. Individual differences and variations must be taken into account when discussing breastfeeding, which is why breastfeeding is an art and not a science.

Many new mothers, however, expect simple and straightforward answers to questions such as: "How often and long does my baby need to breastfeed?" or "When will my baby stop waking at night to nurse?" When a mother asks a general question like this, the most honest response will be, "It depends on your baby." This is because cut-and-dried answers do not take into account individual differences.

Encourage the mother to look to her baby for the answers to these kinds of questions. No one can tell a mother with certainty exactly how often or long her baby will need to nurse or at what age he will "sleep through the night." Babies' nursing patterns vary, and a pattern that is right for one baby may not be right for another. Also, an individual baby's nursing pattern may vary as he grows. Assure the mother that a healthy baby with a good suck will naturally fall into the nursing pattern that is best suited for him. If she is worried about her milk supply, see the later section "Concerns about Milk Supply." Also assure her that by responding to her baby's cues she can be confident that she is doing the best for her baby.

In the Early Days

During the first few days after birth, many babies want to breastfeed often and long—sometimes for an hour or more at a time—until the mother's milk supply becomes more plentiful.

It is normal for a baby to want to breastfeed long and often in the early days. When breastfeeding is unrestricted during the first few days after birth many mothers report that their babies nurse for a couple of hours at a time then sleep for a couple of hours and repeat this pattern until the mother's milk becomes more plentiful (Frantz 1983). Another common pattern is more frequent breastfeeding for shorter periods of time. Occasionally a baby may be uninterested in nursing or very sleepy in the first few days. In this case, suggest the mother encourage her baby to breastfeed at least eight to twelve times per day by trying to rouse the baby when he's in a light sleep cycle. (Look for rapid eye movements under closed eyelids, arm or leg movements, lip movements, and changes in facial expression.) See "How to Rouse a Sleepy Baby" in the chapter "Positioning, Latch-On, and the Baby's Suck."

The colostrum, the yellow or golden first milk the baby receives in his first few days of life, has high concentrations of nutrients and immunities, but it is small in quantity (teaspoons, not ounces). Not feeling full encourages the baby to nurse frequently, which assures that the baby gets the colostrum he needs. Frequent nursing helps to establish a good milk supply early on, as well as providing a variety of health benefits.

The length and difficulty of labor and delivery, the use of medications during labor and delivery, and separation of mother and baby after birth have been found to affect a baby's interest and ability to nurse in the early days.

A mother's labor and delivery may affect breastfeeding at first. For example, a cesarean birth or a difficult labor may make the baby sleepy for several days or may affect the baby's suck.

Recent studies indicate that pain relievers and anesthesia used during labor and delivery may contribute to breastfeeding problems by causing baby's suck and overall coordination to become disorganized and may also delay the first nursing. Sepkoski (1992) found that babies whose mothers received epidurals were less alert, less able to orient themselves, and had less organized movements than babies whose mothers gave birth without medication and that these differences were measurable during the babies' entire first month. Righard and Alade

(1990) concluded that sucking problems were more common among babies whose mothers received pethidine (also known as meperidine or Demerol) during labor than among babies whose births were unmedicated. Nissen (1995) later replicated this finding and concluded that infants whose mothers received pethidine had delayed and depressed sucking and rooting. Crowell (1994) observed that the first effective breastfeeding was delayed an average of more than eleven hours among mothers who received butorphanol or nalbuphine during labor when compared with mothers who received no labor analgesia.

Righard and Alade (1990) found that in addition to the effects of labor medication, separating mother and baby before the first nursing also resulted in sucking problems when mother and baby were reunited to nurse, even though the separation was only about twenty minutes long. Of the babies who had unmedicated births with no separation from mother, 16 out of 17 breastfed well. Of the babies who had unmedicated births and were taken from mother for about twenty minutes for weighing and measuring, only seven out of 15 babies breastfed well. Of the babies who had medicated births and were briefly separated from mother, none of the 19 babies breastfed well at the first nursing. Other studies have correlated early separation with shorter overall duration of breastfeeding (Wimmer-Puchinger and Nagel 1982; deChateau and Wiberg 1977).

Frequent and unrestricted breastfeeding in the early days offers health benefits for both mother and baby.

If the mother and baby are positioned well and the baby is latched on well and sucking effectively, frequent and unrestricted breastfeeding does not cause sore nipples (deCarvalho 1984). It does, however, offer the following advantages for both mother and baby.

Provides the baby with the colostrum he needs. Although colostrum is small in quantity, it is rich in nutrients and immunities. A baby receives most of his immunities to illness while in utero, but a significant portion comes from his mother's colostrum.

Prevents painful engorgement in the mother. When breastfeeding is unrestricted, mothers are less likely to become painfully engorged. While it is normal for the breasts to enlarge, one study found that the more minutes the newborns spent nursing during their first 48 hours the less painful breast engorgement was reported by their mothers (Moon and Humenick 1989).

Stimulates uterine contractions in the mother and lessens the chances of hemorrhage. After birth, the newborn's immediate nursing hastens the delivery of the placenta. The mother will have less blood loss because the baby's sucking causes the uterus to contract (Chua 1994).

Prevents newborn jaundice. Research comparing groups of babies breastfed at varying intervals has confirmed that those fed more frequently have lower bilirubin levels. In one study (deCarvalho 1982), babies who breastfed at least eight times a day had bilirubin levels three mg/dl lower than babies who breastfed less frequently. This is because the colostrum has a laxative effect, stimulating the baby's bowels to expel his bilirubin-rich stool before the bilirubin is reabsorbed by his body.

Gives the baby practice at nursing before his mother's breasts become full. Giving the baby lots of time at the breast in the first few days allows him to learn to breastfeed effectively before his mother's breasts become fuller as her milk supply becomes more plentiful, usually on the third or fourth day after birth. This is especially important for the mother with flat or inverted nipples.

Stimulates the mother's milk to increase more quickly. One study that followed two groups of newborns from birth found that on their third day of life the milk intake of the babies who nursed six or fewer times per day was only about 54% of that of the babies who nursed seven to eleven times per day. The babies who nursed more frequently also lost less weight initially and began regaining their birth weight more quickly. The difference in intake continued to be significant through the fifth day of life, when the group nursing less frequently consumed

83% of the milk consumed by the more frequently nursing group (Yamauchi and Yamanouchi 1990).

If a baby is sleepy or uninterested in nursing during his first few days, suggest the mother encourage him to breastfeed often.

Some babies are sleepy or uninterested in nursing during their first few days, especially if they are small, labor and delivery were difficult, or their mothers received certain medications during labor and delivery.

To ensure that the baby receives the nutrition he needs and to help prevent or minimize maternal engorgement, suggest the mother encourage her sleepy baby to breastfeed at least eight to twelve times every twenty-four hours. Rather than trying to rouse the baby when he is in deep sleep, she should wait until she notices cues that he is in a light sleep cycle, such as eyes moving under eyelids, movement of lips or arms and legs. See "How to Rouse a Sleepy Baby" in the chapter "Positioning, Latch-On, and the Baby's Suck."

One or two wet diapers a day are normal for the exclusively breastfeeding baby during the first two days after birth.

During a newborn's first day or two (while the mother is producing colostrum alone), he will wet only one or two diapers per day. When his mother's milk becomes more plentiful (or "comes in"), the baby's output will gradually increase (over the next day or two) to six to eight wet cloth diapers or five to six disposables and two to five bowel movements every 24 hours.

The baby's first bowel movement, meconium, is dark and tarry.

In the first few days after birth, the baby's dark, tarry stools are called meconium. This is the stool that the baby has been storing since before birth. Colostrum is a natural laxative and is important in helping the infant pass this first stool. Within twenty-four to forty-eight hours of the mother's milk becoming more plentiful, the baby's stools will change in color and consistency.

Weight loss is considered normal during the first three to four days.

Whether breastfed or artificially fed, newborns tend to lose weight during the first three to four days after birth. This is due to the shedding of excess fluids in the baby's tissues at birth and the passage of meconium (the first stool).

A weight loss of 5% to 7% is normal. One study found that when mothers received regular breastfeeding guidance and support, very few babies lost more than 7% of their birth weight (DeMarzo 1991). While a weight loss of 10% is considered acceptable, it may be a sign that breastfeeding is not going smoothly and that the mother needs additional help.

Birth weight should be regained by two to three weeks of age.

Routine supplements during the early days are unnecessary, can interfere with breastfeeding, and can contribute to health problems in mother and baby.

When breastfeeding is going well, water or formula supplements are not needed (Nylander 1991). Early supplements are not only unnecessary, but they can also contribute to health problems in mother and baby and interfere with breastfeeding in the following ways.

Supplements fill up the baby, making him less interested in breastfeeding, and water supplements contribute to weight loss. A baby who fills up on water is not getting the calories he needs. Water and glucose solutions interfere with breastfeeding, and babies who receive these tend to lose more weight than babies who are exclusively breastfeeding (Kurinij and Shiono 1991; Glover and Sandilands 1990; Houston 1984).

Water supplements contribute to newborn jaundice. Studies indicate that the more water a baby receives in the early days, the higher his bilirubin levels (Kuhr and Paneth 1982; Nicoll 1982). The baby's first stool (called "meconium") is rich in bilirubin. Colostrum has a laxative effect, helping babies to pass this meconium more quickly, thereby keeping bilirubin levels down. Water supplements, on the other hand, do not stimulate bowel movements, causing the bilirubin to be reabsorbed into the baby's system and contributing to newborn jaundice.

Formula supplements in the newborn period can sensitize some babies to milk allergy or intolerance. Babies who receive formula in the newborn period are at greater risk of becoming sensitized to cow's milk and going on to develop cow's milk allergy or intolerance during their first year (Host 1988).

When given with an artificial nipple, supplements can cause breastfeeding problems, weakening a baby's suck or causing baby to refuse the breast. Many breastfeeding experts have observed that a newborn may become confused when switched back and forth from bottle to breast in the early weeks (Neifert 1995). This may be because his tongue, jaw, and mouth move differently during breastfeeding than while using a bottle, pacifier (dummy), and most types of nipple shield (Newman 1990). One study found that 30% of mothers whose babies received bottles in the hospital reported severe breastfeeding problems, as compared with 14% of those whose babies did not (Cronenwett 1992).

Kittie Frantz, retired LLL Leader, pediatric nurse practitioner, and instructor for the UCLA Lactation Educator and Consultant Courses, estimates that 95% of babies will become confused if given artificial nipples during the first three to four weeks after birth. For some babies it may take a week of bottles before they become nipple confused; for other babies, only one or two bottles—or other artificial nipples—will cause it. Once a baby has been breastfeeding well for three to four weeks, nipple confusion is less likely to develop, so if a mother plans to give her baby bottles, suggest she wait until after her baby's first month to introduce them.

Supplements contribute to engorgement, because they decrease the amount of time baby spends breastfeeding. More time spent nursing has been associated with decreased engorgement (Moon and Humenick 1989).

Supplements interfere with the establishment of a mother's milk supply. Milk production is dependent upon how often, long, and effectively the baby nurses. If the baby is supplemented, he will go longer between nursings and take less milk at the breast, possibly developing a less effective sucking pattern and delaying the increase in his mother's milk supply.

Early supplementation is strongly correlated with a shorter duration of breastfeeding, which may be caused by the factors listed above as well as by the unspoken, incorrect message the mother receives when her baby is supplemented—that her milk is not enough for her baby. This may lead her to continue supplementing after the early days (Kurinij and Shiono 1991).

Many of the reasons given for supplementary bottles are not valid.

Glucose, plain water, or formula supplements are unnecessary. These are sometimes offered to babies for a variety of reasons.

To detect a possible T-E fistula. The possibility of tracheoesophageal fistula (an abnormal hole between the windpipe and the esophagus) is sometimes given as a reason for postponing the first breastfeeding. Plain or glucose water may be given routinely in some hospitals before putting the baby to the breast. However, the mother can ask her doctor to check for this in other ways. The incidence of T-E fistula in newborns is about 1 in 4,000.

To prevent or "flush out" jaundice. Research has refuted the validity of this belief, demonstrating that water supplements do not reduce bilirubin levels (Kuhr and Paneth 1982) and can actually increase them (Nicoll 1982). See "Avoid Water Supplements" in the chapter "Newborn Jaundice."

To prevent dehydration in the sleepy or uninterested baby. Stimulating a sleepy newborn to nurse frequently is the preferred approach, due to the disadvantages of supplements listed above (See "How to Rouse a Sleepy Baby" in the chapter "Positioning, Latch-On, and the Baby's Suck.") Because babies are born with excess fluids in their tissues at birth, dehydration is rarely an issue in the first few days. However, if the mother has concerns about it, she may appreciate knowing the symptoms of dehydration so she can be certain that her baby is not at risk:

- listlessness,
- lethargy,
- skin losing its resiliency (when pinched, it stays pinched looking),
- dry mouth, dry eyes,
- weak cry,
- minimal urine output (one to two wet diapers is normal during the first two days, after that fewer than three wet diapers would be a danger sign), and
- fever.

To treat or prevent hypoglycemia. Hypoglycemia, or low blood sugar, is usually due to delayed or inadequate feedings. In most cases, frequent nursing (or feedings of human milk) is all that is needed. Unless a blood test indicates that a baby's blood-sugar level is below normal, supplements should not be considered. See "Neonatal Hypoglycemia" in the chapter "Illness—Baby."

Pacifier use has been associated with breastfeeding problems in some babies.

Pacifier (dummy) use has been associated with the following breastfeeding problems:

- slow weight gain,
- thrush,
- nipple confusion,
- mastitis,
- increased risk of early weaning,

and it may contribute to an earlier return of fertility in the mother. For more information, see the section "Pacifier Use" in the section "Common Questions" later in this chapter.

DURING THE EARLY MONTHS

Within two weeks after birth, colostrum is completely replaced by mature milk.

The special first milk, called colostrum, is a concentrated form of nutrition that also contains the specific immunities that a newborn needs. Colostrum alone is present in small amounts until the third or fourth day after birth, when most mothers notice that their milk becomes more plentiful. This is when the body begins to shift into the production of mature milk, a transition that takes about two weeks to complete.

Within the first month of nursing, most mothers notice that their breasts feel softer and not as full as they did at first.

After the first few weeks, a mother will notice her breasts feel softer and not as full. This softening of the breasts is a sign that the mother's milk production is stabilizing to match her baby's needs. It is normal for the engorged or full feeling of the early weeks to pass.

As long as her baby has at least six to eight wet cloth diapers per day (five to six disposable diapers) and at least two to five bowel movements per day, she can be sure that she has not "lost her milk."

Most exclusively breastfed newborns need to nurse on average eight to twelve times in 24 hours in order to get enough milk.

Most newborns need to nurse an average of eight to twelve times in 24 hours. Some babies nurse less frequently while others nurse more frequently. Less or more frequent nursing is not a problem unless the baby has fewer wet diapers or bowel movements than normal and the baby is not gaining well.

The healthy baby with a good suck will naturally settle into the pattern of nursing that is right for him.

Daily nursing patterns will vary from baby to baby, and an individual baby's nursing pattern may change from day to day and vary as he grows. A healthy baby with a good suck will naturally fall into the nursing pattern that is best suited for him. Ideally—to best meet her baby's nutritional and sucking needs—the mother will "watch the baby and not the clock," breastfeeding him on cue.

During the early months, many babies do what is called "cluster nursing," spacing feedings closer together at certain times of the day (typically during the evening) and going longer between feedings at other times. Although most babies need to nurse eight to twelve times in 24 hours to grow and thrive, many babies are not content with the regular two-to-three hour feeding intervals some new parents expect. In areas where artificial feeding is the norm, many parents misinterpret their baby's desire to nurse more often than every two to three hours as a sign that the mother doesn't have enough milk, when cluster nursing is actually a common feeding pattern for most young breastfed babies.

Some babies do nurse at regular intervals early on, but the length of feedings and the intervals between feedings vary from baby to baby. Due to individual differences, healthy breastfed babies may nurse as often as every hour or as infrequently as every four hours and thrive. If the parents are concerned about their baby's feeding pattern, suggest they focus on the number of feedings in 24 hours (see previous point) rather than the intervals between feedings and have their baby's weight checked, as a healthy weight gain is proof that their baby is getting enough milk. See the next section, "Concerns about Milk Supply," and "Normal Growth Patterns during the Baby's First Year" in the chapter "Weight Gain."

As babies grow—and their stomachs grow larger—babies who nursed irregularly may naturally begin to go longer between feedings and develop more regular feeding patterns.

When the baby is allowed to finish the first breast first, before the mother offers the second, he will get the proper balance of fluid and calories.

Allowing the baby to finish the first breast first is preferable to switching the baby from the first breast to the second after a specified length of time. This is because the composition of the milk changes during a feeding and only the baby knows when he has received the right balance of fluid and calories.

The milk the baby receives when he begins breastfeeding is called the "foremilk," which is high in volume but low in fat. As the feeding progresses, the fat content of the milk rises steadily as the volume decreases. The milk near the end of the feeding is low in volume but high in fat and is called the "hindmilk."

By allowing the baby to decide when he is finished with the first breast, the mother can be sure he has received the proper balance of fluid and fat. Switching breasts too soon might mean the baby will receive only foremilk from each breast, filling him up with low-calorie milk. A baby who receives too much foremilk and not enough hindmilk may gain weight slowly, be fussy at the breast and between feedings, and may have a greenish, liquid stool (Woolridge 1988).

Studies have demonstrated that whether babies nurse from one or two breasts at a feeding they take in similar amounts of milk over twenty-four hours, although a baby may nurse slightly longer when he nurses from one breast at a feeding (Righard 1993; Woolridge 1990).

A mother will know when her baby has finished the first breast when he comes off the breast or falls asleep. Then she can burp him and offer him the other breast, which he may or may not take.

Exceptions to this general rule are the sleepy baby, the lazy nurser, and the baby with a weak suck, who may not nurse effectively at the breast and need the stimulation of being switched from breast to breast frequently in order to nurse actively. (See "Sucking Problems—Types and Suggestions" in the chapter "Positioning, Latch-On, and the Baby's Suck.")

Length of feedings vary due to differences among babies and mothers, nursing efficiency at different ages, and degrees of hunger from one feeding to the next.

Length of feedings vary with the baby's personality and age. THE WOMANLY ART OF BREASTFEEDING describes common nursing styles such as "the leisurely diner," "the nip and napper," "the no-nonsense nurser," and "the what-goes-down-tends-to-come-up tyke" to reflect the personality and physical differences among babies (La Leche League International, pp. 73-75). A baby's nursing style also may change as he grows. The baby who is a slow nurser as a newborn may become faster and more efficient as he becomes practiced at breastfeeding.

Differences among mothers may be a factor in length of feedings, too. One study found that the fat content of milk varies among mothers and that babies whose mothers had lower-fat milk tended to nurse longer at feedings and take a greater percentage of the milk in the breast. Both groups of babies gained weight within the normal ranges, but the babies whose mothers had higher-fat milk gained more during their first six weeks. The researchers concluded that the longer feeding times helped the babies whose mothers had lower-fat milk to receive the calories they needed to gain and grow adequately (Tyson 1992).

A baby's appetite is another factor that affects length of feedings. Because human milk becomes higher in fat as the feeding progresses, a baby who is slightly hungry may nurse for a shorter time at one feeding and longer at another feeding when he is hungrier.

"Growth spurts"—or periods of increased nursing—commonly occur at around two or three weeks, six weeks, and three months of age.

When a baby suddenly wants to nurse more often, it is called a "growth spurt" or "frequency days." More frequent nursing is the baby's way of building his mother's milk supply to meet his increasing needs.

More frequent but shorter nursings build and maintain a mother's milk supply more effectively than less frequent but longer nursings.

Twenty minutes of vigorous nursing every hour or two is more effective in building up the mother's milk supply than less frequent but longer sessions at the breast.

A breastfed baby does not need water or formula supplements.

Human milk provides all the nourishment a baby needs until about the middle of his first year of life. Even in hot weather, bottles of water are unnecessary. Studies of babies living in hot, humid climates and hot, dry climates found that exclusive breastfeeding met the infant's need for fluids (Brown 1986; Goldberg 1983).

Concerns about Milk Supply

New mothers may worry about whether or not their babies are getting enough milk.

Mothers often worry about their milk supply, especially if they began breastfeeding with definite expectations about how often or how long their babies would nurse. Babies' nursing patterns vary, and a pattern that is right for one baby may not be right for another.

If the mother is concerned about her milk supply, review the following points so that she can judge for herself whether she has enough milk.

The more often and effectively a baby nurses, the more milk there will be.

The amount of milk the mother produces depends on the frequency and effectiveness of the sucking her baby does at the breast. The baby's effective sucking at the breast causes two hormones, oxytocin and prolactin, to be released by the mother's pituitary gland. Prolactin is the milk-producing hormone. The more often and effectively the baby sucks, the more prolactin the mother's body releases and the more milk her breasts will produce. If the baby needs more milk than the mother is producing, he may need to nurse more frequently or suck more effectively in order to increase her supply. The second hormone, oxytocin, causes contractions within the breasts which squeeze the milk down the milk ducts to the nipple so that the baby can get it. This is called the let-down, or milk-ejection, reflex.

Milk production follows the principle of supply and demand. In the beginning, the mother's body does not know how much milk her baby needs, but by nursing her baby often—at least eight to twelve times every twenty-four hours—

her body will automatically adjust her milk supply to meet her baby's needs.

More frequent but shorter nursings (at least twenty to thirty minutes) build and maintain a mother's milk supply more effectively than less frequent but longer nursings.

After the mother's milk "comes in" on the third or fourth day after birth, she can tell her baby is getting enough fluids if he has at least six to eight wet cloth diapers (five or six disposable diapers) every twenty-four hours.

If the mother is concerned about her milk supply, suggest she keep track of how often and how much her baby urinates. During a newborn's first two or three days (while he is receiving colostrum), he will wet only one or two diapers per day. Once his mother's milk becomes more plentiful (or "comes in"), the baby should have six to eight wet cloth diapers or five to six disposables per day.

Suggest that the mother try to get a sense of a minimally wet diaper by placing one to two ounces (30-60 ml) of water in a dry diaper to see how it feels.

After six weeks, the number of wet cloth diapers may drop to five or six per day and disposables to four to five per day, but their wetness will increase to four or more ounces (116 ml or more). This is because the baby's bladder grows in size and is able to hold more urine. At all ages, urine should be pale in color and mild-smelling.

If the mother is worried about her milk supply or if her supply seems to be low, suggest she keep an "input/output" diary, writing down each nursing and each wet diaper and bowel movement as she increases the number of nursings per day.

During the first six weeks, two to five bowel movements per day indicate the baby is getting enough calories.

In the first few days after birth, the baby's dark, tarry stools are called meconium. This is the stool that the baby has been storing since before birth. Colostrum is a natural laxative and is important in helping the infant pass this first stool. Within twenty-four to forty-eight hours of the mother's milk becoming more plentiful, the baby's stools will change in color and consistency. Once the meconium has been eliminated, the stool of the baby who is receiving only mother's milk will be loose and unformed, often of a pea-soup consistency, and may be yellow to yellow-green to tan in color. An occasional green stool is also normal. The odor should be mild and not unpleasant.

Bowel movements usually become more frequent as the baby regains his birth weight and continues to gain. Most young babies will have at least two to five substantial bowel movements every twenty-four hours. Many babies continue this pattern for as long as they are exclusively breastfed. If bowel movements are small (just a stain on the diaper), there should be many each day. If the baby has only one every few days, it should be very plentiful. (This is more common in the breastfed baby who is older than six weeks of age.) If the baby has fewer than two bowel movements per day during his first four to six weeks, ask the mother how often and how long he nurses, how many wet diapers he has each day, and his weight gain. This may be a normal variation (in which case the baby will be gaining at least 4 to 8 ounces [113 to 226 grams] per week) or it may be a sign that the baby is not nursing long or well enough to get the fatty, calorie-rich hindmilk he needs, or that there are other health problems.

In the baby older than six weeks, less frequent bowel movements may be normal.

Many babies continue to have frequent bowel movements for as long as they are exclusively breastfeeding. Less frequent bowel movements also may be normal in an older breastfed baby. Some breastfed babies may have bowel movements only once a week without signs of constipation (such as hard, dry stools).

From birth to three months, typical weight gain is four to eight ounces (113 to 226 grams) per week.

Typical weight gain for the first three months is 4 to 8 ounces per week (113 to 226 grams). Weight gain should always be figured from the lowest point rather than from birth weight. Refer to "First, Establish Weight Gain and Loss" under "Slow Weight Gain" in the chapter "Weight Gain."

A mother's milk supply may vary at different times of the day.

Some mothers find that their milk supply varies during the course of a day. Most mothers feel fuller in the morning and less full in the evening. If the mother's milk supply seems to be lower in the evening, more frequent breastfeeding will satisfy the baby's needs.

"False alarms" cause some mothers to worry that their milk supply is low.

Some mothers think they do not have enough milk when actually there is no problem with their supply. They worry about behavior or symptoms that have other causes or they're unfamiliar with the variety of patterns that are normal in breastfed babies. If the baby is gaining well and has plenty of wet diapers and bowel movements, assure the mother there is nothing wrong with her milk supply even if she notices any of the following:

- **The baby nurses very often.** Many babies have a strong need to suck or a need for frequent contact with their mothers. If a baby is nursing effectively, frequent nursing means that the baby is getting enough—not that there is a lack of milk.
- **The baby seems hungry an hour or so after being fed.** Human milk digests more quickly than formula and places less strain on a baby's immature digestive system, so the breastfed baby needs to be fed more frequently than the formula-fed baby.
- **The baby suddenly increases the frequency and/or length of his nursings.** Babies who are very sleepy as newborns often "wake up" at about two to three weeks of age and begin nursing more frequently. Babies also go through occasional growth spurts (at around two weeks, six weeks, and three months). During these periods they nurse more often than usual to bring in more milk for their increasing needs.
- **The baby suddenly decreases his nursing time, perhaps down to five to ten minutes per breast.** He may simply be able to extract the milk more quickly now that he is more experienced at nursing.
- **The baby is fussy.** Many babies have a fussy period each day, often at about the same time of the day. Some babies are fussy much of the time. Fussiness can be caused by many things other than hunger, but often there is no discernible reason. Many mothers believe their babies' irritability and fussiness are indications that they are not getting enough milk. Some studies have indicated that breastfed babies may initially tend to be fussier than their formula-fed peers (DiPietro 1987). This may be a way of making sure they will breastfeed as often as they need to. It is the baby who is placid and easygoing who seems to be more likely to go longer between feedings and gain weight slowly.
- **The mother's breasts leak only a little or not at all.** Leaking has no relationship to the amount of milk the mother produces, and the mother whose breasts do leak during feedings usually finds that leaking between feedings is no longer a problem once her supply becomes established and regulated to her baby's needs.
- **The mother's breasts suddenly seem softer.** This happens as the mother's milk production adjusts to her baby's needs and the initial breast fullness or engorgement subsides within the first few weeks.
- **The mother never feels the let-down, or milk-ejection, reflex or it does not seem as strong as it did before.** This may occur as time goes on. Some mothers do not feel a let-down at all, but they can learn to recognize that it is occurring by watching their baby's pattern of sucking and swallowing go from fast sucks with little swallowing to slow deep sucks and more frequent swallows.
- **The baby was weighed before and after a feeding and the mother was told her baby did not receive enough milk.** Studies have shown that test weighing is not a reliable indicator of whether a baby has breastfed well, because most baby scales are not sensitive enough to record such small changes in weight accurately (Whitefield 1981). However, modern elec-

tronic scales that are more sensitive to small weight changes have been found to accurately reflect how much milk a baby receives (Meier 1994). Test-weighing on this type of scale may be helpful to mothers in certain situations. (For more on these special scales, see "Determining a Baby's Readiness to Breastfeed" in the chapter "Prematurity.")

- **The baby takes a bottle after nursing.** Many babies will suck on a bottle even when they are full, because they like to suck. This is not necessarily a sign that the baby did not get enough at the breast.

- **The mother cannot express much milk.** Milk expression is a learned skill and the amount of milk expressed will increase with practice and the mother's ability to let down her milk to the pump. Pumping effectiveness may also vary depending on the type of pump used, as some pumps tend to be more effective than others. The amount of milk a mother expresses may be unrelated to her milk supply.

If the mother's concern about her milk supply seems to be warranted, refer to "Slow Weight Gain" in the "Weight Gain" chapter.

After the Baby Starts Solids

After her baby starts solids and until he is about a year old, encourage the mother to breastfeed before giving solids so that he will receive the milk he needs for growth.

Human milk is recommended as the primary food for the baby's first year. Since solid foods displace human milk in a baby's diet, suggest the mother breastfeed first, before offering solids, until the baby is nine to twelve months old. She can gradually increase the amount of solids she offers her baby.

In one study, researchers observed 141 mother-baby couples. The mothers exclusively breastfed their babies until solid foods were introduced at no earlier than four months of age. They found that the energy value of the human milk the baby consumed when he was exclusively breastfeeding matched closely the combined energy value of human milk plus solid foods he took later. The researchers concluded that rather than increasing their intake of calories when solid foods were started, the babies balanced their mother's milk and solid food intake to maintain a stable intake of calories. The volume of the mother's milk dropped when solid foods were introduced (Cohen 1994).

By breastfeeding the baby before offering solids until he is about a year old, the mother can be sure that he is receiving the milk he needs for growth. At one year of age, it is appropriate to offer solids first. (More information on introducing solid foods can be found in the chapter "Starting Solid Foods.")

If solids become a major part of the baby's diet during his first year, he may eliminate many nursings. Suggest the mother watch for constipation and be sure her baby's nutritional needs are met.

If solids are introduced too quickly and replace many nursings during the baby's first year, he may not get enough fluids, causing constipation. In the breastfeeding baby, constipation means hard, dry stools. Going for several days without a bowel movement or straining while passing a bowel movement are within the range of normal behavior and are not considered signs of constipation. If other fluids, such as juice or water, are given instead of human milk or formula the baby may not have his nutritional needs met (Smith and Lifshitz 1994).

If the baby is constipated, suggest the mother nurse her baby more often. When the baby is nursing more, he will have softer stools.

The Breastfeeding Toddler

It is normal for breastfeeding to continue past infancy.

In cultures where breastfeeding is unrestricted, breastfeeding continues for years, not months. Natural weaning occurs on average when the child is two to four years old. In developed countries, however, extended nursing may be considered unusual. If the mother would like suggestions on how to encourage her toddler to shorten or eliminate nursings, refer to "Approaches to Weaning" in the chapter "Weaning."

Breastfeeding beyond infancy has many benefits for both mother and child. If the mother would like more information on nursing longer than one year, refer her to the book, MOTHERING YOUR NURSING TODDLER by Norma Jane Bumgarner, available from La Leche League International.

Breastfeeding and Infant Sleep Patterns

Typically, newborns have one long four-to-five hour sleep period, which may or may not be at night. Parents can help encourage sleep by keeping all stimulation at night to a minimum.

Typically, a newborn has one long four-to-five hour sleep period, which often occurs during the day. It is common for a newborn to have his days and nights mixed up, because during pregnancy the mother's movements during the day lull the baby to sleep and her stillness at night promotes baby's alertness. Parents can gradually shift this longer sleep period from day to night by keeping stimulation to a minimum during normal sleep hours. Keeping lights low (using a night light only or turning on the closet light and pulling the door partly closed), minimizing movement, and changing diapers only when absolutely necessary (when baby has a bowel movement or clothing is soaked) all lessen the stimulation that promotes wakefulness. Over time this will help a baby learn to sleep at night instead of during the day.

One study of 26 newborns showed that it is possible to "teach" breastfeeding infants to have a long five-hour stretch of sleep from midnight to 5 AM during their first eight weeks of life by gradually lengthening feeding intervals during the night. Instead of nursing, other comfort measures were given, such as swaddling, diapering, and walking. By eight weeks of age, all 13 of the babies who were "trained" to sleep were sleeping five hours at night, while only 3 of the control babies slept that long. According to the researchers, both groups of babies took in equal amounts of milk per day (Pinilla and Birch 1993). While this may work in some families, other families may find that nursing the baby back to sleep is easier than persuading the baby to accept other comfort measures.

During the early months, it is beneficial for both mother and baby to breastfeed at least once during the night.

The young baby is growing at a phenomenal rate and often has a physical need to be fed during the night. Also, the mother's breasts can become engorged and uncomfortable if she goes for five, six, or more hours without a feeding. If her breasts become uncomfortably full, she is at increased risk for mastitis and the baby might have trouble latching on to very full breasts in the morning.

It is common for babies to continue to wake during the night, even after the early months.

Many babies continue to wake at night, even into their toddler years. Some reasons for waking are: hunger, teething, restlessness due to a new developmental stage, individual differences in sleep patterns, and loneliness. Even older babies may be hungry at night.

One study of breastfeeding mothers and babies, who were followed into their second year, found that the breastfeeding babies and toddlers did not conform to the usual sleep patterns of artificially fed babies and that these differences were even more pronounced among babies who slept with their parents. Rather than beginning to have a long stretches of unbroken sleep after about four months of age, as was common among the artificially fed babies, the breastfeeding babies continued to sleep in short bouts with frequent waking. The researchers concluded that as extended breastfeeding becomes more common in Western society, expectations of babies' sleep/wake patterns may need to be revised (Elias 1986).

Studies show that starting solid foods does not cause babies to sleep longer.

The belief that starting solids will help a baby "sleep through the night" motivates many parents to begin solids earlier than they otherwise would. However, this popular belief has no basis in fact. Two studies found no difference in the sleep patterns of babies who received solids before bedtime in comparison to babies who were not given solids (Macknin 1989; Keane 1988).

Although some babies in these studies began sleeping more at night when solids were started, about the same number of babies in the control group also began sleeping more at night. Macknin concluded, "Infants' ability to sleep through the night is a developmental and adaptive process that occurs regardless of the timing of introduction of cereal."

If the mother is having difficulty coping with her baby's night waking, listen to her feelings and discuss ways she can minimize the disruption to her sleep.

In many cultures where breastfeeding is the norm, mothers and babies sleep close to each other at night so that the baby can be nursed with less disruption of sleep. Parents in these cultures expect babies to wake frequently to nurse at night until they have matured enough to naturally outgrow this behavior, a process that may take years. A wakeful baby—even a wakeful older baby or toddler—is not considered unusual or a problem in these cultures (Morelli 1992).

In many Western cultures, however, artificial feeding is the norm and consequently the expectations are different. Babies are expected to sleep for long stretches alone, often in a separate room, by the time they are three to four months old. When a baby's sleep patterns do not conform to these expectations, the parents may feel frustrated and upset. The mother may wonder what she is doing "wrong" to cause her baby's wakefulness. If she spends her nights going back and forth between her bed and her baby's room and nursing sitting up rather than sleeping while she breastfeeds, she may be exhausted from lack of sleep. Listen to the mother's frustrations and worries and rephrase them so that she knows she has been heard and understood.

Assure her that night waking is normal for many babies (see previous points), and encourage her to find ways to make night nursings easier so that she can get more sleep. For example, if the baby sleeps in a crib, bringing the crib into the mother's room might make it easier for her to hear her baby stir before he has fully awakened and begun to cry. Most mothers and babies settle down to sleep again more quickly if they are not fully awakened.

There are many alternatives to the usual sleeping arrangements that can make night nursings easier. The baby's crib could be attached to the parents' bed in a "side-car" arrangement. A mattress or sleeping bag could be put on the floor in the parents' or baby's room, so that the mother can lie down and sleep while nursing the baby back to sleep, and return to her own bed if she wishes after the baby goes back to sleep. Or the parents could simply bring the baby into their bed, either for part of the night—after he awakens—or for the whole night. The mother should be encouraged to do whatever works best for her and her family.

If the mother would like more information on why babies sleep differently than adults and about alternative sleeping arrangements, refer her to the book, NIGHTTIME PARENTING by William Sears, MD, available from La Leche League International.

Keeping mother and baby close at night not only minimizes sleep loss, it may also have health benefits for baby.

James McKenna, professor of anthropology at Pomona College in Claremont, California, calls babies sleeping alone at night "an extremely recent cultural experiment," and questions whether this practice is good for babies. Several of McKenna's studies provide evidence that when mother and baby sleep together, the mother's breathing and movements affect the baby's breathing and arousal patterns. McKenna suggests that in certain vulnerable infants this may help prevent Sudden Infant Death Syndrome (SIDS), also known as cot death (McKenna and Mosko 1993; McKenna 1990; McKenna 1986). Breastfeeding, independent of sleep practices, has also been found to lower the risk of SIDS (Mitchell 1992).

McKenna suggests that scientists and pediatricians rethink the assumptions underlying infant sleep research and the recommendations they give parents about where and how babies should sleep. According to McKenna, the current Western view of normal sleep patterns for babies reflects only how infants sleep under solitary conditions; he expresses concern about "whether our cultural preferences as to how we want infants to sleep push some infants beyond their adaptive limits" (McKenna 1993). In many non-Western cultures, sharing sleep with infants is the norm (Morelli 1992).

Although it may be possible to "train" babies to adopt sleep patterns appropriate for older children and adults, the long-term effects of altering natural sleep patterns have not been studied.

In the United States over the past ten years, "sleep training" methods have risen in popularity. Sleep training proponents warn that children may have sleep problems later unless they learn to fall asleep alone and soothe themselves back to sleep when they wake at night. Due to these warnings, many parents question whether it is healthy to nurse and comfort their child at night. However, the sleep patterns used as norms by these sleep training proponents may not be appropriate for breastfeeding babies (see previous points).

One of these proponents advises parents to put babies as young as four months old in the crib at bedtime and let them "cry it out" until they fall asleep, which may take hours at first. According to this doctor, the crying will diminish over the first week and the child will learn to go to sleep easily in his crib (Weissbluth 1987). Another sleep training proponent takes a similar approach, but encourages parents to go into the baby's room every five minutes to reassure him without picking him up until he falls asleep (Ferber 1985).

Although it may be possible to train infants and young children to adopt sleep patterns that are developmentally appropriate for older children and adults, no research has been done on the long-term effects of these practices. The fact that sleep training methods "work" for many children is no guarantee that the long-term effects are positive.

THE LET-DOWN, OR MILK-EJECTION, REFLEX

Signs of a Healthy Let-Down

The let-down, or milk-ejection, reflex is triggered by hormones. It releases the milk from all parts of the breast so that it is available to the baby.

Some milk accumulates in the milk reservoirs behind the nipple and in the ducts, but most of the milk is made and stored in other parts of the breast. The let-down reflex releases this milk into the milk ducts, making it available to the baby.

During breastfeeding, the baby's suck stimulates the let-down. When a baby begins to nurse, the rhythmic motion of his jaws, lips, and tongue send nerve impulses to the mother's pituitary, the master gland in the brain, by way of the hypothalamus. Two hormones, prolactin and oxytocin, are then released. It is the oxytocin that stimulates the let-down reflex, causing the band-like cells surrounding the milk-producing cells (alveoli) to constrict and squeeze out the milk from all parts of the breast. This muscle action makes the milk available to the baby by sending it through the ducts to the milk reservoirs (lactiferous sinuses) which are located within the breast beneath the areola behind the nipple.

The most reliable signs of a well-functioning let-down are a slowing of the baby's suck-swallow pattern, deep and regular swallowing, and a healthy weight gain.

Any of the following may be signs that the mother's milk is letting down:

- uterine cramps and increased blood flow (during the first few days after birth),
- a "pins-and-needles" or achy feeling in her breast (some women don't feel this at all and some feel it only after the early weeks),
- milk leaking from the other breast,
- a change in the baby's suck-swallow rhythm, from quick sucks to long, slow sucks with regular swallowing and a breath after every one or two sucks,
- gulping,
- milk appearing in the corner of the baby's mouth,
- a feeling of relaxation in the mother.

Some mothers feel a tingling, pins-and-needles sensation with the let-down or a sharp, stabbing pain or cramp. Other mothers do not notice any sensation or feel it only occasionally. While the mother is breastfeeding, the most reliable sign of the let-down is a change in the baby's sucking and swallowing pattern from quick sucks with occasional swallowing to long, slow sucks with regular swallowing or gulping. If the baby is gaining well, the mother can be certain that her let-down is functioning well.

A baby who is sucking well will stimulate several let-downs during the feeding, assuring that he receives the fatty hindmilk, as well as the watery foremilk that comes at the beginning of a feeding.

The let-down reflex may occur many times during a feeding.

Delayed or Inhibited Let-Down

If the let-down is delayed or inhibited, the baby may nurse well for a minute or two and then pull away in frustration and unhappiness. The mother may notice that her baby is sucking rapidly but not swallowing deeply or often.

If the let-down is delayed or inhibited, the baby may become frustrated and upset, because most of the milk in the breast is not being released.

Some milk accumulates in the milk reservoirs near the nipple, but without the let-down reflex, most of the mother's milk will remain in the breast despite the baby's efforts.

Ask the mother if she is under unusual stress or if she feels tense when she puts her baby to breast. Ask her if she has sore nipples or is engorged.

During times of emotional crisis or unusual stress, some mothers find that their let-down is temporarily affected. If the mother has sore nipples, anticipating the pain may make her tense when she puts her baby to breast, delaying or inhibiting her let-down. If her nipples are sore, talk to her about possible causes and what she can do to eliminate or minimize her discomfort. (See the chapter "Positioning, Latch-On, and the Baby's Suck.") If the mother is engorged, her let-down also may be temporarily affected. Warm compresses, gentle breast massage, and expression of a little milk may help encourage the let-down (Lawrence, p. 252).

Use of ice has been found to inhibit the let-down, so encourage the mother to avoid applying ice to her nipples or breasts before nursing or while her let-down is delayed or inhibited (Newton and Newton 1948).

Ask the mother if she smokes, drinks alcohol, drinks caffeinated beverages, has hormonal problems, or is taking any medications.

Stress, smoking (Dahlstrom 1990; Steldinger and Luck 1988), excessive alcohol (Lawrence, p. 375) or caffeine (Berlin 1984), and some drugs taken by the mother (Batagol 1989; Berlin 1989; Atkinson and Biggs 1988) can also delay or inhibit the let-down. If smoking or excessive alcohol or caffeine may be contributing factors, cutting down may improve the mother's let-down. If the mother is taking a drug that may be interfering with her let-down, suggest she talk to her doctor about finding an alternative medication. For more information on smoking, caffeine, and drugs, see the chapter "Drugs, Vitamins, Vaccines, and Diagnostic Tests."

It is normal for a mother's let-down reflex and milk supply to be temporarily affected while she is going through a crisis.

A mother who is going through a serious emotional or physical crisis—such as a sudden death in the family or a car crash—may find that her let-down and milk supply are temporarily affected. In extreme situations, extra adrenalin in the mother's system can reduce or block the release of the hormones affecting let-down and milk production (Lincoln and Paisley 1982).

If this happens, encourage the mother to try to relax and to continue breastfeeding and/or expressing so that her let-down and milk supply will quickly return to normal.

When a baby is premature or very ill, it is normal for the mother's milk supply to fluctuate with her baby's condition. When the mother is very worried about the baby's health or survival, it may not be easy to express much milk. Times of crisis commonly result in a temporary decrease in milk supply. This is normal, a natural part of the complex emotions involved in having a baby in the intensive-care nursery.

If the mother's milk supply decreases during a crisis, unsupportive comments from those around may convince the mother to give up breastfeeding entirely unless she has another source of support. Assure her that her decrease in supply is only temporary and that it will increase again as she is able to relax. Also tell her that however much milk her baby gets by breastfeeding or she is able to express will be enough to stimulate her breasts to continue making milk. It may also be comforting for her to talk to another mother who has had the same experience.

During the early weeks of breast-feeding, a mother's let-down may take a few extra minutes to occur.

During the early weeks of breastfeeding, it is not unusual for a new mother's let-down to take a few minutes to occur when she puts her baby to breast. But as she becomes more experienced at breastfeeding, her let-down reflex will respond more quickly and automatically when her baby sucks. Eventually, it may be triggered by other stimuli—the sight of her baby, the feel of his skin, his smell, his cry (even another baby's cry), as well as his sucking at the breast.

Breast massage, warm compresses, relaxation exercises, a calm setting, or lying down can help the mother stimulate her let-down.

If the mother has recently given birth, assure her that her let-down will function more automatically with time and practice. Allowing unrestricted nursing in a quiet, undistracted setting will help condition the mother's body to let down her milk more automatically.

For any mother whose let-down is inhibited or delayed, relaxation exercises, warm compresses before nursing, breast massage, and a calm, undistracted setting may help encourage her let-down to occur. Focusing on the baby, stroking his hair, enjoying the feel of his skin may help a mother relax and respond to her baby. Sometimes breastfeeding lying down relaxes the mother enough to help her let-down occur more quickly.

COMMON QUESTIONS

Pacifier (Dummy) Use

Many women combine pacifier use with breastfeeding, but there may be unanticipated consequences.

Pacifiers (also known as "dummies") are used in many parts of the world to minimize the time spent nursing and to keep babies quiet and contented between feedings. In areas where an artificial feeding mentality exists, such as the United States, the pacifier has come to be accepted as the primary source of comfort and mothers are cautioned to limit breastfeeding so as "not to let their baby use their breast as a pacifier." However, for as long as there have been mothers and babies—long before the pacifier existed—the breast has provided babies with comfort, as well as with food. Where breastfeeding is the norm, the breast is accepted as the primary source of comfort, and a baby with a pacifier would be seen as "using the pacifier as the breast."

Whenever a substitute is used for the breast, there are consequences, and the pacifier is no exception. The consequences to pacifier use which are listed in the following points—increased risk of early weaning, slow weight gain, thrush, nipple confusion, earlier return of fertility, and mastitis—are direct results of the baby "using the pacifier as the breast."

Research indicates a strong correlation between regular pacifier use and early weaning.

Research conducted in Brazil has established that pacifier use is highly correlated with early weaning. In developing countries, early weaning is also correlated with increased infant mortality, so for many babies, pacifier use may make the difference between life and death. One study found that at six months 65% of the babies who had used pacifiers from one month of age had weaned from the breast as compared with 24% of the babies who had not used pacifiers. This association between pacifiers and early weaning was found whether or not the babies had also been receiving bottles (Victora 1993). Another study confirmed this finding and also found that the more frequently the pacifier was used, the higher the risk for early weaning. The researchers suggested that pacifier use not be recommended for breastfed infants (Barros 1995).

Regular pacifier use may contribute to slow weight gain.

Pacifier use may contribute to slow weight gain in two ways. In the early weeks, while a baby is still learning to nurse, use of a pacifier may affect a baby's suck, making him less effective at milking the breast, affecting weight gain (Newman 1990; Lawrence, p. 371). Also, a baby with a placid temperament may be content to suck on a pacifier without indicating a desire to nurse, even when he is hungry, resulting in fewer feedings per day and slow weight gain.

Pacifier use may contribute to thrush infection or reinfection.

Because the fungus that causes thrush thrives at room temperature on moist surfaces, a pacifier has the potential to transmit thrush. Thrush can be transmitted from child to child when a pacifier is shared or cause reinfection in a child who uses a contaminated pacifier after treatment. A contaminated bowl in which rubber nipples were stored caused an outbreak of thrush among premature babies in a hospital nursery (Cremer and de Groot 1967). Amir (1995) suggests that the raised humidity in a closed mouth during pacifier use may predispose babies to thrush.

If a pacifier is used during a thrush episode, the mother should boil it for five minutes once a day, then discard and replace it after one week of treatment.

Pacifier use increases the incidence of mastitis in some women.

Regular use of a pacifier can contribute to mastitis because the baby spends less time at the breast. If a mother tends to have an oversupply of milk, she may have an even greater risk of mastitis from pacifier use, particularly during the time she introduces the pacifier and her baby's nursing pattern changes.

Use of a pacifier in the early weeks may contribute to breastfeeding problems related to nipple confusion.

During the early weeks of nursing, when a baby is just learning to nurse, some breastfeeding experts believe that the use of artificial nipples may confuse some babies and cause breastfeeding problems (Neifert 1995; Newman 1990).

Ruth Lawrence, MD, cautions about pacifier use in the early weeks due to the possibility of "imprinting" on a pacifier, causing the baby to develop a preference for the firm, unnaturally shaped nipple. The concept of "imprinting" is also used to describe how some animals form attachments to the first object or creature they see. Lawrence writes: "Nonnutritive sucking on thumbs or pacifiers is displacement activity that would normally be directed at imprinting to mother's nipple....Although the term 'nipple confusion' has not yet been accepted in the medical literature, there is strong psychosomatic evidence that human imprinting can be altered by introducing a foreign object during imprinting" (p. 188).

A mother's fertility may return more quickly if her baby uses a pacifier regularly.

A pacifier satisfies a baby's need to suck and so decreases the amount of time spent at the breast, influencing the delicate hormonal balance required to suppress a mother's fertility. A mother may find that her fertility returns more quickly if her baby uses a pacifier than if her baby satisfied all his sucking needs at the breast (Kippley 1989; Kippley and Kippley 1979).

Leaking Milk

Many women leak milk when their milk lets down, especially during their baby's early months.

It is common for a mother to leak milk from one breast when the baby starts to nurse on the other. The mother may also leak when it is nearly time for a feeding. The sight, sound, or even the thought of her baby may trigger leaking. On the other hand, some mothers have ample milk supplies but never leak.

Leaking is more common during the early weeks of breastfeeding, although for some mothers, it goes on for many months. Share the following tips to make leaking more manageable:

If the mother's milk leaks at inopportune moments, offer suggestions for making leaking more manageable.

- **To stop the leaking, apply gentle pressure directly on the nipples.** Suggest the mother fold her arms across her chest and put the heels of her hands directly on her nipples to stop the milk flow, or put her hands under her chin and press against her breasts with her forearms.
- **Wear nursing pads to catch the milk.** Caution the mother that nursing pads with plastic linings can keep air from getting to her nipples, which can contribute to soreness. Some nursing pads are washable and reusable, others are disposable. If she chooses, the mother can make her own using

folded handkerchiefs or circular pieces of absorbent material (such as cloth diapers) sewn together.
- **Wear clothing that will camouflage the wetness**, such as print blouses, or have an extra jacket or sweater ready as a coverup.
- **Breastfeed or express more often.** Leaking may be a sign that the mother's breasts are becoming overly full. If this is the case, rather than trying to hold back the milk, it may be better for the mother to breastfeed or—if she is away from her baby—express her milk when she feels overly full.

If the mother's breasts feel full, suggest she let the milk leak out and catch the overflow.

If the mother's breasts are very full or engorged, rather than hold it back, suggest she let the milk come out in order to relieve the fullness. To catch the overflow and keep herself dry, suggest the mother use a diaper or another absorbent cloth to absorb the milk.

Spitting Up

Some normal, healthy babies spit up regularly after nursing.

It is not unusual for some babies to spit up regularly after nursing. Even if the baby seems to be spitting up a lot of milk, he is probably doing fine. If the mother is worried, suggest she keep track of the number of wet diapers and bowel movements her baby has in a twenty-four hour period. If he has six to eight wet cloth diapers (five to six disposable diapers) and at least two bowel movements (fewer bowel movements are considered normal if he is older than six weeks), she can feel confident that her baby is getting enough. Weight gain is another reliable indicator. If the baby is gaining at least four ounces (113 grams) a week, the mother can be sure that he is getting enough to eat even if he spits up a lot.

Babies spit up for many reasons.

Some of the reasons babies spit up include:

- a strong let-down, or milk-ejection, reflex,
- a strong gag reflex,
- immature muscle control,
- allergy,
- disease,
- consuming too much milk.

Sometimes the reason for spitting up cannot be determined.

The baby will outgrow spitting up, but in the meantime, offer some suggestions for keeping it to a minimum.

Tell the mother that a normal, healthy baby usually outgrows his spitting up within four to six months. Until it clears up on its own, suggest the mother try gentle handling and keeping the baby upright after feedings. Limiting nursing to one breast per feeding may also help, especially if the mother thinks her baby's spitting up may be related to getting too much milk at a feeding.

Some babies spit up because they're getting too much milk too quickly. If the baby gulps or chokes after the mother's let-down occurs, suggest she try taking him off the breast for a minute or two and catching the milk in a towel or diaper, putting the baby back to the breast after the initial flow of milk has passed.

Testing or treatment for gastroesophageal reflux should be considered only if spitting up is accompanied by poor weight gain, weight loss, severe choking, or lung disease.

Gastroesophageal reflux, the flowing back of the stomach's contents into the esophagus, is a potentially serious health problem for some individuals. However, specialists acknowledge that spitting up is normal for many babies during the first year of life, is not necessarily a sign of later reflux problems, and usually stops spontaneously as the baby matures (Sutphen 1990).

Testing or treatment for reflux in the nursing baby who is spitting up may interfere with breastfeeding and result in unnecessary medical intervention. Offering solids to "thicken feeds" in order to prevent spitting up in the baby younger than about six months interferes with breastfeeding by replacing human milk in the baby's diet and decreasing the mother's milk supply. Too early introduction of solids may also endanger the baby by making it possible for regurgitated solids, which are irritating to the body's tissues, to be aspirated into the baby's lungs. According to experts on reflux, medical tests for reflux are not indicated in the baby younger than one year unless, in addition to spitting up, the baby is gaining poorly or losing weight or has episodes of severe choking or signs of lung disease (Sutphen 1990).

Switching from breastfeeding to formula, which is sometimes suggested for the baby suspected of having reflux, may worsen rather than improve a baby's spitting up. Research has found that breastfed babies tend to have fewer episodes of reflux than babies on formula (Heacock 1992). This may be partly because one cause of reflux is delayed emptying of the stomach and human milk has been found to empty from the stomach twice as quickly as formula (Ewer 1994).

Regular projectile vomiting in a newborn could be a sign of pyloric stenosis.

A baby who regularly spits up after feedings should be checked by his doctor to rule out pyloric stenosis, a narrowing of the muscular wall of the tube that passes from the stomach into the intestines. With pyloric stenosis, the milk does not pass easily from the baby's stomach into his intestines and the baby does not get enough nourishment.

The symptoms of pyloric stenosis usually begin when the baby is between two and eight weeks of age. The first sign may be regular spitting up or projectile vomiting, when the baby's stomach muscles force the milk up his throat and shoot it out of his mouth, sometimes as far as several feet away. At first this may happen only occasionally, but in time it occurs more and more often until the baby is projectile vomiting after every feeding.

A baby who has pyloric stenosis may need simple surgery (called a pyloromyotomy) after his fluid balance has been restored. If the procedure is uncomplicated, the baby can begin breastfeeding again as soon as six to eight hours afterwards. Occasional projectile vomiting does not mean a baby has pyloric stenosis, but if it occurs at least once a day, suggest the mother have the baby checked by his doctor.

If there are no other signs of illness, spitting up may be an indication that the baby is sensitive to a food or a medication.

If the baby is not showing other signs of illness, spitting up may indicate that the baby is sensitive to a food or medication he's receiving, especially if the baby suddenly starts spitting up after his first few weeks.

Ask the mother if she has recently started giving the baby vitamin, iron, or fluoride supplements. These cause spitting up in some babies. If so, suggest she stop giving them to see if the spitting up stops. If not, ask the mother if she is taking vitamin or iron supplements or any medication. Sometimes supplements or medications taken by the mother can cause digestive problems in a breastfeeding baby. If so, the mother can try stopping them to see if the spitting up stops.

Ask the mother if the baby is receiving anything other than her milk. An occasional bottle of formula can cause spitting up or vomiting in a sensitive baby. If the baby is eating solid foods, he may be sensitive to a new food that has been introduced. Whether or not a baby shows other signs of illness, if the spitting up started after he began eating solid foods, suggest the mother stop offering any new food until it has passed.

In rare cases, a food eaten by a breastfeeding mother may affect her baby through her milk, causing him to spit up. (See "Sensitivity to a Food or Drug Mother or Baby Has Ingested" in the chapter "Fussy at the Breast and Breast Refusal.")

Some babies who spit up regularly are healthy, continue to gain weight, and outgrow it.

If the baby is doing well in spite of regularly spitting up—gaining weight and having an appropriate number of wet diapers and bowel movements—then, as La Leche League medical advisor Dr. Gregory White says, "in a healthy baby, spitting up is a laundry problem, not a medical problem."

Suggest the mother be patient. In the meantime she can be prepared by keeping a supply of clean-up supplies, protective coverings, and changes of clothes for her baby. He will outgrow his spitting up in time.

If the baby shows other signs of illness, see "Vomiting" in the chapter, "Illness—Baby."

Crying and Colic

Many babies—no matter how they are fed—have a regular fussy period, often in the late afternoon or early evening.

A baby's cries do not necessarily mean he is hungry.

Babies who are carried more tend to cry less.

If the baby's cries are quieted by more frequent nursings, the mother should feel free to do so. If the baby seems full but still wants to suck for comfort, suggest the mother offer the breast he finished last.

When nursing doesn't seem to help, suggest the mother try other comfort measures.

Whether breastfed or formula-fed, during their first months many babies have a regular fussy period, which usually occurs in the late afternoon or evening. Some babies' fussy period comes so regularly, the parents can set their watches by it.

Some breastfeeding mothers worry that their baby's crying means he is hungry and they don't have enough milk. Explain that babies cry for reasons other than hunger and that frequent breastfeeding will ensure that mother's milk supply is ample. (See the previous section, "Concerns about Milk Supply.")

One study (Hunziker 1986) of first-time mothers found that babies who spent more time being held or carried either in their mother's arms or in a baby carrier—even while contented or asleep—cried less. The younger the baby, the more dramatic the results: three extra hours of carrying a day reduced the amount of crying in a four-week-old baby by 45 percent.

Some mothers are told to space out feedings and nurse no more often than certain set intervals, such as every two or three hours. However, many babies will be unhappy if a set pattern of feedings is enforced. A more natural feeding pattern for most babies (especially newborns) is called "cluster nursing," when feedings are spaced closer together at certain times of the day (typically evening) and further apart at other times. A mother should be encouraged to follow her baby's cues and use the feeding pattern that keeps her baby most contented, nursing for comfort as well as to satisfy hunger. There is no advantage to delaying feedings if the baby will be comforted by nursing.

If a baby nurses very frequently, he might take in more milk than he can comfortably hold. If the mother thinks this might be the case, ask if she is switching breasts after a set amount of time or if she is allowing the baby to finish the first breast first and come off on his own before offering the other breast. Allowing the baby to decide when he has finished the first breast usually results in the mother's supply adjusting more quickly to her baby's demand and prevents baby from taking in too much milk. However, if the mother thinks that the baby is getting too much milk even when she uses this approach, suggest she try restricting the baby to one breast at a feeding. If the baby wants to nurse again soon after a feeding, she should again offer the same breast so that the baby can enjoy the comforting closeness and sucking of breastfeeding without taking in too much milk.

Babies cry for many reasons—overtiredness, overstimulation, loneliness, and discomfort. Also babies have different temperaments; some are extremely sensitive to change and stimulation while others are more adaptable. One baby may be calm while another is colicky.

If nursing doesn't seem to help, mention some of the following comfort measures for mother to try.

- Burp him;
- Change his diaper;
- Undress him completely to see if any of his clothing may be bothering him or a thread may be wrapped around one of his toes;
- Undress with him and get into a warm bath together, supporting his head and bottom and moving him back and forth in the water or lying back in the tub with the baby tummy-down on her chest;

- Give him a massage;
- Put him in a sling or soft baby carrier and walk around the house or take a walk outside;
- Swaddle him in a light blanket;
- If he might be overstimulated, take him into a quieter room;
- Rock him in a rocking chair;
- Carry him in the colic hold (lying across the mother's forearm, tummy down, with her hand supporting his chest);
- Lay him across her lap and gently rub his back while she slowly lifts and lowers her heels;
- Lay him tummy-down on the bed and pat his back.

Tell the mother that whatever the reason for the baby's fussiness, he most often needs the comfort of just being held.

A baby who is not easily comforted and who spends a good part of each day crying may be colicky.

William Sears, MD, in his book, THE FUSSY BABY, says, "If you are wondering whether or not you have a colicky baby, you probably don't have one. The colicky baby leaves no doubt in the minds of sympathetic caregivers that he is truly in agony."

For years people have attempted to define colic, and today most agree that colicky babies suffer from intense physical discomfort, although there are many theories as to what causes the discomfort.

A colicky baby's entire body is tense. He usually pulls up his legs toward his abdomen, clenches his fists, and has a look of agony on his face as he screams in a high-pitched voice. Colic usually occurs during the late afternoon or evening and can last for hours. While crying, these babies tend to swallow a lot of air, which may make them feel even worse.

If the mother has a baby who is impossible to calm, tell her that some babies need to "blow off some steam" and continue crying for a while before they can settle down. By holding the baby when he cries, he will feel cared for until he eventually outgrows this sensitive stage.

Research indicates that chiropractic adjustment helps alleviate colic in some babies.

Research from Denmark, where chiropractic has been used since the turn of the century to treat infant colic, indicates that chiropractic adjustment may help reduce or eliminate colic in some babies (Nilsson 1985). One study of 316 babies with colic found that within 14 days and three chiropractic adjustments, 94% of mothers reported that the colic had improved or that the colic was gone (Klougart 1989). The researchers estimate that between 20-40% of all Danish infants with colic are treated by chiropractors.

A mother of an inconsolable baby may feel helpless, frustrated, and incompetent. Good support is important.

In order for the mother to be able to cope lovingly with her fussy baby, she needs support from those around her. The mother and the baby's father need to define priorities together and be realistic about how much time and energy they want to spend on other things while caring for their fussy baby. The mother also needs to find a way to meet her own needs. This is most easily accomplished when she has support people she can trust. If the mother would like more suggestions for caring for a colicky baby, refer her to the book THE FUSSY BABY by William Sears, MD, available through La Leche League International. Dr. Sears also discusses the concept of the high-need baby, one who may not be experiencing the physical discomfort of colic, but who is very sensitive and very persistent in his complaints. The shift to thinking in terms of the baby's needs has helped many parents see their demanding infant in a new light.

Publications for Parents

Boehle, D. *When Babies Cry*. Schaumburg, Illinois: La Leche League International, 1991. Publication No. 20.

Bumgarner, N. Mothering Your Nursing Toddler. Schaumburg, Illinois: La Leche League International, 1982.

Gotsch, Gwen. Breastfeeding: Pure & Simple. Schaumburg, Illinois: La Leche League International, 1994.

La Leche League International. *Increasing Your Milk.* Schaumburg, Illinois: La Leche League International, 1988. Publication No. 85.

La Leche League International. The Womanly Art of Breastfeeding, 35th Anniversary ed., Schaumburg, Illinois, 1991. pp. 73-75.

Mohrbacher, N. *When You Breastfeed Your Baby: The First Week.* Schaumburg, Illinois: La Leche League International, 1993. Publication No. 124a.

Renfrew, M., Fisher, C., and Arms, S. *Bestfeeding: Getting Breastfeeding Right for You.* Berkeley, California: Celestial Arts, 1990.

Sears, W. The Fussy Baby. Schaumburg, Illinois: La Leche League International, 1985.

Sears, W. Nighttime Parenting. Schaumburg, Illinois: La Leche League International, 1985.

Sears, W. *A Parent's Guide to Understanding and Preventing Sudden Infant Death Syndrome.* Boston: Little Brown, 1995.

References

Normal Breastfeeding Patterns

Brown, K. et al. Milk consumption and hydration status of exclusively breast-fed infants in a warm climate. *J Pediatr* 1986; 108:677-80.

Chua, S. et al. Influence of breastfeeding and nipple stimulation on postpartum uterine activity. *Br J Ob Gyn* 1994; 101:804-05.

Cohen, R. et al. Effects of age of introduction of complementary foods on infant breast milk intake, total energy intake, and growth: a randomised intervention study in Honduras. *Lancet* 1994; 344:288-93.

Cronenwett, L. et al. Single daily bottle use in the early weeks postpartum and breastfeeding outcomes. *Pediatrics* 1992; 90(5):760-66.

Crowell, M. et al. Relationship between obstetric analgesia and time of effective breastfeeding. *J Nurse Midw* 1994; 39:150-56.

deCarvalho, M. et al. Does the duration and frequency of early breastfeeding affect nipple pain? *Birth* 1984; 11:81-84.

deCarvalho, M. et al. Frequency of breastfeeding and serum bilirubin concentration. *Am J Dis Child* 1982; 136:737-38.

deChateau, P. and Wiberg, B. Long-term effect on mother-infant behaviour of extra contact during the first hour post partum. II. A follow-up at three months. *Acta Paediatr Scand* 1977; 66:145-51.

DeMarzo, S. et al. Initial weight loss and return to birth weight criteria for breast-fed infants: challenging the 'rules of thumb.' *Am J Dis Child* 1991; 145:402.

DiPietro, J. et al. Behavioral and heart rate pattern differences between breast-fed and bottle-fed neonates. *Develop Psych* 1987; 23(4):467-74.

Frantz, K. Baby's position at the breast and its relationship to sucking problems. Presented at LLLI Conference, 1983 and 1985.

Glover, J. and Sandilands, M. Supplementation of breastfeeding infants and weight loss in hospital. *J Hum Lact* 1990; 6:163-66.

Goldberg, N. and Adams, E. Supplementary water for breast-fed babies in a hot and dry climate—not really a necessity. *Arch Dis Child* 1983; 58:73-74.

Host, A. et al. A prospective study of cow's milk allergy in exclusively breastfed infants. *Acta Paediatr Scand* 1988; 77:663-70.

Houston, M.J. et al. The effect of extra fluid intake by breastfed babies in hospital on duration of breastfeeding. *J Reprod Infant Psych* 1984; i:42-48.

Kuhr, M. and Paneth, N. Feeding practices and early neonatal jaundice. *J Ped Gastro Nutr* 1982; 1(4):485-88.

Kurinij, N. and Shiono, P. Early formula supplementation of breastfeeding. *Pediatrics* 1991; 88:745.

Lawrence, R. *Breastfeeding: A Guide for the Medical Profession,* 4th ed. St. Louis: Mosby, 1994. pp. 267-68.

Meier, P. et al. A new scale for in-home test-weighing for mothers of preterm and high risk infants. *J Hum Lact* 1994; 10(3):163-68.

Moon, J. and Humenick, S. Breast engorgement: contributing variables and variables amenable to nursing intervention. *JOGNN* 1989; 18(4):309-15.

Neifert, M. et al. Nipple confusion: toward a formal definition. *J Pediatr* 1995; 126(6):S125-29.

Newman, J. Breastfeeding problems associated with early introduction of bottles and pacifiers. *J Hum Lact* 1990; 6(2):59-63.

Nicoll, A. et al. Supplementary feeding and jaundice in newborns. *Acta Paediatr Scand* 1982; 71:759-61.

Nissen, E. et al. Effects of maternal pethidine on infants' developing breast feeding behaviour. *Acta Paediatr* 1995; 84(2):140-45.

Nylander, G. et al. Unsupplemented breastfeeding in the maternity ward. *Acta Obst Gyn Scand* 1991; 70:205-09.

Righard, L. et al. Breastfeeding patterns: comparing the effects on infant behavior and maternal satisfaction of using one or two breasts. *Birth* 1993; 20(4); 182-85.

Righard, L. and Alade, M. Effects of delivery room routines on success of first breast-feed. *Lancet* 1990; 336:1105-07.

Riordan, J. and Auerbach, K. *Breastfeeding and Human Lactation*. Boston and London: Jones and Bartlett, 1993, pp. 93-94, 217-23.

Sepkoski, C. et al. The effects of maternal epidural anesthesia on neonatal behavior during the first month. *Dev Med Child Neurol* 1992; 34:1072-80.

Shrago, L. Glucose water supplementation of the breastfed baby in the first three days of life. *J Hum Lact* 1987; 3:82-87.

Smith, M. and Lifshitz, F. Excess fruit juice consumption as a contributing factor in nonorganic failure to thrive. *Pediatrics* 1994; 93(2):438-43.

Tyson, J. et al. Adaptation of feeding to a low fat yield in breast milk. *Pediatrics* 1992; 89(2):215-20.

Whitefield, M. et al. Validity of routine clinical test-weighing as a measure of the intake of breast-fed babies. *Arch Dis Child* 1981; 56:919-21.

Wimmer-Puchinger, B. and Nagel, M. The importance of attitudes during pregnancy and early mother-child contact for breast-feeding behavior: an empirical study. In: Prill, H-J, Stauber, M., eds. *Advances in Psychosomatic Obstetrics and Gynecology*. Berlin: Springer-Verlag 1982; 782-87.

Woolridge, M. et al. Do changes in pattern of breast usage alter the baby's nutrient intake? *Lancet* 1990; 336:395-97.

Woolridge, M. and Fisher, C. Colic, "overfeeding," and symptoms of lactose malabsorption in the breast-fed baby: a possible artifact of feed management? *Lancet* 1988; 2(8605):382-84.

Yamauchi, Y. and Yamanouchi, H. Breast-feeding frequency during the first 24 hours after birth in full-term neonates. *Pediatrics* 1990; 86:171-75.

Breastfeeding and Infant Sleep Patterns

Elias, M. et al. Sleep/wake patterns of breast-fed infants in the first 2 years of life. *Pediatrics* 1986; 77(3):322-29.

Ferber, R. *Solve Your Child's Sleep Problems*. Simon & Schuster: New York, 1985.

Keane, V. et al. Do solids help baby sleep through the night? *Am J Dis Child* 1988; 142:404-05.

Macknin, M. et al. Infant sleep and bedtime cereal. *Am J Dis Child* 1989; 143:1066-68.

McKenna, J. An anthropological perspective on the sudden infant death syndrome (SIDS): the role of parental breathing cues and speech breathing adaptations. *Med Anthropol* 1986; 10(1) Special issue.

McKenna, J. Rethinking "healthy" infant sleep. Breastfeeding Abstracts 1993; 12:27-28.

McKenna, J. et al. Sleep and arousal patterns of co-sleeping human mother/infant pairs: a preliminary physiological study with implications for the study of sudden infant death syndrome (SIDS). *Am J Phys Anthropol* 1990; 83:331-47.

McKenna, J. and Mosko, S. Evolution and infant sleep: an experimental study of infant-parent co-sleeping and its implications for SIDS. *Acta Paediatr* 1993; Suppl 389:31-36.

Mitchell, et al. Four modifiable and other major risk factors for cot death: the New Zealand study. *J Paediatr Child Health* 1992; 28 Suppl.1:S3-8.

Morelli, G. et al. Cultural variation in infants' sleeping arrangements: questions of independence. *Develop Psych* 1992; 28(4):604-13.

Pinilla, T. and Birch, L. Help me make it through the night: behavioral entrainment of breast-fed infants' sleep patterns. *Pediatrics* 1993; 91(2):436-44.

Weissbluth, M. *Healthy Sleep Habits, Happy Child.* New York: Fawcett, 1987.

The Let-Down or Milk-Ejection Reflex

Atkinson, H. and Biggs, E. The binding of drugs to major human milk whey proteins. *Br J Clin Pharmacol* 1988; 26:107-09.

Batagol, R. Drugs and breastfeeding. *Breastfeeding Rev* 1989; 14:13-20.

Berlin, C. Drugs and chemicals: exposure of the nursing mother. *Pediatr Clin North Am* 1989; 36:1089-97.

Berlin, C. et al. Disposition of dietary caffeine in milk, saliva, and plasma of lactating women. *Pediatrics* 1984; 73:59-63.

Dahlstrom, A. et al. Nicotine and cotinine concentrations in the nursing mother and her infant. *Acta Paediatr Scand* 1990; 79:142-47.

Lawrence, R. *Breastfeeding: A Guide for the Medical Profession,* 4th ed. St. Louis: Mosby, 1994. pp. 71-75, 188, 248-53, 375-6.

Lincoln, D. and Paisley, A. Neuroendocrine control of milk ejection. *J Reprod Fertil* 1982; 65:571-86.

Newton, M. and Newton, N. The let-down reflex in human lactation. *Pediatrics* 1948; 33:69-87.

Riordan, J. and Auerbach, K. *Breastfeeding and Human Lactation.* Boston and London: Jones and Bartlett, 1993, pp. 90, 527.

Steldinger, R. and Luck, W. Half lives of nicotine in milk of smoking mothers: implications for nursing (letter). *J Perinat Med* 1988; 16:261-62.

Pacifier Use

Amir, L. et al. Candidiasis & breastfeeding. *Lactation Consultant Series.* Unit 18. Garden City Park, New York: Avery Publishing, 1995.

Barros, F.C. et al. Use of pacifiers is associated with decreased breast-feeding duration. *Pediatrics* 1995; 95:497-99.

Cremer, G. and de Groot, W. An epidemic of thrush in a premature nursery. *Dermatologia* 1967; 135:107-14.

Kippley, J. and Kippley, S. *The Art of Natural Family Planning,* 2nd ed. Cincinnati, Ohio: The Couple to Couple League, Inc., 1979, pp. 196-98.

Kippley, S. *Breastfeeding and Natural Child Spacing,* 2nd ed. Cincinnati, Ohio: The Couple to Couple League, Inc., 1989, pp. 32-34.

Lawrence, R. *Breastfeeding: A Guide for the Medical Profession,* 4th ed. St. Louis: Mosby, 1994. pp. 187-88, 272-73, 371.

Neifert, M. et al. Nipple confusion: toward a formal definition. *J Pediatr* 1995; 126(6):S125-29.

Newman, J. Breastfeeding problems associated with early introduction of bottles and pacifiers. *J Human Lact* 1990; 6(2):59-63.

Victora, C.G. et al. Use of pacifiers and breastfeeding duration. *Lancet* 1993; 341:404-06.

Spitting Up

Ewer, A. et al. Gastric emptying in preterm infants. *Arch Dis Child* 1994; 71:F24-F27.

Heacock, H. et al. Influence of breast versus formula milk on physiological gastroesophageal reflux in healthy, newborn infants. *J Ped Gastro Nutr* 1992; 14:41-46.

Lawrence, R. *Breastfeeding: A Guide for the Medical Profession,* 4th ed. St. Louis: Mosby, 1994. p. 371.

Sutphen, J. Pediatric gastroesophageal reflux disease. *Gastro Clin N Amer* 1990; 19(3):617-29.

Crying and Colic

Hunziker, U. and Barr, R. Increased carrying reduces infant crying: a randomized controlled trial. *Pediatrics* 1986; 77:641.

Klougart, N. et al. Infantile colic treated by chiropractors: a prospective study of 316 cases. *J Manip Physiol Ther* 1989; 12(4):281-88.

Lawrence, R. *Breastfeeding: A Guide for the Medical Profession,* 4th ed. St. Louis: Mosby, 1994. p. 269-72.

Nilsson, N. Infantile colic and chiropractic. *Eur J Chiro* 1985; 33:264-65.

Riordan, J. and Auerbach, K. *Breastfeeding and Human Lactation.* Boston and London: Jones and Bartlett, 1993, pp. 239-40.

Sears, W. THE FUSSY BABY. Schaumburg, Illinois: La Leche League International, 1985.

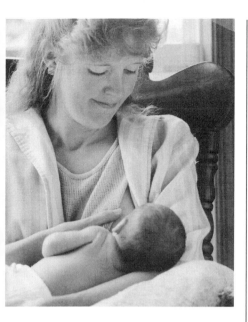

4

Positioning, Latch-On, and the Baby's Suck

POSITIONING
The Mother's Posture—Getting Comfortable
How the Mother Holds the Baby
Common Breastfeeding Positions
Breastfeeding Positions for Special Situations

LATCH-ON—HOW THE BABY GOES ON TO THE BREAST
Support the Breast When Needed
Encourage the Baby to Open His Mouth Wide
Pull the Baby in Close and Keep Him Close
Signs of a Good Latch-On
Coming Off the Breast

THE BABY'S SUCK
Signs of a Good Suck
Sucking Problems

IF BREASTFEEDING HURTS—REVIEW THE BASICS

Encourage the mother to give special attention to positioning and latch-on during the first week or two of nursing. After the early learning period, this is not necessary unless there is a problem.

During the early weeks of breastfeeding, while the mother and her baby are learning the basics, encourage the mother to give special attention to how she positions herself and her baby and how he latches on to the breast.

Good positioning and latch-on will help prevent sore nipples, as well as give the baby more milk for his efforts. A baby who is well-positioned and latched-on will better stimulate the mother's milk supply and get off to a healthier start. If the mother has persistent sore nipples or frequent mastitis or the baby is gaining weight slowly, poor positioning and latch-on may be contributing factors.

If both mother and baby are doing well, she no longer needs to be overly concerned about positioning and latch-on. As mother and baby become more practiced at breastfeeding, they will naturally find themselves nursing comfortably in a variety of positions and settings as they go about their daily activities.

Some babies are able to latch on and suck well from birth, while others need more help and practice. Both mother and baby influence the progress of breastfeeding in the early weeks.

Mother and baby are both active partners in the breastfeeding relationship. Mothers sometimes blame themselves when breastfeeding does not go smoothly, imagining that if they just knew more or did things differently, breastfeeding would have been easier. Although the mother's knowledge and skills can make a difference, the baby's coordination, skill, and temperament—as well as any special physical needs—are all important factors, too. Both mother and baby influence the progress of breastfeeding in the early weeks.

Good latch-on and sucking come easily to some babies. Other babies find it more difficult. For example, a baby who sucked his fingers or tongue *in utero* may need extra help learning to keep his tongue down while latching on to the breast in the early weeks.

If the baby seems to be having a difficult time, assure the mother that it is not her fault and with time, patience, and practice the baby will learn to breastfeed well. The first six weeks are the adjustment period, when mother and baby work together to find a good "fit." For some, a good "fit" comes easily; for others it takes more work.

POSITIONING

The Mother's Posture—Getting Comfortable

The mother needs to be well supported and comfortable so that she can hold her baby close to her breast and relax without straining any muscles.

Since the mother will spend several hours a day breastfeeding her baby, it is important that she position herself so that she can hold the baby close to her breast and relax without any of her muscles straining.

Ask her where she will be nursing at home (in a chair, on a sofa, in bed) and discuss ways she can make herself more comfortable. Encourage her to use pillows, cushions, rolled-up blankets, or other props to support her baby's weight and—if she is sitting up—to use a stool or low table for her feet.

Sitting Up to Breastfeed

Sitting up to breastfeed is usually more comfortable if the mother sits upright and has good support for her arms, back, and feet.

During the early weeks of breastfeeding, when the mother nurses sitting up, suggest she try to find a chair in which she can sit upright. A straight-backed armchair may be more comfortable for breastfeeding than a cushioned chair or sofa. The chair should have good back support so that she doesn't have to lean over her baby or lean too far back. Leaning over the baby may cause back and neck strain and leaning back too far can pull the mother's breast tissue away from her baby, making it more difficult for him to latch on well and keep the breast in his mouth.

For comfort's sake, suggest that she find a chair that's low enough so that her feet are flat on the floor and her knees are slightly raised. Even then, she may find it more comfortable to use a low footstool or table to prop her feet while she nurses.

If the mother prefers to breastfeed on a cushioned chair or sofa, suggest she use pillows behind her back and shoulders, under her arms, and anywhere else that will help her sit upright and feel well-supported. It may take quite a few pillows or cushions to accomplish this.

It is difficult for most women to find a comfortable position to breastfeed while sitting up in bed.

It is difficult to sit upright with legs outstretched or crossed underneath, which is why most women find it difficult to breastfeed sitting up in bed. If the mother wants to breastfeed this way, suggest she put something firm behind her back and a pillow under her knees.

Encourage the mother to use pillows or other props to bring her baby to breast height, so she doesn't have to support his weight throughout the feeding.

Because each mother has different physical characteristics—arms of different lengths and breasts at different heights—encourage the mother to experiment to find the most comfortable position for her.

An important part of this is making sure that the baby is well-supported so that the mother doesn't have to use her arm, shoulder, neck, and back muscles to support his weight throughout the feeding. Even a small baby can feel very heavy within a short time.

When nursing sitting up, most mothers will need to use pillows, cushions, or other props under the baby to support his weight. A mother with high breasts may need several pillows to support her baby at breast height.

Some large-breasted women have difficulty putting their babies to breast because when they are sitting their breasts come down almost to their lap. In this case, suggest the mother roll up a diaper or baby blanket and put it under her breast for support, to lift it high enough to allow the baby to latch on to the nipple more easily. This will also help her to see how the baby is latching on. Supporting and lifting the breast also helps to keep the breast from covering the baby's nose. Some large-breasted mothers find that breastfeeding goes more smoothly when they use the football hold position, because it gives them more control over their baby's head and other movements, as well as a better view of the latching-on process.

Lying Down to Breastfeed

If the mother lies on her side to breastfeed, pillows and other supports can help make nursing more comfortable.

If the mother nurses lying on her side, encourage her to experiment to find a position that is comfortable for her and her baby. A pillow under the mother's head is usually a must. Some mothers prefer several pillows or cushions to raise their upper body even more. Pillows are important behind the mother's back so she can lean back into them for support. Without pillows behind her back, a mother tends to lean forward toward the baby rather than pulling the baby close to her to nurse. A pillow under the mother's upper leg can make a big difference in helping her relax more completely.

The baby's position is also important. The baby's whole body should be facing the mother so that he doesn't have to turn his head or strain his neck to nurse. If the mother is lying on her side, this means the baby should also be lying on his side with his whole body facing his mother. Some mothers find it more comfortable to have the baby positioned with his head on the bed; other mothers rest the baby's head on their upper arm. Encourage the mother to use the position that feels most comfortable to her.

Nursing lying down is sometimes easier for large-breasted women than it is for small-breasted women, because the mother's breast may rest on the mattress, where her baby can easily latch on without the mother having to support her breast or her baby's head with her arm.

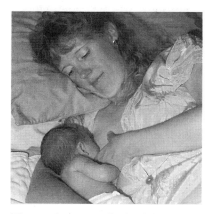

The mother can offer both breasts while lying on one side or roll over to nurse on the other breast.

To offer both breasts without rolling over, the mother can shift her position so she is leaning over her baby or—depending on the shape of the mother's breast—the upper breast may reach her baby's mouth without any change in the baby's position. If the mother wants to roll over to nurse her baby on the other breast, it may make the process easier if she holds her baby to her chest as she rolls over.

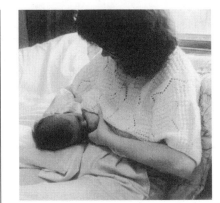

Slide-over position   *Football hold*

How the Mother Holds the Baby

Encourage the mother to bring the baby to the breast, not the breast to the baby.

Suggest the mother hold her baby close so that he directly faces her breast and doesn't have to turn his head or strain to reach the breast.

The baby's ear, shoulder, and hip should be in a straight line and his head tilted slightly back, so that he is not pulling at the breast and can swallow easily.

The baby's body should be well supported, so he feels secure.

The baby's head should be at nipple level or slightly below when he is ready to latch on.

Common Breastfeeding Positions

Cradle Hold

Once the mother is in a comfortable position, encourage her to bring the baby up to breast level, rather than leaning over to him. Leaning over to breastfeed can cause back and neck strain in the mother. In a large-breasted mother, leaning over can also affect latch-on by causing the baby to slip down onto the nipple as he breastfeeds, resulting in sore nipples and less effective breastfeeding.

Whether the mother is sitting up or lying down, the baby will nurse better if he is pulled in close so that his face is directly in front of the breast, with his mouth at nipple height or slightly below. In the cradle hold or the side-lying position, this would mean that he is on his side with his whole body facing hers. In the football hold, this would mean that his body is well-supported at breast height at his mother's side.

 If a baby has to turn his head to reach the breast, it can make swallowing more difficult and can contribute to nipple soreness.

The baby's head should be straight, in line with his body, not arched back or turned sideways. If the baby has to turn his head to breastfeed, it can make swallowing difficult and can contribute to nipple soreness.

 The easiest position for a baby to nurse is with his head slightly back, with his chin pressed gently into the mother's breast. If the baby's chin is tilted down toward his chest, swallowing would be more difficult. (The exception to this is the baby who is using his tongue improperly. He may nurse better if his chin is positioned slightly down toward his chest.)

If the baby feels well-supported and secure, it will enable him to concentrate on breastfeeding, rather than on how he is being held.

The baby should be supported at breast level, or slightly lower, so that the mother is not leaning forward to reach him and he is not straining to reach her nipple or pulling on the nipple once he is on the breast.

 Pillows, cushions, or other supports under the baby will help keep him at breast level without straining the muscles in the mother's arms, shoulders, neck, or back.

The cradle hold is a commonly used nursing position.

 To get comfortable, suggest the mother use pillows behind her back and shoulders, under the elbow of the arm she will be using to hold the baby, and in her lap to support the baby's weight.

 The mother holds the baby securely, with his head resting on her forearm or in the crook of her arm, whichever is more comfortable. His back is supported by her forearm, and her hand cups the baby's buttocks or thigh.

In the cradle hold, the mother sits up. The baby's head is resting on her forearm or in the crook of her arm. He is on his side facing her, pulled in close.

The baby should be positioned on his side with his knees pulled in close to his mother. He should not have to turn his head to take the breast. If he were naked, his umbilicus would not be visible. His ear, shoulder, and hip should be in a straight line.

The baby's bottom arm can be either under the mother's breast or tucked around her waist, depending on which is easier and more comfortable.

Cradle hold

Cross-cradle hold

If gulping and choking are a problem due to forceful let-down or low muscle tone, the baby can be positioned so that his neck and throat are higher than the mother's nipple.

If the mother has a forceful let-down or the baby has low muscle tone, he may tend to gulp and choke more easily. If this is a problem, have the mother try positioning her baby so that his neck and throat are higher than her nipple. She can do this by using the following positions.

- Add a third pillow under the baby and lean back slightly so that her breast is angled upward.
- Lean back in a rocking chair with her feet on a pillow, stool, or low table and her knees drawn up.
- Lie on her side with a folded bath towel under the baby so that his face is angled slightly downward toward her nipple.

Football or Clutch Hold

In the football or clutch hold, the mother is sitting up. Her baby's head faces the breast with his body tucked under her arm at her side. The baby's bottom rests on a pillow near his mother's elbow.

To get comfortable, suggest the mother put a pillow behind her shoulders and firm pillows at her side to raise the baby up to the level of her breast.

The baby faces the mother while his body is tucked under her arm along her side. The baby's bottom rests on the pillow near the mother's elbow with his hips against the back of the chair, sofa, or against the wall, if she is sitting up in bed. The baby's upper back rests along his mother's forearm while she supports his neck with her hand. (With the hypertonic—or arching—baby, it may be necessary to cover the mother's hand with a cloth and tuck up his feet so that nothing touches his soles.)

After the baby latches on, the mother settles back comfortably with her elbow nestled into the pillow at her side. If her arm tires, the mother can support her forearm with her thigh by bending her knee and placing her foot on a footstool or low table. An extra pillow or folded blanket can also help to support the wrist and hand under the baby's head.

The football hold gives better visibility and control over the baby's head and may be preferred in certain special situations.

Because the football hold offers the mother a clearer view of her baby and better control of the baby's head, it works especially well in certain special situations, for example, for the mother with large breasts or flat or inverted nipples.

The football hold is a good choice for a mother who has had a cesarean birth, because it allows her to breastfeed without putting pressure on her incision. (Also see "Finding a Comfortable Nursing Position" in the chapter "Cesarean Birth.") It may also be helpful for the baby who is sleepy or having difficulty learning to breastfeed.

The football or clutch hold works well for premature babies and babies with a weak suck, as it gives a good view of the baby's face, gives the mother control over the baby's head, and allows her to apply gentle pressure to the back of the baby's head, if needed.

Side-Lying

In the side-lying position, the mother and baby lie on their sides facing each other, with the baby's knees pulled in close.

In the side-lying position, the mother lies on her side. To get comfortable, she can put pillows under her head, behind her back, and under the knee of her upper leg. Her body is at an angle to the bed as she leans slightly backward into the pillow behind her back.

The baby is on his side facing his mother with his back resting against his mother's forearm and his knees pulled in close to his mother. (The cesarean mother may need to protect her incision from her baby's kicks with a small pillow, rolled baby blanket, or towel placed between her baby and her abdomen. This can also be tucked under the mother's abdomen to support her sagging muscles if they cause discomfort.)

To keep the baby on his side facing his mother, a folded towel, a rolled receiving blanket, or small pillow may need to be propped behind his back.

The mother can offer both breasts while lying on one side or she may prefer to roll over on her other side while the baby lies on her chest. A cesarean mother can minimize the pulling on her stitches when rolling over by pulling her baby to her chest with her arms and using the muscles in her legs to scoot her hips over to the other side, making sure she gets comfortable before she starts nursing again. (For a step-by-step description, see "Finding a Comfortable Nursing Position" in the chapter "Cesarean Birth.")

The side-lying position allows the mother to rest or sleep while her baby nurses. It is comfortable for cesarean mothers, because it puts no pressure on the mother's incision.

One advantage of the side-lying position is that it allows the mother and baby to rest or sleep while they nurse. Because the baby's weight does not rest on the mother's lap, it may be more comfortable for cesarean mothers than the cradle hold. Some mothers and babies master the side-lying position quickly, others find that it takes time. But even if it takes days or weeks of practice for mother and baby to get comfortable, it is well worth the time and effort. Once a mother learns to nurse in the side-lying position, she can rest or sleep while the baby breast-feeds, day and night, giving her more energy to care for her baby.

Breastfeeding Positions for Special Situations

Slide-Over

The slide-over position can be helpful in persuading a baby who is refusing one breast to nurse on the less preferred breast.

If a baby is refusing one breast or reluctant to nurse on one side, the slide-over position may help persuade him to nurse on the less preferred breast.

Suggest the mother nurse the baby first on the preferred breast, and after the let-down occurs, slide the baby over to the less preferred breast without changing the baby's body position, finishing the feeding with the preferred breast. (For other suggestions, see "Refusal of One Breast" in the chapter "Fussy at the Breast and Breast Refusal.")

Cross-Cradle, Modified Clutch, or Transitional Hold

The cross-cradle, also known as the modified clutch or transitional hold, is an effective position for babies who are having difficulty latching on. It is also effective for most small premies and babies with low muscle tone, a weak rooting reflex, or a weak suck, as the extra head support may help them to stay on the breast.

In the cross-cradle hold, the mother's hand is placed directly behind the baby's head for support and guidance. This is especially useful for a baby who is having difficulty latching on, as this hand gives the mother more control in guiding her baby quickly onto the breast as his mouth opens, which helps a baby latch on more effectively.

This hold may also be helpful for a premature baby (who tends to roll up into a ball when the cradle hold is used) or a baby with low muscle tone, a weak rooting reflex, or a weak suck. These babies will be able to stay on the breast more easily with gentle, steady pressure applied to the back of their heads.

To use the cross-cradle hold, suggest the mother:

- Position herself comfortably, with pillows behind her, leaning slightly back so that she does not have to bend over the baby.

- Support the baby in her lap on a pillow or cushion in a horizontal or semi-upright position.
- Hold the baby using the arm opposite the breast at which he will feed, i.e., the right arm when nursing at the left breast. The mother's hand supports the baby's neck and head; his body extends along the length of her forearm.
- Use her same-side hand to support the breast, i.e., her left hand, if she will be nursing on the left breast.
- Position the baby's mouth at the level of her nipple, or slightly lower, with baby's body on his side facing her.

Unusual Positions

If the mother has a sore spot on her nipple that seems to be aggravated by the usual nursing positions or wants to try new positions for a persistent plugged duct, suggest these unusual ones.

The following positions are rarely, if ever, needed, but there are situations in which they may be useful. If the mother has a sore spot on her nipple that is aggravated by the usual nursing positions or wants to try new positions for a persistent plugged duct, suggest she try these. Some may also be helpful for a baby who is having problems positioning his tongue correctly, such as the baby with a short tongue or frenulum, or the baby who is pulling his tongue up in back. Gravity may help bring the baby's tongue down when the baby approaches the breast with his head down (Marmet and Shell 1993; Maher 1988).

Prone positions. In all of these positions, the mother lies on her back with her head slightly elevated, and the baby lies face down on top of mother. The mother may be more comfortable if she supports her head and knees with pillows and puts pillows along her body on both sides to help support her arms as she holds the baby (Marmet and Shell 1993). In each of these positions, the baby's body position varies in relation to the mother's. In the horizontal prone (also known as the Australian position), the baby lies horizontally across the mother's chest, his body perpendicular to hers. In the vertical prone, the baby's body lies parallel to the mother's, with his feet resting on the same-side leg as the breast he is latched onto. In the lateral prone, the baby's body lies parallel to the mother but slightly off to the side; most of his weight is on the side of his body nearest the mother's arm, and he is cradled by her arm (the mother of twins can use this position with a baby at each arm). In the diagonal prone position, the baby's body is on an angle to the mother's, with his feet against the mother's opposite side. In the over-the-shoulder prone position, the baby lies on a pillow and approaches the breast over the mother's shoulder. This position works best with the older baby who has some head control.

Some mothers have found these positions helpful in the following unusual situations:

- The baby who is having trouble staying on the breast (gravity pulls baby toward the breast),
- The baby who is having trouble extending his tongue, i.e., short tongue, short frenulum, tongue thrust, tongue up in back, or retracted tongue (gravity helps draw down the tongue), and
- The baby who is having problems coping with a fast milk flow (gravity slows the milk flow).

These positions might also be helpful to the mother with a persistent plugged duct who wants to try various positions in order to improve the milk flow from different areas of the breast or the mother who has a sore spot on her nipple and is working to correct her baby's suck.

A disadvantage to positions in which the mother lies on her back is that gravity pulls the mother's breast tissue back, making it more difficult to achieve a good latch-on. To help overcome this disadvantage, suggest the mother hold her breast well behind the areola and compress the breast tissue slightly.

Upside down side-lying. The mother lies on her side with her baby lying on his side upside down in relation to her, with his feet pointing toward the mother's head. This position may offer some relief for nipple soreness, for example, for the mother who is working to correct her baby's poor suck. It is also another choice for the mother with persistent plugged ducts.

Hands and knees. The mother raises herself on her hands and knees above her baby, who lies flat on his back elevated by pillows to breast height. This is another position that offers an unusual angle for the mother with a persistent plugged duct or for nursing twins.

A baby who is having problems coping with milk flow may benefit from nursing in an upright position.

In addition to the prone positions described above, an upright nursing position may also be helpful for the baby who is having problems coping with milk flow. For example, a baby with a cleft palate may find these positions easiest because they can help prevent milk from leaking into his nose. (For other suggestions, see "Cleft Lip and/or Palate" in the chapter "The Baby with Special Needs.") If the mother has a very active let-down (or milk-ejection) reflex, a baby may also find it easier to cope with the fast milk flow if he is more upright. Possible positions to try include:

- **A modified football position**. If the mother is sitting on a sofa, have her sit the baby upright— facing her—at her side, with his legs along her side and his feet at her back. His bottom should be on the sofa or on a pillow (if he needs to be raised to breast level) with a pillow behind his back. The mother can then support the baby's back with her upper arm and his head with her hand. The mother may need to support her breast with her thumb on top and four fingers underneath.
- **Straddle position**. Suggest the mother sit her baby in her lap, facing her, with his legs straddling her abdomen. If the baby is small, it may be necessary to raise him to breast level by putting pillows under him. The mother may need to tip the baby's head back a little as baby latches on so she can position him carefully.

By leaning back when the baby is in the cradle or football hold, the mother can also take advantage of gravity in slowing the milk flow. A rocking chair or lounge chair may make this easier.

LATCH-ON—HOW THE BABY GOES ON TO THE BREAST

Support the Breast When Needed

During the early weeks, most mothers find breastfeeding goes more smoothly if they support their breast while latching on and throughout the feedings.

Suggest the mother support her breast with the C-hold—thumb on top and four fingers underneath— making sure her fingers are well behind the areola, especially underneath the breast.

The purpose of supporting the breast is to make it firmer for easier latch-on and to keep its weight off the baby's chin during feedings so that he stays latched-on well.

Even a mother with small breasts may find that during the early weeks of nursing some breast support helps her achieve better positioning and latch-on. Most mothers find that their breasts are at their largest during the early weeks of nursing and that some support is helpful.

The C-hold—thumb on top and four fingers underneath—allows the mother to gently support her breast without distorting the nipple. It also makes it easier to keep her fingers well behind the areola so that they will not be in the baby's way as he latches on to the breast.

Because a mother cannot easily see where her fingers are in relation to the underside of her areola, suggest that as she begins to support the breast she check carefully to be sure her fingers are far enough back so that they are not covering any part of the areola.

Suggest the mother with large breasts concentrate her efforts on supporting only the part of her breast near the areola. She does not need to be concerned about supporting the rest of her breast, although some large-breasted mothers find it more comfortable to put a rolled-up baby blanket or small towel underneath the breast to raise and support it slightly.

The "cigarette" or "scissors" hold has disadvantages.

Although it has been used for centuries and is often seen in breastfeeding photos or paintings, the "cigarette" or "scissors" hold—with the breast held between the mother's index and middle fingers—has disadvantages. Because the mother's fingers cannot stretch as far apart as the thumb and the fingers in the C-hold, they may get in the baby's way as he tries to latch on, preventing him from taking the breast far enough into his mouth, which can contribute to sore nipples. Some mothers using this hold actually restrict the amount of breast tissue that the baby can take. The extra pressure the fingers put on the breast may cause plugged ducts.

Positioning/Latch-On

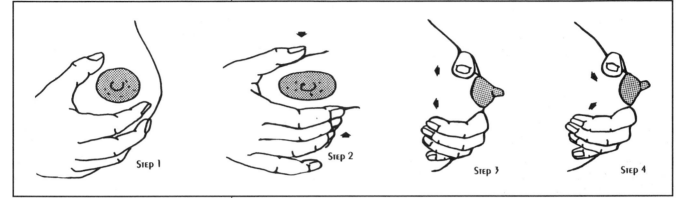

The "nipple sandwich" is another technique that makes latch-on easier for some mothers.

Barbara Heiser, a La Leche League Leader, registered nurse, and board-certified lactation consultant, developed a technique she calls the "nipple sandwich," which makes latch-on easier for some mothers.

The mother first uses the C-hold to support the breast, with her fingers under the breast and her thumb on top. Both fingers and thumb need to be well behind the areola (Step 1).

The mother then gently squeezes her fingers and thumb slightly together. This makes the areola area oblong, instead of round. This means that there is now a narrower part for the baby to latch on to (Step 2).

The mother then pushes in toward her chest wall or ribs. This helps the nipple protrude farther, which makes it easier for the baby to grasp (Step 3).

Finally, the mother pushes in with her thumb more than with her fingers. This makes the nipple point slightly upward toward the roof of the baby's mouth (Step 4).

After making the "nipple sandwich," the mother encourages the baby to open wide and pulls him in close, as described in the following sections.

Mothers with large breasts may need to support their breast beyond the learning period.

Mothers with large breasts may need to support their breast throughout the feeding until their baby is older, so that the weight of their breast does not rest on the baby's chin. Supporting and lifting the breast also helps the mother with large breasts to keep her breast from covering the baby's nose and keeps the breast in the baby's mouth. Unsupported, the weight of the heavy breast would put pressure on the baby's mouth, making it difficult for him to stay well latched-on. If the baby slips down to the nipple, he won't get as much milk for his efforts and may damage the mother's nipple.

Encourage the Baby to Open His Mouth Wide

When the baby is latched-on well, the mother should feel little or no nipple soreness.

After the first day of breastfeeding, it is normal for a mother's nipple to feel a little tender at the beginning of a feeding when the baby's first sucks stretch the nipple and areolar tissue far back into his mouth. This temporary tenderness usually diminishes once the milk lets down and disappears completely within a few days.

Aside from this normal tenderness, breastfeeding is not supposed to hurt. Sore nipples usually indicate that the breast needs to be farther back in the baby's mouth where it cannot be gummed or chewed. If poor latch-on is the cause of the soreness, breastfeeding should be comfortable within a day or two after latch-on is corrected.

If the soreness does not improve after three days of consistently working to correct the cause, it may indicate a sucking problem in the baby, which may mean he is not receiving enough milk. (See the later section "The Baby's Suck.")

The baby needs to open wide and take the breast deeply into his mouth for a good latch-on.

When the mother and baby are positioned comfortably, the baby should already be in front of the mother's nipple. Then he will need to open his mouth wide as he latches on and is pulled in close.

How wide is wide? Descriptions vary. In some parts of the world, breastfeeding counselors tell mothers their baby should open wide, "like a yawn." Because most mothers have seen their babies yawn, this gives them a useful comparison (as well as confidence that their baby can open wide). Although there are important differences between a baby yawning and a baby with a mouth open wide for breastfeeding (tongue placement, for one), this image clearly conveys the idea of "how wide" to many mothers. In England, the expression "wait for the gape" is used to describe not only "how wide" but also the need to wait. It could also be described as "open wide like a baby bird waiting for the worm." Whatever description is used, however, the basic idea is the same. For a good latch-on, the baby needs to open very wide, and the mother needs to wait until he does before pulling him in close.

Opening wide is vital because in order to breastfeed effectively the baby must take the breast far back into his mouth. To release the milk, the baby must compress the milk sinuses which lie well back from the nipple within the breast (about an inch to an inch-and-a-half). To do this, the baby's gums need to bypass the nipple completely and take in a large mouthful of breast. While the baby is opening wide, as the mother pulls him onto the breast, she should center the nipple in the space between the tongue and the baby's upper lip. Since the baby's lower jaw does most of the work during feedings, the baby's lower jaw should be as far back as possible from the nipple and his chin pressed into the breast.

Good latch-on is also important for the mother's comfort. Barbara Heiser suggests an easy way to explain to the mother the importance of proper latch-on. Ask the mother to put her index finger in her mouth just back to the first knuckle and then suck on it. She will feel how her tongue rubs the end of her finger. This is what happens to her nipple when the baby does not get enough of the breast in his mouth. Now ask the mother again to put her index finger in her mouth, but farther back, between the first and second joint, and suck as she did before. This time there is no rubbing. The tongue comes up under the finger, compressing it against the roof of the mouth, and does not touch the end at all. This vividly illustrates why getting the breast farther back into the baby's mouth can make the difference between sore nipples and comfortable breastfeeding.

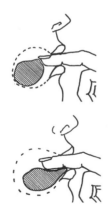

To encourage the baby to open wide, suggest the mother lightly tickle or brush the baby's lips with her nipple.

Babies are born with a reflex that causes them to open their mouths wide when properly stimulated. To trigger this reflex, suggest the mother lightly tickle or brush her baby's lips with the tip of her nipple and wait until the baby opens his mouth. (If the mother uses too much pressure, this will not produce the same response.) For some babies this may take some time, so encourage the mother to keep tickling or brushing and be patient. Some babies respond more quickly if just their bottom lip is lightly brushed or tickled.

Other ways to encourage the baby to open wide are to say the word "open," have the mother open her own mouth, and gently pull down on the baby's chin as he begins to open.

The mother can teach her baby other cues to encourage him to open wide. By saying the word "open" as she tickles or brushes the baby's lips and then opening her own mouth wide, he will learn to associate the word "open" and the mother's open mouth with the desired behavior. Rewarding him with the breast will reinforce this.

If the baby doesn't open his mouth, or doesn't open wide enough, the mother can open the baby's mouth wider by gently but firmly pulling down on the baby's chin with

the index finger of the hand supporting the breast as he is opening. It is important to pull down as the baby is opening because the baby's jaw muscles will be relaxed at that time. If the mother has a helper, suggest the helper pull down on the baby's chin as the mother is latching him on.

Pull the Baby in Close and Keep Him Close

If the baby goes on to the breast well, he will take a large mouthful of breast and be pulled in so close that his chin will be pressed into the mother's breast. His nose may rest on the breast.

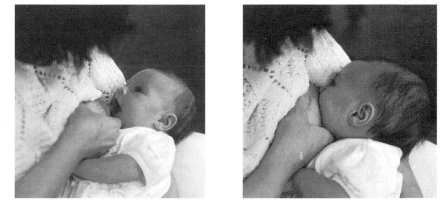

When the baby's mouth is opening wide, encourage the mother to pull him in quickly and gently so that he takes the breast deeply into his mouth. With a good latch-on, a baby's lower jaw (which does most of the work of nursing) should be as far back from the nipple as possible. Although the mother probably will not be able to see this herself, a helper may notice that more of the bottom than the top of the areola is covered (Royal College of Midwives, p. 18-19).

The baby should be pulled in so close that his chin is pressed into the mother's breast. His nose may rest on the breast as well. Some mothers are afraid to pull their babies in this close, because they worry that the baby won't be able to breathe. But a baby's nostrils are flared so that he can easily breathe even when his nose rests against the breast.

If the baby's breathing seems to be blocked by the breast, this is an indication that her positioning probably needs some adjusting. Rather than pressing down on her breast (which could pull the breast to the front of the baby's mouth), the mother should try lifting her breast and dropping her shoulder or pulling in the baby's legs closer to her.

If the baby does not go on the breast well, encourage the mother to gently take him off and try again.

Timing is very important. In order to get the baby latched-on well, the mother needs to pull him in quickly when he opens wide. If she pulls him in while his mouth is closing or before it opens fully, he may not latch on well.

During the early days and weeks of breastfeeding—while mother and baby are both still learning—it may take time and patience for the baby to latch on well. If the baby goes on the breast and the mother feels some discomfort or the baby does not seem to be sucking properly, encourage her to gently take the baby off the breast and try again. Allowing the baby to stay on the breast if it hurts the mother or if the baby is not sucking well may result in sore nipples and ineffective breastfeeding. To remove the baby comfortably, suggest the mother break the suction by using one of the techniques listed at the end of this section under "Coming Off the Breast" so that baby cannot clamp down on her nipple as she removes it from his mouth.

Assure the mother that with time and practice, latching the baby on well will get easier and more automatic.

The baby's body should be tucked in close to the mother.

If the mother is using the cradle hold, the baby should be on his side with his whole body facing hers. If they are breastfeeding lying down, the baby's knees should be pulled in close to the mother's body. In the football hold, the baby's knees should be tucked under mother's arm along her side. Being pulled in close will enable the baby to take the breast deeply into his mouth without his nose being blocked.

Good positioning and support will help assure the baby stays well latched-on throughout the feeding.

To breastfeed well and prevent nipple soreness, the baby will need to keep the breast deeply in his mouth throughout the feeding. Good positioning and support (pillows, cushions, or other props) will help the mother keep the baby at breast height without fatigue or muscle strain.

Without support, the mother's arm muscles may become tired. If the baby gradually drops below the height of the mother's breast, the breast will pull forward in his mouth, where his jaws will chew or gum the nipple.

Some babies need extra help in staying on the breast.

Some babies have a more difficult time than others in latching on and staying on the breast (for example, the baby with a weak suck, low muscle tone, a short tongue, or a short frenulum). For a baby like this, once the baby has opened wide and latched on to the breast, the mother may need to apply steady pressure on the baby's back or his head (see "Cross-Cradle Hold") to help him keep his mouth open wide and the breast deeply in his mouth.

The "Dancer Hand Position" (which is pictured and described in "Cleft Lip and/or Palate" in the chapter "The Baby with Special Needs") gives extra jaw and chin support and is another way to provide extra help for the baby who needs it.

Signs of a Good Latch-On

The baby's body is facing the mother so that he doesn't have to turn his head.

If the cradle hold or side-lying position is used, the baby should be on his side with his shoulders, hips, and knees facing mother. In the football hold, as well as the other holds, the baby's mouth should be directly in front of or slightly below the nipple.

The baby has taken the breast deeply into his mouth.

The baby needs to take a large mouthful of breast—not just the nipple—into his mouth. Although some recommend that the baby take in "all or most of the areola," this is not necessary or practical for women with very large areolae, who may achieve a good latch-on with some of the areola still visible. The suggestion that the baby take in "an inch or more" of the areola has also been called into question because in mothers with very small areolae, the baby may need to take in some of the surrounding breast tissue as well as the areola to achieve a good latch-on.

With a good latch-on, a baby's mouth should be pulled onto the breast so that the lower jaw is as far back from the nipple as possible, so a helper may notice that more of the bottom than the top of the areola is covered (Royal College of Midwives, p. 18-19). (The mother probably will not be able to see this herself.)

The baby is pulled in so close that his chin is pressed into the breast and his nose may rest on the breast.

When a baby is latched-on well, his chin should be pressed into the breast. His nose may be lightly resting on the breast. If the breast blocks his breathing, suggest the mother adjust her positioning by pulling the baby's knees closer to her or by slightly lifting her breast.

If the baby's chin and nose are away from the breast, it is likely that the baby does not have enough breast in his mouth. Suggest the mother break the suction, take the baby off the breast, and try again.

Once he is latched-on, the baby's lips are flanged out and relaxed.

If the mother (or her helper) sees that the baby's upper or lower lip are pulled in rather than flanged out, suggest she gently pull the lip out or take him off the breast and latch him on again with his mouth open wider.

If the baby sucks in either of his lips while nursing, it can cause nipple soreness.

The baby's tongue is cupped beneath the mother's breast.

If nursing is going well and the mother is comfortable, there is no need to check the baby's tongue.

If nursing is uncomfortable and the tongue cannot be seen, the baby may be sucking it along with the nipple or using it incorrectly. It will probably be difficult for the mother to see her baby's tongue while he is nursing, but if she is feeling discomfort, suggest she ask a helper to gently pull down the baby's bottom lip and see if the tongue can be seen between her breast and the baby's gum.

If the baby is retracting his tongue, suggest the mother take the baby off the breast and restart him, being sure his mouth is open very wide and his tongue is down when he latches on (Righard and Alade 1992). (See the later section, "Tongue Sucking, Retracted Tongue, or Tip of Tongue Curled Up.")

Coming Off the Breast

Encourage the mother to let the baby finish the first breast before offering the other breast.

Mothers are sometimes told to limit feedings in the early weeks of breastfeeding to help prevent sore nipples, but if the baby is positioned and latched-on well, there is no advantage to watching the clock. Encourage the mother to watch her baby for cues that he has finished the first breast before offering the other. When the baby has finished that breast, he will come off spontaneously or fall asleep.

Although babies usually nurse for a total of twenty to thirty minutes at a feeding, some babies nurse for shorter periods and others for longer periods. The same baby may nurse longer at one feeding than another.

Allowing the baby to determine when he's finished will ensure that the baby receives the right balance of the watery foremilk and high-calorie hindmilk. The milk increases in fat content as the feeding progresses, and only the baby knows if he's had the right amount of both and is satisfied.

Before taking her baby off the breast, suggest the mother first break the suction.

If the mother decides to take her baby off the breast before he is finished, suggest she first break the suction to avoid damage to sensitive breast tissue. There are several ways to break the suction:

- press down on her breast near the baby's mouth,
- pull down on the baby's chin,
- insert a finger into the corner of the baby's mouth.

THE BABY'S SUCK
Signs of a Good Suck

After a period of quick sucking, the baby's sucking should deepen and the mother should hear regular swallowing. There will be a "wiggle" at the junction of the baby's ears and temples.

A baby usually begins breastfeeding with a period of quick sucking to stimulate his mother's let-down, or milk-ejection, reflex. After the initial let-down occurs, the mother should be able to hear him swallow after every one or two sucks. This suck-swallow pattern should last on average about ten to twenty minutes for most babies, with the baby swallowing less frequently as the feeding progresses.

If the baby is sucking well, the mother should see a "wiggle" at the junction of his temples and ears.

Another sign of a good latch-on and suck is that breastfeeding is comfortable for the mother.

Sore nipples are one of the first symptoms of many of the sucking problems listed in the following section. If a baby is not using his mouth and tongue correctly, it may cause nipple pain, so comfortable breastfeeding, when the other signs are also present, is a good indication that baby is latched-on and sucking well.

A baby who is sucking well will end the feeding when finished.

When a baby is latched-on, positioned, and sucking well, he will come off the breast spontaneously when he is finished, either by falling asleep or popping off on his own. According to the Royal College of Midwives in their 1991 book, *Successful Breastfeeding,* "A baby is able to express satiety, as well as hunger, by his behavior" (p. 18).

To reassure the mother that her baby is latched-on and sucking well, she can keep track of her baby's wet diapers and bowel movements.

Another way for the mother to reassure herself that her baby is latched-on and sucking well is to keep count of his wet diapers and bowel movements. Beginning on the third or fourth day after birth, the baby should wet at least six to eight cloth diapers (five to six disposable diapers) and have two to five bowel movements (fewer bowel movements are normal if the baby is older than six weeks).

To gauge the wetness of a disposable diaper, suggest the mother pour two to four tablespoons (one to two ounces or 30-60 ml) of water on a dry diaper and compare how it feels with her baby's usual wet diaper. Baby's urine should be clear and not concentrated.

Sucking Problems

Questions to Ask

Not all breastfeeding experts agree on how to evaluate and treat sucking problems.

Although the basics of good breastfeeding are the same worldwide, approaches vary. For example, some breastfeeding experts believe that nearly all sucking problems can be alleviated by improving latch-on and positioning (Fisher and Woolridge 1991). While other experts emphasize the importance of latch-on and positioning, in addition, they have evolved various "suck training" techniques, in which a finger inserted in the baby's mouth is used to manipulate his mouth and tongue, teaching him to correct his suck in order to improve breastfeeding (Marmet and Shell 1993; Marmet and Shell 1984). For some babies with sucking problems, other experts turn first to breastfeeding devices, such as the nursing supplementer, to increase weight gain and improve the baby's suck (Riordan and Auerbach, p. 527-31).

Many breastfeeding counselors incorporate variations of some or all of these approaches, tailoring them to the needs and preferences of each mother and baby (McIntyre 1995). For additional help, some also refer parents to a neurodevelopmental therapist (NDT), an occupational, physical, or speech therapist with special certification and training in working with infant muscle and motor problems. (For information on finding an NDT in your area, see the "Resources for Parents" listing at the end of this chapter.)

Helping a mother improve her baby's suck will take time and careful experimentation. Offer a few suggestions at a time, and evaluate them with the mother a day or two later.

Ask the mother about her baby's weight gain and how many wet diapers and bowel movements he has per day.

When discussing the baby's weight gain, refer to the section "First, Establish Weight Gain and Loss" in the "Slow Weight Gain" section of the "Weight Gain" chapter.

Next see "Second, Discuss Breastfeeding Management," also under "Slow Weight Gain." If the baby continues to lose weight even after his mother's milk "comes in" and breastfeeding management is good, this is a strong indication that the baby has a sucking problem.

After the first two or three days, fewer than six wet diapers and/or two bowel movements a day can be another strong indication of an ineffective suck. (Fewer bowel movements are normal for the baby older than six weeks of age.)

If the baby has six or more wet diapers and the baby is younger than six weeks, fewer than two bowel movements a day may also be a sign of a sucking problem. Even with a poor suck, the baby may receive enough of the mother's foremilk to wet six or more diapers a day, but he may not be adequately stimulating his mother's breasts to let down the fatty, high-calorie hindmilk.

If the baby has fewer wet diapers, see the following sections to help determine the problem and for suggestions on how to help him improve his suck. If his suck does not improve immediately, the baby may need to be given a supplement—either expressed mother's milk or formula—until he is able to breastfeed more effectively.

BASIC INFORMATION	BACKGROUND NEEDED
Ask the mother to describe her baby's nursing pattern and his suck. Ask her if anything concerns her about the way he nurses.	If a sucking problem is suspected, the mother's description of her baby's nursing pattern and suck should provide some clues. For example, if the baby nurses more than ten to twelve times a day and longer than thirty to forty-five minutes at each feeding (the mother may say he nurses "all the time") he may not be sucking effectively (Frantz 1992). A sleepy baby sleeps a lot, nurses fewer than ten times a day, and falls asleep during feedings. If the mother says her baby pushes the breast out of his mouth with his tongue, he may have a tongue thrust or protruding tongue, which is especially common in babies with Down Syndrome.
Ask the mother if she hears her baby swallowing while he nurses, and if so, how often.	If the mother is not sure when her baby is swallowing, describe the sound she should listen for—a quiet, exhaled "kaa, kaa, kaa." Typically, a baby begins breastfeeding with a period of quick sucking to stimulate his mother's let-down (milk-ejection) reflex. After her let-down reflex occurs, the mother should be able to hear him swallow after every one or two sucks. This suck-swallow pattern should last at least ten to twenty minutes, with the baby swallowing less frequently as the feeding progresses. If the baby is not swallowing regularly, he will not be getting the milk he needs.
Ask the mother if the baby's cheeks dimple in or if he makes a clicking sound when nursing.	If the baby's cheeks are dimpled or he makes a clicking sound while nursing, he may not be effectively milking the breast. A baby who repeatedly breaks the suction while he is nursing is probably using his tongue incorrectly.
Ask the mother how her nipples feel.	If the baby has a sucking problem, such as a tongue thrust or any of the other incorrect tongue movements, a short frenulum (tongue-tie), or a clenching response, it may cause the mother to develop sore nipples.
Ask the mother if she was engorged during the baby's first week and if she has had persistent sore nipples or frequent mastitis.	When a baby has a sucking problem, the lack of adequate breast stimulation during the first week can result in unrelieved engorgement for the mother, which will rapidly reduce the mother's milk supply. Severe engorgement could be a clue that the baby's suck was incorrect from birth. Another clue is that despite proper positioning, the mother has persistent sore nipples and/or frequent mastitis. This is a sign that the baby is sucking improperly and/or not milking the breast effectively.
Ask the mother if the baby has had any health problems.	A baby born prematurely may have a weak suck due to an immature nervous system. A weak suck can also be caused by illness. In both cases, the baby's suck may grow stronger with time and treatment.
Ask the mother if she would describe her baby as relaxed, like a floppy doll. Is the baby cuddly or hard to hold? Does he frequently arch away from the mother during breastfeeding or at other times?	If the mother describes her baby as "floppy," he may have low muscle tone. If he is "hard to hold" and the mother says he arches away from her whenever she tries to nurse him, the baby may have overactive muscle tone. Both low muscle tone and overactive muscle tone may indicate that the baby's nervous system is temporarily immature or that the baby is neurologically impaired. If you suspect this kind of a problem, suggest the mother have her baby checked by his doctor. (See "The Neurologically Impaired Baby" in the chapter "The Baby with Special Needs.")
Sleepy Baby The baby sleeps a lot, nurses less than ten times a day, and falls asleep during feedings.	It may help the mother to find the reasons for her baby's temporary sleepiness.

Positioning/Latch-On

Ask the mother about her labor and delivery, her baby's health, and when her baby's sleepiness began.	**Labor and delivery.** A difficult labor and delivery, as well as some drugs given during labor and birth, may make a baby sleepy, less interested in nursing, and affect a baby's ability to coordinate sucking, swallowing, and breathing while at the breast (Nissen 1995; Crowell 1994; Righard and Alade 1992; Sepkoski 1992; Righard and Alade 1990).

Medical reasons, such as jaundice or infection. When a baby is sleepy, there may be a medical cause. Ask the mother when the baby was last seen by his doctor.

Jaundiced babies are often sleepy. If the baby is jaundiced, emphasize the need for frequent, round-the-clock breastfeeding. The laxative effect of the mother's colostrum will encourage more frequent bowel movements, which will help the baby pass meconium more quickly, preventing the intestinal reabsorption of bilirubin. (Supplemental water or glucose water do not help lower bilirubin levels.) See the chapter "Newborn Jaundice" for more information.

Mother's milk "coming in." If the baby's sleepiness started after the mother's milk became more plentiful on the third or fourth day of life, the baby may be finding it difficult to get used to the increased volume of milk, and he may be tuning out. Babies sometimes react to this by falling asleep within a minute or two of nursing (Maher 1988).

Too much stimulation. If the environment is too stimulating—too much bright light and noise—the baby may tune out by falling asleep. If so, suggest the mother try breastfeeding in quiet surroundings. |
| A sleepy baby needs to be awakened to breastfeed to get enough milk. | To get enough milk and establish a healthy milk supply during the first weeks of nursing, babies need to breastfeed at least eight to ten times every twenty-four hours. Because newborns tend to "cluster nurse," that is, breastfeed frequently at certain times of the day and go longer between feedings at others (one four- to five-hour sleep period is considered normal), suggest the mother look at each day as a whole, rather than attempting to nurse at certain set intervals.

The mother should also listen to be sure she can hear the baby swallowing during the feedings. The baby needs to nurse actively for at least ten to twenty minutes total in order to get the fatty hindmilk and stimulate the mother's milk production.

If the baby is nursing less than eight to ten times every twenty-four hours, the mother will need to wake and stimulate her baby to nurse more. Suggest she attempt to wake the baby when he shows signs of being in a light sleep, rather than a deep sleep. (See "How to Rouse a Sleepy Baby," which follows, for specific cues to look for.) |
| Encourage the mother to keep trying until she finds a way to wake her baby and keep him alert at the breast. | Different babies will respond differently to the following waking techniques. By experimenting, the mother will find a gentle and effective way to wake her baby and keep him interested in nursing until his sleepiness passes.

Rather than reciting the whole list at once, give the mother two or three ideas at a time. This will make it easier for her to remember them and make breastfeeding sound more manageable. Encourage her to keep in touch to let you know if the techniques don't work so that you can offer more suggestions. |

How to Rouse a Sleepy Baby

Waking Techniques
- Try arousing the baby when he's in a light sleep cycle. Although baby's eyes will be closed, look for rapid eye movements under the eyelids, arm or leg movements, sucking/lip movements, changes in facial expression.
- Dim the lights as bright lights may make the baby close his eyes.
- Loosen or remove blankets.
- Unwrap the baby down to the diaper if the room is warm—sucking activity decreases in temperatures above 80° F (27° C).
- Talk to the baby. Try to make eye contact.
- Hold baby in an upright or standing position.
- Bend the baby into gentle sit-ups on the mother's lap by raising his head, shoulders, and torso, bending him at the hips. Never try to bend the baby at the waist, as this could cause internal damage.

Increasing Stimulation
- Rub or pat the baby's back or suggest the mother walk her fingers up baby's spine.
- Change the baby's diaper.
- Gently rub the baby's hands and feet.
- Increase baby's skin-to-skin contact with mother with a massage or bath.
- Manipulate baby's arms and legs in a gentle "pat-a-cake."
- Wipe the baby's forehead and cheeks with a cool, damp cloth.
- Circle the baby's lips with a fingertip.
- Express milk onto the baby's lips.

Keeping the Baby Interested
- Make sure the hand supporting the breast keeps the weight of the breast off the baby's chin.
- Switch breasts as soon as the baby begins to lose interest in sucking.
- Burp the baby or change his diaper between sides to keep interest high.
- Try nursing using the football hold rather than the cradle hold.
- Massage the baby's crown in a circular motion while nursing.

cusping - winding

Lazy Nurser

The lazy nurser stays attached to the breast but "flutter sucks" rather than nursing vigorously. He may nurse more than ten times a day, cry when taken off the breast, and gain weight slowly.

The lazy nurser has fewer than the usual two to five bowel movements during his early weeks and may or may not have enough wet diapers.

A lazy nurser does not take the breast far enough back into his mouth. Because the nipple is near the front of his mouth, his jaws do not compress the milk sinuses, and he gets little milk for his efforts. In order to get the milk he needs, he may nurse "all the time" and cry when the mother tries to take him off the breast.

The lazy nurser usually nurses with his eyes closed. He sucks at the breast as he would on a pacifier, using only his lips to "flutter suck." The mother will not see a "wiggle" near her baby's temple while he breastfeeds because his jaws do not move vigorously, as they would in a baby with a better suck. Because he does not stimulate the breast well, he gets mostly the watery foremilk and gains weight slowly.

Some lazy nursers do not wake at night to breastfeed.

If the baby has six to eight wet cloth diapers per day (five to six disposable diapers), but fewer than the normal two to five bowel movements, suggest the mother try "super switch nursing" (see next point) to try to improve her baby's suck.

If the baby has fewer wet diapers per day, this may mean that the mother's milk supply is low, especially if the diapers have a strong odor or the urine is concentrated. If so, suggest the mother start "super switch nursing" but also have the baby checked by his doctor. The baby may need a supplement of expressed mother's milk or formula, which can be given via cup, eyedropper, or other alternative feeding method. At the same time, the mother can try "super switch nursing."

"Super switch nursing" may stimulate the baby to breastfeed more effectively, building up the mother's milk supply and increasing the baby's weight gain.

The goal of "super switch nursing" is to stimulate the baby to suck more actively at the breast.

The mother keeps her baby at the breast as long as he is swallowing after every one or two sucks or so. As soon as he begins swallowing less often or closes his eyes and begins drifting off to sleep, the mother takes him off the breast and bends him gently forward from his hips several times to wake him up, and then puts him to the other breast where he continues to nurse as long as he swallows regularly. When he begins to swallow less often, the mother again switches the baby back to the first breast after burping him or bending him at the hips to stimulate him to be more alert. The "wake-and-switch" pattern continues for twenty to thirty minutes at least every two hours during the day, and every four hours at night. With some babies the mother may need to switch sides every thirty to sixty seconds, especially at first.

Within one or two days, the mother will probably notice an increase in wet diapers and bowel movements, as well as more regular swallowing. The mother may also begin noticing signs of increased milk supply, such as leaking and feelings of fullness.

If two or three days of "super switch nursing" do not produce a noticeable improvement, suggest the mother have her baby checked by his doctor to rule out illness or other physical causes.

If "super switch nursing" does not improve a baby's effectiveness at the breast ask the mother how she would feel about using a nursing supplementer.

When a baby swallows, the natural response is to suck. A nursing supplementer—a device that allows the baby to receive supplements through a tube taped to the mother's breast—is designed to stimulate this natural response to help improve a baby's suck while providing needed supplement. (This device is readily available in the USA but may not be an option in some countries.)

Ask the mother how she would feel about using a nursing supplementer. Some women are comfortable using a device at the breast, while others are not. Explain that its use may help the baby to learn to breastfeed more effectively and that she could use it to provide either expressed mother's milk or formula at the breast.

A nursing supplementer may help a baby learn to suck more effectively because the extra milk he gets from the supplementer stimulates him to swallow and consequently suck more often. As the baby's suck becomes more vigorous, he will receive more milk from the breast and further stimulate the mother's milk supply. As a baby begins to take more milk from the breast he automatically takes less from the supplementer. The mother can gauge her baby's progress in part by how much of the supplement is left after nursings.

However, not all babies respond to the nursing supplementer this way. Some babies take the supplement from the nursing supplementer without sucking vigorously; thus they receive the needed supplement but do not improve their suck or stimulate the mother's milk supply. Even so, there may still be advantages to using the nursing supplementer. It allows the mother to supplement her baby without using bottles, which can cause more breastfeeding problems. The nursing supplementer allows the whole feeding time to be spent at the breast, while bottles and other alternative feeding methods are used after nursings.

If breastfeeding does not improve with the use of the nursing supplementer, suggest the mother contact someone with training in sucking problems relating to breastfeeding. Some neurodevelopmental therapists (NDT) are experienced in helping mothers and babies overcome sucking problems. To find an NDT in your area, see the "Resources for Parents" listing at the end of this chapter. (For more information on using the nursing supplementer, see "The Use of Breast Pumps and Other Products.")

Weak Suck

The baby with a weak suck actively nurses, with swallowing, for less than five minutes per breast, never seems satisfied, and has problems staying on the breast.

Although the baby may want to nurse "all the time," the mother cannot hear him swallowing regularly. He may appear to be just mouthing the nipple without regularly swallowing.

Positioning/Latch-On

The baby with a weak suck can be distinguished from a lazy nurser by his difficulty in latching on and staying on the breast. The mother of a baby with a weak suck may say:

- the breast keeps coming out of the baby's mouth, especially when the mother moves even a little,
- milk leaks out of the baby's mouth while nursing,
- the baby chokes on the milk while nursing (this could also be a sign of a forceful let-down reflex).

If a baby is not taking the breast far enough back into his mouth, it may be difficult for him to stay on the breast. If he also has low muscle tone, it may be difficult for him to coordinate sucking and swallowing rhythms, making him more likely to choke or leak milk during breastfeeding. (For suggestions for the baby with low muscle tone, see "Down Syndrome" in the chapter "The Baby with Special Needs.")

Ask the mother if the baby has ever had artificial nipples—bottles, nipple shields, or pacifiers.

Artificial nipples given during a baby's first month can cause a baby's suck to weaken. The mother may notice that the baby keeps the breast near the front of his mouth and purses his lips with his tongue forward. This makes it impossible for the baby to stay on and effectively milk the breast. The mother may develop sore nipples. (Also see the later section, "Tongue Thrust")

A weak suck has several possible causes.

A weak suck may be caused by:

- introduction of bottles or other artificial nipples during the baby's first month,
- an immature nervous system or neurological impairment,
- illness,
- loss of strength due to not getting enough milk.

If a baby is receiving less milk than he needs, he may lose strength, affecting his suck and causing him to breastfeed less effectively. In this case, once a baby is receiving more calories, his suck will become stronger.

Some people believe a weak suck can also be caused by a baby learning to suck improperly *in utero*.

If a weak suck is identified within the first week after birth, encourage the mother to take action as soon as possible.

If the baby has a weak suck, lack of breast stimulation during the first week can result in unrelieved engorgement for the mother, which will rapidly reduce the mother's milk supply. If untreated, the baby's suck may become even weaker due to continuing weight loss.

Identifying and treating the baby's weak suck within his first week allows the mother to begin expressing her milk and offering it to her baby before her milk supply begins to decrease and before the baby begins losing too much weight.

Sometimes a weak suck is not identified until the baby is older.

A weak suck may not become apparent until the baby is several weeks old and he stops gaining well. Sometimes it can be traced to early introduction of bottles or pacifiers. Other times the cause is unknown. Sometimes when a baby is not gaining well and begins to lose strength, his suck will weaken as well.

As with a younger baby, the older baby with a weak suck will spend a lot of time at the breast, but very little of it will be spent effectively sucking and swallowing. Watching and listening to determine if the baby is regularly swallowing will tell the mother whether or not the baby is sucking effectively.

A baby with a weak suck may temporarily need extra help to get the milk he needs.

Once a mother recognizes that her baby has a weak suck, expressing milk into her baby's mouth or giving supplements will ensure the baby receives the nourishment he needs while he is learning to nurse more effectively. There are several options for giving supplements. The mother can:

- hand-express colostrum or milk directly into her baby's mouth while he's nursing, or
- after nursing, she can express her milk to give to her baby during a later nursing or between nursings.

In order to maintain her milk supply, the mother will need to express her milk, which is also the best supplement for her baby. If the mother prefers to use another supplement, she should contact her doctor for a recommendation.

Explain that she can give the baby her expressed milk (or other supplement) during feedings with a nursing supplementer. She can also use the supplementer for finger feeding to get a sleepy baby interested in nursing (see "The Use of Breast Pumps and Other Products."). Or she can supplement between nursings with a cup, bowl, spoon, eyedropper, or feeding syringe. Be sure the mother knows that giving bottles may further weaken the baby's suck. (For suggestions on how and when to offer supplements, see "Working with the Doctor and Supplementation" in the "Slow Weight Gain" section of the "Weight Gain" chapter.)

Explain to the mother that these extra efforts will be necessary only temporarily, that she will be able to stop supplementing gradually when the baby begins gaining well (four to five ounces [113-140 grams] per week), has at least six wet diapers and two bowel movements per day (fewer bowel movements if the baby is older than six weeks), and is nursing more effectively.

A baby whose suck remains weak for more than three to four months, despite all efforts to improve it and good medical care, may have a neurological dysfunction, which would be diagnosed by a doctor.

There are many ways to help the baby improve a weak suck.

For a baby with an immature nervous system, all he may need is time to mature. However, for some babies, the following suggestions can help speed up the process and strengthen the baby's suck.

Suggest the mother have the baby's doctor do a thorough medical evaluation to rule out illness or physical problems. Any baby who is gaining slowly should be evaluated regularly by the doctor until his weight gain improves. A weak suck may be one of the first signs of an illness, such as a urinary tract infection (Marmet and Shell 1993).

Stimulate the baby's lips before breastfeeding. Just before putting the baby to breast, suggest the mother circle the baby's lips with her index finger three times clockwise, then three times counterclockwise, touching them gently but firmly. This may help the baby get a better seal on the breast.

Give careful attention to latch-on and positioning. During latch-on, have baby open wide before pulling him in close. It is important that the baby open his mouth wide (like a yawn) when latching on to the breast. If the baby has received artificial nipples, he may be reluctant to open wide. In this case, suggest the mother pull down gently on the baby's chin as he is opening his mouth and clearly say the word "open" as she is latching him on.

Also, encourage the mother to pull the baby in especially close once his mouth is open in order to get as much of the breast in his mouth as possible. This will stimulate sucking. Tell the mother that the baby should be pulled in so close that his chin is pressed into her breast, and his nose touching her breast. Reassure her that if he has trouble breathing he will let her know so she can adjust his position.

Support the baby's jaw and chin during feedings. If it is difficult for the baby to keep the breast in his mouth during feedings, suggest that the mother use the Dancer Hand Position while nursing to support the baby's chin and hold his jaw steady, freeing him to concentrate his energies on nursing. (For more information, see the section, "Cleft Lip and/or Palate," in the chapter "The Baby with Special Needs.")

Try different nursing positions. If the baby has a weak rooting reflex, it is important for the mother's nipple to be far back in his mouth to stimulate sucking. Experiment with different nursing positions to see if the strength of the baby's suck improves in the football hold or side-lying position. Some babies suck more effectively in the cross-cradle, or transition hold, which is described in the previous section, "Breastfeeding Positions for Special Situations." The constant gentle pressure on the back of the baby's head by the mother's hand enables him to stay on the breast more easily and suck more effectively. It also gives the mother more control over her baby's movements.

Suggest the mother try "super switch nursing." When the mother notices the baby doze off or stop swallowing regularly, she should burp him or bend him at the hips and switch him to the other breast, repeating this several times throughout the feeding. This is the same approach used to encourage more active sucking in a lazy nurser.

Use a nursing supplementer to supplement feedings. When a baby swallows, the natural response is to suck. A nursing supplementer—a device that allows the baby to receive supplements through a tube taped to the mother's breast—is designed to use this natural response to improve a baby's suck while providing needed supplements. A nursing supplementer helps some babies learn a more effective sucking pattern because the extra milk baby gets from the supplementer stimulates him to swallow and consequently suck more often. If the baby's suck becomes more vigorous as a result, he will also receive more milk from the breast and further stimulate the mother's milk supply. As a baby begins to suck more effectively, he automatically takes more milk from the breast and less from the supplementer. The mother can gauge her baby's progress in part by how much of the supplement is left after nursing.

However, not all babies respond to the nursing supplementer this way. The baby with a very weak suck may take the supplement from the nursing supplementer without sucking vigorously, which provides him with the needed supplement, but may not improve his suck or stimulate the mother's milk supply. In this case, the baby's suck may improve with time and maturity. In the meantime, however, the nursing supplementer can help preserve breastfeeding. If the baby's suck does not improve with the nursing supplementer, suggest the mother contact someone with training in sucking problems relating to breastfeeding, such as a neurodevelopmental therapist (NDT). To find an NDT in your area, see the "Resources for Parents" listing at the end of this chapter. (For more information on using the nursing supplementer, see "The Use of Breast Pumps and Other Products.")

Dancer Hand Position

The mother may lack the confidence necessary to stop supplementing when her baby's suck becomes stronger.

A mother needs continuing support while her baby's supplements are gradually discontinued. Even though all the outward signs indicate that her baby is doing well, the mother may lack confidence that her baby can get all the nourishment he needs at the breast, and she may need extra encouragement during this time.

Tongue Thrusting

A baby with a tongue thrust pushes his tongue against the mother's nipple. He may or may not push the breast out of his mouth at the beginning of a feeding. The mother may have sore nipples.

Ask the mother if her baby has been given bottles or a pacifier or if she has used a nipple shield.

Ask the mother if her baby was born early.

Positioning the baby so that his chin is down and he is sitting up while he nurses may help him keep his tongue down.

The mother may be able to help the baby stop thrusting his tongue by tickling his lips with her nipple.

To encourage the baby to use his tongue correctly, suggest the mother try "Pushing the Tongue Down and Out" or "Walking Back on the Tongue."

Soreness at the tip of the nipple may be caused by tongue thrusting. (Other possible causes include a retracted tongue, short frenulum, and poor latch-on.)

If the mother says the baby pushes her breast out of his mouth, this is a sign of tongue thrust, but not all babies with tongue thrust push the breast out of their mouth at the beginning of the feeding. Some babies nurse well while the milk from the first let-down is flowing quickly and begin thrusting their tongue only after the milk flow subsides.

If the mother says the baby has been given artificial nipples, the baby may have learned from them to push out his tongue or to chew at the breast (Lawrence, p. 236-37). (Also see the section, "Nipple Confusion" in the chapter "Fussy at the Breast and Breast Refusal.") In this case, suggest the mother give only the breast while she is teaching the baby to use his tongue correctly. In most cases, after a baby has been breastfeeding well for several weeks, artificial nipples will not affect his suck.

If the mother says her baby has not been given artificial nipples, ask her if the baby has acted this way since birth. He may have sucked his tongue *in utero* and is not dropping it to accept the breast in his mouth.

A baby born early may have an immature neurological system and be more likely to thrust his tongue than a full-term healthy baby.

The baby's tongue may relax if the mother positions him at the breast so that his chin is slightly down toward his chest. Suggest the mother swaddle the baby to pull his shoulders and head forward toward his chest (Maher 1988).

Also, positioning the baby so that he is nursing sitting up may help keep him alert and encourage his tongue to work properly.

Repeatedly tickling or lightly brushing the baby's lips may cause him to bring his tongue out over his lower gum and encourage him to breastfeed correctly. If so, the mother may be able to latch him on well. If not, suggest she try the exercises below.

For the baby with a tongue thrust, suggest that before latching him on the mother try the following exercise.

Pushing the Tongue Down and Out
- Put a clean upturned index finger (with a trimmed fingernail) into the baby's mouth with the fingernail side pressing gently on the baby's tongue.
- Leave the finger in that position for about thirty seconds while the baby sucks on it.
- Turn the finger over slowly so that the finger pad is on the baby's tongue and push down on his tongue while gradually pulling the finger out of his mouth.
- Repeat this exercise several times before latching the baby onto the breast.

If after two or three days, "Pushing the Tongue Down and Out" doesn't seem to be helping, the mother can try the following exercise.

Walking Back on the Tongue
- Touch the baby's cheek with a finger, moving toward his lips. Then brush his lips a few times with a clean index finger (the fingernail should be trimmed) to encourage him to open his mouth.
- Massage the outside of the baby's gums with the index finger, beginning each stroke at the middle of the baby's upper or lower gum and moving toward either side.

- When the baby opens his mouth, use the tip of the index finger to press down firmly on the top of the tip of the baby's tongue and count slowly to three before releasing the pressure.
- Release the pressure, keeping the finger in the baby's mouth, and move back a little farther on his tongue, pressing again to a count of three.
- Move back on the tongue one or two more times.
- Try to avoid gagging the baby. If the baby gags, notice how far back in the baby's mouth the finger was and avoid putting it that far back the next time.
- Repeat the entire "tongue walk" three or four times before each nursing.

Suggest the mother do this gradually less often as her baby learns what to do.

If the baby becomes upset during this exercise, or if little improvement is noticed within three days of doing the "tongue walk" before each nursing, suggest the baby be seen by someone who is trained in working with sucking problems related to breastfeeding. Some neurodevelopmental therapists (NDT) are experienced in helping mothers and babies overcome sucking problems. To find an NDT in your area, see the "Resources for Parents" listing at the end of this chapter.

Some small babies will instinctively nurse correctly while sleeping.

Retracted Tongue, Tongue Sucking, or Tip of Tongue Curling Up

The baby using his tongue incorrectly will have dimpled cheeks or make clicking sounds while he nurses, and the mother will not hear much swallowing. The mother's nipples probably will be sore.

Dimpled cheeks and clicking sounds are signs that suction is being broken and the baby is not effectively milking the breast. A baby who repeatedly breaks the suction while he is nursing is probably using his tongue incorrectly.

The mother may notice little swallowing and the baby may be gaining slowly since he is probably getting only the faster-flowing foremilk. A baby with a more effective suck will stimulate several let-downs during a feeding, giving him the high-calorie hindmilk that comes later in the feeding.

A vertical red stripe on the nipple and the sensation that the baby is chewing while he nurses are also signs of a baby who is using his tongue incorrectly.

The mother may report that after nursing the sides and possibly the tip of her nipples hurt. The baby's tongue, rather than cupping the mother's breast and resting on the top of his lower gum, rubs on the sides or the tip of the mother's nipple.

The next time the baby nurses, ask the mother to have a helper pull down on the baby's lower lip to see if she can see his tongue under her breast.

If the baby has a retracted tongue, is tongue sucking, or is curling up the tip of his tongue, the mother's helper will not be able to see his tongue under the breast.

To encourage the baby to use his tongue correctly, suggest the mother try "Pushing the Tongue Down and Out," which is described in the previous section.

Positioning the baby so that his chin is down while he nurses may also help him keep his tongue down.

The baby's tongue may relax if the mother positions him at the breast so that his chin is down. Suggest the mother swaddle the baby to pull his shoulders and head forward toward his chest. Also, positioning the baby so that he is nursing sitting up will help keep him alert and encourage his tongue to work properly (Maher 1988).

Gravity can help bring down a baby's tongue when the mother nurses him in unusual positions.

If positioning the baby so that his chin is down does not help improve the baby's suck within a day, suggest the mother try nursing positions that use gravity to bring down the baby's tongue. A modified football hold, with the baby positioned so that his head is looking down on the mother's breast, may help the baby's tongue relax and lengthen. The prone positions listed in the previous section, "Unusual Positions," may also be helpful (Marmet and Shell 1993).

Unusual breastfeeding positions may also make nursing more comfortable for the mother if she has sore nipples.

Any of the unusual breastfeeding positions listed in the earlier section, "Breast-feeding Positions for Special Situations," may help the mother breastfeed more comfortably, since the pressure of the baby's tongue would be on different areas of the breast.

If the baby has a retracted tongue, the mother can use a finger exercise between feedings to help her baby learn to use his tongue correctly.

If the baby has been nursing with his chin down while looking down at the breast for a day without improvement, suggest the mother try a finger exercise between feedings that also uses gravity to bring the tongue down.

Suggest the mother lay her baby face down along her forearm, with the heel of her hand supporting the baby's forehead, and then offer the baby a clean finger (with a trimmed fingernail) to suck, pad side against the roof of his mouth. Once in this position, suggest the mother walk with the baby for five minutes, no longer (Maher 1988).

If the baby refuses to suck a finger or if the baby's suck and the mother's soreness do not improve within two or three days, suggest the baby be seen by someone with training in sucking problems relating to breastfeeding, such as a neurodevelopmental therapist (NDT). To find an NDT in your area, see the "Resources for Parents" listing at the end of this chapter.

If the tip of the baby's tongue curls up, the mother may be able to press down with her finger as the baby latches on to keep his tongue down.

To protect her sore nipples and help keep the baby's tongue down, before the mother latches her baby onto the breast suggest that she put the clean index finger (with a trimmed fingernail) of the hand supporting the breast in the baby's mouth. Then suggest she push down on the baby's tongue, position her breast on top of the finger in the baby's mouth, and remove her finger.

Another option is for the mother to prop her baby on pillows at breast height and support her breast with a rolled baby blanket or towel so that she has both hands free. Then she can use one hand to push down on the baby's tongue and the other hand to position her breast. It would be easier for the mother if someone else helps her with this. Once the baby latches on well, the mother can shift to a more comfortable nursing position.

If the baby seems to be struggling at the breast, this is an indication that the baby's tongue is curling up again. Suggest the mother break the suction and latch her baby on again.

Short Frenulum (Tongue-tie) or a Short Tongue

A baby with a short frenulum may breastfeed well or he may have difficulty latching on and breast-feeding effectively, which may cause slow weight gain, mastitis, and sore nipples.

The frenulum is the string-like membrane that attaches the tongue to the floor of the mouth. A short frenulum may or may not cause breastfeeding problems. Some babies with a short frenulum (also known as tongue-tie) breastfeed well from the start or begin to breastfeed well when latch-on and positioning are improved (Jain 1994; Marmet 1990). The baby's ability to breastfeed will depend in part on the characteristics of his mother's breast, as well as on the state of his frenulum. If the mother has small to medium nipples and her breast tissue is elastic rather than taut, a baby with a short frenulum may do well at the breast despite his tongue-tie (Jain 1994).

Some babies have problems latching on and staying on the breast, because their short frenulum prevents the tongue from extending out far enough to prop-erly cup the breast. If the restricted movement of the tongue prevents baby from breastfeeding effectively, he may gain weight slowly, be fussy at the breast, and demand to be nursed almost constantly. Some babies with a short frenulum can suck on a finger or rubber nipple, but not on the breast. Other babies also have difficulty with bottle-feeding (Wilton 1990). Some tongue-tied babies can breast-feed well on one breast but not the other (Huggins 1990).

The mother may have sore nipples, a reduced milk supply, and/or mastitis. If the baby's tongue cannot extend over the lower gum, the breast may be compressed between the gums during feedings, causing nipple trauma. Some mothers' nipples appear distorted after feedings (Notestine 1990).

Positioning/Latch-On

Ask the mother if the baby has difficulty staying on the breast and if she hears a clicking sound as he nurses.

Difficulty staying on the breast and a clicking sound during nursing are signs that the baby is not able to maintain proper suction at the breast and may not be milking the breast effectively. A baby who repeatedly breaks the suction while he is nursing is probably using his tongue incorrectly and should be checked for a short frenulum as well as other possible causes (see the previous section, "Retracted Tongue, Tongue Sucking, or Tip of Tongue Curling Up").

Ask the mother if the baby is able to stick out his tongue past his bottom lip, and if so, is it curled downward?

A short frenulum may make it impossible for the baby to extend his tongue past his bottom gum or lip. In some babies, the frenulum extends to the center of the tip of the tongue, pulling it in, which causes the tongue to look heart-shaped at rest or while extended. In other babies, the tongue may reach past the baby's lower gum or lip, but the tight frenulum causes it to curl downward (Berg 1990b). In less severe cases, these signs may not be as obvious, but the frenulum may still be short enough to affect breastfeeding.

Ask the mother if she knows of anyone in the family who has been tongue-tied or had their tongue (or frenulum) clipped.

Short frenula tend to run in families (Jain 1994; Berg 1990a). Often a mother with a tongue-tied baby will be aware of someone else in the family with this condition.

If a short frenulum causes breastfeeding problems, these may or may not resolve over time. In some cases, in order for the baby to breastfeed effectively, it may be necessary to have the frenulum clipped by a health care professional to release the tongue.

Breastfeeding problems related to a short frenulum may resolve over time without special treatment. The movements of the tongue may cause a short frenulum to stretch (Riordan and Auerbach, p. 526) or the baby may adapt his mouth and tongue movements to improve breastfeeding effectiveness (Ward 1990).

If breastfeeding does not improve over time or the mother does not want to wait, suggest the mother check into the possibility of having her baby's frenulum clipped. The procedure to clip a short frenulum (called a "frenotomy") is a simple one that can be done in a doctor's or dentist's office and involves no stitches or anesthesia (Jain 1994; Marmet 1990; Notestine 1990). But because this procedure has fallen out of favor (Conway 1990), a mother may have to search to find a health care professional who is willing to perform it. If the baby's pediatrician is unwilling, suggest she ask other pediatricians, oral surgeons, dentists, ear-nose-and-throat specialists, or general surgeons in the area.

The Assessment Tool for Lingual Frenulum Function is a method for systematically evaluating the need to have a baby's frenulum clipped (Hazelbaker 1992). A score is assigned to different aspects of the appearance and function of the baby's frenulum (i.e., lift, extension, spread, cupping, snap-back of the tongue and elasticity, length, and attachment of the frenulum), with the function score more heavily weighted than the appearance score. A comparison of the function and appearance scores determines whether a frenotomy should be considered if attempts to correct the breastfeeding problem by improving management fail.

If a short frenulum is contributing to the breastfeeding problem, once the baby's frenulum is clipped the mother may notice immediate improvement, or it may take as long as a week or two before he begins sucking normally (Marmet 1990; Wilton 1990). If a baby with a short frenulum also has a short tongue, it may take more time for breastfeeding effectiveness to improve after clipping (Jain 1994). (See the next point.)

A baby with a short tongue may be unable to latch on and keep hold of the breast. This problem is usually outgrown within four to six weeks.

Rarely, a baby is born with a tongue so short that he cannot latch on well or he repeatedly loses hold of the breast while nursing. This baby usually continues to lose weight after his mother's milk "comes in."

For some short-tongued babies, improving latch-on and positioning may allow them to breastfeed more effectively. Care should be taken that the baby opens very wide and is pulled in quickly and held very close to the breast during feedings so that the nipple is as far back in his mouth as possible. Positions in which the mother has a hand behind the baby's head and can exert gentle pressure throughout feedings may be the best choice until the problem is outgrown.

If despite a good latch the baby is not getting enough milk, the mother will need to express her milk as often as her baby would be nursing and feed it to her baby.

Usually by the time the baby is four to six weeks old, his tongue will have grown enough so that breastfeeding is easier.

If the baby has a large or protruding tongue, which is especially common in babies with Down Syndrome, he may have difficulty latching on to the breast well.

If the baby has a large or protruding tongue, have the mother make sure the baby opens wide before latching on. Pulling down on the chin may be necessary in the early weeks if the baby also has low muscle tone.

A baby who pushes his tongue upward may need some encouragement to keep it down while latching on. See "Pushing the Tongue Down and Out" in the previous section, "Tongue Thrust," for suggestions.

Clamping or Clenching Response

Rarely, a baby may be born with a strong tendency to clench his jaws whenever anything touches the inside of his mouth. This is sometimes incorrectly referred to as "tonic bite reflex."

Rarely, a baby is born with an unusually strong and consistent tendency to clench his jaws, which is triggered whenever anything touches the inside of his mouth. Mothers of these babies describe their babies as "clamping down" or biting the breast, although the term "clenching" is most commonly used by professionals to describe the clenching of the jaws. This clamping, or clenching, response may be more common after a difficult or medicated birth (Jozwiak 1994).

The term "tonic bite reflex" has sometimes been used to describe this response. In the vast majority of babies who clench their jaws during feedings, however, "tonic bite reflex" (which is correctly used to describe a neurological problem associated with cerebral palsy) does not apply. Unlike tonic bite, most of these babies do not have a permanent neurological problem; theirs is a temporary immaturity that fades over the first weeks of life.

If this response persists beyond six to eight weeks, encourage the mother to have her baby evaluated by a pediatric neurologist to rule out neurological problems.

Ask the mother how her nipples look after a feeding. Also ask her if she feels pain, and if so, when the pain occurs.

The mother of a baby who is clenching his jaws during nursing may report that her nipple turns white by the end of the nursing or has a white stripe, due to the blood supply to the nipple being cut off by the pressure of the baby's bite. She may feel as if the baby is clamping down or clenching during most of the feeding. There is intense pain during most of the feeding, which may even increase after the baby comes off the breast as the blood flows back to the nipple. Some mothers report burning nipple pain for up to an hour after nursing (Maher 1988).

Suggest the mother give her baby good support at the breast. A baby may clamp down if he feels unstable.

When a baby feels unstable at the breast, as if he might fall, he may clamp down with his jaws as a reaction. Suggest the mother be sure her baby is well supported at the breast. If she holds her baby in her arms, suggest she use pillows or cushions under the baby to stabilize him.

A baby who is clamping down on the nipple may have overactive muscle tone.

Many babies who clamp down on the nipple also have overactive muscle tone (hypertonia) with frequent arching. The mother may report that he is difficult to cuddle.

A baby who is clenching his jaws and has an overactive muscle tone may be helped to relax with a gentle massage or warm bath just prior to feedings and with breastfeeding positions that flex his body.

A baby with overactive muscle tone who is clenching his jaws may be more relaxed during breastfeeding if the mother first gives him a warm bath or a gentle massage, working from the extremities toward the center of the body.

Using a flexed position for nursing can also be calming to a hypertonic baby. The football hold is one option, being careful that the baby's feet go up rather than pushing against the back of the mother's chair (which will cause arching).

Swaddling the baby in a slightly flexed, tucked position may help him relax and focus on effective breastfeeding (Jozwiak 1994).

For suggestions about breastfeeding the baby with overactive muscle tone, see the section "Arching (Hypertonic) Baby" in the chapter "Fussy at the Breast and Breast Refusal." Also see the next section and "The Neurologically Impaired Baby" in the chapter "The Baby with Special Needs."

Suggest the mother wipe the baby's face with cold then warm water before nursings and apply consistent gentle pressure on the baby's lower lip or chin while he nurses.

To discourage the baby from clamping down his jaws, suggest the mother try wiping the baby's face with cold then warm water several times.

Also suggest the mother control how the baby latches onto the breast by using her thumb or finger to press down firmly on his lower lip or chin to counteract the clenching of his jaws. Continued pressure on the baby's lower lip throughout the feeding may allow her to breastfeed comfortably. If the mother has a problem with her finger or thumb slipping during feedings, suggest she wrap a piece of gauze around it.

If the baby is losing weight and/or pressing down on the baby's lower lip does not relieve the pain, the mother may need to express her milk and feed it to her baby until the clenching relaxes.

If the baby has been nursing ineffectively for some time, he may be uncomfortable and tense because of hunger, making it more difficult for him to latch on and breastfeed well. In this case, it may help for the mother to express some of her milk and give it to the baby before she offers him the breast. (Also see the next section and "The Neurologically Impaired Baby" in the chapter "The Baby with Special Needs.")

Neurologically Impaired Baby

Neurologically impaired babies fall into two general groups—those with overactive muscle tone and those with low muscle tone. If this kind of problem seems evident, suggest the mother have her baby checked by his doctor.

For more information, see the section, "The Neurologically Impaired Baby;" in the chapter "The Baby with Special Needs."

The neurologically impaired baby has a nervous system that does not function normally, either due to immaturity or a physical problem. A neurologically impaired baby may not have the mature suck-swallow reflex of a full-term healthy baby. He may have other symptoms as well. In severe cases, breastfeeding may not be possible, although human milk would still offer many benefits.

Neurologically impaired babies fall into two general groups—those with overactive muscle tone and those with low muscle tone. These babies may exhibit one or more of these symptoms:

- excessive arching of the body,
- overreaction to stimulation,
- excessive rooting and biting movements, including biting/clenching when swallowing,
- low muscle tone,
- weak suck, swallowing, and gag reflexes,
- nonrhythmic sucking.

IF BREASTFEEDING HURTS—REVIEW THE BASICS

Most cases of sore nipples are caused by poor positioning, poor latch-on, or a sucking problem. If the mother's nipples are sore, begin by reviewing the basics.

It is usually necessary to see the mother and baby in person before ruling out positioning, latch-on, or a sucking problem as the cause of the mother's soreness.

Positioning
- The mother is comfortable with arms and back supported.
- The mother does not lean over the baby.

- The baby directly faces the breast without having to turn his head.
- The baby's knees are pulled in close to the mother.
- The baby's ear, shoulder, and hip are in a straight line.
- The baby's body is well-supported.

Latch-On
- The mother supports her breast, as needed, without her hand or fingers covering any part of the areola.
- The mother encourages the baby to open his mouth wide like a yawn.
- The mother waits for the baby's mouth to gape open then quickly brings the baby onto her breast, pulling him in close. He takes the breast deeply into his mouth.
- The baby's chin presses into the breast during the entire nursing. The baby's nose may rest on the breast.
- The baby's lips are flanged out and relaxed.

The Baby's Suck
- The baby's tongue is cupped below the breast.
- A "wiggle" is seen at the baby's temple and ear as he sucks.
- After the mother's milk lets down, the mother can hear the baby swallow after every one or two sucks or so. This pattern continues for at least ten to twenty minutes. Swallowing becomes less frequent as the feeding progresses.
- After the mother's milk becomes more plentiful on the third or fourth day after birth, the baby wets at least six to eight cloth or five to six disposable diapers. During the first six weeks the baby has at least two to five bowel movements a day. (Fewer bowel movements are normal for the baby older than six weeks.)

Resouces for Parents

To find a physical therapist trained in assessing and treating infant feeding problems, contact:

Neurodevelopmental Treatment Association
401 N. Michigan Avenue
Chicago IL 60611-4267 USA
312-321-5151

Publications for Parents

Positioning and Latch-On

Gotsch, G. Breastfeeding: Pure & Simple, Schaumburg, Illinois: La Leche League International, 1993.

Renfrew, M. Fisher, C. and Arms, S. *Bestfeeding: Getting Breastfeeding Right for You*. Berkeley, California: Celestial Arts, 1990.

La Leche League International. *Positioning Your Baby at the Breast*. Schaumburg, Illinois, 1988. Publication No. 107.

La Leche League International. The Womanly Art of Breastfeeding, 35th Anniversary ed., Schaumburg, Illinois, 1991, pp. 50-55, 120-22, 329-31.

Breastfeeding the Neurologically Impaired Baby

Danner, S. and Cerutti, E. *Nursing Your Neurologically Impaired Baby*, Waco, Texas: Childbirth Graphics, 1990.

References

Positioning

Lawrence, R. *Breastfeeding: A Guide for the Medical Profession,* 4th ed. St. Louis: Mosby, 1994, p. 431.

Maher, S. *An Overview of Solutions to Breastfeeding and Sucking Problems.* Schaumburg, Illinois. La Leche League International, 1988. Publication No. 67, pp. 4-5, 8-9.

Marmet, C. and Shell, E. *Lactation Forms: A Guide to Lactation Consultant Charting.* Encino, California: Lactation Institute Publications, 1993, pp. 4-19 to 4-28.

Riordan, J. and Auerbach, K. *Breastfeeding and Human Lactation,* Boston and London: Jones and Bartlett, 1993, pp. 246-48.

Latch-On

Maher, S. *An Overview of Solutions to Breastfeeding and Sucking Problems.* Schaumburg, Illinois. La Leche League International, 1988. Publication No. 67, p. 5.

Marmet, C. and Shell, E. *Lactation Forms: A Guide to Lactation Consultant Charting.* Encino, California: Lactation Institute Publications, 1993, pp. 4-11.

Righard, L. and Alade, M. *Sucking technique and its effect on success of breastfeeding.* Birth 1992; 19(4):185-89.

Royal College of Midwives. *Successful Breastfeeding.* London: Churchill Livingstone, 1991, pp. 18-19.

The Baby's Suck

Royal College of Midwives. *Successful Breastfeeding.* London: Churchill Livingstone, 1991, pp. 18-19.

Sucking Problems

Fisher, C. and Woolridge, M. Infant feeding: the mechanics of breastfeeding. Presented at LLL International Conference, 1991. (Audiocassette available from LLLI.)

Frantz, K. The slow-gaining breastfeeding infant. *NAACOG* 1992; 3(4):647-55.

Maher, S. *An Overview of Solutions to Breastfeeding and Sucking Problems.* Schaumburg, Illinois. La Leche League International, 1988. Publication No. 67, pp. 8-9, 12-13, 23, 25.

Marmet, C. and Shell, E. *Lactation Forms: A Guide to Lactation Consultant Charting.* Encino, California: Lactation Institute Publications, 1993, pp. 4-11.

Marmet, C. and Shell, E. Training neonates to suck correctly. *MCN* 1984; 9:401-07.

McIntyre, E. Management practices in lactation. *Breastfeed Rev* 1995; 3(2):77-86.

Positioning/Latch-On

Riordan, J. and Auerbach, K. *Breastfeeding and Human Lactation,* Boston and London: Jones and Bartlett, 1993, p. 527-31.

Sleepy Baby

Crowell, M.K. et al. Relationship between obstetric analgesia and time of effective breast feeding. *J Nurse Midw* 1994; 39(3):150-56.

Maher, S. *An Overview of Solutions to Breastfeeding and Sucking Problems.* Schaumburg, Illinois. La Leche League International, 1988. Publication No. 67, pp. 6-7.

Nissen, E. et al. Effect of maternal pethidine on infants' developing breast feeding behavior. *Acta Paediatr* 1995; 84(2):140-45.

Righard, L. and Alade, M. Sucking technique and its effect on success of breastfeeding. *Birth* 1992; 19(4):185-89.

Righard, L. and Alade, M. Effect of delivery room routines on success of first breastfeed. *Lancet* 1990; 336:1105-07.

Sepkoski, C. et al. The effects of maternal epidural anesthesia on neonatal behavior during the first month. *Dev Med Child Neurol* 1992; 34:1072-80.

Lazy Nurser

Maher, S. *An Overview of Solutions to Breastfeeding and Sucking Problems.* Schaumburg, Illinois. La Leche League International, 1988. Publication No. 67, p. 25.

Weak Suck

Maher, S. *An Overview of Solutions to Breastfeeding and Sucking Problems.* Schaumburg, Illinois. La Leche League International, 1988. Publication No. 67, pp. 23.

Marmet, C. and Shell, E. *Lactation Forms: A Guide to Lactation Consultant Charting.* Encino, California: Lactation Institute Publications, 1993, p. 4-18.

Tongue Thrusting

Lawrence, R. *Breastfeeding: A Guide for the Medical Profession,* 4th ed. St. Louis: Mosby, 1994, p. 236-37.

Maher, S. *An Overview of Solutions to Breastfeeding and Sucking Problems.* Schaumburg, Illinois. La Leche League International, 1988. Publication No. 67, p. 12.

Marmet, C. and Shell, E. *Lactation Forms: A Guide to Lactation Consultant Charting.* Encino, California: Lactation Institute Publications, 1993, p. 4-17.

Marmet, C. and Shell, E. Training neonates to suck correctly. *MCN* 1984; 9:401-07.

Retracted Tongue, Tongue Sucking, or Tip of Tongue Curling Up

Maher, S. *An Overview of Solutions to Breastfeeding and Sucking Problems.* Schaumburg, Illinois. La Leche League International, 1988. Publication No. 67, pp. 11-13.

Marmet, C. and Shell, E. *Lactation Forms: A Guide to Lactation Consultant Charting.* Encino, California: Lactation Institute Publications, 1993, p. 4-26.

Marmet, C. and Shell, E. Training neonates to suck correctly. *MCN* 1984; 9:401-07.

Short Frenulum (Tongue-Tie) or Short Tongue

Berg, K. Tongue-tie (ankyloglossia) and breastfeeding: a review. *J Human Lact* 1990a; 6(3):109-12.

Berg, K. Two cases of tongue-tie and breastfeeding. *J Human Lact* 1990b; 6(3):124-26.

Conway, A. Ankyloglossia—to snip or not to snip: is that the question? *J Human Lact* 1990; 6(3):101-02.

Fleiss, P. et al. Ankyloglossia: a cause of breastfeeding problems? *J Human Lact* 1990; 6(3):128-29.

Hazelbaker, A. *The Assessment Tool for Lingual Frenulum Function (ATLFF): Use in a Lactation Consultant Private Practice.* (For ordering information, contact The Lactation Institute, 16430 Ventura Blvd., Suite 303, Encino, CA 91436 USA.)

Huggins, K. Ankyloglossia—one lactation consultant's personal experience. *J Human Lact* 1990; 6(3):123-24.

Jain, E. Clinical aspects of the short frenulum. Presented at the International Lactation Consultant Association Conference, 1994. (For ordering information, contact ILCA, 201 Brown Avenue, Evanston, IL 60202-3601 USA, 708/260-8874.)

Lawrence, R. *Breastfeeding: A Guide for the Medical Profession,* 4th ed. St. Louis: Mosby, 1994, p. 267.

Maher, S. *An Overview of Solutions to Breastfeeding and Sucking Problems.* Schaumburg, Illinois. La Leche League International, 1988. Publication No. 67, p. 12.

Marmet, C. et al. Neonatal frenotomy may be necessary to correct breastfeeding problems. *J Human Lact* 1990; 6(3):117-21.

Marmet, C. and Shell, E. Training neonates to suck correctly. *MCN* 1984; 9:401-07.

Notestine, G. The importance of the identification of ankyloglossia (short lingual frenulum) as a cause of breastfeeding problems. *J Human Lact* 1990; 6(3):113-15.

Riordan, J. and Auerbach, K. *Breastfeeding and Human Lactation,* Boston and London: Jones and Bartlett, 1993, p. 526.

Ward, N. Ankyloglossia: a case study in which clipping was not necessary. *J Human Lact* 1990; 6(3):126-27.

Wilton, J. Sore nipples and slow weight gain related to a short frenulum. *J Human Lact* 1990; 6(3):122-23.

Protruding or Large Tongue

Danner, S. and Cerutti, E. *Nursing Your Baby with Down Syndrome.* Waco, Texas: Childbirth Graphics, 1990.

Clenching or Clamping Down

Jozwiak, M. Clampdown bite reflex. LEAVEN 1994; 30(4):53-54.

Maher, S. *An Overview of Solutions to Breastfeeding and Sucking Problems.* Schaumburg, Illinois. La Leche League International, 1988. Publication No. 67, p. 14.

Neurologically Impaired Baby

Danner, S. Breastfeeding the neurologically impaired infant. NAACOG *Clin Is Peri Wom Hlth Nurs* 1992; 3(4):640-46.

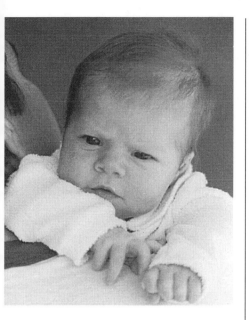

5

Fussy at the Breast and Breast Refusal

THE MOTHER'S FEELINGS

ASKING QUESTIONS AND GATHERING INFORMATION

FUSSY AT THE BREAST
 Fussy at the Breast during the Early Weeks of Breastfeeding
 Fussy at the Breast at Any Stage of Breastfeeding

BREAST REFUSAL
 Breast Refusal during the Early Weeks of Breastfeeding
 Breast Refusal at Any Stage of Breastfeeding

PERSUADING THE BABY TO TAKE THE BREAST

REFUSAL OF ONE BREAST
 Refusal of One Breast from Birth
 Refusal of One Breast at Any Stage of Breastfeeding
 Persuading the Baby to Nurse on the Less Preferred Breast
 One-Sided Nursing

It may take some careful detective work to determine the cause of a baby's fussiness or breast refusal.

Determining the cause of the baby's fussiness or breast refusal will influence what suggestions to give. Babies with an ear infection or thrush may need medical treatment before they can breastfeed comfortably. Babies who are fussy at the breast due to a fussy temperament, distractibility, or teething may breastfeed better if comfort measures are used and they are nursed in a calm environment.

In other cases, an adjustment in breastfeeding management may help. For example, the mother with engorgement will probably find that her baby nurses better if she breastfeeds more often and expresses her milk before feedings for easier latch-on. The baby who is fussy from a foremilk-hindmilk imbalance will be more comfortable if his mother allows him to finish the first breast first. And the mother who is using poor positioning or latch-on may find breastfeeding goes more smoothly when she makes sure her baby's whole body is facing hers and the baby opens wider and takes the breast more deeply into his mouth.

A baby with a weak suck or nipple confusion, an arching baby, and the aggressive non-nurser may require much patience, time, work, and specialized information to get breastfeeding on track. But sometimes, a tincture of time, some common sense suggestions, and good support are all that is necessary, such as in the case of forceful let-down, delayed or inhibited let-down, emotional upset, discomfort when held in the nursing position, or birth injury.

Birth and postpartum interventions, such as medications during labor and delivery and separation of mother and baby after birth, may predispose a baby to be fussy or disorganized at the breast. One study found that the babies of mothers who were given epidurals were disorganized during their first month (Sepkoski 1992). Other labor drugs, such as pethidine (meperidine or Demerol), and separation of mother and baby immediately after birth have been linked to breastfeeding difficulties (Righard and Alade 1990). Fussiness for one or more of these reasons may resolve within days or it may take longer.

Occasionally an outside agent, such as a food, drug, perfume, or other product, may be triggering the baby's fussiness or breast refusal. In this case, some careful detective work and experimentation may be in order.

In rare cases, the cause may never be found, such as an unexplained nursing strike, which is stressful for both mother and baby.

Individual babies respond differently to the same thing.

Not all of the factors listed in this chapter will cause a baby to be fussy at the breast or refuse to nurse. Individual differences in babies account for a wide range of reactions to the same thing. For example, one baby with an ear infection may continue nursing, while a second baby is fussy at the breast and a third refuses to nurse altogether. One baby may switch between the bottle and the breast with no signs of nipple confusion, while another develops breastfeeding problems. A baby whose suck is well-coordinated may be able to cope well with his mother's forceful let-down, while another baby—whose suck is not as well-coordinated—may refuse the breast because he finds his mother's let-down too overwhelming. One baby may nurse well no matter what foods his mother eats, while another baby is sensitive to certain foods in his mother's diet. One baby is easygoing and resilient to stress, while another baby becomes fussy or refuses the breast when there is tension at home.

Also, the intensity of a baby's response may vary. One factor may cause a baby to be fussy at the breast, while the same factor causes another baby to refuse the breast.

THE MOTHER'S FEELINGS

Fussy or Refuse Breast

A mother may feel frustrated and rejected—perhaps also guilty and inadequate—when her baby fusses at or refuses the breast. Listen to and acknowledge her feelings.

When a baby is fussy at the breast or refuses to nurse, the mother may feel frustrated and upset. She may also feel as if her baby is rejecting her as a person. This may affect a mother's feelings about herself and her ability to care for her baby. She may feel anxious about her baby's health. She may feel guilty, believing that her baby's fussiness or refusal to nurse means she has done something wrong or that she has not given him the proper care. If the mother has been told she has to give up breastfeeding, she may feel like a failure.

Listen to the mother and acknowledge her feelings. Giving her an outlet to express her worries, fears, and doubts may make it easier for her to discuss and evaluate her situation and decide how she wants to proceed.

Assure her that there is probably a reason for her baby's behavior and that it is likely her baby can be persuaded to take the breast again, and that her baby needs her now more than ever.

The mother may be worried about her baby getting enough milk.

One of the mother's most pressing worries—especially if her baby totally refuses to nurse—is how to be sure he gets enough milk. Before trying to determine the cause of the baby's behavior, talk to the mother about how she can be sure her baby is getting enough by keeping track of her baby's wet diapers and bowel movements. At least six to eight wet cloth diapers—five to six disposables—and two to five bowel movements a day indicate that the baby is getting enough milk. (Fewer bowel movements are considered normal if the baby is older than six weeks.)

If the baby is younger than six months and is not nursing at all, the mother will no doubt need to express her milk so that she doesn't become uncomfortably full. Suggest the mother give her baby her expressed milk. Avoiding bottles and using alternative feeding methods, such as a cup, spoon, eyedropper, or feeding syringe, will make it easier for the mother to persuade her baby to go back to breastfeeding. (See "The Use of Breast Pumps and Other Products.")

If the baby is older than six months and has started solid foods, the mother may be able to give her baby her expressed milk in a cup and offer other foods. If the mother prefers to give formula, she should check with her doctor.

The mother may be worried about her own comfort.

If the baby is not nursing well, encourage the mother to express her milk whenever she feels full. If the baby is refusing the breast altogether, encourage her to express her milk as often as her baby was nursing. This will prevent mastitis and keep her comfortable. She will also have expressed milk for her baby, as needed.

Some cases of fussiness at the breast or breast refusal resolve themselves quickly. Others require time, patience, and work.

Some cases of breast refusal are quickly resolved. Ear infections and thrush are temporary, short-term conditions that respond quickly to treatment.

Other cases of breast refusal, such as a baby who is severely nipple-confused, a baby on an unexplained nursing strike, or a baby who aggressively refuses the breast from birth, may require much time and patience before breastfeeding is going smoothly. Good support is essential to keep the mother going through this stressful time.

ASKING QUESTIONS AND GATHERING INFORMATION

Ask questions in a calm, relaxed manner, emphasize differences in individual mothers and babies, and look for opportunities to praise the mother for what she is doing right.

In order to help the mother determine the reasons for her baby's fussiness or breast refusal, it is necessary to ask questions and find out more information. Keep in mind that the best way to gather the needed information is to listen attentively, taking notes, and asking pertinent questions in a calm, relaxed manner rather than in rapid succession. A calm and relaxed discussion will put the mother at ease. Some of the questions may deal with sensitive areas, so be sure to word them so they are not threatening to the mother.

Make sure the mother understands that breastfeeding is not a by-the-book procedure; it is an intimate relationship with different dynamics from one nursing couple to the next. (A mother almost always notices differences in breastfeeding when she nurses more than one child.) Although there are general breastfeeding principles with which it is good to be familiar (for example, the more often the baby nurses, the more milk there will be), there are no hard-and-fast rules.

Emphasize the individual differences among mothers and babies as the questions are discussed so the mother does not blame herself for her baby's problems. For example, if the baby is nipple-confused because the mother has been giving bottles, tell her that some babies are able to breastfeed and take bottles with no problems at all, while other babies become nipple-confused. If the mother is asked whether she smokes cigarettes, mention that some mothers smoke and breastfeed with no problems, yet other mothers who smoke find that their let-down is affected or the baby shows some sensitivity to it.

Remember, too, that the mother may have relatives or friends criticizing her efforts to continue breastfeeding. If her baby is refusing to nurse altogether, she may be especially vulnerable. **Be sure to praise her for what she is doing right.**

When the mother's answers give a clue to the reasons behind her baby's fussiness or breast refusal, discuss that area in more depth.

During the course of the questioning, the mother's answers to certain questions may give clues to the cause of her baby's fussiness at the breast or breast refusal. At that point, stop and talk more about this area to allow her to expand on her individual circumstances.

FUSSY AT THE BREAST

Fussy at the Breast during the Early Weeks of Breastfeeding

Questions to Ask

Ask the mother her baby's age and how long he has been fussy at the breast. Also ask if he has been given bottles or if the mother has used a nipple shield.

A baby who is fussy at the breast will take the breast, but does not nurse well or contentedly.

If the baby is younger than a week old and the baby has been fussy since birth, be sure the baby has been thoroughly checked for any medical problem or illness. Then consider poor positioning and latch-on, birth interventions and medications or physical injury at birth, arching (hypertonia), delayed or inhibited let-down, and—if he becomes fussier when held—an aggressive non-nurser.

If the fussiness began between the second and fourth day, consider engorgement, forceful let-down, and delayed or inhibited let-down.

If the fussiness began between one and four weeks, the baby nursed well before then, and the baby has been receiving artificial nipples, consider nipple confusion as a likely cause. Thrush, ear infection, sensitivity to a food or drug given to mother or baby, and a change in the taste of the mother's milk should also be considered. Temperament can also be a factor, as some babies who had previously been placid and easygoing "wake up" at about two to three weeks of age and suddenly become fussy.

Ask the mother if her nipples are sore or her breasts feel engorged.

Sore nipples are a sign of poor positioning or latch-on, which is one common cause of fussiness at the breast. If the baby does not take the breast deeply enough into his mouth, he will be unable to milk the breast well, which may make him fussy. Sore nipples may also be an indication that the baby is using his tongue incorrectly or that the baby has a short frenulum (tongue-tie).

Engorgement may make good latch-on more difficult, causing soreness. If the mother becomes severely and painfully engorged, despite frequent breastfeeding during the early days, this may be a symptom of a baby with a weak or ineffective suck.

Fussy or Refuse Breast

Ask the mother when during the feeding the baby becomes fussy, and if she notices him choking or gagging.

Knowing when during the feeding the baby becomes fussy may provide clues to the cause of his fussiness. If the baby becomes fussy within the first few minutes of the feeding—before the mother's milk lets down—this could be a sign of nipple confusion, poor positioning or latch-on, flat or inverted nipples, delayed or inhibited let-down, discomfort when in the nursing position, ear infection, or a weak suck.

If the baby becomes fussy when the mother notices her milk let down, forceful let-down may be the cause, especially if the baby chokes or has difficulty coping with the milk flow.

If the baby does not become fussy until later in the feeding, consider the possibility that the baby needs to burp or pass a bowel movement. If the baby is a "gulper," that is, the mother hears him loudly gulping as he swallows, he may take in a lot of air during feedings and need to be burped. In this case, the baby tends to get fussier and fussier as the feeding progresses. If the baby passes a bowel movement at the end or right after feedings, this may be the cause of his fussiness.

Ask the mother if her fingers are touching the baby's face or head while he is nursing.

If the mother says that she is touching her baby's face or head while he is nursing, his rooting reflex may cause him to turn away from the breast.

Ask the mother how long she nurses from each breast.

If the mother switches her baby from one breast to the other after a predetermined length of time, ask her about her baby's weight gain, the color of her baby's stools, and if her baby seems gassy. If her baby is gaining weight slowly, has green, watery stools, or seems gassy, consider the possibility of a foremilk-hindmilk imbalance.

Ask the mother how many times a day she has been breastfeeding, how many diapers her baby has been wetting and soiling each day, and how much weight he has gained.

Fewer than six to eight wet cloth diapers (five to six disposables) and fewer than two to five bowel movements per day indicate the baby may not be getting enough milk. This could be due to poor breastfeeding management (such as not nursing often or long enough), poor positioning and latch-on, a weak or incorrect suck, an arching baby, (the arching baby and the baby with a weak suck usually nurse very often), a short frenulum, or any number of other factors. The baby's fussiness at the breast also could be due in part to hunger.

If the baby is not getting enough milk, turn to "Slow Weight Gain" in the chapter "Weight Gain," to try to help the mother determine the cause.

Ask the mother if the baby is fussy when he is not nursing, and if so, how much of the day.

Some babies spend their first few months fussy most of the time. These "high need" or colicky babies also tend to be fussy at the breast.

Ask the mother if she would describe her baby as relaxed, like a floppy doll, or unusually strong and active.

Babies with very low muscle tone (hypotonic) and very high muscle tone (hypertonic) may be fussy at the breast. Both types of babies tend to have an ineffective suck and nurse "all the time."

Poor Positioning or Latch-On

If a baby has to turn his head or strain his neck to nurse or does not have enough of the breast in his mouth, this can cause him to be fussy or refuse the breast.

Good positioning and latch-on are essential for effective breastfeeding. If the baby has to turn his head or strain his neck to nurse, this can make swallowing uncomfortable (as a demonstration, tell the mother to turn her head and try to swallow), which could make him fussy at the breast. Encourage the mother to position the baby so that his whole body faces hers so that he will not have to turn his head.

In order for the baby to get enough milk, he needs to take the breast far back into his mouth, so that his jaws compress the milk sinuses well back from the nipple within the breast. Some babies—especially newborns—will refuse the breast if they cannot get enough of the breast in their mouths. See "Latch-On" in the chapter "Positioning, Latch-On, and the Baby's Suck," for suggestions.

Engorgement

If engorgement makes latching-on difficult, the baby may be fussy at or refuse the breast.

Normal breast fullness may develop into engorgement from the third to fifth day after birth, especially if the baby has not been breastfeeding often or long enough.

Engorgement can present a problem if breast fullness causes the mother's nipples to become flat and the skin on her breasts to become taut, making it difficult for the baby to latch on properly. This may cause some babies to refuse the breast. Others may try to nurse but are unable to latch on well. If the tautness of the areola causes the baby to grasp only the tip of the nipple in his mouth, it will make nursing painful for the mother and make it impossible for the baby to milk the breast well, aggravating the engorgement.

If the mother's areola is engorged, encourage her to express enough milk to soften the areola so that the baby will be able to latch on well. Some mothers are reluctant to express even a little milk for fear that this will increase their milk supply and make their engorgement worse. If the mother mentions this concern, assure her that expressing some milk will make it easier for her baby to remove the milk from her breasts, which will lessen her engorgement. Explain that the engorgement is caused in part by other fluids—lymph and blood—as well as milk, and that removing a little milk will help the baby relieve her fullness. Make sure the mother knows how to treat the engorgement so that it subsides as quickly as possible. (See "Engorgement" in the chapter "Breast Problems.")

Also, suggest the mother give special attention to making sure her baby's mouth is open wide, like a yawn, and to wait for this gape before she puts him to breast. Suggest, too, that she try different nursing positions, such as the football hold, which may give her more control and make latching-on easier. For more information, see "Latch-On" in the chapter "Positioning, Latch-On, and the Baby's Suck," and "Engorgement" in the chapter "Breast Problems."

Nipple Confusion

A baby who is nipple-confused may push the nipple out of his mouth with his tongue and cry in frustration or try to suck at the breast as he does at the bottle, causing sore nipples.

Some breastfeeding experts believe that most babies are at risk of nipple confusion during the early weeks of breastfeeding.

The mother of the nipple-confused baby may report that her baby "doesn't seem to know what to do" at the breast. He may mouth the nipple frantically but not be able to latch on and milk the breast. Or he may go to the breast and suck incorrectly, causing sore nipples and getting little milk for his efforts.

Kittie Frantz, retired LLL Leader, pediatric nurse practitioner, and instructor for the UCLA Lactation Educator and Consultant Courses, estimates that 95% of all babies will become confused if given an artificial nipple during the first three to four weeks after birth (Frantz 1985).

For some babies it may take a week of bottles before they become nipple-confused; for other babies, only one or two bottles or other artificial nipples will cause it. Once a baby has been breastfeeding well for three to four weeks, nipple confusion is less likely to develop.

If a mother plans to introduce bottles, suggest she wait until her baby is at least three to four weeks old.

Although not all breastfeeding experts agree on the existence of nipple confusion, the debate has begun on its existence and its possible causes and risk factors.

Many breastfeeding experts have observed that too early introduction of bottles or pacifiers seems to cause breastfeeding problems (Lawrence, p. 236; Marmet and Shell 1993; Newman 1990a and 1990b; Frantz 1985), but the existence of nipple confusion is not universally accepted. Some health care professionals consider nipple confusion to be a myth, in part because those working in hospitals do not see the consequences of too early introduction of artificial nipples; the resulting breastfeeding problems usually do not become evident until mother and baby go home.

Fussy or Refuse Breast

In a first step toward formally recognizing and defining nipple confusion, the authors of one article offer several theories to explain nipple confusion, suggest possible risk factors in mother and baby, and recommend studies on nipple confusion be conducted (Neifert 1995). The authors list four working theories to explain nipple confusion.

- The newborn has a limited ability to adapt to different sucking patterns and differences in flow in the early weeks.
- A form of "imprinting" may occur at the first feeding, which, if given by bottle, may predispose a baby to breastfeeding problems.
- Because colostrum is available in very small amounts in the first few days, a baby who receives greater amounts of supplement by bottle may become frustrated with the smaller amounts at the breast and become fussy.
- A baby who has trouble nursing may find bottle-feeding easier and therefore be more prone to nipple confusion.

They list several risk factors in the mother, including illness, delayed or reduced milk flow, and nipples that are difficult for the baby to latch onto. Risk factors in the baby include prematurity, illness or other health problems, oral anomalies (such as cleft lip, cleft or high palate, and tongue tie), and neuromotor or development problems (such as Down syndrome, sucking problems, and low muscle tone). They consider mother-baby separation to be another risk factor. The authors suggest that whenever these risk factors are present and supplements are needed that artificial nipples be avoided and alternative feeding methods used instead. The authors also acknowledge that individual babies may be more or less sensitive to the differences in texture, shape, smell, taste, temperature, and elasticity between human and artificial nipples.

In addition to these factors, other authors have observed that from one area to the next differences in breastfeeding knowledge and support as well as labor, delivery, and postpartum practices, may influence the effects of artificial nipples on the early weeks of breastfeeding. Australian breastfeeding expert Maureen Minchin (1989b) writes:

> It was interesting to talk about nipple confusion with midwives in Los Angeles and Philadelphia [USA]. In Los Angeles, such problems were commonplace; in Philadelphia, rarely seen. Both groups tended to think the other wrong to over or underemphasize this problem. Yet the Los Angeles counsellors were seeing women only after birth, when problems had developed; the Philadelphia mothers, educated during pregnancy about early causes of breastfeeding difficulty, probably had few such problems because their postpartum management was so much better.

In areas where conditions are favorable for early breastfeeding, an occasional artificial nipple may not be as likely to cause problems as in areas where mothers do not learn about breastfeeding prenatally, mothers routinely receive labor and delivery medication, separation after birth is the norm, instruction in breastfeeding basics is unavailable or unreliable, and there is no ongoing support.

Ultimately, if a baby is exhibiting symptoms associated with nipple confusion, what it is called is not nearly as important as what is done about it. Some babies can learn to breastfeed while continuing to receive bottles, though eliminating artificial nipples makes the process much easier. Decisions on the use of artificial nipples in breastfeeding babies should be made on a case-by-case basis, with the understanding that early use of artificial nipples may lead to premature weaning. Mothers should be informed and involved in the decision.

Ask the mother if her baby has been given bottles or a pacifier or if she has used a nipple shield.

If a baby has been given bottles or a pacifier or the mother has used a nipple shield, the artificial nipples may have taught the baby to push out his tongue, which pushes the breast out of his mouth, or to chew at the breast.

If the baby has not had artificial nipples, ask the mother if the baby has acted this way since birth. He may have sucked his tongue *in utero* and is not dropping it to accept the breast in his mouth. In this case, suggest the mother use the "Walking Back on the Tongue" exercise described in "Tongue Thrusting" in the chapter "Positioning, Latch-On, and the Baby's Suck."

Many babies find it difficult to switch back and forth between artificial nipples and the breast, especially during the early weeks of breastfeeding.

A newborn becomes confused because his tongue, jaw, and mouth move differently during breastfeeding than while using a bottle, pacifier, or most types of nipple shield. While breastfeeding, baby's jaws and tongue must work together in a coordinated rhythm. Once the baby latches on to the breast, the baby's tongue cups the breast in a rhythmic motion, pressing his mother's breast up against his palate. This flattens and elongates the flesh around his mother's nipple and the back of his tongue drops to form a grooved passageway for the milk to flow from her nipple. Then the baby swallows and takes a breath. The baby's lips should be flanged out and rest against the breast to make a seal.

When a baby tries to nurse from a bottle the way he nurses at the breast, he is immediately met with a flood of liquid. This forces the baby to block the milk with his tongue to prevent him from choking. His lips purse tightly against the firmer artificial nipple and his jaws do not need to move. Milk flows immediately with no waiting for the let-down, giving instant gratification.

If the baby is nipple-confused, suggest the mother stop using artificial nipples and, if needed, use other feeding methods while she works to persuade him to take the breast.

Encourage the mother to stop using bottles, pacifiers, and nipple shields. Most babies will again be able to take bottles or pacifiers without affecting nursing after a few weeks of effective breastfeeding.

The mother may be concerned about how her baby will get enough milk until he is nursing well again. Assure her that there are other ways to supplement a baby without using artificial nipples. A cup, spoon, flexible bowl, feeding syringe, eyedropper, or a nursing supplementer on the finger, known as finger-feeding, can all be used to feed a young baby and will not confuse a baby's suck as a bottle or pacifier would. (See "The Use of Breast Pumps and Other Products.")

Encourage the mother to keep working with her baby, using good positioning and latch-on techniques and praising him whenever he does something right.

The key to persuading the baby to take the breast is patience and persistence, with special care given to good positioning and latch-on.

The baby who is nipple-confused may be reluctant to open his mouth wide, because he is accustomed to holding the firmer artificial nipple tightly between his lips in the front of his mouth. In order to breastfeed effectively, the baby must take the breast far back into his mouth and use his mouth, lips, and tongue differently. He may need help in figuring out what to do.

When positioning the baby, suggest the mother check to be sure she is holding her baby with his mouth directly in front of her nipple so that he doesn't have to turn his head to latch on. His body should be well-supported with his head, shoulder, and hip in a straight line. In the cradle hold or side-lying positions, he should be on his side with his whole body facing hers. Encourage her to use the suggestions in "Latch-On" in the chapter "Positioning, Latch-On, and the Baby's Suck" to help the baby open his mouth very wide.

Once the baby's mouth is open very wide, the mother should pull him quickly onto the breast to make sure he gets as much of her breast in his mouth as possible. The baby should be pulled in so closely that his chin is pressed into the breast and his nose may be lightly resting on the breast. His lips should be flanged out. Taking the breast far back into his mouth ensures that the baby's first sucks will elongate the areola so that his gums can compress the milk sinuses, rewarding him with a satisfying mouthful of milk.

Fussy or Refuse Breast

When a baby is well-positioned and latched-on correctly, he may begin breastfeeding well immediately. More often, though, the nipple-confused baby looks puzzled and pushes the breast out, as if he doesn't know what to do. It may take much time, work, and patience before he gets the idea. Encourage the mother to praise the baby each time he takes a step in the right direction—an open mouth, tongue down, and good latch-on.

The baby may be more willing to take the breast if the mother offers it before he is too hungry and gets her milk flowing first.

Encourage the mother to offer the breast frequently, when the baby is responsive but before he gets too hungry. Most babies are more willing to try nursing when they are not ravenous.

The baby who is given bottles learns to expect an immediate and consistent flow of milk. Suggest the mother express some milk until her milk lets down and then offer her baby the breast so he will receive an instant reward for his efforts. She can do this by using hand-expression, breast massage, heat, or a breast pump.

To encourage the baby to take the breast, it may help to drip some expressed milk or water on the breast during and after latch-on. Use of a nursing supplementer on the breast or a finger may help some babies.

As the baby is attempting to latch on, suggest the mother have a helper drip expressed milk or clean water onto the breast so that it drips into the baby's mouth. This may help to calm the baby and keep him focused on the breast as a source of nourishment. Some babies will be more willing to work at latch-on if they are rewarded in this way. Continuing to drip milk after the baby latches on may encourage him to keep sucking if he has been willing to latch on but pulls off quickly in frustration.

Another approach that applies the same principle is the use of a nursing supplementer to supply instant flow at the breast. If the baby has been willing to latch on but will not stay on, difference in flow between bottle and breast may be a factor and use of a nursing supplementer may help. However, if the baby is unable or unwilling to latch on at all, use of a supplementer at the breast will not be helpful. In this case, finger-feeding the baby by taping the supplementer tube to a finger may make an effective transition to the breast (Ross 1987).

If the baby does not take the breast, does not seem to be swallowing regularly when at the breast, or has been regularly receiving formula, he will probably need a supplement. Suggest the mother keep count of the baby's wet diapers and stools.

When a baby is not taking the breast, some mothers are mistakenly told that they should not give any supplements because baby will nurse when he gets hungry enough. This strategy will not usually work for the baby who is nipple-confused and may put the baby at risk for dehydration. If the baby does not receive proper nourishment, he will become progressively weaker and less able to breastfeed.

It is important that the baby not be stressed by hunger and that he has the energy he needs to learn to breastfeed. If he is not nursing well or at all or has been regularly receiving formula, he will probably need a supplement in order to stay well-nourished. In most cases, the best supplement is mother's milk, and the mother may be expressing her milk already just to stay comfortable. (See "Expression and Storage of Human Milk.") Some mothers will choose to supplement with formula. If so, suggest they contact their baby's health care provider for a recommendation.

Every day the baby should receive approximately 2 to 2½ oz. (60-75 ml) of milk per pound (454 grams) of body weight either at the breast or by another method. A newborn may take about 2 oz. (60 ml) at the breast at a good feeding where regular swallowing is heard for ten minutes or more. Explain the alternative methods of feeding to the mother, and if supplementation is needed, encourage her to use the method with which she feels most comfortable. (See "The Use of Breast Pumps and Other Products.")

One sign that the baby may need a supplement is fewer than the normal number of wet diapers and stools per day. A baby should have at least five or six wet diapers and at least two sizeable bowel movements (fewer stools may be normal in the baby older than six weeks). If the mother does not get the baby to suck and swallow for at least ten minutes at each feeding, the baby may need to be supplemented. Suggest the mother keep a written diary of feedings along with a record of wet diapers and stools while she is working to overcome the nipple confusion. This will help her to gauge when a supplement is necessary.

Mention the suggestions listed in other sections and chapters.

The section later in this chapter "Persuading the Baby to Take the Breast," offers other suggestions, such as giving extra skin-to-skin contact, offering the breast when the baby is sleepy, and when rocking or walking, which may help persuade a reluctant nurser to take the breast.

If the baby is thrusting his tongue forward, the exercise "Walking Back on the Tongue" described in the chapter "Positioning, Latch-On, and the Baby's Suck," may help him keep his tongue down while he nurses.

If a nipple shield has the baby confused, in addition to the previous suggestions, there are several other approaches that can be used.

If the baby refuses to nurse without the nipple shield, the previous suggestions may help. Also mention the following approaches.

Gradually cut off the tip of the shield until it is gone. Some mothers have successfully weaned their babies from a nipple shield by turning the shield inside out and then cutting off a thin strip from the center of the nipple area each day (or before each nursing if the baby will tolerate it) until it is gone, using fine-point cuticle scissors or a razor blade. This method will not work with a silicone nipple shield, because it will leave sharp edges.

Slip the shield off quickly while the baby is nursing. Another approach is to start the baby nursing with the shield and then quickly slip it off.

Stuff the shield with cloth. Some mothers have weaned their babies from the shield by stuffing it with a small piece of clean cloth and putting the shield on as usual to begin a feeding. The baby eventually realizes that he can only get milk from the breast and begins to prefer it over the shield (Maher 1988).

When nipple confusion is severe and the baby fights the breast, the baby may need a time of no bottles and no breast before he can accept the breast.

Susan Meintz Maher, in her booklet *An Overview of Solutions to Breastfeeding and Sucking Problems* (1988), suggests the following progression for the nipple-confused baby who will not take the breast.

First day: no bottles, no breast. Suggest that for one day the mother give the baby her expressed milk from a cup, spoon, flexible bowl, feeding syringe, or eyedropper. If the mother's milk is not available or she chooses to give formula, suggest she call her baby's health care provider for the amount and type of supplement needed for each feeding.

Second day: no bottles, offer the breast for comfort. By now the baby may be ready to accept being positioned close to his mother's bare breast while being fed the supplement. Suggest the mother offer her breast to the baby for comfort after feedings and whenever she notices her baby wants to suck. If he arches away from the breast, suggest she swaddle the baby and calm him before offering the breast again. The baby may need another day of alternative feeding before making the transition to the breast. Encourage the mother to follow her baby's cues.

Transition to the breast. Once her baby accepts the breast for comfort, suggest the mother try to nurse him about half an hour before he is likely to be hungry. Most babies will eventually accept the breast.

Once the baby is breastfeeding, caution the mother to avoid artificial nipples for several weeks to allow him time to learn how to breastfeed well.

If the mother's milk supply is very low or the baby has been receiving regular supplements, caution the mother to reduce the supplements gradually as she builds up her milk supply.

If the mother's milk supply is low or supplements have become a substantial part of the baby's intake, caution the mother not to eliminate the supplements suddenly. Supplements should be eliminated gradually while baby's progress is carefully watched by his doctor. (For more information, see "Working with the Doctor and Supplements," in the "Slow Weight Gain" section of the chapter "Weight Gain.")

Fussy or Refuse Breast

Persuading the baby to take the breast may take time, hard work, and patience. Encourage the mother to get extra help during this period if she is feeling overwhelmed.

Some cases of nipple confusion require much time and patience before breastfeeding is going smoothly. For many babies it takes as long to get back to the breast as it took to become confused.

Good support is essential during this stressful time. Teaching a baby to breastfeed can be very time-consuming and frustrating for both mother and baby. If the mother is feeling overwhelmed, encourage her to get help with household tasks while she is working with her baby.

Flat or Inverted Nipples

If the baby is positioned and latched-on well, most types of flat or inverted nipples will not cause breastfeeding problems.

Babies breastfeed, not "nipple-feed," and if the baby is able to get a good mouthful of breast, most types of flat or inverted nipples will not cause a problem. (For more on different types of nipples, see "Flat and Inverted Nipples" in the chapter "Nipple Problems.")

Suggest that the mother work on good positioning and latch-on techniques. Good latch-on means the baby's mouth and gums will bypass the nipple entirely and take in a large mouthful of breast for effective breastfeeding.

Some types of nipples may be more difficult for baby to latch on to, especially at first, but patience and persistence will pay off.

Getting a "good fit" between mother and baby can take time and patience at first, even for the mother whose nipples are not flat or inverted. If the baby has difficulty latching on and becomes fussy at the breast, go over the suggestions in the section "Latch-On" in the chapter "Positioning and Latch-On."

Most important is patience and persistence. Encourage the mother to keep working with her baby and assure her that gentle persuasion will pay off in time.

There are several ways the mother with inverted or flat nipples can make latching on easier for the baby in the early days of breastfeeding. See "Flat and Inverted Nipples" in the chapter "Nipple Problems."

Touching the Baby's Head

Touching the baby's face or sides of his head while nursing may cause him to turn away from the breast.

A strong rooting reflex causes some babies to move toward a touch anywhere on their face or the sides of the head, unless the pressure is firm and constant. A hand on the back of his head (such as when the football hold is used) does not usually produce the same response.

If the mother has been touching the baby's face or head during nursing, suggest she avoid it during feedings. When using the football hold, it may be less distracting for the baby if the mother covers the hand holding the baby's head with a diaper or a baby blanket. When using the football hold, the mother's hand should be at the base of the baby's head, supporting his head and neck with her fingertips behind and below the level of the baby's ears.

For some babies, touching the back of the head when pulling the baby toward the breast produces an arching reflex. If the baby learns to associate this with the breast, he may then arch whenever the breast is presented.

Forceful Let-Down or Over-abundant Milk Supply

Ask the mother if the baby chokes and pulls away from her breast when her milk lets down.

The baby may gulp, choke, and sputter when the milk lets down. If the mother is not sure when her milk is letting down, see "Signs of a Healthy Let-Down" in the chapter "Breastfeeding Basics."

Suggest the mother try different nursing positions to see what works best.

Some mothers with a forceful let-down or an overabundant milk supply have found that the nursing positions that work best are those that allow the baby to nurse "uphill," with his head and throat higher than the mother's nipple. In the football hold, the mother can lean back. In the cradle hold, the mother can prop the baby in her lap on two pillows and lean back in a rocking chair or recliner.

Other mothers have found that side-lying positions work best, because it is easier for the baby to let the milk dribble out of his mouth if it is coming too fast rather than having to swallow quickly to prevent choking.

When a mother has an overabundant milk supply or a forceful let-down, the baby may be more comfortable nursing on one breast per feeding once the mother's milk supply is established.

If the baby has a difficult time coping with his mother's let-down or milk supply after trying the above suggestions, mention to the mother that many babies do better with one breast per feeding. Nursing the baby from just one breast may help prevent him from being overwhelmed with milk. For the mother with an overabundant supply, nursing on only one side at each feeding helps reduce her milk supply and bring it closer to her baby's demands. If the baby wants to nurse again within an hour to an hour-and-a-half, the mother can continue to offer the same breast. If the mother finds that restricting nursing to one breast leaves her other breast feeling overly full, she can either express just enough milk to make her comfortable or she can offer that breast to her baby and nurse just long enough to alleviate the feeling of fullness.

In order to most effectively stimulate milk production and prevent engorgement, it is best to offer both breasts at each feeding during the early days after birth. The mother's milk supply needs to be established and the baby needs to be gaining weight before suggesting the use of only one breast per feeding.

Other suggestions for the mother with a forceful let-down, include increasing the frequency of nursing, nursing the baby immediately upon waking, burping frequently, and avoiding pacifiers and supplements.

Rather than postponing nursings, which is often the first impulse for the mother whose baby is having problems coping with a fast flow of milk, feedings may be easier if the baby is nursed more frequently. This will reduce the amount of milk accumulated in the breast, making feedings more manageable for the baby.

In many cases the problems associated with a forceful let-down are a result of a combination of characteristics of both mother and baby—a mother who naturally has a fast flow of milk and a baby with a very strong suck. Nursing immediately upon baby's waking—even before the baby is fully awake, if possible—can be helpful because the baby may suck more gently in his relaxed state, making the flow of milk slower and reducing the likelihood of the baby gulping air.

Frequent burping can be helpful to the baby, particularly if he tends to gulp air during feedings, because it will reduce gas and fussiness.

Pacifiers and supplements have not been found to be helpful in dealing with a forceful let-down (Andrusiak and Larose-Kuzenko 1987). Regular pacifier use has been linked to early weaning (Victora 1993), and supplements given by bottle may cause nipple confusion.

The Need to Burp or Pass a Bowel Movement

If the baby gulps loudly during feedings and becomes fussier as the feeding progresses, this may mean the baby needs to burp.

If the baby does not become fussy until later in the feeding, consider the possibility that the baby needs to burp or pass a bowel movement. If the baby is a "gulper," that is, the mother hears him loudly gulping as he swallows, he may take in a lot of air during feedings and need to be burped. In this case, the baby tends to get fussier and fussier as the feeding progresses and feels better after he burps.

If this seems to be a possibility, suggest the mother take the baby off the breast, burp him, and offer him the breast again.

Ask the mother if her baby usually passes a bowel movement while nursing or shortly afterwards.

Some babies' bowels are stimulated by nursing, causing them to strain during nursing as they try to pass a bowel movement. This could cause fussiness at the breast as the baby strains. If the baby usually passes a bowel movement while nursing or shortly afterwards, this may be the cause.

Fussy or Refuse Breast

The "High Need" or Colicky Baby

The mother of a fussy or fretful baby may describe him as difficult to console, demanding, and intense and she may have difficulty helping him settle down enough to breastfeed well.

Ask the mother if the baby is fussy when he is not breastfeeding. If so, does his fussiness make it difficult for him to settle down and breastfeed?

A fretful baby may have difficulty settling down to breastfeed. Mention some of the following suggestions, a few at a time, so that it will not sound overwhelming to the mother.

Offer to give the mother some suggestions for helping a baby to settle down at the breast.

Ways to Soothe a Fretful Baby

Before breastfeeding
- Nurse the baby before he is fully awake.
- If he is already fussing, cuddling or rocking may quiet him enough so that he can latch on and nurse well.
- Swaddling the baby may make him feel safe and allow him to relax.
- Make sure he is warm enough. Some babies are especially sensitive to cold (especially the feet and shoulders).
- Change the baby's clothing to check for something binding.
- Change his diaper.
- Calm him by offering him a clean finger to suck before offering the breast.

During breastfeeding
- Remove competing stimuli (television, radio, even siblings, if possible).
- Sing or speak in a chanting voice to calm him.
- Try different nursing positions. Some babies nurse better in one position than another.
- Use a lot of patience.

General suggestions
- Use a baby carrier or sling between nursings and give lots of skin-to-skin contact. Extra physical closeness may calm him.
- Get extra household help so that the baby can be given extra attention.
- Have the baby checked by the doctor to rule out physical causes for fussiness, such as an ear infection, hypoglycemia (low blood sugar), or hypocalcemia (low blood calcium).

Research indicates that chiropractic adjustment helps alleviate colic in some babies.

Research from Denmark, where chiropractic has been used since the early 1900s to treat infant colic, indicates that chiropractic adjustment may help reduce or eliminate colic (Nilsson 1985) in some babies. One study of 316 babies with colic found that within 14 days and three chiropractic adjustments, 94% of their mothers reported that the colic had improved or that the colic was gone (Klougart 1989). The researchers estimate that between 20-40% of all Danish infants with colic are treated by chiropractors.

Also see the later section, "Sensitivity to a Food or Drug the Mother or Baby Has Ingested."

Foremilk-Hindmilk Imbalance

Switching breasts too soon during the feeding may result in a foremilk-hindmilk imbalance, causing fussiness, gassiness, green stools, and, possibly, poor weight gain.

If the baby's stools are consistently green and watery and the baby is not gaining well, even though the mother's milk supply seems to be plentiful, this could be a sign that the baby is being switched from one breast to the other too soon. Called foremilk-hindmilk imbalance (or "oversupply syndrome"), this sometimes happens when a baby receives too much of the watery lactose-rich foremilk and not enough of the fatty high-calorie hindmilk. Too much lactose stimulates the baby's digestive tract to move the milk along too fast, causing the watery, green stools (Woolridge 1988).

If foremilk-hindmilk imbalance is suspected, suggest the mother wait until the baby finishes the first breast before switching to the second, rather than switching him to the second breast after a predetermined length of time. In some cases, the baby may do best on one breast per feeding.

Consistently green stools may also indicate that the baby is sensitive to a substance he is taking (such as a medication) or something entering the mother's milk from her digestive tract. See the later section, "Sensitivity to a Food or Drug the Mother or Baby Has Ingested." If it persists, this should be discussed with a health care provider as there may be a medical problem.

Delayed or Inhibited Let-Down or Milk-Ejection Reflex

If the let-down, or milk-ejection reflex, is delayed or inhibited, the baby may become frustrated and upset, because most of the milk in the breast is not released.

If the let-down, or milk-ejection reflex, is delayed or inhibited, the baby may nurse well for a few minutes and then pull away with frustration and unhappiness. The mother may notice that her baby is sucking rapidly but not swallowing deeply or often.

Some milk accumulates in the milk reservoirs near the nipple, but without the let-down reflex—which may occur many times during a feeding—most of the mother's milk will remain in the breast despite the baby's efforts. For more information, see "Delayed or Inhibited Let-Down" in the chapter "Breastfeeding Basics."

Sucking Problem

Ask the mother: When the baby is breastfeeding does he suck actively? Does he swallow regularly? Do his jaws move rhythmically, as well as his mouth?

Is there a problem in getting the baby to take the breast? Stay on the breast? Has the mother noticed milk leaking out of the baby's mouth during nursings? Does the baby frequently choke while nursing?

Do the baby's cheeks dimple or does he make a clicking sound when nursing?

Does the mother have sore nipples?

See "Sucking Problems" in the chapter "Positioning, Latch-On, and the Baby's Suck" for suggestions to help the baby improve his suck.

If the mother cannot hear the baby swallowing when the baby is nursing, this is a sign of a sucking problem. Also, if the baby never seems satisfied and wants to nurse "all the time," while just mouthing the nipple without regularly swallowing, this is another sign.

If the baby is not sucking well, hunger could make him fussy at the breast.

If a baby is not taking the breast far enough back into his mouth, it may be difficult for him to stay on during breastfeeding. Also, if his muscle tone is weak, it may be difficult for him to coordinate sucking and swallowing rhythms, making him more likely to choke or leak milk during breastfeeding. (Choking could also be a sign of a forceful let-down.)

Dimpling of the cheeks or clicking sounds are signs of suction being broken, which may mean the baby is not using his tongue properly.

Sore nipples are a common side effect of many types of sucking problems, such as short frenulum (tongue-tie), short tongue, tongue thrusting or sucking, and others.

Arching (Hypertonic) Baby

Ask the mother if the baby arches his head and body away from the breast when he nurses, nurses very often, and swallows a lot of air.

An arching baby has tight muscle tone. He may be described as strong, and he may spend much of his time in an extended position.

To help this baby breastfeed more effectively, suggest the mother calm him before nursing and hold him with his chin down near his chest and in a position in which his feet will not touch anything.

The arching baby may breastfeed more often than the average ten to twelve times a day because he is hungry. He receives little of the high-calorie hindmilk because his sucking is inefficient. The mother may say that her baby won't stay on the breast, that he arches his head and body away from the breast. He may spit up, burp, and pass gas more than the average baby because he swallows air while he nurses.

Fussy or Refuse Breast

The arching baby may spend much of his time with his legs extended straight out. Some babies assume an arching position by extending their bodies strongly at the neck, trunk, and legs. The baby will arch backward if his feet touch anything.

The baby may be developmentally advanced for his age, for example, holding his head up at one to two weeks or rolling over by one month.

Suggest the mother calm the baby before nursing him. Massaging, swaddling, or holding him firmly will all help to relax him. Many of these babies will settle down to nurse after going through the arching behavior three times.

The mother may find it easier to breastfeed the arching baby by making some adjustments in her usual nursing positions. The football hold seems to work especially well with the arching baby because it keeps his head and hips bent in the fetal position, which does not stimulate the arching. Using the football hold—with the baby's buttocks against a hard surface and his legs pointed upward so his feet do not touch anything—may work well. Suggest the mother hold the baby's head down so that his chin almost touches his chest. This helps his tongue move correctly. This position may be more comfortable for the mother if she elevates one leg so that her thigh can support the arm holding the baby. A pillow or folded blanket can also help support the mother's hand and forearm, since her arm may tire easily from the baby's head pushing against her hand.

The mother also can use the cradle position if the baby is held firmly flexed in a cloth sling. The sling helps prevent the mother's arms and shoulders from getting tired.

An arching baby may breastfeed better at night in the side-lying position.

When she is nursing and at other times, suggest the mother move slowly so as not to trigger the baby's arching. (For more information, see "Neurologically Impaired Baby" in the chapter "The Baby with Special Needs.")

Birth or Physical Injury

Ask the mother if her delivery was difficult or if the baby was born with a broken bone, dislocated joint, or any other birth injury.

A long and difficult labor can be stressful for the baby, and the baby may be sore or uncomfortable in the nursing position. If forceps were used, the baby is bruised, or has a large hematoma, he may be in pain, making him less inclined to settle down and nurse well. A dislocated hip or a broken clavicle also are painful and may affect the baby's willingness to nurse. Ask if the baby has been carefully examined by a health care professional to rule out any of these causes.

If the baby has a physical condition that prevents him from nursing well, encourage the mother to experiment with different nursing positions to find one that is more comfortable for the baby. If a comfortable position cannot be found, suggest the mother express her milk for the baby until the injuries have healed enough so that the baby can be held comfortably.

Fussy at the Breast at Any Stage of Breastfeeding

Questions to Ask

Ask the mother if the baby has or recently had a stuffy nose.

Ask the mother her baby's age and if she has recently developed sore nipples or had mastitis.

Ask the mother if she thinks her baby is teething.

Ask the mother if she sees any white patches on the baby's gums, cheeks, or tongue, if the baby has a diaper rash, or if she or the baby have had antibiotics. Also ask the mother if she has sore nipples or is prone to vaginal yeast infections.

Ask the mother if she has recently started a new medication, tried any new foods, or used any new products either on her nipples or on any other part of her body.

Ask if the baby has recently had an injection or hurt himself.

Ask the mother if she thinks that her milk supply is low.

Ask the mother if her baby has ever seemed to have a lot of trouble coping with the fast flow of milk while breastfeeding.

Ask the mother if there have been any unusual stresses in their lives or if the baby is learning a new skill.

Congestion can be caused by a cold or virus and can lead to an ear infection. Persistent congestion may be a symptom of allergy.

Both teething and thrush can cause sore nipples in a mother who had been breast-feeding comfortably. If the baby is four months or older and is drooling and chewing more than usual, consider teething as a strong possibility.

If the mother has recently had mastitis, her baby may be reacting to a change in the taste of her milk.

Swollen and sore gums from teething can make a baby fussy at the breast. (See later section and "Teething and Biting" in the chapter "Nipple Problems.")

White patches in the baby's mouth, diaper rash, antibiotic use, sore nipples, and a vaginal yeast infection in the mother are associated with thrush. If the baby has thrush, his mouth may be sore, making him fussy at the breast. (See later section and "Thrush" in the chapter "Nipple Problems.")

If the mother has started a new medication or eaten an unusually strong or spicy food, this may temporarily change the taste of her milk, causing her baby to be fussy. The baby may also react to a new product, such as a new perfume, deodorant, hair spray, shampoo—even the laundry detergent used to wash her clothes—as well as a nipple cream or ointment.

If it hurts for the baby to be held in the nursing position, due to a sensitive area from an injection or an injury, he may be fussy at the breast. Mouth injuries commonly affect a baby's willingness to nurse.

Overuse of bottles, pacifiers, and solid foods can rapidly decrease a mother's milk supply, causing her baby to be fussy at the breast.

Some mothers with a forceful let-down report that their baby's fussiness at the breast or breast refusal is not confined to the early weeks and months of nursing but may continue as the baby gets older.

Emotional upsets and stress can make a baby fussy. Radical changes in daily routine, moving, or other family tensions are sometimes reflected in a baby's behavior at the breast.

Developmental changes can affect a baby's interest in breastfeeding. If the baby is learning to crawl or walk, for example, he may be unwilling to settle down to nurse at the usual times because he is so preoccupied with his newfound abilities. A younger baby may suddenly become very distractible and may need calmer surroundings to nurse well.

Congestion or an Ear Infection

A congested nose or an ear infection may make breast-feeding difficult or painful.

Keeping the baby upright, with a vaporizer running, and offering short, frequent feedings may make breastfeeding easier.

A baby with a cold or ear infection will benefit from continuing to breastfeed, and a sick baby can almost always cope more easily with breastfeeding than he can cope with taking liquid from a bottle. But breastfeeding may be more difficult if the baby has trouble breathing through his nose or, in the case of an ear infection, if sucking increases the pressure in the baby's ears, making nursing painful.

Fussy or Refuse Breast

The following suggestions may make breastfeeding easier. Suggest the mother:

- Keep the baby in an upright position (by carrying him in arms or positioning him upright in a sling or baby carrier). Elevate his head for a short time before offering him the breast so that the mucus can drain.
- Breastfeed the baby in an upright position.
- Breastfeed the baby in a room where a cool-mist vaporizer is running.
- Try running the water in the shower to steam up the bathroom and breastfeed the baby in there.
- Offer short, frequent feedings.

Suggest the mother call the baby's doctor for medication or other recommended treatments.

If the baby is fussy at the breast or refuses to breastfeed, the mother may need to express her milk and feed it to him another way.

When a baby is congested or has an ear infection, he may become fussy at the breast or refuse to breastfeed because he finds it impossible to breathe while nursing. If he has an ear infection, he may find nursing painful because the sucking increases the pressure in his ears.

If the baby is fussy at the breast and the mother is concerned about how much milk he is getting, suggest she begin counting his wet diapers and bowel movements. Six to eight wet diapers and two to five bowel movements (fewer bowel movements are normal if the baby is older than six weeks) will indicate he is getting enough. While a baby is sick, especially if he is vomiting or has diarrhea, it is not unusual for him to have fewer wet diapers. If he has at least two wet diapers a day, there should be no danger of dehydration.

If the baby refuses to nurse, suggest the mother offer him some of her expressed milk in a spoon or cup and keep offering the breast every hour or so. Assure her that when the baby is feeling better, he will want to nurse again. While her baby is refusing to nurse, encourage the mother to express her milk as often as the baby had been nursing so that her breasts do not become overly full.

Teething

When a baby is teething, his sore gums may cause him to be fussy or refuse the breast.

Assure the mother that this is temporary, and suggest she offer the baby something cold to chew on to numb his gums before trying to nurse.

Teething can make a baby's gums swollen and sore, and he may begin to nurse differently—or even chew on the nipple—during feedings to try to ease the discomfort. He may refuse the breast when the pain is at its peak.

Fussiness at the breast or breast refusal due to teething is temporary and will pass as the baby's teeth erupt. Suggest the mother offer her baby something cold to chew on before offering the breast. This may soothe her baby and make him more willing to nurse. Some possibilities include: a cold, wet washcloth, a refrigerated teething toy, and ice. If the baby is eating solids, chewing on a frozen bagel or any other cold, hard food before breastfeeding may help his gums feel better so that he can nurse more comfortably.

Also share with her the suggestions listed later in the section, "Persuading the Baby to Take the Breast."

Suggest the mother consult her baby's doctor before giving a pain-relieving drug or an over-the-counter preparation to numb his gums.

Reduced Milk Supply

If the mother's milk supply is reduced, the baby may become frustrated due to lack of milk.

If the baby becomes frustrated at the breast, it may be due to a reduced milk supply. Ask the mother if she has been ill or taking any medications or if any of the following common causes of reduced milk supply might apply to her:

- regular supplemental bottles of formula, juice, or water,
- poor breastfeeding management (not nursing often or long enough),
- poor positioning and latch-on,
- overuse of a pacifier,
- too much solid food too soon,
- use of a nipple shield (a flexible artificial nipple worn over the mother's breast during feedings),
- placid, sleepy baby, and
- weak or ineffective suck.

Suggest the mother try to increase her milk supply.

If the mother would like to increase her milk supply, suggest that she:

- **Breastfeed frequently and long enough.** If the baby is younger than six months old, breastfeed ten to twelve times a day for at least twenty to thirty minutes at a feeding.
- **Offer both breasts at each feeding.** If the baby is willing to take both breasts, it will better stimulate the mother's breasts to produce more milk. If the baby is satisfied after one breast, suggest the mother express some milk from the other breast to stimulate her supply.
- **Be sure the baby is positioned and latched-on well**—see the chapter "Positioning, Latch-On, and the Baby's Suck."
- **Try "super switch nursing,"** especially if the baby seems to have a weak or lazy suck. Switching breasts two or three times throughout each feeding may help the baby maintain an effective suck and give more stimulation to the mother's breasts. Suggest the mother watch the baby's sucking and swallowing as he nurses and switch to the other breast as soon as the sucking slows down and he swallows less often. For some babies, this will be several minutes on each side; for others it could be as little as thirty to forty seconds during the first few tries.
- **All the baby's sucking should be at the breast**—avoid bottles and pacifiers since they can confuse the baby and limit the baby's time at the breast.
- **If the baby is younger than six months, give the baby mother's milk only**—avoid solids, water, formula, and juice. If formula supplements have been a significant part of the baby's intake, suggest the mother cut back on the amount gradually as her milk supply increases, counting her baby's wet diapers and bowel movements (he should have at least six to eight wet cloth diapers—five to six disposables—and, if he is younger than six weeks old, two to five bowel movements a day) to be sure he is getting enough.
- **If the baby is between six and twelve months and eating solid foods, suggest the mother nurse first, before offering solids,** so that solids do not replace nursings and so that the baby will get the milk he needs.

Forceful Let-Down

During the first three months of nursing, a baby who is having difficulty handling his mother's forceful let-down may have some of the same symptoms as a colicky baby.

From birth to three months, the baby whose mother has a forceful let-down reflex may swallow a lot of air due to gulping during feeding, may spit up regularly, pass a lot of gas, and soon after falling asleep may wake and behave as if he is very hungry even if he has just nursed. He may have regular periods of fussiness and/or restlessness, may be fussy at the breast, and have difficulty settling down to nurse. He may arch away from the breast when the let-down occurs.

Typically the baby gains weight very rapidly, has frequent very wet diapers, and some green stools. He may have a strong suck, strong muscle tone, and want to nurse frequently. As the mother feels her milk let down, she may notice the baby gulping, choking, and sputtering. Some mothers also report hearing a noise that sounds like milk hitting the bottom of the baby's stomach.

The mother may notice several let-downs during a feeding. She may leak between feedings and from the other breast during feedings, and her let-down may feel painful.

Approaches that may be helpful include:

Fussy or Refuse Breast

- increasing the frequency of breastfeeding,
- nursing on one breast at a feeding,
- nursing the baby immediately upon waking, while he's still sleepy,
- trying different nursing positions, such as side-lying or nursing "uphill" with baby's head higher than the breast,
- burping the baby frequently.

For more information, see "Forceful Let-Down or Overabundant Milk Supply" earlier in this chapter.

From three to six months of age, a baby who is having difficulty handling his mother's forceful let-down may refuse or postpone feedings.

Even if nursing has gone fairly smoothly until this stage, some babies who have had difficulty coping with the mother's forceful let-down may begin to exhibit a reluctance to nurse that may include some of the following symptoms:

- refusal to continue nursing when the mother switches breasts during a feeding,
- refusal to nurse himself to sleep, preferring instead fingers, thumb, or a pacifier,
- refusing some feedings even when obviously hungry,
- "biting" the breast,
- a marked decrease in weight gain or even weight loss,
- refusal to nurse at all (nursing strike).

Some suggestions that may help the mother persuade her baby to nurse more contentedly during this period include:

- offer the breast before the baby is fully awake,
- use nursing positions the baby favors,
- take full advantage of times the baby nurses well,
- nurse on only one breast at a feeding,
- provide as much skin-to-skin contact as possible when not feeding,
- consider supplementation if the baby is not nursing often enough.

If the baby is not nursing often enough, the mother may also need to express her milk to maintain her milk supply.

The baby who continues to have difficulty coping with his mother's forceful let-down may wean earlier than other babies, sometimes before his first birthday.

Some mothers have found that by using the previous suggestions, their babies have begun to enjoy nursing, even becoming eager to nurse and go on to become long-term nursers. However, if a baby does not overcome his discomfort at the breast, he may be more likely to wean early on his own. When a baby cannot nurse for comfort without having to cope with large amounts of milk, he may turn to fingers, thumb, or pacifier for comfort and restrict the breast to feeding only. Once the baby reaches the age when he is taking a variety of other foods, he may be more likely to give up nursing. Some mothers report that their babies wean on their own before their first birthday (Andrusiak and Larose-Kuzenko 1987).

Thrush

Ask the mother if she has sore nipples, a yeast infection, or if she or her baby has recently been treated with antibiotics.

The baby with thrush has a sore mouth. The mother may say that at every feeding the baby starts to nurse but then pulls away and becomes fussy.

To determine whether or not this is the cause of her baby's fussiness, ask the mother if any of the following symptoms of thrush apply to her or her baby. Symptoms of thrush in the mother:

- prolonged or sudden onset of sore nipples during or after the newborn period (the mother may describe her nipples as pink, flaky, and itchy, or red and burning),
- cracked nipples,
- shooting pains in the breast during or after a feeding,
- a vaginal yeast (*monilial*) infection.

Symptoms of thrush in the baby:

- white patches on the inside of his mouth, cheeks, or tongue,
- diaper rash,
- breast refusal or a reluctance to nurse (because his mouth is sore),
- rarely, thrush is a contributing factor in slow weight gain.

Candida albicans, the organism that causes thrush, is a fungus that thrives on milk on the nipples, in the milk ducts, and in the baby's mouth. The baby may carry the organism without showing any symptoms.

For more information, see "Thrush" in the chapter "Nipple Problems."

Discomfort in the Baby's Mouth or When Being Held

Ask the mother if the baby has had an injection recently.

If the baby has recently had an injection, ask the mother where the injection was given and if she may be putting pressure on that area when she holds him to nurse. He may have a sore area that is painful when the mother holds him in the nursing position. If so, suggest she try other nursing positions until the sore area heals.

Ask the mother if her baby has recently been hurt or bruised.

Any sore area from illness or injury could make nursing painful. If the baby has recently had an injury, ask the mother if this may make nursing in the usual position uncomfortable for him. If so, suggest she try other nursing positions until the discomfort goes away.

Ask the mother if the baby has hurt his mouth lately or has sores in his mouth.

A mouth injury or sore (such as a cold sore) can make nursing painful, which may make the baby fussy at the breast or cause him to refuse to nurse.

Gastroesophageal Reflux

Some mothers have found that a baby with gastroesophageal reflux will refuse to nurse.

The baby goes to the breast eagerly, but after the milk begins to flow, the baby cries and pulls away or the baby cries immediately after nursing.

Spitting up and vomiting are the usual symptoms of gastroesophageal reflux, but some mothers have found that a baby's refusal to nurse may be the only indication of this problem. (See "Gastroesophageal Reflux" in the chapter "Illness-Baby.")

Sensitivity to a Food or Drug Mother or Baby Has Ingested

Before discussing the mother's diet, ask her if the baby has been given anything other than her milk to which he might be sensitive.

It is the rare baby who is sensitive to a food or other substance his mother ingests. It is more likely a baby will be sensitive to a food he has been given directly, such as formula, solids, or juice. Occasionally mothers give their babies teas or other remedies that are recommended for colic or fussiness. Sometimes other children in the house are "feeding" the baby without the mother's knowledge.

Fussy or Refuse Breast

Ask the mother if she or anyone else is giving the baby anything other than her milk. Ask specifically if the baby is receiving supplemental feedings from the baby's father or a caretaker when she is not at home, as she may not think of this unless asked.

Ask the mother if she and the baby are taking any medications, vitamins, or other supplements, such as iron or fluoride.

Many medications pass into the mother's milk, although in very small amounts. But a sensitive baby may react to a drug his mother is taking by becoming fussy. Ask if the baby's fussiness began after she started taking the drug. If so, suggest the mother ask her doctor to recommend an alternative drug.

If the baby is taking a drug, he may be experiencing side effects. If the baby's fussiness coincides with his beginning a medication, suggest the mother contact her baby's doctor and discuss finding an alternative medication.

If the mother is taking vitamins, ask her if they contain iron. Some mothers report that when they stop taking iron, their babies' fussiness decreases.

If the baby is being given vitamins, suggest the mother ask her baby's doctor if they are necessary. For the vast majority of breastfed babies, vitamin supplements are unnecessary. In unusual cases, vitamin supplements may be warranted, such as the very premature baby, the baby whose skin is never exposed to sunlight, and the baby whose mother is on a strict vegan diet that excludes meat, fish, eggs, and dairy products.

Some mothers report their babies have reacted to fluoride supplements with symptoms such as fussiness, irritability, and spitting up. It is not known whether this reaction was caused by the fluoride itself or other substances in the drops. Since 1994, however, fluoride is no longer recommended in the US for babies younger than six months (AAP Committee on Nutrition 1995).

Ask the mother if she smokes and if so, how much she smokes each day.

Smoking has been linked to fussiness. In one study, 40% of babies breastfed by smokers were rated as colicky (two to three hours of "excessive" crying) as compared with 26% of babies breastfed by nonsmokers (Matheson and Rivrud 1989). This link between smoking and colic has also been found with artificially fed babies with one or more smokers in the home (Lawrence, p. 519). Smoking has also been linked to earlier weaning (Mansbach 1991) and lower milk production (Hopkinson 1992) in some studies, as well as interference with milk let-down (Lawrence, p. 518).

Some mothers smoke and breastfeed with no apparent problem, yet other mothers and babies may not do well. When a mother smokes a cigarette, the nicotine levels in her blood and milk first increase and then decrease over time. The half-life of nicotine—the amount of time it takes for half the nicotine to be eliminated from the body—is ninety-five minutes (Steldinger and Luck 1988). While it is ideal for the mother to quit smoking entirely, if the mother is unreceptive to this idea or has been unable to quit, suggest she smoke immediately after breastfeeding to cut down on the amount of nicotine in her milk during nursing. Also, encourage her to try to cut down on the number of cigarettes she smokes per day and to avoid smoking in the same room as the baby. The fewer cigarettes smoked, the smaller the chance that difficulties will arise.

Ask the mother if she drinks caffeinated beverages.

The amount of caffeine in five or fewer 5-oz (150 ml) cups of coffee per day will not cause a problem for most breastfeeding mothers and babies (Nehlig and Debry 1994), although some mothers and babies may be unusually sensitive.

When figuring caffeine intake, be sure the mother is counting all her sources, including coffee, iced and hot teas, colas, other soft drinks containing caffeine, and any over-the-counter drugs that contain caffeine. Also, caffeine is found in most cola soft drinks, but it is also in other soft drinks, so encourage her to check the label.

Some over-the-counter drugs also contain caffeine. Examples include:

- stimulants, such as Caffedrine, NoDoz, and Vivarin,
- pain relievers, such as Anacin, Excedrin, and Midol,
- diuretics, such as Aqua-ban, Pre-Mens Fore, and Permathene H2Off,
- cold remedies, such as Coryban-D, Dristan, and Triaminicin, and
- weight-control aids, such as Dexatrim, Dietac, and Prolamine.

Be sure to mention that chocolate contains a substance called theobromine, which is similar to caffeine and can produce the same effect if consumed in large amounts.

Excessive caffeine consumption by a breastfeeding mother may make her baby fussy and wakeful.

If a breastfeeding mother consumes more caffeine in a day than is in five 5-oz cups of coffee (750 ml), caffeine could begin accumulating in her baby's system, causing symptoms of caffeine stimulation.

A baby who is being overstimulated by caffeine is a wide-eyed, active, alert baby who doesn't sleep for long. He may also be unusually fussy. To find out if these symptoms are caused by caffeine, suggest the mother try going without caffeine for a week or two and substituting caffeine-free beverages, both hot and cold, for her caffeinated drinks. (If a mother has been consuming large amounts of caffeine, she may experience headaches when she eliminates it from her diet.)

If caffeine stimulation is the cause of the baby's fussiness, he should begin settling down within a few days to a week after his mother eliminates caffeine from her diet.

When a baby is fussy, many mothers' first thought is that the baby is reacting to something in their diet. Usually this is not the cause.

Most mothers can eat any food they like without it causing any problem for their babies. Even so, many mothers restrict their diets unnecessarily because they have been told that they should avoid certain foods while breastfeeding. If the baby does become fussy, their first thought may be that the fussiness is a reaction to something they ate.

Although many cultures around the world recommend that nursing mothers avoid certain foods, these restrictions vary from place to place. For example, Chinese and Southeast Asian women are advised to avoid cold liquids because they are not good for the baby. Hispanic women may be told to avoid pork, chili, and tomatoes. Some African Americans avoid onions while breastfeeding (Taylor 1985). In Australia, mothers are cautioned to avoid cabbage, chocolates, spicy foods, peas, onions, and cauliflower because these foods are thought to cause colic, gas, diarrhea, and rashes in the breastfeeding baby (Riordan and Auerbach, p. 352).

A mother's varied diet may be an advantage to her breastfeeding baby because it alters the flavor of her milk, providing baby with a variety of tastes which prepares him for the solid foods he'll receive at the family table when he is older. One study found that one to two hours after nursing mothers consumed capsules of garlic extract their milk acquired a garlicky smell, but the babies who received this garlicky milk were not fussier. Instead, they showed a greater interest in nursing and consumed more milk (Menella and Beauchamp 1991).

Some babies do show sensitivity to a food in the mother's diet (see next point), but the foods that cause reactions differ from one mother and baby to the next, so it is not sensible for all nursing mothers to avoid certain foods. In most instances, avoiding particular foods will not cut down on fussiness, and these kinds of "diet rules" have been found to dissuade some mothers from breastfeeding at all (Gabriel 1986).

See the next point to help a mother confirm or rule out a possible food sensitivity as the cause of her baby's fussiness.

Occasionally, a food the mother eats will affect the baby. This is more likely if there is a family history of allergy.

Although most breastfeeding mothers can eat any food in moderation without any effect on their babies, occasionally, a sensitive baby may be affected by a food his mother eats (Lust 1996). The mother may say that her baby is fussy after feedings. He cries inconsolably for long periods, sleeps little, and wakes suddenly with obvious discomfort. He also may have green stools with mucus, eczema, congestion, dry skin, or wheezing. There may be a family history of allergies.

Ask the mother if she has recently had a new food or eaten a large amount of a food. Although it is unusual for a baby to react to a food his mother eats, some mothers notice that their babies become very fussy after they eat a new food (particularly one that is unusually strong or spicy) or when they consume a large amount of one food. To alleviate her baby's fussiness, the mother can simply moderate her intake or avoid that food while continuing to breastfeed. If this is the case, the baby should be back to normal within twenty-four hours.

However, not all food sensitivities are so obvious. Symptoms like congestion, eczema, and wheezing, as well as fussiness, may start gradually and their cause may not be as apparent. Maureen Minchin, Australian breastfeeding expert (1989), suggests asking the following questions to help determine if the baby may be sensitive to a food that is a regular part of the mother's diet.

- Are there foods that you don't like but you are eating while breast-feeding—or ate during pregnancy—for the benefit of your baby?
- Are there foods that you crave? What foods do you feel you have to have when you have had a bad day?

These foods are the most likely suspects, because conscious dislikes or food cravings are signals that the mother's body may be reacting to them in an abnormal way. Suggest to the mother that she eliminate one of these foods from her diet for a minimum of two to three weeks. Eliminating a food for two or three days will be effective in certain situations, such as an acute reaction to a recently introduced food. However, if the baby is responding less acutely or is reacting to long-term exposure to a food that is a regular part of his mother's diet, the baby may not improve immediately when it is eliminated. Although some babies respond within a few days, it is not unusual for the baby to feel worse for about a week after the offending food is eliminated before he feels better. The mother may also have withdrawal symptoms, such as headaches. But over a period of several weeks, the mother will know if she has found the right food because she will see a difference in her baby's disposition. She may even feel better herself.

Suggest the mother eliminate no more than one or two foods at a time so that she can more easily pinpoint the cause. Eliminating more foods at once makes it harder to eat a balanced diet. Encourage the mother to get skilled help in evaluating her diet if she makes major changes in her eating habits.

Cow's milk seems to be a common source of food sensitivity and fussiness in babies, perhaps because many women are encouraged to drink a lot of milk during pregnancy, which can sensitize a baby before birth and while breastfeeding. The protein in cow's milk passes into a mother's milk and if the baby is sensitive to this, it can cause fussiness. One study found that mothers with colicky babies had higher levels of cow's milk protein in their milk than mothers whose babies were not colicky (Clyne and Kulczycki 1991). In another study, thirty-five out of sixty-six mothers of colicky babies reported a decrease in their babies' fussiness when they eliminated milk and milk products from their diets (Jakobsson and Lindberg 1983). It may take ten days to two weeks to eliminate cow's milk protein from the mother's system, so if the mother wants to try eliminating milk and milk products from her diet, encourage her to allow the full two weeks before gauging the results.

If there is a family history of allergies, the baby is more likely to be sensitive to a food in his mother's diet.

Change in the Taste of the Mother's Nipple or Milk

Ask the mother if she is using any creams or ointments on her nipples.

Use of some creams or ointments on the mother's nipples—particularly those that need to be removed before nursing—may change the taste, causing the baby to be fussy at the breast or refuse to nurse.

Ask the mother if her baby's fussiness at the breast or breast refusal coincides with the beginning of her menstrual periods.

Although it is unusual, some babies become fussy or refuse to nurse at the beginning of their mother's menstrual cycles. Ruth Lawrence, MD, reports that "total rejection of both breasts may be due to the return of menstruation. A mother will notice the infant will reject the breast for a day or so with each period."

Mastitis can make the mother's milk taste saltier. This causes some babies to be fussy at the breast.

Sodium and chloride levels may rise in the mother's milk after mastitis, making the milk taste saltier (Thullen 1988; Conner 1979). Some babies react to this change in taste by nursing only reluctantly on that breast—expressing a strong preference for the other breast—or by refusing the affected breast altogether.

If this may be the problem, suggest the mother express her milk as often as her baby had been nursing so that the affected breast does not become overly full. She should continue to offer that breast to the baby. If the mother keeps up her milk supply, her milk will lose its salty taste within a week, and the baby should go back to nursing as usual.

Distractibility and Developmental Changes

A baby's normal developmental behavior may affect how often or how long he breastfeeds.

Normal developmental behavior can affect how often and how long a baby breastfeeds. Each stage of development brings new skills that can distract a baby from breastfeeding and change his usual nursing pattern.

At four to five months of age, a baby loves to look at his changing surroundings. If distractibility causes the baby to consistently fuss at feedings or refuse to nurse, suggest the mother find quiet or darkened surroundings in which to nurse the baby.

At four to six months of age, a baby may begin teething and may be fretful while breastfeeding or refuse to nurse. He may also chew on his hands afterwards.

At five to six months of age, a baby is highly sensitive. Many mothers have found that when they raise their voice to an older sibling during a feeding, the baby becomes upset and stops nursing or may even go on a nursing strike. Encourage the mother to find a quiet and peaceful spot to nurse for most breastfeedings.

From six to twelve months of age. Babies six months and older remain easily distracted. Mother may need to close curtains and eliminate noise as much as possible while nursing. It is not unusual for nine- to twelve-month-olds to become so involved in mastering gross motor skills that they forget to nurse or refuse to settle down for long. Many mothers report at this stage their babies wake up more at night to nurse, because they are "too busy" to nurse during the day. Older babies can also get a lot of milk in a short time, so the baby may only need to nurse for five to ten minutes and the mother may be needlessly concerned.

Reaction to Cosmetics or Other Products

Ask the mother if she has recently started using any new perfumes, shampoos, lotions, laundry detergents, or other products.

Some babies express their dislike of a new soap, deodorant, body powder, lotion, perfume, hair spray, detergent, fabric softener, shampoo, conditioner, or other product the mother uses on her body or her clothes by fussing at the breast or refusing to nurse. Suggest the mother stop using any new product as an experiment to see if the baby will go back to nursing.

Fussy or Refuse Breast

Overstimulation, Stress, or Emotional Upset

Ask the mother if she has been under unusual stress lately or if there have been changes in the household or the baby's routine.

Some babies are fussy at the breast or refuse to nurse when they are overstimulated, upset, or under stress. Each baby has his own level of sensitivity. Some babies do well no matter what is going on around them; other babies balk at nursing at the slightest upset.

Depending on the baby's age and sensitivity, any of the following might affect a baby's willingness to settle down and nurse:

- Breastfeedings are timed, scheduled, or frequently interrupted.
- The mother and baby are often busy outside the home with no quiet time, or the home environment is loud and chaotic.
- The baby is often left to cry.
- There are major changes in the baby's daily routine, such as traveling.
- The mother yells or argues with someone while nursing the baby.
- The baby has bitten the mother and she reacted strongly.
- The mother and baby are separated for an unusually long time.
- The mother is under stress and is unusually tense.
- The family has moved.

BREAST REFUSAL

Breast Refusal during the Early Weeks of Breastfeeding

Questions to Ask

Ask the mother her baby's age, when he started refusing the breast, and other questions listed in the previous section for clues to the cause of the breast refusal.

If the baby is younger than a week old and the baby has been refusing the breast since birth, consider poor positioning and latch-on, birth interventions and medications, birth injury, arching (hypertonia), and—if he becomes more frantic when held—an aggressive non-nurser. Also, be sure the baby has been checked for medical problems or illness.

If the baby began refusing the breast between the second and fourth day, consider engorgement, forceful let-down, and delayed or inhibited let-down.

If the breast refusal began between one and four weeks and the baby has been receiving artificial nipples, consider nipple confusion as a likely cause, although thrush and a change in the taste of the mother's milk should also be considered.

If the baby is older than a month old and suddenly refuses the breast, review the causes listed in the previous section, "Fussy at the Breast at Any Stage of Breastfeeding."

Previously Listed Causes

Most of the factors that can cause fussiness at the breast during the early weeks (see previous section) can also cause breast refusal.

Fussiness at the breast and breast refusal often have the same causes, but individual babies may respond to them differently. Any of the causes listed in the previous section, "Fussy at the Breast during the Early Weeks of Breastfeeding" (with the possible exception of foremilk-hindmilk imbalance) could cause a baby to refuse the breast. Start with the "Questions to Ask" in that section and consider these, as well as the cause that follows.

The Aggressive Non-Nurser

Rarely, a baby is born who aggressively refuses to breastfeed from birth and becomes frantic when held. It takes time, patience, and hard work to persuade the aggressive non-nurser to breastfeed.

Rarely, a baby is born who aggressively fights being held as well as fights being at the breast. What distinguishes this baby from other babies who refuse the breast is that this behavior is evident at birth and no outside cause can be found—there is nothing different or unusual about the birth and there are no detectable medical problems. Barbara Heiser, La Leche League Leader, RN, and IBCLC, has identified and worked with this type of baby. She says that these babies can be breastfed, but that it takes time (sometimes up to several weeks), patience, and hard work to get them to take the breast.

These babies usually spend their time either colicky and overly stimulated or asleep. If the baby is not getting enough milk, he may become sluggish and sleepy.

Reassure the mother and acknowledge that it is the baby who has the problem.

Mothers of aggressive non-nursers are understandably taken aback by their babies' complete rejection of them and of all human contact. While the mother of the reluctant nurser expresses frustration, the mother of the aggressive non-nurser expresses feelings of rejection. These mothers ask, "Why does my baby hate me?" They also worry that their baby is abnormal.

Explain that the problem lies with the baby and assure the mother that hers is not the only baby like this, that there have been others. Tell her that breastfeeding will be possible, but it will take a lot of work and patience from her and her helpers. Describe for her the observed behaviors in the next section so that she will have an idea of what to expect.

The mother needs to decide on a method of feeding until the baby is ready to breastfeed. No matter how the baby is fed, feedings are often difficult.

If the mother decides she wants to breastfeed, encourage her to express her milk for her baby—double-pumping with an automatic electric breast pump will be the fastest and easiest way—so that she can build and maintain her milk supply until the baby is ready to nurse.

The mother also will need to select a method of supplementation. Explain her choices (cup, spoon, feeding syringe, eyedropper, or finger-feeding with a nursing supplementer). Although bottles may cause nipple confusion in a baby younger than a month, this can be overcome later. It is most important during this stressful time that the mother pick a feeding method with which she feels comfortable.

No matter how the baby is fed, feedings are often difficult, because the baby becomes fussier when held and resists any human touch. Encourage the mother to experiment with her baby to find what works best with him. Many of the suggestions that are soothing to colicky babies work well with the aggressive non-nurser. Because the baby fights being held, early feedings often go more smoothly if the baby is fed in an infant seat or carseat. Feedings need to be kept as gentle and non-forceful as possible.

As the baby progresses through the stages, give the mother encouragement and suggestions.

Being aware of the stages of observed behavior can help the mother see the progress her baby is making toward breastfeeding. As he enters each stage, give the mother encouragement and suggestions.

1. **The baby aggressively fights the breast**. In the first stage, assure the mother that the baby is unsettled, but that he is not upset with her. Suggest she allow others to hold the baby so that she can see that she is not the cause of his problem. Within this first stage, the baby may progress from crying uncontrollably to hitting the breast with his fists.

2. **The baby cries more while being held than when he's put down**. Suggest the mother focus on her immediate environment to find ways to calm the baby—turn off the radio, television, bright lights, and keep the running toddler away. The aggressive non-nurser tends to be easily overstimulated, so encourage the mother to modify the surroundings.

3. **The baby is willing to be held in some positions, even if not in a cradle hold**. Tell the mother, "See, he enjoys being with you." Suggest she try the colic hold with baby held face down across her forearm or hold him against her side in the

football or clutch hold with her hand under his head. Some babies prefer to be held with their backs against their mothers' chest, looking out, perhaps in a front carrier.

4. **The baby tolerates being held in the cradle hold.** Suggest the mother begin by holding her baby in the cradle hold with her breast covered at non-feeding times, gradually

Fussy or Refuse Breast

working up to holding the baby with her breast uncovered at feeding times. If the mother has not been finger-feeding up to now and is open to the idea, this is a good time to start, so that the baby gets used to the feel of flesh in his mouth.

5. **The baby will attempt to root.** Encourage the mother to let the baby do anything he likes at the breast. The mother often gets excited at this stage because she thinks her baby may start nursing. But the baby needs time to get used to the breast, and it usually takes a while longer before he is actually nursing.

6. **The baby will lick at the milk on the nipple.** This stage is particularly important because the baby must stick out his tongue in order to lick the nipple—an essential skill needed for sucking. Barbara Heiser says, when the baby licks at the nipple, "This is the home stretch."

7. **The baby will attempt to suck, using an in-and-out movement.** At the beginning of this stage, the baby may just mouth the nipple and then progress to holding it more consistently in his mouth.

   If the baby has been receiving bottles, he may be nipple-confused, waiting for the milk to flow into his mouth. If bottles have been used, suggest the mother begin using another feeding method now, as well as avoiding pacifiers, offering a finger instead if the baby wants to suck between feedings.

8. **The baby will take milk at the breast.** If the mother is willing, using a nursing supplementer at this stage may encourage the baby to take the breast. If he was being finger fed, he will be accustomed to the nursing supplementer and it will help him get into the suck-swallow rhythm he will need to breastfeed. An eyedropper or feeding syringe can also be used. Encourage the mother to praise her baby's efforts at the breast.

   Once the baby has mastered taking milk from the nursing supplementer at the breast, suggest the mother offer the breast alone. First, however, encourage her to express some milk to stimulate her let-down, so that her baby receives an instant reward of milk for his efforts. It is important that the mother keep count of her baby's wet diapers and bowel movements once he is taking the breast alone to be sure that he is getting enough milk.

9. **The baby nurses well, even before the let-down occurs.** In most cases, the baby is breastfeeding by his two- to three-week growth spurt, if not before.

The mother needs consistent support and lots of encouragement during the baby's first few weeks so that she doesn't take her baby's behavior personally.

In addition to coming up with a feeding plan for the baby, the mother needs consistent reassurance so that she doesn't feel as though she is the problem. While the baby is fed using other methods, encourage the mother to allow others to feed the baby occasionally so that she can see that he reacts to others in the same way, and that he is not just upset with her. Also encourage her to keep the baby close to her even when he is asleep and peaceful (such as laying the baby down on a blanket on the floor near her or lying on the bed next to the baby as he sleeps). Being near the baby under calm, peaceful circumstances will help her develop positive feelings for him.

Previously Listed Causes

Most of the factors listed in the previous section, "Fussy at the Breast at Any Stage of Breastfeeding," can also cause breast refusal.

Breast Refusal at Any Stage of Breastfeeding

Questions to Ask

Ask the mother the questions in "Questions to Ask" in the section, "Fussy at the Breast at Any Stage of Breastfeeding."

Fussiness at the breast and breast refusal often have the same causes, but individual babies may respond to them differently. Any of the causes listed in the previous section, "Fussy at the Breast at Any Stage of Breastfeeding," could cause a baby to refuse the breast. So consider these, as well as the causes that follow.

Nursing Strike

A nursing strike occurs when a baby who has been breast-feeding well suddenly refuses to nurse and is unhappy about it.

Occasionally a baby—usually between three and eight months—who has been breastfeeding well will suddenly refuse to nurse for no apparent reason. Some mothers wonder if their baby might be weaning, but it is unusual for a baby to wean entirely on his own during the first year. Another factor that distinguishes a nursing strike from natural weaning is that the baby is obviously unhappy about it. It usually lasts from two to four days and may require some ingenuity to find the cause. Sometimes the cause is never found.

Go over possible causes with the mother to try to find the reason for the nursing strike. If it can't be found, suggest the mother try some of the basic suggestions from the next section.

Finding the cause of the nursing strike will be reassuring to the mother. It will also influence what suggestions are given. But if the cause cannot be determined, offer the mother some basic suggestions from the next section, such as giving the baby more attention, increasing her skin-to-skin contact with the baby, trying to nurse him while he is asleep or drowsy, varying nursing positions, and offering the breast while rocking or walking him. With patience, most babies will return to breastfeeding within two to four days.

While the baby is not nursing, suggest the mother express her milk and give it to her baby in a cup.

The mother will need to express her milk as often as the baby was nursing so that she does not become uncomfortably full. Encourage her to give her baby her expressed milk in a cup until he is ready to take the breast again. A cup will not satisfy a baby's sucking urge like an artificial nipple and so baby may be more motivated to go back to breastfeeding more quickly.

PERSUADING THE BABY TO TAKE THE BREAST

First, try to determine the cause of the baby's fussiness or breast refusal.

Determining the cause of the baby's fussiness or breast refusal will influence what suggestions to give. See the reasons listed previously in this chapter.

No matter what the cause, babies who refuse to nurse usually display certain patterns of behavior as they progress toward breastfeeding.

Barbara Heiser, a La Leche League Leader, registered nurse, and board certified lactation consultant, has observed and noted the following patterns of behavior in "aggressive non-nursers" (babies who from birth aggressively reject the breast, as well as being held) as they progressed toward breastfeeding. These same patterns of behavior may occur in babies who refuse the breast for other reasons or are fussy at the breast, but usually to a lesser degree and some of the stages may be skipped. As the baby advances through the stages, he may follow a "two steps forward, one step back" progression.

Sharing these behavior patterns with the mother may give her an idea of what to expect and help her set some short-term goals. This will enable the mother to gauge her baby's progress, which—even if it happens slowly—can be a morale booster.

Observed Behaviors in Babies Who Refuse the Breast

1. The baby aggressively and physically fights the breast.
   a. The baby cries frantically and uncontrollably.
   b. The baby hits the breast with clenched fists.
2. The baby cries more when he's held than when he's put down.
3. The baby is willing to be held.

4. The baby tolerates being held in the nursing position.
   a. With the breast covered.
   b. With the breast exposed.
5. The baby will try to root.
6. The baby will lick milk on the nipple.
7. The baby will attempt to suck.
   a. The baby will mouth the nipple.
   b. The baby will keep the nipple in his mouth.
8. The baby will take milk at the breast.
   a. Using a nursing supplementer.
   b. From the breast alone, after the let-down is stimulated.
9. The baby breastfeeds well, even before the milk lets down.

Fussy or Refuse Breast

Encourage the mother to keep working with her baby, using good positioning and latch-on techniques.

The key elements in persuading the baby to take the breast are patience and persistence, with special care given to good positioning and latch-on. See the chapter "Positioning, Latch-On, and the Baby's Suck."

Other ways the mother can encourage her baby to nurse are: spend more time skin-to-skin, try different nursing positions, offer the breast when the baby is sleepy or while rocking or walking.

Suggest the mother also try to:

- Nurse the baby when he is asleep or very sleepy. Many babies who refuse to nurse when they are awake will nurse when they are sleepy.
- Use different nursing positions. Some babies will refuse to nurse in one position but take the breast in another.
- Nurse when in motion. Some babies are more likely to nurse when the mother is rocking or walking rather than sitting or standing still.
- Give the baby extra attention and skin-to-skin contact. Focused attention and extra touching are comforting to both mother and baby. When the mother offers the breast, suggest that whenever possible she undress to the waist and clothe her baby in just a diaper. Taking warm baths together can also be soothing.

Also see, "Encouraging the Baby to Take the Breast" in the chapter "Relactation and Adoptive Nursing."

The baby may be more willing to take the breast if the mother gets her milk flowing before offering the breast.

Suggest the mother express some milk, massage her breast, or apply warm compresses to stimulate her let-down reflex before offering her baby the breast so he will receive an instant reward for his efforts.

To encourage the baby to take the breast, it may help to express some milk into his mouth or to drip some expressed milk or water onto the breast or in his mouth after he latches on.

Expressing milk onto the baby's lips may encourage him to take the breast.

Once the baby is on the breast, if he won't stay on, suggest the mother have a helper use an eyedropper, spoon, or feeding syringe to drip expressed milk or warm water on the breast near the baby's mouth or in the corner of his mouth. The baby will swallow the liquid, and the natural response to a swallow is a suck, which may keep him at the breast. More milk or water can be given this way to entice the baby back to the breast if he comes off.

If the baby becomes upset, suggest the mother stop and comfort him. Nursing should not become associated with unhappiness.

The mother or baby may become frustrated during this process. If the mother is feeling overwhelmed or the baby becomes upset, encourage her to stop. Nursing should not become associated with unhappiness.

In some cases of breast refusal, such as severe nipple confusion or the aggressive non-nurser, the baby may actively fight the breast. If so, the baby may need a time of no bottles and no breast before he can accept the breast. (See "Nipple Confusion" in the section "Fussy at the Breast during the Early Weeks of Breastfeeding.")

If her baby will not nurse, encourage the mother to offer her own expressed milk to her baby in a cup.	If the baby will not nurse, the mother will need to express her milk to stay comfortable, so encourage her to offer the baby her milk in a cup or use one of the other alternative feeding methods described in "The Use of Breast Pumps and Other Products." If artificial nipples are avoided, the baby's sucking urge will not be satisfied and he may be likely to return to breastfeeding more quickly.
In rare cases of a nursing strike lasting more than a few days, the baby may take to the breast better if a nursing supplementer is used to give him a continuous flow of milk.	A nursing supplementer will guarantee that the baby receives a continuous flow of milk while at the breast, which may keep him interested in nursing.
	Suggest the mother attach the supplementer tube to the top of the breast with tape so that it extends a quarter-inch (5mm) past her nipple and then situate the tube near the center of the baby's upper lip. To encourage the baby to take the breast, suggest she lightly touch the baby's lips with her nipple so that he opens his mouth. The baby can then grasp the breast and tube together. After each jaw compression, suggest the mother push down slightly on the supplementer bottle to reward the baby's sucking with a small dribble of fluid. Caution the mother not to squeeze too much liquid at once, which may cause choking. At first the baby may need to be tempted with fluid whenever he stops sucking.
If the baby keeps thrusting his tongue forward while taking the breast, suggest the mother do the exercise "Walking Back on the Tongue" before each nursing to help him drop his tongue.	"Walking Back on the Tongue" is an exercise the mother can do with her baby before each nursing to help him drop his tongue so he can latch on to the breast well. See "Tongue Thrusting" in the chapter "Positioning, Latch-On, and the Baby's Suck."

REFUSAL OF ONE BREAST

### Refusal of One Breast from Birth If the baby refuses one breast from birth, suggest the mother ask her baby's doctor to rule out medical reasons.	If a baby refuses one breast from birth, suggest that the mother consult the baby's doctor to rule out any medical reasons that might make nursing on that side uncomfortable for this baby, including congestion in the nose, an ear infection, a hernia, misaligned neck vertebrae, or a broken clavicle. Depending upon how the baby lay *in utero*, he may need a few days after birth for his neck muscles to loosen up so that he can freely move his head from side to side.
### Refusal of One Breast at Any Stage of Breastfeeding #### *Mastitis* Mastitis can make the mother's milk taste saltier. This causes some babies to refuse the breast.	An older baby may suddenly reject one breast for the same medical reasons as the newborn. There may be other reasons, too. Sodium and chloride levels may rise in the mother's milk after mastitis, making the milk taste saltier (Thullen 1988; Conner 1979). Some babies react to this change in taste by nursing only reluctantly on that breast—expressing a strong preference for the other breast—or by refusing the affected breast altogether. If the baby refuses the affected breast, suggest the mother follow the recommendations for a nursing strike and continue breastfeeding on the other breast, expressing her milk as often as her baby had been nursing so that the affected breast does not become overly full. She should continue to offer the affected breast. Within a week the mother's milk will lose its salty taste if the milk supply is maintained and the baby should go back to nursing as usual.
If mastitis makes the areola feel hard, the baby may refuse that breast.	Some babies will refuse one breast if the areola becomes taut from mastitis. This makes the breast feel different in their mouth, perhaps also making it more difficult for them to get milk from that breast. If this happens, suggest the mother express milk from that breast as often as her baby was nursing—more often if her breast becomes overly full—and follow the recommendations for mastitis. (See "Mastitis—Plugged Ducts and Breast Infections" in the chapter "Breast Problems.") When the areola softens, the baby should return to breastfeeding on that breast.

Ear Infection

An ear infection sometimes causes the baby to refuse one breast.

If the baby has an ear infection, he may refuse to nurse when lying on his infected ear. In this case, suggest the mother try using the football hold. Or, when switching the baby to the rejected breast, use the slide-over position so that he lies on the same side at the other breast.

Fussy or Refuse Breast

Differences in the Mother's Nipples or Breasts

If the mother has one flat or inverted nipple—or both nipples are flat or inverted, but to different degrees—the baby may show a preference for one breast.

It is not unusual for a woman to have one flat or inverted nipple while the other protrudes. It is also not unusual for a woman with two flat or inverted nipples to have one nipple that protrudes more than the other. Such a woman may discover at birth that her baby quickly shows a preference for the breast with the more protruding nipple.

Some mothers may benefit from treating flat or inverted nipple(s) during pregnancy to help them protrude for easier breastfeeding. If a mother doesn't notice a flat or inverted nipple until after birth she can begin treatment then (see "Treatments to Draw Out the Nipple" in the chapter "Nipple Problems").

If the baby persistently refuses one breast, encourage the mother to be patient and keep trying. Also assure her that she can breastfeed using one breast if she chooses. (See the last section, "One-Sided Nursing.")

The mother's milk may let down faster or slower in one breast, causing the baby to prefer one breast.

Just as some women have breasts of different sizes and with different types of nipples, some women notice differences in their let-down from one breast to the other.

Suggest the mother stimulate her let-down before putting her baby to the breast. If the baby prefers the breast with the faster let-down, this will get the milk flowing on the other side so that the baby does not have to wait. If the baby prefers the breast with the slower let-down, allowing her milk to let down before she puts her baby to breast will enable her to catch the first flow in a diaper or towel and make nursing more manageable for her baby.

The suggestions in the later section, "Persuading the Baby to Take Both Breasts," may also be helpful.

For suggestions on stimulating the let-down, see "The Key to Successful Milk Expression: Stimulating the Let-Down" in the chapter "Expression and Storage of Human Milk."

Reduced Milk Supply in One Breast

If one breast is given more often, it will produce more milk. This sometimes results in a baby preferring that breast over the other. In some women, one breast produces more milk due to physical differences.

A mother may have more milk in one breast because she nurses more often from that breast. She may favor one breast because she is more coordinated on one side or because one breast is easier for the baby to latch on to. Whatever the reason, when one breast is favored, it receives more stimulation and produces more milk. And the baby may grow to prefer the more bountiful breast over the other.

Some women produce more milk in one breast due to differences in the number of ducts operating, resulting in a faster and more plentiful flow of milk from that breast.

If one breast has been injured or has had surgery, the baby may receive less milk at that breast, causing him to prefer the unaffected breast.

If the mother's milk ducts were cut during surgery or damaged from an injury, this may affect how much milk the baby receives from that breast. Although a full supply of milk will be produced in the milk-producing cells (alveoli), some of the milk will not be able to pass through the severed or damaged ducts to reach the nipple. The more ducts that have been cut or damaged, the less milk the baby will receive. However, there are reported cases of mothers' milk ducts "recanalizing," or growing back, after having been cut. If the mother's milk supply is substantially reduced in one breast, the baby may prefer the unaffected breast.

If the mother's major nerves were cut during surgery or damaged during injury, she will have little or no feeling in her nipple and areola, which would also reduce her milk production. It is the feeling of the baby's suck that sends signals to the mother's pituitary gland to stimulate the hormones prolactin and oxytocin that are necessary for milk production. (See "Breastfeeding after Breast Surgery or Injury" in the chapter "Breast Problems.")

Reaction to Cosmetics or Other Products

If the mother applies deodorant or any other product more heavily on one side than the other, her baby may react to it.

Suggest the mother rinse her breasts with clear water before nursing the baby if she suspects her baby may be reacting to her perfume, deodorant, or other product. Changing from a spray deodorant to a stick or roll-on type may solve the problem.

Breast Tumor

Rarely, a baby's sudden and unexplained refusal of one breast may be a sign of a breast tumor.

If a baby has been nursing well on both breasts for some time and suddenly refuses one breast without any apparent reason, suggest that the mother see her doctor to rule out any medical problem.

Goldsmith (1974) documented the cases of five breastfeeding mothers whose babies suddenly rejected one breast, and weeks or months later a mass was found that proved to be malignant. If a breast tumor is suspected, the mother does not have to stop breastfeeding.

An ultrasound and, if more information is needed, a mammogram can be done without discontinuing lactation (Lawrence, p. 260). Although sudden refusal of one breast is one warning sign of a breast tumor, continued nursing by a baby does not rule out the possibility of cancer.

Persuading the Baby to Nurse on the Less Preferred Breast

With persistence and patience, a baby usually will learn to accept both breasts, although in most cases one breast will produce sufficient milk.

To persuade a baby to nurse on the less preferred breast, get the milk flowing from that side before offering it.

To persuade the baby to nurse on the less preferred breast, suggest the mother nurse the baby first on the preferred breast, and after the let-down occurs, slide the baby over to the less preferred breast without changing the baby's body position (this is known as the "slide-over" position), finishing the feeding with the preferred breast.

For example, if the mother starts nursing on her right breast with her baby in the cradle hold, after the let-down she would slide the baby over to the football hold on the left breast.

Another approach is for the mother to offer the less preferred side first, after she first stimulates her let-down by expressing some milk.

Suggest the mother try nursing the baby in different positions on the less preferred breast.

The baby may be more likely to nurse if he is put to the less preferred breast in different positions. If the mother usually holds him in the cradle hold, suggest she try the football hold or nursing lying down, and experiment with other positions.

Suggest the mother try nursing on the less preferred breast while walking or rocking the baby, in a darkened room, or when he is sleepy.

A baby may be less aware that he is nursing on the less preferred breast when he is sleepy, and therefore be more willing to accept it. While being walked or rocked, he may be distracted by the movement so that he will take the less preferred breast. Nursing in a darkened room may also distract the baby so that he will take the less preferred breast.

Encourage the mother to keep offering the less preferred breast, while regularly expressing milk from it to keep up her milk supply.

Patience and persistence are the keys to persuading the baby to take the less preferred breast, as well as regular expression to keep up the mother's milk supply. Encourage her to express her milk as often as her baby was nursing so that she does not become uncomfortably full.

One-Sided Nursing

It is possible to breastfeed from one breast alone.

Assure the mother that it is possible to breastfeed from one breast alone. However, the mother may find that her baby wants to nurse more often at first. She also may find that the lactating breast will be much larger than the other while she is breastfeeding.

Fussy or Refuse Breast

If milk supply is a concern, suggest the mother keep count of the baby's wet diapers and bowel movements. If the baby has six to eight wet cloth diapers (five to six disposables) and two to five bowel movements a day (fewer bowel movements are normal in a baby older than six weeks), she can be sure the baby is getting enough.

Assure the mother that her breasts will return to the same size when her baby weans.

Publications for Parents

Andrea, J. and Mohrbacher, N. *Nipple Confusion*. Schaumburg, Illinois: La Leche League International, 1992. Publication No. 32.

La Leche League International. THE WOMANLY ART OF BREASTFEEDING, 35th Anniversary ed. Schaumburg, Illinois, 1991. pp. 62, 147, 154-57, 331, 332.

Mohrbacher, N. *How to Handle a Nursing Strike*. Schaumburg, Illinois: La Leche League International, 1992. Publication No. 62.

Renfrew, M., Fisher, C., and Arms, S. *Bestfeeding: Getting Breastfeeding Right for You*. Berkeley, California: Celestial Arts, 1990, pp. 137-44.

Sears, W. THE FUSSY BABY. Schaumburg, Illinois: La Leche League International, 1985.

References

American Academy of Pediatrics Committee on Nutrition. Fluoride supplementation for children: interim policy recommendations. *Pediatrics* 1995; 95(5):777.

Andrusiak, F. and Larose-Kuzenko, M. *The effects of an overactive let-down reflex*. La Leche League International Lactation Consultant Series. Garden City Park, New Jersey: Avery Publishing, 1987.

Clyne, P. and Kulczycki, A. Human breast milk contains bovine IgG; relationship to infant colic? *Pediatrics* 1991; 87(4):439-44.

Conner, A. Elevated levels of sodium and chloride in milk from mastitic breast. *Pediatrics* 1979; 63:910-11.

Frantz, K. Baby's position at the breast and its relationship to sucking problems. Presented at LLL's International Conference, 1983 and 1985. (Audiocassettes available from LLLI.)

Gabriel, A. et al. Cultural values and biomedical knowledge: choices in infant feeding: analysis of a survey. *Soc Sci Med* 1986; 23:501.

Goldsmith, H. Milk-rejection: sign of breast cancer. *Am J Surg* 1974; 127:280-81.

Heiser, B. The aggressive non-nurser. Presented at LLL's International Conference, 1991. (Audiocassette ordering information available from LLLI.)

Hopkinson, J. et al. Milk production by mothers of premature infants: influence of cigarette smoking. *Pediatrics* 1992; 90(6):934-38.

Jakobsson, I. and Lindberg, T. Cow's milk protein causes infant colic in breastfed infants: a double blind study. *Pediatrics* 1983; 71:268-71.

Klougart, N. et al. Infantile colic treated by chiropractors: a prospective study of 316 cases. *J Manip Physiol Ther* 1989; 12(4):281-88.

Lawrence, R. *Breastfeeding: A Guide for the Medical Profession,* 4th ed. St. Louis: Mosby, 1994, pp. 236, 260, 350, 519.

Lust, K. et al. Maternal intake of cruciferous vegetables and other foods and colic symptoms in exclusively breast-fed infants. *Am J Diet Assoc* 1996; 96(1): 46-48.

Maher, S. *An Overview of Solutions to Breastfeeding and Sucking Problems.* Schaumburg, Illinois: La Leche League International, 1988. Publication No. 67, pp. 18-24.

Mansbach, I. et al. Onset and duration of breast feeding among Israeli mothers: relationships with smoking and type of delivery. *Soc Sci Med* 1991; 33(12):1391-97.

Marmet, C. and Shell, E. *Lactation Forms: A Guide to Lactation Consultant Charting.* Encino, California: Lactation Institute Publications, 1993, pp. 4-17, 4-30.

Matheson, I. and Rivrud, G. The effect of smoking on lactation and infantile colic. *JAMA* 1989; 261:42.

Mennella, J. and Beauchamp, G. Maternal diet alters the sensory qualities of human milk and the nursling's behavior. *Pediatrics* 1991; 88(4):737-44.

Minchin, M. Food intolerance and breastfeeding...the connections. Presented at LLL's International Conference, 1989a. (Audiocassette ordering information available from La Leche League International.)

Minchin, M. *Breastfeeding Matters.* Armadale, Victoria, Australia: Alma Publications, 1989b. p. 91.

Nehlig, A. and Debry, G. Consequences on the newborn of chronic maternal consumption of coffee during gestation and lactation: a review. *J Am Coll Nutr* 1994; 13(1):6-21.

Neifert, M. et al. Nipple confusion: toward a formal definition. *J Pediatr* 1995; 126(6):S125-29.

Newman, J. Breast rejection: a little-appreciated cause of lactation failure. *Can Fam Physician* 1990a; 36:449-53.

Newman, J. Breastfeeding problems associated with the early introduction of bottles and pacifiers. *J Hum Lact* 1990b; 6(2):59-63.

Nilsson, N. Infantile colic and chiropractic. *Eur J Chiropract* 1985; 33:264-65.

Righard, L. and Alade, M. Effects of delivery room routines on success of first breastfeed. *Lancet* 1990; 336:1105-07.

Riordan, J. and Auerbach, K. *Breastfeeding and Human Lactation.* Boston and London: Jones and Bartlett, 1993, p. 352.

Ross, M. *Back to the breast: retraining infant suckling patterns.* La Leche League International Lactation Consultant Series. Garden City Park, New York: Avery Publishing, 1987.

Sepkoski, C. et al. The effects of maternal epidural anesthesia on neonatal behavior during the first month. *Dev Med Child Neurol* 1992; 34:1072-80.

Steldinger, R. and Luck, W. Half lives of nicotine in milk of smoking mothers: implications for nursing. *J Perinat Med* 1988; 16:261-62.

Taylor, M. *Transcultural aspects of breastfeeding—USA.* La Leche League International Lactation Consultant Series. Garden City Park, New York: Avery Publishing, 1985.

Thullen, J. Management of hypernatremic dehydration due to insufficient lactation. *Clin Pediatr* 1988; 27:370-72.

Victora, C. et al. Use of pacifiers and breastfeeding duration. *Lancet* 1993; 341:404-06.

Woolridge, M. and Fisher C. Colic, "overfeeding," and symptoms of lactose malabsorption in the breastfed baby: a possible artifact of feed management? *Lancet* 1988:2(8605):382-84.

Fussy or Refuse Breast

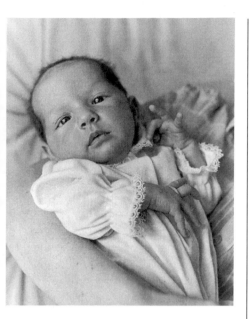

6

Weight Gain

NORMAL GROWTH PATTERNS DURING THE FIRST YEAR

SLOW WEIGHT GAIN DURING THE FIRST YEAR
  The Mother's Feelings
  Asking Questions and Gathering Information
  First, Establish Weight Gain and Loss
  Second, Discuss Breastfeeding Management
  Third, Count Wet Diapers and Bowel Movements
  Other Areas to Explore
  Slow Weight Gain in the Baby Older than Three Months
  Increasing Milk Supply—An Overview
  Working with the Doctor and Supplementation

RAPID WEIGHT GAIN DURING THE FIRST YEAR

NORMAL GROWTH PATTERNS DURING THE BABY'S FIRST YEAR

Weight loss is normal during the first 3 to 4 days after birth.

Whether breastfed or artificially fed, newborns tend to lose weight during the first 3 to 4 days after birth. This is due to the shedding of excess fluids in the baby's tissues at birth and the passage of meconium (the first stool).

Giving extra fluids during these early days may not offset this weight loss or benefit baby. In a study conducted at the University of Rochester, breastfed babies given extra water or formula during the first few days lost more weight and were less likely to start gaining by the fourth day than babies exclusively breastfed or exclusively artificially fed (Lawrence, p. 362).

A weight loss of approximately 5 to 7% is normal. One study found that when mothers received regular breastfeeding guidance very few babies lost more than 7% of their birth weight (DeMarzo 1991). While a weight loss of 10% is considered acceptable by some medical professionals, it is usually a sign that the mother needs additional help with breastfeeding management. If feeding problems are not corrected or if the baby shows signs of dehydration, supplements may be needed.

Most babies regain their birth weight within two to three weeks of age.

Most infants regain their birth weight within 2 to 3 weeks. Weight gain should always be determined from the lowest weight on the third or fourth day after birth. The more weight the baby loses, the longer it can take for him to regain it. Babies who are ill or premature may take longer to regain their birth weight than healthy, full-term babies.

For the first 3 to 4 months, typical weight gain is 4 to 8 ounces (113 to 227 grams) per week.

Typical weight gain for the first 3 to 4 months is 4 to 8 ounces (113 to 227 grams) per week—doubling birth weight by 5 to 6 months. Weight gain should always be figured from the lowest point rather than from birth weight.

During the baby's first year, increases in length and head circumference are also important measures of growth.

Growth in length averages one inch (2.5 centimeters) per month and growth in head circumference is about one-half inch (1.27 centimeters) per month during the first 6 months, and about half that during the second 6 months.

From 4 to 6 months, weight gain typically slows to 3 to 5 ounces (85-142 grams) per week. From 6 to 12 months, weight gain slows to 1½ to 3 ounces (42-85 grams) per week.

The very rapid growth a baby experiences during the first 3 months typically slows down during months 4 to 12. According to recent research (Cohen 1995; Dewey 1992a), an average weight gain for a breastfeeding baby 4 to 6 months is about 3 to 5 ounces (85 to 142 grams) per week. An average weight gain for the breast-feeding baby 6 to 12 months is 1½ to 3 ounces (42 to 85 grams) per week. Growth in length averages about one-half inch (1.27 cm) per month and growth in head circumference is about one-quarter inch (64 mm) per month. At one year, the typical breastfed baby weighs about 2½ times his birth weight, has increased his birth length by 50%, and his head circumference by 33%.

Infant growth charts used to plot babies' growth have shortcomings.

Growth charts can be a useful tool to monitor a baby's growth "at a glance," but they have some shortcomings. For example, they do not take into account regional differences in growth. Also, the charts do not adjust for genetic differences (short parents tend to have shorter children than tall parents) or racial or ethnic differences. Another significant shortcoming is that the current charts are based primarily on the growth of artificially fed babies who for the most part started solids early, so they do not accurately reflect normal growth patterns for exclusively breastfed babies.

More recent studies comparing exclusively breastfed and exclusively formula-fed infants found growth in length and head circumference to be about the same in both groups but found significant differences in energy consumption and weight gain after 3 months of age (see Cohen 1995 and Dewey references). From the fourth month to the twelfth month the breastfed babies gained more slowly, even after solids were started, and at one year the breastfed babies were leaner than the artificially fed babies. The amount of milk consumed during this period by the breastfed babies was also about 20% less than that consumed by the artificially fed babies. Yet the breastfed babies were healthy, active, and thriving. The authors concluded that current growth charts do not accurately reflect the norm for breastfed babies and that new growth charts are needed.

Weight Gain

Growth charts plot a baby's growth against a series of percentile lines. A typical child may be at the 50th percentile for weight. This means that out of 100 children, 49 will weigh less or the same and 50 children will weigh more. It is important to remember that these charts describe the growth of one child by comparing him with others his age. It cannot be said that the 5th percentile is necessarily "bad" nor the 95th percentile necessarily "good." But by comparing growth over a period of days, weeks, or months, a consistent growth pattern can be established. A pattern of consistent weight gain and growth is more important than keeping up with a standard growth chart.

Soft and moist skin tone and normal development are other signs of good health and proper fluid balance.

Baby's skin should be soft and moist. If pinched, the skin should immediately return to its normal appearance and not stay pinched looking. If pressed, the skin should return to normal and not remain dented. Tissue around the eyes and in the baby's mouth should be moist and pink. These are signs that the baby is receiving enough fluids.

The baby who smiles and is socially alert, has good muscle tone, and shows signs of normal development is probably getting enough to eat.

A mother can tell from day to day if her baby is getting enough milk by keeping track of how many wet diapers and bowel movements he has.

One to two wet diapers per day is normal during the first day or two after birth. Beginning about the third or fourth day, the baby's wet diapers and stools should increase until he has at least 6 wet diapers and at least 2 large bowel movements every day. After 6 weeks of age it is normal for some breastfed babies to have fewer bowel movements. See "Third, Count Wet Diapers and Bowel Movements" in the next section.

If the baby does not seem to be receiving enough milk, he should be seen by a doctor immediately.

If after the third or fourth day, the baby is not wetting at least six diapers per day and having at least two good-sized bowel movements, a mother should consult her baby's doctor to have the baby's weight checked. From the third or fourth day onward, baby should begin gaining at least 4 to 8 ounces (113 to 227 grams) per week or at least a pound (454 grams) per month. Weight should be calculated from the lowest weight, not birth weight. (See "First Establish Weight Gain and Loss" in the next section.)

If the baby's output is two wet diapers per day or less after the third or fourth day, suggest the mother watch for the following warning signs of dehydration, which indicate that the baby needs more fluids immediately:

- listlessness,
- lethargy,
- weak cry,
- skin loses its resiliency (when pinched, it stays pinched looking),
- dry mouth, dry eyes,
- the fontanel (or soft spot) on the head is sunken or depressed,
- fever.

If the baby is becoming dehydrated, the mother should consult the baby's doctor immediately.

The baby's disposition or temperament may not be a good indicator of an adequate milk supply.	Many mothers who are concerned about their babies' growth believe their babies' irritability and fussiness are indications that they are not getting enough milk. One study indicated that breastfed babies may initially tend to be fussier than their formula-fed peers (Di Pietro 1987). This may be a way of making sure they will breastfeed as often as they need to. Inadequate weight gain is often seen in infants who are placid and easygoing.

A baby is considered alert if there is a period of time each day when he interacts with his parents, looking squarely at them, takes an interest in his surroundings, and mimics facial expressions. |
| Some mothers worry needlessly about milk supply. | Many mothers think they do not have enough milk when actually there is no problem with their supply. The symptoms they worry about have other causes or they're unfamiliar with the variety of patterns that are normal in breastfed babies. See "Concerns about Milk Supply" under "During the Early Months" in the chapter "Breastfeeding Basics." |

SLOW WEIGHT GAIN DURING THE FIRST YEAR

When babies do not gain well on their mother's milk alone, everyone becomes concerned. Something needs to be done, but inappropriate interventions can lead to premature weaning, depriving the baby of the benefits of breastfeeding. Determining the cause of slow weight gain and taking appropriate action can relieve everyone's concern and boost baby's weight gain.

The Mother's Feelings

The mother may feel worried, guilty, and inadequate when her baby does not gain well. Listen to and acknowledge her feelings.

A baby's weight gain can affect a mother's feelings about herself and her ability to care for her baby. A mother with a slow-weight-gain baby may feel anxious about her baby's health. She may feel guilty, believing that her baby's slow weight gain means she has not given him the proper care. If the mother has been told to give formula, she may feel like a failure.

Listen to the mother and acknowledge her feelings. Giving her an outlet to express her worries, fears, and doubts may make it easier for her to discuss and evaluate her situation and decide how she wants to proceed.

Asking Questions and Gathering Information

In order to help the mother determine the reasons for her baby's slow weight gain, it is necessary to ask questions. The following categories offer a general guide, beginning with questions that need to be asked of all mothers whose babies are gaining slowly and ending with questions that deal with more unusual causes of slow weight gain. Other questions may come to mind as you talk with the mother.

Ask the questions in a calm, relaxed manner, emphasize the differences in individual mothers and babies, and look for opportunities to praise the mother for what she is doing right.

Keep in mind that the best way to gather the needed information is to listen attentively, taking notes, and asking pertinent questions in a calm, relaxed manner rather than in rapid succession. A calm and relaxed discussion will put the mother at ease. Some of the questions may deal with sensitive areas, so be sure to word them so they are not threatening to the mother.

Make sure the mother understands that breastfeeding is not a by-the-book procedure; it is an intimate relationship with different dynamics from one nursing couple to the next. (A mother almost always notices differences in breastfeeding when she nurses more than one child.) Although there are general breastfeeding principles with which it is good to be familiar (for example, the more often the baby nurses, the more milk there will be), there are no hard-and-fast rules. One baby may thrive and gain well by breastfeeding every 4 hours (although this is unusual), while another baby may need to breastfeed every hour to gain well. However, when weight gain is slow, it is wise to consider all the possibilities.

Emphasize the individual differences of mothers and babies as the questions are discussed. For example, if the mother has been giving bottles, tell her that some babies are able to breastfeed and take bottles with no problems at all, while other babies become "nipple-confused." If the mother is asked whether she smokes cigarettes, mention that some mothers smoke and breastfeed with no problems (Little 1994), yet other mothers who smoke have babies who gain slowly (Dahlstrom 1990).

Remember, too, that the mother may have relatives or friends criticizing her efforts to breastfeed. If her baby is not gaining well she is especially vulnerable. Be sure to praise her for what she is doing right.

Weight Gain

When the mother's answers give a clue to the reasons behind her baby's slow weight gain, discuss that area in more depth.

During the course of the discussion, the mother's answers to certain questions may give clues to the cause of her baby's slow weight gain. At that point, it may be helpful to stop and talk more about this area to allow her to expand on her answer and to clarify the mother's understanding of breastfeeding and her individual circumstances.

With each mother, go through the next three sections. Depending on her answers, continue on.

It is not necessary to ask all the following questions of all mothers with slow-gaining babies. With each mother start with "First, Establish Weight Gain and Loss," proceed through "Second, Discuss Breastfeeding Management," and continue with "Third, Count Wet Diapers and Bowel Movements:" These three sections provide the basic information to help the mother evaluate her baby's slow weight gain. If the reasons for the baby's slow weight gain do not become obvious after these sections, continue on.

Pay close attention to the mother's answers, offer suggestions, and follow up after a few days or a week to see if the suggestions have improved the baby's weight gain.

The most common cause of slow weight gain is mismanagement of breastfeeding, that is, not breastfeeding often enough or long enough. A mother may need to breastfeed more often and increase the length of feedings to boost her baby's weight gain. However, it is important to be sure about this before offering suggestions. Breastfeeding more often will not help the baby with a weak suck, for example, so pay careful attention to the mother's answers. It may also be helpful to contact the mother again after a few days or a week to see if the suggestions have helped improve her baby's weight gain.

The baby should be under a doctor's care. Encourage the mother to contact her baby's doctor to discuss any alternatives she plans to take.

In all cases of slow weight gain and failure-to-thrive, the baby should be under the care of a doctor so that his weight gain and overall condition can be regularly assessed and to rule out health problems. Although most cases of slow weight gain are not caused by physical illness, this is a possibility, especially in babies older than one month (Lukefahr 1990).

If the doctor has given the mother instructions to increase the baby's weight gain by supplementing with formula and the mother wants to try other alternatives (such as improving breastfeeding management), encourage her to contact her doctor and discuss her plans. (Also see "The Doctor's Advice and Supplementation" below.)

First, Establish Weight Gain and Loss

The first step is to determine the baby's pattern of weight gain and loss. Ask the mother:

1. How old is the baby now?
2. What is his present weight?
3. What was his birth weight?
4. What was the baby's lowest weight after birth? His age at that time?
5. What other weight checks has he had? What were his age and weight at these times?

Weight gain should be figured from the lowest point. For example:

- Birth weight: 7 pounds, 6 ounces (3345 grams)
- Lowest weight (age one week): 7 pounds (3175 grams)
- Present weight (six weeks old): 8 pounds, 6 ounces (3799 grams)

This baby's weight gain may be considered low because he has only gained one pound (454 grams) over birth weight in six weeks. In reality, the baby's gain for the five-week period was 1 pound, 6 ounces (22 ounces or 624 grams). The baby has had an average weekly weight gain of about 4½ ounces (127 grams).

Normal weight gain for a breastfed baby is 4 to 8 ounces (113 to 227 grams) per week during the first 3 to 4 months, 3 to 5 ounces (85 to 142 grams) per week from 4 to 6 months, and 1½ to 3 ounces (42 to 85 grams) per week from 6 to 12 months (Cohen 1995; Dewey 1992a).

How much has the baby grown in length and head circumference?

Growth in length and head circumference are positive signs of normal development. Growth in length averages one inch (2.54 centimeters) per month and head circumference about one-half inch (1.27 centimeters) per month during the first 6 months. Growth in head circumference indicates brain growth.

Were the same scales used each time, and was the baby undressed or wearing the same weight clothing?

Weight checks can be inaccurate if different scales are used or if the baby wears different weight clothing for different weighings. If this is the case, suggest the mother have the baby weighed again, using the same scale and the same clothing the baby wore at the previous weight check.

What has the doctor said about the baby's health other than weight gain?

If the doctor says the baby is doing well (other than weight gain) this is a good sign. If the baby is developing well and seems healthy and alert, despite the fact that he's gaining slowly, reassure the mother that her baby is doing well and that by discussing her circumstances in more depth there will most likely be specific things she can do to help her baby's weight gain improve.

Has the doctor diagnosed the baby as having slow weight gain or failure-to-thrive?

It is important to clearly distinguish between slow weight gain and failure-to-thrive. Some mothers whose infants fit into the profile of the slow weight gain baby are sometimes mistakenly told that their babies are failure-to-thrive—a serious condition that requires immediate medical intervention. True failure-to-thrive is usually due to organic causes such as infection, anatomical abnormalities, heart defects, malabsorption, gastrointestinal, endocrinological, and chronic diseases or nonorganic causes, for example, breastfeeding mismanagement.

The following characteristics will help to distinguish between slow weight gain and failure-to-thrive.

Slow Weight Gain
- frequent feeds,
- active sucking and swallowing,
- mother experiences regular let-downs,
- pale urine; six or more diapers soaked daily,
- seedy or soft stools, frequency within normal ranges,
- infant is alert and active,
- appropriate developmental milestones met,
- good muscle tone and skin turgor,
- weight gain consistent and continuous although lower than average.

Failure-to-Thrive in a Baby Younger than One Month
- still losing weight after ten days,
- infant does not regain birth weight by two to three weeks,
- weight loss greater than 10% of birth weight by seven to fourteen days,
- little or no growth in length and head circumference,
- evidence of malnutrition, dehydration—sunken fontanel, grayish pallor, lethargy, loss of fat layer under the skin, strong urine, inadequate stools,

- weight below 10th percentile at one month,
- refusal to feed from birth (Tolia 1995).

Failure-to-Thrive in a Baby Older than One Month
- weight below 30th percentile,
- drop in rate of growth of length and head circumference,
- infant falls two standard deviations on the growth chart,
- evidence of malnutrition, dehydration—sunken fontanel, grayish pallor, lethargy, loss of fat layer under the skin, strong urine, inadequate stools.
- infant does not meet developmental milestones,
- infrequent and/or ineffective feeds,
- mother experiences few let-downs,
- erratic or nonexistent weight gain.

Weight Gain

When the baby is accurately diagnosed as failure-to-thrive, immediate supplementation is necessary. See the later section, "Working with the Doctor and Supplementation."

Take note if the mother reports a poor weight gain or weight loss. The baby needs to be checked by a doctor and breastfeeding management evaluated.

The following signs indicate the baby should be checked by a doctor and breastfeeding patterns looked at closely. **This baby may need additional food.**

- The baby has not regained his birth weight within two or three weeks, or
- The baby is younger than 4 months and his weight gain is less than a pound a month.

Second, Discuss Breastfeeding Management

Many mothers assume that nursing a baby successfully is just a matter of putting the baby to the breast and letting nature take care of the rest. They don't realize that it is a learned art for both mother and baby. Ask the mother about her baby's breastfeeding patterns.

How often does the baby nurse during a 24-hour day?

Most newborns need to nurse at least 10 to 12 times every twenty-four hours. Some mothers are told to nurse no more often than every 3 to 4 hours. Others set arbitrary feeding times.

If the mother has been breastfeeding fewer than 10 times per day and the baby's weight gain is low, encourage her to breastfeed more often—every 1½ to 2 hours during the day and every 3 hours at night—until the baby's weight gain has significantly improved.

Explain the principle of supply and demand, that the more often the baby nurses, the more milk there will be. Less frequent nursing is not a problem for the baby who is gaining well.

How long does the baby nurse at each feeding? Who usually ends the feeding?

Ideally, the baby should determine the length of the feeding and finish the first breast before being offered the second breast. Some mothers are told not to nurse for longer than five minutes per breast under the mistaken idea that this will prevent sore nipples or that the baby "gets all the milk in the first five minutes" and does not need to nurse longer than this. During the first few weeks of breastfeeding, the let-down, or milk-ejection, reflex may not be well-conditioned and the baby may need to suck for several minutes just to stimulate the initial milk flow. Limiting nursing to five minutes per breast will not prevent sore nipples and this is not enough time for most babies to get the milk they need. (For information on preventing nipple soreness, see the chapter "Positioning, Latch-On, and the Baby's Suck.")

If the mother has been limiting the length of feedings, explain that this limits the amount of fatty, high-calorie hindmilk the baby receives later in the feeding. The baby may get plenty of fluids from the watery foremilk but not enough of the calories needed for growth. Encourage the mother to allow the baby to determine the length of the feedings. It is not unusual for a baby to nurse 10 to 20 minutes per breast or longer.

Does the baby nurse from both breasts at each feeding?

Some babies need the milk from both breasts to get enough nourishment and to stimulate an adequate milk supply. However, some babies' weight gain improves when they are allowed to nurse from one breast per feeding, instead of switching to the second breast after a predetermined length of time. Weight gain sometimes improves when baby finishes the first breast before offering the second because the baby receives more of the high-calorie hindmilk at each feeding (Woolridge and Fisher 1988).

A study that compared milk intake when nursing from one breast or two found that nursing from both breasts results in an 8.8% greater consumption of milk, but nursing from one breast resulted in a slightly higher daily fat intake. The researchers concluded that neither pattern was better than the other and that mothers should be flexible, taking their lead from the baby (Woolridge 1990). Although the baby may choose to nurse at only breast per feeding, the second breast should be offered, and baby may sometimes take both. Whenever practical and as long as the baby's slow weight gain is not due to a weak or ineffective suck (see next point), the baby should be the one to decide whether to stop the feeding after one breast or to take both breasts.

Can the mother hear the baby swallowing regularly when he breastfeeds? How long does he actively nurse at a feeding?

A baby who is sucking well will usually swallow after every other suck once the milk lets down, perhaps pausing now and then. He will swallow less often after his initial hunger has been satisfied and the flow of milk slows down.

If the mother cannot hear the baby swallowing, it could be a sign of a weak or ineffective suck. Some babies "flutter suck," sucking for comfort rather than for food. If a baby is "flutter sucking" he will only receive the milk that leaks out, rather than milking the breast. (See the section, "The Baby's Suck" in the chapter "Positioning, Latch-On, and the Baby's Suck.")

If the mother notices that her baby stops swallowing early in the feeding—or consistently falls asleep soon after he starts nursing—she can encourage him to breastfeed more actively for longer periods of time by "switch nursing." To "switch nurse," whenever the mother notices that the baby has stopped swallowing, she should take him off the breast and put him on the other breast. (If the baby is sleepy, he may need to be stimulated to stay interested longer. See "How to Rouse a Sleepy Baby" in the chapter "Positioning, Latch-On, and the Baby's Suck.")

Is a pacifier being used? How often and for how long? Does the mother use a baby swing or other soother regularly?

Mothers who limit time at the breast sometimes offer a pacifier between feedings. Overuse of pacifiers, swings, and other soothers can decrease the amount of time baby spends at the breast and contribute to slow weight gain. If this is the case, suggest that the mother offer the breast when the baby wants to suck or be comforted instead of using the pacifier, swing, or other soother.

Is the baby receiving anything other than mother's milk? Water? Formula? Juice? Solids?

Giving artificial nipples in the early weeks can interfere with the baby's ability to suck well at the breast. Sucking on the rubber nipple of a bottle or pacifier can confuse susceptible babies, causing them to breastfeed less effectively or to refuse the breast altogether. (See "Nipple Confusion" in the chapter "Fussy at the Breast and Breast Refusal" for information on how to overcome this difficulty.) Also, time spent sucking on artificial nipples can decrease the time a baby spends at the breast, which will decrease the mother's milk production.

If supplements are necessary in a baby's first few weeks, artificial nipples can be avoided by using a cup, spoon, eyedropper, feeding syringe, or nursing supplementer. (See the section "The Use of Breast Pumps and Other Products" for more information on the use of these alternative feeding methods.)

The breastfed baby does not need water or fruit juice. Human milk supplies all the liquids and nutrients a growing baby needs. Regular water or fruit juice supplements can reduce the calories a baby receives, possibly causing weight gain to slow.

Formula supplements can interfere with the process of supply and demand, causing the baby to take less from the breast so that the mother's milk supply decreases. Because formula is not digested as quickly or completely as human milk, it can leave a baby feeling full longer.

Weight Gain

Low-calorie solids introduced too soon and too rapidly can reduce the quality of nutrition a baby receives, especially if they are given before breast-feeding.

If the baby is less than 6 months old, encourage the mother to replace other foods or liquids with more frequent breastfeedings, if possible. *If the baby is not nursing well and/or the supplements have become a substantial part of the baby's intake, caution the mother not to eliminate the supplements abruptly. In this case, supplements should be eliminated only under the doctor's guidance.* (See the section below, "Working with the Doctor and Supplements," for more information.) In this case, the supplements need to be discontinued gradually while baby's progress is carefully watched.

What are the baby's sleep patterns during the day? At night? Does the baby often fall asleep near the start of a nursing?

Sleepy babies may need to be awakened regularly in order to receive enough milk. Some babies fall asleep while breastfeeding before they've nursed well. Generally newborns need to nurse at least 10 to 12 times every 24 hours.

If the mother has a sleepy baby who is gaining slowly, encourage her to awaken and nurse the baby every 1½ to 2 hours during the day, allowing the baby to sleep for 3-hour stretches at night. Encourage the mother to rest frequently during the day.

A baby who consistently falls asleep early in each nursing may need to be stimulated to breastfeed more actively. For suggestions on rousing and stimulating a sleepy baby, see "Sleepy Baby" in the chapter "Positioning, Latch-On, and the Baby's Suck."

Are the mother's nipples sore? Did she use a nipple shield in the hospital? Is she still using it?

Good positioning and latch-on are important so the baby can milk the breast-most effectively. Poor positioning and latch-on can reduce the amount of milk the baby gets and can cause nipple soreness in the mother. When the baby is well-supported at breast height with his mouth directly in front of the nipple, he will not have to turn his head to nurse, which makes swallowing easier. And if the mother waits until her baby's mouth is wide open before pulling him in close, he'll be able to get more breast in his mouth, allowing for more effective breast-feeding. Pulling baby in close while his mouth is open wide (with chin pressed into the breast) positions the baby's gums so they bypass the nipple and compress the milk sinuses where the milk is stored, giving him more milk for his efforts. (See the chapter "Positioning, Latch-On, and the Baby's Suck" for more details.)

Mother's position during breastfeeding is also important. An uncomfortable mother may not nurse as long, and she may have some difficulty relaxing, which can interfere with the let-down, or milk-ejection, reflex.

Breast shells can be used between feedings postpartum to help bring out inverted nipples. However, nipple shields (used during feedings) rarely help and should only be used with the utmost caution. Besides confusing the baby with the feel of an artificial nipple in his mouth, they decrease direct stimulation to the mother's nipple, decreasing mother's milk production significantly within a short time (Woolridge 1980).

Take note if the mother reports that the baby is not nursing enough or nurses "all the time" but does not gain well. The baby may need to breastfeed more or may have a sucking problem.

The following indicate the baby younger than 3 to 6 months who is not gaining well may not be breastfeeding often enough.

- The baby nurses fewer than 10 times a day,
- The baby is not waking to nurse at night.

The following indicate that the young baby may have a sucking problem.

- The baby nurses often and long but does not gain, or
- The mother has persistent sore nipples and/or mastitis

If the baby is nursing "all the time" but not gaining, is staying at the breast for only a very short time, or is just mouthing the nipple, not actively sucking and swallowing, he may not be sucking effectively. A baby who is not sucking well cannot build up his mother's milk supply to meet his needs.

Persistent sore nipples and/or mastitis in the mother can indicate poor positioning and latch-on or a sucking problem.

For more information, see the next section and "Sucking Problems—Types and Suggestions" in the chapter "Positioning, Latch-On, and the Baby's Suck."

Third, Count Wet Diapers and Bowel Movements

How many wet diapers does the baby have in a 24 hour period? Are they "good and wet"?

The number of wet diapers and bowel movements a baby has every day is an important indicator of how much milk he is getting.

At least six wet cloth diapers a day—five disposable diapers—indicate the baby is getting enough fluids. It can be more difficult to judge wetness in a disposable diaper. If the mother is unsure about how wet her baby's diapers are, have her pour 2 to 4 tablespoons (30-60 ml) of water on a dry diaper, noting its feel and weight.

How often and how much a baby urinates are important considerations, especially for the newborn and the young infant. Typically during his first few days (while the baby is receiving only colostrum), the newborn will wet only one or two diapers per day. Once his mother's milk becomes more plentiful, usually on the third or fourth day, the baby should begin to have six to eight wet cloth diapers (five or six disposable diapers) per day.

As babies get older than 6 weeks of age, the number of wet cloth diapers may drop to five or six per day, but their wetness will increase to 4 or more ounces (120 ml). This is because the baby's bladder grows in size and is able to hold more urine. At all ages, urine should be pale in color and mild-smelling.

When weight gain is a concern, suggest the mother keep an "input/output" diary, writing down each nursing and each wet and/or soiled diaper. Have her keep track over several days to get a clear idea of her baby's intake and elimination patterns.

How many bowel movements does the baby have in a 24-hour period?

At least two to five bowel movements every day indicate the baby younger than 6 weeks is receiving enough calories.

In the first few days after birth, baby's dark and tarry stools are called meconium. This is the stool that the baby has been storing since before birth. Within 24 to 48 hours of his mother's milk becoming more plentiful, the baby's stools will change in color and consistency.

Bowel movements usually become more frequent as baby regains his birth weight and continues to gain. Most young babies will have at least two to five bowel movements every 24 hours for the first several months. (Many babies continue this pattern for as long as they are exclusively breastfed.) If bowel movements are small (just a stain on the diaper), there should be several each day. If the baby has one bowel movement every few days, it should be substantial. (This is more common in the breastfed baby who is past 6 weeks of age.)

If the mother reports less frequent bowel movements during her baby's first 4 to 6 weeks, be sure to note how often the baby nurses and how many wet diapers he has each day. This may be a normal variation (in which case the baby will be gaining well) or it may be a sign that the baby is not nursing long enough to get the fatty hindmilk he needs, which is rich in calories.

Less frequent bowel movements are normal in an older breastfed baby. Some have bowel movements only once a week without signs of constipation. However, if the baby is not gaining well, this may be a clue that he is not getting enough hindmilk.

Weight Gain

Fewer than two bowel movements per day in the poorly gaining young baby may indicate that:

- the baby is not receiving enough milk;
- the baby is not nursing long enough at each breastfeeding to get the high-calorie hindmilk he needs; and/or
- the baby may not be sucking effectively. (See "The Baby's Suck" in the chapter "Positioning, Latch-On, and the Baby's Suck.)

What color are the baby's bowel movements?

For the first few days after birth, a baby's bowel movements (called "meconium") are very dark—greenish black—and sticky. Once the meconium has been eliminated, the stool of the baby who is receiving only mother's milk will be loose and unformed, often of a pea-soup consistency. It may be yellow to yellow-green to tan in color. An occasional green stool is also normal. The odor should be mild and not unpleasant.

If the baby's stools are consistently green and watery and the baby is not gaining well, even though the mother's milk supply seems to be plentiful, this could be a sign that the baby is being switched from one breast to the other too soon. Called foremilk-hindmilk imbalance (or "oversupply syndrome"), this sometimes happens when a baby receives too much of the watery lactose-rich foremilk and not enough of the fatty high-calorie hindmilk. Too much lactose stimulates the baby's digestive tract to move the milk along too fast, causing the watery, green stools.

If foremilk-hindmilk imbalance is suspected, suggest the mother wait until the baby finishes the first breast before switching to the second, rather than switching him to the second breast after a certain length of time. In some few cases, the baby may do best on one breast per feeding, which means he may need to breastfeed more often and the mother may need to express some milk from her other breast at first. so that she does not become overly full.

Consistently green stools may also indicate that the baby is sensitive to a substance he is taking (such as a medication) or something entering the mother's milk from her digestive tract. (See "Sensitivity to a Food or Drug Mother or Baby Has Ingested" in the chapter "Fussy at the Breast and Breast Refusal.")

Take note if the mother reports too few wet diapers or bowel movements. The baby will need to be checked by a doctor and may need additional food.

The following indicates that the baby may not be breastfeeding often or long enough or that he may have a sucking problem (see next section).

- The baby has too few wet diapers or bowel movements.

If this is the case and the baby has not been breastfeeding often or long enough, suggest the mother increase the number or length of nursings. Breastfeeding management should be looked at closely. The baby should also be checked by a doctor. **This baby may need additional food.**

If the baby is nursing at least 10 times a day and still has too few wet diapers or bowel movements, see the next section, "The Baby's Suck."

Other Areas to Explore

The Baby's Suck

Does the baby spend a lot of time at the breast without much swallowing?

Has the mother had persistent sore nipples and/or recurring plugged ducts or mastitis?

Take note if the mother reports that the baby is nursing "all the time," is losing weight after the milk "comes in," or the baby "doesn't look good." The baby should be seen by a doctor and may need additional food.

The Baby's Temperament

Is the baby unusually calm or very fussy?

If calm, how often does the baby indicate he wants to breastfeed?

If the baby is fussy, does his fussiness ever make it difficult for him to settle down and breastfeed?

The Birth and Hospital Stay

If the birth and hospital experience has affected breastfeeding, a less-than-optimal start can be turned around with patience and good breastfeeding management.

Was the baby born more than 2 weeks early?

A baby with a sucking problem may seem to nurse "all the time" but does not gain well or may even lose weight. This is because the baby is not effectively milking the breast. He may only receive the initial milk from the first let-down, which is low in fat, or he may receive little to no milk at the breast, depending on the severity of the problem.

Persistent sore nipples and/or recurring plugged ducts or mastitis in the mother can indicate poor positioning and latch-on or a sucking problem. Some types of sucking problems cause nipple trauma, while other types do not. A baby with a sucking problem is unable to effectively milk the breast, leaving the mother's breasts uncomfortably full, even after nursings. This unrelieved fullness may cause mastitis.

The following indicate the baby should be checked by a doctor and evaluated for a sucking problem. **This baby may need additional food.**

- The baby is losing weight after the mother's milk has "come in,"
- The baby is nursing "all the time" but still does not gain well,
- The baby "doesn't look good" to you or you get this impression from the mother.

For more information, see "Sucking Problems—Types and Suggestions" in the chapter "Positioning, Latch-On, and the Baby's Suck."

Sometimes a baby's temperament can affect breastfeeding.

A placid or fussy temperament can affect a baby's weight gain. The placid baby may not ask to nurse as often as he needs to and mother may forget to offer. The placid slow-weight-gain baby may also sleep a good part of the time and/or use a pacifier often or suck his thumb or fingers routinely.

The mother of a fussy or fretful baby may offer early supplements or solids under the mistaken belief that her baby is fretful because he is hungry. Solids may not provide enough calories for growth and supplements will decrease a mother's milk supply, undermining her confidence.

Suggest the mother be sure to breastfeed at least 10 to 12 times every 24 hours. If the baby is sleepy, he may need to be awakened to nurse often enough, and if he regularly sucks on a pacifier or his fingers or thumb, he may need to be encouraged to take the breast instead. The baby older than 6 months who is exclusively breastfeeding typically needs to nurse at least 6 to 8 times per day. This baby may also be ready to add solids to his diet.

A fretful baby may have difficulty settling down to breastfeed. See "The 'High-Need' or Colicky Baby" in the chapter "Fussy at the Breast and Breast Refusal" for suggestions for helping the baby settle down at the breast.

If the baby is less than 2 months old and has been gaining slowly since birth, the birth and hospital experiences may have affected breastfeeding. Regular supplements can confuse a baby's suck and delayed, scheduled, and/or infrequent feedings can contribute to engorgement and subsequently reduce a mother's milk supply. Reassure the mother that she and her baby can "catch up" by improving breastfeeding management.

Prematurity can affect the baby's ability to nurse, presenting many challenges for the nursing mother. The baby may not suck well, if at all. The baby may tire easily. The baby's mouth may be small in relation to the mother's nipples. Often premature babies lose more than 10% of their birth weight and are prone to jaundice, hypoglycemia, and—if they were born more than 6 weeks before their due date—may need vitamin and mineral supplements. Even so, with time and patience, they can breastfeed. (See the chapter "Prematurity" for more information.)

Did the mother receive analgesia (pain-relieving drugs), labor-enhancing drugs, or anesthesia during labor? How long was her labor? Did she have a cesarean birth? How soon after birth did the baby nurse?

A mother's labor and delivery may affect breastfeeding at first and therefore weight gain. A cesarean birth or a difficult labor may make the baby sleepy for several days or affect his suck.

Weight Gain

Recent studies confirm that pain relievers or anesthesia used during labor and delivery may contribute to breastfeeding problems by delaying the first nursing and by causing baby's suck and overall coordination to become disorganized. Sepkoski (1992) found that babies whose mothers received epidurals were less alert, less able to orient themselves, and had less organized movements than babies whose mothers gave birth without medication and that these differences were measurable during the babies' entire first month. Righard and Alade (1990) concluded that sucking problems were more common among babies whose mothers received pethidine (meperidine or Demerol) during labor than among babies whose births were unmedicated. Nissen (1995) replicated this finding and concluded that infants whose mothers received pethidine had delayed and depressed sucking and rooting. Crowell (1994) observed that the first effective breastfeeding was delayed an average of more than 11 hours among mothers who received labor analgesia when compared with mothers who received no analgesia.

Righard and Alade (1990) found that in addition to the effects of labor medication, separating mother and baby for as little as 20 minutes before the first nursing also resulted in sucking problems when they were reunited to nurse.

If the baby is sleepy in the first weeks after birth, encourage the mother to wake the baby to breastfeed so that he nurses at least 10 to 12 times every 24 hours. (See "How to Rouse a Sleepy Baby" in the chapter "Positioning, Latch-On, and the Baby's Suck.")

Infant illness or need for special medical care may also cause mother and baby to be separated, making it difficult to nurse frequently.

The earlier and more frequently the baby is able to breastfeed after birth, the better start baby will get.

Did the baby suffer birth injuries?

During the process of labor and delivery a baby sometimes suffers an injury, such as a broken bone or a skeletal misalignment. If the baby is in pain after birth, this can make being held at the breast painful or uncomfortable. A baby in pain may not breastfeed well.

Were bottles or pacifiers given to the baby during the hospital stay? Did the mother use a nipple shield? Did the mother have any problems getting the baby to take the breast?

Routine use of bottles and pacifiers in the hospital can cause breastfeeding to get off to a poor start (Newman 1990). Babies who are given bottles and pacifiers during their first month can develop nipple confusion, causing some to nurse less effectively at the breast and others to refuse the breast altogether. Routine use of artificial nipples can deprive mother and baby of opportunities to breastfeed and result in inadequate stimulation of the breasts and a reduced milk supply.

How much time every day did mother and baby spend together while in the hospital? How often did the baby nurse in the hospital? Did the baby nurse well most of the time?

In general, the more time the mother is able to spend breastfeeding her baby, the better start they will both have. If rooming-in was not available or the mother did not choose it, ask her how often the baby was brought to her to nurse.

Limiting how often or how long a baby breastfeeds in the early days can contribute to breastfeeding problems, such as engorgement and low milk supply. Limiting early nursing can also cause or aggravate newborn jaundice.

If a baby is brought to the mother every 3 or 4 hours in the hospital, the mother may assume that is how often she should be nursing at home and attempt to follow that schedule, possibly contributing to slow weight gain.

How long were the mother and baby in the hospital? Did the baby come home with the mother? If not, how much longer was the baby in the hospital?	A long hospital stay can interfere with breastfeeding if mother and baby are separated or feedings are scheduled. A short hospital stay can interfere with breastfeeding if the mother knows little about breastfeeding, receives no help or conflicting advice about getting baby started, and is sent home before her baby has fed well at the breast and no follow-up visits are provided.
Was the baby jaundiced? How was the jaundice treated?	A baby treated for newborn jaundice may have gotten off to a poor breastfeeding start. This is because the jaundiced baby is more likely to have received bottles, been separated from his mother, and/or been too lethargic or sleepy to suck well at first. The jaundice may also be a result of ineffective sucking or poor breastfeeding management, since babies who nurse early and frequently are less likely to have elevated bilirubin levels. (See the chapter "Newborn Jaundice" for treatment options that do not adversely affect breastfeeding.)

The Baby's Health

Has the baby been ill?	Health problems in the baby can sometimes affect weight gain. During their first six months, some babies experience their first illness—a cold, ear infection, bladder or urinary tract infection, or intestinal disorder, which may go untreated and affect weight gain. Babies, like adults, often have less of an appetite when they are ill. In the case of a cold or ear infection, breastfeeding may be difficult or painful. Also, an infection can make a baby sleepy due to the illness itself or from the medications used. Thrush may also curb a baby's desire to nurse or ability to suck effectively. And when a baby breastfeeds less often, weight gain may slow down and milk production decline along with the frequency of nursing. Not all babies who come down with an illness will run a fever or exhibit the symptoms of an older child who is ill. It is important for any baby who is gaining weight slowly to have a thorough physical examination to check for illness. Ear and urinary tract infections are common causes of slow weight gain. An ear check and urinalysis should be done routinely in cases of slow weight gain to rule them out.
Has the baby had any health problems?	Babies who have a cleft lip and/or palate, heart defects, neurological impairments, or Down Syndrome may have breastfeeding problems and/or gain weight slowly. Clefts of the lip or palate can make it difficult for the baby to get enough suction to hold the breast in place and nurse. Babies with heart defects tire easily and use more calories than a healthy baby just to maintain respiration and circulation. A neurologically impaired baby may have problems coordinating his sucking-and-swallowing pattern. (See the chapter "The Baby with Special Needs" for more information on these special circumstances.)
What has the doctor said about the baby's general health? If breastfeeding management and output are normal, slow weight gain may be the first sign of a metabolic disorder or other health problem.	If the baby has been breastfeeding often and long, has plenty of wet diapers and bowel movements, and is still gaining slowly, it may indicate a metabolic disorder or other health problem. Slow weight gain is often the first symptom of cystic fibrosis, as well as other conditions, such as congenital hypothyroidism, heart disease, kidney disease, intestinal malabsorption or obstruction, parasites, neuro-muscular disease, and hypoadrenalism. Breastfeeding continues to offer many benefits to babies with these health problems. (See "The Baby with Special Needs.") Lukefahr (1990) found infant health problems to be the cause of slow weight gain in 18% of the babies studied.

The Mother's Health, Lifestyle, and Emotional Considerations

	There are times when the health or lifestyle choices of the mother can affect her ability to produce milk, to let down her milk, or to breastfeed frequently throughout the day. This can have a direct effect on her baby's weight gain. Ask the mother about her health, lifestyle, and her feelings about motherhood.

Is the mother being treated for an illness or has she felt unusually fatigued lately? Has she ever had thyroid problems or high blood pressure?	Certain illnesses can affect a mother's ability to make milk. Untreated hypothyroidism (underactive thyroid) and untreated diabetes can affect milk production. When these conditions are treated, milk supply usually increases. Anemia can contribute to low milk supply, as well as to fatigue and susceptibility to infections. If the mother has had thyroid problems or anemia at another time in her life, suggest she have blood tests done to rule these out. (See "Thyroid Disease" and "Diabetes" under "Chronic Illness or Physical Limitation" in the chapter "Health Problems—Mother.")

Other illnesses may require mother to take medications that can affect milk supply. Medications for asthma, allergies, depression, hypertension, insomnia, migraine headaches, autoimmune diseases, and heart problems can affect milk supply. |

Weight Gain

Could the mother be pregnant? Is she taking combined oral contraceptives?	Pregnancy can decrease milk supply. Although pregnancy rarely occurs during a baby's first six months if he is fully breastfed, a baby who has been receiving supplements, uses a pacifier, or is not sucking effectively may not fully inhibit ovulation in the mother and a pregnancy could occur. It is usually difficult to maintain a milk supply adequate for a young baby during a pregnancy.

Combined oral contraceptives have been found to decrease milk supply when used during the first three to six months of breastfeeding (Erwin 1994). Current research on progestin-only hormonal contraception, such as the minipill, implants, and injectables, does not indicate a significant effect on milk supply or infant weight gain when lactation is fully established. However, current research seems to suggest that use of progestin-only contraception may cause a compromised milk supply in some women when used during the first 6 to 8 weeks postpartum. For more information, see the chapter "Sexuality, Fertility, and Contraception." |
| Might the mother have retained a fragment of the placenta, or did she have an unusual amount of postpartum bleeding? | Ask the mother about her delivery. Was the placenta delivered intact? Was it necessary for her doctor to remove the placenta using forceps? Has the mother had postpartum bleeding beyond 6 weeks?

If a fragment of the placenta remains in the uterus, the mother's body may react as if she is still pregnant, inhibiting the production of the hormones necessary for establishing a healthy milk supply. If the mother seems to have an unusual amount of postpartum bleeding, she needs to see her doctor. Maternal postpartum hemorrhage has been associated with insufficient milk production (Willis and Livingstone 1995). |
| Is the mother taking any prescription drugs? Over-the-counter medications? | Some prescription drugs and over-the-counter medications may reduce milk supply or delay the let-down, or milk-ejection, reflex. While most medications are compatible with breastfeeding, if a mother needs a prescribed medication she should be sure her doctor knows she is breastfeeding so that its compatibility with breastfeeding can be checked. (See the chapter "Drugs, Vitamins, Vaccines, and Diagnostic Tests.")

Antihistamines and diuretics may reduce milk supply in some mothers. Some over-the-counter drugs can also reduce milk supply, including large doses of certain vitamins (excessive B_6, for example, blocks the release of prolactin from the pituitary), antihistamines, and diet pills (which may contain caffeine and amphetamines, which can make the baby jittery and fussy). |
| Does the mother have a history of hormonal problems? | Hormonal problems can cause an inadequate milk supply or a poor let-down, or milk-ejection, reflex in some mothers, which can compromise the amount of milk a baby receives (Lawrence pp. 378-79). Some women with pituitary disorders may experience an overabundant milk supply (Edge and Segatore 1993; Jewelewicz and Vande Wiele 1980). |

Does the mother smoke cigarettes? (If yes, how many per day?) Does she drink alcoholic beverages? (If yes, how many per day? Per week?) Does she drink caffeinated beverages? (If yes, how much and how often?)

Smoking cigarettes decreases prolactin and slows let-down. Some mothers smoke and breastfeed without problems (Little 1994), but others have babies who do not gain well (Dahlstrom 1990). If the mother smokes, encourage her to smoke in a separate room away from the baby and, if at all possible, smoke no more than ten cigarettes a day.

Alcohol is a depressant and if consumed in large amounts can slow the let-down. Large amounts of caffeine (more than the amount in five 5 ounce cups of coffee per day—750 ml per day) can also affect the let-down in some women.

For more information, see "Alcohol," "Caffeine," and "Nicotine" in the chapter "Drugs, Vitamins, Vaccines, and Diagnostic Tests."

Has the mother taken any recreational drugs since the birth of her baby?

Recreational drugs pose health hazards for both mother and baby. In addition, taking recreational drugs may impair a mother's ability to care for her baby. If the mother has been taking recreational drugs and needs help in stopping, strongly encourage her to contact her doctor for help.

Does the mother feel that she's under a lot of stress? What outside activities is she involved in?

Recent changes, such as returning to work outside the home, moving, marital concerns, family stresses, even an especially hectic week or two, can affect a mother's milk supply. This works in two ways. First, stress can sometimes slow or inhibit the let-down (the baby gets less milk, the mother begins producing less, and the baby's weight gain begins to slow). Second, many mothers find that when there are more demands on their time and energy, they tend to nurse the baby either less frequently or for a shorter time at each feeding. Stress can affect a mother's feelings about breastfeeding and her willingness to respond to her baby's needs.

A mother who goes back to work soon after the birth of her baby needs extra rest, household help, and a diet of nutritious foods. A single mother needs to seek support from family members, the baby's father, and/or friends. Older children can be a help but also need care. Toddlers can become more demanding when a new baby arrives. If the mother and baby are separated frequently or for extended periods (weekends, frequent social engagements), it can affect breastfeeding, as well as contribute to stress.

If she has been tired and under stress, encourage the mother to rest when she can and to enlist the help of the baby's father, relatives, friends—even hired help, if possible. If she feels her let-down is slow, encourage her to breastfeed lying down or in a comfortable chair and to do her best to relax when she is feeding the baby.

Is the mother on a very restricted or inadequate diet?

One study found that when well-nourished women restrict their caloric intake to 1500 calories per day, milk production is not affected for the first week. However, from weeks one through three, infant weight gain was found to decline (Strode 1986). Also, some women's milk supplies may be more sensitive to dieting than others. The US Subcommittee on Nutrition during Lactation of the Institute of Medicine considers 1800 calories per day to be the minimum level a breastfeeding mother should consider when planning to restrict her diet (Subcommittee on Nutrition during Lactation, p. 13). Women with a history of eating disorders or who are obsessively concerned with returning to prepregnancy weight may require nutritional guidance and emotional support to continue eating well during lactation.

Has the mother ever had breast surgery, a breast injury, breast cancer, or deep radiation of her breasts? Has she ever experienced trauma to her breasts from injury, severe engorgement, or milk expression?

Breast surgery, cancer, radiation, injury, trauma, or congenital defects may cause damage to breast and nerve tissue and affect milk supply. (For more information, see the section "Breastfeeding after Breast Surgery or Injury" in the chapter "Breast Problems.")

Did the mother's breasts change in size or shape during pregnancy? Are her breasts very different in size? Did she experience breast fullness or engorgement after birth?

Very rarely, a mother's breasts will not be able to produce sufficient milk for her baby. This is called primary lactation failure and is due to insufficient glandular development, meaning the milk-producing cells and ducts did not develop and are incapable of working properly (Neifert and Seacat 1987; Neifert 1985). Mothers with this condition typically report that their breasts do not change in size or shape during pregnancy. Their breasts may be very different in size, with one breast much larger than the other. They do not experience their milk "coming in" after birth and never feel full or engorged. A mother like this will not be able to fully nourish her baby at the breast. The baby can continue to breastfeed but needs to receive a supplement in addition to his own mother's milk, either with a nursing supplementer or with another feeding method.

Weight Gain

Some mothers who do not notice breast changes during pregnancy or fullness after birth are able to breastfeed without difficulty.

How does she feel about being a mother?

Although rare in breastfed babies, it is possible that slow weight gain may be due to nurturing problems or emotional deprivation (Tolia 1995, Polan and Ward 1994).

Possible clues:

- The mother gives information that is contradictory—on the one hand she feeds her baby all the time and on the other hand the baby nurses 4 to 5 times every 24 hours. (This is also common in mothers who are extremely stressed, fatigued, or experiencing postpartum depression—see "Postpartum Depression" in the chapter "Health Problems—Mother.")
- The mother may talk about having been abused or neglected herself as a child or not mothered well.
- There may be a history of recent separation (mother has gone back to work, baby is in a large, impersonal day-care setting). The mother encourages the baby to soothe himself (fingers, thumb, pacifier) and uses swings, playpens, and other objects to keep the baby quiet without feeding him.

Watching mother and baby interact may help determine if a baby is emotionally deprived. Possible clues:

- A young, emotionally deprived baby will not seek eye contact. His eyes seem to focus on an object far in the distance. Attempts to encourage the baby to maintain eye contact will cause the baby to turn his head or close his eyes in avoidance.
- The mother may offer to nurse the baby, but as soon as baby pauses, she assumes the baby has finished nursing and removes him from the breast, perhaps offering a pacifier.
- The mother may not wish to hold the baby for long—offering him to others to hold or placing him in an infant seat or other carrier—and may not talk to him or interact with him and, if she does, may speak to him in a derogatory way.

If this seems to be the problem, refer the mother to an appropriate health care professional or local social service agency for help. Your local telephone directory will list social service agencies.

Slow Weight Gain in the Baby Older than Three Months

Most babies who have been gaining well during their first three months continue to gain well, although it seems to be normal for a baby who gained very rapidly in the early months to slow down in the 6- to 12-month period (Dewey 1992a). If there seems to be reason for concern, be sure to go over the early sections—

"First, Establish Weight Gain and Loss," "Second, Discuss Breastfeeding Management," and "Third, Count Wet Diapers and Bowel Movements"—and then explore the following possibilities.

Is the baby sleeping through the night?

Western society places a high value on babies sleeping through the night. Some believe that by 4 months of age the breastfed baby should sleep through the night and breastfeed during the day no more often than every three to four hours. However, most babies need to breastfeed more often and will not thrive on this pattern.

Some babies this age begin sleeping through the night while still taking two long naps each day. Suggest the mother pay careful attention to how frequently the baby is nursing.

If the baby who has recently begun sleeping through night slows in weight gain, encourage the mother either to wake the baby at least once during the night to breastfeed or to breastfeed more often during the day so that the baby receives more milk.

Does the baby suck on a pacifier, fingers, or thumb?

If the baby is gaining slowly and spends some time every day sucking on a pacifier or his fingers or thumb, encourage the mother to offer the breast instead whenever the baby indicates a desire to suck. Some babies spend less time at the breast when their sucking needs are satisfied in other ways. Breastfeeding more often may be all that is necessary to improve the baby's weight gain.

Older babies may choose to suck on their fingers or thumbs because they value their increasing mobility and prefer to satisfy their sucking needs without being confined to their mother's lap. These babies need to be watched to ensure that they nurse frequently enough.

Has the baby been ill?

An illness can slow baby's weight gain, especially an illness that affects the baby's appetite or causes the baby to lose his food before it is digested, such as through vomiting or diarrhea.

If the mother reports that her baby was sick and was nursing less often, had been vomiting, or had diarrhea, encourage her to breastfeed more often so that her baby can receive the extra nourishment he needs during recovery. (Also see, "Diarrhea" or "Vomiting" in the chapter "Illness—Baby.")

Has the baby's normal development affected how often or how long he breastfeeds?

Normal developmental changes in behavior can affect how often and how long a baby breastfeeds, affecting weight gain as well. Each stage of development brings new skills that can distract a baby from breastfeeding. For example:

At 2 to 3 months of age, a baby becomes more aware of the world around him. For example, a baby may become intrigued with his mother's face and pause in mid-nursing to examine her features. A mother may misinterpret a pause to indicate that the baby is finished and take him off the breast too soon.

Encourage the mother to offer the breast several times before assuming baby has finished. If distractibility is a problem, suggest she try nursing in quiet or darkened surroundings.

At 4 to 5 months of age, a baby loves to look at his changing surroundings. Some mothers mistake this distractibility for having lost interest in breastfeeding or being full.

If distractibility causes the baby to cut nursings short, suggest the mother find quiet or darkened surroundings in which to nurse the baby.

At 4 to 6 months of age, a baby may begin teething and may be fretful while breastfeeding or may chew on his hands afterwards. Some mothers may interpret this to mean that he's not getting enough.

Suggest the mother offer the baby something cold or hard to chew on before breastfeeding, such as a cold wet washcloth or a teething toy that has been refrigerated or frozen. This may help the baby numb his gums before settling down to breastfeed, making him more comfortable breastfeeding longer. If the mother understands that her baby's chewing behavior is normal, she will be less likely to lose confidence in her milk supply.

At 5 to 6 months of age, a baby is highly sensitive. Many mothers have found that when they raise their voice to an older sibling during a feeding, the baby becomes upset and stops nursing.

Encourage the mother to find a quiet and peaceful spot to nurse for most breastfeedings.

Weight Gain

From 6 to 12 months of age, babies remain easily distracted. Mother may need to close curtains and eliminate noise as much as possible while nursing. It is not unusual for 9- to 12-month-olds to become so involved in mastering gross motor skills that they forget to nurse. Baby's desire to try new things may motivate him to learn to use a cup, and many mothers offer water at this point, which is easy to clean up, but provides no calories. Mother may need to encourage nighttime nursings, as baby may be "too busy" to nurse during the day.

It may be normal for a baby who gained very rapidly in the early months to slow down in the 6- to 12-month period. Adding solids to a baby's diet is appropriate at this age.

Has the baby been receiving low-calorie liquids or solid foods?

Many mothers give their babies water or juice, both of which can fill a baby up but not provide the calories or nutrients he needs to grow and gain weight. If the mother has been giving water or juice to a baby younger than 9 months old, suggest she substitute breastfeeding instead.

Most mothers introduce solids when their babies are between 4 and 8 months of age. What foods mothers add to their babies' diets will vary widely and may contribute to slow weight gain. When given in large amounts—especially if given before breastfeeding—foods low in calories (cereals, vegetables, and fruits) can fill a baby's stomach without providing enough calories to maintain proper growth.

Most dietitians and doctors agree that infants should not be placed on low-fat or low-calorie diets during their first 2 years of life. Iron-rich foods are important because iron deficiency and anemia can cause slow weight gain.

If the baby is younger than 9 months old and the mother has been offering low-calorie solids as a substitute for breastfeeding, suggest she breastfeed first and more often. Because a baby eats varying amounts of solids from one day to the next, human milk should be the principal source of calories, vitamins, and minerals during the first year. (See the chapter "Starting Solid Foods" for more information.)

If the baby is older than nine months, has he been on mother's milk only?

Many babies who receive only human milk well into the second half of their first year slow down in weight gain. In this case, suggest the mother try offering solid foods.

Could the baby have a vitamin deficiency?

A vitamin B_{12} deficiency in the baby may be possible if the mother is on a strict vegan diet without fish, dairy, or eggs, and this can slow weight gain and cause neurological problems. Suggest the mother ask her doctor to order blood tests to check for this deficiency. If the blood test shows a deficiency, the doctor can prescribe treatment with vitamin B_{12} supplements, which may help improve the baby's weight gain.

Increasing Milk Supply— An Overview

When the mother's milk supply is low, she can take positive steps to increase it.

Nurse frequently. If the baby is sucking effectively (the mother hears the baby swallow after every other suck or so during the first 5 to 10 minutes of nursing), suggest the mother plan to spend several days doing little else but nursing and resting. If the baby is younger than six months and if the mother has been breast-feeding fewer than 10 times per day and the baby's weight gain is low, encourage her to breastfeed more often—every 1½ to 2 hours during the day and every 3 hours at night—until the baby's weight gain has significantly improved. A sleepy baby may need to be awakened and encouraged to nurse more frequently. Within a few days the mother's milk supply should show a substantial increase.

Be sure the baby is positioned and latched-on correctly. To get the most milk for his efforts, the baby needs to open wide and be pulled in close, getting as much of the breast in his mouth as possible. See the chapter "Positioning, Latch-On, and the Baby's Suck."

Offer both breasts at each feeding and nurse long enough so that the baby receives the high-calorie hindmilk. This will ensure that the baby gets all the milk available and that both breasts are stimulated frequently. Allowing the baby to nurse well and long from both breasts assures that the baby will receive enough of the high-calorie hindmilk. If the baby is sucking effectively, allow the baby to set the pace. If the baby is sleepy or not sucking effectively, switch nursing may help.

Try switch nursing. If the baby is not sucking actively—he may be sleepy, a lazy nurser, or have a weak suck—try switching breasts several times throughout each feeding to keep the baby interested in nursing and ensure that the baby receives the high-calorie hindmilk. Suggest the mother watch the baby's sucking and swallowing as he nurses and switch to the other breast as soon as the sucking slows down and he swallows less often. For some babies, this will be about 5 minutes on each side, for others it could be as little as 1 or 2 minutes. Both breasts should be offered at least twice at each feeding and the baby should be encouraged to nurse about 30-40 minutes. If the baby does not suck more actively with switch nursing, see "Sucking Problems—Types and Suggestions" in the chapter "Positioning, Latch-On, and the Baby's Suck."

All the baby's sucking should be at the breast. Avoid bottles and pacifiers since they can confuse the baby. If some supplement is necessary temporarily, it can be given by spoon or one of the other alternative feeding methods. (See "The Use of Breast Pumps and Other Products.") Nipple shields can also cut down on the mother's milk supply. If she is using one, discuss ways to wean the baby from it. (See "Nipple Confusion" in the chapter "Fussy at the Breast and Breast Refusal.")

Give only mother's milk, avoiding solids, water, and juice. Cut down on regular formula supplements gradually under the guidance of the baby's doctor. If the baby has been receiving regular formula supplements, encourage the mother to cut these out gradually, with the guidance of her baby's doctor (see next section). The mother can be sure her baby is getting enough by keeping count of his wet diapers and bowel movements. If the baby is six to twelve months old, solids should be offered, given after nursing rather than before.

Encourage the mother to take good care of herself. Eating a well-balanced diet and drinking to thirst, as well as getting enough rest, will help give the mother the energy she needs to care for her baby. Although her milk supply will continue to increase even if she is tired or not eating well or drinking enough fluids, her nutritional reserves and energy level may go down and she may find it more difficult to cope. Also, fatigue and tension sometimes interfere with a mother's let-down, or milk-ejection, reflex, contributing to a decreased milk supply.

Working with the Doctor and Supplementation

The slow-gaining baby should be seen regularly by his doctor, and the mother should discuss any new suggestions with the doctor before trying them.

The terms "slow weight gain" or "failure-to-thrive" may be used to describe the baby's weight gain.

In all cases of slow weight gain, the baby should be under a doctor's care. The doctor should see the slow-weight-gain baby regularly to assess his weight gain and overall condition. If the mother decides to try something to improve the baby's weight gain that she and her doctor have not discussed, suggest she first contact the doctor to talk it over.

Weight Gain

"Slow weight gain" and "failure-to-thrive" are medical terms that doctors use to describe concerns about weight gain and growth, and it may help the mother to understand their differences so she can decide how they apply to her or her baby.

Slow weight gain. This baby usually breastfeeds frequently and has a good suck. The mother notices her breasts letting down their milk and feels less full after a feeding. The baby has at least six wet diapers a day and the urine is pale and mild-smelling. Bowel movements are loose. Weight gain is slow but consistent. The baby is alert, bright, responsive, and developing normally.

Failure-to-thrive. This baby is usually unresponsive or cries weakly and has poor muscle tone and strength. The baby has few wet diapers and concentrated or dark-colored urine. Bowel movements are infrequent and small in quantity. The mother may be scheduling breastfeedings at fewer than 8 times per day and strictly limiting nursing time. The baby may be developmentally delayed. True failure-to-thrive can be a serious health threat to the baby and put breastfeeding at risk.

For more information, see the previous section, "First, Establishing Weight Gain and Loss."

With a healthy but slow-gaining baby, suggest the mother try improving breastfeeding management before giving supplements.

If the baby is healthy, responsive, and alert and the doctor is not adamant about supplementing, suggest the mother contact the doctor to discuss changing her breastfeeding patterns to increase her milk supply (see previous section) before offering supplements. The doctor may agree to check her baby's weight gain for a week or two while the mother improves her breastfeeding management. Give the mother specific suggestions on what to do differently, and suggest she call or see the baby's doctor and discuss her plans.

If the baby is healthy and gaining within the normal range and the doctor insists on supplementing, suggest the mother get a second opinion.

If the doctor insists on a supplement and the baby is healthy, responsive, alert, and gaining at least 3 to 4 ounces (85-113 grams) a week, suggest the mother seek a second opinion. Improved weight gain may be possible with better breastfeeding management or this pattern of weight gain may be normal for her baby.

Occasionally supplements may be needed.

The decision to supplement is one that the mother will make on the recommendation of her baby's doctor. Encourage the mother to evaluate and improve breastfeeding management before starting supplements. Usually supplements will be recommended:

- when the baby has failed to regain birth weight within one month after birth,
- when weight drops below the third percentile on the infant growth chart,
- when baby's weight gain is consistently less than 4 ounces (113 grams) per week or one pound (454 grams) a month during the first 4 months or 3 ounces (85 grams) a week (¾ of a pound [340 grams] per month) from 4 to 12 months, or 1½ ounces (43 grams) per week from 6 to 12 months (Dewey 1992a),
- when baby or mother has health concerns that might make more frequent breastfeeding difficult.

If supplements are needed and the mother is reluctant or unhappy about giving them, acknowledge her feelings.

When a baby is not gaining well or does not seem to be able to nurse effectively from the breast, supplementation may become necessary. Slow weight gain may cause a mother to doubt herself, and she may see supplementation as final proof of her inadequacy.

Listen to and acknowledge her feelings, and explain to the mother that supplementation is not necessarily the end of breastfeeding, but can be a way of getting baby back on track, giving breastfeeding a second chance.

Human milk is the first choice as a supplement for most babies. Formula supplements may be used if the mother is unable or unwilling to express her milk. Solid foods are sometimes recommended as a supplement.

In most cases, the best supplement for the baby is the mother's own milk, especially hindmilk, which is rich in fat and needed calories. The mother can express milk after baby nurses to obtain the hindmilk, although she should not end the feeding prematurely just to express the hindmilk.

See the chapter "Expression and Storage of Human Milk" for information on choosing a method of expression. Many mothers find a fully automatic electric breast pump easiest to use, and the time-saving convenience of being able to express both breasts simultaneously makes it many mothers' first choice. Double-pumping has been found to increase prolactin levels more effectively than single-pumping (Neifert and Seacat 1985) and to produce a greater milk yield (Auerbach 1990). The mother may want to discuss how expressing can be worked into her daily routine. This type of pump is most readily available in Canada and the US. (See "The Use of Breast Pumps and Other Products.")

Some mothers will choose to supplement with formula. If the mother decides to give formula, tell her it is important to make it according to the doctor's recommendations—diluting it would deprive the baby of the calories he needs and making it too strong could be harmful.

Babies with metabolic disorders, such as galactosemia, may need a special formula. In this case, human milk would not be suitable and the mother would have to stop breastfeeding. (See "Galactosemia" in the chapter "The Baby with Special Needs.")

Solids are sometimes recommended as a supplement, but they may not be nutritionally adequate for a baby younger than four to six months. In this case, the goal should be to increase the mother's milk supply through better management techniques.

How much supplement to give and how often to give it will depend upon how much weight the baby was gaining—the more weight gained, the less supplement will be needed.

The mother and her baby's doctor will need to discuss how much supplement to give. It may be helpful for the mother to know that babies need about 2 to 2½ fluid ounces of nourishment per pound of body weight (60-75 ml per 454 grams) every twenty-four hours to maintain a normal weight gain. An additional 1 to 2 ounces (30-60 ml) per pound (454 grams) of body weight per day may be needed to compensate for a previous lack of weight gain.

How much supplement to give and how often to give it will depend upon how much the baby is gaining. Although the supplement could be given in many different ways, certain approaches may encourage the baby to nurse longer and more effectively at the breast, making it easier for the mother to increase her milk supply.

The ideal way to give a supplement is with a nursing supplementer used at the mother's breast. This method of supplementing is ideal because it encourages the baby to suck more effectively, so it can help to increase the mother's milk supply. For more information on the use of the nursing supplementer, see "The Use of Breast Pumps and Other Products."

If another method of supplementing is used, the mother should be advised to breastfeed the baby before offering a supplement or the baby may be too full to nurse well. This works well for most babies, however, the mother should watch her baby to see how he responds. Some babies breastfeed better if the edge is taken off their hunger by giving a little supplement before nursing.

Offer supplements 2 to 5 times every 24 hours, rather than after every nursing. This gives the baby several feedings a day when he will be exclusively breastfeeding. This way the baby will not come to expect the supplement after every feeding.

How many times per day the supplement should be given depends on how much the baby is gaining. For example, if the baby is gaining 3 ounces per week (85 grams), 2 ounces (60 ml) of hindmilk (and/or formula) after 2 or 3 feedings might be recommended. However, if the baby is gaining less than 3 ounces per week (85 grams), 2 ounces (60 ml) of hindmilk after 4 or 5 feedings might be recommended.

Weight Gain

Offer supplements more frequently in smaller quantities (1 to 3 ounces [30-90 ml]), rather than once or twice a day in large quantities (4 to 8 ounces [120-240 ml]). This prevents the baby from becoming overly full and skipping a nursing.

Be sure the mother knows all the feeding methods available to her.

It is important for the mother to know that there are a variety of feeding methods available to her. She may not realize that there are alternatives to bottles, which can cause nipple confusion in the very young baby and weaken the suck of a baby who is not sucking well. Other methods of giving supplements include cup, spoon, bowl, eyedropper, feeding syringe, or nursing supplementer (used at the breast or on a finger). See "The Use of Breast Pumps and Other Products."

When the mother begins giving supplements, encourage her to have realistic expectations and to keep close track of her baby's progress.

It may help the mother to know that babies seldom go from losing weight one week to gaining rapidly the next. They usually stabilize for one or two weeks and then begin to gain slowly (perhaps only 1½ oz or 42 grams initially). This can be disheartening to the mother, but reassure her that the weight gain will come faster.

- Encourage the mother to keep a diary with number of nursings, time and amount of supplements, wet diapers, and bowel movements.
- Have the baby's weight checked every week or two until steady weight gain is shown. Use the same scale every time and similar weight clothing if a baby is not undressed when weighed.

When the baby is gaining well, encourage the mother to wean the baby slowly from the supplements with her doctor's guidance.

When the baby begins to gain more weight, the mother can ask her doctor about decreasing the supplement while she works to increase her milk supply.

When her baby's doctor gives approval, help the mother set appropriate goals for decreasing the supplement while increasing nursing—"8 ounces (240 ml) of supplement this week, 6 to 7 ounces (180-210 ml) next week. A target weight gain of _____." The goals should be reasonable and attainable. By keeping track of her baby's wet diapers and bowel movements, as well as his weight gain, the mother can be sure the baby is getting enough.

Bowel movements will change as the baby receives more human milk.

If the baby has been on formula supplements, remind the mother that his bowel movements will become looser and probably more frequent as he receives more human milk.

The mother will need support and reassurance.

Decreasing supplements while increasing milk supply can be a long process—it may take concentrated time and effort for many weeks as the baby's nursing improves. Reassurance and support will make it easier for the mother to be patient.

RAPID WEIGHT GAIN DURING THE FIRST YEAR

When a baby gains weight more rapidly than the norm, the mother may be worried that her baby is headed for adult obesity. Ask the mother:

- How old is the baby now?
- What is his present weight?
- What was his birth weight?
- What was the baby's lowest weight after birth? His age at that time?
- What other weight checks has he had? What were his age and weight at these times?

Determine weight gain from the lowest weight after birth. Normal weight gain in the breastfed baby is 4 to 8 ounces a week (113 to 227 grams) or one to two pounds (454-908 grams) a month.

Is the baby receiving anything other than mother's milk? Formula? Solids? (If so, what foods does the baby eat regularly?)

If the baby is younger than 6 months old and receiving only his mother's milk, assure the mother that he is receiving a perfect food. Human milk has no "empty calories," as do highly processed foods. There is no evidence that a baby who gains rapidly on human milk will have weight problems as an adult. In fact, one study found that breastfeeding provides significant protection against obesity through adolescence (Kramer 1981).

Also, tell the mother that the fat accumulated in the relatively inactive pre-toddler stage is a preparation for the highly active time when the busy toddler may not want to take time to eat. Usually by age 2 or 3, the rapid gainer slims down naturally.

Nutritional needs vary from baby to baby and limiting nursing may not be in the baby's best interest.

There are hazards in limiting growth by putting a baby on a diet. The young child needs nutrients to produce all types of cells, brain and nerve, as well as fat cells. As with an adult, the nutritional needs of a baby vary from individual to individual.

If the baby is younger than six months and receiving solids, substituting breastfeeding for some of the solids may prevent overfeeding.

If the baby is younger than 6 months old and is receiving solids as well as human milk, point out that an early introduction of solids can contribute to overfeeding. Because a young baby cannot clearly communicate when he has had enough, there is a risk that the mother may inadvertently overfeed him and begin a pattern of feeding that ignores her child's cues.

If the solids have been a substantial part of the baby's diet, and the mother wants to cut back on them, encourage her to cut down on them gradually while breastfeeding more often to assure that her milk supply will be sufficient to meet the baby's nutritional needs.

If the baby is older than six months and receiving high-calorie solids, suggest the mother offer a variety of foods.

If the baby is older than 6 months old, is receiving high-calorie solids, and is gaining exceptionally rapidly, encourage the mother to offer the baby a more natural variety of foods, such as fresh fruits and vegetables. Also, encourage the mother to think of her milk as her baby's primary food for the first year. Solids should be considered a supplement to breastfeeding during this time.

Publications for Parents

La Leche League International. *How to Know Your Healthy Full-Term Breastfed Baby Is Getting Enough Milk.* Schaumburg, Illinois: La Leche League International, 1994. Publication No. 457.

La Leche League International. *Increasing Your Milk.* Schaumburg, Illinois: La Leche League International, 1988. Publication No. 85.

References

La Leche League International. THE WOMANLY ART OF BREASTFEEDING, 35th Anniversary ed. Schaumburg, Illinois, 1991, pp. 144-54 and 329-30.

Mohrbacher, N. *When You Breastfeed Your Baby: The First Week*. Schaumburg, Illinois: La Leche League International, 1993. Publication No. 124a.

Auerbach, K. Sequential and simultaneous breast pumping: a comparison. *Int J Nurs Stud* 1990; 27:257-65.

Cohen, R. et al. Determinants of growth from birth to 12 months among breast-fed Honduran infants in relation to age of introduction of complementary foods. *Pediatrics* 1995; 96(3):504-10.

Crowell, M. et al. Relationship between obstetric analgesia and time of effective breastfeeding. *J Nurse Midwif* 1994; 39:150-56.

Dahlstrom, A. et al. Nicotine and cotinine concentrations in the nursing mother and her infant. *Acta Paediatr Scand* 1990; 79:142-47.

DeMarzo, S. et al. Initial weight loss and return to birth weight criteria for breastfed infants: challenging the 'rules of thumb.' *Am J Dis Child* 1991; 145:402.

DiPietro, J. et al. Behavioral and heart rate pattern differences between breast-fed and bottle-fed neonates. *Dev Psych* 1987; 23:467-74.

Dewey, K. et al. Growth of breastfed infants deviates from current reference data: a pooled analysis of US, Canadian, and European data sets. *Pediatrics* 1995; 96(3):495-503.

Dewey, K. et al. Growth of breastfed and formulafed infants from 0 to 18 months: the DARLING study. *Pediatrics* 1992a; 89(6):1035-41.

Dewey, K. et al. Breastfed infants are leaner than formula-fed infants at one year of age: the DARLING study. *Am J Clin Nutr* 1993; 57:140-45.

Dewey, K. et al. Adequacy of energy intake among breasfed infants in the DARLING study: relationships to growth velocity, morbidity, and activity levels. *J Pediatr* 1991; 119:538-47.

Dewey, K. et al. Growth patterns of breastfed infants in affluent (US) and poor (Peru) communities: implications for timing of complementary feeding. *Am J Clin Nutr* 1992b; 56: 1012-18.

Dewey, K. and Heinig, M. Are new growth charts needed for breastfed infants? BREASTFEEDING ABSTRACTS 1993; 12:35-36.

Edge, D. and Segatore, M. Assessment and management of galactorrhea. *Nurs Practitioner* 1993; 18(6):35-49.

Erwin, P. To use or not use combined hormonal oral contraceptives during lactation. *Fam Plan Perspect* 1994; 26(1): 26-33.

Heinig, M. et al. Energy and protein intakes of breast-fed and formula-fed infants during the first year of life and their association with growth velocity: the DARLING study. *Am J Clin Nutr* 1993; 58:152-61.

Weight Gain

Jewelewicz, R. and Vande Wiele, R. Clinical course and outcome of pregnancy in twenty-five patients with pituitary microadenomas. *Am J Obstet Gynecol* 1980; 136(3):339-43.

Kramer, M. Do breast-feeding and delayed introduction of solid foods protect against subsequent obesity? *J Pediatr* 1981; 98:883-87.

Lawrence, R. *Breastfeeding: A Guide for the Medical Profession,* 4th ed. St. Louis: Mosby, 1994, pp. 359-86.

Little, R. et al. Maternal smoking during lactation: relation to infant size at one year of age. *Am J Epidemiol* 1994; 140:544-54.

Lukefahr, J. Underlying illness associated with failure to thrive in breastfed infants. *Clin Pediatr* 1990; 29:468-70.

McBride, M. and Danner, S. Sucking disorders in neurologically impaired infants: assessment and facilitation of breastfeeding. *Clin Perinatol* 1987; 14:109-30.

Neifert, M. et al. Lactation failure due to insufficient glandular development of the breast. *Pediatrics* 1985; 76:823-28.

Neifert, M. and Seacat, J. Milk yield and prolactin rise with simultaneous breast pumping: Abstract from the Ambulatory Pediatric Association Annual Meeting, Washington, DC, May 7-10, 1985.

Neifert, M. and Seacat, J. Lactation insufficiency: a rational approach. *Birth* 1987; 14:182-88.

Newman, J. Breastfeeding problems associated with the early introduction of bottles and pacifiers. *J Hum Lact* 1990; 6(2):59-63.

Nissan, E. et al. Effects of maternal pethidine on infants' developing breastfeeding behavior. *Acta Paediatr* 1995; 84(92): 140-45.

Polan, H. and Ward, M. Role of the mother's touch in failure to thrive: a preliminary investigation. *J Am Acad Ch Ad Psyc* 1994; 33(8):1098-1105.

Righard, L. and Alade, M. Effects of delivery room routines on success of first breast-feed. *Lancet* 1990; 336:1105-07.

Riordan, J. and Auerbach, K. *Breastfeeding and Human Lactation,* Boston and London: Jones and Bartlett, 1993, pp. 515-33.

Sepkoski, C., et al. The effects of maternal epidural anesthesia on neonatal behavior during the first month. *Dev Med Child Neurol* 1992; 34:1072-80.

Strode, M. Effects of shortterm caloric restriction on lactational performance of wellnourished women. *Acta Paediatr Scand* 1986; 75:222-29.

Subcommittee on Nutrition During Lactation. *Nutrition During Lactation.* Washington, DC: National Academy Press, 1991, p. 13.

Tolia, V. Very early onset nonorganic failure to thrive in infants. *J Ped Gastro Nutr* 1995; 20:73-80.

Willis, C. and Livingstone, V. Infant insufficient milk syndrome associated with maternal postpartum hemorrage. *J Hum Lact* 1995; 11(2):123-26.

Woolridge, M. and Fisher, C. Colic, "overfeeding," and symptoms of lactose malabsorption in the breastfed baby: a possible artifact of feed management? *Lancet* 1988; II(8605):382-84.

Woolridge, M. et al. Do changes in patterns of breast usage alter the baby's nutritional intake? *Lancet* 1990; 336(8712):395-97.

Woolridge, M. et al. Effect of a traditional and of a new nipple shield on sucking patterns and milk flow, *Early Human Dev* 1980; 4:357-64.

Weight Gain

7

Starting Solid Foods

DETERMINING A BABY'S READINESS FOR SOLIDS

HOW TO INTRODUCE SOLIDS

WHAT FOODS TO OFFER

FOODS TO AVOID

INTRODUCING THE CUP

The introduction of solid foods should be a pleasant time for both mother and baby. Encourage the mother to have a positive attitude and let her baby be her guide. Tell the mother that once her baby starts solids there will be changes in baby's stools. She can expect baby to have less frequent stools that smell stronger and are darker in color than the stools of an exclusively breastfeeding baby. They may contain bits of undigested food.

DETERMINING A BABY'S READINESS FOR SOLIDS

The mother's diet changes the taste of her milk, which prepares her baby for the foods he will someday eat at the family table.

Solid foods help meet babies' increased need for iron, protein, and calories as they grow.

The breastfed baby has a richer range of taste experience than his formula-fed counterpart. A mother's milk varies in composition during the course of a day. Its taste also varies, depending on the foods the mother eats. This may prepare her baby for the foods he will someday eat at the family table (Sullivan and Birch 1994).

Most babies show signs of readiness for solids at about the middle of their first year of life.

Signs of readiness for solids include:

- the ability to sit up,
- a fading of the tongue-thrusting reflex so that the baby does not automatically push solids out of his mouth with his tongue,
- readiness to chew,
- the ability to pick up food and put it in his mouth,
- an increased demand to nurse that is unrelated to illness, teething pain, or a change in routine.

If the baby suddenly increases his demand to be fed at around six months of age and this increased demand to be fed continues for four or five days in spite of more frequent nursings, it may be time to offer solids.

If the baby is much younger than six months, however, caution the mother not to rush the start of solids, because this behavior may be due to other causes, such as an illness coming on, a growth spurt, or a change in routine.

There are benefits to waiting until the middle of the baby's first year before introducing solid foods.

Today, medical scientists have verified that human milk is nature's complete food for at least the first six months for the healthy, full-term infant, and there is usually no reason for adding other foods before that time. In its 1980 recommendation, the American Academy of Pediatrics Committee on Nutrition advocates only human milk until four to six months of age. There are many advantages to waiting until the baby is ready for solids.

Decreased risk of allergies. The younger the baby, the more likely it is that any foods other than human milk will cause food allergies. While baby is totally breastfed, components of human milk protect the baby's digestive tract, reducing the risk that foreign proteins could enter the baby's system and cause allergic reactions. At about six months of age, a baby begins producing enough IgA antibodies to prevent the absorption of food antigens through the intestinal wall, reducing the possibility of food allergies (Taylor 1973).

Increased ability of the baby to digest solid foods. The baby's digestive system matures during the first six months. Before his system is ready to handle other foods, most solids are poorly digested and may cause an unpleasant reaction. These same foods, however, will be readily assimilated if they are delayed until the baby is six months or older.

Assurance of proper nutrition through maintenance of the mother's milk supply. The American Academy of Pediatrics recommends that human milk continue to be a baby's primary source of nutrition for the first year. Since solids replace human milk in a baby's diet, the more solids the baby takes, the less milk he takes from the breast and the less milk there will be (Cohen 1994). Early introduction of solids puts baby at risk for premature weaning. By adding solids to her baby's diet before he needs them, the mother substitutes an inferior food for a superior food.

Decreased risk of ear infections. In one study of 1013 babies, researchers found that babies who were exclusively breastfed for four months or more had 40% fewer episodes of acute ear infections than breastfed babies whose diets were supplemented with other foods before four months (Duncan 1993). Because solids take the place of human milk in a baby's diet, starting other foods decreases the amount of protective antibodies the baby receives.

Starting Solids

Decreased health risks from contaminated foods. In areas of the world without safe water supplies, starting solids before six months may present a serious health risk. In these areas, early solids are associated with increased incidence of infections and diarrheal diseases, the number one cause of infant death worldwide. Both the World Health Organization and UNICEF recommend breastfeeding exclusively for six months to protect the health of children in these areas.

Continued effectiveness of breastfeeding as a natural child spacer. The childspacing value of breastfeeding is most effective when the baby is exclusively breastfeeding and receives no supplements, solids, or soothers (pacifiers) that cut down on the baby's time at the breast. (See "Breastfeeding, Fertility, and Contraception" in the chapter "Sexuality, Fertility, and Contraception.")

Ease of feeding. Due to the tongue-thrust reflex of the younger baby—which causes the food to be pushed out of his mouth rather than swallowed—and the baby's inability to sit up alone, feeding solids to a younger baby is much messier and more difficult. As a baby reaches six months old, the tongue-thrust reflex fades and the baby can take a more active part in the feeding.

Studies show that starting solids does not cause babies to sleep longer.

The belief that starting solids will help a baby "sleep through the night" motivates many parents to begin solids earlier than they otherwise would. However, this popular belief has no basis in fact. Two studies found no difference in the sleep patterns of babies who received solids before bedtime when compared to babies who were not given solids (Macknin 1989; Keane 1988).

If the baby is not interested in solids, the mother can try again in a week or two.

Not all babies are ready to begin solids at the same age. Suggest the mother watch her baby, not the calendar, for signs that the baby is ready. If the baby refuses solid foods, encourage the mother to try again another time—after a week or two—perhaps with a different food.

A baby who is susceptible to allergies may refuse solids until he is older.

Some children who are prone to food allergies or intolerances are not interested in solids until they are eight or nine months old or even older. This could be a natural protective reaction in unusually sensitive children. Many babies do well on human milk alone for the first eight or nine months (Borresen 1995). Assure the mother that an adequate hemoglobin count (see next point) and steady weight gain mean that the exclusively breastfed baby is doing well. However, she should continue to offer solids every few days until her child begins to show an interest in them.

Some doctors caution parents that if their babies do not start solids by about six months they may not learn to chew because they have missed the proper developmental stage. However, this concept is questionable because it is based on research on children who received all their feedings for the first year or more via IV or feeding tube into the stomach (Merchant 1987). Although children who have never been fed by mouth have difficulty accepting solids when they are started after one year, this does not mean that breastfed babies who have been taking their mother's milk by mouth from birth will have a similar reaction.

Anemia is uncommon in the breastfed baby, but if the baby refuses solids and there is a concern about iron, suggest the mother request a simple blood test to determine the baby's iron levels.

Anemia is uncommon in the breastfed baby. Reasons for this include:

- The healthy, full-term baby has ample iron stores at birth, enough to last for at least the first six months of life.
- Although the amount of iron in human milk is small, it is well-absorbed—49 percent (Saarinen 1977) as opposed to 10 percent from cow's milk and 4 percent from iron-fortified formula. The high lactose and vitamin C levels in human milk aid in the absorption of iron.
- Breastfed babies do not lose iron through their bowels, as do babies fed cow's milk, which has been found to cause intestinal fissures (Woodruff 1977).

The iron stores the full-term baby has at birth coupled with the readily absorbed iron in human milk are usually enough to keep hemoglobin levels within the normal limits (10.2 to 15 gm/dL) well into the baby's second six months of life (Pisacane 1995; Duncan 1985; Siimes 1984; McMillan 1976). One study of breastfed babies who were not given iron supplements or iron-fortified cereals found that those who were exclusively breastfed for seven months or longer had significantly higher hemoglobin levels at one year than breastfed babies who received solid foods earlier than seven months (Pisacane 1995). The researchers found no cases of anemia within the first year in babies breastfed exclusively for seven months and concluded that breastfeeding exclusively for seven months reduces the risk of anemia and should be recommended in parts of the world where breastfeeding is common and iron supplementation is not available or culturally acceptable.

If the mother or the baby's doctor is concerned about the baby's iron level, suggest the mother ask the doctor to check the blood with a simple hemoglobin test that can be performed in the doctor's office.

Iron levels in human milk are not affected by the mother's iron intake.

The iron levels in a mother's milk are not affected by the amount of iron in a mother's diet or by iron supplements she may take (Vuori 1980).

HOW TO INTRODUCE SOLIDS

Some mothers find the process of starting solids easier if they begin at a quiet time of day, although some babies become more interested in solids when they eat with the rest of the family.

Suggest the mother begin by offering solids during a less rushed time of day—such as mid-morning or mid-afternoon.

If the baby does not seem interested in solids when they are offered mid-morning or mid-afternoon, suggest that the mother try placing the baby's chair next to hers at family mealtimes so the baby sees the rest of the family eating.

Especially at first, suggest the mother breastfeed the baby before offering solids.

The first feedings of solids should be considered an introduction to a new method of eating, not a substitute for mother's milk. Breastfeeding first—before offering solids—will help to ensure that the mother's milk supply continues to be adequate and that baby gets the milk he needs as he learns to eat other foods. Also, a hungry baby will not be very interested in trying anything new.

Rather than increasing a baby's total intake, solids displace human milk in a baby's diet. One study (Cohen 1994) observed 141 mother-baby couples, some of whom breastfed exclusively for six months and some of whom started solids at four months. The researchers found that the energy value of the human milk the baby consumed when he was exclusively breastfeeding matched closely the combined energy value of human milk plus the solids. The researchers concluded that babies balanced their mother's milk and solid foods to maintain a stable intake of calories. The amount of mother's milk consumed daily dropped when solid foods were introduced.

At first it may go more smoothly if the mother feeds the baby in her lap.

The breastfed baby is used to eating in the mother's lap, and this may make the baby more willing to try something new.

Suggest the mother offer one new food at a time.

At first, suggest the mother plan to offer only one food at a time. This means a single food, not a mixed food like stew or soup, or even a mixed-grain cereal. This way the mother will know if her baby is sensitive to a particular food before she starts another.

The single food should be given for a week before introducing another new food so that the mother can watch for allergic reactions.

Suggest the mother also plan to allow about a week between each new food. The reason for this precaution is that although a baby who starts solids after six months of age is not nearly

Starting Solids

as likely to have an allergic reaction as a younger child—because his digestive system is more mature—it is still possible. Allowing a week in between new foods gives the mother a chance to watch for an allergic reaction.

There is no advantage to giving a wide variety of foods in a short period of time. By going slowly, the baby has the opportunity to experience each new food thoroughly before going on to another.

Start with a teaspoon or less (5 ml or 4.7 grams or less) of the new food just once or twice a day, increasing the amount slightly at each feeding.

Encourage the mother to start with a teaspoon or less (5 ml or 4.7 grams or less) of the new food and increase the amount gradually, so that she will notice any allergic reaction before the baby consumes large amounts of it.

Symptoms of allergic reactions, and what to do if they occur.

Allergic reactions include:

- rash, hives, sore bottom,
- wheezing, asthma,
- congestion, cold-like symptoms,
- red, itchy eyes,
- ear infections,
- irritability, fussiness, colic,
- intestinal upsets, vomiting, constipation, and diarrhea.

If the baby has a mild allergic reaction, suggest the mother eliminate that food and try it again later when the baby is older. If the baby's reaction is severe, suggest the mother discuss it with her baby's doctor.

Later, as additional foods are introduced, a combination of foods can be offered.

The mother need not hesitate to "mix and match" foods that have already been introduced. Often a baby will view a new food with suspicion but will accept it if it is mixed with one he is already used to.

Later, as the baby grows, the mother may want to offer a dish with small servings of several foods on it, like the rest of the family.

If necessary, solids can be mashed and moistened at first and then gradually less liquid added until baby is eating them like the rest of the family.

Depending on the age of the baby, the mother may want to mash the food and moisten it with water or her milk. A baby who is six months old, for example, may find softer foods eaten with a spoon easier to manage. An eight-month-old baby, on the other hand, may prefer chunkier finger foods. Encourage the mother to experiment with different textures to see what her baby prefers.

The mother may want to use a blender or food processor to make some table foods easier for the baby to manage. However, a fork works nicely for most foods. The baby who is six months or older when solids are started does not need foods pureed or liquefied.

Some babies, especially babies older than six months, prefer to begin with finger foods.

Finger foods, such as cooked carrots or peas, help a baby gain finger control and coordination, as well as fostering independence. If a baby is eight or nine months old before he is interested in solids, he may be able to start with finger foods and do much of the feeding himself.

Examples of finger foods are:

- grated fruits and vegetables,
- whole-grain bread strips,
- unsweetened cold breakfast cereals,
- cubed soft foods,
- frozen peas and blueberries.

The mother should plan to stay with the baby while he eats in case he gags or chokes.

While the baby is learning to handle food, it is important for the mother to stay with him and not walk away. Most babies have an excellent gag reflex and manage to cough up anything that goes down the wrong way, but in case the baby has a problem and needs help, it is important for the mother to stay close.

To keep mealtimes pleasant, suggest the baby be allowed to stop eating when full and to eat only the foods he likes.

As new foods are introduced and become a regular part of the baby's diet, encourage the mother to offer more as he indicates he wants more. When he doesn't want more, suggest the mother stop.

Caution the mother not to coax, wheedle, cajole, or force the baby to eat. A satisfied baby will probably let the mother know when he has had enough by turning his head, clamping his mouth shut, spitting the food back out, or some other unmistakable gesture.

Babies often like or dislike certain foods just as adults do. If the baby doesn't want to eat a certain food, suggest the mother skip it and try something else. It is also possible for babies to get tired of a food they previously enjoyed.

Babies who are allowed free choice of only good, nutritious foods will tend to balance their own diets.

Within three to six months, most babies will be taking some solids regularly and the mother will not need to be as concerned about mixing foods or starting new foods.

Once solid foods have been introduced, most babies will be eating some solids regularly within three to six months. Once the baby is eating a variety of foods without signs of allergy or distress, the mother can be less concerned about mixing foods or introducing something new. As long as what the mother offers her baby is healthy, nourishing food, she should let the baby's appetite be her guide as to what he wants to eat and when he wants to eat it (Birch 1991).

During the baby's second six months, breastfeeding should continue to be the baby's primary source of nutrition, meeting about three-fourths of his nutritional needs. Gradually and over time, the amount of solids the baby eats will increase to become a major part of his diet during his second year. As the baby grows, human milk continues to provide excellent nutrition.

WHAT FOODS TO OFFER

Whole foods, in as close to their natural state as possible, are the most nutritious and economical foods for baby.

The same basic principles of good nutrition apply to the baby as to the rest of the family. Whole foods in as close to their natural state as possible are the most nutritious—and usually the most economical—foods for baby.

It is not necessary to use commercially prepared baby foods.

Many mothers never use commercial baby foods. They are expensive, as well as being highly processed, which makes them less nutritious than fresh foods. Also, some varieties contain undesirable fillers and preservatives.

Another disadvantage is that the smooth and uniform texture of commercial baby foods makes the transition to regular foods more difficult for some babies. A baby who is six months or older when starting solids does not need foods pureed or liquefied.

A suggested guide for introducing solids.

When starting solids, the following progression works well for most babies.

Ripe banana, avocado, yam, or sweet potato. Banana is a nutritious first food which most babies like because of its smooth consistency. It is also fresh, easy to prepare, contains more food value than cereals, and is less likely to cause allergic reactions. The mother can begin by offering a small amount mashed on a spoon or on her fingertip, or the baby may pick up a small piece of banana to feed himself.

If the baby doesn't like banana, avocado, cooked sweet potato, or yam are nutritious alternatives.

Meat. Meat is suggested early among solid foods because of its high iron and protein content; however, other foods may be substituted in vegetarian families. To reduce meat to a good consistency for the baby, chopped beef, stewed meats, or tender pieces of chicken can be cut into small slivers or mashed with a fork and moistened with meat juices or warm water. Tough connecting fibers should be removed and tender portions gently cooked for baby to eat.

Starting Solids

When the baby has had a week on one meat, the mother can offer a good-sized bone (with no splinters or sharp corners) with a few meat fragments left on it. A chicken drumstick is good and just about the right size to grasp, but the mother needs to be sure to remove the needle-thin splint bone and the gristle cap on the end first. This will give a baby something to teethe on and satisfy the urge to chew and bite, as well as promoting hand-eye coordination.

To make sure the mother has on hand the kind of meat her baby can handle, she can keep individual portions of cooked, chopped, or scraped beef or chicken wrapped and frozen.

If the baby doesn't like meats at first, the mother can try adding a little to the mashed banana.

Whole-grain breads and cereals. Finger-sized pieces of dried or toasted whole-wheat bread are good for the baby to chew and convenient for the mother to offer between meals or while she is preparing dinner.

If the mother regularly serves a cooked, whole-grain cereal, she might want to give her baby some, but encourage her to give the cereal with no added sugar or sweetener and to cook it with water, not milk. Mixed-grain cereals should be avoided until the baby has been introduced to each one.

Baby cereals do not have as much food value as freshly cooked, whole-grain cereals, because they are highly processed.

Fresh fruits. Raw, peeled apple or pear can be grated or scraped with the edge of a spoon and put in a little mound on the baby's tray. An older baby will be able to handle a piece of peeled apple, ripe pear, or peach. Apricots, plums, and melons are good, too. When the baby is eight months or older, other fresh fruits in season may be offered, but with caution. Some berries are allergenic.

Frozen blueberries are a good finger food, and can be soothing when the baby is teething. Citrus fruits can cause allergy, so those are best postponed until children are about a year old, especially in families with a history of allergy. At that time, tangerine segments are good to start with, as long as the seeds are removed.

Suggest the mother avoid canned fruits that contain sugar. They have less food value than fresh fruits, but unsweetened canned fruits are better than no fruit at all. Fruit can be rinsed to remove excess syrup, if desired.

Dried fruits such as raisins, dates, or figs should not be given at all in the first year, and later only on a limited basis. Although they are nutritious, they are very sweet and tend to stick between the teeth, which can cause dental caries.

Vegetables. Sweet potato, as mentioned before, and white potato are both good choices for baby. Dairy products, such as butter, margarine, or sour cream, should not be added to vegetables until they are introduced later.

Finely grated raw carrot can be mixed with grated apple or some of the other foods to which baby has already been introduced. Cooked carrots are good, too.

Other cooked vegetables may be offered from the mother's plate one at a time, as any other new food. Some babies enjoy frozen vegetables right from the package—especially frozen peas that they can pick up and eat one at a time.

Tell the mother that it is not unusual to find little bits of vegetable, virtually unchanged, in the baby's diaper. Even when they are cooked, vegetables appear to be less completely digested than other foods.

Many raw vegetables have more food value than cooked vegetables, but most of them are too hard for a baby to chew and digest. Some raw vegetables—particularly carrots and celery—can be dangerous, as small chunks can be inhaled rather than swallowed and cause choking.

Dairy products. Cottage cheese, yogurt, and natural cheeses can be introduced when the baby is nine or ten months old. These dairy products provide calcium and other nutrients. They are less likely to cause allergies than cow's milk because of the absence of whey proteins. The mother can also add butter or margarine around this time.

FOODS TO AVOID

Some foods are best avoided until the baby reaches one year.

Foods best avoided during the baby's first year are:

Cow's milk. Suggest the mother hold off introducing cow's milk until after the baby's first birthday. Cow's milk is a common food allergen; the baby who is nursing well has no nutritional need for cow's milk or other dairy products during the first year.

Once the baby begins drinking cow's milk, recommend the mother serve whole milk (not skimmed or 2 percent) until the child is two years old. The young child needs some natural fats for optimal growth.

Eggs. Eggs, especially the whites, are another common food allergen. Many physicians recommend waiting until after the baby's first birthday to introduce eggs. Suggest the mother start with a small amount of hard-cooked yolk, not the white, since the white is highly allergenic. Like some vegetables, it is not unusual at first to find bits of egg virtually unchanged in the baby's diaper.

Citrus fruits, berries with seeds, and dried fruits. Citrus fruits are another highly allergenic food and so are best delayed until one year. Berries can be allergenic.

Dried fruits—such as raisins, dates, and figs—are nutritious but very sweet and tend to stick between the teeth, which can contribute to tooth decay. Even after one year they are best given only on a limited basis.

Foods that are high in saturated fat, such as fried foods. Large amounts of saturated fats are not needed and should be consumed in moderation.

Foods that contain added sugar or artificial sweeteners or are high in salt. Sugar contains no vitamins, minerals, or other nutrients, which is why it is sometimes referred to as "empty calories." Sugar seduces the appetite and contributes to poor eating habits, since sweetened foods tend to satisfy hunger and displace healthy foods—no matter what type of sweetener is used.

Remind the mother that in order to make an informed choice when selecting foods, she needs to read labels and watch for sugar under its other names, such as dextrose, sucrose, corn syrup, fructose, and others. Molasses and honey are almost pure sugar and have the same disadvantages. Specifically, advise the mother to avoid sweetened cereals, candy, and sweetened desserts such as puddings, flavored gelatin, cakes, cookies, canned fruits packed in syrup, and teething biscuits. Also, soft drinks should be avoided, carbonated or not, as these are highly sugared, may contain caffeine, and contain no nutrients. Diet beverages are not recommended either.

The sugars found naturally in human milk and in foods such as raw fruits and vegetables are of the kinds and in the proportions that babies (and adults) need and can use. These foods also provide other necessary nutrients.

Foods that are high in salt. Highly salted foods such as canned soups, crackers, chips, and pretzels may foster a taste for salty foods.

Honey. Honey should never be given to babies younger than one year, because it may contain botulism spores that the baby's digestive and immune systems cannot handle.

If the baby has shown signs of being sensitive or allergic or has a family history of allergies, suggest the mother avoid other highly allergenic foods for his first year.

Certain foods may not be suitable for the baby born into a family with a history of allergies. Such a baby should be viewed as potentially allergic. The mother would want to be especially careful to delay solids until at least six months and to be more restrictive as to which foods are introduced before the baby reaches one year.

Highly allergenic foods include wheat, corn, pork, fish (including shellfish), peanuts, tomatoes, onions, cabbage, berries, nuts, spices, citrus fruits and juices, chocolate, and any food that causes allergic reactions in other family members or that the baby has shown sensitivity to through his mother's milk.

Some foods are best avoided because they might cause choking.

Certain foods should not be offered until the baby is older than three years because of the possibility of choking. These include:

- nuts,
- whole grapes,
- popcorn,
- large pieces of hot dog,
- large amounts of peanut butter on a spoon, and
- any food that could break off in large chunks, such as raw carrot or celery sticks.

Starting Solids

INTRODUCING THE CUP

Between six and eight months, many babies enjoy sips of liquid from a cup.

The baby may be ready to begin drinking from a cup between six and eight months. Tell the mother that it may take time for the baby to learn to drink from a cup by himself without making a mess. Assure the mother that there is no need to rush.

Mother's milk, water, homemade soups, and unsweetened fruit or vegetable juices are the healthiest beverages for the baby.

The baby's beverages should consist mainly of:

- mother's milk,
- water,
- homemade soups without added salt or salty seasonings (canned soups may be high in salt and contain preservatives), and
- limited amounts of unsweetened fruit or vegetable juice (suggest the mother check the label on the juice bottle or can for added sugar or salt).

Too much juice can compromise a baby's growth.

Juice, like solids, takes the place of mother's milk in a baby's diet, so intake of juice and other liquids should be kept minimal during a baby's first year. Even after the first year, too much juice can cause nutritional problems. In one study, eight children from 14 to 27 months of age who were malnourished were found to be drinking 12 to 30 ounces of fruit juice every day. This accounted for 25% to 60% of their daily calories. After reducing their juice consumption to four ounces (120 ml) or less a day, giving iron supplements, and improving their diets, the children began growing normally. The researchers concluded that too much fruit juice can displace the foods children need for normal growth (Smith and Lifshitz 1994).

Publications for Parents

Boehle, Debbie. *Your Baby's First Solid Food.* Schaumburg, Illinois: La Leche League International, 1993. Publication No. 105a.

Gotsch, Gwen. Breastfeeding Pure & Simple. Schaumburg, Illinois: La Leche League International, 1993, pp. 97-100.

La Leche League International. The Womanly Art of Breastfeeding, 35th Anniversary ed. Schaumburg, Illinois, 1991, Chapter 13, "Ready for Solids," pp. 239-48.

Sears, William. Growing Together. Schaumburg, Illinois, 1987, Chapter 4, "Feeding Your Baby," pp. 93-96.

References

Birch, L. et al. The variability of young children's energy intake. *N Eng J Med* 1991; 324(4):232-35.

Borresen, H. Rethinking current recommendations to introduce solid food between four and six months to exclusively breastfeeding infants. *J Hum Lact* 1995; 11(3):201-04.

Cohen, R. et al. Effects of age of introduction of complementary foods on infant breast milk intake, total energy intake,and growth: a randomised intervention in Honduras. *Lancet* 1994; 344:288-93.

Committee on Nutrition, American Academy of Pediatrics. On the feeding of supplemental foods to infants. *Pediatrics* 1980; 65:1178.

Duncan, B. et al. Exclusive breast-feeding for at least 4 months protects against otitis media. *Pediatrics* 1993; 91(5):867-72.

Duncan, B. et al. Iron and the exclusively breast-fed infant from birth to six months. *J Ped Gastro Nutr* 1985; 4:412-25.

Keane, V. et al. Do solids help baby sleep through the night? *Am J Dis Child* 1988; 142:404-05.

Lawrence, R. *Breastfeeding: A Guide for the Medical Profession*, 4th ed. St. Louis: Mosby, 1994. pp. 124, 269, 302, 312-14, and 815.

Macknin, M., et al. Infant sleep and bedtime cereal. *Am J Dis Child* 1989; 143:1066-68.

McMillan, J. et al. Iron sufficiency in breast-fed infants and the availability of iron from human milk. *Pediatrics* 1976; 58:686-91.

Merchant, S. Neural development for sucking, swallowing and chewing. In Ballabriga, A. Rey, J., *Weaning: what, why, and when?* Workshop Series, vol. 11, New York: Raven Press, 1987.

Pisacane, A. et al. Iron status in breast-fed infants. *J Pediatr* 1995; 127(3):429-31.

Riordan, J. and Auerbach, K. *Breastfeeding and Human Lactation*, Boston and London: Jones and Bartlett, 1993, pp. 42-43, 115, and 476-80.

Saarinen, U. M. et al. Iron absorption in infants: high bioavailability of breast milk iron as indicated by the extrinsic tag method of iron absorption and by the concentration of serum ferritin. *J Pediatr* 1977; 91(1):36-39.

Siimes, M. et al. Exclusive breast-feeding for nine months: risk of iron deficiency. *J Pediatr* 1984; 104:196-99.

Smith, M. and Lifshitz, F. Excess fruit juice consumption as a contributing factor in nonorganic failure to thrive. *Pediatrics* 1994; 93(2):438-43.

Sullivan, S. and Birch, L. Infant dietary experience and acceptance of solid foods. *Pediatrics* 1994; 93(2):271-77.

Vuori, E. et al. The effects of the dietary intakes of copper, iron, manganese, and zinc on the trace element content of human milk. *Am J Clin Nutr* 1980; 33:227-31.

Woodruff, C. et al. Iron nutrition in the breast-fed infant. *J Pediatr* 1977; 90:36-38.

Taylor, B. et al. Transient IgA deficiency and pathogenesis of infantile atopy. *Lancet* 1973; ii:111-13.

Starting Solids

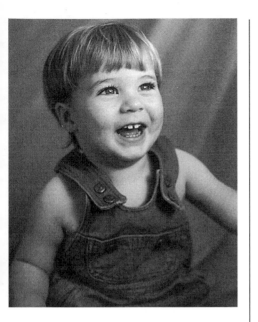

8

Weaning

THE MOTHER'S FEELINGS AND THE DECISION TO WEAN

APPROACHES TO WEANING
    Partial Weaning
    Abrupt Weaning
    Planned Weaning
    Natural Weaning

IF THE BABY REFUSES TO BREASTFEED

PHYSICAL CHANGES THAT OCCUR WITH WEANING

THE MOTHER'S FEELINGS AND THE DECISION TO WEAN

Weaning starts when the baby begins to take anything other than the breast; it is a natural stage in a baby's development. But each mother must decide for herself when she and her baby are ready to take that step. Ideally, the mother will base her decision on her and her baby's needs, not on the expectations of others.

The mother may feel hesitant to ask about weaning and vulnerable to criticism. It is important to acknowledge and accept her feelings and answer her questions.

Some mothers hesitate to ask specific questions about weaning because they are afraid of being judged unfavorably. Be aware that the mother may be feeling vulnerable to criticism. Her feelings must be acknowledged and accepted and her questions answered.

If the mother is sure she wants to wean, this should be respected. This is not the time to point out that continued breastfeeding will keep mother and baby close or to mention its other benefits. However, it is always good to affirm the value of what she has given her child by breastfeeding, no matter how long she has nursed her baby.

When a mother brings up weaning, it may not mean that she is ready to wean, only that she is curious about it and wants more information.

When a mother asks for information about weaning, first give her the information she wants and then ask about her circumstances and her feelings.

The mother who is ready to wean may approach it with mixed feelings. She may find herself wanting to wean and yet being torn between the improvement she expects to see in her life and the fear of depriving her child. Once you have shared with her the specific information she wants, help the mother clarify her own feelings by discussing with her:

- **Her feelings about weaning.** Why does she want to wean? How do others around her feel about it? Is she feeling pressured by someone?

  The mother's feelings about weaning will be a factor in how weaning proceeds. If she is feeling guilty and worried, for example, this may make the child anxious and result in him wanting to nurse more often. On the other hand, if she is feeling confident about her decision and is able to give of herself lovingly to her child in other ways, then her child may have fewer difficulties with weaning.

- **What changes or improvements does she feel weaning will bring about, and are these realistic?** Some mothers believe that weaning will make their child less dependent on them or will make him stop waking at night. Such a mother needs to know in advance that her expectations are unrealistic. In fact, she should know that a baby's fussiness or demands for attention will usually increase, at least temporarily, when a major change such as weaning takes place.

- **Her child's need for nursing.** Talk with her about possible replacements for nursing and how she feels about these. It is important to emphasize that for the older baby and toddler breastfeeding is more than milk, it is also a source of comfort as well as physical and emotional closeness. A child who has been nursing often may have a strong sucking need and may be happier if another outlet for sucking is provided after weaning.

- **What weaning will involve.** Discuss the practical details of a planned weaning at her child's age and stage of development. So that the mother can make an informed decision, be sure she knows about natural weaning, as many mothers are not aware of this option. (See "Natural Weaning" in this chapter.)

Encourage the mother to talk over these considerations and decisions with other family members who may be able to help her and support her during and after weaning.

Mothers are sometimes told to wean when it may not be necessary.

Weaning is sometimes recommended when it is not necessary. For example:

The mother is feeling overwhelmed by caring for her baby. An overwhelmed breastfeeding mother may be told by others that weaning will make life easier for her. Assure her that life with a small baby is a challenge no matter how he is fed and that formula-feeding is not likely to be an answer to her problem. Listen to and acknowledge her feelings before offering information.

The baby's teeth begin to erupt. It is a common misconception that when a baby's teeth come in it is time for him to wean. In most human cultures, however, babies nurse not for months, but for years—long after the baby's teeth have erupted.

The mother develops mastitis. In nearly all cases, a mother who has mastitis should continue nursing rather than wean. In fact, weaning is usually the worst thing a mother in this situation can do, because if her affected breast becomes overly full, her mastitis can worsen into an abscess—a more serious health problem. Contrary to what some mothers are told, the milk of a mother with mastitis is not "bad" for her baby. (See "Mastitis—Plugged Ducts and Breast Infections" in the chapter "Breast Problems.")

Weaning

The mother is planning to return to work. Despite what many women are told, it is possible to breastfeed when mother and baby are regularly separated, and it may even be easier than bottle-feeding, especially during the time they are together. (See the chapter "Employment and Breastfeeding.")

The mother is prescribed a drug or needs to undergo a diagnostic test for which weaning is recommended. Most drugs and diagnostic tests are compatible with breastfeeding. If not, substitutes can often be found. (See the section, "When the Doctor Recommends Weaning" in the chapter "Drugs, Vitamins, Vaccines, and Diagnostic Tests.")

Mother or baby is ill and/or hospitalized. Weaning is not recommended (and may be contraindicated) if the baby is ill or hospitalized, because a sick baby needs the anti-infective properties of his mother's milk. Weaning should be avoided during an already stressful situation such as illness or hospitalization.

If the mother is ill, before a decision about breastfeeding is made, it is important to consider the health complications that can occur with abrupt weaning—such as mastitis. In most cases, breastfeeding can continue. (See the chapter "Health Problems—Mother.")

The mother is pregnant. Although many women choose to wean during pregnancy due to discomforts such as sore nipples, in a normal pregnancy there are no overriding physical reasons to wean. Breastfeeding will not be harmful to the baby growing *in utero,* although the mother may choose to eat more nutrient-dense foods in order to provide for herself and her two growing children. (See the chapter "Pregnancy and Tandem Nursing.")

Mothers' feelings about weaning vary, depending on several factors.

Weaning is a significant change in the way the mother and her baby interact with each other. Like any other major change, there is a whole collection of feelings that tend to go along with it.

In general, mothers' feelings about weaning depend upon:

The age of the child. In one study, researchers found that 65% of the women who weaned at three months or earlier wished they had nursed longer and that more than half of the women who weaned at four to six months were sorry they had weaned their babies so young (Rogers 1987).

A mother's perception of how long is long enough will vary depending upon her cultural norms and her own feelings about breastfeeding. In the US, many mothers set breastfeeding goals of between three and twelve months. In non-Western cultures, a mother may expect to breastfeed for two or three years or longer.

In her book, MOTHERING YOUR NURSING TODDLER (1982), Norma Jane Bumgarner acknowledges the symbiotic nature of breastfeeding, which causes mothers, as well as their babies, to feel frustration and sadness at a premature weaning. After reading letters about nursing from hundreds of La Leche League members and Leaders, she concluded that the mothers who most consistently expressed a sense of loss about weaning were those who weaned before their babies turned two. She says:

> *When nursing continues past two or three, mothers much less frequently describe weaning in the same mixed terms. It seems that a time comes in the growth of the mother-child relationship when it is easier for both to move on and leave baby things behind.*

How weaning came about. When the weaning is a gradual and positive experience for both her child and herself, a mother tends to feel more positively about it. A negative, abrupt, or premature weaning is more likely to leave a mother with regrets.

The closeness of a mother's relationship with her child before, during, and after weaning. Even in the face of a difficult or premature weaning, a strong mother-child relationship can help temper a mother's feelings about weaning.

If the mother is feeling pressured to wean by others, ask her about her own feelings and explore with her how she might handle others' comments.

Some mothers need help in coping with pressures from others about nursing. The closer her relationship with the person pressuring her, the more challenging the situation and the more important it is for them to come to some understanding.

The baby's father. It is especially difficult when the baby's father is pressuring the mother to wean, as the mother may feel herself torn between the two people she loves most. Ask the mother why, in her opinion, he wants her to wean. Some fathers feel jealous or threatened by the intensity of the breastfeeding relationship. Others want more of the mother's time and attention and think that if someone else could give a bottle, it would be easier to find time together.

Suggest that she find some time to talk it through. She can begin by acknowledging that his feelings are important to her and that she knows that he is as concerned as she is about what is best for their child. Then she can talk about her own feelings and opinions about nursing, while listening also to what he has to say.

By taking time to talk about it, and allowing time for him to consider what she has to say and think about it without feeling threatened, the mother increases her chances that he may begin to understand her feelings.

If the father is willing, it may also be helpful to meet with other breastfeeding families, so that he can ask other couples how they fit breastfeeding comfortably into their lives.

If the baby's father continues to apply pressure to wean, ask the mother if a partial weaning may satisfy both their needs. (See "Partial Weaning" in this chapter.)

Family and friends. If relatives are not comfortable with breastfeeding, it may be helpful for the mother to begin—when her baby is small—by breastfeeding discreetly when she is with them.

As with an unsupportive husband, it may also help if the mother acknowledges her relative's concern about her child and their mutual desire to do what's best for him. The mother can also assure the relative that she hopes to have his or her support. Then she can explain about some of the benefits of breastfeeding, so the relative will understand that the mother has made an informed decision. If offered sincerely, compliments about the other person's parenting can be another good way to deflect or prevent criticism.

Sometimes a female relative's reservations about breastfeeding stem from residual bad feelings left over from her own breastfeeding experience. Suggest the mother ask her relative about her own experience, offering her empathy and understanding if she stopped breastfeeding prematurely and was left with feelings of failure.

Also, it may help the mother to keep in mind that some parents feel threatened when others make choices different from their own. Rather than accepting that different choices may be best for different children and different families, they may believe that their way is right for everyone and any other way is therefore wrong. In a case like this, it may be best to agree to disagree and drop the subject.

With friends, as with relatives, there may be a desire to convince everyone to do things "their way." Ideally, in a stable friendship, a friend will be able to understand or accept the other's feelings and decisions when given the chance.

Strangers. The mother may not have the luxury of time to get into long discussions with those outside her family and circle of friends and acquaintances. In this case, humor is sometimes best. When asked while breastfeeding, "How long do you plan to nurse him?" one mother replied, "Oh, about another five minutes." Another mother of a nursing toddler always answered strangers' questions by saying, "We're working on weaning now."

Weaning

Cultural expectations about weaning vary. When all human cultures are considered, two to four years of breastfeeding is the norm.

In most periods of history and in most parts of the world, babies have been breastfed for years rather than months—two to four years being the general norm, according to Margaret Mead and Niles Newton (1967).

It was not until 1800 that most of the popular English writings on child care recommended weaning as young as twelve months. Even in 1725 writers commented on nursing four-year-olds with disapproval, an indication that a significant number of eighteenth-century four-year-olds were still breastfeeding. By 1850 most "experts" were recommending weaning by eleven months. By then it was the nursing two-year-olds who drew official censure. These changes in recommended patterns of child care closely parallel other changes in family life that occurred during the Industrial Revolution in England and the United States.

In other cultures around the world, extended nursing continued for much longer and in some places is still common. Until early in this century, mothers in China and Japan still nursed their little ones for four or five years. A study done in 1945 of sixty-four primitive cultures found only one in which it was clear that a child was ever weaned as young as six months (Mead and Newton 1967).

In an effort to determine the "natural" age of human weaning, independent of cultural considerations, Katherine A. Dettwyler, an anthropologist at Texas A & M University, researched what is known about the weaning ages of primates and other mammals (1994). After examining the criteria used to estimate other mammals' natural weaning age, such as weight gain, relationship to adult body size, relationship to gestational length, and age of eruption of permanent teeth, Dettwyler estimated an appropriate age for human weaning to be between three and seven years.

Although understanding nursing practices of other mammals and other times and places is interesting and offers a broader perspective, it will not necessarily influence a mother's feelings about breastfeeding her own baby at whatever age he is. It can, however, reassure her that—because it appears to be the human norm—extended nursing is not harmful to the growing child.

APPROACHES TO WEANING

Gradual weaning is easiest for both mother and baby.

Whether the weaning is the mother's or baby's choice, gradual weaning will be easiest on them both. If a mother wants to initiate weaning, suggest that she plan to do so gradually. Eliminating one feeding daily no more often than every two or three days allows the mother's milk supply to decrease slowly, without fullness and discomfort. It also gives the mother the opportunity to make sure her baby receives extra loving attention as a substitute for the closeness they shared while nursing.

The practical details of weaning will depend upon the age of the child and the approach the mother takes.

If the baby is younger than about nine months old, weaning primarily involves substituting bottles for breastfeeding (although, since a baby sometimes nurses for comfort, he will probably not need a bottle as often as he was nursed). A mother needs to consult her baby's doctor before starting to give her baby formula.

If the baby is nine months to a year old and is drinking well from a cup and eating other foods, and the mother does not want to use bottles, she may be able to substitute other foods and drinks for breastfeeding, although she should consult her baby's doctor about this.

The planned weaning of a toddler can be a positive experience if the mother is able to find mutually acceptable alternatives to breastfeeding, such as changing routines and anticipating nursings by offering substitutions and distractions. Sometimes bargaining and postponement can also be used with the older nursling.

In a natural weaning, the mother simply encourages her child in his natural growth toward independence and offers mutually acceptable alternatives to nursings as opportunities arise. The mother may need reassurance that her child will wean eventually.

Partial Weaning

If the mother is unhappy with breastfeeding, ask her if it would help to eliminate some nursings or, if her child is at least a year old, to shorten nursings.

When the mother wants to wean because she is unhappy with breastfeeding, ask her if it would help to eliminate certain feedings. It may not be breastfeeding itself that is difficult for a mother, but one or two specific nursing times. Or, if she is nursing a toddler, it may be that nursings last so long that she becomes impatient.

Partial weaning is an alternative to total weaning. The mother may need to consult her baby's doctor about what to substitute for her milk.

Partial weaning allows a mother to eliminate a certain nursing or nursings just as if she were beginning a total weaning, but continue to breastfeed for the rest of the feedings.

If her baby is younger than one year, she should consult with her baby's doctor about what to substitute for her milk. If the baby is exclusively breastfeeding, the mother would need to substitute a formula-feeding for the eliminated breastfeeding. If the baby is drinking well from a cup and is eating other foods, she may be able to substitute other foods or drinks for the eliminated breastfeeding.

For the mother of a breastfeeding toddler, partial weaning may mean cutting down on the length of nursings.

If the mother is unhappy about the length of nursings and her child is older than one year and is eating other foods, she might be able to persuade the child to do something besides nursing after a certain amount of time at the breast. (Cutting nursing time short would be inappropriate for a younger baby because it could result in an inadequate weight gain.) Or she might try offering more frequent, shorter nursing times to see if that might make her feel better about breastfeeding.

Partial weaning can be permanent or temporary.

Partial weaning is one option when a mother is feeling overwhelmed. Another benefit is that it doesn't have to be permanent. The mother may decide later that she wants to go back to breastfeeding more frequently.

Abrupt Weaning

Abrupt weaning is most difficult for both mother and baby.

Although it is sometimes unavoidable—such as in the case of a mother with cancer who must begin chemotherapy without delay—abrupt weaning is most difficult for both mother and baby. There are several reasons for this.

Physical discomfort and potential health complications for mother. Even though a mother stops nursing, her body will continue to produce milk. If some of the milk is not removed, she will become overly full and engorged, which may lead to mastitis or a breast abscess.

Sudden hormonal changes in the mother, which may bring on or worsen depression. The hormone prolactin, which is released during breastfeeding, has been associated with a feeling of well-being. An abrupt weaning will cause a sudden drop in a mother's prolactin levels. During the first few months after birth when a mother's prolactin levels are highest, this may result in feelings of sadness and depression.

These hormonal changes can be particularly overwhelming for a mother who is prone to depression (Susman and Katz 1988). A woman with serious psychiatric problems may be at even greater risk.

Support for continued breastfeeding or assistance with a gradual weaning should be considered an important part of the mother's treatment for depression. If the baby must be taken off the breast immediately, an automatic or semi-automatic electric breast pump can be used to decrease the mother's milk supply slowly, making the hormonal changes more gradual. If the mother chooses to use hand-expression or a manual pump, be sure that she has had enough practice to become skilled at this method. If a gradual weaning is not possible, it is important for the mother's doctor to be aware of the possible effects of an abrupt weaning on her depression. For more information, see "The Mother with Pospartum Depression" in the chapter "Health Problems—Mother."

Weaning

Emotional trauma for the baby. Nursing is more than just a method of feeding. It is also a familiar source of closeness and comfort. Eliminating nursing abruptly may leave a baby feeling as though his mother has withdrawn her love as well as her breast. Gradual weaning, on the other hand, allows the mother to gradually substitute other kinds of attention and affection to compensate for the loss of nursing.

If the mother is considering abrupt weaning, help her explore her feelings and alternatives.

A mother who is considering an abrupt weaning may be feeling pressured and overwhelmed. Whatever her situation, first and foremost listen actively to help the mother clarify her own feelings before offering information.

Ask the mother how much time she has in which to wean. Weaning should occur as slowly as the situation permits.

Ask the mother how much time she has in which to wean. The more time she has, the less abrupt and more gradual the process can be, and the easier it will be for both her and her baby.

Help the mother tailor her weaning plan to her timetable and her baby's nursing pattern. For example, if the mother has five days to wean her three-month-old baby who breastfeeds ten times a day, suggest she begin by replacing two nursings per day with two bottle-feedings, expressing just enough milk when she feels full to relieve any discomfort. If the mother has only two days to wean, suggest she begin by eliminating every other nursing the first day, expressing just enough milk from her breasts to feel comfortable. The following day she can eliminate the rest of the nursings, continuing to express for comfort.

Keep in mind that the baby will probably not need a bottle as often as he was nursed, so that the final number of bottle-feedings will be fewer than the number of times the baby was breastfeeding.

The age of the baby will determine what the mother substitutes for breastfeeding.

If the mother is weaning a baby under a year old who is not drinking well from a cup, she will need to ask her baby's doctor about giving him a bottle and what should be in it.

If the mother is weaning an older baby or toddler who is drinking well from a cup and eating other foods, the mother may be able to replace nursings with other foods or drinks, as well as extra attention and affection. (See the next section on planned weaning for practical suggestions for making weaning easier for the older baby and toddler.)

In order to avoid health complications during an abrupt weaning, suggest the mother express enough milk to feel comfortable, wear a firm—but not binding—bra, restrict salt, and drink to thirst.

Women who wean abruptly are often afraid to relieve their discomfort by expressing milk for fear of encouraging their breasts to make more milk. However, expressing some milk—just enough to relieve fullness but not as much as the baby would take at a feeding—is the most helpful thing a mother can do. Even a few drops may be enough to make the mother more comfortable. The purpose of expressing milk is to alleviate discomfort and to prevent undue accumulation of milk in the ducts, which could lead to mastitis.

If her baby had been nursing about every two hours, the mother may be comfortable expressing her milk every three hours or so to relieve fullness in the beginning. The frequency of expression should be determined by the mother's comfort.

A hot shower or bath is a good preliminary to expressing some milk, as the warm water may help relax the mother and stimulate her let-down. At first the mother may need to express a small amount of milk several times during the day. She may also need to express at night, if she awakens in discomfort. Some women find that ice packs applied to their breasts provide some relief from swelling.

If the mother has problems with leaking, suggest she use nursing pads to absorb leaking milk.

During this time, it may also make the mother more comfortable to wear a firm bra for support. One size larger than usual may be necessary. **Caution: Binding the breasts has not been proven effective by research; it may intensify a mother's discomfort.** Any consistent pressure on the breasts can cause plugged ducts or breast infections.

There is no need for the mother to restrict her fluid intake. The same guideline applies as when she was nursing: drink to thirst.

Since salt causes the body to retain fluids, it may be helpful for the mother to restrict her salt intake until her feelings of fullness are gone.

By gradually expressing her milk less and less often, the mother's milk supply will slowly decrease. Within a couple of weeks she will no longer need to express her milk.

"Dry-up" medication is no longer recommended, as it can have serious side effects.

The use of bromocriptine (Parlodel), a prolactin suppressant, is no longer sanctioned for use as a "dry-up" medication due to increasing reports of serious adverse drug reactions, such as strokes and seizures, including several deaths (FDA 1994). This drug was never effective at reducing milk supply beyond the postpartum period.

Encourage the mother to give her baby extra attention and physical affection while weaning to help compensate for the loss of the closeness of breastfeeding.

Many mothers feel the urge to distance themselves from their babies or toddlers while weaning for fear the child will insist on nursing. However, the child needs reassurance that his mother still loves him. Extra attention and physical affection will help give him this reassurance and help compensate for the loss of breastfeeding. The use of a sling or baby carrier may help a mother keep her baby close.

Once the feeling of fullness is gone, it is normal for the mother's breasts to contain some milk for several months or even for years.

So that the mother does not become needlessly alarmed, be sure she knows that after she has stopped expressing and the feeling of fullness is gone, her breasts will continue to contain milk for some time. It is normal for a nursing mother to have some milk in her breasts for several months or even years after she has stopped breastfeeding.

Planned Weaning

Planned weaning is when the mother decides to stop breastfeeding before receiving cues from her baby that he is ready to stop. Ideally, the mother will approach the weaning process with flexibility and sensitivity to her baby's needs and feelings.

Planned weaning will be easiest on mother and baby if it is gradual—eliminating a daily nursing no more often than once every two or three days.	A gradual weaning is easier on both mother and baby than an abrupt weaning. Weaning gradually—eliminating one daily nursing every two or three days—allows the mother's milk supply to decrease slowly, without fullness and discomfort. It also gives the mother time to make sure her baby is adjusting well to the change and to give her baby the extra loving attention he needs as a substitute for the closeness they shared while nursing.
The planned weaning of a baby younger than about nine months involves primarily substituting bottles of formula for breastfeeding.	If the baby is younger than about nine months old, planned weaning primarily involves substituting bottles of formula for some of the times the baby was breastfed. A baby will probably not need a bottle as often as he was nursed.

If the baby is nine months to a year old and is drinking well from a cup and eating other foods, the mother may be able to substitute other foods and drinks for breastfeeding, although she should consult her baby's doctor about this.

Weaning

Breastfeeding fosters a special emotional closeness between mother and baby, so encourage the mother to provide her baby with extra attention and physical contact during a planned weaning to help compensate for the loss of breastfeeding.

To make the planned weaning of an older baby or toddler a positive experience, the mother needs to consider her child's feelings and find substitutes for nursing that are mutually acceptable.	The planned weaning of an older baby or toddler can be a positive experience if the mother considers her child's feelings throughout the process. Although the older baby or toddler continues to enjoy the nutritional benefits of his mother's milk, the physical and emotional closeness of breastfeeding takes on greater significance as he grows, and this must be provided in other ways in order for a planned weaning to go well.

Also, because the older baby or toddler is a more active partner in the breastfeeding relationship—as he is in all aspects of his daily routine—it is common for him to develop preferences about nursing. As weaning progresses, encourage the mother to consider her child's feelings and preferences. Suggest that when choosing the next step of weaning the mother consider how her child handled the last.

Practical techniques, such as "don't offer, don't refuse," changes in routine, distraction, substitution, postponement, and bargaining, can help the mother find mutually acceptable substitutes for nursing.	The mother who has decided to wean her older baby or toddler may want practical techniques for phasing out breastfeeding in a positive way. Every mother and child couple is different, so encourage the mother to experiment with these methods to find which of them work best for her and her child.

Don't offer, don't refuse. This is a safe and effective weaning technique. The mother breastfeeds whenever the child asks, but does not offer to nurse when the child does not ask. When "don't offer, don't refuse" is used alone, it is not possible to predict how long weaning will take. When used along with the following methods, however, it can help accelerate the weaning process.

Changing daily routines. Most children have certain times and places they ask to nurse. Ask the mother about her child's breastfeeding patterns and brainstorm with her about ways to change her usual routine so that he will not be reminded to nurse as frequently. For example, if he usually asks to nurse when the mother sits down in her favorite chair, she might avoid that chair (or even sitting down!) while she is weaning him.

Fathers can be helpful, too. If the child typically asks to nurse upon waking in the morning, suggest the father be the one to get the child up and bring him to breakfast, making sure that there is something for the child to eat and drink there. (His favorite food might make this change more acceptable.)

Anticipating nursings and offering substitutions and distractions. Some children tend to nurse at certain times of day. If the mother has a general idea of her child's nursing pattern, she might offer a special snack and drink right before a usual nursing time and then take the child out to his favorite place, such as a playground or a friend's house, as a further distraction. When food is used as a substitute for nursing, encourage the mother to use healthy, whole foods that she would be happy to have her child eating.

Other possible distractions include: reading to the child, a new toy, walking and/or singing to the child, outings, bicycle rides, visits from other children.

Distractions are more effective with some children than with others. Some toddlers tend to nurse more often when they are at home with nothing in particular to do and to nurse less frequently when they are out and distracted by new surroundings. For this type of child, the mother might choose to spend as much of the day as possible outside the home in an environment that is interesting to the child. Other toddlers nurse more when they feel overwhelmed by their surroundings. For a child like this, the mother may decide to stay home more and keep distractions to a minimum.

Once the child has asked to nurse, distraction and substitution are far less likely to be effective. They work best when they are offered before the child thinks of breastfeeding.

Postponement. Another effective technique for encouraging weaning is for the mother to postpone breastfeeding whenever she feels her child can handle the delay. If the child nurses irregularly, this may be more practical than trying to eliminate a particular nursing. A drawback, however, is that this will only be comfortable for the child if he is old enough to accept waiting. With some children, this method—which over time may make them feel as though their mother is keeping them at arm's length—will make them even more determined to nurse.

Shortening the length of the nursings. Before eliminating nursings, ask the mother if she would like to try breastfeeding the child whenever he asks but not to nurse as long. This method is usually most effective with children older than two and may serve as a good beginning to a planned weaning. As with all of these techniques, however, encourage the mother to use only those methods that work well with her child.

Bargaining. This can sometimes be used with the older nursling. A child who is close to weaning naturally may be persuaded to give up breastfeeding earlier by mutual agreement, but most children younger than three years old do not have the maturity and perspective to understand the meaning of a promise.

There are many factors that influence how weaning will proceed, including the mother's feelings about weaning.

The relationship the mother and child share, their temperaments, and the child's stage of development will all be factors in how weaning will proceed.

The mother's feelings about weaning will also be a factor—whether she gives of herself lovingly to her child and feels warm, friendly, and cheerful is important. If the mother is feeling guilty about weaning or about pushing weaning too hard, she might find it more difficult to be as loving with her child. This may make the child anxious, and he may demand to nurse more often. If the mother cannot be confident and comfortable with her decision to wean and continue to mother her child lovingly during the process, then her child is likely to have difficulties with weaning.

Encourage the mother to be flexible about weaning.

One of the benefits of a gradual, planned weaning—as opposed to an abrupt weaning—is that the mother can be flexible. Weaning is a big change for both mother and child. There is no advantage to rushing, as it takes time to adjust to change.

Certain nursings may be more important to the child than others. If so, the mother can continue those until the end and allow the child to give them up last. If her child clings to these nursings even after he has given up the others, the mother has the option of continuing to nurse him at those times for a while. Weaning doesn't have to be an "all or nothing" process. For example, some children react strongly to the idea of giving up their nursing at naptime or bedtime. The mother may decide to continue nursing her child to sleep until he is more comfortable giving up those last breastfeedings.

Encourage the mother to be attentive to her child's reactions. For example, when he is ill, he may want to nurse more often. Assure the mother that she can always resume weaning when her child feels better. Or the mother may find that one method is more effective than another; that is, the child may be unhappy with postponement, but do well with distraction and substitution.

Certain behaviors are signs that weaning may be going too fast for the child.

If the child becomes upset and cries or insists upon nursing even when the mother tries to distract him or comfort him in other ways, this may be a sign that weaning is going too fast for the child or that different strategies would be more effective.

Even when the child does not protest at his mother's weaning methods, there are other signs that weaning may be moving too fast. These could be changes or regressions in behavior, such as:

Weaning

- stuttering,
- night-waking,
- an increase in clinginess during the day,
- a new attachment to an object like a stuffed animal or a blanket,
- a new or increased fear of separation,
- biting—when it has never occurred before.

Physical symptoms such as stomach upsets and constipation are other signs that weaning may be going too quickly for the child.

Weaning may or may not be responsible for these changes in behavior. If these behaviors concern the mother, she can try suspending her efforts at weaning for a while and see if the behavior disappears. If the mother notices these behaviors but does not want to slow down her weaning efforts, encourage her to find other ways to meet her child's need for closeness.

If the mother's breasts are uncomfortably full or she is feeling overwhelmed, these may be signs that weaning is moving too fast for her.

Another measure of whether weaning is going too fast is its effect upon the mother. An obvious physical sign is when the mother's breasts become uncomfortably full.

Another sign is when the mother spends large portions of her day and night working hard to keep her child happy without nursing. This can be exhausting and the mother may begin to feel resentful that weaning is taking so much from her. If the mother is feeling overwhelmed or resentful, this can make it harder for her child to cope with weaning.

Each mother will need to evaluate whether what she hopes to gain by weaning is worth the effort she is expending. But if she is feeling strained, it may be time to take another look. This may also be a time to enlist more help from the baby's father and find times during the day when she can meet her own needs.

Some mothers change their minds about weaning during the process.

Sometimes a mother finds during the course of weaning that she has changed her mind. Perhaps her child did not respond well to her efforts to wean, or perhaps she decided she was not ready to give up breastfeeding. In any case, assure the mother that she should do what she feels is best and that she can always try again later.

Some children have a strong need to suck and may find another outlet for sucking after they are weaned.

During or after a planned weaning, it is not unusual for the child to find another outlet for sucking, such as thumbsucking. If the mother would prefer that her child use a bottle or a pacifier, she can offer this instead.

Natural Weaning

The age of weaning will vary from child to child, just like other developmental milestones.

Breastfeeding beyond the first year offers benefits to both mother and baby.

Advantages for Baby

The ages at which children learn to walk, get their first tooth, and learn to use the toilet vary enormously. The same is true for weaning. One child may naturally wean before age two, while another may be going strong at three.

There are many reasons one child may nurse longer than another. One child may have a very strong sucking need. Another may have a great need for closeness and body contact. Still another may have an unrecognized allergy or other physical problem. Natural weaning allows for differences in children by letting them grow at their own rate and give up breastfeeding when they are ready.

Although extended breastfeeding is not as common in Western societies as it is in others, breastfeeding beyond one year offers benefits to both mother and baby.

Breastfeeding for at least one year has been associated with better oral development in children. Breastfeeding provides a natural outlet for the child's non-nutritive sucking needs. The dental arch is wider in the breastfeeding baby, because the mouth and tongue action during nursing differs from bottle-feeding (Labbok and Hendershot 1987). Breastfeeding has been associated with earlier reading in boys and fewer speech problems (Broad 1983).

Research suggests that breastfeeding toddlers enjoy better health. The immunological ingredients of human milk have been found to remain high throughout the first and second years of breastfeeding (Goldman 1983), and studies on toddler health confirm that receiving these immunities confers significant health benefits. Breastfeeding toddlers between sixteen and thirty months old have been found to have fewer types and durations of illness and to require less medical care than their non-breastfeeding age mates (Gulick 1986). Children still breastfeeding at age three have been found to have fewer episodes of illness and lower rates of specific types of illnesses than those weaned earlier (van den Bogaard 1991). In the developing world the health benefits of extended breastfeeding can make the difference between life and death. In Guinea-Bissau, weaned children age one to three years had a mortality rate three-and-a-half times higher than those who were still nursing (Molbak 1994).

Breastfeeding gives comfort when a toddler is tired, upset, ill, or hurt.

Human milk is a readily digested and accepted source of nourishment for a sick child. An older baby or toddler can revert to complete breastfeeding if necessary during an illness, even when other foods cannot be tolerated.

Human milk provides a nutritional cushion for the allergic child, who may need its protection for a longer time in order to develop a tolerance for other foods.

The closeness of breastfeeding enhances the child's relationship with his mother and provides emotional stability during a time of fast growth and development. Allowing a child to wean at his own pace is an expression of trust. It contributes to his self-esteem by letting him wean when it is developmentally right for him.

Advantages for Mother

The child-spacing effect of breastfeeding may continue during the baby's second year. When exclusive breastfeeding is followed by a gradual introduction of solid foods, breastfeeding may continue to suppress fertility during the baby's second year. How long a mother's fertility is suppressed varies from woman to woman and depends on several factors, including how many times a day she nurses, as well as her individual physical makeup. (See "Breastfeeding, Sexuality, and Contraception" in the chapter "Sexuality, Fertility, and Contraception.")

The hormones of breastfeeding continue to relax the mother. For many mothers, the relaxing effect of breastfeeding makes daily life with a toddler more enjoyable.

Breastfeeding guarantees physical closeness. Once a baby begins walking, daily life becomes more hectic for both mother and toddler. If they are still breastfeeding, they are guaranteed that every day they will spend some time relaxing together.

Breastfeeding is an easy way to give comfort. Because breastfeeding gives comfort to a toddler when he is tired, upset, sick, or hurt, extended breastfeeding can make mothering a toddler easier during those often trying times. Continued breast-feeding may also help ease the transition from waking to sleeping at naps and bedtimes. Also, the mother who weans naturally never has to cope with an unhappy child resisting her efforts to wean.

For many mothers, the major challenge of natural weaning is coping
with others' opinions. The mother may
want some suggestions for dealing
with social pressure.

Some mothers need help in coping with pressures from others about extended breastfeeding. The closer her relationship with her critic, the more challenging the situation is, and the more important it is for them to come to some under-standing. (See the first section in this chapter "The Mother's Feelings and the Deci-sion to Wean.")

Weaning

If the mother wants to continue nursing despite a lack of support from her spouse, family, and friends, suggest she contact La Leche League. One researcher (Buckley 1992) interviewed ten US mothers to examine their perceptions about extended breastfeeding and the role of social support on their decision. These women, who nursed their children until they were ready to wean, listed La Leche League as their main source of support and "having to defend self" as the single biggest challenge of extended breastfeeding.

The mother of a nursing toddler may
be able to keep their breastfeeding
relationship private, even in public, by
planning ahead.

Some mothers feel hesitant about natural weaning because they are concerned about others' opinions and the possibility that their child may embarrass them by asking to nurse in public. By planning ahead, the mother may be able to breast-feed discreetly or avoid breastfeeding outside the home, allowing them to keep breastfeeding private.

Carefully choose her clothes. Some mothers find certain coverups—such as ponchos or shawls—allow them to breastfeed their toddlers in public without anyone else knowing. Other mothers wear special nursing clothing with small openings so that their breastfeeding toddlers cannot overexpose them while they are nursing.

The mother may want to keep in mind what kind of fastener her child knows how to use. That way she can avoid being unzipped by a skillful child when she least expects it.

Choose an acceptable "code word" for nursing. Encourage the mother to find a special word her child can use for nursing that she will not find embarrassing when it is spoken clearly in public. Although there is nothing wrong with the child asking to "nurse," as the child grows, the mother may not want everyone in earshot to understand what he is asking for. Some families use variations of the word "nurse," such as "nanny" or "num-num." Others use words related to breastfeeding, such as "side" or "snuggle." An all-purpose word like "mama" could also be used. When the child shouts out, "I want mama!" in the middle of a restau-rant, no one would even turn around.

Be ready with substitutes and distractions. When the mother goes out with her breastfeeding toddler, she may want to bring along some substitutes, such as snacks and drinks, and distractions, such as toys or books. This can help her avoid breastfeeding in places where she would not be comfortable nursing.

Find a private place to nurse. It may not always be possible to distract the child, especially the younger toddler who does not have the patience to wait. In this case, the mother has the option of finding a private place to nurse. If she is visiting a disapproving relative or friend, she can excuse herself and her child to the bedroom. If they are at a shopping mall, a fitting room can be a private haven. The mother need not explain to others why her child needs her for a few minutes alone.

Limiting nursing to certain times and places. Some breastfeeding children are willing to accept limits to nursing and may be comfortable with their mothers' request that they nurse only when they are at home.

Another common concern is whether the breastfeeding toddler is nursing "too much" for his age.

Some nursing toddlers nurse only occasionally, such as to fall asleep or for comfort when they hurt themselves. Sometimes, however, a small child nurses much more avidly. If the mother feels her child wants to nurse "too much" for his age, help her evaluate what is happening in their lives. Ask the mother:

Does her child get a lot of other kinds of attention from her? Has her child spent more time away from her than he is comfortable with or is she home with him but busy with other projects? Is she spending a lot of time on the telephone? Sometimes a mother needs to evaluate her nursing relationship with her child and consider whether nursing has become a substitute for other kinds of attention the child needs. An older baby or toddler may want to nurse simply because he has nothing more interesting to do or because it is the only way to get his mother's attention. As he grows out of the infant stage, the child's need for his mother does not lessen, but it does change.

Is there any kind of major change happening—such as moving—or is the mother going through a stressful time? Children sense tension in the adults around them and any time of major change can make a child feel insecure, increasing his desire to seek comfort through nursing.

Is the child making great strides in some other area of growth or might he be ill? Might he have an ear infection, allergies, or other illness? Times of illness or periods of fast growth are other times children typically seek the familiar comfort of nursing more often.

When her child asks to nurse, if the mother is unsure that he really needs to nurse, she may choose to offer him something else, such as an apple or a story, and see what happens. If the child is happy with this, fine, but if he asks repeatedly or cries to nurse, this would indicate he feels a real need.

Occasionally, a baby may wean naturally before the mother wants or expects it.

Because all children mature according to their own developmental timetables, occasionally a child may wean naturally before the mother wants or expects it. If the mother was looking forward to extended nursing, this might leave her feeling disappointed and unfulfilled. Acknowledge the mother's feelings, but also congratulate her on meeting her child's needs so completely that he was ready to move on. The mother may need time to adjust her expectations and to appreciate the many other ways she can continue to be close to her child.

IF THE BABY REFUSES TO BREASTFEED

If the baby is refusing the breast and is younger than one year, it is unlikely he is weaning naturally and it may be possible for breastfeeding to be resumed.

If the baby younger than one year is refusing to nurse, it is unlikely that he is weaning naturally. See the chapter "Fussy at the Breast and Breast Refusal" to help the mother determine the cause of her baby's refusal and for suggestions on how to resume breastfeeding.

Natural weaning is usually gradual, but occasionally a child may wean naturally all at once.

A child who weans naturally usually weans gradually over a period of weeks or months. When a child abruptly stops nursing after he had been nursing many times a day, a "nursing strike" should first be considered, no matter what the age of the child. Unlike a child who weans naturally, a baby on a "nursing strike" is unhappy about the situation.

If the mother wants to resume breastfeeding, see the chapter "Fussy at the Breast and Breast Refusal" to try to determine the cause of the child's refusal and for suggestions for persuading the child to go back to breastfeeding.

Since every child is unique, it is possible for a sudden weaning to be a natural weaning. If this is the case, the mother's efforts to convince her child to resume breastfeeding will not work and she may need help comfortably decreasing her milk supply (see the previous section "Abrupt Weaning") and accepting her child's sudden step toward independence.

PHYSICAL CHANGES THAT OCCUR WITH WEANING

If the mother's menstrual cycles had not returned before weaning, she can expect them to resume after weaning.

The sucking of the baby at the breast is responsible for suppressing ovulation and therefore menstruation. If weaning occurs before the mother's menstrual cycles have returned, she can expect them to return after weaning. It is very likely that ovulation will occur prior to menstruation, and it is not unusual for the mother's cycles to be somewhat irregular for the first few months after weaning.

Weaning

Some mothers gain weight, others lose weight after weaning.

After weaning occurs, some mothers find that in order to avoid gaining weight, they must cut back on their food intake. Other mothers find that they lose a few pounds, perhaps due to a decreased appetite or a loss of extra water in their body tissues.

The mother's breasts may change after weaning.

After weaning, most mothers find that their breasts return to their pre-pregnancy size. It is also common for the areola to remain darker than before pregnancy and for the Montgomery glands to recede.

Some mothers' breasts become soft and flabby but gradually regain their firmness after several menstrual cycles. In rare cases, some mothers temporarily lose the fatty layer that was in their breasts before pregnancy. This fatty layer is gradually restored over time.

It is not unusual for the mother's breasts to continue producing a few drops of milk for weeks, months, or years after her child has weaned (Barker, p 792). A mother who frequently checks for milk may inadvertently cause a small supply to continue. The same is true for any other type of nipple stimulation.

Publications for Parents

Bumgarner, N. MOTHERING YOUR NURSING TODDLER. Schaumburg, Illinois: La Leche League International, 1982.

Huggins, K. and Ziedrich, L. *The Nursing Mother's Guide to Weaning*. Boston: Harvard Common Press, 1994.

La Leche League International. THE WOMANLY ART OF BREASTFEEDING, 35th Anniversary ed. Schaumburg, Illinois, 1991, Chapter 14, "Weaning Gradually, with Love," pp. 249-64.

Mohrbacher, N. *Approaches to Weaning*. Schaumburg, Illinois: La Leche League International, 1995. Publication No. 125a.

References

Barker, Burton, Lieve, eds. *Principles of Ambulatory Medicine*. Williams & Wilkins, 1982, p. 792.

Broad, F and Duganzich, D. The effects of infant feeding, birth order, occupation and socio-economic status on speech in six-year-old children. *NZ Med J* 1983; 483-86.

Buckley, K. Beliefs and practices related to extended breastfeeding among La Leche League mothers. *J Perinat Ed* 1992; 1(2):45-53.

Bumgarner, N. MOTHERING YOUR NURSING TODDLER. Schaumburg, Illinois: La Leche League International, 1982, p. 196.

Davis, D. et al. Infant feeding practices and occlusal outcomes: a longitudinal study. *J Can Dent Assoc* 1991; 57(7):593-94.

Dettwyler, K. "A Time to Wean: The Hominid Blueprint for the Natural Age of Weaning in Modern Human Populations." in *Breastfeeding: Biocultural Perspectives,* eds. Dettwyler, K. and Stuart-Macadam, P. New York: Aldine de Gruyter, 1995.

Dettwyler, K. A time to wean. BREASTFEEDING ABSTRACTS 1994; 14:3-4.

Food and Drug Administration. Bromocriptine indication withdrawn. *FDA Med Bulletin* 1994; 24(2):2.

Goldman, A. Immunologic components in human milk during the second year of lactation. *Acta Paediatr Scand,* 1983; 72:461-62.

Gulick, E. The effects of breastfeeding on toddler health. *Pediatric Nurs* 1986; 12:51-54.

Labbok, M. and Hendershot, G. Does breast-feeding protect against malocclusion? *Am J Prev Med* 1987; 3:227-32.

Lauwers, J. and Woessner, C. *Counseling the Nursing Mother,* 2nd ed. Garden City Park, New York: Avery Publishing Group, 1990, pp. 285-90.

Lawrence, R. *Breastfeeding: A Guide for the Medical Profession,* 4th ed. St. Louis: Mosby, 1994, pp. 311-21, and 522.

Lewis, P. et al. The resumption of ovulation and menstruation in a well-nourished population of women breastfeeding for an extended period of time. *Fertil Steril* 1991, 55(3):529-36.

Molbak, K. et al. Prolonged breastfeeding, diarrhoeal disease, and survival of children in Guinea-Bissau. *Br Med J* 1994; 308:1403-06.

Mead, M. and Newton, N. Cultural patterns of perinatal behavior, in *Childbearing: Its Social and Psychological Aspects,* ed. S. Richardson and Guttmacher, A. Baltimore, Maryland: Williams & Wilkins Company, 1967.

Riordan, J. and Auerbach, K. *Breastfeeding and Human Lactation,* Boston and London: Jones and Bartlett, 1993, pp. 42-46, 480-81.

Rogers, C. et al. Weaning from the breast: influences on maternal decisions. *Pediatr Nurs* 1987; 13:341-45.

Susman, V. and Katz, J. Weaning and depression: another postpartum complication. *Amer J Psychiatry* 1988; 145(4):498-501.

van den Bogaard, C. et al. The relationship between breast-feeding and early childhood morbidity in a general population. *Family Medicine* 1991; 23:510-15.

9

Expression and Storage of Human Milk

CHOOSING A METHOD OF EXPRESSION

BASICS OF MILK EXPRESSION
    Begin with Realistic Expectations
    The Key to Success: Stimulating the Let-Down
    Hand-Expression

MILK-EXPRESSION STRATEGIES FOR DIFFERENT SITUATIONS
    When Breastfeeding Is Delayed after Birth
    When Breastfeeding Is Temporarily Interrupted
    When Pumping Replaces Breastfeeding
    Regular Separation of Mother and Baby
    Occasional Separations

STORAGE AND HANDLING OF HUMAN MILK
    How Long to Store Human Milk
    Choice and Use of a Storage Container
    Handling and Thawing Human Milk

CHOOSING A METHOD OF EXPRESSION

No method of milk expression will be right for every mother and every situation.

Milk-expression needs vary from mother to mother.

Many breastfeeding mothers never need to express their milk, because they have no reason to be separated from their babies. Others need to rely upon some method of milk expression because breastfeeding is delayed after birth, breastfeeding is temporarily suspended, or they are separated from their babies at feeding times. Mothers all over the world effectively use hand-expression in these situations. On the other hand, mothers who have access to automatic electric breast pumps find them to be effective and easy to use. An automatic electric double pump is more effective than a hand-operated pump, making it a good choice when milk expression must replace breastfeeding for a time or if the mother has regular and lengthy separations from her baby. With an automatic electric pump, a mother does not need to be experienced at pumping in order for it to work well.

Other types of breast pumps, hand-operated and small motorized single pumps, may work well, depending upon the specific pump used and the mother's understanding of how to use it. (For more information, see the chapter "The Use of Breast Pumps and Other Products.") A smaller pump may be all that a mother needs if she plans to express her milk only occasionally. A caution must be given regarding the "bicycle horn" type of pump, as it cannot be sterilized, tends to be ineffective, and can cause tissue damage because its suction cannot be regulated.

Hand-expression is a workable option for almost every mother and learning how to do it provides a mother with a way to relieve fullness or express her milk for her baby in any situation. When a mother asks about pumping her milk, discuss hand-expression as an option and offer to help the mother learn how to do it.

When helping the mother choose a method of expression, ask her about her circumstances and preferences.

Ask the mother how often she plans to express her milk. The mother who is separated from her hospitalized baby will have very different milk-expression needs from the mother who wants to express milk for an occasional outing away from her baby.

Also ask the mother if she is familiar with any of the methods of expression (breast pumps and hand-expression) and if she has a preference. If so, talk to her about the advantages and disadvantages of her preferred method in her situation and mention any other methods that may work well for her, so that she can make an informed choice. If the mother does not have a preference, offer to describe the expression choices that would be appropriate in her situation. (For information on the advantages and disadvantages of the various types of breast pumps under different circumstances, see the section "Features that Affect a Mother's Pump Choice" in the chapter "The Use of Breast Pumps and Other Products.")

Double-pumping with an automatic electric pump is a fast, easy, and effective method of expression for most mothers and should be discussed as an option, particularly if mother and baby are unable to breastfeed due to health considerations or if they are regularly separated for long periods.

Automatic electric piston or diaphragm breast pumps are easy to use because they work automatically; the mother need only put the pump flange to her breast, adjust the suction, sit back, and relax. They do not depend upon the skill of the user to be effective. These pumps automatically alternate suction and release of suction between 30 and 60 times per minute, mimicking the suck of a breastfeeding baby and providing similar breast stimulation to effectively establish and maintain a mother's milk supply.

When a mother uses an automatic electric breast pump, she can minimize her time spent pumping by using the attachments that allow her to pump both breasts simultaneously (double-pump). These pumps also can be used to single-pump (one breast at a time) if the mother prefers. Double-pumping takes 10 to

15 minutes per session as compared with 20 to 30 minutes for single-pumping and has been found to stimulate milk production slightly more than single-pumping (Auerbach 1990).

If this type of pump is available, it is an option to strongly consider if breast-feeding is delayed after birth, if breastfeeding must be temporarily suspended, or if mother and baby are regularly separated for long periods.

Hand-expression and hand pumps require practice and skill, as well as ordinary strength and coordination.

Unlike automatic electric breast pumps—which do not depend upon the mother's skill to be effective—hand-expression and most hand pumps require the mother to manually regulate their rhythm, by either controlling the pressure or providing the pumping action. They take time and practice to master. Be sure the mother understands that it may take several practice sessions for her to express much milk, so that she will have realistic expectations when she begins.

These methods also require that the mother have ordinary strength and hand coordination. Using some pumps

Express/Store Milk

can be tiring, depending on how much physical effort they require and the type of repetitive motion needed to make them work. Methods of expression requiring sustained physical effort would not work well if the mother is in an unusually weakened state, such as immediately following a cesarean birth, has chronic joint pain and weakness in her hands, or has restricted use of her hands.

Some mothers find hand-expression as quick and effective as other methods.

Some mothers prefer hand-expression to using a pump because they feel it is more natural. Also, the feel of skin-to-skin may be more effective at stimulating a let-down, or milk-ejection, reflex for some mothers than the feel of a plastic or glass pump flange. Once the technique is mastered, hand-expression is convenient—nothing to purchase, wear out, break down, wash, store, or transport. When the mother is practiced at it, hand-expression also can be quick and highly effective.

A mother can learn to hand-express her milk while the baby is nursing on the other breast if the baby is propped up to the other breast with pillows. Also, it is possible with practice to learn to hand-express milk from both breasts simultaneously, with the right hand expressing the right breast and the left hand expressing the left breast, provided collection containers are placed on a stable surface at the proper height (Bernard 1996).

In parts of the world where pumps are unavailable or the costs prohibitive, mothers use hand-expression in all situations. The effectiveness of hand-expression is enhanced by good information, support, and encouragement (Armstrong 1995).

The mother who is not comfortable touching her breasts will probably prefer a pump.

BASICS OF MILK EXPRESSION

Begin with Realistic Expectations

Expressing milk is a learned skill that is psychological as well as physical, and effectiveness tends to improve with practice.

Some mothers are able to express only a few drops at their first try. Others express a few ounces (more than 30 ml), although this is unusual. It may help a mother feel better about her first efforts at milk expression if she knows that pumping and hand-expression are learned skills and that effectiveness tends to improve with practice. In order to express effectively, the mother must learn to let down her milk to the feel of her hand or the pump. This process is as much psychological as it is physical.

Suggest the mother think of her first few efforts at expression as practice sessions.

To help the mother begin with realistic expectations, suggest she think of her first few efforts to express her milk as practice sessions. Then any milk she is able to get will seem like a bonus.

Even if she only gets a few drops, congratulate her and tell her she is doing well. This will encourage her to keep practicing. Assure her that with time and practice she will be able to express more.

The amount of milk a mother can express at a sitting will vary, depending on many factors.

The amount of milk a mother is able to pump at a sitting depends on many factors:

- whether she is able to stimulate her let-down, or milk-ejection, reflex,
- how long it has been since she last breastfed or expressed,
- how practiced she is at expressing,
- how comfortable she is in the setting where she is expressing her milk,
- the time of day,
- her milk supply,
- whether she is going through an unusually stressful time (which may inhibit her let-down).

The amount of milk expressed at a sitting (all other factors being equal) also varies from mother to mother.

If the mother is concerned about her inability to pump large quantities of milk, assure her that this does not automatically mean that her milk supply is low. A nursing baby will always be more effective at milking her breast than any method of expression.

Extra fluids will not increase the mother's milk supply or her ability to express milk.

"Drink to thirst" is a nursing mother's best guide to how much fluid she should drink. Most mothers find that they are thirsty more often when they are nursing. Not only is forcing fluids uncomfortable, but one study (Dusdieker 1985) found that mothers did not produce any more milk when they drank 25 percent more fluids than when they drank to thirst.

Encourage the mother not to wait until she is feeling parched to take a drink. Constipation and concentrated urine that is dark in color are both signs that the mother needs to drink more.

Milk expression takes about the same amount of time as breastfeeding, with the exception of double-pumping.

Once the mother is skilled at expression, it usually takes about the same amount of time to express milk as it does to nurse a baby—an average of ten to fifteen minutes per breast.

The exception is double-pumping, when the mother pumps both of her breasts simultaneously using an automatic electric pump with a double-pumping attachment, two small motorized single pumps, or two squeeze hand pumps. This takes half the time of one-sided pumping.

No method of expression will remove the milk from a mother's breasts as effectively as a baby who is nursing well.

A nursing baby with an effective suck is more efficient than any method of expression in stimulating a mother's milk supply and extracting milk. This is partly because mechanical suction and pressure cannot duplicate the synchronized action of the baby's tongue, jaw, and palate. But even more important, the mother's emotional response to her baby is an essential factor in her ability to let down her milk.

The Key to Success: Stimulating the Let-Down

Most milk-expression difficulties are due to a temporary unresponsiveness of the mother's let-down reflex rather than a low milk supply.

If the mother has tried to express without getting much milk, she may worry that her milk supply is low. If the mother has been breastfeeding frequently and her baby is gaining well, this is unlikely.

It is more likely that her efforts to express her milk are not triggering her let-down, or milk-ejection, reflex. If her let-down reflex is not triggered, the mother may have plenty of milk but be unable to express much of it, because she will be able to express only the small fraction of her milk that is in the milk reservoirs near the nipple. Most of her milk will be left in the breast. The let-down usually occurs many times during a feeding or while pumping.

For more information, see "The Let-Down, or Milk-Ejection, Reflex" in the chapter "Breastfeeding Basics."

Suggestions for stimulating the mother's let-down reflex.

Stimulating the let-down, or milk-ejection, reflex is the key to effective milk expression, because the let-down makes the milk in all parts of the breast accessible for nursing or expressing.

The let-down can be psychologically conditioned as well as physically stimulated. For example, some mothers let down their milk when they hear a crying baby or even at the thought of their baby.

Because the sensations of pumping and hand-expressing are not the same as the sensations of nursing a baby, especially at first the mother may need to encourage her let-down, using some of the following methods of physical and psychological stimulation:

Express milk in a familiar and comfortable setting, perhaps in the same place each time, in the same comfortable chair (ideally, one that supports the mother's arms in a comfortable position and allows her to relax her entire body). If the mother is using a pump, resting her pumping arm on a pillow may help her relax. Familiar routines and settings help the mother relax and act as psychological triggers to the mother's let-down reflex.

Minimize distractions. Suggest the mother take her phone off the hook, turn on some relaxing music, and have everything ready that she might need, such as a glass of water or juice, a nutritious snack, or something to read. This will allow her to relax and concentrate on expressing. If the mother has older children who may want her attention while she's pumping, suggest she plan ahead for their needs.

If the mother is pumping or expressing outside the home, suggest she find a comfortable, private setting—such as an unused office, private bathroom or toilet facility, or storage room—where she can relax without having to worry about others interrupting her.

Follow a pre-expression ritual. Following a pre-expression ritual can relax the mother, physically stimulating her let-down, as well as acting as a psychological trigger. Some of the following may not be practical for the mother who expresses away from home.

- Apply heat to the breasts—either moist or dry—using warm, moist compresses, a heating pad, or by taking a warm shower.
- Since warmth is relaxing, suggest the mother put a blanket or sweater around her shoulders or sit near a source of heat.
- Gently massage the breasts, either in the shower or right before expressing. This is especially helpful if the mother is feeling tense.
- Stimulate the nipples, by gently rubbing or rolling the nipples.
- Relax for five minutes, using childbirth breathing exercises or just sitting quietly, using mental imagery to picture a relaxing setting, such as a warm sandy beach with waves lapping at the shore, a mountain stream, or a tropical breeze.
- If the mother is away from the baby, a phone call to see how the baby is doing may help put her in a good frame of mind for expressing.

Use a rhythmic motion while expressing to mimic a baby's suck. When the baby sucks, he applies a gentle rhythmic pressure on the milk sinuses as well as creating suction. To most effectively stimulate her milk let-down, suggest she try to mimic her baby's rhythm at the breast.

Focus all her senses on her baby. While she is expressing, suggest the mother imagine her baby is at the breast, snuggled close to her and warm. It may help to have physical reminders of her baby on hand to stimulate all her senses.

- Look at a photo of her baby while she expresses.
- Listen to a tape recording of her baby's voice.
- Feel and smell a piece of her baby's clothing or one of his blankets.

Express/Store Milk

If she is with her baby, express with the baby close by or while he nurses on the opposite breast. One of the most effective ways to stimulate the let-down is for the mother to express her milk while the baby nurses on the other breast. Some mothers are able to hand-express with their free hand, using pillows to help prop the baby at the other breast. Some mothers find it easier to use a pump on the opposite breast that can be operated with one hand, such as a small motorized single pump or a squeeze hand pump.

If the baby cannot nurse (such as a premature or very ill baby) or if the mother prefers to pump when her baby is not nursing, suggest she try expressing her milk where she can see her baby to encourage her let-down.

Interrupt milk expression several times to massage the breast. The mother should be able to stimulate several let-downs by interrupting her milk expression after about ten minutes, massaging the breast again, and then resuming expression.

Switch breasts when the milk flow lessens, expressing from both breasts several times during each session. Rather than spending ten to fifteen continuous minutes on each breast, the let-down reflex is stimulated more effectively by expressing on each breast until the milk flow decreases and then switching to the other breast, repeating this several times until twenty to thirty minutes have passed.

The mother's emotions may affect her let-down reflex, especially when she is first learning to express milk.

Some women have strong negative feelings when first faced with a breast pump. Others feel odd or awkward. If they have a sick or premature baby and are unable to breastfeed, they may also feel disappointed or discouraged about having to pump for an extended time. Although these feelings will not prevent a mother from pumping, she does need to be relaxed enough to let down her milk.

Encourage the mother whenever possible to express her milk when she is feeling relaxed and unhurried.

It is normal for a mother's let-down reflex and milk supply to be temporarily affected while she is going through a crisis.

A mother who is going through an emotional or physical crisis—such as a sudden death in the family or an auto accident—may find that her let-down and milk supply are temporarily affected. In extreme situations, extra adrenalin in the mother's system can reduce or block the release of the hormones affecting let-down and milk production.

If this happens, encourage the mother to try to relax and to continue breastfeeding and/or pumping so that her let-down and milk supply will quickly return to normal.

When a baby is premature or very ill, it is normal for the mother's milk supply to fluctuate with her baby's condition. When the mother is very worried about the baby's health or survival, it may not be easy to express much milk. Times of crisis commonly result in a temporary decrease in milk supply. This is normal, a natural part of the complex emotions involved in having a baby in the intensive-care nursery.

No matter what the cause, if a mother's let-down is inhibited, suggest she try breathing slowly and deeply to help her relax, or if she took childbirth education classes, try the relaxation techniques she learned there.

Hand-Expression

Whenever a mother plans to save her milk for her baby, encourage her to wash her hands before expressing.

Whatever technique of hand-expression the mother uses, if she plans to save the milk for her baby encourage her to wash her hands thoroughly first. Good hygiene is important.

Descriptions of two techniques for hand-expression follow.

The Marmet Technique©

Hand-expression, like using a pump, takes practice to master.

Like pumping, hand-expression requires the mother to try to duplicate the rhythm of a nursing baby and to learn to let down her milk when her baby is not at the breast. Some mothers, however, find that this is easier with the feel of skin-to-skin, than it is with the feel of the plastic or glass pump flange.

The Marmet technique combines gentle milk expression with breast massage, stroking, and shaking to stimulate the milk-ejection reflex.

The Marmet technique of hand-expression was developed by Chele Marmet, a La Leche League Leader and lactation consultant who is the director of the Lactation Institute in Encino, California. It consists of alternating milk expression with breast massage, stroking, and shaking. This technique can be used to express a little milk (such as to relieve fullness) or to express a full feeding. This technique is reprinted here with permission.

The following is a step-by-step guide that mothers can use to learn this technique. As with any manual skill, practice is important.

If the mother plans to express a full feeding, suggest she follow this twenty- to thirty-minute procedure.

If the mother is expressing her milk in place of a full feeding or needs to establish, increase, or maintain her milk supply when the baby cannot breastfeed, encourage her to follow the procedure below. With practice, many mothers are able to express several ounces of milk very quickly.

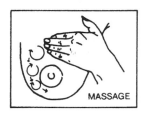

MASSAGE

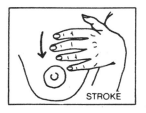

STROKE

Express/Store Milk

- Express each breast until the flow of milk slows down.
- Assist the let-down (or milk-ejection) reflex by massaging, stroking, and shaking both breasts. These can be done simultaneously.
- Repeat the whole process of expressing each breast and assisting the let-down, or milk-ejection, reflex once or twice more. The flow of milk usually slows down sooner the second and third time as the milk reservoirs are drained.

The entire procedure should take about 20-30 minutes.

- Express each breast 5-7 minutes.
- Massage, stroke, shake.
- Express each breast 3-5 minutes.
- Massage, stroke, shake.
- Express each breast 2-3 minutes.

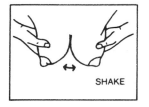

SHAKE

Note: If her milk supply is well established, the mother should use these times only as a guide—watching the flow of milk and changing breasts when the flow dwindles. If the mother has little or no milk yet (such as during the first few days after her baby's birth), suggest she follow the suggested times closely.

Expressing Milk—Draining the Milk Reservoirs
Suggest the mother begin by washing her hands, then:

To express her milk effectively, the mother needs to position, push, and roll her thumb and fingers rhythmically over her milk reservoirs.

1. **Position** her thumb and first two fingers about one to one-and-a-half inches (2.5-3.8 cm) behind her nipple.
   - She should use this measurement, which is not necessarily the outer edge of the areola, as a guide. The areola varies in size from one woman to another.
   - Suggest she place her thumb pad above the nipple and the finger pads below the nipple forming the "C" with her hand, as shown.
   - Note that the fingers are positioned so that the milk reservoirs lie beneath them.
   - Caution her to avoid cupping the breast.
2. **Push** straight into her chest wall.
   - Caution her to avoid spreading her fingers apart.
   - For a mother with large breasts, suggest she first lift and then push into the chest wall.

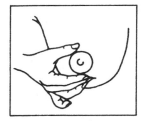

3. **Roll** her thumb and fingers forward as if making thumb and fingerprints at the same time.

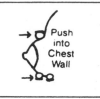 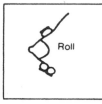 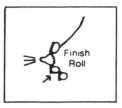

- The rolling motion of the thumb and fingers compresses and empties the milk reservoirs without hurting sensitive breast tissue.
- Note the moving position of the thumbnail and fingernails in the illustration.

4. **Repeat rhythmically** to drain the milk reservoirs.—Position, push, roll; position, push, roll.

5. **Rotate the thumb and finger position to milk the other reservoirs.** Suggest the mother use both hands on each breast in order to reach more of the milk ducts.

Breast Massage, Stroking, and Shaking—Stimulating the Milk Flow
Suggest the mother:
Massage the milk-producing cells and ducts.

Alternating milk expression with breast massage, stroking, and shaking will stimulate the mother's let-down, or milk-ejection, reflex.

- Start at the top of the breast. Press firmly into the chest wall. Move fingers in a circular motion on one spot on the skin.
- After a few seconds move the fingers to the next area on the breast.
- Spiral around the breast toward the areola using this massage.
- The motion is similar to that used in a breast examination.

Stroke her breast area from the top of the breast to the nipple with a light tickle-like stroke.

- Continue this stroking motion from the chest wall to the nipple around the whole breast.
- This will help with relaxation and will help stimulate the let-down.

Shake the breast while leaning forward so that gravity will help the milk eject.

Any technique of hand-expression should first be gentle, so that delicate breast tissue is not damaged. For this reason, certain motions should be avoided:

To avoid damaging delicate breast tissue, caution the mother to avoid squeezing, pulling, and sliding motions while expressing.

- Avoid squeezing the breast, as this can cause bruising.
- Avoid pulling out the nipple and breast, as this can cause tissue damage.
- Avoid sliding the fingers on the breast, as this can cause skin burns.

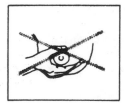 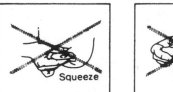 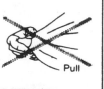 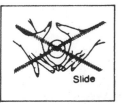

The Traditional Method

Hand-expression is used in many traditional societies.

One technique of hand-expression that is used in many traditional societies is described in the 18-hour breastfeeding management course sponsored by UNICEF and the World Health Organization (1993). It was reprinted with permission from *Helping Mothers to Breastfeed* by F. Savage King (1992).

Tell the mother to expect hand-expression to take about 20 to 30 minutes, especially at first, and to plan for frequent switching from breast to breast as the milk flow slows.

When using this technique, encourage the mother to express from each breast for 3 to 5 minutes until the milk flow slows down, express from the other breast, and repeat both breasts again, using either hand. The entire process usually takes about 20 to 30 minutes. To adequately stimulate the breasts, it is important that the mother spend the full time, especially during the first few days after birth when she may be able to express only a small amount of milk.

Index finger and thumb should be positioned above and below the nipple on the areola.

Index finger and thumb should be placed on the areola above and below the nipple, with finger opposite thumb. Finger and thumb should be far enough apart so that they are away from the nipple.

Using this method, the mother first presses toward the chest wall with finger and thumb then rhythmically presses finger and thumb behind the nipple to stimulate milk flow.

Once the index finger and thumb are positioned away from the nipple on the areola, thumb and finger should be pressed in toward the chest wall and then moved together in a press-and-release rhythm behind the nipple, stimulating milk flow. The mother may need to press and release several times before milk flow begins.

Express/Store Milk

Rotating the hand and pressing the same way from the sides of the areola will allow milk from all parts of the breast to be expressed.

Once the milk flow slows with finger and thumb above and below the nipple, suggest the mother move her fingers to the same position on the sides of the areola away from nipple and repeat the process so that milk is expressed from all parts of the breast.

If hand-expressing hurts, the mother is doing something wrong and needs to change her technique.

Hand-expression should not hurt. If it does, the mother may be squeezing too hard, sliding the fingers along the skin, or squeezing the nipple itself, which is ineffective as well as painful. If the mother says hand-expression is hurting her, talk to her about what she is doing to help her pinpoint what needs to be changed to increase her comfort.

The Warm Bottle Method

The Warm Bottle method uses a wide-mouthed bottle that has been warmed with hot water. It is an option for the engorged mother without access to an effective breast pump whose breast tenderness and nipple tautness make hand expression difficult.

The Warm Bottle method of milk expression is one option for the mother without access to a gentle and effective breast pump who is engorged and finds hand-expression difficult due to tender breasts and taut nipples.

To use this method, suggest the mother find a large glass bottle (a 1 liter bottle or larger is recommended) with a wide mouth (at least 2 inches [5 cm] in diameter) and clean it well (UNICEF/WHO 1993; King 1992). Then suggest the mother:

- Slowly pour hot water into the bottle until it is nearly full and let it stand for few minutes.
- Wrap the bottle in a cloth and pour out the water.
- Cool the neck of the bottle, and then place the bottle's mouth over the nipple to make an airtight seal against the breast. Hold it steady and wait for a few minutes.
- As the bottle cools, it creates gentle suction, which pulls the breast into the neck of the bottle. The combination of the warmth of the bottle and the gentle suction triggers the let-down, or milk-ejection, reflex and causes the milk to be expressed.
- When the milk flow slows, release the suction and remove the breast from the bottle.

Do not leave the bottle on the breast for too long or it may cause nipple pain.

- Pour out the milk and repeat the process on the other breast.

Caution the mother to break the suction immediately if she feels any discomfort. Also, slow cooling of the warm bottle is ideal; too rapid cooling may cause nipple trauma.

MILK-EXPRESSION STRATEGIES FOR DIFFERENT SITUATIONS

When Breastfeeding Is Delayed after Birth

If the Baby Is Unable to Breastfeed

Encourage the mother to select the most effective method of expression that is available, which in most areas is the automatic electric double breast pump.

Breastfeeding may be delayed after birth if the baby is ill or premature or if the mother is unable to breastfeed.

For more information on premature babies, see the chapter "Prematurity."

Use of an automatic electric breast pump with double-pumping attachments is one method of expression that has been proven effective (Lang 1994; Green 1982). In its 1993 *Recommendations for Collection, Storage, and Handling of a Mother's Milk for Her Own Infant in the Hospital Setting,* The Human Milk Banking Association of North America recommends mothers use an electric piston breast pump, because "hand-expression or use of manual, battery, or small electric pumps are not effective for most women to establish and maintain an adequate supply of milk for a hospitalized infant, especially when pumping is required over a long period of time."

If the mother is low-income, tell her that many rental stations or hire agencies offer electric piston pumps at no charge (called "grant pumps") or at reduced fees to low-income women. If the mother cannot locate one of these rental stations or these types of pumps are not available in her area, discuss other methods of milk expression with her.

Encourage the mother to begin expressing her milk as soon as possible after birth.

Encourage the mother to begin expressing her milk as soon as possible after birth, ideally within the first six hours. Even if the mother is not able to breastfeed her baby immediately after birth, assure her that she can bring in and establish her milk supply in preparation for the time when her baby will be ready to breast-feed.

The mother may become discouraged if she is not able to express large quantities of milk immediately.

If the mother is feeling discouraged with the small amounts of milk she is expressing, explain that it takes time and practice to become effective.

If her baby is younger than three days old, be sure the mother knows that during the first few days after birth—before her milk supply becomes more plentiful—it is normal for there to be only very small amounts of colostrum in the breast, but that this colostrum is a concentrated form of nourishment that also offers protection from illness.

Assure her that no amount is too small to save for her baby. Also, be sure she knows that it may take a few days of expressing to be able to collect more milk at a sitting, but that these first sessions will stimulate her milk supply.

The key to establishing and maintaining a milk supply is to establish a daily expression routine and stick to it.

Establishing and maintaining a healthy milk supply while using a breast pump or hand-expressing require regular and frequent expression of milk. If the mother is practiced at hand-expression or is using an effective breast pump, in general, the more often the mother expresses, the more milk she will produce. Short, frequent milk-expression sessions (at least ten to fifteen minutes per breast) tend to stimulate more milk production than longer sessions spaced at wider intervals.

The mother should plan to express 10 to 15 minutes per breast at least 5 to 6 times per day in order to establish and maintain her milk supply. At one time, women were told to pump only as much milk as their baby was taking at the time and plan on increasing their milk supply later, but this advice has been questioned by some experts. Some women have found that when they express only the amount their hospitalized baby needs at first (which may be very little, especially if the baby is not ready to be fed by mouth right away), their breast tissue begins to revert to its prepregnancy state, making it difficult to increase the milk supply later (Woolridge 1995).

Ask the mother how she feels about waking at night to express. Her preferences and comfort will determine what is right for her.

Ask the mother how she feels about waking at night to pump. Some mothers wake at night or in the early morning to pump, especially if their breasts are feeling uncomfortably full. Others find that uninterrupted sleep helps both their milk supply and their ability to cope with the daily pressures that go along with having a hospitalized baby.

If the mother will be expressing her milk for weeks or months, the thought of waking at night to pump may discourage her from continuing. Each mother should be encouraged to make this decision based upon her feelings and her comfort level.

Expressing guidelines vary depending on the baby's intake and condition. These basic principles can help the mother formulate her own daily plan.

In the first few days, the goal is to minimize engorgement and stimulate milk production.

If the mother has other children to care for, it may be difficult for her to find the time she needs for milk expression. Offer to help the mother formulate a daily plan for expressing her milk so that she is able to fit in at least 5 to 6 pumpings per day.

Express/Store Milk

The first three days after birth. Mothers should begin expressing as soon as possible after their baby's birth, ideally within the first 6 hours (Walker 1992). Early and frequent pumping has been correlated with greater milk production (Hopkinson 1988; deCarvalho 1985). Encourage the mother to time her pumpings at regular intervals during the day (ideally at least every 3 hours). It is not necessary for the mother to wake at night to express.

The goal is to minimize engorgement for the mother and stimulate her milk to increase ("come in").

If the baby will not be able to breastfeed for at least two weeks, the goal is to maintain the mother's milk production.

When the baby is three to five days old and the mother's milk supply is becoming more plentiful. Once the mother's milk supply becomes more plentiful, encourage her to express at least five times during the day (ideally, every three hours) for at least ten to fifteen minutes per breast. One study found pumping at least 5 times for a total of more than 100 minutes per day was necessary to maintain milk production (Hopkinson 1988). To increase milk production, pumping more times per day and perhaps at night may be necessary.

If the mother is using an automatic electric double pump, encourage her to start pumping on the minimum pressure setting until the first drops of milk begin to flow and then to move the pressure lever to a comfortable setting and start timing. It is not necessary for the mother to wake at night to express unless she feels uncomfortably full.

The goal is to establish a healthy milk supply.

If the baby will be able to breastfeed within the next two weeks, see the section below.

If the baby is being fed the mother's milk, the goal is to match her milk supply to meet the baby's needs.

The baby is being fed intravenously or is taking small amounts of human milk. Encourage the mother to express at least five times during the day (ideally, every three hours) until her breasts feel softer. If she is pumping this usually takes at least ten to fifteen minutes per breast, beginning at minimum pressure setting and timing the pumping once the first drops of milk begin to flow then adjusting the pressure lever to a comfortable setting. It is not necessary for the mother to wake at night to express unless she feels uncomfortably full.

The goal is to maintain the mother's milk supply.

If the baby will be coming home soon, an ample milk supply will make the transition to breastfeeding easier.

The baby's milk intake is increasing or the baby will be coming home within two weeks. Encourage the mother to express at least seven to eight times during the day and to set her alarm to express at least one time during the night. She should plan to express until her breasts feel softer, which usually takes at least ten to fifteen minutes per breast.

The goal is to increase the mother's milk supply to match the baby's intake. Also, an ample milk supply will make the transition to breastfeeding easier.

When the baby begins to breastfeed, the mother will need to adjust her pumping time.

When the baby begins to breastfeed. Encourage the mother to express at least eight times every 24 hours. If the baby is not yet breastfeeding actively (that is, swallowing regularly during feedings), the mother may need to express after nursing. When the baby will not be nursing, the mother should plan to pump at least ten to fifteen minutes per breast. If she is pumping after a nursing, the mother should subtract the number of minutes the baby spent actively sucking and swallowing at that breast from her pumping time. For example, if the baby nursed actively for four minutes on one breast, the mother will need to pump for six to ten minutes on that breast and ten to fifteen minutes on the other breast.

The goal is to express long enough to soften the breast at least eight times every twenty-four hours to match the nursing frequency of the baby and to provide the baby with the milk he needs as his sucking effectiveness increases.

When the baby is primarily breastfeeding, the goal is to make sure the baby receives enough milk.

When the baby is primarily breastfeeding. Encourage the mother to express after nursing when needed, that is, when the baby does not actively breastfeed for long enough to soften the breast, usually at least ten minutes per breast. The expressed milk can then be given to the baby, if needed. The baby needs to breastfeed eight to ten times a day with at least ten to twenty minutes of rhythmic swallowing at each nursing.

The goal is to make sure the baby receives enough milk.

Some mothers who pump long-term experience a temporary decrease in milk supply. More frequent milk expression should help a mother's supply to increase again.

If a mother notices a decrease in her milk supply, encourage her to express her milk more frequently to increase it again. Whether she breastfeeds or expresses, a mother's milk supply is based on supply and demand—the more often she nurses or expresses, the more milk will be produced.

It is normal for a mother's milk supply to temporarily decrease while she is going through a crisis.

A mother's milk supply often fluctuates with her baby's condition. When the mother is very worried about the baby's health or survival, it may not be easy to pump much milk. Times of crisis commonly result in a temporary decrease in milk supply. This is normal, a natural part of the complex emotions involved in having a baby in the hospital.

If the mother's milk supply decreases during a crisis, unsupportive comments from those around may convince the mother to give up entirely unless she has another source of support. Assure her that her decrease in supply is only temporary and that her milk supply will increase again as the baby's condition improves. Also tell her that however much milk she is able to pump is enough to stimulate her breasts to continue making milk. It may also be comforting for her to talk to another mother who has experienced the same thing.

The next time you speak to the mother, ask her a general question—such as "How are things going with you today?"—rather than focusing on the volume of milk she is able to pump with a question such as, "Were you able to express more milk than yesterday?"

For more information on pumping, see the supplement "The Use of Breast Pumps and Other Products."

Before the mother begins saving her milk for her baby, encourage her to ask about the guidelines used by the hospital.

Different expression and storage precautions may be used if the mother is expressing her milk for a premature or sick infant. Pre-sterilized storage containers may be provided, and containers of expressed milk will need to be labeled with the mother's name, her baby's name, and the date and time of expression.

The mother will need to check with the baby's nurses for the amount of milk to put in each container and their guidelines for storage time for refrigerated and frozen milk.

It is important that refrigerated milk not get too warm and frozen milk not thaw while being transported to the hospital. Suggest the mother pack it in a small ice chest or insulated container. If the mother visits her baby daily, she can take her milk with her then. If she lives far away from the hospital or cannot arrange to visit regularly for some other reason, she may be able to arrange for family, friends, or perhaps a hospital employee who lives nearby to transport her milk.

If the baby remains hospitalized after the mother returns home, she will need to make arrangements for transporting her milk.

In some circumstances, the baby is able to breastfeed but the mother cannot or is isolated away from her baby. For example:

Express/Store Milk

- The mother has a serious illness, such as measles, a high fever, or a serious infection.
- The mother is receiving drugs that are incompatible with breastfeeding.
- Any unusual medical situation that would preclude nursing, for example, if the mother is unconscious.

If the Mother Is Unable to Breastfeed

If the mother is not able to breast-feed after birth, encourage her to express often, simulating the nursing frequency of a newborn.

As soon as the mother is physically able, encourage her to begin breastfeeding. If this is not possible—due to an illness or incompatible drugs—encourage her to express her milk as often as her newborn would nurse—at least six to eight times during the day. The mother who is seriously ill may need help to do this.

Suggest the mother plan to express her milk until her breasts feel softer. If she is using an automatic electric pump, this usually takes at least ten minutes per breast.

The goal is to establish an adequate milk supply and make the transition to breastfeeding easier.

To avoid nipple confusion, suggest the mother request alternative feeding methods be used instead of a bottle until she is able to breastfeed.

To make the transition to breastfeeding easier, the mother may request that her baby not be given bottles or other artificial nipples. Alternative feeding methods include cup, eyedropper, bowl, spoon, feeding syringe, and finger-feeding. For information on using these alternative methods, see the supplement "The Use of Breast Pumps and Other Products."

Putting a breast pad soaked in the mother's milk in the isolette with her baby will accustom him to the smell of her milk and may ease the transition to breastfeeding.

Making the Transition to the Breast

Early feedings take time and patience. Privacy, support, and realistic expectations can help them to go more smoothly.

Early feedings are a learning process for both mother and baby and will require time and patience. The mother may feel awkward, even frustrated at times.

To keep the mother's expectations realistic, explain that it will probably take several breastfeeding sessions before the baby latches on and nurses well. Encourage the mother to expect these first nursings to be "getting acquainted" sessions and to be patient, enjoy the cuddling and closeness, and to keep trying. A reasonable goal for the first nursing is for the baby to respond to the mother's nipple by licking or mouthing it. Also assure her that even if the baby does not receive much milk at the breast, he will not be deprived because he can be fed afterwards.

Privacy and quiet will help. Suggest the mother find out if the hospital has a separate room where she can breastfeed. Other items that may make early nursings more comfortable include:

- a screen or curtains to give mother some privacy if a separate room is not available;
- a comfortable chair with armrests;
- several pillows (one or two to support her elbow and hand on the side she'll be nursing, one or two in her lap to bring the baby up to the level of her nipple, and perhaps one or two behind her back and shoulders for comfort and support);
- suggest the mother wear clothes that allow the baby easy access to the breast.

If the baby is ill or premature, a nurse may be present to monitor the baby.

Good positioning and latch-on are critical for successful breastfeeding.

For a baby to breastfeed effectively, it is important that he be correctly positioned and latched-on to the breast. For more information, see the chapter "Positioning, Latch-On, and the Baby's Suck." For the premature baby, see the section "The First Nursings" in the "Prematurity" chapter.

Suggest the mother determine the length of feedings based on her baby's cues, rather than restricting breastfeeding to a prescribed number of minutes.

Rather than restricting breastfeeding to a prescribed number of minutes, which is sometimes suggested, a mother can ask that she and her baby be evaluated individually, according to how well breastfeeding is going and have the baby's vital signs monitored. Often it takes a baby a little extra time at first to stimulate his mother's let-down, or milk-ejection, reflex and get the milk flowing. Limiting a baby's time at the breast can substantially cut down on the amount of milk he receives.

There are several cues that will tell the mother that her baby is ready to end a feeding:

- he stops sucking;
- he falls asleep at the breast;
- he seems satisfied;
- he shows signs of fatigue or stress.

The length of the early feedings will vary from one feeding to the next. If the baby falls asleep early in the feeding, the mother may be able to hold him while he sleeps and try again when he awakens.

Expressing milk into a baby's mouth encourages some babies to nurse more actively. However, if the baby is sleepy, it may cause him to choke.

The mother can gauge if the baby is nursing well by how her breasts feel after nursing, her baby's nursing pattern, and her baby's wet diapers and bowel movements.

Test-weighing a baby before and after nursings with an ultra-sensitive electronic scale, such as Medela's Baby Weigh or a SMART scale, can accurately measure how much milk the baby gets (see the chapter "Prematurity). There are also other ways to gauge if the baby is nursing well:

- The baby is sucking and swallowing regularly, moving his jaws as well as his lips.
- The mother's let-down, or milk-ejection, reflex is working. Not all women have identifiable sensations when they let down their milk, but a mother can be sure it is occurring when she sees her baby switch from quick sucks to long slow sucks with audible and regular swallowing.
- The mother's breasts feel less full.
- The baby seems satisfied.
- Later the baby has good urine output (six to eight wet diapers every twenty-four hours) and regular bowel movements. (The baby younger than six weeks will usually have at least two bowel movements a day. Fewer bowel movements may be normal in an older baby.)

Test-weighing may be helpful at first in confirming the mother's own impression of how the feeding went. With experience, the mother can begin to rely more on her own judgment and test-weighing will not be necessary.

While the baby is making the transition to breastfeeding, other feedings can be given by cup, spoon, eyedropper, or other alternative methods in order to avoid confusing the baby with artificial nipples.

At first, some babies breastfeed for only one or two feedings a day. A bottle may be used for the other feedings, but since artificial nipples require a different sucking action than the breast, this sometimes causes problems. Some babies become "nipple-confused" when they receive supplemental feedings from bottles. This affects their feeding at the breast, making it more difficult for them to learn to latch on and nurse.

Suggest the mother ask her baby's care providers if it is possible for supplements to be given by alternative feeding methods (or gavage if the baby was receiving previous feedings this way) during the time the baby is learning to breastfeed. Many hospital nurseries are willing to do this, and it will make breastfeeding easier for the baby.

Express/Store Milk

At Kenyatta National Hospital in Nairobi, Kenya, bottles are never used for preterm infants. Any supplemental feedings are given from a cup and the infants are not discharged until they are fully breastfed.

If bottles are unavoidable, breastfeeding may require more patience, but even a baby who is getting bottles will eventually master breastfeeding.

If a bottle has been used for feedings, it may take extra time, practice, and patience for a baby to go from bottle to breast.

If the baby has learned to use a bottle, it may take longer to teach him to latch on and nurse at the breast, because different mouth and tongue movements are used to breastfeed than are used to take liquid from a bottle and the baby has to learn new sucking patterns. If the baby has been breastfeeding well at least several times a week, this transition from bottle to breast will likely be easier.

If a baby has become accustomed to a bottle and will continue to need supplements after he starts breastfeeding, suggest the mother try using an alternative feeding method, so that the baby's effort to breastfeed will not become further confused. (See "The Use of Breast Pumps and Other Products.")

When the mother puts the baby to breast, it is important for her to use good positioning and latch-on (see the chapter "Positioning, Latch-On, and the Baby's Suck"). It may also help for her to express a little milk first in order to stimulate her let-down, or milk-ejection, reflex so that her baby receives an instant reward.

It may take time for the nipple-confused baby to take the breast and nurse well. (See the section, "Persuading the Baby to Take the Breast," in the chapter "Fussy at the Breast and Breast Refusal.") During the transition from bottle to breast, if the baby fusses or cries at the breast, the mother should stop and comfort him, so that the baby does not associate the breast with frustration or unhappiness. Then she can try again.

If after many tries the baby is unable to latch on or nurse well at a particular feeding—or if he seems to be tiring—the mother can supplement him using an alternative feeding method and offer the breast again later. With time, practice, and patience, the baby will learn to nurse.

Breastfeeding will get easier with time and practice.

The mother may feel discouraged if her baby does not take easily and quickly to breastfeeding. It may take several attempts—or several sessions—for the mother to get her baby to latch on to the breast and suck. Assure the mother that the early feedings are the most challenging and that with time and practice it will get easier.

When Breastfeeding Is Temporarily Suspended

Some mothers stop breastfeeding temporarily but plan to resume nursing later.

Under some circumstances, a mother may temporarily stop breastfeeding with the intention of resuming later. For example:

- The mother may need to take a drug or undergo a diagnostic test that could be hazardous for her baby, such as one using a radioactive compound.
- The mother or baby may be separated for a short-term hospitalization.
- The mother may be planning to leave her baby, for example, for a vacation or a business trip.

Temporary weaning is stressful for both mother and baby.

Temporary weaning is stressful, both emotionally and physically, for mother and baby. And if the weaning is abrupt, the stress is compounded. The mother will need support and encouragement during this time, as well as a listening ear.

For the mother, a temporary weaning is a physical stress, since her body is accustomed to regular breastfeeding. It is important during this time that the mother be able to remove the milk from her breasts to reduce her chances of developing mastitis and to help maintain her milk supply. The mother may also experience emotional stress, particularly if the temporary weaning is not her choice and her baby is difficult to comfort without nursing.

For the baby, it is stressful to change abruptly to another feeding method. Also, if the mother does not have a supply of her milk on hand to feed her baby, the baby faces the physical stress of switching to a new food, which carries the risk of allergic reaction.

If the mother is not available to ease this transition—due to hospitalization or a trip away—the baby must also cope with the emotional stress of his mother's sudden absence. If she will be away, encourage the mother to ask whoever will be caring for her baby in her absence to give him lots of cuddling and holding to help compensate for the loss of breastfeeding and her absence.

To keep up her milk supply, encourage the mother to express her milk as frequently as her baby was nursing.

Because milk is produced on a supply and demand basis, encourage the mother to express her milk at least as often as her baby was nursing in order to keep up her milk supply. Her comfort will also be an important guide. If her breasts feel full, she needs to express some milk.

If the mother has been breastfeeding exclusively or has a nearly full milk supply, she will need an effective method of expression in order to stay comfortable and keep up her milk supply during a temporary weaning.

An automatic electric breast pump with double-pumping attachments is a fast, effective method of expression. Other methods of expression are dependent upon the mother's skill and may not be adequate if the mother has a full or nearly full milk supply and the baby is not nursing. If an automatic electric double pump is not available in the mother's area or she has chosen another method, encourage her to become practiced at it before she will need to rely on it for her comfort.

The mother will need to decide on another method of feeding.

Be sure the mother knows all her feeding options when she is deciding how to feed her baby during the temporary weaning. In an older baby, increased amounts of solids and liquid in a cup may be substituted for the missed nursings. If bottles are used, they can sometimes lead to nipple confusion—particularly in a baby younger than one month—or a preference for the bottle.

Alternative feeding methods include cup, spoon, eyedropper, feeding syringe, and finger-feeding. Explain to the mother that these other methods may take more time at first—until the baby becomes practiced at them—but they will make the transition back to breastfeeding easier.

If a mother has not expressed her milk often enough during the temporary weaning, her milk supply may be reduced. In most cases, her supply can be increased by frequent nursing.

If a mother finds after a temporary weaning that her milk supply is reduced, either because her method of expression was ineffective or because she did not express her milk often enough, she may be able to bring back a full milk supply through frequent breastfeeding. This will be more difficult if her supply has been reduced long enough that the breast tissue has begun to involute, or return to its prepregnancy state, which takes about a month to occur.

When she begins breastfeeding again, suggest the mother keep count of her baby's wet diapers. If her baby has at least six wet diapers per day, she can be sure he is getting enough fluids. If her baby has fewer than six wet diapers, suggest she supplement him with whatever food he was receiving while she was gone, using a spoon or eyedropper after nursing. She can reduce the amount gradually as her milk supply increases.

The baby may need some encouragement to go back to breastfeeding after a temporary weaning.

If the baby is reluctant to go back to breastfeeding, give the mother some suggestions from the section, "Persuading the Baby to Take the Breast," in the chapter "Fussy at the Breast and Breast Refusal."

Express/Store Milk

When Pumping Replaces Breastfeeding

Mothers pump instead of breast-feeding for a variety of reasons.

Some mothers express their milk and feed it to their babies by bottle rather than breastfeed. In a survey of 10 mothers who fed their babies this way (Mohrbacher 1996), the mothers gave a variety of reasons for their decision:

- the newborn refused to latch on,
- the baby was unable to latch on due to a cleft palate or other physical abnormality,
- the baby refused to return to breastfeeding after a lengthy temporary weaning,
- the baby preferred bottles after spending the first week in the hospital intensive care nursery,
- the mother's nipples were sore from breastfeeding and the pumping did not hurt,
- the mother found pumping and bottle-feeding more suited to her lifestyle,
- the mother was uncomfortable with breastfeeding in public or with the act of breastfeeding itself.

All ten of the mothers felt positively about their choice primarily because they were able to give their babies the health benefits of human milk.

Mothers pumping one breast at a time took longer at each pumping to express the same amount of milk as mothers who double-pumped.

An automatic electric breast pump with double-pumping attachments, which allows both breasts to be pumped simultaneously, is a fast, effective method of expression (Lang 1994; Green 1982). Mothers surveyed who used this method reported that it took them about 90 minutes of total pumping time per day—an average of 5.3 pumping sessions per day, each averaging 17 minutes in length—to express enough milk to sustain their babies. Mothers surveyed who pumped one breast at a time using an automatic electric breast pump or small motorized single pump reported that it took them an average of about 124 minutes of total pumping time per day—an average of 4.6 pumping sessions per day, each averaging 27 minutes in length (Mohrbacher 1996).

To maintain a milk supply sufficient to sustain their babies on their milk alone, mothers report that they need to pump more than 6 times per day during the first week and between 4 and 6 times per day once their supplies are established.

Whether they double-pumped or single-pumped, mothers surveyed reported pumping an average of 6.3 pumpings per day during the first week (ranging from 4 to 12 times per day). This number dropped to 4 to 6 pumpings per day once their milk had increased to the point that they were getting enough milk to sustain their babies. When the mother with the highest milk yield was eliminated, these mothers had an average milk output of 37 ounces (1100 ml) per day (ranging from 21 oz. [630 ml] to 55 oz. [1650 ml]).

One mother surveyed pumped 6 to 8 times a day in order to build up a milk surplus and averaged about 96 ounces (2830 ml) of milk expressed per day. When she returned her rental pump after 2½ months of pumping, she had enough of her milk stored to feed her baby for the next six weeks without using formula (Mohrbacher 1996).

If a mother is considering this alternative, encourage her to begin by pumping 6 to 8 times a day during the first week and then experiment with her own schedule to determine how often and how long she will need to pump in order to provide for her baby. Individual differences between women, such as differences in milk storage capacity (Daly and Hartman 1995), may mean that one woman with an established milk supply may only need to pump 4 times a day while another may need to pump 6 times per day in order to get the same amount of milk. If a mother wants to increase her supply, she can do so by temporarily increasing the number of pumpings per day, and once her supply is increased, she may be able to cut back to the 4 to 6 pumpings per day to maintain it at that level.

Amount of milk expressed at each session correlated most closely with the length of time since the previous pumping.

The mothers reported that the amount of milk they expressed at each pumping was unrelated to time of day, and correlated most closely with the length of time since the last pumping. The mothers who did not pump during the night reported that their first morning pumping yielded the most milk. The mothers who pumped during the night reported that the amounts were consistent throughout the day and night, irrespective of time of day (Mohrbacher 1996).

A mother will produce milk for as long as she pumps.

As long as a mother continues to express her milk, she will continue to produce milk. Mothers surveyed pumped milk for their babies from 2 to 21 months, with an average pumping duration of 6 months (Mohrbacher 1996). All of the mothers reported being able to maintain their milk supplies until they were ready to discontinue pumping.

When a mother is ready to discontinue pumping, she should do so gradually to avoid discomfort and breast problems. There are several approaches from which she can choose.

When a mother weans a baby from the breast, the standard advice is to eliminate one daily nursing and allow her body 3 to 4 days to adjust before eliminating another feeding. The mother who is pumping instead of nursing can use this approach by eliminating one daily pumping and giving her body time to adjust before eliminating another, but she also has other options that are not available to the mother who is breastfeeding.

An alternative approach is to gradually express less milk at each pumping. For example, if the mother is getting 8 ounces (240 ml) at each pumping, suggest she stop pumping after she gets 7 ounces (210 ml) at each session throughout the day. Suggest she allow several days for her body to adjust and then pump only 6 ounces (180 ml) at each session, and so on. This way she can decrease her supply gradually without discomfort and decrease the risk of a plugged duct or breast infection.

Another approach that allows her to decrease her milk supply gradually is to slowly space pumpings farther apart. For example, if the mother is pumping every three to four hours during the day, she can start by pumping every four to five hours instead. She should then give her body a few days to adjust and begin pumping every five to six hours per day and so on.

Whichever of these approaches is used, tell the mother that if at any time she begins to feel uncomfortably full she should pump just enough milk to make herself comfortable, but not as much as a full pumping. Pumping to comfort will allow her to gradually decrease her milk supply so that she does not become painfully engorged. The goal is a gradual weaning from the pump with a minimum of discomfort.

Regular Separation of Mother and Baby

The mother who is regularly separated from her baby can breastfeed.

Even if a mother is regularly separated from her baby—due to employment outside the home, attending school, or any other outside commitments—she can breastfeed, if she chooses. To make it work, the mother must plan to express her milk or arrange times to breastfeed her baby so that her breasts do not become overly full. She must also make provisions for her baby to be fed while they are apart, either with her milk or another food. For more information, see the chapter "Employment and Breastfeeding."

Express/Store Milk

Occasional Separations

Suggest hand-expression or a hand pump for the mother who plans to express her milk for her baby for their occasional times apart.

A mother who wants to express her milk for occasional times away from her baby does not need a highly efficient automatic electric breast pump. Hand-expression or a hand pump should suit her purposes well.

Refer to the earlier section "Choosing a Method of Expression" and the section "Features that Affect a Mother's Pump Choice" in the supplement, "The Use of Breast Pumps and Other Products" for more information on the advantages and disadvantages of different types of hand pumps. Also, be sure the mother understands that with either hand-expression or a hand pump she will need several practice sessions before she can rely on it. Suggest she allow herself ample learning and practice time before she needs to express milk for the baby.

The mother breastfeeding on cue can choose several approaches to expressing her milk.

If the mother is breastfeeding her baby on cue, she may be concerned about when to express so that there will be enough milk for the baby when he wants to nurse.

Early morning—when the mother is rested and her baby has not nursed for an hour or two—works well for many mothers. They find they can express more milk in a shorter period of time in the morning. In the evening, on the other hand—when they are tired and their babies may be fussy—many mothers report they are able to express less milk. An alternative to expressing once during the day is for the mother to express a little milk several times a day, cooling and combining it.

Another option that may make expression easier is for the mother to express her milk from one breast while her baby is nursing on the other breast. This is possible if a mother is using a method of expression that requires only one hand. An advantage to this is that the baby will stimulate the mother's let-down, or milk-ejection, reflex, making it easier to get the milk flowing and therefore easier to express extra milk.

Assure the mother that even after she expresses her milk, there will be enough for her baby. If she expresses several ounces or milliliters right before the baby wants to nurse, he may want to nurse again a little sooner than usual. Explain that—unlike a bottle—the breast is never empty. In fact, a substantial amount of the milk is produced during the feeding.

Suggest the mother share with the baby's caregiver information on handling human milk and encouraging a baby to take a bottle.

Suggest the mother be sure her baby's caregiver knows about handling of human milk (see the next section). Also, share with her the information in the section, "Feeding Tips for the Baby's Caregiver" in the chapter "Employment and Breastfeeding" if she has questions about how the milk is supposed to look, how much milk to leave, and how to encourage a baby to take a bottle.

Mention to the mother that an alternative to expressing her milk is bringing her baby with her.

After giving the mother all the information she wants on milk expression, mention that rather than leaving the baby with a caregiver while they go out, some mothers choose to bring the baby along. For some mothers, this is less time-consuming than learning to express (and less expensive than buying a pump).

If the mother wants more information, offer to brainstorm with her on ways she could manage her baby and breastfeeding in her situation. For example, if the mother is going shopping, discuss discreet nursing or—if she is uncomfortable nursing in front of others—talk about alternatives, such as using clothing fitting rooms for breastfeeding.

STORAGE AND HANDLING OF HUMAN MILK

How Long to Store Human Milk

Human milk has been found to have properties that protect it from bacterial contamination, which allow it to be stored longer than previously thought.

Recent research indicates that human milk has previously unrecognized properties that protect it from bacterial contamination. These studies indicate that refrigerated human milk can stay fresh longer than the previously recommended 24, 48, or 72 hours (Pardou 1994; Barger and Bull 1987; Sosa 1987) and that milk stored at slightly below room temperature (for example, in a cooler with ice packs) can stay fresh for up to 24 hours (Hamosh 1996). In one study (Barger 1987), there was no statistically significant difference between the bacterial levels of milk stored for 10 hours at room temperature and milk refrigerated for 10 hours. Another study (Pardou 1994) found that after 8 days of refrigeration some of the milk actually had lower bacterial levels than it did on the day it was expressed. The researchers concluded that milk that will be used within 8 days should be refrigerated rather than frozen, because the antimicrobial qualities of human milk are better preserved by refrigeration.

Timetables for human milk storage vary, depending on whether the milk is kept at room temperature, refrigerated, or frozen, and if frozen, where the milk is stored.

The following guidelines apply to mothers who:

- have a healthy, full-term baby;
- are storing their milk for home use (as opposed to hospital use);
- wash their hands before expressing; and
- use containers that have been washed in hot, soapy water and then rinsed well.

Human Milk Storage
At room temperature
   Term colostrum (milk expressed within 6 days of delivery)
   - at 80.6 to 89.6 degrees Fahrenheit (27 to 32 degrees C) 12 hours (Nwankwo 1988)
   Mature milk
   - at 60 degrees Fahrenheit (15 degrees C) 24 hours (Hamosh 1996)
   - at 66 to 72 degrees Fahrenheit (19-22 degrees C) 10 hours (Barger and Bull 1987)
   - at 79 degrees Fahrenheit (25 degrees C) 4 to 6 hours (Hamosh 1996; Pittard 1985)
In a refrigerator
   Mature milk
   - at 32 to 39 degrees Fahrenheit (0 to 4 degrees C) 8 days (Pardou 1994)
In a freezer
   - in a freezer compartment located inside a refrigerator 2 weeks
   - in a selfcontained freezer unit of a refrigerator 3 or 4 months (temperature varies because the door opens and closes frequently).
   - in a separate deep freeze at a constant 0 degrees Fahrenheit (-19 degrees C) 6 months or longer.

All stored milk should be labeled and dated.

Encourage the mother to label each container with the month, date, and year. This will allow the milk to be used in the order in which it was expressed.

If the milk will be given in a setting where more than one baby is being fed (such as a hospital or day-care facility), the baby's name should also be written on each container.

Other guidelines may be used for human milk storage if the baby is ill or premature.

Guidelines may be different for a mother who is expressing and storing milk for a sick or premature baby. Suggest that a mother with an ill or premature baby discuss storage guidelines with her baby's hospital staff.

Choice and Use of a Storage Container

Milk storage containers may be made of glass, plastic, or stainless steel.

If the baby gets most of his nourishment directly from breastfeeding and receives expressed milk only occasionally, the type of storage container is not a major consideration. The makeup of the storage container is of concern only when the baby receives most of his nourishment from expressed human milk.

Express/Store Milk

Research is conflicting about the advantages and disadvantages of storage containers made from different materials. Storage time is also a factor.

For the baby who receives most of his nourishment from expressed human milk, the type of storage container used should be carefully considered. However, research on storage containers composed of different materials is scanty and its conclusions conflicting, with most recommendations based on little information. For example, one study (Paxton and Cress 1979) found that more of human milk's leukocytes adhered to glass as compared to plastic, which led to the recommendation that fresh milk be stored in plastic rather than glass. (Glass was still recommended for freezing, because freezing kills most leukocytes.) A second study (Pittard and Bill 1981) complicated the issue when it found that different types of leukocytes react differently to glass. A third study (Goldblum 1981) convinced many to go back to recommending glass when it was found that length of storage time made a difference, as many of the leukocytes that had adhered to the glass were released over time and that after 24 hours the milk stored in glass had a greater increase in leukocytes than the milk stored in plastic.

Due to the results of one recent study (Williamson and Murti 1996), some are recommending glass over stainless steel (Arnold 1995), which is used for milk storage in some developing countries, because the live cells in milk were found to adhere in greater numbers to stainless steel than those stored in glass.

Milk storage bags, a type of plastic storage container, are used by many women due to their practical advantages. Milk bags take up less storage space than hard-sided storage containers and can be attached directly to a breast pump and used to collect the milk in place of a bottle, cutting down on time spent transferring milk and reducing the number of pump parts that need to be cleaned after each pumping session. However, some recommend against their use, particularly for hospitalized babies, because there is more risk of leakage than with hard-sided containers and they are not as airtight, increasing the possibility of contamination (Arnold 1995). One study (Goldblum 1981) found a 60% decrease in some of the milk's antibodies and a loss of fat that adhered to the plastic sides of the milk bags. However, only the thin, plastic disposable bottle liners were studied, so these findings may not apply to the thicker bags specially designed for freezing human milk. Also, these results have not been duplicated.

Although some consider these bags more difficult to pour milk from (Arnold 1995), some brands have built-in tear spouts. For bags without tear spouts, milk can be removed safely and easily by clipping one corner of the bag with sterile scissors. In some cases, using milk bags may decrease the possibility of milk contamination by reducing the need to transfer milk from one container to another, for example if a mother expresses her milk directly into a milk storage bag and the baby is fed from the same bag with the type of bottle that uses disposable liners.

Some milk storage bags are specially designed for freezing human milk. If disposable bottle liners are used for freezing milk, they need extra protection to prevent leaking and contamination.

Some milk storage bags are pre-sterilized and designed specially for freezing milk. They are thicker than bags made primarily for feeding, include self-sealers, and have areas for labeling. (See "The Use of Breast Pumps and Other Products" for source information.) Others, sold specifically as liners for infant feeding bottles are designed for feeding not storage, and do not include closures (although twist ties can be used). Freezing milk in this less-durable type of plastic liner can be risky. Removing air from the bag can be tricky, the seams may burst during freezing, and the bag may leak during thawing. If the mother chooses to freeze her milk in disposable bottle liners, suggest she follow this procedure for extra protection:

- Put the bag of milk inside another empty bag to avoid tearing.
- Squeeze out the air at the top.
- Roll down the bag to about an inch (2.5 cm) above the milk.
- Close the bag and seal it.
- Place the sealed bag upright in a heavy, plastic container with a lid, and then seal the lid before putting it in the freezer.

When freezing milk in hard-sided containers, glass, which is the least porous, offers the most protection. Suggest the mother use a solid cap for the best seal and to tighten the cap after the milk is frozen.

Glass is the first choice as a storage container for freezing milk. Glass is the least porous, so it offers the best protection for frozen milk. The second choice is clear, hard plastic (polycarbonate). The third choice is cloudy, hard plastic (polypropylene). For maximum protection, the storage container should be sealed with a solid, single-piece cap.

When the milk freezes, it expands. In order to avoid damage to the container and contamination of the milk, it is necessary to leave about an inch (2.5 cm) at the top of the container to allow for expansion. Suggest the mother tighten bottle caps after the milk is completely frozen so that the displaced air can escape.

In one reported case, freezing human milk in brightly colored plastic feeding bottles was believed to have resulted in a chemical odor and the baby refused the affected milk.

Any container used to store milk should be clean.

To avoid bacterial contamination, all storage containers, bottles, nipples, cups, spoons, or any other feeding utensils need to be clean.

To clean a hard-sided milk storage container, use hot, soapy water, rinse well and allow to air dry.

Handling and Thawing Human Milk

Fresh human milk separates, as it is not homogenized, and may appear bluish, yellowish, or brownish.

Some mothers worry when they see their expressed milk separate into milk and cream, because they are used to seeing homogenized cow's milk. Assure the mother that this separation is normal. Suggest the milk be shaken gently to mix it before a feeding.

Also, it is normal for human milk to be either bluish, yellowish, or even brownish in color. Some foods or dyes consumed by the mother have also been shown to change the color of mother's milk. Frozen milk may take on a yellowish color, but this does not mean it is spoiled, unless it smells sour or tastes bad.

Any milk expressed within a 24 hour period can be expressed directly into the same container if the previously expressed milk was stored between 32 and 60 degrees Fahrenheit.

A mother need not keep separate batches of milk expressed at different times during the day, provided the previous batches have been stored between 32 and 60 degrees Fahrenheit (between 0 and 15 degrees C). If the previously expressed milk was stored in this temperature range, the mother can express her milk directly into a container of previously expressed milk for up to 24 hours and then follow the storage recommendations based on the time and date of the first milk expressed. If the previously expressed milk was stored at between 66 and 72 degrees Fahrenheit (19 and 22 degrees C), total storage time should not exceed 10 hours from the time first milk was expressed (Barger and Bull 1987). If the previously expressed milk was stored at 79 degrees Fahrenheit (25 degrees C), total storage time should not exceed 4 to 6 hours from the time first milk was expressed (Hamosh 1996; Pittard 1985). If the previously expressed milk was frozen, see the next point for guidelines.

Freshly expressed milk can be added to already frozen milk if it is cooled first and there is less fresh milk than frozen milk.

Fresh milk can be added to frozen milk provided it is first cooled and there is less fresh milk than frozen milk. After expressing her milk, suggest the mother cool it for about a half hour before adding it to frozen milk, so it does not thaw the top layer. (Human milk should not be thawed and refrozen.)

Frozen human milk should be thawed by running it under cool and then warm running water.

To thaw frozen milk, suggest the mother or caregiver hold the container under cool running water and gradually add warmer water until the milk is thawed and heated to room temperature. If more than one container is being thawed, the caregiver can combine the milk for a feeding. After the milk is thawed, the milk should be shaken before testing the temperature.

    If warm running water is not available, a caregiver can heat a pan of water on the stove and then submerge the container of frozen milk into the warm water. If necessary,

Express/Store Milk

remove the container of milk and reheat the water. A container of milk should not be heated directly on the stove.

    Human milk should not be heated in a microwave oven, as valuable components of the milk will be destroyed if it is heated over 130 degrees F (55 degrees C). (Quan 1992; Sigmen 1989). Also, microwave ovens heat liquids unevenly, causing "hot spots" in the milk that could burn the baby.

Once frozen milk is thawed, it can be kept refrigerated, but not refrozen.

Previously frozen milk that was thawed can be safely kept refrigerated for up to 24 hours (The Human Milk Banking Association of North America 1993). It should not be refrozen.

    Some mothers have reported a slightly soapy smell to their frozen milk after it was thawed. This change in smell has been attributed to changes in the milk fats related to storage in self-defrosting refrigerator-freezers; it has not been found to be harmful to the baby (Lawrence, p. 619).

Suggest the mother store frozen human milk in two- to four-ounce quantities to eliminate waste.

If the mother will be freezing her milk, suggest that she freeze it in two- to four-ounce (60-120 ml) quantities. Small quantities thaw and warm quickly and less milk will be left if the baby does not take it all. This also allows the mother or caregiver to thaw out only the amount of milk the baby is expected to drink. If more is needed, it can be thawed under cool and then warm running water.

The baby may need less human milk than formula.

The baby receiving only mother's milk may need fewer ounces (milliliters) per day than the baby receiving both formula and human milk and the baby receiving formula alone. A study published in the *Journal of Pediatrics* (Butte 1984) found that at four months of age breastfeeding babies consumed 25 percent fewer calories than formula-fed babies of the same age, even though their weight gains were comparable. Some attribute this decreased need for calories to the lower and more organized heart rates of breastfed babies which results in a lower expenditure of energy as compared with babies on formula (Roepke 1995; Zeskind and Goff 1992).

When human milk is stored or used at the workplace and at child-care facilities, it can be kept in a common refrigerator and no special precautions are necessary when handling it.

Both the US Centers for Disease Control (1988) and the Occupational Safety and Health Administration (OSHA) agree that human milk is not among the body fluids that require rubber gloves for handling and feeding or require storage in a separate refrigerator as a biohazardous material. Although concerns have been raised in some areas of the US about the need to use universal precautions for blood-borne pathogens with human milk, as of this writing US federal health agencies do not deem this necessary or beneficial (Simonds and Chanock 1993).

    The American Academy of Pediatrics and American Public Health Association support this position in their joint guidelines for child-care facilities, *Caring for Our Children: National Health and Safety Performance Standards: Guidelines for Out-of-Home Child Care Programs.* (This publication is available from AAP Publications Department, 141 Northwest Point Boulevard, P.O. Box 927, Elk Grove Village IL 60009-0927 USA. Telephone: 800-433-9016 or 847-228-5005. FAX 847-228-1281.)

This means that at the workplace and at childcare facilities, human milk can be stored along with other foods in a common refrigerator and no special precautions are needed when handling or feeding a baby with human milk.

Publications for Parents

Bernshaw, N. *A Mother's Guide to Milk Expression and Breast Pumps.* Schaumburg, Illinois: La Leche League International, 1996, Publication No. 30.

La Leche League International. THE WOMANLY ART OF BREASTFEEDING, 35th Anniversary ed. Schaumburg, Illinois, 1991, pp. 127-37, 168-70, 297, 317-18.

Marmet, C. *Manual Expression of Breast Milk: The Marmet Technique.* Schaumburg, Illinois: La Leche League International, 1988. Publication No. 27.

References

Armstrong, H. Low-tech problem-solving in a high-tech world. Presented at La Leche League 14th International Conference, July 1995. (Ordering information for audiocassettes is available from La Leche League International.)

Arnold, Lois. Storage containers for human milk: an issue revisited. *J Hum Lact* 1995; 11(4):325-28.

Auerbach, K. Sequential and simultaneous breast pumping: a comparison. *Int J Nurs Stud* 1990; 27(3):257-65.

Barger, J. and Bull, P. A comparison of the bacterial composition of breast milk stored at room temperature and stored in the refrigerator. *Int J Childbirth Ed* 1987; 2:29-30.

Bernard, D. Hand-expression. NEW BEGINNINGS 1996; 13(2):52.

Butte, N. et al. Human milk intake and growth in exclusively breast-fed infants. *J Pediatr* 1984; 104:187-95.

Centers for Disease Control. Update. *MMWR* 1988; 37(24):376-88.

Daly, S. and Hartmann, P. Infant demand and milk supply. Part 2: The short-term control of milk synthesis in lactating women. *J Hum Lact* 1995; 11(1):27-37.

deCarvalho, M. et al. Frequency of milk expression and milk production by mothers of nonnursing premature neonates. *Am J Dis Child* 1985; 139:483-87.

Dusdieker, L. et al. Effect of supplemental fluids on human milk production. *J Pediatr* 1985; 106(2):207-11.

Garza, C. et al. Effects of method of collection and storage on nutrients in human milk. *Early Hum Dev* 1982; 6:295-303.

Goldblum, R. et al. Human milk banking I: effects of container upon immunologic factors in mature milk. *Nutr Res* 1981; 1:449-59.

Goldman, A. et al. Effects of storage container upon immunologic factors in mature human milk and colostrum. *HM: Bio & Soc Value* 1980; n:197-205.

Green, D. et al. The relative efficacy of four methods of human milk expression. *Early Human Dev* 1982; 6:153-58.

Hamosh, M. et al. Breastfeeding and the working mother: effect of time and temperature of short-term storage on proteolysis, lipolysis, and bacterial growth in milk. *Pediatrics* 1996; 97(4):492-98.

Hopkinson, J. et al. Milk production by mothers of premature infants. *Pediatrics* 1988; 81:815-20.

The Human Milk Banking Association of North America. *Recommendations for Collection, Storage, and Handling of a Mother's Milk for Her Own Infant in the Hospital Setting.* West Hartford, CT, USA, 1993.

King, F. *Helping Mothers to Breastfeed,* 2nd ed. African Medical and Research Foundation, 1992, pp. 118-25.

Lang, S. et al. Sodium in hand and pump expressed human breast milk. *Early Human Dev* 1994; 38:131-38.

Lawrence, R. *Breastfeeding: A Guide for the Medical Profession,* 4th ed. St. Louis: Mosby, 1994, pp. 599-632.

Mohrbacher, N. Mothers who chose to pump instead of breastfeeding. *Circle of Caring* 1996; 9(2):1.

Nwankwo, M. et al. Bacterial growth in expressed breastmilk. *Ann Trop Pediatr* 1988; 8:92-95.

Pardou, A. et al. Human milk banking: influence of storage processes and of bacterial contamination on some milk constituents. *Biol Neonate* 1994; 65:302-09.

Paxton, C. and Cress, C. Survival of human milk leukocytes. *J Pediatr* 1979; 94:61-64.

Pittard, W. et al. Bacteriostatic qualities of human milk. *J Pediatr* 1985; 107:240-43.

Pittard, W. and Bill, K. Human milk banking: effect of refrigeration on cellular components. *Clin Pediatr* 1981; 20:31-33.

Quan, R. et al. Effects of microwave radiation on anti-infective factors in human milk. *Pediatrics* 1992; 89:667-69.

Riordan, J. and Auerbach, K. *Breastfeeding and Human Lactation.* Boston and London: Jones and Bartlett, 1993, pp. 257, 401-27.

Roepke, J. Growth of breastfed babies—research review. Presented at La Leche League's 14th International Conference, Chicago, Illinois, July 1995. (Audiocassette order information available from LLLI.)

Express/Store Milk

Sigman, M. et al. Effects of microwaving human milk: changes in IgA content and bacterial count. *J Am Diet Assoc* 1989; 89:690-92.

Simonds, R. and Chanock, S. Medical issues related to caring for human immunodeficiency virus-infected children in and out of the home. *Pediatr Infec Dis J* 1993; 12:845-52.

Sosa, R. and Barness, L. Bacterial growth in refrigerated human milk. *Am J Dis Child* 1987; 141:111-12.

UNICEF and WHO. *Breastfeeding management and promotion in a baby-friendly hospital.* New York: United Nations Children's Fund, 1993, pp. 94, 98-99.

Walker, M. Breastfeeding the premature infant. *NAACOG Clin Issues Perinat Women Health Nurs* 1992; 3(4):620-33.

Williamson, M. and Murti, P. Effects of storage, time, temperature, and composition of containers on biologic components of human milk. *J Hum Lact* 1996; 12(1):31-35.

Woolridge, M. Analysis, classification, etiology of diagnosed low milk output. Presented at the International Lactation Consultant Association Conference, Scottsdale, Arizona USA, July 1995.

Zeskind, P. and Goff, D. Rhythmic organization of heart rate in breastfed and bottlefed newborn infants. *Early Dev and Parent* 1992; 1(2):79-87.

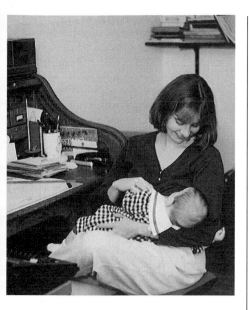

10

Employment and Breastfeeding

THE MOTHER'S FEELINGS
Feeding Options
Breastfeeding and Work Options

MILK EXPRESSION
Why Express?
Basics of Successful Milk Expression
Choosing a Method of Expression
How Often to Express
Expressing Away from Home

HOME STRATEGIES

FEEDING TIPS FOR BABY'S CAREGIVER

STORAGE AND HANDLING OF HUMAN MILK
How Long to Store Human Milk
Choice and Use of a Storage Container
Handling and Thawing Human Milk

THE MOTHER'S FEELINGS

Even if a mother is regularly separated from her baby due to working outside the home, attending school, or any other outside commitments she can breast-feed if she chooses. To make it work, the mother must first decide if she wants to provide her milk for her baby while she is away. If she does, she must plan either to express her milk or breastfeed her baby every few hours to maintain her milk supply and avoid overly full breasts. If she expresses her milk, she must also make arrangements for her baby to be fed while they are apart. If the mother decides to provide another food for her baby while she is away, she will want to avoid uncomfortable fullness by allowing enough time to slowly decrease her milk supply before she begins leaving her baby. Another option would be to express her milk to comfort while she is away, slowly decreasing the amount of expressing until her body comfortably adjusts to her new, lower level of milk production.

Most mothers have concerns about being separated from their babies. Offer to discuss her feelings with her.

Assure the mother that her concerns about being away from her baby are normal.

Even if the mother has made up her mind to breastfeed, there are many other decisions to be made that can add to her anxiety about being away from her baby. For example, the mother may need:

- to find a caregiver she can trust who will support her in breastfeeding,
- to decide on and learn an effective method of milk expression,
- to know more about breastfeeding—for example, the factors that affect her milk supply,
- to make arrangements for a time and place for nursing the baby or expressing milk at work or school,
- to help her baby become comfortable taking feedings from his caregiver while she is away.

Ask the mother what most concerns her, and listen to and acknowledge her feelings. Also, offer to brainstorm with her on the areas that worry her. It may be reassuring for her to discuss her options.

The mother's motivation and determination will be important factors in her continuing to breast-feed. If she begins to have doubts, help her reassess her priorities to determine if they are still valid.

The mother will need motivation and determination to continue breastfeeding. She may receive advice from others to stop breastfeeding "to make it easier on herself." The time she spends expressing her milk at work or school may limit her social time with others and cause her to question her decision.

Because of a demanding lifestyle, some mothers lose sight of their original purpose for wanting to continue breastfeeding. If so, help the mother reassess her reasons for returning to work and continuing to breastfeed to determine if they are still valid.

Also, remind the mother that the need to express does not go on forever. Once the baby begins taking other foods, the mother may be able to slowly increase the time between milk expressions. As the baby gets older, he can be fed solids by the caregiver, while the mother and baby enjoy the breastfeeding relation-ship whenever they are together.

Encourage the mother to seek out those who support her efforts. With support, the mother will be better able to withstand outside pressures.

Feeding Options

The mother may choose to provide her milk for her baby or supplement with formula. If the baby is at least four to six months old, he can receive other foods when they are apart.

When helping the mother consider her options, ask the mother what is most important to her about continuing to breastfeed.

If the mother is motivated to provide her milk to prevent allergies, offer superior nutrition, and provide protection from illness, she may want to avoid formula, which she can do by arranging breastfeeding breaks with her baby during work or school time or by expressing and storing her milk for her baby while she is away.

If the mother wants to breastfeed mainly for closeness, she might not mind if her milk supply decreases and her baby is supplemented with formula. The mother may decide to breastfeed when she and her baby are together and arrange for him to be given formula when they are apart. She would express her milk only when she needs to relieve fullness.

If the baby is four to six months or older when the mother begins work or school it may be possible to substitute some solid food for breastfeeding, depending upon the length of their separations. Suggest the mother talk to her baby's doctor for his or her recommendation.

If the mother finds she is not able to express enough milk for her baby, she can try breastfeeding or expressing more often or supplement with formula or other foods.

If the mother is not able to express enough milk for her baby, she has several options:

Employment

- She can encourage her baby to breastfeed more often when she and her baby are together. Some mothers make an effort to nurse their babies more often during the evening and night so that the baby spends more time sleeping while they are apart and needs less expressed milk or formula.
- She can arrange for more breastfeeding breaks with her baby or express her milk more frequently while at work or school.
- If she is using hand-expression or a hand pump, another option would be for her to use an automatic electric double pump, which is more effective at milking the breast.
- She can supplement her milk with formula, or solid foods if her baby is at least four to six months old.

The mother's milk supply is based on how often the milk is removed from the breast, whether by breastfeeding or expressing. To increase her milk supply, the mother can breastfeed or express more often. Within a day or two she should notice an increase in her supply.

Breastfeeding and Work Options

A mother's work choices have been found to affect breastfeeding.

To find out more specific information about how employment affects breastfeeding, Kathleen Auerbach, PhD, a La Leche League Leader and lactation consultant, surveyed 567 married and single employed nursing mothers. Of the factors Dr. Auerbach analyzed, the following—listed in order of greater to lesser significance—affected the course of breastfeeding (Auerbach and Guss 1984).

1. How soon the mother returned to work. This had the greatest effect on the course of breastfeeding, even more than how many hours a week the mothers worked. Mothers who rejoined the workforce when their babies were at least sixteen weeks old typically nursed longer than those who returned to work sooner.
2. Whether the mother worked full- or part-time. A greater percentage of the mothers working part-time nursed their babies for at least a year. Weaning before one year occurred most often when mothers returned to work full-time before their babies were sixteen weeks old. The longer a mother waited to return to work and the fewer hours she worked, the longer she was likely to nurse.
3. Whether or not the mothers expressed their milk when they missed a feeding. Eighty-six percent of the mothers surveyed expressed milk while they were away from their babies. Mothers who chose to express their milk were more likely to nurse longer than those who did not.

Other studies confirm that these and other factors affect breastfeeding. One study found that women who returned to work before their baby was two months old had more breastfeeding problems and weaned earlier than women who returned to work later (Kearney and Cronenwett 1991). Another study found that women working part-time breastfed longer than women working full-time and that women in professional occupations breastfed longer than women in technical or sales positions (Kurinij 1989). A third study found that women who worked less than 20 hours per week breastfed longer than women who worked more than 20 hours per week (Gielen 1991). A fourth study found that women breastfed longer when their babies were cared for near their workplace and they fed their babies "on demand" rather than on a schedule (even though these women tended to return to work earlier) and that they weaned earlier when they used formula routinely or switched from exclusive breastfeeding to nursing only once or twice a day (Morse 1989). A fifth study found that women breastfed longer when they took longer maternity leave and worked fewer hours (Hills-Bonczyk 1993).

Ask if the mother is interested in exploring work or school options that will give her more time with her baby.

Some mothers have already made a definite commitment as to when and for how long they will be away from their babies. Other mothers, however, may be open to exploring alternatives that will give them more time with their babies and make breastfeeding easier, such as:

- working at home—the mother may spend all her working hours at home or divide her time between home and the workplace;
- job-sharing—dividing one full-time position between two people (perhaps another mother);
- flex-time—allowing the mother to change her work schedule as her baby's needs change, such as arranging to work while her baby is sleeping—for example, the night shift—and adjusting her work hours as her baby grows;
- part-time—arranging to return to work or school on a part-time rather than full-time basis;
- bringing the baby along. Depending on the baby's age and temperament, the mother may be able to work or study with her baby nearby, breastfeeding when needed.

If the mother can arrange to breastfeed her baby during breaks or mealtimes, it may cut down or eliminate her need to express milk.

One alternative that could cut down or eliminate the need to express milk is for the mother to arrange for time with her baby for breastfeeding. There are several possibilities:

- If child care is available at work or school, the mother may be able to go to her baby regularly to breastfeed.
- If the baby's caregiver is located near the mother's work or school, he or she may agree to bring the baby to the mother at breaks and/or mealtimes.
- The mother may make arrangements to go to the baby at breaks and/or mealtimes to breastfeed.

When the mother is arranging for child care, encourage her to consider these possibilities. Many mothers seek child-care arrangements near their homes, without considering the benefit of having their babies near them at work or school.

If the mother wants her baby to be fed only her milk, she can plan ahead to make this easier.

Before the mother begins work or school, she can plan ahead to make it easier to provide her milk for her baby:

Wait as long as possible after the baby's birth to begin regular separations. The first two to three months seem to be most critical for breastfeeding. Breastfeeding tends to go more smoothly and continue longer if a mother first establishes a healthy milk supply. The early months are also important in establishing a strong mother-baby relationship.

Delay introducing a bottle until the baby has been breastfeeding well, ideally for at least three to four weeks. Some mothers are told to begin giving bottles soon after birth "to get the baby used to them," but one study found that the vast majority of babies accept a bottle easily whether it is introduced at one month (70%), two months (63%), or even between three and six months (72%). Only 4% of babies refused the bottle when it was introduced at one month of age (Kearney and Cronenwett 1991). Also, early and consistent use of bottles is no guarantee that a baby will continue to take the bottle over time. Even breastfed babies who take bottles early sometimes refuse bottles when they get older (Frantz 1993b).

Not only is early introduction of bottles unnecessary, it can sometimes bring a quick end to breastfeeding. If the mother feeds her baby a bottle too soon, regardless of what's in it, it may cause breastfeeding problems. If a baby receives both breast and bottle during the early weeks while he is learning how to nurse he may become confused and breastfeed less effectively or refuse the breast altogether (Neifert 1995; Newman 1990).

If formula is given in the early weeks, it can interfere with the establishment of a healthy milk supply. The best way to assure that a mother will have enough milk after she returns to work or school is to breastfeed frequently and exclusively in the early weeks. Establishing a good milk supply early gives the mother more choices later.

Employment

Some breastfeeding experts recommend breastfeeding exclusively until the mother returns to work and then letting the caregiver introduce the bottle at that time (Frantz 1993b). Although this works well for many mothers, some mothers want to be sure their babies will take a bottle before they go back to work. In this case, suggest the mother arrange to have someone else (ideally the baby's future caregiver) introduce the bottle about 10 days before she returns to work. Many babies refuse to take a bottle from their mothers. A baby may also refuse if he knows mother is nearby. If the baby is resistant or refuses to take the bottle after the mother leaves, suggest the caregiver experiment with different types of bottle nipples and other techniques listed in the later section, "Feeding Tips for the Baby's Caregiver."

Start building a reserve supply of frozen milk about two weeks before beginning regular separations. Many mothers find it easiest to express in the morning—about an hour or two after the baby has nursed—when they are most rested and can express more milk in a shorter period of time. Other mothers prefer to express a little milk several times a day and combine these small amounts of milk. Another alternative is for the mother to express from one breast while the baby nurses from the other.

Begin work or school on a Thursday or Friday as the first day. The mother will then have the weekend to recover her strength and plan a strategy for the coming week.

When planning how often to express milk during their separations, count the entire time away from the baby. Mothers often count only the time they spend at work or school, without including time spent driving to the sitter's and then to the workplace or school in the morning and vice versa in the evening. When making plans for expressing, they need to consider the entire time they will be away from their baby and plan to express about every three hours.

Be aware that total time involved is not all time spent expressing. When the mother is calculating the time she needs to express, remind her that she will not only need to allow time for the expressing itself but also for going to and from her expressing place and—if she is using a pump—for setting up the pump and for washing, drying, and putting away the pump accessories.

If the mother will be expressing her milk at work, suggest she talk to her supervisor in advance about her needs, mentioning the benefits to her employer.

Because a relaxed atmosphere at work will make expressing easier, suggest the mother discuss her special needs with her supervisor before returning. Suggest she discuss:

- whether it will be possible to arrange for time with her baby for breast-feeding, either at her workplace or the caregiver's,
- where she can find a comfortable place to express her milk,
- how often she will need to express and how long it will take,
- how she plans to fit this time into her workday.

Many mothers hesitate to ask their employer for time and a place to express milk, because they feel as if they are asking for special favors. Be sure the mother knows that her employer will benefit financially by supporting breastfeeding at the workplace. For example, one study found that when babies receive human milk, mothers are absent fewer days from work (Cohen 1995). Another study of babies cared for in a day-care center (where incidence of illness tends to be higher) found that the higher the percentage of human milk in their diet, the less likely they were to become ill (Jones and Matheny 1993). Healthier babies mean lower health care costs for the company, higher job productivity, employee satisfaction, and morale. Supporting breastfeeding at the workplace may also result in less employee turnover and an earlier return to work after childbirth (Healthy Mothers/Healthy Babies). Being aware of the ways the workplace benefits from breastfeeding allows a mother to approach her supervisor with an attitude of "this is good for my family and good for the company."

Because of the cost savings involved, several large US corporations have begun corporate lactation programs for their employees, with the company providing breastfeeding mothers with a private place to express their milk during work hours and covering the cost of breast pumps and related equipment, as well as the services of a lactation consultant (Cohen 1995; Cohen and Mrtek 1994). In a study that followed 187 employees who chose to take part in a corporate lactation program, 75% of the employees who breastfed after returning to work continued breastfeeding until their child was at least six months old. Average breastfeeding duration was 8.1 months (Cohen and Mrtek 1994). Another study found that without special lactation services, only 10% of employed breastfeeding mothers nursed for six months (Ryan and Martinez 1989).

Suggest the mother look for a caregiver for her baby who is supportive of breastfeeding.

One of the suggestions given by the employed mothers in Auerbach and Guss's study (1984) was to find a child-care provider who is supportive of breastfeeding. Suggest that the mother emphasize to her baby's caregiver that she does not want her baby to be given formula or other foods without her permission and that the baby should be held while being fed.

A caregiver who is supportive of breastfeeding will give the mother the continuing emotional support she needs to provide milk for her baby, as well as helping to make breastfeeding a priority.

MILK EXPRESSION

Why Express?

The mother's milk supply is dependent on how often the milk is removed from her breasts, whether by breast-feeding or expressing.

Milk supply is a frequent concern of mothers who are regularly separated from their babies (Hills-Bonczyk 1993). For them—just as for other mothers—milk is produced on a supply and demand basis. This means that the amount of milk produced is dependent on regular and frequent removal of milk from the breasts, whether it is through nursing, hand-expression, or pumping.

Conversely, regular formula supplementation and fewer expressing sessions and/or nursings contribute to a gradual decrease in milk production.

Regular milk expression offers advantages to the mother, even if she doesn't plan to save her milk for her baby.

Even if the mother does not plan to provide her milk for her baby, regular expression (at least every three hours) during separations offers advantages to the mother:

- It prevents or relieves uncomfortable fullness.
- It minimizes leaking.
- It helps prevent engorgement and mastitis.

Suggest the mother express as often as needed, depending upon the age of the baby and her degree of fullness.

Basics of Successful Milk Expression

Stimulating a milk let-down is crucial to successful milk expression.

Whatever method of expression a mother uses, stimulating a milk let-down is crucial. When a mother nurses her baby at the breast, her baby's sucking naturally stimulates the release of the hormone oxytocin, which causes the muscles around the milk-producing glands to squeeze, forcing the milk from all parts of the breast toward the nipple. This is the milk let-down or milk-ejection reflex.

When a mother puts a pump to her breast or begins to hand-express, many of the physical cues that trigger her milk let-down are missing. A baby at the breast is soft, warm, smells good, and stimulates loving feelings in the mother.

Employment

These cues are missing when a mother hand-expresses or uses a pump, and milk expression may initially feel foreign to the mother. For some mothers, the skin-to-skin contact of hand-expression stimulates a let-down more effectively than a pump.

Without a milk let-down, the mother may be unable to express more than the small fraction of her milk that is in the milk reservoirs near the nipple. Even though she may be producing plenty of milk, most of it will be left in the breast. To make up for the lack of her baby's physical cues while expressing, the mother may need to create other cues to signal her body to let down her milk (see next point).

If the mother will be using a breast pump, tell her that breast pumps that automatically regulate suction and release tend to be considerably more effective at stimulating a milk let-down than pumps that require the mother to regulate the suction and release. However, even with these more effective pumps, the mother's let-down may be affected if she is tense or upset.

Suggest the mother allow herself about ten days to two weeks to practice her method of expression before returning to work.

By giving herself ten days to two weeks to practice her method of expression, the mother can master it and be sure it will work for her. This will also give her time to build a reserve of milk so that she will have extra milk on hand as she adjusts to her new routine.

Once at work, setting up a milk-expression routine and finding a comfortable, relaxed time and place to express can help stimulate a good milk flow.

Successful milk expression is as much psychological as it is physical. If a mother is tense, upset, or uncomfortable, these feelings may delay or inhibit her milk flow even when using a breast pump that automatically regulates suction and release. Many employed mothers have used the following suggestions to maximize their milk expression:

- Allow enough time so as not to feel rushed.
- Express milk in a familiar and comfortable setting. Privacy and comfortable seating promote relaxation, which enhances milk let-down.
- Minimize distractions. Take the phone off the hook and lock the door, if possible.
- Follow a pre-expression routine. Use warmth to relax and stimulate milk flow by applying heat to the breasts or putting a warm wrap around the shoulders. Stimulate the breast and/or nipples through massage. Relax with childbirth breathing or mental imagery, such as envisioning oneself on a warm beach.

- Think about the baby. Make a phone call to check on the baby before expressing. Imagine the baby at the breast while expressing. Bring a picture of the baby to work to look at, a tape recording of the baby's cry to listen to, or a piece of baby's clothing to touch and smell.

For more information, see "Basics of Successful Pumping" in the supplement, "The Use of Breast Pumps and Other Products" and "The Key to Successful Milk Expression: Stimulating the Let-Down" in the chapter "Expression and Storage of Human Milk."

Milk expression should never be painful. If it is, the mother should stop and make changes.

It is possible to damage sensitive breast tissue, so suggest the mother stop what she is doing if her method of milk expression is painful or uncomfortable. Discomfort or pain will also inhibit her milk let-down.

If the mother is hand-expressing, talk to her about how she is doing it. She may need to learn a more comfortable technique. (For more information, see "Hand-Expression" in the chapter "Expression and Storage of Human Milk.")

If the mother is using a breast pump, see the section "What to Do If Pumping Hurts" in the supplement "The Use of Breast Pumps and Other Products."

Choosing a Method of Expression

The speed and effectiveness of the mother's method of milk expression will affect her ability to meet her breastfeeding goals.

A mother who uses a fast and effective method of milk expression will be more likely to meet her breastfeeding goals than a mother whose method is slow or inefficient. One study of employed mothers found the three most frequently cited requirements for successfully combining employment with breastfeeding were: a trusted childcare provider, support, and an efficient method of milk expression (Maclaughlin and Strelnick 1984).

The mother's work situation will affect her choice of method. Ask her how much time she has for expressing, where she will be expressing, and if she has access to an electrical outlet.

The mother's work schedule, her time away from her baby, the amount of time she has for milk expression, her setting, and her access to an electrical outlet will all influence the method of milk expression she selects. If the mother has 30 minutes or less to express, suggest she choose a method that allows her to express milk from both breasts simultaneously (double-pump), such as the automatic electric double pump, the semi-automatic diaphragm pump, or two small battery-operated and squeeze pumps used simultaneously. Because it is necessary for some women who single pump to interrupt milk expression several times to massage the breast and switch from side to side during each session, single-pumping may take more than twice as long as double-pumping (10 to 15 minutes as compared with 20 to 30 minutes for single-pumping). Also, some mothers have found that with practice they can learn to hand-express milk from both breasts simultaneously, with the right hand expressing the right breast and the left hand expressing the left breast, if collection containers are placed on a stable surface at the proper height (Bernard 1996). For more information, see "Hand-Expression" in the chapter "Expression and Storage of Human Milk," and "Pumping Time" under "Features that Affect a Mother's Pump Choice" in the supplement "The Use of Breast Pumps and Other Products."

The mother's access to an electrical outlet and the space available also affect her choice. Although a mother doesn't need much space to express her milk, comfort and privacy are ideal. If the mother's work area does not provide privacy and she is concerned about finding a private place to express, suggest she talk to her supervisor about the possibility of her using a private area during the limited times she will be expressing her milk. If she is unable to arrange for privacy, tell her that many women successfully express milk in less-than-ideal settings, such as bathrooms or toilet facilities and cars. If the mother will be expressing her milk in a toilet stall, she will need a method that she can use comfortably in a confined space. If the mother does not have access to an electrical outlet, she still has many choices: hand-expression, an automatic electric double pump with a rechargeable battery, a mother-powered double pump, a small motorized battery-operated single pump, the Ora'lac, or a manual pump. For the mother who works out of her car or chooses to express in her car for privacy, the mid-size electric piston pumps and Medela's Pump In Style can be powered by the car's battery via an automobile cigarette lighter by using a special cord. For more information, see "Power Source" under "Features that Affect a Mother's Pump Choice" in the supplement "The Use of Breast Pumps and Other Products."

If the mother will be using a pump in a non-private area, the amount of noise a pump makes may also be an important consideration. For more information, see "Noise Level" under "Features that Affect a Mother's Pump Choice" in the supplement "The Use of Breast Pumps and Other Products."

Full-Time Work

Some women who work full-time are able to arrange to breastfeed their babies at breaks and/or mealtimes, which cuts down or eliminates the need to express milk at work.

The amount of time a mother is away from her baby will affect her milk-expression needs. If the mother is planning to work full-time, ask her if it is possible for her to nurse the baby at any time during her workday. If the baby is being cared for near her place of work, she may be able to have the baby brought to her or to go to the baby to breastfeed at breaks and/or meal-times. Nursing breaks during the day will cut down on her need to express milk at work. If she is able to schedule her nursings so that no longer than four hours elapses between breastfeedings, she may not need to express milk at work.

Employment

For the mother away from her baby full-time, a method's effectiveness may be paramount. If the mother is planning to use a breast pump, suggest she ask about the number of suction and releases, or "cycles," it generates per minute.

If the mother will be away from her baby full-time and prefers to avoid giving formula, a method's effectiveness will be of primary importance. For the mother planning to use a breast pump, suggest the mother ask about the number of suction and releases, or "cycles," it generates per minute, which is one good gauge of effectiveness. Full-size automatic electric piston pumps use the preset motion of a metal balancing weight to automatically alternate suction and release of suction between 48 and 60 times per minute, mimicking the suck of a breastfeeding baby. The lighter mid-size electric piston pumps use a plastic piston moving back and forth horizontally to produce suction and release and feature a speed control that allows the mother to make the pump cycle faster or slower, between 30 and 60 cycles per minute, to more closely mimic her own baby's suck. The automatic diaphragm pumps use a diaphragm moving in and out to generate suction and release, with the White River 9050 generating 30 cycles minute and the Medela Pump In Style generating 48 cycles per minute.

The semi-automatic diaphragm pump, such as the Natural Choice or Nurture III, allows the mother to generate about 25 cycles per minute by covering and uncovering a vent with her finger. Some mothers who work part- or full-time find this pump effective in maintaining their milk supply; other mothers do not, probably because it produces fewer cycles per minute than the automatic double pumps.

Most small motorized single pumps allow the mother to generate at most between 4 and 7 suction-and-release cycles per minute (Frantz 1993a). (The exception is Medela's Mini Electric, a small motorized hand pump that automatically generates about 30 cycles per minute.) Fewer cycles per minute provide less breast stimulation, which tends to result in less milk expressed in a longer time, which over the long term may result in a lower milk supply. This is one reason automatic electric double pumps tend to be more effective than small motorized hand pumps at establishing and maintaining a mother's milk supply (Lang 1994; Green 1982).

For more information, see "Effectiveness" under "Features that Affect a Mother's Pump Choice" in the supplement "The Use of Breast Pumps and Other Products."

The way a pump cycles may also influence its effectiveness.

The number of cycles per minute is one measure of a pump's effectiveness, but the way a pump cycles may also influence its effectiveness. Each cycle includes three phases which are known collectively as its suction curve: a steady building of suction, a brief holding of suction at the peak, and a steady decline of suction before the process begins again. In her *Breastfeeding Product Guide 1994,* Kittie Frantz (1993a) notes that some mid-sized pumps have a hesitation in their suction curves due to the action of their pistons. She suggests that this hesitation may make these pumps less effective over the long term in maintaining some mothers' milk supply than the full-size pumps, which cycle more smoothly. According to Frantz, some mothers note an increase in their milk supply when they switch from the mid-size to the full-size pump, which she attributes to these suction-curve differences (Frantz 1993a, p. 109). However, to date, no research has been done to investigate long-term differences in effectiveness among the brands and types of automatic electric double pumps.

Automatic electric double pumps are easy to use, fast, and with regular long-term use they may be one of the most economical choices.

Automatic electric double pumps are easy to use because they work automatically. Unlike hand-expression, small motorized single pumps, or hand pumps, automatic electric double pumps do not depend upon practice or the skill of the user to be effective. The mother need only put the pump flanges to her breasts, adjust the suction control knob, sit back, and relax. The pump does the rest automatically. For more information, see "Ease of Use" under "Features that Affect a Mother's Pump Choice" in the supplement "The Use of Breast Pumps and Other Products."

Automatic electric double pumps are fast because they allow the mother to double pump (both breasts simultaneously), as well as single pump (one breast at a time), depending on the pump attachments the mother uses. Because it is necessary for some women who single pump to interrupt milk expression several times to massage the breast and switch from side to side during each session, single pumping may take more than twice as long as double pumping (10 to 15 minutes as compared with 20 to 30 minutes for single pumping). Double pumping avoids milk loss from leakage, which can occur when only one breast is being pumped and has also been found to stimulate milk production slightly more than single pumping (Auerbach 1990a).

Although an automatic double pump may cost more initially than some of the less-expensive pumps, over the long-term it may prove to be less costly. An automatic electric piston pump can be purchased (1996 purchase prices are between $1030 and $1350 US for full-size pumps and between $575 and $690 US for mid-size pumps), but most mothers find renting this type of pump more cost effective than buying. Most pump rental stations or hiring agencies offer discounted rates for long-term rentals, with long-term rental rates averaging about one-third the cost of exclusive formula-feeding. Medela's Pump In Style, an automatic electric diaphragm pump introduced in 1996, is the first automatic electric double pump that is available for purchase only. Selling at about $200 US (1996 price), this pump is integrated into a carrying case that holds the pump's attachments and stores and cools the mother's expressed milk. Another automatic diaphragm pump is the White River 9050, which is available for rent or purchase (1996 purchase price is $1075 US).

If used two or more times per day, an automatic electric double pump may cost less to use over time than a small motorized battery-powered single pump, which may need its batteries replaced every two to three days. Some mothers have found automatic electric double pumps to be more effective than small motorized single pumps or hand pumps in keeping up their milk supply over time, saving on the cost of formula. Depending on the level of use, a small motorized single pump also may wear out and need to be replaced periodically, further increasing its cost. For more information, see "Cost" under "Features that Affect a Mother's Pump Choice" in the chapter "The Use of Breastfeeding Products and Devices."

Ask the mother if she will be carrying the pump back and forth between home and work every day. If so, size and portability will be major considerations in pump selection.

Some women are able to leave their pump at work. In this case, the size and weight of the pump may not be important. However, if the mother will be carrying the pump to and from work every day, the size and weight of some pumps may make them impractical. Depending on the brand and model, a full-size automatic electric piston pump, for example, weighs between 11 and 22 pounds (4990 to 9980 grams). Another smaller, lighter choice is the mid-size electric piston pump, which weighs between 5 and 6 1/2 pounds (2268 to 2949 grams). Carrying cases are available for purchase through many rental stations that are designed to hold everything the mother needs to carry in one bag: the mid-sized electric piston pump, the bottles and tubing that connect to the pump, and her expressed milk.

Another lightweight option is Medela's Pump In Style, an automatic electric diaphragm pump that weighs about 7 pounds (3175 grams) including case and accessories. The pump is integrated into a carrying case that looks like a purse and holds the collection kit, as well as stores and cools the mother's expressed milk.

Employment

For more information, see "Portability" under "Features that Affect a Mother's Pump Choice" in the supplement "The Use of Breast Pumps and Other Products."

Although hand-expression, hand pumps, and small motorized single pumps work well for some women, other women have found that when they are away from their babies full-time they are unable to maintain a full milk supply with these methods.

Some mothers have found that hand-expression and small motorized single pumps or hand pumps are not as effective as automatic electric double pumps in maintaining a full milk supply, particularly if they are away from their babies full time. If a mother using one of these methods finds her milk supply diminishing despite frequent and regular pumping, suggest she try an automatic electric double pump.

Part-Time Work

A woman away from her baby less than six hours at a time has many milk-expression options.

Some women who work part-time choose the automatic electric double pumps (see previous section), because of their comfort, ease of use, speed, and effectiveness. However, depending upon how long and often she'll be away from her baby, a mother may have other effective options as well.

The mother away from her baby for fewer than four hours at a time may not need to pump at all if she nurses right before leaving her baby and again upon her return.

The mother away from her baby between four and six hours will probably need to express at least once to relieve fullness and keep up her milk supply. If the mother works this schedule three or fewer days a week, hand-expression or a small motorized single pump may work well for her. If her milk supply temporarily decreases, she can nurse more often on her days off to bring her supply back up again. If the mother works this schedule more than three days a week and she finds her milk supply decreasing with these methods, she has the option of nursing more frequently during the hours she's at home to increase her supply.

For more information, see "Features that Affect a Mother's Pump Choice" in the supplement "The Use of Breast Pumps and Other Products."

Many women around the world rely on hand-expression and prefer it to breast pumps.

Some mothers prefer hand-expression to using a pump because they feel it is more natural than a pump. The feel of skin-to-skin may be more effective at stimulating a let-down, or milk-ejection, reflex for some mothers than the feel of a plastic or glass pump flange. Once the technique is mastered, hand-expression is convenient—nothing to purchase, wear out, break down, wash, store, or transport. With practice, some women are able to hand-express both breasts simultaneously. (For more information, see the section "Hand-Expression" in the chapter "Expression and Storage of Human Milk.")

Before relying on hand-expression, a hand pump, or a small motorized single pump at work, suggest the mother take time to practice and master it at home.

If the mother plans to use hand-expression, a hand pump, a small motorized single pump, or a semi-automatic diaphragm pump, suggest that she practice expressing milk before she is separated from her baby.

Unlike the automatic electric double pumps—which do not depend on the mother's skill to be effective—hand-expression, semi-automatic diaphragm pumps, most small motorized single pumps, and hand pumps require the mother to manually regulate their rhythm, either by controlling the suction and release of suction or by providing the pumping action, which is why they take time and practice to master. Be sure the mother knows that it may take several practice sessions for her to express much milk. Suggest she set aside time to master her method of milk expression before relying on it when she returns to work.

For more information, see "Effectiveness" under "Features that Affect a Mother's Pump Choice" in the supplement "The Use of Breast Pumps and Other Products."

If the mother working part-time is away from her baby for long days of eight hours or more, she'll probably need to express every two to three hours to stay comfortable and maintain her milk supply.

Some mothers work part-time, but are away from their babies for long days. If the mother works two or more days of eight hours or more, she'll probably feel the need to express her milk at least two or three times while she is at work. If she is considering using a breast pump, suggest she consider an automatic electric double pump. Double-pumping will cut down on her pumping time at work and be more effective at maintaining her milk supply.

If the mother works one or two long days a week, she will be able to maintain her milk supply by nursing more frequently on her days off. In this case, any method of expression may suit her needs. It will be especially important that she be practiced at it before returning to work, however, because she will be at risk for mastitis if her breasts remain overly full for long periods while she is away from her baby.

Single-pumping may take more than twice as long as double-pumping.

Although with practice some mothers have learned to hand-express both breasts simultaneously or use two pumps that can be operated with one hand, most small motorized single pumps and hand pumps do not give the mother the option of pumping both breasts at once. Because it is necessary for some women who single-pump to interrupt milk expression several times to massage the breast and switch from side to side during each session, single-pumping may take more than twice as long as double-pumping (20 to 30 minutes, as compared with 10 to 15 minutes).

For more information, see "Pumping Time" under "Features that Affect a Mother's Pump Choice" in the supplement "The Use of Breast Pumps and Other Products."

How Often to Express

To help the mother decide how often she needs to express, ask her how many hours she and her baby will be apart, counting from the time she leaves her baby until she returns to him.

How often the mother needs to express will depend on two main factors:

- whether or not she is planning to provide her milk for her baby when they are separated, and
- how many hours she and her baby will be apart—counting travel time.

If the mother plans to give formula while she is away and needs to express her milk to keep from becoming overly full, suggest she use her comfort as her guide. If she has been exclusively breastfeeding, at first she will probably feel the need to express her milk about every three hours. As her milk supply decreases, however, she may feel comfortable expressing less frequently.

If the mother plans to be separated from her baby for fewer than four hours at a time, she may be able to nurse immediately before leaving her baby and immediately upon her return and not need to express her milk while away, unless her breasts become uncomfortably full.

If the mother is separated from her baby between four and six hours at a time, she will need to express her milk at least once during her absence, preferably two to three hours after the last nursing. This would prevent fullness, which may be uncomfortable for the mother and could make latching-on difficult for the baby once they are reunited. Delaying feedings more than four hours without expressing can also lead to mastitis. Suggest that the mother nurse her baby just before leaving him and as soon as possible upon her return to reduce the need for expressing.

If the mother is separated from her baby full-time—eight hours a day or more—encourage her to count the entire time away from her baby and plan to express about every three hours.

When counting time away, be sure the mother includes travel time between home and sitter and between sitter and her destination in the morning and vice versa at the end of the day. Frequently, travel time turns an eight-hour day into a nine- to ten-hour day. Realizing this—and knowing that it's best to express at least every two to three hours—the mother can better calculate her need to express. For example, if the mother will be away from her baby for nine to ten hours, she will need to express three times: in the morning, at lunch, and in the afternoon.

If the mother is not concerned about avoiding formula, she may not need to express her milk so often. She should plan to express whenever she begins to feel full—usually every three to four hours. As her milk supply decreases, she will need to express less frequently.

Employment

Not all women who work away from their babies have access to breast pumps or the time or privacy to express their milk. If the mother wants to avoid giving her baby formula, brainstorm with her about options and encourage her to use her creativity to find a way that will work for her and her baby. For example, some babies reverse their sleep patterns when a mother is gone during the day, sleeping for long stretches during the day and nursing frequently at night when the mother is home. In this case, the mother may be able to maintain her milk supply and leave the milk her baby needs with only minimal milk expression. Or the mother may choose to schedule her work hours during her baby's long sleep period to minimize his need for her milk while she is gone.

Some mothers have developed their own unique approaches. For example, one mother, who worked away from her baby eight hours a day five days a week, decided she did not want to pump at work. Instead she woke an hour before her baby did in the morning and used an automatic electric double pump to express up to 10 to 12 ounces (300 to 360 ml) of milk, which she left for her baby during the day. When the baby woke an hour later, she fed her at the breast, dressed her, and took her to the caregiver. At work, the mother hand-expressed just enough milk during the day to keep herself from becoming overly full, and when she went to pick up her baby after work she fed her at the breast. After this feeding she pumped again, got 3 to 4 more ounces (90 to 120 ml) and stored this milk for the next day. Following this routine, she provided her milk alone for her baby for 3-4 months after returning to work.

A routine like this would work well only for a mother with a large milk storage capacity and an abundant milk supply (Daly and Hartmann 1995). For most mothers, going eight hours between pumpings or feedings would signal their body to produce less milk, and they would be unable to maintain their supply. In many mothers with a full milk supply, going eight hours without pumping or feeding could also trigger mastitis.

Even though weaning may be a long way off, once the baby begins taking solid foods (usually about six months of age), the mother may decide to cut down on her expressing time. Once the baby is taking liquid from a cup and eating a variety of other foods, she may decide to stop expressing entirely and simply breast-feed when they are together.

Although these basic guidelines work well for many mothers, they may not be practical in some situations. Encourage the mother to try other approaches.

As the baby grows and takes other foods, the mother may cut down and eventually stop expressing.

There is no prescribed method for phasing out expressing, although, as with weaning, a gradual approach is best so that the mother doesn't become uncomfortably full. Each mother should be encouraged to make her own decisions based on her and her baby's needs. Emphasize that every nursing couple is unique.

Expressing Away from Home

Encourage the mother to find a comfortable place to express where she will not be disturbed.

Suggest the mother wear clothes that will make expressing easier.

Finding a suitable location for expressing will depend on the mother's individual situation. She may be able to use a private office, an isolated storeroom, or the women's washroom. She'll need to find somewhere she can relax and have some privacy. Some mothers find leaning over a sink helps avoid milk dripping on their clothes and makes use of gravity in removing the milk.

Suggest the mother give some thought to what she is wearing while away from home. Certain clothes make expressing easier, such as two-piece outfits and blouses or dresses that zip or button up the front. Suggest she avoid dresses or blouses that zip or button up the back.

After expressing, the mother may choose to keep her milk at room temperature or cool it for the trip home.

Although it was once recommended that expressed milk be cooled immediately after expressing, recent research (Pardou 1994; Sosa and Barness 1987; Barger and Bull 1987) indicates that human milk has previously unrecognized properties that protect it from bacterial contamination.

The new recommendations give mothers the choice of either cooling their milk after expression and keeping it refrigerated for up to 8 days or keeping it at room temperature for six to ten hours. See the later section, "How Long to Store Human Milk" for guidelines on how long milk can be safely stored at different temperatures.

If the mother decides to cool her milk, she may keep it in a refrigerator, if one is available. If not, she can provide her own insulated thermos or small cooler, with ice or cold packs to cool it. There are several carrying cases especially designed for women who need to express their milk away from home. They contain a milk-storage compartment with coolant and another compartment large enough to hold a breast pump.

If leaking is a problem, gentle pressure, nursing pads, camouflage clothing, and more frequent expression can help.

Some mothers find that their milk leaks when they are away from their babies. This is more common in the early weeks of breastfeeding, although for some mothers, this goes on for many months. Share the following tips to make leaking more manageable:

- **To stop the leaking, apply gentle pressure directly on the nipples.** Suggest the mother fold her arms across her chest and put the heels of her hands directly on her nipples to stop the milk flow, or press against her breasts with her forearms.
- **Wear nursing pads to catch the milk.** Caution the mother that nursing pads with plastic lining can keep air from getting to the nipples and may contribute to soreness. Some nursing pads are washable and reusable, others are disposable. If she chooses, the mother can make her own using folded handkerchiefs or circular pieces of absorbent material (such as diapers) sewn together.
- **Wear clothing that will camouflage the wetness,** such as print blouses, or have an extra jacket or sweater ready as a coverup.
- **Express more often.** Leaking may be a sign that the mother's breasts are becoming overly full. If this is the case, rather than trying to hold back the milk, it may be better for the mother to express her milk more often. More frequent expression will help avoid engorgement and mastitis.

HOME STRATEGIES

The mother may be able to nurse her baby full-time—without supplements or expressing—on the days they are together.

Many breastfeeding mothers find that on weekends or days off they have no problem making the adjustment to nursing full-time. If the mother has been pumping regularly while away, her milk production will be about the same.

Even if the baby's caregiver supplements with formula during the mother's absence, the baby's frequent nursing on her days off will supply him with plenty of milk, probably much more than the mother could remove by expressing. In this case, the mother may experience some fullness during their next separation because of the increased stimulation during the days off. This will make expressing easier.

The baby may want to nurse more during the evening, night, and early morning.

When mother and baby are regularly separated during the day, it is common for the baby to want to nurse more during the evening, night, and early morning to help compensate for their time apart with the closeness of breastfeeding. In fact, some women deliberately encourage an up-at-night, down-during-the-day sleeping pattern for the baby. If the baby sleeps for longer periods while the mother is away, he will need fewer supplements during the day and be more eager to nurse during the evening. More frequent nursing will also help keep up the mother's milk supply to meet her baby's needs.

Employment

If the mother finds this pattern exhausting, suggest she experiment to find ways to get her sleep while still meeting her baby's needs. Some possibilities include:

- bringing the baby into her bed at night.
- having the baby sleep in her room—either in a crib or on a pallet on the floor where she can lie down with him—to minimize getting up and down and going from one room to another.
- setting up a sleeping area for her in her baby's room, so that she can lie down and nurse him there, perhaps spending part of the night there if she falls asleep.

To streamline morning routines, suggest the mother try setting her alarm twenty minutes before she has to get up so she can breastfeed the baby and then breastfeed him again right before she leaves him.

Nursing the baby (even if he is still asleep) before the mother gets up increases her chances that he will be contented while she is dressing and getting ready for work. The baby also may be more interested in nursing again right before the mother has to leave. Organizing her routine so that she nurses her baby right before leaving him offers several advantages:

- It is calming to them both;
- It leaves the baby full so that he will need fewer supplements; and
- It helps minimize the amount of milk the mother will need to express while she is away.

Suggest the mother plan to nurse or play with her baby immediately upon her return rather than attending to the household or meals.

Suggest the mother plan on sitting (or lying) down and nursing or playing with the baby for the first thirty minutes after she arrives home. Spending some relaxed time together can make dinner preparations less chaotic. Keeping nutritious snacks on hand for the whole family will allow them to snack during this time instead of rushing to get dinner on the table.

Encourage the mother to set priorities with her partner and to keep an open mind about lifestyle changes.

The most significant long-term difficulty for employed mothers, which was mentioned by 60 percent of the mothers in Auerbach and Guss's 1984 study, is "role overload"—coping with the multiple demands of work and family life. Surprisingly, this feeling of overload was not any less intense for the married women than for the single women. Although husbands were cited as being helpful by

59 percent of the women, 82 percent of these women said that their husband's help was primarily in the form of encouragement and verbal support, rather than household help or child-rearing responsibilities.

One of the suggestions given in the Auerbach and Guss study was to set priorities, putting essentials (especially the needs of the family members) at the top of the list. Suggest the mother talk to her partner about what household chores he feels are most important and which they could simplify, eliminate, or do less often.

Another suggestion was to have an open mind about lifestyle changes. For instance, many mothers found that keeping their babies close at night made life easier by allowing more time for nursing and extra cuddling. Another suggestion was to encourage greater involvement of fathers in household and child-care responsibilities.

Another study found that full-time employed women with infants reported greater stress in their lives than full-time employed women with older children or full-time homemakers. In order to cope with the stress and cope with work overload, many of the employed mothers of infants neglected their own needs (Walker and Best 1991).

FEEDING TIPS FOR THE BABY'S CAREGIVER

Suggest the mother share information on storage and handling of human milk with the baby's caregiver.

It is important that the baby's caregiver be given information on storage and handling of human milk, so that the milk is used within the proper period of time and none of its special properties are destroyed by excess heating. (See the last section in this chapter.)

The caregiver also needs to know that human milk may not look like formula or cow's milk from the store so that the milk will not be unnecessarily discarded. Because human milk is not homogenized, it naturally separates into layers of milk and cream. Some caregivers mistakenly assume this means that the milk is spoiled. If the milk separates, suggest the caregiver shake it gently to mix.

It is normal for human milk to be bluish, yellowish, or even brownish in color. Frozen milk may take on a yellowish color. The milk is not spoiled unless it smells sour or tastes bad.

Some mothers have reported a slightly soapy smell to their frozen milk after it was thawed. This change in smell has been attributed to changes in the milk fats related to storage in self-defrosting refrigerator-freezers; it has not been found to be harmful to the baby (Lawrence, p. 619).

Babies on human milk alone tend to need less milk than babies on formula.

One study found that at four months of age exclusively breastfeeding babies consumed 25% fewer calories than formula-fed babies of the same age, even though their growth patterns were comparable (Butte 1984). Some attribute this decreased need for calories to the fact that breastfed babies have lower and more organized heart rates than formula-fed babies and so expend less energy (Roepke 1995; Zeskind and Goff 1992).

Usually a small baby will take between two- to four-ounces (60-120 ml) of milk at a feeding.

No one can predict with certainty the exact amount of milk an individual baby will want at a particular feeding, although a regular caregiver will soon get a good idea of how much the baby usually takes. On average, most breastfed babies take between 2 and 4 ounces (60 to 120 ml) about 8 to 12 times per day. It is unlikely that a breastfed baby would consume a full 8-ounce (240 ml) bottle of human milk at one feeding.

Storing human milk in two to four-ounce (60 to 120 ml) quantities minimizes waste and speeds thawing of frozen milk.

A few babies are reluctant to take a bottle, especially at first, Suggest the caregiver be patient and try different ways to encourage the baby.

Most babies take a bottle easily whether it is first offered at one month, two months, or between three and six months (Kearney and Cronenwett 1991), but there are some babies who resist or refuse the bottle.

To begin, suggest the mother find someone else to give the bottle. Most babies will not take a bottle if they know their mother is nearby, because they associate their mother with the pleasure of nursing. Suggest the mother encourage this, as the baby's association of the mother with the breast will decrease the chances that the baby will reject the breast for the bottle.

Some ways that have worked to encourage a baby to take a bottle.

- Try offering the bottle before the baby is likely to be too hungry, before his usual nursing time, as he may be more cooperative then about trying something new.
- Hold the baby lovingly while giving the bottle.
- Wrap the baby in some of the mother's clothing that has her smell on it (a blouse or nightgown, for example) while offering the bottle.
- Instead of pushing the bottle nipple into the baby's mouth, try laying it near his mouth and allow him to pull it in himself, or tickle the baby's mouth with the bottle nipple, as many mothers do with the breast.

Employment

- Try running warm water over the bottle nipple to bring it up to body temperature, like the breast, or—if the baby is teething—try cooling it in the refrigerator, as this may be soothing to his gums.
- Try different types of bottle nipples to find a shape, a substance (rubber or silicone), and a hole size the baby will accept. Some babies prefer a larger or smaller nipple hole or different nipple types and shapes, such as a premie nipple, which is softer than a regular nipple, or an orthodontic nipple.
- Try different feeding positions. Some babies will take a bottle better in the nursing position; others like to sit propped against the caregiver's raised legs (like sitting in an infant seat); still others prefer not to look at the caregiver and will take a bottle better if they are held facing out, with their back against the caregiver's chest.
- Try to feed the baby while moving rhythmically—rocking, walking, or swaying from side to side—because this may be calming to him; some babies who refuse a bottle at other times will take a bottle when they are riding in a carseat.
- Insert the bottle nipple into the baby's mouth when he's sleeping.
- Keep trying, but remember that the baby can be fed the mother's milk using other feeding methods, such as cup, spoon, or eyedropper, if the baby continues to refuse the bottle.

If the baby continues to refuse the bottle, assure the mother that this is not a reflection on her or her choices. Even with early and regular bottles, some babies refuse bottles as they get older (Frantz 1993b). Occasionally even babies who are bottle-fed from birth refuse bottles from anyone other than mother.

Suggest the mother ask her baby's caregiver to give less than a full feeding if the baby is hungry and she is due to arrive soon.

If the baby seems hungry just before the mother is due to arrive, suggest the mother ask her caregiver to try to satisfy him with a small amount of milk until she gets there. The mother's breasts may be full and she may need to nurse the baby for her own comfort. Also, making breastfeeding a priority will help keep the baby nursing well and lessen the likelihood that he will grow to prefer the bottle.

STORAGE AND HANDLING OF HUMAN MILK

**How Long to Store
Human Milk**

Recent research indicates that human milk has previously unrecognized properties that protect it from bacterial contamination. These studies indicate that refrigerated human milk can stay fresh longer than the previously recommended 24, 48, or 72 hours (Pardou 1994; Barger and Bull 1987; Sosa and Barness 1987) and that milk stored at slightly below room temperature can stay fresh for up to 24 hours (Hamosh 1996). In one study (Barger and Bull 1987), there was no statistically significant difference between the bacterial levels of milk stored for 10 hours at room temperature and milk refrigerated for 10 hours. Another study (Pardou 1994) found that after 8 days of refrigeration some of the milk actually had lower bacterial levels than it did on the day it was expressed. The researchers concluded that milk that will be used within 8 days should be refrigerated rather than frozen, because the anti-microbial qualities of human milk are better preserved by refrigeration.

Guidelines for human milk storage vary for milk stored at room temperature, in the refrigerator, or frozen.

The following guidelines apply to mothers who have a healthy, full-term baby, are storing their milk for home use (as opposed to hospital use), wash their hands before expressing, and use containers that have been washed in hot, soapy water and then rinsed well. (Other guidelines may apply to babies who are ill or premature.)

Human Milk Storage

At room temperature
Term colostrum (milk expressed within 6 days of delivery)
- at 80.6 to 89.6 degrees Fahrenheit (27 to 32 degrees C)—12 hours (Nwankwo 1988)

Mature milk
- at 60 degrees Fahrenheit (15 degrees C)—24 hours (Hamosh 1996)
- at 66 to 72 degrees Fahrenheit (19-22 degrees C)—10 hours (Barger and Bull 1987)
- at 79 degrees Fahrenheit (25 degrees C)—4 to 6 hours (Hamosh 1996; Pittard 1985)

In a refrigerator
Mature milk
- at 32 to 39 degrees Fahrenheit (0 to 4 degrees C)—8 days (Pardou 1994)

In a freezer
- in a freezer compartment located inside a refrigerator—2 weeks
- in a self-contained freezer unit of a refrigerator—3 or 4 months (temperature varies because the door opens and closes frequently).
- in a separate deep freeze at a constant 0 degrees Fahrenheit (–19 degrees C)—6 months or longer.

All stored milk should be labeled and dated.

Encourage the mother to label each container with the month, date, and year. This will allow the milk to be used in the order in which it was expressed.

If the milk will be brought to a place where more than one baby is being fed, the baby's name should also be written on each container.

Suggest the mother store her milk in 2 to 4 ounce(60-120 ml) quantities.

No one can predict with certainty the exact amount of milk an individual baby will want at a particular feeding, although a regular caregiver will soon get a good idea of how much the baby usually takes. On average, most breastfed babies take between 2 and 4 ounces (60-120 ml) about eight to twelve times per day. It is unlikely that a breastfed baby would consume a full 8-ounce (240 ml) bottle of human milk at one feeding.

Storing her milk in 2 to 4 ounce (60-120 ml) quantities minimizes waste and speeds thawing of frozen milk.

The baby receiving only mother's milk may need fewer ounces (ml) per day than the baby receiving formula.

One study found that at four months of age exclusively breastfeeding babies consumed 25% fewer calories than formula-fed babies of the same age, even though their growth patterns were comparable (Butte 1984). Some attribute this decreased need for calories to the lower and more organized heart rates of breastfed babies, which results in a lower expenditure of energy as compared with babies on formula (Roepke 1995; Zeskind and Goff 1992).

Choice and Use of a Storage Container

Milk storage containers may be made of glass, plastic, or stainless steel. The material of the container is only of concern when the baby receives most of his nourishment from expressed human milk.

Research is conflicting about the advantages and disadvantages of storage containers made from different materials. Storage time is also a factor.

If the baby gets most of his nourishment directly from breastfeeding and receives expressed milk only occasionally, the type of storage container is not a major consideration. The makeup of the storage container is of concern only when the baby receives most of his nourishment from expressed human milk.

Employment

For the baby who receives most of his nourishment from expressed human milk, the type of storage container used should be carefully considered. However, research on storage containers composed of different materials is scanty and its conclusions conflicting, with most recommendations based on little information. For example, one study (Paxton and Cress 1979) found that more of human milk's leukocytes adhered to glass as compared to plastic, which led to the recommendation that fresh milk be stored in plastic rather than glass. (Glass was still recommended for freezing, because freezing kills most leukocytes.) A second study (Pittard and Bill 1981) complicated the issue when it found that different types of leukocytes react differently to glass. A third study (Goldblum 1981) convinced many to go back to recommending glass when it was found that length of storage time made a difference, as many of the leukocytes that had adhered to the glass were released over time and that after 24 hours the milk stored in glass had a greater increase in leukocytes than the milk stored in plastic.

Due to the results of one recent study (Williamson and Murti 1996) that compared glass and stainless steel, which is used for milk storage in some developing countries (Arnold 1995), some have gone back to recommending glass because the live cells in milk were found to adhere to the stainless steel in greater numbers than those stored in glass.

Milk storage bags, a type of plastic storage container, are used by many women due to their practical advantages. Milk bags take up less storage space than hard-sided storage containers and can be attached directly to a breast pump and used to collect the milk in place of a bottle, cutting down on time spent transferring milk and reducing the number of pump parts that need to be cleaned after each pumping session. However, some recommend against their use, particularly for hospitalized babies, because there is more risk of leakage than with hard-sided containers and they are not as airtight, increasing the possibility of contamination (Arnold 1995). One study (Goldblum 1981) found a 60% decrease in some of the milk's antibodies and a loss of fat that adhered to the plastic sides of the milk bags. However, only the thin, plastic disposable bottle liners were studied, so these findings may not apply to the thicker bags specially designed for freezing human milk. Also, these results have not been duplicated.

Although some consider these bags more difficult to pour milk from (Arnold 1995), some brands have built-in tear spouts. For bags without tear spouts, milk can be removed safely and easily by clipping one corner of the bag with sterile scissors. In some cases, using milk bags may decrease the possibility of milk contamination by reducing the need to transfer milk from one container to another, for example if a mother expresses her milk directly into a milk storage bag and the baby is fed from the same bag with the type of bottle that uses disposable liners.

Some milk storage bags are specially designed for freezing. If disposable bottle liners are used for freezing milk, they need extra protection to prevent leaking and contamination.

Some milk storage bags are pre-sterilized and designed specially for freezing milk. They are thicker than bags made primarily for feeding, include self-sealers, and have areas for labeling. (See the chapter "The Use of Breast Pumps and Other Products" for source information.) Others, sold specifically as bottle liners, are made for feeding and do not include closures (although twist ties can be used). Freezing milk in this less-durable type of plastic liner can be risky. Removing air from the bag can be tricky, the seams may burst during freezing, and the bag may leak during thawing. If the mother chooses to freeze her milk in disposable bottle liners, suggest she follow this procedure for extra protection:

- Put the bag of milk inside another empty bag to avoid tearing.
- Squeeze out the air at the top.
- Roll down the bag to about an inch (2.5 cm) above the milk.
- Close the bag and seal it.
- Place the sealed bag upright in a heavy, plastic container with a lid, and then seal the lid before putting it in the freezer.

When freezing milk in hard-sided containers, glass, which is the least porous, offers the most protection. Suggest the mother use a solid cap for the best seal and to tighten the cap after the milk is frozen.

Glass is the first choice as a storage container for freezing milk. Glass is the least porous, so it offers the best protection for frozen milk. The second choice is clear, hard plastic (polycarbonate). The third choice is cloudy, hard plastic (polypropylene). For maximum protection, the storage container should be sealed with a solid, single-piece cap.

When the milk freezes, it expands. In order to avoid damage to the container and contamination of the milk, it is necessary to leave about an inch (2.5 cm) at the top of the container to allow for expansion. Suggest the mother tighten bottle caps after the milk is completely frozen so that the displaced air can escape.

Any container used to store milk should be clean.

To avoid bacterial contamination, all storage containers, bottles, nipples, cups, spoons, or any other feeding utensils need to be clean.

To clean a hard-sided milk storage container, use hot, soapy water, rinse well and allow to air dry.

Handling and Thawing Human Milk

Any milk expressed within a 24 hour period can be expressed directly into the same container if the previously expressed milk was stored between 32 and 60 degrees Fahrenheit (0-15 degrees C).

Batches of milk expressed at different times during the day need not be kept separate, provided the previous batches have been stored between 32 and 60 degrees Fahrenheit (between 0 and 15 degrees C). If the previously expressed milk was stored in this temperature range, the mother can express her milk directly into a container of previously expressed milk for up to 24 hours and then follow the storage recommendations based on the time and date of the first milk expressed. If the previously expressed milk was stored at between 66 and 72 degrees Fahrenheit (19 and 22 degrees C), total storage time should not exceed 10 hours from the time first milk was expressed (Barger and Bull 1987). If the previously expressed milk was stored at 79 degrees Fahrenheit (25 degrees C), total storage time should not exceed 4 to 6 hours from the time first milk was expressed (Hamosh 1996; Pittard 1985). If the previously expressed milk was frozen, see the next point for guidelines.

Before adding fresh milk to frozen milk, cool the fresh milk and add a smaller amount than that already frozen.

Fresh milk can be added to frozen milk if it is cooled first and if there is less fresh milk than frozen milk. After expressing her milk, suggest the mother cool it for about a half hour before adding it to frozen milk, so it does not thaw the top layer. (Human milk should not be thawed and refrozen.)

When freezing her milk, suggest the mother allow room for expansion and delay tightening any caps until the milk is frozen. One-piece caps provide the best seal.

When milk freezes, it expands. In order to avoid damage to the container and contamination of the milk, it is necessary to leave about an inch (2.5 cm) empty at the top of the container to allow for expansion. For this reason, it is also best not to tighten bottle caps until the milk is completely frozen. One-piece caps are better for freezing than nipple units because they provide a better seal.

Frozen human milk should be thawed under cool then warm running water.

To thaw frozen milk, suggest the caregiver hold the container under cool running water and gradually add warmer water until the milk is thawed and heated to room temperature. If more than one container is being thawed, the caregiver can combine the milk for a feeding. After the milk is thawed, it should be shaken gently before testing the temperature.

If warm running water is not available, the caregiver can heat a pan of water on the stove and submerge the container of frozen milk into the heated water. If necessary, remove the container of milk and reheat the water. A container of milk should not be heated directly on the stove.

Human milk should not be heated in a microwave oven, as valuable components of the milk will be destroyed if it is heated over 130 degrees F (Quan 1992; Sigman 1989). Also, microwave ovens heat liquids unevenly, causing "hot spots" in the milk that may burn the baby.

Employment

Once frozen milk is thawed, it can be kept refrigerated but not refrozen.

Previously frozen milk that was thawed has been safely kept refrigerated for up to 24 hours (The Human Milk Banking Association of North America 1993). It should not be refrozen.

It is not yet known whether it is safe to give a baby milk that was left from a previous feeding or milk that was previously warmed.

Research has not yet been done to determine if it is safe to give a baby milk that was leftover from a previous feeding or milk that was previously warmed but not used.

When human milk is stored or used at the workplace and at child-care facilities, it can be kept in a common refrigerator and no special precautions are necessary when handling it.

Both the US Centers for Disease Control (1988) and the Occupational Safety and Health Administration (OSHA) agree that human milk is not among the body fluids that require rubber gloves for handling and feeding or require storage in a separate refrigerator as a biohazardous material. Although concerns have been raised in some areas about the need to use universal precautions for bloodborne pathogens with human milk, as of this writing US federal health agencies do not deem this necessary or beneficial.

The American Academy of Pediatrics and American Public Health Association support this position in their joint guidelines for child-care facilities, *Caring for Our Children: National Health and Safety Performance Standards: Guidelines for Out-of-Home Child Care Programs.* (This publication is available from AAP Publications Department, P.O. Box 927, Elk Grove Village, IL 60009-0927 USA. Telephone: 800-433-9016 or 847-228-5005. FAX 847-228-1281.)

This means that at the workplace and at child-care facilities, human milk can be stored along with other foods in a common refrigerator and no special precautions are needed when handling or feeding a baby with human milk.

Publications for Parents

Bernshaw, N. *A Mother's Guide to Milk Expression and Breast Pumps.* Schaumburg, Illinois: La Leche League International, 1996. Publication No. 30.

Dana, N. and Price, A. *The Working Woman's Guide to Breastfeeding.* New York: Meadowbrook, 1987.

Healthy Mothers/Healthy Babies. *What Gives These Companies a Competitive Edge? Worksite Support for Breastfeeding Employees.* Washington, DC: National Healthy Mothers/Healthy Babies Coalition.

References

La Leche League International. *Practical Hints for Working and Breastfeeding*. Schaumburg, Illinois, 1991. Publication No. 83.

La Leche League International. THE WOMANLY ART OF BREASTFEEDING, 35th Anniversary ed. Schaumburg, Illinois, 1991, pp. 161-90.

Lowman, K. OF CRADLES AND CAREERS: A GUIDE TO RESHAPING YOUR JOB TO INCLUDE A BABY IN YOUR LIFE. Schaumburg, Illinois: La Leche League International, 1984.

World Alliance for Breastfeeding Action. *Women, work and breastfeeding: Everybody benefits!* WABA Secretariat (PO Box 1200, 10850 Penang, Malaysia).

American Public Health Association and American Academy of Pediatrics; Maternal Child Health Bureau. *Caring for Our Children: National Health and Safety Performance Standards: Guidelines for Out-of-Home Child Care Programs* 1992.

Arnold, Lois. Storage containers for human milk: an issue revisited. *J Hum Lact* 1995; 11(4):325-28.

Auerbach, K. Assisting the employed breastfeeding mother. *J Nurse Midw* 1990a; 35(1):26-34.

Auerbach, K. Sequential and simultaneous breast pumping: a comparison. *Int J Nurs Stud* 1990b; 27(3):257-65.

Auerbach, K. Employed breastfeeding mothers: problems they encounter. *Birth* 1984; 11:17-20.

Auerbach, K. and Guss, E. Maternal employment and breastfeeding: a study of 567 women's experiences. *Am J Dis Child* 1984; 138:958-60.

Barger, J. and Bull, P. A comparison of the bacterial composition of breast milk stored at room temperature and stored in the refrigerator. *IJCE* 1987; 2:29-30.

Bernard, D. Hand-expression. NEW BEGINNINGS 1996; 13(2):52.

Butte, N. et al. Human milk intake and growth in exclusively breast-fed infants. *J Pediatr* 1984; 104:187-95.

Centers for Disease Control. Update. *MMWR* 1988; 37(24):376-88.

Cohen, R. et al. Comparison of maternal absenteeism and infant illness rates among breast-feeding and formula-feeding women in two corporations. *Am J Health Promo* 1995; 10(2):148-53.

Cohen, R. and Mrtek, M. The impact of two corporate lactation programs on the incidence and duration of breastfeeding by employed mothers. *Am J Health Promo* 1994; 8:436-41.

Daly, S. and Hartmann, P. Infant demand and milk supply. Part 2: The short-term control of milk synthesis in lactating women. *J Hum Lact* 1995; 11(1):27-37.

Duckett, L. Maternal employment and breastfeeding. *NAACOG Clin Issues Perinat Women Health Nurs* 1992; 3(4):701-12.

Frantz, K. *Breastfeeding Product Guide 1994*. Sunland California: Geddes Productions, 1993a, pp. 89, 96, 104, 109, 114.

Frantz, K. The working mother and breastfeeding: can both be done? Presented at the EHS Council of Perinatal Nurses 6th Annual Nursing Conference. Oak Brook, Illinois, 1993b.

Frederick, I. and Auerbach, K. Maternal-infant separation and breast-feeding: the return to work or school. *J Reprod Med* 1985; 30:523-26.

Garza, C. et al. Effects of method of collection and storage on nutrients in human milk. *Early Human Dev* 1982; 6:295-303.

Gielen, A. et al. Maternal employment during the early postpartum period: effects on initiation and continuation of breast-feeding. *Pediatrics* 1991; 87:298-305.

Goldblum, R., et al. Human milk banking I: effects of container upon immunologic factors in mature milk. *Nutr Res* 1981; 1:449-59.

Green, D. et al. The relative efficacy of four methods of human milk expression. *Early Human Dev* 1982; 6:153-58.

Greenberg, C. and Smith, K. Anticipatory guidance for the employed breast-feeding mother. *J Pediatr Health Care* 1991; 5(4):204-9.

Hamosh, M. et al. Breastfeeding and the working mother: effect of time and temperature of short-term storage on proteolysis, lipolysis, and bacterial growth in milk. *Pediatrics* 1996; 97(4):492-98.

Healthy Mothers/Healthy Babies. *What Gives These Companies a Competitive Edge? Worksite Support for Breastfeeding Employees*. Washington, DC: National Healthy Mothers/Healthy Babies Coalition, 1993.

Hills-Bonczyk, S. Women's experiences with combining breast-feeding and employment. *J Nurse Midw* 1993; 38(5):257-66.

The Human Milk Banking Association of North America. *Recommendations for Collection, Storage, and Handling of a Mother's Milk for Her Own Infant in the Hospital Setting*, West Hartford, CT USA, 1993.

Jones, E. and Matheny, R. Relationship between infant feeding and exclusion rate from child care because of illness. *J Am Diet Assoc* 1993; 93(7):809-11.

Kearney, M. and Cronenwett, L. Breastfeeding and employment. *JOGNN* 1991; 20(6):471-80.

Kurinij, N. et al. Does maternal employment affect breast feeding? *Am J Public Health* 1989; 79:1247-50.

Lang, S. et al. Sodium in hand and pump expressed human breast milk. *Early Human Dev* 1994; 38:131-38.

Employment

Lawrence, R. *Breastfeeding: A Guide for the Medical Profession,* 4th ed. St. Louis: Mosby, 1994. pp. 387-401, 619.

Lee, K. and DeJoseph, J. Sleep disturbances, vitality, and fatigue among a select group of employed childbearing women. *Birth* 1992; 19(4):208-13.

Loughlin, H. et al. Early termination of breastfeeding: identifying those at risk. *Pediatrics* 1985; 75:508-13.

Maclaughlin, D. and Strelnick, E. Breast-feeding and working outside the home. *Issues Comp Pediatr Nurs* 1984; 7:67-81.

Morse, J. et al. Patterns of breastfeeding and work: the Canadian experience. *Can J Public Health* 1989; 80:182-88.

Newman, J. Breastfeeding problems associated with the early introduction of bottles and pacifiers. *J Hum Lact* 1990; 6(2):59-63.

Neifert, M. et al. Nipple confusion: toward a formal definition. *J Pediatr* 1995; 126(6):S125-S129.

Nwankwo, M. et al. Bacterial growth in expressed breast-milk. *Ann Trop Pediatr* 1988; 8:92-95.

Pardou, A. Human milk banking: influence of storage processes and of bacterial contamnation on some milk consitutuents. *Biol Neonate* 1994; 65:302-09.

Paxton, C. and Cress, C. Survival of human milk leukocytes. *J Pediatr* 1979; 94:61-64.

Pittard, W. et al. Bacteriostatic qualities of human milk. *J Pediatr* 1985; 107:240-43.

Pittard, W. and Bill, K. Human milk banking: effect of refrigeration on cellular components. *Clin Pediatr* 1981; 20:31-33.

Quan, R. et al. Effects of microwave radiation on anti-infective factors in human milk. *Pediatrics* 1992; 89:667-72.

Riordan, J. and Auerbach, K. *Breastfeeding and Human Lactation.* Boston and London: Jones and Bartlett, 1993. pp. 401-27.

Roepke, J. Growth of breastfed babies—research review. Presented at La Leche League's 14th International Conference, Chicago, Illinois, July 1995. (Audiocassette ordering information available from LLLI.)

Ryan, A. and Martinez, G. Breast-feeding and the working mother: a profile. *Pediatrics* 1989; 83:524-31.

Sigman, M. et al. Effects of microwaving human milk: changes in IgA content and bacterial count. *J Am Diet Assoc* 1989; 89:690-92.

Sosa, R. and Barness, L. Bacterial growth in refrigerated human milk. *Am J Dis Child* 1987; 141:111-12.

Walker, L. and Best, M. Well-being of mothers with infant children: a preliminary comparison of employed women and homemakers. *Women & Health* 1991; 17(1):71-89.

Williamson, M. and Murti, P. Effects of storage, time, temperature, and composition of containers on biologic components of human milk. *J Hum Lact* 1996; 12(1):31-35.

Zeskind, P. and Goff, D. Rhythmic organization of heart rate in breast-fed and bottle-fed newborn infants. *Early Dev and Parent* 1992; 1(2):79-87.

Employment

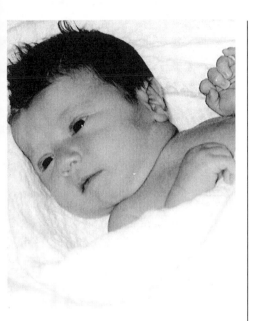

11

Newborn Jaundice

THE MOTHER'S FEELINGS

CAUSES OF NEWBORN JAUNDICE AND ELEVATED BILIRUBIN
    Jaundice during the First Day
    Jaundice Starting on the Second to Fifth Day
    Jaundice and Elevated Bilirubin after the Fifth Day

WHY AND WHEN NEWBORN JAUNDICE MAY NEED TREATMENT

TREATMENT OPTIONS FOR A JAUNDICED BABY
    Breastfeed Frequently
    Increase Baby's Stooling
    Expose the Baby to Indirect Sunlight
    Avoid Water Supplements
    Phototherapy
    Supplement with Formula
    Blood-Exchange Transfusions and Drugs

HELPING THE MOTHER WORK WITH HER BABY'S DOCTOR

Most babies are born with extra red blood cells that break down and are eliminated from the body in the early weeks of life. Bilirubin is a yellow pigment that is a product of this process. Jaundice results when excess bilirubin accumulates in the blood, which occurs for several reasons: the increased production of bilirubin, the limited ability of the newborn liver to handle large amounts of bilirubin, and the increased ability of the intestine to absorb it when the bile enters the intestine. Bilirubin is deposited in the skin, muscles, and mucous membranes of the body, causing the skin to take on a yellowish color. More than half of all newborns become jaundiced within the first week of life. This condition is temporary and usually resolves within a few days without treatment. Although some health care professionals recommend interrupting breastfeeding to bring down bilirubin levels, other effective treatment options will bring down bilirubin levels without putting breastfeeding at risk. Mothers of jaundiced babies are more likely to have stopped breastfeeding by one month than other mothers (Kemper 1989). Because newborn jaundice occurs so frequently, expectant parents should be encouraged to learn something about it before birth and discuss it with their baby's doctor.

THE MOTHER'S FEELINGS

When a mother is told her baby has jaundice, she may be anxious and upset.

When a mother is told that her baby has jaundice, she may react strongly—with feelings of worry, anxiety, and helplessness—especially if she is unfamiliar with newborn jaundice and it is not explained to her clearly or its dangers are overemphasized.

If she is given a technical explanation of her baby's condition while she is upset, it is unlikely that she will be able to understand or remember all of the particulars. If so, encourage the mother to contact her baby's doctor to discuss it with him or her when she is feeling calmer.

Traditional therapy of a jaundiced baby can affect the mother's feelings about breastfeeding and her baby's health. This change in perception is known as the "vulnerable child syndrome."

If mother and baby are separated, supplements are given, or temporary weaning is recommended, these can increase a mother's anxiety and affect her feelings about breastfeeding. Long periods of time away from her baby can add to a mother's anxiety and feelings of helplessness. If the mother of a jaundiced baby is told to stop breastfeeding or give supplements in the early days, this can affect her feelings about nursing her baby. If she is discouraged from spending time with her baby or from nursing him, she may question whether her milk is really good for him. And if her baby becomes confused by the artificial nipple, she may find it difficult to get him back to the breast, adding stress to an already stressful time.

Although it has been documented (Newman and Maisels 1990) that normal, full-term babies who are jaundiced suffer no long-term adverse health effects from physiologic jaundice, research indicates that treatment does affect the behavior and attitudes of the mothers of jaundiced (but otherwise healthy) babies.

In one study (Kemper 1989) of more than two hundred mothers, the researchers found that one month after hospital discharge, mothers of jaundiced babies were more likely to have stopped breastfeeding (42 percent versus 19 percent), even though more mothers of jaundiced babies started out breastfeeding (79 percent versus 61 percent). Although both groups of mothers reported similar numbers of health problems in their babies during the first month, mothers of jaundiced babies were more likely to take their baby to well-baby checkups and were more than twice as likely to bring the baby to the doctor for a sick visit or to the hospital emergency room (bilirubin checks were not counted).

Another study (Kemper 1990) involved a six-month follow-up on mothers of jaundiced and non-jaundiced babies. Again, mothers of jaundiced babies had more feeding problems. They were less likely to be breastfeeding and were more likely to have tried a special formula. They also tended to judge their infant's minor illnesses as serious and to have taken the child to an emergency room.

The authors concluded that traditional therapies for jaundice (which are based on fears of serious long-term effects on babies' health) are unnecessary, have adverse effects on breastfeeding, may affect the mother-baby relationship, and should be reconsidered.

Time together can be calming to both mother and baby.

Physical closeness between mother and baby can be calming and help reduce feelings of anxiety. Encourage the mother to request treatment options that will allow her to spend time with her baby and breastfeed frequently without being rushed or interrupted. This will also help eliminate the bilirubin more quickly from the baby's system. Supplements are not necessary in most cases if the baby is nursing well and often.

Also, mother and baby can usually remain together even when the baby's jaundice requires treatment such as phototherapy. For example, the bili-lights can be set up in the mother's room. Home phototherapy is another option. (See "Treatment Options" below.)

Repeated bilirubin tests can be difficult for both mother and baby.

The baby's bilirubin level is obtained through a blood test, which requires filling a thin tube with blood. Usually the baby is pricked on his heel, toe, or finger. Sometimes obtaining the necessary amount of blood can be painful. Repeated blood tests can become an ordeal for both mother and baby but may be necessary.

Newborn Jaundice

Give the mother support during this stressful time.

Most mothers of a newborn find dealing with a health concern overwhelming. It can be helpful to bolster the mother's self-confidence by encouraging her with statements such as: "I can see you have put a lot of thought into making the best decision for your baby," or "I applaud your taking the time to find out what your options are."

CAUSES OF NEWBORN JAUNDICE AND ELEVATED BILIRUBIN

The timing and the level of a newborn's elevated bilirubin will help determine its cause and whether treatment is needed.

Elevated bilirubin in the newborn may be a symptom of a wide range of problems. Most elevated bilirubin is within acceptable levels and requires no action, however in unusual cases it becomes exaggerated to the point where the baby needs treatment. Both the timing and the level of the newborn's elevated bilirubin provide clues to its cause, which will help determine if any action needs to be taken.

Jaundice during the First Day

High or rapidly rising bilirubin levels evident at birth or within the first day or two are most likely due to a problem unrelated to feeding.

When high or rapidly rising levels of bilirubin are evident at birth or within the first day or two, this is usually an indication of abnormal or pathological jaundice, which is caused by a physical problem unrelated to feeding. If bilirubin levels are rising rapidly (0.5 mg/dl [8.5 µmol/L] or more per hour), the baby may need immediate treatment.

Some causes for pathological jaundice include:

- a disease or condition that results in increased red blood cell breakdown,
- a disease or condition that interferes with the processing of the bilirubin by the liver,
- a disease or condition that increases the reabsorption of bilirubin by the bowel.

The first category includes Rh or ABO blood incompatibilities. While Rh incompatibility has become relatively rare due to preventive methods, ABO incompatibility, a much milder condition, is still common. The mother's doctor will determine if either of these could be the cause of the baby's jaundice by checking the mother's and baby's blood types and by performing other tests. Other causes of increased red cell breakdown can also occur; some are inherited.

The second category includes liver enzyme-deficiency diseases, infections, and metabolic problems, such as galactosemia and hypothyroidism.

The third category would include conditions such as gastrointestinal obstruction.

Whenever pathological jaundice is suspected, these causes should be considered. If one of these health problems is causing the jaundice, the baby will need to be treated for the underlying cause as well as the jaundice itself.

With the exception of the baby with galactosemia, breastfeeding can and should continue during the treatment of pathologic jaundice.

Frequent breastfeeding (10 to 12 times every 24 hours) can and should continue during treatment for pathologic jaundice. The colostrum and mature milk the baby receives will stimulate more bowel movements, speeding the elimination of the bilirubin.

The rare exception to this is the baby whose jaundice is caused by galactosemia, an inherited metabolic disorder that leaves the baby unable to metabolize lactose, or milk sugar, and makes breastfeeding contraindicated. (See "Galactosemia" in the chapter "The Baby with Special Needs.")

Jaundice Starting on the Second to Fifth Day

Because many babies are jaundiced or have elevated bilirubin levels peaking on the third or fourth day after birth, this is considered normal.

More than half of all newborns become jaundiced within the first week of life, which is why this jaundice is called "physiologic," meaning normal. Physiologic jaundice is caused by a rise in blood levels of bilirubin, a yellow pigment that is a product of the breakdown of hemoglobin from the extra red blood cells with which most babies are born. Jaundice results when excess bilirubin accumulates in the blood and is deposited in the skin, muscles, and mucous membranes of the body, causing the skin to take on a yellowish color.

Because bilirubin is initially fat-soluble (indirect bilirubin), it cannot be dissolved in blood or urine. In order to be eliminated by the body, bilirubin must be bound to water-soluble proteins in the blood and processed (conjugated) by the liver. The liver converts the bilirubin into a water-soluble form (called direct bilirubin) that can be carried by bile into the intestines and the stool, where it is excreted from the body.

Normal newborn (or physiologic) jaundice is caused by a combination of three factors: the increased amount of bilirubin produced in the newborn, the increased reabsorption of bilirubin from the intestines, and the limited ability of the newborn's immature liver to process large amounts of bilirubin as effectively as a more mature liver. The newborn's liver commonly takes a week or two to mature sufficiently to handle the build-up of bilirubin in the blood.

This condition is temporary and usually resolves within a few days or weeks without treatment. Some health care professionals recommend interrupting breastfeeding to bring down bilirubin levels, although this is not necessary. Supplementing breastfeeding with formula, however, may be needed if the mother's milk supply is low and bilirubin levels become exaggerated. See the later section "Why and When Newborn Jaundice May Need Treatment" for a chart of the bilirubin levels at which the American Academy of Pediatrics recommends treatment.

Newborn jaundice may be mild or exaggerated.

Bilirubin levels in the baby with physiologic jaundice usually peak between the third and fifth days of life and are usually less than 12 milligrams of bilirubin per deciliter of blood, or mg/dl, (204 μmol/L) and are rarely higher than 15 mg/dl (255 μmol/L). In infants of Asian ancestry, normal bilirubin levels due to physiologic jaundice are often higher (Hodgman and Edwards 1992). Some other ethnic groups also tend to have higher bilirubin levels (see the next-to-last point in this section).

Please note: An average value of 1 mg/dl=17μmol/L is used throughout this chapter unless values are expressed differently in a specific study that is quoted.

Breastfeeding early and often during the first days of life can prevent physiologic jaundice from becoming exaggerated.

Early and frequent breastfeeding will prevent physiologic jaundice from becoming exaggerated. If a baby does not breastfeed often and well, bilirubin levels may rise higher than 15 mg/dl (255 µmol/L). One study found that a minimum of nine nursings every twenty-four hours may prevent normal newborn jaundice from becoming exaggerated and that the number of breastfeedings the first day may be especially critical (Yamauchi and Yamanouchi 1990). Babies who nursed seven to eleven times per day from birth were found to consume substantially more milk (86% more milk on the second day) than babies who nursed six or fewer times.

A baby who does not receive enough colostrum (which acts as a laxative) in the early days may not pass meconium (the bilirubin-rich first stools) quickly (Tudehope 1991; deCarvalho 1985). The bilirubin in the meconium may then be reabsorbed into the baby's bloodstream, resulting in higher bilirubin levels. For an overview of the research on how breastfeeding management affects bilirubin levels during the first week, see Gartner (1994a).

When a jaundiced baby is feeding frequently and effectively, physiologic jaundice will resolve on its own without intervention.

In most cases, physiologic jaundice gradually resolves by itself within several days to a few weeks, as the baby's liver processes the backlog of bilirubin in the baby's system. Physiologic jaundice is not a disease; it is a harmless condition that has no aftereffects, provided the baby's bilirubin does not reach unsafe levels.

Newborn Jaundice

Some newborns are sleepy and may need to be awakened and stimulated to breastfeed often enough (10 to 12 times every 24 hours, or at least every two hours during the day with one sleep period of four to five hours). High bilirubin levels can increase sleepiness. Except for the baby possibly needing extra stimulation to breastfeed often and well, physiologic jaundice need not affect breastfeeding and will resolve on its own without treatment.

If physiologic jaundice becomes exaggerated, there are treatment options available that will not compromise breastfeeding. (See the section "Treatment Options for a Jaundiced Baby.")

Higher bilirubin levels are more common in certain ethnic groups and at higher altitudes.

Physiologic jaundice is more prevalent in certain populations, such as Chinese, Japanese, Korean, Native American, and South American. These babies also tend to have higher levels of bilirubin (Hodgman and Edwards 1992).

One study found that babies at higher altitudes also tend to have higher bilirubin levels (Leibson 1989). Researchers attribute this to the lower oxygen levels at higher altitudes, which may increase the amount of hemoglobin and red cells in the newborn's circulation.

Experts have suggested that research should be done to determine if elevated bilirubin is beneficial to the newborn.

Because breastfed babies tend to have higher bilirubin levels and a greater incidence of normal newborn jaundice, some experts have suggested that research be done to determine if bilirubin levels associated with natural feeding may be beneficial to newborns due to bilirubin's properties as an antioxidant in the newborn infant (Gartner 1994c). Preliminary research indicates that higher bilirubin levels may be associated with a decreased incidence of some diseases in term and preterm babies (Hegyi 1994; van Zoeren-Grobben 1994; Benaron and Bowen 1991).

Jaundice and Elevated Bilirubin after the Fifth Day

Although jaundice rising after the fifth day was once thought to be an unusual and distinct type of newborn jaundice, recent research has found that as many as one-third of breastfed newborns are clinically jaundiced and another one-third have elevated bilirubin levels at two to three weeks of age.

Jaundice rising or continuing past the first week—previously called "late onset" or "breast milk jaundice"—was once believed to be distinct from physiologic jaundice and to affect less than 4% of all breastfed newborns. However, recent research has found that prolonged jaundice and elevated bilirubin levels are more common than previously realized, with one-third of breastfed newborns two to three weeks old being clinically jaundiced (bilirubin levels above 5 mg/dl [85 µmol/L])—with visual signs of jaundice present—and another one-third of breastfed newborns having elevated bilirubin levels without visible jaundice (bilirubin levels between 1.5 and 5 mg/dl [26 to 85 µmol/L]) (Alonso 1991). Artificially fed newborns have bilirubin counts equivalent to adult levels (1.3 to 1.5 mg/dl [22 to 26 µmol/L]) by two to three weeks of age

Rather than being considered abnormal, this late-occurring elevated bilirubin is beginning to be recognized as a "normal extension of physiologic jaundice of the newborn" (Gartner 1994b). The high incidence of prolonged jaundice or elevated bilirubin in healthy breastfed babies is in the process of changing "the view of breast milk jaundice from one of a disease or syndrome to one of normal, expected developmental physiology" (Gartner 1994b). As such, some experts are suggesting that the lower bilirubin levels that are found in artificially fed infants "be considered the aberration or abnormal situation" (Gartner 1994b).

Experts have suggested that research should be done to determine if elevated bilirubin is beneficial to the newborn.

Because breastfed babies have higher bilirubin levels and a greater incidence of normal newborn jaundice, some experts have suggested that research be done to determine if bilirubin levels associated with natural feeding may be beneficial to newborns due to bilirubin's properties as an antioxidant in the newborn infant (Gartner 1994c). Preliminary research indicates that higher bilirubin levels may be associated with a decreased incidence of some diseases in term and preterm babies (Hegyi 1994; van Zoeren-Grobben 1994; Benaron and Bowen 1991).

Prolonged jaundice or elevated bilirubin is thought to be caused by a combination of three factors: a substance in most mothers' milk that increases intestinal absorption of bilirubin, individual variations in the baby's ability to process bilirubin, and the inadequacy of feeding in the early days.

There is evidence that prolonged jaundice may be due to a substance in the milk of most mothers that increases their babies' absorption of bilirubin from their intestines (Alonso 1991). In light of recent research (Alonso 1991), a previous theory that a substance in some mothers' milk inhibits a liver enzyme involved in the processing of bilirubin (Auerbach and Gartner 1987; Bevan 1965) now seems unlikely.

Another factor that influences the degree and duration of prolonged jaundice is the baby's ability to process this as-yet-unidentified factor in the mother's milk. Due to individual differences among mothers and babies, some babies may have exaggerated prolonged jaundice while others may not (Gartner 1996).

Another important factor is the adequacy of feedings in the early days. A healthy baby who receives more milk in the early days and has lower initial levels of bilirubin would be less likely to have prolonged jaundice and elevated bilirubin than the healthy baby whose bilirubin levels become elevated in the early days due to inadequate milk intake (Gartner 1994b).

If a baby is growing well but still jaundiced at 2-3 weeks of age, the doctor may want to do tests to rule out causes of pathological jaundice.

If a baby is growing well and the mother's milk supply is adequate, the doctor may want to do tests to rule out causes of pathological jaundice. Breastfeeding can and should continue unless the jaundice is found to be caused by a metabolic disease such as galactosemia.

Once pathologic causes have been ruled out, treatment is not usually necessary and the jaundice will eventually clear on its own without aftereffects, although in some cases it may take as long as three months.

Prolonged jaundice or elevated bilirubin will eventually clear on its own without interrupting breastfeeding, although it may take up to three months before the bilirubin levels drop to adult levels. If the mother keeps breastfeeding, the bilirubin will continue to be eliminated, more quickly in some babies than in others.

Some doctors recommend temporary weaning to determine whether or not a factor in the mother's milk is causing the jaundice, but this is neither beneficial nor necessary.

In the healthy, full-term baby, bilirubin levels below 23 to 29 mg/dl (400 to 500 µmol/L) have not been associated with short- or long-term health effects (Newman and Klebanoff 1993).

High or rapidly rising bilirubin levels are unusual in a baby with prolonged jaundice, but if they occur, treatment may be required.

Although it is unusual for a baby with prolonged jaundice to have rapidly rising bilirubin levels or levels above 20 mg/dl (340 µmol/L), if levels rise above 20 to 25 mg/dl (340 to 430 µmol/L), treatment may be needed. If so, the same treatments can be used as with elevated levels of physiologic jaundice. (See "Treatment Options for a Jaundiced Baby.")

Because it is rare for bilirubin to reach high levels with prolonged jaundice, the first action some doctors take when this occurs is to order tests to rule out physical causes unrelated to breastfeeding, such as infection, intestinal obstruction, or other disease. Phototherapy can be used to bring down bilirubin levels until the test results are available (L. Gartner, personal communication 1995).

When prolonged jaundice was thought to be a separate and distinct type of jaundice, some treatments were recommended especially for babies with prolonged jaundice, such as supplementing with the mother's expressed breast milk that had been heated to 56 degrees C and then cooled, or supplementing with donor milk. However, with the new understanding of prolonged jaundice as an extension of normal newborn jaundice, these special treatments are no longer recommended (Gartner 1996). If a baby with prolonged jaundice has bilirubin levels rising above 20 mg/dl (340 µmol/L), the same treatments should be considered as for a baby with elevated levels of physiologic jaundice (see next section).

Newborn Jaundice

Because prolonged jaundice is an extension of physiologic jaundice, breastfeeding early and often will help minimize it.

Babies whose physiologic jaundice becomes exaggerated by infrequent feedings in the early days are more likely to have prolonged jaundice. Frequent breastfeeding helps the baby eliminate the excess bilirubin that is normally present soon after birth. By keeping bilirubin at low levels during the first few days, prolonged jaundice will be minimized (Gartner 1994b).

WHY AND WHEN NEWBORN JAUNDICE MAY NEED TREATMENT

Although most cases of jaundice require no treatment, most doctors will take action when the bilirubin exceeds a certain level.

Although it rarely occurs today, excessive bilirubin can cause kernicterus, or brain damage.

High levels of unconjugated (indirect) bilirubin are of serious concern because of the possibility of brain damage. Bilirubin is potentially toxic and can cause cell damage when it circulates in the bloodstream. Unconjugated bilirubin can enter fatty tissues, such as those in the brain and nervous system. Although most cells will grow back, brain cells destroyed by bilirubin do not. The end result of very high untreated bilirubin levels is bilirubin encephalopathy or kernicterus, meaning that bilirubin has crossed into and damaged part of the brain.

Kernicterus is rare today and is of greatest concern in the premature or sick baby with abnormal (pathological) jaundice. Kernicterus has never been reported in an infant with prolonged, also known as "late-onset" or "breast milk" jaundice (Auerbach and Gartner 1987), but it is possible that it could occur at extremely high bilirubin levels.

Safe bilirubin levels in the full-term, healthy baby have recently been revised.

Safe bilirubin levels in the full-term, healthy baby have recently been revised. After reviewing research on more than 30,000 babies, Newman and Maisels (1992) concluded that keeping bilirubin below 20 mg/dl (340 µmol/L), which had been the standard recommendation, is appropriate for premature and ill babies, but not for healthy, full-term newborns. Because health problems resulting from these higher bilirubin levels are rare (Newman and Klebanoff 1993), the risks and costs of treating these babies may outweigh the benefits. Newman and Maisels (1992) suggested raising the maximum safe levels for healthy, full-term newborns to 23 to 29 mg/dl (400 to 500 µmol/L), which they termed "a kinder, gentler approach." In 1994, the American Academy of Pediatrics (AAP) adopted these levels in its recommended management of jaundice in healthy newborns. (See the next point on safe levels for the healthy or ill premature baby.)

The 1994 AAP guidelines recommend that treatment for the full-term healthy baby be considered based on a baby's age and total serum bilirubin level (in mg/dl [µmol/L]). Babies who are clinically jaundiced within their first 24 hours are not considered healthy.

Baby's Age	Consider Phototherapy	Phototherapy	Exchange Transfusion If Intensive Phototherapy Fails	Exchange Transfusion and Intensive Phototherapy
25 to 48 hours	≥12 (204)*	≥15 (260)	≥20 (340)	≥25 (430)
49 to 72 hours	≥15 (260)	≥18 (310)	≥25 (430)	≥30 (510)
> 72 hours	≥17 (290)	≥20 (340)	≥25 (430)	≥30 (510)

Correction of mathematical error in published table.

In addition to the level itself, the rate at which the bilirubin level is rising is also of concern if it is rising more than 0.5 mg/dl (8.5 µmol/L) per hour. Once a baby's bilirubin level has peaked, leveled off, and begun to go down, it is unlikely to increase again, except for a slight rebound effect that may occur after phototherapy (AAP 1994) or when the baby begins breastfeeding again after a temporary weaning, if this has been considered necessary. In these cases, the rise in serum bilirubin should be slight.

Safe maximum bilirubin levels are lower for premature or sick babies.

A premature baby is unable to process bilirubin as effectively as a full-term healthy baby, because his liver is immature. Also, a premie's blood-brain barrier is less effective at blocking the entry of bilirubin into the brain. These considerations put the premature baby at greater risk of brain injury at lower bilirubin levels.

Illness in the premature baby further increases the risks associated with jaundice. Serious infections of any kind including infection of the blood (sepsis), a lack of oxygen or reduced levels of oxygen in the tissues (anoxia or hypoxia), and the accumulation of acids in the body (acidosis) all increase a premature baby's risk of brain injury from jaundice.

Safe bilirubin levels for the premie are determined by the baby's gestational age, weight, and health. For example, according to Gartner (1994b), when the bilirubin of an ill premature baby weighing 1000 to 1249 grams (2 lbs. 3 oz. to 2 lbs. 12 oz.) reaches 10 mg/dl (171 µmol/L) an exchange transfusion is recommended. A bilirubin of 18 mg/dl (308 µmol/L) is considered the upper limit for a healthy premie weighing 2000 to 2500 grams (4 lbs. 6 oz. to 5 lbs. 8 oz.).

TREATMENT OPTIONS FOR A JAUNDICED BABY

With mild-to-moderate jaundice, some doctors simply observe and monitor the baby.

When bilirubin levels are less than 20 mg/dl (340 µmol/L), most doctors will begin by observing the baby and monitoring his bilirubin levels through regular blood tests before considering treatment. Some doctors choose to observe and monitor the baby when bilirubin levels are in the 20-25 mg/dl (340-425 µmol/L) range, particularly if the levels are rising slowly or appear to be peaking.

Research confirms the safety of this approach. In one study that evaluated the effectiveness of four common treatment plans for jaundice, the researchers concluded that most babies require no intervention and can be safely breastfed and observed (Martinez 1993).

Whenever jaundice is a concern, the mother can help bring down her baby's bilirubin levels in the following ways.

Breastfeed Frequently

Breastfeeding frequently helps the jaundiced baby eliminate the bilirubin from his system.

When a baby begins to show signs of jaundice, the mother can help minimize her baby's jaundice by encouraging him to breastfeed as often as possible (at least every two hours), stimulating the baby if he is sleepy or lethargic. (See "How to Rouse a Sleepy Baby" under "Sleepy Baby" in the chapter "Positioning, Latch-On, and the Baby's Suck.") Frequent breastfeeding will help rid the baby of the excess bilirubin in his system by stimulating bowel movements so that the bilirubin in the stool cannot be reabsorbed through the intestines and recirculated in the bloodstream. Frequent breastfeeding in the first few days of life also stimulates the mother's milk supply so that her mature milk comes in sooner, providing the baby with more fluids and calories (Gartner 1994a; Yamauchi and Yamanouchi 1990).

Research comparing groups of infants breastfed at varying intervals has confirmed that those fed more frequently have lower bilirubin levels. In one study (deCarvalho 1982), the researchers found that babies who breastfed at least eight times a day had bilirubin levels three points lower than the babies who breastfed less frequently. Feeding every two hours was associated with even lower bilirubin levels.

Newborn Jaundice

If the baby is sleepy or lethargic, the mother may need to stimulate him so that he breastfeeds frequently and long enough.

High bilirubin levels sometimes make a baby sleepy or lethargic, which may also make him less interested in breastfeeding. If the baby tends to sleep for hours at a time, encourage the mother to wake him to breastfeed at least every two hours and to stimulate him during breastfeedings if he falls asleep early in the feeding. (See "How to Rouse a Sleepy Baby" under "Sleepy Baby" in the chapter "Positioning, Latch-On, and the Baby's Suck.")

In most cases, breastfeeding does not need to be interrupted in order to bring bilirubin levels down.

In its 1994 practice guidelines for pediatricians, the American Academy of Pediatrics (AAP) lists bilirubin levels at which treatment should be considered and five treatment options for those unusual times when a baby's bilirubin rises to the point where treatment is warranted. (For a table listing the bilirubin levels at which treatment is recommended, see the previous section "Why and When Newborn Jaundice May Need Treatment.")

In the unusual event that a baby's bilirubin rises to levels where there is a concern, the AAP lists the following five treatment options:

1. Observe
2. Continue breastfeeding; administer phototherapy
3. Supplement breastfeeding with formula, with or without phototherapy
4. Interrupt breastfeeding; substitute formula
5. Interrupt breastfeeding; substitute formula; administer phototherapy

These guidelines to pediatricians also state: "The AAP discourages the interruption of breastfeeding in healthy term newborns and encourages continued and frequent breastfeeding (at least eight to ten times every 24 hours)." If further treatment is needed, the AAP encourages the pediatrician to discuss with parents the five treatment options.

In a study that confirms the safety of continuing to breastfeed through unusually high levels of newborn jaundice, researchers divided 125 full-term breastfed babies with bilirubin levels of at least 17 mg/dl (289 µmol/L) into four different groups, each with its own treatment plan: 1) continue breastfeeding and observe, 2) continue breastfeeding and begin phototherapy, 3) interrupt breastfeeding and substitute formula, and 4) interrupt breastfeeding, substitute formula, and begin phototherapy (Martinez 1993). The researchers concluded that most babies require no intervention and can be safely breastfed and observed. They noted: "Many mothers do not want to interrupt nursing (if this is at all possible) and the option of doing nothing, or providing phototherapy while they continue nursing, should be offered. In fact, our data show that if the baby receives phototherapy...there is no significant advantage in discontinuing nursing."

Careful monitoring is indicated and treatment should be started if bilirubin levels continue to rise to levels that place the baby at risk of brain injury. With good breastfeeding management, this is rarely necessary.

Increase Baby's Stooling

A baby should have at least two stools per day by the third day of life.

Bilirubin is eliminated primarily via a baby's stools. The more stool a baby passes, the more quickly his bilirubin levels will go down (Tudehope 1991; deCarvalho 1985). If a baby has fewer than two stools per day by the third day of life, or has not yet passed all of the meconium, he should be stimulated to breastfeed more frequently or more actively to help eliminate the bilirubin from his system more quickly.

Receiving enough of the fatty hindmilk assures that the baby will have the stools needed to eliminate the excess bilirubin from his body quickly.

If the baby is nursing actively, encourage the mother to allow her baby to finish the first breast first before offering the second rather than switching breasts after a predetermined length of time. When a baby begins nursing, the first milk, called the foremilk, is low in fat. As he continues nursing, the milk gradually increases in fat content. By not limiting the baby's time at either breast, the mother can be sure that her baby receives the fatty hindmilk he needs, which stimulates bowel movements, eliminating bilirubin more quickly from the baby's intestines.

If the baby is not nursing actively, suggest the mother take the baby off the breast when he stops sucking and swallowing, stimulate him, and put him back to breast as many times as necessary to encourage active sucking and swallowing for at least ten to twenty minutes (known as "super switch nursing").

Another alternative is breast massage during nursing, which has been found to increase milk volume and fat content and keep the baby nursing actively longer (Stutte 1988). This technique is recommended after the baby's sucking pattern changes from long, slow mouth movements to either rapid, shallow mouth movements or no sucking at all. When this change occurs, without removing the baby from the breast, suggest the mother move the hand supporting the breast to the back and middle part of the breast near the armpit and gently massage the breast several times. Typically, the baby pauses while the mother is massaging and takes several long, slow sucks afterwards. When the baby pauses again, repeat the massage. When the area of breast being massaged begins to feel softer, suggest the mother move her fingers to another area, alternating breast massage with active nursing until the entire breast feels soft.

If the baby has fewer than two stools a day and does not respond to more frequent and/or active nursing, the mother can express her milk to offer as a supplement and to stimulate her milk production.

If the baby does not respond to the mother's efforts to stimulate him to breastfeed more often or more actively, the mother may need to express her milk, which can be used as a supplement until the baby is more active at the breast. To avoid confusing the baby with an artificial nipple, the supplement can be given by cup, eyedropper, feeding syringe, or spoon or by using a nursing supplementer at the breast or on a finger. (For more information, see the section "Alternative Feeding Methods" in the chapter "The Use of Breast Pumps and Other Products.")

In addition to providing a supplement for her baby, milk expression will also help a mother stimulate her milk production if her baby is not nursing often or long enough.

Expose the Baby to Indirect Sunlight

Expose the baby to indirect sunlight to help lower his bilirubin levels.

Because bilirubin is broken down in the skin by the light, exposing the baby to indirect sunlight will help lower his bilirubin levels. Suggest the mother keep the baby in a room that gets a lot of daylight and undress the baby down to his diaper so that his skin will be exposed to the light.

To avoid sunburn and overheating, it is important that the mother not put the baby in direct sunlight.

Discontinue the use of any drug that might increase the risk of kernicterus.

Aspirin, other salicylates, and certain sulfa drugs have been shown to increase the risk of brain damage in the presence of jaundice (Drew and Kitchen 1976). If the mother or baby is taking such a drug, it should be discontinued and, if needed, a substitute found. These drugs should never be used by a nursing mother whose baby is jaundiced.

Avoid Water Supplements

Glucose or plain water supplements are offered routinely to newborns in many hospitals, and mothers are sometimes told that water supplements will prevent jaundice or "flush out" the bilirubin in a jaundiced newborn. Research has refuted these widespread beliefs, demonstrating that water supplements are associated with higher bilirubin levels (Nicoll 1982).

Because the type of bilirubin associated with physiologic jaundice is not excreted in the urine, the idea of "flushing out" the jaundice with water supplements is not valid.

Only 2% of a baby's bilirubin is eliminated through his urine, while 98% is eliminated through his bowel movements, so the idea of "flushing out" the jaundice with water supplements is not valid. Water supplements will not stimulate more bowel movements. In fact, water supplements can even decrease the number of bowel movements because the baby fills up on water rather than colostrum or mature milk, which contains fat that increases bowel movements.

Newborn Jaundice

Water supplements have also been recommended in order to prevent dehydration and reduce weight loss, but these have not been found to reduce jaundice.

Another rationale for offering glucose water is to prevent dehydration and reduce weight loss, both of which are commonly believed to be associated with jaundice. Research has shown, however, that dehydration is not a contributing factor in the jaundice of most breastfed babies (Murphy 1981). Receiving fewer calories than needed, however, is a significant contributor to newborn jaundice, and giving water adds to this deficit.

Research has indicated that water supplements can actually increase bilirubin levels by depressing the urge to breastfeed.

In one study (Nicoll 1982), researchers found that glucose water supplements may actually increase bilirubin levels by interfering with breastfeeding and as a consequence delaying the passing of meconium. In another study (Kuhr 1982), researchers found that babies who received large volumes of glucose water during their first three days of life took less milk per feeding by the fourth day and also were more likely to be jaundiced than those who did not. Plain water supplements have been shown to have no effect on bilirubin concentrations (deCarvalho 1981).

In addition to filling up the baby so that he breastfeeds less frequently and has fewer bowel movements, water supplements given by bottle can also interfere with breastfeeding by affecting the baby's suck. Because the baby uses his mouth and jaw muscles differently when he takes liquid from a bottle, he may become nipple-confused if he goes back and forth from breast to bottle in the early weeks of nursing. If a baby becomes confused by the artificial nipple, he may refuse the breast or nurse less effectively when offered the breast, giving him less milk, fewer bowel movements, and higher bilirubin levels.

The American Academy of Pediatrics states that giving breastfed babies water or sugar water supplements does not lower bilirubin levels.

The American Academy of Pediatrics (AAP) published the following statement in its 1994 practice guidelines to pediatricians: "Supplementing nursing with water or dextrose water does not lower the bilirubin level in jaundiced, healthy, breastfeeding infants."

Phototherapy

Phototherapy is the use of light to break down bilirubin through the skin.

Phototherapy is a common treatment for all types of exaggerated jaundice, sometimes in addition to other treatments.

Phototherapy is the use of white, blue, or green fluorescent light to break down bilirubin through the skin. The light is absorbed by the bilirubin, changing the bilirubin to a water-soluble product, which can then be eliminated through the liver without having to be conjugated by the liver.

The baby is placed under the light source—called bili-lights—nearly naked, with his eyes covered to protect his corneas and retinas from damage.

Phototherapy can be given at the hospital or at home and does not require separation of mother and baby. It does not have to be continuous to be effective and can be interrupted for feedings.

Phototherapy in the hospital often means that the baby is kept in the nursery, where the bili-lights are. But a mother can request that the bili-lights be brought to her room, where she may be able to nurse the baby under the lights or take the baby out from under the lights for brief periods when he is wakeful. Or a mother may be permitted to sit with her baby in the nursery, watching for periods of wakefulness when the baby will be interested in nursing. Phototherapy does not have to be continuous to be effective.

Phototherapy units can be rented from sources outside the hospital and brought to the mother's home. One study found that babies who received home phototherapy for jaundice were less likely to wean prematurely than babies who received phototherapy in the hospital (James 1993). If the doctor recommends the baby remain at the hospital when it is time for the mother to be discharged, home phototherapy is an option the mother might want to discuss with her baby's doctor. If it is ordered by the doctor, the costs of home phototherapy may be reimbursed by the mother's medical insurance. Some doctors believe it is safer and more convenient for the phototherapy to be given in the hospital where bilirubin levels can be monitored frequently, the baby can be closely observed, and other treatments are available if they are required.

A baby whose eyes are patched needs regular stimulation.

So that he doesn't feel totally cut off from the world, a baby whose eyes are covered needs contact with his parents, especially their loving touch. He also benefits from having his patches removed regularly so that he can make eye contact, especially during feedings, and see the world around him.

Phototherapy may have side effects.

Although phototherapy is an effective tool in speeding up the elimination of bilirubin from the baby's system, it may have side effects. Babies can become dehydrated under phototherapy due to increased water loss through their stools and from the skin. Frequent breastfeeding should continue during phototherapy to increase fluid intake. The loose stools associated with phototherapy are due to the increased excretion of bilirubin.

Separation of mother and baby is another possible side effect of phototherapy that can have long-term effects on breastfeeding and the mother's feelings about her baby's health and well-being.

The Wallaby phototherapy unit is an alternative to traditional phototherapy that does not require eye patching or separation.

An alternative to traditional overhead phototherapy, the Wallaby phototherapy unit is a fiberoptic blanket that is secured around the baby's trunk and provides continuous treatment from the therapeutic lights. This method does not require eye patching or separation from the mother for treatment. It is considered by most to be as effective as traditional phototherapy lights. (For information on where to find home phototherapy units, see the "Other Resources" section at the end of this chapter.)

Supplement with Formula

In most cases, breastfeeding need not be supplemented or interrupted in order to bring bilirubin levels down.

Although giving formula is sometimes recommended for jaundiced newborns, either in addition to breastfeeding or as a temporary (24 hour) substitute for breast-feeding (AAP 1994; Maisels and Gifford 1986; Amato 1985), there are other effective treatments that will bring down bilirubin levels without putting breastfeeding at risk. In its 1994 practice guidelines for pediatricians, the American Academy of Pediatrics (AAP) lists bilirubin levels at which treatment should be considered and five treatment options for those unusual times when a baby's bilirubin rises to the level where treatment is warranted. (For a table listing bilirubin levels by age at which treatment is recommended, see the previous section "Why and When Newborn Jaundice May Need Treatment.")

In the unusual event that a baby's bilirubin rises to levels where there is a concern, the AAP lists the following five treatment options:

1. Observe
2. Continue breastfeeding; administer phototherapy
3. Supplement breastfeeding with formula, with or without phototherapy
4. Interrupt breastfeeding; substitute formula
5. Interrupt breastfeeding; substitute formula; administer phototherapy

These guidelines to pediatricians also state: "The AAP discourages the interruption of breastfeeding in healthy term newborns and encourages continued and frequent breast-

Newborn Jaundice

feeding (at least eight to ten times every 24 hours)." If further treatment is needed, the AAP encourages the pediatrician to discuss with the parents the five treatment options.

In a study that confirms the safety of continuing to breastfeed through unusually high levels of newborn jaundice, researchers divided 125 full-term breastfed babies with bilirubin levels of at least 17 mg/dl (289 µmol/L) into four different groups, each with its own treatment plan: 1) continue breastfeeding and observe, 2) continue breastfeeding and begin phototherapy, 3) interrupt breastfeeding and substitute formula, and 4) interrupt breastfeeding, substitute formula, and begin phototherapy (Martinez 1993). The researchers concluded that most babies require no intervention and can be safely breastfed and observed. They noted: "Many mothers do not want to interrupt nursing (if this is at all possible) and the option of doing nothing, or providing phototherapy while they continue nursing, should be offered. In fact, our data show that if the baby receives phototherapy...there is no significant advantage in discontinuing nursing."

Careful monitoring is indicated and treatment should be started if bilirubin levels continue to rise to levels that place the baby at risk of brain injury. With good breastfeeding management, this is rarely necessary.

Although some doctors recommend supplementing breastfeeding with formula or substituting formula for breastfeeding for 24 hours, these treatment options have drawbacks.

Although giving formula is sometimes recommended for jaundiced newborns, either in addition to breastfeeding or as a temporary (24-hour) substitute for breast-feeding (AAP 1994; Maisels and Gifford 1986; Amato 1985), these treatment options have drawbacks:

- Babies who receive formula in the newborn period may be at greater risk of becoming sensitized to cow's milk and going on to develop cow's milk allergy or intolerance during their first year (Host 1988).
- Supplements interfere with the establishment and maintenance of a mother's milk supply.
- Early supplementation is strongly correlated with a shorter duration of breastfeeding (Kurinij and Shiono 1991), which in the case of the jaundiced baby, may be due in part to the unspoken, incorrect message that the mother's milk could harm her baby.

- Breastfeeding problems may result when formula is given with an artificial nipple, which can weaken a baby's suck or cause baby to refuse the breast.
- Giving formula puts the mother at increased risk of engorgement and mastitis unless she has access to an effective means of milk expression.

The mother who temporarily interrupts breastfeeding for 24 hours will need to express her milk in order to stay comfortable and to avoid a plugged duct or mastitis, as well as to establish or maintain her milk supply. It may also be necessary for some mothers who are supplementing breastfeeding to express their milk in order to stay comfortable. (For information on choosing a gentle and effective method of expression, see the chapter "Expression and Storage of Human Milk.")

Under some circumstances, supplementing with formula may be necessary.

Exaggerated jaundice is linked to fewer feedings during the first few days, and fewer feedings per day also contribute to a lower milk supply (Yamauchi and Yamanouchi 1990). Formula supplements on a short-term basis may be necessary if the baby's bilirubin level rises to a level where treatment is indicated and the mother does not yet have enough milk to increase her baby's stooling. In this case, supplementing with formula may be helpful in bringing the baby's bilirubin down while the mother builds her milk by increasing the number of effective feedings per day and/or by expressing milk.

Nipple confusion can be avoided if bottles are not used to give formula.

When formula is given for 24 hours (either as a supplement to breastfeeding or as an alternative), the return to complete breastfeeding may be easier if bottles are avoided. The use of artificial nipples during the early weeks—while baby is still learning to breastfeed—is often confusing to a baby, and he may have difficulty going back to breastfeeding (Neifert 1995). This is believed to be because a baby's tongue, jaw, and mouth move differently during breastfeeding than while using a bottle (Newman 1990). In one study, 30% of mothers whose babies received bottles in the hospital reported severe breastfeeding problems, as compared with 14% of those whose babies did not (Cronenwett 1992).

Other feeding methods include cup, spoon, eyedropper, feeding syringe, or a nursing supplementer used on the finger (known as "finger-feeding").

When a supplement is given while continuing to breastfeed, another approach is to use the nursing supplementer to give formula while the baby is nursing at the breast.

See the chapter "The Use of Breast Pumps and Other Products" for more information on the use of these alternative feeding methods.

Blood-Exchange Transfusions and Drugs

A blood-exchange transfusion is a drastic treatment that can bring down bilirubin levels quickly if they are rapidly reaching unsafe levels.

An exchange transfusion is the fastest way to bring down a baby's bilirubin count. It involves a continuous process of removing small amounts of the baby's blood and replacing it with donor blood.

Exchange transfusions are seldom needed to treat jaundice. In the past, the most common reason for doing exchange transfusions was pathologic jaundice due to Rh incompatibility, which is now usually prevented by the routine use of RhoGAM. The availability of phototherapy has also decreased the need for exchange transfusions.

Drugs may be used to treat jaundice, but their use is controversial.

In Europe, phenobarbital has been used to treat newborn jaundice, but it is not used worldwide because of concern over possible side effects. Other drugs, such as cholestyramine, have been used along with phototherapy to reduce jaundice, but their potential side effects preclude general use. New drugs are being tested, but none have been widely used.

HELPING THE MOTHER WORK WITH THE BABY'S DOCTOR

Suggest the mother explain her feelings about breastfeeding.

A mother can help avoid conflicts with her baby's doctor by telling him or her in the beginning what her goals are. She might say something like, "I want to do everything I can to get breastfeeding off to a good start." This may make the doctor more willing to try different approaches.

Encourage the mother to ask her baby's doctor about anything she doesn't understand.

When a mother is told that her baby has jaundice, she may have a strong emotional reaction, especially if she is unfamiliar with newborn jaundice and it is not explained to her clearly.

If the mother is given a technical explanation of her baby's condition while she is upset, it is unlikely that she will be able to understand or remember all of the particulars. If so, encourage the mother to contact her baby's doctor to discuss it when she is feeling calmer.

Throughout her baby's care, encourage the mother to stay well-informed and ask for clarification when she needs it.

Some questions the mother may want to ask are:

Newborn Jaundice

- What is the cause of the baby's jaundice?
- What tests have been done or are planned? What do the results mean?
- What criteria will be used to decide when the baby will be able to come home?
- If breastfeeding is suspended, how long will it be necessary, and at what bilirubin level can breastfeeding be resumed?

Remind the mother that although the doctor is the medical expert, the mother is the expert on her baby and it is she and the baby's father who are ultimately responsible for the decisions made about their baby.

Encourage the mother to ask for treatment options that will allow her to stay close to her baby and breastfeed frequently.

Long periods of time away from her baby can add to a mother's anxiety and feelings of helplessness. Research has shown that mothers who are separated from their newborns are more likely to feel anxious about caring for their babies and are more likely to wean early (Kemper 1990; Kemper 1989).

Also, mother and baby can usually remain together even if the baby needs to be treated for jaundice with phototherapy. See previous sections of this chapter for specific suggestions.

It is important that the mother be open and honest with her doctor.

Honesty is essential to any doctor-patient relationship. The health and well-being of the baby are the goals of both mother and doctor. The doctor cannot treat a patient with incomplete or incorrect information. When mother and doctor disagree, it is important to keep the channels of communication open and try to separate feelings from facts.

If the mother feels pressured to hide things from her baby's doctor, suggest instead she seek another opinion.

If the doctor recommends a treatment that will negatively affect breastfeeding or has been invalidated by research, offer to share references with the mother that she can go over with her doctor.

If the doctor's advice seems counterproductive to breastfeeding or inappropriate, keep these points in mind:

- In a complex medical situation such as jaundice, the mother may not have explained or completely understood everything about her baby's situation. First impressions may not be accurate, and there may be more to it than is apparent.

- Openly disagreeing with the doctor's advice will not help the mother. In fact, it may confuse her even more. What she needs is help in coming to some agreement with her baby's doctor.

In this case, the safest approach is to offer to share references with her that she can go over with the doctor. For example, if the baby's doctor suggests a course of action that is not backed by current research, say to the mother: "Some doctors do take that approach, but research has shown..." and then ask the mother if she would like a reference she can share with her doctor. Here are some specific examples:

- If the mother says her doctor wants her to take her three-day-old baby off the breast for a day or two because of jaundice, say: "Research has shown that nursing at least every two hours helps to prevent or eliminate jaundice. Would you like a reference to an article in a medical journal to share with your doctor?" If she says yes, then ask her to write down the references to studies (Martinez 1993; Auerbach and Gartner 1987; deCarvalho 1982) listed at the end of this chapter.
- If the doctor recommends treatment for jaundice when the baby's bilirubin levels are below 20 mg/dl (340 μmol/L), refer the mother to the American Academy of Pediatrics (1994) practice guidelines for pediatricians.
- If the doctor recommends water supplements to "flush out" the jaundice, refer the mother to the Nicoll (1982) and the deCarvalho (1981) studies.

If the mother is uncomfortable with her doctor's recommendations, suggest ways to discuss her concerns.

Most people, but especially a pregnant woman or new mother, find it very stressful to be in conflict with a doctor. If the doctor advises a treatment that the mother is uncomfortable with, give her the tools she needs to come to some agreement with her doctor. The basic tools are tact, honesty, respect, knowledge, and patience.

Suggest the mother think through her approach before she speaks to the doctor. There are many ways she can make her encounter with the doctor more positive. The mother can:

Practice her responses before she talks to the doctor. Offer to take some time to discuss the mother's concerns and to have her practice expressing them before talking to the doctor.

Ask the doctor for a complete explanation of the treatment. If the mother is unsure of the reasons for the doctor's recommendations, encourage her to ask him or her to take the time to explain it to her thoroughly. In evaluating the doctor's advice, it may help to ask, "Is this your general policy with regard to jaundice or is this specific to my baby?"

Repeat the doctor's statements in her own words. By paraphrasing what the doctor says, the mother can avoid confusion and show the doctor what impact his or her words are having on her.

Share her feelings with the doctor. It is best if a mother has been clear about her feelings from the beginning, but if not, it is never too late to start. A doctor cannot know what an individual mother's preferences and priorities are unless she tells him. The mother might tell the doctor, for example, "Our family has a history of allergies and I feel strongly about exclusive breastfeeding. I would prefer treatment options that allow for continued breastfeeding without giving formula." Or, "I would feel better if I could spend more time with my baby. Would it be possible to have the bili-lights brought to my room so that I can hold and nurse him while he is under the lights?"

Project self-confidence. Writing down questions and concerns in advance can be helpful, as well as a friendly manner and a willingness to consider alternatives.

Make statements in a positive way. Another way to foster a friendly atmosphere is to make statements in a positive way, for example, "I would like to try stimulating my baby to breastfeed more often before offering supplements," rather than "I don't want to give my baby supplements."

Try the "broken record" technique. When disagreements arise, the "broken record" technique can be an effective way of getting a message across. The mother can simply restate her basic position, calmly and quietly to each argument. "I appreciate your concern about her health, but now that she's breastfeeding well, I'd like to wait and monitor her bilirubin level for another day before considering other options."

Use tact, give respect, and expect them in return. If a mother feels that her doctor is being judgmental or overly critical, it may be helpful to recognize his or her concern for her baby (for example, "I understand your concern for my baby's health and well-being") but still calmly insist that the doctor offer current medical information to back up opinions. Most physicians are not inflexible and would be willing to meet a mother halfway.

Keep in mind that the ultimate responsibility for the baby's health lies with the parents. Although the doctor is the medical expert, the parents are the ones who are ultimately responsible for the decisions made about their baby. A mother can shift a discussion to emphasize parental responsibility by saying, "You'd like my permission to... ?" or "Your recommendation is... ?"

If not satisfied, seek a second opinion. If, after discussing her feelings and possible approaches with her baby's doctor, a mother feels that the doctor is not as supportive of breastfeeding or her feelings as she would like, it is her right to get a second opinion.

Newborn Jaundice

Other Resources

Home phototherapy units are available from:
Medela, Inc.
P.O. Box 660
McHenry, IL 60051-0660 USA
1-800-835-5968
1-815-363-1166

The Wallaby phototherapy unit is available from:
Fiberoptic Medical Products, Inc.
Suite 300 Commerce Plaza
5100 Tilghman St.
Allentown, PA 18104 USA

References

Alonso, E. et al. Enterohepatic circulation of nonconjugated bilirubin in rats fed with human milk. *J Pediatr* 1991; 118(3):425-30.

Amato, M. et al. Interruption of breast feeding versus phototherapy as treatment of hyperbilirubinemia in full term infants. *Helv Paediatr Acta* 1985; 40:127-31.

American Academy of Pediatrics (AAP) Provisional Committee for Quality Improvement and Subcommittee on Hyperbilirubinemia. Practice parameter: management of hyperbilirubinemia in the healthy term newborn. *Pediatrics* 1994; 94(4):558-65.

Auerbach, K. and Gartner, L. Breastfeeding and human milk: their association with jaundice in the neonate. *Clin Perinatol* 1987; 14:89-107.

Benaron, D. and Bowen, F. Variation of initial serum bilirubin rise in newborn infants with type of illness. *Lancet* 1991; 338:78-81.

Bevan, B. et al. The effect of pregnanediol and pregnanediol glucuronide on bilirubin conjugation by rat liver slices. *Clin Sci* 1965; 29:353-61.

Cronenwett, L. et al. Single daily bottle use in the early weeks postpartum and breastfeeding outcomes. *Pediatrics* 1992; 90(5):760-66.

deCarvalho, M. et al. Effects of water supplementation on physiological jaundice in breastfed babies. *Arch Dis Child* 1981; 56:568-69.

deCarvalho, M. et al. Fecal bilirubin excretion and serum bilirubin concentrations in breastfeeding and bottle-feeding infants. *J Pediatr* 1985; 107:786-90.

deCarvalho, M. et al. Frequency of breastfeeding and serum bilirubin concentration. *Am J Dis Child* 1982; 136:737-38.

Drew, J. and Kitchen, W. The effect of maternally administered drugs on bilirubin concentrations in the newborn infant. *J Pediatr* 1976; 89:657.

Gartner, L. Professor of Pediatrics, University of Chicago. Personal communication, May 1996.

Gartner, L. Professor of Pediatrics, University of Chicago. Personal communication, September 1995.

Gartner, L. On the question of the relationship between breastfeeding and jaundice in the first 5 days of life. *Sem Perinatol* 1994a; 18(6):502-09.

Gartner, L. Neonatal jaundice. *Pediatr Review* 1994b; 15(11):422-32.

Gartner, L. et al. Neonatal bilirubin workshop. *Pediatrics* 1994c; 94(4):537-40.

Gartner, L. and Auerbach, K. Breast milk and breastfeeding jaundice. *Acta Paediatr* 1987; 34:249.

Hegyi, T. et al. The protective role of bilirubin in oxygen-radical diseases of the preterm infant. J Perinatol 1994; 14(4):296-300.

Hodgman, J. and Edwards, N. Racial differences in neonatal jaundice. *Clin Pediatr* 1992; 719-22.

Host, A. et al. A prospective study of cow's milk allergy in exclusively breastfed infants. *Acta Paediatr Scand* 1988; 77:663-70.

James, J. et al. Discontinuation of breast-feeding infrequent among jaundiced neonates treated at home. *Pediatrics* 1993; 92(1):153-55.

Kemper, K. Neonatal jaundice in the development of the vulnerable child syndrome. Breastfeeding Abstracts 1990; 10:7.

Kemper, K. et al. Jaundice, terminating breast-feeding, and the vulnerable child. *Pediatrics* 1989; 84:773-78.

Kemper, K. et al. Persistent perceptions of vulnerability following neonatal jaundice. *Am J Dis Child* 1990; 144:238-41.

Kuhr, M. and Paneth, N. Feeding practices and early neonatal jaundice. *J Ped Gastro Nutr* 1982; 1:485-88.

Kurinij, N. and Shiono, P. Early formula supplementation of breastfeeding. *Pediatrics* 1991; 88:745.

Lawrence, R. *Breastfeeding: A Guide for the Medical Profession,* 4th ed. St. Louis: Mosby, 1994, pp. 446-54.

Leibson, C., et al. Neonatal hyperbilirubinemia at high altitude. *Am J Dis Child* 1989; 143:983-87.

Maisels, M. and Gifford, K. Normal serum bilirubin levels in the newborn and the effects of breastfeeding. *Pediatrics* 1986; 78:837.

Martinez, J., et al. Hyperbilirubinemia in the breast-fed newborn: a controlled trial of four interventions. *Pediatrics* 1993; 91(2):470-73.

Murphy, J. et al. Pregnanediols and breast milk jaundice. *Arch Dis Child* 1981; 56:474-76.

Neifert, M. et al. Nipple confusion: toward a formal definition. *J Pediatr* 1995; 126(6):S125-29.

Newman, J. Breastfeeding problems associated with early introduction of bottles and pacifiers. *J Hum Lact* 1990; 6(2):59-63.

Newman, T. and Klebanoff, M. Neonatal hyperbilirubinemia and long-term outcome: another look at the Collaborative Perinatal Project. *Pediatrics* 1993; 92(5):651-57.

Newman, T. and Maisels, M. Evaluation and treatment of jaundice in the term newborn: a kinder, gentler approach. *Pediatrics* 1992; 89(5):809-18.

Newman, T. and Maisels, M. Does hyperbilirubinemia damage the brain of healthy full-term infants? *Clin Perinatol* 1990; 17(2):331-58.

Nicoll, A. et al. Supplementary feeding and jaundice in newborns. *Acta Paediatr Scand* 1982; 71:759-61.

Riordan, J. and Auerbach, K. *Breastfeeding and Human Lactation.* Boston and London: Jones and Bartlett, 1993, pp. 333-46.

Stutte, P. et al. The effects of breast massage on volume and fat content of human milk. *Genesis* 1988; 10(2):22-25.

Tudehope, D. et al. Breast feeding practices and severe hyperbilirubinaemia. *J Paediatr Child Health* 1991; 27:240-44.

van Zoeren-Grobben, D. et al. Postnatal changes in plasma chain-breaking antioxidants in healthy preterm infants fed formula and/or human milk. *Am J Clin Nutr* 1994; 60:900-06.

Yamauchi, Y. and Yamanouchi, H. Breast-feeding frequency during the first 24 hours after birth in full-term neonates. *Pediatrics* 1990; 86:171-75.

Newborn Jaundice

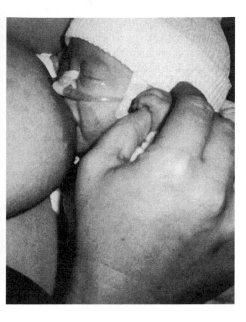

12

Prematurity

THE MOTHER'S FEELINGS

THE ADVANTAGES OF BREASTFEEDING A PREMATURE BABY

BUILDING A RELATIONSHIP BETWEEN MOTHER AND BABY
    Kangaroo Care

THE PREMIE WEIGHING MORE THAN 1500 GRAMS (3.3 LBS.)

THE PREMIE WEIGHING LESS THAN 1500 GRAMS (3.3 LBS.)
    Feeding Methods and Options
    Before Baby Can Breastfeed
    Determining a Baby's Readiness to Breastfeed

THE FIRST NURSINGS
    Setting the Scene
    Putting Baby to Breast
    Making the Transition to Breastfeeding

THE MOTHER'S DIET AND DRUG CONSIDERATIONS

WORKING WITH HOSPITAL PERSONNEL

PREPARING FOR HOSPITAL DISCHARGE

THE FIRST WEEKS AT HOME
    Household Preparations and Realistic Expectations
    Breastfeeding at Home

A premature baby is one who is born at least three weeks before his due date. The term covers a broad spectrum, from a tiny, fragile infant born months too soon to a healthy, robust baby born just a few weeks early. The breastfeeding considerations vary, too, and depend on several factors: the gestational age of the baby, the baby's health, the length of the baby's hospital stay, and how soon he is ready to breastfeed.

THE MOTHER'S FEELINGS

Immediately after giving birth to a premature baby, the mother may be in shock, making it difficult for her to remember information.

When the mother delivers a premature baby—especially one who is considered high risk or who has physical problems—she may go through a grieving period in which she mourns the loss of the healthy full-term baby and the normal pregnancy she had expected and comes to terms with the experience she is now facing. The mother's initial reactions may include shock, denial, and an emotional "numbness" when confronted with her baby's problems.

Even when the baby seems to be doing well, premature labor and delivery can be frightening. The mother may not have had a chance to prepare herself by taking childbirth classes or reading baby-care books. She may be confused, worried, and anxious. Fathers and mothers may be at different stages of dealing with their feelings, and each may feel alone at times.

While the mother is going through these early stages of grief, patience is needed, because she may not be able to accept and understand information unless it is repeated several times. It may help to give her written information to which she can refer.

The mother who has recently given birth prematurely may doubt her ability to breastfeed. Give her the information she needs at this stage.

If the mother doubts her ability to breastfeed her baby, assure her that it can be done and explain to her just what she needs to know at this stage—such as the importance of beginning frequent milk expression as soon as possible to stimulate and establish an ample milk supply. Even small amounts of colostrum expressed in the first few days after birth will be of benefit to the baby. By telling her only what she needs to know at the time, the mother will not be overloaded with too much information.

Encourage the mother to take it one day at a time. Keep information brief and to the point and be available to talk to the mother on a regular basis as her circumstances change and she begins to come to terms with her situation.

The mother may pass through the stages of grief, including shock, denial, anger, bargaining, depression, and finally, acceptance.

Premature birth is a traumatic experience, and the mother may go through a grieving process. Strong feelings are normal, but if the mother feels so overwhelmed that she cannot function, encourage her to seek the help of a mental health specialist.

Once the initial shock passes and the reality of her baby's condition sinks in, the mother's intense feelings may begin to surface. She may deal with them in different ways at different times and experience denial in various forms. The mother may try to block out the reality of her baby's condition. She may refuse to believe her baby's medical caregivers and search for a specialist who will "make the baby better." She may be overly optimistic, believing that "everything will work out fine," or overly pessimistic, feeling that "all is lost."

Other feelings may surface, including anger and depression. For example:

- She may feel overwhelmed.
- She may feel as though her body has failed her and her baby.
- If the baby suffers from serious health problems, she may feel anger, guilt, and depression.
- Her questions may center around finding reasons for the baby's problems.
- She and her husband may blame themselves or each other while searching for a reason why the birth occurred early.
- Their anger may be directed at the hospital staff or the doctor.

- The mother may have feelings of helplessness, loss of control, and isolation.
- She may have crying bouts and develop physical symptoms, such as insomnia, eating problems, or fatigue.

If she goes through a bargaining stage, the mother may look for a magical or quick solution to her problems by doing what she perceives as the "right" thing, such as attending religious services.

It is especially important for the mother to be able to express her feelings and to know that these feelings are normal. It is not unusual for the mother and father to be in different stages of grief at the same time, impairing their ability to communicate with and comfort each other (Walker 1990).

Give the mother positive reinforcement and suggest specific ways she can keep in touch with her baby.

Avoid trying to cheer up the mother or explain away her feelings with facts. Instead, give her positive reinforcement for the things she is doing for her baby, such as providing her milk, and encourage her to maintain as much contact with her baby as she can. When she is with her baby, encourage her to touch him as much as possible, as touching and holding are comforting to both mother and baby and can help reduce anxiety.

Suggest the mother ask the nurses if there is a support group at the hospital for parents whose babies are in the special-care nursery. She may benefit from spending time with others going through the same experiences. Other parents can also be a help in finding sources for premie diapers and clothing, as well as offering ongoing information about a premature baby's development after he is out of the hospital.

Prematurity

La Leche League meetings can also support the mother in her efforts and provide her with the information she needs to breastfeed her baby.

Also, if any of the mother's family members or close friends have breastfed their babies and feel positively about it, encourage the mother to draw on them for ongoing support.

The mother's feelings of grief and loss may influence her feelings about breastfeeding.

The mother's breastfeeding choices will be affected by the process of mourning and attachment. Usually a mother expresses her feelings in one of two ways: deciding to breastfeed for positive reasons or deciding not to breastfeed out of fear of becoming more attached to her baby. Deciding to breastfeed so that she can provide an important health benefit for her baby is a healthy reaction to her feelings of guilt and helplessness. The decision to breastfeed can increase her feelings of being in control and gives her a tangible way to "make it up to her baby" and lessen her feelings of guilt.

Some women choose not to breastfeed because this emotional commitment to their baby makes them feel more vulnerable. They may be afraid to become too attached to their baby in case he dies. If the baby's life is in jeopardy, the mother may decide not to breastfeed or postpone expressing her milk until her baby's condition stabilizes.

If a mother has mixed or negative feelings about breastfeeding, emphasize that the baby receives the greatest benefit from his mother's milk during his first few weeks and that the mother could approach it as a temporary commitment. Assure her that if she decides to quit after a week or two, her milk will already have given her baby valuable protection from infection. Explain that it is much easier to stop expressing milk after two weeks than it is to start expressing then. It is important that this be said in a caring way with respect for the fact that the decision rests with the mother.

The mother may become discouraged if she has difficulty learning to express her milk especially when she contemplates how long it may be before she can bring her baby home.

Some women have strong negative feelings the first time they use a breast pump. Others feel odd, awkward, or disappointed. When contemplating the possibility of having to express their milk for an extended time, many mothers feel discouraged.

Most mothers find these feelings fade quickly, but if the mother has any of these reactions, assure her that they are normal. If her baby has just been born, be sure she knows that during the first few days after birth—before her milk supply becomes more plentiful—she may only be able to express very small amounts of colostrum. Assure her that it usually takes time and practice before a mother is able to express and collect a significant amount of milk at a time. (For more information, see the chapter "Expression and Storage of Human Milk.")

To make milk expression more manageable over the long term, suggest the mother establish a regular routine and offer to talk with her about how she can fit it into her daily life. A mother who needs to express her milk long-term should be encouraged to rent an automatic electric piston pump, because it is most effective at building and maintaining a milk supply. A double-pumping attachment will allow a mother to cut her pumping time in half.

THE ADVANTAGES OF BREASTFEEDING A PREMATURE BABY

Breastfeeding provides advantages over formula for the premature baby.

Mother's milk provides a premature baby with many health, nutritional, and developmental advantages. For example:

- Human milk is easier to digest and better tolerated by the premature baby, because the proteins in human milk are more completely broken down and absorbed by the digestive system than the proteins in formula. Tube feeding tends to be established earlier and with fewer problems in premies fed human milk than in premies fed formula (Gross and Slagle 1993; Lucas 1987; Lucas 1984).
- Human milk contains the enzyme lipase which helps the baby digest milk fat more efficiently. This is significant because fat is an important source of energy for the premature baby's growth (Clandinin 1989).
- Antibodies and other factors in human milk protect the premature baby from potentially serious bacterial infections. Premies receiving formula are more likely than premies fed human milk to develop necrotizing enterocolitis (NEC), an often fatal bowel problem seen in premature babies (Buescher 1994; Parsa 1994; Lucas and Cole 1990). Because the premature baby's immune system is immature, he is at greater risk of developing a variety of infections and less able to cope with them should they occur.
- Human milk contributes to better vision in premies, which may be due to the types of fatty acids in human milk that are absent in formula (Uauy 1990; Carlson 1989).
- Human milk contributes to higher intelligence and improved motor development later in life. At age 7½ to 8 years, even when corrected for confounding factors such as parental education, socioeconomic status, gender, and the need for mechanical ventilation, children who had received human milk as premies scored an average of 8.3 points higher on IQ tests than children who had been fed formula (Lucas 1992). In another study of full-term babies, long-term intelligence and improved motor development directly correlated with duration of breastfeeding (Rogan and Gladen 1993).
- An array of hormones and enzymes in human milk, including various growth factors, may be important to the maturation of the baby's digestive and nervous systems (Gale 1989).
- Breastfeeding brings the mother and her baby closer. Even if the baby receives his milk by tube at first, expressing her milk for her baby can

make the mother feel "connected" to him. Once the baby begins nursing at the breast, many mothers report that the closeness they experience helps them make up for the time they were apart.

The milk of a mother who delivers prematurely (preterm milk) differs from the milk of a mother who delivers at term. The mother's own milk is better for her baby than donor milk.

In some areas, premature babies may be given banked milk from human donors. However, the benefits are greater when a mother takes the time and effort to give her baby her own milk.

- The mother's own preterm milk can be given fresh to her baby. Donor milk must be pasteurized, which kills the live cells that fight infection.
- Preterm milk contains even more infection-fighting antibodies than the milk of mothers who deliver at term (Mathur 1990).
- Preterm milk is more suited to the unique nutritional needs of the premature baby, because early in lactation it is higher in certain nutrients, such as protein, sodium, iron, and chloride (Lemons 1982).

BUILDING A RELATIONSHIP BETWEEN MOTHER AND BABY

It is more challenging for the mother of a premie to form an emotional bond with her baby.

Love between mother and baby does not necessarily occur naturally. Feelings develop and are reinforced through behaviors and cues, and it may take time for love to grow. When a baby is born prematurely, mother and baby are separated, and their bond is at risk. There are several other reasons that forming a close relationship with a premie is more difficult.

Prematurity

If the baby's life is at risk, the mother may be afraid to let herself feel close to her baby. Allowing herself to love her baby may make her feel vulnerable to even greater trauma if he should die. Once the mother feels sure that her baby will live, it may be easier for her to relax and let her feelings for her baby grow.

The mother may find her baby's appearance upsetting, especially if the baby is very different from what the mother expected. A premature baby looks different than a full-term baby. He is thin, with little fat under his translucent skin, and has a protruding abdomen and poor muscle tone. It can also be upsetting for the mother to see her baby surrounded by medical paraphernalia, with tubes and wires coming from his body.

The mother may not be able to touch or hold her baby, especially if the baby is very ill, which will affect her feelings for him.

A premature baby may be unable to respond. Building a relationship is a two-way process. In order to feel close, both people must be open and responsive. A premie, however, may be unable to respond to his mother, giving her little feedback from which to form a relationship. Premies spend much of their time sleeping, in part as a means of protecting themselves from overstimulation in a bright, noisy, and bustling nursery. If the baby is asleep during the mother's visit she misses the chance to establish eye contact.

Some hospitals are changing the environments of their intensive-care nurseries to reduce the amount of stimulation the babies receive by:

- combining medical procedures to minimize disruption to the babies;
- draping blankets over the incubators to reduce the glare of the lighting;
- providing tactile boundaries for the babies and holding and positioning them in special ways.

Touching is comforting to both mother and baby and can help speed a baby's progress.

Medical professionals are becoming increasingly supportive of the mother's need to form an attachment to her premature baby while he is in the hospital. Time apart from her baby can add to a mother's anxiety and feelings of helplessness. If a mother is discouraged by the hospital staff from spending time with and nursing her baby, she may question whether her presence and her milk are really important to him.

Physical closeness can help reduce emotional stress for both mother and baby. Some hospital staffs encourage mothers to help with their premature babies' care. If this is not possible, the mother may still be able to sit beside her baby's incubator and look into his eyes and touch and stroke him. This will let him know that someone loves him, which is very important to his continued progress.

Suggest the mother watch her baby's cues so that he doesn't become overstimulated.

Some premies are very sensitive to stimulation, so suggest the mother watch her baby's cues to discover what kinds of sounds and touches work best with her baby to be sure he does not get more stimulation than he can handle.

In their book, *Kangaroo Care: The Best You Can Do to Help Your Preterm Infant* (1993a), authors Susan Ludington-Hoe and Susan Golant list behaviors that may signal distress in premies:

* clenched fist with white knuckles,
* fingers splayed out wide,
* cheeks and chin sagging—a sign of fatigue,
* furrowed brow,
* ears tucked closely into head,
* an arm bent at the elbow with a raised hand (stop sign),
* legs up as if in a leg lift,
* arching away,
* averting their gaze,
* alert gaze with a worried look,
* turning head away,
* yawns or hiccups.

Als (1994) found that letting the baby rest when these cues occur and adjusting the environment improve infant outcome.

Encourage the mother to spend as much time as she can with her baby.

Encourage the mother to schedule regular visits with her baby, spending as much time as she can with him. If the hospital is a long distance from the mother's home, suggest she look into the possibility of making arrangements to stay in a hotel or with friends so that she can be closer to her baby.

Once she begins breastfeeding, both mother and baby will benefit from breastfeeding frequently without being rushed or interrupted. Nursing is calming and comforting to them both.

Other suggestions may help the mother build a relationship with her premature baby.

Other suggestions may help the mother feel closer to her baby:

* Name the baby and use the name when talking to him and about him.
* Touch and talk to the baby as much as possible.
* Change and feed the baby whenever possible.
* Ask questions and let the staff know what she thinks and how she feels.
* Make observations and offer suggestions to the staff.
* Make a tape recording of the mother's voice and leave it in the baby's incubator.
* Leave a photo of the family in the baby's incubator.
* Take pictures of the baby to keep a record of his progress.
* Keep a record of the baby's changes to make small improvements more obvious.

Kangaroo Care

"Kangaroo care" is becoming increasingly popular as a way to give stable premies warmth and comfort through skin-to-skin contact with their mothers. It also provides opportunities for early breastfeeding, enhances milk let-down (even to the breast pump afterwards), and increases duration and frequency of breastfeeding.

Skin-to-skin contact, nicknamed "kangaroo care" because of its similarity to the kangaroo's pouch, was introduced in 1979 in a hospital in Bogota, Colombia, where many premature babies were being born but incubators were not always available. Death from infection was commonplace, babies under 3 pounds (1350 grams) at birth usually did not survive, and abandonment of premature babies by their mothers had become a serious problem. In the years since then, kangaroo care has been observed and studied by researchers from around the world.

Clad only in a diaper, the baby is held skin-to-skin against his mother between her breasts or cradled against her breast under a loose-fitting blouse or shirt. The baby may look at the mother, respond to her voice, breastfeed at will (if he has begun breastfeeding), or just relax and sleep peacefully. In Colombia, babies cared for this way who are in good condition are discharged early (sometimes within a day of birth) from the infectious environment of the hospital and have their progress regularly monitored at special clinics. Heat loss, a major concern with premies, is avoided by keeping the unwrapped baby completely under the mother's clothing and skin-to-skin (Acolet 1989).

Kangaroo care has been used in Colombia with babies as small as 1,000 grams (about two pounds three ounces). In England, newborns weighing only 700 grams (about one-and-a-half pounds) have maintained stable skin temperature, respirations, and heart rates for up to three hours while being held this way (Whitelaw 1986). Some health care professionals say that the skin-to-skin aspect of kangaroo care can be started while a baby is still on a ventilator and before he is ready to breastfeed (Gale 1993), but others caution that this method has not yet been tested for safety and effectiveness (Ludington-Hoe 1994).

Prematurity

Mothers who give kangaroo care tend to breastfeed longer and more frequently. Kangaroo care has also been found to benefit premature babies and their families in other ways.

Research on kangaroo care indicates it offers many benefits to premies and their families. Babies in kangaroo care have been found to spend less time crying and more time in quiet alertness and deep sleep (Bosque 1995; Ludington-Hoe 1993b). Babies receiving kangaroo care are moved out of incubators and into open cribs sooner, go home sooner, and cry less at six months of age than babies receiving conventional care (Wahlberg 1992; Anderson 1989a; Whitelaw 1988). One large randomized clinical trial found premies given kangaroo care had fewer serious illnesses and fewer readmissions to the hospital (Sloan 1994).

Mothers who give kangaroo care have been found to breastfeed longer and more frequently (Bosque 1995; Wahlberg 1987; Whitelaw 1986). They also report feeling more confident about caring for their babies in the hospital nursery and about bringing their babies home than mothers whose babies receive conventional care (Affonso 1993; Affonso 1989). Fathers can also provide and be an integral part of kangaroo care (Ludington-Hoe 1992).

Kangaroo care can be started early or late, depending on circumstances.

According to Gene Cranston Anderson (1995), who has observed and researched this method of caring for premies, kangaroo care can be started at different times, depending on circumstances.

- Birth. If the baby has an Apgar score of 6 or more, kangaroo care can begin at birth by immediately placing the baby skin-to-skin on the mother and covering them both over the baby's back with a warmed large bath blanket folded in half.
- Very early. Beginning 30 to 40 minutes after birth, kangaroo care can begin as above (Ludington-Hoe 1993b).
- Early. As done in Bogota, Colombia, kangaroo care begins when the baby is stable, which may be within hours after birth. To stabilize the baby, he may be warmed in an incubator and, if needed, given oxygen and intravenous therapy.

- Intermediate. Kangaroo care can also begin about a week after birth for babies who may still need extra oxygen and experience apnea (periodic spells when breathing stops briefly) and bradycardia (slowed heartbeat). Research on apnea in premies has found that kangaroo care causes no increase and may even reduce the frequency and duration of apnea (Bosque 1995; Hadeed 1995).
- Late. Kangaroo care can also begin when the baby no longer requires any intensive care and no longer needs extra oxygen. This may be several days to several weeks after birth.

Other Resources

Parents or others who would like information on how other parents have been assisted with kangaroo care by intensive-care nursery staffs can write to:
Gene Cranston Anderson, PhD, RN, FAAN
Mellen Professor of Nursing
Case Western Reserve University
1009 Euclid Avenue
Cleveland OH USA 44120-4906

THE PREMIE WEIGHING MORE THAN 1500 GRAMS (3.3 LBS.)

The baby weighing more than 1500 grams is usually born at more than thirty weeks gestation. If a baby is heavier than 1500 grams but younger than thirty weeks gestation, refer to the information in the next section.

If he is healthy, the larger premature baby may be able to breastfeed within the first hour or two after birth.

Many premature babies who are born healthy at 1500 grams or more are able to breastfeed within the first hour or two after birth. It is not unusual for a baby in the lower end of this weight range to have a weak suck. Even so, it is still worthwhile to try breastfeeding whenever the baby shows feeding cues.

If the larger premature baby is ill or not yet ready to breastfeed, many of the considerations will be the same as for the tiny premie (see the next section).

The mother of an ill premature baby may be faced with many of the same challenges and considerations as the mother of a tiny premie—an extended hospitalization, a variety of feeding methods and options, the challenge of long-term milk expression, and the decision of when to begin breastfeeding. See the next section for more information.

Larger premature babies tend to grow well on their mother's milk without the need for vitamin or mineral supplements.

As with the tiny premie, his mother's fresh milk is best for the larger premie. Larger premature babies tend to grow well on their mother's milk alone, without the need for vitamin or mineral supplements. Size, age, health, and routine nutritional monitoring will be used to determine if the baby would benefit from extra nutrients added to his mother's milk.

THE PREMIE WEIGHING LESS THAN 1500 GRAMS (3.3 LBS.)

How early a baby is born can affect how the baby is fed and also the number of prematurity-related problems he may experience. In general, the younger the baby's gestational age at birth, the more health problems he may develop and the longer delay there will be in establishing breastfeeding. The baby weighing less than 1500 grams is usually thirty weeks gestation or younger.

Feeding Methods and Options

At first, the baby may be fed intravenously or by tube.

Depending on the baby's physical condition, at first he may get his nourishment through intravenous feedings or by tube.

If the baby is very small or ill, he may be fed through a nasojejunal tube, which sends a continuous stream of milk through a tiny tube inserted through a baby's nose directly into his small intestine. This constant feeding ensures the baby never receives more milk than he can handle at one time.

A larger premie may be fed through a nasogastric tube, which sends the milk through a tiny tube inserted through the baby's nose directly into his stomach. This method is used when the baby can tolerate larger amounts of milk at each feeding. Using this method, the baby is fed a specific amount of his mother's milk every few hours and rests between feedings. The mother's milk supply and the baby's feeding ability can be enhanced by placing the baby skin-to-skin at the mother's breast during feedings (Wahlberg 1992).

When the baby begins tube feeding, colostrum and mature milk have been found to be better tolerated than formula.

Human milk contains special components, called growth modulators, that help the premie's digestive system adjust to oral feedings (Davies 1989). Research indicates that premies fed human milk vomit less and establish tube feeding earlier than premies fed formula (Gross and Slagle 1993; Lucas 1987; Lucas 1984). By beginning with fresh or frozen colostrum and following these feedings with fresh milk, premies also benefit from receiving protection from infection and illness, because of factors contained in human milk that are missing from formulas.

The mother's own fresh milk is generally better for her baby than frozen or donor milk.

The mother's own milk is more suited to her baby's special needs than donor milk, because of the extra antibodies and nutrients it contains and because it changes over time in keeping with her baby's needs, which change as he grows. The mother's fresh milk is also best because it contains live cells and other protective factors that ward off infection.

Freezing destroys some, though not all, of these live cells, but frozen milk still offers many of the other advantages of fresh milk. In order to provide the greatest nutritional benefit, the mother's frozen milk should be given to the baby in the sequence in which it was expressed and frozen. If fresh milk is also available, it can be mixed or alternated with the frozen milk so that the baby receives the live cells in the fresh milk at regular intervals.

Prematurity

If the mother's own fresh or frozen milk is not available, donor human milk is next best. Donor milk is usually mature milk that has been expressed by other breastfeeding mothers. In most parts of the world, donor milk is pasteurized, which kills all the live cells, so it is lacking in fresh milk's anti-infective properties and preterm milk's extra nutrients, but it is superior to formula for the premature baby. Like the mother's fresh and frozen milk, donor milk is easier to digest than formula and thus may help the baby avoid the bowel problems to which premies are prone. The nutrients in human milk are also more completely utilized than those in formula.

When human milk is in short supply or unavailable, special premie formulas can be used.

If the mother is unable to provide enough of her own milk for her baby's needs and donor milk is unavailable, special premie formulas can be used. These are higher in the nutrients that premies require than regular formulas. If formula is given along with the mother's milk, there are two strategies that are recommended. One strategy is to alternate feedings composed entirely of human milk with feedings composed entirely of special formula, which early data indicate may enhance mineral absorption (Schanler 1995). The other strategy is to mix human milk and special formula at feedings so that at every feeding the baby receives the enzymes in human milk that aid in digestion, as well as its immunologic benefits (Lawrence, p. 418). There is currently no data supporting this second strategy.

The Nutrition Committee of the Canadian Paediatric Society (1995) considers premie formulas as a second choice to human milk because: "Formulas do not contain any of the biologically active immune substances, nor some of the enzymes, hormones, or growth factors found in human milk. The long-term significance of the lack of these components has not been determined, however, recent studies suggest that mental and motor development are affected by the type of early feeding provided."

A baby may grow well on human milk alone, or the milk may need to be fortified to meet all the baby's nutritional needs.

Mothers who deliver preterm babies produce milk that is higher in antibodies (Mathur 1990), nitrogen, protein nitrogen, sodium, chloride, iron, and fatty acids than the milk of mothers who deliver full-term babies (Lemons 1982). Beginning about two weeks after birth, the preterm milk gradually begins to change into more mature milk. By the end of a premie's first month, his mother's milk is similar to the milk of a mother whose baby was born at term, although some differences in fatty-acid composition have been documented for as long as six months (Luukkainen 1994).

Although some premature babies grow and develop well on human milk alone (Ramasethu 1993; Jarvenpaa 1983), the milk may have to be fortified with some nutrients in order for extremely early and small premies to grow and develop properly. Experts currently recommend that as soon as tube feeding has been established the mother's milk should be fortified with calcium and phosphorus until the baby reaches a particular weight or goes home (Robertson and Bhatia 1993; Williams 1993). Some experts also recommend fortification with protein, sodium, and some vitamins (Canadian Paediatric Society 1995; Schanler 1995).

The ideal option for fortifying human milk is based on a process called "lacto-engineering," in which specific nutrients are taken from banked human milk to add to the mother's own milk (Lawrence, p. 419). Another option that is more widely available is the use of powdered or liquid human milk fortifiers that are derived from cow's milk and added to the mother's expressed milk. Powdered fortifiers can be used when there is enough human milk to provide the necessary volume of liquid. Liquid fortifiers can be used to increase the volume of a human milk feeding if it is in short supply.

Guidelines on appropriate weight gain for premature babies are being reexamined.

Although it was once recommended that a premature baby be fed in a way that enables him to gain and grow at about the same rate as he would have in utero, these guidelines are in the process of being reexamined. This is occurring in part because the original standards were derived from growth charts developed more than 40 years ago and are not as applicable to the very early premies that are being saved today as they were to larger premies (Wright 1993).

Maintaining an intrauterine rate of growth can be a challenge to these very early premies because they have an immature digestive system that is less able to absorb and digest food than that of a full-term, healthy baby. Also, any extra nutrients must be in a form that is digestible and absorbable so that extra stress is not put on the premature baby's kidneys and other organs.

In some studies, babies fed their own mother's milk (either alone or mixed with donor milk), have been found to grow at intrauterine rates (Ramasethu 1993; Jarvenpaa 1983). Other babies on mother's milk do not. In this case, some doctors recommend human milk be supplemented with fortifiers or premie formula to produce greater weight gains. However, some babies do not gain at intrauterine rates no matter what or how much they are fed (Walker 1990).

If a premature baby is not gaining well on human milk alone, see the next point for options to consider.

If the baby's weight gain is a concern, ask the mother how long she is pumping at each session and assess her milk production.

If the baby's weight gain is a concern, suggest the mother first ask her baby's doctor if the baby would tolerate more milk at each feeding or if the same amount could be given more times per day. Sometimes the prescribed feeding amounts are not increased quickly enough to adjust for a baby's rapid growth.

Also, ask the mother how long she is pumping at each session. Explain that the fat content of her milk increases the longer she pumps or nurses and to get the fattier hindmilk she needs to express at least 10 to 15 minutes per breast, longer if the milk flow continues at a steady rate. If she has been limiting her expressing time, the mother may have inadvertently decreased the amount of fat her baby receives in her milk.

Changing or modifying the milk delivery system used to feed the baby can also increase the amount of fat the baby receives from mother's milk. The type of system that feeds a baby continuously has been found to produce the greater milk fat losses than other methods (Greer 1984). When a continuous feeding system is used, milk fat tends to stick to tubing, so the longer the tubing between the milk and the baby, the more milk fat is lost. If it is not possible to change to another type of system, shortening the tubing has been found to cut down on fat loss. The type of system that feeds a baby intermittently causes less fat loss, but even in this case, milk fat content can be improved. When a syringe and pump are used to tube feed, orienting the syringe in an upright position has been found to decrease fat losses from 48% to 8% (Schanler 1995).

Another approach that has been found to improve weight gain in low birth weight babies is to give more high-fat hindmilk at feedings (Valentine 1994). If the mother is producing more milk than her baby needs, suggest she ask her baby's doctor about the use of hindmilk. Separating the milk into foremilk and hindmilk and giving the baby more of the hindmilk will provide more calories, because the hindmilk is higher in fat.

When premies fed human milk and premies fed formula are compared, long-term differences have been found in bone mineral status, length, and intelligence.

Research has uncovered some long-term differences in length and bone mineral content in premies fed human milk in comparison to premies fed premie formula (Schanler 1992; Raupp 1990). Long-term studies on bone mineral content seem to indicate that although premies fed human milk may initially have lower bone mineral content than premies fed formula, in time these differences equalize

Prematurity

and reverse, with children fed human milk as premies surpassing those fed formula. In one study, even when the human milk the premies received was fortified, those who breastfed a minimum of two months after discharge were found to have lower bone mineral content than the premies fed formula. By two years of age, the bone mineral content of these two groups had equalized (Schanler 1992). Continued fortification of human milk after hospital discharge has been suggested in order to increase the mineral status of these babies (Schanler 1992; Raupp 1990). However, a later study of premies at age five found greater bone mineral content among those fed human milk than those fed formula. Researchers noted that the more human milk these children received, the greater their bone mineral content at age five. In fact, children fed human milk as premies had significantly greater bone mineral content at five years than is normal for babies born at term (Bishop 1996). Low bone mineral content is of concern because it can lead to fractures and bone deformities. As of this writing, there is no evidence that premies fed human milk (whether fortified or unfortified) have a higher incidence of these problems.

Differences in length and intelligence have also been found between premies fed human milk and those fed formula. Premies fed human milk were found to average 1 cm (⅓–½ in) less in length at 18 months when compared with premies fed premie formula (Lucas 1989). Research has also linked human milk feeding in premies to higher intelligence at age 7½ to 8 years (Lucas 1992). Regarding these findings, one British commentator wrote: "If the mother's own milk is used they will probably be slightly shorter but more intelligent at the age of 7 than those fed formula milk" (Williams 1993).

A mother who thinks her milk may not be meeting her baby's needs may feel depressed.

If the mother thinks that her milk is not meeting her baby's needs either in quantity or quality, she may feel discouraged, depressed, and threatened. Although she wants to breastfeed, she may have doubts, especially if her baby's health care professionals convey the attitude that she is being "self-centered," putting her desire to breastfeed above her baby's welfare.

A mother in this situation needs reassurance and support. She also needs help in communicating her feelings and goals to the hospital personnel. (See "Working with Hospital Personnel" later in this chapter.) Be sure the mother knows that her milk is better for her baby than any type of formula and that the need for supplementation is temporary. It may also help her to know that stardard infant formula must also be supplemented with extra nutrients in order to meet a premie's special physical needs.

Before Baby Can Breastfeed—The Challenge of Expressing Milk

For information about choosing a method of expression, see the chapter "Expression and Storage of Human Milk."

Most mothers do not get much milk when they express during the first few days after birth.

Before the mother's milk volume increases on the third or fourth day after birth, the mother may be able to express very little milk, even with an automatic electric piston breast pump. Assure her that no amount is too small to save for the baby and that the early milk is especially valuable. Tell her that it usually takes a few days before she can expect to collect ounces (30 ml or more) of milk rather than drops. Using a 1 cc or 5 cc syringe to measure the milk expressed during the first few days may help the mother feel better about the amount she is expressing.

The mother may become discouraged if she is not able to express large quantities of milk immediately.

Expressing milk is a learned skill that takes practice. And it is a psychological as well as a physical process. The mother's emotions influence how effectively she can express her milk. Some women have strong negative feelings when first faced with a breast pump. Others feel odd, awkward, or disappointed. They may also feel discouraged when contemplating the possibility of having to express their milk for an extended time. Although these feelings need not prevent a mother from expressing milk, it helps to be relaxed in order for her milk to let down.

If the mother mentions any of these feelings, assure her that they are normal. If her baby is less than three days old, be sure she knows that during the first few days after birth—before her milk supply becomes more plentiful—she may only be able to express very small amounts of colostrum. Assure her no amount is too small to save for the baby and that it usually takes time and practice to be able to express and collect a significant amount of milk when she expresses. (See the chapter "Expression and Storage of Human Milk.")

Simplified guidelines for the collection, storage, and handling of human milk for the hospitalized baby have been adopted by many hospitals. Suggest the mother ask the nurses for the guidelines that are used at that hospital.

Many of the procedures recommended in the past for collecting and storing human milk for hospitalized babies have been found to be ineffective at reducing bacterial contamination. Others have been found to significantly reduce the immunological protection the baby receives from mother's milk. Examples of these unnecessary procedures include breast cleansing and nipple lubrication before pumping, sterilizing pump parts after each use, discarding the first milk expressed, screening each mother's milk for bacteria, and pasteurizing the milk. Some of these procedures, while unnecessary for the mother expressing milk for her own baby, may be necessary when women provide donor milk.

To simplify and standardize hospital guidelines, the Human Milk Banking Association of North America has published "Recommendations for Collection, Storage, and Handling of a Mother's Milk for Her Own Infant in the Hospital Setting" (1993). These guidelines have been adopted by many hospitals. These guidelines recommend that:

- Mothers wash their hands thoroughly before expressing their milk.
- An electric piston breast pump be used.
- Each mother use her own collection kit (the bottles and tubing that attach to the pump).

- All parts of the collection kit that touch the milk be cleaned after each use with hot soapy water, thoroughly rinsed, then placed on a clean paper towel, covered with another clean paper towel, and allowed to air dry.
- The expressed milk be labeled with the date, the baby's name, the baby's hospital identification number, any illnesses in the family, and any medication(s) the mother is taking.
- The milk from each pumping be kept in its own container and not mixed with milk from other pumpings.
- Milk be stored in feeding-sized portions.
- Storage containers be made of glass, polycarbonate (clear, hard plastic), or polypropylene (cloudy, hard plastic) with solid caps that provide an airtight seal.

For more information on these guidelines and the research that supports them, contact the Human Milk Banking Association of North America, P.O. Box 370464, West Hartford, CT 06137-0464 USA. These differ from the guidelines recommended for use at home by mothers of healthy full-term babies. See the chapter "Expression and Storage of Human Milk."

Although these guidelines have been adopted by many hospitals, suggest the mother talk to the nursery nurses or the hospital lactation consultant for specific instructions.

Some hospitals occasionally culture expressed milk to check on bacteria levels to be sure the milk is being collected in a safe and clean manner. Some bacteria in the milk is normal. Milk is usually judged acceptable if it does not contain certain disease-causing organisms and contains low levels of other types of bacteria (Meier and Anderson 1987). Currently, there are no accepted, research-based standards for "safe" milk, so the results of this testing are often inconclusive.

Prematurity

If the doctor is concerned about bacteria levels in the mother's expressed milk, the mother may be able to reduce them.

If the baby's health care providers are concerned about bacteria in the milk, there are several things the mother can do to reduce the levels:

- Wash the pumping and milk-storage equipment according to instructions.
- Wash her hands thoroughly before touching the pump and milk-storage equipment.
- Avoid touching the inside of the clean containers.

Discarding the first teaspoon (5 ml) or even the first few drops of milk expressed has been recommended by some to reduce bacteria counts (Meier and Mangurten 1993), but according to the Human Milk Banking Association of North America (1993) "more recent studies and clinical practice in many settings have shown it to be unnecessary." Cleansing the nipple area with sterile water and/or special soaps before milk expression is also controversial. While some continue to recommend it (Meier and Mangurten 1993), the Human Milk Banking Association of North America (1993) considers routine daily hygiene to be sufficient and labels breast cleansing as "unnecessarily harsh."

The key to maintaining a milk supply over time while expressing is to establish a daily routine and stick to it, mimicking the frequency and length of a baby's usual breastfeeding routine.

Establishing and maintaining a healthy milk supply while expressing depends upon regular and frequent expression of milk. If the mother is using an automatic electric piston breast pump, in general, the more often the mother expresses, the more milk she will produce (deCarvalho 1985). Short, frequent expressions (every two or three hours for 10 to 15 minutes per breast) tend to stimulate more milk production than longer sessions spaced at wider intervals.

Pumping both breasts simultaneously ("double-pumping") cuts milk expression time in half and has been found to increase prolactin levels and better stimulate milk production (Auerbach 1990). A mother can double-pump with any automatic electric piston pump if she acquires a double-pumping collection kit (the bottles and tubing that attach to the pump). Some hospitals provide mothers with this kit. If not, she can purchase it where she rents the pump.

Ask the mother how she feels about waking at night to express. Some mothers don't mind waking to express during the night or in the early morning, especially if their breasts feel uncomfortably full. Others prefer uninterrupted sleep and find that this improves both their milk supply and their ability to cope with the daily pressures of having a hospitalized baby.

Mothers should begin expressing as soon as possible after their baby's birth, ideally within the first six hours (Walker 1992). Early and frequent pumping has been correlated with greater milk production (Hopkinson 1988; deCarvalho 1985). One study found pumping at least five times for a total of more than 100 minutes per day was necessary to maintain milk production (Hopkinson 1988). To increase milk production, pumping more times per day may be necessary.

Although it was once suggested that a mother of a premie express only as much milk as her baby is taking at that time, this advice has been questioned by some experts. Some women have found that when they express very little milk at first it is difficult to increase their milk supply later. This may be because their breast tissue partially involutes (or reverts to its prepregnancy state), making it more difficult to increase milk production. For this reason, establishing a full milk supply as early as possible is being suggested as a better strategy than waiting until later (Woolridge 1995). For more information, see, "When Breastfeeding Is Delayed After Birth" in the chapter "Expression and Storage of Human Milk."

Holding and touching her baby may help the mother express more milk.

Encourage the mother to hold her baby before expressing. Most premies can be held, even if they are not yet strong enough to breastfeed. If a mother holds her baby skin-to-skin with the baby's mouth near the breast, it may enhance her let-down the next time she expresses (Anderson 1996).

If the mother experiences a decrease in milk supply over time while expressing, encourage her to express more often to increase her supply.

Whether she nurses or expresses, a mother's milk supply is based on supply and demand—the more often she nurses or expresses the more milk there will be. To establish and maintain a healthy milk supply over the long term, suggest the mother pump more frequently over a period of several days when her baby is between two and three weeks and again at six weeks to mimic the "frequency days" or "growth spurts" of a healthy full-term baby. If her supply begins to decrease at any time, suggest she express more often to increase her supply. With more frequent pumping, a mother's milk supply usually begins to increase within a few days, although it may take a week or more in some mothers.

It is normal for a mother's milk supply to temporarily decrease while her baby is going through a crisis.

A mother's milk supply often fluctuates with her baby's condition. When the mother is very worried about the baby's health or survival, her let-down may be delayed or inhibited and it may not be easy for her to express much milk. Times of crisis commonly result in a temporary decrease in milk supply. This is normal, a natural part of the complex emotions involved in having a baby in the intensive-care nursery.

If the mother's milk supply decreases during a crisis, unsupportive comments from those around her may convince the mother to give up entirely unless she has another source of support. Assure her that her decrease in supply is only temporary and that it will increase again as the baby's condition improves. Also tell her that however much milk she is able to express is enough to stimulate her breasts to continue making milk. It may also be comforting for her to talk to another mother of a premature baby who has gone through a similar experience.

Ask the mother a general question—such as "How are things going with you today?"—rather than focusing on the volume of milk she is able to express with a question such as, "Were you able to express more milk today than yesterday?"

If appropriate, suggest the mother try to arrange more skin-to-skin contact with her baby before milk expression, as this may enhance her milk let-down, making her milk expression more effective.

Having extra collection kits on hand can reduce the amount of time needed to clean equipment.

While the mother is still hospitalized, hospital personnel will clean the pump. When the mother returns home, this can be a way in which the baby's father or other support person helps out. Having more than one collection kit to use with an electric pump cuts down on the time needed to clean equipment.

Pumping sometimes leads to sore nipples.

If the mother's nipples become sore from pumping there are a number of ways she might be able to minimize or alleviate the soreness. Do not suggest all of them at once. Mention three or four from this list for her to try. Ask her to let you know if they do not seem to be helping. Then you can suggest the others, if need be.

- Express a small amount of milk onto the nipple and allow it to air-dry, which can aid healing.
- Apply Lansinoh for Breastfeeding Mothers® to the nipple; other creams or ointments should be avoided, as they would need to be removed before pumping, which could further irritate the nipple.
- Use breast massage to stimulate the let-down, or milk-ejection, reflex before pumping; the soreness often lessens as the milk starts to flow.
- Moisten the flange of the breast pump before beginning.
- Be sure the nipple is centered so that it doesn't rub against the side of the pump flange.
- Try a pump flange with a larger nipple tunnel (for example, the nipple tunnel of Ameda/Egnell's HygieniKits is slightly larger than the nipple tunnel of Medela's kits).
- Pump on the least sore side first.
- Use less suction providing the milk flow is maintained.
- Try pumping more frequently but for shorter periods of time.
- Try a different type of pump; all electric piston pumps start at suction levels of about 100 mmHg except Ameda/Egnell's Elite, which starts at zero and gives the sensitive mother the option of lower suction levels.

Prematurity

Determining a Baby's Readiness to Breastfeed

If the baby is ready to be fed by mouth, breastfeeding is less stressful than bottle-feeding.

Many mothers of premature babies are told that they may not feed their babies directly at the breast until bottle-feedings are going well and their babies reach a certain weight. These recommendations are based on commonly held assumptions, which are not based on scientific research:

- Breastfeeding is too stressful for babies weighing less than 1500 grams (3.3 pounds).
- Babies cannot coordinate sucking and swallowing well enough to breastfeed until they reach thirty-four to thirty-five weeks gestation.
- Babies must be able to bottle-feed before they can breastfeed, because breastfeeding is more "difficult."

Many health care facilities base their policies and procedure on these beliefs. But in recent years, these assumptions have been challenged by research.

In one study (Meier 1988; Meier and Anderson 1987) premature babies whose average weight was 1300 grams (about 2.9 pounds) when oral feedings began were observed during bottle-feedings and breastfeedings, with each baby serving as his or her own control. Signs of physical stress were measured by checking body temperature, apnea and bradycardia, and transcutaneous oxygen pressure (a measure of baby's reaction to stress). The results indicated that breastfeeding is less stressful than bottle-feeding, and the smaller the babies, the greater the difference.

Other findings were that babies can organize sucking and swallowing more easily during breastfeedings than bottle-feedings. In fact, it appears that the ability to breastfeed develops well before the ability to bottle-feed. The premies observed were twenty to fifty days old before they began breastfeeding and were about thirty-two weeks gestation. These babies were able to suck and swallow regularly and predictably while breastfeeding. But when these same babies were given a bottle within 24 hours, their sucking and swallowing pattern was disorganized.

These two studies indicate that breastfeeding is not more difficult than bottle-feeding. In fact, bottle-feeding was actually more difficult for these small premies.

When a baby is ready to be fed by mouth (rather than by tube), many doctors recommend beginning with bottle-feedings. Rather than waiting until that time to see what the doctor says, encourage the mother to ask her baby's doctor in advance about starting with breastfeeding instead of bottle-feeding. Suggest she share with her baby's doctor some of the references listed at the end of this chapter, particularly Meier and Anderson 1987 and Meier 1988. Also see "Helping the Mother Work with Her Doctor" in the chapter "Giving Effective Breastfeeding Help."

By going directly from tube feeding to the breast—without giving bottles—premature babies can avoid nipple confusion. In some parts of the world, premature babies are fed by cup rather than bottle.

If a baby can nurse at the breast, there are good reasons for avoiding bottles at first. When a baby is fed by both breast and bottle—or bottle alone—while he is first learning to take his nourishment by mouth, he may develop nipple confusion. Babies with nipple confusion may have difficulty latching on to the breast and nursing well, which is an additional stress for both mother and baby. A baby who is switched from bottle to breast has to learn new sucking patterns. If a baby can go directly to the breast when he is ready to be fed by nipple, this difficulty can be avoided.

While the baby is making the transition to the breast, other feedings can continue to be given by gavage tube in order to avoid artificial nipples. Cup feeding is used routinely instead of bottles in Kenya (Armstrong 1987) and Tanzania when a baby is born prematurely and is not yet ready for breastfeeding or if the mother and baby are separated. One article (Newman 1990) states, in fact, that nipple confusion appears to be a rare problem in most East African hospitals because bottles are never used. A study of 85 premature babies in Exeter, England, found that babies could successfully feed by cup as young as 30 weeks gestation, earlier than they could either breastfeed or bottle-feed (Lang 1994). In this study, more of the babies who received supplements by cup were fully breastfeeding at hospital discharge than those who received supplements by bottle (81% as compared to 63%). The researchers noted that cup feeding requires little energy, gives the baby more control over milk intake than bottle-feeding, and involves tongue movements that are also important for successful breastfeeding. During cup feedings, the premies were found to maintain satisfactory heart rate, breathing, and oxygen levels. For more information on cup feeding, see the supplement "The Use of Breast Pumps and Other Products."

There is no advantage to delaying breastfeeding until the baby reaches an arbitrarily determined weight or gestational age.

Each baby needs to be evaluated individually for his readiness to breastfeed, which may occur well before he is ready for bottle-feeding.

Each baby must be evaluated individually for readiness to breastfeed. Weight, gestational age, or the ability to take bottle-feedings should not determine if a baby is ready for breastfeeding.

Factors that will need to be taken into account when evaluating a baby's readiness for breastfeeding include:

- the baby's overall condition;
- how well the baby tolerates milk fed by gavage;

- the baby's ability to coordinate sucking, swallowing, and breathing;
- whether the baby can maintain his body temperature outside his incubator.

In a survey of 430 US neonatal intensive care units, 64% lacked a specific policy for starting oral feedings (Siddell and Froman 1994). For those units with a specific policy, the two most common criteria used to determine when to start oral feedings were gestational age (50% used this criterion) and weight (25% used this criterion). Despite the research demonstrating premature babies' ability to breastfeed earlier than previously expected and that breastfeeding is less stressful than bottle-feeding, more than 93% of the staff nurses surveyed reported that standard practice was to start bottle-feeding before breastfeeding, even if the mother had indicated her desire to breastfeed.

In some hospitals, premature babies are breastfed without the use of bottles.

In the US, some innovative hospitals have developed protocols that allow premature babies to go directly from tube feeding to the breast without the use of bottles (Stine 1990). In some developing countries, such as parts of Africa, where bottles cannot easily be sterilized, premies are routinely cup fed until ready to go to the breast (Newman 1990; Armstrong 1987). Cup feeding has also been successfully used with premies in England as an alternative to bottle-feeding when supplementation is necessary (Lang 1994).

Once a baby starts oral feedings, there are benefits to feeding on cue rather than using a fixed feeding schedule.

Saunders (1991) compared two groups of stable premies (weighing at least 1550 grams), one fed formula on cue and the other fed formula on a schedule. She found that the babies **Prematurity** fed on cue ate well, had no problems with overfeeding, and had about the same weight gain as the babies fed on a schedule, despite the fact that they took in less milk, and took longer rest periods. The demand babies were discharged earlier than the schedule babies and the researchers noted that demand feeding allowed parents to learn their babies' hunger cues before they went home, making the first weeks at home easier. Other research also provides strong support for feeding on cue (Collinge 1982).

If feeding on cue is being considered for the hospitalized premie, it is important that the mother be producing enough milk to sustain her baby. Test-weighing before and after feedings with Olympic's SMART scale, Medela's Baby-Weigh scale (which is available for rent for home use), or any well-calibrated electronic scale should be considered for the first week or so to confirm that the baby is nursing effectively enough to get the milk he needs from the breast. Once the baby is breastfeeding successfully, if the mother is not rooming in with her baby, encourage her to work out a schedule with the nurses so that she can breastfeed freely during the hours she is visiting her infant. When the mother is not at the hospital, the nurses can then resume their usual feeding schedule.

Knowing how much milk a baby receives while breastfeeding can be important, and test-weighing using a special electronic scale can allow a baby's intake while breastfeeding to be measured accurately.

Knowing how much nourishment a premature baby is receiving can be important during his early weeks. Some health-care professionals are reluctant to let a mother nurse her premature baby because they believe that it is impossible to know how much milk a premie consumes while breastfeeding.

Weighing a baby before and after nursings (test-weighing) is the usual method of measuring how much human milk a baby receives at the breast, but test-weighing is not very reliable if mechanical scales are used. A sensitive electronic scale, however, can solve this problem. Two scales, Olympic's SMART scale and Medela's BabyWeigh scale have been found accurate enough to measure milk intake during breastfeeding (Meier 1994; Meier 1990). In addition to using one of these scales in the hospital to evaluate the effectiveness of a baby's early nursings, in many areas Medela's BabyWeigh scale is also available for rent, so mothers can use it at home after discharge to alleviate concerns about milk intake, the most significant worry for many mothers of premies (Hill 1994; Meier 1993).

Information gained from test-weighing may help a mother learn to evaluate her baby's effectiveness at nursing and boost her confidence in breastfeeding.

THE FIRST NURSINGS

Setting the Scene

Early feedings take time and patience. Privacy, support, and realistic expectations can help them to go more smoothly.

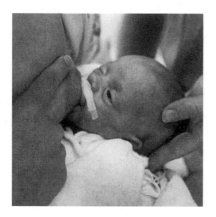

Early feedings are a learning process for both mother and baby and will require time and patience. The mother may feel awkward, even frustrated at times.

To keep the mother's expectations realistic, explain that it will probably take several breastfeeding sessions before the baby latches on and nurses well. Encourage the mother to expect these first nursings to be "getting acquainted" sessions and to be patient, enjoy the cuddling and closeness, and keep trying. A reasonable goal for the first nursing is for the baby to respond to the mother's nipple by licking or mouthing it. Also assure her that it is all right if the baby does not receive much milk at the breast in these early nursing sessions because he will be fed afterwards by other means.

Privacy and quiet help. Suggest the mother find out if the hospital has a separate room where she can breastfeed. Other items that may make early nursings more comfortable include:

- a screen or curtains to give the mother some privacy if a separate room is not available;
- a comfortable chair with armrests;
- several pillows (one or two to support her elbow and hand on the side she'll be nursing, one or two in her lap to bring the baby up to the level of her nipple, and perhaps one or two behind her back and shoulders for comfort and support);
- suggest the mother wear clothes that allow the baby easy access to the breast.

If the baby is small, a nurse may be present to monitor the baby.

Putting the Baby to Breast

The first few feedings may go more smoothly if a nurse or support person applies steady, gentle pressure to the baby's head and helps the mother by opening the baby's mouth as he goes onto the breast.

The cross-cradle, or transitional hold, is an effective position for most small premies, as many need extra head support.

It may make it easier for the mother if a nurse or other support person is there to give her a hand in putting the baby to breast. During the first few feedings, it can be helpful to have another pair of hands to get the baby latched on and keep the baby on the breast. The support person can assist the mother by pulling gently down on the baby's chin as the mother latches him onto the breast and by applying steady, gentle pressure on the back of his head. This gentle, steady pressure keeps the baby on the breast with less expenditure of energy and keeps as much of the breast in his mouth as possible throughout the feeding, minimizing soreness for the mother and maximizing the amount of milk the baby receives.

If the mother does not have the help of a nurse or support person, she will need to find a comfortable way to breastfeed her baby without assistance. The nurse may want to stay as an observer to monitor the baby's condition while he nurses, especially if he is a small premie.

Most pictures of breastfeeding mothers and babies show the baby in the cradle hold, with the baby's head resting on the mother's forearm near the bend of her elbow. This position may be fine for a larger premie or full-term baby but does not generally work well for most small premies, as they tend to roll up into a little ball when held like this. To breastfeed comfortably, most small premies need a hand behind their head for support.

To position the baby for breastfeeding, suggest the mother use what is called the cross-cradle, or transitional hold. She should:

- Position herself comfortably, leaning back in her seat so that she does not bend over the baby with a tight neck and shoulders.

- Put the baby on the pillow in her lap in front of her in a semi-upright position.
- Hold the baby with the arm opposite the breast at which he will feed. The mother's arm extends the length of the baby's back and neck, and the mother's hand holds the baby's head to stabilize its position.
- Use the C-hold to support her breast with the other hand. The C-hold offers the best support of the breast with the least chance of the mother's fingers getting in the way of the baby's mouth. To use the C-hold, the mother's thumb goes on top, her fingers underneath, placed an inch (2.5 cm) or more behind the edge of the areola.
- Pull the baby toward her, rather than moving her body toward the baby.
- Position the baby's mouth at the level of her nipple, with his body facing hers, tummy to tummy, making sure the baby does not have to stretch or turn his head to reach the nipple.
- Apply gentle pressure on the baby's head throughout the feeding in order to support his head and prevent him from pulling away. This gentle pressure also helps the baby keep more of the areola in his mouth, which minimizes soreness and maximizes the amount of milk he will be able to get.

For example, if the mother is breastfeeding on her left breast, she will hold her baby's head with her right hand behind the baby's head to guide and support him and use her left hand to support her breast. On the right side, she would use her left hand to support the baby's head and the right hand to support the breast.

Prematurity

The football or clutch hold also works well for premies, as it gives a good view of the baby's face and gives the mother control over the baby's head.

The football or clutch hold is another position that works well for premies. This position gives the mother a clear view of her baby's face and allows her to apply pressure to the baby's head.

If the mother starts on her left breast, she would get into this position by:

- using her left hand to support the baby's head;
- tucking the baby's body under her left arm at her left side;
- using a pillow or two under the baby and under her forearm to bring the baby up to the level of her nipple;
- using her right hand to support the left breast with the C-hold described above.

If she is nursing on her right breast, her right hand holds the baby at her right side and her left hand supports the breast.

Many small premies need practice and encouragement to open wide—like a yawn—and latch on well to the breast.

When the mother is ready to put her baby to breast, suggest she:

- begin by massaging her breast and pulling gently on the nipple to make it erect and easier to grasp,
- express a few drops of milk to get the baby interested, and
- brush her nipple gently across the baby's lips.

When a baby's lips are tickled, he will usually respond by opening his mouth wide. It is important that before the baby latches on his mouth is open wide—like a yawn—with his tongue down and flat. When the baby does open his mouth wide like yawn, encourage the mother to quickly pull her baby onto her breast, getting as much breast as possible into his mouth.

A baby should take the breast deeply into his mouth. If the baby takes only the nipple, the mother should break the suction, remove him from the breast, calm him down if necessary, and try again. If the baby sucks only on the nipple, he will not get much milk and the mother's nipples will get sore. The mother may need to keep trying. With practice it will get easier.

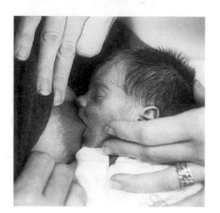

If the baby does not open his mouth wide enough, the mother can use the index finger of the hand supporting her breast to push down gently on his chin. (A nurse or support person can help with this at first if the mother feels as though she needs an extra pair of hands.) Suggest the mother say "open" as she does this, and the baby will learn to associate the sound with the action. Then the mother can guide the breast into the baby's mouth, quickly pulling him in close to her.

When he latches on to the breast, the baby's tongue should be under the breast. His lips should be flanged out, and the baby should be close enough so that his nose and chin are touching the breast. Suggest the mother refrain from pressing her finger down on her breast to make an airway for her premie. Babies have flared nostrils, so they don't need this extra help, and pressing down on the breast can cause the breast to be pulled from the back to the front of the baby's mouth, making the baby's efforts to breastfeed less effective and contributing to nipple soreness.

The baby should not have to stretch or turn his head to reach the mother's nipple.

Some babies latch on well right away. Others just make little sucking movements or lick the nipple at first.

If the baby has trouble staying on the breast, he may need more support. The mother also may need to support her breast throughout the feeding.

Tiny babies sometimes have trouble staying on the breast. The mother can make it easier for her baby to stay on the breast by supporting the weight of her breast so it doesn't rest on the baby's chin. With a small baby, it is usually necessary to support the breast through the whole feeding. The exception would be the mother with very small breasts. The mother can also hold her index finger under the baby's chin to help him stay latched on.

If he needs more support, the mother can use the Dancer Hand position. For photographs and a description, see "Breastfeeding the Baby with a Cleft Lip and/or Cleft Palate" in the chapter "The Baby with Special Needs."

It may take some time and practice before the baby sucks well at the breast.

The baby's first bursts of sucking will be short, but they will lengthen with practice.

Gene Cranston Anderson (1989a), who has worked extensively with premature babies receiving kangaroo (skin-to-skin) care (see previous section), observed, "At first [after birth], the infant may receive milk only passively.... Nursing with only one or two sucks at a time will follow, but the infant will often suck more within a few minutes. All of this seemingly minor activity is necessary. Sucking behavior will gradually increase and lead to significant breastfeeding; however, this process can take days and even weeks for the smallest infants."

Although switching back and forth from breast to breast may be too tiring for a tiny premie, switching may help keep an older or larger baby interested at the breast for a longer time.

Very tiny babies may not be able to tolerate switching from one breast to other; movement, repositioning, and efforts to latch on may tire them out. During early feedings it is common for a baby to nurse well from only one breast. Encourage the mother to watch the baby's cues to avoid overtiring or stressing him. It is better for the baby to nurse well on only one breast than to nurse less effectively on both. However, if the baby is still awake and alert after nursing at the first breast, it is fine to offer the other breast, provided the baby is not showing signs of distress. (For a list of behaviors that signal distress, see the previous section, "Building a Relationship Between Mother and Baby.") If the baby is not yet nursing effectively enough to get all the milk he needs from breastfeeding alone and he takes one breast at a feeding, suggest the mother pump the other breast to keep up her milk supply. Milk volume has also been found to increase when kangaroo care is given. Having a larger milk supply may also improve milk flow, making feedings easier for the baby.

For an older or larger baby, regular switching from breast to breast may keep him interested in nursing for a longer time. After a baby who is nursing effectively has latched on, his first sucks will be rapid, small movements, until the milk begins to flow. After the let-down, or milk-ejection, reflex occurs, the sucking rhythm will change to deeper and slower sucks, and the mother will hear him swallow.

After a few minutes of rhythmic sucking, swallowing, and pausing, the mother may notice the sucking rhythm changing again, as the baby goes back to little sucks with swallows farther and farther apart and longer pauses. The baby may seem to be drifting off to sleep. Then the mother may want to take the baby off the breast (breaking the suction first), burp him, and switch to the other breast. This switching back and forth may help to keep him interested in breastfeeding for a longer time. As long as the baby is not showing signs of distress, she can repeat this switching back and forth several times during a feeding session, so that the baby nurses on each breast at least twice, and perhaps as many as four or five times.

This switching stimulates more let-downs during a feeding and keeps the milk flowing faster, which may also make the baby interested in breastfeeding for longer periods of time than he otherwise would be.

An overheated baby may suck less vigorously.

There is often a tendency to dress a premature baby warmly so that he doesn't become chilled. But when the room is warm and the baby is covered with heavy clothing, the baby may become overheated, which may make him drowsy and weaken his suck.

If the baby's hands get in the way, swaddling may help.

Prematurity

If the baby's hands are active and make it difficult to achieve or maintain a comfortable, effective breastfeeding position during the first few tries, it may help to swaddle the baby snugly with his hands down. Babies don't seem to mind this; it may even help the sleepy baby to awaken or the fussy baby to settle down.

It is best not to restrict the baby's time at the breast to a prescribed number of minutes, as he may need extra time to get the milk flowing.

Rather than restricting breastfeeding to a prescribed number of minutes, which is sometimes suggested in order to prevent the baby from becoming fatigued, suggest the mother ask that she and her baby be evaluated individually, according to how well breastfeeding is going. Often it takes a premature baby a little extra time at the breast to stimulate his mother's let-down reflex and get the milk flowing, and limiting a premie's time at the breast can substantially cut down on the milk he receives.

The baby's cues will tell the mother when to end a feeding.

There are several cues that will tell the mother that her baby is ready to end a feeding.

- the baby stops sucking;
- the baby falls asleep at the breast;
- the baby seems satisfied;
- the baby shows signs of fatigue or stress.

The length of the early feedings will vary from one feeding to the next. If the baby falls asleep early in the feeding, the mother may be able to continue to hold him skin-to-skin while he sleeps and try again when he awakens.

Expressing milk into a baby's mouth encourages some babies to nurse more actively. However, if the baby is sleepy, it may cause him to choke.

Breastfeeding will get easier with time and practice.

The mother may feel discouraged if her baby does not take to breastfeeding easily and quickly. It may take several attempts—or several sessions—for the mother to get her baby to latch on to the breast and suck. Assure the mother that the early feedings are the most challenging and that with time and practice it will get easier.

Making the Transition to Breastfeeding

While the baby is making the transition to breastfeeding, other feedings can be given by gavage in order to avoid confusing him with artificial nipples.

At first, most premies breastfeed for only one or two feedings a day. The other feedings can be given by cup, gavage tube, or bottle. Since artificial nipples require a different sucking action than the breast, nipple confusion can result when babies receive supplemental feedings from bottles. This affects their feeding at the breast, making it more difficult to teach them to latch on and nurse.

Although the mother may begin by breastfeeding once or twice a day, ideally the number of breastfeedings will increase as the number of other feedings decreases. Suggest the mother ask her baby's care providers if it is possible for supplements to continue to be given by cup or gavage during the time the baby is learning to breastfeed. Many nurseries are willing to do this, and it may make the transition to breastfeeding easier for the baby.

At Kenyatta National Hospital in Nairobi, Kenya, bottles are never used for preterm infants. Any supplemental feedings are given from a cup and the infants are not discharged until they are fully breastfed (Newman 1990; Armstrong 1987).

If bottles are unavoidable, breastfeeding may require more patience, but even a baby who is getting bottles will usually master breastfeeding.

After her baby begins breastfeeding, the mother may need to continue expressing for a while.

When a baby begins to take a few feedings at the breast, the mother will still need to continue expressing during the times when she can't be at the hospital for feedings. She may also need to express at the hospital after feedings if her baby does not take much milk at first while he nurses.

If the mother's milk supply is low when the baby starts breastfeeding, his nursing may not be vigorous or frequent enough to stimulate more milk production. Suggest the mother increase her number of pumpings per day. As the baby's suck becomes more effective, more frequent pumping and/or breastfeeding may help increase her supply. Most mothers notice an increase within a few days; with others, it may take a week or more.

At first, it may take some time for the baby's suck to trigger the mother's let-down reflex.

The first time a nursing mother uses a breast pump, it may take a minute or two for her milk to let down and flow, because the feel of a pump on her breast is very different from the feel of the baby nursing. This may be true in reverse for the mother who is used to letting down her milk to the feel of the pump, but has not had much practice at letting down her milk to her baby at the breast. Kangaroo care may be helpful in enhancing the mother's milk let-down when she pumps afterward (Anderson 1996).

The mother who has been expressing her milk may be accustomed to triggering her let-down reflex with a pump. When the mother who has been pumping begins breastfeeding, it is normal for it to take a little longer for the mother's let-down reflex to occur, and it is not unusual for the baby to suck for several minutes and fall asleep before her milk lets down. This can be frustrating, but assure the mother that her body will soon learn to respond to her baby's nursing and her milk will let down more quickly. In the meantime, two ways a mother can stimulate her let-down to occur more quickly when the baby goes to the breast is to use a breast pump or hand-expression to get her milk flowing immediately before putting baby to breast or to use the pump (or have a helper use the pump) on the opposite breast to stimulate a let-down as the baby latches on.

Encourage the mother to let the nurses know when she will be at the hospital, so they can plan for those feedings to be at the breast.

When the baby is learning to breastfeed, encourage the mother to let the nurses know when she will be coming to the hospital each day—posting a sign on the baby's isolette as a reminder—so she won't arrive to find that the baby has just been fed and is sound asleep.

Aside from test-weighing using an electronic scale, there are other ways to gauge if the baby is nursing well.

Test-weighing a baby with an electronic scale that is sensitive enough to accurately measure the amount of milk a baby gets while breastfeeding, such as Olympic's SMART scale or Medela's BabyWeigh scale, is one way to gauge if the baby is nursing well (for more information see the earlier section, "Determining a Baby's Readiness to Breastfeed"). There are also other ways:

- The baby is sucking and swallowing regularly, moving his jaws as well as his lips.
- Some babies make slurping sounds and dribble.
- The baby is sucking and swallowing regularly, moving his jaws as well as his lips.
- The mother's let-down reflex is working. Not all women have identifiable sensations when their milk lets down, but they can be sure it is happening when their babies suddenly begin sucking and swallowing more slowly and deeply.
- The mother's breasts feel less full (if in doubt, the mother can pump her breasts to see how much milk she is able to pump and how it differs from her previous efforts).
- The baby seems satisfied.
- Later, the baby has good urine and stool output.
- The baby's previous rate of weight gain continues.

If a bottle has been used for feedings, it may take extra time, practice, and patience for a baby to go from bottle to breast.

Prematurity

If the baby has learned to use a bottle, it may take longer to teach him to latch on and nurse at the breast, because different mouth and tongue movements are used and the baby has to learn new sucking patterns. If the baby has been breastfeeding well at least several times a week, this transition from bottle to breast will likely be easier.

If a baby has become accustomed to a bottle and will continue to need supplements after he starts breastfeeding, suggest the mother try using an alternative feeding method for supplementing him, so that the baby's effort to breastfeed will not become further confused (Walker 1992). (See "The Use of Breast Pumps and Other Products.")

When the mother puts the baby to breast, it is important for her to use good positioning and latch-on. (See the previous section, "Putting Baby to Breast.") It may also help to express a little milk first to stimulate her let-down reflex so that her baby receives an instant reward.

It may take time for the nipple-confused baby to take the breast and nurse well. (See the section, "Nipple Confusion," in the chapter "Fussy at the Breast and Breast Refusal.") During the transition from bottle to breast, if the baby fusses or cries at the breast, the mother should stop and comfort him, so that the baby does not associate the breast with frustration or unhappiness. She can then try nursing him again. Lots of skin-to-skin contact between mother and baby can comfort and calm them both and help the baby perceive the breast as a pleasant place to be.

If after many tries the baby is unable to latch on or nurse well at a particular feeding—or if he seems to be tiring—the mother can supplement him using an eyedropper, cup, spoon, or feeding syringe and offer the breast again later. With time, practice, and patience, most babies will learn to nurse.

Putting a breast pad soaked in the mother's milk in the isolette with her baby will accustom him to the smell of her milk and may ease the transition to breast-feeding.

THE MOTHER'S DIETARY AND DRUG CONSIDERATIONS

Unless the mother reacts to a food or sees a reaction in her baby after eating a food, she does not need to restrict her diet.

In most cases, it is not necessary for a breastfeeding mother to restrict her diet in any way. Most babies do not react to specific foods their mothers eat, but an occasional baby might. If the mother is allergic to a certain food or if she notices her baby is fussy or gassy after she eats a certain food, she might want to avoid that food for a while.

For the sake of the mother's health, it is wise for her to eat mostly nutritious foods.

The mother's milk continues to contain adequate amounts of nutrients even if the mother's diet is less than ideal. However, the mother will feel the effects of eating poorly: her resistance to disease may go down, she may have less energy, and she may feel less able to cope. So for her own sake, it is wise for her to eat a healthy diet.

If the mother is considering taking any prescribed or non-prescribed drugs, suggest she discuss it with her baby's doctor before she begins taking them.

The premature baby's small size and immature processing systems make him more vulnerable to drugs than a healthy, full-term baby. It is important, therefore, that the mother discuss a drug with her baby's doctor before she begins taking it, so that he can evaluate it in light of her baby's size and condition.

Because alternative drugs are usually available, even if a particular drug would pose hazards to her baby, it may be possible to find a substitute that would be compatible with continued nursing. (For more information, see the chapter "Drugs, Vitamins, Vaccines, and Diagnostic Tests," and the supplement "The Transfer of Drugs and Other Chemicals into Human Milk.")

Cigarette smoking, alcohol consumption, and illegal drug use should also be discussed with the baby's doctor.

Recreational drugs, such as alcohol, nicotine, and illegal drugs, all pass into the mother's milk to some degree. If a mother is a light smoker or occasionally has an alcoholic drink, it is unlikely to have a major effect on breastfeeding or her baby, but a premature baby is less able to process these substances than a healthy, full-term baby. If the mother smokes, drinks, or takes illegal drugs, it is vital that she discuss this with her baby's doctor. Illegal drugs, especially, pose significant health hazards for both mother and baby.

WORKING WITH HOSPITAL PERSONNEL

Hospitals vary in the amount of support and cooperation they extend to breastfeeding mothers of premature infants.

Suggest the mother explain her feelings about breastfeeding as soon as possible.

A mother can help avoid conflicts with her baby's doctor and other hospital personnel by telling them in the beginning what her goals are. She might say something like, "I want to do everything I can to be able to breastfeed my baby." This may make the doctors and nurses more willing to try different approaches.

Encourage the mother to ask about anything she doesn't understand.

The mother may still be in shock when she is first given a technical explanation of her baby's condition. If information is given to her while she is upset, it is unlikely that she will be able to understand or remember all of the particulars. If so, encourage the mother to contact her baby's doctor or other hospital personnel to discuss her baby's condition when she is feeling calmer.

Throughout her baby's care, encourage the mother to stay well-informed and ask for clarification when she needs it.

Remind the mother that although the doctor is the medical expert, it is she and the baby's father who are responsible for the decisions made about their baby.

Suggest the mother notice which doctors and nurses are good at explaining things and are supportive and then seek them out when she has questions or wants to talk.

The technology and terminology of the intensive-care nursery can be frightening and intimidating. Talking to the doctors and nurses can help the mother get a better idea of how her baby is doing. She may find that there are one or two caretakers who are particularly good at explaining things, listening, and responding to her concerns. Encourage her to seek out those people, arrange to visit the nursery while they are working, and share her good moments as well as her worries with them.

Once the baby is past the critical stage, the mother may see less of the doctors and more of the nurses.

Encourage the mother to ask for treatment options that will allow her to stay close to her baby and breastfeed as soon as possible.

Long periods of time away from her baby can add to a mother's anxiety and feelings of helplessness and affect her feelings about nursing her baby. If she is discouraged from spending time with her baby, providing her milk for him, or nursing him, she may question whether she is important to her baby or her milk is really good for him.

Physical closeness can help reduce emotional stress. Encourage the mother to request treatment options that will allow her to spend time with her baby and breastfeed as soon as possible. Once she begins breastfeeding, suggest the mother ask not to be rushed or interrupted.

If the doctor recommends a treatment that will negatively affect breastfeeding or has been invalidated by research, offer to share references with the mother that she can give to her doctor.

If the doctor's advice seems counterproductive to breastfeeding or inappropriate, keep these points in mind:

Prematurity

- In a complex medical situation, the mother may not have explained or completely understood everything about her baby's circumstances. First impressions may not be accurate, and there may be more to the situation than is apparent.
- Openly disagreeing with the doctor's advice will not help the mother. In fact, it may confuse her even more. What she needs is help in coming to some agreement with her baby's doctor.

One approach is to offer to share references with the mother that she can give to the doctor. For example, if the baby's doctor suggests a course of action that is not backed by current research, say to the mother: "Some doctors do take that approach, but research has shown..." and then ask the mother if she would like a reference she can share with her doctor. Most doctors have access to the medical journals cited in the "References" section at the end of this chapter and can refer to articles at their local hospital or medical library. Here are some specific examples:

- If the mother says her doctor wants her baby to be fed by bottle before trying breastfeeding, say: "Some doctors do take that approach, but research has shown that premature babies may be able to breastfeed before they can bottle-feed and that breastfeeding is less stressful than bottle-feeding. Would you like me to give you a reference to give to your doctor?" If she says yes, then ask her to write down the reference to the Meier and Anderson 1987 and Meier 1988 articles listed at the end of this chapter.
- If the mother says her doctor does not want her to begin breastfeeding because he needs to know how much the baby is getting at each feeding, say, "That is a valid concern, but recent research has shown that when a special electronic scale is used to weigh the baby before and after feedings it is possible to know how much the baby receives at the breast. Would you like me to give you a reference to give to your doctor?" If she says yes, then dictate the references to the Meier 1994, Gross 1993, and Meier 1990 studies listed at the end of this chapter.

If the mother is uncomfortable with her doctor's recommendations, discuss how she can raise her concerns.

Most people, but especially a pregnant woman or new mother, find it very stressful to be in conflict with a doctor. If the doctor advises a treatment that the mother is uncomfortable with, give her the tools she needs to come to some agreement with her doctor. The basic tools are tact, honesty, respect, knowledge, and patience.

Suggest the mother think through her approach before she speaks to the doctor. There are many ways she can make her encounter with the doctor more positive. The mother can:

Practice her responses before she talks to the doctor. Offer to take some time to discuss the mother's concerns and to have her practice expressing them before talking to the doctor.

Ask the doctor for a complete explanation of the treatment. If the mother is unsure of the reasons for the doctor's recommendations, encourage her to ask him or her to take the time to explain them to her thoroughly. In evaluating the doctor's advice, it may help to ask, "Is this your general policy with regard to premature babies or is this specific to my baby?"

Repeat the doctor's statements in her own words. By paraphrasing what the doctor says, the mother can avoid confusion and show the doctor what impact his or her words are having on her.

Share her feelings with the doctor. It is best if a mother has been clear about her feelings from the beginning, but if not, it is never too late to start. A doctor cannot know what an individual mother's preferences and priorities are unless she tells him. The mother might tell the doctor, for example, "Our family has a history of allergies and I feel strongly about my baby receiving only human milk, if at all possible. Are there treatment options that allow for continued breastfeeding without giving formula?" Or, "I know my baby is small, but I would like to start breastfeeding him as soon as possible. Would you find this acceptable if we arranged for a nurse to sit with us during nursings to monitor the baby?"

Project self-confidence. Writing down questions and concerns in advance can be helpful, as well as a friendly manner and a willingness to consider alternatives.

Make statements in a positive way. Another way to foster a friendly atmosphere is to make statements in a positive way, for example, "I would like to try extending my pumping time to get more hindmilk before offering supplements," rather than "I don't want my baby to receive formula supplements."

Try the "broken record" technique. When disagreements arise, the "broken record" technique can be an effective way of getting a message across. The mother can simply restate her basic position, calmly and quietly to each argument. "I appreciate your concern about her health, but now that she's beginning to breastfeed well, I'd like to avoid artificial nipples and have her other feedings given by cup or gavage tube rather than bottles."

Use tact, give respect, and expect them in return. If a mother feels that her doctor is being judgmental or overly critical, it may be helpful to recognize his or her concern for her baby (for example, "I understand and appreciate your concern for my baby's health and well-being") but still calmly insist that the doctor offer current medical information to back up opinions. Most physicians are not inflexible and would be willing to meet a mother halfway.

Keep in mind that the ultimate responsibility for the baby's health lies with the parents. Although the doctor is the medical expert, the parents are the ones who must live with the consequences of the decisions made about their baby. A mother can shift a discussion to emphasize parental responsibility by saying, "You'd like my permission to... ?" or "Your recommendation is... ?"

If not satisfied, seek a second opinion. After discussing her feelings and possible approaches with her baby's doctor, if a mother feels that the doctor is not as supportive of breastfeeding or her feelings as she would like, it is her right to get a second opinion.

Encourage the mother to seek out the support she needs.	Many hospitals provide support groups for parents whose babies were born prematurely or are in the special-care nursery. See previous section in this chapter under "The Mother's Feelings."

PREPARING FOR HOSPITAL DISCHARGE

Doctors and hospitals vary in their discharge policies for premature babies.

Some doctors and hospitals will discharge a baby as small as three-and-a-half pounds (1590 grams) if the baby is doing well, which means that he is sucking and swallowing well, has no respiratory problems, has no signs of illness or complications, and is gaining weight well. Others set an arbitrary discharge weight—for example, five pounds (2270 grams)—which the baby must reach before he can go home.

If the baby's doctor or hospital discharges premies based on an arbitrary weight and the mother would like her baby to come home sooner, encourage her to discuss this with her baby's doctor. Often special arrangements can be made if the mother makes her wishes known tactfully and respectfully (see the previous section, "Working with Hospital Personnel.").

The mother may have mixed emotions about bringing the baby home.

Often parents of a premature baby go through a second crisis around the time of hospital discharge that brings feelings similar to those felt when their baby was born. Even after the doctors pronounce a baby healthy and growing well, the fears and difficulties of the past weeks tend to linger in the parents' minds. Feelings of help-lessness and apprehension mixed with joy and happiness are common, particularly among mothers who have not participated actively in their baby's care. The mother may feel overwhelmed at the idea that she will have to care for her special-need baby at home while at the same time feeling eager to be like a "normal" family and start enjoying her baby.

Prematurity

Becoming more involved in the baby's care before he leaves the hospital will increase a mother's self-confidence.

Even if a premie has breastfed well while in the hospital, once the mother takes her baby home, the most commonly reported worry is whether her baby is getting enough milk (Kavanaugh 1995; Hill 1994). Encourage the mother, if possible, to feed her premie on cue at the hospital for at least a day or two before his homecoming. In one US hospital, where premies of mothers planning to breastfeed go from tube feeding to the breast with no bottles, the baby is transferred to the postpartum floor and mother and baby room-in for two to three days before discharge. The mother is not charged for staying at the hospital to care for her baby (Stine 1990).

Also, encourage the mother to begin kangaroo care, especially if she has not done this before.

Learning the signs that a baby has breastfed well will give the mother greater self-confidence when she brings her baby home.

After spending weeks watching health care professionals measure and record every feeding, it may be hard for the parents to believe that breastfeeding can work at home. Learning the basics of breastfeeding can add to their self-confidence. If the mother has begun to breastfeed in the hospital, suggest she notice the signs that her baby has nursed well, as these will be useful when she breastfeeds him at home. Some of these signs are:

- the baby is sucking and swallowing regularly, moving his jaws as well as his lips;
- the mother notices her let-down reflex occur;
- the mother's breasts feel less full;
- the baby seems satisfied;
- the baby wets at least 6-8 cloth or 5-6 disposable diapers;
- the baby has at least 2-5 stools each day during his first six weeks;
- the baby gains more than 4-5 oz. (113-142 g) per week.

If the mother is concerned about her baby's intake, scheduling frequent weight checks with her baby's doctor after discharge will help her know for sure how breastfeeding is going. Some mothers—particularly those whose babies were receiving precisely measured feedings in the hospital—find it reassuring to rent Medela's BabyWeigh scale for the first week or two after baby comes home so they can see how much milk their baby receives at the breast at each feeding.

Another way to know if baby is getting enough is by keeping track of his wet diapers (each day he should have at least six to eight cloth or five to six disposable diapers) and his bowel movements (he should have at least two to five a day for his first six weeks). Also, by scheduling frequent appointments with the baby's doctor after he is discharged, the mother can have her baby's weight gain monitored.

The amount of support and assistance provided by the hospital after discharge varies from place to place.

Some hospitals provide parents with follow-up care once their premature baby has been discharged; others do not. Encourage the mother to find out what services her hospital offers before discharge, so she will know what to expect.

THE FIRST WEEKS AT HOME

Household Preparations and Realistic Expectations

Encourage the mother to plan for household help and to spend the first week or two concentrating on her baby.

Although the mother may have had time to recover physically from childbirth before her baby comes home, the constant, twenty-four hour demands of caring for a small baby can be exhausting. Encourage the mother to plan to spend her first days at home with her baby doing nothing but nursing him and taking care of his needs. Many mothers crave time alone with their babies, especially if they have been separated after birth. This is a normal reaction to their time apart.

Household help with laundry, cleaning, and cooking should be considered a necessity for at least the first week. If there are older children, suggest the mother consider making arrangements with relatives or friends to come over and entertain them. It will also make the transition easier if the baby's father can take time off so the parents can spend quiet, relaxing time together with their baby. Suggest the mother limit visitors and ask those who do come to stay for only a few minutes.

Encourage the mother to plan to eat well and sleep when baby sleeps.

The first weeks at home with a small baby can be stressful. The mother should plan to eat well, drink plenty of fluids, and get enough rest.

Some premature babies tend to sleep for long periods; others are wakeful. Experts disagree on whether it is appropriate to wake and stimulate a sleepy premature baby for frequent feedings. Some who have worked extensively with premies before and after discharge recommend stimulating sleepy premies to feed frequently (8-12 times per day), watching for cues that baby is in a light sleep (such as movements under closed eyelids, sucking motions, and body movements) before waking (Walker 1992). Others believe that waking and stimulating a premie to feed frequently from both breasts may compromise a premie's intake and growth (Meier and Mangurten 1993). The mother's observations of her baby's behavior during and between feedings will help her determine which approach works best for her baby. Behaviors in the baby such as clenched fists with white knuckles, fingers splayed out wide, or furrowed brows are indicators that the baby may need a break (Als 1994). (For a more complete list of behaviors that signal distress, see the previous section, "Building a Relationship Between Mother and Baby.")

Breastfeeding at Home

Most mothers of premies experience a "crisis of confidence" when they take their babies home, even if breastfeeding had been going well in the hospital.

The more fully a mother is able to breastfeed her baby in the hospital, the easier the transition to breastfeeding should be once the baby comes home. Experience with kangaroo care in the hospital has also been found to ease the transition (Affonso 1993; Wahlberg 1992; Affonso 1989). But even when breastfeeding has gone well in the hospital, many mothers of premies have doubts and questions once they are home and nursing.

When a special program to support breastfeeding mothers of premies was started in a US hospital, the program team found that despite objective measures that the babies were breastfeeding well while in the hospital, detailed breastfeeding instructions to the mother before discharge, and telephone follow-up 48 hours after discharge, the mothers reported at least one major breastfeeding problem and serious concerns about their babies' intake (Kavanaugh 1995). In hospitals without special breastfeeding support, worries about milk supply and milk production have also been found to be among the mothers' main concerns after discharge (Hill 1994).

Although some premies may not breastfeed often and long enough at first, with time and patience, breastfeeding tends to improve as babies mature.

Many premies are able to breastfeed well once they get home. Some premies, however, tire at the breast more quickly than a full-term baby, and others are sleepy, napping for several hours at a stretch. With time and patience, many premies learn to breastfeed more effectively. Encourage the mother to give her baby time and to watch for signs of stress or overstimulation during feedings (Als 1994). (For a list of behaviors that signal distress, see the earler section, "Building a Relationship Between Mother and Baby.")

Prematurity

If the baby is not fully breastfeeding at discharge, encourage the mother to keep her electric breast pump for the first week or two at home.

If the baby has a weak suck, takes only one breast at each feeding, or is not taking as much milk at feedings as the mother was expressing, suggest the mother keep her electric piston breast pump for at least the first week or two after her baby comes home. This will make it easier for her to express after feedings, so that she can maintain her milk supply and stay comfortable.

If the baby's suck is weak, the mother may need to keep expressing while his suck improves.

If the mother's milk supply is plentiful enough to meet her baby's needs—because she has been regularly expressing during her baby's hospitalization—but his suck is not effective enough for him to milk the breast well while nursing, the mother will need to continue expressing while her baby's sucking improves in order to keep up her milk supply.

One approach to strengthening a baby's suck is to stimulate him to breastfeed frequently (every two hours) with good positioning and latch-on. Some who have worked extensively with premies before and after discharge recommend stimulating sleepy premies to feed frequently (8-12 times per day), watching for cues that baby is in a light sleep (such as movements under closed eyelids, sucking motions, and body movements) before waking (Walker 1992). Others believe that waking and stimulating a premie to feed frequently from both breasts may compromise a premie's intake and growth (Meier and Mangurten 1993). The mother's observations of her baby's behavior during and between feedings will help her determine which approach works best for her premie. Behaviors in the baby such as clenched fists with white knuckles, fingers splayed out wide, or furrowed brows are indicators that the baby may need a break. (For a more complete list of behaviors that signal distress, see the previous section, "Building a Relationship Between Mother and Baby")

If the baby's suck does not improve quickly, a nursing supplementer—a device that allows the baby to receive supplement through a tube taped to the mother's breast—can be used to produce a faster flow of milk at the breast. This stimulates more active sucking in some babies. Even if the baby's suck is not improved by use of the nursing supplementer, it offers other advantages, such as allowing the baby to be supplemented without bottles, which sometimes cause breastfeeding problems, and allowing the whole feeding time to be spent at the breast.

The mother will want to know if the baby is getting enough.

There are several ways to gauge if the baby is getting enough from the breast alone.

At least six to eight wet cloth diapers (five or six disposable diapers) every twenty-four hours are an indication that the baby is getting enough fluids. Suggest that the mother try to get a sense of a minimally wet diaper by placing two ounces (60 ml) of water in a dry diaper to see how it feels.

The wetness of disposable diapers can be more difficult to gauge than cloth diapers. Five to six wet disposable diapers per day indicates baby is getting enough fluids.

In a healthy full-term baby the number of wet cloth diapers may drop to five or six per day at about six weeks of age, but their wetness will increase to four or more ounces (120 ml). This is because the baby's bladder grows in size and is able to hold more urine. It is not known when this change occurs in a preterm baby. At all ages, urine should be pale in color and mild-smelling.

During the baby's first six weeks, at least two to five bowel movements per day indicate he is getting enough calories. Most young babies will have at least two to five good-sized bowel movements every twenty-four hours. Many babies will continue this pattern for as long as they are exclusively breastfed. If bowel movements are small, there should be many each day. If the baby has only one every few days, it should be substantial. (This is more common in the full-term breastfed baby who is past six weeks of age.) A mother who reports less frequent bowel movements during her baby's first four to six weeks should be asked how often he nurses and how many wet diapers he has each day. This may be a normal variation (in which case the baby will be gaining well) or it may be a sign that the baby is not nursing long enough to get the fatty hindmilk he needs, which is rich in calories.

Less frequent bowel movements are normal in an older breastfed baby. Some have bowel movements only once a week without signs of constipation.

A weight gain of more than 4-5 ounces (113-142 grams) a week also indicates the baby is getting enough. Frequent appointments with the baby's doctor during the first weeks at home can help reassure the mother that her baby is gaining well and thriving under her care.

Another way for a mother to be reassured about her milk supply is to test-weigh the baby using a sensitive electronic scale. Medela's BabyWeigh scale, which is available for rent in some areas, can be used to measure the amount of milk a baby takes at the breast by weighing him before and after feedings. This may be especially reassuring to a mother of a premie during the first week or two after discharge.

In some cases, it may be necessary to give supplements.

If the baby has fewer wet diapers or bowel movements than he should while breastfeeding exclusively or his weight gain is not sufficient, the baby may need to be supplemented until the mother's milk supply increases or until the baby's suck improves.

When choosing a feeding method, it is important that the mother know providing supplements by bottle can cause nipple confusion in the very young baby and weaken the suck of a baby who is not sucking well. Other methods of giving supplements are listed in "The Use of Breast Pumps and Other Products," and include: eyedropper, feeding syringe, cup, spoon, or nursing supplementer. Encourage the mother to pick the method with which she feels most comfortable.

When the supplement is given depends on the feeding method used.

If supplements are given by bottle, eyedropper, feeding syringe, or cup, suggest the mother start by breastfeeding before offering the supplement, otherwise the baby may be too full to nurse well. However, suggest the mother watch her baby to see how he responds. Some babies breastfeed better if the edge is taken off their hunger first. It is best not to let a premie get too hungry.

If supplements are given by nursing supplementer, a device that allows the baby to receive supplement through a tube taped to the mother's breast, the baby will receive the supplement while he nurses at the breast. In many cases, this reduces the total amount of time spent feeding the baby. Because it gives a baby a faster flow at the breast, the supplementer stimulates more active sucking in some babies. As the baby's suck becomes more effective, he may take more from the breast and less from the supplementer. Some babies, however, become dependent on the supplementer and do not naturally wean themselves from it without help.

The choice of feeding method will vary from mother to mother. Some mothers dislike having to use a device like the nursing supplementer while nursing their babies; others prefer using the supplementer because it keeps the baby at the breast.

Also see, "Working with the Doctor and Supplementation" under "Slow Weight Gain" in the chapter "Weight Gain."

The mother's expressed milk is the first choice as a supplement. Formula can also be used.

For many reasons, the mother's own expressed milk is the best supplement, but if this is not available or the mother chooses to use formula, suggest she contact her baby's doctor for a recommendation for a commercial formula.

Prematurity

The baby's doctor will tell the mother how much supplement to give. Feedings should be given in small amounts, but not necessarily at every feeding.

How much supplement to use and when to give it are decisions the mother and her baby's doctor will need to discuss. The baby's nurses or doctor will be able to tell the mother how much expressed milk or formula the baby was getting in the hospital in addition to breastfeeding.

If a nursing supplementer is used, she can determine how much supplement to use during each nursing by estimating the number of nursings a baby has per day (usually around ten) and dividing the recommended amount of supplement by that number.

If the supplement is given by another method, the mother may choose to offer it after every feeding or to offer supplements only after every other feeding or at regular intervals, usually two to five times every twenty-four hours, rather than after every nursing. If the mother is giving supplements by bottle, offering supplements after every feeding increases the likelihood that the baby will become nipple-confused and if his suck is already weak, frequent bottles may weaken it further.

When supplements are given by bottle, cup, spoon, eyedropper, or feeding syringe, supplements are best offered in small quantities (one to three ounces [30-90 ml]), rather than as one or two large quantities (six to eight ounces [180-240 ml]). This prevents the baby from becoming overly full and skipping or delaying a nursing.

The baby's effectiveness at the breast and how often and long he breastfeeds determine how soon the baby will be able to breastfeed without supplements.

It is important for the mother to know that although it may take a few days or a few weeks for her baby to become fully breastfed, her body will produce enough milk for her baby. There are three main variables that determine how quickly this will happen.

How well the mother's milk supply was maintained before breastfeeding was started. Although it was once suggested that the mother of a premie express only as much milk as her baby is taking at that time, some women have found that when they express very little milk at first it is difficult to increase their milk supply later. This may be because their breast tissue partially involutes (or reverts to its prepregnancy state), making it more difficult to increase milk production. For this reason, establishing a full milk supply as early as possible via frequent pumping is now being suggested as a better strategy (Woolridge 1995). For more information, see, "When Breastfeeding Is Delayed After Birth" in the chapter "Expression and Storage of Human Milk."

How effectively the baby breastfeeds. A baby who is breastfeeding effectively sucks vigorously and swallows regularly. The mother should be able to see his jaws moving all the way back to his ears. A baby with a weak suck mouths the nipple weakly without regular swallowing.

If the baby is not sucking and swallowing regularly, suggest the mother try frequent breastfeeding—at least every two to three hours—with switch nursing. Often a baby begins a feeding by sucking well and after a few minutes of rhythmic sucking, swallowing, and pausing, the baby changes his nursing pattern to little sucks with swallows farther and farther apart and longer pauses. When switch nursing, as soon as the mother notices the baby's suck becoming less effective, she takes the baby off the breast (breaking the suction first), burps him, and switches him to the other breast. This switching back and forth may help to keep him interested in breastfeeding effectively for a longer time. She can repeat this switching back and forth several times during a feeding session, so that the baby nurses on each breast at least twice.

This switching stimulates more let-downs during a feeding and keeps the milk flowing faster, which may also keep the baby interested in breastfeeding for longer periods of time than he otherwise would be. However, she should watch the baby for signs of stress; premies tire quickly and are more easily overstimulated than full-term infants.

If switch nursing does not seem to help, the mother can try using a nursing supplementer to supplement the baby and help strengthen his suck.

How often and how long the baby breastfeeds. If a baby is nursing effectively, the more often he nurses, the more milk the mother will produce. The average newborn needs to breastfeed eight to twelve times every twenty-four hours to receive enough milk.

Also, the mother should be encouraged not to limit breastfeedings to a prescribed number of minutes. If her baby is nursing effectively, the baby will indicate when he is finished on each breast by falling asleep, coming off the breast himself, or by stopping actively breastfeeding. By nursing long enough, the mother will be sure that the baby gets the fatty, high-calorie hindmilk that is available later in the feeding.

Supplements should be decreased gradually.

When the baby is breastfeeding effectively and the mother is ready to begin cutting down on the supplements in order to increase her milk supply, there are several ways to make this process easier. Suggest that the mother:

Begin by keeping a written diary of how much supplement her baby takes and when, as well as the number of nursings, wet diapers, and bowel movements. The mother should look for: regular sucking and swallowing for ten minutes or more on each breast at every feeding—with nursings increasing in length as the baby's effectiveness increases—ten or more breastfeedings every twenty-four hours, six to eight wet diapers every day, and several bowel movements a day (fewer with an older baby). As the days go by, she will see the amount of supplement her baby takes decrease as he begins taking more from the breast and as her supply increases.

Plan to cut down on the supplement slowly. With the approval of her baby's doctor, help the mother set appropriate goals for decreasing the supplement while increasing nursing. The goals should be reasonable and attainable.

If a mother is using a nursing supplementer to supplement her baby at the breast, as the baby's suck improves he may begin taking more from the breast and less from the supplementer. In this case, milk left in the supplementer after nursings will tell the mother that the baby is taking more from the breast and it is time to offer less supplement. In some cases, the baby learns to take the supplement from the supplementer without sucking vigorously. If his suck does not seem to be improving, suggest the mother try using one of the other alternative feeding methods to see if the baby will learn to breastfeed more effectively without the supplementer.

If the mother is supplementing her baby using a cup, spoon, eyedropper, feeding syringe, or bottle, there are two ways to approach cutting down. The mother could cut down on the number of feedings at which she offers the supplement, or she could cut down on the amount of supplement she offers at each feeding. Either of these options accomplishes the same goal and has its own advantages and disadvantages. The advantage to offering the supplement less often is that the baby will encounter the supplementing device less often. The advantage to offering less of the supplement at each feeding is that the baby will be less likely to fill up on the supplement and skip or delay the next nursing. Suggest the mother try whichever option she feels most comfortable with, and if she or her baby are not happy with one, to try the other approach. If the baby has been on formula supplements, remind the mother that his stools will become looser as the baby takes more of her milk.

Have the baby's weight checked every week. This will reassure the mother that her baby is growing well. Suggest the same scale be used every time along with similar weight clothing if the baby is not undressed when he is weighed.

Be patient. Helping a premie learn how to breastfeed can sometimes be a long process. Be sure the mother knows as she begins that it may take concentrated time and effort for many weeks until her baby's nursing improves. Her patience and persistence will make it happen.

Prematurity

Making Breastfeeding Easier and More Comfortable

Privacy, a comfortable chair, and pillows for support may make breastfeeding go more smoothly at first.

Especially at first, it may be helpful for the mother to find a private and comfortable place to nurse, away from all activity and with plenty of pillows to support the baby, her back, and her arms.

Suggestions from the previous section, "Putting the Baby to Breast," may be helpful in finding a comfortable and effective position and guiding the baby onto the breast. Also see the chapter "Positioning, Latch-On, and the Baby's Suck."

The best time to breastfeed is before the baby is crying from hunger.

The baby may be more receptive to breastfeeding if he is not too hungry. Frequent feedings help ensure that the baby will not be ravenously hungry and crying when he is offered the breast.

Keeping baby close may make nighttime nursings less disruptive.

Many parents find that the easiest way to handle nighttime nursings is to keep the baby in their room at night and nurse lying down so that their sleep is less disrupted and they can rest during feedings. The baby might sleep in a crib, bassinette, mattress or palette on the floor, or in the parents' bed. If the mother or baby are not yet comfortable breastfeeding lying down, some other suggestions may make night nursings easier.

- Move a big, comfortable chair with a footstool into the mother's room for nighttime nursings and keep an extra blanket nearby to cover mother and baby.
- Sit on the bed to nurse, with extra pillows at the mother's back and elbow and at her side to support the baby at the breast.

When the feeding is over, the mother can either return the baby to his own bed or keep him next to her so she won't have to get out of bed for the next feeding. If the mother decides to keep her baby in bed with her, a bedrail, like those made for toddlers who are learning to sleep in a big bed, will guard against falls. Or the parents can push their bed against the wall.

Publications for Parents

Danner, S. and Cerutti, E. *Nursing Your Premature Baby*. Waco, Texas: Childbirth Graphics.

Gotsch, G. *Breastfeeding Your Premature Baby*. Schaumburg, Illinois: La Leche League International, 1990. Publication No. 26.

La Leche League International. THE WOMANLY ART OF BREASTFEEDING, 35th Anniversary ed. Schaumburg, Illinois, 1991, pp. 261-96.

Ludington-Hoe, S. with Golant, S. *Kangaroo Care: The Best You Can Do to Help Your Preterm Infant*. New York: Bantam Books, 1993.

References

Acolet, D. et al. Oxygenation, heart rate, and temperature in very low birthweight infants during skin-to-skin contact with their mothers. *Acta Paediatr Scand* 1989; 78:189-93.

Affonso, D. et al. Reconciliation and healing for mothers through skin-to-skin contact provided in an American tertiary level intensive care nursery. *Neo Network* 1993; 7(6): 43-51.

Affonso, D. et al. Exploration of mothers' reactions to the kangaroo method of prematurity care. *Neo Network* 1989; 7:43-51.

Als, H. et al. Individualized developmental care for the very low-birth-weight preterm infant: medical and neurofunctional effects. *JAMA* 1994; 272(11):853-58.

Anderson, G. Mellen Professor of Nursing, Bolton School of Nursing, Case Western Reserve University, Cleveland, Ohio. Personal communication, July 1996.

Anderson, G. Touch and the kangaroo method in *Touch in Early Development*. Mahwah, New Jersey: Lawrence Erlbaum Associates, 1995, pp. 35-51.

Anderson, G. Current knowledge about skin-to-skin (kangaroo) care for preterm infants. *Breastfeed Rev* 1993; II(8):364-73.

Anderson, G. Current knowledge about skin-to-skin (kangaroo) care for preterm infants. *J Perinatol* 1991; 216-25.

Anderson, G. Kangaroo care and breastfeeding for preterm infants. BREASTFEEDING ABSTRACTS 1989a; 9:7-8.

Anderson, G. Skin-to-skin: kangaroo care in Western Europe. *Am J Nurs* 1989b; 89:662-66.

Anderson, G. et al. Kangaroo care for premature infants. *Am J Nurs* 1986; 86:807-09.

Armstrong, H. Breastfeeding low birth weight babies: advances in Kenya. *J Hum Lact* 1987; 3(2):34-37.

Auerbach, K. Sequential and simultaneous breast pumping: a comparison. *Int J Nurs Stud* 1990; 27(3):257-65.

Bishop, N. et al. Early diet of preterm infants and bone mineralization at age five years. *Acta Paediatr* 1996; 85:230-36.

Bishop, N. Feeding the preterm infant. *Pediatr Nephrol* 1994; 8:494-98.

Bosque, E. et al. Physiologic measures of kangaroo versus incubator care in a tertiary-level nursery. *JOGNN* 1995; 219.

Buescher, E. Host defense mechanisms of human milk and their relations to enteric infections and necrotizing enterocolitis. *Clin Perinatol* 1994; 21(2):247-62.

Carlson, S. Polyunsaturated fatty acids and infant nutrition. In Galli, C. and Simopoulos, A., eds. *Dietary Omega-3 and Omega-6 Fatty Acids: Biological Effects and Nutritional Essentiality*. New York: Plenum Press, 1989, pp. 147-58.

Clandinin, M. et al. Requirements of newborn infants for long chain polyunsaturated fatty acids. *Acta Paediatr Scand Supp* 1989; 351:63-71.

Collinge, J. et al. Demand vs. scheduled feedings for premature infants. *JOGNN* 1982; 11:362-67.

Davies, D. How suitable is human milk for preterm babies? *Acta Paediatr Japonica* 1989; 31:439-54.

deCarvalho, M. et al. Frequency of milk expression and milk production by mothers of non-nursing premature neonates. *Am J Dis Child* 1985; 139:483-87.

Gale, G. et al. Skin-to-skin (kangaroo) holding of the intubated premature infant. *Neo Network* 1993; 12(6):49-57.

Gale, S. et al. Is dietary epidermal growth factor absorbed by premature human infants? *Biol Neonate* 1989; 55:104-10.

Greer, F. et al. Changes in fat concentration of human milk during delivery by intermittent bolus and continuous mechanical pump infusion. *J Pediatr* 1984; 105:745-49.

Gross, S. and Slagle, T. Feeding the low birth weight infant. *Clin Perinatol* 1993; 193.

Hadeed, A. et al. Skin to skin contact (SSC) between mother and infants reduces idiopathic apnea of prematurity (IAOP). *Pediatr Res* 1995; 37(4):pt 2:1233.

Hill, P. et al. Delayed initiation of breast-feeding the preterm infant. *J Perinat Neonatal Nurs* 1995; 9(2):10-20.

Hill, P. et al. Mothers of low birthweight infants: breastfeeding patterns and problems. *J Hum Lact* 1994:10(3):169-76.

Hopkinson, J. et al. Milk production by mothers of premature infants. *Pediatrics* 1988; 81:815-20.

The Human Milk Banking Association of North America. *Recommendations for Collection, Storage, and Handling of a Mother's Milk for Her Own Infant in the Hospital Setting*. West Hartford, CT, USA, 1993.

Prematurity

Jarvenpaa, A. et al. Preterm infants fed human milk attain intrauterine weight gain. *Acta Paediatr Scand* 1983; 72:239-43.

Kavanaugh, K. et al. Getting enough: mothers' concerns about breastfeeding a preterm infant after discharge. *JOGNN* 1995; 24(1):23-32.

Lang, S. et al. Cup feeding: an alternative method of infant feeding. *Arch Dis Child* 1994; 71:365-69.

Lawrence, R. *Breastfeeding: A Guide for the Medical Profession,* 4th ed. St. Louis: Mosby, 1994, pp. 405-30.

Lemons, J. et al. Differences in the composition of preterm and term human milk during early lactation. *Pediatr Res* 1982; 16:113-16.

Lucas, A. et al. Breast milk and subsequent intelligence quotient in children born preterm. *Lancet* 1992; 339:261-64.

Lucas, A. and Cole T. Breast milk and neonatal necrotising enterocolitis. *Lancet* 1990; 336:1519-23.

Lucas, A. et al. Early diet in preterm babies and developmental status in infancy. *Arch Dis Child* 1989; 64:1570-78.

Lucas, A. AIDS and human milk bank closures. *Lancet* 1987; I:1092-93.

Lucas, A. et al. Multicentre clinical trial of diets for low birthweight infants: interim analysis of short term clinical and biochemical effects of diet. *Paediatr Res* 1984; 18(A):807.

Ludington-Hoe, S. et al. Kangaroo care: research results and practice implications and guidelines. *Neo Network* 1994; 13(1):19-27.

Ludington-Hoe, S. with Golant, S. *Kangaroo Care: The Best You Can Do to Help Your Preterm Infant*. New York: Bantam Books, 1993a, pp. 53-64.

Ludington-Hoe, S. et al. Skin-to-skin beginning in the delivery room for Colombian mothers and their preterm infants. *J Hum Lact* 1993b; 9(4):241-42.

Ludington-Hoe, S. et al. Selected physiologic measures and behavior during paternal skin contact with Colombian preterm infants. *J Develop Physiol* 1992; 18:223-32.

Luukkainen, P. et al. Changes in the fatty acid composition of preterm and term human milk from 1 week to 6 months of lactation. *J Ped Gastro Nutr* 1994; 18:355-60.

Mathur, N. et al. Anti-infective factors in preterm human colostrum. *Acta Paediatr Scand* 1990; 79:1039-44.

Meier, P. et al. A new scale for in-home test-weighing for mothers of preterm and high risk infants. *J Hum Lact* 1994; 10(3):163-68.

Meier, P. and Mangurten, H. "Breastfeeding and the pre-term infant." In *Breastfeeding and Human Lactation,* eds. J. Riordan and K. Auerbach. Boston and London: Jones and Bartlett, 1993, pp. 253-78.

Meier, P. et al. The accuracy of test weighing for preterm infants. *J Ped Gastro Nutr* 1990; 5:50-52.

Meier, P. Bottle and breast feeding: effects on transcutaneous oxygen pressure and temperature in small preterm infants. *Nurs Res* 1988; 37:36-41.

Meier, P. and Anderson G. Responses of preterm infants to bottle and breast feeding. *MCN* 1987; 12:97-105.

Newman, J. Breastfeeding and problems associated with early introduction of bottles and pacifiers. *J Hum Lact* 1990; 6(2):59-63.

Nutrition Committee, Canadian Paediatric Society. Nutrient needs and feeding of premature infants. *Can Med Assoc J* 1995; 152(11):1765-85.

Parsa, N. et al. Role of breastfeeding in necrotizing enterocolitis in preterm infants. *Am J Epidemiol* 1994; 139(11):S73.

Ramasethu, J. et al. Weight gain in exclusively breastfed preterm infants. *J Trop Pediatr* 1993; 39:152-59.

Raupp, R. et al. Biochemical evidence for the need of long-term mineral supplementation in an extremely low birth weight infant fed own mother's milk exclusively during the first 6 months of life. *Eur J Pediatr* 1990; 149(11): 806-08.

Robertson, A. and Bhatia, J. Feeding premature infants. *Clin Pediatr* 1993; n:36-44.

Rogan W. and Gladen, B. Breast-feeding and cognitive development. *Early Human Dev* 1993; 31:181-93.

Saunders, R. et al. Feeding preterm infants: schedule or demand? *JOGNN* 1991; 20(3):212-18.

Schanler, R. Suitability of human milk for the low-birthweight infant. *Clin Perinatol* 1995; 22(1):207-22.

Schanler, R. and Abrams, S. Postnatal attainment of intrauterine macromineral accretion rates in low birth weight infants fed fortified human milk. *J Pediatr* 1995; 126:441-47.

Schanler, R. and Hurst, N. Human milk for the hospitalized preterm infant. *Sem Perinatol* 1994; 18(6):476-84.

Schanler, R. et al. Bone mineralization outcomes in human milk-fed preterm infants. *Pediatr Res* 1992; 31(6):583-86.

Siddell, E. and Froman, R. A national survey of neonatal intensive-care units: criteria used to determine readiness for oral feedings. *JOGNN* 1994; 23(9):783-89.

Sloan, N. et al. Kangaroo mother method: randomised controlled trial of an alternative method of care for stabilised low-birthweight infants. *Lancet* 1994; 344(8925):182-85.

Prematurity

Stine, M. Breastfeeding the premature newborn: a protocol without bottles. *J Hum Lact* 1990; 6(4):167-70.

Uauy, R. et al. Effect of dietary omega-3 fatty acids in retinal function of very-low-birth-weight neonates. *Pediatr Res* 1990; 28:485-92.

Valentine, C. et al. Hindmilk improves weight gain in low birth weight infants fed human milk. *J Ped Gastro Nutr* 1994; 18:474-77.

Wahlberg, V. A retrospective comparative study using the kangaroo method as a complement to standard incubator care. *Eur J Pub Health* 1992; 2(1): 34-37.

Wahlberg, V. Alternative care for premature infants: the kangaroo method, advantages, risks, and ethical questions. *Neonatalogica* 1987; 4:362-67.

Walker, M. Breastfeeding the premature infant. *NAACOG Clin Issues Perinat Women Health Nurs* 1992; 3(4):620-33.

Walker, M. *Breastfeeding Premature Babies*. Unit 14. La Leche League International Lactation Consultant Series. Garden City Park, New York: Avery, 1990.

Whitelaw, A. et al. Skin-to-skin contact for very low birth weight infants and their mothers. *Arch Dis Child* 1988; 63:1377-80.

Whitelaw, A. Skin-to-skin contact in the care of very low birth weight babies. *Mat Child Health* 1986; 7:242-46.

Williams, A. Human milk and the preterm baby: mothers should breastfeed. *BMJ* 1993; 306:1428-29.

Woolridge, M. Analysis, classification, etiology of diagnosed low milk output. Presented at the International Lactation Consultant Association Conference. Scottsdale, Arizona USA, July 1995.

Wright, K. et al. New postnatal growth grids for very low birth weight infants. *Pediatrics* 1993; 91(5):922-26.

Ziemer, M. and George, C. Breastfeeding the low-birthweight infant. *Neo Network* 1990; 9(4)33-38.

13

Illness—Baby

WHEN THE BABY IS ILL
Colds and Ear Infections
Diarrhea
Neonatal Hypoglycemia
Vomiting

HOSPITALIZATION OF THE BREASTFEEDING BABY
General Considerations
When the Baby Is Seriously Ill
When the Baby Is Facing Surgery

WHEN THE BABY IS ILL

The mother may be worried and upset.

Depending on the severity of her baby's illness, the mother may be worried and upset. Ask her how she's doing to get a sense of how well she's coping. Then ask her what her baby's doctor has recommended.

If a sick baby is able to take anything by mouth, it should be his mother's milk.

Human milk provides the baby with perfect nutrition that is easily and quickly digested, as well as antibodies to help him fight his illness. And when he is able to breastfeed, the comfort a sick baby receives at his mother's breast is also an important benefit.

Colds and Ear Infections

Congestion may make breast-feeding difficult.

A sick baby can almost always cope more easily with breastfeeding than he can cope with taking liquid from a bottle (Lawrence, p. 438). Even so, if the baby has trouble breathing through his nose, it may be difficult for him to breastfeed. Offer the mother some suggestions for making breastfeeding more comfortable.

- Keep the baby in an upright position (by carrying him in arms or in a sling or a front or back baby carrier) or elevate his head for a short time before offering him the breast so that the mucus can drain.
- Clear the baby's nose with a soft rubber suction bulb.
- Breastfeed the baby in an upright position.
- Breastfeed the baby in a room where a cool-mist vaporizer is running.
- Offer short, frequent feedings.
- Call the baby's doctor for other suggestions.

Some babies refuse to breast-feed when they have an ear infection or are congested.

When a baby is congested or has an ear infection, he may refuse to breastfeed. A congested baby may find it impossible to breathe while nursing. The baby with an ear infection may find nursing painful, because the sucking increases the pressure in his ears.

If the baby refuses to nurse, suggest the mother offer him some of her expressed milk in a spoon or cup and keep offering the breast every hour or so. Assure her that when the baby is feeling better, he will want to nurse again.

As long as the baby is refusing to nurse, encourage the mother to express her milk as often as she was nursing and give it to her baby using one of the alternative feeding methods, such as a cup, spoon, or eyedropper. This will ensure the baby gets the fluids he needs and the mother's breasts do not become overly full.

Diarrhea

When the mother says her baby has diarrhea, ask her about her baby's symptoms to rule out the possibility that it is the normal stool of a breastfed baby.

Not all frequent and loose stools are diarrhea, but if the baby does have diarrhea, he will almost always benefit by continuing to breastfeed.

For the first few days after birth, a baby's bowel movements (called "meconium") are greenish black and sticky. Once the meconium has been eliminated, the stool of a baby who is receiving only mother's milk is loose and unformed—of pea-soup consistency—and yellow to yellow-green to tan in color. An occasional green stool is also normal. The odor should be mild and not unpleasant.

Bowel movements may be frequent. Most babies younger than six weeks old have at least two to five bowel movements every twenty-four hours. But some normal, healthy babies have more frequent bowel movements—perhaps one with every nursing. After six weeks of age, it is normal for some breastfed babies to have bowel movements as infrequently as once a week (these infrequent bowel movements are usually profuse). If a baby is gaining weight adequately, fewer than two bowel movements per day in a baby younger than six weeks is not a cause for concern.

Diarrhea is at least twelve stools a day that have an offensive odor.

Even though the antibodies in human milk offer a baby protection from many illnesses, breastfed babies sometimes have diarrhea. Diarrhea has the following symptoms:

- twelve to sixteen stools per day,
- watery stools with no substance, or
- stools with an offensive odor.

If there are no other signs of illness, consistently green, watery bowel movements may indicate a foremilk-hindmilk imbalance (also called "oversupply syndrome").

If the baby does not have a fever or other signs of illness and his stools are consistently green and watery, this could be a sign that the baby is being switched from one breast to the other too soon. Called "oversupply syndrome" (Woolridge 1988), this sometimes happens when a baby receives too much of the watery lactose-rich foremilk and not enough of the fatty, high-calorie hindmilk. Too much lactose is thought to stimulate the baby's digestive tract, which then moves the milk along too fast, causing the watery, green stools. Another symptom of oversupply syndrome is slow weight gain, even when the mother's milk supply is plentiful.

When oversupply syndrome is suspected, ask the mother if the baby nurses from both breasts at feedings, and if so, who decides when it's time to switch—mother or baby. If the mother has been switching the baby from the first breast to the second after a predetermined length of time, suggest she allow the baby to finish the first breast before offering the second. (When finished, the baby will either come off on his own or fall asleep.) Another option is to restrict the baby to one breast per feeding and see if this causes a change in the baby's stools.

When a mother who has been nursing her baby from both breasts begins nursing from one breast per feeding, she may feel fullness in the unused breast. If so, suggest she express just enough milk to soften the breast. Soon, however, her milk supply will adjust to her baby's demand and expressing milk will not be necessary.

Illness—Baby

If there are no other signs of illness, consistently green, watery stools or other types of diarrhea may also indicate the baby is sensitive to a food or a medication.

If the baby is not running a fever or showing any other signs of illness, consistently green, watery stools may also indicate a sensitivity to a food or medication the baby is receiving or something that the mother is ingesting that is passing into her milk.

Ruth Lawrence, MD, says in the fourth edition of her book, *Breastfeeding: A Guide for the Medical Profession,* "Occasionally an infant will have diarrhea or an intestinal upset because of something in the mother's diet. It is usually self-limited, and the best treatment is to continue to nurse at the breast. If the mother has been taking a laxative that is absorbed or has been eating laxative foods, such as fruits in excess, she should adjust her diet" (p. 434).

Also see "Sensitivity to a Food or Drug Mother or Baby Has Ingested" in the chapter "Fussy at the Breast and Breast Refusal."

The baby who has diarrhea will benefit from continuing to breastfeed, with rare exceptions.

For the breastfeeding baby with a mild case of diarrhea, special measures are usually not necessary. As always, if a baby is willing to take anything by mouth, it should be his mother's milk (Ruuska 1992). Because human milk is digested so rapidly, even the baby who is vomiting and has diarrhea will absorb some of the fluids and nutrients from the milk (Riordan and Auerbach, p. 487). Only in artificially fed babies is it sometimes beneficial to eliminate milk feedings during bouts of diarrhea (Brown 1991).

When diarrhea is moderate to severe, the baby's doctor might feel it is necessary to give the baby an oral electrolyte solution, such as Pedialyte, or oral rehydration therapy (ORT), as a supplement to breastfeeding. But this is rarely necessary in a breastfeeding baby. If the baby has lost sufficient fluid to be seriously dehydrated, the doctor may need to give fluids intravenously. Even under these circumstances, breastfeeding may continue.

If a baby younger than one month needs to be given an electrolyte oral solution, encourage the mother to give it using one of the alternative feeding methods, such as a cup, spoon, feeding syringe, or eyedropper, as giving it by bottle could cause nipple confusion. (See "The Use of Breast Pumps and Other Products.")

In extremely rare cases, diarrhea and vomiting may be symptoms of metabolic disorders that make human milk unsuitable for the baby. For example, a baby with a primary lactase deficiency is born without any lactase—the enzyme needed to break down lactose, or milk sugar. He will not be able to use the lactose in milk and must be fed a special lactose-free formula to survive. Another metabolic disorder, called galactosemia, means the baby is born without the liver enzyme that breaks down galactose and is unable to metabolize lactose, or milk sugar. (Also see "Galactosemia" in the chapter "The Baby with a Special Physical Need.") Galactosemia, if left untreated, causes vomiting, weight loss, cataracts, liver disease, and mental retardation. Both primary lactase deficiency and galactosemia generally become obvious within a baby's first weeks or months of life.

The danger of diarrhea is dehydration. It may reassure the mother to know its signs and how to prevent it.

Diarrhea in the breastfed baby usually clears up within a few days. But diarrhea occasionally causes more serious problems in babies and young children. The lining of the intestine becomes inflamed and irritated, and it leaks fluids and passes nutrients through the body too rapidly. The loss of water and salt may lead to dehydration and eventually to shock.

Suggest the mother watch for the following signs of dehydration and call her baby's doctor immediately if she suspects her baby is becoming dehydrated.

- listlessness and sleeping through feeding times,
- lethargy,
- weak cry,
- skin loses its resiliency (when pinched, it stays pinched looking),
- dry mouth, dry eyes,
- less than the usual amount of tears,
- minimal urine output (less than two wet diapers in twenty-four hours),
- the fontanel (or soft spot) on the baby's head is sunken or depressed,
- fever.

The best way to prevent dehydration is to make sure the baby gets plenty of fluids. The best way to do this for the ill breastfeeding baby is to offer frequent feedings.

Persistent diarrhea in toddlers (sometimes called "transient lactose intolerance") usually lasts two to four weeks and will pass without interrupting breastfeeding.

One of the most common causes of persistent diarrhea, especially in toddlers, is sometimes referred to as "transient (or temporary) lactose intolerance." In his book, SAFE AND HEALTHY (1989), William Sears, MD, uses what may be a more appropriate term, "nuisance diarrhea" (p. 112).

Nuisance diarrhea may be a reaction to:
- an intestinal illness,
- treatment with antibiotics,
- the process of changing from a milk diet to a diet of adult foods.

These could irritate the lining of the child's intestines and cause persistent diarrhea. With this temporary condition, time—not weaning—is the answer. Nuisance diarrhea will pass—usually within two to four weeks—and it is not necessary or helpful to wean. In fact, as with other types of diarrhea, continued breastfeeding has been found to shorten its course (Vonlanthen 1995; Mahalanabis 1991).

Another possible cause of nuisance diarrhea is overconsumption of fruit juice (AAP Committee on Nutrition 1991). In this case, cutting down or eliminating fruit juice should end the diarrhea. Too much fruit juice has been found to contribute to malnourishment in some toddlers by displacing other foods; research has shown that fruit juice should be limited to no more than four ounces (120 ml) per day for young children (Smith and Lifshitz 1994).

Lactose intolerance cannot be the cause of diarrhea in a child younger than four or five.

Lactose intolerance, which is common in adults in some human populations, is caused by a slow decrease in the body's production of lactase, the enzyme that breaks down lactose, or milk sugar. This occurs gradually, over a period of many years, and would not cause sudden diarrhea. Its symptoms do not appear before age four or five and usually not until young adulthood.

Temporary weaning for diarrhea is not beneficial to the baby.

It was once standard advice to wean the baby temporarily when he is vomiting or has diarrhea and instead give an oral electrolyte solution, sold under the brand name of Pedialyte in the US, or oral rehydration therapy (ORT). But studies have found that temporary weaning offers no benefits for the breastfeeding baby (Brown 1991). Human milk—unlike formula and other milk products that are best avoided while the baby has diarrhea—is a natural fluid that is easily and rapidly digested (Ewer 1994). In 1985, the American Academy of Pediatrics changed its guidelines by recommending the breastfeeding baby continue to nurse freely during acute cases of diarrhea and to alternate nursings with oral rehydration solution (Mauer 1985). Research has shown that continuing to breastfeed significantly reduces the duration and severity of acute diarrhea as compared to formula feeding (Haffejee 1990) and that discontinuing breastfeeding during a diarrheal illness doubles the risk of a baby becoming sicker and dying (Mahalanabis 1991; Clemens 1988).

Illness—Baby

In developing countries, where diarrhea can be a very serious health problem in infants and small children, studies have demonstrated that babies return to health faster when they keep nursing. One study of twenty-six children under the age of two years who had severe diarrhea showed that the children who kept breastfeeding while also receiving oral rehydration therapy (ORT) had fewer bowel movements and recovered more quickly than the children who were weaned from the breast and received only the oral electrolyte solution (Khin-Maung-U 1985).

If the baby's doctor advises temporary weaning, encourage the mother to share some references with her doctor.

If the mother does not want to wean, the first step is for her to let the doctor know that she would rather continue to breastfeed and ask if he or she would be willing to look over some references with her (Vonlanthen 1995). The American Academy of Pediatrics' guidelines support continued breastfeeding through diarrhea (Mauer 1985).

Also see "Helping the Mother Work with Her Doctor" in "Giving Effective Breastfeeding Help." If her doctor is not supportive, the mother has the option of getting a second opinion.

Neonatal Hypoglycemia

Hypoglycemia, or low blood sugar, can occur with or without symptoms in the newborn and is usually due to delayed or inadequate feeding.

Hypoglycemia—or low blood sugar—occurs when the body's rate of use of glucose is greater than the rate of glucose production and the plasma glucose concentration falls (Rudolph 1982). A baby with mild to moderate hypoglycemia may be without symptoms. As hypoglycemia increases in severity, symptoms may include: lethargy, limpness, sweating, jitteriness, tremors, refusal to eat, feeding difficulties, rapid respiration, and pallor. Hypoglycemia with symptoms is usually due to delayed or inadequate feeding, but there are inherited abnormalities of glucose metabolism whose first symptom may be high blood sugar. Some breastfed infants with these inherited abnormalities only develop symptoms after they stop breastfeeding. If hypoglycemia persists, further investigation by the physician is indicated. Hypoglycemia is of concern because moderate to severe hypoglycemia has been associated with reduced mental and motor development scores at 18 months (Lucas 1988).

Risk factors in the mother and/or baby can predispose a baby to hypoglycemia.	A newborn is at risk for hypoglycemia if feedings are delayed or the baby becomes chilled. Other risk factors in the baby include:

A newborn is at risk for hypoglycemia if feedings are delayed or the baby becomes chilled. Other risk factors in the baby include:

- prematurity or postmaturity,
- small- or large-for-gestational age,
- oxygen deprivation,
- meconium staining,
- infection,
- a central nervous system abnormality, and
- a congenital glucose metabolic problem.

Risk factors in the mother that can increase her baby's chances of becoming hypoglycemic include:

- a long, difficult labor,
- toxemia,
- diabetes,
- pregnancy-induced hypertension,
- drug ingestion, and
- a glucose IV used during labor and delivery (Sexson 1984).

A standard definiton of hypoglycemia has not yet been agreed upon.

The definition of hypoglycemia varies among physicians and from place to place. Although a serum/plasma glucose concentration of less than 40 mg/dl or 2.2 mmol/L (whole blood glucose level lower than 35 mg/dl or 1.9 mmol/L) is the guideline used by some, it has been questioned, because research has found that by this standard more than 20% of well term newborns would be considered hypoglycemic (Sexson 1984). Also, research has shown that term infants, particularly when breastfed, can use a variety of body fuels to compensate for initially lower blood glucose levels (Hawdon 1994; Hawdon 1992). Some researchers recommend that hypoglycemia be defined as a serum glucose concentration of less than 30 mg/dl or 1.7 mmol/L during the first day and less than 40 mg/dl or 2.2 mmol/L during the second day, particularly if there are no symptoms (Heck and Erenberg 1987).

Some apply a different standard to premature or small-for-gestational-age babies. Gentz (1969) uses whole blood concentrations of 20 mg/dl or 1.1 mmol/L as the guideline, while Hawdon (1994) supports 46.8 mg/dl or 2.6 mmol/L as the lower limit because premature or small-for-gestational-age infants are less able to compensate for low blood sugar.

There are disadvantages to giving glucose water feedings to prevent or treat hypoglycemia. In most cases, frequent nursing (or feedings of human milk) is all that is needed.

For most babies at risk for hypoglycemia, including premature babies (Gentz 1969; Smallpeice and Davies 1964), at least ten to twelve feedings per day from birth stabilizes blood glucose levels (Wang 1994).

Giving glucose water instead of nursing causes a sudden rise in blood glucose levels and then a sudden drop. Glucose water feedings in the early days have also been found to cause a greater early weight loss and increase infant bilirubin levels (Glover and Sandilands 1990; Kuhr and Paneth 1982; Nicoll 1982). Colostrum has 6.4% milk sugar and in addition contains fat, protein, and calories, which are also important for infant well-being. In adults, treatment for hypoglycemia is small, frequent high-protein meals, which is what a baby receives when he nurses often from birth.

Treatment of hypoglycemia should be considered only if blood tests indicate a need. Giving supplements with alternative feeding methods may help avoid breastfeeding problems.

In order to prevent hypoglycemia, some hospitals routinely give glucose water supplements to all babies whose birth weight falls outside a designated weight range. However, unless a blood test indicates that the baby's blood-sugar level is below normal, glucose water supplements should not be considered.

If a blood test indicates that glucose water is needed, artificial nipples, which have been found to cause breastfeeding problems in some babies in the early weeks (Newman 1990), can be avoided by feeding the baby with one of the alternative feeding methods, such as cup, eyedropper, spoon, feeding syringe, or tube feeding device (see "The Use of Breast Pumps and Other Products").

Vomiting

When the mother says her baby is vomiting, ask her about her baby's symptoms to rule out the possibility that his "vomiting" is the spitting up that many normal, healthy babies do after nursing.

For some babies, it is not unusual to spit up after a nursing. In cases of spitting up, the baby would show no other signs of illness.

Even if the baby seems to be spitting up a lot of milk, he may be doing fine. If the mother is worried, suggest she keep track of the number of wet diapers and bowel movements her baby has in a twenty-four hour period. If he has six to eight wet cloth diapers (five to six disposable diapers) and at least two bowel movements (fewer is normal if the baby is older than six weeks), she can feel confident that her baby is getting enough. Weight gain is another reliable indicator. If the baby is gaining at least four ounces (113 grams) a week, the mother can be sure that he is getting enough to eat even if he spits up a lot. For more information, see "Spitting Up" in the chapter "Breastfeeding Basics."

Testing or treatment of gastro-esophageal reflux should be considered only if spitting up is accompanied by poor weight gain, weight loss, severe choking, or lung disease.

Gastroesophageal reflux, the flowing back of the stomach's contents into the esophagus, is a potentially serious health problem for some individuals. However, specialists acknowlege that spitting up is normal for many babies during the first year of life, is not necessarily a sign of later reflux problems, and usually stops spontaneously as the baby matures (Sutphen 1990).

Testing or treatment for reflux in the nursing baby who is spitting up may interfere with breastfeeding and result in unnecessary medical intervention. Offering solids to "thicken feeds" in order to prevent spitting up in the baby

Illness—Baby

younger than about six months interferes with breastfeeding by replacing human milk in the baby's diet and decreasing the mother's milk supply. Too early introduction of solids may also endanger the baby by making it possible for regurgitated solids, which are irritating to the body's tissues, to be aspirated into the baby's lungs. According to experts on reflux, medical tests for reflux and treatment with medication are not indicated in the baby younger than one year unless, in addition to spitting up, the baby is refusing to nurse, gaining poorly or losing weight, or has episodes of gagging or severe choking or signs of lung disease (Sutphen 1990).

Management suggestions include upright positioning of the baby during and after feedings, thorough burping, and small frequent feedings.

Switching from breastfeeding to formula, which is sometimes suggested for the baby suspected of having reflux, may worsen rather than improve a baby's reflux symptoms. Research has found that breastfed babies tend to have fewer episodes of reflux than babies on formula (Heacock 1992). This may be in part because one cause of reflux is delayed emptying of the stomach and human milk has been found to empty from the stomach twice as quickly as formula (Ewer 1994).

Regular projectile vomiting in a newborn could be a sign of pyloric stenosis.

A baby who regularly spits up after feedings should be checked by his doctor to rule out pyloric stenosis, a narrowing of the muscular wall of the tube that passes from the stomach into the intestines. With pyloric stenosis, the milk does not pass easily from the baby's stomach into his intestines and the baby does not get enough nourishment.

The symptoms of pyloric stenosis usually begin when the baby is between two and eight weeks of age. The first sign may be regular spitting up or projectile vomiting, when the baby's stomach muscles force the milk up his throat and shoot it out of his mouth, sometimes as far as several feet away. At first this may happen only occasionally, but in time it occurs more and more often until the baby is projectile vomiting after every feeding. It is unlikely that a baby has pyloric stenosis if he is gaining well.

A baby who has pyloric stenosis may need simple surgery (called a pyloromyotomy) after his fluid balance has been restored. If the procedure is uncomplicated, the baby can begin breastfeeding again as soon as six to eight hours afterwards (Lawrence, p. 460), although the mother may need to limit the baby to one breast per feeding for a short time (Riordan and Auerbach, p. 494).

Occasional projectile vomiting does not mean a baby has pyloric stenosis, but if it occurs at least once a day, suggest the mother have the baby checked by his doctor.

In rare cases, vomiting may be a symptom of a metabolic disorder that precludes breastfeeding.

In extremely rare cases, vomiting or diarrhea may be symptoms of metabolic disorders that make human milk unsuitable for the baby. For example, a baby with a primary lactase deficiency is born without any lactase—the enzyme needed to break down lactose, or milk sugar. He will not be able to use the lactose in milk and must be fed a special lactose-free formula to survive. Another metabolic disorder, called galactosemia, means the baby is born without the liver enzyme that breaks down galactose and is unable to metabolize lactose, or milk sugar. (See "Galactosemia" in the chapter "The Baby with Special Needs.") Galactosemia, if left untreated, causes vomiting, weight loss, cataracts, and mental retardation. Both primary lactase deficiency and galactosemia, which are rare, would become obvious within a baby's first weeks or months of life. If a baby has been developing normally and gaining well during his first few months, he is not likely to have either of these conditions.

If there are no other signs of illness, vomiting or spitting up may be an indication that the baby is sensitive to a food or a medication.

If the baby is not showing other signs of illness, vomiting may indicate that the baby is sensitive to a food or medication he's receiving, either directly or through his mother's milk. See "Sensitivity to a Food or Drug Mother or Baby Has Ingested" in the chapter "Fussy at the Breast and Breast Refusal."

If the baby is ill and vomiting, he will benefit from continuing to breastfeed.

If the baby can take anything by mouth, it should be his mother's milk. Because human milk is digested rapidly, even the baby who is vomiting will absorb some of the nutrients and fluid from the milk before it comes up. Other foods that are commonly suggested, such as sodas or gelatin water, offer little nourishment and none of human milk's antibodies.

If the sick baby vomits after every nursing, suggest the mother try expressing some milk and offering her baby a less full breast. Offering ice chips is another alternative.

If the baby's stomach is very upset and the baby vomits after every nursing, suggest to the mother that she try expressing most of her milk and offering the baby a less full breast on which he can nurse for comfort. By decreasing the amount the baby gets at each nursing—but nursing more often—the baby will be less likely to throw it all up immediately. After a few hours of tolerating these smaller feedings, the baby may be able to handle larger feedings again.

If the baby is six months or older, suggest the mother try offering ice chips or water from a spoon. The advantage of ice is that it goes down slowly and is distracting as well, so that the baby's stomach stays emptier for longer. But if the baby is insistent on nursing, the mother can continue to nurse him on the less full breast.

The danger of vomiting is dehydration. It may reassure the mother to know its signs and how to prevent it.

Vomiting in the breastfed baby usually clears up within a few days. But if it is severe or if it continues, the loss of water and salt can lead to dehydration, which is a serious problem. Suggest the mother watch for the following signs of dehydration and contact her baby's doctor immediately if she suspects her baby is becoming dehydrated:

- listlessness and sleeping through feeding times,
- lethargy,

- weak cry,
- skin loses its resiliency (when pinched, it stays pinched looking),
- dry mouth, dry eyes,
- less than the usual amount of tears,
- minimal urine output (less than two wet diapers in twenty-four hours),
- the fontanel (or soft spot) on the baby's head is sunken or depressed,
- fever.

The best way to prevent dehydration is to make sure the baby gets plenty of fluids, and the best way to do this for a breastfeeding baby is to offer short, frequent feedings.

Temporary weaning is not beneficial to the baby.

When a baby is ill and vomiting, some doctors routinely advise that the baby be temporarily weaned from the breast and instead be given an electrolyte oral solution, such as Pedialyte or oral rehydration therapy (ORT). If the baby were formula-fed, this would be appropriate advice, but temporary weaning offers no benefits for the breastfed baby. Human milk—unlike formula and other milk products that are best avoided while baby is vomiting—is a natural fluid that is easily and rapidly digested (Ewer 1994).

Temporary weaning can also make life miserable for both mother and baby. When the familiar solace of nursing is abruptly taken away from a sick baby, he becomes frustrated and upset. Meanwhile the mother's breasts continue to produce milk and become fuller and fuller. So in addition to caring for a sick and possibly inconsolable baby, the mother must devote extra time and effort to expressing her milk to keep from becoming overly full.

If the baby's doctor advises temporary weaning, encourage the mother to check the literature with her doctor.

If the mother does not want to wean, the first step is to let the doctor know that she would rather continue to breastfeed and to ask the doctor if he or she would be willing to look at some references. Both Riordan and Auerbach's *Breastfeeding and Human Lactation,* (pp. 486-88) and Ruth Lawrence's *Breastfeeding: A Guide for the Medical Profession,* (p. 371) support continuing to breastfeed through most cases of vomiting. Also see "Helping the Mother Work with Her Doctor" in "Giving Effective Breastfeeding Help." If her doctor is not supportive, the mother has the option of getting a second opinion.

Illness—Baby

HOSPITALIZATION OF THE BREASTFEEDING BABY

General Considerations

A baby may remain hospitalized after birth or return to the hospital with complications, a serious illness, or an injury.

The mother may be frightened and upset.

No matter what the circumstances, this will be an emotionally trying time for the mother. She may feel vulnerable and guilty. Her self-esteem may be badly shaken. Listen carefully to the mother and support her in her choices, whatever they may be.

Ask the mother about her circumstances.

It will be helpful to know:

- the age of her baby,
- whether she has other children and their ages,
- why the baby has been hospitalized,
- if she knows how long the baby will be in the hospital.

Find out how much access the mother has to her baby and the doctor's orders concerning breastfeeding.

What has the baby's doctor said about breastfeeding? If the baby cannot take anything by mouth, the mother can still express and store her milk for the time when her baby is ready to be fed. This will not only provide milk for her baby, but allow the mother to keep up her milk supply and keep her breasts from becoming overly full.

If the baby can take anything by mouth, human milk is best because it is easily and quickly digested. A natural fluid, it also confers immunities to illness that can help a sick baby get well faster.

If the mother wants to breastfeed her baby or provide her expressed milk and the baby's doctor discourages her from doing so, encourage her to express her wishes and work with the doctor to find a mutually acceptable solution. See "Helping the Mother Work with Her Doctor" in "Giving Effective Breastfeeding Help." The mother has the option of getting a second opinion or changing doctors if she feels her doctor is unsupportive.

How far away is the baby's hospital? If the baby is hospitalized far from home—in a high-risk center, for instance—to make it easier for her to spend time with him suggest the mother check into the possibility of having him transferred to a hospital closer to home after his condition has stabilized.

What is the hospital's rooming-in policy? Depending upon the baby's condition, the hospital's policy, and her other responsibilities, the mother may be able to stay with her baby day and night and breastfeed him without restrictions. Many hospitals allow parents to stay with their children and help care for them while they are hospitalized. If twenty-four-hour rooming-in is not the hospital's usual policy but the mother makes special arrangements for it, suggest the mother ask the baby's doctor to tell the nursing staff and write on the hospital orders that the parents' free access to the baby is part of his recommended care.

Staying with baby day and night might not be feasible if the mother has other children at home or other responsibilities. Even if the mother cannot be with her baby twenty-four hours a day, she may still be able to visit him regularly, breastfeed him during her visits, and provide her milk for him when she is not there to nurse him.

If the mother can't be with her baby, discuss how she can express milk for her baby and keep up her milk supply.

If the mother can't stay with her baby at the hospital full-time and breastfeed him, ask her if she wants to provide her milk for him for the times she can't be there. If she does, offer to brainstorm with her about how she might manage the practical details. Go through a typical day with her and help her plan times and places that she can express her milk. Discuss what she might need to know about expressing her milk. (See the chapter "Expression and Storage of Human Milk.")

If the mother prefers that her baby receive formula when she can't be with him to breastfeed, be sure she knows:

1. If she was fully breastfeeding before the baby's hospitalization, she will probably need to express at least some milk to keep from becoming overly full. Even though she will not be with her baby, her breasts will continue to produce milk, and if it is not removed, she may be at risk for engorgement or mastitis.

2. If her baby will be in the hospital for more than a few days and she does not express regularly, her milk supply will decrease. If she wants to resume breastfeeding once her baby is released, expressing at least 5 times a day will keep her milk supply up to the level of her baby's need. If she decides not to express her milk, it will still be possible to increase her milk supply later, once her baby is back home and nursing again.

Simplified guidelines for the collection, storage, and handling of human milk for the hospitalized baby have been adopted by many hospitals.

Many of the procedures recommended in the past for mothers collecting and storing their milk for their hospitalized babies have been found to be either ineffective at reducing bacterial contamination or have been found to significantly reduce the immunological protection the baby receives from mother's milk. Examples of these unnecessary procedures include breast cleansing and nipple lubrication before pumping, sterilizing pump parts after each use, discarding the first milk expressed, screening each mother's milk for bacteria, and pasteurizing the milk. Some of these procedures, while unnecessary for the mother expressing milk for her own baby, may be necessary for donor milk provided by other women.

To simplify and standardize hospital guidelines, *Recommendations for Collection, Storage, and Handling of a Mother's Milk for Her Own Infant in the Hospital Setting* was published in 1993 by the Human Milk Banking Association of North America and has been adopted by many hospitals. These guidelines recommend that:

- Mothers wash their hands thoroughly before expressing their milk.
- A hospital-grade, piston-driven electric breast pump be used.
- Each mother use her own collection kit (the bottles and tubing that attach to the pump).
- All parts of the collection kit that touch the milk be cleaned after each use with hot soapy water and thoroughly rinsed then placed on a clean paper towel, covered with another clean paper towel, and allowed to air dry.
- The expressed milk be labeled with the date and time, the baby's name, the baby's hospital identification number, and the baby's illness and use of medications.
- The milk from each pumping be kept in its own container and not mixed with milk from other pumpings.
- Milk be stored in feeding-sized portions.
- Storage containers be made of glass, polycarbonate (clear, hard plastic) or polypropylene (cloudy, hard plastic) and have solid lids that provide an airtight seal.

For more information on these guidelines and the studies that support them, contact The Human Milk Banking Association of North America, P.O. Box 370464, West Hartford CT 06137-0464 USA.

Illness—Baby

These differ from the guidelines recommended for use at home by mothers of healthy, full-term babies. See the chapter "Expression and Storage of Human Milk."

Some mothers notice a drop in milk supply or a delayed or inhibited let-down reflex when they are under unusual stress.

The mother in a stressful situation may say that she has "lost her milk." Explain that it is not unusual for breastfeeding mothers to notice a temporary drop in their milk supply or a delayed or inhibited let-down, or milk-ejection, reflex when they are under great stress. Encourage the mother to try to relax using the techniques she learned in her childbirth education classes and to keep breastfeeding or expressing. Assure her that her milk supply or let-down will return to normal. (See "Delayed or Inhibited Let-Down" in the chapter "Breastfeeding Basics.")

Offer to give the mother suggestions for making the hospital stay easier.

Small improvements can sometimes make a difficult situation easier. The following are some ideas that may make a baby's hospital stay more pleasant for the mother.

Accommodations
- If the baby is in a semi-private room, request the bed farthest from the door so the mother and baby will get more privacy and less traffic.
- If family finances allow, a private room would mean fewer interruptions.

Comfort measures for mother
- If the mother is spending large amounts of time at the hospital, suggest she bring drinks and nutritious snacks to help sustain her and keep up her stamina. She can also ask the nurses for extra cups and pitchers of water. Since she is a food source for her baby, she may be eligible for hospital meals.
- The mother can bring extra pillows from home to aid in positioning the baby at the breast and to increase her own comfort.
- By wearing comfortable clothes in which she can nurse discreetly, the mother may feel less inhibited when hospital employees enter her baby's room. Comfortable shoes can also help her feel more at ease.

Medical paraphernalia and procedures
- If the baby is on an IV, the mother can ask the nurses to connect extra tubing to the IV to allow for more freedom of movement when the baby nurses.
- The mother can get into an oxygen tent with her baby to nurse.
- If the baby must undergo an uncomfortable medical procedure, the mother may be able to get permission to nurse her baby before the procedure, stay with him during the procedure, and nurse him immediately afterwards.

When the Baby Is Seriously Ill

Breastfeeding can provide needed nutrition, immunities, and comfort.

Illness can sometimes change a baby's nursing pattern.

Human milk offers several important benefits for the seriously ill baby: it is easy to digest, provides immunities to help fight sickness, and offers a familiar taste in unfamiliar surroundings. If the baby is well enough to breastfeed, the sucking and closeness will be a source of comfort as well.

Some babies nurse more frequently—even constantly—when they are very sick. Other babies, especially if they are lethargic from a low-grade infection or other illness, may become less interested in nursing. If a baby loses interest in nursing, the mother may need to express her milk for her own comfort, to keep up her milk supply, and to provide milk for her baby. A lethargic baby can be given his mother's milk in other ways, such as tube feeding, if he is too weak to suck.

When the Baby Is Facing Surgery

When a baby is facing surgery, encourage the mother to ask how close to surgery she can breast-feed her baby and how soon afterwards she will be able to see her baby and breastfeed him.

Although some doctors require that a patient be given nothing by mouth ("NPO") for eight hours before surgery, these guidelines are in the process of changing. Recent studies indicate that a more reasonable fasting time before surgery is six hours for formula (Spear 1992), three hours for human milk, and two hours for clear liquids (Litman 1994; Schreiner 1994). The mother should discuss the NPO orders with the surgeon and anesthesiologist beforehand; many are willing to accommodate the needs of the breastfeeding baby. The mother may also want to plan strategies for comforting and distracting the baby in the hours immediately before surgery when breastfeeding is restricted.

If the mother asks in advance, it may be possible for her to be with her baby after surgery and breastfeed him in the recovery room. Many mothers and babies find nursing comforting during this stressful time.

Expressing her milk before a scheduled surgery can help a mother store extra milk for her baby in case the stress decreases her milk supply.

Some mothers find that stress temporarily affects their milk supply or their let-down, or milk-ejection, reflex, making less milk available during breastfeeding and expressing. If the mother knows several days in advance when her baby's surgery is scheduled, she may wish to express and store extra milk for her baby in case she has trouble expressing during the stressful time before and after her baby's surgery.

Resources for Parents

Children in Hospitals
31 Wilshire Park
Needham, MA 02192 USA

Gastroesophageal Reflux

PAGER Association
PO Box 1153
Germantown MD 20875-1153 USA
Phone: 301-601-9541

Publications for Parents

La Leche League International. THE WOMANLY ART OF BREASTFEEDING, 35th Anniversary ed. Schaumburg, Illinois, 1991, pp. 326-28.

Rooney, K. *Breastfeeding the Chronically Ill Child*. Schaumburg, Illinois: La Leche League International, 1991. Publication No. 51.

Sears, W. Safe And Healthy. Franklin Park, Illinois: La Leche League International, 1989.

Thompson, J. *Persistent Diarrhea: Could It Be Lactose Intolerance?* Schaumburg, Illinois: La Leche League International, 1992. Publication No. 31.

Colds and Ear Infections

Lawrence, R. *Breastfeeding: A Guide for the Medical Profession*, 4th ed. St. Louis: Mosby, 1994, pp. 438-39, 462-63.

Riordan, J. and Auerbach, K. *Breastfeeding and Human Lactation*, Boston and London: Jones and Bartlett, 1993, pp. 488-89.

Diarrhea

American Academy of Pediatrics Committee on Nutrition. The use of fruit juice in the diets of young children. *AAP News* 1991; 7:11.

Brown, K. Dietary management of acute childhood diarrhea: optimal timing of feeding and appropriate use of milks and mixed diets. *J Pediatr* 1991; 118(4)pt 2:S92-S98.

Brown, K. and Lake, A. Appropriate use of human and non-human milk for the dietary management of children with diarrhoea. *J Diarrhoeal Dis Res* 1991; 9(3):168-85.

Clemens, J. et al. Discontinuation of breastfeeding during episodes of diarrhoea in rural Bangladeshi children. *Trans Royal Soc Trop Med Hygiene* 1988; 82:779-83.

Ewer, A. et al. Gastric emptying in preterm infants. *Arch Dis Child* 1994; 71:F24-F27.

Haffejee, J. Cow's milk-based formula, human milk, and soya feeds in acute infantile diarrhea: a therapeutic trial. *J Ped Gastro Nutr* 1990; 10:193-98.

Khin-Maung-U. et al. Effect on clinical outcome of breastfeeding during acute diarrhea. *BMJ* 1985; 290:587-89.

Lawrence, R. *Breastfeeding: A Guide for the Medical Profession*, 4th ed. St. Louis: Mosby, 1994, pp. 371 and 434-38.

Mahalanabis, D. et al. Prognostic indicators and risk factors for increased duration of acute diarrhoea and for persistent diarrhoea in children. *Int J Epidemiol* 1991; 20:1064-72.

Mauer, A. et al. American Academy of Pediatrics Committee on Nutrition: Use of oral fluid therapy and post-treatment feeding following enteritis in children in a developed country. *Pediatrics* 1985; 75:358-61.

References

Illness—Baby

Riordan, J. and Auerbach, K. *Breastfeeding and Human Lactation,* Boston and London: Jones and Bartlett, 1993, pp. 486-88.

Ruuska, T. Occurrence of acute diarrhea in atopic and nonatopic infants: the role of prolonged breastfeeding. *J Ped Gastro Nutr* 1992; 14:27-33.

Sachdev, H. et al. Does breastfeeding influence mortality in children hospitalized with diarrhoea? *J Trop Pediatr* 1991; 37:275-79.

Sears, W. SAFE AND HEALTHY, Franklin Park, Illinois: La Leche League International, 1989, p. 112.

Smith, M. and Lifshitz, F. Excess fruit juice consumption as a contributing factor in nonorganic failure to thrive. *Pediatrics* 1994; 93(2):438-43.

Vonlanthen, M. Management of diarrhea: to continue to breastfeed or not? BREAST-FEEDING ABSTRACTS 1995; 14:26-27.

Woolridge, M. and Fisher, C. Colic, "overfeeding," and symptoms of lactose malabsorption in the breastfed baby: a possible artifact of feed management? *Lancet* 1988; II(8605):382-84

Neonatal Hypoglycemia

American Academy of Pediatrics Committee on Fetus and Newborn. Routine evaluation of blood pressure, hematocrit, and glucose in newborns. *Pediatrics* 1993; 92(3): 474-76.

Gentz, J. et al. On the diagnosis of symptomatic neonatal hypoglycemia. *Acta Paediatr Scand* 1969; 58:449-59.

Glover, J. and Sandilands, M. Supplementation of breastfeeding infants and weight loss in hospital. *J Hum Lact* 1990; 6:163-66.

Hawdon, J. et al. Prevention and management of neonatal hypoglycaemia. *Arch Dis Child* 1994; 70:F60-F65.

Hawdon, J. et al. Patterns of metabolic adaptation for preterm and term infants in the first neonatal week. *Arch Dis Child* 1992; 67:357-65.

Heck, I. and Erenberg, A. Serum glucose levels in term neonates during the first 48 hours of life. *J Pediatr* 1987; 110:119-22.

Kuhr, M. and Paneth, N. Feeding practices and early neonatal jaundice. *J Ped Gastro Nutr* 1982; 1(4):485-88.

Lucas A. et al. Adverse neurodevelopmental outcome of moderate neonatal hypoglycaemia. *BMJ* 1988; 297:1304-08.

Newman, J. Breastfeeding problems associated with the early introduction of bottles and pacifiers. *J Hum Lact* 1990; 6(2):59-63

Nicoll, A. et al. Supplementary feeding and jaundice in newborns. *Acta Paediatr Scand* 1982; 71:759-61.

Rudolph, A. et al. "Hypoglycemia" in *Pediatrics,* 17th ed., pp. 283-88. Norwalk, Connecticut: Appleton-Century-Crofts, 1982.

Sexson, W. Incidence of neonatal hypoglycemia: a matter of definition. *J Pediatr* 1984; 105:149-50.

Smallpeice, V. and Davies, P. Immediate feeding of premature infants with undiluted breastmilk. Lancet 1964; 2:1349-52.

Wang, Y. et al. Preliminary study on the blood glucose level in the exclusively breastfed newborn. *J Trop Pediatr* 1994; 40:187-88.

Vomiting

Ewer, A. et al. Gastric emptying in preterm infants. *Arch Dis Child* 1994; 71:F24-F27.

Heacock, H. et al. Influence of breast versus formula milk on physiological gastroesophageal reflux in healthy, newborn infants. *J Ped Gastro Nutr* 1992; 14:41-46.

Lawrence, R. *Breastfeeding: A Guide for the Medical Profession,* 4th ed. St. Louis: Mosby, 1994, pp. 371, 459-60.

Riordan, J. and Auerbach, K. *Breastfeeding and Human Lactation,* Boston and London: Jones and Bartlett, 1993, pp. 486-88 and 494.

Illness—Baby

Sutphen, J. Pediatric gastroesophageal reflux disease. *Gastro Clin N Amer* 1990; 19(3):617-29.

Hospitalization of the Breastfeeding Baby

Brewster, D. *You Can Breastfeed Your Baby...Even in Special Situations.* Emmaus, Pennsylvania: Rodale Press, 1979, pp. 253-63.

The Human Milk Banking Association of North America. *Recommendations for Collection, Storage, and Handling of a Mother's Milk for Her Own Infant in the Hospital Setting,* West Hartford, CT USA, 1993.

Lawrence, R. *Breastfeeding: A Guide for the Medical Profession,* 4th ed. St. Louis: Mosby, 1994, pp. 463-64.

Litman, R. et al. Gastric volume and pH in infants fed clear liquids and breast milk prior to surgery. *Anesth Analg* 1994; 79:482-85.

Nicholson, S. and Schreiner, M. Feed the babies. Breastfeeding Abstracts 1995; 15(1):3-4

Riordan, J. and Auerbach, K. *Breastfeeding and Human Lactation,* Boston and London: Jones and Bartlett, 1993, pp. 505-08.

Schreiner, M. Ingestion of liquids compared with preoperative fasting in pediatric outpatients. *Anesthesiology* 1990; 72(4):593-97.

Schreiner, M. Preoperative and postoperative fasting in children. *Ped Clinics N Amer* 1994; 4(1):111-20

Spear, R. Anesthesia for premature and term infants: perioperative implications. *J Pediatr* 1992; 120(2 pt 1):165-75.

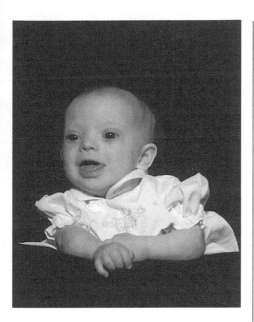

14

The Baby with Special Needs

THE MOTHER'S FEELINGS

CARDIAC PROBLEMS

CLEFT LIP AND/OR PALATE

CYSTIC FIBROSIS

DOWN SYNDROME

GALACTOSEMIA

THE NEUROLOGICALLY IMPAIRED BABY

PKU

THE MOTHER'S FEELINGS

The mother of a baby with special needs may feel overwhelmed and upset. It is normal for the mother to feel conflicting emotions and to have difficulty remembering information.

The parents of a baby with special needs may be coping with feelings of disappointment, anger, helplessness, and guilt. They may need to go through a grieving process of giving up the baby they imagined in order to accept the baby in their arms.

When offering information and options, keep in mind that the mother's strong feelings may make it difficult for her to remember information. It may need to be repeated several times before she can use it. Written information that the mother can refer to may be more helpful.

If breastfeeding is not going well, the mother may take it personally, blaming herself and believing that the difficulties reflect on her own inability to care for her special child. Or she may blame her child's physical problem for normal infant behavior, such as fussiness. When talking to the mother:

- Listen to and acknowledge the mother's feelings. This will help her work through her emotions so that she can better cope with her situation and make necessary decisions.
- Encourage the mother to take it one day at a time, paying close attention to her baby's cues as she tries to find ways that work for them.
- Focus on the normal aspects of the baby. Ask who the baby looks like, how he responds to his parents, and other questions you might ask any new parent. Focusing on the normal can help the mother see her child as a baby first and a baby with a physical problem second.
- If one exists, refer her to a support group for parents of children like hers.

CARDIAC PROBLEMS

The mother of a baby with cardiac problems may feel overwhelmed and have difficulty remembering information.

See the previous section, "The Mother's Feelings."

The baby with cardiac problems tends to gain weight slowly.

Babies with cardiac problems usually gain weight slowly, regardless of how they are fed, because they must breathe more often and their hearts must pump faster to maintain adequate oxygen and circulation. An adequate weight gain is considered to be four ounces (113 grams) a week, although it is not unusual for a baby with cardiac problems to gain more slowly, even if he is receiving enough nourishment.

Research has found that breastfeeding is less stressful and more energy-efficient than bottle-feeding. Babies with cardiac problems who are breastfed are discharged from the hospital sooner and gain weight more readily than babies who are artificially fed.

Although it was once thought that breastfeeding takes more energy than bottle-feeding, research on premature babies (Meier 1988) and babies with congenital heart disease (Marino 1995) indicates that the opposite is true: bottle-feeding is more physically stressful than breastfeeding. Differences between the composition of human milk and formula may also affect the amount of energy expended. One study of healthy two-day-old babies found that the breastfed newborns had more energy-efficient heart rhythms, lower heart rates, and expended less energy than the artificially fed babies, even though the breastfed babies spent less time sleeping than their bottle-fed counterparts (Zeskind 1992). The researchers suggested that formula may have a sedating effect that diminishes behavioral organization.

A study of babies with congenital heart disease (Combs and Marino 1993) found significant differences between those who were breastfed and those who were not. In this study, the researchers considered a baby to be breastfed if he received any mother's milk at all. Even though the breastfed babies may have received very little human milk, the differences in the two groups were significant: the breastfed babies had shorter hospital stays and gained weight more readily than the exclusively formula-fed babies. The researchers theorized that the slower weight gain of the artificially fed babies was a result of decreases in tissue oxygen levels due to breathing interruptions associated with bottle-feeding. The severity of a baby's cardiac defect was found to be unrelated to his ability to breastfeed.

Some babies with cardiac problems can be breastfed exclusively; others may need to be supplemented. If supplements are needed, suggest the mother discuss with her baby's doctor the possibility of using expressed hindmilk.

Some babies with heart problems can breastfeed exclusively. The baby who does not gain well on human milk alone may need a nutrient-dense supplement. Extra calories and nutrients are necessary for some babies to gain weight while maintaining their faster heart and breathing rates, and gaining weight may mean gaining strength as well.

If the baby needs a supplement in addition to breastfeeding, suggest the mother discuss with her baby's doctor the possibility of using her hindmilk, the high-calorie milk at the end of a feeding. If the baby is not able to suck effectively enough or long enough to obtain much hindmilk, additional hindmilk expressed by the mother after feedings can provide the baby with more calories without exposing him to the risks of artificial feeding. (See the chapter "Expression and Storage of Human Milk.")

The mother and her baby's doctor need to discuss how often and how much supplement needs to be given. Depending on the baby's weight gain and the effectiveness of his suck, the mother may give the baby the supplement after every feeding, after every other feeding, or two or three times a day. A nursing supplementer used at the breast may provide the baby with more calories for his sucking efforts. If the mother does not want to use a nursing supplementer at the breast, encourage her to use it on a finger or give the supplement with a cup, spoon, eyedropper, or feeding syringe. (See "The Use of Breast Pumps and Other Products.") Supplements given by bottle may cause nipple confusion in a baby younger than a month.

Special Needs—Baby

If supplementing causes the mother to question the value of her milk or her milk supply, assure her that these are not the problem.

The need for a supplement causes some mothers to question the value of their milk, their milk supply, even their adequacy as mothers. Assure the mother that there is nothing wrong with her, her milk, or her milk supply and that her milk is the best for her baby's health and development.

Increasing the volume of milk the baby receives may not be the answer when cardiac problems exist, because it may require too great a volume of human milk or regular formula to provide the extra nutrients the baby needs.

Some babies with cardiac problems have a weak or uncoordinated suck but their suck improves with medication.

Some mothers have found that once their baby is stabilized on heart medication and the baby becomes more enthusiastic about nursing, an ineffective suck improves noticeably. (For more information see the section "The Baby's Suck" in the chapter "Positioning, Latch-On, and the Baby's Suck.")

CLEFT LIP AND/OR CLEFT PALATE

Breastfeeding a baby with a cleft lip and/or palate offers special advantages to mother and baby.

A cleft of the lip and/or palate is one of the most common birth defects. These two conditions may occur together or separately. A cleft of the lip occurs when parts of the baby's upper lip do not fuse together as the baby is developing *in utero*. A cleft palate occurs when parts of the baby's palate do not fuse. Both of these defects can be corrected through surgery In severe cases of cleft palate, breastfeeding may not be possible, although the baby would still benefit greatly from receiving his mother's milk.

Special benefits of breastfeeding include:

Fewer ear and other types of infections. Babies with a cleft palate tend to have more ear infections than other babies, because the tubes going from the back of the nose to the inner ears may not function properly. The muscles of the palate normally open the ear tubes during swallowing to equalize air pressure. When these do not function adequately, fluid can accumulate in the middle ear and may become infected. Duncan (1993) found that among four-month-olds without cleft palates, exclusively breastfed babies developed half the ear infections as compared with artificially fed babies. Babies with cleft defects who receive human milk have also been found to develop fewer ear infections than those on formula only (Paradise 1994). The immunities in human milk provide protection against all kinds of infections, which is especially important to a baby facing surgery.

Non-irritating fluid. Human milk is a natural body fluid that is less irritating to the body's tissues than formula. Leakage of human milk into a baby's nose (a common problem with an opening in the soft or hard palate) is less irritating to a baby's delicate mucous membranes than formula would be.

Closeness between mother and baby. Because a cleft lip is so apparent, the mother might consciously or unconsciously avoid face-to-face contact with her baby. Breastfeeding assures that mother and baby spend lots of cuddling time with plenty of skin-to-skin contact. This is calming and comforting for both mother and baby and promotes their intimate bond.

Proper development of the baby's mouth and face. The muscles used during breastfeeding become stronger and more developed with practice, contributing to more normal formation of the muscles in the face. This promotes better speech and language development as the baby grows (Broad and Duganzich 1983).

Feeding advantages. Although feedings can be time-consuming, for many of these babies, breastfeeding offers advantages:

- The breast is more flexible than a rubber nipple, allowing it to mold itself to compensate for abnormalities in the lip or mouth.
- The baby has more control over the flow of milk and the position of the breast in his mouth.
- By positioning the baby above or below the breast, the direction of the milk flow can be changed to accommodate how fast the milk is flowing, the baby's individual sucking pattern, and the location of the baby's defect.

Allows baby to suck for comfort as well as for food. Part of each breastfeeding is spent sucking for comfort, which is soothing. When a baby is fed by bottle, there is less comfort sucking, and some babies with cleft defects find it difficult to use a pacifier.

A baby with a cleft lip (whether it is on one side or both) sometimes makes it difficult for the baby to form a seal on the breast. By experimenting with different positions, it is usually possible for the mother to find a way to use her thumb or her breast to fill in the defect and form the seal.

When a baby has an opening in the soft and/or hard palate (on one or both sides), this can affect feedings in several ways:

- With incomplete palates, these babies have to work harder to nurse at first than an infant with a normal palate. They may tire easily and not receive as many calories as they need from the breast. If so, give the mother information on how to supplement her baby's feedings with expressed milk until her baby can nurse more effectively.
- The baby cannot close off the passage between mouth and nose to provide the suction needed to keep the nipple in his mouth. Poor suction also creates a noisy suck.

[Margin notes:]

A baby with a cleft lip can usually nurse at the breast even before surgery is performed to close the cleft.

A baby with a cleft palate may have difficulty breastfeeding, depending on the severity of the cleft.

Experimenting with breastfeeding positions and ways of supporting the breast in the baby's mouth may help keep the breast in its proper place.

- Milk can leak through the opening in the soft or hard palate and enter the baby's nose, causing choking. This may happen less as the baby gets stronger and can better control the flow of milk.
- During breastfeeding the baby presses the mother's nipple against the palate to compress the milk sinuses and extract the milk. If his mouth does not have a fully formed palate, he may have difficulty positioning the breast so that he can milk it well. It may take practice and patience for the baby to learn how to position and milk the breast effectively.

Early nursings are especially valuable, because:

- **The baby will receive the health benefits of his mother's colostrum.**
- **It is easier for the baby to learn the mouth and jaw movements he will need to milk the breast while the breast is still soft.** When the mother's milk becomes more plentiful on the third or fourth day, her breast becomes firmer and fuller and may be more difficult for her baby to grasp, nurse, and stay latched-on if he has not had much practice nursing.
- **This early practice will help the baby remember how to nurse if breast-feeding must be interrupted due to corrective surgery.** This will allow the baby to return to breastfeeding more easily later.
- **The mother benefits from early nursings, too, because the baby's sucking contracts the uterus and reduces bleeding.** Nursing early and often may also minimize or prevent painful breast engorgement. Breastfeeding will also facilitate the attachment process between the mother and baby. It keeps the mother's focus on an important and normal task that requires her to interact with her baby.

Encourage the mother to begin breastfeeding as soon as possible after birth, trying different nursing positions while her breast is still soft.

Special Needs—Baby

Tell the mother to expect that feedings will be time-consuming in the early weeks, no matter how the baby is fed.

During the baby's first few weeks, the mother may need to spend most of her baby's waking hours feeding him. No matter how he is fed, a baby with a cleft lip and/or palate may take up to two or three times longer to feed than a baby without this defect. Although this can be tiring for both mother and baby, this time can also be spent touching, talking, and enjoying each other's presence, which can help build a strong relationship.

Encourage the mother to be patient and to experiment to find the way that works best for her and her baby.

Every nursing couple is unique, and the way they breastfeed will be unique as well. It is important that any breastfeeding position be comfortable for the mother as well as the baby, as they will be spending many hours a day nursing. Depending on the nursing position, pillows and cushions can be used to support the mother's back, legs, and/or the baby's body. Once the baby is settled in and nursing, the mother should be able to relax all her muscles.

The best way to find an effective breastfeeding position is to experiment. And because the breast is soft and more pliable in the first few days, this is the ideal time to start.

Maintaining suction is a challenge for babies with cleft defects. Depending on the location and extent of the baby's cleft, one breastfeeding position may be more effective than another. Some mothers of babies with a unilateral (one-sided) cleft lip have found that they can help their babies form a seal and maintain suction by positioning their nipple to one side of the baby's cleft and using their thumb to fill the space above his upper lip. The mother's thumb can also be used in this way for the baby with an alveolar ridge defect, an incomplete development of the bony ridge under the gums.

One mother of a baby with a cleft of the soft palate tried experimenting with nursing in different positions and at different times, keeping careful track of what

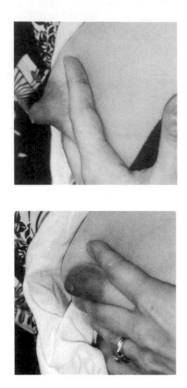

Cleft Palate Hold

A well-supported, upright nursing position may help breastfeeding go more smoothly.

Modified Football Position

Good latch-on is also important for effective breastfeeding.

worked to find an effective approach they could use consistently. She found that her baby did best when her breast was firm and full. If she held the breast firmly in the baby's mouth, the baby could milk the breast using her gums and tongue in the same way the mother used her fingers when she hand-expressed her milk. The problem was that her baby's cleft caused suction to be broken whenever the nipple reached the cleft, causing the nipple to fall back to the front of the baby's mouth, which resulted in less effective breastfeeding. The mother found that by holding the nipple firmly in the baby's mouth (pressing her nipple out between her index and middle fingers with ring and little fingers below, lifting and holding the breast) and pressing the baby's head into her breast, the mother was able to manually hold the nipple far enough back in the baby's mouth to allow for effective nursing. The baby nursed happily and well this way (Grady 1983).

Tell the mother that achieving effective and comfortable breastfeeding can be a challenge even for mothers and babies without cleft defects. It often takes time and patience before nursing is going smoothly. Encourage the mother to seek help and support during stressful times.

For babies with severe clefts, breastfeeding may be very difficult or, in a few cases, impossible. In this instance, suggest that the mother ask the baby's plastic surgeon about the possibility of using a palatal obturator (see later point). If a baby is unable to breastfeed, a mother still has the option of using an effective method of milk expression to provide her milk for her baby (see "When Pumping Replaces Breastfeeding" in the chapter "Expression and Storage of Milk"). Human milk can help keep the baby healthy before undergoing corrective surgery and afterwards speed his recovery. By expressing her milk for her baby and holding him to her breast as she feeds it to him, the mother can share some of the warm closeness of the breastfeeding relationship with her baby.

An upright position is often easiest for the baby with a cleft palate because it can help prevent the milk from leaking into the baby's nose. Possible positions to try include:

- **A modified football position.** If the mother is sitting on a bed, have her sit the baby upright—facing her—at her side, with his legs along her side and his feet at her back. His bottom should be on the bed or a pillow (if he needs to be raised to breast level) with a pillow behind his back. The mother can then support the baby's back with her upper arm and his head with her hand. The mother may need to support her breast with the C–hold (thumb on top, four fingers underneath well back from the nipple) or the alternate breast hold described in the previous point. It may also help to lean forward until the baby latches on, but once the baby is nursing, lean back again to avoid backaches.
- **Straddle position.** Suggest the mother sit her baby in her lap, facing her, with his legs straddling her abdomen. If the baby is small, it may be necessary to raise him to breast level by putting pillows under him. The mother may need to tip the baby's head back a little as baby latches on so she can position him carefully.

When a baby goes onto the breast, it is important for him to open his mouth wide (like a yawn) and take the breast deeply into his mouth. To encourage him to open wide, try lightly tickling his lips with the nipple. If this doesn't work after about a minute, try tickling even more lightly. A good latch-on helps him to get more milk for his efforts and makes breastfeeding more comfortable for mother. A baby who latches on closer to the tip of the nipple will not get as much milk and a poor latch-on may cause sore nipples.

The baby may need jaw and chin support to nurse well.

Dancer Hand Position

Suggest the mother set the feeding pace by making sure she breastfeeds her baby long enough and frequently enough.

If the baby is swallowing a lot of air during breastfeeding, he may need to take frequent breaks and be burped often.

Babies with cleft palates tend to gain weight slowly, no matter how they are fed.

If the baby is not gaining well, the mother can supplement by expressing her high-calorie hindmilk after nursing and giving it to her baby.

Some babies need jaw and chin support to hold their jaws steady while on the breast. If the baby's cheeks become hollow in an effort to hold his jaw steady, jaw and chin support would be beneficial. One way to provide this extra support during nursing is to use the "Dancer Hand Position" (see photo).

To use this position, suggest that the mother:

1. Support her breast with the C-hold (thumb on top, four fingers underneath).
2. Slide the hand supporting the breast forward, supporting the breast with three rather than four fingers. Her index finger and thumb should now be free in front of her nipple.
3. Bend her index finger slightly so it gently holds the baby's cheek on one side while the thumb holds the other cheek. The index finger and thumb form a "U" with the baby's chin resting on the bottom of the "U."

As the baby grows and practices nursing, his muscle tone will improve and he may not need as much support. As the baby gains muscle tone, suggest the mother try supporting the baby's chin just using her index finger.

Because feedings can be tiring, the baby may not nurse long enough to get the high-calorie hindmilk he needs for growth. The mother may need to encourage the baby to nurse long enough and often enough (at least ten minutes of sucking and swallowing on each breast every two to three hours). If the baby nurses this often during the mother's waking hours, she can let him sleep for a longer time (four or five hours) during the night.

Suggest the mother be sure her baby is fully awake before beginning to breast-feed. (See "How to Rouse a Sleepy Baby" in the chapter "Positioning, Latch-On, and the Baby's Suck.")

Special Needs—Baby

Because a baby with a cleft palate may swallow a lot of air during breastfeeding, he may need to take frequent breaks and be burped often. Use the baby as a guide.

One position that is good for burping and will also help strengthen the baby's muscles is sitting up in the mother's lap. For the small baby whose neck muscles are still weak, the mother can support the baby's chin between her thumb and index finger while he is sitting. Patting the baby's back while gently bending him slightly forward will usually bring up a burp. Whatever burping position is used, it will be easier to get up a burp if there is gentle pressure on the baby's stomach.

In babies with cleft palates, slow weight gain may be only partly due to feeding difficulties. One study (Avedian 1980) of thirty-seven cleft palate babies with no other physical abnormalities reported that in the first two months, the babies' weights fell slightly on the growth charts and did not regain their original position on the charts until they were six months old.

If the baby is not gaining well, the mother can use her high-calorie hindmilk as a supplement by expressing her milk after the baby nurses and giving it to him. Depending on the baby's weight gain, the effectiveness of his suck, and his stamina, the mother can give the baby her hindmilk after every feeding, after every other feeding, or two or three times a day. Supplements can be given by spoon, cup, or feeding syringe, as well as by bottle. If suction is a problem, a nursing supplementer may not work well. (See "The Use of Breast Pumps and Other Products.")

When deciding how to give a supplement, keep in mind that the baby must be able to gulp the milk quickly between breaths to prevent its flowing into his nose. This will not be possible unless the milk goes immediately to the back of his mouth where it can be quickly swallowed.

A special mouth appliance, called a palatal obturator, can help some babies with a cleft palate breastfeed more normally. Suggest the mother request that a smooth rather than rough plate be used so it will be less irritating to her nipples during breastfeeding.

Some health care teams recommend that newborns with cleft palates be fitted with a mouth appliance called a palatal obturator (Markowitz 1979). The palatal obturator is a plastic plate that is placed over the opening in the palate and shaped to fit the baby's upper mouth. It is used before corrective surgery to keep the cleft in the baby's hard palate from closing in an improper way. It may be put in the baby's mouth as early as 24 hours after birth or as late as several weeks after birth. This appliance may be costly, needs to be replaced as the baby's mouth grows, and may or may not be covered by health insurance.

Sarah Danner, a certified pediatric nurse practitioner who has worked extensively with breastfeeding babies with cleft defects, believes that "there is great benefit to feeding with an obturator in place." She writes, "Health care teams that use this approach think that there is better feeding, that crying and later speech sound more normal, that there is a reduction in the size of the defect, and a positive effect on the family.... More normal sucking assists growth and helps with feeding" (Danner 1992).

Before the baby's obturator is made, suggest the mother tell the baby's plastic surgeon that she is breastfeeding and ask that the obturator be made with a smooth rather than a rough surface. If the surface is rough, it can be irritating to the mother's nipple during breastfeeding.

When an obturator is first placed in the baby's mouth, it may feel uncomfortable and the baby may be reluctant to breastfeed. For the first day or two, it may take patience to encourage the baby to breastfeed while wearing it, but the baby will adjust to it with time and practice. In the meantime, if the baby refuses the breast he can be fed with a syringe or other special feeding device, such as a Breck or Haberman Feeder, until he is willing to nurse. The Haberman Feeder is designed for babies with feeding problems. The special nipple does not require suction, and it has a slit valve that allows the milk flow to be controlled so that the baby is not overwhelmed with milk. (For more information, see "The Use of Breast Pumps and Other Products.")

At first some babies change their nursing pattern by latching on closer to the tip of the nipple, so that they don't have to press the nipple against the obturator. If this happens, encourage the baby to open wide and take more of the breast into his mouth while keeping his head firmly tucked in close to the breast. Changing nursing positions can also ease discomfort if the mother's nipples become sore. Patience is needed while the baby learns to nurse with the obturator.

Cleft lip surgery may be done after 48 hours of age, while cleft palate repair is usually performed between ages one and two years.

Surgery for a cleft lip may be performed any time after 48 hours of age. Although it was once believed that surgery should be delayed until the baby reached an age of 10 weeks and a weight of 10 pounds (4.5 kg), research has found no health disadvantages to early repair and no difference in the success of the surgery (Weatherly-White 1987). No complications occurred in babies allowed to breastfeed immediately following the surgery.

Repair of the cleft palate is usually scheduled when the baby is between one and two years of age, after the face and mouth have grown more mature but before the baby has begun to do much talking.

If the baby's doctor agrees, breastfeeding may be allowed within three hours before the surgery and be resumed when the baby leaves the recovery room.

Although some doctors routinely advise that a patient facing surgery be given nothing by mouth ("NPO") for eight hours before surgery, guidelines for presurgical fasting are in the process of changing. Recent studies indicate that a more reasonable fasting time before surgery for children is six hours for formula (Spear 1992), three hours for human milk, and two hours for clear liquids (Nicholson and Schreiner 1995; Litman 1994; Schreiner 1994). Suggest the mother discuss the NPO orders with the surgeon and anesthesiologist beforehand; many are willing to accommodate the needs of the breastfeeding baby.

With cleft lip repair, breastfeeding may only be interrupted for a few hours. If the interruption is longer, suggest the mother express her milk to maintain her milk supply and ask that her milk be given to her baby. Some surgeons allow babies to nurse as soon as they leave the recovery room after surgery, and reserach has confirmed the safety of this practice (Cohen 1992; Weatherly-White 1987). These arrangements need to be made in advance with the baby's doctor.

If the doctor is uncomfortable with the idea of breastfeeding after surgery, suggest the mother share with the doctor the Cohen and Weatherly-White references at the end of this chapter. Doctors who have never had patients breastfeed soon after surgery will sometimes agree if the mother breastfeeds in the presence of a nurse, who can watch for any damage to the stitches. Different doctors have different approaches to cleft repair surgery, and if parents have misgivings about a doctor's recommendations, a second opinion is in order.

With cleft palate repair, if the surgery is performed on a nursing toddler, breastfeeding may be uncomfortable for him immediately after the operation because the roof of his mouth will be sore. He will also have a newly structured palate, and sucking, even if the pain is tolerable, will be accomplished differently. The new sensation may be unsettling to him. Even so, holding the mother's nipple in his mouth may be comforting. But as he recovers—in a week or so—he'll probably return to nursing, perhaps even more enthusiastically than before, as the surgery makes breastfeeding easier. If the mother maintains her supply during this time with an effective method of milk expression, she will be able to stay comfortable and have a ready milk supply available when her toddler comes back to the breast.

Resources for Parents

United Kingdom

The Cleft Lip & Palate Association
National Secretary, Mrs. Cy Thirlaway
1 Eastwood Gardens, Kenton
Newcastle upon Tyne NE3 3DQ
England
24-hour answer phone: 091 2859396

Special Needs—Baby

United States

American Cleft-Palate-Craniofacial Asociation (professional association)
Cleft Palate Foundation (parent support arm)
1218 Grandview Avenue
Pittsburgh, PA 15211 USA
(412) 481-1376; FAX (412) 481-0847
Cleftline: 1-800-24-CLEFT (24-hour-a-day support line)
Cleft Palate Foundation offers informational pamphlets for parents.

AboutFace, USA (newsletter and support groups)
P.O. Box 93
Limekiln, PA 19535 USA
Telephone: 1-800-225-FACE

National Cleft Palate Asociation (NCPA)
906 Hillside Lane Flower Mound, TX 75028 USA
Has local chapters throughout the US.

Wide Smiles (newsletter)
P.O. Box 5153
Stockton, CA 95205-0153 USA

Publications for Parents

Danner, S. and Cerutti, E. *Nursing Your Baby with a Cleft Palate or Cleft Lip.* Waco, Texas: Childbirth Graphics, 1990.

La Leche League International. THE WOMANLY ART OF BREASTFEEDING, 35th Anniversary ed. Schaumburg, Illinois, 1991, pp. 298-301.

Mohrbacher, N. *Nursing a Baby with a Cleft Lip or Cleft Palate.* Schaumburg, Illinois: La Leche League International, 1994, Publication No. 122.

CYSTIC FIBROSIS

A baby with cystic fibrosis "tastes salty" and tends to gain weight slowly, despite lots of wet diapers and bowel movements.

Cystic fibrosis is a congenital disease that affects a baby's breathing and digestion. The baby with cystic fibrosis secretes unusually thick, gluey mucus and his sweat is unusually salty. The thick mucus clogs the bronchial tubes in the lungs, causing breathing difficulties, and blocks the digestive enzymes from leaving the pancreas, causing incomplete digestion.

There are many degrees of severity of cystic fibrosis, from cases that can only be detected through laboratory tests to cases that are extremely serious. Depending on the seriousness of the disease, babies with cystic fibrosis may have a constant cough and regular respiratory infections. They may look thin, pale, and undernourished.

The first clues that a baby has cystic fibrosis may be his "salty" taste, which the mother notices when she kisses him, and his slow weight gain, despite plenty of wet diapers and bowel movements. Slow weight gain is caused by the baby's incomplete digestion of his food and is unrelated to the amount of mother's milk the baby is getting.

Breastfeeding is recommended for babies with cystic fibrosis because it offers special advantages for these babies.

In a survey of US cystic fibrosis centers (Luder 1990), most recommended breastfeeding, either alone or supplemented with special enzymes (see next point). Some of the advantages of breastfeeding include:

- **Improved growth.** One study of babies with cystic fibrosis found that exclusively breastfed babies were heavier and taller than exclusively formula-fed babies (Holliday 1991).
- **Delay in the onset of symptoms.** Due to human milk's ease of digestion and the protection from infection it offers, some babies do not develop symptoms until after weaning (Rooney 1988).
- **Fewer respiratory infections.** Because babies with severe cystic fibrosis are more susceptible to respiratory infections than other babies, breastfeeding's protection from infection is particularly beneficial to them.

In order to gain weight properly, some babies with cystic fibrosis may need to be given special enzymes in addition to breastfeeding.

If a baby's cystic fibrosis is severe enough that excess mucus blocks the flow of digestive enzymes, he may need replacement enzymes in order to gain weight properly. These enzymes can be dissolved in soft foods, such as applesauce, and given by spoon after nursing. The baby may also need extra vitamins and, in hot weather, salt (Gaskin and Waters 1994).

DOWN SYNDROME

Down Syndrome is a genetic birth defect caused by the presence of an extra chromosome. Although babies with Down Syndrome will experience developmental delays, love, care, and support will help them grow up to lead interesting, useful lives.

The mother of a newborn with Down Syndrome may feel overwhelmed and upset, which can make it difficult for her to remember information.

See the first section in this chapter "The Mother's Feelings."

In addition to coping with her own feelings, the mother may not receive much support from others. Family and friends may feel awkward about mentioning the baby and avoid visiting because they "don't know what to say." Others may expect that the parents of a child with Down Syndrome soon will come to accept their situation. Adjusting to the situation takes time. Learning to take one day at a time and to focus on the baby as a unique individual will help the parents cope in the short and long run (Cooley 1993).

Breastfeeding offers special physical advantages to the baby with Down Syndrome and can enhance the closeness between mother and baby.

Special benefits of breastfeeding include:

- **Protection from infection and bowel problems.** Babies with Down Syndrome are especially prone to respiratory tract infections and bowel problems. Human milk provides immunities to infection and an ease of digestion that formula cannot.
- **Improved mouth and tongue coordination.** The act of breastfeeding benefits facial muscle tone and improves mouth and tongue coordination. Breastfed babies as a whole have been found to have fewer speech problems later in life (Broad and Duganzich 1983).
- **Extra stimulation.** The extra skin-to-skin contact that is an automatic part of breastfeeding gives babies extra stimulation to more fully develop their capabilities.
- **Closeness between mother and baby.** Breastfeeding, when it goes well, can enhance the bond between mother and baby by giving baby the closeness and comfort all babies need. It assures that the mother spends lots of her time cuddling and getting to know her baby better. Breastfeeding can also help a mother feel that she is doing something meaningful for her child's well-being—as indeed she is.
- **Enhanced mothering skills.** The skills a mother uses in her baby's early weeks to help him learn to breastfeed—the encouraging, the coaxing, and responding to his cues—are the same skills that she will need over the years to help her child learn to use his full potential.

Special Needs—Baby

When physical problems require that the baby be cared for in a special or intensive-care nursery, colostrum or mature milk can be given by tube or bottle until the baby is ready to nurse.

Many babies with Down Syndrome have heart problems or respiratory tract infections and may need special medical care early in life. Even when a baby must be cared for in a special nursery, the mother can provide her colostrum or mature milk for him. For information on choosing an effective method of milk expression, see the chapter "Expression and Storage of Human Milk."

When a baby is able to take anything by mouth, he can be given colostrum or mature milk, which are natural fluids and therefore less irritating than formula. Colostrum and mature milk are also complete foods that are easy to digest.

If a baby is fed at first by tube, some doctors will suggest a baby go directly from tube feeding to the breast. Others may want to start by giving a bottle.

The first time the mother offers her breast, she may feel unsure of herself and nervous about how it will go. Encourage the mother to express a little milk onto her nipple so the baby can taste it. Most important, tell her to enjoy her time with her baby and not worry too much about how well the baby nurses. Suggest she think of these first nursings as practice sessions and tell her that she and her baby will have many opportunities to keep trying even if the baby doesn't catch on at first. (For more ideas, see the section "The First Nursings" in the chapter "Prematurity.")

Breastfeeding may take longer than usual in the early weeks if the baby has low muscle tone and a weak suck.

A study (Aumonier 1983) of fifty-nine breastfed babies with Down Syndrome reported that thirty-one (52%) had no sucking problems. But most babies with Down Syndrome tend to be "floppy," or have low muscle tone (called muscular hypotonicity), and some may not be able to breastfeed effectively at first. A baby like this may need extra help in finding, latching on, and remaining on the breast. Tell the mother that the baby's muscle tone and sucking will improve with time and practice.

A baby with low muscle tone may have difficulty cupping his tongue around the breast while nursing. A flattened tongue can cause the milk to slide to the sides of the baby's mouth, rather than being immediately swallowed, resulting in more effort for less milk. So the mother of a baby with low muscle tone may need to allow more time for feedings in the early weeks.

Because babies with Down Syndrome are often placid and sleepy, the mother may need to set the pace for feedings.

It is also common for the baby with Down Syndrome to be very sleepy in the first few weeks. It may be difficult to wake him for feedings and keep him interested in breastfeeding for very long. If he does not breastfeed often or long enough, he may not gain well.

Suggest the mother:

- **Try to interest her baby in frequent nursings throughout the day.** Explain that short, frequent feedings (at least ten minutes of active nursing at each breast every two to three hours) will be better for her baby than longer, more infrequent feedings.
- **Try to fully awaken the baby before offering the breast and stimulate him to stay interested throughout the nursing.** (See "How to Rouse a Sleepy Newborn" in the chapter "Positioning, Latch-On, and the Baby's Suck.")
- **Give the baby lots of touching and attention to stimulate him.** A baby sling or carrier might make this easier. Encourage the mother to spend lots of time talking to her baby, carrying him, and enjoying his cuddliness.

In the early weeks when positioning baby at the breast try to keep the baby's body horizontal, using pillows as support.

When positioning the baby at the breast, make sure the baby is in a well-supported position. The baby needs to devote his energy to nursing, rather than holding his head and body up. Two pillows under the baby may make it easier for him to nurse by keeping his body horizontal, which encourages better sucking with less effort. Either the cradle hold, the transitional hold, or the football hold can work well. (See "Positioning, Latch-On, and the Baby's Suck.") Encourage the mother to experiment to see what works best for her and her baby.

If gulping and choking are a problem, the baby can be positioned so that his neck and throat are higher than the mother's nipple.

Babies with Down Syndrome tend to gulp and choke more easily than other babies because their low muscle tone leaves their airway unprotected when swallowing. If this is a problem, have the mother try positioning her baby so that his neck and throat are higher than her nipple. She can do this by using the following positions.

- Add an extra pillow under the baby and lean back slightly so that her breast is angled upward.
- Lean back in a rocking chair with her feet on a pillow, stool, or low table and her knees drawn up.
- Lie on her side with a folded bath towel under the baby so that his face is angled slightly downward toward her nipple.

If low muscle tone in the tongue causes it to protrude, the baby may have difficulty latching on to the breast properly.

As with all babies, have the mother make sure the baby opens wide before latching on (pulling down on the chin may be necessary in the early weeks for the baby with low muscle tone).

A baby who pushes his tongue upward may need some encouragement to keep it down while latching on. Suggest the mother try the exercise "Pushing the Tongue Down and Out" (see "Tongue Thrusting" in the chapter "Positioning,

Latch-On, and the Baby's Suck") before putting the baby to the breast. She may need to repeat this movement several times before breastfeeding.

The baby may need jaw and chin support to nurse well.

Some babies need jaw and chin support to hold their jaw steady while on the breast. If the baby's cheeks become hollow in an effort to hold his jaw steady, jaw and chin support would be beneficial. One way to provide this extra support during nursing is to use the "Dancer Hand Position." (See the previous section, "Cleft Lip and/or Palate," for a description and photo.) As the baby grows and practices nursing, his muscle tone will improve and he may not need as much support. As the baby gains muscle tone, suggest the mother try supporting just the baby's chin using her index finger. Chin support may be necessary for quite a while.

If the baby swallows a lot of air during breastfeeding, he may need to be burped often.

Suggest the mother use her baby as her guide. If the baby is gulping, choking, or she notices he is swallowing a lot of air, suggest she stop breastfeeding after five minutes or so and burp the baby.

One position that is good for burping and will also help strengthen the baby's muscles is sitting up in the mother's lap. With a small baby whose neck muscles are still weak, the mother can support the baby's chin between her thumb and index finger while he is sitting. Patting the baby's back while gently bending him slightly forward will usually bring up a burp. Whatever position is used, it will be easier to get up a burp if there is gentle pressure on the baby's stomach.

If the baby is not nursing effectively and gaining less than four ounces (113 grams) a week, suggest the mother try expressing her hindmilk and offering it as a supplement.

A baby who is not nursing effectively or often enough may not be getting enough of his mother's high-calorie hindmilk. Gaining weight may mean gaining strength as well. An adequate weight gain is considered to be four ounces (113 grams) a week, although it is not unusual for a baby with Down Syndrome to gain slowly even when receiving enough nourishment. In this case slow

Special Needs—Baby

weight gain may be due to a physical abnormality, such as a heart defect, which requires the baby to spend extra energy and calories just maintaining adequate circulation. One study (Aumonier 1983) of babies with Down Syndrome reported that the more severe the baby's heart defect, the less effectively the baby was able to suck.

By expressing her milk after the baby has finished nursing, the mother can obtain her high-calorie hindmilk. Then she can give it to her baby with a nursing supplementer or by other methods. The nursing supplementer has the advantage of allowing the entire feeding to take place at the breast. Also, some babies respond to the increased flow by sucking more effectively at the breast, which stimulates the mother's milk supply as it improves their suck. However, if achieving a good latch-on is already difficult, adding the tube from a nursing supplementer to the equation can make this process even more challenging. Also, the nursing supplementer will not be a good option if the mother is uncomfortable with its use. If the mother does not want to use a nursing supplementer, encourage her to give the hindmilk with a cup, spoon, eyedropper, or feeding syringe. (See "The Use of Breast Pumps and Other Products" for suggestions on using these alternative feeding methods.) Supplements given by bottle can cause nipple confusion during the first month and may also be difficult for a baby with low muscle tone to take without choking.

Patience is the key.

Breastfeeding the baby with Down Syndrome can be a challenge, but assure the mother that patience and persistence will go a long way. As the baby grows and gains in strength and muscle tone, breastfeeding will get easier. And in the meantime the baby will be enjoying all the special benefits breastfeeding has to offer.

Resources for Parents

March of Dimes Birth Defects Foundation
1275 Mamaroneck Avenue
White Plains, NY 10605 USA
Telephone: 914-428-7100

National Association for Down Syndrome
P.O. Box 4542
Oak Brook, IL 60522-4542 USA
Telephone: 630-325-9112

National Down Syndrome Congress
1605 Chantilly Drive, Suite 250
Atlanta, GA 30324 USA
800-232-6372

National Down Syndrome Society (NDSS)
666 Broadway
New York, NY 10012-2317 USA
Telephone: 212-460-9330

Parents of Children with Down Syndrome
ARCMC
11600 Nebel Street
Rockville, Maryland 20852
Telephone: 301-984-5792

Publications for Parents

Danner, S. and Cerutti, E. *Nursing Your Baby with Down Syndrome*. Waco, Texas: Childbirth Graphics, 1990.

La Leche League International. THE WOMANLY ART OF BREASTFEEDING, 35th Anniversary ed. Schaumburg, Illinois, 1991, pp. 297-98.

Good, J. *Breastfeeding the Baby with Down Syndrome*. Schaumburg, Illinois: La Leche League International, 1985, Publication No. 23.

GALACTOSEMIA

Blood tests for galactosemia produce many false-positive results.

Galactosemia is a rare inherited metabolic disorder in which the liver enzyme that breaks down galactose is absent, leaving the baby unable to metabolize lactose, or milk sugar. Too much galactose in a baby's system can cause a variety of symptoms, usually starting with vomiting and diarrhea and progressing to failure-to-thrive, malnutrition, liver problems, and mental retardation. Since human milk is high in lactose, breastfeeding is not possible if a baby has galactosemia. The baby must be fed a special galactose-free formula.

Because the enzyme in question is sensitive to heat, babies who do not have this disorder may test positive for galactosemia (especially during the summer months when blood samples may not be kept cool).

Suggest the mother ask her baby's doctor to evaluate the baby's health and have her baby tested again as soon as possible. Often, by being assertive with the doctor and the testing agency a mother can greatly reduce the time needed to get results. For example, the mother can ask the baby's doctor to call the testing facility and request special handling of the test. If the mother is within driving distance of the testing facility, one option would be for her or someone she trusts to drive her baby's blood sample to the testing facility. Overnight delivery would be another option. Once the sample reaches the testing facility, results may be obtained within a day or two.

After evaluating the baby's health, the baby's doctor can advise the mother whether or not she should wean her baby to a special galactose-free formula until the baby's second test results are received.

THE NEUROLOGICALLY IMPAIRED BABY

The mother of a neurologically impaired baby may feel overwhelmed and upset, which can make it difficult for her to remember information.

The neurologically impaired baby has a nervous system that does not function normally. A neurologically impaired baby may not have the mature suck-swallow reflex of a full-term healthy baby. He may have other symptoms as well. McBride and Danner (1987) state: "There is no evidence that neurologically impaired babies with sucking problems learn feeding better at the bottle than at the breast." In severe cases, the baby may have to be fed through a tube, although human milk would still offer many benefits.

See the first section in this chapter "The Mother's Feelings."

Neurologically impaired babies can exhibit a variety of symptoms.

Neurologically impaired babies fall into two general groups—those with uncoordinated sucking and overactive muscle tone (for example, arching, or "hypertonic" babies or babies with a clenching or clamping down response), and those with a weak suck and low muscle tone. Neurologically impaired babies may exhibit one or more of the following symptoms:

- nonrhythmic sucking,
- excessive arching of the body,
- overreaction to stimulation,
- excessive rooting and biting movements, including biting when swallowing,
- low muscle tone,
- weak suck, swallowing, and gag reflexes.

Special Needs—Baby

Breastfeeding offers special advantages to the neurologically impaired baby.

Special benefits of breastfeeding include:

Improved neuro-muscular coordination. The jaw and mouth movements necessary for effective breastfeeding help the baby develop and improve coordination of his muscles and nervous system.

Protection from infection. Human milk provides a perfect first food, which will keep the neurologically impaired baby well nourished and offer protection from infection.

Closeness between mother and baby. Breastfeeding enhances the relationship between mother and baby, which can help the mother appreciate her baby as an individual first and a child with a disability second.

Encourage the mother to choose doctors and therapists for her baby who are supportive of breastfeeding and aware of breastfeeding's benefits for the neurologically impaired baby.

Any nursing mother will benefit from working with a doctor who is knowledgeable and supportive of breastfeeding, but the mother of a neurologically impaired baby may have to work with an entire medical team, possibly including a neonatologist, a pediatrician, and a speech or occupational therapist or physical therapist with neurodevelopmental training. Because the mother needs to rely on her baby's medical team to give her advice and evaluate her baby's progress as the baby grows, it is important that they respect and support her desire to breastfeed.

When her baby's medical team is being assembled, encourage the mother to ask its members how they feel about breastfeeding. If a member of the team has reservations, perhaps that person would be willing to recommend another specialist who would be more supportive. Neurodevelopmental therapists, just like doctors, have varying amounts of knowledge about breastfeeding. Encourage the mother to ask her local breastfeeding support people for recommendations.

The mother may need to set the pace in feeding.	Encourage the mother to be sure her baby nurses often enough and long enough (at least ten minutes of sucking and swallowing on each breast every two to three hours). Some neurologically impaired babies tire quickly and may not be able to nurse for as long as they need to.
The low-muscle-tone baby with a weak suck and gag reflex may breast-feed more effectively if his lips and tongue are stimulated before nursing.	Weak or absent suck and gag reflexes are associated with low muscle tone in the mouth and face. The tongue may stay in the back of the mouth most of the time and not cup around the nipple to carry the milk to the throat. (See the section in this chapter on "Breastfeeding the Baby with Down Syndrome" for more suggestions for breastfeeding the baby with low muscle tone.) The mother can help her baby learn to nurse more effectively by: • tapping or stroking his lips, cheeks, and tongue before putting him to the breast. • stroking the baby's tongue to increase his awareness of it and help him learn to use it more effectively while nursing.
The high-muscle-tone baby who arches or is easily excitable may breastfeed more effectively if he is kept flexed and there are few distractions.	A high-muscle-tone baby may arch away from the mother when she holds him, which can pose a challenge to breastfeeding. Encourage the mother to keep her baby flexed, with his chin down and spine rounded, as much as possible. Wrapping him securely in a blanket while in a flexed position may be helpful. The arching baby may also be easily excitable, moving or jerking suddenly and overreacting to loud noises, bright lights, or sudden movement. If the mother notices this in her baby, suggest she try sitting still during feedings. Talking to the baby in a soothing voice may be calming. The baby might also do best in a quiet, darkened room. Also see "The Arching (Hypertonic) Baby" in the chapter "Fussy at the Breast and Breast Refusal."
A baby who clamps his jaws down as he swallows may be encouraged to breastfeed more effectively if the mother wipes his face with cold then warm water before nursing.	A hyper-reflexive baby may bite and root more than the average baby. He may grimace, pull back, and clamp his jaws as he swallows. He may also move his tongue too much, even pushing the mother's nipple out of his mouth. To discourage this, before nursings have the mother try wiping the baby's face with cold then warm water several times. Also, suggest the mother control how the baby latches on to the breast by using her thumb or finger to press down firmly on his chin to counteract the clenching of his jaws. Continued pressure on the baby's chin throughout the feeding may allow her to breastfeed comfortably. If the mother has a problem with her finger or thumb slipping during feedings, suggest she wrap a piece of gauze around it. If the baby is losing weight, the mother may need to express her milk and feed it to her baby until the clenching relaxes.
The baby who does not suck rhythmically may do better at breastfeeding if the mother gives special attention to good positioning and latch-on and supports his chin while he nurses.	Non-rhythmic sucking can be a problem for both kinds of neurologically impaired babies—those with low muscle tone and those with overactive muscle tone. A baby who sucks non-rhythmically may have difficulty keeping his mother's nipple in his mouth and may swallow more air than usual. Suggest that the mother: • **Find a comfortable nursing position.** Make sure the mother is well-supported by pillows and relaxed (suggest she sit slightly back rather than leaning over the baby) and that the baby is well-supported so that he can use his energy for breastfeeding, not holding up his head or body. The mother may need to use two pillows to prop baby up in her lap. Either the cradle hold or the football hold may work well. • **Express some colostrum or milk to encourage the baby to latch on.** This will also motivate the baby to suck once his mouth is on the breast. • **Support her breast while she nurses.** This can help the baby keep the breast in his mouth.

- **Pull down gently on baby's chin as he latches on** to be sure his mouth is open wide enough to get as much of the breast as possible in his mouth.
- **Make sure the baby's lower lip is turned out** and his tongue is under the nipple. The mother's helper should be able to see the baby's tongue over his lower gum while he is nursing by gently pulling down on the baby's lower lip.
- **Give the baby extra jaw and chin support**, if necessary. This can be done using the Dancer Hand position. (See the description and photo in the section, "Cleft Lip and/or Palate.")

As the baby grows and practices nursing, he may not need as much support. Then suggest the mother try supporting just the baby's chin using her index finger.

If the baby swallows a lot of air during breastfeeding, he may need to be burped often.

Suggest the mother use her baby as her guide. If the baby is gulping, choking, or she notices he is swallowing a lot of air, suggest the mother stop breastfeeding after five minutes or so and burp the baby.

One position that is good for burping and will also help strengthen the baby's muscles is sitting up in the mother's lap. With a small baby whose neck muscles are still weak, the mother can support the baby's chin between her thumb and index finger while he is sitting. Patting the baby's back while gently bending him slightly forward will usually bring up a burp. Whatever burping position is used, it will be easier to get up a burp if there is gentle pressure on the baby's stomach.

If the baby is not nursing effectively and gaining less than four ounces (113 grams) a week, suggest the mother try expressing her hindmilk and offering it as a supplement.

A baby who is not nursing effectively may not be getting enough of his mother's high-calorie hindmilk. Gaining weight may mean gaining strength as well. An adequate weight gain is considered to be four ounces (113 grams) a week, although it is not unusual for a neurologically impaired baby to gain slowly even if he is receiving enough nourishment.

Special Needs—Baby

By expressing her milk after the baby has finished nursing, the mother can obtain her high-calorie hindmilk. Then she can give it to her baby with a nursing supplementer or by other methods. The nursing supplementer has the advantage of allowing the entire feeding to take place at the breast. Also, some babies respond to the increased flow by sucking more effectively at the breast, which stimulates the mother's milk supply as it improves their suck. However, if achieving a good latch-on is already difficult, adding the tube from a nursing supplementer to the equation can make this process even more challenging. The nursing supplementer will also not be a good option if the mother is uncomfortable with its use. If the mother does not want to use a nursing supplementer at the breast or on a finger, encourage her to give the hindmilk with a cup, spoon, eyedropper, or feeding syringe. Supplements given in bottles can cause nipple confusion and may also be difficult for a baby with low muscle tone to take without choking.

Patience is the key to breastfeeding the neurologically impaired baby.

Breastfeeding the neurologically impaired baby can be a challenge, but assure the mother that patience and persistence will go a long way. As the baby grows and gains in strength and coordination, breastfeeding will get easier. And in the meantime the baby will be enjoying all the special benefits breastfeeding has to offer.

For help in finding a neurodevelopmental specialist in your area, contact:

Resources for Parents

The Neurodevelopmental Treatment Association
401 N. Michigan Avenue
Chicago, IL 60611-4267 USA
Telephone: (312) 321-5151

Publications for Parent

Danner, S. and Cerutti, E. *Nursing Your Neurologically Impaired Baby.* Waco, Texas: Childbirth Graphics, 1990.

PKU

Phenylketonuria (PKU) is a rare metabolic disorder in which a liver enzyme is lacking. As a result an essential nutrient, the amino acid phenylalanine, is not broken down and accumulates in the blood, interfering with normal brain development. If not detected and treated, PKU can cause mental retardation.

Blood tests for PKU produce many false-positive results. The baby who tests positive for PKU should be retested to confirm the diagnosis.

The test for PKU will not be accurate unless the baby has had some phenylalanine in his diet. So to be effective, the test should not be administered until the baby is at least 24 hours old and has been breastfeeding well. It is not necessary for the baby to receive cow's milk or formula before being tested for PKU.

Many babies who test positive for PKU do not have the disorder. However, continuing to exclusively breastfeed a baby with PKU can cause serious problems, so if a baby tests positive for PKU, encourage the mother to have the baby tested again as quickly as possible to confirm the diagnosis.

By being assertive with the doctor and the testing agency a mother may be able to greatly reduce the time needed to get results. For example, the mother can ask the baby's doctor to call the testing facility and request special handling of the test. If the mother is within driving distance of the testing facility, one option would be for her or someone she trusts to drive her baby's blood sample to the testing facility. Overnight delivery would be another option. Once the sample arrives at the testing facility, results may be obtained within a day or two.

Sometimes several re-tests are needed before PKU can be ruled out.

A baby with PKU can be breastfed along with the use of a special low-phenylalanine formula.

A baby with PKU cannot get enough protein from his diet without also getting too much phenylalanine. But continued breastfeeding is possible because the baby with PKU also needs *some* phenylalanine for normal growth. This means that in addition to being fed Lofenalac, a special low-phenylalanine formula, the baby also needs some other protein in his diet. The mother can continue breastfeeding while supplementing her baby's diet with Lofenalac. Human milk is lower in phenylalanine than cow's milk formula.

A baby with PKU needs to be carefully monitored to be sure the amount of phenylalanine in his blood does not rise above safe levels. Some mothers use a special electronic scale to weigh their babies before and after breastfeeding to get an accurate measure of how much human milk baby consumed, however, research has found this procedure to be unnecessary.

In one recent study (Greve 1994), estimates of average daily human milk intake were used to calculate how much low-phenylalanine formula should be given per day to maintain safe blood levels, and mothers gave this amount of special formula, either offering it before nursing or alternating feedings with breast and bottle. Twice weekly blood tests were used to monitor blood levels and the results were used to adjust the amount of special formula given. Because human milk is lower in phenylalanine than regular formula, less low-phenylalanine formula was needed for the breastfed babies than the artificially fed babies, saving money and providing improved nutrition. The researchers concluded that although health professionals must spend more time at first monitoring blood levels and assessing weight gains while breastfeeding is being established, "eventually breastfeeding decreases the need for complicated formula mixtures and can make overall management easier."

One study found that children who were breastfed before their PKU diagnosis and treatment (which usually occurred before six weeks of age) scored an average of 14 points higher on intelligence tests during elementary school than the children who were fed formula from birth (Riva 1996). The researchers concluded that breastfeeding may offer a "positive nutritional benefit on later childhood neurodevelopmental performance," in part because human milk contains less phenylalanine than formula, resulting in lower blood levels of phenylalanine in breastfed babies before treatment begins. Also, human milk contains long-chain polyunsaturated fatty acids, which have been found to enhance neural functioning. Artificially fed babies have been found to have decreased levels of these fatty acids in their brain membranes after a few weeks of life.

Babies with PKU who were breastfed before diagnosis and dietary treatment have been found to score an average of 14 points higher on intelligence tests than babies formula-fed from birth.

References

Cardiac Problems

Combs, V. and Marino, B. A comparison of growth patterns in breast and bottle-fed infants with congenital heart disease. *Pediatr Nurs* 1993; 19(2):175-79.

Marino, B. et al. Oxygen saturations during breast and bottle feedings in infants with congenital heart disease. *J Pediatr Nurs* 1995; 10(6):360-64.

Meier, P. Bottle and breast feeding: effects on transcutaneous oxygen pressure and temperature in small preterm infants. *Nurs Res* 1988; 37:36-41.

Special Needs—Baby

Riordan, J. and Auerbach, K. *Breastfeeding and Human Lactation*. Boston and London: Jones and Bartlett, 1993, p. 492-94.

Zeskind, P. et al. Rhythmic organization of heart rate in breast-fed and bottle-fed newborn infants. *Early Dev Parent* 1992; 1(2):79-87.

Cleft Lip and/or Palate

Avedian, L. and Ruberg, R. Impaired weight gain in cleft palate infants. *Cleft Palate J* 1980; 17:24.

Broad, F. and Duganzich, D. The effects of infant feeding, birth order, occupation and socio-economic status on speech in six-year-old children. *NZ Med J* 1983; 96:483-86.

Cohen, M. et al. Immediate unrestricted feeding of infants following cleft lip and palate repair. *J Craniofac Surg* 1992; 3(1):30-32.

Danner, S. Breastfeeding the infant with a cleft defect. *NAACOG Clin Issues Perinat Women Health* 1992; 3(4):634-39.

Danner, S. and Wilson-Clay, B. *Breastfeeding the infant with a cleft lip/palate*. Unit 10. La Leche League International Lactation Consultant Series. Garden City Park, New York: Avery Publishing, 1986.

Duncan, B. et al. Exclusive breast-feeding for at least 4 months protects against otitis media. *Pediatrics* 1993; 91(5):867-72.

Grady, E. *Nursing my baby with a cleft of the soft palate.* Schaumburg, Illinois: La Leche League International, 1983.

Lawrence, R. *Breastfeeding: A Guide for the Medical Profession,* 4th ed. St. Louis: Mosby, 1994, pp. 454-58.

Litman, R. et al. Gastric volume and pH in infants fed clear liquids and breast milk prior to surgery. *Anesth Analg* 1994; 79:482-85.

Markowitz, J. et al. Immediate obturation of neonatal cleft palates. *Mt Sinai J Med* 1979; 46:123-29.

Mohrbacher, N. *Nursing a Baby with a Cleft Lip or Cleft Palate.* Schaumburg, Illinois: La Leche League International, 1994, Publication No. 122, pp 7-8.

Nicholson, S. and Schreiner, M. Feed the babies. Breastfeeding Abstracts 1995; 15(1):3-4.

Paradise, J. et al. Evidence in infants with cleft palate that breast milk protects against otitis media. *Pediatrics* 1994; 94(6):853-60.

Riordan, J. and Auerbach, K. *Breastfeeding and Human Lactation.* Boston and London: Jones and Bartlett, 1993, p. 495-97.

Schreiner, M. Preoperative and postoperative fasting in children. *Ped Clinics N Am* 1994; 41(1):111-20.

Spear, R. Anesthesia for premature and term infants: perioperative implications. *J Pediatr* 1992; 120(2 pt 1):165-75.

Weatherly-White, R. et al. Early repair and breastfeeding for infants with cleft lip. *Plas Reconstruc Surg* 1987; 79:886-87.

Cystic Fibrosis

Gaskin, K. and Waters, D. Nutritional management of infants with cystic fibrosis. *J Paediatr Child Health* 1994; 30:1-2.

Holliday, K. et al. Growth of human milk-fed and formula-fed infants with cystic fibrosis. *J Pediatr* 1991; 118:77-79.

Lawrence, R. *Breastfeeding: A Guide for the Medical Profession,* 4th ed. St. Louis: Mosby, 1994, pp. 441-42.

Luder, E. et al. Current recommendations for breastfeeding in cystic fibrosis centers. *Am J Dis Child* 1990; 144:1153-56.

Riordan, J. and Auerbach, K. *Breastfeeding and Human Lactation.* Boston and London: Jones and Bartlett, 1993, p. 501, 523.

Rooney, K. Breastfeeding a baby with cystic fibrosis. New Beginnings 1988; 4:43-44.

Down Syndrome

Aumonier, M. and Cunningham, C. Breast feeding in infants with Down's Syndrome. *Child Care Health Development* 1983; 9:247-55.

Broad, F. and Duganzich, D. The effects of infant feeding, birth order, occupation and socio-economic status on speech in six-year-old children. *NZ Med J* 1983; 96:483-86.

Cooley, W. Supporting the family of the newborn with Down Syndrome. *Compreh Therapy* 1993; 19(3):111-15.

Lawrence, R. *Breastfeeding: A Guide for the Medical Profession,* 4th ed. St. Louis: Mosby, 1994, p. 443-45.

Riordan, J. and Auerbach, K. *Breastfeeding and Human Lactation.* Boston and London: Jones and Bartlett, 1993, p. 490-91.

Timko, S. et al. *Breastfeeding the baby with Down Syndrome.* Unit 9, La Leche League International Lactation Consultant Series. Wayne, New Jersey: Avery Publishing, 1986.

Galactosemia

Lawrence, R. *Breastfeeding: A Guide for the Medical Profession,* 4th ed. St. Louis: Mosby, 1994, p. 439.

Riordan, J. and Auerbach, K. *Breastfeeding and Human Lactation.* Boston and London: Jones and Bartlett, 1993, p. 499.

Special Needs—Baby

The Neurologically Impaired Baby

Danner, S. and McBride, M. Sucking disorders in neurologically impaired infants. BREASTFEEDING ABSTRACTS 1988; 7:13.

Lawrence, R. *Breastfeeding: A Guide for the Medical Profession,* 4th ed. St. Louis: Mosby, 1994, p. 430-32.

McBride, M. and Danner, S. Sucking disorders in neurologically impaired infants. *Clin Perinatol* 1987; 109-30.

Riordan, J. and Auerbach, K. *Breastfeeding and Human Lactation.* Boston and London: Jones and Bartlett, 1993, p. 490-92.

PKU

Greve, L. et al. Breastfeeding in the management of the newborn with phenylketonuria: a practical approach to dietary therapy. *J Am Diet Assoc* 1994; 94:305-09.

Lawrence, R. *Breastfeeding: A Guide for the Medical Profession,* 4th ed. St. Louis: Mosby, 1994, p. 440.

McCabe, L. The management of breast feeding among infants with phenylketonuria. *J Inher Metab Dis* 1989; 12:467-74.

Riordan, J. and Auerbach, K. *Breastfeeding and Human Lactation*. Boston and London: Jones and Bartlett, 1993, p. 499.

Riva, E., et al. Early breastfeeding is linked to higher intelligence quotient scores in dietary treated phenylketonuric children. *Acta Paediatr* 1996; 85: 56-58.

15

Multiples— Breastfeeding Twins, Triplets, or More

BEFORE BIRTH—FEELINGS ABOUT HAVING MORE THAN ONE BABY

ADVANTAGES OF BREASTFEEDING MULTIPLES

PREPARATIONS DURING PREGNANCY

AFTER BIRTH—ADJUSTING TO LIFE WITH MULTIPLES

BREASTFEEDING BASICS

MOTHER CARE FOR THE MOTHER OF MULTIPLES

BREASTFEEDING TRIPLETS AND QUADRUPLETS

Listen to and accept the mother's feelings, which may be intense, and keep an open mind.

The mother of multiples is like any other breastfeeding mother—only more so. Her joys, her experiences, her feelings, her problems are intensified by having more than one baby. As always, listen carefully and accept her feelings, whatever they may be. And keep an open mind. What works well for a mother of one baby may not be practical for the mother of multiples. In the United States one out of every ninety births is a multiple birth.

BEFORE BIRTH—FEELINGS ABOUT HAVING MORE THAN ONE BABY

When a woman discovers she is pregnant with more than one baby, it is common to react at first with negative or ambivalent feelings. Acknowledge these feelings and let her know they are normal.

Many mothers react to the news that they are expecting more than one baby with dismay, which may scare them. A common response to a confession of ambivalent feelings is: "Don't worry. Everything will be fine." A better response is to acknowledge the feelings and to let the woman know that these feelings are normal.

Early diagnosis of a multiple pregnancy is an advantage because it gives the mother time to adjust to the idea. Mothers who find out early that they are expecting more than one baby tend to have an easier time bonding with their babies as a unit.

The expectant mother may be upset if her normal pregnancy is reclassified as high-risk, changing her birth plan and her daily routine. If a mother is unhappy with her doctor's advice, encourage her to seek another opinion.

A woman who believed her pregnancy to be normal and healthy may be upset when she is told that she must submit to repeated tests, spend weeks or months on bedrest, and plan for a high-risk birth.

A twin pregnancy may increase the chances of cesarean birth. Although some doctors plan an automatic cesarean in cases of multiple births, others do not. If a mother is unhappy with her doctor's advice, encourage her to seek another opinion. Repeated tests may carry risks and be intimidating, and a cesarean can cause breastfeeding to get off to a slower start.

Extended bedrest can cause feelings of helplessness and depression, making the expectant mother more vulnerable to others' advice.

If a woman is confined to bed for an extended time during her pregnancy, she may feel helpless and depressed. Often it is necessary during a difficult pregnancy to ask relatives or friends to help care for the expectant mother. If she is depressed, the expectant mother may feel emotionally distant from others and concerned about the prospect of motherhood. In this state she may be especially vulnerable to advice from those around her.

Sometimes—out of concern for her—these helpers may try to convince the woman to bottle-feed rather than breastfeed her babies so that they can continue to help her after the babies are born. Although these offers are made out of kindness, having a helper take over primary care of the babies may cause more harm than good. After a difficult pregnancy, a mother needs more contact, not less, with her babies so that she can feel needed and emotionally close to them. If she is treated like an invalid while her babies are cared for by others, it can deepen her depression by making her feel useless.

Encourage the mother to talk to her helpers about how they can be of most help after the babies are born with such household tasks as laundry, housework, and meals. If a helper is insistent that the expectant mother consider bottle-feeding (and this may be especially awkward if the helper is a relative), the mother may need the help of the babies' father in explaining her wishes.

ADVANTAGES OF BREASTFEEDING MULTIPLES

Breastfeeding offers special advantages for the mother of multiples.

Like all aspects of mothering multiples, the advantages of breastfeeding are the same as for other mothers—only more so.

Breastfeeding contracts the mother's uterus, which is especially important to a mother of multiples because her uterus has stretched even more than usual to accommodate more than one baby.

Breastfeeding ensures the mother will spend lots of time every day holding the babies, which promotes feelings of closeness. Many mothers of multiples find that they naturally feel closer to one baby over another, especially if there is some separation after birth. Breastfeeding guarantees that the mother will give both babies the skin-to-skin contact and holding that they need to develop a loving relationship.

Breastfeeding saves eight to ten hours a week. This is based on the assumption that the babies will sometimes breastfeed simultaneously and sometimes separately. These saved hours represent time that the mother will not have to spend shopping for formula and preparing bottles.

The hormones released during breastfeeding relax the mother. This is especially important when she is dealing with two crying babies.

Human milk, the perfect food, also provides the babies with immunities to illness. Studies have shown that breastfed infants are sick less often during the first year of life. This is another time-saver for the mother of multiples.

The mother's milk is immediately available. There is no waiting while babies cry and formula is warmed.

Substantial financial savings. The breastfeeding mother of multiples saves two to three times more money (depending on whether she is breastfeeding twins or triplets) than the breastfeeding mother of one baby. It is estimated that breastfeeding will save a mother of twins more than $1600 (US) during the babies' first year.

PREPARATIONS DURING PREGNANCY

An expectant mother of multiples has different nutritional needs than a mother expecting one baby. However, she may find it difficult to eat as much high-quality food as she needs.

A well-nourished mother will have an easier start at motherhood and breastfeeding. To ensure proper development and a higher birth weight, good nutrition is crucial. But the mother expecting multiples may find it difficult to eat as much food as she needs. If she is unable to meet her daily requirements by eating three meals a day, encourage the mother to eat many small meals frequently during the day. She should try to eat foods high in nutritional value and eliminate foods containing empty calories.

Multiples

A weight gain double that of a single pregnancy is not unusual. Most doctors now agree that restricting weight gain will result in lower birth weights for the babies. Since multiple pregnancies are more likely to end in premature birth, a healthy diet is especially important to give these babies the best start possible.

Encourage the mother to make a well-informed choice when selecting her own and her babies' doctors.

An unmedicated, natural birth is the ideal. Encourage the mother to make a list of her priorities and discuss them with prospective doctors. A doctor who has had experience in delivering multiples vaginally would be less likely to schedule a cesarean birth automatically.

When interviewing a doctor for her babies, suggest she ask these questions:

- What are your feelings about breastfeeding in general, and about breastfeeding multiples?
- Do you believe multiples can be totally breastfed for the first several months?
- If one or more babies require special care, could my expressed milk be given to them?
- Would you encourage me to spend time with them in the special-care nursery?

Suggest the mother find out who is the neonatologist on staff at her hospital. Often this doctor is required to be present at all multiple births and may be put in charge of the case. By making an appointment with the neonatologist before her babies are born, the mother can get to know this doctor and his or her standard procedures before birth.

Encourage the mother to attend childbirth education classes early in her pregnancy in case she is on bedrest later on.

Arranging for household help during the babies' first few months is essential.

Any new mother can use extra help, but it can be crucial for the mother of multiples. Encourage the mother to find help from those who are supportive of her choices, rather than someone who will be critical. Suggest she make it clear that she needs help with household chores, not with baby care, so she can give her babies her full attention.

Suggest she learn in advance about expressing her milk, as there is a greater likelihood that she will be separated from one or more of her babies after birth.

Before her babies are born, encourage the mother to learn about expressing her milk, as her chances of being separated from one or more of her babies at birth are greater than the mother expecting one baby.

Suggest she call the hospital where she is to give birth to find out if a lactation consultant is on staff to help her with breastfeeding and if an automatic electric piston breast pump will be available to her in case she is separated from one or more of her babies after birth (Biancuzzo 1994). If one is not available at the hospital, give her information on where she can rent one.

Talk about how the automatic electric piston breast pump works and how often she will need to pump her breasts to stimulate her milk supply and provide milk for her babies. Also, be sure she understands that in the first few days after birth it is normal not to produce large quantities of milk, but that once her milk supply becomes more plentiful on the third or fourth day she will see a dramatic increase. (See "When Breastfeeding Is Delayed after Birth" in the chapter "Expression and Storage of Human Milk.")

AFTER BIRTH—ADJUSTING TO LIFE WITH MULTIPLES

It is common for a mother to feel emotionally closer to one of her babies and for it to take longer to feel close to twins, as opposed to a baby who is born singly.

When unexpected multiples are born, it is not unusual for the mother to feel more motherly toward the firstborn. Subconsciously, the mother may see the first baby as the baby she wanted and the other(s) as an intruder. Even when multiples are expected, if one baby comes home and another stays at the hospital, the mother may feel closer to the baby she is with and feel as if the other baby is a stranger. In some cases, without even realizing it, the mother may express her more distant feelings toward one baby by perceiving that he has difficulty breastfeeding and weaning him to a bottle—while continuing to breastfeed the other baby.

If a mother is worried because her feelings toward her babies differ, reassure her that this will pass with time. In the meantime, rather than wasting time feeling guilty, she can begin to make an effort to give extra attention to the baby she does not feel as close to. Encourage her to look into his face and talk to him, use a baby carrier to keep him close, breastfeed him skin-to-skin, or take a bath with him.

A mother who has older children who were born singly may be upset that she does not feel as intimate a bond with her multiples as quickly as she did with her other children. This, too, is normal. It is naturally more difficult to fall in love with two or more babies than one. Reassure her that the bond will develop in time. For some women it may take months, or even a year or two, which may be disappointing to the mother. Acknowledge her feelings and point out that breastfeeding will make forming a loving relationship with the babies easier.

Some mothers—especially those who have had the advantage of knowing early in pregnancy that they were expecting multiples—become emotionally attached to their babies first as a unit and only later as individuals. Such a mother may dress her babies alike and give them similar sounding names. This is normal, too, and a mother who becomes attached to her babies in this way may have less ambivalence about caring for multiples. It is not necessary for her to make an effort to focus on them as individuals when they are tiny. This perception will naturally change as they grow and mature.

One study found that mothers of twins were more likely to become depressed than mothers of single babies, even those with closely spaced children. The researchers attributed these findings in part to the simultaneous demands of two children, the extra financial stress, and the difficulties getting out with two babies (Thorpe 1991).

BREASTFEEDING BASICS

Breastfeeding early and often is especially important with multiples. If mother and babies are separated, expressing can help build her milk supply and provide nourishment for the babies.

To establish a plentiful milk supply, the mother needs to know that the more often she breastfeeds, the more milk she will have (Saint 1986). If she is separated from one or more of her babies due to health problems, encourage her to express milk and store it to be given to the baby or babies. See "When Breastfeeding Is Delayed after Birth" in the chapter "Expression and Storage of Human Milk."

If the babies are healthy, suggest that while in the hospital the mother ask that both babies be brought to her for all feedings. Rooming-in would give her even more access to her babies.

Avoiding bottles and pacifiers during the babies' early weeks will help establish a healthy milk supply and encourage the babies to suck effectively.

Artificial nipples can cause nipple confusion and interfere with the mother's milk supply. However, if the babies receive bottles, assure the mother that she can still breastfeed. It may mean, however, that she will need to be more patient and persistent to get the babies to take the breast.

If the babies receive supplements, be sure the mother knows about the alternative feeding methods, such as cup, spoon, eyedropper, feeding syringe, and finger feeding. (See "The Use of Breast Pumps and Other Products.")

The babies can breastfeed simultaneously or separately.

Most mothers of multiples find that at times it is easier to nurse the babies together and at other times it is easier to nurse them separately. If a baby is having difficulty latching on or sucking, it may be best for the mother to give him her full attention during breastfeeding. Simultaneous nursing usually becomes easier as the babies get older and are more practiced at latching on to the breast.

Multiples

Simultaneous nursing may cause a greater increase in the mother's prolactin levels, increasing her milk production. This may be especially important to the mother who is trying to increase her milk supply. However, the babies may not always be interested in nursing at the same time. Also, some mothers prefer to breastfeed separately because they can give each baby more individual attention. As far as a tiny baby is concerned, however, he may not realize or care that there is a baby at the other breast. The mother will need to experiment to find out what works best for her and her babies (Gromada 1992).

If the mother would like to breastfeed her babies together but is finding it difficult, suggest that she use pillows to support the babies at breast height. If the mother is sitting on a couch, suggest she put one baby next to her while she settles the other baby at the breast, putting pillows under him to support him. Then she can position the other baby at the breast, with pillows under him as well.

There are several nursing positions that can be used to breastfeed both babies simultaneously.

It will be much easier to get into a comfortable simultaneous nursing position —especially when the babies are tiny—if the mother has a helping hand. Extra pillows under arms, legs, and babies can add to mother's comfort. The mother can breastfeed on a bed, couch, chair, or floor. Possible simultaneous nursing positions include:

Combination Cradle and Football Hold. The mother is sitting upright. One baby is in the cradle hold. The other baby is in the football hold with his head on his sibling's abdomen. Pillows under the mother's elbows and the babies will make

Parallel Position

Double Football Hold

Good latch-on is important for avoiding sore nipples.

Criss-Cross

this easier. This position is the most inconspicuous for nursing outside the home and one of the most easily mastered if one or both babies have difficulty latching on to the breast.

Criss-Cross. The mother is sitting upright. Both babies are in the cradle hold criss-crossed in her lap. One baby's body is pressed against the mother, the other baby's body is pressed against his sibling. Their heads are in the crooks of the mother's arms. A pillow under the mother's elbow helps to support the lower baby. This position could also be used outside the home without pillows if the mother clasps her hands to support the babies' weight. Without pillows it is more tiring.

Parallel. The mother is sitting upright, and the babies' bodies extend in the same direction. One baby is in the cradle hold with his head in the crook of his mother's arm and his body across his mother's lap. The other baby's body extends in the same direction as his sibling's off the mother's lap, with his head supported by his mother's hand and arm. Pillows supporting the mother's elbows and on her lap will make this position more comfortable.

Double Football Hold. The mother is sitting upright. Both babies are in the football hold, lying on firm pillows at the mother's sides. The higher the pillows, the easier this position is on the mother's back. It may also be more comfortable if the mother props her feet on a footstool, chair, or low table. This position may be especially comfortable for a mother who has had a cesarean birth, because the babies' weight will not be resting on her incision.

Babies at Side. The mother is sitting upright. The babies lie at the mother's sides, partly on their sides facing each other with their feet in her lap. Pillows need to be placed behind the mother's back and under each baby's head to support him at the breast. The mother's hands are free in this position.

V-Position. The mother is lying nearly flat on her back with two pillows under her head. The babies' heads are at their mother's breasts, forming a V with their knees touching in her lap. This can be a safe and comfortable position for simultaneous night nursings.

Stomach. The mother lies on her stomach propped on her elbows. The babies lie on their backs underneath her. This is the least-used simultaneous nursing position.

Sore nipples are a common concern of mothers of multiples. Tell the mother that sore nipples are not caused by how often or how long the babies breastfeed. The most common cause of soreness is improper latch-on and positioning.

Suggest the mother be sure that when the babies go on the breast that their mouths are open very wide (like a yawn) and that she pulls them in very close to her so they each get a large mouthful of breast tissue. This will be easier on her nipples and will also help them get more milk for their efforts. (See "Latch-On—How the Baby Goes on to the Breast" in the chapter "Positioning, Latch-On, and the Baby's Suck.")

Also, whatever position the mother uses, suggest she make sure that the babies do not have to turn their heads to nurse, that they are directly facing the nipple. If a baby has to turn his head, he will pull on the nipple as he nurses, possibly contributing to soreness.

If soreness persists, see, "If Breastfeeding Hurts—Review the Basics" in the chapter "Positioning, Latch-On, and the Baby's Suck" and "Sore Nipples" in the chapter "Nipple Problems."

If the mother has persistent nipple soreness and her babies are less than one month old, ask her if the babies are also receiving bottles. When receiving both bottle and breast, some babies try to nurse at the breast as they do at the bottle, causing sore nipples. The mother can determine if this is the cause by eliminating bottles and instead giving supplements using one of the alternative feeding methods.

Every mother of multiples needs to work out for herself the practical details of breastfeeding, such as which breast to offer which baby.

Unless a baby is not gaining well, it is fine to allow the babies to breastfeed on cue according to their own needs. (If a baby is not gaining well, he may need to be encouraged to breastfeed more often. See "Slow Weight Gain" in the chapter "Weight Gain," for more information.) Every mother of multiples has to work out for herself the practical details of breastfeeding according to the needs of her babies and her own preferences. While keeping in mind that milk is produced according to supply and demand, the mother may decide to encourage the babies to nurse simultaneously at certain times of the day to save time. Or she may prefer to nurse the babies separately because she enjoys that one-on-one time with each baby. She may also find that the babies fall into their own nursing patterns, with one baby wanting to breastfeed more often than the other.

There are different approaches to deciding which baby gets which breast. Some mothers never think about which baby gets which breast. They just offer whichever breast feels most full to whichever baby is hungriest at the moment. Other mothers keep each baby on the same breast for an entire day, alternating breasts at least every day. Switching breasts gives the babies the varied visual stimulation they need. Some mothers of twins assign each baby a certain breast, which he gets at every feeding and never varies. However, the disadvantage to this is that the babies' eyes are not stimulated as optimally as if they nursed on both breasts.

If one baby has a weaker suck, it is important to regularly switch breasts so that both breasts are well-stimulated to keep up the mother's milk supply.

Some mothers of multiples keep careful track of which baby nursed when on which breast, and count each baby's wet diapers and bowel movements every day. This gives them daily reassurance that both babies are getting enough. Other mothers don't keep track of either feedings or diapers. If both babies are gaining well, such record-keeping is unnecessary. If a baby is not gaining well, suggest to the mother that she keep a journal for a few days to record frequency and length of nursings and number of wet and soiled diapers. Life with multiples is hectic, and if a baby is placid or sleepy it is possible he will not breastfeed often or long enough to meet his needs.

Multiples

There are many ways to handle night nursings.

When nursing at night, suggest the mother try nursing one baby in the side-lying position. Many mothers find this position difficult with a newborn, but as the baby grows, it becomes easier. When a mother can nurse lying down, it allows her to accomplish two things at once (always a plus for mothers of multiples!)— breastfeeding while getting her sleep. Until she can comfortably breastfeed in this position, the mother may need to sit up for night nursings, with pillows for support. Some mothers routinely wake the second baby after the first awakens to nurse, so that they will get a longer stretch of uninterrupted sleep.

Many mothers of multiples have both babies sleep in one crib, because they find the babies sleep better when they are touching. If a crib is used, it may make night nursing easier if it is in the same room where mother sleeps so there is less moving around (which usually means waking up more fully) when the babies need to nurse at night. Some mothers of multiples fasten the crib to the side of their bed, adjust the mattress level to theirs, and remove the side rail closest to their bed. This makes for easier access to the babies at night. The mother then brings into bed with her whichever baby wants to nurse, breastfeeds him while lying on her side, and returns him to the crib after he's finished or—if she falls asleep—when the other baby awakens to nurse.

An alternative is to have a mattress on the floor, either in the babies' room or the mother's room so that the mother can lie down with the babies and sleep during feedings. Another option that would have this same advantage is to bring the babies in the mother's bed (with the bed pushed against the wall or a guard rail on the side where the babies sleep) just for nursings or for the whole night.

Support the mother in using whatever way works best for her. Encourage her to use her creativity and to keep an open mind.

Sometimes, supplements may be needed.

A mother may need to give her babies supplements if breastfeeding got off to a slow start. Some of the common reasons for this are:

- only one baby was brought at feeding times in the hospital;
- night nursing was restricted in the hospital;
- the mother was separated from one or more of the babies because he needed to be in the special-care nursery;
- one or more babies have a weak suck (common in babies born prematurely) or are nipple confused.

If only one baby seems to have difficulty breastfeeding and is being supplemented, help the mother explore her feelings to see if lack of emotional attachment to that baby could be part of the problem. (See previous section on "After Birth—Adjusting to Life with Multiples.")

For the nipple-confused baby, simultaneous nursing will increase the milk flow and encourage him to suck more effectively.

If a baby is nipple-confused, suggest the mother try breastfeeding him simultaneously with his sibling. The baby with the more effective suck will stimulate the let-down, or milk-ejection, reflex, and the faster flow of milk will encourage the confused baby to suck and swallow correctly.

If this doesn't work, suggest the mother offer her own expressed milk as a supplement while the confused baby is learning how to take the breast. She may find it easy to express milk from one breast while the other baby nurses on the other breast (a pump that can be operated with only one hand is a necessity for this unless the mother is able to support the baby at the breast with pillows while she hand-expresses her milk). To avoid further confusion, suggest the mother consider using a spoon, cup, eyedropper, or feeding syringe to give the supplements instead of a bottle.

Growth spurts can mean an increase in nursing for several days.

It is especially important for the mother of multiples to know that all babies experience growth spurts at around three weeks, six weeks, and three months of age. During these growth spurts babies usually nurse more frequently to increase their mother's milk supply to meet their growing needs. If the mother expects increased nursing at these times she will not panic and incorrectly assume that she does not have enough milk for her babies.

Encourage her to nurse more frequently for several days, after which her babies' nursing patterns should return to normal. In the meantime, she can be confident that her babies are getting enough by keeping track of the babies' wet diapers and bowel movements. (Each baby should have six to eight wet cloth diapers—five to six disposables—and two to five bowel movements per day; fewer bowel movements are considered normal if the babies are older than six weeks.)

Regular supplements can contribute to breastfeeding difficulties.

Some mothers may feel tempted to give (or have someone else give) their babies regular supplements. It is important to let each mother find the way that works best for her in her individual circumstances, but if she asks about the pros and cons of occasional supplements, tell her:

- Supplements given by bottle during the babies' first month can cause nipple confusion, which may make one or both babies refuse the breast or contribute to nipple soreness.
- Her milk supply is dependent upon how often her babies breastfeed. If she routinely supplements to replace a breastfeeding, her milk supply will go down. Because formula may keep the babies full longer (since it is not as quickly digested as human milk), this can further extend the time

between feedings, decreasing her milk supply even more, making more supplements necessary and starting a downward cycle of fewer breastfeedings and more formula.

- Skipping nursings when the mother's breasts are full makes the mother more susceptible to mastitis.
- Water supplements are not needed and can produce more wet diapers without providing any nutrition. This would make a wet-diaper count inaccurate, leaving the mother without a way to gauge whether or not her babies were getting enough.
- Solids given at bedtime have not been proven to eliminate night-waking.

Supplements should be eliminated gradually.

If the babies are breastfeeding effectively (that is, neither baby has a weak suck), the mother can cut down on the supplements gradually with the guidance of her babies' doctor while breastfeeding more often to build up her milk supply.

In order to stimulate more milk production, encourage the mother to breastfeed first, before offering a supplement. (See "Working with the Doctor and Supplementation" in the chapter "Weight Gain.") Also, suggest she keep a record of frequency and length of nursing, as well as number of wet diapers and bowel movements, to be sure the babies are getting enough as she decreases the amount of supplement. Also, explain the importance of not limiting feeding times so that the babies get the fatty hindmilk they need.

Explain that babies do not need water or juice and that giving anything other than her milk will affect her milk supply and may confuse her babies in the early weeks. Also, suggest the mother avoid giving pacifiers while she is trying to increase her milk supply, because pacifiers can satisfy a baby's sucking need and cut down on his time at the breast.

MOTHER CARE FOR THE MOTHER OF MULTIPLES

Encourage the mother to drink to thirst, eat nutritious foods, and sleep when the babies sleep.

As with any breastfeeding mother, it's not necessary for the mother of multiples to drink a certain, specific amount of fluids. Suggest, instead, that the mother drink to thirst. The mother will be able to tell if she is not getting enough fluids if her urine becomes concentrated or she is constipated. If she notices either of these symptoms, she should make sure to drink more. It may help to keep a pitcher of water and a glass near the place she usually nurses so she will have a drink handy when she is thirsty.

Multiples

Suggest the mother have nutritious snacks on hand that she can eat during the day that require a minimum of preparation, such as fresh fruits and vegetables, cheese slices or cubes, nuts, hard-cooked eggs, meat slices, and whole-grain bread and crackers. Although meal preparation may need to be simplified while the babies are small, encourage the mother to eat nutritiously. Nature ensures—for the babies' sake—that human milk is produced at the same high quality even if the mother's diet is less than ideal. But if the mother does not eat well, she will deplete her own nutritional stores, which may make her tired, irritable, and decrease her resistance to illness. So it is in her own best interest to eat well.

Fatigue is a fact of life for any mother of a small baby. Encourage the mother to sleep when her babies sleep and not use this time to catch up on housekeeping. Especially in the early months, her rest should be a higher priority.

Suggest the mother limit visitors in the early weeks, arrange for household help for several months, accept help from friends and relatives, streamline housekeeping, and set priorities.

If at all possible, encourage the mother to plan to have full-time help when she comes home from the hospital. This could be the babies' father, if he is able to take time off from work, a relative, a friend, a teenage neighbor, a retiree, someone from a social service agency, or a full-time housekeeper, depending on the family's resources. Some churches provide volunteer mother's helpers to mothers of multiples. Whoever is there to help should understand that his or her job is to "mother the mother" and help with household chores, not to take over the care of the babies.

Limiting visitors during the babies' first few weeks can simplify life. Once friends and relatives begin to visit, their first question is usually what they can do to help. Suggest the mother take them up on their offer to help and ask them to:

- Bring food when they visit.
- Change the babies.
- Give her a back rub or foot massage while she nurses the babies.
- Watch the babies while she takes a fifteen-minute walk, bath, or shower.
- Listen if she is feeling scared, tired, or overwhelmed.
- Do laundry, fold clothes, or put them away.
- Do grocery shopping for her.
- Clean up the kitchen, do dishes, vacuum, pick up.

Also suggest—before the visitors arrive—that the mother tell them that she is breast-feeding.

The mother may also appreciate some suggestions for simplifying routine baby care:

- Use a diaper service.
- Have baby-changing areas in all parts of the house and change the babies assembly-line style.
- Give weekly instead of daily baths, making sure the diaper areas and faces are clean each day.

She might also like some tips for streamlining housework and shopping:

- Use laundry baskets to collect clutter and put things away later.
- Buy only easy-care clothing and enlist the regular help of older children or other helpers with putting away clothes and doing laundry.
- Clean the bathroom after a shower by wiping with a damp towel when everything is steamy.
- Soak dirty dishes in hot, soapy water in the sink until they can be washed.
- Collect recipes that can be prepared in stages.
- Shop from catalogues.
- Find drug stores and grocery stores that deliver.
- Within the family's budget do or buy anything that simplifies household tasks and allows more time to enjoy the babies.

It is especially important for the mother and father of multiples to set priorities together. People's needs come first, especially the babies'. After that comes food and clothing. Encourage the mother to discuss with the babies' father what household tasks he feels are important and what he feels can be set aside. They need to establish priorities together to decide how best to manage from day to day.

Suggest the mother surround herself with people who are supportive of her decision to breastfeed. This will keep her confidence high.

Many mothers of multiples receive criticism from relatives who do not share their enthusiasm for breastfeeding. They may pressure the mother to give bottles or begin solid foods earlier than usual or to wean before she is ready. Sometimes innocent questions, such as "Are you sure you have enough milk?" or "Isn't it hard on you?" are enough to undermine a mother's confidence in her ability to breastfeed.

It is important that the mother has someone she can call to reassure her when she begins to doubt herself. Even better, if possible, is to surround herself with people who are supportive of breastfeeding.

BREASTFEEDING TRIPLETS AND QUADRUPLETS

Triplets and quadruplets can be breastfed.

Some mothers of triplets and quadruplets have fully breastfed their babies (Duggin 1994; Gromada 1992; Mead 1992). Supplements may be needed if the babies get off to a slow start (see the previous section, "Breastfeeding Basics"). The mother may be interested to know that in 17th century France, wet nurses in foundling homes were allowed to nurse up to six infants at one time (Lawrence, p. 433).

When the babies breastfeed often and effectively, a healthy milk supply usually follows. One mother of quadruplets reported that her milk supply was so copious that when the babies slept for two hours at a stretch she was able to pump enough milk for supplemental feedings (Mead 1992). But even when milk supply is no problem, finding the time to nurse can be. Breastfeeding two babies simultaneously can help keep the time spent nursing each day more manageable.

Frequency and effectiveness of breastfeeding are the keys to building a plentiful milk supply. The more often a baby nurses, the more milk there will be. Tell the mother to expect to breastfeed each baby about eight to twelve times every twenty-four hours. With three or four babies it may be wise, especially in the first two to three months, to keep track of who nurses when, for how long, and how many wet diapers and bowel movements each baby has per day. (Each baby should have six to eight wet cloth diapers—five to six disposables—and two to five bowel movements; fewer bowel movements are considered normal if the babies are older than six weeks.) This can help the mother be sure each baby is getting enough.

Encourage the mother to experiment to find comfortable routines for breastfeeding.

Some mothers of triplets routinely breastfeed two babies at a time, others breastfeed the babies separately. A king-size chair may be helpful, so the mother can keep one baby at her side and one on her lap while the third baby nurses.

Multiples

Resources for Parents

Center for Study of Multiple Births
333 E. Superior Street, Room 464, Chicago IL 60611 USA
Telephone: (312)266-9093

National Organization of Mothers of Twins Clubs
P.O. Box 23188, Albuquerque NM 87192-1188 USA
Telephone: (800)243-2276

The Triplet Connection
P.O. Box 99571, Stockton CA 95209 USA
Telephone: (209)474-0885

Publications for Parents

Double Talk Newsletter, P.O. Box 412, Amelia OH 45102. Telephone: (513) 231-TWIN (Twin Bookshop).

Fleming, M. *Breastfeeding Twins.* Schaumburg, Illinois: La Leche League International, 1991. Publication No. 52.

Gromada, K. MOTHERING MULTIPLES: BREASTFEEDING AND CARING FOR TWINS. Schaumburg, Illinois: La Leche League International, 1991.

La Leche League International. THE WOMANLY ART OF BREASTFEEDING, 35th anniversary ed., Schaumburg, Illinois, 1991, pp. 305-12.

Noble, E. *Having Twins*. Boston: Houghton Mifflin, 1991.

Twins Magazine, P.O. Box 12045, Overland Park, KS 66212 USA. Telephone: (800) 821-5533.

Twin Services Reporter, P.O. Box 10066, Berkeley, CA 94704.

References

Biancuzzo, M. Breastfeeding preterm twins: a case report. *Birth* 1994; 21(2):96-100.

Duggin, J. Breastfeeding triplets—it can be done! *Breastfeed Rev* 1994; II(10):469-70.

Gromada, K. Breastfeeding more than one: multiples and tandem breastfeeding. *NAACOG* 1992; 3(4):656-66.

Lawrence, R. *Breastfeeding: A Guide for the Medical Profession,* 4th ed. St. Louis: Mosby, 1994, p. 433.

Mead, L. et al. Breastfeeding success with preterm quadruplets. *JOGNN* 1992; 21(3):221-27.

Riordan, J. and Auerbach, K. *Breastfeeding and Human Lactation*. Boston and London: Jones and Bartlett, 1993, pp. 243-44.

Saint, L. et al. Yield and nutrient content of milk in eight women breast-feeding twins and one woman breast-feeding triplets. *Br J Nutr* 1986; 56:49-58.

Thorpe, K. et al. Comparison of prevalence of depression in mothers of twins and mothers of singletons. *BMJ* 1991; 302:875-79.

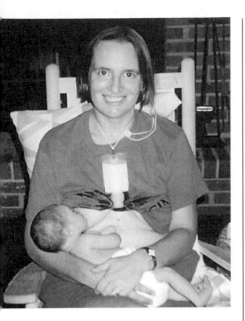

16

Relactation and Adoptive Nursing

TALK ABOUT FEELINGS, GOALS, AND REALISTIC EXPECTATIONS

RELACTATION—STIMULATING A MILK SUPPLY

INDUCED LACTATION—STIMULATING A MILK SUPPLY

ENCOURAGING THE BABY TO TAKE THE BREAST

MAKING THE TRANSITION—HOW TO BE SURE THAT BABY IS GETTING ENOUGH

Relactation is rebuilding a birth mother's milk supply after it has been reduced or dried up. Adoptive nursing—or induced lactation—is attempting to produce milk when the mother has not recently given birth.

Relactation is the process of rebuilding a birth mother's milk supply, which has been reduced or dried up after weeks or months of not breastfeeding. The mother may or may not have begun breastfeeding after birth. A mother may decide to relactate because her baby has a physical need for her milk—a formula intolerance, allergy, or other serious medical condition—or for other reasons. It is possible—assuming the baby eventually takes the breast—that with effort and perseverance she will be able to produce a full milk supply for her baby.

Induced lactation, or adoptive nursing, is the process of stimulating the adoptive mother's body to produce milk even though she has not experienced a recent birth or pregnancy. In many cases, the amount of milk produced, although beneficial to the baby, may be less important to the mother than establishing a satisfying nursing relationship. Bringing in a full milk supply may be possible, but will require more intense effort and much support.

When a mother who is breastfeeding an older baby or toddler wants to increase her milk supply for an adopted baby, this is called partially induced lactation and the approach is the same as induced lactation.

TALK ABOUT FEELINGS, GOALS, AND REALISTIC EXPECTATIONS

First ask the mother why she wants to breastfeed.

Discussing her reasons for wanting to relactate or induce lactation can help a mother clarify her feelings, evaluate her motivations, and assess whether or not her goals are likely to be met.

A mother considering relactation may feel guilty, either because her choice to bottle-feed caused problems for her baby or for other reasons. Her feelings, which may be intense, can affect her reactions to relactation.

For the mother considering relactating, ask her why she stopped breastfeeding or chose bottle-feeding.

When exploring the possibility of relactation, talk to the mother about why she stopped breastfeeding or decided to bottle-feed. Whatever circumstances or feelings led her to wean or to choose bottle-feeding may still exist and need to be resolved.

If the mother weaned her baby because she had breastfeeding problems, ask her what happened. Her difficulties may have been due to a misunderstanding that needs to be clarified. For example, a mother may have been told to breast-feed on a schedule. Because the baby was not nursing often enough, he did not gain well, so supplements were recommended and gradually increased until the baby was no longer breastfeeding. This mother would need to understand the supply-and-demand principle on which milk production is based or she would face the same problem again. The mother who stopped breastfeeding because she had sore nipples needs to understand proper positioning and latch-on. No matter what caused her to give up on breastfeeding, make sure she knows how to avoid the problem this time.

If a mother chose to bottle-feed, discuss why she made this choice. Are these reasons still a consideration? How does she feel about breastfeeding? If she was uncomfortable with the idea of breastfeeding when her baby was born, those feelings may still exist and need to be addressed.

Ask the mother about her baby and her circumstances.

Find out more about the mother and the baby. It will be helpful to know:

- the age of the baby,
- the baby's response when offered the breast,
- if the baby has ever breastfed (if so, how long has he been weaned from the breast?),

- if the mother or baby has any medical problems (if the baby is hospitalized, the mother may have limited control over how he is fed),
- if the mother is taking any medications that may affect breastfeeding,
- if the mother has inverted nipples,
- if the mother has other children (if so, their ages),
- what other daily obligations and activities the mother has,
- if the family is under any unusual stress.

The younger the baby and the more willing he is to take the breast, the more likely it is that relactation or induced lactation will go smoothly. A healthy mother and baby will also make the process easier. A mother with inverted nipples may have to work a little harder at getting the baby well latched-on to her breast. (For suggestions, see "Flat and Inverted Nipples" in the chapter "Nipple Problems.")

Daily obligations and activities, as well as older children, can make it more difficult for the mother to find the extra time she needs for relactation or induced lactation. If the mother has a busy schedule and other children to care for, ask her if it would be possible to take some time out from other obligations and find help with her older children while she focuses on bringing in her milk.

Ask the mother how much help and support she will have.

Relactation and induced lactation require much time and effort, and the mother's motivation and self-confidence are vital to the process. Explain the value of support and ask the mother who among her family and friends will give her the day-to-day help she will need, as well as emotional support and encouragement. This is especially vital if the mother has other children.

Ask the mother how the baby's father feels about her desire to breastfeed, as his feelings may have a major impact on the mother.

Encourage the mother to contact other mothers who have had similar experiences.

Help the mother develop realistic expectations.

Relactation. In one survey of 366 women who relactated, most women reported not being as concerned with the amount of milk they produced as they were with having the opportunity to nurture their baby through breastfeeding (Auerbach and Avery 1980). Although some mothers made the decision to relactate based on their baby's intolerance of formula or other health problems, most did so because of the effect breastfeeding would have on their relationship with their baby. In hindsight, 75% of the women surveyed felt relactation had been a positive experience and the amount of milk they produced was unrelated to their feelings of success.

Relactate/Adopt

In this survey, the majority of mothers were able to successfully relactate. More than half of the mothers surveyed established a full milk supply within a month. It took another 25% of the mothers more than a month to fully relactate. The remaining mothers both breastfed and gave supplements until their babies weaned. Mothers who attempted relactation within two months of childbirth reported greater milk production than those who attempted it later on. Although every situation is unique, many women have found the length of time it takes to relactate fully (i.e., establishing a milk supply that completely meets her baby's needs) is about equal to how long it has been since breastfeeding was discontinued. Several weeks would be a realistic expectation for most mothers.

Tell the mother to expect that her efforts to get her baby back to the breast will require her to adjust her priorities and devote most of her time for the next two weeks or so. Ask her if she will be able to make it a top priority in her life. If not, she may need to reevaluate her desire to relactate or her other commitments.

Induced lactation. Different mothers approach adoptive nursing with different goals and expectations. To clarify the mother's goals, ask her how important the amount of milk is to her. Some mothers—particularly in developing countries where artificial feeding is dangerous—approach induced lactation with bringing in a full milk supply as their top priority. Other mothers focus primarily on the emotional benefits of nursing, although they consider the milk important for their babies and they want to try to bring in a full supply. Still other mothers may see induced lactation as first and foremost a way to enhance their relationship with their baby and give little thought to the amount of milk produced. When comfort and closeness are an important consideration, adoptive nursing is almost always a satisfying experience for both mother and baby.

When a mother says closeness is her top priority, suggest she concentrate on the emotional closeness breastfeeding offers her and her baby and think of any milk she might produce as an added bonus. In this case, "success" is best evaluated by whether or not the baby will suckle the breast and achieve the comfort and security of a close relationship with his new mother.

If bringing in a full milk supply is the mother's top priority, explore the reasons behind this goal. Help the mother evaluate her situation realistically and weigh the intense effort needed to bring in a full milk supply against her baby's and her own needs and the relative risks of supplementing with formula. While information from developing countries suggests that many adoptive mothers can bring in a full milk supply, cultural differences may make it difficult to achieve the same results in other circumstances. If appropriate, share with the mother information from developing countries, where there has been a long history of mothers' inducing full lactation (Slome 1956; Wieschhoff 1940).

In one study conducted in Papua, New Guinea, a combination of milk-stimulating drugs given to the mother and frequent suckling by the baby resulted in a full milk supply in 24 of 27 adoptive mothers (Nemba 1994). Cultural differences and the baby's willingness to take the breast play important roles in a woman's success in inducing full lactation. Where breastfeeding is the norm, mothers expect to be able to nurse their babies and they are supported to this end. In the New Guinea study, for example, the birth mothers breastfed the babies during the time the adoptive mothers were bringing in their milk. Bottles were not used, eliminating that as a complicating factor in the baby accepting the breast. Any supplements were given by cup or spoon. Also, because breastfeeding is a matter of life and death in these areas, health care providers strongly urged the mothers to induce lactation in order to insure their baby's survival and provided practical help to accomplish this. The mothers' families supported them as well.

In areas where artificial feeding is the norm and even birth mothers receive mixed or negative messages about their ability to breastfeed, inducing lactation is likely to be perceived as an oddity. Health care providers and society-at-large may know little about adoptive nursing, and mothers may receive no information or encouragement. They may even be discouraged from trying. Use of bottles and pacifiers is accepted and encouraged, which complicates convincing babies to take the breast. The mother may not be able to put her adopted baby to the breast until he is days, weeks, or months old. Because in these areas supplements are less likely to cause serious illness or death, an adoptive mother may feel less motivated to devote the intensive time and energy required to induce full lactation.

Whether a mother decides to breastfeed primarily for the closeness or primarily for the milk, induced lactation is time-consuming and challenging. As many mothers have found, however, it can be done, provided the baby takes the breast. Usually the younger the baby is, the more willing he will be to learn to breastfeed. However, older babies have been known to take willingly to breastfeeding (Phillips 1993). Every baby is different, and there is no way to know until the mother puts the baby to the breast how he will accept it.

If a mother wants to know how much milk she can expect to produce for her baby, see the later section, "Induced Lactation—Stimulating a Milk Supply."

Tell the mother what is involved before she begins, and suggest she learn about the basics of breastfeeding and the physical changes that accompany lactation.

To make an informed decision, the mother will need to have a realistic idea of what relactation or induced lactation will require of her so she can decide if it is something she wants to do or will be able to do within the context of her family situation. (For the details, see the section, "Induced Lactation—Stimulating a Milk Supply.")

It will also be helpful for her to know the basics of breastfeeding so she will understand the reasons behind the suggestions. For a mother who is relactating or inducing lactation, knowing the principle of supply and demand will help her understand why she needs to put her baby to the breast frequently to stimulate her milk supply. Understanding the basics will also help her determine if her baby is getting enough milk at the breast and whether or not he will need supplementation. Understanding proper positioning and latch-on will help her avoid nipple soreness and assure that the baby will be able to take milk from the breast most effectively. A good, basic understanding of breastfeeding will give her greater flexibility to adapt specific suggestions to her unique baby and her individual circumstances.

Understanding the normal physical changes that take place in a lactating woman will reassure her should she experience them. The following physical changes may occur:

- changes in menstrual patterns—irregular cycles or suppression of menstruation and ovulation due to the hormonal effects of the baby's sucking,
- breast and nipple changes—such as darkening of the areola, breast tenderness or fullness, and
- the appearance of colostrum when milk production begins.

Some women also experience mood swings once their milk production begins to increase, due to lactation-related hormonal changes. These changes often cause depression, fatigue, tears, or anger. Some mothers feel uncomfortably warm, anxious, or nervous. These feelings—coupled with the tiring job of working with the baby—may make some mothers feel like giving up. This is when good support becomes crucial. Tell a mother who is experiencing these feelings that it is usually around this time that she'll notice an increase in her milk supply.

Relactate/Adopt

Suggest the mother contact her baby's doctor.

The mother may wish to have her baby's weight checked regularly while she makes the transition to the breast. She will also need the doctor to rule out illness and other health problems in the baby. The doctor does not need to be completely convinced of the value of relactation in order to be consulted. However, if the doctor is strongly opposed to the mother relactating or inducing lactation, the parents may want to change to a doctor who will be supportive of the mother and her decision to breastfeed.

For the mother considering induced lactation, suggest she use discretion in informing the adoption agency of her plans to breastfeed.

Different social service agencies have different attitudes about adoptive nursing. Some agencies are supportive, even holding meetings for mothers who plan to nurse their adopted babies, but others may view the idea with skepticism or suspicion.

RELACTATION—STIMULATING A MILK SUPPLY

The more often a baby breastfeeds, the more milk will be produced.

The average baby breastfeeds for twenty to thirty minutes every two to three hours during the day. At night, a baby may go four to five hours between nursings.

Ideally, a mother who is relactating will put the baby to the breast at least this often and for this long—assuming her baby is willing. Breastfeeding for comfort should also be encouraged. As milk is produced by supply and demand, the more often the baby breastfeeds, the more milk there will be. Encourage the mother to keep the baby close to her at night so he can suckle for comfort and enhance milk production.

A baby with a weak suck may appear contented at the breast, but may not be actively stimulating his mother's milk production. See "Sucking Problems— Types and Suggestions" in the chapter "Positioning, Latch-On, and the Baby's Suck."

Encourage the mother to care for herself as well.

To keep up her strength and to keep her outlook positive, it is important that the mother get adequate rest, proper nutrition, and enough fluids. The mother will know she needs more fluids if her urine becomes concentrated or dark in color or she becomes constipated.

Expressing milk may help the mother increase her milk supply.

If the baby is unwilling or unable to breastfeed often, the mother may decide to further stimulate her milk supply by expressing her milk. Be sure she knows that milk expression is a learned skill and that the amount of milk she expresses is not a reliable indication of how much milk she has, since a baby who is actively breastfeeding will always be more effective at taking milk from the breast than any method of milk expression. It takes time and conditioning for a woman's body to respond to hand-expression or a hand pump as it does when a baby breastfeeds. Most women find that with practice they can increase the amount of milk they express at a sitting.

An automatic electric double breast pump is the easiest and fastest way to express milk. Double-pumping allows the mother to pump both breasts simultaneously, cutting pumping time in half. There is also evidence that double-pumping may be more effective than single pumping at stimulating a mother's milk supply (Auerbach 1990).

For information on selecting a method of expression, encouraging the let-down, or milk-ejection, reflex, and getting the most milk for the time spent expressing, see the chapter "Expression and Storage of Human Milk."

A slight, temporary drop in milk supply sometimes accompanies menstruation.

Some women experience a slight decrease in milk supply at the onset of menstruation. After a few days their milk supply increases again.

Some medications have been found to increase milk supply.

When used in combination with frequent nursing and/or milk expression, certain medications have been found to increase milk supply. One of the most commonly used medications is metoclopramide (Reglan), which when given at 10 mg doses three times per day for 7 to 14 days has been found to increase milk production an average of 110% in mothers with one-month-old babies (Ehrenkranz and Ackerman 1986) and 72% in mothers with 8- to 12-week-old babies (Kauppila 1983). When the metoclopramide is discontinued, a mother's milk supply may drop, but not usually to the level it was before treatment. Other medications that have been used to increase milk production are thyrotropin-releasing hormone (TRH), which is given as a nasal spray, and human growth hormone, but neither of these have been studied as extensively as metoclopramide (Anderson and Valdes 1993).

Some herbal preparations have been reported to increase milk supply, but these claims have not been proven.

Some mothers report that herbal preparations have helped them increase their milk supply. Because herbs may be potent, they should not be used casually. If the mother would like to explore this possibility, suggest she contact someone knowledgeable in their use.

INDUCED LACTATION—STIMULATING A MILK SUPPLY

Regular expression or pumping of the breasts will stimulate milk production. Ask the adoptive mother if she wants to begin expressing before her baby arrives.

An adoptive mother may know her baby's due date weeks or months in advance and know approximately when he will join the family. Depending on her feelings and her individual circumstances, she may want to begin stimulating her breasts to produce milk immediately or she may want to wait until about two to four weeks before her baby's expected arrival.

An automatic electric double breast pump will be more effective at stimulating milk production than a smaller pump, and regular expressing will be more effective than occasional expressing. Double-pumping (pumping both breasts simultaneously) has been found to be more effective at stimulating milk production than single-pumping (Auerbach 1990) and makes frequent pumping more practical since it takes half the time.

A mother who is unsure about when her baby will be arriving may want to start with just a few sessions per day and gradually add more sessions until she is expressing every two to two-and-a-half hours during the day. When she begins pumping, suggest she start at the lowest suction setting and begin pumping between five and fifteen minutes per breast, depending on her comfort, working up to about fifteen minutes per breast. She would not need to express at night unless she wants to mimic a baby's nursing pattern and she knows her baby will be arriving within a few days.

It may take a few days to a few weeks for the breasts to begin producing milk.

If the mother has no idea when the baby might be arriving, expressing her milk may not be practical. Some mothers find that their milk supply continues to increase over time with regular expressing, but others find that without a baby to nurse, the milk gradually decreases, even with continued expressing.

If the mother begins expressing, suggest she plan to discontinue it once her baby arrives and begins nursing well at the breast. A nursing baby is more effective than any method of expression, and once she has her baby, any time spent expressing is better spent nursing the baby.

Relactate/Adopt

Some medications have been found to stimulate milk production and increase milk supply.

When used in combination with frequent nursing and/or milk expression, certain medications have been found to increase milk supply. In some parts of the world, medications are used to prepare an adoptive mother's body for lactation and help establish her milk supply. In a study of adoptive mothers in Papua, New Guinea, with the help of medication 24 out of 27 mothers were able to fully lactate. The mothers who had never breastfed received a single injection of 100 mg of medroxyprogesterone (Depoprovera) a week before beginning their efforts to induce lactation then took 10 mg of metoclopramide (Reglan) or 25 mg of chlorpromazine (Thorazine) four times daily until they had enough milk to sustain their babies. The mothers who had previously breastfed received the oral medication without the injection until adequate lactation was established (Nemba 1994).

In another study, metoclopramide (Reglan), given in 10 mg doses three times per day for 7 to 14 days, was found to signficantly increase milk production from an average of 110% in birth mothers with one-month-old babies (Ehrenkranz and Ackerman 1986) to 72% in birth mothers with 8- to 12-week-old babies (Kauppila 1983). When metoclopramide is discontinued, a mother's milk supply tends to drop, but not usually to the level it was before treatment. Other medications that have been used to increase milk production are thyrotropin-releasing hormone (TRH), which is given as a nasal spray, and human growth hormone, but neither of these have been studied as extensively as metoclopramide (Anderson and Valdes 1993).

Some herbal preparations have been reported to increase milk supply, but these claims have not been proven.

Some mothers report that herbal preparations have helped them increase their milk supply. Because herbs may be potent, they should not be used casually. If the mother would like to explore this possibility, suggest she contact someone knowledgeable in their use.

It is not possible to predict exactly how much milk an adoptive mother will be able to produce, although most mothers produce some milk.

Unlike a birth mother, an adoptive mother does not have the benefit of nine months of hormonal changes to cause her breast tissue to grow and physically prepare her body for breastfeeding. More sucking is needed to induce lactation than it takes to establish and maintain lactation after birth.

An adoptive mother may or may not eventually produce enough milk to breast-feed her baby completely without supplementing, depending upon how effectively and frequently the baby nurses and her individual body chemistry. A few women respond quickly to expressing and breast stimulation and produce a full milk supply. The majority of women produce some milk. A few women don't produce any milk. Previous breastfeeding does not seem to be a major factor.

In one survey of 65 adoptive mothers from Western countries (Hormann 1977), the mothers were asked to calculate what percentage of their babies' intake they were able to supply by subtracting the amount of formula the baby took from the amount of formula the baby would need if he was completely formula-fed, based on the assumption that a baby needs about two-and-a-half ounces (74 ml) of formula per pound (.45 kg) of body weight. According to these calculations, most mothers reported that they provided between 25% to 75% of their babies' intake. Two mothers induced a full milk supply, and two mothers (who suffered from types of pituitary disorders, which could affect their ability to produce milk) produced no milk. These estimates may be inaccurate, however, because a more recent study found that at four months of age breastfed babies growing and gaining normally consume on average about 25% fewer calories than babies on formula (Butte 1984).

A mother's milk supply depends on several factors.

How much milk a mother produces is dependent upon:

- The baby. His willingness to nurse at the breast and his ability to suck effectively will be affected by age, interest, adaptability, sucking needs, distractibility, basic temperament, and previous feeding experiences.
- The frequency and effectiveness of breast stimulation. The effectiveness of the baby's suck or the mother's method of expression as well as how often the mother nurses or expresses, will affect the amount of milk produced. The more effective the breast stimulation and the more frequently the mother nurses or expresses, the more milk will be produced.
- The mother's response to breast stimulation. Each mother's physical response to breast stimulation will vary.
- How long the mother has been nursing or expressing. An induced milk supply may build very slowly or reach plateaus (periods where it stays at one level) only to increase later. Some mothers' milk supplies continue to increase even into their babies' second year.

Depending on how often she is nursing, a mother who is currently nursing a toddler may or may not be able to quickly build up her milk supply to meet the needs of a newborn.

A mother with an avidly nursing toddler younger than twelve to eighteen months old may be able to increase her milk supply to meet the needs of a newborn in just a few weeks.

However, if the mother is nursing an older toddler or a toddler who nurses only infrequently, her situation will be similar to the mother who is totally inducing lactation. It may not be possible for her to stimulate a full milk supply. If the mother has expected to increase her milk quickly, she may be disappointed and discouraged.

Many mothers report that around the time of their menstrual period their milk supply decreases slightly and they experience restlessness while nursing.	Due to the hormonal changes of menstruation, some mothers find that during this time in their cycle, their milk supply temporarily decreases slightly and their emotions run high. Jimmie Lynne Avery writes in Jan Riordan's book, *A Practical Guide to Breastfeeding*, "Typically, [the mothers] reported that lactation progressed steadily but then seemed to plateau or diminish suddenly. They described their breasts as feeling full, firm, and painfully tender to the touch. Emotional status was described as irritable, depressed, often on the verge of tears.... They felt certain that 'milk is there, but it isn't coming out,' and they often said they felt like giving up the effort.... We learned that within a day or two, the women had a menstrual period, in some cases only a slight spotting on one day. Within two to three days after the onset of menses, lactation again increased at a fairly steady pace."

Some mothers also report feeling restless or "antsy" while nursing during the time around their menstrual periods. These feelings usually subside within a day or two.

The more often a baby nurses, the more milk there will be. Depending upon her circumstances, the mother may prefer to focus on making breastfeeding a happy, comforting time, rather than focusing on the amount of milk she produces.	As with relactation, the more often an adopted baby breastfeeds the more milk there will be. Depending on the relative safety of supplementation in her area, however, the main goal of a mother who is inducing lactation may vary. Where breastfeeding can mean the difference between life and death, it may be necessary to use an intense regimen of continuous nursing combined with milk-stimulating medications to bring in the mother's milk quickly (Nemba 1994). However, for the mother whose main goal is to develop a satisfying nursing relationship, any amount of milk produced may be perceived as an extra bonus for the baby's health. In this case, the more intense methods of inducing lactation may run counter to her goal of establishing a comfortable nursing relationship with her baby. This mother should be encouraged to concentrate on the physical and emotional bonds she is establishing with her baby.

Offering the breast for comfort will increase a mother's milk supply and enhance her relationship with her baby.	Offering the breast for comfort will enhance the relationship between the mother and baby and also stimulate the mother's milk supply. The mother can use the breast for comfort in many ways.

Relactate/Adopt

- Use breastfeeding—rather than a pacifier—between feedings to comfort the baby.
- Pick a time to nurse when the baby is not too hungry or too sleepy.
- Choose a warm and private place to nurse, free from distractions for mother or baby.
- Give lots of cuddling and skin-to-skin contact, along with offering the breast.
- Try breastfeeding when baby is sleeping.
- Breastfeed in the bathtub with the baby's face above water and his body submerged.
- Make nursing sessions times of special attention and closeness, and don't feel pressured about how the baby responds.
- If the mother is using a bottle, wait until the baby is almost asleep and full from the bottle and then slip out the bottle and replace it with the breast. After a few of these sleepy feedings, the baby may be more likely to take the breast while fully awake.

A nursing supplementer allows the adoptive mother to use the breast for feedings and stimulate her milk supply at the same time.	A nursing supplementer, which allows the baby to receive extra nourishment as well as comfort at the breast, can make adoptive nursing go more smoothly because some babies become confused when switched back and forth between breast and bottle.

The supplementer is designed to give less supplement as the baby takes more of the mother's milk. And the sucking the baby does at the breast in order to receive the supplement stimulates the mother's own milk supply. For more information, see "The Use of Breast Pumps and Other Products."

If the mother does not want to use a nursing supplementer or does not have access to one, cup feeding and other alternative feeding methods are less likely than bottles to interfere with the establishment of breastfeeding. Because an artificial nipple is not used, the baby will be unable to satisfy his sucking urge at feedings and will be more likely to accept the breast for comfort and for food.

Establishing a satisfying breastfeeding relationship and building her milk supply will be easier if the mother breastfeeds often and takes good care of herself.

Some basics for establishing a satisfying nursing relationship and building a milk supply include:

- Relax and enjoy the baby—the mother's emotions are important to her milk supply.
- Nurse before, after, and between feedings for as long as the baby is willing—no matter how the supplement is given.
- Avoid pacifiers—encourage all the baby's sucking to be at the breast.
- Nurse during the night—keep the baby close.
- Nurse on both breasts at every feeding, if possible. This may be difficult if a nursing supplementer is used and the baby has a hard time latching on well.
- Drink enough fluids and eat a well-balanced diet.
- Get enough rest.
- Give up smoking (which can decrease milk supply) or keep it to a minimum, cutting down as much as possible.

ENCOURAGING THE BABY TO TAKE THE BREAST

A baby who has been receiving bottles regularly may need encouragement to take the breast.

A baby nursing actively at the breast will stimulate a mother's milk supply more effectively than any method of milk expression. But if a baby has been receiving bottles regularly, he may be reluctant to take the breast. Liquid flows from a bottle quickly, with no special effort from baby. At the breast, baby needs to be more actively involved—drawing the nipple far back into his mouth and coordinating his jaws and tongue to milk the breast.

Some babies switch to the breast easily; others need lots of encouragement. In one survey of 366 women who relactated, 39% reported that their baby nursed well on the first attempt, 32% said their babies were ambivalent about breastfeeding, and 28% refused the breast. But within a week, 54% of the babies had taken the breast well, and by ten days the number rose to 74%. Although babies younger than three months and those who had previously breastfed tended to be more willing (see next point), the most crucial factors were time, patience, and persistence (Auerbach and Avery 1980).

The baby's age and his past breastfeeding experience may affect his willingness to take the breast.

Usually, the younger the baby, the more willing he will be to nurse at the breast. Whether or not the baby has ever breastfed and the length of time that has elapsed before he is first put to the breast or has last breastfed are also factors that may affect a baby's willingness to nurse. Keep in mind, though, that every baby is unique and that with time and patience most babies will take the breast, even if they do not seem interested at first.

According to one report, although some children appear to lose the ability to breastfeed well within several weeks of weaning, some retain that ability (Phillips 1993). In this report six children between 12 and 48 months who had been weaned for up to six months stimulated their mothers to at least partially relactate through sucking alone.

Instead of relying solely on bottles to supplement, encourage the mother to learn about and try other feeding methods.

Babies like to suck for comfort, and many babies satisfy their sucking need at the bottle. If they are given their nourishment (either mother's milk or formula) with alternative feeding methods, such as a spoon, cup, eyedropper, feeding syringe, or finger-feeding, they may be more likely to accept the breast for comfort, which will help to stimulate the mother's milk supply. Using bottles regularly may mean the baby will be less willing to nurse at the breast for comfort. Some babies also have difficulty switching back and forth between breast and bottle.

A nursing supplementer, which allows a mother to supplement her baby while at the breast, can help avoid nipple confusion and stimulate the mother's milk supply at the same time. If a mother's milk supply is very low, the nursing supplementer will offer a baby instant reward at the breast. In order to avoid the baby becoming overly dependent upon the nursing supplementer, suggest the mother try using the supplementer on one breast only and after the baby's initial hunger has been satisfied switching to the breast without the supplementer. A baby who refuses the breast may sometimes be willing to take supplements from a nursing supplementer taped to the mother's finger, which is called finger-feeding. This can serve as a transition—as the baby becomes comfortable with the supplementer and his mother's skin—until the baby is ready to accept the breast. Suggest the mother think of finger-feeding as a short-term feeding method and not plan to use it longer than a week.

If a mother prefers to continue using the bottle, encourage her to hold the bottle to her breast so that the baby becomes comfortable in that position. After beginning the feeding with the bottle, she might be able to switch over to the breast. Another approach that may help make the transition to the breast go more smoothly is if during feedings the mother holds the baby in the nursing position and wraps the bottle with a cloth so that the baby cannot touch the bottle.

There are many ways to encourage a baby to take the breast.

To encourage a baby to take the breast, suggest the mother try the following:

Times and Places to Try Breastfeeding
- when the baby is not too hungry or too sleepy,
- when the baby is asleep or relaxed,
- while walking,
- in the bathtub,
- in a darkened room,
- in a place that is free of distractions for mother and baby,
- while rocking in a rocking chair,
- while soothing music is playing.

Relactate/Adopt

Increase Touching
- Give the baby lots of skin-to-skin contact.
- Spend more time each day stroking and cuddling.
- Use a sling or baby carrier to keep baby close between feedings.
- Take baths together.
- Sleep together.

At the Breast
- Make sure to use effective positioning and latch-on, so the mother's nipples will not get sore and her baby will get more milk for his efforts.
- Apply mother's milk or formula to the nipple and areola to encourage baby to latch on. (Do not use honey, as it may contain botulism spores.)
- Drip expressed human milk or formula over the nipple or in the corner of the baby's mouth while at the breast, using an eyedropper or feeding syringe.
- Talk to the baby. Although babies cannot understand the words, they do understand tone of voice. Give the baby a pep talk and congratulate him when he is doing well.

- Try to keep breastfeeding as pleasant as possible, so the baby will associate nursing with positive feelings. When the baby starts to fuss, try to calm him before offering the breast again. If he adamantly refuses to nurse, give him human milk or formula with a spoon, eye-dropper, cup, or feeding syringe and try again later.
- Be patient. It is stressful for both mother and baby to change to another way of feeding. Patience and perseverance will go a long way during the transition.

Also see "Persuading the Baby to Take the Breast" in the chapter "Fussy at the Breast and Breast Refusal."

MAKING THE TRANSITION—HOW TO BE SURE THAT BABY IS GETTING ENOUGH

Keep a record of baby's feedings, wet diapers, bowel movements, and weight gain.

Changing from one feeding method to another can be stressful for a baby. To be sure a baby is receiving enough nourishment during the transition, a mother will need to keep track of:

- frequency and length of breastfeeding sessions,
- the baby's reaction to breastfeeding (Does he suck actively? Is he happy to take the breast?),
- amount of supplement being offered and how it was given,
- number of wet diapers per day (cloth diapers feel wetter, but a mother can learn to judge wetness in disposable diapers by pouring two to four tablespoons (30-60 ml) of water on a dry disposable diaper and seeing how it feels),
- number and volume of bowel movements,
- weight gain and growth (the mother may want to schedule weekly weight checks with her baby's doctor).

A baby should have at least six to eight wet diapers (if disposable diapers are used, five to six) every twenty-four hours. If there are fewer wet diapers or if the baby's urine is concentrated and dark in color, the mother may need to give more supplement. A baby should not be stressed by hunger. When formula is given, it should never be diluted. If the baby is less than six weeks old, he should have at least two bowel movements a day. Weight gain of about four ounces (113 grams) a week is another indication that baby is getting enough.

Some—but not all—babies increase the time between feedings once milk supply increases.

A few ounces (28-56 grams) of weight loss might occur during this transitional period, but the baby's weight should stabilize and begin to climb within about five days.

It may be reassuring to the mother to know the signs of dehydration.

Knowing the signs of dehydration may reassure the mother that her baby is doing well and act as a warning if he's not. The signs include:

- few wet diapers (two or less per day),
- poor skin tone (when pinched, the skin stays pinched looking),
- lethargy (the baby becomes less responsive), and
- dry mouth and dry eyes.

As the baby takes more from the breast, the mother can cut down on the supplement.

Keep track of how much supplement the baby is taking, his weight gain, and the number of wet diapers and bowel movements. It is impossible to know exactly how much milk a mother is producing, but there will be certain signs when her milk supply increases.

For relactation. When the baby begins actively breastfeeding and begins losing interest in finishing the supplement, gradually reduce the amount of supplement given. (Decreasing the supplement one-half ounce (15 ml) per feeding per day works well for some mothers and babies.) Make sure that the baby continues to have at least six to eight wet cloth diapers (five to six disposable diapers) a day.

A baby's bowel movements are a good indicator of how much human milk he is getting. Changes in the color, odor, and consistency—and possibly frequency of bowel movements—will tell the mother that her milk supply is increasing. As the baby receives more human milk, his bowel movements will lighten, the odor will decrease, the consistency will soften, and—especially if he is under six weeks of age—he will probably have bowel movements more often.

A baby's health and disposition may also improve as he receives more of his mother's milk. A diaper rash or other skin condition may improve, along with the baby's general skin tone. The baby may become more alert and active, or if he was very active before, he may relax. Many babies begin to take more interest in their surroundings.

For induced lactation. When the amount of supplement begins to level off but the baby continues to gain, it means the mother's milk supply is filling the gap. If at any time the baby regularly nurses more slowly, lets milk dribble out while sucking, or otherwise seems full, **stop giving supplement for that feeding.** If there is supplement left after several feedings in a row, cut back a little on the amount put in the nursing supplementer or bottle. Suggest the mother also try using the nursing supplementer for only part of the feeding, such as only on the second side or only near the end of the feeding.

If the baby seems comfortable with the reduced amount, gradually reduce the amount offered. Continue to gradually reduce the amount offered, but avoid leaving the baby feeling too hungry after a feeding. Just make sure not to give him more supplement than he actually wants.

Suggest the mother watch the baby's bowel movements to see if he is getting more mother's milk. Human milk bowel movements are thinner, more yellow, and smell better than formula bowel movements. Count the number of wet diapers—if he has six to eight wet cloth diapers (five to six disposable diapers) he is getting enough.

Publications for Parents

Anderson, K. *Nursing Your Adopted Baby.* Schaumburg, Illinois: La Leche League International, 1986. Publication No. 55a.

Relactate/Adopt

Peterson, D. *Breastfeeding the Adopted Baby.* San Antonio, Texas: Corona, 1994.

References

Anderson, P. and Valdes, V. Increasing breast milk supply. *Clin Pharmacy* 1993; 12:479-80.

Auerbach, K. Sequential and simultaneous breast pumping: a comparison. *Int J Nurs Stud* 1990; 27(3):257-65.

Auerbach, K. and Avery, J. Relactation: a study of 366 cases. *Pediatrics* 1980; 65:236-48.

Butte, N. et al. Human milk intake and growth in exclusively breast-fed infants. *J Pediatr* 1984; 104:187-95.

Ehrenkranz, R. and Ackerman, B. Metoclopramide effect on faltering milk production by mothers of premature infants. *Pediatrics* 1986; 78(4):614-20.

Hormann, E. Breastfeeding the adopted baby. *Birth Fam J* 1977; 4:165.

Kauppila, A. et al. Metoclopramide and breast feeding: transfer into milk and the newborn. *Eur J Clin Pharmacol* 1983; 25:819-23.

Lawrence, R. *Breastfeeding: A Guide for the Medical Profession,* 4th ed. St. Louis: Mosby, 1994, pp. 565-72.

Nemba, K. Induced lactation: a study of 37 non-puerperal mothers. *J Trop Pediatr* 1994; 40:240-42.

Phillips, V. Relactation in mothers of children over 12 months. *J Trop Pediatr* 1993; 39:45-48.

Riordan, J. *A Practical Guide to Breastfeeding*. St. Louis: Mosby, 1983, pp. 275-93.

Riordan, J. and Auerbach, K. *Breastfeeding and Human Lactation*. Boston and London: Jones and Bartlett. pp. 357-61.

Ross, M. *Back to the breast: retraining infant suckling patterns*. La Leche League International Lactation Consultant Series. Unit 15. Garden City Park, New York: Avery Publishing, 1987.

Slome, C. Nonpuerperal lactation in grandmothers. *J Pediatr* 1956; 49:550-52.

Sutherland, A. and Auerbach, K. *Relactation and induced lactation*. La Leche League International Lactation Consultant Series. Unit 1. Wayne, New Jersey: Avery Publishing, 1985.

Wieschhoff, H. Artificial stimulation of lactation in primitive cultures. *Bull Hist Med* 1940; 8(10):1403-15.

17

Pregnancy and Tandem Nursing

BREASTFEEDING DURING PREGNANCY

    Sorting Out Feelings

    Concerns about the Unborn Baby

    Physical and Emotional Changes during Pregnancy

TANDEM NURSING

    Before Birth—Expectations and Plans

    After Birth—Practical Details

    The Mother's Feelings about Nursing Two

BREASTFEEDING DURING PREGNANCY

The decision whether or not to continue breastfeeding through a pregnancy is an individual one.

Sorting Out Feelings

Talk to the mother about her feelings and help her to separate her feelings from the feelings and expectations of others.

When a woman becomes pregnant while nursing she may have mixed feelings. Continuing to nurse a toddler or older child through a pregnancy and after the new baby is born is not something that most mothers plan to do, and it is considered unusual or unacceptable in many societies. The mother may be feeling pressure from others to wean, or she may be feeling pressure to continue nursing. It can be helpful to talk over her situation and help her separate her own feelings from the attitudes and advice of others.

Discuss her feelings in light of her circumstances and the needs of her child.

After talking to her about her feelings, discuss her circumstances and her child's needs. In addition to the mother's feelings, some other important considerations will be:

- the age of the nursing child,
- the child's need to nurse (both physical and emotional),
- whether the mother is experiencing any breastfeeding-related discomforts (such as sore nipples) and the degree of her discomfort,
- the mother's past nursing experience(s),
- health concerns relating to the pregnancy, such as uterine pain or bleeding while breastfeeding, a history of premature delivery, or loss of weight by the mother during pregnancy, and
- the father's feelings about breastfeeding through a pregnancy.

The mother should also know that many children wean during pregnancy. Two studies of women who became pregnant while nursing found that most of their nursing children (57% and 69%) weaned before their sibling was born (Moscone and Moore 1993; Newton and Theotokatos 1979). This may be due to several factors:

- the changes in the mother's milk during pregnancy (most weanings initiated by children took place during the second trimester, when the milk decreases in amount and changes in flavor),
- the hormonally caused nipple soreness many women experience during pregnancy, which may motivate them to cut back on their child's nursing,
- the child's readiness to wean, unrelated to the pregnancy.

It is not possible to predict by a child's age whether he will wean during pregnancy. Children mature at different rates, and while one child may be ready to stop nursing, another child of the same age may want to continue.

One option for the mother who is unsure about nursing during pregnancy is not to decide about weaning at all and simply take it one day at a time.

Help the mother who is considering weaning evaluate whether breastfeeding fills a real need for her child or can easily be replaced by other kinds of attention or activities.

A mother may question whether her child's continued nursing is a need or a habit. Consider the child's age. Only rarely will a child under one year be ready to wean on his own.

For the older child, suggest the mother try to anticipate her child's need to nurse by substituting the child's favorite pastimes for nursing and then note his reaction. Also suggest she try changing their usual daily routines to see if her toddler may be receptive to spending their time doing other things, rather than nursing.

If the child still wants to nurse in spite of the distractions and substitutions, it is possible that breastfeeding still meets a genuine need. In this case, a positive weaning will require a lot of time and energy on the mother's part. See the chapter "Weaning" for more specific suggestions. Depending on the child's age, the mother may want to consider providing him with a substitute, such as a bottle or pacifier. The child may also begin sucking his thumb for comfort instead.

Some mothers decide to continue breastfeeding through a pregnancy.

If the mother wants to continue breastfeeding through her pregnancy, encourage her to avoid rigid expectations about how breastfeeding will go during the coming weeks and months. Emotions and comfort levels for both mother and child can be unpredictable during pregnancy. Flexibility, along with a respect for changing needs, is the key to making breastfeeding during pregnancy a positive experience.

Many mothers have found that by continuing to nurse they are better able to meet their child's emotional needs during a somewhat stressful time.

Some mothers decide to wean during a pregnancy.

The mother who decides to wean needs support and acceptance. Assure her that her child's needs can be met in many ways, and offer to talk about the other ways she can meet her child's need for love and closeness.

Concerns about the Unborn Baby

Breastfeeding during a pregnancy will not deprive the unborn child of needed nutrients if the mother is eating well.

A well-nourished mother should have no difficulty providing for both the unborn baby and the nursing child, if he is more than a year old. But it is important for her to gain weight at the appropriate rate and eat nutritious foods, as well as get sufficient rest. For some mothers, it may be necessary to consume extra calories while breastfeeding during pregnancy. Some mothers take extra vitamin supplements as a precaution.

In fact, one study found the babies of 57 mothers who breastfed during pregnancy to be healthy and the appropriate weight at birth (Moscone and Moore 1993). Another study of 253 women found no significant difference in babies' birth weight when mothers who had weaned their older sibling more than six months before conception were compared with mothers who breastfed into the second or third trimester of pregnancy (Merchant 1990). Although the growth of the baby *in utero* was not affected, this second study noted that the mothers who breastfed during pregnancy took more of the nutritional supplements made available to them and still showed evidence of reduced maternal fat stores.

Pregnant/Tandem

Uterine contractions stimulated by breastfeeding usually pose no danger to the unborn baby and do not increase the risk of premature delivery.

There is no documented danger to mother or fetus when mothers breastfeed through a healthy pregnancy. Although uterine contractions are experienced during breastfeeding, they are a normal part of pregnancy. (Stimulation of the nipples causes secretion of small amounts of the hormone oxytocin which, in turn, can cause contractions of the uterus and the alveoli in the breasts.) Uterine contractions also occur during sexual activity, which most couples continue during pregnancy.

Even though some breastfeeding mothers notice stronger and more frequent contractions in later pregnancy, this does not seem to pose a danger to the unborn baby during a normal pregnancy. One study confirmed that breastfeeding does not appear to adversely affect the course of pregnancy (Moscone and Moore 1993).

The hormones of pregnancy will not be harmful to a breastfeeding baby or toddler.

The hormones that maintain a pregnancy are found in very small quantities in human milk, but they are not harmful to the breastfeeding child. The amount of these hormones the child receives will decrease as the mother's milk supply decreases. The baby *in utero* is exposed to the hormones produced by pregnancy at a much higher level than the nursing child.

A difficult pregnancy may be a reason to consider weaning.

Medical reasons to consider weaning during pregnancy may include:

- uterine pain or bleeding,
- a history of premature delivery,
- continued loss of weight by mother during pregnancy.

Physical and Emotional Changes during Pregnancy

While it is true that many mothers who breastfeed during pregnancy experience sore nipples, a decrease in milk supply, and emotional ups and downs about their decision to continue to breastfeed, there are also mothers who experience none of these. It's important to listen carefully to the mother and not attempt to predict what a particular mother's experience will be like.

Fatigue is a normal part of pregnancy, but breastfeeding will not necessarily be an extra drain on a mother's physical energy.

Breastfeeding, in and of itself, is not a drain on physical energy, although most women do feel fatigued when pregnant.

One advantage to breastfeeding is that it may be easier to convince a baby or toddler to lie down with mother and nurse when she feels the need to get some extra rest.

Nausea during pregnancy may decrease a mother's enjoyment of nursing.

It can be difficult to manage an energetic child while experiencing nausea. Some mothers report that nursing is not the real problem—holding a squirming child is, which would be difficult whether the mother was nursing or not. Other mothers report that feelings of nausea increased while they were nursing, whether their child was active or not. This may be in part because a mother is less distracted by outside stimulation while nursing and more aware of her body.

If nausea occurs during the early months, a mother may want to try sharing frequent small meals with her child each day. This may help the nausea and may reduce her little one's need to nurse.

The mother's growing abdomen may make nursing awkward.

In late pregnancy, a mother's abdomen may become so large that it is difficult for her child to reach the nipple. It may help to experiment with different nursing positions, such as side-lying. An older toddler may be able to nurse comfortably in an amazing variety of positions, such as leaning over his mother's side while she is lying down or over her shoulder while sitting. If a toddler is motivated to nurse, he will most likely find a way.

Sore nipples often occur during pregnancy.

Nipple tenderness is often one of the first symptoms of pregnancy and is caused by hormonal changes. Therefore, the usual recommendations given to the mother of a newborn for sore nipples will not be helpful. The onset of sore nipples is individual and can vary. Some women notice soreness before they miss their first menstrual period. Others never experience it or notice it only late in pregnancy. The duration of soreness is also individual. In one study, women reported sore nipples mostly during the first trimester (Moscone and Moore 1993), while in another study the majority of mothers reported it lasting almost the entire pregnancy, disappearing only after the birth of their baby (Newton and Theotokatos 1979).

Some mothers choose to wean because of sore nipples. Mothers who continue breastfeeding during pregnancy learn to cope with nipple soreness in a variety of ways. To make the soreness more manageable, a mother with sore nipples could try these suggestions:

- Use the breathing techniques from her childbirth classes.
- Vary nursing positions.
- Ask the older nursing child to nurse more gently and/or for shorter periods of time, while assuring the child the soreness is not his fault.

- Hand-express enough milk to start the milk flowing before the child begins to nurse, as a decrease in milk production is sometimes a factor in nipple discomfort.

The research reflects the differences in women's experiences. In one study, 74% of women who became pregnant while still nursing experienced varying degrees of nipple pain or soreness, 65% noticed a decrease in their milk supply, and 57% felt some degree of discomfort, such as restlessness or irritation while nursing (Newton and Theotokatos 1979). In another study, 39% of the women reported nipple soreness, 60% noticed a decrease in their milk supply, and 22% reported irritability while nursing (Moscone and Moore 1993).

Feelings of restlessness while breastfeeding are common.

Some mothers experience a type of emotional discomfort while nursing and pregnant—a feeling of restlessness or irritation with the older child during nursing. Many mothers refer to this as an "antsy" feeling. If this occurs, it may help if the mother tries to distract herself by directing her thoughts elsewhere, for instance, by reading a book, listening to music, or watching television.

A decrease in milk supply—as well as a change in the flavor of the milk—is common during pregnancy.

The hormones that maintain a pregnancy also cause a decrease in the amount of milk produced. This usually happens during the last four months of the pregnancy.

During the last few months of pregnancy the milk changes to colostrum in preparation for the birth. The mother need not be concerned that the nursing child will "use up" all the colostrum—no matter how much he nurses, colostrum will still be available at birth for the newborn.

If the nursing baby is younger than a year old, suggest the mother watch his weight gain to be sure he is getting enough to eat.

If the nursing baby is younger than a year old, the natural decrease in milk supply that occurs during pregnancy could compromise his nutritional needs. Suggest the mother keep track of her baby's weight gain and offer supplements if they are needed.

Some children wean on their own during pregnancy. Others who wean during pregnancy want to nurse again once the baby is born.

Some nursing babies or toddlers cut down on breastfeeding or wean when the mother's milk supply decreases. Some mothers report during this time that their nursing child suddenly begins eating more of other foods, one sign of decreased milk production. The flavor of the milk also may change, which convinces some children to wean. Other toddlers continue to nurse despite the changes in quantity and taste.

Although a child may wean during pregnancy, this does not guarantee he won't want to nurse once the baby is born. However, if the mother does not want to resume nursing the older sibling, suggest she offer the older sibling a taste of her milk in a spoon or cup.

Pregnant/Tandem

TANDEM NURSING

When a mother finds herself pregnant before her child is ready to stop nursing, she may decide to continue nursing the older child after the baby is born. Tandem nursing, as it is sometimes called, can be joyful, but it can also be stressful.

Before Birth— Expectations and Plans

Discuss with the mother her feelings about tandem nursing.

Some mothers approach tandem nursing with positive feelings, others with trepidation. Assure the mother—no matter what her feelings are now—that when her baby is born it is best to take it one day at a time, without too many preconceived ideas about how it will go.

Discuss the needs of the expected baby with the older child.

Many children past early toddlerhood can begin to learn the concept of waiting. If the mother takes the time to talk to the older child about his needs as a baby and how she responded to them, it can help him begin to understand the new baby's needs.

When planning for the baby's birth, minimize separation from the older child, if possible.

Encourage the mother to look into arrangements for the birth that will involve the least amount of separation from the older child. Whether or not the older child still needs to nurse, separation can be emotionally hard on him during an already stressful time.

Encourage the mother to arrange for help after her baby is born and to establish ground rules.

Extra help is important whenever a new baby is born. Sometimes the father is able to take on this job, but if another family member (such as the mother's mother or mother-in-law) offers to stay with the family to help, make sure the helper understands his or her role. Before the baby arrives, make it clear to the helper that he or she can be of most help by taking care of the house and helping with the older child while the mother concentrates on the baby .

After Birth—Practical Details

During the baby's early weeks, he needs the nutritional and immunological benefits provided by the colostrum.

The special first milk, called colostrum, is a concentrated form of nutrition that also contains the specific immunities that a newborn needs. Colostrum alone is present in small amounts until the third or fourth day after birth, when most mothers notice that their milk becomes more plentiful. This is when the body begins to shift into the production of mature milk, a transition that takes about two weeks to complete.

If the older child nurses only occasionally, the mother will not need to take special measures to make sure the newborn receives the colostrum he needs. If the older child is nursing often, however, the mother may want to be sure that the newborn gets first priority at the breast. If a mother has extra help at home during the newborn's first weeks, the baby's father or other household helper can give the older child extra attention so that it will be easier for the mother to see that the baby's nutritional needs are met.

For the older child, an increased desire to nurse is common after a new baby is born.

When the older child sees his new brother or sister nursing, he may temporarily increase his requests to nurse. Breastfeeding for the older child is more than food, it is a source of comfort and closeness. When he feels anxious or threatened by the new addition to the family, he may turn to nursing as a reassurance that he is still loved and that there is still a place for him at his mother's breast. Especially when he senses his mother's deepening attachment to the baby, he may feel the need to reestablish his own relationship with her by asking to nurse and making other demands for her attention.

The older child may have looser and more frequent stools during the early weeks after birth, due to the laxative effect of colostrum. This will disappear as colostrum is replaced by mature milk.

Tandem nursing can minimize engorgement and ensure a bountiful milk supply.

Even though the older child nursed through the pregnancy, some engorgement may still occur, especially if the newborn does not nurse often during his early days. If he is willing to nurse, the nursing older child can be of help in reducing and relieving engorgement once the mother's milk becomes more plentiful on the third or fourth day after birth. Some older nursing siblings refuse to nurse until the breast is softer and more "familiar" once again, while others are thrilled by the new bounty.

While tandem nursing, normal hygiene is sufficient in most cases.

Normal hygiene is sufficient while tandem nursing. Regular baths or showers, clean clothes, and reasonable standards of cleanliness are good enough. The glands around the nipple secrete an anti-bacterial fluid and babies are born with an immunity to most household (and sibling) germs. Mother's milk also contains these same immunities.

If one of the siblings is ill, it is not necessary for the mother to limit each child to one breast, because the germs that cause colds and other infections are communicated before symptoms appear. Once an illness is apparent, the siblings will have already been sharing their mother's breasts for several days.

Exceptions to this rule include thrush, a fungus infection that is passed between mother and baby, and any other illness that is serious or highly contagious. At these times, a mother may want to limit each child to one breast.

The tandem nursing mother has an increased need for fluids, nutritious foods, and rest.

A mother who is nursing two may find she is hungrier and thirstier than when she was nursing just one baby. To satisfy her increased hunger, it can be helpful to keep nutritious snacks on hand and to eat something every two to three hours. Preparing and freezing meals before the baby is born will help the mother get the nutrients she needs. It also makes mealtimes simpler during the baby's early weeks.

Encourage the mother to drink to thirst. She can gauge whether she is getting enough fluids by watching her urine. If her urine is concentrated or dark in color, or if she becomes constipated, she will need to drink more.

In order to get the rest she needs, encourage the mother to accept all offers of household help from family and friends. If it's possible, she may want to hire household help. If this is not within her budget, perhaps a high school girl could come after school to play with the older children, fold laundry, set the table, or start dinner. This would allow the mother to get some extra rest.

How the baby and older child share the breast is best worked out by each family, taking into account the older child's age and other aspects of their situation.

Each mother has to decide how she wants to manage nursing two within the context of her own family. While it is essential that the baby receives the milk he needs, tandem nursing may be easier for some mothers if they can be flexible about who nurses first, on what breast, and for how long (Gromada 1992).

The needs of the baby. A mother may feel anxious about whether her newborn is getting enough milk when he and the older child share the breast. A mother may have a strong desire to restrict the older child's nursing to certain times or only after the baby has finished. If the older child does well with this arrangement it is fine. But if this causes conflict, assure the mother that most women who tandem nurse find that—because milk is produced on a supply-and-demand basis—they produce plenty of milk to nurse both children, each whenever he likes.

Explain that for the baby's sake it can be best to vary nursing patterns—not always nursing one child first and the other second—because the milk is different at different times during the feeding. Because the baby has a physical need for the milk, it is best for him to nurse first most of the time. Switching from one breast to the other—rather than restricting each child to a side—is good for the baby, too, as it promotes proper development of eye-hand coordination.

If the mother is worried about her baby's intake, suggest that she keep count of the baby's wet diapers and stools. At least six to eight wet cloth diapers (five to six disposables) and two or more bowel movements a day during the first six weeks (fewer bowel movements are normal after six weeks) indicate the baby is getting enough.

The needs of the older child. How the older child feels about sharing the breast and any restrictions placed on nursing will depend largely on his age, his temperament, and his sucking need. Some tandem nursing mothers find that their older child can handle restricting nursing to certain times and places. Other mothers find that asking their older child to wait, even for a few minutes, is unbearable to the child. Also, the same child may react differently at different times of the day. Encourage the mother to experiment, to try different patterns of nursing—such as nursing her baby and older child together, varying who nurses when throughout the day, or giving her older child consistent nursing times he can count on—

Pregnant/Tandem

until she finds what works best for them. It is important to consider the mother's feelings as well as those of the child in reaching these decisions.

The mother may want to encourage some regularity in her older child's nursing—as opposed to nursing nonstop one day and not at all the next—so that her milk supply does not vary greatly from day to day. If a mother's breasts are emptied irregularly, she may develop mastitis.

The needs of the mother. Encourage the mother to discuss her feelings about tandem nursing. Talk about ways to balance these feelings with the needs of her children and see if she can think of ways to make tandem nursing more enjoyable for her, as well. For example, some mothers feel better about tandem nursing if they nurse both children together and are not nursing "all the time." However, other mothers become restless or irritable when their children nurse at the same time and find tandem nursing more enjoyable if they nurse their children separately. Some mothers feel most comfortable allowing baby and older child to nurse whenever they want, because it decreases the level of conflict. Others feel better when they restrict their older child's nursing to certain times and places. Brainstorm with the mother to find practical ways she can make tandem nursing subjectively better for her within her own family situation.

If a mother finds tandem nursing overwhelming or unpleasant, encourage her to find gradual and positive ways to wean her older child. (For suggestions, see "Weaning.")

There are many possible positions for nursing two simultaneously.

When nursing two together, some mothers find it easiest to start nursing the newborn in the football or clutch hold supported by a pillow. If the mother is using the cradle hold, the toddler may enjoy having the newborn lying across his lap. Other mothers start nursing the newborn in any position that's comfortable for them and then let the toddler arrange himself. Nursing toddlers can usually find a way to reach the breast under almost any circumstances. When mother nurses the newborn lying on her side, some toddlers are comfortable leaning over the mother's other side to nurse.

A baby sling or carrier can make it easier to meet both children's needs.

A baby sling or carrier can make it easier for the mother to keep her baby close and still have a free hand for her older child. A sling or carrier in which the baby can also nurse will help the mother breastfeed the baby while giving the older child other kinds of attention.

The father can help make tandem nursing more manageable for the mother.

The father can be a big help in making tandem nursing more manageable for the mother by entertaining the older child and introducing him to more "grown-up" activities.

Nursing while away from home can present challenges.

Many older children are too busy enjoying themselves while away from home to be interested in nursing. But if the older child asks to nurse somewhere the mother is not comfortable nursing him, she can ask him to wait until they are in a more private place, such as a dressing room or the car. Allowing the child to nurse when the location is appropriate teaches him that his mother can be counted on. This may make waiting easier to accept the next time. (See "Natural Weaning" in the chapter "Weaning.")

Should the mother need to nurse both children at once while out, wearing clothing that permits discreet nursing will make it easier. A shawl or blanket to throw over one or both children can also make it less obvious.

Nursing both children before leaving home and offering snacks and drinks to the older child while out can cut down on requests to nurse.

The Mother's Feelings about Nursing Two

Mothers' feelings about tandem nursing vary.

Whatever her expectations before birth, a mother's feelings may change after the baby arrives, and talking about them—and knowing they are normal—can help.

Mothers react differently to tandem nursing. Some feel positively about it, other do not. Because emotions can vary from mother to mother and from day to day, listen carefully, and do not presume that one mother's experience will necessarily be the same as another's or that the same mother's feelings will stay the same during the coming days, weeks, and months.

Many mothers are motivated to tandem nurse because they feel strongly about continuing to satisfy their older child's needs through breastfeeding. Their primary focus is on the child they know rather than on the unborn baby, who is still a stranger.

However, once a baby is born, many mothers find their feelings shift dramatically. Nature programs mothers—especially if mother and newborn get off to a good start in the early days and weeks—to become infatuated with the little one in their arms. The older child suddenly looks so big, and many mothers find that they resent taking time away from their newborn to nurse their older child.

Not every mother experiences such a dramatic shift in feelings. But when she does, she may feel guilty and alarmed—especially if she decided to tandem nurse for the sake of the older child and then feels waves of resentment at his wanting to nurse. Assure her that these feelings are normal. These opposing feelings—first protective of the older child, then resentful of his demands—are common when a new baby joins the family.

If the mother has these negative feelings, assure her that she might still have these feelings about her older child's demands even if he was not nursing. When nursing is part of the picture, however, it is common for negative feelings to focus there. This does not mean, however, that she will never enjoy nursing her older child again.

Mood swings are common, especially in the early weeks.

An emotional roller coaster is often part of the process of rearranging lives and redefining priorities after a baby is born. Assure the mother that, in time, these strong feelings will settle down. The emotional adjustments, along with hormonal swings a woman experiences in the postpartum period, make it difficult to be rational and objective all the time.

Physical sensations sometimes make tandem nursing uncomfortable for mother.

Some mothers find that when they nurse the baby and older child together they become restless or irritable.

Some mothers are disturbed by the sensations they feel when the older child nurses. Tandem nursing mothers sometimes describe how different their older child's nursing feels in comparison to their newborn's suck. An older child sucks differently, and his teeth and gums may cause friction on the nipple and areola. Some mothers may not notice these differences; others, however, find them disturbing. Sometimes these sensations of the older child nursing are experienced as erotic feelings. Or they may make the mother feel irritable or restless, even when the older child nurses alone. Assure the mother that these feelings are common and encourage her to try varying her older child's nursing positions to alleviate these feelings.

Pregnant/Tandem

Some mothers cope with these feelings by limiting their older child's time at the breast, keeping each nursing short but not necessarily eliminating or postponing nursings. Other mothers cut down on nursings by distracting their older child with other activities, postponing nursing times, or anticipating the older child's request to nurse by offering substitutions, such as snacks or drinks.

It is common to feel "touched out" when tandem nursing.

"Touched out" is what a mother sometimes feels when she has been cuddling, holding, and nursing all day long and wants some physical space to herself. Both children need her, her husband is interested in her, and she may wonder if she will ever have her body to herself again.

Assure the mother that these feelings are common. Although she may indeed spend more time holding her children because she is tandem nursing, remind the mother that even if she were not, her older child would still need her for closeness and comfort.

Suggest that she try to find a few minutes for herself each day—with her partner's help—perhaps to take a bath or shower alone or a short walk. Even a small amount of "alone time" can go a long way in raising a mother's spirits.

Encourage the mother to draw on others for support.

Tandem nursing calls for creativity, a positive attitude, and a sense of humor. When one or all of these can't be mustered, encourage the mother to call on someone who will listen sympathetically: her husband, a friend, other mothers who have tandem nursed, or those who are supportive of breastfeeding.

If the mother wants to wean the older child, talk about gradual and loving ways to make this process easier.

It is not unusual for a mother to approach tandem nursing with a positive attitude and then find that the actual experience is not what she imagined. If a mother has experimented with different ways of nursing both children and is still uncomfortable—or decides suddenly she no longer wants to continue and is not open to experimenting—talk to her about how to wean her older child in a gradual and loving way. For more information, see the chapter "Weaning."

Publications for Parents

Bumgarner, N. MOTHERING YOUR NURSING TODDLER. Schaumburg, Illinois: La Leche League International, 1982, pp. 110-22.

Berke, G. *Nursing Two: Is It for You?* Schaumburg, Illinois: La Leche League International, 1989. Publication No. 53.

La Leche League International. THE WOMANLY ART OF BREASTFEEDING, 35th Anniversary ed. Schaumburg, Illinois, 1991, pp. 261-64.

References

Gromada, K. Breastfeeding more than one: multiples and tandem breastfeeding. *NAACOG* 1992; 3(4):656-66.

Lawrence, R. Breastfeeding: *A Guide for the Medical Profession,* 4th ed. St. Louis: Mosby, 1994, pp. 561, 568, 594-95.

Merchant, K. et al. Maternal and fetal responses to the stresses of lactation concurrent with pregnancy and of short recuperative intervals. *Am J Clin Nutr* 1990; 52:280-88.

Moscone, S. and Moore, J. Breastfeeding during pregnancy. *J Hum Lact* 1993; 9(2):83-88.

Newton, N. and Theotokatos, M. Breastfeeding during pregnancy in 503 women: does a psychobiological weaning mechanism exist in humans? *Emotion and Reproduction* 1979; 20B:845-49.

Riordan, J. and Auerbach, K. *Breastfeeding and Human Lactation.* Boston and London: Jones and Bartlett, 1993, pp. 351.

18

Sexuality, Fertility, and Contraception

BREASTFEEDING AND SEXUALITY

Changes in Sexual Desire

Breastfeeding and Sexual Relations

Making Adjustments as a Couple

BREASTFEEDING, FERTILITY, AND CONTRACEPTION

How Breastfeeding Affects Fertility

Contraception and the Breastfeeding Mother

Non-Hormonal Methods

Lactational Amenorrhea Method (LAM)

Natural Family Planning (NFP)

Barrier Methods (Condoms and Diaphragms) and Spermicides

Non-Hormonal Intrauterine Devices (IUD)

Sterilization

Progestin-Only Methods

Methods Containing Estrogen

BREASTFEEDING AND SEXUALITY

Changes in Sexual Desire

Many women feel less sexual desire after the birth of a baby.

Although research is scarce, many women report feeling less sexual desire after their baby's birth. There are many possible reasons for this:

- Caring for a newborn is a physically taxing job with non-stop days and sleepless nights. The sheer amounts of time and physical energy invested can result in jangled nerves and extreme fatigue.
- Intense feelings of love and the sense of oneness with a baby can consume nearly all of a woman's emotional energy. By its very nature, the mother-baby relationship in the early weeks tends to be exclusive of others.
- The woman's relationship with her baby's father is likely going through a period of adjustment as they cope with the changes a new baby brings. Some new parents, for example, have difficulty thinking of their partners as both parents and lovers.
- Time for the couple to be alone may be at a premium.
- Physical or emotional complications from the birth, such as painful stitches from an episiotomy or feelings of grief, ineffectiveness, and vulnerability from a disappointing birth experience, can affect a woman's desire for sex.
- Any baby-related difficulties, such as health problems or colic, can put additional strain on a couple's relationship.
- Hormonal fluctuations may cause mood swings and/or postpartum depression, which also affect a woman's sexual desire.

Some women report a heightened sexual responsiveness while breastfeeding.

For some women, the deep glow of inner peace that has been associated with breastfeeding throughout the ages spills over into their sexual relationship with their partners. The feelings of warmth and tenderness that are among the byproducts of caring for an infant can translate into an enhanced sexual desire and a deeper sexual bond between husband and wife. As one woman said, "There's something about nursing a baby that gives you an all's-right-with-the-world feeling. I feel so loving toward my whole family, not just toward my baby. Sex just seems to be a natural expression of this good feeling" (Kenny 1973).

Researchers agree that breastfeeding affects a woman's postpartum sexuality, but they do not agree on how.

Masters and Johnson (1966) say that breastfeeding mothers are more comfortable with their own sexuality and therefore are more anxious to resume sexual relations with their husbands than are their bottle-feeding counterparts. Other researchers point out that the low levels of estrogen present in the lactating mother create a correspondingly lowered interest in sex, and that sexual desire decreases as nursing hormones increase.

There is also some evidence to suggest that an increase in sexual desire is linked to the resumption of a woman's menstrual periods. This is thought to be due to the presence of the hormones that cause ovulation, but research is too sparse to warrant any firm conclusions.

Breastfeeding and Sexual Relations

The low estrogen level present during breastfeeding may cause vaginal dryness.

Low estrogen levels associated with breastfeeding may cause vaginal dryness, tightness, and tenderness. If intercourse is painful or uncomfortable for the mother, more foreplay may help. Suggest she try using a water-based lubricant, such as K-Y jelly. Another possibility is using estrogen-based creams or suppositories, which are available by prescription. One study found these to be helpful and showed no apparent effect on lactation (Wisniewski and Wilkinson 1991).

Some women experience a let-down of their milk during sexual relations.

The hormonal changes that occur during lovemaking stimulate a let-down in some women. If this bothers the man or the woman, suggest the mother feed the baby or express some milk before making love. Applying pressure to the nipples when the milk begins to let down will stop the milk flow. Having a towel handy to catch the milk may also be helpful.

There is no need for couples to restrict their fondling or lovemaking while the woman is breastfeeding. A mother's partner need not consider her breasts "off limits." Some men enjoy the presence of mother's milk during lovemaking.

Jan Riordan, EdD, says in her book, *A Practical Guide to Breastfeeding,* "Pressures and problems of sexual relations while lactating are as ancient as woman herself. Physicians during the 17th Century recommended breastfeeding, but insisted that sexual relations during lactation would spoil the milk and endanger the life of the child." Because artificial feeding was not safe at that time, wet nurses became popular and allowed women to stop breastfeeding to accommodate their husbands' desires without compromising their babies' health.

Some cultures place a high value on child-spacing and insist on total abstinence from sex for a certain period of time—from a few weeks to a year, or even longer. In some cases, resumption of sexual relations is determined by a developmental milestone, such as when the baby's teeth begin to erupt or when he begins crawling or walking.

When sex becomes a lower priority for weeks or months, the baby's father may feel hurt and confused. Caring for a baby involves a tremendous investment of time from the mother, as well as fatigue from interrupted sleep, feelings of being "touched out" at the end of the day, and less interest in sex. These are all reasons why the birth of a baby is widely recognized as being one of the most stressful times in a couple's life.

During times of change and adjustment it is important for couples to keep channels of communication open. Whenever vague feelings of unhappiness surface, it is time to talk. A father may need reassurance that the mother's lack of sexual desire is not a rejection of him, but a byproduct of the immediate postpartum period. The mother, for her part, may feel better if she knows that her baby's father will not insist on what she cannot comfortably give, and will work with her to strengthen and deepen their relationship in other ways that are acceptable to both of them.

Many believe that there is an almost psychic link between mothers and babies, particularly those who are breastfeeding, that results in their being so closely attuned to each other that the baby frequently wakes up when the mother is experiencing strong emotions, including sexual arousal. But this type of "radar" only lasts for a short time while the baby is small. The intensity of the mother-baby relationship diminishes as the baby matures and becomes less totally dependent on the mother.

Sexuality/Fertility

Time spent together as a couple, regardless of how frequently or infrequently it involves sex, is of utmost importance. Changes occur very rapidly after the birth of a baby, and it is best if mother and father can help each other adjust to these changes. Particularly if sexual relations occur less frequently, their relationship will stay strong if they make it a priority to be intimate in other ways. If nursing and caring for the baby have left the mother feeling "touched out," suggest something else romantic, such as a favorite meal served by candlelight.

In the early months after birth, many women consider the time the father spends doing housework a true sign of caring and love—perhaps the best foreplay. Keeping up with household chores while also caring for a tiny baby can be overwhelming. If the father does the housework, rather than commenting on all the chores that are left undone, the mother may be able to relax and feel more positively about finding time for sex. It is important for a woman to communi-

There are no physical restrictions on the breastfeeding woman during sexual relations.

Different cultures have different attitudes about breastfeeding and sexual relations.

Making Adjustments as a Couple

If the mother has less interest in sex, she needs to talk with her partner about her feelings and listen to his.

Two common challenges for many couples are finding a time and place to make love and finding time to be together as a couple.

cate her need for assistance to her partner. He may be oblivious to unfinished household tasks.

Suggest that the mother be openly appreciative of everything her partner does to make her life easier—whether it's household chores or waiting patiently during periods when the baby is consuming nearly all of her time and energy.

Although some couples think they need to plan outings away from the baby for their time together, time as a couple does not have to mean time away from the baby. Many breastfeeding mothers are more comfortable and relaxed when they are close to their babies and schedule their private time at home or take their babies along when they go out.

BREASTFEEDING, FERTILITY, AND CONTRACEPTION

How Breastfeeding Affects Fertility

Breastfeeding delays the return of a woman's fertility after childbirth.

In many countries, breastfeeding has a greater impact on birth rates than all other contraceptives combined. Miriam Labbok of Georgetown University's Institute for Reproductive Health estimates that if all breastfeeding were to stop, within a year there would be a 20-30% rise in the birthrate worldwide (Labbok 1995).

The child-spacing effect of breastfeeding depends primarily upon the pattern of breastfeeding used. Because breastfeeding practices vary from place to place, the length of natural child-spacing also varies. In some traditional societies, births are naturally spaced several years apart by breastfeeding alone. In the !Kung tribe of Botswana, Africa, children were spaced an average of forty-four months apart despite having no taboos about sexual relations during lactation. The mothers breastfed intensively for several years, allowing babies and young children to breastfeed for a few minutes several times each hour and sleeping with them at night (Konner and Worthman 1980).

Breastfeeding's effect on fertility is nature's way of preventing a mother from having another child immediately, enabling her to give her full attention to the baby she already has and giving her body a chance to recover from pregnancy and childbirth. In developing nations, adequate child-spacing can be crucial to the survival of both mother and child.

Research has clarified the relationship between breastfeeding behavior and the return of fertility.

In the past, the likelihood of becoming pregnant while breastfeeding was studied mainly by studying birth rates in large populations. More recent research, however, has focused on individual mothers and babies and the relationship between breastfeeding behavior and the mother's nutritional status on the return of fertility. By measuring hormones in urine and in saliva, scientists are able to follow closely what is happening in a woman's reproductive system and can pinpoint whether she is ovulating and whether sufficient hormones are present to support a pregnancy. Researchers then analyze this information along with data about how frequently the mother nurses her baby, the length of feedings, the length of time between feedings, the intensity of the baby's sucking, the use of supplements and solids, and the mother's nutrition.

The baby's frequent and effective sucking, day and night, is primarily responsible for the delay in the mother's return to fertility.

In August of 1988, researchers met in Bellagio, Italy to evaluate research on breastfeeding and fertility from developed and developing countries. The meeting led to a better understanding of the way breastfeeding suppresses fertility and to the development of a set of guidelines in 1990 called the Lactational Amenorrhea Method (LAM) of child-spacing at the Institute for Reproductive Health at Georgetown University (1994). Offering more than 98% protection from pregnancy during the first six months postpartum, LAM has since been extensively tested and its effectiveness verified around the world.

According to the LAM guidelines, a mother has less than a 2% chance of becoming pregnant if:

- her menses have not returned (no vaginal bleeding after the 56th day after birth), **and**
- she is not supplementing regularly nor going longer than four hours between feedings during the day or longer than six hours between feedings at night, **and**
- her baby is younger than six months old.

Every mother must be informed that when any of these parameters is no longer true, she is at increased risk of unplanned pregnancy.

In Rwanda, where women average 12 months before return of menses postpartum, use of LAM has been extended from six to nine months with no reported pregnancies (Cooney 1994).

The key to suppression of fertility through breastfeeding is frequent nursing day and night. Research has found that fertility will be reliably suppressed during amenorrhea as long as the vast majority of feedings are at the breast (supplements comprise no more than 5-15% of the baby's intake and are given after breastfeeding) and mother and baby go no longer than four hours during the day or six hours at night between feedings (Institute for Reproductive Health 1994). Once the baby begins sleeping through the night there is an increased likelihood of fertility returning. See the next section for more information.

In addition to suppressing ovulation, the hormones of breastfeeding may decrease a mother's ability to support a pregnancy during the first cycle or more after menses return.

Research has found that breastfeeding increases the likelihood that a mother's first menstruation will be anovulatory (not preceded by ovulation), particularly if it occurs during the first six months of breastfeeding (Campbell and Gray 1993; Diaz 1992; Lewis 1991). The longer a mother's menses are delayed by breastfeeding, the more likely she is to ovulate before her first menstruation. In one study, mothers whose babies were older than one year were more than two-and-a-half times more likely to ovulate before their first menstrual period than mothers whose babies were less than three months old (Lewis 1991). Another study found that ovulation before the first menstrual period also occurred more often in women who were supplementing their babies by bottle (Diaz 1992).

Even if ovulation does occur before a nursing mother's first menstruation, in many cases, the hormones of lactation cause mothers to have deficient eggs and luteal phases, that is, the hormonal levels in the second half of the menstrual cycle are too low to maintain a pregnancy (Campbell and Gray 1993; Diaz 1992; Lewis 1991). In some cases, this can happen during more than one cycle, further lengthening a woman's natural period of infertility.

Even after menses return, breastfeeding continues to reduce fertility. Although mothers should consider themselves fertile once they have any vaginal bleeding after 56 **Sexuality/Fertility** days postpartum, or when supplementation replaces breastfeedings, according to one study (Singh 1993) continuing to breastfeed appeared to suppress ovulation in mothers whose menses returned when their babies were 3 to 9 months old. The younger the baby when the mother's menses returned, the more anovulatory cycles the mother was likely to have. No differences in fertility were associated with continuing to breastfeed in women whose menses returned after 9 months postpartum.

Studies have found that maternal nutrition has little effect on return of fertility.

Although some older studies equated better maternal nutrition with an earlier return to fertility, these studies did not take into account the effect of breastfeeding frequency on fertility (Frisch 1988; Prema 1981). More recent studies that have included data on frequency of breastfeeding found that a mother's nutritional status appears to have little or no effect on her return to fertility (Kurz 1991; Lewis 1991).

Mothers who nurse their babies unrestrictedly (for comfort as well as for nutrition, night as well as day) generally go for many months without their menses returning.

The key to delaying the return of menstruation and fertility through breastfeeding is frequent nursing day and night. Research has found that optimal breast-feeding—full breastfeeding without any supplements for the first six months—is not only best for mother's and baby's health, it is also most effective in maximizing the natural period of infertility.

Fertility will be most effectively suppressed when the vast majority of feedings are at the breast and mother and baby go no longer than four hours during the day or six hours at night between feedings (Institute for Reproductive Health 1994). Once the baby begins sleeping more than six hours at night, goes longer than four hours without nursing during the day, or the mother increases supplements, the mother's hormonal balance may be altered sufficiently to permit ovulation and menstruation to resume. However, if the baby sucks frequently at the breast, for comfort as well as for food, and nurses during the night as well as the day, the period of infertility will almost always be lengthened accordingly. See LAM in the next section for more information.

Differences in mothers' return to fertility vary from place to place, depending upon local breastfeeding practices. In Rwanda, for example, where breastfeeding is the norm, breastfeeding mothers average a return to menses at 12 months. However, in the United States, the breastfeeding rates and duration are much lower. In 1992, only about 20% of mothers were breastfeeding at all at six months, so the vast majority of breastfeeding women return to fertility much sooner. Even in areas where age of weaning is similar, return to fertility has been found to vary due to differences in breastfeeding patterns (Gray 1994).

The woman's body chemistry is also a factor in the duration of her infertility.

While the pattern of breastfeeding is a key factor in the length of infertility, the woman's own body chemistry also influences the duration of infertility. Some few mothers nurse their babies without supplements and nevertheless resume their menses within the first three months postpartum. Other mothers whose babies sleep through the night or who give some supplements do not resume having menstrual cycles for 12 months or more. Individual differences in both mothers and babies can either lengthen or shorten the period of natural infertility. Some women go as long as two years or more without menstruating.

When solid foods are started, the mother's menses may continue to be delayed. By breastfeeding before giving solids, introducing foods gradually, and continuing to nurse at night, she may be able to prolong her infertility.

Once a baby starts solids, if the mother's menses have not returned, there are several things she can do that may help to prolong her natural period of infertility:

- breastfeed first, before offering solids,
- introduce solids gradually, and
- continue to breastfeed unrestrictedly at night.

Solids replace mother's milk in a baby's diet (Cohen 1994). In some cases, the reduced amount of sucking at the breast due to solids will be enough to cause fertility to return. In other cases, the mother's natural infertility may continue. If the baby is still enjoying frequent, prolonged nursings during the day, even though he sleeps through the night or has begun to eat a substantial amount of solid foods, the absence of menstrual periods may last for many more months. But the longer a mother breastfeeds without menstruating, the greater the likelihood that she will ovulate before menstruating.

When the baby begins nursing less, the mother's chances of ovulating before menstruation increase even more.

When the baby is nursing less, because he is taking more solid foods, because he is sleeping through the night, or because the mother has started weaning, ovulation is more likely to occur prior to menstruation. Be sure the mother who does not wish to conceive again is aware that these changes may increase her risk of unplanned pregnancy.

When a mother has any vaginal bleeding after 56 days postpartum, she should consider herself fertile.

In many cases, the first menstrual period during breastfeeding is anovulatory, that is, not preceded by ovulation. Because pregnancy is impossible without ovulation, some women refer to this as their "warning" period. Even if ovulation does occur before a mother's first menstrual period, the hormones of breastfeeding may cause a deficient egg and follicle and a deficient luteal phase, making the hormonal levels too low to maintain a pregnancy (Campbell and Gray 1993; Diaz 1992; Lewis 1991), further lengthening a woman's natural period of infertility, sometimes by as much as two or three more cycles.

In some women light bleeding or spotting is the first indication of their return to fertility. Although one study found that ovulation was nearly 10 times more likely to precede "regular" or "heavy" bleeding as opposed to "spotting" or "light" bleeding (Campbell and Gray 1993), the mother with light bleeding or spotting of two days or more should consider herself fertile (Bellagio 1995).

Once a mother's menses have returned, increased nursing and/or milk expression may suppress menstruation again. The mother should still consider herself fertile.

Occasionally, mothers who have resumed their menstrual cycles have reported that a sudden increase in the baby's nursing or in milk expression lengthened the time between menses. The amount of additional sucking needed to cause menstruation to be suppressed varies from woman to woman. If this occurs, the mother should still consider herself potentially fertile.

Sometimes a woman who wants to conceive finds it difficult or impossible to do so while breastfeeding, even after her menses have returned.

In some cases, even infrequent breastfeeding is enough to prevent pregnancy in a woman who had previously practiced more intensive breastfeeding patterns (Gray 1990). One such woman reported that her periods had returned at eighteen months postpartum. Her son continued to nurse for another year and even though there were signs that she was ovulating, she was unable to conceive. She consulted a fertility specialist who mentioned that research has indicated that some breastfeeding women who are ovulating may remain infertile for a time due to subtle hormonal changes caused by breastfeeding. She became pregnant within weeks of completely weaning her son (Gotsch 1991).

Contraception and the Breastfeeding Mother

Questions about contraceptives should be handled with respect for cultural and religious differences as well as differences in family values and priorities.

When a mother asks about contraceptives and breastfeeding, her cultural, religious, and family values will influence her choices. A method that is popular and effective in one part of the world may be unacceptable in another. A method that works well in one family may be unworkable in another. While respecting these differences, share current information on contraceptives and breastfeeding with the mother and encourage her to discuss this information with her health care provider before making a decision.

Because many physicians are not well informed on breastfeeding's natural effects on fertility, be sure the mother has this information so that she can make an informed choice.

Sexuality/Fertility

Non-Hormonal Methods

The contraceptive methods in this section are considered to be the first choice for the breastfeeding mother because they do not involve the use of artificial hormones.

The methods of contraception listed in this section do not involve the use of artificial hormones, which may pass into the milk and affect milk composition or production. Non-hormonal methods are the first-choice methods for the breastfeeding mother.

A mother needs to be aware of LAM (see next section), so that when she is making decisions about contraception she is aware that certain patterns of breastfeeding offer effective protection from pregnancy for the first six months. LAM can be used as an interim method while the mother is considering other alternatives.

Lactational Amenorrhea Method (LAM)

LAM is a family planning method that offers a mother who is exclusively or almost exclusively breastfeeding more than 98% protection against pregnancy during the first six months after birth.

Developed in 1989 at the Institute for Reproductive Health at Georgetown University, the Lactation Amenorrhea Method (LAM) is based on the Bellagio Consensus, the combined opinion of two dozen scientists in lactational infertility, about how an individual woman can use lactational amenorrhea for contraception (Kennedy 1989; Family Health International 1988). An interim family planning method that provides more than 98% protection against pregnancy during the first six months after birth, the effectiveness of LAM has been replicated in many studies around the world (Kazi 1995; Kennedy 1992; Perez 1992; Diaz 1991).

LAM is an effective alternative to other family planning methods during this first six months as long as the mother can answer "no" to the following questions:

1. Have your menses returned?
2. Are you supplementing regularly or allowing long periods without breastfeeding, either during the day (more than four hours) or at night (more than six hours)?
3. Is your baby more than six months old?

If the mother answers "yes" to any of these questions, her risk of pregnancy is increased. If she wants to avoid pregnancy, she should consider using an additional method.

In Rwanda, where women average 12 months before return of menses postpartum, use of LAM has been extended from six to nine months with no reported pregnancies (Cooney 1994).

To use LAM effectively, the mother needs to understand what is meant by exclusive or almost exclusive breastfeeding and be willing to breastfeed her baby for the vast majority of feedings.

To help mothers and their health care providers more clearly understand the impact of feeding choices on fertility, the researchers who developed LAM categorized and defined various breastfeeding patterns. Three main categories—full, partial, and token breastfeeding—were subdivided into the following six subcategories:

Full breastfeeding
- **Exclusive breastfeeding**—The baby receives no liquids or solids other than mother's milk.
- **Almost exclusive breastfeeding**—In addition to breastfeeding, the baby receives vitamins, minerals, water, juice, or any other foods infrequently (no more than one or two mouthfuls per day).

Partial breastfeeding
- **High partial breastfeeding**—The vast majority of feedings are breastfeedings.
- **Medium partial breastfeeding**—About half of the feedings are breastfeedings.
- **Low partial breastfeeding**—The vast majority of the feedings are not breastfeedings.

Token breastfeeding
- **Token breastfeeding**—The baby is minimally breastfed on an occasional, irregular basis.

The mother who adopts exclusive or almost exclusive breastfeeding patterns (both of which fall into the "full breastfeeding" category) can rely on LAM with confidence until her menses return, her breastfeeding pattern changes, or her baby reaches six months of age. Research indicates that a high partial breastfeeding pattern (with supplements comprising no more than 5-15% of a baby's feedings) can also effectively suppress a mother's fertility, especially if she breastfeeds first before giving the supplements. However, if the mother increases supplementation or her baby begins going longer between feedings day or night, she is at increased risk for return of her fertility (Gray 1990). Medium partial breastfeeding delays return of fertility for some mothers, but cannot be relied upon to prevent pregnancy. Low partial or token breastfeeding has little impact on fertility.

LAM improves the health of mother and baby, saves money, and gives the mother control over her fertility.

Choosing breastfeeding patterns that enhance a mother's natural infertility after birth promotes good breastfeeding management and saves money that would otherwise be spent on supplements and contraceptives. Research indicates that mothers who use LAM tend to breastfeed longer and return to fertility later than other breastfeeding mothers, even in parts of the world where breastfeeding is the norm (Labbok 1993). LAM is acceptable to virtually all religious groups, and it has the advantage of giving the mother control over her fertility. LAM not only helps a mother prevent pregnancy and avoid the side effects of other contraceptive methods, it gives both mother and baby the optimal health benefits of breastfeeding.

Under certain circumstances LAM can be used if mother and baby will be regularly separated, however, her risk of pregnancy will be slightly higher.

A mother can use LAM if she is regularly separated from her baby for generally less than four to six hours at a time, as long as she is expressing her milk at least as often as her baby was nursing and never less often than every four hours. In one study done in Chile, LAM was found to be 95% effective for women who hand-expressed their milk at work (Labbok 1995).

Natural Family Planning

A woman who wants to reduce her chances of becoming pregnant without using artificial contraceptives can learn to recognize her body's signs of ovulation and abstain from intercourse during fertile times. When used correctly, NFP has been found to be highly effective.

Natural Family Planning (NFP) is a method of child-spacing that involves noting and interpreting a woman's body signs to determine times of fertility and to use that information to prevent or achieve pregnancy by timing intercourse accordingly. Body signs of ovulation include changes in temperature, in the cervical mucus, and in the opening of the cervical os (the mouth of the cervix). The breastfeeding mother may notice an obvious mucus pattern prior to the first postpartum ovulation, thus providing ample indication of the onset of fertility. However, some women find their mucus pattern confusing. If a woman is also taking her temperature upon waking in the morning, she may watch for the rise in her temperature that indicates ovulation has occurred. However, if a mother's sleep is disturbed during the night, temperature readings may not be as reliable.

For the mother who wants to prevent pregnancy without using artificial contraceptives, one of her options is to start by using LAM (see previous section) and begin NFP after her baby is six months old or whenever LAM no longer applies (see also next point). NFP, when used correctly, has been found to be 91-99% effective (Institute for Reproductive Health 1994). When used incorrectly, however, NFP is, of course, far less effective. One study (Kennedy 1995) found that breastfeeding mothers using NFP (but not LAM) were nearly always able to determine their fertile period but misinterpreted many nonfertile days as fertile, resulting in more abstinence from intercourse than was necessary to avoid pregnancy. By using LAM during the first 6 months, it was found that much of the unnecessary abstinence could be avoided (Kennedy 1991).

Sexuality/Fertility

Books available on the subject include *The Art of Natural Family Planning* by John and Sheila Kippley and *Your Fertility Signals: Using Them to Achieve or Avoid Pregnancy, Naturally* by Merryl Winstein (for more information, see "Publications for Parents" at the end of this chapter).

If a mother has not learned to use NFP before becoming pregnant, it may be more difficult to gauge her return to fertility if she starts using this method while breastfeeding.

The body signs indicating a return to fertility during breastfeeding are more subtle than the changes during a regular monthly cycle. Whether or not a mother has previously been instructed in NFP, suggest she consult with an instructor to better understand how her symptoms will differ while she is breastfeeding. Local instructors can be located through the Couple to Couple League, P.O. Box 11084, Cincinnati, Ohio 45211 USA or the National Office of Natural Family Planning, 8514 Bradmoor Drive, Bethesda, MD 20817-3810 USA.

NFP does not affect breastfeeding and is free from side effects. Training is necessary. To be effective, the mother and her partner must agree to abstain from intercourse when she is fertile.

Because no drugs or products are involved, NFP is safe for mother and baby and does not affect breastfeeding. Training in NFP involves time and may cost money, and in order to effectively prevent pregnancy, both the mother and her partner must agree to abstain from intercourse during the mother's fertile times, which may be more difficult to determine while the mother is breastfeeding.

Barrier Methods and Spermicides

Barrier methods, such as condoms, diaphragms, and others, can be used alone or as a supplement to other methods.

Barrier methods—which include condoms, diaphragms, contraceptive sponges, and cervical caps—offer several advantages. They are generally available in many areas, some offer protection from sexually transmitted diseases, they are fairly inexpensive, and they can be used in conjunction with other methods. For example, if the mother is using NFP to determine her fertile times (see previous section), barrier methods can be used when she is fertile rather than abstaining from intercourse. When used correctly, condoms and diaphragms are generally considered to be effective in preventing pregnancy.

Barrier methods also have some disadvantages. Unless lubricated condoms are used, they can be irritating to the vagina due to the dryness caused by low estrogen levels during the early months of breastfeeding. Diaphragms require a physical exam and need to be refitted whenever the mother's weight fluctuates more than 10 pounds (4.5 kg).

Barrier methods and spermicides, used together or separately, have no effect on breastfeeding.

Barrier methods without spermicides have no effect on breastfeeding. When spermicides are used, extremely minute amounts may be absorbed into the mother's blood and pass into the milk, but no problems in babies have been documented (USPDI 1996). Use of spermicides is considered compatible with breastfeeding, and spermicides provide extra lubrication when, due to a woman's low levels of estrogen during breastfeeding, she may be experiencing some vaginal dryness.

Non-Hormonal Intrauterine Devices (IUD)

Non-hormonal IUDs are highly effective in preventing pregnancy and are considered compatible with breastfeeding.

An intrauterine device (IUD), as its name describes, is a device inserted into a woman's uterus and left in place for months or years. Although the IUD is highly effective in preventing pregnancy, there is controversy about how it works.

A non-hormonal IUD has no effect on breastfeeding (Koetsawang 1987).

Breastfeeding women have less pain and less bleeding on IUD insertion and lower removal rates. Recent studies have found no increased risk of uterine perforation in breastfeeding women using the IUD when compared with non-breastfeeding women.

Although one early study showed an increased risk of uterine perforation when breastfeeding women used the IUD (Heartwell and Schlesselman 1983), other large studies found that when experienced clinicians inserted the IUDs, no increased risk of uterine perforation was found in breastfeeding women (Farr and Rivera 1992; Chi 1989; Cole 1983). In one study, no uterine perforations were reported among any of the 2275 women followed. The breastfeeding women, however, were found to have lower incidence of pain at the time of IUD insertion and fewer removals for bleeding and pain than the women who were not breastfeeding. The researchers concluded that these differences were due to the hormonal effects of lactation (Farr and Rivera 1992).

Timing of insertion has also been found to be a factor in expulsion rates. To reduce the risk of expulsion, at this writing experts recommend that an IUD insertion be performed either within the first two to four days after birth or after about six weeks postpartum (Chi 1989).

Sterilization

Vasectomy and tubal ligation are popular in some parts of the world and highly effective in preventing pregnancy. They do not directly affect breastfeeding, although a tubal ligation can complicate early breastfeeding if it is performed right after birth.

A full or partial hysterectomy will not affect breastfeeding, other than the breastfeeding complications that can occur with any surgical procedure.

Progestin-Only Methods

Progestin-only methods of contraception are considered compatible with breastfeeding, but are the second choice for nursing mothers because small amounts of the hormones pass into the mother's milk and there may be slight changes in the composition of the milk and the mother's milk supply.

Progestin-only methods include a variety of contraceptives, including the minipill, progestin-IUDs, progestin-releasing vaginal rings, injectables (Depo-Provera), and implants (Norplant).

Sterilization is now a popular method of family planning in the United States (Kennedy 1993) and is highly effective in preventing pregnancy. Although vasectomies and tubal ligations can sometimes be reversed, they should be considered permanent, and as with any surgery, carry the risk of side effects.

Neither mother nor child is affected when the mother's partner has a vasectomy, however, as with any surgery on the mother, a tubal ligation can indirectly affect breastfeeding, particularly if it is performed immediately after birth. The time it takes to recover from the anesthesia can interfere with the early establishment of breastfeeding, and the drugs that pass into the milk may decrease the nursing baby's interest and effectiveness in breastfeeding. The pain from the surgery may also complicate the mother's efforts and desire to breastfeed.

Breastfeeding is regulated by hormones secreted by the hypothalamus and the pituitary glands. These hormones affect the function of the ovaries by suppressing ovulation during the early months of breastfeeding, but removal of the uterus and/or ovaries during a full or partial hysterectomy does not affect milk production.

As with any mother who undergoes surgery, the breastfeeding mother who has a partial or full hysterectomy will need help in maintaining breastfeeding through her hospital stay. But her milk production will not be directly affected by the removal of the uterus or ovaries.

While small amounts of hormones pass into the milk of a mother using hormonal contraception (Harlap 1987; Hull 1981), progestin-only methods are considered by most experts to be compatible with breastfeeding (see the last point in this section).

Many studies have found that progestin-only methods have little effect on breastfeeding. Some studies have found no effect on the volume and composition of milk (McCann 1994; WHO 1994a), while other studies found slightly improved milk supplies and greater duration of breastfeeding in mothers using specific progestin-only injectables (Emery 1993).

Regarding changes in milk composition, it is uncertain whether the slight changes noted in the milk of mothers using hormonal contraception have any significance. In a review of the literature, Fraser (1991) noted that infant growth and development among babies of mothers using either progestin-only methods or others that included estrogen were comparable to those of babies of women who were not using hormonal contraception. However, no distinction was made as to exclusive or partial breastfeeding. The similarity among the groups and the natural variability in milk composition from feeding to feeding and day to day led Fraser to conclude that the significance of changes in milk composition related to hormonal contraception is unclear.

Sexuality/Fertility

One study found that use of progestin-only methods offered some protection against bone loss in breastfeeding women (Caird 1994).

Progestin-only methods administer progestin in a variety of ways, but they all prevent pregnancy in the same way: by blocking ovulation, thickening cervical mucus, making sperm penetration more difficult, and thinning the uterine lining. One noteworthy difference among these methods is that timed-released methods result in higher levels of progestin circulating in the mother's bloodstream as compared with the minipill (Kennedy 1993). Timed-released methods are many public health departments' methods of choice because they offer continuous highly effective protection from pregnancy over a long period of time, independent of the woman's actions. The differences in these methods may make one method more suitable to a particular mother than another; however, all of them are not available in all areas.

The progestin-only minipill is taken daily and should ideally be taken at about the same time each day. Its effectiveness is dependent upon regular use, and it is slightly less effective (as well as being less forgiving of missed pills) than the combined oral contraceptive. Irregular bleeding, a commonly reported side effect of the minipill, does not normally occur during lactation.

The progestin-releasing vaginal ring is inserted in the vagina, worn continuously, and prevents pregnancy for three months. Like other progestin-only methods, research has found that the progestin-releasing vaginal ring does not effect the duration of breastfeeding or the growth of the baby (Shaaban 1991).

Other timed-released progestin-only methods include:

- progestin-IUD—works like a non-hormonal IUD and also releases small amounts of progestin into the mother's system over time,
- the progestin-only injectable (Depo-Provera)—each injection prevents pregnancy for three months, and
- the progestin-only implant (Norplant)—an implant inserted under a woman's skin that prevents pregnancy for up to five years.

It is recommended that progestin-only methods not be started until after the first six to eight weeks of breastfeeding, as earlier introduction may decrease milk supply, or may affect the infant's immature liver.

Timing of the introduction of progestin-only methods is controversial and research results are mixed. While one study found no effect on breastfeeding or infant growth and development when these methods were started at one week after birth (Moggia 1991), other research and anecdotal reports suggest waiting until breastfeeding has been established for at least six to eight weeks before starting these methods (Institute for Reproductive Health 1994; WHO Task Force 1994a; WHO Task Force 1994b).

Two concerns related to early introduction of progestin-only methods are:

- possible negative effect on milk supply, and
- lack of information on the baby's ability to metabolize the hormones during the first weeks of life, while his liver is still immature (Institute for Reproductive Health 1994).

When considering appropriate timing for progestin-only methods, suggest the breastfeeding mother and her health care provider take into account the period of natural infertility the mother will receive in the early months if her baby is primarily breastfeeding. (For more information, see the previous section on LAM.)

Although small amounts of progestin do pass into mother's milk, research has found no long-term effects on the children of nursing mothers.

As of this writing, research has followed the breastfed children of mothers who used progestin-only methods for up to seventeen years. No long-term effects have been found on sexual development during puberty or in any other area. The researchers concluded that use of progestin-only methods during breastfeeding does not adversely affect the long-term growth and development of children (Pardthaisong 1992). However, these studies do not fully report on individual patterns of breastfeeding and the total amount of exposure to the hormones.

Progestin-only methods are considered compatible with breastfeeding by the American Academy of Pediatrics (AAP Committee on Drugs 1994).

Methods Containing Estrogen

Hormonal contraceptives containing estrogen are considered the third choice for breastfeeding mothers because they have been found to have the greatest effect on breastfeeding. However, breastfeeding can still continue if they are used.

Contraceptives containing estrogen are considered the third choice for breastfeeding mothers because estrogen has been found to decrease milk supply and duration of breastfeeding. Some studies have found that use of combined oral contraceptives during the first few weeks after birth can decrease milk supply from 20-40% (Fraser 1991; Croxatto 1983; Borglin and Sandholm 1971). This led to a belief that use of oral contraceptives was not compatible with breastfeeding. However, much of the earlier research was done on mothers taking the older, higher-dose oral contraceptives during the early weeks after birth. Newer combined oral contraceptives with lower doses of estrogen appear to have less effect on both duration of breastfeeding and milk supply, particularly when they are started after breastfeeding has been established (Erwin 1994; Madhavapeddi and Ramachandran 1990).

It is uncertain whether the slight changes in milk composition noted in mothers using hormonal contraception have any significance. In a review of the literature, Fraser (1991) noted that infant growth and development among babies of mothers using either progestin-only methods or those containing estrogen were comparable to those of babies of women who were not using hormonal contraception. This similarity among the groups and the natural variability in milk composition from feeding to feeding and day to day led him to conclude that the significance of changes in milk composition is unclear.

If a breastfeeding mother chooses a method containing estrogen, she can continue breastfeeding and watch for any signs of a reduction in her milk supply. Regular checkups will allow her health care provider to monitor her baby's weight gain. Most experts agree that the known benefits of breastfeeding outweigh potential risks of hormonal contraceptives.

Two methods containing estrogen include the combined oral contraceptive pill and the combined injectable.

The most commonly used method containing estrogen is the combined oral contraceptive, a pill taken daily that contains a combination of estrogen and progestin. Another recent option is the combined injectable, which like Depo-Provera (see previous section) gives continuous highly effective protection from pregnancy that is independent of the woman's actions.

If chosen, it is recommended that methods containing estrogen not be started until after the baby is at least six months old and consuming other foods.

Because methods containing estrogen have been found to decrease milk supply (see the first point in this section), it is recommended that mothers wait to start them until their babies are at least six months old, when other foods will also be a major part of baby's diet (Institute for Reproductive Health 1994; WHO Task Force 1994a).

Estrogen and progestin are considered compatible with breastfeeding by the American Academy of Pediatrics (AAP Committee on Drugs 1994).

Although small amounts of estrogen do pass into mother's milk, there is no indication of any long-term effects on breastfed children.

Mothers have been using methods containing estrogen for several decades and except for indications of reduced milk supply when high-estrogen methods are used in the early postpartum period, there are no case reports of long-term effects of estrogen on breastfeeding babies.

Resources for Parents

Couple to Couple League
P.O. Box 11084
Cincinnati, Ohio 45211 USA

Sexuality/Fertility

National Office of Natural Family Planning
8514 Bradmoor Drive
Bethesda, MD 20817-3810 USA
Telephone: 301-897-9323

Institute for Reproductive Health
Breastfeeding Publications List
2115 Wisconsin Avenue #602
Washington DC 20007 USA

Publications for Parents

Gotsch, G. *Breastfeeding and Fertility.* Schaumburg, Illinois: La Leche League International, 1991. Publication No. 87.

Kippley, J. and Kippley, S. *The Art of Natural Family Planning.* Cincinnati, Ohio: Couple to Couple League International, Inc., 1979.

Kippley, S. *Breastfeeding and Natural Child Spacing*. Cincinnati, Ohio: Couple to Couple League International, Inc., 1989.

La Leche League International. *Breastfeeding and Sexuality*. Schaumburg, Illinois, 1985. Publication No. 82.

La Leche League International. THE WOMANLY ART OF BREASTFEEDING, 35th Anniversary ed., Franklin Park, Illinois, 1991. pp. 115-18, 377-80

Winstein, M. *Your Fertility Signals: Using Them to Achieve or Avoid Pregnancy, Naturally*. St. Louis, Missouri: Smooth Stone Press, 1994.

Institute for Reproductive Health. *Guidelines: breastfeeding, family planning, and the Lactational Amenorrhea Method—LAM*. Washington, DC: Georgetown University, 1994.

References

Breastfeeding and Sexuality

Kennedy, K. "Fertility, sexuality and contraception during lactation." In *Breastfeeding and Human Lactation*, eds. J. Riordan and K. Auerbach. Boston and London: Jones and Bartlett, 1993. pp. 438-46.

Kenny, J. Sexuality of pregnant and breastfeeding women. *Arch Sex Behav* 1973; 2:215-29.

Lawrence, R. *Breastfeeding: A Guide for the Medical Profession,* 4th ed. St. Louis: Mosby, 1994. pp. 591-97.

Masters, W. and Johnson, V. *Human Sexual Response*. Boston: Little, Brown & Company, 1966.

Riordan, J. *A Practical Guide to Breastfeeding*. St. Louis: Mosby, 1983, p. 339.

Wisniewski, P. and Wilkinson, E. Postpartum vaginal atrophy. *Am J Obst Gynecol* 1991; 165: 1249-54.

Breastfeeding, Fertility, and Contraception

AAP Committee on Drugs. The transfer of drugs and other chemicals into human milk. *Pediatrics* 1994; 93:141.

Bellagio, Italy. Press Release, December 14, 1995. Family planning method endorsed. Family Health International; World Health Organization; Georgetown University. Institute for Reproductive Health.

Borglin, N. and Sandholm, L. Effect of oral contraceptives on lactation. *Fertil Steril* 1971; 22:39-41.

Caird, L. et al. Oral progestogen-only contraception may protect against loss of bone mass in breast-feeding women. *Clin Endocrinol* 1994; 41:739-45.

Campbell, O. and Gray, R. Characteristics and determinants of postpartum ovarian function in women in the United States. *Am J Obstet Gynecol* 1993; 169:55-60.

Chi, I. et al. Performance of the copper T-380A intrauterine device in breastfeeding women. *Contraception* 1989; 39(6):603-18.

Cohen, R. et al. Effects of age of introduction of complementary foods on infant breast milk intake, total energy intake, and growth: a randomised intervention study in Honduras. *Lancet* 1994; 344:288-93.

Cole, L. et al. Effects of breastfeeding on IUD performance. *Am J Public Health* 1983; 73:384-88.

Cooney, K. Assessment of the nine-month lactational amenorrhea method in Rwanda (MAMA-9). Occasional paper. Washington, DC: *Institute for Reproductive Health*, 1994.

Croxatto, H. et al. Fertility regulation in nursing women: IV. Long-term influence of a low-dose combined oral contraceptive initiated at day 30 postpartum upon lactation and infant growth. *Contraception* 1983; 27:13-25.

Diaz, S. et al. Relative contributions of anovulation and luteal phase defect to the reduced pregnancy rate of breastfeeding women. *Fertil Steril* 1992; 58(3):498-503.

Diaz, S. et al. Contraceptive efficacy of lactational amenorrhea in urban Chilean women. *Contraception* 1991; 43(4):335-52.

Emery, M. Can a woman breastfeed while using Depo-Provera as an agent for birth control? *J Hum Lact* 1993; 9(3):187-88.

Erwin, P. To use or not use combined hormonal oral contraceptives during lactation. *Fam Plan Perspect* 1994; 26(1):26-33.

Family Health International. Consensus statement: breastfeeding as a family planning method. *Lancet* 1988; 1204-5.

Farr G. and Rivera, R. Interactions between intrauterine contraceptive device use and breast-feeding status at time of intrauterine contraceptive device insertion: analysis of TCu-380A acceptors in developing countries. *Am J Obstet Gynecol* 1992; 167:144-51.

Fraser, I. A review of the use of progestogen-only minipills for contraception during lactation. *Reprod Fertil Dev* 1991; 3:245-54.

Frisch, R. Fatness and fertility. *Sci Am* 1988; 258:88-95.

Gotsch, G. *Breastfeeding and Fertility.* Schaumburg, Illinois: La Leche League International, 1991. Publication No. 87.

Gray, R. et al. The risk of ovulation during lactation. *Lancet* 1990; 335:25-29.

Gray, S. Comparison of effects of breast-feeding practices on birth-spacing in three societies: nomadic Turkana, Gainj, and Quechua. *J Biosoc Sci* 1994; 26:69-90.

Harlap, S. Exposure to contraceptive hormones through breast milk: are there long-term health and behavioral consequences? *Int J Gyn Ob* 1987; 25(suppl):47-55.

Sexuality/Fertility

Heartwell, S. and Schlesselman, S. Risk of uterine perforation among users of intrauterine devices. *Obstet Gynecol* 1983: 61(1):31-36.

Howie, P. and McNeilly, A. Effect of breastfeeding patterns on human birth intervals. *J Reprod Fertil* 1982; 65:545-57.

Hull, J. The effects of hormonal contraceptives on lactation: current findings, methodological considerations, and future priorities. *Studies in Fam Plan* 1981; 12:134-55.

Institute for Reproductive Health. *Guidelines: breastfeeding, family planning, and the Lactational Amenorrhea Method—LAM.* Washington, DC: Georgetown University, 1994.

Kazi, A. et al. Effectiveness of the lactational amenorrhea method in Pakistan. *Fertil Steril* 1995; 64(4):717-23.

Kennedy, K. et al. Breastfeeding and the symptothermal method. *Studies in Fam Plan* 1995; 26(2):107-15.

Kennedy, K. "Fertility, sexuality and contraception during lactation." In *Breastfeeding and Human Lactation,* eds. J. Riordan and K. Auerbach. Boston and London: Jones and Bartlett, 1993. pp. 429-38, 446-57.

Kennedy, K. and Visness, C. Contraceptive efficacy of lactational amenorrhoea. *Lancet* 1992; 339:227-30.

Kennedy, K. et al. The natural family planning—lactational amenorrhea method interface: observations from a prospective study of breastfeeding users of natural family planning. *Am J Obstet Gynecol* 1991; 165(6):2020-26.

Kennedy, K. et al. Consensus statement on the use of breastfeeding as a family planning method. *Contraception* 1989; 39(5):477-96.

Koetsawang, S. The effects of contraceptive methods on the quality and quantity of breastmilk. *Int J Gynaecol Obstet* 1987; 25(suppl):115-28.

Konner, M. and Worthman, C. Nursing frequency, gonadal function, and birth spacing among !Kung hunter-gatherers. *Science* 1980; 207:788-91.

Kurz, K. et al. Influences of maternal nutrition and lactation on length of postpartum amenorrhoea. *J Trop Ped* 1991; 37(Suppl 1):15-18.

Labbok, M. Breastfeeding and Child Spacing—The Lactational Amenorrhea Method. Presented at LLLI 14th International Conference, July 1995. (Audiocassette ordering information available from LLLI).

Labbok, M. The lactational amenorrhea method (LAM): another choice for mothers. BREASTFEEDING ABSTRACTS 1993; 13:3-4.

Labbok, M. and Laukaran, V. "Breastfeeding and family planning." In *Gynecology and Obstetrics,* ed. J. Sciarra. Philadelphia: Lippincott 1994.

Lawrence, R. *Breastfeeding: A Guide for the Medical Profession,* 4th ed. St. Louis: Mosby, 1994. pp. 575-91.

Lewis, P. et al. The resumption of ovulation and menstruation in a well-nourished population of women breastfeeding for an extended period of time. *Fertil Steril* 1991; 55(3):529-36.

Madhavapeddi, R. and Ramachandran, P. Growth and morbidity of breastfed infants whose mothers were using combination pills. *Breastfeed Rev* 1990; 11(2):66-68.

McCann, M. and Potter, L. Progestin-only contraception: a comprehensive review. *Contraception* 1994; 50(6)Suppl 1:S138-51.

McCann, M. et al. The effects of a progestin-only oral contraceptive (levonorgestrel 0.03 mg) on breastfeeding. *Contraception* 1989; 40:635-48.

Moggia, A. et al. A comparative study of a progestin-only oral contraceptive versus non-hormonal methods in lactating women in Buenos Aires, Argentina. *Contraception* 1991; 44(1):31-43.

Nilsson, S. et al. Long-term follow-up of children breast-fed by mothers using oral contraceptives. *Contraception* 1983; 27:27-38.

Pardthaisong, T. et al. The long-term growth and development of children exposed to Depo-Provera during pregnancy or lactation. *Contraception* 1992; 45:313-24.

Peralta, O. et al. Fertility regulation in nursing women: V. Long-term influence of a low-dose combined oral contraceptive initiated at day 90 postpartum upon lactation and infant growth. *Contraception* 1983; 27:27-38.

Perez, A. et al. Clinical study of the lactational amenorrhoea method for family planning. *Lancet* 1992; 339:968-70.

Prema, K. et al. Nutrition-fertility interaction in lactating women of low income groups. *Br J Nutr* 1981; 45:461-67.

Shaaban, M. Contraception with progestogens and progesterone during lactation. *J Steroid Biochem* 1991; 40(4-6):705-10.

Singh, K. et al. Effects of breast feeding after resumption of menstruation on waiting time to next conception. *Human Bio* 1993; 65(1):71-86.

US Pharmacopeial Convention. *United States Pharmacoepia Dispensing Information: Drug Information for the Health Care Professional,* 16th ed. Rockville, Maryland: US Pharmacopeial Convention, 1996. p. 2687.

World Health Organization (WHO) Task Force. Progestogen-only contraceptives during lactation: I. Infant growth. *Contraception* 1994a; 50:35-53.

World Health Organization (WHO) Task Force. Progestogen-only contraceptives during lactation: II. Infant development. *Contraception* 1994b; 50:55-68.

Sexuality/Fertility

19

Nutrition, Weight Loss, Exercise, and Personal Grooming

NUTRITION FOR THE NURSING MOTHER
    Nutritional Needs
    No Need to Eat or Avoid Certain Foods
    Is Baby Reacting to a Food in the Mother's Diet?
    The Vegetarian Mother
    Fluids—Drink to Thirst

WEIGHT LOSS AND EATING DISORDERS

EXERCISE

PERSONAL GROOMING
    Hair Dyes and Permanents, Tanning Beds, and Nipple Piercing

NUTRITION FOR THE NURSING MOTHER

Nutritional Needs

Choose Nutritious Foods

The same principles of good nutrition apply to the nursing mother as to the rest of the family.

Keep nutrition information simple. Complex dietary rules are unnecessary and may dissuade some women from breastfeeding.

Emphasize that choosing nutritious foods does not necessarily mean spending more time in the kitchen.

Research indicates that a less-than-perfect diet will not affect a mother's milk supply. Her milk is still the best food for her baby.

Encourage the mother to follow a basic approach to good nutrition by eating a well-balanced and varied diet of foods in as close to their natural state as possible. As is true for the rest of the family, the breastfeeding mother should eat fresh fruits and vegetables, whole grain breads and cereals, as well as calcium-rich and protein-rich foods. Naturally, the mother's choices within these categories will vary, depending on her cultural heritage, economic situation, and food preferences.

The more simply this approach to good nutrition is stated, the better. Ruth Lawrence, MD, explains in the fourth edition of her book, *Breastfeeding: A Guide for the Medical Profession* (1994): "Most writings for the nursing mother regarding maternal diet during lactation set up complicated 'rules' about dietary intake that fail to consider the mother's dietary stores and normal dietary preferences. Thus, one barrier to breastfeeding for some women is the 'diet rules' they see as being too hard to follow or too restrictive" (p. 279). One survey found that some mothers chose not to breastfeed for this reason (Gabriel 1986).

For many breastfeeding mothers, knowing what to eat is not nearly as challenging as finding the time for shopping and cooking. But good nutrition doesn't have to mean spending more time in the kitchen. Many foods are both nutritious and handy for snacking and quick meals. Cheese, yogurt, whole-grain bread or crackers, tomatoes, sprouts, fresh fruits, whole or sliced raw vegetables, hard-cooked eggs, and nuts can be eaten with little or no preparation. More frequent smaller meals can be just as nutritious as three larger meals. Rather than preparing three large meals a day, some nursing mothers try to have a healthy snack and something to drink every time they sit down to nurse.

Planning meals a week at a time cuts down on trips for food. Cleaning and cutting up vegetables in large batches will make it easy to eat them by the handful as a snack or add to a salad or casserole. Making double batches of main dishes or casseroles takes only a little more time and freezing half gives the mother a supply of quick-to-fix meals for hectic days.

Research from developing countries and other parts of the world indicates that even mothers who are mildly malnourished produce plenty of good quality milk for their babies and that only under famine or near famine conditions will a mother's nutrition affect her milk supply or the composition of her milk (Perez-Escamilla 1995; Prentice 1994). Even in famine conditions, milk production may be only slightly affected if the mother has body stores from which to draw energy for milk production (Smith 1947). In some developing countries where food supplies are limited, babies of women given nutritional supplements have not been found to gain more weight than babies of women whose diets were not supplemented (Prentice 1983).

Among generally well-nourished mothers, milk composition tends to remain stable even when they do not eat well. However, chronically undernourished women with low body stores and inadequate diets may produce milk that is lower than normal in some vitamins, including A, D, B_6, or B_{12} (see the section "The Vegetarian Mother"). In this case, if the mother's diet improves or she takes vitamin supplements, the vitamin levels in her milk would return to normal.

The types of fatty acids in human milk have been found to vary, depending upon the mother's diet. For example, mothers who eat more unsaturated fats tend to produce milk that is higher in unsaturated fats than the milk of mothers who eat more animal products (Sanders 1992). These appear to be normal variations.

Eat to Hunger

Suggest the mother "eat to hunger." It is recommended that lactating women consume 2700 calories per day, however, many nursing mothers actually take in closer to 2200 calories per day or less.

Although the Subcommittee on Nutrition during Lactation (1991) recommends that a breastfeeding mother consume about 2700 calories per day (about 500 calories a day more than a non-pregnant, non-nursing woman), studies have found that nursing mothers actually consume between 2200 (Butte 1984) and 2460 (English and Hitchcock 1968) calories per day and experience a safe, gradual weight loss at this level (Butte 1984). The minimum safe intake for an average-sized breastfeeding mother is considered to be 1800 calories per day, and it is recommended that mothers who restrict their diet to this level eat foods high in nutritional value and consider a vitamin and mineral supplement (see later section, "Weight Loss and Eating Disorders").

Many women are not in the habit of counting calories, so suggest the nursing mother "eat to hunger." Most mothers tend to feel hungrier when they are breastfeeding, so encourage a mother to trust her appetite and choose nutritious foods that will help her feel energetic.

A mother who is less active, has more fat stores from pregnancy, and eats more foods high in nutritional value may need fewer calories per day than the more active mother with fewer fat stores who eats more processed foods.

A nursing mother's caloric requirements are influenced by her body stores and her activity level. While it is often recommended that nursing mothers consume an extra 500 calories per day, research indicates that these recommendations may be too high for many mothers. For example, a mother who is less active will need fewer calories per day than a more active mother. Also, a mother who was well-nourished during pregnancy can draw from the fat stores laid down during pregnancy, as well as the food she eats daily, to meet her energy requirements (Goldberg 1991). On the other hand, a mother who was not well-nourished during pregnancy may need to eat more. Research also indicates that a mother's metabolism may be more efficient during breastfeeding, possibly decreasing her need for extra energy from food (Illingworth 1986).

Also, because the 2700-calorie-per-day recommendation is based upon the nutritional content of the typical American diet, which includes many processed foods, a mother who consumes more foods that are higher in nutritional value may be able to fulfill her nutritional needs with fewer calories (Subcommittee on Nutrition during Lactation, p. 224).

If the mother is eating poorly, she may feel tired and run down and have a decreased resistance to illness.

Although a mother who is eating poorly will produce the milk her baby needs, she can compromise her own health and energy by depleting her own nutritional stores. Encourage the mother to eat well so that she will have more energy and be more resistant to illness.

If a low-income mother is malnourished to the extent that it affects her milk supply, it is healthier and less expensive to feed the mother nutritious foods than to buy formula for her baby.

Some low-income mothers are discouraged from breastfeeding by health professionals, social workers, and others who question whether their diets are adequate. But if the mother is malnourished to the extent that it affects her milk supply, it is much less expensive to feed the mother nutritious food than to buy formula for her baby. Human milk is also healthier for the baby and increases his resistance to illness.

Nutrition/Exercise

If the low-income mother is given free formula, Dr. Jack Newman, pediatrician and member of LLL's Health Advisory Council from Toronto, Canada, suggests that she consume it herself in baked goods. In this way the mother will receive extra nutrition and her baby will receive the perfect food—human milk.

Supplements

Routine vitamin-mineral supplements are not necessary for the nursing mother if she eats a healthy, balanced, and varied diet.

As a general rule, well-nourished mothers don't need to take vitamin supplements while breastfeeding. While supplements may be of benefit to mothers who are malnourished or on a restricted diet (see next point), the best way for a well-nourished breastfeeding mother to get the nutrients she needs is through a balanced diet.

A woman on a restricted or extremely poor diet may benefit from taking supplements.

If a woman is chronically malnourished or on a very restricted diet, some vitamin deficiencies will eventually affect the levels of some vitamins in her milk, including A, D, B_6, or B_{12} (see the section "The Vegetarian Mother"). In this case, vitamin-and-mineral supplements may be warranted.

No Need to Eat or Avoid Certain Foods

Contrary to popular belief, there are no foods that must be eaten or avoided by the nursing mother. Moderation is the key.

The natural variations in a nursing mother's diet alter the flavor of her milk, which may better prepare her baby for eating solids when he is older.

If the mother has healthy eating habits, there is usually no reason to change them when she is breastfeeding. There are no foods (such as cow's milk) that must be consumed while a mother is breastfeeding, and there are no foods that all nursing mothers should avoid. Although there are exceptions, most breastfeeding mothers find they can eat anything they like in moderation—including chocolate and spicy foods—without any effect on their babies.

A mother's varied diet may be an advantage to her breastfeeding baby because it alters the flavor of her milk, providing the baby with a variety of tastes which prepares him for the solid foods he'll receive at the family table when he is older (Sullivan and Birch 1994). One study found that one to two hours after nursing mothers consumed capsules of garlic extract their milk acquired a garlicky smell, but the babies who received this garlicky milk were not fussier. Instead, they showed a greater interest in nursing and consumed more milk (Menella and Beauchamp 1991). This variability in the flavor of the milk may be one reason why children who were breastfed as babies tend to have fewer feeding problems as they get older (Lawrence, p. 305).

Caffeine

Moderate intake of caffeine causes no problems for most breastfeeding mothers and babies.

The amount of caffeine in five or fewer 5 oz. cups of coffee per day (a total less than 750 ml) has not been found to cause a problem for most breastfeeding mothers and babies (Nehlig and Debry 1994), although some mothers and babies may be more sensitive than others.

When figuring caffeine intake, be sure the mother is counting all her sources, including coffee, iced and hot teas, colas, other soft drinks containing caffeine, and any over-the-counter drugs that contain caffeine (see next point).

Excessive caffeine consumption by a breastfeeding mother may make her baby fussy and wakeful.

If a breastfeeding mother consumes more caffeine in a day than is found in five 5 oz. cups of coffee (more than 750 ml), caffeine could begin accumulating in her baby's system, causing symptoms of caffeine stimulation. A baby who is being overstimulated by caffeine is a wide-eyed, active, alert baby who doesn't sleep for long and may also be unusually fussy. To find out if these symptoms are caused by caffeine, suggest the mother cut down on caffeine gradually for a week, substituting caffeine-free beverages, both hot and cold, for her caffeinated drinks. Abrupt withdrawal may cause headaches or other discomfort.

If the mother wants to cut down on her caffeine intake, be sure she knows which drinks and non-prescribed drugs contain caffeine.

If the baby is reacting to the caffeine ingested by the mother, be sure she knows the usual sources of caffeine so she can avoid them. Common sources are coffee and tea, including iced tea. If the mother drinks a lot of coffee or tea, suggest she use decaffeinated coffee and tea for a week or two while she observes her baby's behavior. Also, caffeine is found in most cola soft drinks, as well as in other soft drinks. Suggest the mother read the labels and avoid those containing caffeine.

Some over-the-counter drugs sold in the US also contain caffeine. Examples include:

- stimulants, such as Caffedrine, NoDoz, and Vivarin,
- pain relievers, such as Anacin, Excedrin, and Midol,
- diuretics, such as Aquaban, PreMens Fore, and Permathene H2Off
- weight-control aids, such as Dexatrim, Dietac, and Prolamine.

If caffeine stimulation is the cause of a baby's sleeplessness, he should begin settling down to more normal sleeping patterns within a few days to a week after his mother gradually eliminates caffeine from her diet.

The mother who is eliminating caffeine from her diet should know that theobromine, which is in chocolate and cocoa, is similar to caffeine.

If a baby is showing signs of caffeine stimulation, in addition to talking to the mother about her sources of caffeine, be sure to mention that chocolate contains a substance called theobromine, which is similar to caffeine and can produce the same effect if taken in large amounts (Berlin and Daniel 1981).

Chocolate

Most nursing babies are not affected if their mothers consume chocolate in moderation.

Although the theobromine in chocolate is similar to caffeine (see previous point), there is much less theobromine in chocolate than caffeine in coffee. A 5 oz. cup (150 ml) of brewed drip coffee contains about 130 mg. of caffeine, a 5 oz. cup (150 ml) of decaffeinated coffee contains about 3 mg of caffeine, and one ounce (28 grams) of milk chocolate contains 6 mg of theobromine (Behan, p. 130). Although one study found a link between chocolate consumption and colic symptoms (Lust 1996), most breastfeeding experts believe that moderate consumption of chocolate does not usually cause problems in breastfeeding babies (Renfrew, pp. 97-98; Lawrence, p. 305).

Is Baby Reacting to a Food in the Mother's Diet?

When a baby is fussy, a mother's first thought may be that the baby is reacting to something in her diet. Usually this is not the cause.

Most mothers can eat any food without causing fussiness in their babies. Even so, many mothers restrict their diets unnecessarily because they have been told that they should avoid certain foods while breastfeeding. If their baby does become fussy, a mother's first thought may be that the fussiness is a reaction to something she ate.

Although many cultures around the world recommend that nursing mothers avoid certain foods, these restrictions vary from place to place. For example, Chinese and Southeast Asian women are advised to avoid cold liquids because they are not good for the baby. Hispanic women may be told to avoid pork, chili, and tomatoes. Some African Americans avoid onions while breastfeeding (Taylor 1985). In Australia mothers are cautioned to avoid cabbage, chocolate, spicy foods, peas, onions, and cauliflower because these foods are thought to cause colic, gas, diarrhea, and rashes in the breatfeeding baby (Riordan and Auerbach, p. 352).

Some babies do develop a sensitivity to a food in the mother's diet, but the foods that cause reactions differ from one mother and baby to the next, so it is not sensible to advise all nursing mothers to avoid certain foods. In most instances, avoiding particular foods will not cut down on fussiness, and these kinds of "diet rules" have been found to dissuade some women from breastfeeding (Gabriel 1986).

There is little scientific basis to the notion that eating "gassy" foods will make a baby gassy or that citrus eaten by mother is "too acid" for baby.

Nutrition/Exercise

Although many mothers have heard that eating "gassy" foods will cause gas in their breastfeeding babies, this idea is suspect. Gas is produced when intestinal bacteria act upon fiber in the intestines. Gas and fiber do not pass into breast milk, even if the mother suffers from excess gas. Neither do high-acid foods change the pH of the mother's milk (Lawrence, p. 305).

Although spices and strong flavors such as garlic have been found to change the smell and flavor of the milk, this does not necessarily cause problems in babies. In one study, when nursing mothers were fed garlic capsules, their babies nursed more and took more milk than they did before the milk took on a garlicky smell (Mennella and Beauchamp 1991).

Another study found a correlation between colic symptoms in the baby and the mother's consumption of certain foods (cruciferous vegetables, cow's milk, onion, and chocolate), however, this study was based upon the mothers' recollection of their previous week's diet and their babies' subsequent behavior (Lust 1996). A retrospective survey like this may be questionable in its reliability in establishing a connection between diet and infant reaction, because the mothers' responses may be influenced by the cultural messages they receive about how particular foods affect a breastfeeding baby.

Before assuming a baby is reacting to something in the mother's milk, ask if the baby has been given anything else he might be sensitive to, if the mother is taking a medication or nutritional supplement, or if she smokes cigarettes or drinks alcohol.

Although some rare babies are sensitive to a food in their mothers' diet (see next point), it is more likely that a baby will be sensitive to a food he has been given directly, such as formula, solids, or juice. Occasionally mothers give their babies teas or other remedies that are recommended for colic or fussiness. Sometimes children in the house or caregivers feed the baby other foods without the mother's knowledge.

Ask the mother if she or anyone else is giving the baby anything other than her milk. Ask specifically if the baby is receiving supplemental feedings by the baby's father or a caregiver when the mother is not at home, as she may not think of this unless asked.

Ask if the mother is on any medication or taking any nutritional supplements. If so, ask if the baby's reaction began after she started taking the drug or supplement. If so and the mother is on medication, suggest the mother ask her doctor to recommend an alternative drug. If the mother is taking vitamins, vitamin-mineral supplements, or other supplements, such as brewer's yeast, suggest she eliminate them for a week to see if they may be causing the reaction.

Ask the mother if the baby is getting vitamin supplements directly. If so, ask the mother if they were recommended for a specific aspect of the baby's health. Although vitamins are not necessary in most cases and can be eliminated, they may be necessary in unusual situations, such as the very premature baby, the baby whose skin is not exposed to sunlight, or the baby whose mother is on a diet that includes no animal products.

Ask the mother if she smokes cigarettes or if she drinks alcohol or caffeinated beverages. A baby may react to the mother's intake of nicotine, alcohol, or caffeine. (See "Caffeine" in the previous section and "Alcohol" and "Nicotine" in the chapter "Drugs, Vitamins, Vaccines, and Diagnostic Tests".)

Occasionally, a food the mother eats will affect the baby. This is more likely if there is a family history of allergy. The baby may have physical symptoms associated with food sensitivity.

Although most breastfeeding mothers can eat any food in moderation without any effect on their babies, occasionally, a sensitive baby may be affected by a food his mother eats. Food sensitivity may be the cause if the baby has some or all of the following signs:

- fussiness after feedings,
- inconsolable crying for long periods,
- sleep disturbances,
- sudden waking with obvious discomfort,
- green stools with mucus,
- eczema,
- congestion,
- dry skin,
- wheezing.

There also may be a family history of allergies.

To determine what food is causing the problem, ask the mother if she has recently eaten a new food or has eaten an unusually large amount of a food. If so, eating less of that food or eliminating it for two or three days may solve the problem.

Ask the mother if she has recently tried a new food or has eaten a large amount of a food. Although it is unusual for a baby to react to a food his mother eats, some mothers notice that their babies become very fussy after they eat a new food (particularly one that is unusually strong or spicy) or when they consume a large amount of a food. To alleviate her baby's fussiness, the mother can simply moderate her intake or avoid that food while continuing to breastfeed. If a new food or overconsumption of a food is the cause of the problem, the baby should be back to normal within 24 hours (Lawrence, p. 305).

If the mother has not eaten a large amount of a food, the baby may be reacting to a food that is a regular part of the mother's diet. If so, ask her if she has food cravings or if she is eating a food she dislikes because she thinks it is good for the baby.

Not all food sensitivities are obvious. Symptoms like congestion, eczema, and wheezing, as well as fussiness, may start gradually and their cause may not be easily identified. Australian breastfeeding expert Maureen Minchin (1989) suggests asking the following questions to help determine if the baby may be sensitive to a food that is a regular part of the mother's diet.

- Are there foods that you don't like but you are eating while breast-feeding—or ate during pregnancy—for the benefit of your baby?
- Are there foods that you crave? What foods do you feel you have to have when you have had a bad day?

These foods are the most likely suspects, because according to Minchin, conscious dislikes or food cravings are signals that the mother's body may be reacting to them in an abnormal way.

If the baby may be sensitive to foods that are a regular part of the mother's diet, suggest the mother avoid one or two of the suspected foods for two to three weeks.

Suggest to the mother that she eliminate one of these regular foods from her diet for a minimum of two to three weeks. Eliminating a food for two or three days will be effective in certain situations, such as an acute reaction to a recently introduced food. However, if the baby is responding less acutely or is reacting to long-term exposure to a food that is a regular part of the mother's diet, the baby may not improve immediately when it is eliminated. Although some babies respond within a few days, it is not unusual for the baby to feel worse for about a week after the offending food is eliminated before he feels better. The mother may also have withdrawal symptoms, such as headaches. But over a period of several weeks the mother will know if she has found the right food because she will see a difference in her baby's disposition. She may even feel better herself.

Suggest the mother eliminate no more than one or two foods at a time so that she can more easily pinpoint the cause. Eliminating more foods at once makes it harder to eat a balanced diet. Encourage the mother to get skilled help in evaluating her diet if she makes major changes in her eating habits.

Cow's milk in the mother's diet is a common cause of food sensitivity in babies.

Cow's milk seems to be a common source of food sensitivity and fussiness in babies, perhaps because many women are encouraged to drink a lot of milk during pregnancy and lactation, which can sensitize a baby before birth and while breast-feeding. Research has found that cow's milk antibodies in the form of protein pass into a mother's milk and if the baby is sensitive to these, it can cause fussiness. One study found that mothers with colicky babies had higher levels of this cow's milk protein in their milk than mothers whose babies were not colicky (Clyne and Kulczycki 1991). In another study, 35 out of 66 mothers of colicky babies reported a decrease in their babies' fussiness when they eliminated milk and milk products from their diets (Jakobsson and Lindberg 1983). It may take ten days to two weeks to eliminate cow's milk protein from the mother's system, so if the mother wants to try eliminating milk and milk products from her diet, encourage her to allow the full two weeks before gauging the results.

Nutrition/Exercise

If the mother chooses to eliminate milk and milk products from her diet, encourage her to get skilled help in evaluating her diet. A cup (227 grams) of cooked bok choy, a type of cabbage, is an alternative source of calcium that provides 86% as much calcium as a cup (240 ml) of milk. Half a cup (113 grams) of ground sesame seeds—which can be added to baked goods, pancake batter, or sprinkled on salads or cereals—contains twice as much calcium as a cup (240 ml) of milk. Other sources of calcium include blackstrap molasses, calcium-enriched tofu, collards, spinach, broccoli, turnip greens, kale, liver, almonds, and Brazil nuts, as well as canned sardines and salmon, both of which are normally eaten with the soft bones.

Color Changes in the Mother's Milk

Pink or pink-orange milk has been linked to food dyes in orange soda in the mother's diet.

Sometimes, a food or drug a mother ingests may affect the color of her milk and/or the color of her baby's urine. Usually this is not cause for concern.

In one report, drinking Sunkist orange soda, which contains red and yellow dyes, turned a mother's milk to a pink-orange color. In another report, the mother's consumption of Sunkist orange soda turned her breastfeeding baby's urine to a pink-orange color (Roseman 1981). Food dyes are used in many other sodas, gelatin desserts, and fruit drinks, so if a mother reports this type of color change in her milk or her baby's urine, ask if she has consumed foods containing these dyes.

Green milk and green urine in the baby have been linked to mothers' ingestion of Gatorade (a drink containing green food dye), as well as kelp, other seaweed, and vitamins.

According to Ruth Lawrence, MD, over the years several mothers have approached the breastfeeding experts at the University of Rochester with concerns about green milk. After a careful review of the mothers' diets, the suspected foods were eliminated from their diets and then reintroduced to confirm the effect. Foods that were found to color the milk green included Gatorade (a drink containing green food dye), kelp, other seaweed, especially seaweed tablets, and the type of natural vitamins found in health food stores (Lawrence, p. 306).

Black milk has been linked to a mother's long-term use of the drug minocycline hydrochloride.

One case of black milk was reported in a woman who had been taking minocycline hydrochloride for four years (Basler and Lynch 1985).

The Vegetarian Mother

If a mother says she is a vegetarian, ask her what foods she avoids, as there would be no special considerations for vegetarian diets that include animal protein.

Many types of vegetarian diets include animal products, and these present no special problems in relation to breastfeeding. For example, semivegetarians avoid red meat but eat poultry, seafood, milk products, and eggs. Ovo-lacto-vegetarians avoid all flesh foods (red meat, seafood, and poultry) but eat milk products and eggs. Lacto-vegetarians avoid flesh foods and eggs but eat milk products. Ovo-vegetarians avoid flesh foods and milk products but eat eggs. All of these diets include some form of animal protein.

Diets that include no animal protein, such as the vegan and macrobiotic diets, may require supplementation to avoid vitamin B_{12} deficiency (see next point).

Nursing mothers who eat a diet with no animal products may need to supplement their diet to avoid a vitamin B_{12} deficiency in their nursing baby.

Vegetarian diets that include no animal products, such as vegan and macrobiotic diets, may lead to a vitamin B_{12} deficiency in mother or baby, because vitamin B_{12} is primarily available from animal protein. In one reported case, the breastfeeding baby of a mother who consumed no animal products developed a severe vitamin B_{12} deficiency. Symptoms included loss of appetite, regression in motor development, lethargy, muscle atrophy, vomiting, and blood abnormalities. The mother showed no signs of vitamin B_{12} deficiency (Kuhne 1991). Two studies found lower concentrations of vitamin B_{12} in the milk or other signs of a vitamin B_{12} deficiency in mothers on a macrobiotic diet (Specker 1994; Dagnelie 1992).

If the mother on a vegan or macrobiotic diet does not want to consume animal products, suggest she consider taking a vitamin B_{12} supplement and/or adding fermented soybean foods and yeast to her diet, both of which contain some B_{12}. Another alternative would be to give her baby vitamin B_{12} supplements.

Vegetarian mothers have been found to consume less calcium and vitamin D than other mothers, but this does not affect the levels in their milk.

One study found that while vegetarian mothers tended to consume less calcium than other mothers, this did not affect the levels of calcium in the milk. Also, although the vegetarian mothers had low vitamin D levels, supplements were not recommended because most mothers and babies receive adequate vitamin D through exposure to the sun (Specker 1994). Exposure to sunlight for only a few minutes per day is sufficient for breastfed babies in most parts of the world. Another study found the calcium level in the milk of mothers on a macrobiotic diet to be lower than the calcium level in the milk of nonvegetarian mothers (Dagnelie 1992).

Suggest the vegetarian mother who does not consume milk or other dairy products give special care to taking in enough calcium. A cup (227 grams) of cooked bok choy, a type of cabbage, is an alternative source of calcium that provides 86% as much calcium as a cup (240 ml) of milk. Half a cup (113 grams) of ground sesame seeds—which can be added to baked goods, pancake batter, or sprinkled on salads or cereals—contains twice as much calcium as a cup (240 ml) of milk. Other sources of calcium include blackstrap molasses, calcium-enriched tofu, collards, spinach, broccoli, turnip greens, kale, almonds, and Brazil nuts.

The milk of vegetarian mothers tends to be lower in environmental contaminants than the milk of mothers who eat animal products.

Research has found the milk of vegetarian mothers to be lower in environmental contaminants, such as PCBs, than the milk of other mothers (Dagnelie 1992). Environmental contaminants are stored primarily in fat, and vegetarian diets tend to be lower in fat than diets including more animal products.

Fluids—Drink to Thirst

The nursing mother should be encouraged to drink to thirst. Drinking more than that is not beneficial and will not increase her milk supply.

"Drink to thirst" is a nursing mother's best guide to how much liquid she should drink. Most mothers find that they are naturally more thirsty when they are nursing. Encourage the mother not to wait until she is feeling parched to take a drink. If the mother finds that she often overlooks her feelings of thirst, suggest she have a drink waiting for her whenever she sits down to nurse.

Good sources of fluids include water, fruit and vegetable juices, milk, soups, and other liquids.

It is not beneficial for the mother or her milk supply to force extra fluids. Not only is forcing fluids uncomfortable, but one study (Dusdieker 1985) found that mothers did not produce any more milk when they drank 25 percent more fluids than when they drank to thirst.

If the mother is not drinking enough fluids, her urine will be concentrated and she may become constipated.

If the mother is producing large amounts of pale yellow urine, she is probably drinking enough. Constipation (hard, dry stools) and concentrated urine (darker in color with a stronger smell) are both signs that a mother needs to drink more.

If the mother is constipated, she can avoid having to use commercial remedies by increasing her liquid intake and her consumption of fresh fruits and raw vegetables (prunes and pears are especially effective), as well as whole grains.

The nursing mother does not have "to drink milk to make milk," although it is important for her to have other sources of calcium in her diet if she does not drink milk or eat dairy products.

Many women worry about getting enough calcium in their diets, especially since medical science has learned that calcium deficiencies may contribute to osteoporosis, a degenerative bone disease.

Milk is one possible source of calcium, but if the mother does not like milk or if she or her baby is sensitive to milk, there are other sources. Yogurt and cheeses are possible alternatives that some mothers and babies can tolerate better because they are processed. If the mother consumes no milk or milk prod-

Nutrition/Exercise

ucts, encourage her to get skilled help in evaluating her diet. (See previous section "Is Baby Reacting to a Food in the Mother's Diet?" for additional sources of calcium.)

WEIGHT LOSS AND EATING DISORDERS

Most breastfeeding mothers gradually lose weight while "eating to hunger."

Breastfeeding mothers who eat to hunger tend to lose weight gradually. The Subcommittee on Nutrition during Lactation (1991) reports: "On average, lactating women who eat to appetite lose weight at the rate of 0.6 to 0.8 kg (1.3 to 1.6 pounds) per month in the first 4 to 6 months of lactation, but there is a wide variation in the weight loss experience of lactating women (some women gain weight during lactation). Those who continue breastfeeding beyond 4 to 6 months ordinarily continue to lose weight, but at a slower rate than during the first 4 to 6 months" (p. 74).

Breastfeeding mothers tend to lose more weight when their babies are three to six months old than formula-feeding mothers who consume fewer calories (Dewey

1993; Heinig 1992). One study of mothers at one month postpartum found that mothers who breastfed (either exclusively or partially) had slimmer hips and weighed less than women whose babies received only formula (Kramer 1993).

If the mother wants to lose weight more quickly, suggest she wait until her baby is at least two months old.

Extra pounds are added during pregnancy to store energy for producing milk and breastfeeding makes it easier to shed these extra pounds, according to Judith Roepke, a nutritionist at Ball State University in Indiana. Dr. Roepke considers lactation an ideal time to lose weight, as it seems to mobilize even fat accumulated before pregnancy. However, it is important to lose weight slowly. Dr. Roepke suggests that nursing mothers do nothing purposely to bring about weight loss during the first two months postpartum. During that time the mother's body needs to recover from childbirth and establish a good milk supply.

Weight loss should be gradual— no more than 4 lbs. (2 kg) per month—to minimize the release of stored environmental contaminants into the mother's milk.

Crash diets, fad diets, and quick weight loss present problems for nursing mothers. Environmental contaminants including PCBs and pesticides are stored in body fat. Losing weight rapidly—more than about four pounds (2 kg) per month, or a pound (.45 kg) per week—may release these contaminants into the mother's bloodstream quickly and increase the levels in her milk.

Gradual weight loss—no more than 4 lbs. (2 kg) per month—has not been found to affect milk supply.

Gradual weight loss has not been found to affect a mother's milk (Dewey and McCrory 1994). One study found that nursing mothers who lowered their calorie intake by 25% safely lost about 1 lb. (.45 kg.) per week without affecting their baby's growth (Dusdieker 1994).

If the mother decides to cut more calories to lose weight, encourage her to eat foods high in nutritional value and consume at least 1800 calories per day.

To promote slow weight loss, suggest the mother begin by increasing her activity level and eliminating 100 calories per day from her diet. If she wants to cut more calories to lose weight, suggest she plan to eat at least 1800 calories per day or more of foods that are high in nutritional value and consider taking a vitamin and mineral supplement.

The Subcommittee on Nutrition during Lactation (1991) writes: "Advise women who choose to curb their energy intake to pay special attention to eating a balanced, varied diet and to including foods rich in calcium, zinc, magnesium, vitamin B_6, and folate. Encourage intake of at least 1800 kcal/day. Calcium, multivitamin-mineral supplements, or both may be advised when dietary sources are marginal and it is unlikely that appropriate dietary practices will or can be followed. Intakes below 1500 kcal/day are not recommended at any time during lactation, although fasts lasting less than 1 day have not been shown to decrease milk volume. Liquid diets and weight loss medications are not recommended" (p. 15).

Women who reduce their intake to less than 1800 calories per day or who are currently suffering from an eating disorder are at risk for nutritional deficiencies.

When a breastfeeding mother does not get the nourishment she needs, she runs the risk of using up her own nutritional stores to provide for her baby's nourishment, although her milk will still be best for her baby. Depleting her own reserves may lower her energy level and her resistance to illness. If she becomes chronically malnourished, the levels of vitamin A, D, B_6, and B_{12} in her milk may be reduced (Subcommittee on Nutrition during Lactation, p. 140) and her milk supply may eventually decrease.

A history of anorexia, bulimia, or other eating disorders does not necessarily preclude successful breastfeeding. In one case report, a woman who overcame anorexia and bulimia went on to regain normal weight, become pregnant, and was still breastfeeding her baby at five months (Bowles 1990). However, some women with a history of eating disorders report a worsening of symptoms after birth (Weekly 1992). If the mother is suffering from an eating disorder, suggest she seek nutritional guidance as well as help in overcoming her eating problems.

EXERCISE

Moderate exercise is beneficial and appropriate for the breast-feeding mother.

Exercise is invigorating, an excellent change of pace, and a great stress reliever. Some mothers are concerned that exercise might interfere with milk production, but one recent study (Lovelady 1990) indicates that exercise has little effect on milk production. In fact, when eight vigorously exercising mothers of exclusively breastfeeding babies between nine and twenty-four weeks were compared with breastfeeding mothers who did not exercise, the exercising women had slightly higher milk volume. However, because the number of women studied was so small, this slight increase in milk may not be significant.

Another study that compared two groups of mothers—one group who participated in supervised aerobic exercise 5 days per week for 12 weeks and one group who did not exercise—found no differences between the two groups in the mothers' body weight, fat loss, prolactin levels, in the volume or composition of the mothers' milk, or in the babies' weight gain (Dewey 1994).

Despite reports in the popular press, there is no reason to postpone breastfeeding after exercise.

In 1992, the popular press reported on a study in which researchers analyzed mothers' milk before and after strenuous exercise and compared the babies' acceptance of the before-exercise milk with the milk expressed after their mothers exercised (Wallace 1992). The mothers' milk was found to be higher in lactic acid after exercise, and the babies were judged to be less accepting of the after-exercise milk. Wide publicity was given to the researchers' conclusions: that breastfeeding mothers should nurse their babies before exercising or express milk for later feedings, and they should avoid nursing right after exercise, perhaps for as long as 90 minutes.

These conclusions were questionable for several reasons. First, the babies were fed the before- and after-exercise milk via medicine dropper, a new feeding method for them, but the researchers did not consider this change in feeding method as affecting the babies' acceptance of the milk. In their review of the literature on exercise and breastfeeding, Dewey and McCrory (1994) cited several other limitations of the study. The mothers in the study exercised to their maximum, but the researchers' recommendations did not distinguish between moderate and maximal exercise. Lactic acid concentrations in the milk are likely to be much lower in women who exercise moderately. Also, although the mothers rated their babies' acceptance of the after-exercise milk lower than the before-exercise milk, there was not much difference between these ratings. On a scale of 1 (cry) to 9 (laugh), the average before-exercise milk rating was 6.7 while the average after-exercise milk rating was 4.7. In addition, none of the mothers in the study reported that their babies reacted negatively to nursing after exercise on previous occasions.

Nutrition/Exercise

After reviewing many studies, Dewey and McCrory concluded that exercise gives breastfeeding mothers better cardiovascular fitness and that exercise during breastfeeding is safe for most women. Also, "altered acceptance of breast milk due to higher lactic acid concentrations post-exercise is not likely to be a problem in most cases."

A breastfeeding woman who exercises regularly should keep track of her weight to be sure she isn't losing weight too quickly.

Most breastfeeding mothers experience a slow weight loss even if they are not exercising. The lactating mother who exercises regularly may need to keep track of her weight to be sure she doesn't lose too much weight too soon—more than about four pounds (2 kg) a month (or a pound [.45 kg] a week). Many women who exercise regularly, however, find that their appetites increase along with their energy demands.

If losing weight too quickly is a concern, suggest the mother snack between meals. Nutrient-dense snacks will help her keep her weight loss gradual and provide extra energy.

If lack of time is a concern, suggest ways she can combine exercise with other activities.

Lack of time may make exercising seem impossible for the new mother. If so, suggest ways she might combine exercise with other activities she can do with her baby. For example, walking outside with her baby in a stroller or in a baby carrier can provide exercise along with a change of scene. If the weather is bad, walking through the shopping mall is another alternative. There are special strollers designed for a mother to use if she wants to run or jog with her baby. Exercise videotapes can be rented or purchased and played at home. Books are also available that feature exercise routines in which the mother can exercise along with her baby.

A supportive bra may make exercising more comfortable for the breastfeeding mother.

PERSONAL GROOMING

Hair Dyes and Permanents, Tanning Beds, and Nipple Piercing

There is no evidence that hair dyes and permanents used by the nursing mother have any effect on her breastfeeding baby.

No evidence exists that the nursing mother's use of hair-care products, such as hair dyes and permanents, has any effect on her breastfeeding baby. When a mother uses hair-care products, some of the chemicals will be absorbed through her skin. If her scalp is healthy and intact, less will be absorbed than if the skin on her scalp is scratched or abraded.

There is no evidence that the nursing mother's use of tanning beds affects her breastfeeding baby.

No evidence exists that the nursing mother's use of tanning beds has any effect on her breastfeeding baby.

There is no evidence that nipple piercing affects breastfeeding.

No evidence exists that nipple piercing, which has become fashionable among some, has any effect on breastfeeding. Some women report normal breastfeeding after nipple piercing. A mother who had one of her two nipple rings removed and restricted breastfeeding to the breast without a ring reported that a "painless, large milk blister" developed in the pierced hole of the breast with the remaining nipple ring. This blister gradually resolved without treatment after several weeks (Lee 1995).

Publications for Parents

Behan, E. *Eat Well, Lose Weight While Breastfeeding*. New York: Villard Books, 1994.

La Leche League International. THE WOMANLY ART OF BREASTFEEDING. 35th Anniversary ed., Franklin Park, Illinois, 1991. pp. 86-87, 230, 233, 272, 333

Mohrbacher, N. *Nutrition & Breastfeeding*. Schaumburg, Illinois: La Leche League International, 1994. Publication No. 159a.

References

Nutrition for the Nursing Mother

Butte, N. et al. Human milk intake and growth in exclusively breast-fed infants. *J Pediatr* 1984; 104:187-95.

English, R. and Hitchcock, N. Nutrient intakes during pregnancy, lactation and after the cessation of lactation in a group of Australian women. *Br J Nutr* 1968; 22:615-24.

Gabriel, A. et al. Cultural values and biomedical knowledge choices in infant feeding: analysis of a survey. *Soc Sci Med* 1986; 23:501.

Goldberg, G. et al. Longitudinal assessment of the components of energy balance in well-nourished lactating women. *Am J Clin Nutr* 1991; 54:788-98.

Illingworth, P. et al. Diminution in energy expenditure during lactation. *BMJ* 1986; 292:437-40.

Lawrence, R. *Breastfeeding: A Guide for the Medical Profession,* 4th ed. St. Louis: Mosby, 1994, pp. 279-310, 313.

Perez-Escamilla, R. et al. Maternal anthropometric status and lactation performance in a low-income Honduran population: evidence for the role of infants. *Am J Clin Nutr* 1995; 61(3):528-34.

Prentice, A. et al. Body mass index and lactation performance. *Eur J Clin Nutr* 1994; 48 Suppl 3: S78-89.

Prentice, A. et al. Dietary supplementation of lactating Gambian women. I. Effect on breast-milk volume and quality. *Human Nutr Clin Nutr* 1983; 37C:53-64

Riordan, J. and Auerbach, K. *Breastfeeding and Human Lactation.* Boston and London: Jones and Bartlett, 1993, pp. 349-53.

Sanders, T. The influence of a vegetarian diet on the fatty acid compositon of human milk and the essential fatty acid status of the infant. *J Pediatr* 1992; 120(4)pt.2:S94-95.

Smith, C. Effects of maternal undernutrition upon newborn infants in Holland (1944-1945). *J Pediatr* 1947; 30:229-43.

Subcommittee on Nutrition during Lactation, Food and Nutrition Board, Institute of Medicine, National Academy of Sciences. *Nutrition during Lactation.* Washington, DC: National Academy Press, 1991.

No Need to Eat or Avoid Certain Foods

Gabriel, A. et al. Cultural values and biomedical knowledge choices in infant feeding: analysis of a survey. *Soc Sci Med* 1986; 23(5):501-09.

Lawrence, R. *Breastfeeding: A Guide for the Medical Profession,* 4th ed. St. Louis: Mosby, 1994, p. 305.

Mennella, J. and Beauchamp, G. Maternal diet alters the sensory qualities of human milk and the nursling's behavior. *Pediatrics* 1991; 88(4):737-44.

Riordan, J. and Auerbach, K. *Breastfeeding and Human Lactation.* Boston and London: Jones and Bartlett, 1993, pp. 37-42, 350-53.

Sullivan, S. and Birch, L. Infant dietary experience and acceptance of solid foods. *Pediatrics* 1994; 93(2):271-77.

Nutrition/Exercise

Taylor, M. *Transcultural aspects of breastfeeding—USA*. Unit 2. La Leche League International Lactation Consultant Series. Garden City Park, New York: Avery Publishing, 1985.

Caffeine

Berlin, C. and Daniel, C. Excretion of theobromine in human milk and saliva. *Pediatr Res* 1981; 15:492.

Lawrence, R. *Breastfeeding: A Guide for the Medical Profession,* 4th ed. St. Louis: Mosby, 1994, pp. 342, 754-55.

Nehlig, A. and Debry, G. Consequences on the newborn of chronic maternal consumption of coffee during gestation and lactation: a review. *J Am Coll Nutr* 1994; 13(1):6-21.

Riordan, J. and Auerbach, K. *Breastfeeding and Human Lactation*. Boston and London: Jones and Bartlett, 1993, p. 351.

Chocolate

Behan, E. *Eat Well, Lose Weight While Breastfeeding*. New York: Villard Books, 1994, p. 130.

Berlin, C. and Daniel, C. Excretion of theobromine in human milk and saliva. *Pediatr Res* 1981; 15:492.

Lawrence, R. *Breastfeeding: A Guide for the Medical Profession,* 4th ed. St. Louis: Mosby, 1994, pp. 305.

Lust, K. et al. Maternal intake of cruciferous vegetables and other foods and colic symptoms in exclusively breast-fed infants. *J Am Diet Assoc* 1996; 96(1):46-48.

Renfrew, M., Fisher, C. and Arms, S. *Bestfeeding: Getting Breastfeeding Right for You*. Berkeley, CA: Celestial Arts, 1990, pp. 97-98.

Is Baby Reacting to a Food in the Mother's Diet?

Clyne, P. and Kulczycki. Human breast milk contains bovine IgG; relationship to infant colic? *Pediatrics* 1991; 87(4):439-44.

Gabriel, A. et al. Cultural values and biomedical knowledge choices in infant feeding: analysis of a survey. *Soc Sci Med* 1986; 23:501.

Jakobsson, I. and Lindberg, T. Cow's milk protein causes infant colic in breastfed infants: a double blind study. *Pediatrics* 1983; 71:268-71.

Lawrence, R. *Breastfeeding: A Guide for the Medical Profession,* 4th ed. St. Louis: Mosby, 1994, p. 305.

Lust, K. et al. Maternal intake of cruciferous vegetables and other foods and colic symptoms in exclusively breast-fed infants. *J Am Diet Assoc* 1996; 96(1):46-48.

Mennella, J. and Beauchamp, G. Maternal diet alters the sensory qualities of human milk and the nursling's behavior. *Pediatrics* 1991; 88(4):737-44.

Minchin, M. Food intolerance and breastfeeding...the connections. Presented at LLLI International Confrence, 1989. (Audiocassette order forms available from La Leche League International.)

Riordan, J. and Auerbach, K. *Breastfeeding and Human Lactation.* Boston and London: Jones and Bartlett, 1993, pp. 239-40, 352.

Color Changes in a Mother's Milk

Basler, R. and Lynch P. Black galactorrhea as a consequence of minocycline and phenothiazine therapy. *Arch Dermatol* 1985; 121:417.

Lawrence, R. *Breastfeeding: A Guide for the Medical Profession,* 4th ed. St. Louis: Mosby, 1994, pp. 305-06.

Riordan, J. and Auerbach, K. *Breastfeeding and Human Lactation.* Boston and London: Jones and Bartlett, 1993, p. 41.

Roseman, B. Sunkissed urine. *Pediatrics* 1981; 67:443.

The Vegetarian Mother

Dagnelie P. et al. Nutrients and contaminants in human milk from mothers on macrobiotic and ominivorous diets. *Eur J Clin Nutr* 1992; 46:355-66.

Kuhne, T. et al. Maternal vegan diet causing a serious infantile neurological disorder due to vitamin B_{12} deficiency. *Eur J Pediatr* 1991; 150:205-08.

Lawrence, R. *Breastfeeding: A Guide for the Medical Profession,* 4th ed. St. Louis: Mosby, 1994, pp. 104-05, 290-91, 300-02, 657.

Riordan, J. and Auerbach, K. *Breastfeeding and Human Lactation.* Boston and London: Jones and Bartlett, 1993, p. 41-42.

Specker, B. Nutritional concerns of lactating women consuming vegetarian diets. *Am J Clin Nutr* 1994; 59(Suppl): 1182S-86S.

Fluids—Drink to Thirst

Blaauw, R. et al. Risk factors for development of osteoporosis in a South African population. *SAMJ* 1994; 84:328-32.

Cumming R. and Klineberg, R. Breastfeeding and other reproductive factors and the risk of hip fractures in elderly women. *Int J Epidemiol* 1993; 22(4):684-91.

Dusdieker, L. et al. Effect of supplemental fluids on human milk production. *J Pediatr* 1985; 106(2):207-11.

Lawrence, R. *Breastfeeding: A Guide for the Medical Profession,* 4th ed. St. Louis: Mosby, 1994, pp. 287-88.

Riordan, J. and Auerbach, K. *Breastfeeding and Human Lactation.* Boston and London: Jones and Bartlett, 1993, p. 349-50.

Nutrition/Exercise

Weight Loss and Eating Disorders

Bowles, B. et al. Pregnancy and lactation following anorexia and bulimia. *JOGNN* 1990; 19(3):243-48.

Dewey, K. and McCrory, M. Effects of dieting and physical activity on pregnancy and lactation. *Am J Clin Nutr* 1994; 59(Suppl):446S-59S.

Dewey, K. et al. Maternal weight-loss patterns during prolonged lactation. *Am J Clin Nutr* 1993; 58:162-66.

Dusdieker, L. et al. Is milk production impaired by dieting during lactation? *Am J Clin Nutr* 1994; 59:833-40.

Heinig, M. et al. Lactation and postpartum weight loss. *Mechanisms Regulating Lactation and Infant Nutrient Utilization* 1992; 30:397-400.

Kramer, F. et al. Breast-feeding reduces maternal lower-body fat. *J Am Diet Assoc* 1993; 93(4):429-33.

Lawrence, R. *Breastfeeding: A Guide for the Medical Profession,* 4th ed. St. Louis: Mosby, 1994, pp. 304-05.

Riordan, J. and Auerbach, K. *Breastfeeding and Human Lactation.* Boston and London: Jones and Bartlett, 1993, p. 350.

Subcommittee on Nutrition during Lactation, Food and Nutrition Board, Institute of Medicine, National Academy of Sciences. *Nutrition during Lactation.* Washington, DC: National Academy Press, 1991, p. 15, 74, 140.

Weekly, S. Diets and eating disorders: implications for the breastfeeding mother. *NAACOG Clin Issues Perinat Women Health Nurs* 1992; 3(4):695-700.

Exercise

Dewey, K. et al. A randomized study of the effects of aerobic exercise by lactating women on breast-milk volume and composition. *N Engl J Med* 1994; 330(7):449-53.

Dewey, K. and McCrory, M. Effects of dieting and physical activity on pregnancy and lactation. *Am J Clin Nutr* 1994; 59(Suppl):446S-59S.

Lawrence, R. *Breastfeeding: A Guide for the Medical Profession,* 4th ed. St. Louis: Mosby, 1994, pp. 30-34.

Lovelady, C. et al. Lactation performance of exercising women. *Am J Clin Nutr* 1990; 52:103-09.

Wallace, J. et al. Infant acceptance of post-exercise breast milk. *Pediatrics* 1992; 89(6):1245-47.

Personal Grooming

Lee, N. More on pierced nipples (letter). *J Hum Lact* 1995; 11(2):89.

20

Nipple Problems

SORE NIPPLES
    Sore Nipples in the Early Weeks
    Sore Nipples at Any Stage of Breastfeeding

TREATMENT OF SORE, CRACKED, OR BLEEDING NIPPLES

FLAT AND INVERTED NIPPLES
    Types of Nipples
    Treatments to Draw Out the Nipple
    The Early Weeks of Breastfeeding

TEETHING AND BITING

THRUSH

NIPPLE BLISTERS AND SORES

SORE NIPPLES

A mother with sore nipples may be in pain and feel discouraged about breastfeeding.

Sore Nipples in the Early Weeks

Experts disagree on how much, if any, nipple soreness is normal at first.

The mother with sore nipples may begin to dread feedings and feel discouraged with breastfeeding. If her nipples are cracked and bleeding, she may be in great pain.

Breastfeeding experts differ in the amount and duration of early nipple soreness they consider normal. At one end of the spectrum, some, such as British breastfeeding expert Chloe Fisher, believe that only a minimal amount of nipple soreness is normal: "Breastfeeding should not hurt, other than a brief pain during the first few sucks of each feed in the first few days." (Renfrew, p. 58). At the other end, is Australian breastfeeding expert Maureen Minchin, who considers initial soreness normal for the first week or two (Minchin, p. 131). In between fall US experts Jan Riordan and Kathleen G. Auerbach, who write: "Transient nipple soreness...occurs in a majority of breastfeeding mothers in the first week postpartum, peaks between the third and the sixth day, and then recedes," (Riordan and Auerbach, p. 229) and Ruth Lawrence, MD: "It is common for the initial grasp of the nipple and first suckles to cause discomfort in the first few days of lactation" (Lawrence, p. 242). Unfortunately, most of the studies attempting to shed light on nipple soreness (Ziemer 1993; Ziemer 1990) reach questionable conclusions since they do not address the effects of positioning and latch-on—the most important factors in breastfeeding comfort—or the use of artificial nipples, including pacifiers.

Nipple tenderness at the beginning of a feeding may be normal in the first two to four days of breastfeeding. Soreness that is more intense or continues for a longer time indicates that some adjustment needs to be made.

During the first two to four days, the mother's nipples may feel tender at the beginning of a feeding when the baby's first sucks stretch the nipple and areolar tissue far back in his mouth. This temporary tenderness usually diminishes once the milk lets down and disappears completely within a day or two after birth if a baby is positioned and latched-on well at the breast.

Aside from this early tenderness, breastfeeding is not supposed to hurt. Persistent sore nipples indicate that some adjustment needs to be made. A mother with sore nipples should be encouraged to seek help as soon as possible, especially when:

- it hurts to breastfeed after the first day,
- she has a burning sensation in her nipples during feedings, at the end of feedings, or between feedings, or
- the soreness does not improve after three days of consistently working to correct the cause. (Persistent soreness may indicate a sucking problem in the baby, which could also mean he is not receiving enough milk.)

Ask the mother when and where her nipple hurts the most, as this information may provide clues to the cause. Also ask her what she thinks is causing the pain.

Ask the mother when during the feeding she feels the pain. Her answer will provide clues to the cause of the soreness.

- **Soreness at the beginning of the feeding,** but not after the milk begins to flow, indicates the mother's latch-on technique could be improved.
- **Soreness on the first day after birth** indicates a latch-on or sucking problem, which is usually easier to correct in the early days before it becomes a habit.
- **Soreness during the entire nursing** could be a positioning and latch-on problem, a sucking problem in the baby, or the soreness may be caused by thrush, especially if she describes the pain as burning or itching. In any case, she needs help immediately.

Ask the mother which area of the nipple is sorest. Her answer to this question will also provide clues.

- **Soreness at the top of the nipple** indicates the baby is not latched-on to enough breast tissue or the baby is raising up the back of his tongue while he nurses.
- **Soreness at the bottom of the nipple** may mean the baby is sucking in his lower lip while nursing (if so, encourage the mother to gently pull it out) or is taking in too much of the top of the breast and not enough of the underside.
- **Soreness at the tip of the nipple**, with or without a horizontal red stripe, could be due to the breast not going deeply enough into the baby's mouth, the nipple pointing up or down at latch-on (rather than pointing straight as it goes into the baby's mouth), tongue thrusting by the baby, or the baby having a short frenulum (tongue-tie) or short tongue.
- **If the entire nipple is sore**, it may be due to poor positioning and latch-on in a baby with a vigorous suck, the baby retracting his tongue during breastfeeding, or the baby curling up the tip of his tongue (which may produce a vertical red stripe on the mother's nipples after nursing). It may also be that the mother is not breaking the suction when removing the baby from the breast or is leaning over her baby while nursing. Thrush is another possibility.

The mother may have some idea about the cause of her soreness. Be sure to ask her what she thinks.

Poor positioning or latch-on is the most common cause of sore nipples, especially in the early weeks.

A mother who learns how to position her baby well and latch him on properly can expect little or no nipple tenderness as her baby begins to nurse. In most cases, sore, cracked, or bleeding nipples can be alleviated by adjusting the way the baby is positioned and latches on to the breast. (For more information, see "If Breastfeeding Hurts—Review the Basics" in the chapter "Positioning, Latch-On, and the Baby's Suck.")

If the baby's position and latch-on change during the course of the feeding, this can also cause sore nipples.

If the mother has sore nipples and is confident her baby is positioned and latched-on well at the beginning of the feeding, suggest she also check these later in the feeding. For example, if the baby falls asleep at the breast or slips down on the nipple, this can cause soreness.

Engorgement can contribute to sore nipples if it makes the breast so full and hard that proper latching on is difficult.

Engorgement can present a problem if breast fullness causes the mother's areolae to become flat and taut, making it difficult for the baby to latch on properly. If the tautness of the areola causes the baby to grasp only the nipple in his mouth, it will make nursing painful for the mother and make it impossible for the baby to milk the breast well, aggravating the engorgement.

Nipple Problems

If the mother's areola is engorged, encourage her to express enough milk to soften the areola so that the baby will be able to latch on well. Some mothers are reluctant to express even a little milk for fear that this will increase their milk supply and make the engorgement worse. If the mother mentions this concern, assure her that expressing some milk will make it easier for her baby to remove the milk from her breasts, which will lessen her engorgement. Explain that the engorgement is caused in part by other fluids—lymph and blood—as well as milk, and that removing a little milk will help the baby relieve the fullness.

Also, suggest the mother try other nursing positions, such as the football hold, which may give her more control and make latching on easier. (For more information on the treatment of engorgement, see the chapter "Breast Problems.")

If the baby receives artificial nipples (bottles, pacifiers, or nipple shields) in the early weeks it may affect his suck, causing sore nipples.

Sucking differs from bottle to breast. If the baby receives artificial nipples, such as bottles or pacifiers, he may try to nurse from the breast using the same jaw, tongue, and mouth motions he uses with the artificial nipple, causing the mother's nipples to become sore. Most types of nipple shields (flexible artificial nipples worn over the mother's nipples during feedings) also cause the baby's suck to change. Although the ultra-thin latex nipple shield has not been shown to alter sucking patterns (Woolridge 1980), babies may still become nipple confused when it is used and refuse the breast without it.

If the mother has been giving the baby artificial nipples, suggest she stop using them until the baby has a chance to learn to breastfeed well. If the baby has been receiving formula regularly, caution the mother against reducing the amount of supplement too rapidly. It may take time to rebuild the mother's milk supply and teach the baby to nurse at the breast effectively. In the meantime, the mother can offer expressed milk or formula with one of the alternative feeding methods described in "The Use of Breast Pumps and Other Products." (For more information on persuading a reluctant baby to take the breast, see the section, "Nipple Confusion," in the chapter "Fussy at the Breast and Breast Refusal.")

If either of the baby's lips is sucked in while he nurses, this can cause sore nipples.

Suggest the mother take special note of how the baby's lips are positioned while nursing. If either his top or bottom lip is sucked in, suggest she gently pull it out.

If the baby's tongue is improperly positioned during nursing or he has other sucking problems, this can cause sore nipples.

An improper suck—especially when the baby is not using his tongue properly while nursing—can cause sore nipples. Have the mother or her helper pull down the baby's lower lip to see if the baby's tongue is visible while he is breastfeeding. The mother's helper should be able to see his tongue on top of the lower gums.

If the mother's helper can't see the baby's tongue, this may mean the baby is not sucking correctly, causing the mother's nipples to become sore and the baby to receive less milk for his efforts.

For suggestions on helping the baby improve his suck, see the chapter "Positioning, Latch-On, and the Baby's Suck."

Taking the baby off the breast without first breaking the suction can contribute to nipple soreness.

If the mother regularly takes the baby off the breast without first breaking the suction, this can damage the delicate skin on the nipple and areola, contributing to sore nipples.

If the mother decides to take her baby off the breast before he comes off on his own, encourage her to first break the suction, which can be done by gently inserting a finger in the corner of the baby's mouth, pulling down on the baby's chin, or pressing down gently on the breast.

Inverted nipples sometimes contribute to nipple soreness, especially during the early weeks.

Inverted nipples may make it more difficult for the baby to latch on well, especially during the early weeks. See the section, "Flat and Inverted Nipples," later in this chapter for more information.

A baby with a short frenulum or a short tongue may have difficulty latching on well to the breast, which can cause sore nipples.

The mother says her nipples feel sore after the baby has latched on to the breast. The baby may have difficulty staying on the breast. She may hear a "smacking" or clicking sound as the suction is repeatedly broken.

Ask the mother if the baby is able to stick out his tongue past his bottom lip. If he can't, he may have a short tongue or a short frenulum, the string-like membrane that attaches the tongue to the floor of the mouth. A short tongue or frenulum may prevent the infant from cupping and pulling enough of the breast into his mouth to nurse well and may also cause sore nipples in the mother. A short tongue or short frenulum may make it impossible for the baby to extend his tongue past his bottom lip. In some babies with a short frenulum, the membrane extends to the center of the tip of his tongue, causing the tip of the tongue to look heart-shaped. A baby with a short frenulum may be able to suck on a finger or a rubber nipple but not be able to cup the breast with his tongue. Some tongue-tied babies can breastfeed on one breast but not the other.

A baby with a short frenulum or a short tongue may breastfeed more effectively if latch-on and positioning are improved. Time and growth will also make breastfeeding easier. A short frenulum can be clipped by a doctor to release the tongue and make breastfeeding easier. For more information, see "Short Frenulum or a Short Tongue" under "The Baby's Suck" in the chapter "Positioning, Latch-On, and the Baby's Suck."

Rarely, a baby is born with a strong clenching response. One symptom is that the mother's nipple turns white by the end of the nursing.

Rarely, a baby is born with an unusually strong and consistent clenching response, which causes him to clamp down whenever anything touches the inside of his mouth. One symptom of this is that the mother's nipple turns white by the end of the nursing. The baby may outgrow this quickly (within days) or it may persist for some time.

For suggestions on alleviating this problem, see "The Baby's Suck" in the chapter "Positioning, Latch-On, and the Baby's Suck."

Sore Nipples at Any Stage of Breastfeeding

Thrush can cause sore nipples.

The nipple pain associated with thrush is often described as an itching or burning sensation. See the section, "Thrush," later in this chapter for more information.

Teething can contribute to sore nipples if the baby begins chewing on the nipple or changes his nursing pattern.

It may hurt the baby to nurse when his gums are tender from teething, or he may find comfort in chewing and biting down after his hunger is satisfied. Some babies chew or bite down toward the end of a nursing to signal to the mother that they are finished. (See the section, "Teething and Biting," later in this chapter.)

Improper breast pump use can cause sore nipples.

Improper breast pump use can cause nipple and/or breast pain. The "bicycle-horn" hand pump can cause injury to the nipple and breast tissue because there is no suction regulator. Hand pumps that provide constant suction—such as a battery-operated, AC/DC, or semi-automatic electric pump—can also cause nipple soreness or injury if the mother neglects to relieve the suction. Cylinder-type pumps can be used too vigorously and cause soreness or nipple damage. In some women, excessive suction from a breast pump has caused hemorrhages under the skin, which look like tiny, flat, perfectly round, purple-red spots.

Chapped nipples may feel sore. Possible causes of chapping are: washing the nipples with soap, applying an irritating substance, or rubbing them roughly.

Bathing with plain water is all that is necessary to clean the breastfeeding mother's nipples. Suggest the mother avoid using soap on her nipples as it can remove the natural protective oils, predisposing the nipples to cracking and chapping. Scrubbing the nipples or applying any irritating substance (such as alcohol) on them can cause chapping and irritation, especially in sensitive women.

Skin problems such as eczema, dermatitis, impetigo, bacterial infections of the skin, and others can develop on the nipple, causing or contributing to nipple soreness. The mother needs to seek medical treatment for these.

Skin problems sometimes occur on the nipple as they do on other parts of the body. If the mother develops a rash, flaking, oozing, or any other unusual skin condition, find out more information.

Nipple Problems

Ask the mother if she has applied any creams or ointments to her nipples recently. Eczema and other types of dermatitis—skin inflammations characterized by red, itchy, flaking skin—can develop on the mother's nipples as a result of the use of irritating nipple creams. In one study, researchers suggest that some women develop nipple inflammation as a reaction to the preservatives or other ingredients found in certain brands of nystatin creams (a medically prescribed treatment for thrush), which have been associated with a high incidence of contact dermatitis (Huggins and Billon 1993).

There are also reports of women developing impetigo and other types of infections on the nipple. In this case, treatment by a doctor may be necessary.

Huggins and Billon (1993) found that with appropriate treatment mothers with these unusual skin conditions were able to resume breastfeeding without pain within a few days. They suggest in their study that a mother see a doctor (possibly a dermatologist) when:

- she continues to complain of pain when she has her baby latched-on well and her baby's suck is normal, especially if she describes the pain as burning or stinging;
- her cracked nipple is not healing or is healing extremely slowly;
- she has other skin conditions on her nipple, such as scaling, crusting, sores, or fluid-filled sacs, such as blisters;
- she does not respond to treatment for thrush after several days.

Ask the mother if she has any other health problems, as some conditions can make a mother more prone to skin problems. One study found that a woman with celiac disease (which is associated with an increased incidence of some types of dermatitis) developed eczema on her nipple while breastfeeding both of her babies. With appropriate medical treatment, the eczema cleared and she was able to continue breastfeeding her second child (Amir 1993).

Ask the mother if her baby is eating solid foods. If the mother is sensitive to certain foods, eczema can develop on the mother's nipples if the baby breast-feeds with particles of these foods in his mouth. This can sometimes be allevi-ated by rinsing the baby's mouth with water before nursings or by temporarily eliminating the irritating food from the baby's diet.

Ask the mother if she has begun using a new product, such as cologne, deodorant, hair spray, or powder anywhere near the sensitive skin of the nipple and surrounding areola. Also ask if she has started using a new laundry detergent. Rarely, detergents used on a mother's clothing have caused nipple irritation. Also suggest the mother avoid using soap on her nipples, which can remove natural protective oils and predispose the nipples to cracking.

Eczema on one nipple that does not respond to treatment may be a symptom of Paget's disease of the nipple, an uncommon form of breast cancer (Amir 1995). A mother with this symptom should see her health care provider to rule out this possibility.

Wearing a bra that is too tight or one with a rough seam can cause nipple soreness.

A bra that is too tight can compress the nipple causing it to become sore. A rough seam can rub against the nipple causing it to become irritated.

The hormonal changes of pregnancy can cause sore nipples.

Nipple tenderness is often one of the first symptoms of pregnancy and is caused by hormonal changes. Therefore, the usual recommendations given to the mother of a newborn for sore nipples will not be helpful. The onset of sore nipples during pregnancy is individual and can vary. Some women notice the soreness before they miss their first menstrual period. Others never experience it or notice it only late in pregnancy. The duration of soreness is also individual, but the majority of mothers report it lasts almost the entire pregnancy and disappears almost immediately after birth.

Some mothers choose to wean during pregnancy because of sore nipples. Mothers who continue breastfeeding during pregnancy learn to cope with nipple soreness in a variety of ways. To make the soreness more manageable, a mother with sore nipples could try these suggestions:

- Use the breathing techniques from her childbirth classes.
- Vary nursing positions.
- Ask the older nursing child to nurse more gently and/or for shorter periods of time, while assuring the child the soreness is not his fault.

- Hand-express enough milk to start the milk flowing before the child begins to nurse, as a decrease in milk production is sometimes a factor in nipple discomfort.

In a study of 503 women who became pregnant while still nursing, 74 percent experienced varying degrees of nipple pain or soreness, 65 percent noticed a decrease in their milk supply, and 57 percent felt some degree of discomfort, such as restlessness or irritation while nursing (Newton and Theotokatis 1979). For more information, see the chapter "Pregnancy and Tandem Nursing."

Some creams and ointments contain ingredients that can contribute to soreness. If a cream must be removed before the baby nurses, the extra rubbing can also contribute to soreness.

If a mother's nipples became sore when she began using a cream or ointment, suggest she stop using it to see if it may be a contributing factor. Some creams and ointments contain ingredients that may cause a reaction in a sensitive mother. Creams or ointments with many ingredients are a greater risk than products containing one ingredient.

Also if a nipple cream or ointment needs to be removed before the baby nurses, the rubbing during removal may contribute to soreness. If the mother wants to use a cream or ointment, suggest she choose one that can be safely left on the nipple for feedings. Lansinoh for Breastfeeding Mothers® is one such product. (See next section for more details.)

Some preservatives added to nystatin creams, a treatment for thrush, have been found to cause dermatitis in some sensitive mothers (Huggins and Billon 1993). In this case, rather than discontinuing the cream, the mother may need to ask her doctor about the possibility of substituting another brand of nystatin cream.

Mothers of older babies and toddlers sometimes develop sore nipples due to increased nursing or unusual nursing positions that stretch the nipple.

Sore nipples sometimes occur in the mother of an older baby or toddler. Ask the mother if she has any idea why she may be sore. It could be that her child has begun nursing in unusual positions that stretch her nipple. If the mother thinks this may be the cause, suggest she encourage her child to find nursing positions that are more comfortable for her.

Occasionally, an older baby or toddler will go through a period when he suddenly nurses much more often than usual, which may contribute to nipple soreness. There may be many possible causes for increased nursing: illness, a major transition, such as moving, or the beginning of a new stage of development, such as walking. If increased nursing seems to be the cause of the mother's soreness, review with her the basics of good latch-on and positioning. No matter what the baby's age, good latch-on and positioning will contribute to more comfortable breastfeeding. Also see the previous point on eczema if a mother of an older baby or toddler suddenly develops sore nipples. It may be a reaction to food particles left in the child's mouth when he nurses.

Whenever the mother of an older baby suddenly develops sore nipples, be sure to discuss the possibility of thrush. (See the section, "Thrush," later in this chapter.)

Nipple Problems

TREATMENT OF SORE, CRACKED, OR BLEEDING NIPPLES

Breastfeeding is not supposed to hurt. If the mother has sore, cracked, or bleeding nipples, the first step is to find the cause.

Go through the above section and help the mother determine the cause of her soreness, beginning with positioning and latch-on, which is the most common cause of nipple problems, especially in the first weeks of nursing.

First, find the cause of the sore, cracked, or bleeding nipples and, if possible, discuss ways to correct it before discussing comfort measures.

Once the cause has been found, if possible, help the mother correct the problem to stop the trauma to her nipples. Some minor adjustment of positioning and latch-on may be all that is needed or the mother may need to work with her baby if an improper suck is the cause. For thrush, the mother will need to see her doctor for treatment. If pregnancy is causing the mother's soreness, explain that there are no easy solutions and discuss the management suggestions in the previous section.

Once the cause is determined and corrected, short-term comfort measures will help make nursing more comfortable while the nipple is healing.

Most cases of sore, cracked, or bleeding nipples are due to poor positioning or latch-on. Assure the mother that if the baby is latched-on well—so that the nipple goes deeply into the baby's mouth—this will protect the nipple from further damage. Then discuss the following comfort measures that will encourage healing. Suggest the mother:

- hand-express some milk before a feeding to stimulate the let-down reflex before putting the baby to breast, or if just one nipple is sore, begin to nurse on the least sore side until the let-down occurs, then switch the baby gently to the affected breast, paying careful attention to good positioning and latch-on;
- express a little milk or colostrum onto the nipples after nursings and let it dry (this is not recommended if the soreness is due to thrush, as thrush thrives on milk);
- apply enough Lansinoh for Breastfeeding Mothers® to keep the nipple moist between feedings. This has been found to soothe and speed the healing of sore, cracked, and bleeding nipples due to poor positioning and latch-on or sucking problems (Spangler and Hildebrandt 1993).
- If the mother's nipples are so sore that she cannot tolerate the pressure of her bra or clothing on them and it is painful for her to hold her baby, suggest she apply Lansinoh after feedings then use breast shells with large nipple openings and holes for air circulation, or tea strainers, with the handles removed, in her bra to protect her nipples.
- The mother may also wish to talk to her doctor about taking an analgesic that is compatible with breastfeeding.

Keeping skin dry is no longer recommended for nipple soreness.

Suggestions for healing sore, cracked, and bleeding nipples once included drying techniques, such as use of a hair dryer on low on the nipples after feedings, keeping bra flaps down, and use of a sun lamp on the nipples. Although keeping skin dry was once standard practice, researchers on moist wound healing discovered that wounds actually heal 50% faster and scabbing and crusting can be avoided when the internal moisture of the skin is maintained (Hinman and Maibach 1963). This information has convinced many breastfeeding experts to change their sore nipple recommendations to reflect this understanding.

Internal moisture is not the same as surface wetness, such as that of milk-soaked breast pads against the skin, which can cause chapping and ultimately slow healing. To maintain internal moisture, the nipple needs to be covered by a moisture barrier to prevent evaporation and avoid drying and scab formation. Nipple scabs tend to be pulled off when the baby nurses, requiring the healing process to begin all over again.

One way to retain a moisture barrier and promote healing of sore nipples is to apply Lansinoh for Breastfeeding Mothers,® the purest and safest brand of USP modified lanolin.

To maintain this moisture barrier, the mother needs to apply enough Lansinoh for Breastfeeding Mothers® to the injured nipple after feedings to maintain the normal moisture present in the skin. If she uses too little or neglects to apply it often enough, the moisture barrier will be lost and the area will dry out.

Many creams and ointments sold for the treatment of sore nipples may actually contribute to the problem.

Some creams and ointments change the taste of the nipple, causing the baby to be fussy at the breast or refuse to nurse. Others—such as vitamin A and D ointments, baby oil, Vaseline, and other petroleum-based products—may not be safe for baby to ingest. Creams or ointments containing alcohol are drying to the skin.

Ointments containing astringents or anesthetic agents are not recommended because they are potentially harmful to both mother and baby. Also, numbing the nipples may inhibit the let-down, or milk-ejection reflex. Some creams or ointments may irritate a sensitive mother's nipple, causing dermatitis, an inflammation of the skin.

Too much cream or ointment applied to the nipple may make it so slippery that latch-on is difficult for the baby. Repeated use of some creams and ointments may clog the pores of the nipple, the areola, and the Montgomery glands.

If a nipple cream or ointment needs to be removed before the baby nurses, the rubbing may further damage the nipple and contribute to soreness. If the mother wants to use a cream or ointment, suggest she choose Lansinoh for Breastfeeding Mothers® which can be safely left on the nipple for feedings.

In the past, some breastfeeding experts have recommended a drop or two of vitamin E oil squeezed from the capsules onto the nipples to help promote healing. Some have expressed concerns about the possibility of side effects if babies ingest too much vitamin E. In one study of full-term babies and their mothers, after the mothers applied liberal amounts of vitamin E on their nipples, their babies' blood levels of vitamin E rose, but not out of the normal range (Marx 1985). Another concern about vitamin E is possible skin reactions in the mother. Although vitamin E almost never produces allergic reactions when swallowed, vitamin E preparations used to treat burns have been found to produce contact dermatitis and hives in some individuals (Fisher 1986; Aeling 1973; Minkin 1973; Brodkin 1965). A product less likely to cause skin reactions would be a better choice for use on the nipples.

Creams, ointments, lubricants, or moisturizers should never be used as a substitute for finding and correcting the cause of a mother's soreness.

If the mother wants to apply something to her nipple to speed healing, human milk expressed at the end of the feeding can be used.

An alternative to creams and ointments is the mother's own milk. Encourage her to express a few drops of her milk after the baby has finished nursing and rub it gently into the skin, allowing her nipples to air dry afterwards. In many cultures, skin irritations are commonly treated with human milk, probably due to its anti-bacterial properties.

If the mother wants to apply something to her nipple other than her milk, suggest she choose a product that is safe for the baby.

When choosing a product to use on her nipples, suggest the mother carefully read the label and choose one that is safe for human consumption, as her baby may ingest some of it when he nurses. Lansinoh for Breastfeeding Mothers® is one such product.

In general, USP modified lanolin does not need to be removed before breastfeeding. However, it is important to know there are many refinements of modified lanolin and some contain higher levels of pesticides, free lanolin alcohols, and detergents than others; these components have been identified as the cause of lanolin allergy.

Nipple Problems

Lansinoh for Breastfeeding Mothers,® is the purest and safest brand of USP modified lanolin available. It does not need to be removed before feeding, guarantees pesticide levels below 1 part per million, free lanolin alcohols at 1.5% and below, and is the only lanolin to test for detergent levels which are held below 0.05%. When modified lanolin is produced to these specifications, clinical studies conducted on lanolin sensitive patients failed to elicit a single allergic response (Clark 1981).

The use of Lansinoh for Breastfeeding Mothers® on sore nipples may also decrease pain, perhaps because it maintains a more "normal" environment for the free nerve endings that signal pain and protect them from external stimuli (Mann Mertz 1990). (See "The Use of Breast Pumps and Other Products." for more information on Lansinoh.)

Suggest the mother with sore nipples avoid bras or breast pads with plastic liners or synthetic fabrics.

While sore nipples are healing, suggest the mother avoid breast pads with plastic liners and bras made with synthetic fabrics. If dried milk causes a bra or breast pad to stick to the mother's nipples, suggest she first moisten it with water before trying to remove it.

A nipple shield—a flexible artificial nipple worn over the mother's breasts during feedings—usually causes more problems than it solves.

A nipple shield is sometimes recommended for mothers with sore nipples, but it usually causes more problems than it solves. Just like any other artificial nipple, it can confuse the baby, making him reluctant to nurse without it. Also, because nipple shields reduce the amount of stimulation to the breast, their regular use decreases the mother's milk supply and the amount of milk the baby receives.

Interrupting breastfeeding is rarely necessary, even in cases of extreme soreness.

In most cases, mothers with sore or cracked nipples will find that breastfeeding is no longer painful once they have achieved good positioning and latch-on.

In the rare instances when the mother feels her nipple soreness is interfering with her relationship with her baby, she can express her milk and feed the milk to her baby for a short time, preferably avoiding bottles by using one of the alternative feeding methods described in "The Use of Breast Pumps and Other Products" so that there is no danger of nipple confusion. Make sure that the method of expression she chooses is gentle but effective and will not contribute to her soreness.

Swallowing blood from damaged nipples will not harm the baby.

Assure the mother that any blood her baby swallows from damaged nipples will not be harmful to him. Emphasize that finding the cause of her nipple damage will allow her to correct it, so that her damaged nipples can heal and the bleeding will no longer be a concern.

Assure the mother that sore nipples do heal and that she and her baby can go on to enjoy the benefits of breastfeeding for many months.

A mother who is experiencing a lot of discomfort from sore nipples will need reassurance about the benefits of breastfeeding that make it worthwhile to continue. It may take patience and determination to discover the cause of her nipple soreness and help the nipples to heal if they have been seriously injured.

FLAT AND INVERTED NIPPLES

Types of Nipples

Flat nipples are those that do not protrude or become erect when stimulated or cold.

A true flat nipple is one that cannot be compressed outward (see the next point) and does not protrude or become erect when stimulated or cold. If the mother discovers during pregnancy that she has flat nipples, encourage her to use the treatments mentioned in the next section to help draw out her nipples.

If the mother first notices a flat nipple after her baby's birth, consider the possibility that it may be due to engorgement, as this can flatten a protruding nipple.

If the nipple becomes erect or protrudes when stimulated or compressed, it needs no treatment before breastfeeding begins.

Inverted nipples retract rather than protrude when the areola is compressed.

The mother can determine whether or not she has true inverted nipples by gently compressing the areola about an inch (2.5 cm) behind the base of the nipple. If her nipple protrudes, it is not truly inverted and no special treatment is needed. If the nipple retracts, or becomes concave, it is a true inverted nipple.

Inverted Nipple

If the mother's nipple is only slightly inverted, it may not affect breastfeeding, but a moderately to severely inverted nipple may.

A woman's nipples may differ; one may be flat or inverted while the other nipple protrudes. Or they may both be flat or inverted, but to different degrees. The baby may show a preference for one breast because of the shape of the mother's nipple or the size of her breast.

Treatments to Draw Out the Nipple

Breastfeeding experts disagree on whether pregnant women should be screened for flat or inverted nipples and whether treatments to draw out the nipple should be routinely recommended.

There are different types of inverted nipples, which may explain in part why the literature offers different explanations of their causes. According to one widely held theory, nipple inversion is caused by tiny bands of connective tissue, called adhesions, which attach the nipple to the inner breast tissue and pull in the nipple. Another theory attributes nipple inversion to very short lactiferous sinuses, which draw the nipple inward (Chandler 1990). Another theory holds that nipples invert because there is less dense connective tissue beneath the nipple than is found in women with everted nipples (Terrill and Stapleton 1991; Schwager 1974).

If the mother discovers an inverted nipple during pregnancy, she can try the treatment options listed in the next section to draw out her nipple before her baby is born. She should also concentrate on learning good positioning and latch-on skills and plan to get good breastfeeding help in the early weeks of breastfeeding.

A certain type of inverted nipple, known as a dimpled or folded nipple—in which only a part of the nipple is inverted—will not protrude or harden when stimulated, but it can be pulled out with the fingers, although it won't stay out. The dimpled nipple may also benefit from treatment during pregnancy.

There are different degrees of nipple inversion. Some nipples are only slightly inverted, and a baby with a normal suck will bring out the nipple with no difficulty (although a premature baby or a baby with a weak suck may have difficulty at first). Other nipples are moderately to severely inverted, which means that when compressed they retract deeply, to a level even with or behind the surrounding areola. A deeply buried nipple may make latching-on and breastfeeding difficult. In this case, treatment during pregnancy to stretch out the nipple may be helpful. If the inverted nipple is not discovered until after the baby is born, explain the treatment options to the mother and let her decide if she would like to try any or all of them or focus simply on good positioning and latch-on.

It is not unusual for a woman to have one flat or inverted nipple while the other protrudes. It is also not unusual for a woman with two flat or inverted nipples to have one nipple that protrudes more than the other. Such a woman may discover at birth that her baby quickly shows a preference for the breast with the more protruding nipple.

Encourage the mother to treat her flat or inverted nipple during pregnancy to help it protrude for easier breastfeeding. If she doesn't notice it until after birth, she can begin treatment then (see the next section).

If the baby persistently refuses one breast, encourage the mother to be patient and keep trying. Also assure her that she can breastfeed using one breast if she chooses. (See "One-Sided Nursing" in the chapter "Fussy at the Breast and Breast Refusal.")

Nipple Problems

Although the treatments that follow have been developed to help women draw out flat or inverted nipples, not all breastfeeding experts agree that they should be recommended. In *Successful Breastfeeding* (1991), the British Royal College of Midwives discourages routine screening for flat and inverted nipples because hormonal changes during pregnancy and childbirth cause many mothers' nipples to protrude naturally. They believe that a diagnosis of flat or inverted nipples "will only serve to damage [a mother's] confidence and can be a self-fulfilling prophecy" (p. 7). Rather than focusing on "inadequate nipples," they encourage mothers to get skilled help in latch-on and positioning. In *Bestfeeding* (Renfrew 1990), the baby's ability to draw out the nipple when he latches on well is emphasized and mothers are reminded that "babies do not nipple-feed: they breastfeed!"

In addition, none of these treatments have been proven in controlled studies to be effective. One recent study found no benefit to the use of breast shells during pregnancy for women with at least one inverted or flat nipple (MAIN Trial Collaborative Group 1994), and one study found that women with at least one inverted nipple who were assigned to wear breast shells during pregnancy were less successful at breastfeeding than women who did not treat their nipples during pregnancy (Alexander 1992). In their conclusion, researchers expressed concern that drawing attention to a woman's nipple problems before birth may "act as a disincentive" to successful breastfeeding for women with nipple problems because it calls into question their ability to breastfeed (Alexander 1992). Others have questioned the conclusions of this study, asserting that the breast shells used in England, where the study was conducted, have holes with diameters too large to effectively draw out small-to-average size nipples (Stark 1994). More research is needed to determine whether the hole size of different types of breast shells influences their effectiveness.

Despite the current controversy, many women over the years have found these treatments helpful and many breastfeeding experts continue to recommend them (Marmet and Shell 1993; Riordan and Auerbach, pp. 380; Lawrence, pp. 229-30). Although their use during pregnancy is being debated, the woman whose newborn is having difficulty latching on to a flat or inverted nipple may find some or all of these treatments help her baby latch on and breastfeed more easily.

Wearing breast shells may help draw out flat or inverted nipples.

The hormonal changes of pregnancy increase the elasticity of a woman's skin. Breast shells were designed to take advantage of this natural stretchiness by applying gentle but steady pressure to stretch underlying adhesions and draw out the nipple.

Also called milk cups, breast cups, breast shields, or Woolwich shields, breast shells are made of hard, lightweight plastic. Some are constructed with flexible silicone backs. They are meant to be worn in the mother's bra. The inner ring applies gentle but steady pressure on the areola, causing the nipple to protrude and stretching the adhesions that pull it in. The dome—which may or may not have holes—holds the bra away from the emerging nipple. The mother may need to wear a bra one cup size larger than usual to comfortably accommodate the shells. If the mother's bra is not large enough, the shells may put too much pressure on the areola, making her uncomfortable and placing her at risk for mastitis.

Those who recommend breast shells suggest they be used during the last trimester of pregnancy, starting with a few hours a day and gradually increasing the time, with the mother using her comfort as a guide.

If flat or inverted nipples are not discovered until after the baby is born, breast shells can be worn about a half hour before nursings to draw out the nipple.

When in use, breast shells should be washed daily.

Use of breast shells has not been shown to be of benefit in two recent studies.

The effectiveness of breast shells in drawing out flat or inverted nipples has not been proven in controlled studies. One recent study found no benefit to the use of breast shells during pregnancy for women with at least one inverted or flat nipple (MAIN Trial Collaborative Group 1994), and one study found that women with at least one inverted nipple who were assigned to wear breast shells during pregnancy were less successful at breastfeeding than women who did not treat their nipples during pregnancy (Alexander 1992). In this second study, after birth the women in the breast shells group were less likely to begin breastfeeding and less likely to be breastfeeding at six weeks than women who did not treat their breasts. Some women complained that the breast shells caused pain, discomfort, skin rashes, milk leakage, and embarrassment (Alexander 1992). Some have questioned the conclusions of this study, asserting that the breast shells used in England, where the study was conducted, have holes with diameters too large to effectively draw out small-to-average size nipples (Stark 1994).

More research is needed to determine whether the hole size of different types of breast shells influences their effectiveness and whether other long-standing practices, such as the Hoffman technique (which follows), are really effective. In the meantime, these treatments should be considered optional for pregnant women.

The Hoffman technique may help to draw out flat or inverted nipples.

Doing the Hoffman technique several times a day may help loosen the adhesions at the base of the nipple. To do the Hoffman technique, the mother places a thumb on each side of the base of the nipple. Her thumbs should be directly at the base of the nipple, not at the edge of the areola. She should press in firmly against the breast tissue and at the same time pull the thumbs away from each other. She'll be stretching out the nipple and loosening the tightness at the base, which will make the nipple move up and outward. This should be repeated five times a day, moving the thumbs around the base of the nipple (Hoffman 1953).

Some breastfeeding experts caution against the use of the Hoffman technique due to the possibility of damaging delicate breast tissue and stimulating uterine contractions during pregnancy (Lawrence, p. 230). One study found no difference in breastfeeding success between a group of women who practiced the Hoffman technique daily and a group of women who did not treat their nipples (Alexander 1992).

Use of a breast pump or other suction device just prior to feedings may help some women draw out flat or inverted nipples so that the baby can latch on to the breast more easily.

After birth, the use of a breast pump or other suction device can help to draw out a flat or inverted nipple immediately before breastfeeding, making latching on easier for the baby.

An alternative to a breast pump is a modified disposable syringe, which is available worldwide, but may be especially helpful in parts of the world where breast pumps are unavailable or unaffordable. In one study, Kesaree (1993) describes how to alter a 10ml syringe to create a small suction device that a mother can use prior to feedings to draw out an inverted nipple. (A 20ml syringe can be used for the mother with large nipples.) The piston is removed from the syringe and the nozzle cut off with a sharp blade. The piston is reinserted through the cut end of the syringe. The mother can put the smooth end of the syringe over her nipple and onto her areola. By gently pulling the piston to maintain steady but gentle pressure for 30 to 60 seconds, the mother can draw out her nipple, adjusting the pressure according to her own comfort.

Kesaree followed eight mothers with inverted nipples who had been unable to latch their babies onto the breast after birth and had been bottle-feeding for between 28 and 103 days. After they began using this device several times a day and received help at positioning their babies, seven of eight mothers were able to successfully latch their babies onto the breast. Six of these eight women were able to establish exclusive breastfeeding within four to six weeks.

Because flat or inverted nipples may return to their prepregnancy state after breastfeeding, suggest the mother check her nipples during each pregnancy.

Flat or inverted nipples may be drawn out during breastfeeding but return to their prepregnancy state after the baby weans. If the mother has breastfed before, suggest during

Nipple Problems

her next pregnancy she check her nipples by gently compressing the areola about an inch (2.5 cm) from the base of the nipple to determine if breastfeeding has drawn out her nipples permanently or whether they have retracted and would benefit from treatment before the baby is born.

The Early Weeks of Breastfeeding

If the baby is positioned and latched-on well, most types of flat or inverted nipples will not cause breastfeeding problems.

Some types of nipples may be more difficult for baby to latch on to, especially at first, but patience and persistence will pay off.

Every mother with inverted or flat nipples should learn the basics of making latching-on easier in the early days of breastfeeding.

There are other suggestions to try if a mother needs more than the basics of latching-on.

Babies breastfeed, not "nipple-feed," and if the baby is able to get a good mouthful of breast, most types of flat or inverted nipples will not cause a problem. Suggest that the mother work on good positioning and latch-on techniques. Good latch-on means the baby's mouth and gums will bypass the nipple entirely and latch on to the areola for effective breastfeeding.

Getting a "good fit" between mother and baby can take time and patience at first, even for the mother whose nipples are not flat or inverted. If the baby has difficulty latching on, go over the suggestions in the section "Latch-On" in the chapter "Positioning, Latch-On, and the Baby's Suck." Also see the suggestions in the following section.

Most important of all is patience and persistence. Encourage the mother to keep working with her baby and assure her that her gentle persuasion will pay off in time.

Getting skilled help with positioning and latch-on is critical for the mother with inverted or flat nipples. The baby needs to learn how to open his mouth wide to bypass the nipple and close his gums farther back on the breast.

Suggest the mother experiment with different nursing positions to find those that make latching on easier. Some mothers find that the football hold gives them more control, making it easier for the baby to latch on well.

If the baby becomes upset, stop and calm him, and take a break whenever needed. Working with a baby who is having trouble latching on can be tense for everyone. If the baby gets upset, stop immediately and calm him. Do not allow him to associate breastfeeding with unpleasantness. Offer him a finger to suck on or walk him, waiting until he is calm before trying again.

Avoid artificial nipples—bottles, nipple shields, and pacifiers—in the early weeks. If the baby is not nursing well and needs nourishment, encourage the mother to give the baby her expressed milk or formula by using any of the alternative feeding methods described in "The Use of Breast Pumps and Other Products." Artificial nipples may confuse the baby and make it more difficult for him to take the breast.

Recommend the mother plan to breastfeed early and often to avoid engorgement and to give the baby practice at breastfeeding while her breasts are still soft. It will be much easier for the baby to learn to breastfeed while the mother's breasts are still soft after delivery and before her milk "comes in." Encourage the mother to breastfeed her baby as soon as possible after birth and at least every two to three hours thereafter to give him plenty of practice at nursing well before her breasts become fuller and heavier, which usually happens between the second and fourth day after birth. Many babies continue to do well when the breasts become fuller if they have already spent lots of time nursing.

When making suggestions, be careful not to overwhelm a new mother with too many things to do at once. Also, be sensitive to her reaction. If any of these suggestions sound unappealing to her, do not push. Use of breast shells and the Hoffman technique, while long-standing practices, have not been proven effective in controlled studies.

Use a breast pump or other suction device before a feeding to soften the areola and draw the nipple out. The suction, or negative pressure, generated by the breast pump or other suction device (such as the modified disposable syringe described in the previous section) will pull out the nipple uniformly from the center, which may make latch-on easier for the baby (Kesaree 1993).

Stimulate the nipples before feedings. If the nipple can be grasped, suggest the mother roll the nipples between her thumb and index finger for minute or two and then try to make the nipple erect by quickly touching it with a moist, cold cloth or ice wrapped in a cloth. (Avoid prolonged use of ice, because numbing the nipple and areola can inhibit the let-down reflex.)

Wear breast shells about a half hour before nursing. Breast shells—hard plastic shells that are designed to draw the nipple out—can be worn in the mother's bra about a half hour before feedings.

Do the Hoffman technique several times a day to loosen the adhesions at the base of the nipple. Suggest the mother follow the instructions in the previous section.

Express some milk onto the nipple or into the baby's mouth to entice him. If the mother has a helper, suggest the helper drip some of the mother's milk or sterile water onto the breast near the nipple with a spoon or eyedropper while the mother works with the baby. This may keep him focused on latching-on. (Never use honey on the nipple, as it has been associated with infant botulism.) Using an eyedropper, the helper could also try dripping some milk into the corner of the baby's mouth while he is at the breast to make him swallow. The baby's natural response to a swallow is to latch on and suck.

When latching on, try pulling back slightly on the breast tissue to help the nipple protrude. As the mother holds her breast, thumb on top, fingers underneath and behind the areola, suggest she pull back slightly on the breast tissue toward the chest wall to help the nipple protrude. Rarely, a mother may benefit from pulling back on the breast tissue through the entire feeding.

If the mother decides to use a nipple shield, suggest she remove it within the first few minutes of the feeding. As a last resort some mothers decide to use a nipple shield—a flexible nipple that is worn over the mother's nipple during feedings—so that the sucking can pull out the nipple and the baby can receive some nourishment at the breast. To prevent the baby from becoming dependent on the nipple shield, suggest the mother remove it within the first few minutes of the feeding so that the baby can nurse directly on the breast. Also suggest the mother decrease the length of time the shield stays on at each feeding so that she is no longer using it within two or three days. Although a thin latex nipple shield has been found to have less of an effect on the mother's milk supply (Woolridge 1980), a baby can become "hooked" on it just as easily as any other type of nipple shield. All nipple shields decrease the amount of milk the baby receives and decrease the mother's milk supply. (For suggestions on weaning a baby from a nipple shield, see "Nipple Confusion" in the chapter "Fussy at the Breast and Breast Refusal.")

Some types of inverted nipples contribute to nipple soreness.

A true inverted nipple or dimpled nipple may make the mother prone to nipple soreness, depending on its type and severity. Breastfeeding may cause trauma in some types of inverted nipples, because the adhesions are stretched when the nipple is drawn into the baby's mouth. If the nipple retracts between feedings, the skin may stay moist, contributing to chapping. Patting the nipples dry after feedings, and applying Lansinoh for Breastfeeding Mothers® can help avoid this. (See earlier section on treatment of sore nipples.)

Nipple Problems

A device called a Velcro Dimple Ring was designed to hold the dimpled nipple out between feedings. For more information, contact Chele Marmet, Lactation Institute, 16430 Ventura Blvd. Suite 303, Encino CA 91436 USA; Telephone: 818-995-1913.

If the mother has continuing nipple pain despite good positioning and latch-on, look for other solutions.

Some mothers experience nipple soreness for about two weeks as their baby's sucking gradually draws out their nipples. Other mothers have persistent sore nipples for a longer period of time. Sometimes, instead of stretching, the adhesions remain tight, creating a point of stress that can cause cracks or blisters.

Using an automatic electric double pump can help draw out the nipple when the usual methods fail. When a nipple is deeply inverted and the baby tries to latch on, rather than compressing the mother's milk sinuses under her areola, his gums compress the buried nipple instead. Because the baby is unable to get the nipple correctly positioned in his mouth, he will not receive much milk and nursing will be painful for the mother. The automatic electric double pump helps because, rather than compressing the mother's areola, it provides a uniform suction from the center of the nipple, drawing the nipple out and, eventually, breaking the adhesions that hold it in.

When offering suggestions and options, consider each mother's individual needs. For example, most mothers have one nipple that is easier for the baby to grasp. If the baby nurses well on one breast, suggest the mother continue to nurse on that breast while she pumps the breast with the deeply inverted nipple until the nipple is drawn out and the baby can grasp it normally. Rarely, a mother may have two deeply inverted nipples. In this case, suggest she pump both breasts for fifteen to twenty minutes about every two hours (a double-pumping attachment will allow the mother to pump both breasts simultaneously, cutting pumping time in half) until her nipples are drawn out. In the meantime, she can feed her baby her milk using one of the alternative feeding methods described in "The Use of Breast Pumps and Other Products."

How long the mother will have to pump in order to draw out her nipples will depend on the strength of the adhesions and the degree of inversion. For some mothers, one pumping is enough. If the nipple stays out after pumping, the mother can begin nursing on that breast immediately. However, if the nipple inverts again, the mother may need to continue pumping at feeding times. Rarely, a mother may need to pump for days or weeks before her nipple is drawn out. If the mother's nipples do not respond immediately to pumping, offer to help her determine a pumping schedule that will be practical for her.

When the mother's nipple can be drawn into the baby's mouth correctly, the baby will be able to breastfeed effectively and the mother should be able to discontinue pumping and breastfeed without discomfort. On rare occasions, a mother will continue to feel some discomfort even after the baby has begun nursing properly, because her nipple has undergone a radical correction. Rarely, after a mother's nipple has been drawn out by the pump, it may invert again when the baby pauses during nursing. In this case, the mother may need to pump for a few minutes to draw out the nipple and then use a nursing supplementer to encourage continuous sucking and swallowing as a temporary transition to exclusive breastfeeding.

TEETHING AND BITING

When a baby is teething, his sore gums may make him nurse differently, causing sore nipples.

Assure the mother that the change in nursing is temporary, and suggest she offer the teething baby something cold to chew on to numb his gums before nursing.

Teething can make a baby's gums swollen and sore, and he may begin to nurse differently, or even chew on the nipple during feedings to try to ease his discomfort.

Nipple soreness due to teething is a temporary discomfort which will pass as the baby's teeth erupt. Assure the mother that it is not necessary to wean, and give her other suggestions to soothe her baby and make nursing more comfortable.

Offer the baby something cold to chew on before nursing, for example, a cold, wet washcloth, or a cold teething toy. If the baby is eating solids, chewing on a frozen bagel or any other hard, cold food before breastfeeding may help his gums feel better so that he can nurse more comfortably.

Suggest the mother consult her baby's doctor before she gives her baby a pain-relieving drug or an over-the-counter preparation to numb his gums. These products may also numb the baby's tongue (and occasionally the mother's areola), making breastfeeding difficult.

It is not necessary to wean when a baby's teeth begin to erupt.

Many mothers are told to wean when their babies get their first tooth, but this is not necessary. Many babies never even attempt to bite and those who try once usually respond to a mother's startled reaction by never biting again.

If a baby is biting, he's not breastfeeding.

When a baby breastfeeds, the mother's nipple is positioned far back in his mouth, and the baby's lips and gums are positioned well behind the nipple on the outer edge of the areola. The baby's tongue extends beyond the gums, between his lower teeth and the breast. Therefore, even after a baby's teeth erupt, he cannot bite while he is actively nursing.

If the baby begins to bite, suggest the mother try to stay calm and pull him in close, rather than pulling him off the breast.

Most mothers' natural reaction to biting is to startle and pull the baby off the breast. For many babies this reaction is enough to discourage them from ever biting again.

If the baby bites more than once, however, encourage the mother to try to stay calm. Pulling the baby abruptly off the breast after he has clamped down can cause more damage to the mother's nipple than the bite itself. Also, many babies will be startled if the mother yells or reacts strongly. This sometimes backfires in sensitive babies, who react by refusing the breast. (For more information, see the chapter "Fussy at the Breast and Breast Refusal.") Because it takes much coaxing to persuade a baby who has been "on strike" to go back to nursing, suggest the mother try to moderate her response to biting.

Instead of pulling the baby off, encourage the mother to pull the baby in as close as possible to her breast. If she pulls him in close enough to partially block his airway, this will cause him to release the nipple. Babies are very sensitive to even a slight blockage of their nose. Some mothers do this by gently pinching the baby's nose so that he opens his mouth and releases the nipple. Other mothers use a slightly different approach by slipping a finger between the baby's gums or teeth, which will also cause him to release the nipple.

Offer to discuss ways to anticipate and prevent biting.

If a mother is concerned about her baby biting or if the baby has begun to bite persistently, offer to discuss ways to prevent and anticipate biting.

Give the baby her complete attention while he is nursing. Eye contact, touching, and talking make it less likely that the baby will bite to get the mother's attention. Being alert also means the mother will be more likely to notice when the baby is becoming uninterested and may be ready to stop nursing.

Learn to recognize the end of a nursing. Most biting occurs at the end of a nursing when the baby loses interest. While she is watching her baby, the mother may notice that tension develops in his jaw before he actually bites down. This is a signal to the mother to break the suction and take the baby off the breast before he gets a chance to bite. Some babies chew or bite down toward the end of a nursing to signal to the mother that they are finished.

Don't force a nursing. If the baby is wriggling, rolling, or pushing against the mother with his arms, this indicates he is not hungry or really interested in nursing. Sometimes, lying down with the baby in a quiet room will help him settle down enough to breast-feed.

Nipple Problems

Give extra attention to good positioning and latch-on. Being well-positioned and latched-on will help a baby focus on sucking and lessen the chance of biting. Women with large breasts may need to be especially careful to support the breast with their free hand while the baby is latching on and during the entire nursing. Suggest the mother make certain that the baby's mouth is open wide before pulling him in close.

If the baby falls asleep, remove him from the breast. When removing the baby from the breast, suggest the mother insert her little finger into the corner of the baby's mouth past the gums and then take out the nipple. This way, if the baby inadvertently bites in an attempt to resume nursing, he'll bite the mother's finger instead of her nipple.

Keep her milk supply plentiful. If the baby gets frustrated at the breast from too little milk, it may increase the odds that he will bite. Human milk is the only food a baby needs until the middle of the first year. If other foods are started too early or used too frequently in place of breastfeeding, the mother's milk supply can diminish. Bottles of water or juice given regularly can also interfere with the mother's milk supply.

Be aware of behaviors that lead to biting. Some babies respond to teasing, cajoling, or the mother yelling at older siblings by biting. Suggest the mother take note of what preceded her baby's biting. Pinpointing the cause will allow her to avoid behaviors that provoke biting.

Keep breastfeedings relaxed and pleasant. Some babies are sensitive to their mother's emotional state and body tenseness. If the mother is upset or tense, the result may be an anxious nip. If circumstances have the mother frazzled, suggest she try some deep breathing, put on some relaxing music, or nurse lying down in a darkened room.

Offer positive reinforcement when the baby doesn't bite. Suggest the mother lavish her baby with praise when he latches onto or releases the breast properly. "Thank you" and "good baby," smiles, hugs, and kisses will go a long way toward gently teaching the baby the proper way to nurse.

Persistent biting can be discouraged in other ways.

If the biting becomes persistent, in addition to pulling the baby closer to partially block his airway, encourage the mother to try other strategies to discourage biting.

Stop the feeding, so the baby is not tempted to see if he can make the mother jump again.

Offer an acceptable teething object. As soon as a bite or "near miss" occurs, offer baby a teething ring or toy so that he will know what is acceptable to use his teeth on.

Quickly put the baby on the floor. Some mothers may want to take firmer action after a bite. After a few seconds of distress after being put down, the baby can then be comforted and should get the message that biting brings negative consequences.

Keep a finger poised near the baby's mouth to quickly break the suction in case he turns his head. Some babies like to take the nipple with them whenever they are distracted and turn their heads. Keeping a finger poised to break the suction can discourage the baby from doing this. It won't take long for him to learn that turning away means losing the nipple.

The baby associates feelings of comfort and security as well as satisfaction of hunger with his mother. He does not understand that putting his teeth on her nipple causes her pain. Babies do not bite out of "meanness." A baby has to learn what to do with new teeth while nursing, and this is sometimes learned by trial and error.

THRUSH

Thrush is a fungus that can cause symptoms in the mother and the baby.

Candida albicans, the one-celled organism that causes both thrush and vaginal yeast infections, is a fungus that thrives in moist, dark environments, such as on the nipples, in the milk ducts, in the mother's vagina, and in the baby's diaper area.

In the mother, possible symptoms of thrush include:

- intense nipple or breast pain that occurs from birth, lasts throughout the nursing, and is not improved with better latch-on and positioning,
- sudden onset of nipple and/or breast pain after the newborn period,
- nipples that are itchy or burning and appear pink or red, shiny, flaky, and/or have a rash with tiny blisters,

- cracked nipples,
- shooting pains in the breast during or after feedings,
- nipple and/or breast pain with correct use of an automatic electric breast pump,
- vaginal yeast *(monilial)* infections.

In the baby, possible symptoms of thrush include:

- diaper rash,
- creamy white patches inside baby's mouth, cheeks, or tongue,
- a whitish sheen to the saliva or the inside of the lips,
- baby repeatedly pulling off the breast, making a clicking sound while nursing, or refusing the breast (because his mouth is sore),
- gassiness and fussiness,
- rarely, thrush is a contributing factor in slow weight gain.

The baby also may be **without visible symptoms.**

A secondary yeast infection may invade either the milk ducts or areas of the breast surrounding the milk ducts and cause pain during or between feedings. This seems to be more common if the mother or baby has been on antibiotics (because antibiotics kill the beneficial bacteria in the body that keep yeast under control) or if the mother has had cracked nipples (the fungus can enter the breast through the cracks). For more information on secondary yeast infections within the breast, see the section, "Deep Breast Pain," in the chapter "Breast Problems."

In addition to taking antibiotics, there are other factors that predispose mother and baby to thrush.

Mothers who have been given antibiotics are at higher risk of developing thrush. A mother who has had a cesarean birth may have received antibiotics in her IV to prevent infection without being aware of it.

Other predisposing factors to thrush in the mother include:

- nipple damage,
- use of nursing pads, which creates a warm, moist environment (Amir 1995),
- heavy consumption of dairy products, heavily sweetened foods, and artificial sweeteners (Horowitz 1984),
- nutritional deficiencies of iron, folic acid, and vitamins A, B, C, and K (Odds 1988),
- diabetes,
- mastitis that has been treated with antibiotics (Amir 1991),
- continuous use of antibiotics for longer than one month, even in the distant past (Amir 1991),
- use of estrogen-containing oral contraceptives (Odds 1988),
- use of long-term steroids, such as for asthma (Lawrence, p. 494).

Nipple Problems

In the baby, greater incidence of thrush has been associated with treatment with antibiotics and pacifier (dummy) use (Manning 1985).

If thrush is suspected, suggest the mother contact her doctor for diagnosis and treatment.

If thrush is diagnosed, both mother and baby will need to be treated simultaneously with medication prescribed by their health care providers. Standard treatment varies in different parts of the world. In the US, nystatin nipple cream for the mother and oral nystatin suspension for the baby's mouth are commonly prescribed. Oral nystatin is sometimes prescribed for the mother if there is a recurrence (Lawrence, p. 265). Some strains of *Candida albicans* have become nystatin-resistant, and in this case, other medications may be needed. In Australia, a combination of oral nystatin for the mother and topical miconazole or clotrimazole gel for both mother and baby are recommended by some medical practitioners (Amir 1995).

Breastfeeding need not be affected by thrush treatment. In mild cases of thrush, once treatment has begun relief may be felt in twenty-four to forty-eight hours. In other cases, the symptoms may take three to five days or longer to disappear.

Encourage the mother to continue with her medication for the full course, since the thrush may recur if she stops taking the medication when the symptoms disappear.

During treatment, there are ways the mother can ease the symptoms of thrush and make breastfeeding more comfortable.

When the mother is being treated for thrush, the symptoms may seem worse for a day or two before they improve. Suggest she rinse her nipples with clear water and air dry them after each nursing, as thrush thrives on milk and moisture. Before the pain has gone, the following suggestions may help make nursings less painful:

- offer short, frequent feedings,
- nurse first on the least sore side (if there is one), and
- break the baby's suction before taking him off the breast by gently pulling on the baby's chin or by pulling on the corner of his mouth.

Once thrush has been confirmed, encourage the mother to take precautions so that the thrush does not recur.

Because thrush can be harbored in many places, including milk, encourage the mother to wash her hands frequently and take the following precautions so that the thrush does not recur.

- Expressed milk can be fed to the baby, but milk expressed during a thrush outbreak should not be saved and frozen. Freezing deactivates yeast but does not kill it (Rosa 1990). So if the frozen milk is given to the baby after treatment is completed, it could cause the thrush to recur.
- If the baby uses pacifiers, bottle nipples, or teethers, boil them once a day for twenty minutes to kill the thrush. After one week of treatment, discard them and buy new ones.
- If the mother uses a breast pump, suggest she boil daily all parts that touch the milk (except the rubber gaskets).
- Disposable nursing pads should be discarded after each feeding. Cloth nursing pads should be changed after each feeding and not be used again until they've been washed in hot, soapy water.
- If the baby is old enough to play with toys, anything the baby puts into his mouth should be washed frequently with hot, soapy water, so that he does not reinfect himself with thrush or spread it to other children.

If recurring thrush is a problem, all members of the family may need to be treated.

Men can have thrush without exhibiting any symptoms. Thrush can be passed back and forth between husband and wife during sexual relations and from child to child if shared toys are put in their mouths or in a tandem nursing situation. If thrush continues to recur after mother and baby have had two full courses of treatment, all members of the family may need to be treated simultaneously.

NIPPLE BLISTERS AND SORES

A nipple blister or sore can make breastfeeding extremely painful.

If the mother has a nipple blister or nipple sore, keep in mind that breastfeeding may be very painful for her. Do not try to minimize her discomfort. Empathize with her and help her find a way to alleviate her pain.

A white or clear nipple blister may be caused by a plugged milk duct or skin blocking a milk duct.

White or clear nipple blisters (also known as "milk blisters") may be caused by a plug, such as a granule of thickened milk, blocking the milk flow near the opening to the nipple, or a thin layer of skin blocking the opening of a milk duct from the outside.

For both causes, the treatment is the same: apply very warm compresses and then immediately put the baby to breast, paying careful attention to good positioning and latch-on.

Whether the white or clear blister is caused by a plug from within the duct or a blockage of skin over the opening, the treatment is the same. Suggest the mother apply very warm compresses to the blister to soften it and then immediately put the baby to breast, paying careful attention to good positioning and latch-on. The heat will cause the duct to expand slightly, which may allow the plug to pass through. If the skin over the duct is the cause of the problem, the heat will thin the skin as it expands.

In most cases, once heat has been applied, the force of the mother's let-down, or milk-ejection, reflex in combination with the baby's suck will be enough to open the blister. After that, the comfort measures recommended for sore nipples may help speed healing.

If the blister persists, it can be opened by a health care professional.

If the above treatment does not bring quick relief, suggest the mother go to her health care professional to open the blister. If she tries to open it herself, it may result in an infection.

Herpes sores—which can occur on the nipple—are spread through contact and can be dangerous to the newborn.

Herpes simplex I (cold sores) and II (genital herpes) are spread by the herpes virus through contact with the sores. Herpes has proved fatal to newborn babies up to three weeks of age (Riordan and Auerbach, p. 172). Genital herpes sores can be transferred to the breast. A pregnant woman should talk to a doctor knowledgeable about herpes and breastfeeding to decide what precautions to take if she or her husband has recurrent herpes, either cold sores or genital sores.

If a herpes sore appears on the mother's breast, she must cover it or—if it is on or near the nipple or areola—stop breastfeeding on the affected breast and express her milk until the sore is healed.

If the herpes sore on the mother's breast can be covered so that the baby does not touch it, breastfeeding can continue. But if the sore is on the nipple or areola, or anywhere the baby might come in contact with it while he nurses, the mother needs to express her milk from that breast until the sore heals. She can, however, continue to nurse on the unaffected breast.

If the mother's hand or breast pump touches the sore while the mother is expressing, the milk should be discarded because it could be contaminated with the virus. If the mother's hand or breast pump does not touch the sore, the expressed milk can be given to the baby.

A culture of the sore can confirm herpes within a few days.

Babies older than five months may not be as susceptible to herpes complications as younger babies.

Two babies older than five months have reportedly touched their mother's herpes sores while breastfeeding without developing complications. This may not be sufficient proof to conclude that it is safe to allow an older baby to come in contact with a herpes sore (Riordan, p. 130).

Nipple sores and rashes may sometimes be caused by dermatitis, eczema, impetigo, scabies, infections, or other skin conditions that need to be evaluated by a doctor.

Sores on the nipple should be evaluated for treatment by a doctor. There are many possible causes, such as dermatitis, eczema, impetigo, scabies, and infections. For more information, see the previous section, "Sore Nipples at Any Stage of Breastfeeding."

Nipple Problems

Publications for Parents

Gotsch, G. Breastfeeding: Pure & Simple. Schaumburg, Illinois: La Leche League International, 1994, pp. 42-47.

La Leche League International. *Preparing Your Nipples*. Schaumburg, Illinois: La Leche League International, 1990. Publication No. 106.

La Leche League International. *Sore Nipples*. Schaumburg, Illinois: La Leche League International, 1992. Publication No. 28a.

La Leche League International. THE WOMANLY ART OF BREASTFEEDING, 35th Anniversary ed. Schaumburg, Illinois, 1991. pp. 29-31, 52, 120-24, 126, 127, 154-58.

Renfrew, M., Fisher, C., and Arms, S. *Bestfeeding: Getting Breastfeeding Right for You*. Berkeley, California: Celestial Arts, 1990.

Taylor, B. If your baby bites. NEW BEGINNINGS 1990; 6:163-67.

References

Sore Nipples

Aeling, J. et al. Allergic contact dermatitis to vitamin E aerosol deodorant. *Arch Dermatol* 1973; 108:579-80.

Amir, L. et al. *Candidiasis & breastfeeding*. La Leche League International Lactation Consultant Series. Unit 18. Garden City Park, New York: Avery Publishing, 1995, p. 11.

Amir, L. Eczema of the nipple and breast: a case report. *J Hum Lact* 1993; 9(3):173-75.

Brodkin, R. et al. Sensitivity to topically applied vitamin *E. Arch Derm* 1965; 92:76-77.

de Carvalho, M. et al. Does the duration and frequency of early breastfeeding affect nipple pain? *Birth* 1984; 11:81-84.

Clark, E. et al. Lanolin of reduced sensitizing potential. *Contact Dermatitis* 1981; 80-83.

Fisher, A. *Contact Dermatitis*. Philadelphia: Lea & Febiger, 1986, p. 151.

Hinman, C. and Maibach, H. Effect of air exposure and occlusion on experimental human skin wounds. *Nature* 1963; 200:377-88.

Huggins, K. and Billon, S. Twenty cases of persistent sore nipples: collaboration between lactation consultant and dermatologist. *J Hum Lact* 1993; 9(3):155-60.

Huml, S. Cracked nipples in the breastfeeding mother. *ADVANCE for Nurse Practitioners* 1995: 29-31.

Lawrence, R. *Breastfeeding: A Guide for the Medical Profession,* 4th ed. St. Louis: Mosby, 1994, pp. 242-47.

Mann Mertz, P. Intervention: dressing effects on wound healing. *New Directions in Wound Healing. Convatec* 1990; 7:83.

Marx, C. et al. Vitamin E concentrations in serum of newborn infants after topical use of vitamin E by nursing mothers. *Am J Obstet Gynecol* 1985; 152:668-70.

Minchin, M. *Breastfeeding Matters*. Armadale, Victoria, Australia: Alma Publications, 1989. pp. 130-36.

Minkin, W. et al. Contact dermatitis from deodorants. *Arch Dermatol* 1973; 107:774-75.

Newton, N. and Theotokatos, M. Breastfeeding during pregnancy in 503 women: does a psychobiological weaning mechanism exist in humans? *Emotion and Reproduction* 1979; 20 B:845-49.

Renfrew, M., Fisher, C., and Arms, S. *Bestfeeding: Getting Breastfeeding Right for You.* Berkeley, California: Celestial Arts, 1990, pp. 58, 128-31.

Riordan, J. and Auerbach, K. *Breastfeeding and Human Lactation.* Boston and London: Jones and Bartlett, 1993, pp. 229-34.

Royal College of Midwives. *Successful Breastfeeding.* London: Churchill Livingstone, 1991, pp. 56-60.

Sharp, D. Moist healing for cracked nipples. BREASTFEEDING ABSTRACTS 1992; 12(2):19.

Spangler, A. and Hildebrandt, E. The effect of modified lanolin on nipple pain/damage during the first 10 days of breastfeeding. *IJCE* 1993; 8(31):15-19.

Woolridge, M. et al. Effect of a traditional and a new nipple shield on sucking patterns and milk flow. *Early Human Dev* 1980; 4:357-62.

Ziemer, M. and Pigeon, J. Skin changes and pain in the nipple during the 1st week of lactation. *JOGNN* 1993; 22(3):247-56.

Ziemer, M. et al. Methods to prevent and manage nipple pain in breastfeeding women. *West J Nurs Res* 1990; 12(6):732-44.

Flat and Inverted Nipples

Alexander, J. et al. Randomised controlled trial of breast shells and Hoffman's exercises for inverted and non-protractile nipples. *BMJ.* 1992; 304:1030-32.

Chandler, P. A direct surgical approach to correct the inverted nipple. *Plast Reconstr Surg* 1990; 86(2):352-54.

Hoffman, J. A suggested treatment for inverted nipples. *Am J Obstet Gynecol* 1953; 66(2):346-48.

Kesaree, N., et al. Treatment of inverted nipples using a disposable syringe. *J Hum Lact* 1993; 9(1):27-29.

Lawrence, R. *Breastfeeding: A Guide for the Medical Profession,* 4th ed. St. Louis: Mosby, 1994, pp. 225-31.

Nipple Problems

MAIN Trial Collaborative Group. Preparing for breast feeding: treatment of inverted and non-protractile nipples in pregnancy. *Midwifery* 1994; 10:200-14.

Marmet, C. and Shell, E. *Lactation Forms: A Guide to Lactation Consultant Charting.* Encino, California: Lactation Institute Publications, 1993, pp. 56, 57, 58, and 59.

Renfrew, M., Fisher, C., and Arms, S. *Bestfeeding: Getting Breastfeeding Right for You.* Berkeley, California: Celestial Arts, 1990, pp. 58, 128-31.

Riordan, J. and Auerbach, K. *Breastfeeding and Human Lactation*. Boston and London: Jones and Bartlett, 1993, pp. 379-80.

Royal College of Midwives. *Successful Breastfeeding*. London: Churchill Livingstone, 1991, pp. 6-7, 72-73.

Schwager, R. Inversion of the human female nipple with a simple method of treatment. *Plast Reconstr Surg* 1974; 54(5):564-69.

Stark, Y. *Human Nipples: Function and Anatomical Variations in Relationship to Breastfeeding,* 1994. For ordering information, contact The Lactation Institute, 16430 Ventura Blvd., Suite 303, Encino, CA 914-36 USA.

Terrill, P. and Stapleton, M. The inverted nipple: to cut the ducts or not? *Br J Plast Surg* 1991; 44: 372-77.

Woolridge, M. et al. Effect of a traditional and a new nipple shield on sucking patterns and milk flow. *Early Human Dev* 1980; 4:357-62.

Teething and Biting

Lauwers, J. and Woessner, C. *Counseling the Nursing Mother,* 2nd ed. Garden City Park, New York: Avery Publishing, 1990. pp. 271-72.

Taylor, B. If your baby bites. NEW BEGINNINGS 1990; 6:163-67.

Thrush

Amir, L. et al. *Candidiasis & breastfeeding*. Lactation Consultant Series. Unit 18. Garden City Park, New York: Avery Publishing, 1995.

Amir, L. Candida and the lactating breast: predisposing factors. *J Hum Lact* 1991; 7(4):177-81.

Danforth, D. Could it be thrush? LEAVEN 1990; 26:56.

Hancock, K. and Spangler, A. There's a fungus among us! *J Hum Lact* 1993; 9(3): 179-80.

Horowitz, B. et al. Sugar chromatography studies in recurrent candida vulvovaginitis. *J Reprod Med* 1984; 29:441-43.

Huggins, K. and Billon, S. Twenty cases of persistent sore nipples: collaboration between lactation consultant and dermatologist. *J Human Lact* 1993; 9(3):155-60.

Lawrence, R. *Breastfeeding: A Guide for the Medical Profession,* 4th ed. St. Louis: Mosby, 1994, pp. 264-65, 492-94.

Manning, D. et al. Candida in mouth or on dummy? *Arch Dis Child* 1985; 60:381-82.

Odds, F. Factors that predispose the host to candidiasis, chapter 8 in *Candida and Candidiasis: A Review and Bibliography,* 2nd ed. London: Baillere Tindall, 1988.

Riordan, J. *A Practical Guide to Breastfeeding*. St. Louis: Mosby, 1983, p. 130.

Riordan, J. and Auerbach, K. *Breastfeeding and Human Lactation*. Boston and London: Jones and Bartlett, 1993, pp. 384-87.

Rosa, C. et al. Yeasts from human milk collected in Rio de Janeiro, Brazil. *Rev Microbiol* 1990; 21(4):361-63.

Nipple Blisters and Sores

Lawrence, R. *Breastfeeding: A Guide for the Medical Profession,* 4th ed. St. Louis: Mosby, 1994, pp. 259-60.

Maher, S. *An Overview of Solutions to Breastfeeding and Sucking Problems*. Schaumburg, Illinois: La Leche League International, 1988. Publication No. 67. p. 15.

Noble, R. Milk under the skin (milk blister) a simple problem causing other breast conditions. *Breastfeed Rev* 1991; II(3):118-19.

Riordan, J. and Auerbach, K. *Breastfeeding and Human Lactation*. Boston and London: Jones and Bartlett, 1993, p. 387.

Nipple Problems

21

Breast Problems

ENGORGEMENT

MASTITIS—PLUGGED DUCTS AND BREAST INFECTIONS
    Recurring Mastitis

BREAST ABSCESS

BREAST LUMPS

BLOOD IN THE MILK

DEEP BREAST PAIN
    Deep Breast Pain during the First Six Weeks
    Deep Breast Pain at Any Stage of Breastfeeding

BREASTFEEDING AFTER BREAST SURGERY OR INJURY
    General Considerations
    Breast Augmentation Surgery
    Breast Reduction Surgery
    When Milk Ducts or Major Nerves Have Been Cut or Damaged

ENGORGEMENT

Some breast fullness
is normal after birth.

It is normal for a mother's breasts to become larger, heavier, and a little tender when they begin producing greater quantities of milk on the second to sixth day after birth. This is due to the extra blood and lymph fluids traveling to the breasts to prepare them for producing milk, as well as to the increased volume of the milk itself.

This normal fullness usually decreases within the first two or three weeks after birth if the baby is breastfeeding regularly and well. After the initial fullness disappears, the mother's breasts will feel softer, even when her milk supply is plentiful.

Uncomfortable engorgement can
be minimized and even prevented
if the baby is positioned and
latched-on well and breastfeeds
frequently after birth.

The secret to minimizing engorgement is making sure the newborn is positioned and latched-on well at the breast (see the chapter "Positioning, Latch-On, and the Baby's Suck") and nurses frequently and unrestrictedly after birth. Frequent nursing (eight to twelve times every twenty-four hours) removes the colostrum and incoming milk so that normal postpartum fullness is less likely to develop into painful engorgement.

A baby who is allowed to
breastfeed without restrictions
after birth may breastfeed very
frequently or very long.

A baby who is allowed to breastfeed unrestrictedly in the early days may breastfeed frequently for short periods of time, as often as a few minutes every hour, or for long stretches, even hours at a time, until the mother's milk becomes more plentiful, or "comes in." A mother whose baby breastfeeds often and well is less likely to experience painful engorgement.

A sleepy baby should be
awakened at least every two to
three hours to breastfeed.

If the baby is sleepy in the early days and does not seem interested in breastfeeding, encourage the mother to awaken him frequently to breastfeed (at least every three hours with one longer four- to five-hour sleep period), so that he gets the nourishment he needs and the mother can avoid uncomfortable engorgement. (For tips on waking a sleepy baby, see "Sleepy Baby" in the chapter "Positioning, Latch-On, and the Baby's Suck.")

Engorgement, when it occurs, usually
begins on the third to fifth day and, if
promptly treated, lasts between
twelve and forty-eight hours.

Normal breast fullness may develop into engorgement between the third and sixth day after birth. In many cases, painful engorgement can be avoided by breastfeeding long and often from birth. One study found that the risk of engorgement increased when the baby was given supplements and that the risk of engorgement decreased when the nursings lasted as long as mother and baby wanted (Moon and Humenick 1989). But there are some women who become painfully engorged no matter how well and often their babies breastfeed. If engorgement is promptly treated, its most extreme manifestation usually subsides within 12 to 48 hours. Engorgement that is not treated will also subside, usually within 7 to 10 days.

Engorgement can vary in one woman from one child to the next and also vary from one woman to another. One study found that mothers who had breastfed previous children became engorged sooner and more severely than first-time breastfeeding mothers (Hill and Humenick 1994). Another study (Humenick 1994) identified four distinct patterns of engorgement:

Pattern 1: An increasing level of engorgement building to a peak between the third and sixth day and then decreasing.

Pattern 2: Minimal engorgement with little variation over time.

Pattern 3: More than one peak of engorgement with periods of less engorgement in between the peaks.

Pattern 4: Intense engorgement for the entire two-week period of the study.

The length of time between nursings and the frequency and duration of nursings were similar across these four patterns. Whichever engorgement pattern is observed, mothers should be encouraged to nurse long and often and follow the treatment plans described below.

If the mother says she's engorged, ask her about her symptoms and her breastfeeding patterns.

To find out more about the mother's symptoms, ask her:

- **How old is your baby?** If her baby is three to six days old, this is the usual time for engorgement to start. If the baby is older, engorgement may be due to missed or delayed feedings. (For suggestions, see the last point in this section.)
- For the mother experiencing postpartum engorgement: **How often and for how long has your baby nursed since birth?** Her answer to this question will offer a clue as to her degree of engorgement. The longer and more frequently the mother nurses right after birth, the less likely she is to become painfully engorged.
- **How do your breasts feel?** If her breasts are hard, the mother is probably engorged.
- **Is the skin on your breasts soft and elastic or stretched tight?** Taut skin is a sign of engorgement.
- **Does your areola feel soft and elastic like your earlobe or hard like the tip of your nose?** If she says her areola is soft and elastic, she may not need to express milk before putting her baby to the breast. If her areola is hard, expressing a little milk may help her baby to latch on.

Possible symptoms of engorgement include breast swelling, tenderness, warmth, redness, throbbing, pain, low-grade fever, and flattening of the nipple.

Infrequent breastfeeding causes the breasts to become congested with milk, slowing circulation. When blood and lymph move through the breasts slowly, fluid contained in the blood vessels can seep into the breast tissues, causing swelling. This swelling causes breast tenderness, warmth, and throbbing, which may extend up into the mother's armpit. The mother's skin may appear taut, shiny, and transparent.

Engorgement may also cause a low-grade fever, which is sometimes confused with a postpartum infection, resulting in unnecessary separation of mother and baby.

Engorgement may occur only in the areola (called "areolar engorgement"), only in the body of the breast (called "peripheral engorgement"), or in both. It can also occur in one or both breasts, depending on the baby's nursing pattern.

Engorgement should be treated promptly to prevent possible complications.

Prompt treatment of engorgement will prevent possible complications, which include:

- feeding problems or slow weight gain if the baby is unable to latch on well to the breast;
- sore nipples when a baby fumbles on and off an areola that is too firm to grasp;
- increased risk of mastitis due to pressure within the breast and inadequate milk flow;
- damage to the milk-producing cells, in the rare case when excessive pressure from engorgement is unrelieved and so severe that it causes a decrease in the mother's milk supply.

Breast Problems

To treat engorgement, massage and apply heat before breastfeeding, and breastfeed frequently, making sure both breasts soften with each feeding. Cold compresses between feedings reduce swelling and pain.

Before breastfeeding. Suggest the mother begin by applying warm moist compresses right before she breastfeeds, which will stimulate her let-down, or milk- ejection, reflex and help the milk to flow. Gentle breast massage—massaging from the chest wall toward the nipple area in a circular motion—may also help stimulate the let-down. Sometimes the engorged area is mainly in one part of the breast, perhaps high up toward the arm. Depending on how engorged the mother is, suggest she use her fingertips to gently knead the breast, again starting near the chest wall and working toward the nipple area. It may be more effective if the mother tries this while under the shower or while leaning over a bowl or sink of warm water and splashing the water over her breasts.

Frequent breastfeeding—at least every one-and-a-half to two hours, timed from the beginning of one feeding to the beginning of the next—will remove the milk and help prevent further congestion. The more frequently the baby breast-feeds, the sooner the engorgement will subside. Suggest the mother encourage her baby to breastfeed from both breasts until they feel softer, which usually takes about ten to twenty minutes per breast. Limiting the feedings to a certain prescribed number of minutes, which is sometimes erroneously recommended to prevent sore nipples, can contribute to engorgement.

If the baby will not breastfeed long enough to soften both breasts, encourage the mother to hand-express or pump her milk after nursing. (If a pump is used, be sure it is a gentle and effective pump, not the "bicycle-horn" type, which has no suction regulator and can cause damage to breast tissue.)

Cold compresses between feedings can reduce swelling and relieve pain. Suggest that the mother place a handkerchief or small towel on her breasts to protect her skin and then use ice packs or ice "flowers" (crushed ice in three small plastic bags joined by a twist tie) for about twenty minutes, or however long the mother is comfortable. The mother should switch to heat treatment about ten to fifteen minutes before the next feeding.

Cabbage leaves are used by some as a home remedy for engorgement. Their effectiveness has not been scientifically proven, but many women find them soothing (Roberts 1995a; Nikodem 1993; Rosier 1988).

To use, rinse either refrigerated or room temperature cabbage leaves (Roberts 1995b), strip the large vein, and cut a hole for the nipple. The mother should apply the cabbage leaves directly to her breasts, wearing them inside her bra. When they wilt, usually within two to four hours, she should remove them and reapply fresh leaves. Mothers who attributed some engorgement relief with the use of cabbage leaves reported this to occur within eight hours of application (Roberts 1995a).

If the mother's areola is engorged and the baby has difficulty latching on, suggest the mother express a little milk to soften the areola before putting the baby to breast.

Engorgement can present a problem if breast fullness causes the mother's nipples to become flat and taut, making it difficult for the baby to latch on properly. If the tautness of the areola causes the baby to grasp only the nipple in his mouth, it will make nursing painful for the mother and make it impossible for the baby to milk the breast well, aggravating the engorgement.

If the mother's areola is engorged, encourage her to express enough milk to soften the areola so that the baby will be able to latch on well. The warm bottle method of milk expression is one option for the mother who is engorged and does not have access to a gentle and effective breast pump. (For more information on this technique and other methods of milk expression, see the chapter "Expression and Storage of Human Milk.")

Some mothers are reluctant to express even a little milk for fear that this will increase their milk supply and make their engorgement worse. If the mother mentions this concern, assure her that expressing some milk will make it easier for her baby to remove the milk from her breasts, which will lessen her engorgement. Explain that the engorgement is caused in part by other fluids— lymph and blood— as well as milk, and that removing a little milk will allow the baby to nurse well, which will relieve her congestion. If the mother uses a breast pump to express her milk, gentleness should be a primary consideration when selecting it.

Also, suggest the mother try other nursing positions, such as the football hold, which may give her more control and make latching-on easier.

Wearing breast shells thirty minutes before feedings may help soften the areola.

Breast shells (also called milk cups, breast shields, or Woolwich shields) can be worn inside a bra large enough to accommodate them for thirty minutes before nursings in order to soften the areola and bring out the nipple.

Caution the mother to avoid nipple shields and bottles, which can contribute to feeding problems and make her engorgement worse.

When a mother is engorged, nipple shields—flexible artificial nipples placed over the mother's nipple during feedings—are sometimes recommended to make it easier for a baby to latch on. However, a nipple shield can cause more problems than it solves by contributing to nipple confusion, a feeding problem common among babies who receive artificial nipples within their first three to four weeks. The baby will probably not be able to nurse as effectively through a nipple shield, which will add to the engorgement. The nipple shield also decreases the amount of nipple stimulation the mother receives from breastfeeding, causing a significant reduction in her milk supply over time.

When a baby is having difficulty latching on and breastfeeding well, it may be tempting to supplement him with a bottle, but this can contribute to nipple confusion. A baby who is nipple-confused breastfeeds less effectively or may refuse the breast altogether, contributing to the mother's engorgement.

If the baby cannot breastfeed, suggest the mother express her milk until he can and use an alternative feeding method until then.

The goal is for the baby to nurse directly from his mother's breast. Milk expression will not be as effective at removing the milk as a baby who is nursing well. But if the baby is sick or premature or cannot breastfeed for some other reason, the mother will need an effective method of expression to keep her breasts from becoming overly full and to relieve congestion. The engorged mother's breasts are tender, so it is important that the mother use a gentle method of expression.

If the engorged mother must express her milk instead of nursing and she is not practiced at hand-expression or a hand pump, suggest she rent an automatic electric breast pump, as its effectiveness and comfort do not depend on the skill of the user. Suggest the mother use the pump at the minimum pressure setting to avoid bruising the skin and underlying breast tissues. (For more information, see the chapter "Expression and Storage of Human Milk.")

If the baby is hungry and refuses the breast, suggest the mother express some milk and give it to him using one of the alternative feeding methods—spoon, cup, eyedropper, bowl, or feeding syringe—which will not cause nipple confusion. She can then keep trying to breastfeed, expressing her milk and giving it to him in other ways if her baby continues to refuse. (For more information on how to use these alternative feeding methods, see "The Use of Breast Pumps and Other Products.")

There is no advantage to restricting fluids when a mother is engorged.

Restricting fluids has not been shown to reduce engorgement. Encourage the mother to drink to thirst.

Breast Problems

A well-fitting, supportive bra may make the mother more comfortable. A bra that does not fit properly can cause mastitis.

If the mother is wearing a bra, it should fit well and not be too tight or pinch, as this can constrict milk ducts, causing mastitis. A well-fitting, supportive bra may make the engorged mother more comfortable.

If the mother notices hard areas in her breasts after frequent nursings, suggest she try taking off her bra when she breastfeeds to be sure her bra is not constricting her milk ducts and that her milk is flowing freely through all parts of the breast.

BASIC INFORMATION	BACKGROUND NEEDED
If the mother is in pain, suggest she ask her doctor about pain medication.	Some mothers experience severe pain with engorgement. If the mother's discomfort prevents her from nursing her baby frequently, suggest she ask her doctor to recommend a pain medication that is compatible with breastfeeding.
If the mother's engorgement persists in one breast for more than 48 hours of consistent treatment with no obvious reason, suggest she see her doctor to rule out other causes.	Continued engorgement in one breast after consistent treatment is one warning sign of a breast tumor (Auerbach 1995). If there is no other obvious cause, such as one inverted nipple or the baby refusing one breast, suggest that the mother see her doctor to rule out this possibility.
Engorgement can occur when the baby is older if feedings are missed or if weaning occurs too abruptly.	Although engorgement is most common within the first week or two after birth, it may also occur later if feedings are missed and the mother's breasts become overly full. The same treatment recommended above for the new mother is also appropriate for the mother of an older baby. Particular emphasis should be given to frequent breastfeeding or—if the engorgement occurs during weaning—milk expression to avoid mastitis.

MASTITIS—PLUGGED DUCTS AND BREAST INFECTIONS

A mother suffering the pain or illness of mastitis, whether it is from a plugged duct or a breast infection, may feel discouraged about breastfeeding and worried about herself and her baby.	The mother who develops mastitis is usually feeling some discomfort or pain and may be running a fever or feeling achy and run down. In addition to coping with her own symptoms, she may be concerned about her baby. She may also be feeling discouraged about breastfeeding.

Reassure the mother that continued breastfeeding is best for her and her baby. Frequent nursing will prevent mastitis from becoming worse and aid in its treatment. Discuss treatment and causes to help the mother determine why it happened and how to prevent it from happening again. |
| Mastitis refers to any inflammation of the breast, whether or not the mother has a fever or whether or not she has a bacterial infection. | Mastitis is a general term used to refer to any inflammation of the breast. "Itis" means inflammation. It is not always possible to determine if the mother's breast inflammation is due to an infection or a plugged duct, as it is possible for a mother to run a low-grade fever even without a bacterial infection. The term mastitis covers both possibilities. |
| A tender spot or lump in the breast that is not accompanied by a fever is usually a plugged duct. | If a breastfeeding mother notices a tender spot, redness, or a sore lump in her breast and she does not have a fever, the most likely cause is a plugged milk duct. This means that a milk duct is not draining properly and has become inflamed. Pressure builds up behind the plug, causing inflammation in the surrounding tissues. This is also sometimes referred to as "caking," and usually occurs in only one breast. |
| A tender spot or lump in the breast that is accompanied by a fever and sometimes other symptoms may be a breast infection. | If the mother's breast soreness or lump is accompanied by a fever and/or flu-like symptoms (feeling tired and achy or run-down), she may have a breast infection, although it is not always possible to tell if it is a true bacterial infection or whether the fever is a general symptom of the inflammation. The mother's breast may feel hot and look red and swollen. Usually it occurs in only one breast. (If the inflammation is in both breasts, the mother's symptoms are severe, and the baby is less than two weeks old, see the last point in this section about hospital-acquired breast infections.) Other symptoms, such as nausea and vomiting, may also occur. A breastfeeding mother will sometimes develop a breast infection when other members of the family suffer from colds or the flu.

The following symptoms may indicate that the mother has a bacterial breast infection. She should be encouraged to contact her doctor for treatment if she has:

- a cracked nipple with obvious signs of infection, |

- pus and blood in her milk,
- red streaks from the site of the infection back into her breast,
- sudden and severe symptoms with no identifiable cause.

Ruth Lawrence, MD, in the fourth edition of her book, *Breastfeeding: A Guide for the Medical Profession* (p. 261), differentiates between a plugged duct and a breast infection in the following ways.

A plugged duct:

- comes on gradually,
- may shift in location,
- the mother feels little or no warmth in the area,
- the pain is mild and localized,
- the mother feels generally well, and
- her temperature is lower than 101° F (38.4° C).

A breast infection, on the other hand:

- comes on suddenly,
- is localized,
- the mother's breast is red, hot, and swollen,
- the pain is intense but localized,
- the mother has flu-like symptoms, and
- her temperature is 101° F (38.4° C) or higher.

If a mother has the symptoms of a breast infection, encourage her to contact her doctor for treatment. Breastfeeding can and should continue.

Treatment of mastitis consists of heat, gentle massage, frequent breastfeeding—especially on the affected breast—and rest.

Suggest the mother treat mastitis with heat, gentle massage, frequent breastfeeding, and rest.

Apply wet or dry heat to the affected area—gently massaging the area while it is warm—and remove any dried milk secretions on the nipple by soaking it with plain water. Suggest the mother lean over a basin of warm water or lie on her side in a warm bathtub and soak her breasts for ten minutes or so three times a day. Also recommend she take warm showers, use hot wet packs, a heating pad, or a hot water bottle between nursings.

Suggest she massage the affected area gently while it is warm, working over the lump using the palm of her hand and all her fingers in a gentle but firm circular motion. If she can do it comfortably, also suggest the mother use her fingertips to knead her breast as part of the massage, starting at the armpit and working toward the nipple.

Encourage her to breastfeed the baby or hand-express some milk immediately after treating the area with warmth and massage. Getting the milk to flow while the breast is warm will help unplug the affected duct.

Breastfeed the baby frequently on the affected side. Encourage the mother to breastfeed at least every two hours—including during the night—as long as the breast is tender or warm to the touch, nursing on the affected side first at each feeding. Frequent nursings will keep the breast from becoming overly full and keep the milk flowing freely.

Breast Problems

Loosen constrictive clothing, especially her bra. The mother may benefit from not wearing a bra for a few days. If she is more comfortable with a bra, suggest she wear one that is a size larger or one that has a different cut or style. This should relieve any pressure that her usual bra may have been putting on the milk ducts.

Make sure the baby is well-positioned at the breast and opens his mouth wide enough when he latches on so that the breast goes deeply into his mouth. Whatever nursing position is used, when the baby is breastfeeding, he should be well-supported with his mouth at nipple height and facing the breast so that he doesn't have to turn his head to nurse. Encourage the mother to wait for the baby to open wide before putting him to breast and then quickly pull him in very close so that the breast goes deeply into his mouth as he latches on. Once on, his chin should be pressed into the breast and his nose may be lightly touching. A good latch-on will enable him to drain all the milk ducts more effectively at every feeding.

Vary nursing positions. Varying nursing positions may help to relieve a plugged duct, if the mother is able to latch the baby on well in all the positions she uses, for example, side-lying, football hold, and cradle hold. Proper latch-on is essential to effective breastfeeding. Riordan and Auerbach (p. 381) suggest that at least once during each feeding the mother position the baby so that his nose points toward the plug.

Rest. Mastitis may be the first sign that the mother is trying to do too much. Encourage the mother, if possible, to go to bed with the baby and stay there until she is feeling better. If she can't do this, suggest, at the very least, that she eliminate all extra activities and spend an extra hour or two relaxing with the baby at her breast and her feet off the floor. Be sure she understands that rest is an important part of the treatment.

Discuss with the mother the main causes of mastitis so she can avoid a recurrence,

Mastitis has several main causes:

Missed or shortened feedings and irregular breastfeeding patterns. Anything that reduces a baby's time at the breast can leave a mother with overly full or engorged breasts and increase the risk of mastitis. Ask the mother:

- **Has she just brought her newborn home from the hospital?** Hospital schedules may prevent mother and baby from nursing as often as they should, leading to engorgement and overly full breasts.
- **Is she limiting her baby's time at the breast or is he falling asleep early in the feedings?** If the mother ends the nursings before the baby has had the chance to soften the breast, she can become overly full. If the baby is sleepy, he may not be nursing actively for long enough to soften the mother's breasts at each feeding. Suggest the mother stimulate the baby to nurse actively for longer periods or express her milk to relieve her fullness. (For more information on stimulating a sleepy baby, see "Sleepy Baby" in the chapter "Positioning, Latch-On, and the Baby's Suck.")
- **Has her baby begun sleeping through the night, either consistently or irregularly?** When a baby begins sleeping for longer stretches at night, the mother's breasts can become overly full. If the baby breastfeeds many times during one night and none at all the next night, the mother's breasts may be stimulated to produce more milk and then abruptly become overly full.
- **Has she been giving her baby supplementary bottles?** Whether the mother is giving water, juice, formula, or her own milk in a bottle, it can increase the time between nursings.
- **Does her baby use a pacifier?** If so, how often? Overuse of a pacifier can contribute to mastitis because the baby spends less time at the breast. If her baby has just started using a pacifier every day, this could be a contributing factor.
- **Has her schedule been unusually busy?** A busy schedule (such as around holidays) can distract the mother and baby from breastfeeding as often as usual.
- **Has there been any abrupt change in her baby's nursing pattern?** Examples: a teething baby who suddenly cuts feedings short, a baby who is refusing the breast (see the chapter "Fussy at the Breast and Breast Refusal"), the mother beginning work or school outside the home.

- **Does the baby breastfeed irregularly or frequently go for longer than two to three hours between nursings?** Some babies breastfeed more often during one part of the day and less often at other times (such as the baby who sleeps long hours at night and breastfeeds every hour during the day or the mother who breastfeeds often when she's at home but is away from her baby for part of the day). Some babies go longer than average between feedings yet still have a healthy weight gain and thrive. Suggest the mother try encouraging her baby to nurse more often or more regularly, waking the baby if necessary. If this does not work or is not practical, suggest the mother express her milk whenever she begins to feel full in order to stay comfortable and avoid mastitis. A working mother may need to express her milk more often while she is away from her baby.

Consistent pressure on the breast. Any consistent or sustained pressure on any part of the breast can restrict the flow of milk and cause mastitis. Some possibilities include:

- a tight bra or one that does not support well, causing the weight of the breast to put pressure on the milk ducts,
- a tight bathing suit,
- a baby carrier, heavy purse, or diaper bag with straps that put pressure on the breasts,
- thick breast pads or breast shells that cause her bra to be too tight,
- the mother who sleeps on her stomach, putting pressure on her breasts,
- the baby resting on the mother's breasts,
- the mother gripping her breast tightly during feedings or pressing down on her breast during nursings to form an airway,
- the baby pressing on the breast with his hands during feedings.

Poor latch-on, positioning, or sucking at the breast. If the baby is not latching on well—if he is grasping the nipple rather than taking a large amount of breast tissue into his mouth— he may not be milking the breast effectively, causing the breast to become overly full or the ducts to be emptied unevenly. Poor positioning and latch-on can also cause sore nipples, which can result in overly full breasts if the mother postpones feedings, as well as providing a site for bacteria to enter the breast. (For more information, see the chapter "Positioning, Latch-On, and the Baby's Suck.")

A baby with a weak suck may not be able to milk the breast well enough to soften it during feedings. Reduced milk flow contributes to mastitis, as well as poor weight gain in the baby. In this case, the mother's breasts would feel full even after nursing.

See the next section, "Recurring Mastitis," for other possible causes of mastitis.

An antibiotic may be needed for mastitis if the mother's fever has not disappeared within twenty-four hours of home treatment or if her fever increases suddenly.

When the mother has a fever or flu-like aching along with a sore spot on her breast, it is important she begin treatment (described above) for her mastitis immediately. If after twenty-four hours of treatment the mother still has a fever, she should contact her doctor. The doctor may want to give her a prescription for an antibiotic. Encourage her to contact her doctor immediately if she has already been running a fever for some time, if she has obvious signs of a bacterial infection, such as pus, or if her temperature increases suddenly.

Breast Problems

If the mother needs medication, suggest she request a drug that is compatible with breastfeeding.

Antibiotics are usually compatible with breastfeeding, as the baby receives much less from his mother's milk than he would if he were given a treatment dose. Some antibiotics are more effective than others for treatment of a breast infection. If a doctor is wary about the effects of a specific antibiotic, suggest the mother ask that he or she prescribe one that is known to be effective in the treatment of mastitis and compatible with breastfeeding. (See the chapter "Drugs, Vitamins, Vaccines, and Diagnostic Tests," and the supplement "Transfer of Drugs and Other Chemicals into Human Milk.")

Continued breastfeeding during mastitis is beneficial for both mother and baby.

Continued breastfeeding during mastitis will not harm the baby. Antibodies in the mother's milk protect the baby from any bacteria. Even temporary weaning is an unnecessary hardship at a time when the mother is not feeling well.

At one time it was standard procedure to recommend weaning with mastitis. However, the mastitis clears up more quickly when the breast is not allowed to become overly full, and there is less risk of developing an abscess (Marshall 1975). Also, the mother is much more comfortable when she continues to breastfeed.

Mastitis could make the mother's milk taste saltier. This causes some babies to refuse the breast.

Sodium and chloride levels may rise in the mother's milk after mastitis, making the milk taste saltier (Thullen 1988; Conner 1979). Some babies react to this change in taste by nursing only reluctantly on that breast—showing a strong preference for the other breast—or by refusing the affected breast altogether.

If the baby is reluctant to nurse on or refuses the affected breast, suggest the mother follow the recommendations in "Persuading the Baby to Take the Breast" in the chapter "Fussy at the Breast and Breast Refusal," and continue breastfeeding on the other breast, expressing her milk when needed so that the affected breast does not become overly full. Within a week the mother's milk will lose its salty taste if the mother has kept up her milk supply, and the baby should go back to nursing as usual.

The mother with a plugged duct may be able to express the plug from her breast.

In many cases of a plugged duct, the mother never notices a physical plug. But occasionally, a mother is able to express a plug. When the plug is drawn out through the duct's opening in the nipple, the coagulated milk may look like a crystal, a grain of sand, or a long, thin strand of spaghetti and may be accompanied by mucus. This will not harm the baby.

If both of the mother's breasts are affected and/or her baby is less than two weeks old, she may have hospital-acquired mastitis.

Occasionally a mother contracts mastitis through exposure to virulent bacteria at the hospital after giving birth. This was once a major problem—for both breastfeeding and bottle-feeding mothers—when hospital stays were longer. Hospital-acquired mastitis may be more severe than other types (Lawrence, p. 261).

If the hardened area or lump has not begun to shrink within several days of consistent treatment, suggest the mother see her doctor to rule out other causes.

A lump that does not respond within several days to the usual treatment for mastitis should be checked by a doctor. A lump that does not shrink may be a more serious problem (Auerbach 1995). Although most breast lumps are not tumors, this possibility needs to be ruled out if standard treatments do not bring improvement. Suggest the mother see her doctor.

For prolonged or recurring mastitis, some health care professionals use breast stripping to avoid abscess and speed recovey.

Breast stripping, a technique used by some health care professionals to manually remove pus from the breast, has long been used in animal husbandry. For serious cases of mastitis, such as those in which treatment has been delayed, the mastitis does not respond to the usual treatment, or it is recurring (see next section), breast stripping may be used in conjunction with antibiotics to help avoid abscess and speed recovery (Bertrand and Rosenblood 1991). The breast stripping, which may be very painful, is initially done by a health care professional after the mother nurses her baby to reduce the amount of milk in the breast. The procedure can continue to be done at home by the mother after feedings.

If no pus is extracted during the stripping, the infection may be in the connective tissue between the ducts and breast stripping will not be helpful. For a detailed description of the technique, see Cantlie 1988.

Recurring Mastitis

Recurring mastitis can be demoralizing to the mother.

The cycle of pain and illness associated with recurring mastitis can demoralize any mother, even one who is strongly committed to breastfeeding. Although some mothers struggle through many bouts without considering weaning, chronic recurrence leaves many mothers questioning their commitment to breastfeeding.

Listen to and acknowledge the mother's feelings. Offer to talk to her in more depth to try to determine the cause of her continuing problem. Assure her that in most cases of recurring mastitis the cause can be found and eliminated or treated, breaking the cycle of recurrence. Also caution her that weaning while she has mastitis may make it worse.

If the mother has recurring mastitis, despite careful attention to the main causes (listed in the above section), discuss other risk factors.

To help the mother determine the cause of her recurring mastitis, first talk to her in depth about the main causes listed in the previous section. Then offer to discuss the following risk factors. The list is long, and for some mothers it may be overwhelming to talk about all of these in one or even two conversations. It may be necessary to go through them a few at a time over the course of several conversations.

Failure to fully recover from mastitis. Any time a woman has mastitis that has not completely cleared up, she is at greater risk of having a recurrence. If she has used home treatment, encourage the mother to be vigilant in treating her mastitis until it is gone.

If the mother's mastitis recurs even after treatment with antibiotics, chances are good that the original mastitis did not clear up completely. Repeated mastitis does happen occasionally, but it is almost always a recurrence of the original mastitis rather than a new case.

The mother is likely to suffer a recurrence if she does not take antibiotics for at least ten days (either because her doctor prescribed a shorter course or because she stopped taking them sooner), if an inappropriate antibiotic was prescribed, or in the rare case that the baby is carrying an infection in his mouth and he reinfects the mother after she finishes her medication. If her mastitis recurs after at least ten days on antibiotics, suggest the mother ask her doctor to culture her milk and her baby's throat to determine the appropriate antibiotic treatment for her and/or her baby.

Fatigue and stress. It may be important for the mother to find a way to get more rest, even if this means changing some of her basic expectations about her life. In a survey of ninety-one breastfeeding mothers, the one-third of the women who said they had had mastitis (defined as the presence of breast soreness and redness, accompanied by flu-like aching and a fever above 100.4° F) ranked fatigue first and stress second as major contributing factors (Riordan 1990). Several of the mothers described family trips, holidays, christenings, parties, and household moves as precipitating factors.

Lowered resistance to infection and anemia. If the mother is run-down or tired, suggest she have a medical checkup with a blood count. Anemia is a common contributor to repeated mastitis. Some doctors suggest taking supplemental vitamins and iron or, perhaps, extra vitamin C to combat infections. Also, cigarette smoking can lower a woman's resistance to infection, as well as inhibit her let-down, or milk-ejection, reflex.

An overabundant milk supply. The mother who produces an overabundant milk supply is at increased risk, because it may not be possible for the baby to soften both breasts at each nursing, contributing to overly full breasts.

Encourage the mother to allow the baby to finish nursing at the first breast before offering the second. If the baby isn't interested in nursing on the second

Breast Problems

breast, or only nurses briefly, suggest the mother offer it after an hour or two or—if it feels full—to express just enough milk from that breast so that she feels more comfortable, offering the second breast first at the next feeding.

Nipple damage. Nipple damage can offer a point of entrance for infective organisms that can contribute to plugged ducts and infections. If the mother has sore, cracked, or bleeding nipples (or had them at one time) be sure she knows about proper positioning and latch-on so she can avoid further damage. Also, discuss other treatments for sore nipples. (See the chapter "Nipple Problems.")

Dried milk secretions on the nipple. Occasionally, a plugged duct is caused by dried milk secretions covering one of the nipple openings. In this case, suggest the mother apply moist, warm compresses to her nipple until the dried milk peels off. Also suggest she try expressing some milk to encourage that opening to clear. Some mothers report that a thick, yellowish plug emerges with gentle expression, clearing the duct. Once the mother is able to freely express milk through the opening, the dried milk should no longer cause a problem.

Use of a nipple shield. Nipple shields—flexible artificial nipples that are worn over the mother's nipple during feedings—can slow the flow of milk through the breast, increasing the risk of mastitis.

A baby who breastfeeds reluctantly or refuses the breast periodically. If the baby is reluctant to breastfeed or refuses the breast outright, this puts the mother at increased risk. Some babies, for example, refuse the breast right before or during their mother's menstrual period or after mastitis, due to changes in the taste of the milk. Other babies cut feedings short abruptly when they suffer from teething pain or ear infections. (See the chapter "Fussy at the Breast and Breast Refusal.")

Constrictive clothing. Encourage the mother to wear comfortable clothing that does not bind the breast when she nurses and avoid bras that are overly tight or whose inner band constricts the breast, such as some underwire bras. Ask the mother to check to be sure that neither her bra straps nor any other parts of her clothing are blocking circulation to any part of the breast. If the mother is wearing a regular, non-nursing bra and pulling it up over the breast to nurse, this can put pressure on the breast.

Breast abnormalities. Any breast surgery—such as a biopsy, breast reduction, breast augmentation, tumor, or cyst removal—increases the risk of mastitis due to scarring and/or pressure on the milk ducts. An anatomical problem in a particular duct may cause recurring plugged ducts. Women with breast lumps may also be at increased risk. Past injuries, such as severe bruising or abscess, may also pose problems. If any of these are the cause, the mastitis will recur in the same area of the breast. In the very rare cases when this happens, the mother may choose to breastfeed only on the unaffected breast, gradually allowing the milk supply to dry up completely on the affected side.

Too much saturated fat in the diet. Dr. Ruth Lawrence recommends that a mother with recurring plugged ducts limit her fat intake to polyunsaturated fats and take one tablespoon per day of lecithin. Dr. Lawrence says this has offered dramatic improvement to women she has treated with "repeated lumps in their breasts with poor flow of milk, often as if the ducts were plugged" (p. 258).

Sodium intake. Excessive amounts of sodium in the diet may cause fluid retention in body tissues, which can make women susceptible to infections of any type, including mastitis. The opposite situation, a chronic salt deficiency, can also contribute to recurring mastitis.

Exposure to allergens. In her book *Breastfeeding Matters*, Maureen Minchin theorizes that if a mother has allergies, recurring mastitis might be caused by the "complex immune responses" that occur when she is exposed to an allergen. In a group of food-intolerant women, Minchin observed that their plugged ducts, "which rarely progressed to overt infection and which often recurred either premenstrually or before ovulation," were "often accompanied by other symptoms of allergy intolerance—some of them indicating that blood vessels were affected, e.g., migraine, easy bruising...hives, premenstrual tension.... In some cases, breast refusal, PMT [premenstrual tension] and mastitis all ended after the mother identified and was avoiding her allergens."

Excessive upper-arm exercise. Excessive and repetitive movements of the upper arm—although usually not a problem for breastfeeding mothers—should be considered a risk factor when women have recurrent mastitis, as they may restrict the flow of milk.

Attitudes and emotions, especially in the early weeks postpartum. The early weeks at home are a period of adjustment for the mother and her baby. Getting off to a good start can help prevent mastitis. Encourage the mother to depend on family members or friends for help and support and to act as buffers against too many visitors and extra activities. Encourage her to structure her life to put her and her baby's needs first.

If mastitis recurs after a ten-day antibiotic treatment, suggest the mother ask her doctor to take a culture of her milk and the baby's throat to determine the appropriate antibiotic.

If the mother has followed through with a course of antibiotics for at least ten days and her mastitis recurs, suggest she see her doctor again and have her treatment reevaluated. Suggest the mother ask her doctor to take a culture of her milk and her baby's throat. Then the doctor can evaluate whether a different antibiotic should be prescribed. A culture of the baby's throat will determine if the baby is reinfecting the mother and needs to be treated as well.

Recurring mastitis has been successfully treated with long-term, low-dose antibiotic therapy.

For some women, the cycle of chronic recurring mastitis has been broken by preventive long-term antibiotic treatment. Following the ten-day course of antibiotics to treat the current mastitis, these women were given low doses of antibiotics to take once a day for two to three months to prevent recurrence. (Cantlie 1988; Hoffman and Auerbach 1986.)

If the mother's recurring mastitis is always in the same breast and the same location, suggest she see her doctor to rule out other causes.

Recurring mastitis in the same location is one of the warning signs of a breast tumor. Although most recurring mastitis is not caused by a breast tumor, this possibility needs to be ruled out when the mastitis is always in the same breast and the same spot. Suggest the mother see her doctor.

BREAST ABSCESS

A breast abscess is a serious medical condition that is usually the result of untreated mastitis or—rarely—one that does not respond to treatment,

Breast abscesses happen rarely. When they do, they are usually the result of untreated mastitis, a delay in treatment, or incorrect treatment. The abscess—a localized collection of pus—forms in an area of the breast that has no opening for drainage and so it must be surgically drained to the outside. It is a serious and painful condition that needs immediate medical attention.

Ultrasound can be an effective tool in diagnosing and locating an abscess without interfering with breastfeeding.

In some cases, it may not be possible for the mother's doctor to confirm the existence and/or location of an abscess by examination alone. A mammogram, which can be used as a diagnostic tool for many breast problems, does not clearly show the difference between an abscess and other masses, such as a tumor. Ultrasound, however, when performed by a technician familiar with the lactating breast, has been found to be helpful in distinguishing a breast abscess from other breast masses (Hayes 1991). By confirming the existence and location of the abscess before attempting drainage, the mother can avoid unnecessary incisions in the breast.

Breast Problems

A breast abscess requires surgical drainage, as well as treatment with antibiotics and rest, but in most cases breastfeeding can continue.

Breastfeeding can continue even when the breast abscess must be surgically drained. The mother can breastfeed on the unaffected side, and if the incision is far enough from the nipple so that the baby's mouth does not touch it when he breastfeeds, the mother may also be able to nurse on the affected side. Antibiotics and rest are also part of the treatment.

If the mother does not nurse on the affected side, encourage her to express her milk from that breast while her incision is healing to prevent engorgement. (See the chapter "Expression and Storage of Human Milk.")

Continued breastfeeding on the affected breast will not prevent it from healing, and it has several advantages.

Some women are told after surgical drainage of a breast abscess that continued nursing on the affected breast will prevent healing. Although milk may seep out of the incision, healing will continue. The incision may heal more slowly if the mother continues to nurse on the affected breast, but continued breastfeeding also has several advantages:

- It prevents engorgement;
- It helps prevent mastitis from recurring;
- It decreases the likelihood that the baby will develop a preference for the unaffected breast once the incision is healed.

BREAST LUMPS

When breastfeeding, a mother's breasts normally feel lumpier than when she is not lactating.

A mother's breasts will feel differently when she is lactating than when she is not, because during lactation there is more blood and lymph in her breasts and because her milk ducts fill and empty many times each day.

Encourage the mother to examine her breasts every month so that she can become familiar with the way her breasts feel during lactation. She can learn to distinguish normal breast lumpiness from a lump that might need medical attention by observing whether or not it decreases in size after nursing. A lump that stays constant in size or enlarges needs to be checked by a doctor.

If the mother has a breast lump that does not go away after a week of careful treatment for a plugged duct, suggest she see her doctor.

Most lumps in a nursing mother's breasts are either milk-filled glands or inflammation, such as a plugged duct or a breast infection. Some are benign tumors (fibromas) or milk-retention cysts (galactoceles). Only in the rarest cases are they due to cancer. (For more information on breast cancer, see the section "Cancer," in the chapter "Health Problems—Mother.")

If the mother's doctor is not familiar with the lactating breast, encourage the mother to ask her doctor to consult with a knowledgeable colleague or to find another doctor who has had experience with breastfeeding mothers.

Suggest the mother breastfeed immediately before an examination or medical procedure.

Breastfeeding immediately before an examination or medical procedure reduces the amount of milk in the breasts. This makes it easier to feel a lump and to perform other medical procedures (such as fine-needle aspiration).

If the mother brings the baby with her to the doctor's office or medical facility, she can breastfeed while she is waiting, keeping the amount of milk in her breasts at a minimum when she sees the doctor.

Breastfeeding can continue through most diagnostic tests.

There are several diagnostic tests that might be used when breast lumps are found:

X-rays. The mother's milk will not be affected by an x-ray, and she may safely nurse immediately afterward.

Ultrasound and computer axial tomography (CAT) scanning. These noninvasive imaging techniques can be used without interfering with breastfeeding or affecting the milk. Unlike mammograms, ultrasound has been found to be effective in distinguishing solid breast lumps from cysts and abscesses (Hayes 1991). Ultrasound has also detected breast implant leaks not visible by mammography (Beekman 1996; Skolnick 1992).

Magnetic resonance imaging (MRI) is a noninvasive imaging technique that will not affect breastfeeding or the mother's milk. However, as part of an MRI the mother is injected with a dye that has not been investigated to date in pregnant or lactating women, although no adverse reactions have been reported. Contact La Leche League International's Center for Breastfeeding Information for the latest information regarding this dye.

Mammograms. A mammogram—which x-rays the breast using very low levels of radiation—can be performed on a lactating breast, although it may be more difficult to read due to the density of the extra tissue present during lactation. When a woman is breastfeeding, a mammogram can be useful in determining the size and location of a known lump but may not be able to show early lumps or soft-tissue changes in the lactating breast. A mammogram is also of limited use in screening the breasts of non-lactating younger women, because their breast tissue is denser than the breast tissue of older women.

How often the baby nurses can make a difference in the quality of the mammogram. If the mother has a sizable milk supply with all of its accompanying breast tissue changes, she would have to stop breastfeeding for at least a month to make a difference in the quality of her mammogram. The mother who is breastfeeding infrequently, however, will have less milk and extra breast tissue, so her mammogram would be more easily read.

If the mother needs to have a mammogram, encourage her to look for a radiologist who has had experience reading mammograms of breastfeeding women. Also, suggest that she bring her baby with her to the testing site and nurse him right before the mammogram to minimize the amount of milk in the breast during the procedure.

Fine-needle aspiration cytologic study. This procedure may be recommended for the mother with a breast lump to determine the nature of a solid mass. This is a quick, nearly painless procedure, which can be performed in a physician's office with the use of local anesthetic. Breastfeeding would not need to be interrupted. This procedure can sometimes be used to avoid a biopsy.

Breastfeeding can continue after a biopsy or other surgery.

The mother can continue breastfeeding after a breast biopsy, as with any other surgery, although she will want to be sure to let her doctor and surgeon know that she is breastfeeding so they can select medications that are compatible with nursing. Also, suggest she ask her surgeon to avoid cutting her milk ducts whenever possible. (For ways to make her hospital stay easier, see "When Mother Is Hospitalized" in the chapter "Health Problems—Mother.")

The mother with fibrocystic disease can breastfeed, and it may delay the return of her symptoms.

There is no generally agreed upon definition for fibrocystic disease and its existence is the subject of controversy. Some describe it simply as breast lumpiness (Love 1995). Many women also have other symptoms, which may or may not be related to their breast lumps, such as breast pain and tenderness. Many women report that their symptoms are most severe during the time around their menstrual period.

Many women find that their breast lumps are fewer and that the pain and tenderness is reduced or relieved during pregnancy. For some women, breastfeding delays the return of their symptoms. Some women have found relief by eliminating all caffeine and related products from their diet.

Breast Problems

A galactocele is a cyst that fills with milk, causing a lump in the breast that doesn't respond to the treatment for a plugged duct.

Dr. Ruth Lawrence says in the fourth edition of her book, *Breastfeeding: A Guide for the Medical Profession:* "Milk-retention cysts are uncommon and, when found, are almost exclusively a problem in lactating women. The contents at first are pure milk. Owing to absorption of the fluid they later contain thick, oily material. The swelling is smooth and rounded, and compression of it may cause milky fluid to exude from the nipple. Galactoceles are believed to be caused by the blockage of a milk duct. The cyst may be aspirated to avoid surgery but will fill up again. It can be removed surgically under local anesthesia without stopping the breastfeeding. Its presence does not require cessation of the lactation. A firm diagnosis can be made by ultrasound; a cyst and milk will appear the same, and a tumor will be distinguishable" (p. 259).

Fine-needle aspiration of the breast—a procedure done under local anesthetic in the doctor's office that allows the contents of the cyst to be removed and checked—may be an alternative to surgery and a useful diagnostic tool if the doctor is unsure of the cyst's contents.

BLOOD IN THE MILK

The mother with blood in her milk may be upset and worried about herself and her baby.

Blood in the milk without nipple soreness or damage can be upsetting to a mother, who may worry that it indicates a serious medical problem, such as breast cancer. She may also worry that the blood in her milk will harm her baby.

Suggest the mother talk to her doctor about the bleeding, but assure her that bleeding from the breast in late pregnancy and the first two weeks postpartum is usually due to more harmless causes, such as broken capillaries and intraductal papillomas. Also assure her that the bleeding will not harm her breastfeeding baby and that it is fine to continue nursing.

Blood in the milk may be due to several causes.

Blood in the milk without nipple soreness or damage may be due to several causes. One cause of blood in the milk of pregnant or lactating women has been referred to as "vascular engorgement," a slight internal bleeding caused by a combination of increased blood flow to the breast and rapid development of the milk-producing glands. This is reported to be most common in first-time mothers, usually occurs in both breasts (although in some mothers it occurs in only one breast at first), and there is little or no discomfort (Lawrence, p. 526). In a survey of 32 Australian women who reported blood in the milk during pregnancy and lactation that could not be explained by other causes, most reported the blood clearing within three to seven days after the onset of lactation (O'Callaghan 1981).

Other common causes of blood in the milk include intraductal papillomas and fibrocystic disease (Lawrence p. 526). An intraductal papilloma is a benign tumor in a milk duct. An intraductal papilloma usually occurs in only one breast, cannot be felt as a lump, and may or may not be accompanied by pain or discomfort. The bleeding often stops spontaneously without any treatment (Riordan and Auerbach, p. 392).

Another possible cause is broken capillaries within the breast from too vigorous nipple preparation, rough handling of the breasts, or the improper use of a breast pump.

Encourage the mother with blood in her milk to consult her doctor.

It is not unusual for blood in the milk to clear up without treatment. If it doesn't stop within two weeks after birth, however, the mother should be checked by her doctor.

Breastfeeding can continue without harm to the baby.

The blood in the milk will not hurt the baby, and the baby can continue to breastfeed.

DEEP BREAST PAIN

The mother with deep breast pain may feel worried and upset.

The mother experiencing deep breast pain may be worried that her pain is an indication of a serious physical problem, such as breast cancer. Recurring pain may also hamper her enjoyment of her baby and give her second thoughts about breastfeeding.

Listen to and acknowledge the mother's feelings. Offer to talk to her in more depth to try to determine the cause of her pain. Assure her that in most cases the cause of deep breast pain can be found and the pain relieved. Reassurance and support can make the discomfort less frightening and more bearable.

Deep breast pain has many possible causes. To help determine the cause, ask the baby's age and if the pain comes during or between feedings and if it is in one or both breasts.

Occasionally a breastfeeding mother reports a sharp, shooting pain within her breast that is unrelated to nipple pain or soreness. If the pain comes during feedings, suspect a forceful let-down or mastitis. These are the most common causes of deep breast pain. To confirm this, ask the mother if there is a hard, sore area in her breast that hurts when she presses it or if the pain radiates throughout the entire breast and is not localized. If she has a hard, sore area in her breast, see the previous section, "Mastitis—Plugged Ducts and Breast Infections." If her pain radiates throughout the breast or mastitis does not seem to be the cause, see the following sections for other possibilities.

Deep Breast Pain during the First Six Weeks

Deep breast pain occurring within the first six weeks of nursing may resolve itself with time and the establishment of breastfeeding.

When deep breast pain occurs during the first six weeks of nursing, it may be due to causes that will resolve themselves with time—(i.e., muscle strain during delivery) or with the establishment of breastfeeding (engorgement and forceful or delayed let-down). However, if the deep breast pain is due to mastitis, it is important the mother begin treatment immediately.

Knowing if the pain occurs during or between feedings (or both) and if the pain is in one or both breasts will help to determine its cause.

Engorgement, especially if it's severe, can produce extreme pain and a feeling of tight, bursting fullness usually in both breasts during and between feedings, although the pain may diminish after the baby has nursed well. Severe engorgement usually occurs when the mother and baby are separated by hospital routines or medical procedures during the early weeks after birth. (For more information, see the first section in this chapter.)

Engorgement may also occur when the baby is older if feedings are missed or delayed, for example when mother and baby are separated, when the baby begins sleeping through the night, when the baby is given supplemental bottles, or for any other reason.

Muscle strain incurred during delivery, especially a pulled back muscle, is sometimes perceived as breast pain during or between feedings in one or both breasts, depending on the location of the strained muscle. If this is a possibility, encourage the mother to use pillows to support the baby's weight while she is holding or breastfeeding him. It may also make the mother more comfortable during breastfeeding to prop her feet on a stool or low table so that her knees are higher than her hips—leaning back into her chair, rather than leaning over her baby to breastfeed. A heating pad placed between her shoulder blades and a well-fitted bra may also help bring relief. It will usually take less than two weeks for the injury to heal.

Forceful let-down can cause breast pain during feedings in the breast from which the baby is nursing. This occurs especially in mothers with an overabundant milk supply. Pain from forceful let-down may be due to the stretching of the ducts as the milk passes through them. Sometimes the severity of the pain can be reduced by offering only one breast at each feeding, and/or nursing more frequently to prevent engorgement. This type of breast pain usually clears up spontaneously within the first months of breastfeeding.

Breast Problems

Until the pain disappears, suggest the mother use her childbirth relaxation techniques or ask her doctor for a mild pain reliever that is compatible with breastfeeding.

Delayed or inhibited let-down is usually experienced as pain during a feeding in one or both breasts. It may be the result of engorgement during the first days and weeks of breastfeeding or stress during times of emotional crisis. Along with extreme stress, other factors that can interfere with a mother's let-down, or milk-ejection, reflex are: sore nipples (which make the mother feel tense when she puts her baby to breast), excessive caffeine in her diet, smoking, and certain drugs. (See "Delayed or Inhibited Let-Down" under "The Let-Down or Milk-Ejection Reflex" in the chapter "Breastfeeding Basics.")

If the mother has sore nipples, talk to the mother about the possible causes and cures to eliminate or minimize her discomfort. See "If Breastfeeding Hurts—Review the Basics" in the chapter "Positioning, Latch-On, and the Baby's Suck."

Sudden refilling of milk ducts may cause a deep, pervasive pain, sometimes described as "shooting" pains between feedings, usually soon after a nursing. This pain may occur intermittently during the early weeks of breastfeeding and usually disappears gradually as breastfeeding becomes established .

Hospital-acquired mastitis can cause intense, localized throbbing pain, redness, swelling, heat, and a fever or flu-like symptoms. The pain occurs in both breasts during and between feedings. For more information, see the section earlier in this chapter "Mastitis—Plugged Ducts and Breast Infections."

Deep Breast Pain at Any Stage of Breastfeeding

Other causes of deep breast pain are not limited to the first six weeks. Again, ask the mother if she notices the pain during or between feedings and in one or both breasts.

Some causes of deep breast pain can occur at any stage of breastfeeding.

Mastitis can cause a consistent, localized sore area in the breast with or without other symptoms. Mastitis usually occurs in one breast and the pain is most intense during a feeding. Immediate treatment is important. For more information, see the previous section, "Mastitis—Plugged Ducts and Breast Infections."

Leaning over to breastfeed can create tension in the mother's back and shoulders, which can cause pain that radiates to the breast. The pain is felt in one or both breasts during feedings. Leaning over the baby may also cause the baby to pull on the mother's breast tissue, increasing the pain.

Encourage the mother to find a comfortable chair in which she is well-supported while she breastfeeds, and to bring the baby up to the breast, rather than leaning over to bring the breast to the baby. To make this easier, suggest she put pillows in her lap and under her elbows—to support the baby's weight—and rest her feet on a stool or low table so that her knees are higher than her hips. Once the mother has found a more comfortable nursing position, a heating pad placed between her shoulder blades and a gentle back and shoulder massage can also help bring relief.

Injury to the breast or an ill-fitting bra can cause breast pain, which may be described as soreness, bruising, or stabbing pain. The pain is usually localized in one breast in the area where the injury occurred or where the bra pinches or the underwires dig into the breast.

Improper breast pump use can cause breast pain during or between feedings in one or both breasts, depending on the location and degree of damage. The "bicycle-horn" hand pump can cause injury to the nipple and breast tissue because there is no suction regulator. Hand pumps that provide continuous suction, such as a battery-operated or semi-automatic electric pump, can also cause breast injury if the mother neglects to relieve the suction. In some women, excessive suction from a breast pump has caused hemorrhages under the skin, which look like flat, round, purple-red spots.

Back injury or muscle strain. Ask the mother if she has recently injured her back or engaged in vigorous exercise. If so, she may be experiencing muscle strain or injury as breast pain **during or between feedings in one or both breasts**. The muscle injury in her back may produce a sharp, shooting pain radiating to the breast or arm, depending on which nerves are affected.

Suggest the mother apply warm compresses to her back before nursing and use pillows under her arms to support the baby during nursing. It may also make her more comfortable to prop her feet on a stool or low table so that her knees are higher than her hips—leaning back into her chair, rather than forward.

A yeast infection can cause stabbing or burning pain in one or both breasts.

A yeast infection of the milk ducts can cause an intense stabbing or burning pain in one or both breasts during or shortly after feedings. The following are clues that a yeast infection (*Candida albicans*) may be causing the mother's breast pain:

- The mother was recently treated with antibiotics (which kill the beneficial bacteria in the body that keep the yeast in check);
- The mother has had cracked nipples (the fungus can enter the breast through the cracks);
- The mother has had thrush (burning, itchy, flaky, or red nipples) and/or a vaginal yeast infection; and
- The baby has had thrush (white spots on the inside of his cheeks, a diaper rash, or no symptoms).

Thrush may be diagnosed when any or all of these conditions are present. Culturing of the mother's milk or nipples is usually not recommended, because even when thrush is present, the results of a culture are often negative (Amir 1995).

If thrush is diagnosed, the mother and baby will need simultaneous treatment with medication prescribed by their health care providers. Standard treatment varies in different parts of the world. In the US, nystatin nipple cream for the mother and oral nystatin suspension for the baby's mouth are commonly prescribed. Oral nystatin is sometimes prescribed for the mother if there is a recurrence (Lawrence, p. 265). Some strains of *Candida albicans* have become nystatin-resistant, and in this case, other medications may be needed. In Australia, a combination of oral nystatin for the mother and topical miconazole or clotrimazole gel for both mother and baby are recommended by some medical practitioners (Amir 1995). For information on how to avoid recurrence, see "Thrush" in the chapter "Nipple Problems."

Adhesions from a previous breast surgery or scarred breast tissue can cause pain when they are stretched during breastfeeding. The pain is usually **felt in one breast**. If the mother's scars are on the nipple or areola, suggest the mother try wearing breast shells between feedings to stretch and loosen adhesions and scars. In the very rare cases when the pain or discomfort is too intense for the mother to tolerate, the mother may choose to breastfeed on the unaffected breast only, expressing only for comfort and gradually allowing the milk supply to dry up completely on the affected side.

Premenstrual pain, a cyclical feeling of heavy fullness and tenderness, is usually at its peak during the days leading up to a menstrual period. The pain is felt **during or between feedings in both breasts**, and it occurs because the breasts are swollen with blood and lymph fluid before menstruation. This is perfectly normal in many women. The symptoms typically disappear soon after the start of menstruation.

Very large breasts are heavy and can pull on the connective tissues above the breast. In this case, **when the mother applies gentle pressure, tenderness would be felt above the breasts where they join the chest wall and near the third rib. Pain is independent of feedings**. A different style or size of bra— for example, one with a fuller or deeper cup—may help relieve the pain. Using a folded towel under a large breast can help to support its weight during feedings.

Breast Problems

Fibrocystic disease does not have a generally agreed-upon definition and its existence is the subject of controversy. Some describe it simply as breast lumpiness (Love 1995). Many women have other symptoms, which may or may not be related to their breast lumps, such as breast pain and tenderness. The pain could be **in one breast or both during or between feedings but it usually only occurs or is at its worst in the days preceding a menstrual period**. If the mother feels this may be causing her deep breast pain, suggest she see her doctor. Reducing or eliminating caffeine from their diet has brought relief for some women.

Crash dieting. Some women have reported deep breast pain during crash diets. Once they stopped dieting, the pain stopped. There is no explanation for this occurrence at the present time.

After considering possible causes, if the cause of the breast pain is still unclear and the pain continues, suggest the mother see her doctor.	Unexplained breast pain is the one of the warning signs of a breast tumor. If no other causes can be determined and the pain continues, suggest the mother see her doctor to rule out this possibility.

BREASTFEEDING AFTER BREAST SURGERY OR INJURY

General Considerations

When a woman who has had previous breast surgery or a breast injury is considering breastfeeding, her first concern may be whether her surgery or injury will affect her ability to produce enough milk for her baby.

If the mother has had breast surgery, ask her where her incisions are located and if she knows what was done during her surgery. If her milk ducts and major nerves are intact, she should be able to breastfeed.

A woman who has had breast surgery may be worried about her ability to produce enough milk for her baby. If her milk ducts and major nerves were not cut or damaged, her milk supply may not be affected. If her incisions are located exclusively in the fold under her breast, chances are no milk ducts or nerves were cut. If her incisions are near the armpits and the surgeon took care not to damage any major nerves, breastfeeding will probably not be affected.

Incisions around the areola almost always indicate some cut milk ducts and possible nerve damage. In one study (Neifert 1990), researchers found that women with incisions around the areola were nearly five times more likely to have insufficient milk than were those who did not have breast surgery. Another study (Hurst 1996) found that none of the 11 women with incisions around the areola produced sufficient milk to exclusively breastfeed their babies. Half of the women with incisions in the fold under the breast and near the armpit produced sufficient milk.

If the mother is unsure about how her surgery was performed, suggest she ask her surgeon.

If the mother has had a breast injury, ask her to describe her injury. The same general principles apply to her as apply to the woman who has had breast surgery.

A woman who has had a breast injury may be worried about her ability to produce enough milk for her baby. The same principles apply to her as apply to the woman who has had breast surgery. If her milk ducts and major nerves were not damaged, her milk supply should not be affected. A loss of sensation in one or both breasts may indicate that there is nerve damage, and there is a possibility that her let-down, or milk-ejection, reflex might be affected in that breast. A loss of sensation may reduce the nerve stimulation from the nipple to the mother's pituitary. Adequate nerve stimulation is necessary to stimulate the let-down reflex, as well as the release of prolactin, which maintains milk production.

Nipple injuries or burns can sometimes affect breastfeeding.

If the mother's nipples were injured—for example, if they were burned—her ability to breastfeed would depend on how well the milk was able to flow through them.

The only way for the mother to know for sure if she can breastfeed is to try. Attempting to express colostrum during pregnancy is not a reliable gauge of how breastfeeding will proceed, as many mothers who are unable to express colostrum go on to breastfeed with no problems. If the mother can express colostrum during her pregnancy, however, it would be an indication that her breasts are functioning normally.

Some mothers with burned nipples have scar tissue that makes breastfeeding painful. Again, the only way the mother will know if she can breastfeed comfortably is to try. If breastfeeding is painful, the mother will need to decide if she is willing to continue breastfeeding in spite of the pain.

If only one breast is affected, the mother should be able to breastfeed using the unaffected breast only.

If the mother has had surgery or sustained an injury on one breast only, breast-feeding may not be affected, as most mothers are capable of nursing twins and even women who have had one breast removed due to mastectomy can produce enough milk for their babies by nursing frequently on the remaining breast. (See "One-Sided Nursing" in the chapter "Fussy at the Breast and Breast Refusal.")

Encourage the mother who is worried about her ability to breast-feed to learn as much as she can about breastfeeding before her baby is born to increase her self-confidence and her ability to evaluate her own experience.

Many women find after surgery or an injury that they lose confidence that their bodies will function normally. Even if the mother is told that her surgery or injury will not affect breastfeeding, she may still feel insecure about her ability to breast-feed. Once a mother who has had breast surgery or a breast injury gives birth, she may be more likely than the average mother to doubt that breastfeeding is going well and blame her surgery or injury for any concern or difficulty.

Before her baby is born, encourage the mother to:

- learn as much as she can about the normal course of breastfeeding by reading about breastfeeding from reliable sources,
- find a doctor who is supportive of breastfeeding and can help her evaluate how breastfeeding is going on the basis of accurate, up-to-date information, and
- attend local La Leche League Group meetings, so that she can hear the experiences of other breastfeeding mothers and better gauge whether her own experiences fall within the norm.

Emphasize the importance of learning the basics of breastfeeding, not just information relating to her special situation. If she feels uncertain about her ability to breastfeed—even more than the average mother—she will need to know before her baby is born:

- what she can do to get breastfeeding off to a good start;
- the factors that affect milk production, especially the principle of supply and demand;
- the benefits of unrestricted breastfeeding in her baby's first days and, if she plans to have her baby in a hospital, how to increase the likelihood she will not be separated from her baby during this time;
- the reasons for avoiding supplements and artificial nipples and how to make arrangements so that her baby can avoid them; and
- how to tell if her baby is getting enough milk.

If the mother is concerned about producing enough milk for her baby, explain that she will be able to tell if her baby is getting enough simply by counting her baby's wet diapers and bowel movements. In the first few days after birth, one to two wet diapers per day are average. Once her milk becomes more plentiful on the third or fourth day, six to eight wet cloth diapers (five or more disposable diapers) and two or more bowel movements each day are considered adequate. (In babies older than six weeks, fewer bowel movements may be normal.)

Breast Problems

Some women are concerned about whether loss of feeling in their breasts will affect their ability to breastfeed.

Whenever surgery is performed on the breast, loss of sensation is common. Typically, most of the feeling comes back to the breasts within six months to two years after the surgery. Some women experience unusual sensations or extra sensitivity after breast surgery. Usually, the more extensive the surgery, the greater the loss of sensation.

Women who have a breast injury sometimes experience a loss of sensation, too.

If the areola has some feeling, breastfeeding should not be affected, as it is the nerve stimulation of the baby's suck that sends the signals to the brain that initiate milk production. But if there is no sensation at all, this may indicate that major nerves have been damaged. (See the later section, "When Milk Ducts or Major Nerves Have Been Damaged.")

If the woman is making plans for breast surgery and is concerned about how her breast surgery will affect breastfeeding in the future, encourage her to explore options with her surgeon that will be least destructive of milk ducts and breast tissue.

In most types of breast surgery, there is more than one way for the surgery to be performed. Suggest that the mother tell her surgeon about her desire to breastfeed and ask him which of her options involves the least destruction of milk ducts and major nerves.

For the mother considering **breast augmentation surgery**, she can ask her surgeon where he plans to make the incision. An incision around the areola would cut milk ducts and possibly major nerves. An incision in the fold under the breast is less likely to affect breastfeeding, as the milk ducts and major nerves would not be involved. If the surgeon carefully avoids major nerves, an incision near the armpit is less likely to affect breastfeeding. Another consideration is the type of implant. Saline-filled implants do not carry the same possibility of health risks to the mother as silicone-filled implants if the implants should leak.

If the mother is planning to have **breast reduction surgery**, tell her that the surgery may affect her ability to breastfeed, because sections of the breast (including the milk ducts) would be removed. If her nipple is surgically removed and repositioned, the odds of producing a full milk supply are further reduced, as all the milk ducts and major nerves would be cut. However, if the mother explains her desire to breastfeed, her surgeon may be able to use one of the several surgical procedures that leave the nipple connected to the duct system while other tissue is removed (Widdice 1993). The procedures are less destructive of milk ducts and major nerves and will increase her chances of being able to fully breastfeed her baby (Marshall 1994).

If the mother needs to have a breast biopsy performed or a tumor or cyst removed, encourage her to talk to her surgeon about her desire to breastfeed and ask him to try to avoid—as much as he can—cutting milk ducts and major nerves during the surgery.

Breast Augmentation Surgery

Breast augmentation surgery, also known as augmentation mammoplasty, is a procedure that has been performed on more than two million women. Silicone- or saline-filled sacs are implanted under the surface of the breast through an incision that is usually made in the fold under the breast, near the armpit, or around the edge of the areola.

Silicone injections, which were once used to increase breast size, are no longer recommended because they can cause breast inflammation, which results in extensive scarring and milk duct destruction.

Ask the mother where her incisions are located.

If the mother's incisions are in the folds under the breasts or near the armpits, the implants were most likely inserted behind the milk ducts, leaving them undisturbed. If the milk ducts and major nerves have not been cut, breastfeeding may not be affected.

If the mother's incisions are around the areolae, it is likely that at least some of the milk ducts and perhaps the major nerves have been cut. In one study (Neifert 1990), researchers found that women with incisions around the edge of the areola were nearly five times more likely to have insufficient milk than were those without surgery. Another study (Hurst 1996) found that none of the 11 women with incisions around the areola produced sufficient milk to exclusively breastfeed their babies. Half of the women with incisions in the fold under the breast and near the armpit produced sufficient milk. If the mother's incisions are across the areola and nipple, her chances of breastfeeding are low, because milk ducts and nerves had to be cut during surgery (Riordan and Auerbach, p. 389). (See the later section, "When Milk Ducts Have Been Cut or Breast Tissue Damaged.")

Women have scarring inside the breasts after breast augmentation surgery, which sometimes causes breast discomfort.

Although two case reports have raised health concerns about the breastfed children of women with implants, as of this writing, silicone breast implants are considered by most to be compatible with breastfeeding.

All women who have breast augmentation surgery develop scarring inside the breasts, as this is the body's natural reaction to the surgery. In severe cases, it can cause pain and discomfort when the mother breastfeeds.

Two 1994 case reports raised health concerns about the breastfed children of women with silicone implants. Although the authors of one report (Levine and Ilowite 1994) suggested a link between breastfeeding with silicone implants and an unusual gastrointestinal disorder, the report's flaws call this link into question. The US Food and Drug Administration published four responses (1996; 1995; 1994a; 1994b) that called the report "inconclusive and preliminary" due to its small size (eleven children from six families) and selection bias (only children with gastrointestinal disorders were chosen).

The second case report included two initially breastfed children with joint and muscle pains and other autoimmune symptoms (Teuber and Gershwin 1994). The mothers had similar rheumatic symptoms, and there were multiple health problems in other relatives. Once again, small sample size and no comparison group, plus a possible genetic predisposition to these health problems, limit this report's relevance to the population of children at large breastfed by mothers with implants (Berlin 1994).

A follow-up study by Levine, Ilowite, and Teuber (1996) found no significant differences in the level of auto-antibodies in the blood of 122 children born to mothers with or without silicone implants. All the children in the study had rheumatic and/or gastrointestinal problems, but their symptoms did not correlate with their auto-antibody concentrations. There was no difference in the presence of auto-antibodies between the 29 breastfed children and those artificially fed. The authors wrote in their conclusion: "Failure to find any association between clinical symptoms and humoral antibody expression makes one consider whether the symptoms in these children are unrelated to the mothers' silicone implants."

Although one source cautions against breastfeeding with silicone implants (Briggs 1994), other articles and commentaries have concluded that "breast, whether augmented or not, is still best" (Berlin 1994; Flick 1994; Mohrbacher 1994).

It is unlikely that silicone leaks into a mother's milk.

If a mother is concerned about potential silicone leakage into her milk, explain that physical constraints make it unlikely this could happen. The very large size (molecular weight) of the silicone used in breast implants (McEvoy, p. 17-20) is considered too large to pass through the small water-filled pores in the lining of the mother's alveoli, or milk-producing cells (Lawrence, p. 326). In addition, silicone does not dissolve in water, another characteristic that decreases the likelihood of it passing into the milk (Anderson 1991).

There are currently no available standardized tests to detect silicone in a mother's milk or body, but even if there were, their results would be inconclusive because normal levels have not yet been established and because silicone can enter the body from a variety of sources.

Mothers with implants often ask if their milk can be tested for the presence of silicone. However, as of this writing, there is no widely available standardized test to detect silicone in the mother's body or her milk (FDA 1996). Some laboratories test human milk for silicon, a naturally occurring element in the human body and the diet and an indirect measure of silicone. But there is no clear **Breast Problems** connection between the presence of silicon and the presence of silicone. Even if a simple test for silicone were available, however, neither normal nor safe levels of silicone have been determined. Without this information, test results would be meaningless.

Also, because silicone enters our bodies from many sources, if silicone was detected in a woman's body or her milk, there would be no way to determine if the silicone came from her implants (which ordinarily "bleed" silicone even if no rupture exists) or from other sources (FDA 1996). Silicone is commonly used as a coating on fresh fruits and vegetables. Silicone is also routinely ingested from cosmetics and over-the-counter drugs, including antacids. Silicone is used to lubricate syringes. Some pacifiers (dummies) and bottle nipples (teats) are made from silicone. Even infant colic medications contain the same form of silicone as silicone breast implants and are given directly to babies as a gas reducer and to help alleviate colic by coating the babies' digestive system. For these reasons, many individuals without silicone implants also have silicone in their bodies.

Saline implants are considered compatible with breastfeeding.

Saline, or salt water, is a natural body fluid, so if a mother's saline implants leak or rupture, there should be no health risk to mother or baby. Saline implants are encased in a silicone envelope, however. The potential for a reaction to silicone remains, but to a much lesser degree.

It is not known if there are any special breastfeeding considerations for women with polyurethane-coated implants.

About 10% of women with silicone breast implants have a type with polyurethane coating. Media reports raised some concerns about the safety of these implants when it was found that under laboratory conditions the coating of these implants could chemically break down to release small amounts of a substance called TDA, which can cause cancer in animals. There has been no association made with TDA and cancer in humans (FDA 1994b).

It is not known whether women with polyurethane-coated implants need to have any special concerns about breastfeeding their babies. Although according to one report TDA had been found in a single sample of human milk, questions were immediately raised about whether the testing procedure itself had caused the contamination. To answer these concerns, the US FDA has required the manufacturer to conduct studies on these implants, but the results of these studies are not yet known (FDA 1996).

Breast Reduction Surgery

Ask the mother how her surgery was done, how much breast tissue was removed during her surgery, and if her nipples were involved.

Breast reduction surgery, also known as reduction mammoplasty, involves removing part of the breast tissue in order to decrease the size of the breasts. Some milk ducts are almost always cut during a breast reduction. Sometimes the nipple is removed and replaced in a different location, so the breasts look more symmetrical. If the nipple is removed, all milk ducts and major nerves are cut.

The more breast tissue that was removed, the less likely it is that the mother will be able to fully nourish her baby through breastfeeding. If her nipples were removed and repositioned, her chances decrease even more, although there are women whose milk ducts have "recanalized," or grown back. In one reported case (Marmet and Shell 1987), a woman who had breast reduction surgery and whose nipples were removed and repositioned went on to fully breastfeed her baby, but this is rare.

The odds of a mother who has had breast reduction surgery being able to fully nourish her baby by breastfeeding are unknown.

At least some milk ducts are almost always cut during breast reduction surgery, which—depending on how many ducts were cut and whether or not they have "recanalized," or grown back—may reduce the amount of milk available to the baby. The only way the mother can find out if her baby will receive enough milk through breastfeeding is to give it a try. One study evaluated the breastfeeding experiences of 30 women who had undergone breast reduction surgery and found that the women who had surgical procedures in which moderate amounts of breast tissue had been left attached to the nipple sustained their babies more completely on their milk than the women in which little or no breast tissue had been left attached to the nipple (Marshall 1994). For an overview of the research on breast reduction surgery through 1992, see Widdice 1993.

When Milk Ducts or Major Nerves Have Been Cut or Damaged

If a mother's milk ducts were cut during surgery or damaged during injury, this may affect how much milk the baby receives. Although a full supply of milk will be produced in the milk-producing cells (alveoli), some of the milk will not be able to pass through the damaged ducts to reach the nipple. The more ducts that have been damaged, the less milk the baby will receive. However, there are reported cases of mothers' milk ducts "recanalizing," or growing back, after having been cut and the babies satisfying all their nutritional needs through breastfeeding.

Concerns before the Baby's Birth

If some of the mother's milk ducts or major nerves were cut during surgery or damaged from an injury, it may affect the amount of milk the baby receives when he breastfeeds.

If the mother's major nerves were cut during surgery or damaged during injury, she will have little or no feeling in her nipple and areola, which would also reduce her milk production. It is the nerve stimulation of the baby's suck that sends signals to the mother's pituitary gland to release the hormones prolactin and oxytocin that are necessary for the let-down reflex and milk production.

If some or all of the mother's milk ducts or major nerves have been cut or damaged, it is not possible to know before her baby's birth whether or not her baby will receive enough milk at the breast. The only way the mother can know for sure is to try breastfeeding. To prepare herself for breastfeeding, encourage the mother to learn as much as she can about breastfeeding before her baby is born. (See the earlier section, "General Considerations.")

Tell the mother that if her baby does not receive enough milk by breastfeeding alone that partial breastfeeding is possible and that supplementation can be given at the breast or with other methods.

Mention the availability of the nursing supplementer, which would allow the mother to supplement at the breast if her baby is not receiving enough milk from breastfeeding alone. The nursing supplementer offers several advantages:

- the mother and baby can continue to enjoy the closeness of breastfeeding, and
- along with the supplement, the baby would receive whatever mother's milk was available from the breast, so that the baby could continue to receive health benefits from breastfeeding.

If the baby needs a supplement and the mother wants to continue breastfeeding, another option is for her to supplement using any of the alternative feeding methods described in "The Use of Breast Pumps and Other Products." After the early weeks when artificial nipples can lead to nipple confusion, the mother may find it easiest to use bottles to supplement.

When the Mother Begins Breastfeeding

The mother whose milk ducts were cut during surgery or damaged in an injury may have engorged areas in her breasts that do not soften with nursing.

After her baby is born and she begins breastfeeding, the mother may have engorged areas in her breasts that do not soften with nursing. If so, it is likely that some of the milk ducts were cut or damaged and the milk cannot flow through them. Within a few days, the engorged areas should return to normal even if the mother continues to breastfeed. Since the milk is not emptied out, milk production will stop in these areas and the milk will be reabsorbed by the mother's body.

If the mother is uncomfortable, suggest she use cold packs between feedings to help reduce the swelling (see "Engorgement" at the beginning of this chapter) and ask her doctor to recommend pain medication that is compatible with breastfeeding.

The baby's weight should be checked one week after birth. If the baby has fewer than normal wet diapers and bowel movements before then, his weight should be checked earlier.

The mother should plan to have her baby's weight checked when he is one week old. During the first three or four days after birth, the mother should look for one or two wet diapers each day. If, after her milk "comes in," the baby has fewer than six wet diapers and two bowel movements each day despite effective sucking and frequent breastfeeding, the baby may need supplements.

Breast Problems

Assuming breastfeeding is well managed, there are several possible outcomes when a mother's milk ducts have been cut or damaged.

When a mother's breast surgery or injury causes milk ducts to be cut or damaged, there are several possible outcomes when breastfeeding is well managed:

- Breastfeeding progresses normally, because not enough milk ducts or major nerves were cut or damaged to make a significant difference in the

amount of milk the baby receives or because the mother's milk ducts have grown back since being cut or damaged.
- The baby gains well for the first few weeks because the mother's increased levels of hormones after childbirth stimulate extra milk production. Then the baby's weight gain drops off and supplements become necessary (Hatton and Keleher 1983).
- The mother's milk supply is low from the beginning, and the baby needs supplementation early on.

Publications for Parents

Engorgement

La Leche League International. THE WOMANLY ART OF BREASTFEEDING, 35th Anniversary ed. Schaumburg, Illinois, 1991, pp. 56-57, 137-44.

Mohrbacher, N. *When You Breastfeed Your Baby: The First Week.* Schaumburg, Illinois: La Leche League International, 1993. Publication No. 124.

Plugged Ducts and Breast Infections

La Leche League International. THE WOMANLY ART OF BREASTFEEDING, 35th Anniversary ed. Schaumburg, Illinois, 1991, pp. 137-41.

Mohrbacher, N. *Sore Breasts.* Schaumburg, Illinois: La Leche League International, 1993. Publication No. 29.

Breast Lumps

La Leche League International. THE WOMANLY ART OF BREASTFEEDING, 35th Anniversary ed. Schaumburg, Illinois, 1991, pp. 141-43.

Breastfeeding after Breast Surgery or Injury

La Leche League International. THE WOMANLY ART OF BREASTFEEDING, 35th Anniversary ed. Schaumburg, Illinois, 1991, p. 144.

Mohrbacher, N. *Nursing with Breast Implants.* Schaumburg, Illinois: La Leche League International, 1993. Publication No. 24.

References

Engorgement

Auerbach, K. Common signs and symptoms with uncommon outcomes. Presented at Breast Pathology and Lactation Workshop, Rush University, College of Nursing and The Comprehensive Breast Center, Chicago, Illinois, February 24, 1995.

Hill, P. and Humenick, S. The occurrence of breast engorgement. *J Hum Lact* 1994; 10:79-86.

Humenick, S., et al. Breast engorgement: patterns and selected outcomes. *J Hum Lact* 1994; 10:87-93.

Lawrence, R. *Breastfeeding: A Guide for the Medical Profession,* 4th ed. St. Louis: Mosby, 1994, pp. 238-42.

Livingstone, V. Too much of a good thing: maternal and infant hyperlactation syndromes. *Can Fam Phys* 1996; 42: 89-99.

Maher, S. *An Overview of Solutions to Breastfeeding and Sucking Problems.* Schaumburg, Illinois: La Leche League International, 1988. Publication No. 67, pp. 18-19.

Moon, J. and Humenick, S. Breast engorgement: contributing variables and variables amenable to nursing intervention. *JOGNN* 1989; 18:309-15.

Nickodem, V. et al. Do cabbage leaves prevent breast engorgement? A randomized, controlled study. *Birth* 1993; 20:61-64.

Riordan, J. and Auerbach, K. *Breastfeeding and Human Lactation,* Boston and London: Jones and Bartlett, 1993, pp. 227-29, 395-96.

Roberts, K. A comparison of chilled cabbage leaves and chilled gelpaks in reducing brest engorgement. *J Hum Lact* 1995a; 11(1):17-20.

Roberts, K., et al. A comparison of chilled and room temperature cabbage leaves in treating breast engorgement. *J Hum Lact* 1995b; 11(3):191-94.

Rosier, W. Cool cabbage compresses. *Breastfeeding Rev* 1988; 12:28.

Mastitis—Plugged Ducts and Breast Infections, Breast Abscesses

Bertrand, H. and Rosenblood, L. Stripping out pus in lactational mastitis: a means of preventing breast abscess. *Can Med Assoc J* 1991; 145(4):299-306.

Cantlie, H. Treatment of acute puerperal mastitis and breast abscess. *Can Fam Phys* 1988; 34:2221-26.

Conner, A. Elevated levels of sodium and chloride in milk from mastitic breast. *Pediatrics* 1979; 63:910-11.

Foxman, B. et al. Breastfeeding practices and lactation mastitis. *Soc Sci Med* 1994; 38(5):755-61.

Hayes, R. et al. Acute inflammation of the breast—the role of breast ultrasound in diagnosis and management. *Clin Radiology* 1991; 44:253-56.

Hoffman, K. and Auerbach, K. Longterm antibiotic prophylaxis for recurrent mastitis. *J Hum Lact* 1986; 1(4):72-75.

Kaufmann, R. and Foxman, B. Mastitis among lactating women: occurrence and risk factors. *Soc Sci Med* 1991; 33(6):701-05.

Lawrence, R. *Breastfeeding: A Guide for the Medical Profession,* 4th ed. St. Louis: Mosby, 1994, pp. 258 and 260-66.

Breast Problems

Livingstone, V. Too much of a good thing: maternal and infant hyperlactation syndromes. *Can Fam Phys* 1996; 42: 89-99.

Maher, S. *An Overview of Solutions to Breastfeeding and Sucking Problems.* Franklin Park, Illinois: La Leche League International, 1988. Publication No. 67, p. 16.

Marshall, B., Hepper, J. and Zirbel, C. Sporadic puerperal mastitis: an infection that need not interrupt lactation. *JAMA* 1975; 233:1377-79.

Minchin, M. *Breastfeeding Matters: What We Need to Know about Infant Feeding.* Australia: Alma Publications, 1989. p. 156.

Riordan, J. Mastitis: a new look at an old problem. BREASTFEEDING ABSTRACTS 1990; 10:1.

Riordan, J. and Auerbach, K. *Breastfeeding and Human Lactation,* Boston and London: Jones and Bartlett, 1993, pp. 381-98.

Riordan, J. and Nichols, F. A descriptive study of lactation mastitis in long-term breastfeeding women. *J Hum Lact* 1990; 6(2):53-57.

Thullen, J. Management of hypernatremic dehydration due to insufficient lactation. *Clin Pediatr* 1988; 27:370-72.

Breast Lumps

Beekman, W. et al. Silicone breast implant bleed and rupture: clinical diagnosis and predictive value of mammography and ultrasound. *Ann of Plas Surg* 1996; 36(4):345-47.

Hayes, R. et al. Acute inflammation of the breast—the role of breast ultrasound in diagnosis and management. *Clin Radiology* 1991; 44:253-56.

Lawrence, R. *Breastfeeding: A Guide for the Medical Profession,* 4th ed. St. Louis: Mosby, 1994, pp. 259 and 527-28.

Love, S. *Dr. Susan Love's Breast Book.* Reading, Massachusetts: Addison-Wesley, 1995. pp. 73-84.

Riordan, J. and Auerbach, K. *Breastfeeding and Human Lactation,* Boston and London: Jones and Bartlett, 1993, pp. 390-91.

Skolnick, A. Ultrasound may help detect breast implant leaks. *JAMA* 1992; 267(6):786.

Blood in the Milk

Kline, T. and Lash, S. The bleeding nipple of pregnancy and postpartum period: a cytologic and histologic study. *Acta Cytol* 1964; 8:336.

Lawrence, R. *Breastfeeding: A Guide for the Medical Profession,* 4th ed. St. Louis: Mosby, 1994, pp. 525-27.

O'Callaghan, M. Atypical discharge from the breast during pregnancy and/or lactation. *Aust NZ Obstet Gynaecol* 1981; 21:214-16.

Riordan, J. and Auerbach, K. *Breastfeeding and Human Lactation,* Boston and London: Jones and Bartlett, 1993, pp. 391-92.

Deep Breast Pain

Amir, L. et al. *Candidiasis & Breastfeeding*. Lactation Consultant Series. Garden City Park, New Jersey: Avery Publishing, 1995.

Johnstone, H. and Marcinak, J. Candidiasis in the breastfeeding mother and infant. *JOGNN* 1990; 19:171-73.

Lawrence, R. *Breastfeeding: A Guide for the Medical Profession,* 4th ed. St. Louis: Mosby, 1994, pp. 264-65, 266-67.

Love, S. *Dr. Susan Love's Breast Book.* Reading, Massachusetts: Addison-Wesley, 1995. pp. 73-84.

Riordan, J. and Auerbach, K. *Breastfeeding and Human Lactation,* Boston and London: Jones and Bartlett, 1993, p. 387.

Breastfeeding after Breast Surgery or Injury

Anderson, P. Drug use during breastfeeding. *Clin Pharmacy* 1991; 10:595.

Berlin, C. Silicone breast implants and breastfeeding. *Pediatrics* 1994; 94(4):547-49.

Briggs, G., Freeman, R., and Yaffe, S. Update to Drugs in Pregnancy and Lactation 1994; 7:13-15.

Courtiss, E. and Goldwyn, R. Breast sensation before and after plastic surgery. *Plast Reconstr Surg* 1976; 58:1.

Flick, J. Silicone and espophageal dysmotility: are breastfed infants at risk? *JAMA* 1994; 271:240-41.

Food and Drug Administration. Study of children breastfed by women with breast implants. *FDA Talk Paper,* January 21, 1994a. T94-6.

Food and Drug Administration. Breast implants: an information update. Rockville, Maryland USA: *US FDA,* July 1995. pp. 14, 17, 30-31.

Food and Drug Administration. Breast implants: an information update. Rockville, Maryland USA: *US FDA,* June 1994b. pp. 1011, 19-20.

Food and Drug Administration. Breast implants: an information update. Rockville, Maryland USA: *US FDA,* March 1996. pp. 15, 22-23, 30-31.

Hatton, M. and Keleher, K. Breastfeeding and breast reduction mammoplasty. *J Nurse-Midwife* 1983; 28(4):19-22.

Hurst, N. Lactation after augmentation mammoplasty. *Obstet Gynecol* 1996; 87(1):30-34.

Lawrence, R. *Breastfeeding: A Guide for the Medical Profession,* 4th ed. St. Louis: Mosby, 1994, pp. 326 and 528-31.

Levine, J. et al. Lack of auto-antibody expression in children born to mothers with silicone breast implants. *Pediatrics* 1996; 97(2):243-45.

Breast Problems

Levine, J. and Ilowite, N. Scleroderma-like esophageal disease in children breast-fed by mothers with silicone breast implants. *JAMA* 1994; 271:213-16.

Marmet C. and Shell, E. Breastfeeding in Unusual Circumstances: An Overview. Presented at LLLI's 11th International Conference, 1987. (Audiocassette available from La Leche League International.)

Marshall, D. et al. Breastfeeding after reduction mammaplasty. *Br J Plast Surg* 1994; 47:167-69.

McEvoy, G. *American Hospital Formulary Service Drug Information,* 3rd ed. Bethesda, Maryland: American Society of Hospital Pharmacists, 1992, p. 17-20.

Mohrbacher, N. Breastfeeding with silicone breast implants: are there risks? *Rental Roundup,* Medela, Inc. 1994; 11:8-9.

Neifert, M. et al. The influence of breast surgery, breast appearance, and pregnancy-induced breast changes on lactation sufficiency as measured by infant weight gain. *Birth* 1990; 17:31-38.

Riordan, J. and Auerbach, K. *Breastfeeding and Human Lactation,* Boston and London: Jones and Bartlett, 1993, pp. 387-91.

Soderstrom, B. Helping the woman who has had breast surgery: a literature review. *J Hum Lact* 1993; 9(3): 169-71.

Teuber, S. and Gershwin, M. Autoantibodies and clinical rheumatic complaints in two children of women with silicone gel breast implants. *Int Arch Allergy Immunol* 1994; 103:105-08.

Widdice, L. The effects of breast reduction and breast aumentation surgery on lactation: an annotated bibliography. *J Hum Lact* 1993; 9(3):161-67.

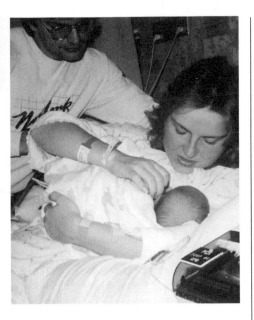

22

Cesarean Birth

THE MOTHER'S FEELINGS
  The Unexpected Cesarean
  The Planned Cesarean

ADVANTAGES OF BREASTFEEDING TO THE MOTHER

BREASTFEEDING IN THE HOSPITAL
  Choice of Anesthetic
  Access to Baby
  Avoid Supplements and Artificial Nipples
  Medication
  Finding a Comfortable Nursing Position

THE FIRST WEEKS AT HOME

The cesarean mother can breast-feed, but her hospital experience and her feelings may be different from the mother who gives birth vaginally.

Research has found that regardless of how her baby was born, a woman's commitment to breastfeeding is the most important factor in her success (Janke 1988). However, the hospital and postpartum experiences of the mother who gives birth by cesarean will differ from those of the mother who gives birth vaginally. The mother who has a cesarean has a longer hospital stay, her discomfort is greater, she may not have easy access to her baby while she is in the hospital, and she may be more dependent upon hospital personnel for assistance. Also, her feelings about herself and her baby may be different, especially if the cesarean was unexpected.

THE MOTHER'S FEELINGS

Having a cesarean can affect how a mother feels about herself, her baby, and breastfeeding.

The Unexpected Cesarean

A mother who has an unexpected cesarean may have strong feelings of guilt, inadequacy, anger, and disappointment.

Most cesareans are unplanned. A woman who had expected a natural birth but ends up with a cesarean may feel guilty, inadequate, or angry for not living up to her own and her partner's expectations. She may feel regret over the loss of her birth plan and cheated out of the experience she had wanted. She may even feel "disfigured" or less attractive.

Her feelings about her baby can be affected, too. She may feel angry with her baby if the cesarean was performed because he was "too big" or turned the wrong way. She may feel detached from her baby if she was unconscious during the birth or if she and the baby were separated for many hours after birth.

She may also have negative feelings about others. She may be angry at her doctor for choosing to do the cesarean or her husband for not understanding her feelings.

Touching and holding her baby can help the mother feel better.

Time spent touching and holding her baby can be comforting to the mother and help mother and baby establish their relationship.

Whatever the mother's feelings, encourage her to talk about them and seek support.

Emotional scars are more likely to form if the mother keeps her feelings bottled up inside. So that she has an outlet to express her feelings and feel supported, encourage the mother to contact her closest cesarean support group. (See "Other Resources" at the end of this chapter.)

The Planned Cesarean

A mother who knows she will be having a cesarean is more likely to come to terms with it emotionally before birth. She will also have the opportunity to make plans with her doctor and hospital.

If a mother has time to adjust emotionally to the idea of a cesarean birth it is likely that she will be more comfortable with the reality. She will also have the time and opportunity to make plans for her birth and postpartum period and discuss with her doctor any individual arrangements she would like concerning the birth and her hospital stay.

When choosing a health care facility and a doctor for her baby, suggest the mother ask about routine policies that may affect breastfeeding.

Hospital policies have a greater effect on breastfeeding if the mother has a cesarean, because her hospital stay will be longer than a mother who delivers vaginally and she will be more dependent on hospital personnel for assistance. The first week after birth can be a sensitive time for both mother and baby, so the environment during this time should be supportive. Policies that promote breastfeeding include:

- no routine pacifiers or bottles;
- regular educational programs for nurses on how to help mothers breast-feed;

- no routine separation of mother and baby after birth if both are healthy (some hospitals and doctors require a mandatory observation period in the nursery for all babies born by cesarean);
- optional twenty-four-hour rooming-in.

Hours of rooming-in vary widely, even among hospitals in the same area. When checking on rooming-in policies, suggest the mother ask specific questions, such as, "Can the baby stay with me at night?" "Can someone stay overnight with me to help with the baby?" and "Can I keep my baby during visiting hours?" In some hospitals, rooming-in is available only in private rooms, so the mother may want to ask if there may be restrictions based on the accommodations.

Suggest the mother also talk to her baby's doctor about these concerns, as they may fall under the doctor's, rather than the hospital's, jurisdiction. If the hospital does not have a policy against routine bottles or pacifiers, suggest the mother have the doctor give her orders in writing that her baby is to receive no bottles and pacifiers. Then suggest she make copies of these written orders and bring them with her to the hospital when she gives birth.

ADVANTAGES OF BREASTFEEDING TO THE MOTHER

Breastfeeding offers advantages to the mother who has had a cesarean.

No matter how a baby is delivered, breastfeeding early and often offers many health advantages to both mother and baby (see "In the Early Days" in the chapter "Breastfeeding Basics."), but there are some advantages that may be particularly important to the mother who has had a cesarean.

- The baby's sucking stimulates the mother's uterus to contract more quickly and speeds her healing.
- Breastfeeding can bring mother and baby emotionally closer, which may be especially important if they are separated after birth or the birth was traumatic.
- Breastfeeding can help the mother feel competent and whole.

BREASTFEEDING IN THE HOSPITAL

Choice of Anesthetic

The type of anesthetic that is used during a cesarean affects how soon the mother can begin breastfeeding.

If a regional anesthetic was used and both mother and baby are alert and healthy, the baby can breastfeed in the delivery room.

Unless an emergency cesarean is performed, where every second counts, the mother may be given the choice of a general or regional anesthetic. If a regional (spinal or epidural) is used, a mother can be awake for her baby's birth and can breastfeed for the first time right on the delivery table in the operating room although she will need help in putting the baby to breast.

During the time after her baby is delivered but before the regional anesthetic wears off, the mother will be alert, free of pain, and excited about the baby, which is an especially good time to start breastfeeding. Focusing on the baby will also help decrease the mother's anxiety and foster her attachment to her baby.

If the mother decides to breastfeed on the delivery table, she may have to nurse while lying on her back. If she has had a spinal anesthetic, she will need to remain flat to prevent a spinal headache. Also, one or both arms may be restrained if an IV is still in place.

The mother may be able to turn to one side and breastfeed in a side-lying position once her incision has been closed. The baby's father or a nurse can help the mother get the baby into position and arrange pillows for the mother's comfort. Or, if pillows are not available, the baby's father could physically support her while she nurses.

Cesarean Birth

If a general anesthetic was used, the mother may breastfeed as soon as she feels able and the baby is ready to take nourishment by mouth.

If a mother is given a general anesthetic, she may be unconscious for a while after her baby's birth and may be groggy for some time after that, delaying the beginning of breastfeeding. As soon as the mother feels able to breastfeed, she should be encouraged to. Little anesthetic will remain in her system at that point and will not be harmful to her baby (Spigset 1994).

Access to the Baby

Breastfeeding Is Easier If Mother and Baby Can Be Together

Breastfeeding goes more smoothly when mother and baby can be together around the clock and nurse unrestrictedly.

Early and unrestricted breastfeeding offers health benefits for both mother and baby and prevents many common difficulties, such as engorgement in the mother and nipple confusion in the baby. For more information, see "In the Early Days" in the chapter "Breastfeeding Basics."

Although one study found that the first feeding tends to occur later when a baby is born by cesarean (Kearney 1990), early and unrestricted breastfeeding is not as impractical as it may seem for the mother who has had a cesarean if she has extra help in the early days. Many hospitals offer the option of having the baby's father or another helper stay in the mother's room around the clock, although in some hospitals this may be possible only if the mother arranges for a private room.

Twenty-four-hour rooming-in makes unrestricted breastfeeding easier, although the mother would need to arrange for extra help at first.

If the father or another helper stays with the mother (hiring a private-duty nurse who is knowledgeable about breastfeeding is another option if family or friends are unavailable), the mother will receive the help she needs with changing the baby's diapers, putting the baby to breast, and switching the baby from side to side while she is lying down. Hospital nurses may be available to fill in if a helper can't be there for a time.

In addition to the satisfaction of caring for her baby, rooming-in offers other advantages to the mother who has had a cesarean.

- If the baby is sleepy, the mother can be aware of her baby's sleeping and waking cycles and take advantage of the times baby is alert or stirring to nurse him.
- Since the baby does not spend time in the nursery, she can be sure the baby is not receiving bottles or other artificial nipples, which could confuse him and interfere with breastfeeding.

If the mother and baby are separated after birth, they can still breastfeed.

If the mother and baby cannot be together after birth, due to health problems or hospital policies, they can still breastfeed when they are together, and in the meantime the mother can express her milk for her baby, which can be given to him when he is ready to take his nourishment by mouth. (See "When Breastfeeding Is Delayed after Birth" in the chapter "Expression and Storage of Human Milk.")

A fever in the mother—whether it is low-grade or high—need not always mean separation of mother and baby.

Some hospitals or doctors routinely isolate a mother from her baby when the mother begins to run a fever. But a low-grade fever is common in mothers in the early days of breastfeeding and should not be considered a health risk to the baby.

As a result of their surgery, mothers who have had a cesarean tend to develop more infections and run more fevers during their postpartum period than mothers who deliver vaginally. The most common sites of infection are the incision and the mother's urinary tract, resulting from the use of the catheter following surgery.

There is no advantage to separating mother and baby when the mother is running a fever—even if her incision is infected—as long as she cleans her hands before holding her baby. If the doctor recommends the mother be isolated away from her baby, suggest the mother ask that she and her baby be isolated together.

Avoid Supplements and Artificial Nipples

Weight loss during the first three to four days after birth is normal.

Water and formula supplements are not needed and should not be given.

When artificial nipples are given to a baby during his early weeks, they can cause nipple confusion.

If the doctor recommends water supplements, suggest the mother offer to breastfeed more frequently instead.

Medication

Antibiotics and medications used for pain relief are almost always compatible with breastfeeding.

Suggest the mother take pain medication as needed, rather than the standard amount.

Finding a Comfortable Nursing Position

There are several breastfeeding positions that will allow a mother to nurse without putting pressure on her incision.

Most infants lose weight until their mothers' milk becomes more plentiful on the third or fourth day. A weight loss of 5% to 7% is considered normal (DeMarzo 1991). This normal weight loss is due to the shedding of excess fluids in the baby's tissues at birth and the passage of meconium (the first stool).

If the mother breastfeeds her baby frequently (at least every two to three hours) and the baby is breastfeeding well, there is no need for routine supplements (Sozmen 1992). Glucose or plain water supplements are offered routinely to newborns in many hospitals, but they are not needed and should not be given as they offer no benefits and can cause breastfeeding problems. (For more information, see "In the Early Days" in the chapter "Breastfeeding Basics.")

Encourage the mother to nurse frequently and give her baby all his feedings at the breast. Artificial nipples—bottles, pacifiers, and nipple shields (rubber nipples placed over a mother's nipples while she breastfeeds)—do more harm than good while a baby is learning to breastfeed. A baby who receives both artificial nipples and the breast during his first three or four weeks is at risk of becoming confused.

Suggest that the mother ask her baby's doctor to give her written orders saying that her baby is not to receive artificial nipples.

If the doctor is concerned about the amount of fluids the baby is receiving, suggest the mother offer to breastfeed more often to increase her milk supply and the amount of fluids the baby receives.

Although most medications given to a breastfeeding mother pass into her milk to some degree, most antibiotics and medications used for pain relief have not been shown to affect the baby. Because the first milk, colostrum—although very concentrated—is small in quantity, the amount of medication the baby will receive through his mother's milk will also be small.

If there is any question about a particular medication, a doctor can almost always find information on its concentration in human milk or effect on the baby and, if necessary, prescribe a substitute. (For more information, see the chapter "Drugs, Vitamins, Vaccines, and Diagnostic Tests.")

Because the pain medication taken by a breastfeeding mother may sometimes make her baby drowsy, encourage the mother to take the minimum amount of pain medication she needs to stay comfortable. Often pain medication is distributed routinely in standard amounts without regard for individual needs.

After a cesarean, many mothers find it difficult at first to find a comfortable nursing position, because they have to work around a painful incision and an IV, either in the hand or arm. Each mother needs to experiment to find the positions that feel best to her. There are several alternatives that will not put pressure on the mother's incision:

- Side-lying—with the mother and baby lying on their sides facing each other.
- The football or clutch hold—with the mother sitting upright in the bed or on a chair and the baby resting on a pillow held along the mother's side with his legs bent at the hips and his bottom against the back of the chair or bed.
- The cradle or cross-cradle hold—with the mother sitting up in the bed or on a chair and the baby facing mother chest-to-chest horizontally while resting on a pillow covering the mother's abdomen.

Cesarean Birth

Many mothers find nursing while lying on their side the most comfortable during the first day or so. It's also an easy way to nurse and rest at the same time. (Also see "Common Breastfeeding Positions" in the chapter "Positioning, Latch-On, and the Baby's Suck.")

Some mothers find it more comfortable to breastfeed in a chair than in bed.

Extra pillows and rolled up baby blankets or towels may add to a mother's comfort in the early days.

Suggest the mother bring with her or request several extra pillows to support the different parts of her body—her legs, back, feet, and head—while she tries to get comfortable. A small pillow or a rolled-up baby blanket or towel can also help protect her incision while she nurses lying down. A rolled-up baby blanket or towel can also be helpful if the mother has large breasts, as she can put it under her breasts for extra support when she nurses sitting up.

How to get into the side-lying position and shift from side to side using the bed rails for support.

Here is a step-by-step guide for getting into the side-lying position:

- Begin with the bed in a flat position and side rails up.
- Use extra pillows behind the mother's back for extra support.
- Then carefully roll to one side while grasping the side rail and relaxing the abdominal muscles. Move slowly to avoid strain.
- To protect the incision from the baby's kicking, cover the abdomen with a small pillow, a towel, or a rolled-up blanket.
- To minimize the strain on stomach muscles, flex the legs and place a pillow between them for more support.
- Lean back into the pillows behind the back.

To shift from side to side, the mother can either hold her baby to her chest with one arm and use the other arm to grasp the side rails or ask her helper or a nurse to move the baby to her other side before she begins. Then she should:

- Turn her hips a little at a time with her feet positioned flat on the bed.
- Move slowly, being careful not to pull suddenly, as it could pull on the incision.
- Hold on to the side rails for support.
- Reposition the pillows.

When using the side-lying position, the baby should be placed on his side facing the mother's body—chest to chest—so he doesn't have to turn his head to nurse. The baby's knees should be drawn in close to the mother's body with his head either lying on the bed or on the mother's arm, whichever feels more comfortable. The mother can either roll her body toward her baby to latch him on or she can pull her baby toward her.

If the baby latches onto the breast well, the mother will be able to avoid or minimize sore nipples in the early days.

If the baby nurses only on the tip of the nipple, soreness is almost sure to result. Making sure the baby opens his mouth wide and latches on well behind the nipple itself will help avoid soreness for the mother and the baby will more effectively stimulate milk production and receive more nourishment for his efforts. (See "Latch-On" in the chapter "Positioning, Latch-On, and the Baby's Suck.")

The mother can request her IV be repositioned if it restricts her freedom of movement.

If the mother's IV is inserted into the back of her hand, she may find it restricts her movement, making it more difficult to maneuver her baby into a comfortable nursing position. Also, a supporting board is sometimes attached to the mother's hand to keep her IV in place.

If the mother feels her IV or supporting board is interfering with her ability to handle her baby comfortably, she can request the IV be inserted into her forearm and have the supporting board be removed, with extra tape used to secure the IV tubing.

Encourage the mother to ask for help when she needs it, as she will need assistance in the early days after her surgery.

If the mother doesn't bring her own helper with her to the hospital, or if her helper is not available twenty-four hours a day, the mother will need to ask the hospital staff for help when lifting or changing her baby and in moving from side to side while she is lying down.

THE FIRST WEEKS AT HOME

Once she gets home, the mother should plan to spend most of her time resting and leave household tasks to others while she recuperates.

Because she has had major abdominal surgery as well as having given birth, the mother will need plenty of rest when she goes home. To avoid having to get up and down often, suggest the mother keep the baby close, either in bed with her or in a cradle or bassinette near her bed. With diapers and changing equipment at hand and a pitcher of juice or water and a snack, the mother may not have to get up for several hours, yet she'll get the rest she needs while getting to know her baby better.

Suggest that the mother—if at all possible—find someone to help with cooking and other household tasks. Her doctor will tell her when she is ready to ease into normal activities.

Good nutrition and plenty of fluids are important to the quick healing of the mother who has had a cesarean.

A nutritious diet and plenty of fluids are important for recovery. Surgery tends to deplete the body of vitamins, minerals, and other nutrients, and the mother will need to be sure to eat healthy foods in order to replenish her nutritional reserves so that her tissues will heal quickly.

Resources for Parents

ICAN (International Cesarean Awareness Network),
1304 Kingsdale Avenue, Redondo Beach CA 90278.
Telephone: 310-542-6400
Fax: 310-542-5368

Publications for Parents

Rosen, M. and Thomas, L. *The Cesarean Myth*. New York: Penguin, 1989.

La Leche League International. THE WOMANLY ART OF BREASTFEEDING, 35th Anniversary ed., Schaumburg, Illinois, 1991, pp. 23-25, 282-86.

Mohrbacher, N. and Stock, J. *Breastfeeding after a Cesarean Birth*. Schaumburg, Illinois: La Leche League International, 1988. Publication No. 80.

References

DeMarzo, S. et al. Initial weight loss and return to birth weight criteria for breastfed infants: challenging the 'rules of thumb.' *Am J Dis Child* 1991; 145:402.

Janke, J. Breastfeeding duration following cesarean and vaginal births. *J Nurs Midwif* 1988; 33:159-64.

Kearney, M. et al. Cesarean delivery and breastfeeding outcomes. *Birth* 1990; 17(2):97-103.

Lawrence, R. *Breastfeeding: A Guide for the Medical Profession,* 4th ed. St. Louis: Mosby, 1994, pp. 473-74.

Riordan, J. and Auerbach, K. *Breastfeeding and Human Lactation*. Boston and London: Jones and Bartlett, 1993, pp. 223-27.

Sozmen, M. Effects of early suckling of cesarean-born babies on lactation. *Biol Neonate* 1992; 62:67-68.

Cesarean Birth

Spigset, O. Anaesthetic agents and excretion in breast milk. *Acta Anaesthesiol Scand* 1994; 38:94-103.

Victora, C. et al. Caesarean section and duration of breast feeding among Brazilians. *Arch Dis Child* 1990; 65:632-34.

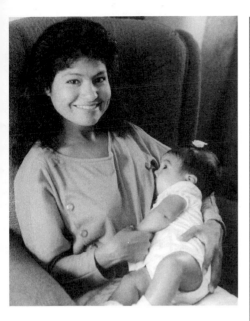

23

Health Problems—Mother

WHEN MOTHER IS ILL
    Listen, Accept the Mother's Feelings, and Discuss Options
    Specific Illnesses

WHEN MOTHER IS HOSPITALIZED
    Planned Hospitalization
    Unexpected Hospitalization

CHRONIC ILLNESS OR PHYSICAL LIMITATION
    General Considerations
    Specific Conditions

POSTPARTUM DEPRESSION

WHEN MOTHER IS ILL

Listen, Accept the Mother's Feelings, and Discuss Options

The mother may be feeling over-whelmed and worried, both about herself and her baby.

When a breastfeeding mother is ill, both mother and baby will benefit from continuing to breastfeed in almost all cases.

When a mother becomes ill, her entire household may be disrupted. If she is breastfeeding, she not only has her own health problems to contend with, she also may worry about how her illness or her medication(s) may affect her nursing baby.

If her illness is serious or life-threatening, the mother may also be coping with her fear of death.

If the mother has a serious or life-threatening illness, she may be grieving. Listen to her concerns and accept her feelings.

When listening to the mother, it's important to accept her feelings. If her illness is serious, she may be working through her fears and the normal, healthy stages of grief identified by Dr. Elizabeth Kubler-Ross:

- denial,
- anger,
- bargaining,
- depression, and
- acceptance or resignation.

Regardless of her stage of grief, listening is always helpful. Acknowledging a mother's feelings (with comments such as, "You are going through a rough time" or "Go ahead and cry. What a lot to cope with!") lets her know that you are listening and are not uncomfortable with her strong feelings.

The mother's fears and worries are real to her. Expressing them and knowing that her feelings are accepted and that she is being heard may help her move on to the next step: sorting information and decision-making.

Answer her questions and discuss options for keeping her household running and continuing to breastfeed.

Once a mother's feelings have been heard, she may be ready to discuss options and make decisions.

If caring for her baby and family presents a challenge during her illness, discuss ways to simplify housework while continuing to meet the needs of the people in the family. If she has a large family and many responsibilities, suggest getting some outside help in order to keep the household running smoothly.

Talk about ways she can continue to breastfeed and meet her baby's need for her. For example, if her baby is young, it may be practical for the mother to tuck baby into bed with her while she recuperates, breastfeeding him while lying down and keeping supplies nearby for changing his diaper. If her baby is older and more active, she may be able to keep him with her in a closed room along with toys to amuse him while she gets her rest. A nursing toddler may want to spend some time with other family members and come back to the mother every so often to nurse and to "touch base."

If the mother has gotten into a habit of putting others' needs before hers, she may have to make some mental adjustments to make her own needs a priority. If so, encourage her to do what she must to get well, for her family's sake as well as her own.

The mother may be concerned that her medication may not be compatible with breastfeeding.

If a mother is concerned about her medication, suggest she discuss it with her doctor and her baby's doctor. (See the chapter "Drugs, Vitamins, Vaccines, and Diagnostic Tests" and the supplement "The Transfer of Drugs and Other Chemicals into Human Milk" for more information.)

Weaning is rarely necessary, but if it is, discuss ways to make it less stressful for mother and baby.

Weaning is rarely necessary when a breastfeeding mother is ill. But if the mother must wean her baby, either temporarily or permanently, talk to her about how to make this process less stressful both physically and emotionally for her and her baby.

If she must suspend breastfeeding temporarily, talk to her about the how-to's of milk expression (see "When Breastfeeding Is Temporarily Interrupted" in the chapter "Expression and Storage of Human Milk"). Even if she can't give her milk to her baby, regular expressing will keep her comfortable and keep up her milk supply until her baby can breastfeed again.

If she must wean her baby permanently (for example, if she will be undergoing chemotherapy for cancer), find out how soon her baby must be weaned and help her come up with a timetable for eliminating nursings that will allow weaning to be as gradual as possible. (See the chapter "Weaning.")

Specific Illnesses

Cancer

Breastfeeding can continue through most diagnostic tests.

Cancer is a disease in which malignant body cells multiply rapidly. Treatment often controls them. Except for blood cancers such as leukemia, these cells then develop into a malignant tumor that is likely to invade nearby tissues. Many types of cancer, if detected early and treated promptly, can be completely cured. As the cancerous cells spread from the original tumor through the body, the chances for cure decrease.

There are several diagnostic tests that might be used when cancer is suspected:

X-rays. Human milk is not affected by a diagnostic x-ray, and the mother may safely nurse immediately afterward.

Ultrasound and computer axial tomography (CAT) scanning. These noninvasive imaging techniques can be used without interfering with breastfeeding or affecting the milk. Unlike mammograms, ultrasound has been found to be effective in distinguishing solid breast lumps from cysts and abscesses (Hayes 1991).

Magnetic resonance imaging (MRI) is a noninvasive imaging technique that will not affect breastfeeding or the mother's milk. However, as part of an MRI the mother is injected with a dye that has not been investigated to date in pregnant or lactating women, although no adverse effects have been reported. If there is concern about the dye, briefly discarding the milk expressed after receiving the dye is usually all that is necessary. Contact La Leche League International's Center for Breastfeeding Information for the latest information regarding this dye.

Mammograms. A mammogram—which x-rays the breast using very low levels of radiation—can be performed while a mother is lactating, although it is more difficult to read due to the density of a young woman's breast and the extra tissue present during lactation. For more information, see "Breast Lumps" in the chapter "Breast Problems."

Fine-needle aspiration cytologic study. This procedure may be recommended for the mother with a breast lump to determine the nature of a solid mass. This is a quick, nearly painless procedure, which can be performed in a physician's office without the use of local anesthetic. Breastfeeding would not need to be interrupted.

If the suspected cancer is in the mother's breast, see "Breast Lumps" in the chapter "Breast Problems."

Breastfeeding can continue through a biopsy or other surgery.

The mother can continue breastfeeding through a biopsy, as with any other surgery, although she will want to be sure to let her doctor and surgeon know that she is breastfeeding so they can select medications that are compatible with breastfeeding.

If the biopsy is being done on her breast, suggest she ask her surgeon to avoid cutting her milk ducts whenever possible.

Health Problems—Mother

(See "Unexpected Hospitalization of Mother" and "Planned Hospitalization of Mother" later in this chapter for ways to continue breastfeeding through a hospitalization.)

If radioactive compounds are used for cancer diagnosis, the baby would need to be temporarily weaned.

If the mother's doctor feels that radioactive isotope testing is necessary before she can be treated, the baby would need to be temporarily weaned. Because certain radioactive materials tend to accumulate in the milk and are passed on to the baby, the use of radioactive compounds is incompatible with breastfeeding. For more information, see "Diagnostic Tests" in the chapter "Drugs, Vitamins, Vaccines, and Diagnostic Tests."

If the mother must temporarily wean, encourage the mother to regularly express her milk during this time and discard it. (For more information, see "When Breastfeeding Is Temporarily Interrupted" in the chapter "Expression and Storage of Human Milk.") The radioactivity will decline over time, and frequent expressing will help the mother eliminate the radioactivity from her body more quickly. The expressed milk can and should be tested periodically to determine when it is free of radioactivity.

When the mother's cancer is confirmed, she will need to decide about breastfeeding in light of her circumstances and feelings and the type of treatment needed.

Even if no further treatment is needed, some doctors recommend any mother with cancer wean her baby on the theory that breastfeeding is "draining" to the mother. One study (Illingworth 1980) refutes this notion, indicating that breastfeeding may actually take less energy than previously thought by making a mother's metabolism more efficient.

Many mothers feel that breastfeeding makes caring for a baby easier. Breastfeeding can make it easier to calm a fussy baby and make nighttime feedings less disruptive. Also, a mother with cancer may be reluctant to wean prematurely, because the extra closeness of breastfeeding provides needed comfort during an anxious time.

If the mother is told to stop breastfeeding and there are no compelling medical reasons to do so, suggest she first ask herself these questions: Does she want to stop breastfeeding? Does she feel that weaning her baby will make her life easier?

If she wants to continue nursing, suggest she talk with her doctor and share her feelings. If he is still insistent she stop breastfeeding, suggest she ask him for references that support his position. If her doctor is not open to discussion, encourage the mother to seek another opinion, starting first with an obstetrician or pediatrician, in addition to an oncologist.

Breastfeeding can continue while the mother undergoes radiation therapy, provided both breasts are not being radiated.

Like diagnostic x-rays, radiation therapy does not cause human milk to become radioactive, so breastfeeding can continue.

Radiation of the breast, however, damages a woman's breast tissue, which may affect breast development and lactation in that breast at the time of treatment and with subsequent pregnancies (Neifert 1992). One study showed that breast radiation causes "ductal shrinkage, condensation of cytoplasm in cells lining the ducts, atrophy of the lobules, and perilobar and periductal fibrosis" (David 1985).

Studies on women who had undergone radiation therapy to one breast and later became pregnant indicate that some women will produce enough milk to sustain their babies. In one study of thirteen pregnancies, the treated breast produced milk in four cases and failed to produce milk in six cases; milk production was suppressed with drugs in the other three. All reported little or no change in the treated breast during pregnancy (Higgins and Haffty 1994). In another study, eighteen of the fifty-three women (34%) reported some milk production from the irradiated breast and thirteen (24.5%) breastfed, with five (9%) describing their treated breast as smaller. Two-thirds of the nine women who commented on milk production in the treated breast described it as "less but adequate." One baby refused to nurse from the treated breast (Tralins 1995).

Like a mother who has had breast reduction surgery, a mother who has undergone radiation treatments to one breast will not know before her baby's birth if she will produce enough milk to sustain her baby. The only way she can find out is to give breastfeeding a try. If her baby needs more milk than she can produce, she can continue breastfeeding and supplement at the breast with a nursing supplementer or give supplements using other feeding methods.

If only one breast is receiving radiation treatments, breastfeeding can continue on the unradiated breast. The treatments will not affect the function of the other breast.

Chemotherapy and treatment with radioactive compounds is incompatible with breastfeeding, and temporary or permanent weaning will be necessary.

Because radioactive materials are passed on to the baby, the use of radioactive compounds is incompatible with breastfeeding. It may be possible, however, for the mother to return to breastfeeding after her treatment is over. (Some women have gone back to breastfeeding after a break of as long as three or four months.) The mother can begin breastfeeding again after her milk has been tested for radioactivity (a Geiger counter can be used), and it has reached a normal level. Expressing milk frequently will more quickly eliminate the radioactivity from the mother's system. (For information on helping a mother stay comfortable and maintain her milk supply during a temporary weaning, see the section, "When Breastfeeding Is Temporarily Interrupted," in the chapter "Expression and Storage of Human Milk.")

Chemotherapy is the treatment of cancer by powerful anticancer drugs and is considered hazardous to the nursing baby. It is always necessary to wean the baby before chemotherapy is started.

Cardiac Problems or Hypertension

The relaxation of breastfeeding is a special advantage for the woman with cardiac problems or hypertension.

The milk-producing hormone, prolactin, relaxes and soothes the breastfeeding mother, which may be of particular benefit to the woman with cardiac problems or hypertension.

Breastfeeding has not been found to cause extra stress on the heart.

Research on the cardiovascular effects of breastfeeding has found no significant differences in blood pressure or cardiac output in lactating as compared with non-lactating mothers (Robson and Hunter 1989; Robson 1987).

Many medications for cardiac problems and hypertension are considered compatible with breastfeeding.

Diuretics, which promote the passing of urine and keep fluid levels down in the body, are frequently used to treat hypertension. While certain high-dose diuretics suppress lactation, some low-dose diuretics are considered compatible with breastfeeding. Some beta-blockers and other drugs used for cardiovascular treatment are also considered compatible with breastfeeding (Lawrence, pp. 345-48, 512).

Carpal Tunnel Syndrome

Carpal tunnel syndrome occurs when the nerves leading to the hand are compressed by a swelling of the tissues in the wrist as a result of repetitive movements or other causes. Symptoms include numbness and tingling in the hand, along with pain from wrist to shoulder.

Some women develop carpal tunnel syndrome during pregnancy and/or breastfeeding.

When a pregnant woman develops carpal tunnel syndrome, it tends to clear up completely after childbirth, though it may remain a problem during the first month or two of lactation. There are also some cases reported of carpal tunnel syndrome during breastfeeding that begin within a month of birth and only completely resolve after weaning (Wand 1990; Wand 1989; Snell 1980). The majority of these women reported relief from their symptoms through treatments such as wearing a splint at night, keeping the hand elevated, and the use of diuretic drugs.

Health Problems—Mother

Since the mothers had no residual signs or symptoms, continuing to breastfeed while using this type of conservative treatment is appropriate (Yagnik 1987).

Chickenpox

Chickenpox—a common childhood disease that rarely causes complications if a baby catches it after birth—can be fatal in an unborn baby, a very premature baby, or a newborn when contracted *in utero* (congenital chickenpox).

The incubation period for chickenpox is from 11 to 21 days and it is contagious for about seven days.

The incubation period of chickenpox is from 11 to 21 days and the mother will be contagious for about seven days, beginning about two days before the sores, or lesions, appear.

Chickenpox is no longer considered contagious when:

- there have been no new eruptions for seventy-two hours, and
- all the lesions have become crusted.

As most women have had chickenpox during childhood, cases of a mother catching chickenpox before birth are relatively rare.

A blood test will tell an exposed woman whether or not she has immunities to chickenpox.

If a pregnant woman has been exposed to chickenpox and is uncertain whether or not she had it as a child, her doctor can order a blood test to determine if she has immunity to the disease.

If the mother contracts chickenpox within five days before childbirth, the doctor may recommend she and her baby be separated after birth. About half of the babies exposed to chickenpox prenatally will develop a mild case of the disease despite the separation.

If the mother comes down with chickenpox within five days before giving birth and her baby is not born with the disease, some doctors recommend the mother and baby be separated to minimize the chance of infection. About half of the babies will develop a mild case of the disease despite the separation.

When a baby catches chickenpox after birth, it is usually a mild case. If the doctor recommends that the mother and baby be separated, encourage the mother to talk to her baby's doctor about alternatives.

If the mother and doctor agree on separating her from her baby, encourage the mother to regularly express her milk and have it given to her baby. If the mother has chickenpox, the baby will also be given a zoster immune globulin (ZIG) shot, if it is available. (See "When Breastfeeding Is Delayed after Birth" in the chapter "Expression and Storage of Human Milk.")

There is no benefit to delaying breastfeeding after the mother is no longer contagious. For example, if the mother breaks out with the chickenpox rash four days before birth, the baby and mother can be reunited and the baby can breastfeed on his second day with no chance of contagion if the mother's lesions have crusted.

If siblings have chickenpox when baby is ready to come home, the mother can bring the baby home but should keep the siblings away from the baby while they are contagious.

If the baby's siblings have chickenpox when the baby is born, the mother should keep the siblings away from the baby. If the mother has previously had chickenpox herself, the risk of the newborn catching chickenpox is greatly reduced.

Cholera and Typhoid Fever

Breastfeeding protects the baby from cholera and very likely gives protection from typhoid fever as well.

Cholera is caused by bacteria that damage the intestinal lining and cause severe diarrhea and vomiting. The bacteria is spread through polluted water or raw fruits and vegetables in places where sanitation and hygiene are poor. Typhoid fever is an infectious disease spread under unsanitary conditions through contaminated food, drink, or water, but it can also be spread from person to person.

Breastfeeding protects a baby from cholera in two ways. First, if the mother has been exposed to cholera, her breastfed baby will receive protection from the symptoms of cholera through her milk, although the *Vibrio cholerae* bacteria may be found in the exposed baby's system. Second, if the baby is exclusively breastfeeding he will not ingest the polluted water or foods or use feeding implements that have been washed in unclean water, so it is unlikely the baby will contract the disease.

Typhoid fever is also spread in part through unsanitary conditions, so the exclusively breastfed baby would avoid contact with the bacteria through food, drink, or feeding implements. The antibodies in human milk would also offer some protection from diarrhea.

There is no evidence that cholera or typhoid fever can be transmitted through breastfeeding.

A mother with cholera or typhoid fever may be too ill to care for her baby during the acute phase.

Although the breastfeeding mother will not infect her baby, during the acute phase of the illness she may not have the physical strength to care for her baby.

A mother who is too ill to breastfeed on her own will need help in either putting her baby to breast or regularly expressing her milk, so that she does not become engorged or develop mastitis. If her milk is expressed, it could be given to her baby.

Cold, Flu, or Mild Infections

It is best for the baby to keep breastfeeding when his mother has a cold, the flu, or a mild infection.

When the mother is exposed to an illness, such as a cold or the flu, her body very quickly begins producing specific antibodies that protect her breastfeeding baby. By the time the mother begins to feel sick, her baby has already been exposed to her illness. Continuing to breastfeed will help the baby fend off the mother's illness. And if he does get sick, the breastfeeding baby almost always has a milder case because of the antibodies he receives from his mother's milk.

Continuing to breastfeed also has advantages for the mother.

Many mothers find it easy to conserve their strength by tucking the baby into bed with them and breastfeeding lying down when the baby gets hungry. For the sick mother who has to care for her baby alone, breastfeeding makes this easier. She does not have to go out and buy formula or get up and prepare bottles. If the mother has household help, encourage her to breastfeed the baby in bed and then ask her helper to change and entertain the baby while she rests.

Breastfeeding through an illness can add to a mother's feeling of normalcy through a difficult time. Breastfeeding is one way she can contribute to her baby's well-being when she can do little else for him.

On the other hand, abrupt weaning during an illness can compound a mother's physical problems by causing discomfort, engorgement, or even mastitis. In addition to making her physically uncomfortable, sudden weaning can be hard on a mother emotionally.

Abrupt weaning is also difficult for a baby. If his familiar source of nourishment and comfort is suddenly taken away, the baby may be difficult to console, disrupting the household even more. Weaning also increases the baby's risk of becoming ill.

The mother with a fever may need to drink extra fluids.

Fever can reduce the mother's body fluids, which increases her chances of becoming constipated and dehydrated.

The mother can decrease the baby's chances of catching her illness by practicing good hygiene.

Illnesses are usually transmitted through skin contact and secretions from the nose and mouth, not through breastfeeding. When a mother is ill, good hygiene can decrease the baby's chances of catching her illness.

Regular hand-washing, for example, will help prevent transmission through skin contact. Limiting face-to-face contact will help the mother avoid breathing on her baby. In extreme cases, if the mother's illness is highly contagious or potentially serious, wearing a face mask whenever the mother holds the baby will help prevent transmission through breath or nose-and-mouth contact.

Health Problems—Mother

Cytomegalovirus (CMV)

If the baby is exposed to CMV in utero, it is unlikely to cause serious health problems, even if it is transmitted to him through his mother's milk after birth.

Cytomegalovirus (CMV) is one of the five known herpes viruses that infect humans. By the age of fifty, nearly all adults are infected with CMV but few ever show its symptoms, which include fatigue, fever, swollen lymph glands, pneumonia, or liver or spleen defects.

If the mother has CMV during pregnancy, the virus and antibodies to the virus are transmitted to her baby *in utero*. According to studies, CMV appears in the milk of mothers who test positive for the disease, and the virus may also be transmitted through human milk (Hotsubo 1994; Minamishima 1994). One study (Dworsky 1983) found that more than two-thirds of the babies of CMV-positive mothers became infected, even though their mother's milk also contained antibodies that fight CMV. The full-term, healthy babies with CMV exhibited no symptoms of the illness, even though tests confirmed the presence of CMV in their bodies. Two premature babies, however, developed serious health problems.

A premature or otherwise compromised CMV-negative baby is at risk of serious health problems if he is fed milk from a CMV-positive donor.

A baby who is CMV-negative has not received antibodies to the disease from his mother while *in utero*. When a CMV-negative baby, particularly one who is premature or otherwise compromised, is exposed to the virus via human milk from a CMV-positive donor, a serious CMV infection can result (Yeager 1983). There are no reported incidents of health problems in healthy, full-term babies through the transmission of CMV through another mother's milk. Pasteurizing donated milk, as milk banks do, destroys the virus and eliminates the risk of infection. Freezing the milk at -20 degrees C (0 degrees F) for seven days before use has also been reported to destroy the virus. Some experts recommend freezing for only three days (Committee on Infectious Diseases, pp. 74-76; Lawrence, p. 485).

Food Poisoning

As long as the mother's symptoms are confined to her gastrointestinal tract, breastfeeding can continue without interruption.

When a mother eats a food that is contaminated with certain bacteria or toxins, she may develop "food poisoning," which can cause vomiting, abdominal cramps, and diarrhea. Depending on the situation, food poisoning may be caused by botulism, listeriosis, salmonella, shigella, cigutera, *E. coli,* or others.

When the mother has food poisoning, it usually stays localized in her intestinal tract and does not pass into her milk. In the vast majority of cases, food poisoning is a temporary condition and passes within a few days causing no further problems. In this case, it poses no danger to the breastfeeding baby.

The breastfeeding mother with diarrhea and vomiting needs to be sure to drink enough liquids to maintain her fluid balance and avoid dehydration.

Vary rarely, food poisoning may become systemic and breastfeeding should be interrupted until blood tests are negative.

In rare cases, food poisoning becomes systemic (meaning the bacteria have passed into the mother's bloodstream and her milk), and the mother becomes extremely ill. If a blood culture shows a systemic infection, antibiotics are usually given. In this case, breastfeeding should be interrupted until blood tests are negative.

If the mother stops breastfeeding and becomes engorged, suggest that her caregivers help her regularly express her milk to avoid engorgement or mastitis. While her food poisoning is systemic, her milk should be discarded.

Giardia

Giardia itself is not dangerous to the nursing baby, but one medication used to treat it is controversial when used during breastfeeding.

Giardia is a parasitic infection that causes diarrhea and may interfere with the absorption of food. Parasites have caused serious health problems in underdeveloped countries, and parasitic disease is increasing in industrialized countries.

The drug commonly used to treat giardia is Flagyl (metronidazole) and is often prescribed as a single 2-gram dose. Although this drug is prescribed for both premature and full-term babies who have giardia or other infections, the 1994 American Academy of Pediatrics' "Transfer of Drugs and Other Chemicals into Human Milk" places Flagyl in the category "Drugs Whose Effect on Nursing Infants Is Unknown But May Be of Concern" and recommends the mother "discontinue breastfeeding 12-24 h[ours] to allow excretion of dose when single-dose therapy [is] given...." The baby who continues to breastfeed through the single-dose therapy receives 25.3 mg. over the next 48 hours, or about 40% of the newborn treatment dose (Passmore 1988; Drinkwater 1987).

A lower dose of metronidazole taken for a longer course is an alternative to single-dose therapy that research indicates may be compatible with breastfeeding. Passmore (1988) found that 400 mg of metronidazole taken three times per day caused no serious reactions in the infants studied. With this treatment, the babies monitored were found to receive a dose of 6.25 mg per day, or "less than 10% of the recommended daily dose for infants of equivalent age and weight" who are given this drug for giardia or other infections (Passmore 1988). When breastfeeding is interrupted following the 2-gram single-dose therapy, infants who resume nursing after 12 hours and 24 hours receive 9.8 mg and 3.5 mg of metronidazole respectively over the next 48 hours through their mother's milk (Drinkwater 1987; Erickson 1981). The USP DI (1996) lists 250 mg of metronidazole taken three times per day over a five-to-seven day course as one of the standard treatments for giardia. Suggest the mother ask her health care provider if this alternative to single-dose therapy would be appropriate for her and her baby.

Another alternative to temporary weaning is treatment with another drug. According to Ruth Lawrence, MD (personal communication, Lactation Study Center, University of Rochester, NY, 1995), the drug furazolidone can be used to treat giardia and is compatible with breastfeeding in the infant over one month of age. Furazolidone is not considered compatible with breastfeeding in the infant under one month of age and in the infant with the rare G6PD deficiency. Suggest the mother discuss furazolidone as an alternative to metronidazole with her health care provider to determine whether this option would be appropriate for her and her baby.

If the mother temporarily weans during her treatment for giardia, encourage her to regularly express her milk to avoid uncomfortable fullness. She will need to discard her milk during this time. (For more information, see "When Breastfeeding Is Temporarily Interrupted," in the chapter " Expression and Storage of Human Milk.)

Hepatitis A

The mother with hepatitis A can breastfeed.

Hepatitis A is the short-incubation form of viral hepatitis, also called "infectious hepatitis." It is a viral infection of the liver, which causes the liver to become tender and swollen and bilirubin to accumulate in the bloodstream, causing jaundice. It is transmitted through contact with infected blood or bowel movements.

There is no benefit to withholding breastfeeding in hepatitis A.

If the mother is in an acute phase, she may temporarily feel too ill to nurse.

When the mother with hepatitis A is in an acute phase of her illness and symptomatic, the mother may feel too ill to nurse. Breastfeeding may be temporarily suspended until her symptoms subside.

If she must temporarily wean or postpone beginning breastfeeding, talk to the mother about how to express her milk while she is not breastfeeding, so that she can keep up her milk supply and avoid uncomfortable fullness. (See "When Breastfeeding Is Temporarily Interrupted" in the chapter "Expression and Storage of Human Milk. ")

Regardless of maternal clinical symptoms or stage of maternal infection with hepatitis A, the American Academy of Pediatrics Committee on Infectious Diseases (1994) recommends that the infant be treated with one dose of standard gamma globulin intramuscularly. There is no reason for the mother not to breastfeed. In fact, antibodies found in human milk may protect the baby.

Hepatitis B

If a mother is diagnosed with hepatitis B, her baby can be given a vaccine that will allow him to continue breastfeeding without interruption.

Hepatitis B is the virus that causes the long-incubation form of viral hepatitis, also called "serum hepatitis." Hepatitis B has symptoms that are similar to hepatitis A, but they are usually longer lasting. It is spread through contact with saliva, mucus, blood, and other body fluids, as well as from contaminated food. It is also transmitted by sexual activity.

Health Problems—Mother

If a mother has hepatitis B during pregnancy, the newborn may be exposed to the disease by coming in contact with maternal fluids at birth. The American Academy of Pediatrics Committee on Infectious Diseases (1994) recommends that the baby be given hepatitis B hyperimmune gamma globulin within the first twelve hours of life, followed by three doses of hepatitis B vaccine. The baby may be breastfed.

If a mother contracts the illness after pregnancy, her baby (and other members of her family) should be vaccinated and breastfeeding can continue.

Hepatitis C

Hepatitis C is a virus that usually begins with a mild infection (although it may begin without symptoms) and then progresses to jaundice. About half of those who contract hepatitis C develop chronic liver disease, including cirrhosis of the liver. It is spread through needles, blood, and sexual contact. There is no currently known effective treatment for the acute infection.

The risk of transmission of hepatitis C through breastfeeding is considered minimal.

The risk of transmission of the hepatitis C virus (HCV) through breastfeeding is not known (Ruff 1994) but considered minimal. According to the US Food and Drug Administration (1994), there is "no evidence...to support any special treatments or precautions for pregnant women [who are carriers of HCV] and their offspring." The US Centers for Disease Control give no recommendations concerning breastfeeding with hepatitis C, but when contacted, an official stated that under normal circumstances (e.g., mother's nipples not bleeding, no open sores in baby's mouth) breastfeeding is not contraindicated (Eng 1994; Lawrence, p. 208).

Currently available research confirms the minimal risk of contracting HCV infection through breastfeeding. Lin (1995) found no evidence of infection in 11 breastfed babies of HCV-infected mothers during their first year. Ogasawara (1993) found no HCV in the milk of 26 carrier mothers. In one study, however, researchers found the HCV in the milk of two of the seven carrier mothers, one whose baby acquired the infection at ten months of age. Due to the unusual timing of the onset of infection, the researchers attributed this transmission to breastfeeding (Uehara 1993). According to the medical literature to date, the incidence of hepatitis C infection in breastfed infants is the same as that in artificially fed infants born to hepatitis C carrier mothers (Gartner 1996).

A mother in an inactive phase of her illness will need to discuss with her doctor the risks and benefits of breastfeeding.

An HCV-positive mother considering breastfeeding needs to compare the risk of her baby acquiring HCV from breastfeeding with the risks of artificial feeding to her baby's health. According to Lawrence M. Gartner, MD, Professor, Department of Pediatrics, University of Chicago (personal communication, 1994), "While considering the 'theoretical' risk of transmission of hepatitis C in breast milk, one must also consider the equally important theoretical possibility that the breastfed infant of a mother with hepatitis C virus may actually be protected from the development of hepatitis C liver disease....Studies of hepatitis B in China many years ago suggested that breastfed infants of hepatitis B carrier mothers were less likely to develop chronic hepatitis than artificially fed infants. It was believed that a passive-active immunization occurred in these breastfed infants. Clearly, for hepatitis C we have no definite data on this, but the possibility of this occurring is as good as the possibility that breastfeeding increases the risk."

The mother in an active phase of hepatitis C may need to suspend breastfeeding.

When a mother is in an acute phase of her illness, breastfeeding may have to be suspended until her symptoms subside.

If she must temporarily wean, talk to the mother about how to express her milk so that she can keep up her milk supply and avoid uncomfortable fullness. (See "When Breastfeeding Is Temporarily Interrupted" in the chapter "Expression and Storage of Human Milk.")

Other Hepatitic Diseases

Nothing is known about the transmission of hepatitis D, E, F, or G through human milk. It is not known whether human milk offers protection against these viruses.

Hepatitis D, E, F, and G are recently discovered types of hepatitis. Hepatitis D occurs only in those already infected with hepatitis B.

Hepatitis E is transmitted primarily via contaminated water. It is currently found in Asia, Africa, and the Middle East and has a 15-20% mortality rate among women who contract it during pregnancy (Fanous and Balart 1994; Purdy and Krawczynski 1994; Krawczynski 1993).

Nothing is known regarding the transmission of hepatitis D, E, F, or G through human milk or if human milk offers any protection to the babies of women who are carriers of these infections.

Herpes Simplex I (Cold Sores) and II (Genital Herpes)

Breastfeeding can continue if the newborn does not touch the sores.

The herpes virus, which is spread through contact with the sores, has proven fatal to newborn babies up to three weeks of age. Genital herpes sores can be transferred to the breast. A pregnant woman should talk to a doctor knowledgeable about herpes and breastfeeding to decide what precautions to take if she or her husband has recurrent herpes, either cold sores or genital sores.

When a new mother develops a herpes sore, breastfeeding can continue as long as the baby does not touch the sore. Any sores must be covered so that the baby does not touch them. Until all the sores are dried, the mother needs to follow strict precautions:

- wash her hands before holding the baby and after she touches the sores,
- put clean coverings over the sores, and
- avoid kissing the baby when she has a cold sore on or near her mouth.

If a sore appears on the mother's breast, she must cover it. If it is on or near the nipple or areola, she must stop breastfeeding on the affected breast and regularly express her milk until the sore is healed.

If a sore on the mother's breast can be covered so that the baby does not touch it, breastfeeding can continue. But if the sore is on the nipple or areola, or anywhere the baby might come in contact with it while he nurses, the mother may need to express her milk from that breast until the sore heals. She can, however, continue to nurse on the unaffected breast.

If the mother's hand or breast pump touches the sore while the mother is expressing, the milk could become contaminated with the virus. In this case, the milk should be discarded. If the mother's hand or breast pump does not touch the sore, the expressed milk can be given to the baby. One study indicates that mother's milk may offer the newborn some protection from herpes simplex II (Lopez 1990).

A culture of the sore can confirm herpes within a few days.

A herpes infection in a baby younger than four weeks can be a serious and sometimes fatal illness. Older babies rarely develop complications.

Herpes can easily be passed among family members, father to mother, sibling to sibling, mother to baby. In one recorded case, a nursing toddler with a cold sore in his mouth passed herpes to his mother via nursing (Sealander and Kerr 1989).

A herpes infection is serious or life-threatening only if it is acquired *in utero,* at birth, or during the first few weeks of life (Sullivan-Bolyai 1983; Quinn and Lofberg 1978). Following the previously listed precautions can help avoid this possibility.

HIV (AIDS)

Breastfeeding is considered to be a possible route of transmission for HIV, which causes AIDS.

Human immunodeficiency virus (HIV) is transmitted through the exchange of blood and other body fluids. Infection with HIV eventually results in the development of Acquired Immune Deficiency Syndrome (AIDS), which destroys the immune system and allows the invasion of opportunistic infections, which cause death.

Although many HIV-positive women around the world have breastfed without transmitting HIV to their babies, breastfeeding is considered to be a possible route of transmission. One researcher isolated the virus in human milk (Thiry 1985), and a number of case reports document the presumed transmission of HIV via human milk in mothers who acquired the

Health Problems—Mother

virus after childbirth (Palasanthiran 1993; Van de Perre 1992; Malaviya 1992; Van de Perre 1991; Lepage 1985; Ziegler 1985).

About one-third of the babies born to HIV-positive women become infected whether or not they are breastfed. For babies who become HIV-positive, breastfeeding appears to slow the progression of the disease (Ryder 1991;Tozzi 1990). Antibodies to HIV have been found in the milk of healthy HIV-positive women. A study of both HIV-positive and HIV-negative mothers identified a factor in human milk that inhibits the binding of HIV to specific receptor sites on human T-cells in the laboratory (Newburg 1995), thus potentially inhibiting the virus from taking hold in the baby (Newburg 1992).

Unfortunately, it is impossible to predict at birth which babies will ultimately become infected with HIV. All babies whose mothers are HIV-positive during pregnancy are born with high HIV antibody levels, which prevent the accurate diagnosis of the disease in the months after birth. Most babies lose these antibodies within the first 15 to 18 months and those who are not infected will eventually test negative.

The inability to identify which babies are already infected at birth makes it difficult to calculate the transmission rate of HIV through breastfeeding. By comparing the infection rate among babies who were not breastfed with babies who were breastfed, Dunn (1992) estimates the transmission rate through breastfeeding to be about 14%. The European Collaborative Study (1992) estimates it to be about 20%. Although some studies have found no greater incidence of HIV among breastfed babies, babies who died during their first year were dropped from these studies, which may have influenced the results (Semba 1994; Halsey 1990). Van de Perre (1995), Ryder and Behets (1994), Ruff (1994), and Goldfarb (1993) offer reviews of the literature to date and perspectives on the conflicting data.

Further complicating attempts to determine a transmission rate is the suggestion from preliminary research results that the risk of transmitting HIV through breastfeeding may depend upon the stage of the mother's infection, the duration of breastfeeding, as well as an unknown number of other factors, including the mother's vitamin A status (Semba 1994). The transmission rate may be higher if the mother acquires the HIV infection during the course of breastfeeding (Cutting 1994; Van de Perre 1993; Rubini and Passman 1992; Van de Perre 1991) or if the mother is in an active phase of the disease (Ryder 1989). The transmission rate may also increase as a baby nurses longer, particularly after six months (Datta 1994). Therefore, if a study includes a large percentage of mothers in one or more of these higher-risk categories, the transmission rate may be markedly higher than the transmission rate calculated by a study in which a large percentage of the mothers are HIV-positive but are at lower risk for transmission.

Breastfeeding recommendations vary for women who are HIV-positive, depending on whether safe alternatives to breastfeeding are available.

Recommendations on breastfeeding for the HIV-positive mother vary, depending upon whether safe alternatives to breastfeeding are available. In 1985 in the US, the Centers for Disease Control published its guidelines for HIV-infected mothers in developed countries. "HIV-infected women should be advised against breastfeeding to avoid postnatal transmission to a child who may not yet be infected....The recommendation is intended for the United States where alternative, safe and effective infant nutrition is widely available....Women considered at increased risk simply because of country of origin, residence in a high prevalence community, or sexual activity should not be discouraged from breastfeeding in the absence of a positive antibody test..." (Oxtoby 1988; Centers for Disease Control 1985).

In 1992, experts from the World Health Organization (WHO) and UNICEF issued the following recommendations: "Where the primary causes of infant deaths are infectious diseases and malnutrition, infants who are not breastfed run a particularly high risk of dying from these conditions. In these settings, breastfeeding should remain the standard advice to pregnant women, including those who are

HIV-infected, because their baby's risk of becoming infected through breast milk is likely to be lower than its risk of dying of other causes if deprived of breast-feeding....In settings where infectious diseases are not the primary causes of death during infancy, pregnant women known to be infected with HIV should be advised not to breastfeed but to use a safe feeding alternative for their babies. Women whose infection status is unknown should be advised to breastfeed" (World Health Organization 1992).

Ultimately, each woman must make her own decision about infant feeding based upon her circumstances and in conjunction with her family and her health care provider.

Because it is possible for a baby to acquire HIV from unpasteurized human milk, cross nursing (wet nursing) and the use of fresh unpasteurized donor milk may pose a risk of infection.

In some parts of the world, it is commonplace for women other than the biological mother to donate fresh expressed human milk for ill babies and for women to nurse other women's babies (also known as cross nursing or wet nursing). However, with the possibility of transmitting HIV through human milk, these practices carry risks (Nduati 1994; Colebunders 1988).

HTLV-I

One to five percent of those infected with human T-cell leukemia virus type 1 (HTLV-1) develop adult T-cell leukemia and lymphoma, a highly malignant disease which is nearly always fatal (Tajima 1988). However, this disease has a long latency period and symptoms do not appear in this small percentage of those infected until some time in adulthood. Discovered in 1977, HTLV-1 is spread through blood, sexual activity, and breastfeeding. It is not yet common in the US or Europe but is on the rise in parts of the Caribbean, Africa, South America, and southwestern Japan, where in the city of Nagasaki, 5 to 10 percent of adults are carriers of HTLV-1 (Ichimaru 1991).

Studies have found that breastfeeding is a major route of transmission of HTLV-I.

Studies have shown that HTLV-1 can be transmitted by breastfeeding. Hino (1989) found that about 30% of exclusively breastfed babies born to HTLV-1 positive mothers became infected, as compared with 10% who received both breast and bottle, and 0% who were artificially fed. Tsuji (1990) found that 39% of the breastfed babies became infected as compared with 0% of the artificially fed babies. Results such as these have led to recommendations that HTLV-1 carrier women, particularly those living in areas where HTLV-1 is prevalent, should refrain from breastfeeding (Committee on Infectious Diseases 1994, p. 75; Ichimaru 1991).

However, more sensitive DNA testing has identified infection routes other than through breast milk (Kawase 1992). In both retrospective and prospective studies of HTLV-1 seropositive women, Oki (1992) found a significant difference between seroconversion rates of short-term (less than 7 months) and long-term (7 months or more) breastfed infants of 3.8% and 25% respectively. The short-term breastfeeding seroconversion rate (3.8%) was nearly equal to that of artificially fed infants (5.6%). Hirata (1992) found the overall prevalence of anti-HTLV-1 among children breastfed more than 3 months was significantly higher (27.6%) than that of those breastfed for less than 3 months (5.1%). The data also suggested that 12.8% of artificially fed infants born to carrier mothers were infected with HTLV-1. Wiktor (1993) found HTLV-1 transmission was associated with breast-feeding for more than 6 months. Because the disease typically does not manifest until decades after infection, it is also not known if transmission through breast-feeding results in disease later (Lawrence, p. 211).

As with the transmission of other viruses through breast-feeding, there are some risk factors that appear to increase the chance of infection. Studies show that the higher the mother's blood levels of the virus, the older the mother, and

Health Problems—Mother

the longer the baby nurses, the greater the likelihood of HTLV-1 being transmitted to the breastfeeding baby (Wiktor 1993; Hirata 1992; Oki 1992; Takahashi 1991). Ichimaru (1991) found that transmission was most likely to occur when infected cells were found in the mothers' blood and/or milk. When no infected cells were found in the carrier mothers' blood or milk, none of the babies became infected.

An alternative to short-term breast-feeding or artificial feeding for the mother who is HTLV-I positive is to express her milk and freeze and thaw it before giving it to her baby.

Studies have shown (Ando 1989a; Ando 1989b) that the HTLV-1 virus is killed when human milk is frozen to -20 degrees C (0 degrees F) and thawed. If an HTLV-1 positive mother wants to express her milk and use this freeze-and-thaw method as an alternative to artificial feeding, talk to her about methods of expression that will establish and maintain her milk supply without putting the baby to breast. (See "Pumping as an Alternative to Breastfeeding" in the chapter "Expression and Storage of Human Milk.")

Leprosy

The mother with leprosy can breastfeed.

Leprosy is a chronic infectious disease that attacks the skin, the tissues, and the nervous system. It is characterized by ulcers, scabs, deformities, and wasting of body parts and can be transmitted only after long and close contact.

There is no evidence that leprosy is transmitted by human milk, and the medications given for leprosy are compatible with breastfeeding (Lawrence, p. 482).

Lyme Disease

There is no evidence that Lyme disease can be transmitted by breastfeeding.

Lyme disease is caused by a microorganism known as a spirochete, which is carried by ticks. Symptoms include a circular rash (usually appearing within three to thirty-two days after being bitten by an infected tick), fever, headache, chills, and fatigue. In the US, the incidence of Lyme disease is increasing.

Although the Lyme spirochete can be transmitted to an unborn baby from his mother via the placenta, there is no evidence that it can be transmitted by breastfeeding.

According to the US Centers for Disease Control (1992), if a nursing mother is suspected of being infected with Lyme disease, she should be treated with an appropriate antibiotic, her baby should be observed for signs of infection, and his blood tested for evidence of infection if illness develops.

Malaria

The mother with malaria may continue breastfeeding.

Malaria, which occurs in tropical and semi-tropical climates, is typically caused by a parasite that is spread from one person to another by a certain type of mosquito. About eight to thirty days after being bitten by an infected mosquito, the symptoms begin: headache, fatigue, and nausea, followed by the "febrile paroxysm" of malaria—a sudden chill followed by a fever with rapid breathing but no sweating and ending with a sweating stage accompanied by a drop in temperature. In some types of malaria, these bouts recur. In one type of malaria, there is only one extremely severe bout.

There is no evidence that malaria can be transmitted by breastfeeding, and treatments including antimalarial drugs are available for the nursing mother that are compatible with breastfeeding (Fulton and Moore 1992).

Measles

The incubation period for measles is seven to sixteen days, and it is contagious until the rash and other symptoms disappear.

Like chickenpox, measles can be fatal in an unborn or newborn baby when contracted *in utero* (congenital measles). The mother who is contagious with measles at the time of birth may be separated from her baby after birth to reduce the chances of infection.

During the first three to four days of measles, there is no rash. The symptoms are the same as a bad cold—fever, red and watery eyes, congestion, and a cough. The rash usually appears on about the fourth day. Measles are no longer contagious when the rash has disappeared and the cold symptoms are gone.

Most women have either had measles or received a measles vaccine during childhood, so cases of a mother catching measles before birth are relatively rare.

A blood test will tell an exposed woman whether or not she has immunity to measles.

If a pregnant woman has been exposed to measles and is uncertain whether or not she had it or received the measles vaccine as a child, her doctor can order a blood test to determine if she has immunity to the disease.

If the mother contracts measles within five days before childbirth, the doctor may recommend she and her baby be separated. About half of the babies exposed to measles prenatally will develop the disease despite the separation.

If the mother comes down with measles within five days before giving birth and her baby is not born with the disease, the doctor may recommend the mother and baby be separated to minimize the spread of the disease. About half of the babies will develop the disease despite the separation.

If the doctor recommends that the mother and baby be separated, encourage the mother to regularly express her milk so it can be given to her baby. The mother's milk will not transmit her illness, and it contains antibodies that will help the baby fight it off. (See "When Breastfeeding Is Delayed after Birth" in the chapter "Expression and Storage of Human Milk.")

The baby may begin breastfeeding as soon as the mother is no longer contagious. For example, if the mother comes down with measles just before birth, the baby may be allowed to breastfeed as soon as his mother's rash disappears and cold symptoms are gone.

Measles contracted by baby after birth will usually be mild.

If the baby catches measles after birth (as opposed to catching it *in utero*), it will usually be mild (Lawrence, p. 487). If the mother catches measles after the newborn period, no special precautions are necessary.

Rubella, or German Measles

The mother with rubella can continue breastfeeding.

Rubella is a mild infectious disease that is usually no more serious than a common cold. If a woman catches rubella during pregnancy, however, the disease may cause damage to the baby through infection *in utero*.

If mother contracts rubella, she will have already exposed her baby to the virus long before she exhibits any symptoms. As with any illness, if the baby comes down with rubella he will do better if he is breastfeeding. Human milk may even provide a natural immunization to rubella if the mother has had rubella or been immunized (Krogh 1989; Losonky 1982).

Sexually Transmitted Diseases

If a mother has a sexually transmitted disease, such as chlamydia, gonorrhea, syphilis, or trichomonas, during pregnancy, she may infect her newborn during delivery, so both mother and baby may need treatment immediately postpartum. If the mother contracts one of these diseases while she is breastfeeding, she will need to seek medical advice.

Chlamydia

The mother with chlamydia can continue breastfeeding.

Chlamydia cannot be transmitted through breastfeeding, and the treatment is compatible with breastfeeding. The mother with chlamydia can continue to breastfeed without interruption.

Gonorrhea

The mother with gonorrhea can continue breastfeeding.

Gonorrhea cannot be transmitted through breastfeeding and the treatment is compatible with breastfeeding, so the mother with gonorrhea can continue to breastfeed without interruption.

Syphilis

If the mother has syphilis, breastfeeding can continue if the newborn does not touch the sores.

The treatment for syphilis consists of antibiotics, which are compatible with breastfeeding.

If a mother has syphilis when her baby is born, the same precautions are used as would be if she had herpes. (See the earlier section, "Herpes.")

Trichomonas

Trichomonas is not dangerous to the nursing baby, but the medication used to treat it may be contraindicated during breastfeeding.

The drug commonly used to treat trichomonas is Flagyl (metronidazole) and is often prescribed as a single 2-gram dose. Although this drug is prescribed for both premature and full-term babies who have trichomonas infections, the 1994 American Academy of Pediatrics' "Transfer of Drugs and Other Chemicals into Human Milk" places Flagyl in the category "Drugs Whose Effect on Nursing Infants Is Unknown But May Be of Concern" and recommends the mother "discontinue breastfeeding 12-24 h[ours] to allow excretion of dose when single-dose therapy [is] given...." The baby who continues to breastfeed through the

Health Problems—Mother

single-dose therapy receives 25.3 mg. of metronidazole over the next 48 hours, or about 40% of the newborn treatment dose (Drinkwater 1987).

A lower dose of metronidazole taken for a longer course is an alternative to single-dose therapy that research indicates may be compatible with breastfeeding. Passmore (1988) found that 400 mg of metronidazole taken three times per day caused no serious reactions in the infants studied. With this treatment, the babies monitored were found to have blood concentrations of 6.25 mg per day, or "less than 10% of the recommended daily dose for infants of equivalent age and weight" who are given this drug (Passmore 1988). When breastfeeding is interrupted following the 2-gram single dose therapy, infants who resume nursing after 12 hours and 24 hours receive 9.8 mg and 3.5 mg of metronidazole respectively over the next 48 hours through their mother's milk (Drinkwater 1987; Erickson 1981). The USP DI (1996) lists 250 mg of metronidazole taken three times per day for seven days as one of the standard treatments for trichomonas. Suggest the mother ask her health care provider if this alternative to single-dose therapy would be appropriate for her and her baby.

If the mother temporarily weans during her treatment for trichomonas, encourage her to regularly express her milk to avoid uncomfortable fullness and to maintain her milk supply. She will need to discard her milk during this time. (For more information, see "When Breastfeeding Is Temporarily Interrupted," in the chapter "Expression and Storage of Human Milk.")

Shingles

Shingles is usually an adult illness and is a relative of chickenpox. It is contracted through direct contact with the breath, the rash, or droplets from the nose or mouth. Although shingles and chickenpox are related, they are not treated alike. If a mother has shingles when her baby is born, the same precautions are used as if she had herpes. (See the earlier section, "Herpes.")

Toxic Shock Syndrome

The mother with toxic shock syndrome will probably be too ill to breastfeed and will need help expressing her milk until she feels well enough to nurse.

Toxic shock syndrome occurs when a particular bacterium (*staphylococcal enterotoxin*) colonizes and infects the body, producing a toxin that is spread by the bloodstream. Symptoms include watery diarrhea, vomiting, muscle aches, and chills. Body temperature increases, while blood pressure decreases.

In its severest form, the mother with toxic shock syndrome may be so ill as to be admitted to the intensive care unit. In this case, she will probably be too ill to nurse and will need help expressing her milk so that she can avoid uncomfortable fullness and decrease her risk of mastitis. (See "When Breastfeeding Is Temporarily Interrupted" in the chapter "Expression and Storage of Human Milk.") Because the toxin associated with toxic shock syndrome has been found in the milk of a mother suffering from this illness (Vergeront 1982), any expressed milk should be discarded during this time. If toxic shock syndrome is caught early and treated with appropriate antibiotics, the toxin may be eliminated from a mother's milk within a few days. In more severe cases, elimination of the toxin from the milk may take longer. When the mother who has been on appropriate antibiotics feels well enough to nurse she should consult her doctor to determine when breastfeeding can safely be resumed. In one case report, a mother was able to safely breastfeed her baby 14 days after the onset of symptoms (Vergeront 1982).

Toxoplasmosis

Toxoplasmosis can be dangerous to an unborn baby if his mother contracts it during pregnancy.

Toxoplasmosis is one of the most common infections in the world and can cause a variety of symptoms that are often attributed to other causes. The percentage of individuals who test positive to toxoplasmosis increases with age.

Although toxoplasmosis carries few risks for a child or adult, it can cause serious health problems if a baby contracts it from his mother *in utero* during early pregnancy. By late pregnancy, however, the consequences are usually less serious.

Toxoplasmosis is most commonly acquired in three ways:

- through drinking unpasteurized cow's milk,
- eating uncooked or undercooked meat, and
- through contact with cat feces, such as by cleaning a litter box.

To be on the safe side, the pregnant or nursing woman should not clean up after a cat, especially a cat under one year who goes outside.

The mother with toxoplasmosis can breastfeed.

There is no evidence that toxoplasmosis can be transmitted by breastfeeding, and the mother provides her baby with antibodies to this infection in her milk. So if the mother has been infected with toxoplasmosis, breastfeeding can and should continue.

Tuberculosis

If a mother with tuberculosis is allowed to be with her baby, it is safe for her to breastfeed.

Tuberculosis is an infectious disease caused by bacteria that is usually transmitted from person to person through the air, although cow's milk is another possible source. Tuberculosis may develop slowly and can cause chronic poor health and death if not treated. The bacteria usually attack the lungs, but they can also spread to other parts of the body.

If it is safe for a mother to be with her baby, it is safe to breastfeed (Lawrence, p. 482). If the mother's tuberculosis is active in the lung and can be transmitted by close nose-and-mouth contact, mother and newborn would have to be separated whether baby was breastfed or artificially fed. (See "When Breastfeeding Is Delayed after Birth" in the chapter "Expression and Storage of Human Milk.") During this period, to establish and maintain her milk supply, the mother will need to express and discard her milk. Once the mother with active tuberculosis has been on effective drug therapy for a week or two, she and her baby can usually be reunited and breastfeeding safely begun or resumed (Lawrence, p. 482).

If a mother develops an active case of tuberculosis during pregnancy and receives appropriate drug therapy, she need not be separated from her baby after birth.

Antitubercular drug therapy is generally considered to be compatible with breastfeeding, but since drug treatment may last for years, both mother's and baby's blood levels may need to be monitored (Committee on Drugs 1994; Snider and Powell 1984; Lawrence, p. 482).

WHEN THE MOTHER IS HOSPITALIZED

When either mother or baby is hospitalized, the needs of both should be taken into consideration.

Planned Hospitalization

Discuss the mother's feelings, circumstances, and options.

If a mother knows in advance that she will be hospitalized, she has the opportunity to explore her feelings and options and make choices that will best meet her needs and the needs of her baby.

A breastfeeding mother who is told she needs to be hospitalized may be in a state of emotional upheaval. She is concerned about her own health and concerned about her baby. She may have been advised to wean. She may need help thinking through her feelings and options.

Discuss the mother's circumstances.

Ask the mother:

Health Problems—Mother

- The age of her baby.
- Her baby's usual nursing patterns.
- Does she have any other children?
- Why did the doctor recommend hospitalization?
- Who will be caring for the baby while she is hospitalized?
- How long does she expect to be in the hospital?

- Does her doctor know she is breastfeeding? If so, has she discussed continuing to breastfeed? What did he or she say?
- Are the baby's father and other family members available to help with the baby in the hospital?
- How do the baby's father and other family members feel about her continuing to breastfeed the baby through a hospital stay?

Discuss her feelings about continuing to breastfeed.

Ask the mother:

- How she feels about continuing to breastfeed her baby through a hospital stay.
- If she were not facing hospitalization, would she consider weaning her baby now?

If the mother wants to wean, talk to her about the practical details. (See "Weaning.")

Discuss whether the hospitalization is necessary, whether the procedure could be done on an outpatient basis, or whether the stay could be shortened.

Ask the mother:

- Has she asked the doctor about an alternative to hospitalization?
- Has she received a second opinion, or would she like to?
- If hospitalization is necessary, could it be postponed until the baby is older?
- Might it be possible to arrange for the treatment or procedure to be done on an outpatient basis and/or with a local anesthetic?
- If she needs to be admitted for a hospital stay, would early discharge be possible if she arranged for nursing care at home?

If the mother needs to be hospitalized, discuss her options concerning breastfeeding.

If a hospital stay is necessary, what options are available at her hospital for continuing to breastfeed? Suggest the mother ask if the hospital has a specific policy concerning breastfeeding mothers and babies. Many hospitals now have policies that allow and even encourage breastfeeding mothers to keep their infants with them and continue breastfeeding as long as there is no medical contraindication for mother or baby. Suggest the mother talk to the hospital lactation consultant or the patient liaison first. A contact person may be able to pave the way. Discuss the range of possibilities, from twenty-four hour rooming-in of baby (with an extra adult to help care for him) to visits from her baby to total separation of mother and baby.

If the baby would not be allowed to room-in with the mother, discuss other options. Ask the mother:

- Would arranging for a room in another area of the hospital (such as the maternity or pediatrics floor) make a difference in the hospital's willingness to allow the baby to stay with her?
- If the baby will not be allowed to room-in with her, will the hospital allow him to be brought to her room to nurse, and if so, how often could someone bring the baby?
- If the hospital will not allow the baby to be brought to her room, would she be allowed to nurse the baby in another part of the hospital?

If the mother will have to miss nursings, talk about what arrangements need to be made.

Some questions to ask:

- If the mother must miss nursings, will the hospital provide access to a full-size automatic electric breast pump or would she need to hand-express her milk or bring her own pump?

- If she finds it difficult to express her milk herself, and the baby is not available to breastfeed, are the nurses on the floor knowledgeable in the use of the pump and willing to help her?

Discuss the principle of supply and demand and explain that by regularly expressing the mother will be able to keep up her milk supply. Another important benefit to expressing is that it will help her avoid uncomfortable engorgement and the possibility of mastitis.

If the mother is concerned about her baby's acceptance of a bottle, share with her the suggestions under, "Feeding Tips for the Baby's Caregiver," in the chapter "Expression and Storage of Human Milk." Also mention that there are other alternative feeding methods (see "The Use of Breast Pumps and Other Products") and that if the baby is reluctant to take a bottle any of these could be used.

If the mother wants to continue breastfeeding, suggest that she explain her feelings to her doctor and be assertive about her wishes.

It is important that the mother's doctor understand the mother's desire to continue breastfeeding. Ideally they should work together. The doctor can help the mother:

- evaluate her condition to determine whether or not her hospitalization is necessary at this time, if it could be postponed, if her treatment could be performed on an outpatient basis, or if an early discharge might be possible;
- look into hospital policy with her to see how breastfeeding can best be managed;
- check into necessary medications and their compatibility with breastfeeding, looking into alternatives as necessary.

Suggest that the mother contact the hospital herself to learn about hospital policies and procedures. Sometimes exceptions to policy can be made.

The better informed the mother is about hospital policies, the less anxious she will feel and the more confident she will be in her plans. Suggest she put her plans in writing, have her doctor sign them, and bring them with her to the hospital so everything is clear when she arrives.

Sometimes hospitals are willing to make exceptions to policy when asked. It helps to be flexible and polite when making requests. If the mother is willing to cooperate with hospital personnel, chances are greater that they will cooperate with her. (See "Helping the Mother Work with Her Doctor" in "Giving Effective Breastfeeding Help.")

Even with major surgery, breastfeeding can continue.

After major surgery, the mother's medical condition or discomfort may make nursing and caring for her baby difficult, but if the mother has planned ahead, is motivated, and has help, it can be done.

Suggest the mother ask her doctor how she will be feeling after surgery. Some mothers will be alert and in little pain; others will be completely incapacitated and may require a lot of medical intervention. Knowing this will help the mother decide how she wants to proceed. Some mothers may be able to nurse right after surgery, while others may have to wait several days. If there will be a wait, suggest the mother consider making arrangements to have an automatic electric breast pump available.

After a general anesthetic, a mother can nurse as soon as she is alert enough to handle her baby.

Drugs used to give general anesthesia do not remain in the mother's system or affect her milk. She can breastfeed as soon as she is alert enough to handle her baby (Spigset 1994).

Health Problems—Mother

Unexpected Hospitalization

The mother will be anxious about her baby and may worry about whether or not she will be able to resume breastfeeding.

When a mother is hospitalized unexpectedly, she may suddenly find herself in a situation where her and her baby's needs are not easily met. The emotional pain the mother feels at the sudden separation from her baby may be as difficult for her as the physical problem that caused her hospitalization.

The mother who is suddenly taken away from her baby during a medical emergency may not have the opportunity to make sure that her baby's needs will be met or to discuss with her doctor or hospital personnel her desire to continue breastfeeding. The emotional stress she is experiencing from her illness or injury will probably be intensified by her worries about her separation from her baby.

Reassure the mother that after a brief separation breastfeeding can usually be resumed with few problems.

Most babies will return to the breast after a separation from their mothers, some willingly and others with some coaxing. Tell the mother that even if her baby is reluctant to go back to the breast at first, with patience and persistence it is very likely she will be able to convince him to resume nursing. (For specific suggestions see "Persuading the Baby to Take the Breast" in the chapter "Fussy at the Breast and Breast Refusal.")

Reassure the mother that she will be able to make up for her time away from her baby.

The mother may be concerned about her baby's emotional state and his need for her presence. Reassure the mother that the loving care she gave her baby before her hospitalization and the love she will give him after she returns will help her baby overcome any upset he might experience while she is away.

Help the mother explore her options.

The mother who is hospitalized unexpectedly will not have the luxury of time to make arrangements, research alternative treatments, or compare hospitals or doctors before she is treated. But she—or her advocate, if she is unable—can still make her wishes known and discuss with her doctor and hospital personnel alternative treatments and her options regarding breastfeeding and/or expressing. (See previous section, "Planned Hospitalization of Mother" for specific questions to ask and possibilities to explore and "Helping the Mother Work with Her Doctor" in "Giving Effective Breastfeeding Help.")

Discuss how the mother can maintain her milk supply and stay comfortable.

The mother may find herself in a hospital with no baby, no pump, and breasts that are rapidly becoming overly full. In most cases, milk production will continue even if the mother is very sick or anesthetized; in some cases the milk supply decreases. Suggest the mother—or her advocate—find out:

- if the baby can be brought to her to breastfeed, or
- if there is a full-size automatic electric breast pump in the hospital that she can use or, if she is unable, that the hospital staff or her advocate can use to pump her breasts.

The mother—or her advocate—should let her doctor and nurses know that breastfeeding her baby or expressing her milk will help her avoid medical complications, such as mastitis.

If her baby cannot be brought to her and a full-size automatic electric breast pump is not available through the hospital, suggest that the baby's father, a relative, or a friend look into the possibility of renting a pump from an outside source and bringing it into the hospital for her to use. If this is not possible, suggest she hand-express her milk or get a hand pump to help relieve engorgement and to keep up her milk supply.

If the mother will not be able to breastfeed her baby for all feedings and is concerned about her baby's willingness to take a bottle, tell her about other feeding methods.

See "Feeding Tips for the Baby's Caregiver," from the chapter "Expression and Storage of Human Milk" for suggested ways to encourage the baby to take a bottle.

Missed feedings can also be given using alternative feeding methods, such as cup, spoon, bowl, eyedropper, feeding syringe, or finger feeding. (See "The Use of Breast Pumps and Other Products.")

With most serious illnesses, the mother will not transmit her illness to her baby by breast-feeding or through her milk.

A mother does not need to be afraid of transmitting most illnesses to her baby by breastfeeding or giving him her expressed milk. Tell the mother:

- Her baby was exposed to her illness even before her symptoms were apparent.
- Antibodies are automatically produced in the mother's body to any infectious illness to which baby is exposed, and these are transmitted to the baby through her milk. These antibodies may help her baby fend off the illness or make his reaction less severe. Some illnesses in the acute stage may require temporary weaning. (See the previous section "When Mother Is Ill" for more information on specific illnesses.)
- Continuing to breastfeed may ease the mother's worries and help her get extra rest.
- Sudden weaning can be physically and emotionally traumatic to both mother and baby.

The chances of a baby catching an infection in the hospital are slim, especially if mother and baby are in a private room.

Physicians, nurses, family members, and the mother may be concerned that the young baby may catch an infection in the hospital. Any risk is extremely minimal, especially if mother and baby are in a private room. Plus, whenever a mother is exposed to a hospital infection, her body will begin making antibodies that immediately pass into her milk, rapidly protecting her breastfeeding baby from any infectious agents.

Medications that are compatible with breastfeeding can be found for almost every situation.

A mother needs to be sure her doctor knows she is breastfeeding so he can evaluate the medications she needs to take in light of their compatibility with breastfeeding. Usually the amount of medication found in the mother's milk is so small it is unlikely to affect the baby. If her doctor is uncertain about whether a particular drug might be harmful for her nursing baby, the mother can ask her doctor to check into other alternatives that may be more compatible with breastfeeding. (See the chapter "Drugs, Vaccines, Vitamins, and Diagnostic Tests" and the supplement "The Transfer of Drugs and Other Chemicals into Human Milk" for more information.)

If the mother needs help in discussing the situation with her doctor, see "Helping the Mother Work with Her Doctor" in the chapter "Giving Effective Breastfeeding Help."

CHRONIC ILLNESS OR PHYSICAL LIMITATION

General Considerations

A chronic illness is a disorder that usually develops slowly and persists for long periods of time, often a lifetime. When talking to a woman with a chronic illness or physical limitation, keep in mind that many women have breastfed in these special situations and that breastfeeding offers advantages to them and their babies.

The mother may need help in sorting out her own feelings about breastfeeding from the opinions and advice of others.

Studies have shown that about the same percentage of mothers with a chronic illness choose to breastfeed as healthy mothers. But the mother with a chronic illness or physical limitation may be advised by others not to breastfeed. The mother may be told to arrange for other family members to take over some of the baby's care to relieve her from fatigue or stress, "to make it easier on herself." This advice may be offered out of concern for the mother's well-being. However, allowing others to take over her baby's care could compromise the mother's self-esteem and her relationship with her baby. By breastfeeding, the mother can do something for her baby that no one else can do, as well as enhance the closeness between them.

Health Problems—Mother

If the mother seems uncertain about whether she wants to breastfeed, try to help her clarify her feelings on the basis of her own desires and correct information, rather than misconceptions and the advice of others. Encourage her to do what feels right for her and, if she chooses to breastfeed, offer to brainstorm with her on ways she can fit breastfeeding into her daily life.

It is not necessary to know everything about a mother's physical problem to help her with breastfeeding.

In most cases, the questions and concerns a mother has will be the same as those of any other mother. However, if she questions how her condition will affect breastfeeding, it may be necessary to ask her for more information about her illness and the limitations it presents. A mother who has a chronic illness or physical limitation is usually well educated about it.

The mother with a chronic illness may worry that her baby will contract her illness through breastfeeding.

Babies cannot contract their mother's chronic illness through breastfeeding. Most chronic illnesses, such as lupus, diabetes, multiple sclerosis, and rheumatoid arthritis, are caused by alterations in the mother's immune system or are genetic and cannot be passed on through the mother's milk.

Breastfeeding offers advantages for the mother with a physical limitation or chronic illness.

Breastfeeding offers special advantages to mothers with physical limitations or chronic illness, which will vary, depending on individual circumstances. Advantages common to all these mothers include:

- Breastfeeding saves energy, as it is not necessary to prepare or buy formula. There is also evidence that breastfeeding alters a woman's metabolism, producing more energy at less physical cost.
- The breastfed baby is statistically healthier, saving many trips to the doctor's office with ear infections, digestive problems, and allergies.
- Unlike bottle-feeding, the mother can breastfeed lying down, allowing her to rest while she feeds her baby.
- Breastfeeding helps build a close emotional bond between mother and baby, which might be more difficult to develop if others take over the baby's care.

When the mother has physical limitations and/or discomforts, offer to talk about how she can make breastfeeding more comfortable.

The mother may wonder how to manage breastfeeding if her activity and/or mobility are limited by pain, fatigue, or loss of function of body parts. (For information about mothers who have breastfed with the loss of one or more limbs, see Dunne and Fuerst 1995 and Thomson 1995.)

No matter how the baby is fed, caring for a newborn is bound to be challenging. Offer to brainstorm with her about how she can manage breastfeeding within her physical limitations. Begin by asking her for details about her specific situation. Then discuss options that may make breastfeeding easier or more comfortable. See the following sections for more specific ideas. Modify suggestions according to the mother's particular situation. For example, should she need to care for her baby alone, a mother with physical limitations might benefit by setting up a "nursing station," a special area stocked with everything she might need for the day. A pitcher of water or juice and a glass, snacks, lots of pillows, a place to lay the baby down, clean diapers and a receptacle for dirty ones, baby wipes, a phone, and possibly some books or magazines, a radio, or the remote control for the television would help make it possible for a mother challenged by even the most severe symptoms to manage most of the day alone with her baby.

Talk about ways to simplify household tasks and the value of lowering expectations of what really needs to be done to keep a household running. Encourage the mother to accept offers of assistance with housework from family or friends or hire household help.

Fatigue may be a continuing challenge.

For mothers with a chronic illness, fatigue can be a continuing challenge. Be sure to mention that with practice she will be able to nurse lying down, so she can rest while feeding her baby.

| Breastfeeding may cause a temporary remission of the mother's illness. | In some chronic illnesses, hormonal changes may cause the remission of illness during pregnancy and breastfeeding (for example, rheumatoid arthritis and lupus). |

Breastfeeding may cause a temporary remission of the mother's illness.

In some chronic illnesses, hormonal changes may cause the remission of illness during pregnancy and breastfeeding (for example, rheumatoid arthritis and lupus).

During pregnancy, diabetic women may need to increase their caloric intake or change their insulin dosage. Many women find they need less insulin while they are breastfeeding. The mother needs to be sure her blood-glucose levels are closely monitored.

When her symptoms return, the mother may worry.

When a chronic illness goes into remission during pregnancy, symptoms usually reappear two to eight months postpartum.

Since the symptoms of the illness may return while the mother is still breastfeeding, she may think breastfeeding is causing the return of her symptoms. Assure her that breastfeeding is not the cause. In fact, for many mothers, the hormonal changes of breastfeeding actually help to extend their remission after their babies are born.

Many mothers also complain that the symptoms, when they reappear, are "worse than they ever were." Gently explore with the mother the possibility that after a time of remission and relief, she may have forgotten how severe the symptoms used to be.

Medications and treatments that are compatible with breastfeeding can almost always be found if mother and doctor work together.

Medications that are not harmful to the nursing baby can be found for almost every illness. A breastfeeding mother who regularly takes prescribed medication needs to inform her doctor that she is breastfeeding and to inform her baby's doctor what medication(s) she is taking, along with the dosage(s).

Encourage the mother to let her doctor and her baby's doctor know how important nursing is to her. She needs their help in finding medications that will be compatible with breastfeeding. Encourage her to be honest and maintain an attitude of partnership with her doctors while determining appropriate medication and treatment. If a mother has never questioned her doctor before, this may be difficult for her. If so, ask the mother if she would like to role play with you, so she can practice her responses.

If any of the doctors are unsupportive of the mother's desire to breastfeed, encourage her to seek another opinion. (See the chapter "Drugs, Vitamins, Vaccines, and Diagnostic Tests" for more information.)

Specific Conditions

Blindness

Breastfeeding offers the same advantages to the blind mother as to the sighted mother.

Breastfeeding offers advantages to all mothers. For the blind mother the following advantages may be particularly appreciated:

- Breastfeeding makes things simpler; there is nothing to measure, prepare, pour, or sterilize.
- Breastfeeding makes going out with baby and traveling easier, as no preparation is necessary in an unfamiliar environment.
- The breastfed baby is statistically healthier with fewer ear infections, digestive problems, and allergies.
- Breastfeeding helps build a close emotional bond between mother and baby, which might be more difficult to develop if others took over the baby's care.
- Breastfeeding can increase a blind mother's sense of self-reliance, competence, and self-esteem.

Practical tips can make breast-feeding and baby care easier

A baby sling or carrier and books on audio tape could be of special help to the visually impaired mother.

La Leche League International has materials for the visually handicapped, which include publications on audio tape and in Braille. Contact La Leche League International Headquarters for more information.

Health Problems—Mother

Chronic Joint Pain, Swelling, and Weakness

Breastfeeding offers special advantages to the mother with chronic joint pain, swelling, and weakness.

When the mother has physical limitations and/or discomforts, offer to talk about how she can make breastfeeding more comfortable.

Several chronic illnesses can cause joint pain, swelling, and weakness, making baby care and breastfeeding a challenge. Some of these illnesses are: arthritis, systemic lupus erythematosus (SLE or lupus), and myasthenia gravis (MG).

Advantages of breastfeeding for the mother with chronic joint pain, swelling, and weakness are listed in the previous section, "General Considerations."

No matter how the baby is fed, caring for a newborn is bound to be challenging. Offer to brainstorm with her about how she can manage breastfeeding within her limitations. Begin by asking her for details about her specific situation. Then discuss ideas for making breastfeeding easier or more comfortable.

For example, a mother with lupus, arthritis, or myasthenia gravis may suffer from weakness, joint pain, and swelling, which may make holding the baby difficult or painful. Suggest the mother try using lots of pillows as support for her arms and to nurse lying down. Ask her if a baby sling might take the pressure off her arms and make nursing more comfortable. A nursing station, as described in the previous section, "General Considerations," may also be of help.

Fatigue may be a continuing challenge.

For a mother suffering from chronic fatigue, be sure to mention that with practice she will be able to nurse lying down, so she can rest while feeding her baby.

Cystic Fibrosis

Cystic fibrosis is a congenital disease that affects breathing and digestion. Until recent years those with cystic fibrosis rarely survived into adulthood, but with improved treatment, women with cystic fibrosis are having babies.

The individual with cystic fibrosis secretes unusually thick, gluey mucus and the sweat is unusually salty. The thick mucus clogs the bronchial tubes in the lungs, causing breathing difficulties, and blocks the digestive enzymes from leaving the pancreas, causing incomplete digestion. Cystic fibrosis can be mild to severe. Some cases can be detected only through laboratory tests, while some are extremely serious.

With incomplete digestion and absorption of nutrients, maintenance of proper weight is a major concern and special enzymes are sometimes taken to aid in digestion. (For information on breastfeeding the baby with cystic fibrosis, see the chapter "The Baby with Special Needs.")

Women with cystic fibrosis can produce normal milk and breastfeed, but they need careful nutritional monitoring.

Although information is scarce, studies have found that mothers with cystic fibrosis can breastfeed their babies and produce milk with normal concentrations of protein, fats, and minerals (Michel and Mueller 1994; Shiffman 1989). Several case reports confirm that women with cystic fibrosis have breastfed babies who have maintained normal growth (Michel and Mueller 1994; Smith 1992). Although one case report described a mother whose milk had elevated sodium levels, this mother had not been breastfeeding and had expressed her milk for study purposes only. Elevated sodium levels are normal during breast involution and may have been unrelated to her cystic fibrosis (Alpert and Cormier 1983).

Because cystic fibrosis impairs normal digestion, a mother should have her nutritional needs carefully monitored before, during, and after pregnancy, as well as during lactation. If the mother is having difficulty maintaining her weight or her health, or her baby is not gaining well, breastfeeding may not be recommended. Michel and Mueller (1994) suggest that women with adequate weight and stable cystic fibrosis be considered candidates for breastfeeding.

Diabetes Mellitus

Diabetes is one of the most common serious metabolic disorders. A diabetic's body does not make enough insulin, a hormone needed to convert sugars and starches to energy. This causes an abnormally high blood-sugar level. Insulin-dependent diabetics must have daily injections of insulin and carefully follow a prescribed diet.

Breastfeeding offers advantages for the woman with diabetes.

Breastfeeding offers special advantages to diabetic mothers:

- Breastfeeding can reduce stress, which aggravates diabetes. By breast-feeding lying down, the mother can get extra rest while feeding her baby. Also, the hormones released during breastfeeding relax the mother.
- Studies indicate that breastfeeding may reduce the baby's risk of developing diabetes later in life (Karjalainen 1992; Metcalfe 1992; Virtanen 1991). Since susceptibility to Type I diabetes is inherited, it is of particular benefit to the baby of an insulin-dependent diabetic mother to be breastfed.
- The breastfed baby is statistically healthier, saving many trips to the doctor's office with ear infections, digestive problems, and allergies.
- The hormones released during breastfeeding and the extra energy used during milk production may decrease the amount of insulin the mother needs.
- Many diabetic mothers report increased feelings of health and well-being while they are breastfeeding.
- Breastfeeding enhances feelings of love and closeness between mother and baby, an important benefit if mother and baby must be separated for a time after birth.
- Breastfeeding, in general, tends to make diabetes more easily managed after the birth of a baby, because it is the body's natural response to childbirth and the hormones responsible for lactation cause the physiological changes to occur more gradually.
- Breastfeeding can help the mother feel normal, because like every other mother, she is able to give her baby the best.

Preparation for Birth

During pregnancy, encourage the mother to choose her doctor and her baby's doctor carefully, as well as the hospital where she will give birth.

It is important that the diabetic woman and her doctors work together in harmony, with confidence in each other, and with complete understanding of what is in the best interest of both mother and baby.

Suggest that the mother talk with several doctors early in pregnancy to discuss whether the doctor has had experience in the care of diabetic women and how the physician managed their care. Other areas the mother might want to cover:

- Discuss with the obstetrician how she would like labor and childbirth managed. Also, discuss the importance of early, frequent contact with the baby.
- Discuss her desire to breastfeed with her obstetrician, pediatrician, and diabetes specialist, who will advise her on adjusting her diet during pregnancy and lactation.
- Discuss with the obstetrician procedures used during a high-risk pregnancy.
- Discuss with the baby's doctor his or her care of premature babies, as well as his or her standard procedures for newborn jaundice and hypoglycemia.

Since most diabetic women are considered high risk during pregnancy, many doctors choose large medical centers for delivery where sophisticated monitoring facilities are available. However, in some large hospitals, when a baby needs observation, he may be taken to an intensive-care nursery in a different area of the hospital, far from where the mother will be. Some mothers find that a smaller but well-equipped hospital allows them to spend more time with their babies after birth. Suggest the mother check into her local options.

Health Problems—Mother

The diabetic mother needs to be carefully monitored during pregnancy and childbirth.

The hormonal changes of pregnancy and childbirth cause fluctuations in the mother's blood-glucose levels, which means she needs to be carefully monitored by her doctor.

The first few days after birth, the mother will probably experience drastic changes in blood-glucose and acetone levels. These sudden metabolic shifts need to be closely monitored. Once the mother's diet and insulin are adjusted and control achieved, the diabetic mother should have no further problems if she continues to follow good management practices.

Whether or not the mother breastfeeds, she will still undergo these metabolic changes. Breastfeeding, in general, tends to make diabetes more easily managed after the birth of a baby, because it is the body's natural response to childbirth and the hormones responsible for lactation cause the natural physiological changes to occur more gradually.

Suggest the mother discuss with her doctor and her baby's doctor how she can minimize separation from her baby after birth.

Keeping mother and baby together can help breastfeeding go more smoothly. Encourage the mother to discuss with her doctor and the baby's doctor how soon she can breastfeed her baby.

Ferris (1988) found that fewer newborns of mothers with diabetes are put to the breast during their first few days than babies of non-diabetic mothers. Webster (1995) found that 74% of the babies born to diabetic mothers were admitted to the special care or intensive-care nurseries after birth as compared with 17% of the babies of non-diabetic mothers. This separation of mother and baby not only postpones the start of breastfeeding but also increases the likelihood that the baby will receive bottles or artificial nipples, which can make the baby less interested in nursing. Another study (Whichelow and Doddridge 1983) followed forty-two insulin-dependent diabetic mothers and concluded that the most important factor in breastfeeding success was how much time passed before the first breastfeeeding. Ferris (1993), who studied thirty-three diabetic women, also noted longer delays in the first feeding, less frequent feedings, increased use of supplemental feedings, and less time spent together in the first few days. Webster (1995), who observed nineteen diabetic mothers, found no correlation between timing of the first nursing and length of time breastfed.

Since fewer than half of babies with diabetic mothers actually have physical problems after birth, the mother could suggest to her doctors that if she and the baby are healthy and capable of breastfeeding they need not be routinely separated.

Milk production during pregnancy and lactation can affect the accuracy of different types of blood-glucose monitoring.

Some blood-glucose monitoring methods are affected by milk production. The two-drop Clinitest is accurate only for the first twenty weeks of pregnancy. After that, during the rest of pregnancy and while breastfeeding, only Diastix and Tes-Tape are accurate for testing urine. They are the only tests that do not react to the lactose (milk sugar) a woman starts producing later in pregnancy and while breastfeeding.

The mother may be able to decrease the baby's risk of developing hypoglycemia after birth.

About half of all babies born to diabetic mothers develop hypoglycemia, or low blood sugar. The chances of this are decreased if the mother maintains good diabetic control during pregnancy. The fetus of the diabetic mother may be exposed to higher than normal levels of glucose *in utero,* which he stores in body organs as fat. This also causes the baby to produce excessive insulin. At birth, the excess circulating insulin is responsible for a rapid drop in blood glucose, which is called hypoglycemia. Many newborns adjust quickly. Others, especially premature babies, require milk feeding or intravenous glucose to raise the blood glucose. Breastfeeding is the first choice, but expressed human milk or formula can be given by cup, eyedropper, spoon, or feeding syringe to avoid nipple confusion. Intravenous glucose is usually necessary only for those infants with symptoms or those resistant to feeding by mouth.

Some doctors have found that putting the baby to breast immediately after birth (if the mother is feeling fit) can moderate or prevent hypoglycemia.

The glucose-and-water IVs, often routinely given to mothers in labor, may contribute to the baby's becoming hypoglycemic following birth (If fluids are necessary for the mother, non-glucose liquids can be used in the IV.) If the mother wants to avoid a routine IV, suggest she discuss this with her obstetrician before birth.

Encourage the mother to be well informed about newborn jaundice before her baby is born.

The baby of a diabetic mother is at higher risk of developing newborn jaundice (Sirota 1992). Encourage the mother to discuss with her baby's doctor how he or she handles newborn jaundice. In most cases, jaundice disappears without treatment. Also, tell the mother that breastfeeding early and often is an effective way of preventing jaundice. (See the chapter "Newborn Jaundice" for ways to treat jaundice without affecting breastfeeding.)

Getting Started Breastfeeding

Assure the mother that the insulin she takes will not harm her breastfeeding baby.

Insulin is considered compatible with breastfeeding. Insulin has not been found in human milk because its molecules are too large to pass into it. Also, when taken by mouth, insulin is destroyed in the digestive tract.

If mother and baby are separated after birth, encourage the mother to express her milk so it can be given to the baby when he is ready for it.

Even if the newborn cannot be given his mother's milk, regular expressing will help the mother avoid engorgement and establish a plentiful milk supply.

If the baby is unable to nurse but ready to take food by mouth, to avoid nipple confusion suggest the mother request her milk be given by cup, eyedropper, feeding syringe, or gavage tube rather than by rubber nipple.

If the baby is sleepy or lethargic, encourage the mother to stimulate him, keep offering the breast, and be patient.

If the baby is sleepy, he may need to be stimulated to nurse well. Suggest the mother make sure he isn't too warmly dressed or wrapped, loosen his clothes and move him around before putting him to the breast. Before switching him to the other side, suggest she burp him and change him. (For more suggestions, see "How to Rouse a Sleepy Baby" in the chapter "Positioning, Latch-On, and the Baby's Suck.")

Some diabetic mothers report that their milk "comes in" two to three days later than usual.

A mother's milk usually becomes more plentiful (or "comes in") by about the third or fourth day after birth. Some diabetic mothers, however, report a delay until the fifth or sixth day. Neubauer (1993) measured the milk composition of mothers with insulin-dependent diabetes and found that the diabetic mothers with good control had milk with similar composition to the mothers without diabetes, suggesting no delay in milk production. However, the diabetic mothers without good control had milk composition that suggested a delay in milk production up to about the seventh day after birth. These results may have been influenced, though, by the fact that the babies of the diabetic mothers received more formula supplements during the first week, possibly delaying increased milk production. Arthur (1989) reported in his study of diabetic and non-diabetic mothers that the diabetic mothers felt their milk "coming in" between the second and fourth day after birth, which was later than the non-diabetic mothers, but not significantly later.

Early and frequent nursing will help stimulate the mother's milk supply. However, even with early and unrestricted nursing, fluctuating insulin requirements and other physical changes related to the mother's diabetes may cause a delay. If so, the mother can continue to nurse and feel confident that her milk supply will eventually increase.

If the baby's doctor recommends the baby be given a supplement until the mother's milk supply increases, it is best to avoid using an artificial nipple, as newborns are susceptible to nipple confusion, which can complicate breastfeeding. Suggest that the mother request that the supplement be given using one of the alternative feeding methods, such as feeding syringe, eyedropper, or nursing

Health Problems—Mother

supplementer, rather than by bottle. (See "The Use of Breast Pumps and Other Products.")

Increasing her daily calories will provide the mother with the extra energy necessary for milk production.

One study found that diabetic mothers planning to breastfeed nursed longer when they followed a recommended diet of increased calories (Ferris 1988). This extra food provides the energy needed for milk production. The mothers who consistently ate less than recommended amounts stopped breastfeeding earlier than planned. Ferris concluded that a diabetic mother needs a knowledgeable dietary counselor, as well as other support people, for breastfeeding to go well.

Encourage the mother to follow her recommended diet from her baby's birth.

After Breastfeeding Is Established

The hormonal changes of pregnancy and breastfeeding may reduce the amount of insulin required by the diabetic mother.

Many diabetic mothers enjoy a partial or total remission from their diabetes that may last for as long as they breastfeed. During breastfeeding, a mother's insulin requirement may be significantly less than it was before she became pregnant (Butte 1987). Davies (1989) found that after birth breastfeeding mothers needed to decrease their insulin dose by 27% of their prepregnancy dose to avoid hypoglycemic reactions. However, each mother's response to the physical changes of pregnancy, childbirth, and breastfeeding will be individual.

For women with gestational diabetes, breastfeeding has been found to enhance glucose metabolism during lactation and offer some protection from the development of subsequent diabetes unrelated to pregnancy during the follow-up period of the study (Kjos 1993). It is not known whether or not this benefit is long-term.

The mother may need to adjust her diet during times when the baby nurses more or less.

The mother can often compensate for changes in her baby's nursing pattern by eating more (if the baby nurses more) or less (if the baby nurses less). Some mothers may also need to adjust their insulin dosage. This is individual and varies from mother to mother.

Some mothers with diabetes are prone to sore nipples and breast infections.

Diabetics, in general, are prone to infections of all kinds, including fungal, such as yeast (monilial) infections of the vagina and nipples, which can cause sore nipples (Buchanon 1985). Suggest the mother carefully monitor her blood-glucose levels, as the risk of contracting a yeast infection increases when her blood-glucose levels are elevated. Also suggest the mother keep her nipples clean (by rinsing them with clear water after feedings) and dry, as yeast thrives on milk and moisture. Good hygiene, such as hand-washing, is important. If the mother has persistent sore nipples, she may have thrush. For a diagnosis, she can consult her doctor, who may prescribe a topical fungicidal cream or a systemic medication. The baby must also be treated for thrush. (See "Thrush" in the chapter "Nipple Problems.")

Encourage the mother to recognize and treat plugged milk ducts promptly and be aware of the symptoms of mastitis. Any lumps or sore spots in the breast should be treated immediately with heat, frequent nursing on that breast, gentle breast massage, and rest. Gagne (1992) confirmed a greater incidence of breast infections in diabetic mothers. If recurring mastitis becomes a problem, encourage the mother to breastfeed regularly (so that her breasts do not become overly full due to missed feedings), avoid fatigue, and be sure to take any prescribed antibiotics for the full ten-to-fourteen day course. Suggest the mother ask her doctor if it would be appropriate to use an antifungal as a preventive measure along with the antibiotic, since diabetic mothers are prone to yeast infections and antibiotics kill the beneficial bacteria that keep the yeast in check. By being alert to symptoms, the mother can prevent most problems. (See "Mastitis—Plugged Ducts and Breast Infections" in the chapter "Breast Problems.")

Gradual weaning makes maintaining diabetic control easier.

If the weaning process is gradual, adjustments of insulin and diet during weaning can be equally slow and smooth. Encourage the mother to avoid abrupt weaning. She should plan either to wean her baby naturally as he outgrows the need to nurse or, if she chooses planned weaning, to eliminate nursings gradually—reducing by no more than one daily feeding per week.

Epilepsy

Breastfeeding offers advantages for the mother with epilepsy.

Epilepsy is a disorder of the central nervous system that can cause seizures. Its cause is unknown and there is no cure, but at least half of all epileptics are able to completely control their seizures with medication and most of the rest achieve at least partial control.

Special preparations and safety tips can make breastfeeding easier for the mother with epilepsy.

Preparations can be made to ensure the baby's safety in case the mother has a seizure.

- Suggest the mother breastfeed in a big easy chair, if one is available. If a seizure should occur suddenly, the padding will help keep the mother in the chair and protect the baby.
- If the mother nurses in a rocking chair or any other chair that does not have padded arms, suggest she pad the arms. One way would be to fold two towels thickly and wrap one around each arm, pinning them to keep them in place. This makes a pillow for baby's head and provides padding in case of a seizure. Extra pillows and cushions can also help the mother avoid bruises.
- When the mother is breastfeeding sitting up, suggest she elevate her feet with a small stool. With her legs elevated, the baby would roll into her lap if she has a seizure.
- If the mother wants to sleep with the baby, she can use guardrails and pillows for padding. Resting on the floor on a blanket would also be safe for both mother and baby.
- Have a playpen or portable crib on each level of the house. If the mother feels a seizure coming on, she can lay the baby down where he will be safe.
- For a crawling baby or toddler, put gates across doorways and stairs, so in the event of a seizure the baby will be kept in a safe area.
- When on an outing with her baby, suggest the mother attach a tag or sticker to her stroller or carriage explaining that she has epilepsy and listing the baby's name and the name of a relative or friend who can be reached to help care for the baby.

If the mother has questions about her medication, see "Drugs, Vitamins, Vaccines, and Diagnostic Tests."

Multiple Sclerosis

Multiple sclerosis causes the covering surrounding the nerves to become inflamed and swollen. Weakness, clumsiness, and numbness of limbs are common symptoms, as well as blurring of vision and slurred speech. Multiple sclerosis can be mild or severe. In mild cases, the woman may completely recover after her symptoms have passed and have long periods of remission. In severe cases, she may have repeated attacks that leave her permanently and progressively disabled.

The mother may be worried that her baby will contract her illness through breastfeeding.

A baby cannot contract multiple sclerosis through breastfeeding, as it is caused by alterations in the mother's immune system and cannot be transmitted through her milk.

Health Problems—Mother

Breastfeeding longer than six months may offer the baby some protection from multiple sclerosis later in life.

One study (Pisacane 1994) found lower rates of multiple sclerosis among individuals breastfed for more than six months as compared with those never breastfed or breastfed for six months or less. The researchers suggest possible reasons for this:

- Because cow's milk has lower amounts of unsaturated fatty acids than human milk, the brain of artificially fed babies may have a different composition that makes it more prone to contracting multiple sclerosis.
- Human milk strengthens the immune system in ways that may protect the infant from multiple sclerosis later in life.

Breastfeeding offers special advantages for the mother with multiple sclerosis.

Advantages for the mother with multiple sclerosis are listed in the earlier section, "General Considerations."

Breastfeeding does not cause the mother's symptoms to improve or worsen.

Studies show that the number of pregnancies and births are unrelated to the long-term disability from a woman's multiple sclerosis (Poser and Poser 1983). Typically, a woman has some remission of symptoms during pregnancy and then a worsening of her symptoms, especially during the first three months postpartum. One study of 191 pregnancies of women with multiple sclerosis (Nelson 1988) found that breastfeeding does not seem to make mothers' symptoms during the postpartum period more or less severe.

When the mother has physical limitations and/or discomforts, offer to talk about how she can make breastfeeding more comfortable.

No matter how the baby is fed, caring for a newborn is bound to be challenging. Offer to brainstorm with her about how she can manage breastfeeding within her limitations. Begin by asking her for details about her individual situation. Then discuss options that may make breastfeeding easier or more comfortable.

For example, if the mother suffers from weakness, holding the baby may be difficult. Suggest the mother try using lots of pillows as support for her arms and to nurse lying down. Ask her if a baby sling might make nursing easier. If the mother has no help and can't lift the baby, she may be able to lean over the baby's crib to breastfeed or keep the baby safely on a bed where she can get to him easily without lifting. She may also need outside help. Modify suggestions to fit the mother's particular situation. A nursing station, as described in the previous section, "General Considerations," may also be of help.

Fatigue may be a continuing challenge.

Be sure to mention that with practice the mother will be able to learn to nurse lying down, so she can rest while feeding her baby.

If the mother has questions about her medication(s), see the chapter "Drugs, Vitamins, Vaccines, and Diagnostic Tests."

Thyroid Disease and Other Endocrine Problems

The thyroid gland controls the rate of all the body's metabolic processes. Any nursing mother with thyroid disease should be under the care of a doctor who is supportive of her desire to breastfeed.

Pregnancy and postpartum changes can temporarily alter a mother's thyroid levels.

Hormonal changes during pregnancy and during the postpartum period can cause thyroid levels to temporarily increase or decrease, even in a mother who has never had thyroid irregularities before (Lazarus and Othman 1991). Encourage the mother who has a history of thyroid problems to have her thyroid levels monitored regularly so that her medication can be adjusted.

Radioactive testing—for which temporary weaning is necessary—may be recommended to diagnose thyroid problems.

While most cases of hypothyroidism (underactive thyroid) or hyperthyroidism (overactive thyroid) can be diagnosed based on symptoms the mother is experiencing and simple blood tests, there are occasions when radioactive testing and visualization of the thyroid gland are recommended to determine the location and cause of the problem, especially when a goiter (enlarged thyroid gland) is present.

If radioactive testing is recommended, suggest the mother ask her physician whether the test can be postponed or another, non-radioactive alternative can be found.

If radioactive testing is unavoidable, temporary weaning is necessary. The length of time the mother needs to suspend breastfeeding will depend on the type and dosage of radioactive material used for the test. Her milk can be tested to determine when it is safe to resume breastfeeding. (See "Diagnostic Tests" in the chapter "Drugs, Vitamins, Vaccines, and Diagnostic Tests.")

Tell the mother that during her temporary weaning regular expressing can prevent her breasts from becoming overly full and keep up her milk supply. Expressing milk will also help remove the radioactive materials from her body more quickly. This milk will have to be discarded. (See "When Breastfeeding Is Temporarily Interrupted" in the chapter "Expression and Storage of Human Milk.")

Underactive Thyroid

Symptoms of underactive thyroid may be wrongly attributed to breastfeeding.

An underactive thyroid is a fairly common problem. The symptoms may seem vague to the mother and come on slowly. It is not unusual for the mother with an underactive thyroid to be misdiagnosed.

Hypothyroidism—underactive thyroid—often causes fatigue, poor appetite, and depression. The mother or her doctor may wrongly attribute these symptoms to breastfeeding. If the mother is experiencing these symptoms, suggest she ask that her doctor test her for thyroid function, as well as anemia.

Low thyroid levels can decrease milk production.

Women with a history of thyroid problems may need to be retested if their nursing baby is slow in gaining weight, as changes in metabolism can affect milk production.

Thyroid supplements taken by the mother will not harm her breastfeeding baby.

Thyroid supplements are not contraindicated during breastfeeding. They simply bring the mother's thyroid up to a normal level (Lawrence, p. 506). Thyroid-deficient mothers usually find that while taking thyroid supplements they feel better and have better milk supplies.

Overactive Thyroid

Thyroid suppressants can be found that are compatible with breastfeeding.

An overactive thyroid is a serious health problem, putting a strain on the mother's heart, muscles, and nervous system. If the mother's condition is severe, immediate treatment may be necessary.

Certain antithyroid medications are not concentrated in milk and result in minimal doses to the breastfeeding baby (Lazarus and Othman 1991; Lawrence, p. 506). If the mother takes a thyroid suppressant, she needs to inform the baby's doctor so her baby can be monitored.

If the baby's thyroid levels are lowered by the mother's thyroid suppressant, an alternative to weaning would be to give the baby a thyroid supplement.

Encourage the mother to let her doctor and her baby's doctor know how important nursing is to her. She needs their help in finding medications that will be compatible with breastfeeding. Encourage her to be honest and maintain an attitude of partnership with her and her baby's doctor while determining appropriate medication and treatment. If a mother has never questioned her doctor before, this may be difficult for her. If so, ask the mother if she would like to role play with you, so she can practice her responses.

If the doctor is unsupportive of the mother's desire to breastfeed, encourage her to seek another opinion. (See "Exploring Options When the Doctor Recommends Weaning" in the chapter "Drugs, Vitamins, Vaccines, and Diagnostic Tests.")

Health Problems—Mother

If radioactive treatment is required, temporary weaning will be necessary.

Radioactive compounds are sometimes used to treat an overactive thyroid. Because radioactive materials tend to accumulate in the milk and are passed on to the baby, the use of radioactive compounds is incompatible with breastfeeding.

It may be possible, however, for the mother to return to breastfeeding after her treatment is over. (Some women have gone back to breastfeeding after a break of three to four months.) The mother can begin breastfeeding again after her milk has been tested for radioactivity (a Geiger counter can be used), and it has reached a normal level. Expressing her milk more frequently will lower radioactivity levels more quickly, as the radioactivity is eliminated from the body through the excretion of fluids.

For information on helping a mother stay comfortable and maintain her milk supply during a temporary weaning, see the section, "When Breastfeeding Is Temporarily Interrupted," in the chapter "Expression and Storage of Human Milk."

Sheehan's Syndrome

Caused by postpartum hemorrhage so severe that the blood loss irreversibly damages the pituitary gland, Sheehan's syndrome is responsible for breastfeeding failure. Other symptoms include loss of pubic and underarm hair, inability to tolerate cold, low blood pressure, and atrophy of vaginal tissue, as well as subsequent infertility.

The mother with Sheehan's syndrome usually does not produce milk or enough milk to sustain her baby after birth.

In the mother with Sheehan's syndrome, extreme loss of blood due to severe hemorrhage causes the malfunction of the pituitary gland, which interferes with production of the milk-producing hormone, prolactin. Failure to lactate is considered to be the primary symptom of this rare syndrome in the immediate postpartum period.

In the fourth edition of her book, *Breastfeeding: A Guide for the Medical Profession* (p. 499), Ruth Lawrence, MD, reports that at the University of Rochester in New York, a mother who was presumed to have Sheehan's syndrome was able to build her milk supply by using syntocin nasal spray and a nursing supplementer at each feeding for two weeks. Over the next two weeks she gradually weaned from the drug and the supplementer and went on to breastfeed fully for six months. One study followed ten women who suffered postpartum hemorrhage and found an association between excessive maternal postpartum blood loss and insufficient milk intake in their babies (Willis and Livingston 1995).

POSTPARTUM DEPRESSION

Many new mothers have the "baby blues" after birth, but if the symptoms intensify, it may be postpartum depression.

Many new mothers experience the "baby blues" during the first week or two after birth. In fact, some studies indicate that more than half of all new mothers have one or more of the following symptoms: crying, irritability, fatigue, and insomnia (O'Hara 1987). The "blues" are probably caused by a combination of factors: hormonal changes, exhaustion from labor and delivery, and the emotional ups and downs that accompany a major life change such as birth and a new role such as motherhood.

However, if these symptoms intensify rather than fade, and last longer than about four weeks, the mother may be suffering from postpartum depression. Late-onset postpartum depression can develop weeks or months after giving birth. If the mother is isolated from others—either due to a recent move or an isolated living situation—she will be at higher risk of developing postpartum depression (Hopkins 1984).

Postpartum depression has many possible symptoms.

A mother with postpartum depression may suffer from any or all of the following symptoms, although the most severe symptoms occur only rarely.

- feelings of sadness and helplessness,
- anxiety,
- headaches,
- mood swings,
- insomnia,

- general lack of interest in life,
- fear of hurting the baby or worry over inability to care for the baby,
- loss of appetite,
- ankle swelling or a sudden weight increase,
- vomiting,
- panic,
- distorted perception of reality,
- hallucinations or delusions,
- suicidal or homicidal thoughts.

The last three are symptoms of postpartum psychosis, the most severe form of postpartum depression. Postpartum psychosis affects one to two of every 1000 postpartum women (O'Hara 1987), most commonly begins during the first two weeks after childbirth, and requires immediate treatment.

Although the mother may feel embarrassed or ashamed, encourage her to express her feelings.

A mother with postpartum depression may feel embarrassed, ashamed, or guilty and be tempted to downplay her problem. However, this can make her feel even more isolated—as she may come to see all other mothers as blissfully happy and in control of their lives and believe that she is the only one who has negative feelings.

Offer her emotional support. Praise her for the good care she has given her baby and let her know that her negative feelings are normal. Encourage her to talk to other mothers so she can understand that others have their down moments, too.

Sometimes a mother who is depressed may begin to believe that breastfeeding is the cause of all her problems. Encourage her to keep her expectations realistic. Tell her that problems such as a fussy baby, fatigue, and feelings of being overwhelmed are not confined to nursing mothers. Tell her, too, that breastfeeding makes the hormonal changes that occur after birth more gradual. One study from Australia found a lower rate of postpartum depression in breastfeeding women (Astbury 1994).

A depressed mother may describe her nursing sessions with her baby in negative terms. One study found differences in mother-baby interactions during feedings when the mother was depressed. As compared with a group of breastfeeding mothers who were not depressed, the depressed mothers tended to see their baby's fussiness when hungry as a rejection of them or their milk rather than viewing it as having a physical cause. The depressed mothers also expressed less satisfaction in their interactions with their babies and appeared less sensitive to their babies' needs and cues (Tamminen and Salmelin 1991).

It may be difficult to listen to the mother suffering from mild postpartum depression, because unlike most helping situations, there may not be anything concrete that can be done for her or any specific information that will help her solve her problem. Conversations with her may be emotionally draining. But taking the time to listen can be of real help to her by giving her the opportunity to sort through her feelings and providing her with the warm, human contact she needs during a difficult time.

Some self-help measures can be suggested.

To help overcome her depression, suggest the mother:

- Enlist household help from the baby's father (ask if he could take more time off from work), relatives, friends, or hired help.
- Get some physical exercise every day, such as taking walks with the baby.
- Eat nutritious snacks and meals and drink to thirst.

Health Problems—Mother

- Try to sleep when the baby sleeps, which can be made easier by taking the phone off the hook and attaching a piece of paper to the front door where unexpected visitors can leave notes.
- Learn to breastfeed lying down so that she can get some sleep while nursing at night as well as during the day.
- Get together regularly with other mothers of small babies, especially those who have experienced postpartum depression or are sympathetic to it.
- Call trusted friends and family for moral support during her most difficult times of the day.
- Encourage her to write down those things on her "good days" that helped her feel better so that when she's not feeling good she can try them.
- Believe that she will feel better again.

There are a wide range of treatment options for postpartum depression.

Tincture of time. In time, a mild case of postpartum depression may clear up on its own. By using the self-help measures above, many women overcome their depression without needing further treatment.

Counseling. A knowledgable and sympathetic therapist can help. A preliminary report shows that short-term interpersonal psychotherapy brought significant improvement for a small group of non-randomly selected depressed postpartum women (Stuart 1995). Counselors can be found at women's health centers, churches, hospitals, community health centers, and local organizations such as the YWCA, as well as through physician referral and health care provider lists. If a mother finds that her counselor is not supportive of breastfeeding or her mothering style, encourage her to seek another.

Medication. Doctors sometimes prescribe antidepressant medication as part of the treatment for postpartum depression. The medication recommended is dependent upon the needs of the individual mother, as each woman reacts differently to this type of drug. The American Academy of Pediatrics' Committee on Drugs (1994) classifies antianxiety and antipsychotic drugs, as well as antidepressants, under the category "Drugs Whose Effect on Nursing Infants Is Unknown But May Be of Concern." The Committee writes "Although there are no case reports of adverse effects in breastfeeding infants, these drugs do appear in human milk and thus could conceivably alter short-term and long-term central nervous system function."

Specific information is slowly becoming available on these drugs from case reports of mothers and their babies whose blood and milk levels were monitored while the mother was taking the drug. For more information on fluoxetine (Prozac), see Briggs, Freeman, and Yaffe (1994) and for information on this and other antidepressants, see Hatzopoulos and Albrecht (1996). If a mother is reluctant to take medication, encourage her to express her feelings to her doctor so they can find a course of treatment with which she will be comfortable.

If the mother is told that the medication is incompatible with breastfeeding and she does not want to wean, it is important that she express to her doctor her desire to continue breastfeeding. It may be possible for her doctor to find a medication that is more compatible with breastfeeding. Some questions the mother could discuss with her doctor which could help clarify her need for medication include:

- Does the depression seem to be caused by external pressures, such as housework, isolation, exhaustion, or inner pressures, such as self-doubt, anxiety, lack of self-esteem, or fear?
- If external pressures seem to be contributing to the depression, could self-help measures and counseling be tried before resorting to medication?
- Might a better diet and more exercise improve her emotional state?
- If the depression is thought to be organic in origin, are there any alternative treatments or combination of treatments that would enable her to continue to breastfeed?

- Could the physical, hormonal, and emotional changes the mother would experience by weaning abruptly make her depression worse?

If the doctor feels strongly that the mother must wean in order to be treated for her depression, the mother has the option of seeking another opinion. She could also ask her doctor:

- Since abrupt weaning increases the risks of mastitis, would it be possible to begin treatment and wean gradually?

One option, which is recommended by the American Academy of Pediatrics Committee on Drugs (1994) when there is a question about a drug, is to have her doctor regularly monitor her and her baby. (For more information, see the section, "Exploring Options When the Doctor Recommends Weaning," in the chapter "Drugs, Vitamins, Vaccines, and Diagnostic Tests.")

Hospitalization. A severe case of postpartum depression or postpartum psychosis may require the mother to be hospitalized. In England and some other countries, hospitals provide mother-baby units where women can receive treatment while continuing to care for their babies. This allows a mother to get the help she needs without disrupting the mother-baby relationship. Giving a hospitalized mother the option of having her baby with her can be a boost to her flagging self-esteem by acknowledging her baby's need for her and her adequacy as a mother. It also allows breastfeeding to continue without interruption. This option is just beginning to be offered in some hospitals in the United States. Encourage the mother to look into this possibility, as keeping the mother and baby together has been found to decrease the mother's recovery time and her incidence of relapse (Waletzky 1981).

If at all possible, abrupt weaning should be avoided.

Breastfeeding is not a physiological contributor to postpartum depression. The hormonal changes after birth occur more gradually when a mother breastfeeds. However, the management of weaning should be considered an important part of the treatment of the breastfeeding mother with postpartum depression, as there are physical, hormonal, and emotional changes that take place during weaning that can affect the mother's depression.

Abrupt weaning increases a mother's risk for mastitis and breast abscess, physical problems that could complicate her treatment. Abrupt weaning also causes a change in a mother's hormonal balance, and since her depression may be hormonally related, this may deepen her depression. These hormonal changes can be particularly overwhelming for a mother who is prone to depression (Susman and Katz 1988). A woman with serious psychiatric problems may be at even greater risk.

Weaning may also be experienced as an emotional loss, because for most women, breastfeeding is more than a means of feeding a baby; it is also a way of giving and receiving love and comfort. For many women, breastfeeding is one of the few positive things they alone can do for their babies, even though they are going through a difficult time. To have this taken away suddenly can leave them feeling useless and incompetent, interchangeable with any other caregiver.

If weaning is truly necessary, encourage the mother to find a way to wean gradually, replacing one daily nursing with a formula feeding every three to four days. A gradual weaning should be considered an important part of the mother's treatment for depression. If the baby must be taken off the breast immediately, an automatic electric double pump is recommended to decrease the mother's milk supply slowly, making the hormonal changes more gradual. If a gradual weaning

Health Problems—Mother

is not possible, it is important that the mother have good support and that her doctor be aware of the possible effects of an abrupt weaning on her depression.

Depression may also influence a mother's decision to wean. One study noted an association between depression and early weaning, with the depression occurring before the weaning in the overwhelming majority of the cases (Cooper 1993). It is unclear whether the mother's depression influenced her decision to wean, whether feeding problems contributed to her depression, or whether the weaning was related to a third factor not accounted for in the study.

The mother's depression may make it especially difficult for her to be assertive with her doctor.

Even under the best of circumstances, most patients are uncomfortable questioning their doctors' recommendations and being assertive about their own desires. This is intensified for the woman with postpartum depression, who feels vulnerable and weak and may be ashamed or embarrassed about her condition. If the prospect of being assertive with her doctor seems overwhelming to the mother, encourage her to bring along her husband or a supportive relative or friend who would be willing to help her express her point of view.

Publications for Parents

When Mother Is Ill

La Leche League International. THE WOMANLY ART OF BREASTFEEDING. 35th Anniversary ed. Schaumburg, Illinois, 1991, pp. 318-25.

Mohrbacher, N. *When a Nursing Mother Gets Sick*. Schaumburg, Illinois: La Leche League International, 1996. Publication No. 21a.

Diabetes

Good, J. *The Diabetic Mother and Breastfeeding*. Schaumburg, Illinois: La Leche League International, 1987. Publication No. 17.

Postpartum Depression

Dunnewold, A. and Sanford D. *Postpartum Survival Guide*. Oakland, California: New Harbinger Publications, 1994.

Other Resources

Depression After Delivery
P.O. Box 1282
Morrisville, PA 19067
Telephone: 215-295-3994
800-944-4PPD

References

Cancer

David, F. Lactation following primary radiation therapy for carcinoma of the breast. *Int J Rad Onc Biol P* 1985; 11(7):1425.

Hayes, R. et al. Acute inflammation of the breast—the role of breast ultrasound in diagnosis and management. *Clin Radiology* 1991; 44:253-56.

Higgins, S. and Haffty, B. Pregnancy and lactation after breast-conserving therapy for early stage breast cancer. *Cancer* 1994; 73(8):2175-80.

Illingworth, P. et al. Diminution in energy expenditure during lactation. *BMJ* 1980; 292:437-40.

Lawrence, R. *Breastfeeding: A Guide for the Medical Profession,* 4th ed. St. Louis: Mosby, 1994, pp. 203-06, 511.

Neifert, M. Breastfeeding after breast surgical procedure or breast cancer. NAACOG *Clin Issues Perinat Women Health Nurs* 1992; 3(4):673-82.

Riordan, J. and Auerbach, K. *Breastfeeding and Human Lactation.* Boston and London: Jones and Bartlett, 1993, pp. 392-94.

Tralins, A. Lactation after conservative breast surgery combined with radiation therapy. *Am J Clin Oncol* 1995; 18(1):40-43.

Cardiac Problems or Hypertension

Lawrence, R. *Breastfeeding: A Guide for the Medical Profession,* 4th ed. St. Louis: Mosby, 1994, pp. 345-48 and 512-13.

Robson, S. et al. Haemodynamic changes during the puerperium: a Doppler and M-mode echocardiographic study. *Br J Ob Gyn* 1987; 94:1028-29.

Robson, S. and Hunter, S. Haemodynamic effects of breast-feeding. *Br J Ob Gyn* 1989; 96:1106-08.

Carpal Tunnel Syndrome

Lawrence, R. *Breastfeeding: A Guide for the Medical Profession,* 4th ed. St. Louis: Mosby, 1994, pp. 517.

Snell, N. et al. Carpal tunnel syndrome presenting in the puerperium. *Practitioner* 1980; 224:191.

Wand, J. Carpal tunnel syndrome in pregnancy and lactation. *J Hand Surgery* 1990; 15-B(1):93-95.

Wand, J. The natural history of carpal tunnel syndrome and lactation. *J R Soc Med* 1989; 82:349.

Yagnik, P. Carpal tunnel syndrome in nursing mothers. *South Med J* 1987; 80:1468.

Chickenpox

Lawrence, R. *Breastfeeding: A Guide for the Medical Profession,* 4th ed. St. Louis: Mosby, 1994, pp. 203-06, 486-89.

Riordan, J. and Auerbach, K. *Breastfeeding and Human Lactation,* Boston and London: Jones and Bartlett, 1993, pp. 172-73, 175.

Cholera and Typhoid Fever

Lawrence, R. *Breastfeeding: A Guide for the Medical Profession,* 4th ed. St. Louis: Mosby, 1994, p. 169.

Health Problems—Mother

Cytomegalovirus (CMV)

Committee on Infectious Diseases: Report of the Committee, *Red Book,* ed. 23. Elk Grove Village, Illinois: American Academy of Pediatrics, 1994, pp. 74-76.

Dworsky, M., et al. Cytomegalovirus infections of breast milk and transmission in infancy. *Pediatrics* 1983; 72:295.

Hotsubo, T. Detection of human cytomegalovirus DNA in breast milk by means of polymerase chain reaction. *Microbiol Immunol* 1994; 38(10):809-11.

Lawrence, R. *Breastfeeding: A Guide for the Medical Profession,* 4th ed. St. Louis: Mosby, 1994, pp. 484-85.

Minamishima, I. et al. Role of breast milk in acquisition of cytomegalovirus infection. *Microbiol Immunol* 1994; 38(7):549-52.

Riordan, J. and Auerbach, K. *Breastfeeding and Human Lactation.* Boston and London: Jones and Bartlett, 1993, pp. 173-75.

Yeager, A. et al. Sequelae of maternally derived cytomegalovirus infections in premature infants. *J Pediatr* 1983; 102:918.

Food Poisoning

Lawrence, R. *Breastfeeding: A Guide for the Medical Profession,* 4th ed. St. Louis: Mosby, 1994, pp. 169, 478-79, 484.

Giardia

Briggs, G., Freeman, R. and Yaffe, S. *Drugs in Pregnancy and Lactation,* 4th ed. Baltimore: Williams & Wilkins, 1994, pp. 587-89.

Committee on Drugs, American Academy of Pediatrics. The transfer of drugs and other chemicals into human milk. *Pediatrics* 1994; 93:139.

Drinkwater, P. Metronidazole. *Aust NZ J Obst Gyn* 1987; 27:228-30.

Erickson, S., et al. Metronidazole in breast milk. *Obstet Gynecol* 1981:57:48.

Lawrence, R. *Breastfeeding: A Guide for the Medical Profession,* 4th ed. St. Louis: Mosby, 1994, p. 339, 495-96.

Lawrence, R. Lactation Study Center, University of Rochester, New York. Personal communication, 1995.

Morrow, A. et al. Protection against infection with Giardia lamblia by breastfeeding in a cohort of Mexican infants. *J Pediatr* 1992; 121:363-70.

Passmore, C., et al. Metronidazole excretion in human milk and its effect on the suckling neonate. *Br J Clin Pharmac* 1988; 26:45-51.

US Pharmacopeial Convention. *United States Pharmacoepia Dispensing Information: Drug Information for the Health Care Professional,* 16th ed. Rockville, Maryland: US Pharmacopeial Convention, 1996, p. 2058.

Hepatitis

Committee on Infectious Diseases: Report of the Committee, *Red Book*, ed. 23. Elk Grove Village, Illinois: American Academy of Pediatrics, 1994, pp. 74-76, 223, 236.

Eng, D. Epidemiologist, US Centers for Disease Control. Personal communication, December 2, 1994.

Fanous, E. and Balart, L. Recent developments in viral hepatitis. *Curr Opinion Gastroenterology* 1994; 10:237-42.

Gartner, L. Professor, Department of Pediatrics, University of Chicago, Illinois. Personal communication, April 1996 and December 1994.

Krawczynski, K. Hepatitis E. *Hepatology* 1993; 17:932-41.

Lawrence, R. *Breastfeeding: A Guide for the Medical Profession,* 4th ed. St. Louis: Mosby, 1994, pp. 206-08, 490-91, 611.

Lin, H-H., et al. Absence of infection in breast-fed infants born to hepatitis C virus-infected mothers. *J Pediatr* 1995; 126(4):589-91

Ohto, H. Transmission of hepatitis C virus from mothers to infants. *N Engl J Med* 1994; 330:744-50.

Ogasawara, S. et al. Hepatitis C virus RNA in saliva and breastmilk of hepatitis C carrier mothers. *Lancet* 1993; 341:561.

Purdy, M. and Krawczynski, K. Hepatitis E. *Gastroenterol Clin N Am* 1994; 23:537-46.

Riordan, J. and Auerbach, K. *Breastfeeding and Human Lactation,* Boston and London: Jones and Bartlett, 1993, pp. 174-76.

Ruff, A. Breastmilk, breastfeeding, and transmission of viruses to the neonate. *Sem Perinatol* 1994; 18(6):510-16.

Uehara, S. et al. The incidence of vertical transmission of hepatitis C virus. *J Exp Med* 1993; 171:195-202.

US Food and Drug Administration. *FDA Med Bulletin* 1994; 24(2):4.

Herpes Simplex I (Cold Sores) and II (Genital Herpes)

Lawrence, R. *Breastfeeding: A Guide for the Medical Profession,* 4th ed. St. Louis: Mosby, 1994, pp. 485-86.

Lopez, I. et al. Neutralising activity against herpes simplex virus in human milk. *Breastfeeding Rev* 1990; 11(2):56-58.

Quinn, P. and Lofberg, J. Maternal herpetic breast infection: another hazard of neonatal herpes simplex. *Med J Aust* 1978; 2:411-12.

Health Problems—Mother

Riordan, J. and Auerbach, K. *Breastfeeding and Human Lactation*. Boston and London: Jones and Bartlett, 1993, pp. 171-73, 175.

Sealander, J. and Kerr, C. Herpes simplex of the nipple: infant-to-mother transmission. *Am Fam Phys* 1989; 39:111-13.

Sullivan-Bolyai, J. et al. Disseminated neonatal breast lesion. *Pediatrics* 1983; 71:455-57.

HIV (AIDS)

Centers for Disease Control. Recommendations for assisting in the prevention of perinatal transmission of human T-lymphotropic virus type III/lymphadena lymphadenopathy-associated virus and acquired immunodeficiency syndrome. *MMWR* 1985; 34:721-6, 731.

Colebunders, R. et al. Breastfeeding and transmission of HIV. *Lancet* 1988; 2:(8626/8627):1487.

Cutting, W. Breast-feeding and HIV—a balance of risks. *J Trop Pediatr* 1994; 40:6-11.

Datta, P. et al. Mother-to-child transmission of human immunodeficiency virus type 1: report from the Nairobi study. *J Infect Dis* J 1994; 170:1334-40.

Datta, P. et al. Resumption of breast-feeding in later childhood: a risk factor for mother to child human immunodeficiency virus type 1 transmission. *Ped Infect Dis* J 1992; 11(11):974-76.

Dunn, D. Risk of human immunodeficiency virus type 1 transmission through breastfeeding. *Lancet* 1992; 340: 585-88.

European Collaborative Study: Risk factors for mother-to-child transmission of HIV-1. *Lancet* 1992; 339:1007-12.

Goldfarb, J. Breastfeeding AIDS and other infectious diseases. *Clin Perinatol* 1993; 20(1):225-43.

Halsey, N. et al. Transmission of HIV-1 infections from mothers to infants in Haiti. *JAMA* 1990; 264(16):2088-92.

Lawrence, R. *Breastfeeding: A Guide for the Medical Profession,* 4th ed. St. Louis: Mosby, 1994, pp. 174, 208-11, 611.

Lepage, P., et al. Postnatal transmission of HIV from mother to child. *Lancet* 1985; 2(8555):400.

Malaviya A. et al. Circumstantial evidence of HIV transmission via breast milk. *J Acquir Immun Defic Syndr* 1992; 5:102-06.

Nduati, R. et al. Postnatal transmission of HIV-1 through pooled breast milk. *Lancet* 1994; 344:1432.

Newburg, D. et al. Human milk glycosaminoglycans inhibit HIV glycoprotein gp120 binding to its host cell CD4 receptor. *J Nutr* 1995; 125:419-24.

Newburg D. et al. A human milk factor inhibits the binding of HIV to the CD4 receptor. *Pediatr Res* 1992; 3(1):22-28.

Oxtoby, M. Human immunodeficiency virus and other viruses in human milk: placing the issues in broader perspective. *J Pediatr Infect Dis* 1988; 7:825-35.

Palasanthiran, P. et al. Breast-feeding during primary maternal human immunodeficiency virus infection and risk of transmission from mother to infant. *J Infec Dis* 1993; 167:441-44.

Riordan, J. and Auerbach, K. *Breastfeeding and Human Lactation.* Boston and London: Jones and Bartlett, 1993, pp. 167-71, 175.

Rubini, N. and Passman, L. Transmission of human immunodeficiency virus infection from a newly infected mother to her two year old child by breastfeeding. *Ped Infect Dis J* 1992; 11:682.

Ruff, A. Breastmilk, breastfeeding, and transmission of viruses to the neonate. *Sem Perinatol* 1994; 18(6):510-16.

Ryder, R. and Behets, F. Reasons for the wide variation in reported rates of mother-to-child transmission of HIV-1. *AIDS* 1994; 8(10):1495-97.

Ryder, R. et al. Evidence from Zaire that breast-feeding by HIV-1-seropositive mothers is not a major route for perinatal HIV-1 transmission but does decrease morbidity. *AIDS* 1991; 5(6):709-14.

Ryder, R. et al. Perinatal transmission of the human immunodeficiency virus type 1 to infants of seropositive women in Zaire. *N Engl J Med* 1989; 320:1637-42.

Semba, R. et al. Maternal viatmin A deficiency and mother-to-child transmission of HIV-1. *Lancet* 1994; 343:1593-97.

Thiry, L. et al. Isolation of AIDS virus from cell-free breast milk of three healthy virus carriers. *Lancet* 1985; 2:891-98.

Tozzi, A. et al. Does breast-feeding delay progression to AIDS in HIV-infected children? *AIDS* 1990; 4:1293-1304.

Van de Perre, P. et al. Infective and anti-infective properties of breastmilk from HIV-1-infected women. *Lancet* 1993; 341:914-18.

Van de Perre, P. et al. Postnatal transmission of human immunodeficiency virus type 1: the breast-feeding dilemma. *Am J Obstet Gynecol* 1995; 173(3):483-87.

Van de Perre, P. et al. Mother-to-infant transmission of human immunodeficiency virus by breast milk: presumed innocent or presumed guilty? *Clin Infect Dis* 1992; 15:502-07.

Van de Perre P. et al. Postnatal transmission of human immunodeficiency virus type 1 from mother to infant. *N Engl J Med* 1991; 325(9):593-98.

World Health Organization. Consensus statement from the WHO/UNICEF consultation on HIV transmission and breast-feeding, Geneva, 30 April - 1 May 1992.

Health Problems—Mother

Ziegler, J. et al. Postnatal transmission of AIDS-associated retrovirus from mother to infant. *Lancet* 1985; 1:896-97.

HTLV-I

Ando, Y. et al. Bottle-feeding can prevent transmission of HTLV-I from mothers to their babies. *J Infect* 1989a; 19:25-29.

Ando, Y et al. Effect of freeze-thawing breast milk on vertical HTLV-I transmission from seropositive mothers to children. *Jap J Cancer* Res 1989b; 80:405-07.

Committee on Infectious Diseases: Report of the Committee, *Red Book;* ed 23. Elk Grove Village, Illinois: American Academy of Pediatrics, 1994, p. 75.

Hino, S. Milk-borne transmission of HTLV-I as a major route in the endemic cycle. *Acta Paediatric Jap* 1989; 31:428.

Hirata, M., et al. The effects of breastfeeding and presence of antibody to P40tax protein of human T cell lymphotropic virus type-I on mother to child transmission. *Int J Epidemiol* 1992; 21(5):989-94.

Ichimaru, M. et al. Mother-to-child transmission of HTLV-I. *Cancer Detect Prev* 1991; 15:177-81.

Kawase, K-i., et al. The effects of breastfeeding and presence of antibody to p40tax protein of human T-cell lymphotropic virus type-I on mother to child transmission. *Jpn J Cancer Res* 1992; 83(9):968-77.

Lawrence, R. *Breastfeeding: A Guide for the Medical Profession,* 4th ed. St. Louis: Mosby, 1994, p. 211.

Oki, T. et al. A sero-epidemiological study on mother-to-child transmission of HTLV-I in southern Kyushu, Japan. *Asia-Oceania J Obstet Gynaecol* 1992; 18(4):371-77.

Ruff, A. Breastmilk, breastfeeding, and transmission of viruses to the neonate. *Sem Perinatol* 1994; 18(6):510-16.

Tajima, K. Malignant lymphomas in Japan epidemiological analysis of adult T-cell leukemia/lymphoma. *Cancer Metastasis Rev* 1988; 7:223-24.

Takahashi, K. et al. Inhibitory effect of maternal antibody on mother-to-child transmission of human T-lymphotrophic virus type I. *Int J Cancer* 1991; 49:673-77.

Tsuji, Y. et al. Prevention of mother-to-child transmission of human T-lymphotropic virus type-I. *Pediatrics* 1990; 86(1):11-17.

Wiktor, S. et al. Mother-to-child transmission of human T-cell lymphotrophic virus type I (HTLV-I) in Jamaica: association with antibodies to envelope glycoprotein (gp46) epitopes. *J Acquir Immun Defic Syndr* 1993; 6:1162-67.

Leprosy

Lawrence, R. *Breastfeeding: A Guide for the Medical Profession,* 4th ed. St. Louis: Mosby, 1994, p. 482.

Lyme Disease

Centers for Disease Control. General facts about Lyme Disease and its transmission. Document #351701, November 19, 1992.

Lawrence, R. *Breastfeeding: A Guide for the Medical Profession,* 4th ed. St. Louis: Mosby, 1994, p. 483.

Malaria

Fulton, B. and Moore, L. Anti-infectives in breastmilk, Part II: sulfonamides, tetracyclines, macrolides, aminoglycosides, and antimalarials. *J Hum Lact* 1992; 8(4):221-23.

Measles

Lawrence, R. *Breastfeeding: A Guide for the Medical Profession,* 4th ed. St. Louis: Mosby, 1994, pp. 487-89.

Rubella, or German Measles

Krogh, V. et al. Postpartum immunization with rubella virus vaccine and antibody response in breastfeeding infants. *J Lab Clin Med* 1989; 113:695.

Lawrence, R. *Breastfeeding: A Guide for the Medical Profession,* 4th ed. St. Louis: Mosby, 1994, p. 484.

Losonsky, G. et al. Effect of immunization against rubella on lactation products. I. Development and characterization of specific immunologic reactivity in breast milk. *J Infec Dis* 1982; 145:661-66.

Riordan, J. and Auerbach, K. *Breastfeeding and Human Lactation,* Boston and London: Jones and Bartlett, 1993, pp. 174-75.

Sexually Transmitted Diseases

Committee on Drugs, American Academy of Pediatrics. The transfer of drugs and other chemicals into human milk. *Pediatrics* 1994; 93:139.

Briggs, G., Freeman, R. and Yaffe, S. *Drugs in Pregnancy and Lactation,* 4th ed. Baltimore: Williams & Wilkins, 1994, pp. 587-89.

Drinkwater, P. Metronidazole. *Aust NZ J Obst Gyn* 1987; 27:228-30.

Erickson, S., et al. Metronidazole in breast milk. *Obstet Gynecol* 1981:57:48.

Lawrence, R. *Breastfeeding: A Guide for the Medical Profession,* 4th ed. St. Louis: Mosby, 1994, p. 339, 480-81, 494-95.

Passmore, C., et al. Metronidazole excretion in human milk and its effect on the suckling neonate. *Br J Clin Pharmac* 1988; 26:45-51.

Riordan, J. and Auerbach, K. *Breastfeeding and Human Lactation,* Boston and London: Jones and Bartlett, 1993, pp. 174-76.

Health Problems—Mother

US Pharmacopeial Convention. *United States Pharmacoepia Dispensing Information: Drug Information for the Health Care Professional,* 16th ed. Rockville, Maryland: US Pharmacopeial Convention, 1996, p. 2058.

Toxic Shock Syndrome

Lawrence, R. *Breastfeeding: A Guide for the Medical Profession,* 4th ed. St. Louis: Mosby, 1994, pp. 477-80.

Vergeront, J. et al. Recovery of staphylococcal enterotoxin F from the breast milk of a woman with toxic-shock syndrome. *J Infec Dis* 1982; 146:456-59.

Toxoplasmosis

Lawrence, R. *Breastfeeding: A Guide for the Medical Profession,* 4th ed. St. Louis: Mosby, 1994, p. 492.

Tuberculosis

Committee on Drugs, American Academy of Pediatrics. The transfer of drugs and other chemicals into human milk. *Pediatrics* 1994; 93:137-50.

Lawrence, R. *Breastfeeding: A Guide for the Medical Profession,* 4th ed. St. Louis: Mosby, 1994, pp. 478-79, 481-82.

Riordan, J. and Auerbach, K. *Breastfeeding and Human Lactation,* Boston and London: Jones and Bartlett, 1993, p. 357.

Snider, D. and Powell, K. Should women taking antituberculosis drugs breast-feed? *Arch Intern Med* 1984; 144:589-90.

When Mother is Hospitalized

Lawrence, R. *Breastfeeding: A Guide for the Medical Profession,* 4th ed. St. Louis: Mosby, 1994, pp. 520-23.

Spigset, O. Anaesthetic agents and excretion in breast milk. *Acta Anaesthesiol Scand* 1994; 38:94-103.

Physical Limitation or Chronic Illness

Dunne, G. and Fuerst, K. Breastfeeding by a mother who is a triple amputee: a case report. *J Hum Lact* 1995; 11(3):217-18.

Thomson, V. Breastfeeding and mothering one-handed. *J Hum Lact* 1995; 11(3):211-15.

Blindness

Brewster, D. *You Can Breastfeed Your Baby...Even in Special Situations.* Emmaus, Pennsylvania: Rodale Press, 1979. pp. 476-80.

Cystic Fibrosis

Alpert, S. and Cormier, A. Normal electrolyte and protein content in milk from mothers with cystic fibrosis: an explanation for the initial report of elevated milk sodium concentration. *J Pediatr* 1983; 102:77.

Lawrence, R. *Breastfeeding: A Guide for the Medical Profession,* 4th ed. St. Louis: Mosby, 1994, pp. 507-09.

Luder, E. et al. Current recommendations for breastfeeding in cystic fibrosis centers. *Am J Dis Child* 1990; 144:1153-56.

Michel, S. and Mueller, D. Impact of lactation on women with cystic fibrosis and their infants: a review of five cases. *J Am Diet Assoc* 1994; 94(2):159-65.

Riordan, J. and Auerbach, K. *Breastfeeding and Human Lactation,* Boston and London: Jones and Bartlett, 1993, p. 356.

Shiffman, M. et al. Breast-milk composition in women with cystic fibrosis: report of two cases and a review of the literature. *Am J Clin Nutr* 1989; 49:612-17.

Smith, P. et al. Breastmilk and cystic fibrosis. *Med J Aust* 1992; 157:283.

Diabetes Mellitus

Arthur, P. et. al. Milk lactose, citrate, and glucose as markers of lactogenesis in normal and diabetic women. *J Ped Gastro Nutr* 1989; 9:488-96.

Buchanon, T. et al. Medical management of diabetes in pregnancy. *Clin Perinatol* 1985; 12:625.

Butte, N. et al. Milk composition of insulin-dependent diabetic women. *J Ped Gastro Nutr* 1987; 6:939.

Davies, H. et al. Insulin requirements of diabetic women who breast feed. *BMJ* 1989; 298(6684):1357-58.

Ferris, A. et al. Lactation outcome in insulin-dependent diabetic women. *J Am Dietetic Assoc* 1988; 88: 317.

Ferris A. et al. Perinatal lactation protocol and outcome in mothers with and without insulin-dependent diabetes mellitus. *Am J Clin Nutr* 1993; 58:43-48.

Gagne, M. et al. The breast-feeding experience of women with type I diabetes. *Health Care Women Int* 1992; 13:249-60.

Karjalainen, J. et al. A bovine albumin peptide as a possible trigger of insulin-dependent diabetes mellitus. *N Engl J Med* 1992; 327(5):302-07.

Kjos, S. The effect of lactation on glucose and lipid metabolism in women with recent gestational diabetes. *Obstet Gynecol* 1993; 82(3):451-55.

Lawrence, R. *Breastfeeding: A Guide for the Medical Profession,* 4th ed. St. Louis: Mosby, 1994, pp. 499-505.

Health Problems—Mother

Metcalfe, M. et al. Family characteristics and insulin dependent diabetes. *Arch Dis Child* 1992; 67(6):731-36.

Neubauer, S. et al. Delayed lactogenesis in women with insulin-dependent diabetes mellitus. *Am J Clin Nutr* 1993; 58:54-60.

Riordan, J. and Auerbach, K. *Breastfeeding and Human Lactation,* Boston and London: Jones and Bartlett, 1993, pp. 353-54.

Sirota, L. Beta glucuronidase and hyperbilirubinemia in breastfed infants of diabetic mothers. *Arch Dis Child* 1992; 76:120.

Virtanen, S. et al. Infant feeding in Finnish children <7 years of age with newly diagnosed IDDM. *Diabetes Care* 1991; 14(5):415-17.

Webster, J., et al. Breastfeeding outcomes for women with insulin dependent diabetes. *J Hum Lact* 1995; 11(3):195-200.

Whichelow, M. and Doddridge, M. Lactation in diabetic women. *BMJ* 1983; 287:649.

Epilepsy

Brewster, D. *You Can Breastfeed Your Baby...Even in Special Situations.* Emmaus, Pennsylvania: Rodale Press, 1979. pp. 484-87.

Lawrence, R. *Breastfeeding: A Guide for the Medical Profession,* 4th ed. St. Louis: Mosby, 1994, pp. 516-17.

Riordan, J. and Auerbach, K. *Breastfeeding and Human Lactation,* Boston and London: Jones and Bartlett, 1993, pp. 364-65.

Multiple Sclerosis

Lawrence, R. *Breastfeeding: A Guide for the Medical Profession,* 4th ed. St. Louis: Mosby, 1994, p. 534.

Nelson, L. Risk of multiple sclerosis exacerbation during pregnancy and breast-feeding. *JAMA* 1988; 259:3441-43.

Pisacane, A. et al. Breast feeding and multiple sclerosis. *BMJ* 1994; 308:1411-12.

Poser, S. and Poser, W. Multiple sclerosis and gestation. *Neurology* 1983; 33:1423-27.

Riordan, J. and Auerbach, K. *Breastfeeding and Human Lactation.* Boston and London: Jones and Bartlett, 1993, pp. 361-62.

Thyroid Disease and Other Endocrine Problems

Lawrence, R. *Breastfeeding: A Guide for the Medical Profession,* 4th ed. St. Louis: Mosby, 1994, pp. 498-99, 505-07.

Lazarus, J. and Othman, S. Thyroid disease in relation to pregnancy. *Clin Endocrinol* 1991; 34:91-98.

Riordan, J. and Auerbach, K. *Breastfeeding and Human Lactation*. Boston and London: Jones and Bartlett, 1993, pp. 354-55.

Willis, C. and Livingstone, V. Infant insufficient milk syndrome associated with maternal postpartum hemorrhage. *J Hum Lact* 1995; 11(2):123-26.

Postpartum Depression

Astbury, J. et al. Birth events, birth experiences and social differences in postnatal depression. *Aust J Public Health* 1994; 18(2):176-84.

Committee on Drugs, American Academy of Pediatrics. The transfer of drugs and other chemicals into human milk. *Pediatrics* 1994; 93:139.

Cooper, P. J. et al. Psychosocial factors associated with the early termination of breast-feeding. *J Psychosom Res* 1993; 37(2):171-76.

Briggs, G., Freeman, R. and Yaffe, S. *Update [on Drugs in Pregnancy and Lactation]* 1994; 7:9-11.

Hatzopoulos, F. and Albrecht, L. Antidepressant use during breastfeeding. *J Hum Lact* 1996; 12(2):139-41.

Hopkins, J., Marcus, M. and Campbell, S. Postpartum depression: a critical review. *Psychol Bull* 1984; 95:498-515.

Lawrence, R. *Breastfeeding: A Guide for the Medical Profession,* 4th ed. St. Louis: Mosby, 1994, pp. 189-92, 315, 522.

O'Hara, M. Post-partum "blues," depression, and psychosis: a review. *J Psychosom Ob Gynecol* 1987; 7:205-27.

Riordan, J. and Auerbach, K. *Breastfeeding and Human Lactation*. Boston and London: Jones and Bartlett, 1993, pp. 365-68.

Stuart, S. Treatment of postpartum depression with interpersonal psychotherapy. *Arch Gen Psychiatry* 1995; 52:75-76.

Susman, V. and Katz, J. Weaning and depression: another postpartum complication. *Am J Psychiatry* 1988; 145(4):498-501.

Tamminen, T. and Salmelin, R. Psychosomatic interaction between mother and infant during breast feeding. *Psychother Psychosom* 1991; 56:78-84.

Waletzky, L. Emotional illness in the postpartum period. In Ahmed, P., ed. *Pregnancy, Childbirth and Parenthood*. Elsevier North-Hooland, Inc.: New York, 1981.

Health Problems—Mother

24

Drugs, Vitamins, Vaccines, and Diagnostic Tests

PRESCRIPTION AND OVER-THE-COUNTER DRUGS
Encourage the Mother to Work Openly with Her Doctor
General Considerations about Drugs and Breastfeeding
Information Needed Before Checking on a Specific Drug
Giving Information on Specific Drugs
Exploring Options When the Doctor Recommends Weaning
Where to Find Information on Specific Drugs

SUBSTANCES OF CONCERN
Alcohol
Caffeine
Herbal Remedies and Teas
Nicotine

SUBSTANCES OF ABUSE
Amphetamines
Marijuana
Cocaine
Heroin

VITAMIN AND MINERAL SUPPLEMENTS FOR BABIES

VACCINES

DIAGNOSTIC TESTS

PRESCRIPTION AND OVER-THE-COUNTER DRUGS

The vast majority of prescription and over-the-counter medications are compatible with breastfeeding, although most pass into the mother's milk in minute quantities.

Only a licensed medical professional can prescribe or evaluate the safety of a drug for a nursing mother, but there are other ways to be of help.

Only a licensed medical professional can prescribe or recommend a drug to a breastfeeding mother or evaluate the safety of a drug for an individual mother and baby. But there are other ways to be of help to a mother who is faced with the possibility of taking a drug while breastfeeding:

- Help her frame questions to ask her doctor, her baby's doctor, or other health care professional.
- Help her explore her feelings about what she really wants to do.
- Provide her with information and resources.
- Support and encourage her to accept responsibility for the health and well-being of her baby and herself.

When discussing a mother's questions about drugs, keep in mind that the information the mother gives may be incomplete.

Often questions about drugs and breastfeeding are more complicated than they seem. When a mother calls with a question about a drug, keep in mind that the mother may only be telling part of the story, either because she chooses not to share everything or because she does not completely understand the medical situation.

Discuss with the mother why the drug is needed.

If a mother has a minor ailment or discomfort that will quickly clear up on its own, she may be able to avoid or delay taking the drug. Many health problems are routinely dealt with by prescribing or recommending drugs when other methods of easing discomfort or hastening recovery may be substituted for the drug. The mother may wish to discuss with her doctor whether it is really necessary for her to take the drug.

If the drug is considered necessary, the next step is to encourage the mother to work with her doctor.

Encourage the Mother to Work Openly with Her Doctor

The mother should always consult with a doctor (either her own or her baby's) when taking a drug while breastfeeding, because the doctor will need to evaluate the drug's compatibility with breastfeeding in light of the baby's age, medical history, the mother's health, and possible alternatives.

Ask the mother if her doctor knows that she is breastfeeding.

If the mother and her doctor believe the drug is necessary, the next question should be: "Does your doctor know that you are breastfeeding?" Some mothers hesitate to tell their doctors that they are breastfeeding when a drug is prescribed or recommended because they are afraid that mentioning breastfeeding may cause a conflict.

The mother may decide, rather than discussing it with her doctor, to ask someone else to check on the drug for her. In reality, however, the mother needs more than just a reference or a citation in a book. She also needs this information to be interpreted and applied to her own situation. Doing this herself would be self-diagnosing, which may be risky.

If the mother's doctor has given her a prescription for a drug or recommended an over-the-counter drug without knowing she is breastfeeding, encourage the mother to call her own or her baby's doctor to discuss it. Also, offer to check the written resources on the drug.

If the mother has not told the doctor that she is breastfeeding and the doctor has prescribed a drug for her to take or recommended an over-the-counter drug, suggest that *before* she begins taking the drug she call her own or her baby's doctor and discuss it. Even though most drugs are compatible with breastfeeding, it would be wise to have a health professional evaluate the drug in light of the baby's age, medical history, the mother's health, and other alternatives.

If the mother is reluctant to call her own doctor, suggest she talk to her baby's doctor. Offer to spend some time helping her formulate her concerns and responses before she speaks to the doctor directly.

Also, offer to check the written resources concerning the drug's compatibility with breastfeeding (see "Additional Resources" later in this chapter). Caution the mother, however, that this information will need to be interpreted in light of her own situation.

Although most drugs are considered compatible with breastfeeding, doctors do not always evaluate a drug's compatibility with breastfeeding in the same way, so the mother may need to contact more than one doctor.

Different doctors take different approaches to evaluating a drug's compatibility with breastfeeding.

If no information is available about a drug, for example, (and this is likely with a new drug) one doctor may recommend weaning as a precaution, while another doctor would simply prescribe a different drug about which there is more information.

The written resources the doctor uses also may affect his or her advice. For example, some drug information, such as *The Physicians' Desk Reference* (PDR), which consists of information provided by drug companies, takes an overly cautious approach to drugs and breastfeeding due to concern about lawsuits, whereas written resources from independent sources list many more drugs as being compatible with breastfeeding.

Personal opinions about breastfeeding and drugs also may differ among doctors. Some doctors believe that the breastfeeding mother should not take any drugs, despite objective research to the contrary, while other doctors are comfortable prescribing the drugs that have been shown to be compatible with breastfeeding.

So if either the mother's doctor or her baby's doctor has reservations about a drug's compatibility with breastfeeding, suggest she contact the other doctor to discuss it further. (Also, see "Helping the Mother Work with her Doctor" in the chapter "Giving Effective Breastfeeding Help.")

Many factors influence a doctor's choice of drug.

If the doctor knows the mother is breastfeeding, it might affect his or her choice of drug or its form. When a choice is available, the preferred drug for the breastfeeding mother would be:

- time-tested, that is, it has been used by nursing mothers for long enough to be known to be compatible with breastfeeding.
- least toxic to the baby,
- short half-life (which means the drug will be eliminated more quickly from mother's body),
- least concentrated in the mother's milk, and
- given in the smallest effective dose for the shortest course.

The doctor also needs to weigh other factors. For example, how the medication is given can affect its concentration in the mother's milk. A drug given intravenously enters the bloodstream directly and may be more concentrated, whereas the same drug given by injection or by mouth takes longer to reach the bloodstream and becomes more dilute in the process. For most drugs, there will be a greater concentration in the mother's

Drugs/Vaccines/Tests

bloodstream than in her milk. In fact, the amount of drug in milk is usually no more than 1 to 2 percent of the maternal dosage taken.

The characteristics of the drug itself also affect how much of it passes into the mother's milk. For example, some drugs bind to proteins in the mother's blood and others do not. A protein-binding drug would have fewer molecules circulating freely in the mother's bloodstream, resulting in fewer in her milk. Also, slightly alkaline drugs pass into the milk more freely than acidic drugs. Drugs made up of large molecules, such as insulin and heparin, are unable to enter the milk supply at all because they are too large to pass through the membranes and into the milk.

How well the baby can break down and excrete the drug is another important consideration. A small amount of a drug that accumulates in the baby's system may be more of a problem than a larger amount that is quickly eliminated.

Choosing a prescribed or over-the-counter drug for a mother is not as simple as it may seem. Because individuals react differently to the same drug, what works well for one mother might not work well for another. Also, when prescribing or recommending a drug, a doctor needs to take into account how it will react with the mother's diet or any other drugs the mother is taking.

If the mother has not yet seen her doctor but is concerned in advance about a drug she thinks her doctor will prescribe or recommend, check the written resources and encourage her to discuss it with her doctor.

Occasionally, a mother may ask about a drug that is routinely prescribed or recommended for a health problem she is having, even though she has not yet seen her doctor.

Offer to check the written resources about the drug's compatibility with breastfeeding and encourage the mother to discuss this information with her doctor or her baby's doctor.

If the mother has told her doctor she is breastfeeding, ask what information she has already received about the drug.

A mother with a question about a drug may have already been told by others (i.e., her doctor, her baby's doctor, her pharmacist) that the drug is compatible with breastfeeding, and she is double- and triple-checking this for her own peace of mind.

In this case, it may set the mother's mind at ease to have the drug checked again. She might also need a listening ear to work through her own feelings and doubts about taking the drug while breastfeeding.

General Considerations about Drugs and Breastfeeding

A mother may not realize until after she has left her doctor's office that she has unanswered questions about the drug prescribed or recommended. If so, help her frame her questions so she will receive the information she wants when she talks to the doctor.

Ask the mother her concerns about taking the drug.

Most concerns about breastfeeding and drugs fall into several categories:

- Will the drug affect the breastfeeding baby?
- Will the drug affect lactation?
- What are the risks of weaning?
- What are the options?

Will the drug affect the baby?

Although most drugs pass into a breastfeeding mother's milk, the amount is very small, usually about 1 to 2 percent of the mother's dose (Anderson 1991). Because the baby receives such a minuscule amount of the drug, there are few verified reports of a prescribed or over-the-counter drug harming a nursing baby. With few exceptions (such as radioactive compounds), the baby is nearly always unaffected by the medications taken by the mother. **Encourage the mother to ask the doctor what are the reports in the medical literature regarding this drug.**

Some drugs do not pass into the mother's milk at all. Examples include:

- drugs that are not absorbed into the mother's bloodstream from her digestive tract (such as nonabsorbable laxatives), and
- drugs with very large molecules, such as insulin and heparin, that cannot pass through the membranes and into the milk.

If the drug is not present in mother's milk or is known to be safe from a long history of use in nursing mothers, it is compatible with breastfeeding.

The baby's age will affect his ability to eliminate the drug from his system.

The younger the baby, the less able he will be to eliminate most drugs from his system.

A premature baby will be less able to metabolize a drug than a full-term baby, in part because his digestive and renal systems are immature and his liver cannot easily break down and excrete drugs from his system.

A full-term newborn will be better able to metabolize a drug than a premature baby but less able to metabolize a drug than an older baby. Even two weeks of maturity can make a difference in the permeability of a baby's gut. A drug that is considered compatible with breastfeeding for the mother of a full-term newborn may not be considered compatible for the breastfeeding mother of a premature baby. The same is true when comparing the full-term newborn with an older baby. For example, sulfa drugs, although safely given to older babies, would not be the best choice for the breastfeeding mother of a newborn. Sulfa drugs promote newborn jaundice, which is why they are not recommended during the first month of life.

After one month of age most babies are better able to handle certain drugs, such as sulfa medications, that they could not metabolize earlier. An older baby will be better able to metabolize most drugs than a one-month-old.

A heavier baby will be less affected by a drug he receives through the mother's milk than a lighter baby of the same age.

Drug dosage in children is usually calculated by weight. The heavier the child, the larger the dose that is prescribed for him. So, too, the baby's weight is a factor when considering the effect of a drug taken by the breastfeeding mother. A heavier baby will be less affected by a drug he receives through the mother's milk than a lighter baby of the same age.

In general, the baby who is exclusively breastfeeding will receive more of the drug than a baby who is also receiving other nourishment.

A baby who is receiving solid foods or formula as well as human milk will receive less of the drug than one who is exclusively breastfeeding, because mother's milk comprises a smaller percentage of the baby's diet. A breastfeeding toddler who nurses infrequently will receive less of the drug than a toddler who nurses more often.

A drug given to babies is usually a good choice for a breastfeeding mother.

In general, a drug that is safe for babies is a good choice for a breastfeeding mother. The amount the baby receives through the mother's milk is considerably less than he would receive if he were given it directly. Drugs in the penicillin family, such as amoxicillin which is prescribed for babies, are often given to breastfeeding mothers needing an antibiotic.

On the other hand, some drugs that are given to older babies might not be appropriate for the mother of a premature baby or a newborn, because a younger baby is unable to metabolize the drug as well as an older baby. Also certain drugs that are given directly to babies, such as phenobarbital, might still be a concern when taken by a breastfeeding mother because of the amount of the drug passing into the milk. In this case, the mother may need to watch for side effects in her baby, such as changes in feeding and sleeping patterns.

A drug that is given during pregnancy may or may not be compatible with breastfeeding.

In general, when a mother takes a drug, the baby receives a smaller amount during breastfeeding than he would during pregnancy (Anderson 1991). However, drugs that may be considered safe during pregnancy are not necessarily considered compatible

Drugs/Vaccines/Tests

with breastfeeding. During pregnancy the mother's liver and kidneys may detoxify and excrete the drug before it reaches the baby through the placenta, whereas during breastfeeding the baby must process the drug on his own once it reaches his bloodstream. On the other hand, the baby *in utero* receives more of the drug—because it reaches him through his bloodstream—whereas the breastfeeding baby receives only what reaches him through the milk. So the considerations during pregnancy are not necessarily the same as those during breastfeeding.

Doctors do not agree among themselves about whether a mother on long-term drug therapy during pregnancy can safely breastfeed while taking the same drug. Some health professionals believe that if the drug has been taken during nine months of pregnancy it will be less of a problem for a breastfeeding baby, while others believe this may compound its effects.

A drug that is time-tested is usually a better choice than a new drug.

A drug that has been given to other breastfeeding mothers over the years can usually be prescribed or recommended by a doctor with more confidence than a drug that is newly available.

A short-acting form of a drug is preferable to its long-acting form.

If a short-acting form of the drug is available, it is almost always preferable to its long-acting form. An advantage of a short-acting drug is that it is quickly eliminated by both the mother and the baby. A long-acting drug stays in the mother's system and her milk for a longer period of time and is more likely to accumulate in the baby's system.

A drug with a short half-life may be a better choice than a drug with a long half-life.

Half-life refers to the length of time it takes for the drug concentration in the mother's blood to be decreased by half. Drugs vary greatly in their half-lives. On average, penicillin has a half-life of about an hour while phenobarbital has a half-life of about 85 hours (Hale, pp. 309, 314-15). A drug with a short half-life is taken more often than a drug with a long half-life, and it is preferable because it clears the mother's system more quickly. Once a mother has started taking a drug, it usually takes about four or five half-lives to keep the drug levels steady in her blood.

How long the mother takes the drug affects its compatibility with breastfeeding.

A drug taken for weeks or months may have a greater potential impact on a breastfeeding baby than one that is taken only for a few days.

The way a drug is given affects how quickly the drug appears in the mother's milk and its level in the milk.

The speed at which a drug reaches the mother's milk and its level in the milk will depend in part on how it is given. The following methods of drug delivery are listed from fastest and highest levels in the milk to the slowest and lowest levels in the milk:

- intravenous,
- intramuscular or subcutaneous injection,
- oral,
- topical.

If the drug needs to be given by injection because it would be destroyed by the mother's digestive system, then it is likely to be compatible with breastfeeding because in most cases the baby's digestive system renders it harmless as well.

Characteristics of the drug itself can affect its concentration in the mother's milk.

The drug's characteristics, such as whether or not it binds to protein in maternal circulation, its pH, its molecular weight, and others, can affect its concentration in the mother's milk.

For example, a protein-bound drug is less concentrated in the milk than one that does not bind protein, because only the freely circulating molecules (those that are not bound to the protein) pass into the mother's milk. A fat-soluble drug will pass faster and more completely into the milk than a water-soluble drug. An alkaline drug (with a high pH value) will pass into the milk more freely than an acidic drug (with a low pH value). A drug with very large molecules (a high molecular weight) may not appear in the milk at all because its molecules are too large to pass through the membranes and into the milk, whereas a drug with smaller molecules would appear in the milk.

How well the baby can break down and excrete the drug affects its compatibility with breastfeeding.

A small amount of a drug that accumulates in the baby's system is more of a problem than a larger amount of a drug that is quickly eliminated. When a drug accumulates in a baby's system and cannot be excreted, it may build to toxic levels.

Age is a factor in a baby's ability to eliminate some drugs from his system. In general, the older the baby, the better able he will be to metabolize and excrete drugs. Certain drugs, however, tend to accumulate in a baby's system irrespective of the baby's age, and these would need to be used with caution by a breastfeeding mother.

The baby's absorption of the drug affects its compatibility with breastfeeding.

A drug that passes into the milk but is poorly absorbed by the baby would be more compatible with breastfeeding than one that is readily absorbed by the baby. How well a drug is absorbed by the baby is known as its "oral bioavailability."

Some drugs pass into the mother's milk but are not absorbed at all by the baby's system. For example, a drug that is given by injection because it would be destroyed by the mother's digestive system, such as insulin, is also likely to be destroyed by the baby's digestive system if it appeared in the mother's milk.

For some mothers, it may be possible to coordinate breastfeeding with their medication schedule to minimize the amount of the drug their babies receive.

If her baby's breastfeeding pattern is fairly regular, the mother may be able to coordinate breastfeeding with her medication schedule to minimize the amount of the drug her baby receives. This may not be practical, however, for the mother of a newborn or young baby who breastfeeds often and at unpredictable times.

In general, the best time to take a drug is right after breastfeeding, so that the drug can begin clearing from the mother's system before she breastfeeds again. If the mother is taking a once-a-day medication, suggest she take it right before her baby's longest sleep period, if her doctor agrees.

If the mother is concerned about possible side effects in her baby, suggest she watch for symptoms in the baby.

If the mother is concerned about the drug's effect on her breastfeeding baby, suggest she ask her doctor what symptoms to watch for in her baby. Any change in feeding or sleeping patterns, fussiness, rash, constipation, or diarrhea should be reported to the doctor. On the other hand, the baby's symptoms may indicate he is coming down with his mother's illness.

Some drugs are best avoided because they affect breastfeeding itself.

Although they may not present a risk to the baby, some drugs are best avoided by a breastfeeding mother because they affect the quantity or quality of her milk, affect the secretion of prolactin (the milk-producing hormone), or inhibit the mother's let-down, or milk-ejection, reflex.

Along with concerns about taking the drug, the mother also needs to weigh the risks of giving formula.

When considering the risks and benefits of continuing to breastfeed while taking a drug, it is important to point out the risks of weaning—even temporary weaning. There are difficulties and sometimes dangers in taking the baby off the breast and substituting formula, even for a few days.

If the mother already has a health problem, abrupt weaning can compound it by causing painfully engorged breasts or mastitis. Weaning can also change the complexion of the whole mother-baby relationship. Caring for the baby and keeping him happy may become difficult or impossible.

Drugs/Vaccines/Tests

Weaning can be risky for the breastfeeding baby as well. If there is a family history of allergy the baby may develop asthma or eczema when exposed to cow's milk (or any other) formula at too early an age. Also, weaning will deprive the baby of the mother's antibodies and immune factors that protect him from illness.

Information Needed before Checking on a Specific Drug

Ask about the drug itself.

Gathering complete and accurate information is essential to researching a drug and its compatibility with breastfeeding.

In order to locate information about the drug, ask the mother:

- the name of the drug (have the mother spell it, reading from the pharmacy label, if possible), and
- the generic name of the drug, if she has it.

Ask why and how much of the drug is being given and how long she will be taking it.

Ask the mother:

- why she is taking this drug,
- the dosage prescribed,
- if she has been given the usual dosage, as far as she knows.

Most written information on drugs and breastfeeding is based on the usual dose. If a mother is taking a higher-than-usual dose, it may mean that more of the drug will pass into her milk.

- how long she will be taking the drug.

Some drugs that are considered compatible with breastfeeding when given for less than two weeks are considered questionable if given for weeks or months at a time. Two examples are tetracycline and cortisone.

Ask about the baby's age, weight, how much of his intake is human milk, and his general health.

Ask the mother:

The age of the baby. The age of the baby can affect how much of the drug he will receive through the mother's milk. A newborn, for example, is likely to be less able to get rid of a drug, weigh less, and nurse more often than an older baby and so would be more affected by a drug than an older baby. A toddler, who is more mature, heavier, nursing less often, and eating other foods, would be least affected by a drug.

The baby's weight. A heavier baby would be less affected by the same amount of the drug as a lighter baby of the same age.

About how often the baby nurses in twenty-four hours and whether or not he is eating or drinking anything other than mother's milk. A baby who is exclusively breastfed would probably receive more of the mother's milk (and more of the drug) than a baby breastfeeding less often and receiving some nourishment from formula or solid foods.

The baby's general health. A baby in poor health or one who is premature may be more affected by the drug than a baby in good health.

Giving Information about Specific Drugs

Be familiar with written resources on drugs and breastfeeding before using them.

When a mother asks for information on a specific drug, keep in mind that information on new drugs may not exist.

Keep in mind that different resources may approach the issue of drugs and breastfeeding with different slants, so be familiar with whatever source you are using and its approach before sharing information from it.

Medical literature contains studies on individual drugs and breastfeeding. When referring to a study, read it critically. Not all studies are unbiased, well-constructed, and offer valid conclusions. When evaluating a study consider these questions:

- Is the study current (five years or less)? If the study is more than five years old, is it still pertinent or considered a classic study?
- Was the study done by qualified researchers?
- Was the study financed or published by a drug manufacturer or formula company?
- Was the study based on anecdotal or testimonial information or on a large, well-controlled sample? (A study based on the experiences of only a few individuals or on events that occurred before the study began is considered of less value.)
- Are the conclusions supported by the findings and validly drawn?

Before drawing conclusions from a study or sharing it with a mother, it is important to read it critically first and to be familiar with it.

Drug lists and review articles can be helpful, offering an easy-to-read, quick review of a wide variety of drugs, but they also have their limitations. They do not describe the conditions for which the drug is given. They do not list dosage, frequency, or length of therapy. They do not list every drug available, and it can be hazardous to draw conclusions about an entire class of drugs based on one or two drugs. While they list references, they often do not tell whether the research has been well constructed. With some drugs, it may be necessary to look for further information. The American Academy of Pediatrics Committee on Drugs' "Transfer of Drugs and Other Chemicals into Human Milk (1994)," which is included as a supplement to this book, falls into this category.

Books such as *The Physicians' Desk Reference* (PDR), **which consists of information provided by drug companies** should be used with caution, as their recommendations are influenced by the companies' legal liability. In some of these sources, drug evaluations are based largely on fear of litigation rather than an objective weighing of the benefits of breastfeeding against the potential risks of the drug. The information is often overly cautious, with the underlying premise being that drugs that have not been absolutely proven safe should not be taken by a breastfeeding mother.

When sharing information from a written resource, read it verbatim, without personal opinion or interpretation, and give the mother the name of the source and any references listed to share with her doctor.

When sharing information with the mother about a drug's compatibility with breastfeeding, it is important to read verbatim from the written resource. Any interpretation or personal opinion is inappropriate and falls in the category of giving medical advice, which can only properly be given by licensed health care professionals. To allow the mother to look into the information in more depth, give her the name of the source and any references listed, so she can share these with her doctor.

Even when a mother asks directly for an opinion or interpretation, it is still possible to stick to the facts. Here is an example:

MOTHER: I just got home from my doctor's office. I have "Health Problem A" and my doctor prescribed "drug B" for me. I want to know if I can take "drug B" while breastfeeding.

COUNSELOR: Have you told your doctor that you are breastfeeding?

MOTHER: No, he has given me a hard time about breastfeeding ever since my baby turned six months old, and I didn't want to mention it. I thought I'd ask you instead.

COUNSELOR: You sound uncomfortable with the idea of talking to your doctor. I'll be glad to share what's in my written resources with you, but it is also important that a doctor evaluate the drug in light of your and your baby's medical history. If you don't want to tell your doctor you are breastfeeding, would you be more comfortable talking to your baby's doctor?

MOTHER: Yes I would. He is much more supportive of breastfeeding. But first, what do you have on the drug? I'd like to know before I talk to him.

Drugs/Vaccines/Tests

COUNSELOR: In the American Academy of Pediatrics Committee on Drugs' 1994 statement, "Transfer of Drugs and Other Chemicals into Human Milk," "drug B" is listed in the section "Maternal Medication Usually Compatible with Breastfeeding," and in the column "Reported Sign or Symptom in Infant or Effect on Lactation," it says, "None."

MOTHER: Does that mean it's safe for me to take?

COUNSELOR: You'll need to ask your baby's doctor that question. I'd be glad to give you the source and the references to share with your baby's doctor, if you think that would be helpful. (Dictates source and references.... Mother writes them down.)

MOTHER: Do you know of any other drugs I can take for "Health Problem A" that are safe for my baby?

COUNSELOR: I'm not qualified to answer that, but there are almost always choices. Be sure to tell your baby's doctor that you want to continue breastfeeding and you would like to take a drug that is most compatible with breastfeeding. Then the doctor can discuss your options with you in more detail. It is rare that breastfeeding is affected when a mother needs to take a drug, but let me know if there seems to be a problem and we can talk more about your options.

Exploring Options When the Doctor Recommends Weaning

Ask the mother how she feels about weaning.

If the mother's doctor advises her to stop breastfeeding while she is taking a drug, it is important for the mother to be open with him or her about her feelings and priorities. Often alternatives to weaning can be found.

If the mother has decided that she wants to wean, ask her how long she would need to stop breastfeeding to take the drug. If she is interested in resuming nursing once this period is up, give her information on how to effectively express her milk during the temporary weaning (see "When Breastfeeding Is Temporarily Suspended" in the chapter "Expression and Storage of Human Milk"). Whether she intends to wean temporarily or permanently, talk to her about how to make this process less stressful for her and her baby. (See the chapter "Weaning.")

If the mother wants to continue breastfeeding, suggest the mother discuss it further with her doctor.

If the doctor recommends the mother wean and the mother wants to continue breastfeeding, suggest the mother talk further with her doctor. Often alternatives to weaning can be found. Encourage the mother to:

- Make it clear to the doctor that she wants to continue breastfeeding.
- Ask the doctor why the drug is thought to be unsafe. (Is there research that documents the risks of taking the drug? Is the recommendation based on an absence of research? On personal opinion?)
- If the doctor does not base his or her opinion on research, ask what reports in the medical literature say about the drug.
- Ask the doctor whether further information on the drug would be useful.
- Ask the doctor if there is an alternative drug or treatment that would allow the mother to continue breastfeeding.
- Ask the doctor what will happen if she doesn't take the drug.

Another option would be for the mother to discuss with the doctor the suggestion given by the American Academy of Pediatrics Committee on Drugs in their 1994 updated policy statement: "If there is a possibility that a drug may present a risk to the infant, consideration should be given to monitoring blood concentrations of the drug in the nursing infant."

Some doctors may recommend weaning when written resources indicate the drug is compatible with breastfeeding.

There are several reasons a doctor may recommend weaning when written resources indicate the drug is compatible with breastfeeding.

The baby's health or age. A baby who is premature or in poor health may be more susceptible to the effects of the drug than a healthy, full-term baby. A drug that would be considered safe for a mother of a full-term, healthy baby may not be appropriate for the mother of a premature or sick baby. Also, a drug that may be appropriate for the mother of an older baby may be more risky when taken by the mother of a newborn.

A lack of research coupled with a concern about legal liability. If no information is available about a drug (this is likely with a new drug) the doctor may recommend weaning as a precaution. In this case, encourage the mother to ask the doctor if another drug could be prescribed about which there is more information—something that is time-tested, has been effective in similar cases, and is compatible with breastfeeding.

It may also help to point out to the doctor that there are health risks associated with weaning to formula, such as allergic reactions in the baby and, if weaning is abrupt, mastitis in the mother.

Slanted information. Some written resources—such as those compiled by drug companies—take an overly cautious approach to drugs and breastfeeding, warning that any drug that has not been scientifically proven safe should not be taken by a breastfeeding mother. Their evaluation may be based more on fear of litigation than an objective comparison of the benefits of breastfeeding with the risks of the drug. If the doctor has checked only one source, encourage the mother to ask her doctor if other sources would be useful. (See the list below.)

Personal opinion. Some doctors believe that the breastfeeding mother should not take any drugs, despite objective research to the contrary. In this case, if the mother wants to continue breastfeeding, a second opinion may be necessary.

Where to Find Information on Specific Drugs

American Academy of Pediatric Committee on Drugs. The transfer of drugs and other chemicals into human milk. *Pediatrics* 1994; 93(1)137-50. (Reprinted as a supplement to this book.)

Briggs, B., Freeman, R. and Yaffe, S. *Drugs in Pregnancy and Lactation,* 4th ed. Baltimore/London: Williams and Wilkins, 1994.

Hale, T. *Medications and Mother's Milk,* 5th ed. Amarillo, Texas: Pharmasoft, 1996.

Lawrence, R. *Breastfeeding: A Guide for the Medical Profession,* 4th ed. St. Louis: Mosby, 1994, pp. 668-791.

US Pharmacopeial Convention. *United States Phamacoepia Dispensing Information: Drug Information for the Health Care Professional,* 16th ed. Rockville, Maryland: US Pharmacopeial Convention, 1996.

SUBSTANCES OF CONCERN

Alcohol

Occasional or light drinking of alcoholic beverages has not been found to be harmful to the nursing baby.

The American Academy of Pediatrics Committee on Drugs considers alcohol consumption compatible with breastfeeding, although side effects are noted if alcohol is taken in large amounts (see next point). An occasional drink or regular light drinking (one or fewer drinks per day) has not been found to be harmful to the nursing baby.

Alcohol passes freely into mother's milk and has been found to peak about 30 to 60 minutes after consumption, 60 to 90 minutes when taken with food (Lawton 1985). Alcohol also passes freely out of a mother's milk and her system. It takes a 120 pound woman about two to three hours to eliminate from her body

Drugs/Vaccines/Tests

the alcohol in one serving of beer or wine (Schulte 1995). However, the more alcohol that is consumed, the longer it takes for it to be eliminated. It takes up to 13 hours for a 120 pound woman to eliminate the alcohol from one high-alcohol drink. The effects of alcohol on the breastfeeding baby are directly related to the amount the mother consumes.

Although drinking beer was once recommended to help a mother relax and stimulate her milk supply, two studies found that after mothers consumed alcoholic or non-alcoholic beer, the babies whose mothers received the alcoholic beer nursed more frequently but consumed less milk than the babies whose mothers consumed the non-alcoholic beer (Mennella and Beauchamp 1993; Carlson 1985). In a similar study, babies whose mothers drank orange juice with added alcohol sucked more frequently at first but consumed an average of 27% less milk than the babies whose mothers drank plain orange juice (Mennella and Beauchamp 1991). This study also found a change in the odor of the mother's milk that paralleled the changes in alcohol concentration in the milk.

Moderate-to-heavy alcohol consumption by the nursing mother may interfere with the let-down, or milk-ejection reflex, inhibit milk intake, affect infant motor development, slow weight gain, and cause other side effects in the baby.

Although the American Academy of Pediatrics Committee on Drugs (1994) considers alcohol compatible with breastfeeding, it also lists possible side effects when it is taken in large amounts, such as "drowsiness...deep sleep, weakness, decrease in linear growth, abnormal weight gain." And it notes that "maternal ingestion of 1 g/kg daily decreases milk-ejection reflex."

One study found that the babies of nursing women who consistently drank moderately to heavily (the amount of alcohol in 2 or more drinks per day) scored slightly lower on motor development at one year of age than the norm (Little 1989). Mental development was normal in both groups. One flaw of this study is that "breastfed" was defined as receiving up to 16 ounces (480 ml) per day of supplemental milk or formula. Also, binge drinking, which is more likely to cause damage, was not adequately factored into the results.

Regular abuse of alcohol by a nursing mother can result in slow weight gain or failure-to-thrive in her baby. An alcoholic mother may not breastfeed often enough, and the baby may become so sleepy from the alcohol in the mother's milk that he may sleep through feedings or suck less effectively.

To confirm alcohol abuse, it may be necessary to ask specific questions.

A mother with a drinking problem may not readily volunteer this information. When asked how much she drinks, she may admit only to drinking occasionally. Ask the mother specifically how much she drinks each day, each week, and each month. If you suspect there is a problem, refer her to a substance abuse counselor or her health care provider.

Caffeine

Moderate intake of caffeine causes no problems for most breastfeeding mothers and babies.

The amount of caffeine in five or fewer 5 oz. cups of coffee per day (less than 750 ml) will not cause a problem for most breastfeeding mothers and babies (Nehlig and Debry 1994), although some mothers and babies may be more sensitive than others.

When figuring caffeine intake, be sure the mother is counting all her sources, including coffee, iced and hot teas, colas, other soft drinks containing caffeine, and any over-the-counter drugs that contain caffeine (see below for more details).

Excessive caffeine consumption by a breastfeeding mother may make her baby fussy and wakeful.

If a breastfeeding mother consumes more caffeine in a day than is found in five (5 oz.) cups of coffee (more than 750 ml), caffeine could begin accumulating in her baby's system, causing symptoms of caffeine stimulation.

A baby who is being overstimulated by caffeine is a wide-eyed, active, alert baby who doesn't sleep for long. He may also be unusually fussy. To find out if these symptoms are caused by caffeine, suggest the mother try going without caffeine for two to three weeks, substituting caffeine-free beverages, both hot and cold, for her caffeinated drinks. A mother may experience headaches or other symptoms if she abruptly stops consuming caffeine.

If the mother wants to cut down on her caffeine intake, be sure she knows which drinks and non-prescribed drugs contain caffeine.

If the baby is reacting to the caffeine ingested by the mother, be sure she knows all the usual sources of caffeine so she can avoid them. Common sources of caffeine are coffee and tea, including iced tea. If the mother drinks a lot of coffee or tea, suggest she use decaffeinated coffee and tea for a week or two while she observes her baby's behavior. Also, caffeine is found in most cola soft drinks, and also in some other soft drinks. Suggest the mother read the labels and avoid those containing caffeine.

Some over-the-counter drugs also contain caffeine. Examples include:

- stimulants, such as Caffedrine, NoDoz, and Vivarin,
- pain relievers, such as Anacin, Excedrin, and Midol,
- diuretics, such as Aqua-ban, Pre-Mens Fore, and Permathene H2Off
- cold remedies, such as Coryban-D, Dristan, and Triaminicin, and
- weight-control aids, such as Dexatrim, Dietac, and Prolamine.

If caffeine stimulation is the cause of the baby's sleeplessness, he should begin settling down to more normal sleeping patterns within a few days to a week after his mother eliminates caffeine from her diet.

Theobromine, which is found in chocolate and cocoa, is similar to caffeine and can have similar effects on mother and baby.

If a baby is showing signs of caffeine stimulation, in addition to talking to the mother about her sources of caffeine, be sure to mention that chocolate contains a substance called theobromine, which is similar to caffeine and can produce the same effect, though it has also been found to stimulate milk supply in some mothers.

The theobromine in chocolate is similar to caffeine, but there is much less theobromine in chocolate than caffeine in coffee. A 5 oz. cup (150 ml) of brewed drip coffee contains about 130 mg. of caffeine, a 5 oz. cup (150 ml) of decaffeinated coffee contains about 3 mg of caffeine, and one ounce (28 gr.) of milk chocolate contains 6 mg of theobromine (Behan, p. 130). Although one study found a link between chocolate consumption and colic symptoms (Lust 1996), most breastfeeding experts believe that moderate consumption of chocolate does not usually cause problems in breastfeeding babies (Renfrew, pp. 97-98; Lawrence, p. 305).

Herbal Remedies and Teas

Just as drugs can have side effects, so can herbs.

Like drugs, herbs can produce side effects. Some herbs act as stimulants, others as tranquilizers. Certain herbs can also affect breastfeeding. Sage, for example, can reduce a mother's milk supply if taken in large amounts. Herbs can also affect other body processes. Licorice, for example, can increase blood pressure (Lawrence, pp. 346-47).

Many of today's modern medicines come from the natural herbs that are used for teas and home remedies. Because these herbs may be potent, they should not be used casually. They should be thought of as drugs and recommended **only** by individuals knowledgeable in their use.

Major brands of herb teas pose little risk to nursing mothers and babies, but "private" brands or herbs brewed as tea should be used with caution.

Major brands of herbal teas are considered safe for nursing mothers. However, teas marketed as "private" brands or teas brewed from individual herbs should be used with caution, as poisonous alkaloids may render them toxic (Berlin 1996).

A tea's strength depends on its preparation.

If the mother is concerned about her herbal tea consumption, mention that the strength of tea depends on its preparation. The longer the tea leaves are steeped, the stronger the tea. By decreasing her steeping time the mother can also decrease the potency of the tea.

Excessive consumption of herbal teas should be avoided.

When a mother is breastfeeding, it is sensible to avoid excesses in any food or drink. A mother who drinks a few

Drugs/Vaccines/Tests

cups of herbal tea a day is unlikely to encounter any difficulties. But if the mother is regularly drinking a quart (.946 liter) or more of herbal tea each day or if the tea contains active or potent ingredients (see previous point), it may produce unexpected reactions in the mother or her breastfeeding baby.

Herbal teas that promise to increase a mother's milk supply may also contain other active agents and should be taken in moderation.

"Mother's Milk" tea is a blend of herbs that many generations have believed will increase a mother's milk supply. The mix of herbs in this tea—fennel seeds, coriander seeds, chamomile flowers, lemongrass, borage leaves, blessed thistle leaves. star anise, comfrey leaves, and fenugreek seeds—is free of caffeine, but taken in excess, it can have possible side effects, including vomiting, vertigo, insomnia, and rest-lessness.

If a mother is concerned about her milk supply, be sure she knows more effective ways she can increase it. (See "Slow Weight Gain" in the chapter "Weight Gain.")

Nicotine

If a mother smokes cigarettes, her baby can still enjoy the benefits of breastfeeding. But the more cigarettes a mother smokes, the greater the health risks for both her and her baby—whether he is breastfed or bottle-fed. If the mother can't or doesn't want to stop smoking, encourage her to cut down.

If the mother smokes fewer than twenty cigarettes a day, the risks to her baby from the nicotine in her milk are small.

The fewer cigarettes the mother smokes each day, the more she decreases the health risks to her and her baby. Smoking has been linked to earlier weaning (Mansbach 1991), fussiness (Matheson and Rivrud 1989), and lower milk produc-tion (Hopkinson 1992), as well as interference with milk let-down (Lawrence, p. 518).

Some mothers smoke and breastfeed with no apparent problem, yet other mothers and babies do not do well. When a mother smokes a cigarette, the nico-tine levels in her blood and milk first increase and then decrease over time. The half-life of nicotine—the amount of time it takes for half the nicotine to be elim-inated from the body—is ninety-five minutes (Steldinger and Luck 1988). While it is ideal for the mother to quit smoking entirely, if the mother is unreceptive to this idea or has been unable to quit, suggest she smoke immediately after breast-feeding to cut down on the amount of nicotine in her milk during nursing. Also, encourage her to try to cut down on the number of cigarettes she smokes per day and to avoid smoking in the same room with the baby. The fewer cigarettes smoked, the smaller the chance that difficulties will arise.

When a breastfeeding mother smokes more than twenty to thirty cigarettes a day, the risks increase.

Heavy smoking can reduce a mother's milk supply and on rare occasions has caused symptoms in the breastfeeding baby such as nausea, vomiting, abdom-inal cramps, and diarrhea. (Vorherr 1974).

The effect of cigarette smoking on the nursing mother may be more serious and subtle. Smoking lowers prolactin levels in nursing mothers. The hormone prolactin promotes a good milk supply and is a natural tranquilizer that makes nursing more pleasurable for mothers. This may be why one study (Lyon 1983) found that smoking mothers on the average tend to wean their babies from the breast earlier than non-smoking mothers. The heaviest smokers tend to wean the earliest.

Mothers who smoke also have slightly higher metabolic rates and may be leaner than non-smoking mothers, therefore, caloric stores for lactation may be low and the mother may need to eat more.

Encourage the mother not to smoke cigarettes immediately before or during breastfeeding.

Cigarette smoking has been shown to interfere with the let-down, or milk-ejec-tion, reflex. For this reason, encourage the mother not to smoke immediately before or during breastfeeding.

Whether breastfed or bottle-fed, second-hand (or "side-stream") smoke poses health hazards to the baby.

No matter how the baby is fed, breathing second-hand or "side-stream" smoke poses health risks. Researchers have documented the health hazards to children when one or both parents smoke. In one study (Colley and Corkhill 1974) researchers monitored the respiratory health of 2,205 babies and found a significant correlation between parents' smoking habits and the incidence of pneumonia, bronchitis, and SIDS during their babies' first year of life.

If a mother cannot quit smoking, encourage her to try to cut down and avoid smoking in the same room with the baby.

Because smoking is so physically addictive, many smokers find it difficult to quit despite their best intentions. If the mother wants to stop smoking, suggest she join a support group of others who are trying to quit smoking or attend a "stop smoking" clinic.

If the mother can't or doesn't want to quit, cutting down the number of cigarettes she smokes each day may seem more within reach. One way to cut down that works for some is to cut out the cigarettes that are not really needed, such as the ones smoked while talking on the phone or while eating or drinking. When the mother does smoke, encourage her to smoke in a different room or outdoors, away from her baby or other children.

SUBSTANCES OF ABUSE

The American Academy of Pediatrics Committee on Drugs (1994) states: "The Committee on Drugs believes strongly that nursing mothers should not ingest any of these compounds. Not only are they hazardous to the nursing infant but they are detrimental to the physical and emotional health of the mother."

If a mother reveals that she is abusing any of the following drugs, refer her to a substance abuse counselor and her baby's doctor. Her health and her baby's health may be at risk.

Amphetamines

When abused, amphetamines can cause irritability and sleeplessness in the breastfeeding baby.

When used in the usual prescription dosages, amphetamines are compatible with breastfeeding. When used in excessive amounts, however, amphetamines tend to accumulate in the milk and can pose hazards to the breastfeeding mother and her baby, causing symptoms such as jitteriness, irritability, and sleeplessness. (AAP Committee on Drugs 1994).

Marijuana

Use of marijuana is contraindicated during breastfeeding.

The active ingredient in marijuana, THC, is concentrated in human milk. After a breastfeeding mother uses marijuana, THC is evident in her baby's urine and stools (Perez-Reyes and Wall 1982). Any second-hand smoke the baby would be exposed to increases the amount of the drug he receives. Because "street drugs" are rarely pure, marijuana may be laced with other drugs or substances that also may be harmful to the breastfeeding baby. One study found that during a baby's first month of life marijuana exposure through mother's milk was associated with decreased motor development at age one year (Astley and Little 1990).

Another concern, unrelated to how the baby is fed, is the probability that marijuana intoxication will impair a mother's ability to care for her baby.

Marijuana is on the American Academy of Pediatrics Committee on Drugs (1994) list of "Drugs of Abuse Contraindicated During Breastfeeding."

Cocaine

Use of cocaine is contraindicated during breastfeeding.

Cocaine passes into the mother's milk in significant amounts and can cause cocaine intoxication in her breastfeeding baby (AAP Committee on Drugs 1994). Reported symptoms in the baby include: irritability, vomiting, dilated pupils, tremors, and increased heart and respiratory rates. After exposure, cocaine has been found in mother's milk for as long as 36 hours and in the baby's urine for as long as 60 hours (Chasnoff 1987). Because "street drugs" are rarely pure, cocaine may be laced with other drugs or substances that also may be harmful to the breastfeeding baby.

Drugs/Vaccines/Tests

In one reported case, a mother applied cocaine to her nipples to help relieve soreness. Three hours after the baby nursed through a nipple shield, the baby had convulsions and developed breathing problems (Chaney 1988).

Another concern, unrelated to how the baby is fed, is the probability that cocaine intoxication will impair a mother's ability to care for her baby.

Cocaine is on the American Academy of Pediatrics Committee on Drugs (1994) list of "Drugs of Abuse Contraindicated During Breastfeeding."

Heroin

Use of heroin is contraindicated during breastfeeding.

When the mother abuses heroin, the amount of the drug that passes into her milk is significant and can cause heroin addiction in her breastfeeding baby.

Also, because "street drugs" are rarely pure, there is the additional concern that the heroin may be laced with other drugs or substances that may be harmful to the breastfeeding baby.

Another concern, unrelated to feeding method, is the probability that heroin intoxication will impair a mother's ability to care for her baby.

Heroin is on the American Academy of Pediatrics Committee on Drugs (1994) list of "Drugs of Abuse Contraindicated During Breastfeeding."

On the other hand, methadone, the drug that is used to treat heroin addiction, is considered compatible with breastfeeding when the mother is consuming 20 mg per day or less (AAP Committee on Drugs 1994). In fact, methadone use by the addicted nursing mother has been found to prevent withdrawal symptoms in her addicted baby (Briggs 1994).

VITAMIN AND MINERAL SUPPLEMENTS FOR BABIES

Human milk is the perfect food for babies. As long as a baby is thriving on his mother's milk alone, he has no need for extra vitamins, fluoride, iron, or other supplements in the early months.

Fluoride

Fluoride supplements are no longer recommended for babies younger than six months.

The American Academy of Pediatrics' 1995 policy statement recommends that fluoride supplements not be given to babies younger than six months (AAP 1995). Previously, the AAP recommended fluoride supplements for breastfed babies in areas where drinking water contains less than 0.3 ppm of fluoride. This recommendation was changed due to an increased incidence of fluorosis (a discoloration of the teeth occurring during tooth formation when a child takes in too much fluoride).

In some areas, fluoride supplements may be recommended for babies older than six months.

In its 1995 policy statement, the American Academy of Pediatrics recommends that fluoride supplements be limited to children from six months to three years living in areas where the drinking water has fluoride levels of less than 0.3 ppm. In areas where fluoride levels are higher than this, fluoride supplements are not recommended (American Academy of Pediatrics 1995).

Iron

In the full-term, healthy, breastfed baby, extra iron is usually not needed until the baby is old enough to eat solid foods, and then foods naturally rich in iron can be given.

The full-term, healthy newborn is born with iron stores that, in combination with the iron he receives from his mother's milk, will last him well into the second half of his first year. Although human milk does not contain large amounts of iron, the iron is well absorbed—49 percent (Saarinen 1977)—because mother's milk contains the right proportion of lactose and vitamin C levels to promote iron absorption. Only 10 percent of the iron in cow's milk is absorbed, and 4 percent from iron-fortified formula. In addition, breastfed babies do not lose iron, as can happen to babies whose intestines bleed as a result of irritation from cow's milk.

A full-term, breastfed baby will not usually need extra iron until he is ready for solid foods, around the middle of his first year. At that time, foods naturally rich in iron can be offered.

One study of breastfed babies not given iron supplements or iron-fortified cereal found that those who were exclusively breastfed for seven months or longer had significantly higher hemoglobin levels at one and two years than breastfed babies who received solid foods earlier than seven months (Pisacane 1995). Although some of the breastfed babies who received solids before seven months were found to be anemic by their first birthday, the researchers found no cases of anemia within the first year among babies breastfed exclusively for seven months.

A premature baby, however, may need iron supplementation before starting solids, as he will not have received as much stored iron before birth.

If there is concern about a baby's iron levels, a simple blood test can be done.

If the mother or the baby's doctor is concerned about the baby's iron levels, a simple blood test can be done that measures the hematocrit. At birth, a baby's iron levels (measured as hemoglobin) are normally high—between 13.7 and 20.1 gm/dl and then drop over time. The following lists the normal hemoglobin levels, which vary according to age:

- At three months, 9.5 to 14.5 (average 12).
- At six months to six years, 10.5 to 14.0 (average 12).

(from Behrman, Kliegman, and Arvin. *Nelson Textbook of Pediatrics,* 15th ed. Philadelphia: W.B. Saunders, 1996, p. 1379.)

Iron drops and iron-fortified foods sometimes cause digestive upsets in babies and can reduce the efficiency of iron absorption.

When iron supplements are given, the baby's delicately balanced use of iron may be jeopardized and digestive problems, such as vomiting and diarrhea, can result. Two specialized proteins in mother's milk, lactoferrin and transferrin, pick up and bind iron from the infant's intestinal tract. In binding this iron, they stop harmful bacteria from multiplying by depriving them of the iron they need for growth. When iron supplements are given to the breastfed baby, the iron-binding abilities of lactoferrin and transferrin are overwhelmed, allowing the bacteria to thrive.

Vitamins

For the vast majority of breastfed babies, vitamin supplements are unnecessary.

It is generally agreed that vitamin supplements are unnecessary for almost all healthy, full-term babies.

Human milk was designed by nature for the special needs of the human baby and has long been recognized as the superior infant food for the first six months of life. It contains all the nutrients a baby needs in the ideal proportions. For the average, healthy, full-term baby, vitamin and mineral supplements are unnecessary.

Some very premature babies may need extra vitamins and minerals, which can be added to the mother's milk when it is given to the baby. A blood test will indicate if the baby will benefit from added nutrients.

The nutritional needs of premature babies are different from babies born at term. Nature provides for these babies by adding higher concentrations of certain nutrients in the milk of mothers whose babies are born early (Lemons 1982). Now that medical technology is able to save babies born as much as three months early, it is sometimes necessary to fortify human milk with extra vitamins and minerals. Even though fortification is sometimes beneficial, human milk offers many advantages over special formulas, such as its ease of digestion and the protection it offers against disease.

Experts do not agree on a precise gestational age and weight at which premies begin to benefit from adding extra nutrients to their mother's milk. Generally, it appears that babies weighing less than 1000 grams are likely to need fortifiers, whereas babies weighing between 1000 and 1500 grams (2.2 to 3.3 pounds) may or may not. If there is doubt, blood tests will tell the mother and the baby's doctor if extra vitamins and minerals are needed. (See the chapter "Prematurity" for more information.)

Drugs/Vaccines/Tests

There are some other rare, special circumstances when vitamin supplements may be indicated.

In rare cases, some breastfed babies benefit from vitamin supplements. If the mother is undernourished, she and her baby are dark-skinned, they both go for months without sunlight, and the mother does not consume enough vitamin D, they may be at risk for rickets (a condition caused by a lack of sufficient vitamin D), and so a vitamin D supplement may be indicated (Sills 1994; Bhowmick 1991). Exposure to sunlight for just a few minutes per day provides plenty of vitamin D for most babies (Specker 1994, Specker 1985).

Babies whose mothers are on strict vegetarian diets that exclude meat, fish, and dairy products may benefit from vitamin B_{12} supplements, although cases of deficiency are rare, especially in North America. Thiamine deficiencies have been reported in exclusively breastfed babies in Africa when the mother is severely undernourished and in parts of Asia where women consume raw fish containing a thiamine-splitting enzyme. Cooked fish is not a problem. When a mother is deficient in a particular nutrient, improving the mothers' nutrition and/or providing her with supplements may be as or more effective than giving her baby vitamin supplements (Stoltzfus 1993).

VACCINES

Immunizing the Breastfeeding Mother

Most vaccines can safely be given to the breastfeeding mother.

According to the US Centers for Disease Control (1994), "neither killed nor live vaccines affect the safety of breastfeeding for mothers or infants." The following is a list of vaccines considered compatible with breastfeeding:

- cholera
- diphtheria
- influenza
- measles
- oral polio and injected polio
- pertussis (whooping cough)
- rabies
- rubella (German measles)
- tetanus
- typhoid
- typhus
- yellow fever

Because both killed and live vaccines are considered compatible with breastfeeding, the new chickenpox vaccine should be compatible with breastfeeding. Since the chickenpox vaccine can be given to children over 12 months old as well as adults, if the mother or doctor is concerned about its effect on the breastfeeding baby, suggest the mother ask the baby's doctor about giving the vaccine to the baby when she receives it (Centers for Disease Control 1996).

The rubella vaccine should not be given to a woman who might be pregnant or might become pregnant within two months, as it can cause serious health problems in an unborn baby. For this reason, if the pregnant mother's blood test shows no immunity to rubella, it is often recommended that she be vaccinated immediately after giving birth (AAP Committee on Infectious Disease 1994).

An Rh-negative mother can be given an injection of Rh antibodies (RhoGAM) without harm to her breastfeeding baby.

An Rh-negative mother who gives birth to an Rh-positive baby will probably receive an injection of Rh antibodies (RhoGAM) after her baby is born. RhoGAM is used widely to prevent Rh complications and is not harmful to a breastfeeding baby (Lawrence, p. 354).

Immunizing the Breastfeeding Baby

The same schedule of immunizations is recommended for the breastfeeding baby as for the formula-fed baby.

Breastfeeding appears to enhance a baby's response to some immunizations.

It is recommended that the breastfeeding baby receive the same immunizations following the same timetable as the formula-fed baby. There is no need for the mother to refrain from breastfeeding her baby before or after any vaccine has been given, including the oral polio vaccine (AAP Committee on Infectious Disease 1994).

Studies have found that some immunizations tend to produce a more active immune response in babies who are breastfeeding as compared with babies who are artificially fed (Hahn-Zoric 1990; Pabst and Spady 1990).

DIAGNOSTIC MATERIALS AND TESTS

Breastfeeding can continue through most diagnostic tests, the exception being tests that use radioactive compounds.

Barium testing will not affect breastfeeding.

Barium, used in diagnostic tests on the digestive system, is not absorbed by the mother or baby and so will not affect breastfeeding.

X-rays will not affect breastfeeding.

Human milk is not affected by an x-ray, and the mother may safely nurse immediately afterward.

Mammograms will not affect breastfeeding, but a mammogram on a lactating breast will be more difficult to read.

A mammogram—which x-rays the breast using very low levels of radiation—can be performed while a mother is lactating, although the mammogram will be more difficult to read due to the density of the tissue in a younger woman's breast and the extra tissue present during lactation. When a woman is breastfeeding, a mammogram can be useful in determining the size and location of a known lump but may not be able to show early lumps or soft-tissue changes in the lactating breast. A mammogram is also of limited use in screening the breasts of non-lactating younger women, because their breast tissue is denser than the breast tissue of older women.

The frequency of nursing can make a difference in the quality of the mammogram. If the mother is breastfeeding often and has a sizable milk supply with all of its accompanying breast tissue changes, she would have to stop breastfeeding for at least a month to make a difference in the quality of her mammogram. The mother who is nursing infrequently will have less milk and less breast tissue, so her mammogram might be more easily read.

If the mother needs to have a mammogram, encourage her to look for a radiologist who has had experience reading mammograms of lactating women. Also, suggest that she bring her baby with her to the testing site and nurse him right before the mammogram to minimize the amount of milk in the breast during the procedure, which may make her mammogram easier to read.

Noninvasive imaging techniques, such as ultrasound, CAT scanning, and magnetic resonance imaging (MRI) will not affect breastfeeding, although the dye that may be used in an MRI has not been studied in nursing mothers.

Ultrasound and computer axial tomography (CAT) scanning are noninvasive imaging techniques that can be used without interfering with breastfeeding or affecting the milk. Unlike mammograms, ultrasound has been found to be effective in distinguishing solid breast lumps from cysts and abscesses (Hayes 1991).

Magnetic resonance imaging (MRI) is a noninvasive imaging technique that will not affect breastfeeding or the mother's milk. However, as part of an MRI the mother is injected with a dye that has not been investigated to date in pregnant or lactating women, although no adverse reactions have been reported.

Contact La Leche League International's Center for Breastfeeding Information for the latest information regarding this dye.

Drugs/Vaccines/Tests

Fine-needle aspiration for cyto-logic study of breast tissue will not affect breastfeeding.

Fine-needle aspiration of cells for questionable breast tissue may be recommended for the mother with a breast lump to determine the nature of the mass. This is a quick, nearly painless procedure that can be performed in a physician's office without the use of local anesthesia. Breastfeeding would not need to be inter-rupted.

Radio-opaque dyes, such as iopanoic acid (Telepaque), will not affect breastfeeding.

Telepaque (iopanoic acid) is a radio-opaque dye that is used in some diagnostic tests. Although it contains an iodine radical, it is not radioactive. When used in a single dose, radio-opaque materials are compatible with breastfeeding.

The tuberculin test will not affect breastfeeding.

The agent in the tuberculin test has not been found in milk (Rothermel and Faber 1975). If the mother is sensitive to the tuberculin agent in the test, then it may provoke an immune response, which will cause her body to produce antibodies to fight tuberculosis. These antibodies will provide her baby with an immunity to tuberculosis that may last for several years.

If radioactive materials are used in a diagnostic test, the baby would need to be temporarily weaned.

If radioactive testing is performed, the baby would need to be temporarily weaned. Because radioactive materials tend to accumulate in the milk and are passed on to the baby, their use is incompatible with breastfeeding. The length of weaning depends on the type of radioactive material used and how much is needed.

The accuracy of radioactive testing on a breastfeeding mother has been questioned by scientists.

Also, some scientists question the accuracy of radioactive testing when a mother is breastfeeding, because a disproportionate amount of the radioactive material is diverted to the milk by the mammary gland, which could affect the test results. Ruth Lawrence, MD, writes in the 1994 edition of her book, *Breastfeeding: A Guide for the Medical Profession,* "The excretion by the breast may alter the validity of the test result" (p. 353).

If the mother is facing radioactive testing and does not want to wean temporarily, help her formulate questions to ask her doctor.

If the mother's doctor recommends a test using radioactive materials, and she does not want to wean even temporarily, encourage her to tell her doctor how she feels and find out if there are any options that will allow her to continue breastfeeding without interruption. The following are some questions that the mother may want to ask her doctor:

- **What will happen if the procedure or therapy is not done or is delayed?**
- **Can an alternative procedure be found?** Possible alternatives to radioactive testing include ultrasound, CAT scanning, and magnetic resonance imaging (MRI).
- **Can the procedure be delayed until the mother is able to express enough milk so that her baby will not have to receive formula during the interrup-tion?** If there is a family history of allergy, this may be a significant issue.
- **Is the radioactive material being used for diagnosis or therapy?** If radioactive materials are used as a therapeutic treatment (for example, for the mother with cancer) rather than for testing, the mother would need to suspend breastfeeding for a much longer time—weeks or months, depending on the compound and the dose—and not resume breastfeeding until her milk is tested and found to be clear of radioactivity.
- **Has the radioactive material been selected that will clear the mother's milk in the shortest possible period of time?** See the last point in this section for the current recommendations for several radioactive materials.
- **Is a hospital or clinic available that can test the mother's milk to determine when it is clear of excess radioactivity?**
- **Will the radioactive material be concentrated in a specific organ of the mother's body (for example, the thyroid), and if so, will the mother need to keep her baby away from that part of her body until the radioactivity is at**

safe levels? In some cases, the baby may be exposed to excess radioactivity just by being close to his mother.
- **Is the mother interested in getting another medical opinion?**

If the mother weans temporarily, encourage her to express her milk and discard it.

If the mother and her doctor decide to go ahead with the radioactive testing and she must temporarily wean, encourage her to express her milk during this time and discard it. Radioactivity of the milk declines over time, and frequent milk expression will help the mother eliminate the radioactivity from her body more quickly (Rose 1990). While this is true of radioactive substances, frequent milk expression will not hasten the elimination of other drugs from the mother's milk (Anderson 1991).

Assure the mother that most babies will return to breastfeeding after a brief interruption and that if her baby does refuse the breast at first, there are many ways to persuade a baby to return to breastfeeding. (See "Nursing Strike" in the chapter "Fussy at the Breast and Breast Refusal.")

How long the mother must wean depends upon which radioactive material is used and the dose.

The length of time the mother must suspend breastfeeding varies, depending on the specific radioactive material and the dose used, the age of the baby, and whether he is taking other foods, as well as how frequently the mother expresses her milk. As noted in the point above, radioactivity has been found to clear from mother's milk in less time when a mother expresses her milk frequently. Research has found that when mothers expressed their milk as frequently as the baby had been breastfeeding the shorter periods listed below were sufficient to clear radioactivity from the milk (Rose 1990).

- Radioactive iodine (I-123) for diagnostic purposes—suspend breastfeeding for 8 to 48 hours, depending on the compound used and how frequently the mother expresses her milk (Rose 1990).
- Radioactive iodine (I-125 and I-131) for diagnostic testing—suspend breastfeeding until milk is clear; this may take 2-14 days (AAP Committee on Drugs 1994; Lawrence, p. 354).
- 67-Gallium citrate—suspend breastfeeding for 72 hours to 2 weeks (AAP Committee on Drugs 1994; Lawrence, p. 354; Rubow 1991).
- 99m-Technitium MIBI—no suspension of breastfeeding needed (Rubow 1991).
- 99m-Technitium MAA—suspend breastfeeding for 6 to 36 hrs. (AAP Committee on Drugs 1994; Rose 1990).

Publications for Parents

Mohrbacher, N. *When a Nursing Mother Gets Sick.* Schaumburg, Illinois, La Leche League International. 1996. Publication No. 21.

La Leche League International. THE WOMANLY ART OF BREASTFEEDING, 35th Anniversary ed. Schaumburg, Illinois, 1991, pp. 235, 320-22.

References

Prescription and Over-the-Counter Drugs

American Academy of Pediatrics Committee on Drugs. The transfer of drugs and other chemicals into human milk. *Pediatrics* 1994; 93(1):137-50.

Anderson, P. Drug use during breastfeeding. *Clin Pharmacy* 1991; 10:594-623.

Briggs, G., Freeman, R. and Yaffe, S. *Drugs in Pregnancy and Lactation,* 4th ed. Baltimore/London: Williams & Wilkins, 1994.

Hale, T. *Medications and Mother's Milk,* 5th ed. Amarillo, TX: *Pharmasoft,* 1996, pp. 309, 314-15.

Drugs/Vaccines/Tests

Lawrence, R. *Breastfeeding: A Guide for the Medical Profession,* 4th ed. St. Louis: Mosby, 1994, pp. 323-58.

O'Dea, R. Medication use in the breastfeeding mother. *NAACOG Clin Issues Perinat Women Health Nurs* 1992; 3(4):598-604.

Riordan, J. and Auerbach, K. *Breastfeeding and Human Lactation.* Boston and London: Jones and Bartlett, 1993, pp. 135-66.

Substances of Concern

Alcohol

American Academy of Pediatrics Committee on Drugs. The transfer of drugs and other chemicals into human milk. *Pediatrics* 1994; 93(1):137-50.

Carlson, H. et al. Beer-induced prolactin secretion: a clinical and laboratory study of the role of Salsolinol. *J Clin Endocrinol Metab* 1985; 60:673.

Lawrence, R. *Breastfeeding: A Guide for the Medical Profession,* 4th ed. St. Louis: Mosby, 1994, p. 75-76, 343-44.

Lawton, M. Alcohol in breast milk. *Aust NZ J Obst Gyn* 1985; 25(1):71-73.

Little, R. et al. Maternal alcohol use during breast-feeding and infant mental and motor development at one year. *New Engl J Med* 1989; 321:425-30.

Mennella, J. and Beauchamp, G. Effect of beer on breastfed infants. *JAMA* 1993; 269(13):1637.

Mennella, J. and Beauchamp, G. The transfer of alcohol to human milk: effects on flavor and the infant's behavior. *New Engl J Med* 1991; 325(14):981-85.

Riordan, J. and Auerbach, K. *Breastfeeding and Human Lactation.* Boston and London: Jones and Bartlett, 1993, p. 147.

Schulte, P. Minimizing alcohol exposure of the breastfeeding infant. *J Hum Lact* 1995; 11(4):317-19.

Caffeine

Behan, E. *Eat Well, Lose Weight While Breastfeeding.* New York: Villard Books, 1994, p. 130.

Berlin, C. et al. Disposition of dietary caffeine in milk saliva and plasma of lactating women. *Pediatrics* 1984; 73:59-63.

Berlin, C. and Daniel, C. Excretion of theobromine in human milk and saliva. *Pediatr Res* 1981; 15:492.

Lawrence, R. *Breastfeeding: A Guide for the Medical Profession,* 4th ed. St. Louis: Mosby, 1994, pp. 305, 342, 754-55.

Lust, K. et al. Maternal intake of cruciferous vegetables and other foods and colic symptoms in exclusively breastfed infants. *J Am Diet Assoc* 1996; 96(1):46-48.

Nehlig, A. and Debry, G. Consequences on the newborn of chronic maternal consumption of coffee during gestation and lactation: a review. *J Am Coll Nutr* 1994; 13(1):6-21.

Renfrew, M., Fisher, C. and Arms, S. *Bestfeeding: Getting Breastfeeding Right for You.* Berkeley, CA: Celestial Arts, 1990, pp. 97-98.

Riordan, J. and Auerbach, K. *Breastfeeding and Human Lactation.* Boston and London: Jones and Bartlett, 1993, p. 351.

Herbal Remedies and Teas

Berlin, C., Hershey Medical Center, Hershey, PA USA. Personal communication, May 1996.

Lawrence, R. *Breastfeeding: A Guide for the Medical Profession,* 4th ed. St. Louis: Mosby, 1994, pp. 346-47.

Riordan, J. and Auerbach, K. *Breastfeeding and Human Lactation.* Boston and London: Jones and Bartlett, 1993, pp. 40, 143.

Nicotine

Colley, J. and Corkhill, R. Influence of passive smoking and parental phlegm on pneumonia and bronchitis in early childhood. *Lancet* 1974; 2:1031.

Hopkinson, J. et al. Milk production by mothers of premature infants: influence of cigarette smoking. *Pediatrics* 1992; 90(6):934-38.

Lawrence, R. *Breastfeeding: A Guide for the Medical Profession,* 4th ed. St. Louis: Mosby, 1994, pp. 518-19, 760-61.

Lyon, A. Effects of smoking on breastfeeding. *Arch Dis Child* 1983; 58:378.

Mansbach, I. et al. Onset and duration of breast feeding among Israeli mothers: relationships with smoking and type of delivery. *Soc Sci Med* 1991; 33(12):1391-97.

Matheson, I. and Rivrud, G. The effect of smoking on lactation and infantile colic. *JAMA* 1989; 261:42.

Riordan, J. and Auerbach, K. *Breastfeeding and Human Lactation.* Boston and London: Jones and Bartlett, 1993, pp. 87, 368-69.

Steldinger, R. and Luck, W. Half lives of nicotine in milk of smoking mothers: implications for nursing. *J Perinat Med* 1988; 16:261-62.

Vorherr, H. *The Breast: Morphology, Physiology, and Lactation.* New York: Academic Press, 1974, p. 117.

Substances of Abuse

Wilton, J. Breastfeeding and the chemically dependent woman. *NAACOG Clin Issues Perinat Women Health Nurs* 1992; 3(4):667-82.

Drugs/Vaccines/Tests

Amphetamines

American Academy of Pediatrics Committee on Drugs. The transfer of drugs and other chemicals into human milk. *Pediatrics* 1994; 93(1):137-50.

Lawrence, R. *Breastfeeding: A Guide for the Medical Profession,* 4th ed. St. Louis: Mosby, 1994, pp. 712-13.

Riordan, J. and Auerbach, K. *Breastfeeding and Human Lactation.* Boston and London: Jones and Bartlett, 1993, p. 147.

Marijuana

American Academy of Pediatrics Committee on Drugs. The transfer of drugs and other chemicals into human milk. *Pediatrics* 1994; 93(1):137-150.

Astley, S. and Little, R. Maternal marijuana use during lactation and infant development at one year. *Neurotoxicol Teratol* 1990; 12(2):161-68.

Lawrence, R. *Breastfeeding: A Guide for the Medical Profession,* 4th ed. St. Louis: Mosby, 1994, pp. 520, 750-51.

Perez-Reyes, M. and Wall, M. Presence of delta-9-tetrahydrocannabinol in human milk. *New Engl J Med* 1982; 307:819-20.

Riordan, J. and Auerbach, K. *Breastfeeding and Human Lactation.* Boston and London: Jones and Bartlett, 1993, p. 146.

Cocaine

American Academy of Pediatrics Committee on Drugs. The transfer of drugs and other chemicals into human milk. *Pediatrics* 1994; 93(1):137-150.

Chaney, N. et al. Cocaine convulsions in a breast-feeding baby. *J Pediatr* 1988; 112:134-35.

Chasnoff, I. et al. Cocaine intoxication in a breast-fed infant. *Pediatrics* 1987; 80:836-38.

Lawrence, R. *Breastfeeding: A Guide for the Medical Profession,* 4th ed. St. Louis: Mosby, 1994, pp. 750-51.

Riordan, J. and Auerbach, K. *Breastfeeding and Human Lactation.* Boston and London: Jones and Bartlett, 1993, pp. 146-47.

Heroin

American Academy of Pediatrics Committee on Drugs. The transfer of drugs and other chemicals into human milk. *Pediatrics* 1994; 93(1):137-150.

Briggs, G., Freeman, R. and Yaffe, S. *Drugs in Pregnancy and Lactation,* 4th ed. Baltimore: Williams & Wilkins, 1994.

Lawrence, R. *Breastfeeding: A Guide for the Medical Profession,* 4th ed. St. Louis: Mosby, 1994, pp. 337-38, 750-51.

Vitamin and Mineral Supplements for Babies

Fluoride

American Academy of Pediatrics. *Pediatrics* 1995; 95:777.

Iron

Behrman, Kliegman, and Arvin. *Nelson Textbook of Pediatrics,* 15th ed. Philadelphia: W.B. Saunders, 1996, p. 1379.

Lawrence, R. *Breastfeeding: A Guide for the Medical Profession,* 4th ed. St. Louis: Mosby, 1994, pp. 302.

Riordan, J. and Auerbach, K. *Breastfeeding and Human Lactation.* Boston and London: Jones and Bartlett, 1993, pp. 350-51.

Saarinen, Y. et al. Iron absorption in infants: high bioavailability of breast milk iron as indicated by the extrinsic tag method of iron absorption and by the concentration of serum ferritin. *J Pediatr* 1977; 91(1):36-39.

Pisacane, A. Iron status in breast-fed infants. *J Pediatr* 1995; 127(3):429-31.

Woodruff, C. Iron nutrition in the breast-fed infant. *J Pediatr* 1977; 90:36-38.

Vitamins

Bhowmick, S. et al. Rickets caused by vitamin D deficiency in breast-fed infants in the southern United States. *Am J Dis Child* 1991; 145:127-30.

Lawrence, R. *Breastfeeding: A Guide for the Medical Profession,* 4th ed. St. Louis: Mosby, 1994, pp. 813-15.

Lemons, J. et al. Differences in the composition of preterm and term human milk during early lactation. *Pediatr Res* 1982; 16:113-17.

Riordan, J. and Auerbach, K. *Breastfeeding and Human Lactation.* Boston and London: Jones and Bartlett, 1993, p. 350.

Sills, I. et al. Vitamin D deficiency rickets: reports of its demise are exaggerated. *Clin Pediatr* 1994; n:491-93.

Specker, B. Do North American women need supplemental vitamin D during pregnancy or lactation? *Am J Clin Nutr* 1994; 59(Supl):4845-915.

Specker, B. et al. Sunshine exposure and serum 25-hydroxyvitamin D concentrations in exclusively breast fed infants. *J Pediatr* 1985; 107:372-76.

Stoltzfus, R. et al. High dose vitamin A supplementation of breastfeeding Indonesian mothers: effects on the vitamin A status of mother and infant. *J Nutr* 1993; 123:666-75.

Vaccines

Drugs/Vaccines/Tests

AAP Committee on Infectious Disease: Report of the Committee on Infectious Disease. In *The Red Book,* 23rd ed., Elk Grove Village, Illinois: American Academy of Pediatrics, 1994.

Centers for Disease Control. General recommendations on immunization. *MMWR* 1994; 43(RR-1):1-38.

Centers for Disease Control. Establishment of VARIVAX® pregnancy registry. *MMWR* 1996; 45:239.

Chirico, G. et al. Hepatitis B immunization in infants of hepatitis B surface antigen-negative mothers. *Pediatrics* 1993; 92(5):717-19.

Lawrence, R. *Breastfeeding: A Guide for the Medical Profession,* 4th ed. St. Louis: Mosby, 1994, pp. 354-55.

Hahn-Zoric, M., et al. Antibody responses to parenteral and oral vaccines are impaired by conventional and low protein formulas as compared to breastfeeding. *Acta Paediatr Scand* 1990; 1137-42.

Pabst, H. and Spady, D. Effect of breast-feeding on antibody response to conjugate vaccine. *Lancet* 1990; 336:269-70.

Riordan, J. and Auerbach, K. *Breastfeeding and Human Lactation.* Boston and London: Jones and Bartlett, 1993, pp. 474-75.

Diagnostic Tests

American Academy of Pediatrics Committee on Drugs. The transfer of drugs and other chemicals into human milk. *Pediatrics* 1994; 93(1):137-50.

Anderson, P. Drug use during breast-feeding. *Clin Pharmacy* 1991; 10:594-623.

Hayes, R. et al. Acute inflammation of the breast—the role of breast ultrasound in diagnosis and management. *Clin Radiol* 1991; 44:253-56.

Lawrence, R. *Breastfeeding: A Guide for the Medical Profession,* 4th ed. St. Louis: Mosby, 1994, pp. 203, 353-54, 730-35.

Riordan, J. and Auerbach, K. *Breastfeeding and Human Lactation.* Boston and London: Jones and Bartlett, 1993, pp. 369-73.

Rose, M. et al. Excretion of iodine-123-hippuran, technetium-99m-red blood cells, and technetium-99m-macroaggregated albumin into breast milk. *J Nucl Med* 1990; 31:978-84.

Rothermal, P. and Faber, M. Drugs in breast milk: a consumer's guide. *Birth and Family J* 1975; 2:76-88.

Rubow, S. et al. Excretion of gallium 67 in human breast milk and its inadvertent ingestion by a 9-month-old child. *Eur J Nucl Med* 1991; 18(10):829-33.

Skolnick, A. Ultrasound may help detect breast implant leaks. *JAMA* 1992; 267(6):786.

The Transfer of Drugs and Other Chemicals Into Human Milk

Committee on Drugs

This statement was first published in 1983,[1] with a revision published in 1989.[2] Information about the transfer of drugs and chemicals into human milk continues to become available. This current statement is intended to revise the lists of agents transferred into human milk and describe their possible effects on the infant or on lactation, if known (Tables 1 through 7). The fact that a pharmacologic or chemical agent does not appear on the lists is not meant to imply that it is not transferred into human milk or that it does not have an effect on the infant; it only indicates that there were no reports found in the literature. These tables should assist the physician in counseling a nursing mother regarding breast-feeding when the mother has a condition for which a drug is medically indicated.

The following question and options should be considered when prescribing drug therapy to lactating women. (1) Is the drug therapy really necessary? Consultation between the pediatrician and the mother's physician can be most useful. (2) Use the safest drug, for example, acetaminophen rather than aspirin for analgesia. (3) If there is a possibility that a drug may present a risk to the infant, consideration should be given to measurement of blood concentrations in the nursing infant. (4) Drug exposure to the nursing infant may be minimized by having the mother take the medication just after she has breast-fed the infant and/or just before the infant is due to have a lengthy sleep period.

Data have been obtained from a search of the medical literature. Because methodologies used to quantitate drugs in milk continue to improve, this current information will require continuous updating. Drugs cited in Tables 1 through 7 are listed in alphabetical order by generic name; brand names are listed in Tables 8 and 9 in accordance with the current *Physicians Desk Reference, AMA Drug Evaluation*, and the *USAN and the USP Dictionary of Drug Names*. The reference list is not inclusive of all articles published.

Physicians who encounter adverse effects in infants fed drug-contaminated human milk are urged to document these effects in a communication to the American Academy of Pediatrics Committee on Drugs and to the Food and Drug Administration. This communication should include the generic and brand name of the drug, the maternal dose and mode of administration, the concentration of the drug in milk and maternal and infant blood in relation to the time of ingestion, the method used for laboratory identification, the age of the infant, and the adverse effect. Such reports may significantly increase the pediatric community's fund of knowledge regarding drug transfer into human milk and the potential or actual risk to the infant.

ACKNOWLEDGMENT

The Committee would like to thank Linda Watson for her work in reference identification, document retrieval, and manuscript preparation.

COMMITTEE ON DRUGS, 1992 to 1993
Ralph E. Kauffman, MD, PhD, Chairperson
William Banner, Jr, MD, PhD
Cheston M. Berlin, Jr, MD
Jeffrey L. Blumer, MD, PhD
Richard L. Gorman, MD
George H. Lambert, MD
Geraldine S. Wilson, MD

LIAISON REPRESENTATIVES
Donald R. Bennett, MD, PhD,
    American Medical Association
Jose F. Cordero, MD, MPH,
    Centers for Disease Control and Prevention
Paul Kaufman, MD,
    Pharmaceutical Manufacturers' Association
Sam A. Licata, MD,
    National Health and Welfare, Health
    Protection Branch, Canada
Paul Tomich, MD,
    American College of Obstetricians and
    Gynecologists
Gloria Troendle, MD,
    Food and Drug Administration
Sumner J. Yaffe, MD,
    National Institute of Child Health and
    Human Development, National Institutes of
    Health

AAP SECTION LIAISON
Charles J. Coté, MD,
    Section on Anesthesiology

CONSULTANT
Anthony R. Temple, MD

TABLE 1. Drugs That Are Contraindicated During Breast-Feeding

Drug	Reason for Concern, Reported Sign or Symptom in Infant, or Effect on Lactation	Reference No.
Bromocriptine	Suppresses lactation; may be hazardous to the mother	3, 4
Cocaine	Cocaine intoxication	5
Cyclophosphamide	Possible immune suppression; unknown effect on growth or association with carcinogenesis; neutropenia	6, 7
Cyclosporine	Possible immune suppression; unknown effect on growth or association with carcinogenesis	8
Doxorubicin*	Possible immune suppression; unknown effect on growth or association with carcinogenesis	9
Ergotamine	Vomiting, diarrhea, convulsions (doses used in migraine medications)	10
Lithium	One-third to one-half therapeutic blood concentration in infants	11–13
Methotrexate	Possible immune suppression; unknown effect on growth or association with carcinogenesis; neutropenia	14
Phencyclidine (PCP)	Potent hallucinogen	15
Phenindione	Anticoagulant: increased prothrombin and partial thromboplastin time in one infant; not used in United States	16

* Drug is concentrated in human milk.

TABLE 2. Drugs of Abuse: Contraindicated During Breast-Feeding*

Drug Reference	Reported Effect or Reasons for Concern	Reference No.
Amphetamine†	Irritability, poor sleeping pattern	17
Cocaine	Cocaine intoxication	5
Heroin	Tremors, restlessness, vomiting, poor feeding	18
Marijuana	Only one report in literature; no effect mentioned	19
Nicotine (smoking)	Shock, vomiting, diarrhea, rapid heart rate, restlessness; decreased milk production	20–26
Phencyclidine	Potent hallucinogen	15

* The Committee on Drugs strongly believes that nursing mothers should not ingest any compounds listed in Table 2. Not only are they hazardous to the nursing infant, but they are also detrimental to the physical and emotional health of the mother. This list is obviously not complete; no drug of abuse should be ingested by nursing mothers even though adverse reports are not in the literature.
† Drug is concentrated in human milk.

TABLE 3. Radioactive Compounds That Require Temporary Cessation of Breast-Feeding*

Drug	Recommended Time for Cessation of Breast-Feeding	Reference No.
Copper 64 (^{64}Cu)	Radioactivity in milk present at 50 h	27
Gallium 67 (^{67}Ga)	Radioactivity in milk present for 2 wk	28
Indium 111 (^{111}In)	Very small amount present at 20 h	29
Iodine 123 (^{123}I)	Radioactivity in milk present up to 36 h	30
Iodine 125 (^{125}I)	Radioactivity in milk present for 12 d	31
Iodine 131 (^{131}I)	Radioactivity in milk present 2–14 d, depending on study	32–35
Radioactive sodium	Radioactivity in milk present 96 h	36
Technetium-99m (^{99m}Tc), ^{99m}Rc macroaggregates, ^{99m}Tc O4	Radioactivity in milk present 15 h to 3 d	37–42

* Consult nuclear medicine physician before performing diagnostic study so that radionuclide that has shortest excretion time in breast milk can be used. Before study, the mother should pump her breast and store enough milk in freezer for feeding the infant; after study, the mother should pump her breast to maintain milk production but discard all milk pumped for the required time that radioactivity is present in milk. Milk samples can be screened by radiology departments for radioactivity before resumption of nursing.

TABLE 4.   Drugs Whose Effect on Nursing Infants Is Unknown But May Be of Concern

Psychotropic drugs, the compounds listed under antianxiety, antidepressant, and antipsychotic categories, are of special concern when given to nursing mothers for long periods. Although there are no case reports of adverse effects in breast-feeding infants, these drugs do appear in human milk and thus could conceivably alter short-term and long-term central nervous system function.[43]

Drug	Reported or Possible Effect	Reference No.
Antianxiety		
Diazepam	None	44–46
Lorazepam	None	47
Midazolam	. . .	48
Perphenazine	None	49
Prazepam*	None	50
Quazepam	None	51
Temazepam	. . .	52
Antidepressants		
Amitriptyline	None	53, 54
Amoxapine	None	55
Desipramine	None	56, 57
Dothiepin	None	58, 59
Doxepin	None	60
Fluoxetine	. . .	61
Fluvoxamine	. . .	62
Imipramine	None	56
Trazodone	None	63
Antipsychotic		
Chlorpromazine	Galactorrhea in adult; drowsiness and lethargy in infant	64, 65
Chlorprothixene	None	66
Haloperidol	None	67, 68
Mesoridazine	None	69
Chloramphenicol	Possible idiosyncratic bone marrow suppression	70, 71
Metoclopramide*	None described; dopaminergic blocking agent	72, 73
Metronidazole	In vitro mutagen; may discontinue breast-feeding 12–24 h to allow excretion of dose when single-dose therapy given to mother	74, 75
Tinidazole	See metronidazole	76

* Drug is concentrated in human milk.

TABLE 5.   Drugs That Have Been Associated With Significant Effects on Some Nursing Infants and Should Be Given to Nursing Mothers With Caution*

Drug	Reported Effect	Reference No.
5-Aminosalicylic acid	Diarrhea (1 case)	77, 78
Aspirin (salicylates)	Metabolic acidosis (1 case)	79–81
Clemastine	Drowsiness, irritability, refusal to feed, high-pitched cry, neck stiffness (1 case)	82
Phenobarbital	Sedation; infantile spasms after weaning from milk containing phenobarbital, methemoglobinemia (1 case)	83–87
Primidone	Sedation, feeding problems	83, 84
Sulfasalazine (salicylazosulfapyridine)	Bloody diarrhea (1 case)	88

* Measure blood concentration in the infant when possible.

TABLE 6. Maternal Medication Usually Compatible With Breast-Feeding*

Drug	Reported Sign or Symptom in Infant or Effect on Lactation	Reference No.
Acebutolol	None	89
Acetaminophen	None	90–92
Acetazolamide	None	93
Acitretin	. . .	94
Acyclovir†	None	95, 96
Alcohol (ethanol)	With large amounts drowsiness, diaphoresis, deep sleep, weakness, decrease in linear growth, abnormal weight gain; maternal ingestion of 1 g/kg daily decreases milk ejection reflex	20, 97–100
Allopurinol	. . .	101
Amoxicillin	None	102
Antimony	. . .	103
Atenolol	None	104–106
Atropine	None	107
Azapropazone (apazone)	. . .	108
Aztreonam	None	109
B₁ (thiamin)	None	110
B₆ (pyridoxine)	None	111–113
B₁₂	None	114
Baclofen	None	115
Barbiturate	See Table 5	
Bendroflumethiazide	Suppresses lactation	116
Bishydroxycoumarin (dicumarol)	None	117
Bromide	Rash, weakness, absence of cry with maternal intake of 5.4 g/d	118
Butorphanol	None	119
Caffeine	Irritability, poor sleeping pattern, excreted slowly; no effect with usual amount of caffeine beverages	120–125
Captopril	None	126
Carbamazepine	None	127, 128
Carbimazole	Goiter	129, 130
Cascara	None	131
Cefadroxil	None	102
Cefazolin	None	132
Cefotaxime	None	133
Cefoxitin	None	133
Cefprozil	. . .	134
Ceftazidime	None	135
Ceftriaxone	None	136
Chloral hydrate	Sleepiness	137
Chloroform	None	138
Chloroquine	None	139–141
Chlorothiazide	None	142–143
Chlorthalidone	Excreted slowly	144
Cimetidine†	None	145
Cisapride	None	146
Cisplatin	Not found in milk	9
Clindamycin	None	147
Clogestone	None	148
Clomipramine	. . .	149
Codeine	None	92, 107
Colchicine	. . .	15
Contraceptive pill with estrogen/progesterone	Rare breast enlargement; decrease in milk production and protein content (not confirmed in several studies)	151–158
Cycloserine	None	159
D (Vitamin)	None; follow up infant's serum calcium level if mother receives pharmacological doses	160–162
Danthron	Increased bowel activity	163
Dapsone	None; sulfonamide detected in infant's urine	141, 164
Dexbrompheniramine maleate with d-isoephedrine	Crying, poor sleeping patterns, irritability	165
Digoxin	None	166, 167
Diltiazem	None	168
Dipyrone	None	169
Disopyramide	None	170–171
Domperidone	None	172
Dyphylline†	None	173
Enalapril	. . .	174
Erythromycin†	None	175
Estradiol	Withdrawal, vaginal bleeding	176

TABLE 6. *Continued*

Drug	Reported Sign or Symptom in Infant or Effect on Lactation	Reference No.
Ethambutol	None	159
Ethanol (cf. alcohol)	. . .	
Ethosuximide	None, drug appears in infant serum	127, 177
Fentanyl	. . .	178
Flecainide	. . .	179, 180
Flufenamic acid	None	181
Fluorescein	. . .	182
Folic acid	None	183
Gold salts	None	184–188
Halothane	None	189
Hydralazine	None	190
Hydrochlorothiazide	. . .	142, 143
Hydroxychloroquine†	None	191, 192
Ibuprofen	None	193, 194
Indomethacin	Seizure (1 case)	195–197
Iodides	May affect thyroid activity; see miscellaneous iodine	198
Iodine (providone-iodine/vaginal douche)	Elevated iodine levels in breast milk, odor of iodine on infant's skin	198
Iodine	Goiter; see miscellaneous, iodine	198
Iopanoic acid	None	199
Isoniazid	None; acetyl metabolite also secreted; ? hepatotoxic	159, 200
K_1 (vitamin)	None	201, 202
Kanamycin	None	159
Ketorolac	. . .	203
Labetalol	None	204, 205
Levonorgestrel	. . .	206–209
Lidocaine	None	210
Loperamide	. . .	211
Magnesium sulfate	None	212
Medroxyprogesterone	None	148
Mefenamic acid	None	213
Methadone	None if mother receiving ≤20 mg/24 h	214, 215
Methimazole (active metabolite of carbimazole)	None	216
Methocarbamol	None	217
Methyldopa	None	218
Methyprylon	Drowsiness	219
Metoprolol†	None	104
Metrizamide	None	220
Mexiletine	None	221
Minoxidil	None	222
Morphine	None; infant may have significant blood concentration	223, 224
Moxalactam	None	225
Nadolol†	None	226
Nalidixic acid	Hemolysis in infant with glucose-6-phosphate dehydrogenase (G-6-PD) deficiency	227
Naproxen	. . .	228
Nefopam	None	229
Nifedipine	. . .	230
Nitrofurantoin	Hemolysis in infant with G-6-PD deficiency	231
Norethynodrel	None	232
Norsteroids	None	233
Noscapine	None	234
Oxprenolol	None	235, 236
Phenylbutazone	None	237
Phenytoin	Methemoglobinemia (1 case)	85, 127, 238
Piroxicam	None	239
Prednisone	None	241
Procainamide	None	242
Progesterone	None	243
Propoxyphene	None	244
Propranolol	None	245–247
Propylthiouracil	None	248
Pseudoephedrine†	None	249
Pyridostigmine	None	250
Pyrimethamine	None	141, 251
Quinidine	None	252
Quinine	None	223
Riboflavin	None	110

TABLE 6. *Continued*

Drug	Reported Sign or Symptom in Infant or Effect on Lactation	Reference No.
Rifampin	None	159
Scopolamine	...	107
Secobarbital	None	253
Senna	None	254
Sotalol	...	180, 255
Spironolactone	None	256
Streptomycin	None	159
Sulbactam	None	257
Sulfapyridine	Caution in infant with jaundice or G-6-PD deficiency, and ill, stressed, or premature infant; appears in infant's milk	258, 259
Sulfisoxazole	Caution in infant with jaundice or G-6-PD deficiency, and ill, stressed, or premature infant; appears in infant's milk	260
Suprofen	None	261
Terbutaline	None	262
Tetracycline	None; negligible absorption by infant	263, 264
Theophylline	Irritability	120, 265
Thiopental	None	86, 266
Thiouracil	None mentioned; drug not used in United States	267
Ticarcillin	None	268
Timolol	None	236
Tolbutamide	Possible jaundice	269
Tolmetin	None	270
Trimethoprim/sulfamethoxazole	None	271, 272
Triprolidine	None	249
Valproic acid	None	127, 273, 274
Verapamil	None	275
Warfarin	None	276
Zolpidem	None	277

* Drugs listed have been reported in the literature as having the effects listed or no effect. The word "none" means that no observable change was seen in the nursing infant while the mother was ingesting the compound. It is emphasized that most of the literature citations concern single case reports or small series of infants.

† Drug is concentrated in human milk.

TABLE 7. Food and Environmental Agents: Effect on Breast-Feeding

Agent	Reported Sign or Symptom in Infant or Effect on Lactation	Reference No.
Aflatoxin	None	278–280
Aspartame	Caution if mother or infant has phenylketonuria	281
Bromide (photographic laboratory)	Potential absorption and bromide transfer into milk; see Table 6	282
Cadmium	None reported	283
Chlordane	None reported	284
Chocolate (theobromine)	Irritability or increased bowel activity if excess amounts (16 oz/d) consumed by mother	120, 285
DDT, benzenehexachlorides, dieldrin, aldrin, hepatachlorepoxide	None	286–293
Fava beans	Hemolysis in patient with glucose-6-phosphate dehydrogenase (G-6-PD) deficiency	294
Fluorides	None	295, 296
Hexachlorobenzene	Skin rash, diarrhea, vomiting, dark urine, neurotoxicity, death	297, 298
Hexachlorophene	None; possible contamination of milk from nipple washing	299
Lead	Possible neurotoxicity	300–301
Methyl mercury, mercury	May affect neurodevelopment	302–304
Monosodium glutamate	None	305
Polychlorinated biphenyls and polybrominated biphenyls	Lack of endurance, hypotonia, sullen expressionless facies	306–310
Tetrachlorethylene-cleaning fluid (perchloroethylene)	Obstructive jaundice, dark urine	311
Vegetarian diet	Signs of B_{12} deficiency	312

TABLE 8. Generic Drugs and Corresponding Trade Names*†

Generic	Trade	Generic	Trade
acebutolol	Sectral	fentanyl	Sublimaze
acetaminophen	Tylenol, Anacin-3, Panadol, Tempra, Phenaphen	flecainide	Tambocor
		flufenamic acid	Arlef (foreign)
acetazolamide	Diamox	fluoxetine	Prozac
acitretin	Soriatane	fluvoxamine	. . .
acyclovir	Zovirax	gold sodium thiomalate	Myochrysine
allopurinol	Zyloprim	haloperidol	Haldol
aminosalicylic acid	Rowasa	hydralazine	Apresoline
amitriptyline	Elavil, Endep	hydrochlorothiazide	HydroDIURIL
amoxapine	Asendin	hydroxychloroquine	Plaquenil
amoxicillin	Amoxil	ibuprofen	Advil, Motrin
amphetamine (dextroamphetamine)	Dexedrine	imipramine	Tofranil, Janimine
		indomethacin	Indocin
aspartame	NutraSweet	iopanoic acid	Telepaque
atenolol	Tenormin	isoniazid	INH
azapropazone (apazone)	Not available in United States	kanamycin	Kantrex
aztreonam	Azactam	ketorolac	Toradol
baclofen	Lioresal	labetalol	Normodyne, Trandate
bendroflumethiazide	Naturetin	levonorgestrel	as Levlen, as Nordette, as Norplant, as Tri-Levlen, as Triphasil
bishydroxycoumarin	Dicumarol		
bromocriptine	Parlodel		
butorphanol	Stadol		
captopril	Capoten	lidocaine	Xylocaine
carbamazepine	Tegretol	loperamide	Imodium
carbimazole	Neo-mercazole (foreign)	lorazepam	Ativan
cefadroxil	Duricef	medroxyprogesterone	Provera, Depo-Provera
cefazolin	Ancef, Kefzol	mefenamic acid	Ponstel
cefotaxime	Claforan	mesoridazine	Serentil
cefprozil	Cefzil	methadone	Dolophine
ceftazidime	Fortaz	methimazole	Tapazole
ceftriaxone	Rocephin	methocarbamol	Robaxin
chloramphenicol	Chloromycetin	methotrexate (amethopterin)	Folex, Rheumatrex
chloroquine	Aralen		
chlorothiazide	Diuril, Chlotride (foreign)	methyprylon	Noludar
chlorpromazine	Thorazine	metoclopramide	Reglan
chlorprothixene	Taractan	metoprolol	Lopressor
chlorthalidone	Hygroton, as Combipres	metrizamide	Amipaque
cimetidine	Tagamet	metronidazole	Flagyl, Protostat
cisapride	Benzamide (foreign)	mexiletine	Mexitil
cisplatin	Platinol	midazolam	Versed
clemastine	Tavegil (foreign), Tavist	minoxidil	Loniten, Rogaine
clindamycin	Cleocin	monosodium glutamate	MSG, Accent
clomipramine	Anafranil	moxalactam	Moxam
colchicine	(Generic only)	nadolol	Corgard
cyclophosphamide	Cytoxan	nalidixic acid	NegGram
cycloserine	Seromycin	naproxen	Naprosyn
danthron	Dorbane, Istizin	nefopam	Acupan (unavailable in United States)
dapsone	(Generic only)		
desipramine	Norpramin, Pertofrane	nifedipine	Procardia
dexbrompheniramine maleate with *d*-isoephedrine	as Disophrol, as Drixoral	nitrofurantoin	Furadantin, Macrodantin
		[³H]Norethynodrel	as Enovid
dextroamphetamine	Dexedrine	noscapine	Tusscapine
diazepam	Valium	oxprenolol	Trasicor (foreign)
digoxin	Lanoxin, Lanoxicaps	perphenazine	Trilafon, as Etrafon, as Triavil
diltiazem	Cardizem		
dipyrone	Diprofarn, Novaldin (unavailable in United States)	phenindione	Hedulin, Indon (unavailable in United States)
disopyramide	Norpace		
domperidone	Motilium (unavailable in United States)	phenylbutazone	Azolid, Butazolidin
		phenytoin	Dilantin
		piroxicam	Feldene
dothiepin	Prothiaden (unavailable in United States)	prazepam	Centrax
		prednisolone	Delta-Cortef, Meti-Derm, Prelone
doxepin	Sinequan		
doxorubicin	Adriamycin	prednisone	Deltasone, Meticorten, Sterapred
dyphylline	Dilor		
enalapril	Vasotec	primidone	Mysoline
ergotamine tartrate with caffeine	as Cafergot	procainamide	Pronestyl
		propoxyphene	Darvon, Dolene, SK65
estradiol	Estrace	propranolol	Inderal
ethambutol	Myambutol	propylthiouracil	(Generic only)
ethosuximide	Zarontin	pseudoephedrine	as Actifed, Novafed, as Sudafed

TABLE 8. *Continued*

Generic	Trade	Generic	Trade
pyridostigmin	Mestinon	thiopental	Pentothal
pyrimethamine	Daraprim	thiouracil	Thiouracil (no longer marketed in United States)
quazepam	Dormalin		
quinine	as Quinamm	ticarcillin	as Timentin
rifampin	Rifadin, Rimactane	timolol	Blocadren, Timoptic
		tinidazole	Fasigyn, Simplotan (unavailable in United States)
secobarbital	Seconal		
senna	Senokot		
sotalol	(Investigational)	tolbutamide	Orinase
spironolactone	Aldactone	tolmetin	Tolectin
sulbactam	as Unasyn	trazodone	Desyrel
sulfasalazine (salicylazosulfapyridine)	Azulfidine	trimethoprim with sulfamethoxazole	Bactrim, Septra
sulfisoxazole	Gantrisin	triprolidine	Actidil, as Actifed
suprofen	Suprol	valproic acid	Depakene
temazepam	Restoril	verapamil	Calan
terbutaline	Bricanyl, Brethine		
tetracycline	Achromycin	warfarin	Coumadin, Panwarfin
theophylline	Bronkodyl, Elixophyllin, Slo-Phyllin, Theo-Dur	zolpidem	Ambien

* For convenience, one or more examples of the trade name are given.
† Inclusion of drug names in Table 8 does not constitute an endorsement by the American Academy of Pediatrics of the products listed. Names are included for informational purposes only.

TABLE 9. Trade Names and Generic Equivalents*

Trade	Generic	Trade	Generic
Accent	monosodium glutamate	Coumadin	warfarin
Achromycin	tetracycline	Cytoxan	cyclophosphamide
Actidil	triprolidine	Daraprim	pyrimethamine
as Actifed	triprolidine	Darvon	propoxyphene
as Actifed	pseudoephedrine	Delta-Cortef	prednisolone
Acupan (unavailable in US)	nefopam	Deltasone	prednisone
Adriamycin	doxorubicin	Depakene	valproic acid
Advil	ibuprofen	Depo-Provera	medroxyprogesterone
Aldactone	spironolactone	Desyrel	trazodone
Ambien	zolpidem	Dexedrine	dextroamphetamine
Amipaque	metrizamide	Diamox	acetazolamide
Amoxil	amoxicillin	Dicumarol	bishydroxycoumarin
Anacin-3	acetamethophan	Dilantin	phenytoin
Anafranil	clomipramine	Dilor	dyphylline
Ancef	cefazolin	Diprofarn (foreign)	dipyrone
Apresoline	hydralazine	as Disophrol	dexbrompheniramine maleate
Aralen	chloroquine	Diuril	chlorothiazide
Arlef (foreign)	flufenamic acid	Dolene	propoxyphene
Asendin	amoxapine	Dolophine	methadone
Ativan	lorazepam	Dorbane	danthron
Azactam	aztreonam	Dormalin	quazepam
Azolid	phenylbutazone	as Drixoral	dexbrompheniramine maleate
Azulfidine	sulfasalazine	Duricef	cefadroxil
Bactrim	trimethoprim with sulfamethoxazole	Elavil	amitriptyline
		Elixophyllin	theophylline
Benzamide (foreign)	cisapride	Endep	amitriptyline
Blocadren	timolol	Enovid	[³H]Norethynodrel
Brethine	terbutaline	Estrace	estradiol
Bricanyl	terbutaline	as Etrafon	perphenazine
Bronkodyl	theophylline	Fasigyn	tinidazole
Butazolidin	phenylbutazone	Feldene	piroxicam
as Cafergot	ergotamine tartrate with caffeine	Flagyl	metronidazole
Calan	verapamil	Folex	methotrexate (amethopterin)
Capoten	captopril	Fortaz	ceftazidime
Cardizem	dilitiazem	Furadantin	nitrofurantoin
Cefzil	cefprozil	Gantrisin	sulfisoxazole
Centrax	prazepam		
Chloromycetin	chloramphenicol	Haldol	haloperidol
Chlotride (foreign)	cholothiazide	Hedulin	phenindione
Claforan	cefotaxime	HydroDIURIL	hydrochlorothiazide
Cleocin	clindamycin	Hygroton	chlorthalidone
as Combipres	chlorthalidone	Imodium	loperamide
Corgard	nadolol	Inderal	propranolol

TABLE 9.   *Continued*

Trade	Generic	Trade	Generic
Indocin	indomethacin	Rheumatrex	methotrexate
Indon	phenindione	Rifadin	rifampin
INH	isoniazid	Rifamycin	rifampin
Istizin	danthron	Rimactane	rifampin
Janimine	imipramine	Robaxin	methocarbamal
		Rocephin	ceftriaxone
Kantrex	kanamycin	Rogaine	minoxidil
Kefzol	cefazolin	Rowasa	mesalamine
Lanoxicaps	digoxin		
Lanoxin	digoxin	Seconal	secobarbital
as Levlen	levonorgestrel	Sectral	acebutolol
Lioresal	baclofen	Senokot	senna
Loniten	minoxidil	Septra	trimethoprim with
Lopressor	metoprolol		sulfamethoxazole
Macrodantin	nitrofurantoin	Serentil	mesoridazine
Mestinon	pyridostigmine	Seromycin	cycloserine
Meticorten	prednisone	Simplotan (unavailable	tinidazole
Meti-Derm	prednisolone	in US)	
Mexitil	mexiletine	Sinequan	doxepin
Motilium	domperidone	SK65	propoxyphene
Motrin	Ibuprofen	Slo-Phyllin	theophylline
Moxam	moxalactam	Soriatane	acitretin
MSG	monosodium glutamate	Sotalol	sotalol
Myambutol	ethambutol	Stadol	butorphanol
Myochrysine	gold sodium thiomalate	Sterapred	prednisone
Mysoline	primidone	Sublimaze	fentanyl
Naprosyn	naproxen	as Sudafed	pseudoephidrine
Naturetin	bendroflumethiazide	Suprol	suprofen
NegGram	nalidixic acid	Tagamet	cimetidine
Neo-mercazole (foreign)	carbimazole	Tambocor	flecainide
Noludar	methyprylon	Tapazole	methimazole
as Nordette	levonorgestrel	Taractan	chlorprothixene
Normodyne	labetalol	Tavegil (foreign)	clemastine
Norpace	disopyramide	Tavist	clemastine
as Norplant	levonorgestrel	Tegretol	carbamazepine
Norpramin	desipramine	Telepaque	iopanoic acid
Novafed	pseudoephedrine	Tempra	acetomethophan
Novaldin (unavailable in US)	dipyrone	Tenormin	atenolol
Nutrasweet	aspartame	Theo-Dur	theophylline
		Thiouracil (no longer	thiouracil
Orinase	tolbutamide	marketed in US)	
Parlodel	bromocriptine	Thorazine	chlorpromazine
Panadol	acetomethophan	as Timentin	ticarcillin
Panwarfin	warfarin	Timoptic	timolol
Pentothal	thiopental	Tofranil	imipramine
Pertofrane	desipramine	Tolectin	tolmetin
Phenaphen	acetomethophan	Toradol	ketorolac
Plaquenil	hydroxychloroquine	Trandate	labetalol
Platinol	cisplatin	Trasicor (foreign)	oxprenolol
Ponstel	mefenamic acid	Triavil	perphenazine
Prelone	prednisolone	Trilafon	perphenazine
Procardia	nifedipine	as Tri-Levlen	levonorgestrel
Pronestyl	procainamide	as Triphasil	levonorgestrel
Propacil	propylthiouracil	Tusscapine (foreign)	noscapine
Prothiaden (unavailable in US)	dothiepin	Tylenol	acetaminophen
		as Unasyn	sulbactam
Protostat	metronidazole	Valium	diazepam
Provera	medroxyprogesterone	Vasotec	enalapril
Prozac	fluoxetine	Versed	midazolam
as Quinamm	quinine	Xylocaine	lidocaine
Quine	quinine	Zarontin	ethosuximide
Reglan	metoclopramide	Zovirax	acyclovir
Restoril	temazepam	Zyloprim	allopurinol

* Inclusion of drug names in Table 9 does not constitute an endorsement by the American Academy of Pediatrics of the products listed. Names are included for informational purposes only.

REFERENCES

1. American Academy of Pediatrics, Committee on Drugs. The transfer of drugs and other chemicals into human breast milk. *Pediatrics.* 1983;72: 375–383

2. American Academy of Pediatrics, Committee on Drugs. Transfer of drugs and other chemicals into human milk. *Pediatrics.* 1989;84: 924–936

3. Kulski JK, Hartmann PE, Martin JD, et al. Effects of bromocriptine mesylate on the composition of the mammary secretion in non-breast-feeding women. *Obstet Gynecol.* 1978;52:38

4. Katz M, Kroll D, Pak I, et al. Puerperal hypertension, stroke, and seizures after suppression of lactation with bromocriptine. *Obstet Gynecol.* 1985;66:822–824

5. Chasnoff IJ, Lewis DE, Squires L. Cocaine intoxication in a breast-fed infant. *Pediatrics.* 1987;80:836–838

6. Wiernik PH, Duncan JH. Cyclophosphamide in human milk. *Lancet.* 1971;1:912

7. Amato D, Niblett JS. Neutropenia from cyclophosphamide in breast milk. *Med J Aust.* 1977;1:383

8. Fletcher SM, Katz AR, Rogers AJ, et al. The presence of cyclosporine in body tissue and fluids during pregnancy. *Am J Kidney Dis.* 1985;5:60

9. Egan PC, Costanza ME, Dodion P, et al. Doxorubicin and cisplatin excretion into human milk. *Cancer Treat Rep.* 1985;69:1387

10. Fomina PI. Untersuchungen uber den Ubergang des aktiven agens des Mutterkorns in die milch stillender Mutter. *Arch Gynecol.* 1934;157:275

11. Schou M, Amdisen A. Lithium and pregnancy, III: lithium ingestion by children breast-fed by women on lithium treatment. *Br Med J.* 1973;2:138

12. Tunnessen WW Jr, Hertz C. Toxic effects of lithium in newborn infants: a commentary. *J Pediatr.* 1972;81:804

13. Sykes PA, Quarrie J, Alexander FW. Lithium carbonate and breast-feeding. *Br Med J.* 1976;2:1299

14. Johns DG, Rutherford LD, Leighton PC, et al. Secretion of methotrexate into human milk. *Am J Obstet Gynecol.* 1972;112:978

15. Kaufman, KR, Petrucha RA, Pitts Jr FN, et al. PCP in amniotic fluid breast milk: case report. *J Clin Psychiatry.* 1983;44:269

16. Eckstein HB, Jack B. Breast-feeding anticoagulant therapy. *Lancet.* 1970; 1:672

17. Steiner E, Villen T, Hallberg M, et al. Amphetamine secretion in breast milk. *Eur J Clin Pharmacol.* 1984;27:123

18. Cobrinik RW, Hood RT Jr, Chusid E. The effect of maternal narcotic addiction on the newborn infant: review of literature and report of 22 cases. *Pediatrics.* 1959;24:288

19. Perez-Reyes M, Wall ME. Presence of tetrahydrocannabinol in human milk. *N Engl J Med.* 1982;307:819

20. Bisdom W. Alcohol and nicotine poisoning in nurslings. *JAMA.* 1937; 109:178

21. Ferguson BB, Wilson DJ, Schaffner W. Determination of nicotine concentrations in human milk. *AJDC.* 1976;130:837

22. Luck W, Nau H. Nicotine and cotinine concentrations in the milk of smoking mothers: influence of cigarette consumption and diurnal variation. *Eur J Pediatr.* 1987;146:21–26

23. Luck W, Nau H. Nicotine and cotinine concentrations in serum and milk of nursing mothers. *Br J Clin Pharmacol.* 1984;18:9–15

24. Luck W, Nau H. Nicotine and cotinine concentrations in serum and urine of infants exposed via passive smoking or milk from smoking mothers. *J Pediatr.* 1985;107:816–820

25. Labrecque M, Marcoux S, Weber J-P, et al. Feeding and urine cotinine values in babies whose mothers smoke. *Pediatrics.* 1989;83:93–97

26. Schwartz-Bickenbach D, Schulte-Hobein B, Abt S, et al. Smoking and passive smoking during pregnancy and early infancy: effects on birth weight, lactation period, and cotinine concentrations in mother's milk and infant's urine. *Toxicol Lett.* 1987;35:73–81

27. McArdle HJ, Danks DM. Secretion of copper 64 into breast milk following intravenous injection in a human subject. *J Trace Elem Exp Med.* 1991;4:81–84

28. Tobin RE, Schneider PB. Uptake of ^{67}Ga in the lactating breast and its persistence in milk: case report. *J Nucl Med.* 1976;17:1055

29. Butt D, Szaz KF. Indium-111 radioactivity in breast milk. *Br J Radiol.* 1986;59:80

30. Hedrick WR, Di Simone RN, Keen RL. Radiation dosimetry from breast milk excretion of radioiodine and pertechnetate. *J Nucl Med.* 1986;27: 1569–1571

31. Palmer KE. Excretion of ^{125}I in breast milk following administration of labelled fibrinogen. *Br J Radiol.* 1979;52:672

32. Honour AJ, Myant NB, Rowlands EN. Secretion of radioiodine in digestive juices and milk in man. *Clin Sci.* 1952;11:447

33. Karjalainen P, Penttila IM, Pystynen P. The amount and form of radio-

activity in human milk after lung scanning, renography and placental localization by ^{131}I labelled tracers. *Acta Obstet Gynecol Scand.* 1971;50:357

34. Bland EP, Crawford JS, Docker MF, et al. Radioactive iodine uptake by thyroid of breast-fed infants after maternal blood-volume measurements. *Lancet.* 1969;2:1039

35. Nurnberger CE, Lipscomb A. Transmission of radioiodine (I^{131}) to infants through human maternal milk. *JAMA.* 1952;150:1398

36. Pommerenke WT, Hahn PF. Secretion of radioactive sodium in human milk. *Proc Soc Exp Biol Med.* 1943;52:223

37. O'Connell MEA, Sutton H. Excretion of radioactivity in breast milk following ^{99}Tcm-Sn polyphosphate. *Br J Radiol.* 1976;49:377

38. Berke RA, Hoops EC, Kereiakes JC, et al. Radiation dose to breast-feeding child after mother has 99^{m}Tc-MAA lung scan. *J Nucl Med.* 1973; 14:51

39. Vagenakis AG, Abreau CM, Braverman LE. Duration of radioactivity in the milk of a nursing mother following 99^{m}Tc administration. *J Nucl Med.* 1971;12:188

40. Wyburn JR. Human breast milk excretion of radionuclides following administration of radiopharmaceuticals. *J Nucl Med.* 1973;14:115

41. Pittard WB III, Merkatz R, Fletcher BD. Radioactive excretion in human milk following administration of technetium Tc 99 m macroaggregated albumin. *Pediatrics.* 1982;70:231

42. Maisels MJ, Gilcher RO. Excretion of technetium in human milk. *Pediatrics.* 1983;71:841

43. American Academy of Pediatrics, Committee on Drugs. Psychotropic drugs in pregnancy and lactation. *Pediatrics.* 1982;69:241–244

44. Patrick MJ, Tilstone WJH, Reavey P. Diazepam and breast-feeding. *Lancet.* 1972;1:542

45. Cole AP, Hailey DM. Diazepam and active metabolite in breast milk and their transfer to the neonate. *Arch Dis Child.* 1975;50:741

46. Dusci LJ, Goods M, Hall RW, et al. Excretion of diazepam and its metabolites in human milk during withdrawal from combination high dose diazepam and oxazepam. *Br J Clin Pharmacol.* 1990;29:123–126

47. Summerfield RJ, Nielson MS. Excretion of lorazepam into breast milk. *Br J Anaesth.* 1985;57:1042

48. Matheson I, Lunde PK, Bredesen JE. Midazolam and nitrazepam in the maternity ward: milk concentrations and clinical effects. *Br J Clin Pharmacol.* 1990;30:787–793

49. Olesen OV, Bartels U, Poulsen JH. Perphenazine in breast milk and serum. *Am J Psychiatry.* 1990;147:1378–1379

50. Brodie RR, Chasseaud LF, Taylor T. Concentrations of N-descyclopropylmethylprazepam in whole-blood, plasma, and milk after administration of prazepam to humans. *Biopharm Drug Dispos.* 1981;2:59

51. Hilbert JM, Gural RP, Symchowicz S, et al. Excretion of quazepam into human breast milk. *J Clin Pharmacol.* 1984;24:457

52. Lebedevs TH, Wojnar-Horton RE, Yapp P, et al. Excretion of temazepam in breast milk. *Br J Clin Pharmacol.* 1992;33:204–206

53. Bader TF, Newman K. Amitriptyline in human breast milk and the nursing infant's serum. *Am J Psychiatry.* 1980;137:855

54. Erickson SH, Smith GH, Heidrich T. Tricyclics and breast feeding. *Am J Psychiatry.* 1979;136:1483

55. Gelenberg AJ. Amoxapine: a new antidepressant appears in human milk. *J Nerv Ment Dis.* 1979;167:635

56. Sovner R, Orsulak PJ. Excretion of imipramine and desipramine in human breast milk. *Am J Psychiatry.* 1979;136:451

57. Stancer HC, Reed KL. Desipramine and 2-hydroxydesipramine in human breast milk and the nursery infant's serum. *Am J Psychiatry.* 1986; 143:1597

58. Rees JA, Glass RC, Sporne GA. Serum and breast milk concentrations of dothiepin. *Practitioner.* 1976;217:686

59. Ilett KF, Lebedevs TH, Wojnar-Horton RE, et al. The excretion of dothiepin and its primary metabolites in breast milk. *Br J Clin Pharmacol.* 1992;33:635–639

60. Kemp J, Ilett KF, Booth J, et al. Excretion of doxepin and N-desmethyldoxepin in human milk. *Br J Clin Pharmacol.* 1985;20:497

61. Burch KJ, Wells BG. Fluoxetine/norfluoxetine concentrations in human milk. *Pediatrics.* 1992;89:676–677

62. Wright S, Dawling S, Ashford JJ. Excretion of fluvoxamine in breast milk. *Br J Clin Pharmacol.* 1991;31:209

63. Verbeeck RK, Ross SG, McKenna EA. Excretion of trazodone in breast milk. *Br J Clin Pharmacol.* 1986;22:367

64. Polishuk WZ, Kulcsar SA. Effects of chlorpromazine on pituitary function. *J Clin Endocrinol Metab.* 1956;16:292

65. Wiles DH, Orr MW, Kolakowska T. Chlorpromazine levels in plasma and milk of nursing mothers. *Br J Clin Pharmacol.* 1978;5:272

66. Matheson I, Evang A, Fredricson Overo K, et al. Presence of chlorprothixene and its metabolites in breast milk. *Eur J Clin Pharmacol.* 1984;27: 611

67. Stewart RB, Karas B, Springer PK. Haloperidol excretion in human milk. *Am J Psychiatry*. 1980;137:849

68. Whalley LJ, Blain PG, Prime JK. Haloperidol secreted in breast milk. *Br Med J*. 1981;282:1746

69. Ananth J. Side effects in the neonate from psychotropic agents excreted through breast-feeding. *Am J Psychiatry*. 1978;135:801

70. Havelka J, Hejzlar M, Popov V. Excretion of chloramphenicol in human milk. *Chemotherapy*. 1968;13:204

71. Smadel JE, Woodward TE, Ley HL Jr, et al. Chloramphenicol (Chloromycetin) in the treatment of tsutsugamushi disease (scrub typhus). *J Clin Invest*. 1949;28:1196

72. Gupta AP, Gupta PK. Metaclopramide as a lactogogue. *Clin Pediatr*. 1985;24:269

73. Kauppela A, Arvela P, Koivisto M, et al. Metaclopramide and breast-feeding: transfer into milk and the newborn. *Eur J Clin Pharmacol*. 1983; 25:819

74. Erickson SH, Oppenheim GL, Smith GH. Metronidazole in breast milk. *Obstet Gynecol*. 1981;57:48

75. Heisterberg L, Branebjerg PE. Blood and milk concentrations of metronidazole in mothers and infants. *J Perinat Med*. 1983;11:114

76. Evaldson GR, Lindgren S, Nord CE, et al. Tinidazole milk excretion and pharmacokinetics in lactating women. *Br J Clin Pharmacol*. 1985;19:503

77. Nelis GF. Diarrhoea due to 5-aminosalicylic acid in breast milk. *Lancet*. 1989;383

78. Jenss H, Weber P, Hartmann F. 5-Aminosalicylic acid its metabolite in breast milk during lactation. *Am J Gastroenterol*. 1990;85:331

79. Clark JH, Wilson WG. A 16-day-old breast-fed infant with metabolic acidosis caused by salicylate. *Clin Pediatr*. 1981;20:53

80. Levy G. Salicylate pharmacokinetics in the human neonate. In: Marselli PL, ed. *Basic and Therapeutic Aspects of Perinatal Pharmacology*. New York, NY: Raven Press; 1975:319

81. Fakhredding J, Keshavarz E. Salicylate excretion in breast milk. *Int J Pharm*. 1981;8:285

82. Kok THHG, Taitz LS, Bennett MJ. Drowsiness due to clemastine transmitted in breast milk. *Lancet*. 1982;1:914

83. Nau H, Rating D, Hauser I, et al. Placental transfer and pharmacokinetics of primidone and its metabolites phenobarbital, PEMA and hydroxyphenobarbital in neonates and infants of epileptic mothers. *Eur J Clin Pharmacol*. 1980;18:31

84. Kuhnz W, Koch S, Helge H, et al. Primidone and phenobarbital during lactation period in epileptic women: total and free drug serum levels in the nursed infants and their effects on neonatal behavior. *Dev Pharmacol Ther*. 1988;11:147

85. Finch E, Lorber J. Methaemoglobinaemia in the newborn: probably due to phenytoin excreted in human milk. *J Obstet Gynaecol Br Emp*. 1954; 61:833

86. Tyson RM, Shrader EA, Perlman HH. Drugs transmitted through breast milk, II: barbiturates. *J Pediatr*. 1938;13:86

87. Knott C, Reynolds F, Clayden G. Infantile spasms on weaning from breast milk containing anticonvulsants. *Lancet*. 1987;2:272

88. Branski D, Kerem E, Gross-Kieselstein E, et al. Bloody diarrhea–a possible complication of sulfasalazine transferred through human breast milk. *J Pediatr Gastroenterol Nutr*. 1986;5:316

89. Boutroy MJ, Bianchetti G, Dubruc C, et al. To nurse when receiving acebutolol: is it dangerous for the neonate? *Eur J Clin Pharmacol*. 1986; 30:737

90. Berlin CM Jr, Yaffe SJ, Ragni M. Disposition of acetaminophen in milk, saliva, and plasma of lactating women. *Pediatr Pharmacol*. 1980;1:135

91. Bitzen PO, Gustafsson B, Jostell KG, et al. Excretion of paracetamol in human breast milk. *Eur J Clin Pharmacol*. 1981;20:123

92. Findlay JWA, DeAngelis RL, Kearney MF, et al. Analgesic drugs in breast milk and plasma. *Clin Pharmacol Ther*. 1981;29:625

93. Soderman P, Hartvig P, Fagerlund C. Acetazolamide excretion into human breast milk. *Br J Clin Pharmacol*. 1984;17:599

94. Rollman O, Pihl-Lundin I. Acitretin excretion into human breast milk. *Acta Derm Venereol (Stockh)*. 1990;70:487–490

95. Lau RJ, Emery MG, Galinsky RE. Unexpected accumulation of acyclovir in breast milk with estimation of infant exposure. *Obstet Gynecol*. 1987; 69:468

96. Meyer LJ, de Miranda P, Sheth N, et al. Acyclovir in human breast milk. *Am J Obstet Gynecol*. 1988;158:586–588

97. Binkiewicz A, Robinson MJ, Senior B. Pseudo-cushing syndrome caused by alcohol in breast milk. *J Pediatr*. 1978;93:965

98. Cobo E. Effect of different dose of ethanol on the milk-ejecting reflex in lactating women. *Am J Obstet Gynecol*. 1973;115:817

99. Kesaniemi YA. Ethanol and acetaldehyde in the milk and peripheral blood of lactating women after ethanol administration. *J Obstet Gynaecol Br Commonw*. 1974;81:84

100. Little RE, Anderson KW, Ervin CH, et al. Maternal alcohol use during breast-feeding and infant mental and motor development at one year. *N Engl J Med*. 1989;321:425–430

101. Kamilli I, Gresser U, Schaefer C, et al. Allopurinol in breast milk. *Adv Exp Med Biol*. 1991;309A:143–145

102. Kafetzis DA, Siafas CA, Georgakopoulos PA, et al. Passage of cephalosporins and amoxicillin into the breast milk. *Acta Paediatr Scand*. 1981;70:285

103. Berman JD, Melby PC, Neva FA. Concentration of Pentosam in human breast milk. *Trans R Soc Trop Med Hyg*. 1989;83:784–785

104. Liedholm H, Melander A, Bitzen P-O, et al. Accumulation of atenolol and metoprolol in human breast milk. *Eur J Clin Pharmacol*. 1981;20:229

105. Schimmel MS, Edelman AI, Wilschanski MA, et al. Toxic effects of atenolol consumed during breast feeding. *J Pediatr*. 1989;114:476–478

106. Thorley KJ, McAinsh J. Levels of the beta-blockers atenolol and propanolol in the breast milk of women treated for hypertension in pregnancy. *Biopharm Drug Dispos*. 1983;4:299–301

107. Sapeika N. The excretion of drugs in human milk—a review. *J Obstet Gynaecol Br Commonw*. 1947;54:426

108. Bald R, Bernbeck-Betthauser E-M, Spahn H, et al. Excretion of azpropazone in human breast milk. *Eur J Clin Pharmacol*. 1990;39:271–273

109. Fleiss PM, Richwald GA, Gordon J, et al. Aztreonam in human serum and breast milk. *Br J Clin Pharmacol*. 1985;19:509

110. Nail PA, Thomas MR, Eakin R. The effect of thiamin and riboflavin supplementation on the level of those vitamins in human breast milk and urine. *Am J Clin Nutr*. 1980;33:198

111. Roepke JLB, Kirksey A. Vitamin B6 nutrature during pregnancy lactation: I. vitamin B_6 intake, levels of the vitamin in biological fluids, condition of the infant at birth. *Am J Clin Nutr*. 1979;32:2249

112. West KD, Kirksey A. Influence of vitamin B_6 intake on the content of the vitamin in human milk. *Am J Clin Nutr*. 1976;29:961

113. Greentree LB. Dangers of vitamin B_6 in nursing mothers. *N Engl J Med*. 1979;300:141

114. Samson RR, McClelland DBL. Vitamin B_{12} in human colostrum milk: quantitation of the vitamin its binder the uptake of bound vitamin B_{12} by intestinal bacteria. *Acta Paediatr Scand*. 1980;69:93

115. Eriksson G, Swahn CG. Concentrations of baclofen in serum and breast milk from a lactating woman. *Scand J Clin Lab Invest*. 1981;41:185

116. Healy M. Suppressing lactaton with oral diuretics. *Lancet*. 1961;1:1353

117. Brambel CE, Hunter RE. Effect of dicumarol on the nursing infant. *Am J Obstet Gynecol*. 1950;59:1153

118. Tyson RM, Shrader EA, Perlman HH. Drugs transmitted through breast milk, III: bromides. *J Pediatr*. 1938;13:91

119. Pittman KA, Smyth RD, Losada M, et al. Human perinatal distribution of butorphanol. *Am J Obstet Gynecol*. 1980;138:797

120. Berlin CM Jr. Excretion of the methylxanthines in human milk. *Semin Perinatol*. 1981;5:389

121. Tyrala EE, Dodson WE. Caffeine secretion into breast milk. *Arch Dis Child*. 1979;54:787

122. Hildebrandt R, Gundert-Remy V. Lack of pharmacological active saliva levels of caffeine in breast-fed infants. *Pediatr Pharmacol*. 1983;3:237

123. Berlin CM Jr, Denson HM, Daniel CH, Ward RM. Disposition of dietary caffeine in milk, saliva and plasma of lactating women. *Pediatrics*. 1984;73:59–63

124. Ryu JE. Caffeine in human milk and in serum of breast-fed infants. *Dev Pharmacol Ther*. 1985;8:329

125. Ryu JE. Effect of maternal caffeine consumption on heart rate and sleep time of breast-fed infants. *Dev Pharmacol Ther*. 1985;8:355

126. Devlin RG, Fleiss PM. Captopril in human blood and breast milk. *J Clin Pharmacol*. 1981;21:110

127. Nau H, Kuhnz W, Egger JH, et al. Anticonvulsants during pregnancy and lactation. *Clin Pharmacokinet*. 1982;7:508

128. Pynnonen S, Kanto J, Sillanpaa M, et al. Carbamazepine: placental transport, tissue concentrations in foetus newborn, level in milk. *Acta Pharmacol Toxicol*. 1977;41:244

129. Cooper DS. Antithyroid drugs: to breast-feed or not to breast-feed. *Am J Obstet Gynecol*. 1987;157:234

130. Lamberg B-A, Ikonen E, Österlund K, et al. Antithyroid treatment of maternal hyperthyroidism during lactation. *Clin Endocrinol*. 1984;21: 81–87

131. Tyson RM, Shrader EA, Perlman HH. Drugs transmitted through breast milk, I: laxatives. *J Pediatr*. 1937;11:824

132. Yoshioka H, Cho K, Takimoto M, et al. Transfer of cefazolin into human milk. *J Pediatr*. 1979;94:151

133. Dresse A, Lambotte R, Dubois M, et al. Transmammary passage of cefoxitin: additional results. *J Clin Pharmacol*. 1983;23:438

134. Shyu WC, Shah VR, Campbell DA, et al. Excretion of cefprozil into human breast milk. *Antimicrob Agents Chemother*. 1992;36:938–941

135. Blanco JD, Jorgensen JH, Castaneda YS, et al. Ceftazidine levels in human breast milk. *Antimicrob Agents Chemother*. 1983;23:479

136. Kafetzis DA, Brater DC, Fanourgakis JE, et al. Ceftriaxone distribution between maternal blood and fetal blood and tissues at parturition and between blood and milk postpartum. *Antimicrob Agents Chemother*. 1983;23:870

137. Lacey JH. Dichloralphenazone breast milk. *Br Med J*. 1971;4:684

138. Reed CB. A study of the conditions that require the removal of the child from the breast. *Surg Gynecol Obstet*. 1908;6:514

139. Soares R, Paulini E, Pereira JP. Da concentracao e eliminacao da cloroquina atraves da circulacao placentaria e do leite materno, de pacientes sob regime do sal loroquinado. *Rev Bras Malariol Doencas Trop*. 1957;9:19

140. Ogunbona FA, Onyizi CO, Bolaji OO, et al. Excretion of chloroquine and desethylchloroquin in human milk. *Br J Clin Pharmacol*. 1987;23:476

141. Edstein MD, Veenendaal JR, Newman K, et al. Excretion of chlorquine, dapsone and pyrimethamine in human milk. *Br J Clin Pharmacol*. 1986;22:733

142. Werthmann MW Jr, Krees SV. Excretion of chlorothiazide in human breast milk. *J Pediatr*. 1972;81:781

143. Miller EM, Cohn RD, Burghart PH. Hydrochlorothiazide disposition in a mother her breast-fed infant. *J Pediatr*. 1982;101:789

144. Mulley BA, Parr GD, Pau WK, et al. Placental transfer of chlorthalidone and its elimination in maternal milk. *Eur J Clin Pharmacol*. 1978;13:129

145. Somogyi A, Gugler R. Cimetidine excretion into breast milk. *Br J Clin Pharmacol*. 1979;7:627

146. Hofmeyr GJ, Sonnendecker EWW. Secretion of the gastrokinetic agent cisapride in human milk. *Eur J Clin Pharmacol*. 1986;30:735

147. Smith JA, Morgan JR, Rachlis AR, et al. Clindamycin in human breast milk. *Can Med Assoc J*. 1975;112:806

148. Zacharias S, Aguillern E, Assenzo JR, et al. Effects of hormonal and nonhormonal contraceptives on lactation and incidence of pregnancy. *Contraception*. 1986;33:203

149. Schimmell MS, Katz EZ, Shaag Y, et al. Toxic neonatal effects following maternal clomipramine therapy. *J Toxicol Clin Toxicol*. 1991;29:479–484

150. Milunsky JM. Breast-feeding during colchicine therapy for familial Mediterranean fever. *J Pediatr*. 1991;119:164

151. Nilsson S, Mellbin T, Hofvander Y, et al. Long-term followup of children breast-fed by mothers using oral contraceptives. *Contraception*. 1986;34:443

152. Nilsson S, Nygren KG. Transfer of contraceptive steroids to human milk. *Res Reprod*. 1979;11:1

153. American Academy of Pediatrics, Committee on Drugs. Breast-feeding and contraception. *Pediatrics*. 1981;68:138–140

154. Barsivala VM, Virkar KD. The effect of oral contraceptives on concentration of various components of human milk. *Contraception*. 1973;7:307

155. Borglin NE, Sandholm LE. Effect of oral contraceptives on lactation. *Fertil Steril*. 1971;22:39

156. Curtis EM. Oral-contraceptive feminization of a normal male infant: report of a case. *Obstet Gynecol*. 1964;23:295

157. Kora SJ. Effect of oral contraceptives on lactation. *Fertil Steril*. 1969;20:419

158. Toaff R, Ashkenazi H, Schwartz A, et al. Effects of oestrogen and progestagen on the composition of human milk. *J Reprod Fertil*. 1969;19:475

159. Snyder DR Jr, Powell KE. Should women taking antituberculosis drugs breast-feed? *Arch Intern Med*. 1984;144:589

160. Cancela L, LeBoulch N, Miravet L. Relationship between the vitamin D content of maternal milk and the vitamin D status of nursing women and breast-fed infants. *J Endocrinol*. 1986;110:43

161. Rothberg AD, Pettifor JM, Cohen DF, et al. Maternal-infant vitamin D relationships during breast-feeding. *J Pediatr*. 1982;101:500

162. Greer FR, Hollis BW, Napoli JL. High concentrations of vitamin D2 in human milk associated with pharmacologic doses of vitamin D2. *J Pediatr*. 1984;105:61

163. Greenhalf JO, Leonard HSD. Laxatives in the treatment of constipation in pregnant and breast-feeding mothers. *Practitioner*. 1973;210:259

164. Dreisbach JA. Sulphone levels in breast milk of mothers on sulphone therapy. *Lepr Rev*. 1952;23:101

165. Mortimer EA Jr. Drug toxicity from breast milk? *Pediatrics*. 1977;60:780

166. Loughnan PM. Digoxin excretion in human breast milk. *J Pediatr*. 1978;92:1019

167. Levy M, Granit L, Laufer N. Excretion of drugs in human milk. *N Engl J Med*. 1977;297:789

168. Okada M, Inoue H, Nakamura Y, et al. Excretion of diltiazem in human milk. *N Engl J Med*. 1985;312:992

169. Zylber-Katz E, Linder N, Granit L, et al. Excretion of dipyrone metabolites in human breast milk. *Eur J Clin Pharmacol*. 1986;30:359

170. MacKintosh D, Buchanan N. Excretion of disopyramide in human breast milk. *Br J Clin Pharmacol*. 1985;19:856

171. Hoppu K, Neuvonen PJ, Korte T. Disopyramide and breast feeding. *Br J Clin Pharmacol*. 1986;21:553

172. Hofmeyr GJ, van Idlekinge B. Domperidone and lactation. *Lancet*. 1983;1:647

173. Jorboe CH, Cook LN, Malesic I, et al. Dyphylline elimination kinetics in lactating women: blood to milk transfer. *J Clin Pharmacol*. 1981;21:405

174. Redman CW, Kelly JG, Cooper WD. The excretion of enalapril and enalaprilat in human breast milk. *Eur J Clin Pharmacol*. 1990;38:99

175. Matsuda S. Transfer of antibiotics into maternal milk. *Biol Res Pregnancy*. 1984;5:57

176. Nilsson S, Nygren KG, Johansson EDB. Transfer of estradiol to human milk. *Am J Obstet Gynecol*. 1978;132:653

177. Koup JR, Rose JQ, Cohen ME. Ethosuximide pharmacokinetics in a pregnant patient and her newborn. *Epilepsia*. 1978;19:535

178. Steer PL, Biddle CJ, Marley WS, et al. Concentration of fentanyl in colostrum after an analgesic dose. *Can J Anaesth*. 1992;39:231–235

179. McQuinn RL, Pisani A, Wafa S, et al. Flecainide excretion in human breast milk. *Clin Pharmacol Ther*. 1990;48:262–267

180. Wagner X, Jouglard J, Moulin M, et al. Coadministration of flecainide acetate and sotalol during pregnancy: lack of teratogenic effects, passage across the placenta, and excretion in human breast milk. *Am Heart J*. 1990;119:700–702

181. Buchanan RA, Eaton CJ, Koeff ST, et al. The breast milk excretion of flufenamic acid. *Curr Ther Res*. 1969;11:533

182. Mattern J, Mayer PR. Excretion of fluorescein into breast milk. *Am J Ophthalmol*. 1990;109:598–599

183. Retief EF, Heyns ADuP, Oosthuizen M, et al. Aspects of folate metabolism in lactating women studied after ingestion of ¹⁴C-methylfolate. *Am J Med Sci*. 1979;277:281

184. Bell RAF, Dale IM. Gold secretion in maternal milk. *Arthritis Rheum*. 1976;19:1374

185. Blau SP. Metabolism of gold during lactation. *Arthritis Rheum*. 1973;16:777

186. Gottlieb NL. Suggested errata. *Arthritis Rheum*. 1974;17:1057

187. Ostensen M, Skavdal K, Myklebust G, et al. Excretion of gold into human breast milk. *Eur J Clin Pharmacol*. 1986;31:251

188. Bennett PN, Humphries SJ, Osborne JP, et al. Use of sodium aurothiomalate during lactation. *Br J Clin Pharmacol*. 1990;29:777–779

189. Cote CJ, Kenepp NB, Reed SB, et al. Trace concentrations of halothane in human breast milk. *Br J Anaesth*. 1976;48:541

190. Liedholm H, Wahlin-Boll E, Hanson A, et al. Transplacental passage and breast milk concentrations of hydralazine. *Eur J Clin Pharmacol*. 1982;21:417

191. Ostensen M, Brown ND, Chiang PK, et al. Hydroxychoroquine in human breast milk. *Eur J Clin Pharmacol*. 1985;28:357

192. Nation RL, Hackett LP, Dusci LJ, et al. Excretion of hydroxychloroquine in human milk. *Br J Clin Pharmacol*. 1984;17:368

193. Townsend RJ, Benedetti T, Erickson SH, et al. A study to evaluate the passage of ibuprofen into breast milk. *Drug Intell Clin Pharm*. 1982;16:482

194. Townsend RJ, Benedetti TJ, Erickson SH, et al. Excretion of ibuprofen into breast milk. *Am J Obstet Gynecol*. 1984;149:184

195. Eeg-Olofsson O, Malmros I, Elwin CE, et al. Convulsions in a breast-fed infant after maternal indomethacin. *Lancet*. 1978;2:215

196. Fairhead FW. Convulsions in a breast-fed infant after maternal indomethacin. *Lancet*. 1978;2:576

197. Lebedevs TH, Wojnar-Horton RE, Yapp P, et al. Excretion of indomethacin in breast milk. *Br J Clin Pharmacol*. 1991;32:751–754

198. Postellon DC, Aronow R. Iodine in mother's milk. *JAMA*. 1982;247:463

199. Holmdahl KH. Cholecystography during lactation. *Acta Radiol*. 1955;45:305

200. Berlin CM Jr, Lee C. Isoniazid and acetylisoniazid disposition in human milk, saliva and plasma. *Fed Proc*. 1979;38:426

201. Dyggve HV, Dam H, Sondergaard E. Influence on the prothrombin time of breast-fed newborn babies of one single dose of vitamin K₁, or synkavit given to the mother within 2 hours after birth. *Acta Obstet Gynecol Scand*. 1956;35:440

202. Kries RV, Shearer M, McCarthy PT, et al. Vitamin K₁ content of maternal milk: Influence of the stage of lactation, lipid composition, vitamin K₁ supplements given to the mother. *Pediatr Res*. 1987;22:513

203. Wischnik A, Manth SM, Lloyd J, et al. The excretion of ketorolac tromethamine into breast milk after multiple oral dosing. *Eur J Clin Pharmacol*. 1989;36:521–524

204. Lunell HO, Kulas J, Rane A. Transfer of labetalol into amniotic fluid

and breast milk in lactating women. *Eur J Clin Pharmacol.* 1985;28:597

205. Atkinson H, Begg EJ. Concentration of beta-blocking drugs in human milk. *J Pediatr.* 1990;116:156

206. Díaz S, Herreros C, Juez G, et al. Fertility regulation in nursing women, VII: influence of Norplant levonorgestrel implants upon lactation and infant growth. *Contraception.* 1985;32:53–74

207. Shaaban MM, Odlind V, Salem HT, et al. Levonorgestrel concentrations in maternal and infant serum during use of subdermal levonorgestrel contraceptive implants, Norplant by nursing mothers. *Contraception.* 1986;33:357–363

208. Shikary ZK, Betrabet SS, Patel ZM, et al. Transfer of levonorgestrel (LNG) administered through different drug delivery systems from the maternal circulation into the newborn infant's circulation via breast milk. *Contraception.* 1987;35:477–486

209. McCann MF, Moggia AV, Higgins JE, et al. The effects of a progestin-only oral contraceptive (levonorgestrel 0.03 mg) on breast-feeding. *Contraception.* 1989;40:635–648

210. Zeisler JA, Gaarder TD, DeMesquita SA. Lidocaine excretion in breast milk. *Drug Intell Clin Pharm.* 1986;20:691

211. Nikodem VC, Hofmeyr GJ. Secretion of the antidiarrhoeal agent loperamide oxide in breast milk. *Eur J Clin Pharmacol.* 1992;42:695–696

212. Cruikshank DP, Varner MW, Pitkin RM. Breast milk magnesium and calcium concentrations following magnesium sulfate treatment. *Am J Obstet Gynecol.* 1982;143:685

213. Buchanan RA, Eaton CJ, Koeff ST, et al. The breast milk excretion of mefenamic acid. *Curr Ther Res Clin Exp.* 1968;10:592

214. Blinick G, Inturrisi CE, Jerez E, et al. Methadone assays in pregnant women and pregnancy. *Am J Obstet Gynecol.* 1975;121:617

215. Blinick G, Wallach RC, Jerez E, et al. Drug addiction in pregnancy and the neonate. *Am J Obstet Gynecol.* 1976;125:135

216. Cooper DS, Bode HH, Nath B, et al. Methimazole pharmacology in man: studies using or newly developed radioimmunoassay for methimazole. *J Clin Endocrinol Metab.* 1984;58:473

217. Campbell AD, Coles FK, Eubank LLK, et al. Distribution and metabolism of methocarbamol. *J Pharmacol Exp Ther.* 1961;131:18

218. White WB, Andreoli JW, Cohn RD. Alpha-methyldopa disposition in mothers with hypertension in their breast-fed infants. *Clin Pharmacol Ther.* 1985;37:387

219. Shore MF. Drugs can be dangerous during pregnancy and lactations. *Can Pharm J.* 1970;103:358

220. Ilett KF, Hackett LP, Paterson JW. Excretion of metrizamide in milk. *Br J Radiol.* 1981;54:537

221. Lownes HE, Ives TJ. Mexiletine use in pregnancy and lactation. *Am J Obstet Gynecol.* 1987;157:446

222. Valdivieso A, Valdes G, Spiro TE, et al. Minoxidil in breast milk. *Ann Intern Med.* 1985;102:135

223. Terwilliger WG, Hatcher RA. The elimination of morphine and quinine in human milk. *Surg Gynecol Obstet.* 1934;58:823

224. Robieux I, Koren G, Vandenbergh H, et al. Morphine excretion in breast milk and resultant exposure of a nursing infant. *J Toxicol Clin Toxicol.* 1990;28:365–370

225. Miller RD, Keegan KA, Thrupp LD, et al. Human breast milk concentration of moxalactam. *Am J Obstet Gynecol.* 1984;148:348

226. Devlin RG, Duchin KL, Fleiss PM. Nadolol in human serum and breast milk. *Br J Clin Pharmacol.* 1981;12:393

227. Belton EM, Jones RV. Haemolytic anaemia due to nalidixic acid. *Lancet.* 1965;2:691

228. Jamali F, Tam YK, Stevens RD. Naproxen excretion in breast milk and its uptake by suckling infant. *Drug Intell Clin Pharm.* 1982;16

229. Liu DTY, Savage JM, Donnell D. Nefopam excretion in human milk. *Br J Clin Pharmacol.* 1987;23:99

230. Ehrenkranz RA, Ackerman BA, Hulse JD. Nifedipine transfer into human milk. *J Pediatr.* 1989;114:478–480

231. Varsano I, Fischl J, Tikvah P, et al. The excretion of orally ingested nitrofurantoin in human milk. *J Pediatr.* 1973;82:886

232. Laumas KR, Malkani PK, Bhatnagar S, et al. Radioactivity in the breast milk of lactating women after oral administration of ³H-norethynodrel. *Am J Obstet Gynecol.* 1967;98:411

233. Pincus G, Bialy G, Layne DS, et al. Radioactivity in the milk of subjects receiving radioactive 19-norsteroids. *Nature.* 1966;212:924

234. Olsson B, Bolme P, Dahlstrom B, et al. Excretion of noscapine in human breast milk. *Eur J Clin Pharmacol.* 1986;30:213

235. Sioufi A, Hillion D, Lumbroso P, et al. Oxprenolol placental transfer plasma concentrations in newborns and passage into breast milk. *Br J Clin Pharmacol.* 1984;18:453

236. Fidler J, Smith V, DeSwiet M. Excretion of oxprenolol and timolol in breast milk. *Br J Obstet Gynaecol.* 1983;90:961

237. Leuxner E, Pulver R. Verabreichung von irgapyrin bei Schwangeren und Wochnerinnen. *MMW.* 1956;98:84

238. Mirkin B. Diphenylhydantoin: placental transport, fetal localization, neonatal metabolism, possible teratogenic effects. *J Pediatr.* 1971;78:329

239. Ostensen M. Piroxicam in human breast milk. *Eur J Clin Pharmacol.* 1983;25:829

240. McKenzie SA, Selley JA, Agnew JE. Secretion of prednisolone into breast milk. *Arch Dis Child.* 1975;50:894

241. Katz FH, Duncan BR. Entry of prednisone into human milk. *N Engl J Med.* 1975;293:1154

242. Pittard WB III, Glazier H. Procainamide excretion in human milk. *J Pediatr.* 1983;102:631

243. Diaz S, Jackanicz TM, Herreros C, et al. Fertility regulation in nursing women, VIII: progesterone plasma levels and contraceptive efficacy of a progesterone-releasing vaginal ring. *Contraception.* 1985;32:603

244. Kunka RL, Venkataramanan R, Stern RM, et al. Excretion of propoxyphene and norpropoxyphene in breast milk. *Clin Pharmacol Ther.* 1984;35:675

245. Levitan AA, Manion JC. Propranolol therapy during pregnancy and lactation. *Am J Cardiol.* 1973;32:247

246. Karlberg B, Lundberg D, Aberg H. Excretion of propranolol in human breast milk. *Acta Pharmacol Toxicol.* 1974;34:222

247. Bauer JH, Pape B, Zajicek J, et al. Propranolol in human plasma and breast milk. *Am J Cardiol.* 1979;43:860

248. Kampmann JP, Johansen K, Hansen JM, et al. Propylthiouracil in human milk: revision of a dogma. *Lancet.* 1980;1:736

249. Findlay JWA, Butz RF, Sailstad JM, et al. Pseudoephedrine and triprolidine in plasma and breast milk of nursing mothers. *Br J Clin Pharmacol.* 1984;18:901

250. Hardell L-I, Lindstrom B, Lonnerholm G, et al. Pyridostigmine in human breast milk. *Br J Clin Pharmacol.* 1982;14:656

251. Clyde DF, Shute GT, Press J. Transfer of pyrimethamine in human milk. *J Trop Med Hyg.* 1956;59:277

252. Hill LM, Malkasian GD Jr. The use of quinidine sulfate throughout pregnancy. *Obstet Gynecol.* 1979;54:366

253. Horning MG, Stillwell WG, Nowlin J, et al. Identification and quantification of drugs and drug metabolites in human breast milk using GC-MS-COM methods. *Mod Probl Paediatr.* 1975;15:73

254. Werthmann MW, Krees SV. Quantitative excretion of senokot in human breast milk. *Med Ann DC.* 1973;42:4

255. Hackett LP, Wojnar-Horton RE, Dusci LJ, et al. Excretion of sotalol in breast milk. *Br J Clin Pharmacol.* 1990;29:277–278

256. Phelps DL, Karim A. Spironolactone: relationship between concentrations of dethioacetylated metabolite in human serum milk. *J Pharm Sci.* 1977;66:1203

257. Foulds G, Miller RD, Knirsch AK, et al. Sulbactam kinetics and excretion into breast milk in postpartum women. *Clin Pharmacol Ther.* 1985; 38:692

258. Jarnerot G, Into-Malmberg MB. Sulphasalazine treatment during breast feeding. *Scand J Gastroenterol.* 1979;14:869

259. Berlin CM Jr, Yaffe SJ. Disposition of salicylazosufapyridine (Axulfidine) and metabolites in human breast milk. *Dev Pharmacol Ther.* 1980; 1:31

260. Kauffman RE, O'Brien C, Gilford P. Sulfisoxazole secretion into human milk. *J Pediatr.* 1980;97:839

261. Chaiken P, Chasin M, Kennedy B, et al. Suprafen concentrations in human breast milk. *J Clin Pharmacol.* 1983;23:385

262. Lindberberg C, Boreus LO, DeChateau P, et al. Transfer of terbutaline into breast milk. *Eur J Respir Dis.* 1984;65:87

263. Tetracycline in breast milk. *Br Med J.* 1969;4:791

264. Posner AC, Prigot A, Konicoff NG. Further observations on the use of tetracycline hydrochloride in prophylaxis and treatment of obstetric infections. In: Welch H, Marti-Ibanez F, eds. *Antibiotics Annual 1954–1955.* New York, NY: Medical Encyclopedia Inc; 1955:594

265. Yurchak AM, Jusko WJ. Theophylline secretion into breast milk. *Pediatrics.* 1976;57:518

266. Anderson LW, Qvist T, Hertz J, et al. Concentrations of thiopentone in mature breast milk and colostrum following an induction dose. *Acta Anaesthesiol Scand.* 1987;31:30

267. Williams RH, Kay GA, Jandorf BJ. Thiouracil: its absorption, distribution, excretion. *J Clin Invest.* 1944;23:613

268. Von Kobyletzki D, Dalhoff A, Lindemeyer H, et al. Ticarcillin serum and tissue concentrations in gynecology and obstetrics. *Infection.* 1983; 11:144

269. Moiel RH, Ryan JR. Tolbutamide (Orinase) in human breast milk. *Clin Pediatr.* 1967;6:480

270. Sagranes R, Waller ES, Goehrs HR. Tolmetin in breast milk. *Drug Intell Clin Pharm.* 1985;19:55

271. Arnauld R. Etude du passage de la trimethoprime dans le lait maternel. *Ouest Med.* 1972;25:959

272. Miller RD, Salter AJ. The passage of trimethoprim/sulpha-methoxazole into breast milk and its significance. Proceedings of the 8th International Congress of Chemotherapy, Athens. *Hellenic Soc Chemother.* 1974;1:687

273. Alexander FW. Sodium valproate and pregnancy. *Arch Dis Child.* 1979;54:240

274. Von Unruh GE, Froescher W, Hoffman F, et al. Valproic acid in breast milk: how much is really there? *Ther Drug Monit.* 1984;6:272

275. Anderson P, Bondesson U, Mattiasson I, et al. Verapamil and norverapamil in plasma and breast milk during breast feeding. *Eur J Clin Pharmacol.* 1987;31:625

276. Orme ML'E, Lewis PJ, deSwiet M, et al. May mothers given warfarin breast-feed their infant? *Br Med J.* 1977;1:1564

277. Pons G, Francoual C, Guillet P, et al. Zolpidem excretion in breast milk. *Eur J Clin Pharmacol.* 1989;37:245–248

278. Wild CP, Pionneau FA, Montesano R, et al. Aflatoxin detected in human breast milk by immunoassay. *Int J Cancer.* 1987;40:328

279. Maxwell SM, Apeagyei F, de Vries HR, et al. Aflatoxins in breast milk, neonatal cord blood and sera of pregnant women. *J Toxicol Toxin Rev.* 1989;8:19–29

280. Zarba A, Wild CP, Hall AJ, et al. Aflatoxin M_1 in human breast milk from The Gambia, West Africa, quantified by combined monoclonal antibody immunoaffinity chromatography HPLC. *Carcinogenesis.* 1992;13:891–894

281. Steginik LD, Filer LJ Jr, Baker BL. Plasma, erythrocyte human milk levels of free amino acids in lactating women administered aspartame or lactose. *J Nutr.* 1979;109:2173

282. Mangurten HH, Kaye CI. Neonatal bromism secondary to maternal exposure to a photographic laboratory. *J Pediatr.* 1982;100:596

283. Radisch B, Luck W, Nau H. Cadmium concentrations in milk and blood of smoking mothers. *Toxicol Lett.* 1987;36:147

284. Miyazaki T, Akiyama K, Kaneko S, et al. Chlordane residues in human milk. *Bull Environ Contam Toxicol.* 1980;25:518

285. Resman BH, Blumenthal HP, Jusko WJ. Breast milk distribution of theobromine from chocolate. *J Pediatr.* 1977;91:477

286. Wolff MS. Occupationally derived chemicals in breast milk. *Am J Ind Med.* 1983;4:259

287. Egan H, Goulding R, Roburn J, et al. Organo-chlorine pesticide residues in human fat human milk. *Br Med J.* 1965;2:66

288. Quinby GE, Armstrong JF, Durham WF. DDT in human milk. *Nature.* 1965;207:726

289. Bakken AF, Seip M. Insecticides in human breast milk. *Acta Paediatr Scand.* 1976;65:535

290. Adamovic VM, Sokic B, Smiljanski MJ. Some observations concerning the ratio of the intake of organochlorine insecticides through food and amounts excreted in the milk of breast-feeding mothers. *Bull Environ Contam Toxicol.* 1978;20:280

291. Savage EP, Keefe TJ, Tessari JD, et al. National study of chlorinated hydrocarbon insecticide residues in human milk, USA. *Am J Epidemiol.* 1981;113:413

292. Wilson DJ, Locker DJ, Ritzen CA, et al. DDT concentrations in human milk. *AJDC.* 1973;125:814

293. Bouwman H, Becker PJ, Cooppan RM, et al. Transfer of DDT used in malaria control to infants via breast milk. *Bull World Health Organ.* 1992;70:241–250

294. Emanuel B, Schoenfeld A. Favism in a nursing infant. *J Pediatr.* 1961;58:263

295. Simpson WJ, Tuba J. An investigation of fluoride concentration in the milk of nursing mothers. *J Oral Med.* 1968;23:104

296. Esala S, Vuori E, Helle A. Effect of maternal fluorine intake on breast milk fluorine content. *Br J Nutr.* 1982;48:201

297. Dreyfus-See G. Le passage dans le lait des aliments ou medicaments absorbes par denourrices. *Rev Med Interne.* 1934;51:198

298. Ando M, Hirano S, Itoh Y. Transfer of hexachlorobenzene from mother to newborn baby through placenta and milk. *Arch Toxicol.* 1985;56:195

299. West RW, Wilson DJ, Schaffner W. Hexachlorophene concentrations in human milk. *Bull Environ Contam Toxicol.* 1975;13:167

300. Rabinowitz M, Leviton A, Needelman H. Lead in milk and infant blood: a dose-response model. *Arch Environ Health.* 1985;40:283

301. Sternowsky JH, Wessolowski R. Lead and cadmium in breast milk. *Arch Toxicol.* 1985;57:41

302. Koos BJ, Longo LD. Mercury toxicity in the pregnant woman, fetus, and newborn infant: a review. *Am J Obstet Gynecol.* 1976;126:390

303. Amin-Zaki L, Elhassani S, Majeed MA, et al. Studies of infants postnatally exposed to methylmercury. *J Pediatr.* 1974;85:81

304. Pitkin RM, Bahns JA, Filer LA Jr, et al. Mercury in human maternal and cord blood, placenta, and milk. *Proc Soc Exp Biol Med.* 1976;151:565

305. Steginik LD, Filer LJ Jr, Baker GL. Monosodium glutamate: effect on plasma and breast milk amino acid levels in lactating women. *Proc Soc Exp Biol Med.* 1972;140:836

306. Miller RW. Pollutants in breast milk. *J Pediatr.* 1977;90:510

307. Rogan WJ, Bagniewska A, Damstra T. Pollutants in breast milk. *N Engl J Med.* 1980;302:1450

308. Wickizer TM, Brilliant LB, Copeland R, et al. Polychlorinated biphenyl contamination of nursing mothers in Michigan. *Am J Public Health.* 1981;71:132

309. Brilliant LB, Van Amburg G, Isbister J, et al. Breast milk monitoring to measure Michigan's contamination with polybrominated biphenyls. *Lancet.* 1978;2:643

310. Wickizer TM, Brilliant LB. Testing for polychlorinated biphenyls in human milk. *Pediatrics.* 1981;68:411–415

311. Bagnell PC, Ellenberg HA. Obstructive jaundice due to a chlorinated hydrocarbon in breast milk. *Can Med Assoc J.* 1977;117:1047

312. Higginbottom MC, Sweetman L, Nyhan WL. A syndrome of methylmalonic aciduria, homocystinuria, megaloblastic anemia neurologic abnormalities in a vitamin B_{12}-deficient breast-fed infant of a strict vegetarian. *N Engl J Med.* 1978;299:317

LLLI Editor's Note: The 1994 edition of the AAP's "Transfer of Drugs and Other Chemicals into Human Milk" raised some questions among physicians whose concerns were published in "Letters to the Editor," *Pediatrics* 1995;95(6):956-58. Suggestions were made to remove the following drugs from Table 6, "Maternal Medications Usually Compatible with Breastfeeding" and be placed as follows:

acebutolol and atenolol, table 1; clomipramine, table 4.

According to a printed response from Cheston Berlin Jr., MD, Chairperson, AAP Committee on Drugs, these changes may be reflected in future editions of AAP's list.

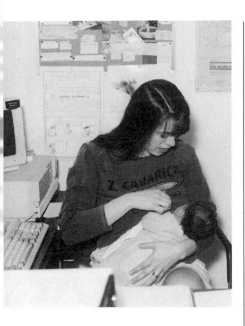

Supplement B

The Use of Breast Pumps and Other Products

ALTERNATIVE FEEDING METHODS
    Cup or Bowl Feeding
    Spoon Feeding
    Eyedropper or Feeding Syringe
    Nursing Supplementer

BREAST PUMPS
    Getting Started with a Breast Pump
    Basics of Successful Pumping
    What to Do If Pumping Hurts
    Features that Affect a Mother's Pump Choice
    Types of Breast Pumps
    A Comparison Chart of Double Pumps and Small Motorized
        Single Pumps

BREAST SHELLS

CREAMS AND OINTMENTS

MILK STORAGE BAGS

NIPPLE SHIELDS

NURSING PADS

NURSING PILLOWS

NURSING STOOLS

OTHER PRODUCTS
Electronic Scales
Hand-Expression Funnel
InstaHeat

ALTERNATIVE FEEDING METHODS

When the baby younger than four to six weeks old needs to be fed other than from the breast, an alternative feeding method may be preferable to bottles.

If the mother cannot feed her baby at the breast or if the baby needs a supplement in addition to breastfeeding, be sure the mother knows that there are a variety of feeding methods available. Bottles are the most common, but they have disadvantages, particularly for the baby younger than three to four weeks old. Because a baby does not have to open his mouth as wide when he takes a bottle and uses his mouth and tongue differently during bottle-feeding, bottles can cause nipple confusion in the very young baby and weaken the suck of a baby who is not sucking well.

The mother may not realize that there are alternatives to bottles, such as a cup, eyedropper, feeding syringe, spoon, bowl, or nursing supplementer (used at the breast or on a finger).

Explain all her options so the mother can pick the feeding method with which she is most comfortable.

Some women have strong feelings about one feeding method or another, so it is important to explain all the options. This allows the mother to choose the one with which she feels most comfortable.

After all the alternatives have been explained, some women will still prefer to use a bottle. If the mother is aware of all her options, this will be an informed choice. Although bottles can cause nipple confusion in a very young baby, the mother's feelings about feeding her baby are important, too, and nipple confusion can be overcome. (See "Nipple Confusion" under "Fussy at the Breast during the Early Weeks of Breastfeeding" in the chapter "Fussy at the Breast and Breast Refusal.")

It may take some practice at first to learn to feed the baby with another feeding method.

Although it takes some practice to use a cup, bowl, spoon, eyedropper, feeding syringe, or nursing supplementer to feed a newborn, it also takes some practice to learn how to bottle-feed a baby. Tell the mother to expect that it will get easier over time and that within a few days she and her baby will have mastered it.

Cup or Bowl Feeding

A newborn—even a premature baby—can be fed by cup or bowl.

Cup feeding is used routinely instead of bottles in Kenya and Tanzania when a baby is born prematurely and is not yet ready for breastfeeding or if the mother and baby are separated. Nipple confusion appears to be a rare problem in most East African hospitals because bottles are never used (Newman 1990).

A study of 85 premature babies in Exeter, England, found that babies could successfully feed by cup as young as 30 weeks gestation, earlier than they could either breastfeed or bottle-feed. This study also found that more of the babies who received supplements by cup were fully breastfeeding at hospital discharge than those who received supplements by bottle (81% as compared with 63%). The researchers noted that cup feeding requires little energy, gives the baby more control over milk intake than bottle-feeding, and involves tongue movements that are also important for successful breastfeeding. During cup feedings, the premies were found to maintain satisfactory heart rate, breathing, and oxygen levels (Lang 1994).

Any type of straight-edged or flexible cup or bowl may be used. The baby should be held upright and small amounts of milk given slowly.

A small cup or glass—like a shot glass—or a flexible bowl may be a little easier to maneuver than an adult-sized cup, drinking glass, or bowl, but any clean cup, glass, or bowl can be used. By feeding slowly and using the following suggestions, the baby should be able to drink the milk.

- Be sure the baby is awake and alert.
- Swaddle the baby to keep his hands from bumping the cup.
- Protect baby's and mother's clothing from spills with a cloth.
- Hold the baby in an upright sitting position.
- Fill the cup at least half full with the supplement.
- Bring the container to the baby's lips, gently tilting it so that when he opens his mouth the cup rests lightly on his lower lip and the milk just touches his lips.
- Tip the cup slightly so that a few drops of milk flow onto the baby's lips.
- Leave the cup in this position and let the baby set his own sipping rhythm, pause when needed, and end the feeding when ready.

Some babies feed continuously; some prefer to have the cup tilted back between swallows. Some babies extend their tongue as they cup feed; others do not. Suggest the mother note and respect her own baby's cup-feeding style.

Although any ordinary cup or bowl can be used, special baby feeding cups are also available.

Baby feeding cups are available from both Ameda/Egnell and Medela (see "Product Information" at the end of this chapter). The Ameda Baby Cup is a straight-sided, two-ounce cup calibrated in ounces and milliliters that includes a snap-on cap. Because it can be sealed, the Ameda Baby Cup can be used as both a milk-storage cup and a feeding cup, which cuts down on the risk of contamination.

Medela's SoftCup is designed to feed but not to store milk. The SoftCup consists of several parts: an 80 ml container, a flow regulator, and a soft silicone spout with a built-in fluid reservoir. To deliver the milk to the spout, the person feeding the baby squeezes the milk reservoir at the base of the spout, which sends a mouthful of milk from the container to the spout. Rhythmically squeezing the reservoir sends the milk mouthful by mouthful to the feeding spout. The flexible spout can also be narrowed by the feeder's fingers for easier feeding.

La Leche League International sells a feeding cup with a cut-out portion to help mother see the liquid as she feeds. Also, some use small 3-ounce (90 ml) plastic disposable cups ("Dixie" cups).

In areas where hygiene is an issue, such as in some developing countries, a simpler baby cup would be a better choice, because it would be easier to keep clean.

Spoon Feeding

A baby can be fed by spoon by tilting the spoon to his mouth so that the liquid goes in, giving him time to swallow before offering more.

Any type of clean spoon can be used. By feeding slowly, using the following suggestions, the baby should be able to take the milk.

- Be sure the baby is awake and alert.
- Swaddle the baby to keep his hands from bumping the spoon.
- Protect baby's and mother's clothing from spills with a cloth.
- Hold the baby in an upright sitting position.
- Fill the spoon with a mouthful of the supplement.
- Bring the spoon to the baby's lips, gently tilting it so that when he opens his mouth it rests lightly on his lower lip and the milk just touches his lips.
- Tip the spoon slightly so that the milk flows into the baby's mouth.
- Give the baby time to swallow, refill the spoon, and repeat as needed.

Eyedropper or Feeding Syringe

An eyedropper and feeding syringe are used in the same way, although a feeding syringe holds more fluid. To avoid choking, make sure the baby is upright and give small amounts at a time.

Both eyedroppers and feeding syringes are available at most drug or discount stores.

When choosing an eyedropper, a soft plastic one is preferred, because it is unbreakable. A feeding syringe (also known as a peridontal or orthodontic syringe) is used the same way but holds more fluid. By feeding slowly and using the following suggestions, the baby should be able to drink the milk.

- Be sure the baby is awake and alert.
- Swaddle the baby to keep his hands from bumping the syringe.
- Protect baby's and mother's clothing from spills with a cloth.
- Hold the baby in an upright sitting position.
- Fill the syringe with the supplement.
- Bring the syringe to the baby's mouth, gently dripping in the milk slowly enough so that he has a chance to swallow it before more is given.

The feeding syringe can also be used to finger feed the baby. To do so, the feeder should first wash his or her hands, then gently introduce the index finger pad side up into the baby's mouth until the baby sucks it back to a comfortable spot. The filled feeding syringe can then be inserted just inside the corner of the baby's mouth. (The syringe should not be extended along the length of the finger.) When the baby sucks the finger, the plunger should be slowly depressed. When the baby pauses, the feeder should also pause, depressing the plunger again when the baby starts to suck.

Nursing Supplementer

The nursing supplementer provides a supplement to the baby along with whatever milk his mother is producing while he nurses at the breast.

The nursing supplementer can be used for finger-feeding, which also promotes proper sucking.

The nursing supplementer should not be recommended casually for short-term use. First, basic breastfeeding management should be discussed and other alternatives considered.

The nursing supplementer encourages proper sucking at the breast and stimulates milk production while avoiding the use of bottles.

The nursing supplementer consists of a container for the supplement (either a plastic bag or bottle), which hangs on a cord around the mother's neck and rests between her breasts. Thin tubing, leading from the container, is taped to the mother's breast, extending about a quarter-inch (6 mm) past the mother's nipple. Some models feature a tie-off in the cap that prevents the milk from flowing until the baby sucks. Some models include two tubes which can be taped to both breasts at once to make it easier to switch sides while breastfeeding. Some models also come with different sizes of tubing—the larger the tubing, the faster the milk flow. The choice of tubing will depend upon the effectiveness of the baby's suck and his need for supplements. (See the last point in this section for a comparison of different brands of nursing supplementers and where they can be ordered.)

When used at the breast, the nursing supplementer allows the baby to stimulate milk production while he receives the supplement. But if the baby will not or cannot take the breast—for example, if the baby refuses the breast or the mother is not available—it can be used to feed the baby by taping the tubing to the pad of the index finger and introducing it gently, pad side up, into the baby's mouth. When finger-feeding, the baby uses his mouth and tongue properly, so it will not confuse his suck the way a bottle can.

In general, other alternative feeding methods are preferable to the nursing supplementer when the baby needs supplements for only a short time. Other methods are less expensive and involve less paraphernalia.

Also, some mothers and babies become "hooked" on the nursing supplementer. The baby may become accustomed to the steady, even flow of milk and refuse to breastfeed without the tube present. The mother may be so reassured by watching the milk flowing into her baby's mouth that she hesitates to stop using the supplementer, even after the need has passed.

Before suggesting the nursing supplementer, discuss basic breastfeeding management (refer to "Slow Weight Gain" in the "Weight Gain" chapter, beginning with "Asking Questions and Gathering Information" and proceeding through the other sections). Improved breastfeeding management will solve most breastfeeding problems.

The nursing supplementer makes breastfeeding seem unnatural to some mothers.

It is important that the nursing supplementer be mentioned as only one of several options. Some mothers react favorably to the idea of using the nursing supplementer, but some mothers are uncomfortable with it and will choose not to continue breastfeeding if it is the only option offered.

Possible situations for using the nursing supplementer.

Possible uses of the nursing supplementer include:

- an adopted baby;
- a baby with a special physical need who requires extra supplements, such as some neurologically impaired babies, some babies with cardiac problems, some babies with Down Syndrome, some premature babies, and some babies with a cleft palate (if maintaining suction is a problem, the nursing supplementer may not work well at the breast);
- a baby who needs an immediate supplement because his mother's milk supply is low (such as a baby who is failure-to-thrive and/or a baby whose mother is relactating) or because he is unable to suck effectively at the breast (such as a baby who is refusing the breast or a baby with a weak suck that has not improved after trying other suggestions).

The length of time the nursing supplementer is used varies from a few days or weeks to several months, depending on the baby and the circumstances. Discuss realistic expectations with the mother.

The mother of an adopted baby may need to use the nursing supplementer until her baby starts solids and is drinking well from a cup.

But under the following circumstances the length of use will vary, depending on the development of the baby's suck and his physical condition:

- a premature baby,
- a baby with Down Syndrome,
- a baby with cardiac problems,
- a baby with a cleft palate,
- a baby with failure-to-thrive,
- a baby who is neurologically impaired,
- a baby whose mother is relactating,
- a baby with a weak suck.

It may not be possible to tell the mother when she begins using the nursing supplementer exactly how long her baby will need to use it. Short-term use (less than three to four days) can usually be assumed when the baby refuses to nurse due to nipple confusion or other reasons.

Talk with the mother about what she can reasonably expect.

Although feeding and clean-up take longer with a nursing supplementer, its use avoids nipple confusion and stimulates the mother's milk supply while the baby nurses.

The nursing supplementer is an excellent alternative to bottles when supplements must be given for weeks or months, because it keeps the baby at the breast, stimulating the mother's milk supply and decreasing the likelihood that the baby will grow to prefer the bottle.

Human milk is the best supplement, followed by formula. Some types of formula may clog the supplementer tubing.

In most cases, the best supplement for the baby is the mother's own milk. See the chapter "Expression and Storage of Human Milk" for information on choosing a method of expression. Many mothers find a full-size automatic electric piston pump easiest to use. Many models feature attachments that allow the mother to simultaneously express both breasts at once, cutting pumping time in half. Double-pumping also most effectively stimulates the breasts to produce more milk. The mother may want to discuss how expressing can be worked into her daily routine.

Some mothers will choose to supplement with formula. If this is the mother's choice, suggest she ask her baby's doctor for a recommendation and be sure she knows that she should prepare it according to the instructions—diluting it would deprive the baby of the calories he needs and making it too strong could be harmful. Some formulas do not flow through the tubing easily because they are so thick. If the mother uses powdered formula, suggest she shake it well to avoid clogging the tubing.

The tubing size and the placement of the supplement container in relation to the baby's mouth will determine how quickly the supplement flows to the baby.

Each brand of nursing supplementer is slightly different. Becoming familiar with the available models will make it easier to help mothers learn to use them.

Certain basic principles may be helpful for the mother to understand. For example, the tubing size and the placement of the supplement container will determine how quickly the supplement flows to the baby. The larger the tubing, the faster the flow. If the mother has a choice of tubing size, encourage her to start with the medium-size tubing and experiment to see which size works best for her baby. The higher the supplement container is placed on the mother's body, the faster the flow. When the bottom of the supplement container is above the level of the mother's nipple, the supplement will flow non-stop, which may cause the baby to gulp or choke. The lower the container is placed, the harder it will be for the baby to extract the supplement.

Good positioning and latch-on will help encourage stimulation of the breast and discourage the baby's dependence on the supplementer tube.

Be sure the mother is aware of the importance of good positioning and latch-on, as well as the proper positioning of the tubing. If the baby opens his mouth wide when going onto the breast and takes the breast far back into his mouth, he will learn to breastfeed correctly, getting the maximum amount of milk directly from the breast and better stimulating his mother's milk supply. On the other hand, if he tries to nurse at the tip of the nipple—where the tubing ends—he may learn to suck from the tube instead of breastfeeding properly, which means he will not receive much milk directly from the breast and he may also give his mother sore nipples.

When the mother tapes the tubing to her breast, the tape should be near the outer edge of her areola—not too near the nipple—or it may interfere with good latch-on. Also, the skin on the areola is very sensitive, and applying and removing tape may be irritating.

Encourage the mother to consult with her baby's doctor, and if the baby's suck doesn't seem to be improving, to seek a referral for further evaluation.

Suggest the mother inform her baby's doctor that she is using a nursing supplementer. The doctor should be consulted to evaluate the baby's health when she begins using the supplementer and as her baby takes less supplement.

If the baby's suck does not improve after he has been using the nursing supplementer for several weeks, ask the mother if she would like a referral to an occupational therapist or physical therapist with neurodevelopmental training or other accredited health-care provider for a professional evaluation of the baby's suck and general development. This person should be experienced in working with breastfed babies. Neurodevelopmental therapists, just like doctors, have varying amounts of knowledge about breastfeeding. Encourage the mother to ask her local breastfeeding support people for recommendations. (To find a local neurodevelopmental specialist, contact the Neurodevelopmental Treatment Association, 401 N. Michigan, Chicago IL 60611-4267 USA. Telephone 312-321-5151.)

Some babies wean from the nursing supplementer spontaneously, others need more active encouragement, and some few continue to need the supplementer until they can drink from a cup.

The nursing supplementer is designed so that when the baby begins sucking more effectively, he will take less supplement. Some babies simply take less and less supplement as their sucking becomes more effective and their mother's milk supply increases. Weaning from the supplementer in this way is automatic.

Some babies need more help in weaning from the nursing supplementer. The mother can encourage this process in two ways: by switching to a smaller size tubing (if this is an option with her model of supplementer) and by lowering the container of fluid. These will encourage a stronger suck for less reward. Suggest the mother listen for her baby's swallowing (he should be swallowing at least after every second or third suck during the first five minutes of nursing) and keep track of how many wet diapers and bowel movements he has a day to be sure he is getting enough. (The baby should have six to eight wet cloth diapers a day— five to six disposables—and, if he is younger than six weeks old, two to five bowel movements a day. Fewer bowel movements are considered normal in the older baby.) As the mother weans her baby from the nursing supplementer, suggest she have her baby's doctor carefully monitor his progress.

Some few babies will not be able to wean from the supplementer until they are able to take their supplementation by cup.

Different brands of nursing supplementers have different features.

Axicare Nursing Aid. Available in the United Kingdom from Colgate Medical, Ltd., Fairacres Estate, Edworth Road, Windsor, Berks SL4LE. Telephone: Windsor 60378.
Type of container and size—4-ounce (120 ml) plastic bottle.
Easy to assemble?—Yes.
Obvious under clothing?—Yes, bulky and visible.
Tubing—Two tubing sizes, but only one fits on the unit at a time.
Also includes—Cleaning syringe.
Other considerations—Features a stop-cock device in the tube to regulate the milk flow.

Lact-Aid®. Available from Lact-Aid® International, P.O. Box 1066, Athens, Tennessee 37303 USA. Telephone: 615-744-9090.
Type of container and size—4.5-ounce (135 ml) disposable plastic bag.
Easy to assemble?—No, the mother may need help at first.
Obvious under clothing?—No, lies flat and hides under clothing.
Tubing—One tubing size. Only one tube fits on the unit at a time.
Also includes—Cleaning syringe; instructions for adjusting rate of flow.
Cost—Approximately $38 US (1996 price).
Other considerations—Basic kit includes 2 complete units; additional bags may be ordered separately.

Medela Supplemental Nursing System (SNS). Available from Medela, P.O. Box 660, McHenry, Illinois 60051-0660 USA. Telephone: 1-800-835-5968. (From Alaska, or Hawaii, call collect 815-363-1166.) Also available from La Leche League International's Catalogue and many local La Leche League Leaders. For information, call 1-800-LA LECHE, 847-519-9585, or write to: LLLI, P.O. Box 4079, Schaumburg IL 60168-4079 USA.
Type of container and size—5-ounce (150 ml) rectangular bottle.
Easy to assemble?—Yes.
Obvious under clothing?—Yes, bulky and visible.
Tubing—Three tubing sizes for variety of flow regulation. Two tubes fit on the unit at once, so the mother can switch the baby to the other breast without moving the tubing.
Cost—Approximately $40 US (1996 prices).
Other considerations—No cleaning syringe necessary, as the unit is cleaned by squeezing the bottle. Extra components can be ordered separately. Packaged sterile and assembled.

Medela Starter SNS. Also available from Medela (see previous product for order information).
Type of container and size—80 ml (2.6 ounce) round bottle
Easy to assemble?—Yes
Obvious under clothing?—Yes, bulky and visible.

Pumps/Products

Tubing—One tubing size. Only one tube extends from the unit.

Cost—approximately $12.50 US (1996 price).

Other considerations—Recommended for 24 hours of total use. Bottle clips to clothing rather than hanging around neck.

Supply Line Mark II. Available from the Nursing Mothers' Association of Australia, P.O. Box 231, Nunawading 3131, Victoria, Australia. Telephone: 61-3877-5011 FAX: 61-3894-3270

Type of container and size—Thin 4-ounce (120 ml) bottle with pouch.

Easy to assemble?—Yes.

Obvious under clothing?—Yes, bulky and visible.

Tubing—One tubing size. Only one tube fits on the unit at a time.

Also includes—Cleaning syringe.

BREAST PUMPS

Getting Started with a Breast Pump

If the pumped milk will be given to the baby, the mother needs to begin by washing her hands and making sure the pump and storage container are clean.

Good hygiene is important when the expressed milk will be given to the baby. Before the mother begins pumping, she will need to wash her hands and follow the pump manufacturer's directions for cleaning the pump or the pump collection kit (the bottles and tubing that connect to the pump). Bacteria can accumulate if dried particles of milk are left in the breast shield, pump parts, or collection bottle.

When expressing milk for a healthy baby, it is necessary to sterilize the pump or pump collection kit only once—before its first use. If the pump is sterile when the mother receives it, she need not sterilize it. Once sterile, after each pumping session the mother should wash the parts that touch the milk in the dishwasher or with hot, soapy water and rinse well (The Human Milk Banking Association of North America 1993). If the mother is pumping for a hospitalized baby, there may be other guidelines she needs to follow. Suggest the mother ask the hospital nurses who care for her baby.

The mother will get the best results if she follows the pump directions, centers her nipple in the proper size nipple adapter, moistens her breast, and begins at the lowest pressure setting.

To get the best results with her pump, the mother needs to stimulate her milk let-down (see next section). Suggest she follow these steps:

- Follow the manufacturer's directions for the pump.
- To improve suction, suggest the mother moisten her breast with water to create a "seal" before applying the pump shield or flange.
- The mother should be sure that her nipple is centered in the breast flange, with the flange closely surrounding the nipple but not rubbing against the sides.
- Encourage the mother to go easy at first by using the lowest pressure setting, or the least amount of suction, to get started, and then increase it to the highest comfortable level. If suction is increased past the point of comfort, a mother's let-down reflex may be inhibited. Some mothers get better results by varying the pressure setting of the pump while they are expressing.

Motor-operated pumps use a "regular-suction-and-release" method of pumping; with some hand pumps the mother also can use a "draw-and-hold" method.

Automatic pumps, semi-automatic pumps, and small motorized single pumps use a "regular-suction-and-release" method of pumping. The automatic pumps use a regular rhythm of suction and release to closely mimic the rhythm of the baby's suck, while the other motorized pumps generate fewer suction and release cycles per minute.

Cylinder-type and squeeze pumps can be used to manually generate regular suction and release or the mother can use a "draw-and-hold" method, in which she uses a rhythmic motion to stimulate her let-down reflex and then—after the let-down occurs—gently pulls the cylinder to draw out the milk until the milk flow slows down. She then repeats this process on the other breast, going back and forth from breast to breast until she is finished. Some mothers find that this switching seems to stimulate the let-down reflex more effectively than pumping each breast continuously for 10 to 15 minutes. Encourage the mother to experiment to see what works best for her.

Basics of Successful Pumping

Stimulating a milk let-down is crucial to successful milk expression.

Whatever method of expression a mother uses, stimulating a milk let-down is crucial. When a mother nurses her baby at the breast, her baby's sucking naturally stimulates the release of the hormone oxytocin, which causes the muscles around the milk-producing glands to squeeze, forcing the milk from all parts of the breast toward the nipple. This is the milk let-down or milk-ejection reflex.

When a mother puts a pump to her breast, many of the physical cues that trigger her milk let-down are missing. Unlike a baby at the breast, who is soft, warm, smells good, and stimulates loving feelings in the mother, a pump is cold and inanimate and may initially feel foreign to the mother.

Without a milk let-down, the mother may be unable to express more than the small fraction of her milk that is in the milk reservoirs near the nipple. Most of her milk will be left in the breast. To make up for the lack of her baby's physical cues while expressing, the mother may need to create other cues to signal her body to let down her milk (see next point).

Breast pumps that automatically regulate suction and release tend to be more effective at stimulating a milk let-down than pumps that require the mother to regulate the suction and release. However, even with these more effective pumps, the mother's let-down may be affected if she is tense or upset.

Suggest the mother think of her first few pumpings as practice sessions, particularly if she chooses a pump that requires her to regulate the suction and release.

Encourage the mother to think of the first few pumpings as practice sessions. This will help her be more relaxed and not as focused on the amount of milk she gets at first, which will enhance her pumping success. A pump that automatically regulates suction and release will take much less practice than a pump that requires the mother to regulate suction and release.

Setting up a milk-expression routine and finding a comfortable, relaxed time and place to express can help stimulate a good milk flow.

Successful milk expression is as much psychological as it is physical. Even when using a breast pump that automatically regulates suction and release, if a mother is tense, upset, or uncomfortable, these feelings may delay or inhibit her milk flow. Many mothers have used the following suggestions to maximize their milk expression:

- Allow enough time so as not to feel rushed.
- Express milk in a familiar and comfortable setting. Privacy and comfortable seating promote relaxation, which enhances milk let-down.
- Minimize distractions. Take the phone off the hook and lock the door, if possible.
- Follow a pre-expression routine. Use warmth to relax and stimulate milk flow by applying heat to the breasts or putting a warm wrap around the shoulders. Stimulate the breast and/or nipples through massage. Relax with childbirth breathing or mental imagery, such as envisioning oneself on a warm beach.
- Think about the baby. Make a phone call to check on the baby before expressing. Imagine the baby at the breast while pumping. If the baby is with the mother, suggest she look at or touch the baby. If the baby is not there, suggest she look at a picture of the baby, listen to a tape recording of the baby's cry, or touch and smell a piece of clothing.

The amount of milk a mother gets at a pumping will vary, depending on a number of factors.

The amount of milk a mother is able to pump at a session depends upon many variables:

- how long it has been since she nursed or pumped,
- whether she has missed a nursing or is pumping between regular nursings,

- her milk supply (is she exclusively breastfeeding or is her baby taking other foods?),
- whether she is tense or relaxed, comfortable or uncomfortable,
- the time of day (some women find they get more milk early rather than later in the day),
- the effectiveness of her pump.

Any of these variables can have a major effect on the amount of milk a mother gets at a pumping session.

If the mother is pumping between regular nursings rather than missing feedings, under ideal conditions (the mother is using an effective breast pump early in the day, is exclusively breastfeeding, and is comfortable in her pumping setting) an average amount of milk to expect is about half as much milk as she would get if she were pumping for a missed feeding at a regular feeding time, or about half a feeding.

Suggest the mother who is not missing feedings try pumping about an hour after the first morning nursing. Mothers tend to get more milk at that time of day. Waiting for an hour after a nursing is usually long enough to allow her to get some milk without affecting her baby's next feeding.

If after reading the instructions and practicing with the pump, the mother continues to be unable to get much milk, talk with her about realistic expectations and, if necessary, suggest she try a different type of pump.

Mothers respond differently to different types of pumps, and a pump that works wonderfully well for one mother may be ineffective for another. If the mother has followed the manufacturer's instructions, has given herself several relaxed practice sessions, and tried without success all the suggestions in the previous points, talk to her about her expectations. Make sure that she isn't trying to pump right after a feeding, late in the day, or while feeling tense. Try to discuss all possible factors that might be affecting her ability to pump milk.

If all the other variables have been ruled out as the cause, suggest to the mother that she try a different pump. Many mothers who are unsuccessful with one pump, erroneously conclude that it is somehow their fault, that they don't have enough milk (even when they have a thriving baby), or that they are using the pump incorrectly. Some mothers in this situation even give up on breastfeeding.

Due to individual differences, occasionally a mother will get very little milk with an electric piston pump, which tends to be the most effective type. If this happens, suggest she try another model or another brand. For example, some mothers find that the speed control feature on some mid-size electric piston pumps helps stimulate their milk let-down more effectively than the full-size pumps (which are set at one standard speed), whereas other women find that they get better pumping results with the smoother cycling of a full-size pump (see the next section). If a mother is using a type of pump that requires her to regulate suction and release, suggest she try an automatic double pump, which tends to be more effective. Don't assume that just because a particular pump worked well for one mother that it will work well for all.

What to Do If Pumping Hurts

Milk expression should never be painful. If it is, the mother should stop and make changes.

It is possible to damage sensitive breast tissue, so if the breast pump is hurting the mother tell her to stop what she is doing. Discomfort or pain will also inhibit her milk let-down.

First read the instructions, then decrease suction.

Suggest the mother first read the pump instructions to be sure she is using the pump according to the manufacturer's instructions. If she is, suggest she decrease the amount of suction. Some sensitive mothers feel discomfort even at the lowest setting of some electric piston pumps, which tend to be the gentlest breast pumps. In this category of pumps, the Ameda/Egnell Elite is the only pump to start at zero pressure and increase from there. All the others start at 75-100 mmHg as their lowest setting. If the mother is using another automatic electric piston pump and she has eliminated all the other possibilities in this point, suggest she switch to the Elite.

Have the mother make sure her nipple is centered in the breast flange and that her nipple is not too large for the nipple tunnel.

Suggest she check to make sure that her nipple is centered in the breast flange and not rubbing against the sides of the nipple tunnel. If her nipple is too large for the nipple tunnel, she may be more comfortable with a collection kit with a larger nipple tunnel. (The nipple tunnel of the Ameda/Egnell Hygienikits is slightly larger than the nipple tunnel of the Medela kits). Women with very large nipples may need to use a special breast flange such as the Medela Extra Large Glass Breastshield Kit.

Other changes may make pumping more comfortable.

If soreness persists, suggest the mother try the following:

- Apply Lansinoh for Breastfeeding Mothers®; other creams or ointments should be avoided, as they would need to be removed before pumping, which could further irritate the nipple. (See later section "Creams and Ointments.")
- Use breast massage to get the let-down, or milk-ejection, reflex started before pumping, as the soreness usually lessens as the milk starts to flow.
- Moisten the breast before beginning.
- Start pumping on the least sore side first and pump for less time on the sore breast.
- Try pumping more frequently but for shorter periods of time.

Soreness can sometimes be caused by the slow cycling time of most small motorized single pumps. Using another type of pump may eliminate the discomfort.

If the mother is using a small motorized single pump, her soreness may be due to the longer cycling time of these pumps. Even under ideal circumstances, most small motorized single pumps can only generate between 4 and 7 suction and releases, or "cycles," per minute, as compared with the 30 to 60 cycles of the automatic electric pumps (Frantz, p. 89). Fewer cycles per minute mean the breast is drawn into the nipple tunnel of the pump flange for a longer time before it is released, which causes nipple pain in some women. Fewer cycles per minute also mean less breast stimulation, which may result in less milk expressed over the long term and a lower milk supply. If longer cycling time is the reason for the mother's soreness, using a pump with more cycles per minute should make pumping more comfortable.

If the mother is using an automatic double pump at the lowest setting and pumping is still uncomfortable, thrush should be ruled out as a contributing factor.

Nipple pain when using an automatic electric breast pump correctly is one of the symptoms associated with thrush, also known as *Candida albicans*, a fungal infection of the breast and nipple (Amir 1995). If the mother is unable to make pumping more comfortable in spite of trying all the above suggestions, see the section "Thrush" in the chapter "Nipple Problems" to rule out thrush as a contributing factor.

Features that Affect a Mother's Pump Choice

Effectiveness

More suction and releases, or "cycles," per minute are associated with greater effectiveness, fewer cycles per minute with less effectiveness.

A pump's effectiveness can be judged in part by how closely the number of suction and releases per minute, or "cycles," approximates a baby at the breast. A baby actively nursing generates an average of 1.28 sucks per second (Ramsey and Gisel 1996). The full-size automatic electric piston pumps use the preset motion of a metal balancing weight to automatically generate between 48 and 60 cycles per minute. The lighter mid-size automatic piston pumps use a plastic piston moving back and forth horizontally to automatically generate suction and release, with the models featuring speed control allowing the mother to speed up or slow down the pump's cycling (within a range of 30-60 cycles per minute) to more closely mimic her own baby's suck. The automatic diaphragm pumps use a diaphragm moving in and out to produce 30-48 cycles per minute, with the number of cycles varying with the make and model of pump.

Other types of pumps tend to be less effective because they cannot generate as many cycles per minute. The semi-automatic diaphragm pump produces at most about 25 cycles per minute, which is regulated when the mother covers and uncovers a vent with her finger. Some mothers who work part- or full-time find this pump effective in maintaining their milk supply; other mothers do not.

Even when a mother is practiced at their use, most small motorized single pumps are capable of generating only 4 to 7 cycles per minute, as compared with the 30 to 60 cycles of the automatic electric piston pumps (Frantz, p. 89). Medela's Mini Electric Breast Pump is the exception, a small motorized single pump that automatically generates between 30-38 cycles per minute.

Fewer cycles per minute mean the breast is drawn into the nipple tunnel of the pump for a longer time before it is released, which has been associated with nipple pain. Fewer cycles per minute also mean less breast stimulation, which may result in less milk expressed and over the long term a lower milk supply. This is one reason full-size electric piston pumps tend to be more effective than the smaller pumps at establishing and maintaining a mother's milk supply (Lang 1994; Green 1982). In addition, more cycles per minute may be the reason that milk expressed with a full-size electric piston pump has been found to be higher in fat content than milk expressed with other types of pumps or via hand-expression (Garza 1982).

The way a pump cycles can also influence its effectiveness.

Number of suction and releases per minute, or "cycles," is one gauge of a pump's effectiveness, but the way a pump cycles may also influence its effectiveness. Each cycle includes three phases which are known collectively as its suction curve: a steady building of suction, a brief holding of suction at the peak, and a steady decline of suction before the process begins again. In her *Breastfeeding Product Guide* 1994, Kittie Frantz notes that some mid-sized pumps have a hesitation in their suction curves due to the action of their pistons. She suggests that this hesitation may make these pumps less effective over the long term in maintaining some mothers' milk supply than the full-size pumps, which cycle more smoothly. According to Frantz, some mothers note an increase in their milk supply when they switch from the mid-size to the full-size pump, which she attributes to these suction-curve differences (Frantz, p. 109). No research is available on the differences in effectiveness of different types and brands of automatic electric double pumps.

Although small motorized single pumps and hand pumps work well for some women, many women who substitute pumping for nursing two or three times a day or more find it difficult to maintain a full milk supply with their use.

Because the small motorized single pumps and hand pumps do not allow the mother to generate the same number of cycles per minute as the automatic double pumps, many women who substitute pumping for nursing two or three times per day or more (such as the mother who is working full-time or whose baby is not breastfeeding) find it difficult to maintain a full milk supply with their regular use.

However, there are always exceptions. A woman whose milk supply is larger than average and whose milk lets down easily may find almost any method of expression effective in expressing milk and maintaining her supply.

Double-pumping is not only faster, it also stimulates slightly more milk production than single-pumping.

Double-pumping (pumping both breasts simultaneously) cuts pumping time in half (as little as 10 minutes as compared with 20 to 30 minutes for single-pumping) and avoids milk loss from leakage, which can occur when only one breast is being pumped. In addition, double-pumping has also been found to stimulate milk production slightly more than single-pumping (Auerbach 1990).

A pump that quickly and easily stimulates a mother's milk let-down will be more effective than a pump that takes longer to stimulate milk flow.

Breast pumps that automatically regulate suction and release tend to be considerably more effective at stimulating a milk let-down, because their suction and release is more similar to a baby breastfeeding than pumps that require the mother to regulate the suction and release.

Comfort

Automatic pumps tend to be more comfortable than pumps that require the mother to regulate suction and release.

Automatic pumps are specially designed to limit suction to safe levels and to automatically release the suction at regular intervals. This differs significantly from the small motorized single pumps, most of which apply continuous suction until the mother releases the suction by pressing a button or bar. If the mother does not release the suction quickly enough, it is possible for suction to exceed safe levels and cause breast tissue damage (Frantz 1993). Some mothers have erroneously left the suction on without interruption throughout a pumping because they did not read the instructions and wrongly assumed that "electric" or "battery-operated" meant that the pump worked automatically.

Even when the mother releases the suction at regular intervals, however, the small motorized single pumps tend to cause more nipple soreness, because with fewer cycles per minute the nipple spends more time drawn into the nipple tunnel.

Milk expression should never be painful. If it is, the mother should stop and make changes.

It is possible to damage sensitive breast tissue, so if the breast pump is hurting the mother suggest that she stop what she is doing. Discomfort or pain will also inhibit her milk let-down. See the previous section, "What to Do If Pumping Hurts."

Ease of Use

Automatic double pumps are the easiest pumps to use.

With automatic double pumps, the mother need only adjust the suction (and on some pumps, the speed), sit back, and relax. Because the pump works automatically, the mother simply puts the pump flanges to her breasts and the pump does the rest.

All pumps other than the double automatics require the mother to regulate the suction and release, and some of these pumps require more effort than others. For example, many of the cylinder pumps require repeated arm movements that make them tiring to use. The squeeze pumps vary in the amount of effort required. Medela's PedalPump requires that the mother rhythmically press and release a foot pedal to power its double-pumping kit. The semi-automatic double pump and the small motorized single pumps involve less effort; the mother presses a button or plugs a hole to generate or release the suction, which involves less physical effort, but still requires attention to the process.

Most mothers can operate most automatic electric double pumps with one hand (or no hands) and do other things while they pump.

When using most double-pumping kits, many women find that with practice they can use one hand and the same-side forearm to position and hold the breast flanges to their breasts, leaving one hand free. Once the breast flanges are in position and the pump is turned on and properly adjusted, they can do other things while the pump works automatically. It is also possible to hold both breast flanges to the breasts with one hand, giving the mother a hand free to do other things while she pumps. The exception to this is the White River Pump collection kit, which features flexible silicone breast flanges that require two hands to hold in place.

Medela's Pumping Free attachment kit allows a mother to attach a Medela collection kit to a specially designed Medela bra so that the mother can pump with both hands free.

Variations in the collection kits used with the electric piston pumps can affect a pump's ease of use.

Most of the electric piston pumps available for rent are similar in operation. The most noticeable differences are in the collection kits: the bottles and tubing that attach to the pump. Whenever a mother rents a pump, she must have her own collection kit, which she keeps after the rental is over, so there is no mixing of milk from one pump user to the next. Some women are given these kits at the hospital, others purchase them where they rent the pump.

In 1996 Medela introduced its advanced collection kit, which allows a mother to switch from single- to double-pumping or vice versa by moving a dial.

Also, the tubing that attaches the collection bottles to the pump was made thinner and easier to work with than the tubing on the previously available standard kits.

The tubing with Ameda/Egnell's HygieniKits is even lighter and more flexible, and the collection units of the double kits operate independently of each other, so the mother can switch from double- to single-pumping or vice versa without changing anything. The Ameda/Egnell Hygienikits feature a diaphragm under the cap that prevents the milk from touching the cap or the tubing, even if it is turned upside down. The cap snaps on, so the tubing does not pull loose during pumping.

Collection kits for both Medela and Ameda/Egnell pumps can be purchased with parts that convert them to hand pumps, and features of the hand pump may influence a mother's choice. Medela's Manualectric Breast Pump requires two hands to operate and may be tiring to use. Ameda/Egnell's One-Hand Breast Pump is a squeeze pump that can be operated with one hand and requires less effort.

Pumping Time

If pumping time is a concern, ask the mother how much time she has for pumping.

Double-pumping may take as little as 10 minutes; single pumping usually takes 20-30 minutes.

The amount of time the mother has for pumping will influence her choice of pump. If the mother is limited to less than 30 minutes per pumping, suggest she choose a pump that allows her to double-pump (pump both breasts at the same time).

Pumps that allow the mother to either double-pump (both breasts simultaneously) or single pump (one breast at a time) give the mother the opportunity to cut her pumping time substantially, as little as 10 minutes as compared with 20 to 30 minutes for single-pumping.

A pump that most easily stimulates a mother's milk let-down will work faster than a pump that takes longer to stimulate milk flow.

Breast pumps that automatically regulate suction and release tend to stimulate a mother's milk let-down more quickly than pumps that require the mother to regulate the suction and release. If pumping time is an issue for the mother, an automatic double pump is usually fastest.

Portability

If a mother plans to take the pump with her when she goes out, portability may be a major consideration in her choice of a pump.

Both the mid-size electric piston pumps and the automatic electric diaphragm pumps are lightweight enough to carry easily.

Some women pump in the same place each time. In this case, the size and weight of the pump may not be important. But if the mother plans to carry her pump with her when she goes out, its portability will be important, and she has many options.

If the mother prefers the features of an automatic double pump, the mid-size electric piston pump is light enough to carry easily, weighing 5 to 6 1/2 pounds (2268 to 2949 grams). Examples include the Ameda/Egnell Elite and the Medela Lactina. If no electrical outlet is available, the Ameda/Egnell Elite features a model with a built-in rechargeable battery and the Medela Lactina can be powered with a separate rechargeable battery pack.

Carrying cases are available through many rental stations that are designed to hold everything the mother needs to carry in one bag: the pump, the bottles and tubing that connect to the pump, and her expressed milk. Some also contain a special compartment that can keep the milk cool when freezer packs are used. Costing between $575 and $710 US (1996 prices), some mothers purchase them, but most find renting more cost-effective, particularly at the discounted long-term rental rates.

Another lightweight option is Medela's Pump In Style, an automatic diaphragm pump that weighs about 7 pounds (3175 grams) including case and accessories and which is available for purchase only (1996 price is approximately $200 US). The pump is integrated into a carrying case that holds the collection kit and stores and cools the mother's expressed milk. This pump can also be powered with a separate rechargeable battery pack (available for rent or sale from Medela distributors) if no electrical outlet is available.

Semi-automatic electric double pumps are small, light, and easy to carry.

The semi-automatic electric diaphragm pump, the Nurture III, the Double-Up, and Natural Choice, weigh only 1.6 pounds (642 grams), making them light enough for a woman to carry in a large purse or a tote bag.

Small motorized single pumps and hand pumps are also small and light, although they tend to rank lower in effectiveness, comfort, and pumping time.

Although the small motorized single pumps and hand pumps are smaller and lighter than the previously listed pumps, they tend not to be as effective at establishing and maintaining a milk supply for women who substitute pumping for nursing more than two times per day. They also take longer to use than double pumps, and mothers find some models contribute to nipple soreness.

The need to pump in a confined space, such as a toilet stall, will influence a mother's choice of pumps.

If the mother will be using her pump in a very confined space, she may prefer to use a pump that she can hold in one hand, such as a small motorized single pump or a hand pump. If she prefers to double-pump, suggest she consider two small motorized single pumps or two hand pumps that can be operated with one hand, such as Ameda/Egnell's One-Hand Breast Pump.

Noise Level

Some pumps make no noise at all and some are relatively loud. Ask the mother if the noise level of the pump is important to her.

The Ora' Lac, which is powered by the mother's sucking on a tube, is a virtually noiseless pump. Hand pumps, such as cylinder and squeeze pumps, tend to make very little noise.

Automatic electric mid-size piston pumps range from 54 to 57 decibels, and full-size piston pumps range from 60-64 decibels. The sounds made by these pumps are described as "whirring" or "breathing" (Frantz, p. 109). Most mothers find them soothing.

Of the automatic diaphragm pumps, the White River 9050 pump is reportedly in the quiet range (Frantz, p. 116). No decibel readings are available for the Medela Pump In Style.

The noise level of the small motorized single pumps range from a quiet 54 (Evenflo) to a somewhat loud 71 decibels (Medela Mini Electric). Frantz (pp. 99 and 115) describes the sounds these pumps make as a "quiet hum" (Evenflo), a "steady buzz" (Gentle Expressions at 67 decibels), and a "wavy buzz noise" (Medela Mini Electric). For the pumps at the upper range, noise level is a concern for some mothers. The sound the Medela Mini Electric makes is comparable in volume and pitch to a man's electric razor.

Power Source

Access to an electrical outlet will influence a mother's pump choice.

The mother's access to an electrical outlet will influence her choice of pump. If there is no outlet available, her choices include: an automatic double pump with a built-in rechargeable battery (or separate rechargeable battery pack), a mother-powered double pump (such as the Medela PedalPump), a small battery-powered, motorized single pump, a hand pump, or the Ora' lac. The mid-size electric piston pumps and Medela's Pump In Style can be powered by an automobile battery via a special cord used in the cigarette lighter.

Her choice among these will depend upon the other features that are important to her.

Some full-size automatic electric double pumps require a three-pronged outlet or plug adapter.

If the mother is considering a full-size automatic electric double pump, be sure she knows that some of the Medela Classic and the Ameda/Egnell SMB pumps require a three-pronged outlet or a plug adapter.

Pumps/Products

Cost

If the mother is working full-time or her baby is not breastfeeding, an automatic double pump may be the most cost-effective choice.

For the mother who is working full-time or whose baby is not breastfeeding, an automatic double pump tends to be the most effective pump at establishing and maintaining her milk supply, because it most closely mimics the suck of a breast-feeding baby (see the information on "cycling" in the section on "Effectiveness").

An automatic electric piston pump can be rented at considerably less than the cost of artificial feeding. Although this type of pump can be purchased (1996 purchase prices are between $1030 and $1350 US for full-size pumps and between $575 and $710 US for mid-size pumps), most mothers find renting more cost-effective than buying. Most pump rental stations or hiring agencies offer discounted rates for long-term rentals, with long-term rental rates averaging about one-third the cost of exclusive formula-feeding.

When rented long-term and used regularly, an automatic electric piston pump may cost less to use than a battery-operated small motorized single pump, which may need the batteries replaced every couple of days. For most women, automatic electric piston pumps will be more effective than small motorized single pumps or hand pumps in keeping up their milk supply, saving on the cost of formula. Depending on the amount of use, a small motorized single pump also may wear out and need to be replaced periodically.

Another option for a mother who is substituting pumping for nursing more than twice a day is an automatic electric diaphragm double pump, such as Medela's Pump In Style, which is available for purchase only (1996 price is approximately $200 US). This pump is integrated into a carrying case that holds the collection kit, as well as stores and cools the mother's expressed milk. Another automatic diaphragm pump is the White River 9050, which is available for rent or purchase (1996 price is $1075 US).

The PedalPump offers a less expensive alternative for women wanting to double-pump.

Medela's PedalPump consists of a wooden footpedal designed to allow women to use the strong muscles of their leg to power Medela's double-pumping kit. Retailing at approximately $85 US (including the footpedal plus double-pumping kit), this provides another choice for women who want to keep their pump costs low and yet be able to double-pump, as well as women with no electrical outlet available.

If the mother is considering a small battery-operated pump, suggest she include in her cost calculations regular battery and pump replacement.

When considering the cost of various methods of expression, be sure the mother who is considering a small battery-operated pump knows that with regular use the batteries need to be replaced as often as every few days.

Unlike automatic double pumps, small electric or battery-operated pumps have only a 90-day warranty (Frantz, p. 98); depending on the amount of use they get, the pumps themselves may need periodic replacement.

Retail prices of hand pumps range between $3 and $50 US. Retail prices of small motorized single pumps range between $35 and $87 US.

The least expensive types of pumps are the hand pumps, which range in price from $3 US for the Davol rubber bulb pump (not recommended) to $50 US for the Loyd-B pump. Next in price are the small motorized pumps, which range between $35 US for the Gentle Expressions pump to $75 to $87 US for Medela's Mini Electric.

Price does not necessarily reflect effectiveness or ease of use among the hand pumps. The Loyd-B at $50 US is not necessarily more effective or easier to operate than another squeeze pump, the Ameda/Egnell One-Hand Breast Pump at $28 US.

Among the small motorized single pumps, the highest priced, the Medela Mini Electric ($75 to $87 US) does offer several advantages. Unlike the other pumps in this category, which require the mother to manually regulate the suction by pressing a button, the Mini Electric automatically regulates suction and release. The Mini Electric also produces 30 cycles per minute as compared with the Evenflo, Gentle Expressions, and MagMag, which produce at most 7 cycles per minute.

Types of Breast Pumps

Full-Size Automatic Electric Piston Pumps

Mechanism: The preset motion of a metal balancing weight automatically alternates suction and release of suction at a set speed of between 48 and 60 times per minute

Examples:
- Ameda/Egnell SMB
- Ameda/Egnell Lact-E
- Medela Classic (015)

Cost:

Rental—short-term rental rate: $2.65 US/day (price varies)

   long-term rental rate: as low as $30 US/month (price varies)

   (Cost doesn't include purchase of collection kit and a refundable pump deposit.)

Purchase—$1030 to $1350 US (1996 prices)

Advantages:
- Effective; some mothers find these pumps more effective than others at expressing milk and keeping up their milk supply over the long term.
- Comfortable; suction control allows mother to adjust to her own comfort level.
- Automatic; pump regulates suction and release.
- Double- or single-pumping.
- Quiet.

Disadvantages:
- Heaviest type of pump:
  Ameda/Egnell SMB—22 pounds (9980 grams)
  Ameda/Egnell Lact-E—11 pounds (4990 grams)
  Medela Classic (015)—16 pounds (7258 grams)
- Requires an electric outlet (some require three-pronged outlet or plug adapter).

Mid-Size Automatic Electric Piston Pump

Mechanism: A plastic piston moves back and forth horizontally to automatically generate suction and release of suction from 30 to 60 times per minute (some models feature speed control, which allows the mother to vary the number of cycles per minute).

Examples:
- Ameda/Egnell Elite—6½ pounds (2949 grams)
- Medela Lactina Select—5 pounds (2268 grams)

Cost:

Rental—Suggested short-term rental rate: $2.65 US/day (price varies)

   Suggested long-term rental rate: as low as $30 US/month (price varies)

   (Cost doesn't include purchase of collection kit and a refundable pump deposit.)

Purchase—$575 to $710 US (1996 prices)

Advantages:
- Some models offer speed control (faster or slower cycling), which enhances let-down in some women.
- Comfortable; suction control allows mother to adjust to her own comfort level.
- Automatic; pump regulates suction and release.
- Double- or single-pumping.
- Lighter than full-size:
  Ameda/Egnell Elite—6½ pounds (2949 grams)
  Medela Lactina Select—5 pounds (2268 grams)
- Quiet.
- Electrical outlet not needed in those models with an integrated rechargeable battery or if a separate battery pack is used (available for rent at additional cost).

Disadvantages:
- Not as effective as full-size pumps over the long-term for some mothers.
- Some models require electrical outlet.

Automatic Electric Diaphragm Pumps

Mechanism: A diaphragm moves within a container to automatically generate suction and release of suction from 30 to 48 times per minute.

Examples:

- Medela Pump In Style
- White River 9050

Cost:

Rental (White River 9050 only): price varies, contact White River rental station. (Cost doesn't include purchase of collection kit and a refundable pump deposit.)

Purchase: White River 9050—$1075 US (1996 price).

Medela Pump In Style (purchase only): $200 US (1996 price)

Advantages:

- Comfortable; suction control allows mother to adjust to her own comfort level.
- Automatic; pump regulates suction and release.
- Carrying case and built-in cooler included as part of Medela Pump In Style.
- Double- or single-pumping.
- Medela Pump In Style lighter than full-size piston pumps—7 pounds (3175 grams)
- Quiet.
- No electrical outlet needed for Medela Pump In Style if powered by rechargeable battery pack (available for rent at additional cost).

Disadvantages:

- White River 9050 generates 30 cycles per minute maximum.
- Double-pumping with one hand is not possible with the soft, flexible silicone breast flanges of the White River 9050 collection kit.
- White River 9050 as heavy as full-size electric piston pumps—12 pounds (5443 grams).

Semi-Automatic Diaphragm Pump

Mechanism: A small motor, similar to those used with fish tanks, provides power; the mother intermittently generates suction and release by covering and uncovering a hole to mimic a baby's sucking pattern.

Examples:

- Nurture III
- Double-Up
- Natural Choice

Cost:

- $100 to $150 US (1996 price), may also include video, case, and nursing pads.

Advantages:

- Double- or single-pumping.
- Small, light (1.6 pounds [642 grams]), portable.
- Quiet.

Disadvantages:

- Mother regulates suction and release, so takes time and practice to master.
- Generates at most 25 suction-and-release cycles per minute.
- Needs an electrical outlet.

Mother-Powered Pumps

Mechanism: A double-pumping collection kit is attached to a specially designed wooden foot pedal, which allows the mother to power the suction and release by pressing the pedal with her foot.

Example:

Medela PedalPump

Cost:

$85 US (1996 price) for footpedal plus double-pumping kit.

Advantages:

- Powered by the muscles of the leg, which are stronger than hand or arm muscles.
- Double- or single-pumping.
- Portable (weighs about 5 pounds [2268 grams]).
- Quiet.
- Needs no electric outlet, as powered by the mother.

Disadvantages:

- Mother regulates suction and release, so takes time and practice to master.
- Larger, bulkier, and heavier than most hand pumps.

Small Motorized Single Pumps

Mechanism—Small electric and/or battery-powered motor provides continuous suction and release, which the mother intermittently interrupts to mimic a baby's sucking pattern by putting her finger over the suction-release valve or depressing a lever or button. (See exception at end.)

Examples:

- Gentle Expressions
- MagMag
- Evenflo Soft Touch Ultra
- Medela Mini Electric

Cost:

- $35 to $87 US (1996 prices), plus cost of batteries in battery-powered models (with regular daily use, batteries will need replacement as often as every few days).

Advantages:

- Small, light (ranging from 7 to 17 ounces [198 to 482 grams]), portable.
- Some are quiet (Evenflo Soft Touch Ultra operates at 54 decibels).
- No electric outlet needed for battery-powered models.

Disadvantages:

- Mother regulates suction-and-release so takes time and practice to master. Exception: Medela Mini Electric, which has automatic cycling.
- Few suction-and-release cycles (most in 4 to 7 cycles per minute range). Exception: Medela Mini Electric, which generates 30 cycles per minute.
- Sore nipples may be caused by limited cycling.
- Single-pumping only unless the mother has two pumps that can be operated with one hand.
- Some are loud (Medela Mini Electric operates at 71 decibels, comparable in volume and pitch to a man's electric razor).
- 90-day warranty. May need periodic replacement with consistent daily use. Medela states that their Mini Electric can be relied upon for about 150 hours of use.

Cylinder Pumps

Mechanism: One cylinder fits inside another with a rubber gasket acting as a seal between them. Suction is created when the inner cylinder is pulled out, drawing the milk into the outer cylinder or a separate collection bottle.

Examples:

- Comfort Plus Kaneson Pump
- White River Breast Pump Kit Model 500
- Medela Manualectric or Spring Express Breast Pump (features separate collection bottle)
- Ameda/Egnell Cylinder Hand Pump

Cost:

- $12 to $28 US (1996 prices).

Advantages:

- Small, light, portable.

Pumps/Products

- Different brands have nipple tunnels of different diameters for mother with different nipple sizes:

    Small: Comfort Plus Kaneson Pump (Marshall Baby Care)—⅝ to ⅞ inch (2 cm)

    Medela Manualectric or Spring Express—¾ or ⅞ inch (2 cm), with or without optional nipple adapter

    Large: Ameda/Egnell's Cylinder Hand Breast Pump (1⅛ inches [2.8 cm]).

- White River has a soft silicone flange.
- Powered by the mother, so needs no electrical outlet.

Disadvantages:

- Mother regulates suction and release, so takes time and practice to master.
- Takes two hands to operate.
- Some designs tip over easily.
- Most have no suction control.
- When milk flows directly into outer cylinder, suction can be affected.

Exception: Medela Manualectric and Spring Express have air holes in the cylinder and a pressure relief valve where the bottle connects that prevents pressure from going too high, have a suction control adjustment, the milk flows into a bottle that is separate from the cylinder, and come with a stand to help prevent the pump from falling over.

Rubber Bulb Pumps (not recommended)

Mechanism: The bulb is squeezed, causing suction, which provides pressure and draws the milk into the bulb itself. (Also known as the "bicycle-horn pump.")

Example:

- Davol rubber bulb pump

Cost:

- $3 US (1996 price)

Not recommended:

- Suction cannot be regulated, and damage to the breast can result.
- Ineffective at expressing milk.
- Difficult to clean
- High risk of milk contamination.
- No collection bottle for saving milk.
- Requires two hands to operate.

Trigger Squeeze Pumps

Mechanism: A trigger (like those on household cleaning products) is pulled and released to generate suction and release, and the expressed milk is drawn into a separate collection bottle.

Example:

- Loyd-B

Cost:

- $50 US (1996 price)

Advantages:

- Small enough to fit into a large purse or tote bag, although larger than other hand pumps.
- Quiet.
- Tends to be effective after mother becomes practiced.
- Powered by the mother, so needs no electrical outlet.

Disadvantages:

- Mother regulates suction and release, so takes time and practice to master.
- The trigger mechanism is designed as if someone facing the mother is doing the pumping, making it awkward and tiring to operate.
- Requires more strength and energy to operate than other hand pumps.
- Larger and bulkier than other hand pumps.
- Some models have a breakable glass breast flange.
- Requires two hands to operate.

Handle Squeeze Pumps

Mechanism: A handle is squeezed and released, moving a piston with a rubber seal that generates suction and release and drawing expressed milk into a separate bottle.

Example:
- Ameda/Egnell One-Hand Breast Pump

Cost:
- $28 US (1996 price)

Advantages:
- Small, light (4 ounces [113 grams]), portable
- Quiet.
- Can be operated with one hand, allowing the mother to double-pump with two pumps or to operate while the baby is nursing on the other breast.
- Handle swivels, allowing the mother to keep her wrist straight.
- Suction remains within safe levels due to air vents in the pump.
- No change in pressure as the bottle fills with milk.
- Soft silicone nipple adapter allow nipple tunnel diameter to be reduced if needed.
- Standard size bottle can be used.
- Powered by the mother, so needs no electrical outlet.

Disadvantages:
- Mother regulates suction and release, so takes time and practice to master.

Ora' Lac

Mechanism: The mother sucks on one of the two tubes extending from the top of the collection bottle, creating a vacuum in the bottle which provides the suction and pressure to stimulate the breast and draw the milk from the breast into the other tube and the collection bottle.

Cost:
- $30 US (1996 price)

Advantages:
- Small, light, portable.
- Quiet.
- Powered by the mother, so needs no electrical outlet.

Disadvantages:
- Low levels of suction generated (60 mmHg, compared with the minimum suction setting of 75 mmHg on most electric piston pumps).

Glossary of Terms

Automatic pump—A pump that automatically generates suction and release of suction, without any action by the mother. If a motorized pump requires the mother to cover a hole or depress a button or bar to generate and/or release suction, it is considered "semi-automatic."

Cycle—One suction plus one release of suction is a cycle. A baby actively nursing generates approximately 1.28 sucks per second. A pump's effectiveness can be evaluated in part by how closely the number of cycles per minute approximate a baby at the breast. See also "suction curve."

Cylinder pump—The mother generates the suction by pulling the inner cylinder, which fits inside the outer cylinder with a rubber gasket acting as a seal between them, drawing the milk into the outer cylinder or a separate collection bottle. Examples: Ameda/Egnell's Cylinder Hand Breast Pump, Comfort Plus Kaneson Pump, Medela Spring Express or Manualectric, White River Breast Pump Kit Model 500.

Diaphragm pump—A pump that uses a diaphragm moving in and out to generate suction and release of suction. Both automatic and semi-automatic diaphragm pumps are available.

Double pump—A pump that allows mothers to pump both breasts simultaneously, which cuts pumping time in half, avoids milk loss from leakage, and has also been found to stimulate milk production slightly more than single-pumping (Auerbach 1990).

A COMPARISON CHART OF DOUBLE PUMPS AND SMALL MOTORIZED SINGLE PUMPS

	Automatic?	# cycles/min.	Suction levels	Weight	Needs outlet?	rental?/purchase $
Double Pumps						
Full-Size Automatic Piston						
Ameda/Egnell SMB	yes	48-60	110-220 mm Hg	22 lbs. (9980 g)	yes	rental
Ameda/Egnell Lact-E	yes	48-60	70-220 mm Hg	11 lbs. (4990 g)	yes	rental/$1030 US
Medela Classic	yes	48-60	80-240 mm Hg	16 lbs. (7258 g)	yes	rental/$1350 US
Mid-Size Automatic Piston						
Ameda/Egnell Elite	yes	30-60	0-250 mm Hg	6.5 lbs. (2949 g)	no	rental/$710 US
Medela Lactina Select	yes	30-60	80-240 mm Hg	5 lbs. (2268 g)	yes	rental/$650 US
Automatic Diaphragm						
Medela Pump In Style	yes	48	80-240 mm Hg	7 lbs. (3175 g)	yes	$200 US
White River 9050	yes	30	76-190 mm Hg	12 lbs. (5443 g)	yes	rental/$1075 US
Semi-Automatic Diaphragm						
Nurture III/ Double-Up	no	25	to 240 mm Hg	1.6 lbs. (642 g)	yes	$100-150 US
Mother-Powered Pump						
Medela PedalPump	no	varies	to 240 mm Hg	5 lbs. (2268 g)	no	$85 US
Small Motorized Single Pumps						
Evenflo Soft Touch Ultra	no	5	250 mm Hg	14.5 oz. (411 g)	no	$40 US
Gentle Expressions	no	5	50-280 mm Hg	8 oz (227 g)	no	$35 US
MagMag (Pigeon)	no	5	50-220 mm Hg	8.6 oz (244 g)	no	$70 US
Medela Mini Electric	yes	30	80-240 mm Hg (with AC adapter)	17 oz. (482 g)	no	$75.87 US

Draw and hold method of pumping—Can be used with a squeeze pump or a cylinder pump. The mother uses a rhythmic motion to stimulate her let-down reflex and then—after the let-down occurs—gently pulls the cylinder or squeezes the handle to draw out the milk until the milk flow slows down. She then repeats this process on the other breast, going back and forth from breast to breast until she is finished.

Flange—The bell-shaped part of the pump collection unit that is placed over the breast during pumping.

Full-size automatic electric piston pump—This pump, which can be used to double- or single-pump, uses the preset motion of a metal balancing weight that swings from side to side to automatically generate suction and release of suction. Cycles per minute: 48 to 60. Examples: Ameda/Egnell Lact-E, Ameda/Egnell SMB, Medela Classic.

Handle squeeze pump—The mother squeezes and releases a handle, which moves a piston fitted with a rubber seal that generates suction and release and draws expressed milk into a separate bottle. Example: Ameda/Egnell One-Hand Breast Pump.

Mid-size automatic electric piston pump—This pump, which can be used to double- or single-pump, uses a plastic piston moving back and forth horizontally to automatically generate suction and release. Some models, such as the Ameda/Egnell Elite and the Medela Lactina Select, feature speed control, which allows the mother to speed up or slow down the pump's cycling to more closely mimic her baby's suck and better stimulate milk let-down. Cycles per minute: 30-60. Examples: Ameda/Egnell Elite, Medela Lactina Plus, Medela Lactina Select.

Nipple adapter—The plastic or silicone piece that fits into the nipple tunnel of the pump flange to narrow the nipple tunnel and give mothers with very small nipples a better fit. Suggest the mother discontinue its use if it makes the nipple tunnel so narrow that her nipple rubs along its sides during pumping.

Nipple tunnel—The part of the pump flange into which the mother's nipple is drawn by suction. Ideally the mother's nipple should fit comfortably in the nipple tunnel without rubbing along the sides. If not, the mother needs to discontinue use of the nipple adapter (see previous point), get a pump or pump collection kit with a larger nipple tunnel (Ameda/Egnell kits have a slightly larger nipple tunnel than Medela kits), or buy a pump flange specially made for women with large nipples (i.e., the Medela Extra Large Glass Breastshield Kit).

Semi-automatic—A motorized pump that requires the mother to cover a hole or push a button or bar to generate and/or release suction.

Semi-automatic diaphragm pump—A pump with a small motor, similar to those used with fish tanks. The mother intermittently generates suction and release by covering and uncovering a hole to mimic a baby's sucking pattern. Can be used to double or single pump. Cycles per minute: 25. Examples: Nurture III, Double-Up, Natural Choice.

Single pump—A pump that requires the mother to pump one breast at a time, as opposed to a double pump, which can pump both breasts simultaneously. Single-pumping may take more than twice as long as double-pumping (20-30 minutes as opposed to 10-15 minutes).

Small, motorized single pump—A small electric and/or battery-powered hand-held pump, most of which are semi-automatic. Maximum cycles per minute: 4-7 (except the Medela Mini Electric, which provides 30-38 automatically). Examples: MagMag, Evenflo Soft Touch Ultra, Gentle Expression, Medela Mini Electric.

Speed control—A feature on some mid-sized automatic electric piston pumps that allows the mother to cycle the pump faster (to better stimulate milk let-down) or slower (to mimic the longer, slower drawing action of a baby after the milk lets down).

Suction control—The knob or lever that allows the mother to control the amount of suction, or negative pressure, the pump generates. More suction does not necessarily equal faster or more effective pumping. If the suction is high enough to be uncomfortable, the mother's let-down reflex may be inhibited. Encourage her to use the highest setting that is comfortable.

Suction curve—Each suction-and-release cycle includes three phases, which are known collectively as its suction curve: a steady building of suction, a brief holding of suction at the peak, and a steady decline of suction before the process begins again. It is thought that some mothers respond better to one automatic double pump over another because of the differences in their suction curves. Also, see "cycle."

Trigger squeeze pump—The mother pulls and releases a trigger (like those on household cleaning products) to generate suction and release, and the expressed milk is drawn into a separate collection bottle. Example: Loyd-B

BREAST SHELLS

Composition, design, and care of breast shells.

Also called milk cups, breast cups, breast shields, or Woolwich shields, breast shells are made of hard, lightweight plastic. Some are constructed with flexible silicone backs. They can be worn inconspicuously in the mother's bra. The mother may need to wear a bra one cup size larger than usual to accommodate them comfortably. If the mother's bra is not large enough, the pressure may cause mastitis.

Each shell has two sections: the inner ring, with an opening for the nipple, fits directly over the breast, and the dome, which may or may not have holes, holds the bra away from the nipple.

When in use, breast shells should be washed daily.

Breast shells have long been recommended to draw out flat or inverted nipples, but their effectiveness has not been proven.

The hormonal changes of pregnancy increase the elasticity of a woman's skin. Breast shells were designed to take advantage of this natural stretchiness by applying gentle but steady pressure to stretch underlying adhesions and draw out the nipple. (For more information, see the section "Flat and Inverted Nipples" in the chapter "Nipple Problems.")

Those who recommend breast shells suggest they be worn during the last trimester of pregnancy, starting with a few hours a day and gradually increasing the time, with the mother using her comfort as a guide.

If flat or inverted nipples are not discovered until after the baby is born, breast shells can be worn about a half hour before nursings to draw out the nipple.

Although thousands of women have used breast shells to draw out their flat or inverted nipples, the effectiveness of breast shells has not been proven in controlled studies. One recent study found no benefit to the use of breast shells during pregnancy for women with at least one inverted or flat nipple (MAIN Trial Collaborative Group 1994), and one study found that women with at least one inverted nipple who were assigned to wear breast shells during pregnancy breastfed less successfully than women who did not treat their nipples during pregnancy (Alexander 1992). More research is needed to determine whether the hole size of different types of breast shells influence their effectiveness (Stark 1994). In the meantime, the use of breast shells should be considered optional for mothers with inverted nipples. Any mother with inverted nipples, whether she uses breast shells or not, may need assistance in getting the baby latched-on after birth.

Breast shells can be used to protect sore nipples.

If the mother's nipples are so sore that she cannot tolerate the pressure of her bra or clothing on them and it is painful for her to hold her baby, breast shells that have larger nipple openings and holes in the dome will protect them while allowing for air circulation. They also prevent the mother's clothing from sticking to her nipples. Tea strainers with the handles removed can also be used for this purpose.

The cause of the soreness also needs to be determined and corrected. (See "If Breastfeeding Hurts—Review the Basics" in the chapter "Positioning, Latch-On, and the Baby's Suck.")

Breast shells can be used to soften an engorged areola.	When a mother is engorged, wearing breast shells (with the smaller hole in the inner ring) thirty minutes before feedings may help soften the areola, but they should be used with caution. (See the next point.)
Overuse of breast shells after birth can contribute to plugged ducts and promote nipple soreness.	After birth, breast shells should be used with caution. Consistent use of breast shells without air holes can promote nipple soreness. Continuous use may also compress tissue behind the nipple, causing mastitis. (See "Engorgement" in the chapter "Breast Problems.")
Milk that collects in a breast shell should be discarded.	Some women leak milk into the breast shell while it is worn. Since the milk is kept warm and close to the mother's body, there is concern that bacteria can grow. Any milk collected in a breast shell should be discarded.
Sources of breast shells.	Pharmacies and independent pump rental depots may also carry breast shells. They are available from Ameda/Egnell, La Leche League International, and Medela. (See addresses at the end of this chapter.)

CREAMS AND OINTMENTS

The Montgomery glands surrounding the areola secrete a natural cleansing lubricant, making nipple creams and ointments unnecessary for most mothers.	The Montgomery glands are small oil-producing glands surrounding the areola that provide lubrication and discourage growth of bacteria on the skin of the nipple and areola by altering the skin's pH (Williams 1992). This natural, cleansing lubricant makes nipple creams and ointments unnecessary for most mothers.
Creams and ointments are not helpful in preventing sore nipples.	Creams and ointments do not prevent nipple soreness. If the mother has sore nipples, see the chapter "Nipple Problems" to find the cause of the soreness so it can be corrected.
If the mother wants to apply something to her nipple to speed healing, human milk can be used.	If the mother's nipples are sore or cracked and she wants to apply something to promote healing, encourage her to express a few drops of her milk after the baby has finished nursing and rub it gently into the skin, allowing her nipples to air dry afterwards. Many cultures use human milk as a healing agent, probably due to its anti-bacterial properties. The only exception to this is if a mother's nipple soreness is due to thrush, a fungal infection. In this case, rather than expressing some milk on the nipple and letting it dry, as thrush thrives on milk, suggest the mother rinse her nipples with clear water after feedings.
Some creams and ointments change the taste of the nipple, slow healing, or are harmful or irritating to mother and baby.	Some creams and ointments change the taste of the nipple, causing the baby to be fussy at the breast or refuse to nurse. Others, such as vitamin A and D ointments, baby oil, and Vaseline, are petroleum-based products that may not be safe for the baby to ingest. Creams or ointments containing alcohol are drying to the skin. Too much cream or ointment applied to the nipple may make it so slippery that latch-on is difficult for the baby. Ointments containing astringents or anesthetic agents are not recommended, because they are potentially harmful to both mother and baby. Numbing the nipples may inhibit the mother's let-down, or milk-ejection, reflex and may also numb the baby's mouth, affecting sucking. Some creams or ointments may irritate a sensitive mother's nipple, causing dermatitis, an inflammation of the skin.
Avoid creams or ointments that must be removed before nursing.	If the mother wants to use a cream or ointment on her nipples, suggest she choose one that does not need to be wiped off before the baby nurses. If the label suggests wiping it off, this means it contains ingredients the baby should not be ingesting. The friction of rubbing it off can further irritate sore nipples.

Lansinoh for Breastfeeding Mothers® is one form of lanolin that can be recommended.

USP modified lanolin does not need to be removed before nursing. However, it is important to know that there are many refinements of modified lanolin and that some formulations contain higher levels of pesticides, free lanolin alcohols, and detergents, the components that have been identified as the cause of lanolin allergy. Lansinoh for Breastfeeding Mothers® is recommended as the purest and safest lanolin available.

For many years, lanolin use was discouraged because some women reported skin reactions and there were increasing concerns about its ingestion by the baby due to reports of high levels of pesticides. In 1992, the US Pharmacopoeia (USP) set minimum standards of purity for lanolin used by breastfeeding mothers. These standards set upper limits for free lanolin alcohols (one of the factors that caused skin reactions) and pesticides. Most companies who now sell "USP modified lanolin" meet these minimum standards.

One company, Lansinoh Laboratories, Inc., was the first to sell this improved lanolin as Lansinoh for Breastfeeding Mothers,® and this product is recommended because its formula is considerably purer than the minimum acceptable USP standards. The free lanolin alcohols and measurable pesticides are less than half the amount found in other brands. Since some ingestion by the baby occurs, this added degree of purity is desirable.

Research has found that free alcohol levels and pesticides are only part of the cause of skin reactions. Although reducing free lanolin alcohols to a level of 6% reduces skin reactions in many people, 41% of those sensitive to lanolin will still have an allergic response. Even when the level is reduced to 2.2%, reactions occur. According to one study (Clark 1981), low levels of both free lanolin alcohols and detergent residues appear to be necessary to avoid skin reactions. In this study, when levels of both free lanolin alcohols and detergent residues were kept low, virtually no reactions occurred in a lanolin-sensitive population. Lansinoh for Breastfeeding Mothers® keeps free lanolin alcohols to 1.5% and detergent residues below 0.05%. No other company controls for detergent residues nor reports the levels present in their products, making Lansinoh for Breastfeeding Mothers® the purest and safest lanolin available.

Lansinoh for Breastfeeding Mothers® is sold by La Leche League International and Ameda/Egnell distributors. It is also available in retail outlets.

If a mother with sore nipples wants to apply something to her nipples other than her milk, Lansinoh for Breastfeeding Mothers® may be helpful in soothing and speeding the healing of sore nipples.

Creams, ointments, lubricants, or moisturizers should never be used as a substitute for finding and correcting the cause of a mother's soreness. However, when nipples are extremely sore, cracked, or bleeding, use of Lansinoh for Breastfeeding Mothers® to keep the nipple moist between feedings has been found to soothe and speed healing while the cause of the soreness is being determined and corrected (Spangler and Hildebrandt 1993).

In the past, suggestions for healing sore nipples included drying techniques, such as the use of a hair dryer on a low setting on the nipples after feedings, keeping bra flaps down, and the use of a sun lamp on the nipples. However, research on moist wound healing has found that wounds heal 50% faster and scabbing and crusting are avoided when the internal moisture of the skin is maintained (Sharp 1992; Hinman and Maibach 1963). To maintain the moisture barrier that prevents evaporation and avoids drying and scab formation, the mother needs to apply enough Lansinoh for Breastfeeding Mothers® to the nipple after feedings to keep the area moist, reapplying as needed.

Use of Lansinoh may also decrease pain, because it maintains a more "normal" environment for the free nerve endings that signal pain and protects them from external stimuli (Mann Mertz 1990).

Although vitamin E was once recommended for use on the nipples, it may not be the best choice, due to concerns about changes in babies' vitamin E levels and possible skin irritation in mother.

In the past, some breastfeeding experts have recommended mothers squeeze a drop or two of vitamin E oil from a capsule onto the nipples to help promote healing. However, concerns have been expressed about the possibility of side effects if babies ingest too much vitamin E. In one study of full-term babies and their mothers, after the mothers applied liberal amounts of vitamin E to their nipples, their babies' blood levels of vitamin E rose, but not out of the normal range (Marx 1985). Another concern about using vitamin E on the nipples is possible skin reactions in the mother. Although vitamin E almost never produces allergic reactions when swallowed, vitamin-E preparations used to treat burns have been found to produce contact dermatitis and hives in some individuals (Fisher 1986; Aeling 1973; Minkin 1973; Brodkin 1965). A product less likely to cause skin reactions would be a better choice for use on the nipples.

If the mother uses anything other than her milk or Lansinoh for Breastfeeding Mothers® to lubricate her nipples, suggest she apply it sparingly and discontinue use immediately if any rash or other irritation develops.

If the mother uses anything other than her milk or Lansinoh for Breastfeeding Mothers® on her nipple, suggest she carefully read the label and choose something that is safe for human consumption, as her baby may ingest some of it when he nurses. Also suggest the mother begin by using it sparingly to test for possible skin reactions. If a rash or other irritation develops, suggest she discontinue using it immediately.

Creams, ointments, lubricants, or moisturizers should never be used as a substitute for finding and correcting the cause of a mother's soreness.

MILK STORAGE BAGS

Composition and design of milk storage bags vary from brand to brand.

Milk storage bags, or freezer milk bags, are specifically designed for freezing and storing human milk. (See the last point in this section for product information.) Other milk bags, sold as disposable bottle liners, are not as durable and may be sold without their own closures (in this case, twist ties or clips can be used).

Freezing milk in the less-durable type of plastic liner can be risky.

Using the less-durable type of milk bag carries risks:

- removing air from the bag without spilling milk can be tricky;
- the seams may burst during freezing;
- the bag may leak during thawing.

If the mother is expressing her milk for a hospitalized baby, it may be more difficult for nurses to remove the milk from the bag without accidentally touching the milk, increasing the possibility of contamination. One way to avoid contamination is for the nurses to snip off the bottom corner of the bag with a sterile scissors and pour the milk out.

If the mother decides to use the less-durable type of plastic liner to store her milk, she can decrease the risks by following certain procedures.

If the mother wants to freeze her milk in disposable bottle liners, suggest she follow this procedure:

- use double bags to avoid tearing,
- squeeze out the air at the top,
- roll down the bag to about one inch (2.5 cm) above the milk,
- close the bag and seal it.

Another commonsense precaution is to place the sealed bag upright in a heavy, plastic container with a lid, and seal the lid before putting it in the freezer.

Sources of freezer milk bags designed to store human milk.

Durable milk storage bags are made specifically for freezing and storing human milk. One brand, called Mother's Milk Freezer Bags, is sold by La Leche League International and Ameda/Egnell distributors. Another brand, called CSF Bags (for

Collection, Storage, and Freezing) is made by Medela and sold by Medela distributors. (See the "Product Information" section at the end of this chapter.)

These milk storage bags are two-ply, coated with polyethylene, and lined with nylon, so the fat cells in human milk will not adhere. They are self-sealing and pre-sterilized and have areas for labeling.

NIPPLE SHIELDS

Composition and design of nipple shields.

Nipple shields are soft latex, silicone, or rubber nipples that are designed to be worn over the mother's nipples during feedings.

Nipple shields do not prevent and are not recommended to treat sore nipples.

Nipple shields usually cause more problems than they solve. Nipple shields do not prevent sore nipples or correct their cause. And rather than helping the baby take the breast, nipple shields condition the baby to the feel of the artificial nipple in his mouth instead of skin. Many mothers who have used nipple shields report that their babies grow to prefer nursing with the shield on, refusing to breastfeed when they take it off.

The baby sucks on most types of nipple shield the same way he sucks on a bottle nipple, contributing to nipple confusion. Even though the ultra-thin latex nipple shield has not been shown to alter sucking patterns (Woolridge 1980), some babies still refuse to nurse without it, perhaps because they grow accustomed to the feel of the latex in their mouth.

Also, with some types of nipple shield, the baby cannot compress the milk sinuses as well, which prevents adequate drainage of the breast and can lead to mastitis.

Consistent use of the nipple shield can reduce a mother's milk supply because it decreases stimulation of the mother's areola during breastfeeding.

Different types of nipple shields have differing effects on the amount of milk the baby receives. For example, in one study (Woolridge 1980), use of a red rubber nipple shield reduced the amount of milk the baby received by 58 percent. A thin latex shield, on the other hand, reduced the amount of milk the baby received by 22 percent and "had no significant effect on sucking patterns." This study, however, observed only one feeding, so conclusions cannot be drawn on the long-term effects of the use of the ultra-thin latex nipple shield.

If the baby refuses to nurse without the nipple shield, offer suggestions for weaning him away from it.

If the baby refuses to nurse without the nipple shield, mention the following approaches, as well as the other suggestions listed in the section, "Nipple Confusion," under "Fussy at the Breast during the Early Weeks of Breastfeeding" in the chapter "Fussy at the Breast and Breast Refusal."

Gradually cut off the tip of the shield until it is gone. Some mothers have successfully weaned their babies from a nipple shield by turning the shield inside out and then cutting off a thin strip from the center of the nipple area each day (or before each nursing if the baby will tolerate it) until it is gone, using fine-point cuticle scissors or a razor blade. This method will not work with a silicone nipple shield, because it leaves sharp edges.

Slip the shield off quickly while the baby is nursing. Start the baby nursing with the shield and then, after the let-down, quickly slip it off and latch him onto the breast.

Stuff the shield with cloth. Some mothers have weaned their baby from the shield by stuffing it with a small piece of clean cloth and putting the shield on as usual to begin a feeding. The baby eventually realizes that he can get milk only from the breast and begins to prefer it over the shield.

NURSING PADS

Some mothers wear nursing pads in their bra to protect their clothing from leaking milk. Disposable and reusable pads are sold, but some mothers make their own.

Features to look for in a nursing pad.

Features to avoid in a nursing pad.

During an outbreak of thrush, nursing pads should be changed after each feeding and not be reused unless they have been washed in hot, soapy water.

Rather than buying nursing pads, another option is for the mother to make her own by using folded handkerchiefs or circular pieces of absorbent material (such as diapers) sewn together.

When shopping for nursing pads, suggest the mother look for:

- All-cotton or all-paper pads, which allow maximum air circulation.
- White or natural rather than colored pads, because the dyes may be irritating to the mother's skin.
- Pads that are large enough for effective absorbency.

Suggest the mother avoid nursing pads with the following features:

- A plastic or waterproof lining, which may trap wetness near the mother's skin, keep air from getting to the mother's nipples, and cause the pad to stick to the mother's skin.
- Synthetic materials which restrict air circulation.
- Dyes which may be irritating to the mother's skin.

Candida albicans, the organism that causes thrush, is a fungus that thrives on milk on the nipples, in the milk ducts, and in the baby's mouth. It can also live and grow in the milk absorbed by nursing pads. Because thrush can be harbored in many places, encourage the mother to wash her hands frequently and take precautions so that the thrush does not recur. In addition to changing and washing nursing pads after every feeding, other precautions are listed under "Thrush" in the chapter "Nipple Problems."

NURSING PILLOWS

A nursing pillow can make breastfeeding more comfortable for some mothers and babies. Different types of pillows are available.

A nursing pillow can provide needed support for mother and baby, if the pillow is a good fit for them. A variety of nursing pillows are available, some large, some small. Some pillows are designed to support the mother's arm at the elbow, while others bring baby up to breast height. If the mother is interested in a nursing pillow, suggest she try different sizes and designs to see what works best for her and her baby. A mother with a long torso or high breasts, for example, may find that no nursing pillow brings her baby up to breast height and she needs to add regular pillows under her nursing pillow to achieve the right height. She may prefer using the type of nursing pillow that provides arm support (Frantz 1993).

The use of a nursing pillow can make all the difference in some special situations. For example, babies with low muscle tone and premies tend to breastfeed better with firm body support. Mothers with disabilities may find that they need the extra support of a nursing pillow to manage breastfeeding comfortably. Mothers of twins (or more) find a nursing pillow invaluable in supporting two babies for simultaneous feedings.

NURSING STOOLS

A nursing stool can help some mothers breastfeed more comfortably by elevating their knees, so that they sit back in a more relaxed position.

Some mothers find that a nursing stool helps them to sit back and relax during breastfeeding. Elevating a mother's knees can help lessen the stress on her back, shoulders, and arms as she breastfeeds.

OTHER PRODUCTS

Electronic Scales

Two electronic baby scales are available for rent that are helpful to breastfeeding mothers in some situations.

Although test-weighing is not recommended for most breastfeeding mothers and babies, in some special situations, such as when a baby has a medical problem or was born prematurely, test-weighing with an accurate electronic baby scale can be helpful. Medela's BabyWeigh scale, which is available for home rental in many areas through Medela distributors, has been found accurate to 2 g, which is precise enough to accurately measure milk intake during breastfeeding (Meier 1994). The BabyWeigh scale is used by some hospitals to measure the effectiveness of a premature baby's early nursings. Some mothers—particularly those whose babies were receiving precisely measured feedings in the hospital—find it reassuring to rent Medela's BabyWeigh scale for the first week or two after baby comes home so they can see how much milk their baby receives at the breast at each feeding. When parents know how much their baby is getting at the breast, they can have confidence that their baby is getting enough to eat. On the other hand, if the baby is not getting enough, they will know exactly when a supplement is necessary.

An alternative to the BabyWeigh is Medela's BabyChecker scale, which is not used to monitor intake but can be helpful in monitoring weight gain. It is also available for rent in some areas and is accurate to one ounce (28 g). The BabyChecker scale can be used for daily weight monitoring in situations where the BabyWeigh's precise accuracy is not needed to monitor intake.

Hand-Expression Funnel

Composition and care of the hand-expression funnel.

The hand-expression funnel is made of lightweight, hard plastic.

If the milk is being expressed for home use, the funnel and collection bottle should be sterilized before their first use. At other times, the funnel and the collection bottle can be washed in lukewarm, soapy water, rinsed in clear water, and air dried. If the milk is being expressed for a hospitalized baby, the mother should follow the instructions given by the doctor or hospital.

Design and purpose of the hand-expression funnel.

The deep, cup-shaped opening of the hand-expression funnel is large enough to accommodate a mother's hand and breast, and the inward rolled rim is designed to catch all the sprays of expressed milk to prevent waste, save time, and keep clothing and surrounding areas dry. The funnel is threaded and sized to screw onto any standard feeding bottle.

Sources of the hand-expression funnel.

The hand-expression funnel is available from Medela, La Leche League International, and many La Leche League Leaders.

InstaHeat

InstaHeat reusable heating pads can be used whenever warmth applied to the breast would be beneficial, such as during mastitis, engorgement, or to facilitate milk expression.

InstaHeat reusable heating pads can be used by the breastfeeding mother to apply warmth to the breasts before pumping or nursing or for engorgement, a plugged duct, or a breast infection. Like other reusable heating pads, they can be recharged between uses in the microwave or in boiling water and then activated as needed. Unlike other pads, however, they are shaped to fit comfortably over the breast or to fit around a breast pump flange during pumping and their flat bottom helps keep them in place if they are worn inside a mother's bra.

Sources of InstaHeat pads

InstaHeat pads are available from Medela, La Leche League International, and many La Leche League Leaders.

Product Information

Contact these sources for a catalog of available products.
Ameda/Egnell
755 Industrial Drive
Cary, Illinois 60013 USA

Telephone: 1-800-323-8750

Bailey Medical Engineering (Nurture III, Double-Up, or Natural Choice pump)
2020 11th Street
Los Osos, CA 93402 USA
Telephone: 805-528-5781
FAX: 805-528-1461

Evenflo Products, Co.
771 N. Freedom Street
P.O. Box 1206
Ravena, OH 44266-1206 USA
Telephone: 1-800-356-2229
        1-216-292-3465
FAX: 1-216-8588

La Leche League International
1400 N. Meacham Rd.
P.O. Box 4079
Schaumburg, IL 60168-4079 USA
Telephone: 1-800-525-3243 (1-800-LALECHE)
        1-847-519-9585 and 1-847-519-7730
FAX: 1-847-519-0035

Lopuco, Ltd. (Loyd-B pump)
1615 Old Annapolis Road
Woodbine, MD 21797 USA
1-800-634-7867

Marshall Baby Products (Comfort Plus Kaneson pump)
Division, Omron Health Care, Inc.
300 Lakeview Parkway
Vernon Hills, IL 60061 USA
Telephone: 1-800-922-2959
        1-847-680-6206
FAX: 1-847-680-6269

Medela
P.O. Box 660
McHenry, Illinois 60051-0661 USA
1-800-835-5968

Pigeon Corporation (MagMag pump)
5-1, Tomlymae, Kanda
Chiyoda-Ku, Tokyo 101
JAPAN
Telephone: 81-03-32524111
FAX: 81-03-32524029

White River Corporation
Natural Technologies, Inc.
924 "C" Calle Negocio
San Clemente, CA 92673 USA
1-800-824-6351
1-714-366-8960
FAX: 1-714-366-1664

Publications for Parents

Bernshaw, N. *A Mother's Guide to Milk Expression and Breast Pumps*. Schaumburg, Illinios: La Leche League International, 1996. Publication No. 30.

La Leche League International. THE WOMANLY ART OF BREASTFEEDING, 35th Anniversary ed. Schaumburg, Illinois, 1991, pp. 127-37, 168-70, 317-18.

References

Alternative Feeding Methods

Armstrong, H. Feeding low birthweight babies: advances in Kenya. *J Hum Lact* 1987; 3:34-37.

Frantz, K. *Breastfeeding Product Guide* 1994. Sunland, California: Geddes Productions, 1993, pp. 118-24.

Lawrence, R. *Breastfeeding: A Guide for the Medical Profession,* 4th ed. St. Louis: Mosby, 1994, pp. 571-72, 792-94.

Riordan, J. and Auerbach, K. *Breastfeeding and Human Lactation*. Boston and London: Jones and Bartlett, 1993, pp. 317-22.

Newman, J. Breastfeeding problems associated with early introduction of bottles and pacifiers. *J Hum Lact* 1990; 6(2):59-63.

Lang, S. et al. Cup feeding: an alternative method of infant feeding. *Arch Dis Child* 1994; 71:365-69.

Breast Pumps

Amir, L. et al. *Candidiasis & breastfeeding*. La Leche League International Lactation Consultant Series. Unit 18. Garden City Park, New York: Avery Publishing, 1995.

Auerbach, K. Sequential and simultaneous breast pumping: a comparison. *Int J Nurs Stud* 1990; 27(3):257-65.

Frantz, K. *Breastfeeding Product Guide* 1994. Sunland, California: Geddes Productions, 1993, pp. 47-117.

Garza, C. et al. Effects of method of collection and storage on nutrients in human milk. *Early Human Dev* 1982; 6:295-303.

Green, D. et al. The relative efficacy of four methods of human milk expression. *Early Human Dev* 1982; 6:153-58.

The Human Milk Banking Association of North America. *Recommendations for Collection, Storage, and Handling of a Mother's Milk for Her Own Infant in the Hospital Setting*. West Hartford CT USA, 1993.

Lang, S. et al. Sodium in hand and pump expressed human breast milk. *Early Human Dev* 1994; 38:131-38.

Lawrence, R. *Breastfeeding: A Guide for the Medical Profession,* 4th ed. St. Louis: Mosby, 1994, pp. 604-07.

Ramsey, M. and Gisel, E. Neonatal sucking and maternal feeding practices. *Dev Med Child Neurol* 1996; 26(3):34-47.

Riordan, J. and Auerbach, K. *Breastfeeding and Human Lactation*. Boston and London: Jones and Bartlett, 1993, pp. 279-311.

Breast Shells

Alexander, J. et al. Randomised controlled trial of breast shells and Hoffman's exercises for inverted and non-protractile nipples. *BMJ* 1992; 304:1030-32.

Frantz, K. *Breastfeeding Product Guide 1994*. Sunland, California: Geddes Productions, 1993, pp. 4-12.

Lawrence, R. *Breastfeeding: A Guide for the Medical Profession,* 4th ed. St. Louis: Mosby, 1994, pp. 228-29.

MAIN Trial Collaborative Group. Preparing for breast feeding: treatment of inverted and non-protractile nipples in pregnancy. *Midwifery* 1994; 10:200-14.

Riordan, J. and Auerbach, K. *Breastfeeding and Human Lactation*. Boston and London: Jones and Bartlett, 1993, pp. 316-17.

Stark, Y. *Human Nipples: Function and Anatomical Variations in Relationship to Breastfeeding,* 1994. (For ordering information, contact The Lactation Institute, 16430 Ventura Blvd., Suite 303, Encino, CA 91436 USA.)

Creams and Ointments

Aeling, J. et al. Allergic contact dermatitis to vitamin E aerosol deodorant. *Arch Dermatol* 1973; 108:579-80.

Brodkin, R. et al. Sensitivity to topically applied vitamin E. *Arch Derm* 1965; 92:76-77.

Clark, E. et al. Lanolin of reduced sensitizing potential. *Contact Dermatitis* 1981; 80-83.

Fisher, A. *Contact Dermatitis*. Philadelphia: Lea & Febiger, 1986, p. 151.

Frantz, K. *Breastfeeding Product Guide 1994*. Sunland, California: Geddes Productions, 1993, pp. 29-38.

Hinman, C. and Maibach, H. Effect of air exposure and occlusion on experimental human skin wounds. *Nature* 1963; 200:377-88.

Lawrence, R. *Breastfeeding: A Guide for the Medical Profession,* 4th ed. St. Louis: Mosby, 1994, p. 247.

Mann Mertz, P. Intervention: dressing effects on wound healing. *New Directions in Wound Healing. Convatec* 1990; 83.

Marx, C. et al. Vitamin E concentrations in serum of newborn infants after topic use of vitamin E by nursing mothers. *Am J Obstet Gynecol* 1985; 152:668-70.

Pumps/Products

Minkin, W. et al. Contact dermatitis from deodorants. *Arch Dermatol* 1973; 107:774-75.

Riordan, J. and Auerbach, K. *Breastfeeding and Human Lactation*. Boston and London: Jones and Bartlett, 1993, pp. 231-33.

Sharp, D. Moist wound healing for sore or cracked nipples. Breastfeeding Abstracts 1992; 12(2):1.

Spangler, A. and Hildebrandt, E. The effect of modified lanolin on nipple pain/damage during the first 10 days of breastfeeding. *J Childbirth Educ* 1993; 8(31):15-19.

Williams, J. Anatomy and physiology of breastfeeding: assessment of the mother. Presented at the International Lactation Consultant Association Conference, Chicago, Illinois, July 1992.

Milk Storage Bags

Frantz, K. *Breastfeeding Product Guide* 1994. Sunland, California: Geddes Productions, 1993, pp. 125-34.

Nipple Shields

Frantz, K. *Breastfeeding Product Guide* 1994. Sunland, California: Geddes Productions, 1993, pp. 39-46.

Lawrence, R. *Breastfeeding: A Guide for the Medical Profession,* 4th ed. St. Louis: Mosby, 1994, p. 245.

Riordan, J. and Auerbach, K. *Breastfeeding and Human Lactation*. Boston and London: Jones and Bartlett, 1993, pp. 311-16.

Woolridge, M. et al. Effect of a traditional and a new nipple shield on sucking patterns and milk flow. *Early Human Dev* 1980; 4:357-62.

Nursing Pads and Pillows

Frantz, K. *Breastfeeding Product Guide* 1994. Sunland, California: Geddes Productions, 1993, pp. 13-28.

Scales

Meier, P. et al. A new scale for in-home test-weighing for mothers of preterm and high risk infants. *J Hum Lact* 1994; 10(3):163-68.

Other Products

Frantz, K. *Breastfeeding Product Guide* 1994. Sunland, California: Geddes Productions, 1993, pp. 153-54.

About La Leche League

La Leche League is an international organization that was founded in 1956 to give information and encouragement, mainly through personal help, to all mothers who want to breastfeed their babies. While complimenting the care of the physician and other health care providers, it recognizes the unique importance of one mother helping another to perceive the needs of her child and to learn the best means of fulfilling those needs.

LLL believes that breastfeeding, with its many important physical and psychological benefits, offers advantages for both mother and child and is the ideal way to initiate healthy family relationships.

PUBLICATIONS

La Leche League International is also a resource for accurate information on all aspects of breastfeeding. La Leche League publishes a wide variety of books, pamphlets, and periodicals for parents as well as for those involved in health care and counseling the nursing mother.

THE WOMANLY ART OF BREASTFEEDING, with more than two million copies in print, has faithfully served breastfeeding mothers for four decades by answering questions and offering reassurance.

BREASTFEEDING ABSTRACTS, an 8-page quarterly publication for health professionals, features abstracts of breastfeeding research with articles and book reviews emphasizing clinical applications of new knowledge.

PAMPHLETS on topics such as *Positioning the Baby at the Breast, Breastfeeding Does Make a Difference,* and *Breastfeeding after a Cesarean Birth,* and more, are available at discounted rates for distribution to parents. *Facts About Breastfeeding* provides summaries of current research and is updated annually. Also available are tear-off sheets to provide basic information in an inexpensive format.

BREASTFEEDING RESOURCE CENTERS have been established to provide the opportunity for health care providers and others interested in supporting breastfeeding to act as independent sources for LLL's breastfeeding information in places where LLL Groups are not practical.

TRANSLATIONS of many La Leche League books and pamphlets are available, along with original material in other languages.

La Leche League International's **CENTER FOR BREASTFEEDING INFORMATION** has compiled a collection of research documentation strictly related to breastfeeding and lactation. The material available includes more than 12,000 full-length research articles from 1,300 professional journals, with a range of 200 different categories. Write or call to request a list of breastfeeding research categories available and information about subscribing to this service.

HEALTH ADVISORY COUNCIL

La Leche League works with an advisory council of health professionals who are consulted when new medical situations or research studies need to be evaluated.

MEDICAL ASSOCIATES

In addition to La Leche League's Professional Advisors, doctors who are interested and supportive may serve as Medical Associates of La Leche League.

LA LECHE LEAGUE INTERNATIONAL serves as a Non-Governmental Organization consultant to UNICEF and WHO, acts as a registered Private Voluntary Organization for the Agency of International Development, and is an accredited member of the US Healthy Mother/Healthy Baby Coalition and the World Alliance for Breastfeeding Action (WABA).

INTERNATIONAL CONFERENCES are held biennially for parents and professionals. Speakers include experts from all parts of the world who present information on breastfeeding, parenting, childbirth, nutrition, childcare, and related topics.

PHYSICIANS' SEMINARS are held annually and are cosponsored by the American Academy of Pediatrics and the American College of Obstetricians and Gynecologists. They are also accredited by the American Medical Association—Category 1 of the Physician's Recognition Award, the American Academy of Family Practices, and the American Osteopathic Association.

LACTATION SPECIALIST WORKSHOPS are sponsored by La Leche League International for lactation specialists, nurses, LLL Leaders, and others who work with breastfeeding mothers.

LA LECHE LEAGUE'S 900 LINE offers recorded information for parents on a variety of topics. This Breastfeeding Helpline can be accessed 24 hours a day so mothers can get information when they need it. 1-900-448-7475 ext. 88.

WORLD WIDE WEB SITE. La Leche League International's web site includes pertinent breastfeeding information, answers to frequently asked questions, announcements of upcoming conferences, seminars, and workshops, and the complete LLLI catalogue of books, publications, breast pumps, and other products. Orders can be faxed directly to the LLLI Order Department. Web site address listed below.

For further information about La Leche League's programs or a free copy of the LLLI Catalogue, write to:

La Leche League International
1400 North Meacham Road
P.O. Box 4079
Schaumburg IL 60168-4079 USA

1-800-LA LECHE or 847-519-7730 or 847-519-9585
Fax 847-519-0035
http://www.lalecheleague.org/

Photo Credits

Photos on these pages taken by:
J. J. Anderson, 153
David Arendt, 1, 45, 47, 48, 49, 54, 169, 195, 279, 371, 387, 413, 573
Jean Hoelscher, © Association for Breastfeeding Fashions, 19, 451
Betsy Liotus, 221, 353
Cindi Russell, 78, 113, 499
Ginger Sall, 343
Judy Torgus, 443
Dale Pfeiffer, 48, 55, 61, 65, 301

Photos on these pages provided by:
Gene Cranston Anderson, 241
Linda Flores, 317
Gwen Gotsch, 295
Pamela Maher, 300
Sallie Miller-Howe, 329

Illustrations:
Basics of Breastfeeding, 17
Barbara Heiser, 53
© Chele Marmet, 175, 176
Paul Torgus, 322, 397
Cleft Palate Foundation, 300

Index

A

AAP Drug List, 525-31

Abscess, 155, 422, 425-26

Active listening, 2-7

Adolescent mothers, 7-8

Adoptive nursing, 329-41

Aggressive non-nurser, 102-04

AIDS, and breastfeeding, 461-63

Alcohol, 128, 509

Allergy, to foods mother eats, 97-99, 281; to solid foods, 142, 148-49

Alternative feeding methods, 62, 65, 120, 211, 234, 256, 262, 269, 280, 337-38, 540-46

Alveoli, 16

Amphetamines, 513

Anatomy of the breast, 16-18

Anderson, Gene Cranston, 247-48

Anemia, 144, 423

Anesthetics, for cesarean, 445-46

for surgery, 290, 302-03, 469

for labor, 20-21, 78, 125

Antibiotics, contribute to thrush, 405-07

for mastitis, 421-22, 425

Arching baby, 91, 310-11

Areola, 17, 415-17, 433

Asking questions, 3-5, 80, 154, 170

Aspirin, risks of taking, 231

Auerbach, Kathleen, 197, 210, 287, 388

Augmentation surgery, breast, 434-36

Automatic electric pumps, 170-71, 202-06, 546-62

Avery, Jimmie Lynne, 337

B

Baby with special needs, 296-313

Bacteria in mother's milk, 252-53, 288

Balancing foremilk and hindmilk, 25, 90, 123, 281

Barrier methods of contraception, 362

Basics, if breastfeeding hurts, 71-72

Battery-operated pumps, 546-62

Bedrest, with multiple pregnancy, 318, 321

Bicycle-horn pumps, 558

Bilirubin levels, 223-37

exaggerated, 225-27

treatment levels, 228

Biopsy, 427, 453

Biting, as cause of sore nipples, 402-04

See also Clenching Response

Bleeding nipples, 393-96

Blindness, 473

Blisters, on nipple, 406-07

Blood in milk, 396, 428

Bonding to multiples, 320-21

Bottles, avoiding, 23, 120, 135, 234, 338-40, 324-25, 447, 540

for premature baby, 255-57, 263

introducing, 199, 210-12

weaning from, 86-87, 263

Bowel movements, 27

eliminate bilirubin, 230

normal patterns, 122-23, 280-81

Bra, too tight, 394, 417, 419, 421, 424

Breast anatomy, 16-18

augmentation, 107, 434-36

engorgement, 414-18

implants, 434-38
infection, 418-25
injury, 107, 432-34
lump, 426-28, 422
pain, 428-32
problems, 414-38
pumps, 170-72, 202-06, 546-62
reduction, 107, 152, 436-38
refusal, 101-08, 166, 424
shells, 397-99, 417, 562-63
size, 107, 167
softness, 24
stripping, 422
tumor, 108, 422
Breastfeeding
benefits to employers, 200
delays fertility, 356-61
ending a feeding, 57, 261, 390
helping mothers effectively, 1-14
in the early days, 20-24, 414-18
multiples, 318-27
patterns, 20-31, 420
positions, 46-52, 322, 420
products, 540-69
soon after birth, 20-24
toddlers, 29, 157, 164-66, 347-52
when it doesn't work out, 13-14
Bumgarner, Norma Jane, 29, 155-56
Burp, need to, 61, 88-89
positions for, 311

C

Cabbage leaves, 416
Caffeine, 97-98, 128, 374-75, 510-11
Calcium, 377, 379
Caloric needs,
after starting solids, 29, 131, 144
of breastfeeding mother, 128, 372-74, 379-80
of premature baby, 257
when breastfeeding twins, 325
when pregnant and nursing, 345
Cancer, 453-55
Cardiac problems, 296-97, 455
Caregiver, 200
feeding tips for, 210-12
Carpal tunnel syndrome, 455-56
CAT scans, 426, 453
Cereals, for baby, 147
Cesarean birth, 443-49
care at home, 449
effects of medications, 445, 447
hospital stay, 445-48
need for supplements, 447
positions for nursing, 447-49
Chapped nipples, 391

Chart, comparing pumps, 560
Chickenpox, 456; vaccine, 516
Child spacing, 356-65
Chlamydia, 465
Chocolate, 375, 511
C-hold, to support the breast, 52, 175
Cholera, 456-57
Chronic illness, mother's, 471-82
joint pain, 474
"Cigarette" hold, 53
Cleft lip or palate, 297-03
resources, 303-04
Clenching or clamping response, 70, 309-11, 391
Clutch, or football, hold, 49-50
Cocaine, 513
Code word for nursing, 165
Coffee, 97-98, 374-75
Colds, 92-93, 280, 457
Colic, 38-39, 89-90
Colostrum, 20-24, 244-45, 348
Comfort, mother's, 46-51, 72, 394, 447, 551
when baby is hospitalized, 289
Commercial baby foods, 146
Communication skills, 1-14, 355
Communicating with doctor, 10-13, 133-35, 235-37, 264-67, 283-84, 297, 302, 309-10, 447, 508-10
Concerns about milk supply, 26-29
for adopted baby, 340-41
Congestion or ear infection, 92-93, 280
Containers to use, for storing milk, 187-90, 213-14, 565-66
Contraception, 359-65
Contraceptives, hormonal, 127
Cosmetics, reaction to, 101
Cow's milk, for baby, 148; in mother's diet, 99-100, 377
Cradle hold, 48-49
Creams and ointments, 394-96, 563-65
Cross-cradle hold, 50, 259
Crying baby, 38-39, 89-90
Cultural expectations, about weaning, 157
differences, 9-10
Cup, introducing, 149
for supplements, 256, 540-41
Cylinder pumps, 554-59
Cystic fibrosis, 304, 474
Cytomegalovirus (CMV), 458

D

Dairy products, for baby, 148; in mother's diet, 99, 377
Dancer Hand position, 56, 65, 301, 311
Decrease in milk supply, 26-28, 33, 94
as cause of biting, 404

due to pregnancy, 344-47

when pumping, 174, 205, 548

Decreasing supplements, 121, 134-35

for adopted baby, 340-41

Deep breast pain, 428-32

Dehydration, signs of, 23, 115, 282, 286-87, 340-41

Depression, 321, 482-86

Dettwyler, Katherine, 157

Developmental behavior, 100, 130, 164-66

Diabetes mellitus, 197-201, 474-79

Diagnostic testing, of mother, 426-27, 453, 517-19

of baby, 312, 308

for causes of jaundice, 223-24, 226

Diarrhea, 280-83

Diet, mother's, 97-99, 264, 372-80

Distracting toddlers, 161-62

Distractibility, 100-01, 130

Doctor, dialogue with, 10-13, 133-35, 235-37, 283-84, 297, 302, 309-10, 454

Double-pumping, 170-71, 185, 202-04, 552, 559

Down syndrome, 304-07

resources, 308

Drug information, sources of, 507-09

Drug List, 525-31

"Dry-up" medication, 160

E

Ear infections, 92-93, 280, 298

Eating disorders, 379-80

Economic differences, 10

Eczema, as cause of sore nipples, 391-92, 408

Effects on breastfeeding, of drugs taken by mother, 20-21, 127, 231, 332-34, 447, 473, 484, 500-09

See also Drug List

Electronic scales, 568

Emotional deprivation, 129

Employed mothers, 195-219, 546-62

Employers, 200

Encouraging the baby to take the breast, 86-87, 104-09, 166-67, 338-40

Engorgement, 21, 82, 177, 389, 414-18, 563

Epilepsy, 479

Estrogen, 17, 354, 363-65

Exchange transfusions, 234

Exercise, 381-82, 425

Expectations when pumping, 171-72, 548

Expressing milk, 170-87, 200-08, 546-62

for a premature baby, 252-58

to soften areola, 389, 416

to stimulate a milk supply, 334-35

Eyedropper, 542

F

Failure-to-thrive, 118-19

"False alarms" about milk supply, 26-29

Features, pumps, 549-59

Feeding the baby expressed human milk, 190-91, 297, 301, 307

Feeding options, 197, 540-46

Feeding syringe, 542

Feelings, mother's, 2-3, 5-6, 154-57, 196-200, 222-23, 242-44, 296, 318-21, 330-33, 344-45, 354-56, 444-45

Fertility, 356-62

Fibrocystic disease, 427, 431

Fine-needle aspiration, 427, 453

Finger-feeding, 542

Finger foods, 146

Fisher, Chloe, 388

Flat or inverted nipples, 396-402

Flu, colds, mild infections, 457

Fluctuations in milk supply, 26-29, 346, 420, 547-48

Fluid needs, of breastfeeding mother, 172, 379, 417

with twins, 325

Fluoride, 514

Food poisoning, 458

Foods to avoid, for baby, 148

for mother, 97-99, 374-77

Football hold, 49-50, 259; modified, 52, 300

Forceful let-down, 49, 94-95, 429

Foremilk-hindmilk imbalance, 25, 90, 123, 281

Fortification of human milk, for premie, 250

Frantz, Kittie, 23, 82

Freezing human milk, 188-90, 214-15

Frenulum, short, 68-70, 392-93; clipping, 69

Frequency of feedings, 24, 122, 229, 269

of pumping, 178-80, 207-09, 254

to suppress ovulation, 356-61

Fruits for baby, 147

Fussy baby, 38-39, 78-100

at the breast, 78-101

reacting to mother's diet, 97-99, 376-77

G

Galactocele, 426-28

Galactosemia, 224, 282, 286, 308-09

Gartner, Dr. Lawrence, 226

Gastroesophageal reflux, 36, 96, 285

German measles (rubella), 465

Giardia, 458-59

Glucose supplements, 22-24, 231, 477

for hypoglycemia, 283-85

Gonorrhea, 465

Grief, working through, 242, 452

Growth charts, 115

Growth spurts, 26, 324

Guidelines for pumping, 170-87, 201-10, 546-62

for adopted baby, 334-35

for freezing and thawing milk, 188-91, 212-15

for storing milk, 188-91, 212

H

Hair care products, 382

Hand-expression, 171, 174-77, 186, 202-03; funnel, 568

Health care professionals, working with, 10-13, 264-67, 33

Health problems, mother, 452-86

baby, 223, 280-90

Heiser, Barbara, 53, 54, 104

Helping mothers, 1-14

Hepatitis, 459-61

Herbal remedies and teas, 334, 336, 511-12

Heroin, 514

Herpes simplex I and II, 461; sores, 407

High need baby, 89

Hindmilk, need for, 25, 230, 281, 325

as a supplement, 134, 230, 297, 301, 307, 311

HIV virus, 461-63

Hoffman technique, 399-401

Hormonal methods of contraception, 363-65

Hormones, 17-18, 347, 354-55, 475

Hospitalization,

after a cesarean, 445-49

of baby, 287-90

of mother, 467-71

pumping, 288-89

How to soothe a fussy baby, 89

HTLV-1, 463-64

Human milk, healing effects, 394-95

as a supplement, 134

color changes, 378

composition, 372

handling, 190, 215

storage guidelines, 188-91

Hypertension, 455

Hyperthyroidism, 481-82

Hypertonic babies, 91, 309-11

Hypoglycemia, 24, 283-84, 476-77

Hypothyroidism, 481

Hysterectomy, 363

I

Illegal drugs, 513-14

See also Drug List

Illness,

as cause of slow weight gain, 126-27

baby's, 280-90, 296-313

mother's, 452-86

Imbalance of foremilk-hindmilk, 25, 90, 123, 281

Immunizations, 516

Increasing milk supply, 26-28, 132, 254

for adopted baby, 330-41

Induced lactation, 330-41

Infections, breast, 418-26

mild, 457

Infertility, 356-58

Injury, to baby's mouth, 96

to breasts or nipples, 430, 432-36

Insta Heat, 568

Insufficient milk syndrome, 128

Insulin, 479, 505

Intensive care nursery, 264-68

Introducing solids, 141-49

Inverted nipples, 87, 396-402, 562-63

Iron, baby's need for, 144; supplements, 514-16

IUD, 362

J

Jaundice, 21-23, 221-37

AAP treatment guidelines, 227-29, 233

causes, 223-27

in premature babies, 228

treatment, 227-34

Joint pain or weakness, 474

K

Kangaroo care, 245-48

Kernicterus, 227

L

Labbok, Miriam, 356

Lact-Aid®, 545

Lactiferous ducts, 16, 397

Lactose intolerance, 282-83

La Leche League programs, 573-75

Lansinoh for Breastfeeding Mothers®, 394-96, 564-65

Large-breasted mothers, 47, 53

with pain in breast, 431

LAM, 360-61

Latch-on, 52-57; of premature baby, 258-60

Late-onset (or "breast milk") jaundice, 226-27

Lawrence, Dr. Ruth, 35, 281, 287, 372, 388, 419, 427, 482

Lazy nurser, 61-62

Leaking milk, 35, 208-09, 567

Length of nursing, 25-26, 90

Leprosy, 464

Let-down reflex, 18, 32-34

delayed or inhibited, 33-34, 90, 429

encouraging, 32-34

overactive, 49, 94, 429
  signs of, 32
  stimulating when pumping, 172-74, 201-02, 547
Loss of weight, newborn, 114
Lifestyles, 7-9, 126
Low muscle tone, 306-07
Lumps, breast, 426-28
Lyme disease, 464

M

Maher, Susan Meintz, 86
Malaria, 464
Malnourished mothers, 372-73
Mammary gland, 16-18
Mammogram, 426
Marijuana, 513
Marmet technique of hand-expression, 174-76; Chele, 401
Mastitis, 418-26
  causes of, 420-21
  recurrent, 423-25
  treatment of, 418-25
McKenna, James, 31
Measles, 464-65
Meats, for baby, 147
Meconium, baby's first stool, 22, 27, 123, 225, 230, 280
Medical situations, 12-13, 280-90, 296-313, 452-86, 500-09
Medications, 97, 127, 445-47, 452, 500-09
  used during labor, 20-21, 78, 125
  used to stimulate milk supply, 332-36
  See also Drug List
Menstrual periods (menses), 357-61
  affect milk supply, 334, 337, 431
Milk-ejection reflex, 18, 32-34
  See also Let-Down
Milk supply, concerns about, 26-29, 477-78
  decreasing, 33, 346
  increasing, 26-29, 94, 331-33
  insufficient, 129, 434-38
  reduced, 26-29, 94, 205
Milk storage bags, 188, 213, 565
Minchin, Maureen, 83, 388
Modified football hold, 52, 300
Moist wound healing, 394-96
Montgomery glands, 17, 167
Mother's feelings,
  about a baby with special needs, 296
  about a premature baby, 242-44, 267-69
  about jaundice, 222-23
  about multiples, 318-21
  about nursing during pregnancy, 344-46
  about relactation, 330-33
  about tandem nursing, 347-49, 351-52

  about weaning, 154-56
  about working, 196-200
  after a cesarean birth, 444-45
  when baby is ill, 280
  when baby refuses the breast, 78-80
  when mother is ill, 452-53
Mother who is unable to breastfeed, 308, 436-38, 482, 540
MRI screening, 426, 453
Multiple sclerosis, 479-80
Multiples
  advantages of breastfeeding, 318-19
  breastfeeding, 321-25
  caring for, 320-27
  expecting, 318-20
  mother's feelings, 318-21

N

Natural Family Planning, 361-62
Natural weaning, 164-66
Neonatal hypoglycemia, 24, 283-85, 476-77
Neurodevelopmental therapists, 58, 62, 72, 311-12, 544
Neurologically impaired baby, 68-69, 309-311
Newborn jaundice, 21-23, 221-37
Newton, Niles, 157
Newman, Jack, 373
Nicotine, 97, 128, 512-13
Nighttime nursing, 30-32; of multiples, 323
Nipple,
  blisters, 406-07
  confusion, 23, 66, 82-87, 390; and slow weight gain, 120-21
  injury, 432
  inverted, 87, 396-402, 562-63
  piercing, 382
  problems, 388-407
  shields, 390, 396, 401, 417, 566; weaning from, 86, 566
  soreness, 388-96; due to pregnancy, 346-47, 392-93; due to pumping, 202, 255, 391, 548-49
"Nipple sandwich," 53
Normal growth patterns, 114-15
"Nuisance diarrhea," 282
Nursing patterns,
  after baby starts solids, 29, 142-44
  at night, 30-32
  newborn, 20-25, 420
  of breastfeeding toddlers, 158-59
  to induce lactation, 337-39
  when mother works, 209
Nursing pads, 567; pillows, 567; stools, 567
Nursing strike, 104, 166
Nursing supplementer, 297, 337-40, 542-46
Nutrition, 372-82

O

Obesity, 136
Obturator, palatal, 300, 302
Occasional separations, pumping for, 186-87
Ointments, for sore nipples, 393-96
One-sided nursing, 106-09
Opening wide, getting baby to, 54-57
Options to regular separation from baby, 187
Oral contraceptives, 365
Oral rehydration therapy (ORT), 281, 283, 287
Overabundant milk supply, 281, 423
Overactive letdown, 49, 81, 88, 429
Overactive thyroid, 481-82
Overstimulation, of a premature baby, 246, 263, 268
"Oversupply syndrome," 281, 423, 429
Over-the-counter-drugs, 500-09
   See also Drug List
Ovulation, 356-62
Oxytocin, 17, 32

P

Pacifier, use of, 24, 35, 120
Paget's disease, 392
Painful breastfeeding, 71-72, 388-96
Pain, in the breast, 428-32
Parenting styles, 10, 30-31
Pathologic jaundice, 223-24, 226
Pedal Pump, 554, 556
Pedialyte, 281, 283, 287
Persuading baby to take the breast, 86-87, 104-09, 166-67, 258-62
Phototherapy, 232
   home units, 232, 237
Physical changes,
   from weaning, 167
   induced lactation, 333
   limitations, mother's, 471-73
   problems, baby, 295-313
Physiologic jaundice, 223-37
Pillows,
   nursing, 567
   to support the baby, 48, 479
   to support the mother, 46
   to support twins, 321-22
PKU, 312-13
Placenta fragment, 127
Plugged ducts, 418-25
Positioning, 46-52
   after cesarean, 447-49
   lying down, 47, 50
   multiples, 321-33
   tandem nursing, 350
   transitional, or cross cradle, 50, 259
   unusual, 51-52

Postpartum depression, 321, 482-86
Pregnancy, avoiding, 356-65
   as cause of sore nipples, 346-47, 392
   as cause of slow weight gain, 127
   breastfeeding during, 344-47
   with multiples, 319-20
Premature baby,
   advantages of breastfeeding, 244-45
   effects of jaundice, 227-28
   ending a feeding, 261
   first nursings, 181-84, 258-62
   growth rate, 250
   going home with, 267-73
   kangaroo care, 245-48
   need for supplements, 249-52
   pumping for, 178-82
   readiness to breastfeed, 255-58
Prescription drugs, 127, 264, 500-09
   See also Drug List
Primary lactation failure, 129
Products, where to obtain, 545-46, 568-69
Progesterone, 17
Progestin-only contraceptives, 363-65
Projectile vomiting, 285-86
Prolactin, 17, 32, 128, 321, 455, 482
Pumps, comparison chart, 560
Pumping instead of breastfeeding, 185-86
Pumping tips, 170-74, 201-09, 547-59
   for hospitalized baby, 288-90
Pushing the tongue down and out, 66, 306
Pyloric stenosis, 37, 285-86

Q

Quadruplets, 327

R

Radiation therapy, 454-55
Radioactive materials, 454-55, 481-82
Rapid weight gain, 136
Reaction to foods in mother's diet, 97-99, 375-77
Readiness for solids, 142-44
Recreational drugs, 513
   See also Drug List
Reduction surgery, breast, 432-38
Reflux, 36, 96, 285
Refusing to breastfeed, 101-09, 166
Relactation, 330-41
Riordan, Jan, 287, 355, 388
Rubber bulb pumps, 558
Rubella, or German measles, 465
Regular separation, pumping for, 201-09
Relationship as a couple, 355
   with adopted baby, 338
   with breastfeeding counselor, 13
   with twins, 320-21

Renting breast pumps, 554
Replacing breastfeeding with pumping, 185-86
Routines for pumping milk, 170-87, 201-09, 547

S

Salty taste of mother's milk, 100, 422
    of baby, 304
Sears, Dr. William, 39, 282
Seizures, 479
Separation of mother and baby, 21, 196-200, 222-23, 288, 415, 446, 468-69, 476
Sexuality, 354-56
Sexually transmitted diseases, 465-66
Sheehan's syndrome, 482
Shingles, 466
Side-lying position, 47, 50, 447
Single mothers, 7-8
Sleep patterns, 30-32
Sleepy baby, 23, 60-65
    and jaundice, 225, 229
    and slow weight gain, 121
    how to rouse, 61
Slide-over position, 50-51
Slow weight gain,
    in early months, 116-129
    past three months, 129-131
Small motorized pumps, 550-61
Smoking cigarettes, 376, 512-13
    and fussiness, 97
    and slow weight gain, 128
Solid foods, 141-49
    affecting weight gain, 131, 136, 144
    introducing, 144-46
    nursing patterns, 29
    readiness for, 142-44
    what to avoid, 148
    what to offer, 146-48
Soothers, 120
Sore nipples, 388-408
    caused by pumping, 202, 255, 391, 548-49
    caused by pregnancy, 346-47
Special needs, baby, 295-312
Spitting up, 36-37, 285
Spoon feeding, 286, 541
Staying on the breast, 56, 298-300, 390
Sterilization, 363
Stimulating a milk supply, 330-41, 547
Storage of human milk, 188-91, 212-15
Streamlining housework, with multiples, 326
Stress, 7, 33; reaction to, 101, 128, 289
Sucking patterns, 57-59
    as cause of sore nipples, 391-92
    problems, 58-70
Sudden Infant Death Syndrome, 31

Sunlight, to treat jaundice, 231
    for vitamin D, 515
Super switch nursing, 62, 65, 94
Supplementary Nursing System, 545-46
Supplements,
    after a cesarean, 447
    alternative feeding methods, 62, 65, 120, 540-46
    eliminating gradually, 121, 134-35
    for adopted baby, 340-41
    for jaundice, 233-34
    for multiples, 324-25
    for premature babies, 248-52, 267-73
    formula, 22-24, 121, 134, 233-34
    glucose or water, 22-24, 283-84
    hindmilk, 134, 230, 297, 301, 307, 311
    when baby is gaining slowly, 119, 133-35
    when baby is sucking incorrectly, 63, 120
Supporting the breast, 52-53, 431
Surgery, breast, 432-38
    mother's, 469
    on baby, 290, 302-03
Switch nursing, 62, 65, 94
Syphilis, 465

T

Taking baby off the breast, 57, 390
Tandem nursing, 347-52
Taste of milk, 39-40, 97-99, 347, 422
    of nipple, 100, 394-96
Teen mothers, 7-8
Teething, 93, 155; as cause of sore nipples, 402-04
T-E fistula, 23
Test-weighing, 28-29, 267-73, 568
Thawing and warming human milk, 190, 210-12
Thrush, 96, 404-06, 478; as cause of deep breast pain, 431
Thyroid disease, 480-82
Toddler nursing, 29, 154-65, 347-52
Tongue, exercises, 66
    problems, 66-70, 306, 390
    retracted, 67
    thrusting, 66-67
    -tie, 68-69, 390
Touching baby's head, 87
Toxic Shock Syndrome, 466
Toxoplasmosis, 466-67
Transfer of drugs into milk, 525-31
Transfusions, 234
Transitional hold, 50
Transition to breastfeeding,
    for adopted baby, 338-41
    for babies who are nipple-confused, 84-87
    for premature baby, 181-84

Treatment of jaundice, 228-34
    discussing with doctor, 235-37
Treatment of sore nipples, 393-96
Trichomonas, 465
Trigger-action pumps, 558
Triplets, breastfeeding, 327
Tubal ligation, 363
Tuberculosis, 467
Twins
    breastfeeding, 321-24
    caring for, 320-27
    expecting, 318-20
    mother's feelings, 318-21
    resources, 327
Typhoid fever, 456-57

U

Ultrasound scanning, 425-26, 453
Unborn baby, 345-46
Uncoordinated sucking, 309-11
Underactive thyroid, 481
Universal precautions, 190, 215
Unusual breastfeeding positions, 51-52
    for cleft palate baby, 300
    for twins, 322

V

Vaccines, 516
Vegetarian (vegan) diet, 131, 378-79, 516
Velcro dimple ring, 401
Vitamin E oil, for sore nipples, 395
Vitamin supplements, 515
    deficiency, 131, 515
    for baby, 97, 515
    for mother, 372-74, 378-79
Vomiting, 37, 285-87
"Vulnerable child syndrome," 222

W

Waking a sleepy baby, 61
Walking back on the tongue, 66
Wallaby home phototherapy units, 232, 237
Warm bottle method, 177
Water, need for, 22-24, 26
    avoid, 231
Weak suck, 63-65
Weaning, 154-66, 344-47
    abrupt, 158-59, 166-67
    because mother is taking a drug, 155
    before surgery, 290
    gradual, 157-60
    natural, 164-66
    partial, 158
    planned, 160-63
    when mother is ill, 155, 453
    when mother is pregnant, 155, 344-47

Weight gain, 27-29, 114-39
    in premature baby, 250
    rapid, 136
    slow, 116-32
Weight loss in newborn, 22, 114; in mother,
    372-82
White, Dr. Gregory, 37
Working mothers, guidelines for pumping,
    201-09
Work options, 197-200
Wet diapers, normal, 22; gauging wetness,
    58, 122
Working with doctor, 10-13, 133-35, 235-37,
    297, 302-03, 309-10, 312, 445-48, 500-09

X

X-ray, 426, 453

Y

Yeast infections, 96, 404-06